Developing Windows NT Device Drivers

Device Drivers

A Programmer's Handbook

Edward N. Dekker
Joseph M. Newcomer

ADDISON-WESLEY

An imprint of Addison Wesley Longman Inc.
Reading, Massachusetts • Harlow, England • Menlo Park, California
Berkeley, California • Don Mills, Ontario • Sydney
Bonn • Amsterdam • Tokyo • Mexico City

Many of the designations used by manufacturers and sellers to distinguish their products are claimed as trademarks. Where those designations appear in this book and Addison Wesley Longman Inc., was aware of a trademark claim, the designations have been printed in initial caps or all caps.

The authors and publisher have taken care in the preparation of this book, but make no expressed or implied warranty of any kind and assume no responsibility for errors or omissions. No liability is assumed for incidental or consequential damages in connection with or arising out of the use of the information or programs contained herein.

The publisher offers discounts on this book when ordered in quantity for special sales. For more information, please contact:

AWL Direct Sales
Addison Wesley Longman, Inc.
One Jacob Way
Reading, Massachusetts 01867
(781) 944-3700

Visit AW on the Web: www.awl.com/cseng/

Library of Congress Cataloging-in-Publication Data

Dekker, Edward N.
    Developing Windows NT device drivers : a programmer's handbook /
Edward N. Dekker, Joseph M. Newcomer.
      p.   cm.
    Includes bibliographical references and index.
    ISBN 0-201-69590-1
    1. Microsoft Windows NT device drivers (Computer programs)
    I. Newcomer, Joseph M. II. Title.
  QA76.76.D49D45   1999
  005.7'126--dc21   98-38017
                                     CIP

Executive Editor: J. Carter Shanklin
Project Editor: Krysia Bebick
Editorial Assistant: Kristin Erickson
Project Manager: Sarah Weaver
Copyeditor: Laura Michaels
Proofreader: Maine Proofreading Services
Composition: Octal Publishing, Inc.

Text printed on recycled and acid-free paper.

ISBN 0-201-69590-1

2 3 4 5 6 7 ARF 02 01 00 99

2nd Printing June 1999

Contents

Appendix B   Error Codes and NTSTATUS Codes   1001

Appendix C   BugCheck Codes   1107

Index   1119

List of Figures

List of Tables

Code Listings

Preface

This is a book about how to write NT Device Drivers. Device Drivers are those very specialized pieces of software that live inside the operating system and allow it, and thus your programs, to communicate to the outside world. *Every* communication NT makes to the outside world, including the keyboard, mouse, display, disks, CD-ROMS, and printers requires a Device Driver. Most of the key ones have been written by Microsoft, and NT supports all of the "standard" devices.

But what about "nonstandard" devices? By nonstandard, we don't mean that devices don't conform to a standard; we mean that they are that are not found on "standard" PCs. Often they are specialized devices whose market is far too small for Microsoft to devote any energy to support. These could be devices such as drivers that support IEEE-488 communications (used for laboratory equipment and test equipment), analog-to-digital data input boards, digital-to-analog data output boards, and specialized communications boards.

The core problem in Windows NT is that *if you don't have a Device Driver, you can't talk to a device*. In Windows 3.*x* and Windows 9*x*, you can cheat; you can write an application program that goes "for the bare metal" and directly manipulates the hardware interface to the device. But in Windows NT, because of the requirements for being certified at C2 Security (an important certification commercially and for government sales), an application program is simply not permitted to manipulate the hardware directly. So you are confronted with the problem of writing a Device Driver.

That's what this book is all about.

How This Book Happened

One evening after a long day at Comdex, Ed and I (*jmn*) were sitting around discussing our Latest Adventures. Ed was telling me about all of the really cool, largely nonobvious (not undocumented, but obscurely documented) things he'd learned about writing Device Drivers. I said to him, "Ed, you should write a book". (At this point, I was well into the writing of *Win32 Programming*, so writing books was at the top of my consciousness.) He looked at me and said, "Joe, I don't know how to write a book". I immediately responded "Well, *I* don't know how to write a Device Driver!" The conclusion was obvious. So we wrote a proposal to Addison Wesley Longman, and you are holding the result.

xxxix

What We Cover

The purpose of this book is to show you how to write NT Device Drivers for a new device that can connect to an NT machine. These include polled, programmed I/O, interrupt-driven, and DMA devices. Modern interrupt drivers add complexity because interrupts can be shared by several devices. DMA has changed from the use of the PC's onboard DMA controller to external DMA controllers and bus master controllers. Many drivers for modern devices need access to onboard memory, and we show how to provide that. In some cases, you might want to write a "user-level" system that does most of the work and that calls the I/O subsystem only to initiate certain input or output transactions and to handle interrupts. We show how to construct these types of drivers.

We talk about how to build drivers that are robust, portable, multithread-safe, and multiprocessor-safe. We talk about what you must do to ensure that your driver won't bring the system crashing down around the user. And we lay out the protocols you must use in communicating to the rest of the system. If you don't follow these fairly exactly, the system won't work as expected. It may crash, it may corrupt the disk, it may ignore the device, it may lose information on input or output, or it may misinterpret the intention of the application programmer who calls the services of the driver. Writing a Device Driver is fairly exacting. We try to capture here much of the Art of building a Device Driver, as well as the Technology.

In addition, we talk about how to actually build drivers, that is, the mechanics of compilation and linking; what they must do to register themselves with the system; and most important, how to debug them. Most of the useful techniques for debugging Device Drivers are either undocumented or difficult to find; we've summarized our experiences in this book.

What We Don't Cover

There is only so much that one book or set of books can cover. We've chosen our goals to cover what most Device Driver writers want or need. But there are several types of drivers we don't cover.

- Graphics drivers

    These include display drivers and printer drivers. The graphics driver contains the code to render an image into the internal frame buffer of the video adapter or printer engine. Most of the effort goes into understanding the incredibly clever hacks needed to get optimal efficiency on a particular piece of hardware. Graphics drivers are in the range of tens of thousands of lines of code. Generally, unless you work for a display card vendor or printer vendor, you will never encounter a need to write one of these. And while there is often a desire to support some old printing or plotting device, frankly, the cost of developing one of these drivers would buy several modern equivalents of those old printers. Chapter 25 contains a very high-level overview of graphics drivers. To do them justice would take another book about the size of this one.

- File system drivers

    These drivers, too, would be worthy of an entire book on their own. In fact, this has already been done (see the Further Reading section at the end of the preface). To write an entire file system is far more complex and is beyond the scope of this book. We've never written a file system and are not now qualified to write about how to do it.

- Network drivers

    As with graphics and system drivers, network drivers are worthy of an entire book devoted just to that subject (there is a pattern here). The chances that most device writers will ever need to write a full network driver are fairly slim. At the lowest level (for example, the card driver), a network card driver bears a strong resemblance to most other devices, but there are some additional complications that require a deep understanding of network protocols. There is just not enough space available in this book to cover network drivers.

- Various User Mode drivers

    There are components which run in user space, and which NT calls "device drivers". Prior to NT 4.0, these included the graphics driver, GDI, which in NT 4.0 is in the kernel. Included in NT 4.0 are the Telephony API (TAPI) drivers, major parts of the Windows Sockets support, and the Virtual DOS Drivers (VDD) that support MS-DOS compatibility. These are actually application programs, often running as *System Services*, and have entirely different rules and protocols from the Kernel-mode drivers we deal with in this book.

In addition, recognize that this is *software*. So there are *dozens* of ways to do *anything*. We present the core methods and possibly one or two interesting alternatives. We cannot tell you every possible way to do every possible thing (if only because we haven't done every possible thing in every possible way ourselves!). Many techniques are unique to particular devices, and in some cases, our ability to talk about some of the more interesting advanced techniques is circumscribed by various nondisclosure agreements we have signed. What we hope to give you here is a sound footing in basic driver technology and illustrations of a few of the more interesting advanced techniques that you might need. But the coverage here is not "complete". If we started to write a "complete" book on version *n* of NT, we would not have delivered the manuscript before version *n* + 1 was released. This wouldn't help anyone.

The Physics Model for Software

No, not "Software Physics". That's something else entirely. The "Physics Model" refers to a comment by a physics professor, who said, "We have an advantage in physics; we teach it by an ever more refined set of lies". What he was referring to is that when physics is first taught, you learn about Newtonian physics. In this model are such phenomena as the wave model of light and the particle model of light. Physical objects are real, and their masses interact according to specified laws of gravity or of energy transfer. But relativity theory tells us that Newtonian physics is really relative to a particular inertial frame, and what is *really* going on is something different. In quantum mechanics, you learn that at a certain scale, physical objects don't exist and phenomena like the Heisenberg Uncertainty Principle come into play; you get an explanation of what is *really* going on. Then there's quantum electrodynamics, in which the *real* model of what is going on is explained, and then . . . well, it's been too long since our physics courses and anyway, you should have the idea by now.

We apply this same principle to teaching software. So don't be surprised if there are some apparent discrepancies between the illustrations and text on one page and the illustrations and text on a later page. We're trying to avoid giving you infinite detail too early and thus avoid being too confusing. Ideally, the earlier text or illustration is a subset of the later one.

About URLs

While many people know about URLs, not everyone might be familiar with them. A *URL* is a *Universal Resource Locator*, a designator for a page of information on the World Wide Web. A URL has a form like the following three examples:

```
http://www.mumble.com/here/and/there/and/everywhere.html
http://www.mumble.com/here/and/there/and/everywhere.htm
http://www.mumble.com
```

To access a Web page for which we give a URL, you must have a *Web browser*, such as Microsoft Internet Explorer or NetScape Navigator (to name the two most popular browsers for Win32 platforms), and a connection to the Internet. We do not explain those details here, but if you don't have a connection, you want to find an *Internet Service Provider* (ISP) who can provide this service to you.

We have investigated a number of interesting Web sites that provide useful information for Device Driver writers. We have included these URLs in various places in the book.

Once you have your Internet connection, you bring up your browser and you type a URL, and as if by magic, the Internet tells you it doesn't exist[1]. Well, actually, if you typed the URL correctly and the Web page wasn't removed, you will get the page. *However, we can't guarantee that all of the URLs we give will continue to exist.* When we give you URLs, we're giving you the best information we have as we went to press. But the Web changes daily, so it is impossible to be instantly current in a print publication.

Documents on the Web

We often cite URLs as a source of documents. The Web page will usually give you a link, such as the name of the document or a button, that allows you to download the document. Downloadable documents come in a variety of formats, but the most popular are Microsoft Word (`.doc`) files and Adobe Acrobat (`.pdf`) files. If you have Microsoft Word, it is easy to read the documents; if you don't, you will need to download the Microsoft Word Viewer. For Acrobat, you need an Acrobat Viewer, available as a download from Adobe. We give their URLs under the Further Reading section at the end of the preface.

---

[1] A *program* is defined as "a magic spell cast over a computer allowing it to turn one's input into error messages" (*The New Hacker's Dictionary*). The World Wide Web is a mechanism that turns URLs into "404: Page Not Found" messages.

Documents on the Web are often compressed, usually using the PKZip utility from PKWare. If you download such a document, you will need the PKZip utility. This is available in both public-domain versions and registered versions. The folks at PKWare have done Good Things for the computing community. Support them by buying a licensed version. The licensed version is not that expensive; if you're a Device Driver writer, you can recover the cost very quickly.

Icons for Insertions

We have included a number of text insets, sidebar-like annotations that elaborate on points that have specific audiences. Rather than put everything inline in the text, we put some discussions into these insets. To clue you as to their relevance, we have a series of icons that we use to indicate the contents.

This Bug Icon indicates a potential bug. Sometimes the bug is in the documentation, and sometimes it is in a particular release of the operating system.

This Information Icon indicates an informational aside. The information may be useful to you, but it is not as important as the main-line text.

This Caution Icon indicates a potential pitfall. Often the pitfall is a compatibility issue such as an obscurely documented feature. Occasionally, we use it to indicate other possible failures that would otherwise be hard to discover. These failures include obscure or undocumented limitations or places where you are likely to get into trouble. In some cases, the behavior of an operation is not intuitively obvious, and if you do what you think is "right", it won't work as expected.

This Opinion Icon indicates that we are expressing a (usually controversial) opinion. We want you to know it is an opinion, rather than a statement of fact. You can disagree with the opinion, but one advantage of being an author is that we get to say, in public, how we feel about certain issues.

A Note on "Hungarian Notation"

This whole section should have one of the Opinion insets, but it is too long and too important to reduce to a mere sidebar.

The so-called "Hungarian Notation" (developed by a Hungarian programmer at Microsoft) is one of the worst ideas to have hit software development in many years. It is that horrid notation that tries to encode the data type in the name, for example, "nCount" indicating an integer count. This is a mistake; only two other popular languages in history ever encoded data type in a name, FORTRAN and BASIC, and both of them abandoned it as a fundamentally Bad Idea. Fortunately, the coders of the NT kernel had the good sense to avoid this notation. You will not find it used in any of our examples, except those user-level examples where we must interface to Microsoft's data structures that use the convention or when some published standard has fallen prey to this insidious notation.

Why is Hungarian Notation bad? Aesthetics aside (it is singularly ugly), it creates maintenance nightmares, which, in our opinion, is a cardinal sin. Software is hard enough to maintain without introducing artifices that make maintenance more difficult. For example, you might declare a short signed integer counter and call it "nCount". But you might then discover that you need more than 32,767 values, but fewer than 65,535 values in the counter. So in a sane world, you would do the obvious: Change the declaration from "short" to "unsigned short" or equivalently "WORD" (the declaration WORD *always* means "unsigned short"). But according to Microsoft's standards, you now need to change the name to "wCount". A global substitution won't work because there might be other contexts in which the variable "nCount" is simply a short. If you don't change it, you'll wonder why you get a compiler warning if you compare what is "obviously" a signed number with another signed value. And if you need more than 64K values, you might want to redeclare it a "long" or "unsigned long" ("DWORD"), in which case you need to change the name to "lCount" or "dwCount". If you don't change the name, you'll wonder why assigning a 16-bit variable wCount to another 16-bit variable wOldCount or passing it to a function that requires a 16-bit parameter generates a compiler warning about value truncation. If the names did not encode the type, you would not make this kind of error because you would have to refer to the declaration to find the type.

You say that changing a single name is trivial? Not so. And the possibility of making an error and *not* changing the name, or perhaps changing the name in too many places, introduces an unnecessary complication to maintenance. It is important to understand how real maintenance is done by real programmers in the real world, rather than legislating how a theoretical model of maintenance *ought* to be, in some ideal but unrealizable world.

But there are other, even more significant, maintenance headaches. If this value was in a structure, *you couldn't change the name* because doing so would force all users of the structure to change their code. So you will find in the Microsoft interfaces names such as "wCount" that were 16-bit unsigned integers in Win16 but changed to 32-bit unsigned integers in Win32. But for compatibility, the prefix had to remain the same. (The classic one for GUI programmers is "wParam", which suggests it is a 16-bit unsigned value but which is really a 32-bit unsigned value! And, in the world of 64-bit NT, it will be a 64-bit unsigned value!) It is not uncommon in the Microsoft interfaces to find declarations in structures such as "int dwCount", "LPVOID dwData", "DWORD lpszData", "WORD nCount", and "int wCount". Many of these represent the failure to fully transition from the 16-bit world to the 32-bit world. None of these would have been a problem if Hungarian Notation had not existed.

By using a naming convention that says the name *does* encode the type, then by violating that convention, you create programs that require additional care in maintenance. If that additional care—which should be completely unnecessary—is not exercised, you can get unmaintainable code or code that contains subtle bugs.

Historically, this naming convention arose in the days before compilers did cross-module type-checking on function calls. It enabled programmers to "visually check" that parameters had the correct types. With the use of ANSI compilers with full function prototypes, this need is gone (and has been gone for many years) and there is little reason to use this convention. We *strongly* discourage introducing *any* Hungarian Notation to any component you write. It is an unfortunate historical aberration that has no place in modern programming practice.

Perhaps the best summary we saw of this was in a book on programming, where the author titled the section "Hungarian Notation: Just Say No". We loved this heading and considered plagiarizing it, but we decided not to. It is too good, and he deserves to have it to himself. But we'll leave you with our expression: "Friends don't let friends program in Hungarian Notation".

NULL and NUL

The value NULL is a *pointer* to nothing. Although it is traditionally 0, the ANSI C Standard does *not* require it to be 0.[2] And while nearly every C program would break if it were changed from 0, that is because people like to write code of the form "if(!pointer)" instead of the (actually, only correct) form "if(pointer == NULL)". (The reason for the former is that on the first PDP-11 compilers, which had no optimization, the compiler could generate one fewer instruction for that form. This was important when the application had only 64K of address space to share for code and data. In modern compilers on modern architectures, there is no difference in the code generated, and the former is simply a type-unsafe computation based on a tradition that a NULL pointer is the same as a 0 value.)

NUL, on the other hand, is a *character* value. *There is no character value NULL.* In fact, the use of the NULL macro to represent a character NUL is incorrect, although we see it all of the time. An example is the assignment string[i] = NULL when string is a char (ANSI) or wchar_t (Unicode) array. The value NUL is the three-letter abbreviation for the character whose value is 0x00.[3] When used in the context of Unicode, it represents the character whose value is 0x0000. In fact, many C compilers formally define NULL as ((void *)0) in conformance with the ANSI standard, thereby making it impossible to actually assign it to a character lvalue. Thus the assignment just given would actually cause a compilation error, and in any decent C compiler, this would be an error, not a warning. Instead, the correct assignment would be either string[i] = '\0' (ANSI) or string[i] = L'\0' (Unicode).

The INs and OUTs of Parameters

You will find that all of the function headers specified by Microsoft have an apparent keyword attached to them: IN, OUT, or both. Starting with NT 5.0, some parameters may be followed by the keyword OPTIONAL. These keywords don't really exist; in fact, they are macros that have empty bodies, so they are effectively thrown away by the preprocessor. They are, however, incredibly useful as documentation aids. A reference parameter that is declared OUT means it

---

[2] Yes, really. Check the language in §7.1.6, which specifies that the macro NULL "expands to an implementation-defined null pointer constant". This phrasing was chosen specifically to *not* require that this value be 0. I used *The Annotated ANSI C Standard*, from Osborne/McGraw-Hill. See the Further Reading section at the end of the preface. *–jmn*

[3] See any reference on the ANSI character set. The one I have is by Hummel (see the Further Reading section at the end of the preface). On page 17, he lists the first 32 characters of the ANSI character set, which are, in order, NUL, SOH, STX, ETX, EOT, ENQ, ACK, BEL, BS, HT, LF, VT, FF, CR, SO, SI, DLE, DC1, DC2, DC3, DC4, NAK, SYN, ETB, CAN, EM, SUB, ESC, FS, GS, RS, and US. *–jmn*

will be written but not read. If it is declared IN OUT, you must initialize it before making the call; it will be updated on return. Little things like this help a lot. You will find that much of our code uses these keywords.

Unicode

Internally, Windows NT uses the *Unicode character set*. This is a 16-bit "universal" character code designed to support multiple languages concurrently. The familiar 8-bit character set is the *ANSI character set* and is a proper subset of the Unicode set. This introduces some interesting wrinkles you must be aware of. For example, there is no longer a one-to-one relationship between the number of bytes and the number of characters. Furthermore, even Microsoft is a bit inconsistent at the driver level. At the application level, the phrase "characters" *always* means "the number of characters", and an application running as a native Unicode application requires 2 bytes per character, but the APIs always use or return character counts. In the kernel, sometimes character counts are used and sometimes byte counts are used. We even point out where Microsoft has incorrectly confused characters and bytes in documenting a critical data structure (the UNICODE_STRING). But basically, you will want to "think Unicode" while within the kernel.

Unicode is *not* the same as the *multibyte character set* mechanism (MBCS) supported by Microsoft and other C libraries. The MBCS allows for embedded "shift" bytes that indicate whether the string is current in 1-byte, 2-byte, or potentially longer encodings. Unicode strings are always 16-bit characters and contain no embedded shift sequences.

Indentation Style

Yes, we recognize indentation style is an issue of deeply held beliefs, defended in general with incredible ferocity. The style used largely throughout the book is one that I (*jmn*) developed over many years. I strongly favor this style. Ed and I actually have quite different styles of indentation (but since I got to annotate all of the code, I got to choose the style). I believe that unlike many of the competing styles of indentation, this is the only one based on fundamental principles of human cognition.[4] While I don't expect to convert anyone to this style, I believe that understanding the principles may encourage thinking more deeply about indentation styles and how they are used in practice.

Think about this: How many times have you had to draw little arrows connecting the { }s of a C program? How many times have you had to print out a hard copy solely for this purpose? How many times have you gotten it wrong? Many years ago, I used a compiler for a language called SAIL, developed at the Stanford AI Lab. It was a classic Algol-class language with additional features that supported backtracking search, associative memory, and many other bells and whistles. The compiler, and its executables, ran on a 256K (roughly 1MB) DECSystem-10

---

[4] There is a piece of history that goes with this. In the early 1970s, I spent a couple years taking courses in Cognitive Psychology, since I was deeply interested in how debugging works intellectually and had hopes of applying this knowledge to the design of debugging tools. My actual dissertation ended up covering the application of AI pattern-matching to identify code patterns for an optimizing compiler. I did this because I decided I needed several more years of study before I could apply Cognitive Psychology principles to debugging. Also, graduate students have finite deadlines for completion. *–jmn*

or DECSystem-20. This language had an incredibly useful feature: You could follow any **begin** keyword with a string that was the "block name" and any **end** keyword with the same string. If the strings didn't match, *the compiler complained and included both names and line numbers in the error message.* This Was Wonderful.

After struggling with trying to find a "C style" that was right for me, I recalled how useful the block name feature was. So I programmed my editor so that when I typed an open-brace, I got a comment following it, into which I could type the "block name". When I typed a close-brace, the editor would find the matching open brace, indent the close brace to be directly under it, *and copy the comment.* While not as good as the checking done by the compiler, this has made brace errors in my code virtually nonexistent even on the first compilation. It also has reduced to single-digit seconds the time to finding the mismatched braces in those few cases where I get sloppy. But more significant is that it enables easy reading of large blocks of code, such as switch statements and loops, that span many screens or printed pages. I *know* that if I see a comment on a closing brace that there is a corresponding open brace with the same comment, and the open brace is trivial to find. This conforms to the human cognitive processes that don't handle counting and nesting very well but that can trivially match "flat" patterns. Since many of our examples span many pages, a bare close-brace is virtually incomprehensible without these annotations.

So think about it. Does your indentation style match human perception, or is it a representation of a machine-oriented perception? I, for one, have little interest in making life easy for machines. I'd rather optimize my own time.

Acknowledgments

No book this complex can be written by only two people in the time we had to write it. We are grateful to a large number of people for their help, support, suggestions, and tolerance during this process.

Mike Hendrickson and Ben Ryan of Addison Wesley Longman between them saw the book through its initial stages. Carter Shanklin, our current editor, helped us through to completion. Laura Michaels, copy editor *extraordinaire*, who took our clear, unambiguous, grammatically-correct prose and turned it into clear, unambiguous, and *actually* grammatically-correct prose (while we thought we knew how to write, having a True Expert read our prose taught us a lot). We are deeply grateful for her considerable efforts. Don Burn, Avinash Chopde, Alan Feuer, Ron Reeves, Bruce Rosen and Scott Thieret added comments on the book that helped us write more clearly on some topics. Special thanks go to Brian Catlin, Tom Carr, Rick Jones and Richard Page, whose suggestions and comments helped make this a far better book, and to the folks at OSR, whose NT Newsletter is full of useful tips. Jim McCollum allowed us to use his example of a driver that detected a subtle problem in DPC queuing that would cause a system crash (and the entire driver community should thank him for having discovered this and the workaround! A Nice Bit Of Work). We also wish to thank Brian Bussey and Frank de Alderete of Technology Exchange Company. The folks in the comp.os.ms-windows.programmer.nt.kernel-mode newsgroup offered answers to many of our questions without our asking, just by our searching the archives. Jim Boemler (jboemler@halcyon.com) maintains the file pcicode.h, which we used for our PCI Explorer, discussed in Chapter 21. And we thank especially the folks of MindShare, most notably Tom Shanley and Don Anderson, who have produced an utterly invaluable series of books on PC architecture. We *needed* some of that data to get our explanations right. (I think that we now each own the complete series, and as they extend it, we will extend our collections. This is a *great* set of books! Run, do not walk, to your nearest technical bookstore and get them.) We also thank them for their permission to include much of the detailed technical data that appears in our USB chapter from their book on the USB architecture. We apologize to anyone we missed in this list.

Our cover photo is by Cliff Wassman. We recommend a visit to his Web site `http://www.mysteriousplaces.com` to see some of his other photos.

We also want to particularly thank Jeff Ross, of VMetro, Incorporated, for the loan of the VMetro board we used for illustrations in the debugging chapter.

end: I need to thank my coauthor. Without his encouragement (and strong push), I never would have started this project. Joe has clearly done the hard part of this book. I also need to thank Joe for all he has taught me over the years we have worked together. I can name few people who have taught me as much.

I also thank my parents; they started me on the path to this book. When I was a small boy, long before first grade, my father started asking me how things work. This would continue for many years. Sometimes we would be in the car and drive past something, say, a road building machine or a factory, and he would ask me to explain how it worked, or how the factory built a product, or how the product the factory built worked. After I answered the question, he would give his answer. When he started, he didn't expect me to have the right answer. He taught me how to come up with possible answers, and construct the thought experiment to test my answer. This also inspired me to read more so that I would know the answers to the next question. My answers have been getting better as I got older. (He may have regretted this. When I started college, he observed that if asked for the time, I would give a monologue on clock building.) It was my mother who put up with my early book addiction (three trips to the library a week was about right, since I could take only 10 books at a time), as well as my electronics habit and the need for small electronic parts (not all of them were tangled in the carpet).

It seems to be tradition for an author to thank his dog, so I will thank mine, who has been as understanding as possible. He would clearly have preferred walking (well, running in circles) through the woods instead of sleeping in my office as I worked on this book. He helped provide the comic relief I needed at times. And he has appeared with his Kong[5] at the times I needed a break from the book and has been satisfied if I spent just a few minutes playing fetch. Well, it resembles fetch. I throw the Kong once, and he is happy if I just move my arm to attempt to take it from him as he runs past at high speed.

jmn: As usual, I need to thank my Little Gray Cat (a.k.a. Bernadette G. Callery) for her patience and endurance during Yet Another Book (this is my third). Mew! She also provided invaluable assistance for this book by providing the lower trace shown on the oscilloscope of Figure 9.27 (by holding the Channel 2 probe), and by keeping stacks of paper near the printer.[6] And for making life worthwhile in so many other ways.

---

[5] Kong is a dog toy available in several sizes, produced by the Kong Company. It is highly recommended by Ed's dog.

[6] One thing Ed and I learned about writing a book: you don't buy paper a case (10 reams) at a time. A case doesn't last long enough. Even with printers that print double-sided. However, Ed has also discovered that shredded laser printer paper makes excellent mulch for his corn crop.

I also want to thank my coauthor for some truly amazing spicy meals during the assorted weeks we spent working together at his place.[7] His years of experience in writing NT Device Drivers are what made this book possible, and his many hours of research on the topics we covered has been invaluable. He has clearly done the hard part of this book. I suspect that any errors of fact left in the book are the result of my misinterpretation of his knowledge.

Like Ed, my parents, and my uncle, William E. Newcomer, set me on this path many years ago by encouraging reading and experimentation; Erector Sets and TinkerToy sets were an important part of my life, as were the salvaged TV sets (a source of cheap electronic parts). These days, I just have a bigger TinkerToy set to play with, called a computer.[8]

About the Authors

Edward N. Dekker offers consulting services through his company Eclectic Engineering, Inc. He specializes in systems programming and real-time systems and has over 20 years' computer software experience. He has spent the majority of his time in the past few years focusing on Device Driver work for Windows NT. He has written Device Drivers for a variety of operating systems including Windows NT, Windows (3.0 and 3.1), DOS, VMS, RSX-11M, UNIX, and VXWORKS. Ed's experience also includes the programming and design of real-time systems, networking systems, databases, programming tools, electronic mail systems, and application programs. He has also consulted on software design and architecture.

Dr. Joseph M. Newcomer is a consultant, instructor, and author with 33 years' experience in computers. His first device driver was for a magnetic ink check reader (MICR) for the IBM 1440, in 1966. He has been a contributor to *Dr. Dobb's Journal,* published over 70 articles and technical reports, and written several books, including *Win32 Programming* (co-authored with Brent Rector; Addison Wesley Longman, 1997). He has worked on operating systems, device drivers, compilers, computer music (MIDI), real-time and embedded systems, and programming tools. Joe has been active in the Microsoft online forums and has been named a Most Valuable Professional (MVP) by Microsoft for several years.

Contacting Us

If you find errors or have suggestions for clarifications or material you'd like to see in future editions, we'd love to hear from you. We will probably be putting up errata sheets, new software, and the like on our Web sites as well. While we've done our best to interpret some very complex documentation on a very complex problem, we too are fallible. And while we think we've found all of the problems (especially with those paragraphs written late at night or early in the morn-

---

[7] We seriously considered a recipe appendix, since if this food helped us through writing this book, it might help you through writing a driver, but somehow we never got around to writing it.

[8] For more of this history, see a letter I wrote a few years ago, which is republished in the book *Legacies*, cited in the Further Reading section at the end of the preface.

ing, depending on your viewpoint), a book, like the software it describes, can't be proved correct—it can only be tested. We hope we have made your job of writing a Device Driver easier.

Edward N. Dekker
New Ipswich, NH
`dekker@eclectic-eng.com`
`http://www.eclectic-eng.com`

Joseph M. Newcomer
Pittsburgh, PA
`newcomer@flounder.com`
`http://www3.pgh.net/~newcomer`

Further Reading/Software Sources

Adobe Systems, *Acrobat Viewer*, available from
`http://www.adobe.com/prodindex/acrobat`

Campbell, Mary K. (ed.), *Legacies,* Institute of Electrical and Electronic Engineers, 1994. ISBN 0-7803-9996-X

Hummel, Robert L., *Programmer's Technical Reference: Data and Fax Communication,* Ziff-Davis, 1993. ISBN 1-56276-077-7

Microsoft Corporation, *Word Viewer*, available from
`http://www.microsoft.com/word/internet/viewer/viewer97`

Nagar, Rajeev, *Windows NT File System Internals*, O'Reilly and Associates, 1997. ISBN 1-56592-249-2

Newcomer, Joseph M., Letter to the Editor, "Post-Gazette", November 27, 1991, quoted in *Legacies.*

> *Legacies* was a special publication of the IEEE celebrating their life members. One of the contributors, who lives in Pittsburgh, saw my letter and said that it characterized much of how engineers became engineers. He asked permission to reprint it. I was particularly pleased because this book is a set of interviews with some of the greatest engineers of the century, all of whom are Life Members of the IEEE, on how they became engineers and what their careers meant to them.

Open System Resources, Inc., *The NT Insider*, currently available by free subscription as follows.

> Open System Resources, Inc.
> 105 State Route 101A, Suite 19
> Amherst, NH 03031

PKWARE, Incorporated, *PKZip*, available as follows.

> PKWARE, Inc.
> 9025 N. Deerwood Dr.
> Brown Deer, WI 53223
> (414) 354-8699
> `http://www.pkware.com`

Raymond, Eric S. *The New Hacker's Dictionary (third edition)*, MIT Press, 1996. ISBN 0-262-68092-0.

> This is a collection of the definitions of jargon based on the original MIT "jargon file" and updated to modern usage, including Microsoft and Unix terms. No, these are not formal definitions. But they are words we often use. (Besides, *jmn* had a lot of input to the first edition, and several of the definitions are his contributions.)

Schildt, Herbert, *The Annotated ANSI C Standard*, Osborne/McGraw-Hill, publication date unknown but, from the notes in the Introduction, suspected to be 1993. ISBN 0-07-881952-0

> VMetro, Inc.
> VMETRO, Inc.
> 1880 Dairy Ashford
> Suite 535
> Houston, TX 77077
> `http://www.vmetro.com`

For More Help

We hope this book will effectively introduce you to NT Device Drivers. If you need additional help, we are consultants and instructors. In addition to this book, we have also written and teach a course on Windows NT Device Drivers. Visit our Web sites or contact us for additional information on the course. We offer consulting and software development services through our own companies.

Course Description: Windows NT 4.0 Device Drivers

A five-day hands-on course or a four-day lecture-only course.

Key Benefits

- Learn the basic principles of Windows NT Device Driver programming.
- Understand how Device Drivers fit into the Windows NT system.
- Use the Microsoft driver build environment and Numega's SoftICE to produce a Device Driver (hands-on course only).
- Develop strategies for solving driver problems.
- Write demonstration Windows NT Device Drivers (hands-on course only).

Who Should Attend

This course is designed for programmers responsible for developing new Windows NT Device Drivers. Students must be fluent in C and must understand peripheral interface hardware and I/O programming for at least one hardware platform. Knowledge of operating systems principles is helpful, but issues such as interrupt services, memory management, DMA, Intel and Alpha Hardware Architecture, Symmetric Multiprocessor (SMP) machines, caches, and virtual memory are covered int the course overview.

Course Overview

This course presents an accelerated introduction to programming Windows NT Device Drivers. Students learn the basic principles of Windows NT I/O system architecture. Course content encompasses Drivers, Class Drivers, MiniDrivers, the Hardware Abstraction Layer (HAL), I/O Request Packets (IRPs), Deferred Procedure Calls (DPCs), Interrupt Service Routines (ISRs), the I/O Manager, and the use of the Registry to maintain device information. Knowledge gained in this course is a prerequisite for writing WDM Drivers for Windows NT 5 and Windows 98.

Chapter

1 *Overview of Drivers*

The term *device driver* has had many meanings in the history of operating systems, and device drivers have been used for many purposes. For Windows NT, *device driver* has several very specific meanings. Why *several*? Because, as we will show you in this chapter, there are many kinds of NT Device Drivers and the exact meaning depends on the context.[1] But first, let's look at the problem that device drivers in general are supposed to solve and why such drivers are important.

Historical Overview

Back in the Bad Old Days of mainframes, people who wanted to read a punched card issued a "read card" instruction (Figure 1.1). The application is, in effect, directly connected to the peripherals and manipulates them with direct hardwired instructions. Sometimes the person issuing the read card instruction could specify the address where the data was to be placed, and sometimes the data went to a specific, hardwired address in memory. This was all well and good,

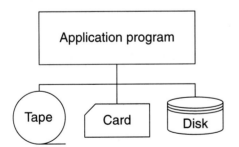

Figure 1.1: *Application program manipulating devices directly.*

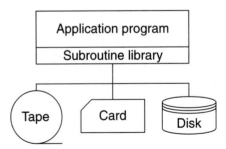

Figure 1.2: *Application program using a subroutine library.*

---

[1] We restrict the discussion of Windows NT Device Drivers in this book to "Kernel Mode" Device Drivers. This book covers the topics common to Kernel Mode Device Drivers and some of the details related to specific Kernel mode device drivers. Other components of NT are also referred to as "device drivers" (e.g., TAPI drivers, Virtual DOS drivers). These execute in User mode and are outside of the scope of this book.

until someone discovered that tying up a multimillion dollar mainframe by having it read cards was a Bad Idea. So, a much cheaper system was used to read the cards and write them to magnetic tape. The application program on the mainframe would then read from the tape. This was *much* faster . . . except for a few minor details. First, the mainframe program had to be rewritten, and all of the "read card" instructions had to be replaced by "read tape" instructions. Second, tapes were notoriously balky—a read may not succeed. In this case, the tape had to be backspaced and the operation retried. So programmers were discouraged from putting actual "read tape" instructions in their code. Instead, they called a subroutine library that was linked to their application (Figure 1.2). You may ask, why didn't they use the operating system? *What* operating system? You cleared memory, loaded your application, let it run, and then started the next job by clearing memory and loading the new executable image!

Gradually, it became obvious that the same subroutines were being used all of the time, so it made sense to consolidate them. This was a Good Idea for another reason. When the site upgraded from Model T tape drives to Model A tape drives, all of the applications needed to be relinked with the new subroutine library. Instead of having to relink, a set of subroutines was preloaded into the computer and *then* the application was loaded (Figure 1.3). The application called the "read tape" subroutine, whichever one was actually loaded, by means of a protocol, such as calling a specific location in memory that contained the call to the tape read subroutine, was now independent of the actual subroutine addresses. (Don't worry about the effects on the stack—there wasn't one!) These systems were prototype operating systems—the precursors of the modern operating system. Their bones can still be discovered in modern systems, after a fair amount of digging.

As time went on, these subroutine libraries became more and more sophisticated. For example, "read tape" became "read input" and read input could be dynamically reassigned to read physical punched cards, magnetic tape, or even those newfangled rotating magnetic storage devices. By the time IBM's OS/360 appeared in the mid-1960s, dynamic reassignment of input had become a fine art. OS/360 could dynamically load privileged segments of code to handle devices that were not yet a glimmer in the hardware designers' eyes, and it didn't require a recompilation of the entire operating system to do so. That is, the user could assign input or output to devices that didn't exist at the time the operating system was first written. Furthermore, the device drivers had an abstract interface to the application. On low-end machines with simple channels that could be used only one at a time, the device might have quite a different driver than on a high-end machine with a sophisticated controller that allowed multiple concurrent input/output (I/O) operations. The application continued to work identically on all machines of

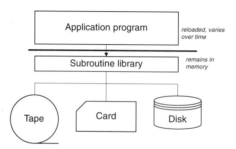

Figure 1.3: *Fixed subroutine library resulting in a proto-Operating System.*

the family. (Well, it did more or less. The system-generation, or SYSGEN, task assembled the operating system out of discrete components. It was complex enough that it sometimes failed, but it worked well enough that it represented a major milestone in operating system architecture.)

Other operating systems were not so fortunate. For example, adding a device driver to Digital's TOPS-10 or TOPS-20 required writing the device driver module in assembly code, relinking the entire operating system, and then rebooting. On UNIX, drivers are written in C, but until the most recent versions, they still had to be linked with the system to form a complete system image.

Versions of Digital's RSX-11 operating system (for the PDP-11) provided the concept of *loadable device drivers*. This concept was carried forward to the VMS operating system (for the Digital VAX).

UNIX, in its later versions,[2] popularized the notion of *configurable* device drivers. Unfortunately, like much of UNIX, this was not so much designed as hacked together. Configuration scripts had idiosyncratic syntax and would crash the system if a comma was misplaced or a blank line was present or no linefeed was at the end of the last line. Further, commenting conventions were nonexistent or ignored (and were inconsistent from driver to driver, including whether "commenting out" a line actually worked).[3]

Manually editing a table in the device driver was actually a system administration function: for example, to partition the physical disk into logical partitions. A system administrator (well, the on-site systems programmer) would edit the desired partition sizes into the driver source code. All disks of the same physical type were forced to use the same partition scheme. Nonetheless, it was a great idea, even if poorly executed. UNIX device drivers also assumed that you would have the entire kernel source available for perusal. After AT&T raised the commercial source license fee of UNIX to $100,000, interest in writing UNIX device drivers began to wane.

UNIX also introduced the notion of *portability*. Unlike the more-or-less homogeneous IBM 360 line, UNIX would run on a variety of disparate platforms, including the PDP-11, Digital VAX, IBM RISC 6000 (in the guise of AIX), Motorola 680x0, National Semiconductor, and Intel 80x86. While the device drivers were never really portable (often they had to be completely rewritten), the *interface* from the application to the device drivers was essentially constant. Thus, if an application program was recompiled for a new machine, it could successfully access the devices it had on the previous machine. What made UNIX interesting in its heyday was the fact that despite the incredible problems of portability, it was still cheaper to port UNIX to a new architecture than to write a complete new operating system. (For years, parts of the kernel were generated by running an editor [sed] script across the generated assembly code to change that code to what was required. This made the whole kernel-generation process sensitive to insane issues such as how the compiler allocated registers.)

The development of the first microprocessors led to the development of the first microprocessor operating system, CP/M. CP/M introduced a new concept, the *Basic Input/Output System*, or BIOS. While the BIOS had severe limitations, it is hard to overstate its importance. The BIOS

---

[2] Earlier versions of Unix, up to and including the Berkeley bsd 4.2 release, required editing the driver source to make changes, even in simple parameters like disk size information.

[3] Yes, really. We Were There. A comment line that resembled a device specification line was interpreted as a device specification line, even though it started with a this-line-is-a-comment symbol. You can lose hours trying to debug this sort of thing!

was a small amount of code that controlled the system devices. The only access to these devices was through the BIOS, so CP/M did not care about how your floppy disk or display was implemented—it always called the same BIOS routine. The BIOS was located on a few dedicated blocks of every boot floppy. There was even a procedure to write the BIOS to a CP/M boot disk to make it work on your new computer.

When IBM (and Microsoft) first produced the personal computer (PC), the BIOS was moved to ROM (read-only memory). The PC industry quickly outgrew the capabilities of the BIOS for programs, but the BIOS still provides the support needed for the PC operating systems to boot and load device drivers.

The IBM/Microsoft collaboration produced MS-DOS. MS-DOS is probably the most important operating system in history (so far). Not because it had any new ideas (it didn't) or because it was sophisticated (it wasn't) or portable (it was written in 8088 assembly code) or reliable (insert giggle here) or secure (insert belly-laugh here). Rather, it simply represented the most widely distributed operating system in the world. Right now (and for Right Now for many years to come), there are more copies of MS-DOS running in the world *than there are of all other operating systems in the history of the field combined over the entire history of operating systems*. Actually, this is an understatement. There are probably individual Fortune 500 companies who, even as you read this, have more copies of MS-DOS running than there are copies of all other operating systems in the history of operating systems.

It is considered fashionable among operating system aficionados (especially UNIX users) to attach disparaging names to MS-DOS. "Messy-DOS" is probably the most popular and most printable. Yet, in spite of its considerable deficiencies as an operating system (actually, it really is a set of preloaded subroutines for doing device management, as shown in Figure 1.3) and in spite of the universal disdain in which it is held by UNIX people, it did something that no other operating system in the history of the field ever has. It made it possible for millions of people who otherwise could never have used a computer to actually use one. Microsoft shipped more copies of MS-DOS in one week than most well-established vendors had sold of their proprietary operating systems in the entire lives of their products. Anyone who ignores this kind of force in the world is going to be left in the dust. Many companies were.

MS-DOS had a really interesting feature: the *loadable device driver*. This wasn't even a *new* idea (OS/360, RSX-11, and VMS already had it, as did several other operating systems). But MS-DOS made it visible to millions of people. You didn't need to be a systems programmer, site administrator, or technical guru to install a device driver. You could put a line in CONFIG.SYS and cause a device driver to be loaded. Almost no one ever wrote a "real" MS-DOS "device driver". The protocol for interacting with a "real" device driver was complex, inefficient, and largely undocumented. Instead, you loaded most "device drivers" by using the DEVICE= line of CONFIG.SYS to load a program that supported some *ad hoc* interface to a device or by running a program from AUTOEXEC.BAT, which initialized itself and then terminated, while overriding the normal program unload. These AUTOEXEC-loaded programs, called Terminate-and-Stay-Resident (TSR) programs, left the code, which was often a device driver, in memory (Figure 1.4). TSRs became one of the important features of MS-DOS, as well as one of the nightmares of users and system administrators everywhere. This was because there were no well-documented, established policies regarding how a TSR would take control. Thus, two or more TSRs could end up contending for the same resources in the same way. Usually, this would crash the system.

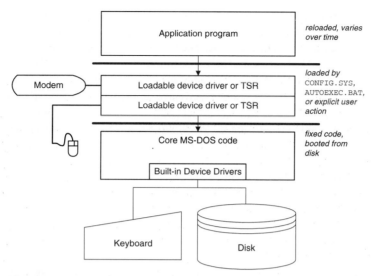

Figure 1.4: *MS-DOS architecture (ideal).*

Another major problem with most MS-DOS drivers was that they each used an *ad hoc* interface that nominally was supposed to be a standard but, in fact, often was not. Only a few device drivers, such as that for the mouse, ever attained a standard to which most vendors adhered. Generally, device independence existed only across a single vendor's product line, and then only if you were lucky. One of the most important set of drivers, beyond that for the mouse, came late in the life of MS-DOS: the ASPI standard (Advanced SCSI Programming Interface) for SCSI devices. Promulgated by Adaptec, a leading vendor of SCSI devices, the ASPI standard presented a device-independent SCSI interface so that all application programs or file systems could talk a single, uniform protocol to all SCSI devices. This was an open standard and was adopted by many other SCSI vendors. (There is an NT version of ASPI, which we discuss in Chapter 25.)

A few vendor-independent subroutine libraries flourished. In particular, serial I/O libraries were popular. These gave the programmer independence from the particular serial I/O chip[4] in use or even supported the many (nonstandard) multiport serial cards in a uniform fashion. Many of these were like the early subroutines-linked-into-the-application model (Figure 1.2), but some used a TSR driver that could be extended as new devices were introduced.

The real value of the MS-DOS implementation, however, was that you could *dynamically extend* the operating system's features without having to relink the operating system. Later operating systems, such as that for the Apple Macintosh, did the same thing. Mainstream UNIX has caught on to this idea only in the last few years.

But did developers use the ability to extend the operating system with TSRs? Many applications, particularly those delivered with specific add-on boards, didn't bother, not even with their own device drivers. Instead, the program just reached out and did the moral equivalent of the

---

[4] While all of the serial I/O chips used on PC motherboards are compatible for the core functionality, later chips provided a FIFO. The support libraries determine which chip is installed and use the optimal operating parameters for the serial chip.

"read-card" instruction. This worked because there was no protection in MS-DOS-based systems; any program could execute any instruction at any time. Most of these applications "programmed to the bare metal", ignoring the existence of MS-DOS entirely for their specific device handling. Thus they ended up more closely resembling the style of Figure 1.1.

Then came Windows. Windows 3.1 was probably the most important member of the 16-bit Windows series because it ran in a 32-bit (segmented) protected address space. (Windows 3.0 still supported the 8088, which had no memory protection.) This made it more difficult to write an application that could modify an interrupt vector. In Windows 3.1, it was necessary to use the `INT 21h` Function 25 or Function 35 (or a DPMI function) to map the interrupt. It was no longer possible to allow applications or drivers to directly modify the hardware interrupt vector (to write "to the bare metal"). Windows 3.1 retained the device drivers used by Windows 3.0, the ".`drv`" drivers, but also introduced a new kind of device driver called the *Virtual Device Driver*,[5] or VxD. The VxD was originally thought to be of limited use; however, VxDs became the popular vehicle for writing Windows 3.1 device interfaces. In addition, certain devices simply could *not* be accessed in any way other than via a genuine, interface-conforming *device driver*.

Windows 95 and Windows 98 are continuations of Windows 3.1. Using a code base consisting of a lot of 16-bit support code, Windows 95 and 98 add such features as a flat 32-bit address space, preemptive multitasking, and a 32-bit-oriented API (Application Program Interface). This API is nominally a subset of the "Reference API", the 32-bit Windows NT API. The relationship between these APIs is actually more complex than space allows us to discuss in this book, simply because the discussion is not terribly relevant to writing Device Drivers. Windows 95 and 98 continue the notion of the ".`drv`" and VxD drivers as the workhorses of device drivers.

Finally, we get to Windows NT. Windows NT represents a sophisticated level of maturity found in few other contemporary operating systems (notable exceptions are OS/2 and modern implementations of UNIX). It owes much of its maturity to the fact that its lead architect, Dave Cutler, was also the lead architect of Digital's VMS operating system, which itself was a quite mature system. Many of the core implementors of NT had VMS experience. For a good history of Windows NT, we recommend the book *Showstopper!*, whose citation we give in the Further Reading section at the end of this chapter.

In Windows NT, a program *cannot* be written "to the bare metal". It was the intent of the designers of Windows NT to obtain a "C2" security level. One of the security requirements to achieve C2 security is that no application program can write to any device register. So if you have an interesting piece of hardware that doesn't already have a Device Driver written for it, you can't communicate with it until you've written a Device Driver for it. Period.

Windows NT follows the tradition that device drivers are dynamically loadable. Some are loaded when the system starts up; some may not be loaded until an application requiring that device is loaded. And they can be *unloaded* as well, provided they are properly coded. For the end user, the capability to unload a device driver means that a server may not need to be shut

---

[5] Windows 3.1 was implemented as a multiple level operating system. The Virtual Machine Manager operated at the lowest level. It managed Virtual 8088 environments. The Windows subsystem ran in the first Virtual 8088 environment. Concurrent DOS processes ran in other Virtual 8088 virtual environments. Interrupts from hardware were first processed by the lower level, the Virtual Machine Manager. If the interrupt processing was not completed in the lower level, the interrupt was passed to each virtual 8088 environment. The VxD is a device driver which executes as a component of the lower level, the Virtual Machine Manager. The ".`drv`" drivers execute as a component of the Windows system. Interrupt latency for the drv drivers was considerably longer than the interrupt latency for ".`drv`" drivers.

down so that the next latest revision of a device driver can be installed. Instead, the device driver, ideally, can be "hot-swapped" for a newer one. (This doesn't always work in practice because the applications using the device driver might not be willing to relinquish it.)

In Windows NT, all Device Drivers follow specific protocols. In fact, in many cases the challenge is not to get the device to communicate to the driver but to get the driver to communicate properly with the rest of the system. The requirements for the protocols are very specific and very strict. Failure to follow them will result in erratic behavior, unsuccessful completion of the I/O request, or, more typically, the infamous Blue Screen of Death as the operating system crashes down about you.

A pilot friend of ours once observed that learning to fly under Instrument Flight Rules (IFR) is seen by the novice as the challenge of learning to fly without external reference points, that is, to keep the airplane on the correct flight path using only the instruments in the cockpit. She observed that the *real* challenge to IFR flight is learning the *protocols*: dealing with the centers that are controlling the IFR traffic, knowing how to read an approach chart, knowing when to abort a landing if the airport isn't where you thought it should be, and knowing how to abort (for example, it is a really bad idea to make a climbing turn to the left if there are mountains on that side). Writing NT Device Drivers has many of the same considerations. It is not enough that your driver can talk to the device. You must follow all of the protocols, or your driver will end up hitting the side of a mountain.

The developers of NT observed that many of the boilerplate tasks are common to all devices. For example, most of the code that handles a SCSI tape drive interface at the lowest level of SCSI commands is identical to the code that handles a SCSI disk or a SCSI CD-ROM. When multiple SCSI controllers are plugged into a computer—possibly multiple SCSI controllers from different vendors—the only change is to the lowest-level details of how to get these SCSI commands to the cards. So NT has a *layered* device structure; see Figure 1.5. Once you've implemented a particular layer, you need only to connect it to the correct lower layers and your work is done. So the controller for a SCSI disk can be written entirely at the SCSI level. The details regarding which register to write what bytes to in order to get the SCSI command to the drive can be handled differently for each SCSI card.

This is very important, so let's look at the example in Figure 1.5 in more detail. At the top of the diagram are two *class drivers*, one for a CD-ROM file system and one for a magnetic disk file system. The kinds of concerns these drivers have are the organization of the media, for example, how the directories are stored and how the data should be retrieved. For example, a CD-ROM File System Driver understands the structure of an ISO-9660 CD-ROM. The FAT File System Driver understands how one particular file system, the FAT file system, is organized.

Say the CD-ROM Driver needs to look up a file. It figures out what has to be done *in the abstract* to read the directory of a CD-ROM. But the details of how that is *actually* done depend on whether the SCSI CD-ROM or the IDE CD-ROM is being read. The driver knows just enough about the request to know which *Port Driver* to call. The SCSI Port Driver knows how to issue SCSI commands to a device, and the IDE Port Driver knows how to issue IDE commands to the device. But neither knows how to actually hand off these commands to the particular device! To do this, a *Miniport Driver* is supplied, either by the vendor or by Microsoft, that knows how to take the SCSI command or IDE command and tweak the actual device registers on the controller card to communicate that command to the device.

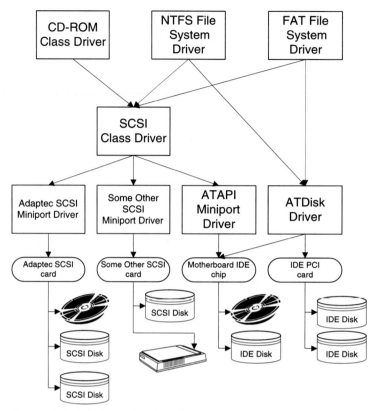

Figure 1.5: *The layered look in drivers.*

Figure 1.5 shows a flatbed scanner on the SCSI chain. This could not be accessed unless we had a defined class driver for flatbed scanners.[6]

Layered drivers are an advanced topic for most Windows NT 4.0 Device Driver programming. But when you move to Windows 2000, layers become so basic to the driver structure that they cannot be ignored. And while a simple, monolithic NT 4.0 driver will work in Windows 2000, you won't be able to take advantage of the cool Windows 2000 features such as Plug-and-Play or power management. So while most of the technology we cover for NT 4.0 applies directly to Windows 2000, the newer operating system adds some restrictions and limitations on how that technology is used in order to gain the power of the extensions. The protocols of how you interact with the NT components will change in some ways. We cover many of these issues in Chapter 28.

One problem that had serious implications for the adoption of Windows NT was that the Windows NT Device Driver Model was completely and mutually incompatible with the Windows 95 Device Driver Model. NT has complex protocols for talking to the device and to the rest

---

[6] Strictly speaking this is not true; you *could* use the SCSI "pass-through" mode, which allows an application program to directly control a SCSI device. Not all devices can be accessed using the pass-through mode, and some with timing sensitivities will not work at all because the delays in scheduling the application can cause the device to malfunction.

of the operating system. Windows 95 had protocols for talking to the operating system, but an application could talk directly to the hardware. Real Programmers Talk Directly To The Hardware. Also, the market for Windows 95 was much larger than the market for Windows NT at that time, so vendors of interesting devices would write Windows 95 device drivers and not bother writing Windows NT Device Drivers.

As part of a push to make devices easier to install, Microsoft created something called the Win32 Driver Model (WDM). The WDM is a uniform approach to writing a device driver. It imposes certain limitations on what can be done and how it is done, but the same device driver binary can execute on both Windows 98 and Windows 2000. We discuss the WDM extensively in Chapter 30.

Ultimately, this book is all about how to get all of those layers right, how to get the protocols right, and how to build reliable, robust, correct Device Drivers for Windows NT.

Overview of the NT Architecture

Windows NT started as an ambitious project to build a state-of-the-art operating system for the Intel 80386 and MIPS platforms. Several goals became obvious.

- The Intel platform was thought to have a limited, short lifespan, so the operating system had to be *portable to other processor architectures*. This meant that most of the code would be written in C.

Prediction has a way of biting the predictor—the Intel architecture is still strong and is a major force in shaping the PC world. Other architectures that held promise, such as the MIPS and PowerPC, on which NT ran, have proven less popular, and Microsoft announced plans to drop support for these two platforms with Windows 2000. In one case this was because Motorola and IBM, two major proponents of the PowerPC architecture, decided to drop their lines of PowerPC-based servers. This leaves only two architectures to run Windows NT: Intel's *x86* family and the Alpha. The forthcoming "Merced" chip, a 64-bit architecture jointly developed by Hewlett-Packard and Intel, will be running Windows NT.

- By implication, most Device Driver code would be written in C.

This is largely true. No assembly code is required to write Device Drivers. The really hairy machine-dependent parts are handled by a specific component we discuss in more detail throughout this book, the Hardware Abstraction Layer, or HAL. Only the VGA (not the SuperVGA) display driver was written largely in assembler,[7] and that was because the performance improvement justified the difficulty and expense.

- The operating system had to be *reliable*. This meant that no one application should be able to interfere with another.

---

[7] 1.42MB of assembly code, 360KB of C code.

- The operating system had to be *secure*, meaning that no one user can manipulate any resource for which he or she has not been granted the right to do so. This included both operating system security, meaning that all operating system objects are safe from the user, and interuser security, meaning that no user can access or modify the resources belonging to another user unless explicitly permitted to do so.

 Traditionally, security has been a feature of *file systems*, and the *file* was the basic unit of protection. In Windows NT, many different kinds of resources, all managed by the operating system, are subject to the same security paradigm, which is implemented at a level far below the level of "file". This security is enforced even on devices, but at a level that you, as a Device Driver writer, will not be concerned with. If your Device Driver gets called, then you can assume the caller had the right to call it.

- The operating system had to be a *multiprocessor operating system*. The multiprocessor architecture is Symmetric Multiprocessor (SMP) with common shared memory. You, as a Device Driver writer, must be excruciatingly conscious of this design requirement, as it has significant implications in how you write the code. We show you how to do this correctly.
- The operating system had to have *specific performance requirements*. For example, there has to be a minimum amount of time in which the machine is "deaf" to interrupts. This means that you must follow specific protocols to guarantee that this specification is met. Otherwise, other device drivers that depend on this specification, such as real-time audio devices, may seriously malfunction if you have not coded your driver properly. This violates the principle that one program must not interfere with another. We show you how to do this correctly.

The Priority System

Windows NT has a two-level priority model. The higher-level priorities are controlled by the hardware and software interrupts and the lower-level priorities are the scheduler priorities.

At any time the executing code will be running with a particular *IRQL* (Interrupt ReQuest Level). The level at which it is running determines what it is permitted to do, whether or not it is subject to the whims of the timeslicing scheduler, and what its relationship is with other threads of execution.

The highest of the IRQL levels are *Device Interrupt ReQuest Levels* (DIRQLs). These are the IRQL levels that correspond to hardware interrupts. The other IRQL levels are implemented in software.

The IRQL level of an interrupt controls when the interrupt may be processed. An interrupt will never be processed when the processor is busy processing a higher-level interrupt. The IRQL levels range from HIGH_LEVEL down to PASSIVE_LEVEL. Levels in the subset from HIGH_LEVEL to APC_LEVEL are referred to as *elevated IRQLs*. DISPATCH_LEVEL and APC_LEVEL are software artifacts.

The lower-level priority model controls the execution of threads running at PASSIVE_LEVEL IRQL. This level is controlled by the *scheduler*, which schedules *threads* (not processes). The scheduler will schedule execution of application and system threads. The scheduler will use the system clock to monitor and control the execution of threads.

There are two major divisions of scheduler priorities within PASSIVE_LEVEL: The "normal" and "real-time" priority classes.

The lowest scheduler priority is reserved for the *Zero Page Thread*, the thread that is run if there is absolutely nothing else to do. The Zero Page Thread is a component of the memory manager that will fill pages in the free list with zeros. When the memory manager receives a request for a zeroed page of memory (typically a page fault on a demand-zeroed page) the memory manager will first attempt to allocate a page zeroed by the Zero Page Thread, and only if none is available will it take the time to zero a page before returning.

Above this are the scheduler priority classes. There are two important classes: The normal class[8] and the real-time class. In Figure 1.6, there are four groups of related priorities. Above the Zero Page Thread is the normal idle priority. Above this are the default application priority levels. The usual background job priority is 7, and the usual foreground job priority is 9. The highest normal priority is 15 (Normal maximum). Above this is the band of real-time priority classes. The lowest real-time priority class, the real-time idle priority[9], is higher than the highest normal priority class. The highest priority real-time class runs at 31 and is of higher priority than any other user thread, so high that if it is compute-bound, *nothing* except I/O can be at higher priority. Note that parts of the file system execute as threads in the real-time priority class at priorities *lower* than the maximum possible value, so a time-critical thread can preempt even some file system operations.

There are two critical differences between the normal and real-time priorities.

If more than one thread is ready to run at the same priority level within the normal priority class, the scheduler will switch between threads whenever a thread has used an entire quantum. The *quantum* is a time interval, a multiple of the system clock interrupt interval. If a normal class thread is still running when a quantum expires, the scheduler will check for a thread of equal priority to run. This assures that all the runnable threads of the highest normal priority will have an opportunity to run. If there is no thread of equal priority that is runnable, the thread whose quantum expired is run for another quantum. Lower-priority threads will run only when all higher-priority threads have blocked.

Additionally, in the normal priority class, the scheduler may alter the priority of a thread. The thread will be given an increased priority to "make up" for processing time not used, given up to start an I/O operation. The thread priority may be reduced whenever a thread uses an entire quantum. The priority will never be increased by more than 2 above the base priority, and will never be decremented to less than 2 below the base priority. The increase in priority will take place at the completion of an I/O operation. The decrease in priority will take place at a quantum expiration. A thread may continue to run after it has had its priority reduced at the quantum expiration, if it remains the highest priority ready to run thread.[10]

Threads running at a priority within the real-time class will run to completion, excluding all threads of equal priority. The scheduler will not change the priority of a real-time thread. Real-

---

[8] Windows NT provides two subclasses of the Normal Class: the IDLE_PRIORITY_CLASS, and the HIGH_PRIORITY_CLASS. These may be used in place of NORMAL_PRIORITY_CLASS for somewhat finer control of application priority. Windows NT 5.0/Windows 2000 adds two additional subclasses of NORMAL, the ABOVE_NORMAL_PRIORITY_CLASS and the BELOW_NORMAL_PRIORITY_CLASS.

[9] While priority levels are named the "realtime idle" and "normal idle" there is no "idle job" executing at this priority. No normal priority thread can run if a thread at realtime idle is always ready to run. The Zero Page Thread will never run if a thread at normal idle is always ready to run.

[10] For more on the Windows NT Scheduler, see David Solomon's book *Inside Windows NT (Second Edition)* cited in the Further Reading section at the end of this chapter.

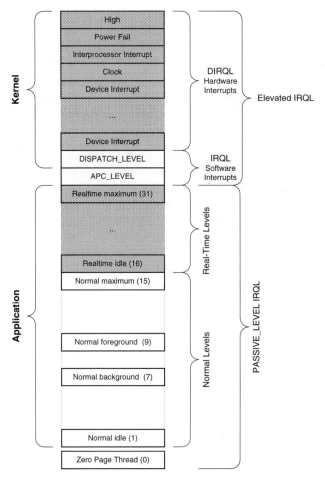

Figure 1.6: *Priority levels.*

time threads are not subject to timeslicing. Thus a real-time thread *must* block at some point, whether on an I/O operation or on some other synchronization primitive like a Semaphore, Mutex, or Event, or the machine will be "locked up".

Note that in all cases a thread will be preempted if a higher priority thread becomes runnable.

PASSIVE_LEVEL is the IRQL level at which an I/O call is dispatched from the I/O Manager in response to a user I/O request. Any deferred processing runs at a higher level, DISPATCH_LEVEL. At the highest priorities are the physical hardware priority levels established by the processor, DIRQL0 through DIRQLn, where n is the highest priority supported by the hardware. For Intel platforms, n is 15.

One feature of the IRQL levels is that certain kernel functions can be called only from certain priority levels. Thus it is essential that a Device Driver writer understand exactly at which level a piece of code is running. A naive approach to *code reuse*—the sharing of a subroutine that might be called from two different levels of operation of the driver—is a sure recipe for disaster. (IRQL_NOT_LESS_OR_EQUAL will become a familiar Blue Screen message.) This is complicated by the fact that a routine may usually be called at one level but may occasionally be called at another. (A dispatch routine will be called at `PASSIVE_LEVEL` if the I/O Manager is passing a request from an application program. The same dispatch routine may be called at elevated IRQL if the I/O routine was called from a completion routine of another device driver.)

When your application program calls an I/O function such as `CreateFile`, `ReadFile`, `WriteFile`, `DeviceIoControl`, or `CloseHandle`, your thread switches from running in your application space to running in the kernel (at that point, while it is your *thread* running, it is not your *code* running). Your thread retains the same `PASSIVE_LEVEL` IRQL that it was running at in the user level. However, the page map has changed so that the kernel memory is now mapped into your upper 2GB. Your thread can access the internal kernel data structures that are normally inaccessible and invisible to the application-level code. Your thread is also now running with kernel privileges. The issue of the memory map is critical to writing Device Drivers, and we devote considerable space to it.

A device driver may create a separate thread, called a *system thread*, to handle low-priority processing (`PASSIVE_LEVEL` and some scheduler priority), or to call system functions accessible only at `PASSIVE_LEVEL` (for example, functions to do file I/O). The system thread created by the driver will by default run at `PASSIVE_LEVEL` with a Real-time scheduler priority. The scheduler priority and IRQL may be explicitly changed by the driver code. Such a thread may be preempted by a higher-priority Real-time thread.

NT System Architecture

The overall architecture of Windows NT 4.0 (and later) is shown in Figure 1.7. This figure concentrates on the classic Win32 system, which executes the Win32 API. Unlike the earlier versions of Windows NT, some important code has been moved from User mode into Kernel mode. The most significant change for Windows NT 4.0 was that the window manager and graphics functions (formerly called USER and GDI) were moved into the kernel. These components were implemented as threads in the user mode CRSS process. In the kernel, they are known collectively as the Win32k (Win32 Kernel) subsystem. This also moved a major portion of the Display Driver into the Kernel.

This change was made for performance reasons. Previous versions of Windows NT were elegant in theory because the USER and GDI components lived in the user space, but in practice they had significant performance problems, particularly with respect to graphics output to the screen. Microsoft's *The Microsoft Windows NT Workstation Resource Kit* contains an evaluation of this change (page 99). According to Microsoft, an access to the GDI under the old architecture took 70 *micro*seconds on a Pentium 90 processor, while under the new architecture it takes 4 to 5 microseconds.

The Windows NT architecture is much more general than Figure 1.7 suggests. Multiple subsystems can live above the NT Executive, including emulators for popular niche-market interfaces such as POSIX. The support for the Virtual DOS Machine (VDM) and support for legacy Win16 applications, called Windows-On-Windows (WOW), also exist as User-mode subsystems above the NT Executive. However, a device opened from any of these subsystems ends up looking the same to your Device Driver, so you will see no difference.

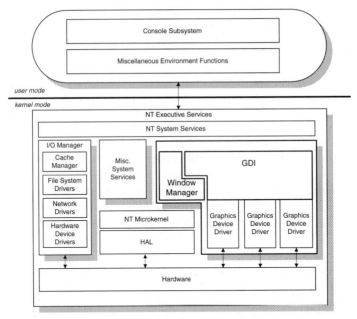

Figure 1.7: *NT system architecture.*

Kernel versus User Modes

In *Kernel* mode, the processor can execute all instructions, including those designated "privileged", and can access all of memory. On an Intel platform, I/O instructions and memory management instructions are all considered privileged. On some other platforms, I/O is done by modifying the contents of memory locations; there are no special I/O instructions. This memory is unavailable to any program not running in Kernel mode.

In *User* mode, an attempt to execute a privileged instruction causes a *processor exception*. Generally, a processor exception causes the user program to terminate. A User-mode program can access only the memory to which the operating system has granted it permission. It can have either read-only or read/write permission to such memory, but it cannot change the map that defines what memory it can access. A User-mode program, can, of course, *ask* the operating system to please change the map, but it is the operating system, running in Kernel mode, that actually makes the change, if it decides the change is permissible.

These protection levels correspond to the Intel *x*86 "Ring 0" (Kernel mode) and "Ring 3" (User mode).

The Hardware Abstraction Layer

Because NT was designed to operate on multiple processor architectures (originally, *x*86, MIPS, PowerPC, and Alpha) and multiple implementations of each architecture, there were some problems that had to be solved to make the operating system code as platform-independent as possible. The platform dependencies are captured in a component called the *Hardware Abstraction Layer* (HAL). This component contains a fairly large percentage of assembly language code. It handles the platform-specific details of timers, I/O busses, device registers, interrupt controllers, Direct Memory Access (DMA) controllers, and the lowest level of interrupt mapping. Most of the traditional low-level interactions are mediated by the HAL.

The BIOS and ARC

On the *x*86 PC platform, the BIOS provides support for booting the system. The BIOS ROM code reads the boot block from the hard drive into memory and executes it. The boot block contains code for a second level bootstrap, NTLDR, which loads the NT system from disk. On this platform, the NT secondary bootstrap and the NT system may be on either a FAT or NTFS disk. The secondary loader reads boot.ini on the root partition of the boot disk and uses information in that file to display a menu of NT configurations that can be booted. The secondary loader uses the information in this file to determine the path of the directory containing the desired NT instance. Parameters for NT startup are also in this file, those for enabling the kernel debugger, setting the debug COM port, and so on.

On RISC platforms, the ARC—a ROM (or NVRAM) resident piece of code named for the Advanced RISC Computing specification—is used to replace both the BIOS and boot.ini. The ARC loads the secondary loader and passes the path to NT and the configuration information as parameters. This information is set through the user interface of the ARC and stored in NVRAM.

The complete boot process is explained in more detail on page 17.

The Kernel

The *kernel* provides a set of services that the rest of the system can use. Its services look the same and have the same interfaces independent of the hardware platform. It calls the HAL to handle any necessary platform-specific operations. Note that in Figure 1.7, the kernel uses the HAL facilities to access the hardware.

The kernel provides services for interrupt dispatching (above the hardware level), thread scheduling, synchronization primitives (Semaphores, Mutexes, and Events), multiprocessor management, and time management. It also provides services represented by *objects*. The ones we are most concerned about in this book are *Device Objects*, which represent distinguishable devices to the user level or intermediate layers within the I/O system; *Driver Objects*, which represent classes of devices; *Controller Objects*, which we need if we have separate Device Objects that share some hardware state; *Adapter Objects* that can be used to simplify our use of DMA; *Timer Objects*, which support timers; *Interrupt Objects,* which let us get interrupts dispatched to our drivers; and *Deferred Procedure Call objects* (DPC), which we use to handle the asynchronous nature of most devices. There are many other types of objects. We will discuss those relevant to writing Device Drivers throughout the book.

The Executive Services

Executive Services include a common interface between user space and kernel space, an object manager, the process manager, and the Local Procedure Call mechanism. Although a Device Driver writer sees very few of this type of service, and thus has little interest in most of them, the following are of interest to the writer.

- The *Configuration Manager*, which handles the inventory of Device Drivers via the Registry database.

- The *Memory Manager*, which handles all of the memory allocation and management. Device Drivers must interact with the Memory Manager for all memory-related activities, including allocating and deallocating blocks of storage, accessing memory on a device, managing DMA buffers, and directly accessing data in the application space.

- The *Service Control Manager*, which handles the starting and stopping of Device Drivers after NT has loaded.

- The *I/O Manager*, which, for a Device Driver writer, is where all the action is.

Getting from Here to There

Applications execute in User mode, yet Device Drivers and other services live in the kernel and execute in Kernel mode. How does control get to the kernel? Or back to the application? Via *interrupts*.

When an *interrupt* occurs, the hardware goes through a specific protocol to transfer control from whatever was running to a specific point in the operating system (in NT, within the kernel). One side effect of this transfer is that the processor is put into Kernel mode. When an I/O device requires attention, or the clock ticks, or a number of other conditions occur, then the processor receives an interrupt and control passes to the kernel and then from the kernel to the Executive, Device Driver, or whatever other kernel component is designated to handle that interrupt. For all practical purposes you may assume this happens Entirely By Magic (if you really want to know, get a standard book on operating systems principles; NT is nearly a textbook case of what happens). The one condition where you must pay attention to the Man Behind the Curtain is in Device Drivers, where you must whisper an incantation to tell the Magical Mechanism how to route an interrupt to your driver. You do not need to understand the details of this mechanism; indeed, this mechanism will be different on different platforms.

When the processing on behalf of the interrupt has completed, the code must complete by executing a return-from-interrupt instruction (on the Intel platforms, an IRET). This restores the processor to the state it was in when the interrupt was taken. From the application level, the effect of the interrupt is unnoticed (except for the time delay).

NT is unusual compared to many older operating systems in that not only can the application level be interrupted, but also even the kernel itself can be interrupted. This has some serious implications for the Device Driver writer that we discuss in great detail. If the kernel is interrupted, the return-from-interrupt instruction returns from the kernel back to the kernel, but to *another part* of the kernel, the part that was running when the interrupt came in.

One last question remains: How does an application-level program transfer control to the kernel when it needs to have some kernel-level function performed? Again, via interrupts. Or, to be perfectly precise, via an interrupt-like mechanism.

There is a software instruction in almost every machine (for the Intel platforms, it is the instruction INT) that generates an interrupt. Historically, this type of instruction has had many names: "supervisor call", "executive call", "kernel call", "system call", "gateway call", and others (some unprintable). They all have the same effect: They cause the hardware to execute a sequence of operations that will eventually transfer control to the kernel. NT on an Intel platform uses the same interrupt mechanism that I/O devices do, except it just interrupts at a different interrupt vector location. All of these entry calls have a matching return-to-application-level mechanism, which, for NT on an Intel platform, is the IRET instruction. However, NT is *porta-ble*. If a new processor architecture came out, a new kernel and a new HAL would be required. The new kernel would handle the features of the processor architecture, and the HAL would handle the details of the implementation of that architecture (the support chips, motherboard organization, and the methods for addressing I/O devices).

But what about all of those places that call the kernel from user space? Wouldn't they have to change, too? It turns out that any call to the kernel is actually specified by a subroutine address that is called with an ordinary subroutine call instruction. That's all the application-level code sees. That subroutine is an address in the application space. The fact that it executes an INT instruction, or does something else entirely, is of no concern to the application-level code. And note that we said *application-level code*, not *the application*. The *application* sees only the calls to its subsystem; for example, Win32 API calls. It doesn't know if they are executed entirely in application space, entirely in kernel space, or partially in application space and partially in kernel space. So the abstraction is carefully maintained.

The Boot Process

The process by which NT starts up is reasonably complex, and for some Device Drivers (those which must be loaded at boot time) it is essential that you understand the steps of the boot process.

The boot process consists of several steps (phases), which are designated by the terms below. In each of the following sections we will explain each phase briefly. Not all of these steps will necessarily be comprehensible at this point because we have not yet explained all of the concepts. You may find it convenient to refer back to this description from later chapters.

1. Firmware
2. OS Loader
3. Kernel Startup
4. Configuration Manager Initialization
5. Executive Loader
6. Free Loader Blocks
7. Session Manager
8. Service Controller

1. Firmware

On *x*86 systems, the *boot ROM* (part of the BIOS) scans memory to determine its size and if it is working correctly, scans the PCI Bus to locate the devices and assign their initial configuration information, and calls any device-specific ROM initialization (such as the VGA extensions, the SCSI BIOS, etc.). Using the BIOS INT 13 mechanisms, it loads the boot sector from the disk. Control is transferred to the code loaded from the boot sector. This will load the component called NTLDR, the OS loader for *x*86 systems.

On Alpha systems, the firmware loads the ARC (the RISC BIOS) drivers, acquires hardware configuration data, and loads the component called OSLOADER, the OS loader on the Alpha.

2. OS Loader

The OS loader (NTLDR or OSLOADER) sets up memory, captures hardware configuration information data, and constructs a description of the hardware in memory. (On *x86* systems, this
hardware description is built by the NTDETECT phase; on RISC platforms, the hardware description is built using the ARC Query Config functions). The OS Loader creates an information
structure called the *loader block* and puts a pointer into this structure referencing the hardware
description it has detected.

The OS Loader then loads the kernel image, the HAL, and any device drivers and file system drivers required at boot time. It then loads any drivers whose START key is 0.[11] When this
process is completed, control proceeds to the Kernel Startup step.

3. Kernel Startup

During the Kernel Startup phase, load-control information is read from the Registry. The Registry can have parameters that control how much memory is available for the Nonpaged Pool, for
page table entries, and other uses. Another important parameter established at this time is the
Registry quota, which tells NT how much kernel space to reserve for keeping frequently-used
Registry structures in memory. Once this phase has completed, control proceeds to the Configuration Manager Initialization phase.

4. Configuration Manager Initialization

A kernel component called CmInitSystem initializes two of the Registry subtrees under
HKEY_LOCAL_MACHINE\Hardware and HKEY_LOCAL_MACHINE\System. It is very
important to understand that until a much later phase in the processing, these are the *only* Registry subtrees you can access. Next, the Registry API is enabled, which allows application-level
components, such as System Services, to access the Registry. Of course, kernel access to the
Registry is also supported at this point. The CurrentControlSet symbolic link is established
to the selected Control Set.

A *Control Set* is a mechanism to collect information in the Registry about a configuration of
the Executive component of NT. NT maintains three Control Sets: the current Control Set and
two older Control Sets. When NT boots, it uses the Control Set to determine the set of drivers to
load, their load time, and their load order and/or dependencies. The current Control Set also
defines the type of keyboard layout to be used, the current time zone, the name of the computer,
information about desired memory allocation (such as Nonpaged Pool size or number of page
table entries), and assorted other information too detailed to worry about here.

5. Executive Loader

A kernel component called IoInitSystem initializes and loads the remaining components of
the NT Executive. By looking at the Control Set specified by the CurrentControlSet key,
IoInitSystem determines which drivers are to be loaded. It also initializes the key kernel

---

[11] This will make more sense when we talk about the Registry entries for a driver in Chapter 8 and Chapter 9.

drivers that were loaded during the OS Loader phase. The effect of the Executive Loader phase is that all the base drivers required for booting the system are loaded.

Note that some drivers which are loaded at this point *must* successfully initialize. At the end of this phase, all of the system's key drivers are initialized and ready to go. If a driver *fails* to initialize, and it is not marked to allow the boot to continue, the system reverts to what is called the "Last Known Good" configuration (see step 8) and tries to reboot using that Control Set. If this reboot fails, NT is unbootable. You may be able to salvage it by using the "emergency repair disk", but it is more likely that at this point you will simply have to re-install NT.[12]

If this phase completes successfully, control proceeds to the next phase.

6. Free Loader Blocks

A kernel component called `MmFreeLoaderBlock` releases the block of information, the loader block, created when the boot process started. In addition, the initial copy of the Registry entry for `HKEY_LOCAL_MACHINE\System` created in step 3 is discarded. The in-memory copy of `HKEY_LOCAL_MACHINE\Hardware` created in step 3 is retained until the next phase.

7. Session Manager

This phase of startup runs certain startup-specific programs, whose details don't matter much to a Device Driver writer (and in any case are not discussed in much detail in the documentation). This phase also opens the paging file. It then initializes the remainder of the Registry, so at this point, all of the Registry entries are available. Some of the requests to write the Registry have also been deferred to this phase, and the write operations to the `HKEY_LOCAL_MACHINE` entries are now written back to the Registry. All of the necessary `HKEY_LOCAL_MACHINE` information is now available.

8. Service Controller

At this point, all remaining drivers in the `CurrentControlSet` that are marked for automatic startup are loaded and initialized. Generally, these drivers have their error response set so that their failure at worst produces a warning message and perhaps produces nothing at all (drivers are permitted, if you choose, to "fail silently"). When this phase completes successfully, the current Control Set is known to produce a successful boot, and becomes the "Last Known Good" Control Set. An index to this Control Set is entered in the Registry as the `HKEY_LOCAL_MACHINE\System\Select\LastKnownGood` key.

At this point, the NT boot process is complete.

---

[12] A very useful product is one called NTRecover, from the folks at www.sysinternals.com. This is a standalone program that boots off a floppy disk and allows a host program running on an NT machine to connect to the file system of the target machine via a serial port. You can mount the disk drives (including NTFS drives) of the target machine as drive letters on the host machine, and use ordinary applications (particularly NT Explorer) to examine and/or modify the files. If you have kept a working copy of the boot-time driver you are working on squirreled away somewhere, you can use this handy program to re-install it, making the system bootable again. You can also completely delete an incorrect driver that is marked as boot-time loadable but also as being allowed to fail (such as a network driver). I've done it. *–jmn*

Overview of Device Drivers

An NT Device Driver can be simplified to the schema shown in Figure 1.8. The arrows indicate the flow of control, or in the case of the hardware, control effected by signals to and from the device. In practice, there are several more-complex drivers that you can write, including those that use internal queueing, those that have multiple internal queues (the simplest example is bidirectional devices such as serial ports), and those that share facilities with other drivers. In fact, drivers can be as elaborate and complex as you can imagine (and possibly a few more complex than you *can* imagine, or even want to!).We look at many of these more complex drivers later in the book. However, now, for this "view-from-35,000 feet", we concentrate on the simple driver shown in the figure.

An NT 4.0 driver has five major states:

1. Initialization
2. Initiating individual operations on the device
3. Handling interrupts from the device
4. Processing the interrupt
5. Unloading

Initialization, the first state, is a relatively simple task, at least in Windows NT 4.0. The special function called `DriverEntry` is called by the I/O Manager after the drive is loaded. `DriverEntry` creates Device Objects to represent the actual hardware. A Device Object represents all of the states of the device; we discuss them in more detail in Chapter 3. `DriverEntry` then sets up the initial state for each device and makes the device available by name to the application level. Rarely, `DriverEntry` will operate on the hardware itself (although `DriverEntry` typically *reads* information from some hardware in order to configure itself). This is shown in Figure 1.9. Note that `DriverEntry`, if it touches the hardware at all, does not do so directly. Rather, it interacts with the hardware via the HAL.

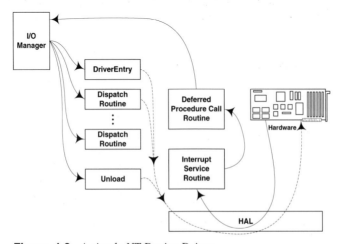

Figure 1.8: *A simple NT Device Driver.*

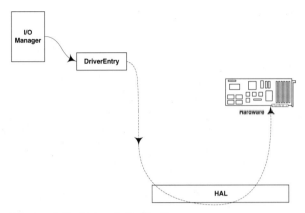

Figure **1.9:** *Driver initialization.*

The second state is to initialize the individual operations on the device. As the application code requests such operations as Open, Close, Read, and Write, NT routes these requests through the I/O Manager, which calls the appropriate *Dispatch Routine* to handle the function. Depending on the operation, the Dispatch Routine may or may not touch the actual hardware. A Close routine, for example, often requires no overt action on the hardware itself (if this seems counterintuitive, don't worry; we explain all of this in exquisite detail in later chapters). A Read operation, though, may touch the hardware (via the HAL) to initiate a transfer. But it doesn't want to sit around and wait for the data to arrive. So it returns and waits for the operation to complete. This is shown in Figure 1.10. For drivers that support queueing, the Dispatch Routine will not touch hardware. Instead, the hardware is manipulated by the code that dequeues the request. We don't go into that level of detail here.

The third and fourth states together are one of the interesting features of NT Device Drivers. (If you come from a VMS background, you will recognize them as being quite similar to what VMS calls a "fork level". The similarity to VMS is not surprising; Dave Cutler is the architect of

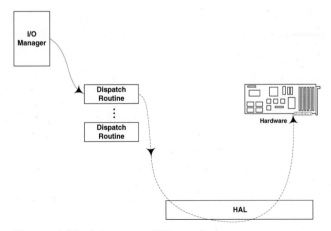

Figure **1.10:** *Initiating an I/O transfer.*

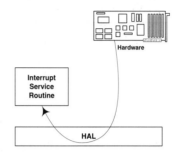

Figure 1.11: *Fielding an interrupt.*

both systems.)[13] Unlike with most traditional device drivers in most traditional operating systems, Windows NT splits the task of responding to the hardware into two separate phases: handling the interrupt and processing the interrupt.

Handling the interrupt is done when the device notifies the processor that it needs attention. The HAL intercepts this signal and activates the Interrupt Service routine (ISR), an entry point that is called to process the interrupt request. This routine does as little as possible—handling perhaps a dozen instructions in the simplest case—and then queues up a request for interrupt *processing* and returns. This is shown in Figure 1.11.

Processing the interrupt is when all of the "real" work of dealing with the interrupt happens. Buffers may get copied if the request was for input. If an error occurred, error recovery may be initiated if it is appropriate for the device. A new I/O operation may be started. Kernel memory that was dynamically allocated may be freed. All of these relatively lengthy operations are handled by a function that is logically "called" by the ISR but which in fact executes at some later time. Because the actual execution of the procedure is deferred, this is called a *Deferred Procedure Call* (DPC) and the procedure itself is called the *DPC Routine*. The DPC Routine is significant in that it executes at a lower priority than any physical device, so consequently it can be interrupted. This means that a device that requires unusually long processing will not impact the interrupt service of some other device. Experienced driver writers for other systems may have experienced putting "priority windows" in a driver to lower the interrupt level so that other devices could interrupt. This is intrinsic to the design of NT and doesn't have to be the cut-and-try, bash-it-till-it-fits approach that had to be used in the past to retrofit priority windows. If this is new to you, this feature means that complex device A will not unduly retard the response to time-critical-device B, even if both are running concurrently. In a world of real-time multimedia, ensuring this is important. And while this feature introduces some complexity, the complexity is *structured* complexity for which there are well-defined approaches. This is better than the ad hoc approach often required in the past.

---

[13] It is said to be entirely coincidental that "WNT" is ("VMS")+1 (using the "distributive law" of addition).

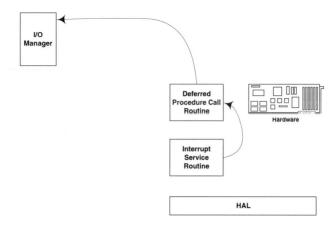

Figure 1.12: *The Deferred Procedure Call.*

The DPC Routine is called, indirectly, by the ISR and when it completes, it notifies the I/O Manager that the I/O transfer has completed (or, perhaps, has failed). The I/O Manager can then release the application program that has been waiting for the I/O operation. The path from the ISR to the DPC Routine to the I/O Manager is shown in Figure 1.12.

The situation is, of course, usually much more complex. The application may have been running, waiting for a notification that the I/O operation had completed, rather than blocked, waiting for the operation to complete. The I/O Manager will hide all of this detail from you. What you will see, and have to deal with, are the many details of what to do once an operation has completed. Perhaps you must do nothing. Perhaps the DPC realizes that the current interrupt represents only a partial transfer and instead of telling the I/O Manager that the request is complete, it initiates additional I/O on the device. Perhaps you have written the Dispatch Routines to queue up additional requests while the device was busy and the DPC has to dequeue them. There are many themes and variations we explore in the rest of this book, building from a simple "Hello World" Device Driver that requires no hardware to more-complex examples of multi-queued devices.

Ultimately, the driver needs to be unloaded. This is done in the fifth state. It can be the consequence of the system's shutting down or of the driver's being explicitly stopped either by the program or by the user. For Windows 2000, unplugging the last instance of a device from the USB or 1394 bus will cause the driver to be unloaded. The Unload operation is called by the I/O Manager and may or may not touch the hardware in the process of being unloaded. A Device Driver may, in the process of unloading, need to "shut down" the device (for example, to tell the hydraulic pump for a robotic arm to turn off). The structure of the Unload operation is shown in Figure 1.13.

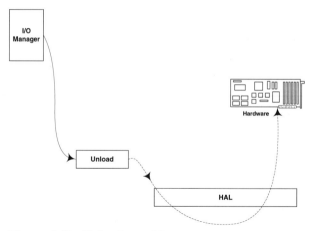

Figure 1.13: *Unloading a driver.*

There's Lots More

There is far more detail than what we've given so far for the Windows NT 4.0 world, and even more (and more capability) in the Windows 2000 world. So now you need to get started.

Driver Writing: Getting Started

To write Device Drivers, you need the following.

- A Microsoft Developer Network (MSDN) subscription

  While, strictly speaking, you no longer need an MSDN subscription to obtain the Driver Developer Kit (DDK), you will need it if you have to program an application or do anything else outside the Device Driver area. In our estimation, it is impossible to program Windows without an MSDN subscription.

  Microsoft over the years has changed the packaging and names of developer network subscriptions. For us, the most cost-effective subscription is the top-of-the-line MSDN Universal Subscription, which provides Windows NT Workstation, Windows NT Server, SQL Server, Microsoft Office, BackOffice, Enterprise editions of NT Server, Visual Studio, and Visual Basic, and many other (well, almost *all* other) Microsoft products.

- A copy of the Windows NT 4.0/NT 5.0 beta/Windows 2000 DDK.

  The DDK is part of the MSDN subscription, but is also downloadable, free, from the Microsoft Web Site. Go to `http://www.microsoft.com/ddk`. You can select the DDK download you want. These are *large* downloads.

- A C compiler and development environment

  We use Microsoft's Visual C++ environment, although there are many others. We have no experience with competing development environments. All of the code in this book was written and tested under VC++ version 4.2. Microsoft offers little support or sympathy if you are writing a Device Driver using other than the Microsoft compiler.

- A second computer, one that will be used as a debugging computer

  Seriously, really, truly. You can't debug a Device Driver if you have only one machine. Don't even bother trying. Furthermore, you have to treat this second machine as sacrificial. Don't put anything important on it because you will regularly have to reinstall the operating system from scratch and will probably lose some or all of the files on the disk fairly often. You'll need enough RAM to run Windows NT, at least 16MB. Large disks are cheap, so just put one on. But this machine must be dedicated to debugging Device Drivers, or you'll end up regretting it.

Several reviewers pointed out to us that you can use NuMega's SoftICE debugger to debug on a single machine. This is true, and it is a fine product. But when we use it, we use it on our second, debugging, machine. There are two major reasons you wouldn't want to debug on your main development machine.

First, if that machine is your *development* machine and you don't back everything up right before each test, you *will* be sorry. On really bad days, especially when writing a File System Filter Driver, you might get at most one test per NT installation. SoftICE does not and cannot protect you from your driver's running amok and corrupting your disk. Even if you debug using only one machine, *don't let this machine be your development machine*. Look at the economics. Losing your development machine can cost you hours, assuming that the *only* thing you have on it is the development environment. If you have an application for e-mail or for, say, Microsoft Word and you are on a network, you can lose a *whole lot* of time. Which is cheaper? A second machine, or a few lost months in the development process (ignoring, entirely, opportunity cost and time-to-market issues). Buy a second machine. They're cheap. You Have Been Warned.

Second, you generally want your development machine to be full-featured, with Internet connectivity, high-performance storage, backup tape units and their controller cards, sound cards, and the like. Testing new silicon in this sort of environment means there are many gratuitous devices on the bus, interrupts coming in all of the time, and a number of parallel events occurring at once. All of this contributes to the complexity of the debugging task and the instability of your debugging platform. *Especially* when debugging new silicon, you want as few extra problems as possible. Of course, you will eventually have to stress-test your driver in real environments, but that comes much later in the development process.

- A network

  Even if you are a one-machine site, you need to be on a network. This is because as soon as you start debugging Device Drivers, you become a two-machine site (see the previous point), and it is vastly simpler to move your files around if there is a network between the two machines. It may also be convenient for you to debug your applications that run using your new driver using the development environment on your host machine. You can debug a remote user program using the network. This saves having to reinstall the development environment on your debugging machine each time you reinstall the system.

- A serial port available on your development machine (host) as well as one available on the debugging machine (target), since you want to run the debugger on a separate machine

  You may also find it convenient to debug applications that test your device with the remote development environment debugger, which can run over serial ports or over the network. You may want to invest in a serial port switch box rather than keep switching cables between an external modem and the debugging computer.

- An optional but very nice piece of software called NuMega's (www.numega.com) SoftICE for Windows NT

  This is a sophisticated debugger that lets you debug on a single machine, with seamless integration between the application and the driver levels. Too often, there is absolutely no substitute for this debugger. However, while it has many useful features, we feel that it has an inhumane user interface. We find it hard to recommend it as the primary debugger for Device Driver development, but that is a matter of personal taste in interfaces. However, it is often more reliable than WinDbg, which can sometimes require far too much coaxing to act as a real debugger. We use both. There appears to be no four-gold-star debugger; each of the main debuggers has strengths and weaknesses. (Note, however, that if you don't have SoftICE, then when you really, really need it, you are in very deep trouble.) SoftICE also comes as part of a complete suite of development tools, which are very much worth looking at.

- Lots of books

  This book is about how to write NT Device Drivers. But you will probably need a book on the underlying architecture, one or more on the particular internal bus structure(s) that you are using (PCI, EISA), and some on the external bus structures you are using (SCSI, IDE, USB, PC-Card [PCMCIA] or IEEE-1394). Many of these topics would each need an entire book to cover well, so we could not hope to cover in a single volume *everything* about these external or internal busses as well as the art and technology of writing Device Drivers. You may even need books on the C programming language, the processor architecture, and the C development environment. If you have access to the logic diagrams for the device, an understanding of digital logic and hardware design can be very valuable. Don't expect to find all of the answers in our book, just the important ones for getting started writing Device Drivers.

  We *highly* recommend the Mindshare series on hardware. We have the complete set, and they are an invaluable reference.

- Lots of paper and, if possible, access to a fast laser printer, preferably one that can print double-sided

  The *preliminary* research on the WDM resulted in our printing almost ten inches of (single-sided) paper on a 6 ppm printer. Actually, two copies, one for each of us. Think of how thick we *could* have made this book![14]

---

[14] There are many reasons for needing paper. One, it can be annotated. Also, it provides an alternative to buying that third 20" display screen so as to get enough "screen real estate" so that you can read the material and type something about it at the same time. Further, it can be read in bed and on the plane between Pittsburgh, Pennsylvania, and Manchester, Hew Hampshire. And it can be hyperlinked by Post-It™ notes stuck in the edges.

Other options to consider are a comfortable chair (you'll be spending a lot of time in it) and a sleeping bag under your desk (unless, like us, you are a self-employed consultant with an office in the home. . . and even then the number of times we have been discovered asleep in our respective computer chairs is astounding). Also, we recommend a contract with a wholesale dealer in caffeinated beverages, a psychic (to help you find out what that hardware interface specification *really* means), and a psychiatrist (for when you begin to question your sanity).

Using C++

As you read this book, you may wonder why we used C instead of C++. After all, Device Drivers are, as you will see, quite object-oriented and, in most cases, lower-level drivers seem somehow to be derived classes of the upper-level drivers. This superficial analysis can lead you down a garden path to doom. While it probably would be nice to write Device Drivers in C++, several factors work against this.

The problem we see is that C++ makes the easy parts of writing a driver easy, but it doesn't make the hard parts any easier, and it introduces complexities that ultimately make your life more difficult. This is not a Real Programmers Don't Use C++ attitude. We feel that the technical challenges of using C++, combined with the lack of support from Microsoft cited below, currently work against this approach.

- Microsoft does not support the use of C++ in the kernel. This affects not only issues such as "name mangling", but serious ones such as the implementation of default constructors. (And if you fail to properly override a default constructor, you will be doomed.) Furthermore, Microsoft will not answer support questions if you are using C++ in the kernel.

- Microsoft does not support the basic structures of C++ as part of how a device is implemented. So you would be constantly "unwrapping" the abstractions provided by C++ to force them into a C world. Even minor details such as how the C and C++ standards require structures to be packed can cause problems.

- The "object-oriented" nature of device drivers actually uses a technique called "late binding" to bind the dispatch tables to the code. The binding is done at the time each driver is loaded. However, C++ requires "early binding", done by the compiler, for much of its functionality. This discrepancy in binding times can lead to complete disaster.

- The binding time issue relates to how drivers inherit from their parent. In fact, in C++ the early binding requires that the parent be compiled (even if only the class definition is part of a header file) before the derived class is compiled. In Device Drivers, not only is this not possible, it isn't even desirable. As long as the interface specifications remain constant, a lower-level driver could be compiled months before, or after, a higher-level driver and still work. Perhaps this is a criticism of the implementation of C++ rather than the language, but it still is a serious limitation.

- When executing in the kernel, the amount of stack space available is severely limited. C++ exhibits a tendency to consume large amounts of stack space. The use of C++ therefore increases the likelihood of a kernel stack overflow, which will crash the system.

One misguided client of ours demanded, seriously, that Device Drivers be written using the Microsoft Foundation Class (MFC) library. This is a serious lapse in technical judgment. MFC is a user-level library system predicated on executing in pure user space, calling API functions for both explicit and implicit operations. It does not allow the user to call API functions when in the kernel. Attempting to circumvent MFC's base assumptions is a pointless waste of time. It is critical to avoid cult-faith issues such as the glories of object-oriented MFC programming (which is perfectly fine for applications). In addition, Microsoft has, at least so far, made it utterly impossible to override the `new` and `delete` operators for any MFC classes, even those unrelated to GUI programming. This makes MFC singularly useless in the driver world, since almost everything that gives MFC its power requires overriding these operators to make the code work in kernel space. Thus virtually nothing of MFC is actually usable for writing Device Drivers, while its core assumptions result in wasting incredible amounts of effort for little gain. If you work for someone who thinks Device Drivers should be written in MFC, you might seriously consider circulating your resumé.

You might also consider reading Richard Feynman's article on "Cargo Cult Science" cited in the Further Reading section at the end of this chapter.

C++ simply does not provide enough leverage to justify writing your own C++ library for Device Drivers.

For a small C++ example defining only a piece of the DDK in C++, and a counterargument to our position, see the *Microsoft Systems Journal* article by John Elliot and Jeff Huckins, cited in the Further Reading section at the end of the chapter. They developed a C++ library for writing Device Drivers. A column in *The NT Insider* by Peter Viscarola and a rebuttal in the subsequent issue by Steve Lewin-Berlin are worth reading if you are considering using C++ to write Device Drivers.

Vendors of C++ libraries for writing Device Drivers are Blue Water Systems (`www.pds-site.com/Bluewatersystems/BlueWaterSystems.htm`) and Vireo Software, Inc. (`www.vireo.com`). Both also have products for access to hardware devices without a driver.

WinRT and Driver::Agent provide a driver and an API that allow the development of code to access simple hardware without any Kernel mode programming. Both are worth investigating for simple hardware and low-data-rate applications. We cannot recommend these products (at least in their current versions) for complex drivers, complex devices, or high-data-rate applications.[15] However, if your driver falls within what these packages do well, you should certainly look at them.

Vireo Software offers the following (quoting from the Vireo Software Web site):

Driver::Works for Windows NT and WDM uncovers the secrets of NT drivers with a new and powerful Wizard integrated into the MSVC development environment. The Driver::Works class library, framework, and Wizard provide access to tens of thousands of lines of working, debugged code that will bring you up to speed on Device Driver development faster than you imagine.

Driver::Agent tears down the wall between user and Kernel mode, giving applications direct hardware access and control on Windows 98, Windows 95, and Windows NT. Ideal for commercial applications, fast prototypes, lab use, diagnostics and test software, and much more; Driver::Agent features Kernel Agents for optimal performance.

---

[15] But times and versions change.

Blue Water Systems offers the following (quoting from the Blue Water Systems Web site):

WinDK 2.5 — WinDK 2.5 is a NT and WDM Driver Development Library. This toolkit is for hard-core kernel driver creation. WinDK breaks down the barriers to the NT DDK in three ways: by encapsulating the thousands of lines of startup code required in NT drivers, with the toolkit's clear sample code for the kinds of drivers you need to write and with its comprehensive 700+ page manual. Drivers created using WinDK execute as fast drivers written solely with the NT DDK. Typical applications include PCI bus master adapters, custom serial drivers, parallel port interfaces, USB, etc. WinDK supports both C and C++ based drivers.

WinRT for NT and Windows 95 — WinRT allows a Win32 application to perform Port I/O, Memory I/O and Interrupt handling. Typical applications include A/D, D/A, digital I/O and PLC cards with moderate data throughput and interrupt rates. This toolkit is very easy to use, with many customers porting their drivers in a day. The resulting hardware control application is binary compatible between NT and Windows 95. (C, C++ and Delphi)

WinRT OCX for NT and Windows 95 — This OLE Control (or ActiveX control) allows a Visual Basic 5 (32-bit) application to handle Port I/O, Memory I/O and Interrupt handling. It is intended for low data and interrupt rate cards. (VB5, Delphi).

Planning a Device Driver

When you confront a Device you need to program, you need to ask the following questions (among many others).

- How can I find the base of the I/O register space?
- How many device registers are there in the I/O register space of my device?
- How many device registers are there, really?
- What device registers are utterly crucial to my driver?
- (Devices with memory attached) How can I find the base address of the memory?
- (Devices with memory attached) How can I find the size of the memory?
- (Devices that do Direct Memory Access) Does the device require one or more of the system DMA channels?
- (Devices that do Direct Memory Access) Is the device a bus mastering device?
- (Enumerable busses) How does the system enumerate the devices on a bus, and how does it locate and load the appropriate drivers?

The chapters that follow show you how to answer these questions.

Further Reading

Custer, Helen, *Inside Windows NT*, Microsoft Press, 1993. ISBN 155615481X.

   Although this book is historically important, for NT 4.0 it has been supplanted by the Solomon book cited below, which is the second edition of this book.

Elliot, John and Jeff Huckins, "Our Exclusive Class Library Speeds Building Windows NT Kernel-Mode Device Drivers", *Microsoft Systems Journal*, Vol. 11, No. 9 (September 1996).

Feynman, Richard, "Cargo Cult Science", from a Caltech commencement address given in 1974. Also published in *Surely You're Joking, Mr. Feynman!*, W. W. Norton & Company, 1997. ISBN 0393316041 (Paperback reprint edition).

Lewin-Berlin, Steve, "Pontifical Perturbation: I Want My C++", in *The NT Insider*, Vol. 4, No. 2 (March 1997), p. 5.

This is a letter in rebuttal to Peter Viscarola's article in the previous issue of *The NT Insider*, cited later in this list.

Microsoft, *Microsoft Windows NT Workstation Resource Kit*, Microsoft Press, 1996. ISBN 1-57231-343-9.

Solomon, David A., *Inside Windows NT (Second Edition)*, Microsoft Press, 1998. ISBN 1-57231-677-2.

The Solomon book is the revision of the Custer book and is considered now to be the definitive edition.

Viscarola, Peter G., "Peter Pontificates: Flavor of the Month! NT Drivers in Java?", in *The NT Insider*, Vol. 4, No. 1 (January 1997), p. 4.

This is a column in which Peter talks about writing NT Drivers in Java and C++. He is quite negative on these possibilities. However, one of us (*jmn*) remembers an international conference in which Alan J. Perlis was advocating LISP for its elegance and simplicity. He was challenged, "If LISP is so good, why don't we write operating systems in it?" Perlis lifted a nonexistent eyebrow and said, "If LISP is so good, why don't we pave roads with it?" This was in the era in which *nobody* wrote operating systems in anything but assembler, and Perlis was pointing out that you must choose the tool that is appropriate. Perlis lived to see operating systems written in LISP, for the Lisp Machines from MIT. Given the current and planned enhancements for Java in embedded systems, Device Driver writers might well find themselves writing Device Drivers in Java some years from now. Or maybe not. (If you read Peter's article, you should also read the rebuttal by Steve Lewin-Berlin, of Vireo Software, cited previously.)

Zachary, G. Pascal, *Showstopper!* The Free Press, 1994. ISBN 0-02-935671-7.

The legendary story of the Legendary Dave Cutler and his legendary Operating System.

Chapter

2 *I/O: User-Level Overview*

In Chapter 1, we showed you some of the details of how a Device Driver interacts with the rest of Windows NT and the hardware to perform an I/O operation. But the point of the operating system is to *protect* the poor user from all of this detail by providing a high-level abstraction that can access any device. Before we can show how the pieces fit together, we need to look at how the user-level code sees the I/O system.

You can't ignore the user level; it is an intrinsic part of the design of your driver. In this chapter, we present the design space you will see and discuss some of the implications of your driver on the user level. While the application-level I/O is occasionally discussed in the literature, very little of this discussion suggests what design decisions go into the definition of that application level.

You also need to know what to do to write user-level test programs to test your driver. We show you how.

User-Level I/O Basics

Synchronous versus Asynchronous I/O

I/O can be either *synchronous* or *asynchronous*. In *synchronous* I/O, the program makes a request to send or receive data. The operation does not return until the data transmission either is complete or has been terminated due to an error that must be reported to the caller. Thus the program is blocked until the operation completes. In particular, it cannot respond to the user.

In Windows NT, the *program* does not block on the I/O operation. What blocks is the *thread* that issues the I/O request. This is very important to understand. Most programs simplistically have exactly one thread running, so the perceived effect is that the program itself is blocked, However, this is not true, except when there is only one thread. We show shortly why this makes a difference.

In *asynchronous* I/O, the program makes a request to send or receive data. The return code indicates if the operation was properly *accepted*, but not necessarily that it has *completed*. In particular, when you get control back from an asynchronous input operation, the contents of any input buffer are likely to be whatever they were before you issued the API call. Further, you had better leave the contents of any output buffer alone. This is because there is an excellent chance you could corrupt the output by modifying a buffer that is being actively read from. Consequently, when using asynchronous I/O you must be very careful to make sure that you manage your buffers properly. You can't, for example, put an I/O buffer on the stack, initiate an operation, and then return from the function that defines the buffers, all while waiting for an asynchronous I/O operation to complete. The result will be either corruption of your stack (for input operations) or the writing of random trash to the output (for output operations). Generally, for asynchronous I/O you want your buffers heap-allocated or statically allocated.

This sounds complicated, and in fact it is. You can handle the notification in one of several ways, including the following.

- You can provide an *Event handle* in an associated (OVERLAPPED) data structure. The Event will be *signaled* upon completion of the I/O operation.

- You can provide a *callback function* that is called when the I/O operation is complete. In the callback function, you do whatever is needed to take note of the completion.

- You can have the driver establish a *named Event*. The application then can open a handle on this Event. Note that while the application can *wait* on this Event, no other information can be passed back with this mechanism.

The first two methods, using the Event handle and callback function, are intrinsically supported by the I/O Manager. The latter method requires special work by the Device Driver writer, as it is an unusual method in the world of drivers.

The goal of asynchronous I/O is to introduce more parallelism to your program by allowing I/O operations to fully overlap the computation. However, there are a couple of catches. First, asynchronous I/O is difficult to write, miserable to debug, and hard to maintain. Second—and this is the real surprise—it is actually slower than synchronous I/O, even in the simplest case. This data comes from Johnson Hart's book *Windows System Programming*. He actually made the measurements and has the data to prove it! See the citation in the Further Reading section at the end of this chapter. He recommends using only synchronous I/O, but to perform the I/O from dedicated I/O threads. Doing this gives all of the advantages of asynchronous I/O, but with fewer problems (there *is* parallelism, and that doesn't go away!). Synchronous I/O also is easier to write, debug, maintain, and use, as well as being more efficient. The use of synchronous I/O is not a fully general solution, and there are conditions under which the trade-offs of doing asynchronous I/O mitigate against it (we discuss one of these shortly).

Synchronous I/O also is more flexible. For example, the I/O thread can have its priority set to be somewhat higher, or even much higher, than the priority of the GUI thread. Thus, once the thread becomes feasible because the I/O operation has completed and control has returned, this thread will get control of the processor nearly immediately and can operate on the data. It may send a message to the main GUI thread and thus have to wait for a reply that the message has been processed. Or it can post a message to the main GUI thread, thus allowing the I/O thread to make a new I/O request and wait for it to complete. These are only a couple of sketches of the many I/O strategies available that will give the effect of overlapped I/O without adding undue complexity to the application.

Asynchronous I/O is most useful when you need to handle *many* outstanding requests; typically, this occurs with some sort of server application that has hundreds of clients. Using threads and synchronous I/O within threads to manage hundreds of (possibly transient) client connections would impose greater overheads than the nominal overheads of using asynchronous I/O. In such cases, asynchronous I/O allows a few threads to have many outstanding I/O requests. This is a key example of when using asynchronous I/O is the better choice.

We do not need to talk about asynchronous I/O from the driver's viewpoint. For the asynchronous I/O operations at the API level, the asynchronous nature of the call is totally masked from the Device Driver by the I/O Manager.

For some high-throughput devices, the key to maximizing throughput is to exploit as much concurrency as possible at the hardware level. Instead of handling requests in a FIFO manner, the driver can use any of a variety of techniques for handling the requests in a way that produces the fastest response. Mechanisms such as multiple queues, priority queues, and sorted queues (by some critierion other than priority) are all possible ways to increase the throughput. Typical examples are usually disk-oriented, such as seeking on multiple drives concurrently or scheduling reads and writes to minimize seek time, but other optimizations for other devices may be appropriate.

User-Level APIs

When designing the application level, you need to consider the API functions described below. A given device will use `CreateFile` and `CloseHandle`, and one or more of the remaining functions, depending on what it does and how you choose to specify the interface to your driver. Note that the application level makes no distinction between a handle to a file (on some storage device) and a handle to a device; they are, at the application level, indistinguishable. Consequently, although it is common to talk about the application level "referencing a file", in all cases this is equivalent to the phrase "referencing a file or a device".

- `CreateFile`

    Creates a file or opens an existing file or device when given a path description. The result, if successful, is a *file handle*. The application program uses the file handle to access the file or device for all subsequent operations. For your device, this is the "ticket" the application program presents to the I/O Manager. The I/O Manager, in turn, eventually initiates the appropriate interactions with your driver. We show how that happens in Chapter 3.

- `ReadFile/ReadFileEx`

    Reads information from a file handle. `ReadFile` is the ordinary synchronous Read operation. `ReadFileEx` has parameters to permit the use of an asynchronous I/O callback function if the file was opened in asynchronous mode.

- `WriteFile/WriteFileEx`

    Writes information to a file handle. `WriteFile` is the ordinary synchronous Write operation. `WriteFileEx` has parameters to permit the use of an asynchronous I/O callback function if the file was opened in asynchronous mode.

- `DeviceIOControl`

  Sends a control operation to the file. A *control operation* is a request that the device perform some operation other than simple sequential I/O. Information is sent to the device via an *input* buffer, whose size depends on the nature of the operation. Information is returned from the device via a different, *output*, buffer, whose size also depends on the nature of the operation. The actual I/O buffer sizes must be supplied and must be at least as large as required to support the operation. The operation may be asynchronous if the file was opened in asynchronous mode.

- `CloseHandle`

  Closes the handle. *Closing the handle does not necessarily close the device.* You may have passed this handle on to a child process or duplicated the handle. Only when *all* of the outstanding handles to a device are closed does the device receive a formal notification that it has closed.[1]

These are discussed in further detail in the following subsections.

CreateFile

The `CreateFile` function is used to obtain a handle to a file or, of more interest to us, to a device.

```
HANDLE CreateFile(
    LPCTSTR FileName,                        // pointer to the name of the file
    DWORD DesiredAccess,                     // access (read-write) mode
    DWORD ShareMode,                         // share mode
    LPSECURITY_ATTRIBUTES Attributes OPTIONAL, // pointer to security attributes
    DWORD CreationDistribution,              // how to create
    DWORD FlagsAndAttributes,                // file attributes
    HANDLE TemplateFile OPTIONAL             // handle with attributes to copy
);
```

The *FileName* parameter is a pointer to a string that is the name of a file. This can be a local disk filename in the traditional sense, but unless you are writing a driver that integrates into the disk file system, you typically won't see a name like this. Nor will an application programmer who uses your driver. *FileName* also can be a UNC (Universal Naming Convention) name for a local or remote device. We illustrate the *FileName* options in Table 2.1.

---

[1] This is the Truth From 10,000 Feet. The Real Truth, particularly for a device that can be open concurrently by several applications, is much more complex and includes having to account for pending I/O operations as well as open file handles. We discuss this in much greater detail when we talk about closing a device.

Table 2.1: *FileName formats for* `CreateFile`

FileName **Format**	**Meaning**
`d:\path...\filename`	Device is addressed by a device letter (optional), path (optional), and filename.
`devicename`	Device is on the local machine.
`\\machine\devicename`	The UNC descriptor of a remote device.
`\\.\devicename`	The UNC descriptor of a local device.

The first form in the table shows how to open a device addressed by a drive letter, pathname, and filename. This requires the presence of a *redirector* that maps the drive letter to a UNC descriptor. You will not see this form for most devices for which you write drivers.

The second form you can use, `devicename,` is the "DOS-compatible" device name. Examples of existing devices are `LPT1`, `COM2`, `AUX`, and `NUL`. You can specify your device name to `CreateFile`, and it will be opened.

The third form you also will typically never use. In this form, you specify the UNC name on a remote machine. Again, since most devices you will be writing for will not have redirectors that make them work across the network, you cannot actually use a remote device directly by this method. (You could, for example, open a named pipe on a remote machine and have a server application on that machine that mediates for you, but you can't open the device directly.)

The final form is equivalent to the second, except that it is the UNC representation. Note that there is a real difference between using the third form with your local machine name and using the last form using "dot" as the machine name. The latter form knows explicitly that the device is local.[2] But if you use the machine name, even if it is your own machine, `CreateFile` will try to use a nonexistent redirector.

Where do these names come from? When a Device Driver loads, it registers itself with the system. One of the names it registers is its DOS-compatible device name. If the Device Driver isn't loaded, you can't open it. Normally, Device Drivers load at boot time, except when you're debugging. You can call the Service Control Manager from an application to load and unload a Device Driver. We discuss normal loading in Chapter 3 and Chapter 16 and the use of the Service Control Manager in Chapter 26.

The next parameter of `CreateFile`, *DesiredAccess*, is one of the values from Table 2.2 and indicates the nature of the desired access (read/write mode). To get both read and write access, you can combine the values `GENERIC_READ` and `GENERIC_WRITE` using the bitwise logical OR operation (|). If neither is specified, only operations that query device status are permitted.

---

[2] Note that some devices cannot be opened unless you use the "dot" form of naming. For example, an attempt to open the *device* `"COM10"` will actually attempt to open the *file* `COM10` in the currently connected directory! COM ports above `COM9` *require* that the device name be specified explicitly as a device on the local machine, for example, `"\\\\.\\COM10"` (remember that "\" is an escape character in C strings and must be doubled to get a single "\" in the actual string value). It is important to know this if you happen to have more than nine COM ports on your machine. This is described in Knowledge Base article Q115831. It is not clear if this same requirement applies to other device names, for example, whether or not a printer server with more than nine printers might have to use the same solution if it had to name `LPT10`.

Table 2.2: *Access Codes for* `CreateFile`

Code	Access
0	Allows only operations that query the device status and selected `DeviceIoControl` codes.
`GENERIC_READ`	Allows data to be read from the device with `ReadFile` or `ReadFileEx`.
`GENERIC_WRITE`	Allows data to be written to the device with `WriteFile` or `WriteFileEx`.

The *ShareMode* parameter is normally used by file systems to control simultaneous access to a file by multiple users. This parameter has no meaning for a device which is defined to be exclusive-only and should be set to 0 for such a device. Otherwise, the I/O Manager controls concurrent access by using the information provided in this parameter. As a Device Driver writer, if you wish to support shared access, you may have to do additional work to handle concurrent access while maintaining integrity of the information.

The *SecurityAttributes* parameter is either a pointer to a SECURITY_ATTRIBUTES structure or NULL. If it is NULL, you will not be able to pass the handle to a child process. Security is handled by the I/O Manager, and in any case is outside the scope of this book. Following are the usual simple forms of the parameter:

```
// No ability to pass handle to child process
HANDLE h;
h = CreateFile(_T("MYDEV"), 0, 0, NULL, 0, 0, NULL);

// Able to pass handle to child process
SECURITY_ATTRIBUTES sa = {sizeof(SECURITY_ATTRIBUTES), NULL, TRUE};
HANDLE h;
h = CreateFile(_T("MYDEV"), 0, 0, &sa, 0, 0, NULL);
```

The *CreationDistribution* parameter deals with named files on a file-oriented device and has no meaning when opening a device. For a device it will always be OPEN_EXISTING.

The *FlagsAndAttributes* parameter has little meaning for most Device Drivers. Most of the flag values apply only to file-based systems. The only interesting value unrelated to the actual file system is FILE_FLAG_OVERLAPPED, which indicates that the user wants to use asynchronous I/O.

ReadFile

```
BOOL ReadFile(
    HANDLE hFile,                      // handle of file to read
    LPVOID Buffer,                     // address of buffer that receives data
    DWORD NumberOfBytesToRead,         // number of bytes to read
    LPDWORD NumberOfBytesRead,         // address of number of bytes read
    LPOVERLAPPED Overlapped OPTIONAL   // address of structure for overlapped I/O
);
```

If the device supports simple sequential input, the `ReadFile` operation can be used to read information. This operation takes the handle of a file (device), *hFile*, obtained from `CreateFile`, a pointer to a *Buffer*, a byte count of the number of bytes (maximum) to read, a pointer to a place to put the actual number of bytes read, and, if asynchronous I/O is being used, a pointer to an OVERLAPPED structure. The latter value is usually NULL for synchronous I/O, although it can be used to pass an additional 64 bits of parameter information to the Read operation.

ReadFile will read no more than *NumberOfBytesToRead* bytes, but depending on the device, it may read fewer. For synchronous I/O, it will block until either *NumberOfBytesToRead* have been read, the transaction has completed by encountering an end-of-file condition, or the semantics of the device permit the reading of fewer bytes than requested. For example, a serial I/O port may deliver only as many bytes as have been received since the last ReadFile operation. The actual number of bytes read will be stored in *NumberOfBytesRead*. The operation returns a nonzero value if it is successful and FALSE if it failed. If it returns a nonzero value for synchronous I/O, the number of bytes actually read still could be 0, depending on the semantics of the device. The *NumberOfBytesRead* is not modified when the function returns from an asynchronous I/O operation, and for asynchronous I/O, this parameter can be NULL.

If there is a failure, the specification is that the GetLastError function will return an error code explaining the reason. As a device driver writer, it is your responsibility to return an appropriately informative error code to the I/O Manager. The I/O Manager then translates this error code to an application-level error code for GetLastError (a summary of the kernel-level codes and their corresponding application-level codes appears in Appendix B).

ReadFileEx

```
BOOL ReadFileEx(
    HANDLE hFile,                       // handle of file to read
    LPVOID Buffer,                      // address of buffer that receives data
    DWORD NumberOfBytesToRead,          // number of bytes to read
    LPOVERLAPPED Overlapped,            // address of structure for overlapped I/O
    LPOVERLAPPED_COMPLETION_ROUTINE CompletionRoutine
                                        // address of completion routine
);
```

The ReadFileEx function is used when the device supports simple sequential I/O and you want to get a callback notification on the completion of asynchronous I/O. Note that the *NumberOfBytesRead* parameter of ReadFile is missing. This is because for asynchronous I/O it has no meaning; the number of bytes read is found in the OVERLAPPED structure. The functionality of ReadFileEx is equivalent to that of ReadFile, except that on completion, the *CompletionRoutine* is called. The primary advantage of this function is that you don't need to deal with issues of blocking on the file handle (using WaitForSingleObject(Ex) or WaitForMultipleObjects(Ex)), with the additional complications of dealing with time-outs and other complexities. Typically, the completion routine will use PostMessage to post the completion to another thread. This has little advantage over using a separate thread and synchronous I/O.

These callbacks can occur only when the thread is in an *alertable wait state*, that is, waiting on one of the functions WaitForSingleObjectEx, WaitForMultipleObjectsEx, or SleepEx. If you are familiar with other operating systems such as UNIX or VMS, be aware that the callback is *not* equivalent to a UNIX signal or a VMS AST (Asynchronous System Trap), which can cause a transfer to the callback routine no matter what the application is doing.

WriteFile

```
BOOL WriteFile(
    HANDLE hFile,                    // handle to file to write to
    LPCVOID Buffer,                  // pointer to data to write to file
    DWORD NumberOfBytesToWrite,      // number of bytes to write
    LPDWORD NumberOfBytesWritten,    // pointer to number of bytes written
    LPOVERLAPPED Overlapped OPTIONAL // pointer to structure for overlapped I/O
    );
```

If the device supports simple sequential output, the WriteFile operation can be used to write information. It takes the handle of a file (device), *hFile*, obtained from CreateFile, a pointer to a *Buffer*, a byte count of the number of bytes to write, a pointer to the place to put the actual number of bytes written, and, if asynchronous I/O is being used, a pointer to an OVERLAPPED structure. The latter value is usually NULL for synchronous I/O, although it can be used to pass an additional 64 bits of parameter information to the Write operation.

For synchronous I/O, WriteFile will block until the output operation has completed or reached a failure point. The actual number of bytes written is stored in *NumberOfBytesWritten* and upon completion should be the same value as *NumberOfBytesToWrite*. The operation returns a nonzero value if it is successful and FALSE if it fails. *NumberOfBytesWritten* is not modified when the function returns from an asynchronous I/O operation, and for asynchronous I/O, it can be NULL.

If there is a failure, the specification is that the GetLastError function should return an error code explaining the reason. As a device driver writer, it is your responsibility to return an appropriately informative error code to the I/O Manager. The I/O Manager then translates this error code to an application-level error code for GetLastError (a summary of the kernel-level codes and their corresponding application-level codes appears in Appendix B).

WriteFileEx

```
BOOL WriteFileEx(
    HANDLE hFile,                    // handle to file to write to
    LPCVOID Buffer,                  // pointer to data to write to file
    DWORD NumberOfBytesToWrite,      // number of bytes to write
    LPOVERLAPPED Overlapped,         // pointer to structure for overlapped I/O
    LPOVERLAPPED_COMPLETION_ROUTINE CompletionRoutine
                                     // address of completion routine
    );
```

The WriteFileEx function is used when the device supports simple sequential I/O, and you want to get a callback notification on the completion of asynchronous I/O. Note that the *NumberOfBytesWritten* parameter of WriteFile is missing. This is because for asynchronous I/O, it has no meaning; the number of bytes written is found in the OVERLAPPED structure. The functionality of WriteFileEx is equivalent to that of WriteFile, except that on completion the *CompletionRoutine* is called. The primary advantage of this function is that you don't need to deal with issues of blocking on the file handle (using WaitForSingleObject(Ex) or WaitForMultipleObjects(Ex)), with the additional complications of dealing with time-outs and other complexities. Typically, the completion routine will use PostMessage to post the completion to another thread. This has little advantage over using a separate thread and synchronous I/O.

These callbacks can occur only when the thread is in an *alertable wait state*, that is, waiting on one of the functions `WaitForSingleObjectEx`, `WaitForMultipleObjectsEx`, or `SleepEx`. If you are familiar with other operating systems such as UNIX or VMS, be aware that the callback is *not* equivalent to a UNIX `signal` or a VMS AST (Asynchronous System Trap), which can cause a transfer to the callback routine no matter what the application is doing.

DeviceIoControl

```
BOOL DeviceIoControl(
    HANDLE hDevice,             // handle to device of interest
    DWORD IoControlCode,        // control code of operation to perform
    LPVOID InBuffer,            // pointer to buffer to supply input data
    DWORD InBufferSize,         // size of input buffer
    LPVOID OutBuffer,           // pointer to buffer to receive output data
    DWORD OutBufferSize,        // size of output buffer
    LPDWORD BytesReturned,      // pointer to variable to receive output byte count
    LPOVERLAPPED Overlapped OPTIONAL
                                // pointer to overlapped structure for asynch I/O
);
```

For many of the devices you will write drivers for, the `DeviceIoControl` function is where all of the action is. In fact, you will often discover that I/O is actually done via `DeviceIoControl` instead of `ReadFile(Ex)` or `WriteFile(Ex)`. This is because, for many specialized devices, you must pass in some parameter to describe the nature or properties of the I/O operation. There is only one parameter you can set for file-based I/O, and that is the file pointer position (set via the `SetFilePointer` API function). Specialized devices often have many parameters to set. Since `SetFilePointer` applies only to file systems, you can't even do "random" I/O on a device of your own unless you use `DeviceIoControl`.

The *hDevice* parameter is the handle for a device, obtained from `CreateFile`.

The *IoControlCode* parameter is created by using the CTL_CODE macro defined in `winioctl.h` (for applications) and `ntddk.h` (for drivers). CTL_CODE is defined as follows:

```
#define CTL_CODE( DeviceType, Function, Method, Access ) ( \
    ((DeviceType) << 16) | ((Access) << 14) | ((Function) << 2) | (Method)  )
```

The resulting structure is shown in Figure 2.1. The *DeviceType* parameter is a 16-bit value that identifies the device. There are a number of predefined codes representing predefined devices such as modems, keyboards, scanners, and floppy disks. As of the most recent Windows 4.0-compatible header file we have, just over 40 of these codes are defined. These are all in the range 0..32767. The values 32768..65535 are reserved for use by "the customer", specifically, you, the Device Driver writer. There is no documented mechanism we have seen for the assignment of these values, but in some sense, it doesn't matter. For example, if you choose

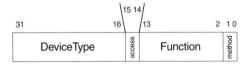

Figure 2.1: CTL_CODE *layout.*

DeviceType 40,000 for your device, and someone else's driver on your machine *also* uses 40,000 as a *DeviceType*, it is unlikely that someone opening your device will erroneously send you a control code (commonly called an IOCTL) destined for the other device. There is nothing that prevents someone's sending an IOCTL for *DeviceType* 40,000, Function 1 to your device just because another open file also supports *DeviceType* 40,000 *Function* 1. Since the IOCTLs are sent to distinct handles, they cannot confuse the I/O Manager (it doesn't look at the *DeviceType* or *Function* fields anyway, only the *Method* and *Access* fields).

Microsoft defines the *Function* codes that the driver, if it implements a standard device, must support. The Microsoft-defined *Function* codes provide the functionality needed by the operating system and standard utility programs. Often, additional functions are provided in drivers for enhanced devices to support enhanced functions in new hardware. The new I/O operations are then used by utility programs provided with the device.

For example, the *Function* codes that Microsoft defines for disk devices allow a program to query the disk geometry, get and set disk partition information, get disk performance statistics, and dozens of other disk-related functions. This book is not about writing file systems (that's another topic as large as or larger than that of this book; see, for example, *Windows NT File System Internals*, cited in Further Reading), so most of the predefined control functions have very little application to most Device Driver writers. Microsoft reserves *Function* codes in the range 0..2047 for their own purposes, so your *Function* codes must be in the range 2048..4095. You should use a code in the lower range only if your device actually supports that function in a fashion identical to that intended by Microsoft.

The *Method* code indicates the way in which the buffers should be handled. It can be one of the codes listed in Table 2.3. Generally, you will want to use METHOD_BUFFERED for small data transfers, and one of the METHOD_..._DIRECT methods for very large blocks of data. You, the Device Driver writer, get to specify which methods your driver will accept for each function

Table 2.3: *Method Codes for* CTL_CODE

Method Code		Meaning
METHOD_BUFFERED	0	The contents of the user's input buffer are copied to a kernel buffer managed by the I/O system. The driver works on this copy of the user's input buffer. Output is generated to the same kernel buffer, and the contents of the kernel buffer are copied back to the user's output buffer when the operation is completed.
METHOD_IN_DIRECT	1	The contents of the user's input buffer are copied to a kernel buffer managed by the I/O system. The driver is passed the information required to directly access the user's output buffer from kernel space. The driver writes its results directly to the mapped output buffer.
METHOD_OUT_DIRECT	2	The contents of the user's input buffer are copied to a kernel buffer managed by the I/O system. The driver is passed the information required to directly access the user's output buffer from kernel space. The driver reads its data directly from the mapped "output" buffer. The user's "output" buffer is write-protected.
METHOD_NEITHER	3	The decision is made on the fly by the device driver as to how to access the user's input and output buffer.

Table 2.4: *Access Codes for* CTL_CODE

Access Code		Meaning
FILE_ANY_ACCESS	0	Read or write access is desired.
FILE_READ_ACCESS	1	Read access is desired.
FILE_WRITE_ACCESS	2	Write access is desired.

code. While it is *possible* to support more than one method for a specific function code, it is uncommon. Normally, your driver decodes the entire 32-bit IOCTL code. We talk more about these methods in Chapter 10 when we discuss how user I/O buffers are handled. We also discuss there why METHOD_NEITHER will make your life really unpleasant if you need to use it.

The *Access* code indicates the type of access: read or write. It can be one of the values from Table 2.4. Ideally, a request for access should correspond to the parameter values GENERIC_READ and GENERIC_WRITE supplied with the CreateFile call. If the device is opened with write access, then any CTL_CODE that specifies write access should be permitted (provided its other values are correct, of course). Likewise, any device opened with read access should permit any CTL_CODE that specifies read access. If both are required for a single operation, you can specify either FILE_ANY_ACCESS or FILE_READ_ACCESS | FILE_WRITE_ACCESS (although they have different values, they ultimately have the same effect).

Almost everything interesting you want to do to your device is done by the DeviceIoControl function. While this means that the interface to your device is going to be specific to your device (including, in most cases, how data is read and written), most devices (other than disk drives) simply have no standards for the expected DeviceIoControl functions. What is done with DeviceIoControl functions include the following:

- Setting the initial status of the device
- Starting and stopping devices for which the notion of "starting" and "stopping" makes sense (or you can think of this as "enabling" or "disabling" device functions that may be visible to the user or to whatever external electronics the device is connected)
- Mapping parts of the device memory into the user's address space
- Specifying large ranges of user-space addresses to be used by the device, that is, in effect mapping the user address space into the Device Driver's address space
- Querying the status of the device
- Causing the device to eject media
- Setting the status of the device while it is in operation

CloseHandle

```
BOOL CloseHandle(HANDLE hObject );   // handle to object to close
```

CloseHandle is a generic function that closes all kinds of handles; file (device) handles are only one case. This releases the handle that is passed in as the parameter. The handle closed may not be the only existing instance of a handle to its object. For example, a child process might issue a CloseHandle while the parent still has an active copy of the handle, or, more typically, a parent process may close its copy of the handle after successfully launching a child process. You cannot close the same handle twice.[3] You can, however, create another handle to the same object either implicitly via process creation of a child process or via the `DuplicateHandle` function.

Closing a handle cleans up any data structures related to the handle itself. An internal structure called the *File Object* is referenced by that handle, and closing the handle decrements the File Object's handle count and reference count by 1. When the reference count goes to 0, the object represented by the handle will be destroyed. This is when you, as a Device Driver writer, receive the notification that the device is finally closed.

Other I/O Operations

Less commonly used functions are `CancelIo`, `SetErrorMode`, and `SetFilePointer`.

CancelIO

```
BOOL CancelIo(HANDLE hFile);
```

The `CancelIo` function is called if there is potentially incomplete asynchronous I/O pending. It is up to the Device Driver to determine how in-process I/O operations (for example, already-initiated DMA transfers) are to be cancelled. In some cases, this might be device-dependent, so if you need to support asynchronous I/O, you'll have to figure out how your driver will do this. In addition, operations that would destroy the File Object associated with the device handle will call the cancellation entry point of your Device Driver. If the operation succeeds, it should return `TRUE`, and if it fails, it should return `FALSE`. In the latter case, `GetLastError` is supposed to return an explanation code of why it failed. As a device driver writer, it is your responsibility to return an appropriately informative error code to the I/O Manager. The I/O Manager then translates this error code to an application-level error code for `GetLastError` (a summary of the kernel-level codes and their corresponding application-level codes appears in Appendix B).

SetErrorMode

The `SetErrorMode` function sets how a Device Driver should respond to what are called *critical errors*. The value passed in is a set of bit flags, one or more from Table 2.5. These bit flags establish the proper response to certain kinds of errors. The return value is the previous setting of the error mode. This mechanism applies only to File System drivers; we can find no documentation on how other types of drivers might use it.

```
UINT SetErrorMode(UINT Mode); // set of bit flags that specify
                              // error-handling properties
```

Critical errors usually are errors that are serious and may require action by the user to correct. They include a missing floppy disk, a missing CD-ROM, or similar conditions. In some cases, the condition to be reported simply is an "unrecoverable" error condition, such as a corrupted disk structure. These latter types of critical errors are normally reported via a message

---

[3] Although the documentation states that closing the same handle twice raises an exception, it doesn't tell what exception is raised. A bit of experimentation reveals that the exception code is `0xC0000008`, `STATUS_INVALID_HANDLE`.

Table 2.5: `SetErrorMode` *Options*

Bit Flag	Meaning
SEM_FAILCRITICALERRORS	If this flag is set, the system does not pop up a message box for critical errors. Instead, it simply returns the error to the caller.
SEM_NOALIGNMENTFAULTEXCEPT	This flag applies only to RISC-based processors, such as the Digital Alpha. It is a request to the Device Driver to fix any errors caused by "misaligned" data references. These are references that are not on the proper byte-alignment boundary.
SEM_NOGPFAULTERRORBOX	This flag is used only by debuggers.
SEM_NOOPENFILEERRORBOX	If this flag is set, the system will not pop up a file open box if the file cannot be found. It has little application to most Device Drivers.

box, sometimes with options like Yes/No/Cancel or OK/Retry/Cancel and sometimes with simply an OK response (indicating there are no additional actions that the user may or must take).

For RISC machines, you can get an *alignment exception* if the user passes in to you an address that is not on the proper word or double-word boundary. You may choose to reflect this exception back to the user, or you may go through some additional work to fix the exception. The SEM_NOALIGNMENTFAULTEXCEPTION flag selects this option.

SetFilePointer

```
DWORD SetFilePointer(  ...  );
```

The SetFilePointer function, which may appear to have utility, is strictly a file-system function. For most devices, the only way to get the functionality of this operation is to use the DeviceIoControl function.

Further Reading

Hart, Johnson M., *Win32 System Programming*, Addison Wesley Longman, 1997. ISBN 0-201-63465-1.
Nagar, Rajeev, *Windows NT File System Internals*, O'Reilly & Associates, 1997. ISBN 1-56592-249-2.

3 *Planning a Device Driver*

This chapter gives a summary and an overview of the entire driver development process. Later chapters plunge into great depth on many of these topics, such as interrupt management, device initialization, and memory management.

Planning the User-Level Interface

Often when you start, you have, at best, an *instance* of the device. You also have an instance of what purports to be complete documentation about the device. It probably isn't complete, as you will discover when you actually try to get the driver running, but it is usually a good first approximation of what is going on. It is important to note, however, that the *application interface* to the device might well be at a much higher level than the device primitives themselves. Thus, after determining the capabilities of the device, you need to design the API to it.

For some devices, the design of the interface is simple. If the device is known to NT, you must implement the standard interface for the device type. For example, every mouse must implement the standard mouse interface, and every disk driver must implement the disk driver interface. The DDK (Device Driver Kit) documentation defines the standard operations for each of the standard devices. In practice, you will use the documentation with the sample sources in the DDK.

With standard devices, you may add functionality unknown to the other similar devices. You would do this by implementing additional Device Control operations that are unique to your device. These Device Control operations may then be accessed by your custom application programs. These operations must not impair the operation of the device with other applications that use the standard operations.

If the device is a specialized, unique device that will be accessed by custom application programs, it is more complex. There might not be a one-to-one mapping between the functions the device performs and the requests as seen by the application. Perhaps one of the most common examples of this is a file system in which a `CreateFile` call may generate many internal requests to support certain activities. An example activity is finding out the disk address of the device's master file directory and then using that information to perform one or more operations to read from the directory, followed by operations that operate on subdirectories, and finally the operation that creates the actual file. Operations that write to the file may generate several similar internal requests, including those that update the file system's allocation information.

The characteristics of the Device Driver interface will be heavily influenced by the performance requirements of the device/driver combination. With low speed/low throughput devices, there is no performance pressure on the choice between a high-level (composite operation) driver and a low-level (map each hardware function) driver. No matter which you choose, the driver will use a small fraction of the available CPU bandwidth. With a high speed/high throughput device, you likely will be inclined to pick a higher-level interface so as to reduce the number of transitions into Kernel mode. To illustrate these trade-offs, we will examine three representative scenarios for devices.

Device Scenario 1

As an example, consider two devices with a similar interface but different data rates. The first device is monitoring a hot water heater and takes one sample per second. The second is a high-performance audio sampler running at 44.1K samples per second (standard CD sampling rate). Each returns data measured from an external device. To support these devices under NT, you need to design the driver-to-application interface. You are concerned with the ability of the Device Driver to return data to the application reliably, in a timely manner, and with an acceptable level of driver and operating system overhead. You must provide the application program sufficient flexibility in the interface so that the planned application programs can be written. You should provide sufficient generality and flexibility in the interface to allow future applications (or version 2) to be written without driver changes.

The first device is easy to deal with. You could simply return individual samples in response to the application by doing a `ReadFile` operation with a buffer length sufficient to hold one sample (or use a `DeviceIoControl` operation in a similar fashion). The application can generate one request at a time as needed. A slight error in the timing, or even a missed sample, will have no effect on the nature of the application or its reliability (the time to change the temperature of a tank of water being significant). It would make no significant difference in the ability to deliver data to the application if the I/O operation read 1, 2, 5, or 50 samples per operation. There would be no measurable difference if the data was buffered in the driver and copied by the I/O Manager to the applications program's buffer (an overhead of one memory read and one write per second) or written directly to the application program's buffer.

The second device is quite different. A missed sample would generate an unacceptable error; several missed samples would create an audible defect. A buffer of data must be passed because there is no practical way to pass each sample individually (or 2 or 5 or 500 samples). Since data must be handled continuously, you need multiple buffers or multiple I/O operations pending to allow the continuous monitoring of the audio data. Further, the data must be written directly to the application program's buffer. A Copy operation would consume enough time to be a potential problem (44.1K 16-bit reads per second and 44.1K 16-bit writes per second). For this device to meet the performance requirements, you must use a far larger buffer (16K, 32K, or possibly 1M samples). The size would depend in part on the application program. However, the smaller the buffer, the greater the number of transitions required between User mode and Kernel mode, and therefore the greater the overhead.

These two devices suggest entirely different strategies. Waiting to fill a buffer with 44.1K samples from the hot water heater monitor produces one sample per second and delivers one buffer per month—clearly not good for anyone taking a shower.

Device Scenario 2

Consider another scenario. You have a device that, for reliability, sends and receives check summed packets of information to and from the host. Each packet requires that a reply be sent for successful or unsuccessful receipt. This device sends one packet per second. Your design could be quite reasonable if it supported operations such as *read packet* and *send packet* and had the application perform the checksum and send the reply. Now consider the case in which the data rate is 1,000 packets per second. What worked well at one packet per second might be a total disaster at 1,000 packets per second. Either packets would get lost due to overruns or the device might time out because if it is sending data at that rate, it might have a very short timeout on the reply wait. In any case, the application likely could not handle a sustained rate of 1,000 packets per second with a simple read-packet operation. For this latter case, you would probably have your DPC (Deferred Procedure Call) compute the checksum and send the reply packet; the application would not have to worry about checksumming at all. It would probably have operations such as *get packets*, whereby an integral number of packets was returned in the input buffer, rather than one at a time. You might even want to couple it to a timeout so that it returns either when the buffer is filled with packets or if some "long" time interval (perhaps 500 ms) passes without a packet's having been received.[1]

Device Scenario 3

Consider yet another scenario. This one is particularly important for multimedia. Events come in that must be time-stamped so that various audio, video, and/or MIDI data streams are kept in synchronization and can be played back. You cannot possibly hope to get the precision of timing required if you simply send the information to the application; the scheduling features of NT means there could *typically* be a difference of tens to hundreds of milliseconds between the timestamps and the actual time of the output. In music, an error of rhythm of 30 ms is detectable by an untrained listener. A performer (particularly a percussionist) can easily detect a 10 ms error in rhythm, while an untrained person can detect a 2-ms skew in nominally concurrent percussive sounds. Your driver, however, could timestamp these in the ISR (Interrupt Service routine), with errors down in the tens to hundreds of microseconds level, well below the threshold of perception. So, where you do work, how much you do, and the interface you present to the application are very problem-domain-dependent. There is no one-driver-fits-all model of the "right" NT driver.[2]

---

[1] A really high-speed interface (an ATM adapter) must compute checksums in hardware. Computing checksums could consume a large fraction of the CPU and memory bandwidth.

[2] Some early reviewers said, in effect, "User-level design is a nonissue. Just give access to the core functionality of the hardware, and the application can put the pieces together any way it wants." But the fundamental question is often not "can it put the pieces together" but "can it put the pieces together in such a way that makes them work to effectively solve the problem?" And that's why you have to worry about the user level.

Even More Design Decisions

Your design choices affect what the application can do. Giving direct access to the hardware by designing a driver that has nothing but low-level operations is useless if the application cannot, due to its own limitations or the limitations NT imposes, provide enough data—and at the right time—or read data fast enough or do time correlation. Remember that there must be enough time to process device I/O not only in isolation but in the application environment. Your driver will run with one or more user applications using the driver, with other drivers for the system hardware and other drivers in the client environment, and with other applications' hardware.

A broad range of system speeds runs under Windows NT, from a 60MHz Pentium to a 450MHz Pentium II. Which will run your driver? Can you require a minimum processor speed?

Systems may be used as a dedicated device controller or be heavily used for other tasks. You may need a different design if your driver will operate while the user is doing software MPEG playback.[3] What restrictions are acceptable on applications that a user may run concurrent with your driver? If you are producing a driver for a new mouse or disk drive, no restrictions are acceptable. How much memory does the target system have, and how much can your driver consume?

Windows NT: Not a Real-Time System

The term *real-time* has many meanings, most of them meaningless marketing hype. In Windows NT, real-time is a class of scheduler priorities. This should not be confused with classifying NT as a real-time system.

There are many different criteria for the designation real-time. Generally, real-time is divided into *hard* real-time and *soft* real-time.[4] Hard real-time has bounded latency for driver response to interrupts and for task response to interrupts. No lateness beyond well-defined limits is considered tolerable. For these goals to be achieved, bounds on the execution time for all elevated-IRQL code must exist so that the processing of the real-time interrupt can occur and also so that the task triggered by the interrupt may start execution within the defined task latency time. Soft real-time presents a far easier constraint. Some lateness is tolerable as long as the system can keep up *on average* with the load. (Note that the definition of "some" is very application-dependent. What programmer A means by "some" and programmer B means by "some" may vary by a factor of a thousand, yet each thinks that he/she is allowing only "some" lateness. And for some systems, 100 ms is "some" time, but in others, 1 ms is more than "some" time.) In soft real-time, a degraded performance level is an acceptable consequence of missing a timing window. Often, the degradation is manifested by the entire operation's having to be retried.

We can illustrate the difference between hard and soft real-time with an example. If a robot arm is putting parts on an assembly moving down an assembly line, there can be two kinds of lines. One is the assembly line on which every assembly is constantly moving at constant speed down the line. The other is the line on which each assembly pauses at each work station for work, resuming motion after the operation is completed. The robot working on the first line is an example of a hard real-time problem. If the arm is a little early or a little late, the arm will punch

---

[3] In this case, hardware may need to provide a higher-level interface.

[4] Ignoring the use of the term *real-time* as marketing hype.

a new (unintended) hole in the assembly or the assembly line itself. The second line could pose a soft real-time problem. In this case, the part can wait a little while at the station for the arm as long as the arm can keep up with the *average* arrival rate of assemblies and not force a backup into the previous station. If there is a bit of buffering between the stations, slight errors can be accommodated. Serious degradation would occur if the entire line preceding a given station came to a stop, but if this stop was brief and happened infrequently, this could be acceptable degradation.

Windows NT meets the requirements of a soft real-time system. However, it does not, by itself, meet the requirements for a hard real-time system, although with the addition of third-party hardware or software, it can. Hard real-time performance levels on NT can be achieved via a number of alternatives:

- A programmable I/O adapter
- A system that places a Win32 interface over a true real-time OS
- A system that replaces the Windows NT HAL with a real-time scheduler or OS

The programmable I/O adapter is programmed with the hard real-time code buffering the data for the remaining code running under Windows NT (driver and application). This technique removes the real-time load entirely from the NT platform. Putting a Win32 interface on top of a real-time OS is the technique used by QNX and VxWorks. This technique provides an NT-like environment and allows some application-level programs to execute, but not NT Device Drivers. Only a limited number of devices are supported (for example, display adapters), and application compatibility is a problem. Replacing the HAL is the technique used by Imagination Systems, Radisys, and Venturcom. This technique allows all NT programs and most Device Drivers to operate. The real-time OS will pass interrupts to NT only after the real-time interrupts and tasks have completed their necessary processing.

Understanding the Application(s)

A significant consideration in designing a Device Driver is how the application needs to access the device. For example, an application might *always* perform operation 1, then wait a short period of time, and then perform operation 2. Or it might perform operation 1 to read some information and, based on that information, always then either perform operation 2 or declare an error condition. When patterns like this exist, it is best to take advantage of them. In particular, note that two I/O operations require two user-to-kernel ring transitions, whereas one composite operation from the application requires only a single user-to-kernel ring transition. In the latter case, not only is the application code simplified, but the whole system is more efficient.

So part of designing a driver is determining the atomic operations that the application should see, the operations that are independent of the actual implementation of the device. By choosing these carefully, you can also make the application program be independent of the underlying device, thereby allowing for future enhancements. Perhaps the most extreme case of this is the Graphics Device Interface (GDI) component, which provides high-level operations such as draw line, draw circle, and fill polygon. Depending on how much you've spent for your graphics card, these might all be implemented by the GDI itself drawing one pixel at a time or by the device, that is, the display card, performing these operations. So you should plan for future, smarter devices by specifying what the *application* wants to see, not necessarily what the device actually provides.[5]

The design of this part of the interface is one of the most crucial steps in designing the Device Driver. This step requires a great deal of care. If you get this part wrong, the whole rest of your driver effort will be a waste. This is because although you are creating a driver that works and meets a specification, the specification may be completely useless. A problem with this design is that it may well require much more information than is contained in the hardware manual. One way to think about this is that the hardware manual is the *syntax*, but the way the application needs to use the hardware is the *semantics*. This latter information can be obtained only from the programmers who want to program the application. If you don't talk to them, you may, at best, produce a Device Driver whose semantics are almost but not quite completely unsuited for the application.

The need to maximize throughput can profoundly influence the design of a driver. It not only changes the buffering strategy; it might also mean that you must supply both high-level composite operations to minimize the user-to-kernel-to-user transitions and low-level operations closely modeled on the hardware functionality to handle the odd cases or other applications. You also might need to provide for I/O that goes directly to user space instead of using buffered Kernel modes that involve additional copying. You further might need to provide for massive kernel buffers that the application can map into its address space or even to map device memory directly into the application space so that the application can work directly on the device memory, thereby minimizing the copying as much as possible.

Understanding the Hardware

The hardware (or firmware) designer may have had in mind a particular way in which the device should be used, and the design is optimized to support one or a small number of paradigms of use. If you are not aware of these intentions, you may be writing a driver that works in an opposed paradigm, one that will make your life miserable as you try to fit it to the device.

Unfortunately, unless you are working for the company that produces the device, you probably have no chance whatsoever of actually talking to the designer(s) of the hardware and firmware. Worse still, your only opportunity to speak with them may be *after* the device is fully committed to silicon and is about to go into production. All too many hardware designers do not have the foggiest notion of the reality of operating system programming and have built devices that are actually completely unsupportable in any modern operating system. If at all possible, you should make sure that Device Driver writers (such as yourself) are involved in the hardware design at its earliest stages, before irrevocable decisions are made that make the device unusable.

There are some considerations that make devices difficult or impossible to use in NT.

- Devices that have timing sensitivities of the form "write the register and then wait at least *n* bus cycles before writing this other register so that the device has time to respond to the first write"

---

[5] It is worth noting that the original NT GDI was implemented as a User-mode driver. This required *four* context transitions: user-to-kernel, kernel-to-user (getting the request to the GDI), user-to-kernel, and kernel-to-user (returning the result to the application). This had serious performance problems. GDI is now part of the NT kernel.

As modern architectures evolve, it is harder and harder to control such fine timings. Timings that could be accomplished on a 386 by inserting a NOP instruction between the two writes simply won't work on a 200MHz Pentium. Some RISC architectures give the programmer no control over the timing of when values are written to registers on the device; these architectures schedule Write operations independent of the program flow. Many devices, such as PCI devices (which we discuss in Chapter 21), are interchangeable between classic Intel and RISC architectures, so it is hard to write a driver that can handle all of these odd timing requirements while still being platform-independent at the source level (other than by introducing far longer delays than may be necessary between the operations, which sometimes presents other problems).

- Devices that have fine timings or seriously short timing windows

    The clock resolution under NT is nominally 10 ms; this makes it almost impossible to perform any critical operations less than 10 ms apart. But realistically, because of the nature of NT, higher-priority interrupts coming in can introduce serious jitter into your Events, thereby making it very, very difficult to guarantee that you can meet a window smaller than 100 ms. This means that you must have sufficient buffering to compensate for this, particularly if you are doing something that requires real-time response.

- Devices that require massive DMA (Direct Memory Access) buffers

    It seems not uncommon today for certain kinds of real-time, high-speed, or high-volume devices such as analog-digital convertors, ATM networks, or full-motion video to require 100MB, 200MB, or even larger DMA buffers. NT is particularly intractable in this regard. It is even worse if the DMA buffers must be in contiguous physical memory (this is discussed in more detail in Chapter 17).

- Devices that do not support the full range of functionality normally specified for the bus to which they are connected

    Particularly intractable are PCI devices that do not allow interrupt or register window reassignment, USB devices that do not support full USB functionality (the most common violation is probably power management), SCSI devices that do not properly support Logical Unit Numbers (LUNs), and the like. Another example is a major manufacturer who produced a PCI device that does not meet the PCI specifications for configuration transactions (because the designer misinterpreted the specification). This confuses the standard HAL.

- Architectures that do not support the full range of functionality specified for the bus

    This is independent of the device and affects all devices that are plugged into it. We have some experience with a PCI bus that does not support bus-mastering PCI devices. It is basically impossible to write drivers that will work correctly if the manufacturer does not meet the specification, particularly if it is only one manufacturer on one model of motherboard or bus.

If you encounter a device (or system) with any of these features, you can be assured that you are in for a long, difficult, expensive, and perhaps even fruitless development effort.

Sometimes we wonder about the types of rewards that have been given to the designers of some of these boards. At times, we feel that 10 to 20 with no hope of parole is the *least* that should be given. However, if you run across one of these boards and you are an independent contractor, you may find that your sanity and your reputation will best be preserved by walking away from a bad job. At least make sure the client *knows* that their problem is difficult so that when you run late and over budget, they can't say that they weren't warned.

How Does It Work, Really?

In most cases, you won't have the option of talking to the designers of the device. So you will be reduced to using experimentation to deduce the behavior. You can often tell a lot just by writing code that attempts to do something simple and discovering that it really does or does not do what the operating manual suggests. In extreme cases, you may be reduced to learning how to use a logic analyzer and hooking probes on the bus, or on the bus and the output of the device, to attempt to deduce what is really happening. This is really not what should be required, but in some cases, the operating manual is somewhere between science fiction and fantasy (not always intentionally).

In addition, "new silicon" often suffers from unsuspected bugs and interactions. For example, you may read in your device's documentation that setting values in Register A and Register B sets up the configuration for doing something when the data is written to Register C. This may even lead you to suspect that A and B can be set up in any order. In fact, *and this often cannot be deduced from reading the documentation*, Register A *must* be set up before Register B is set up, or there will be unexpected side effects on the output. (The classic historical case concerned setting up the registers for the old monochrome display cards. Done in the wrong order, it would cause a critical transistor to burn out from overload, physically destroying the monitor.) In other cases, the designer either simply never considered the issue of how the registers were set up or assumed that "everyone knows" the correct order. And then unexpected things would happen. You may well have to experiment to determine if such dependencies exist.

The need to introduce delay comes up all too often. You will have to experiment to determine if introducing a known delay between two events makes them work as specified. This is even more complex when there is an upper bound on the acceptable delay.

More serious problems exist for some devices in which even the act of *reading* a register can have side effects. For example, reading the status register resets the status and clears the interrupt, but a second read of that register will return something quite different. While we can all hope that no more devices of these properties will ever again be designed, hardware engineers who are taught to "save every gate" will probably continue to create such bogus designs based on the assumptions that "it is easy to get around these limitations in software".

Designing the Driver

Driver design involves many different decisions. There is no "one model fits all" solution. You have to choose not only the functions you will present to the application writer, but the data formats you will present. Having chosen the functions the application writer can use, you can choose how they will be implemented, such as whether you will let the I/O Manager copy data between the kernel and application, or you will directly access the application data. The following sections discuss some of these design issues. In later chapters, we will present all the details of how you implement particular decisions.

Choosing among `ReadFile, WriteFile, DeviceIoControl,` *and* `CancelIo`

Having determined what the atomic operations should be, you next have to map them to operations that the driver itself can support at the application interface. These operations are `ReadFile, WriteFile,` and `DeviceIoControl`. Only one kind of read (`ReadFile(Ex)`) and one kind of write (`WriteFile(Ex)`) is available, but any number of `DeviceIoControl` operations are possible.

If possible, use the `ReadFile(Ex)` and `WriteFile(Ex)` functions. They work well for ordinary sequential I/O. However, for most custom devices you need to pass in additional parameters that control the operations of reading and writing. Even something as simple as a "seek" must be done as a `DeviceIoControl` operation because the actual Seek operation is a file system operation, not a device operation. The `DeviceIoControl` operation has the ability to pass data into the driver and receive data from the driver in a single operation. Furthermore, that data can be arbitrarily structured, whereas operations such as `ReadFile` and `WriteFile` are byte-stream oriented. For example, an operation that writes a waveform to an audio device may also specify volume, sampling rate, bandpass filters, and anything else as appropriate in a single `DeviceIoControl` operation. An operation that reads a waveform from an audio input stream may specify, as output data, the sampling rate, dynamic range clipping, bandpass filters, and so on, and receive as input data the appropriately processed input waveform data.

A driver may have a cancel entry point. You should implement the Cancel operation because the kernel may wish to cancel any pending I/O operations, for example, at application thread exit, at shutdown time, or when the last handle to the device is closed. However, it is also legitimate for the application to cancel an I/O request. The request could have been started in a helper thread and should be cancelled due to timeout, change of task, or application shutdown. Note that the Cancel operation is implicitly synchronous; that is, it will not return until the I/O operation is successfully cancelled. This also requires that a device have a way of cleanly cancelling a lengthy I/O operation that is already in progress or performing the proper response when an I/O operation in progress finally finishes.

Address Mapping

When a `ReadFile, WriteFile,` or `DeviceIoControl` operation is first passed to the I/O system, it is passed in the address context and thread of the calling process. Thus the addresses passed in are directly accessible at this level of the driver. However, the most typical case is that these operations initiate some device activity that will later generate an interrupt. The interrupt takes place in the thread of some process—almost certainly not the one that initiated the operation (often because it has blocked waiting for the operation to complete). In this case, the addresses passed in are no longer accessible in the thread in which the interrupt or the DPC (which we discuss shortly) are executed. The I/O Manager has two ways to deal with this. If the device does *Buffered I/O*, the I/O Manager allocates an internal buffer. For output, it copies the user data to this internal buffer; for input, it copies the contents of this buffer back to the application on completion. If the device does *Direct I/O*, the I/O Manager creates some process-independent memory references, called the Memory Descriptor Lists, or MDLs (pronounced "muddles"). MDLs are the basis of how a Device Driver gets hold of user memory and makes it available in contexts other than the initiating thread. They are passed as part of the I/O request packet, or IRP (pronounced "urp"), which is the basis of all transactions within the I/O system.

We discuss IRPs in greater detail in Chapter 5. MDLs allow some thread that never heard of the initiating process to correctly access the memory of the initiating process and read or write the referenced areas. This saves the extra buffer copy, but at the cost of increased complexity of the driver.

However, it is often convenient at the application level to provide for *lists* of control blocks or control blocks that themselves contain *pointers* to buffers. In these cases, the driver must create MDLs that represent these additional addresses and map them into the address space as needed. So, for example, the `DeviceIoControl` call delivers two pointers—an input and an output—and the I/O Manager creates MDLs for them. Mapping additional pointers is somewhat cumbersome and highly error-prone; you will have to learn an awful lot about the Win32 memory system to actually accomplish this. The usual penalty for error is a Blue Screen of Death. However, you might also corrupt programs you never heard of and/or critical parts of the disk. The decision to use such structures should not be made casually, since it introduces additional cost and complexity to the driver. But it is equally important to realize that if it is the best possible application interface, it may well be the correct decision.

Note also that if the device can make immediate use of the information in the linked structure, that is, it does not have to depend on any kind of deferred processing, then there is no cost to using such a linked list structure. No MDLs need to be created because all of the information is directly accessible in the thread that is processing the `DeviceIoControl` operation. In this case, the decision to use any kind of pointer structure is much easier to make.

Paged and Nonpaged Memory

There are two kinds of memory in a Win32 system: *paged* and *nonpaged* (we discuss these in detail in Chapter 6). Paged memory is memory whose contents can be copied to the paging file and then whose physical memory space can be reallocated for some other purpose. When the contents are again needed, the paging system allocates a page of physical memory and copies back in the data from the paging file. Then it maps that physical page into the appropriate virtual address for the thread that needed the information. This is the usual way in which pages are managed in a multitasking system that has virtual memory.

However, some pages must *always* be in memory and must be fixed, or locked, in the same physical page. Certain key parts of the operating system—for example, the code that performs paging—are in the Nonpaged Pool. The Nonpaged Pool holds critical system data. Device Drivers are usually not paged; for example, an interrupt routine cannot be paged out because you don't know when an interrupt will be coming in. Buffers used for DMA transfers must not be paged out because DMA controllers use physical bus addresses to transfer the data and once a DMA operation has been configured, the pages involved cannot be moved. Such memory is kept in the Nonpaged Pool. As you might expect, the size of the Nonpaged Pool can significantly affect system performance. This is because if you have too many nonpaged (or locked) pages, there is less space left over for paged information. In the extreme case, you could tie up so much memory in the Nonpaged Pool that only one pageable page frame would be available for any computation. Win32 avoids that extreme case by establishing a Nonpaged Pool *quota* based on the physical memory size. The sum of all nonpaged memory used by the operating system and Device Drivers cannot exceed this quota.

Within certain limits, you can change the amount of space that is usable by the Nonpaged Pool by modifying the following Registry entry:
```
\HKEY_LOCAL_MACHINE\System\CurrentControlSet\Control
\Session Manager\Memory Management
```
The value is `NonPagedPoolSize` and is the number of bytes (REG_DWORD). The maximum value this can have will be less than 80% of physical memory. If the value is 0, a default based on the memory size is chosen.
To make this change, you must use the Registry Editor program `RegEdt32` and then reboot.

Generally, the quota is based on the amount of physical memory actually available. For modest machines, adding more physical memory may make half of that additional memory available to the Nonpaged Pool. But for larger machines, a greater percentage of additional physical memory will be available for the Nonpaged Pool, up to 80% of the additional physical memory on very large machines. Adding 128MB to a 128MB machine could add as much as 100MB to the Nonpaged Pool.

In addition to the total amount of Nonpaged Pool, there is a problem getting large blocks of contiguous physical memory in the Nonpaged Pool. This is because the Nonpaged Pool can quickly become fragmented during initialization. The only known solution to this problem is to add massive amounts of physical memory and then try to adjust the load order of drivers so that the drivers that require huge amounts of contiguous nonpaged memory load early, before serious fragmentation has occurred. It is *much* better to design the device so that it can do scatter/gather I/O on noncontiguous memory blocks, a topic discussed in greater depth in Chapter 17, but as a Device Driver writer you may not have the option of using a sensibly designed card.

Actually, *any* massive buffer allocation strategy is inconsistent with some of the basic assumptions of the Windows NT driver support. In our opinion, the best strategy for devices that require massive buffers is to put the memory in the device and then map it to the virtual memory as needed. The cost of putting 200MB on-card is fairly small, and the result is a guaranteed reliable system, not one that depends on features that may change in the next release of Win32. One downside of this is that we have taken the memory off the high bandwidth memory bus and placed it on a far lower bandwidth I/O bus (for example, a PCI bus). Depending on the operation to be performed, the bus bandwidth may not be sufficient. This may require a copy from the device memory into main memory before some intensive operations may be performed (such as a Fourier transform on the data in the buffer).

Another downside to putting massive amounts of onboard memory on a device, at least in NT 4.0, is that there is an aggregate limit for all mapped device memory of 300MB. We anticipate that this limit will change in Windows 2000.

There are serious hazards in letting hardware engineers make design decisions about hardware. For example, one notable coprocessor board came with its onboard 68000 and memory, but the memory had no refresh line because "refresh can be done in software, and it will save $2.35. We will just use the nonmaskable interrupt". So memory-refresh interrupts could occur at any time, including during timing-critical operations of the coprocessor (for example, timing intrapacket and interpacket gaps in a communications protocol). There was no timer for this critical timing because "that can be done in software" (another $2 saved). Imagine trying to write a high-resolution timing loop *that can be interrupted for memory refresh*. Furthermore, the Event this loop was timing had a very, very small window of response, which could be totally disrupted by the memory-refresh interrupt. (The solution was to reroute the refresh interrupt into a maskable interrupt line and use a refresh memory loop as the timing loop with this interrupt disabled.)

The board also had the property that when its processor hung or otherwise went into a bad state, it hung the host processor bus. This meant that recovery could be done *only* by power-cycling the host processor, thus destroying any information that might have helped identify the cause of the problem.

I can't say I wasn't warned. Another project was planning to use this board first, until the project leader of that team refused to use the board for anything at all. When I picked up the communications project, he warned me, "The only acceptable solution is to collect every one of these boards ever made and put them into a single pile. Grind the entire pile into a powder at least as fine as flour, and dispose of the powder in a hazardous waste landfill." Months later, I realized this was an understatement.

This is one of those examples of a design whose superficial flaws completely masked its fundamental flaws. For example, its interrupt vectors tended to go to random locations in memory.
—*end*

Buffered and Direct Access

One component of the design is how the driver accesses data in the application. You have three choices:

- *Buffered I/O* makes a copy of the data in the application space into buffers that are private to the kernel.

- *Direct I/O* accesses the data in the application space.

- *Neither* leaves this decision of what to do with the data up to the Device Driver.

Buffered I/O is the simplest to implement. For `WriteFile`, the I/O Manager allocates kernel memory to hold the data and copies the output data to the kernel. The Device Driver can then access this data directly because the references are to nonpaged memory in kernel space. When the output operation is complete, the kernel space is released. For input data, the kernel allocates a buffer as large as the user buffer and again sets up a kernel-address-space pointer to it. Upon successful completion of the operation, the data will be copied back to the user space and the Kernel-mode space will be released.

Direct I/O does not make a copy of the user data. Instead, the I/O Manager creates MDLs to point to the data in the user space. All that is required of the driver is to call the necessary mapping operations on the MDLs to make the data accessible in the kernel.

Note that for asynchronous I/O, in which `ReadFile` or `WriteFile` returns immediately, the user must not modify any buffers that are used by direct I/O. This is because they are still being shared with the active I/O operation. However, if Buffered I/O was used, there is no problem with immediately modifying the output buffer, since a copy has been made.

Generally, the choice between using Buffered I/O or Direct I/O can be based on the amount of data being transferred. For small amounts of data, Buffered I/O makes more sense, and not only because it reduces the driver development cost. In terms of performance, letting the I/O Manager do the data copy is faster than setting up explicit MDLs and doing the mapping. But for large amounts of data, avoiding the copy may improve performance. If the device is a DMA device, you will need MDLs anyway to perform the transfer, so it is often just as easy to use Direct I/O for a DMA device. So which is better, Buffered I/O or Direct I/O? This is one of those decisions that is based on the Device Driver writer's experience.

In the Neither mode, however, the I/O Manager transparently passes the address of the buffer to the Device Driver. It is up to the Device Driver to decide what to do. It now is responsible for allocating kernel memory and/or constructing MDLs to the data. While this does not appear terribly complex, the reality is that you are doing the memory management equivalent of jumping up and down while patting your head and rubbing your stomach. You must get every single detail right or the world will crumble to dust, usually resulting in Blue Screen and possible overall system corruption.

There are, nonetheless, good reasons for dealing with the Neither mode. If the I/O request involves some sort of scatter/gather in the user space, uses chained control blocks of some sort, or would choose to use Buffered or Direct I/O based on the size of the transfer, then you will have to implement the Neither mode. However, because of the cost of developing a driver using this mode, you should think about it carefully before deciding that it is the only alternative that will work.

`DeviceIoControl` operations *always* use buffered data for passing data from the user's input buffer to the driver, unless the I/O method Neither is chosen. The type of transfer for the data being returned from the driver can be selected as part of the IOCTL defined by the `CTL_CODE` macro and can be Buffered, In Direct, Out Direct, or Neither. This means that each IOCTL could handle it differently, and if the device supports `ReadFile` and `WriteFile`, the mode selected for read/write has no effect on how the data is transferred for `DeviceIoControl`.

If the data buffer contains pointers to memory locations within the data buffer, it will be necessary to do address fixup in the dispatch routine. The pointers will not be directly useable outside the caller context portions (outside the dispatch routines) of the device driver. If the buffer contains pointers to data outside the data buffer and this memory will be accessed outside the dispatch routines, a MDL must be prepared and locked in the dispatch routine to assure that the linked buffers will be present when accessed. This is exactly the process which makes Neither mode access complex.

You should avoid passing complex structures to the device driver if at all possible.

Handling I/O Request Packets

The `ReadFile`, `WriteFile`, and `DeviceIoControl` operations dispatch to separate entry points in the Device Driver. A Device Driver that does not support one or more of these operations must set the entry points in the Device's dispatch vector to `NULL` so that the I/O Manager can reject as "not supported" any unsupported operation.

Note that all `DeviceIoControl` operations go to a single entry point. You must implement your own dispatch mechanism to handle the types of `DeviceIoControl` operations.

Once the I/O Request Packet (IRP) has been received at one of these entry points, you could actually start touching the I/O device to set up the registers and other device-specific locations for the I/O operation. Alternatively, you could defer this processing to a Start I/O routine; this is typically used when DMA will be done.

For very, very simple devices (of which there are very few instances), you could perform all of the device I/O operations in the `ReadFile`, `WriteFile`, or `DeviceIoControl` IRP handlers. No additional processing would be required. This will work for devices that either have no interrupts or that are being used in a noninterrupting mode. In these routines, you have available the complete user-level address space, as well as the kernel address space.

You can also pass the IRP down to a lower-level driver, with or without making modifications to it. This is done quite often in *layered drivers*. A layered driver allows a driver to work at a higher level of abstraction than the bare hardware. For example, a driver for a SCSI-based device rarely talks to the SCSI board itself. Instead, it creates the appropriate sequences of SCSI commands and passes them down to a driver that talks to the SCSI bus. Layered drivers are central to the WDM (Win32 Driver Model) of Windows 2000. You can also create one or more new IRPs and send them down to a lower-level driver to perform lower-level functions that accomplish what the higher-level IRP requested. This pattern can be repeated at each level in the WDM layered model.

Whenever an IRP is handed off to a lower-level driver, the current level returns an indication that the IRP that was sent to it is pending. Later, when the lower-level driver completes, the IRP will be marked as *completed* (either successfully or unsuccessfully) and returned to its sender. A pending IRP will be retained for additional processing. When a lower-level driver completes, it can call an *I/O Completion routine* in the parent driver to notify it that the IRP has completed. If there is no I/O Completion routine established, control passes upward in the layers of drivers until it hits the I/O Manager. The I/O Manager then returns control to the application that initiated the I/O request, either by allowing the thread to resume (in the case of synchronous I/O) or by calling the application's I/O completion callback function or signalling the Event (in the case of asynchronous I/O).

Devices and Device Objects

Each Device has an associated *Device Object*. Recall that a Device Object represents all of the state of the Device. Some of this state is predefined by the operating system, but much of it is device-specific. The device-specific information is in a block of space whose size and layout you determine. This space is allocated when you create the Device Object and is called the *Device Extension*. It is referenced by a pointer in the Device Object.

You must keep all local state for a device in the Device Object, the Device Extension, or some other device-specific location. A driver that contains static or global variables is an *Erroneous Driver*. In addition, a device might have to provide for synchronization if two different IRQLs can be accessing the Device Object or Device Extension in parallel. This includes synchronization between higher levels and lower levels (such as the ISR), as well as synchronization required because the structures could be accessed independently by individual processors in a multiprocessor environment.

Devices and Controllers

Most devices can be represented by a single Device Object. However, some devices share their control on a single adapter (for example, SCSI devices on a SCSI controller), so there is also a *Controller Object* that represents the controller. The Device Objects will contain a reference to the Controller Object. Note that since several Device Objects could be executing concurrently, possibly at several different levels (one executing a setup; another handling an Interrupt Request, or IRQ; a third handling a DPC, for example), you must provide interlocks so that they do not corrupt shared data in the Controller Object. Each Device Object, as mentioned earlier in the chapter, has a device-specific Device Extension area in which all of its local state is stored (which would include a pointer to its Controller Object). A Controller Object may have a Controller Extension that can contain one or more Kernel Spin Locks to synchronize multiprocessor and multithreaded access to its shared data. A driver that does not implement proper synchronization is an Erroneous Driver.

Adapter Objects

An *Adapter Object* is an object used to manage DMA requests. Adapter objects synchronize the usage of the DMA channel. There are two kinds of DMA: System, using the old-style DMA controller chips on the motherboard, and Bus Master, in which the device has its own DMA controller. For older-style cards that require System DMA, there can be more cards in the system requiring DMA than there are controllers to provide it. In this case, the Adapter Object is used to allocate and deallocate System DMA channels and synchronize the usage of System DMA across all drivers. For Bus Master DMA, the Adapter Object provides serialization of the device's DMA channel. This is particularly important on a multifunction card, where the DMA channel may be used by more than one of the functions, but only one function at a time can use it. We discuss Adapter Objects in more detail in Chapter 17.

Handling Interrupts

Most devices require that after an operation is initiated, some indeterminate amount of time will go by before the operation completes. It is unacceptable for the machine to simply lock up and wait for this to happen, so most devices will ultimately use the *interrupt mechanism* to notify the processor when the operation has completed (this can include the case in which the operation completed unsuccessfully). During device initialization, you will establish which interrupt is used for this notification. This establishes the DIRQL (Device Interrupt Request Level) that is used to service the interrupt.

The Interrupt Service Routine

When a device interrupts, the interrupt is routed to the device's Interrupt Service Routine (ISR). At this point, the processor suspends whatever thread is executing (it may be a user thread or even a kernel thread) and transfers control to the ISR. The processor is now running at an elevated IRQL, that is, no interrupt at the same or lower priority will be seen. However, that ISR may itself be preempted by a *higher* priority interrupt request. All software priority levels of the system execute at a lower level than the lowest-priority DIRQL. However, there are IRQLs that are lower than all DIRQLs but higher than the highest user-accessible priority level. We discuss these shortly.

The Deferred Processing Routine

Unlike in many operating systems, an ISR in Windows NT is small and fast. Normally, it does just enough to determine if the interrupt is for its device. If the interrupt is, the ISR removes the pending IRQ state from the hardware device (this then allows other interrupts to be seen, even on the same [shared] IRQ line) and immediately queues a request for its lower-priority handler by using a *DPC Object*. The ISR then exits. At this point, any pending DPCs will be dispatched when the IRQL drops to DPC level. A DPC Routine runs at one of the software priorities less than the lowest DIRQL, but preempts any user threads that may have been executing. But since it is processing at a level lower than any DIRQL, any device can interrupt the DPC Routine. The effect is that devices are locked out from the processor as briefly as possible (a good ISR is from 10 to 100 instructions in length), thus minimizing device latency and the chances of losing data because the processor is not responding.

The DPC Routine completes the processing of the interrupt. This means that it will detect if the operation was successful or if an error occurred. If an error occurred, the IRP will be completed with an appropriate error code and returned to the caller, and probably eventually (the higher level is always free to initiate retries or alterative actions) to the I/O Manager, which will at some time return control to the application program. If there was no error, the driver must determine if the operation completed. For programmed I/O, the DPC will do one of two things. It will initiate the next programmed I/O transfer, or, if the input buffer has been filled or some other criteria for completion has been met (for example, "a complete packet has been received", whatever that might mean for your device), it will complete the IRP and return the completion status to the sender of the IRP, the driver that initiated that device action. In the layered driver model, the IRP may be returned to a higher-level driver, which as a consequence may generate many more IRPs before it ultimately completes its own IRP and returns control upwards.

A DPC might not complete an IRP. For example, the IRP may request that some large number of bytes be read, but the device may deliver only one byte, or a small number of bytes, per interrupt. In such a case, the IRP is not returned but merely continued until the requisite number of bytes have been delivered by the device.

A DPC executes in some thread that most likely is different from the thread that initiated the I/O operation and possibly even different from the thread that was executing the ISR. Thus, if Direct I/O is used, the DPC also must have the application memory mapped into System Logical Address Space. Otherwise, the application-level memory will not be available when the Direct mode is used to access data.

A driver can have more than one DPC handler. To handle a timeout, for example, you can set up a timer so that a timer DPC is called. If the timer DPC is called before the interrupt is taken, then the device can be detected as nonresponsive and the pending IRP can be completed with a completion code that indicates an error and an error code that indicates a timeout.

Polled Devices and Interrupt Frequency

A device that cannot interrupt or that is being used in a noninterrupting mode can be *polled* to determine its completion status. There are, however, limits to how frequently this polling can be done. The resolution of the NT timer is platform-dependent. Currently, on a uniprocessor *x*86 HAL, it is 10 ms; on a multiprocessor *x*86 HAL, it is 15 ms; and on an Alpha, it is 7.5 ms. For Windows 95 it is 55 ms.[6] These intervals can change if an application program has specified a timer resolution using the multimedia timer functions. These resolution limitations set minimum limits on the polling frequency. However, when the issues of interrupt latency, scheduling,

---

[6] Why would you care about Windows 95? Or 98? After all, this is a book about *NT* drivers. However, with Windows 2000, using the Win32 Driver Model (WDM), a driver executable can run on both Windows 2000 and Windows 98. If you write such a driver and make it dependent on the Windows NT timer resolution, it might not work in Windows 98.

higher-priority interrupts, and the like are considered, it is hard to poll much more often than once every 100 ms, even on Windows NT. This also sets a limit on how often a device interrupts. Devices that interrupt at very high frequency (more often than once every 100 ms) require extremely complex drivers to cope with the high interrupt rate and still maintain small ISR times. The serial port driver for NT, for example, handles both input and output and can handle data rates of at least 56Kbits/sec (5.6KB/sec). This translates to less than 200 μsec per character. Even with a 16-deep FIFO on input and responding only to the FIFO-full condition, this is an interrupt about every 3 ms, a serious strain on the NT system. (The calculation of interrupt rate for a 115Kbits/sec serial line is left for the reader.)

> One driver had a requirement that something had to happen every 1 ms, with very little skew. There is no way in the NT driver environment that a 1-ms timing interval can be obtained. In addition, because of the nature of the interrupt system, even if it were possible to generate an interrupt every 1 ms, there is no guarantee as to how long it would be before the interrupt was serviced. Thus a requirement that an interrupt be processed within no more than, say, a 1.2-ms interval would be impossible to achieve or implement without doing something very unusual. In this case, the machine was locked up in a 1-ms busy loop. There is no other alternative that is feasible. There is no guaranteed-on-time delivery of timer interrupts in the kernel.

Synchronization and Serialization

Obviously, if there is any part of the Device Driver touching the hardware, another part of the driver cannot interfere with this "critical section", not even the ISR. Since Windows NT is a multiprocessor system, the driver must be multiprocessor-safe. *Without synchronization, the only operation you can assume is atomic is the memory cycle.* And by "memory cycle", we do *not* mean a *read-write* cycle. A memory *read* is one atomic operation, and a memory *write* is one atomic operation. An "increment" instruction requires *two* such operations, and is *not* an atomic operation.[7]

You must deal with conflicting objectives. You want to optimize the performance of your driver and that of the entire system, and you want to maximize the concurrency of your hardware without resource conflicts. The proper synchronization in a driver is a balancing act. You must stay on the wire without going off on either side (poor performance for your driver or unreliable operation of your driver, or good performance of your driver at the cost of poor system performance).

In different situations within the driver, you can use different techniques for synchronization. NT provides a broad range of synchronization operations. The simplest are the Spin Lock—the basic interprocessor lock in NT—and interlocked equivalents of simple operations such as exchange or add. Interlocked routines provide a multiprocessor-safe way to access a shared variable.

The driver must *serialize* operations and determine the proper order and starting points for each pending operation. The Controller and Adapter Objects provide a method for accessing shared hardware. The system-managed queueing of IRPs (the `StartIo` routine) and more com-

---

[7] This may come as a surprise to those who are familiar with some architectures, notably the PDP-11, in which there was a "read-pause-write" memory access that blocked access to the bus until an updated result was written back. This notion is not supported on the *x86* as a default mode for any instruction.

plex driver queuing of IRPs provide the mechanisms for safely maximizing concurrency. These routines help you serialize the I/O operations that have been specified by the application program (or a higher-level driver). Extremely complex reordering is possible in situations such as the use of the "elevator algorithm" in a disk driver (in which I/O operations are reordered to minimize total head motion of the disk drive).

You also will implicitly export a synchronization model to your application programs. You must implement this inside your driver. The driver might create a single *exclusive device*, a device that may be opened only by one application. Or, it might create some specific number of "devices", each with a unique name and exclusive access, and allow application programs to open all of these concurrently. Or, you can make the device *shared*, thereby allowing multiple programs to have the same device open concurrently.

In more complex drivers, you might have to implement file-system-like locking of driver or hardware resources, thus concurrently allowing multiple shared locks or a single exclusive lock on a resource. NT provides synchronization primitives that allow you to implement shared and exclusive locks on resources.

In the extreme case, layered drivers are used to serialize operations and prevent conflict. The use of the "bus drivers" in Windows 2000 to access busses such as the SCSI, IEEE-1394, and USB prevents the Device Driver for each peripheral from directly accessing hardware and interfering with each other. Without the bus driver, each peripheral driver would have to set up the bus controller hardware, and thereby possibly interfere with a pending operation from another driver. With a lower-level driver, NT will provide a documented interface to the shared resource, the bus, and the bus controller.

Driver Threads

A driver can create one or more threads to use as "helper threads". A relatively expensive operation, it is used most often for "slow" devices. In addition, a limited number of threads are available for immediate use, called *System Worker Threads*. We cover threads extensively in Chapter 24.

A driver thread allows computations to be deferred to a fully schedulable (not just interruptible) level and allows a driver to perform certain operations that cannot be performed at the ISR or DPC level.

Full-Duplex Devices

A *full-duplex device* is a device that can have both input and output pending simultaneously. A serial port is such a device, as is a MIDI (Musical Instrument Digital Interface) port, and many multimedia sound cards. In these cases, the driver must be exceptionally clever. It must sort out input and output operations as they arrive. Also, it might well have a feasible output operation, although it has queued input operations pending, or vice versa.

A driver for a full-duplex device that does not handle separate queueing for input and output operations is another example of an Erroneous Driver. Unless, of course, you believe that a driver for a full-duplex device that would block all output while waiting for input, or all input while waiting for output, is somehow "correct".

Bus Enumeration

For certain busses, such as the PCI, PCMCIA, SCSI, IEEE-1394, and USB, you will have to find the devices on the bus and possibly initialize them. This action is called *bus enumeration*.

Bus enumeration is handled in two ways, depending on the version of NT and the bus:

1. The "old" way, which is all you have available in NT 4.0.
2. The Windows 2000 way (via a bus-specific Bus Driver).

In the "old" way (Windows NT 4.0 and earlier), each driver had to enumerate the bus and determine, for each device it found, if it was the driver to handle that device. This was handled during the device initialization. Each such driver used the HAL (Hardware Abstraction Layer) calls to read the "device configuration" information from the device (for a PCI device, this would be the PCI Configuration Memory).

One useful feature of doing device enumeration of busses such as PCI is that the driver can actually change the assignment of interrupts and I/O addresses of a card by changing the configuration information. This is extremely important when the BIOS has arbitrarily chosen to assign these addresses in an incorrect, incompatible, or infeasible fashion. (This is why Plug-and-Play does not always work correctly on these busses.)

You can even add entries to the Registry database to cause your driver to force a particular configuration. To do this, you must specify the Registry entries (there are no standard entries in this case) and write code in your driver to read these entries and force the desired configuration. There is no magic here; you must write the code yourself.

The second way to do bus enumeration, the Windows 2000 way, is to use a bus-specific Bus Driver. This driver finds each device on the bus in turn and uses information stored in the Registry and elsewhere to determine, for currently inactive devices, what driver to load to support the device. This is a much cleaner model than the PCI, EISA, or PCMCIA models provided by Windows NT 4.0 and earlier versions. Furthermore, because the enumeration is done by the Bus Driver, the driver can detect when a device is either hot-plugged into the bus or removed from the bus. This allows USB or IEEE-1394 devices to be plugged and unplugged without the system's having to be powered down or even rebooted. A driver whose device has been unplugged will get a notice that it has been removed from the system, and a new device that is plugged in will have its driver loaded and activated at its initialization point.

Power Management

The bus-specific Bus Driver (such as PCI, USB, and IEEE-1394) also concentrates all of the information about power management in one place. When a bus is about to be powered down, the enumerator can locate all of the devices, and for those not already powered down, it can initiate power-down notifications. WDM drivers all have a power management entry point that is called to indicate power changes, such as going from fully active to standby to low-power-standby to powered-off and from any of the low-power states back to full power.

Unloading Drivers

A driver should also contain an *unload* entry point. This allows the driver to power down its device and unload itself. The code itself will also be unloaded.

In addition, a driver is normally nonpageable. However, a driver can flag code or data sections within itself as being pageable. Further, it can do this dynamically. Thus a driver may determine that the device is inactive and mark the ISR as now being pageable. When the device again becomes active, the ISR can be marked as nonpaged and thus again be locked down. This means that a very large driver or one that consumes massive amounts of Nonpaged Pool memory can be paged out if the device is not in use. (Keep in mind that there is no guarantee that the non-paged memory will again be accessible when it is needed. And certainly there is no guarantee that if large contiguous blocks of nonpaged memory are needed, they will be available.)

The Registry

The Registry contains some specifications about the Device Driver that are parameters to Windows itself and that are used by the kernel at boot time, such as

- the name of the driver
- the file that implements the driver
- whether the driver is a bootstrap-critical device (such as a disk driver)
- whether the driver is loaded at boot time or can be loaded later by explicit user command or application call
- the load order

The entry in the Registry must be created *before* the driver can be executed for the first time. The NT-required entries have very specific formats which must be followed exactly.

In addition, there are parameters that are device-specific. These are often stored under a `Parameters` subkey within the driver entry in the Registry. Since these parameters are device-specific, there is no particular set of standards that govern what names and value types are used, and you are free to create as many of these parameters as you need for your driver.

In NT 4.0, you can load only those drivers whose Registry entries have been created before the last boot or that have been created by using the Service Control Manager API (discussed in Chapter 26 on page 596).

Event Logging and Journaling

A properly designed driver will log useful and interesting data to the Event Log. Most important, before a driver fails in some unexpected way, it should log as much information as it can so that it generates an intelligible and useful diagnostic log, in particular, one suitable for effective field support. It is also useful for it to log even simple information. When a driver starts up, it should log a start-up Event, including its version, date, or any other identifying marks.

Strictly speaking, a driver should never Blue Screen unless things are utterly hopeless. Most of the time, it should just mark the pending operation as failing and log an Event to the Event

Log to indicate why the failure occurred. There is usually no justification for an explicit call to the KeBugCheck function (which is what causes a Blue Screen of Death), unless there appears to be some uncorrectable situation (possible memory damage) such that, if NT were permitted to continue running, additional damage to the system would result.

Note that even if KeBugCheck is called, you should write key information to the Event Log first. If a crash dump file is to be preserved, there must be a paging file on the boot drive at least as large as physical memory. There is a button on the System Control Panel that, when clicked, selects the record of the information. The Event, as it is logged, does not give a stack dump in the Event Log. It is not actually written to disk until *after* the system reboots. This minimizes the amount of disk activity on a potentially damaged system. The memory dump itself is stored in the paging file. On a reboot, it is copied from the paging file to a memory.dmp file (or the name selected in the Control Panel). This option and several others are shown in Figure 3.1.

Normally, you might even consider adding Event logging under the _DEBUG conditional compilation for logging other Events during debugging. However, we strongly believe that if it was worth logging once, it is worth logging again. Instead of putting the code under a conditional compilation, put it under a Boolean variable. You can then specify a set of Boolean values in the Registry that enable or disable selective logging. This is a *wonderful* field maintenance tool! You can include, as part of your distribution, a little program that just modifies the Registry to set these Boolean values (they should be treated as FALSE if not present) and thus enable all sorts of useful diagnostics. The end user can then send you a printout of the Event Log, or the Log itself, and you will be able to see what caused a failure mode, including all of the events leading up to it (for example, in a "verbose" mode you might log all of the IRPs coming into

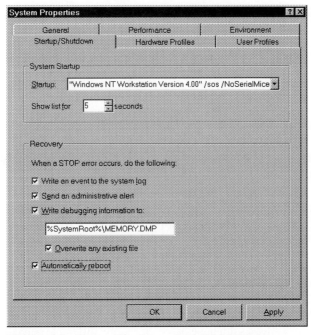

Figure 3.1: *Startup/Shutdown tab in NT 4.0 System Control Panel applet.*

your driver). This will be of immense assistance in determining the cause of the failure, particularly when it may be system-configuration-specific and unreproducible on your own machines. You might also consider building diagnostics into an application that can retrieve the internal state of the driver using special `DeviceIoControl` calls. You will see an example of this later in the sample WDM driver from Microsoft.

Journaling is another useful technique. You can log to a journal file the input or output data as it flows through your driver. For drivers whose high-level components expect structured data of some sort and need to parse it, this will help uncover the most recent message that caused a failure. A good journaling system would log all of the same information as the Event Log, as well as all of the data going out or coming in, and often might include timestamps so that you can determine if there is a time sensitivity involved. Of course, such a journaling system should *never* be removed from the product; it is one of your key field maintenance tools! Just provide a way to turn it on and off.

Of course, there are those who argue that "efficiency" dictates that those little `if`-tests are clearly introducing unacceptable overhead to the driver and that in any case keeping all of that code around is clearly a Bad Idea. Some years ago, I worked on a system that used 16-bit pointers (no, not Win16; this example predates that by at least a decade). The Clever Programmer decided that setting two 16-bit pointers to NULL by assigning 0 to a LONG in a union was a Really Clever Idea. (Well, to be completely honest, the language wasn't C, and the pointers were 18-bit, but the basic idea is the same.) In those days of timesharing, the system actually tracked how much CPU time we used. I was converting the application—over 100K lines of code—to the moral equivalent of 32 bits (well, 36 bits), and the pointers now occupied a full word. So the Clever Idea now set *one* of the pointers to NULL, but not the other. Of course, this caused bizarre storage damage that later manifested itself in some unrelated piece of the program crashing. After 14.5 hours of CPU time and 20 hours of straight debugging, I finally found the problem. When I confronted the Clever Programmer with this, he said, "It saved one instruction and made the initialization more efficient". I computed that if we ran this program, sequentially, based on its running time and the fact that this clever hack saved 1 microsecond *once, during initialization*, it would take *14 years* to break even with the CPU cost of finding the bug! I have been deeply suspicious of all Clever Hacks ever since and avoid them as much as I can.

In considering those little `if`-tests, remember that the single most expensive maintenance point in the lifetime of a product is when it is in the field. The question is, what is the trade-off between the little `if`-tests and flying an engineer to your most important client to locate the problem? They look pretty cheap by comparison. *–jmn*

You also must ensure that the journaled file is complete; that is, if a Blue Screen occurs, you want to ensure that all of the data in the journal file is actually out on the disk. While Microsoft does not provide a synchronization mechanism to flush files, a third-party product provides this capability as a user utility. This was, as we went to press, downloadable from the Web site `www.sysinternals.com` (formerly known as `www.ntinternals.com`) as the "sync" program.

International Drivers

In addition to the "domestic" version of Win32 (for whatever country you are in), there are international releases. These releases might be based on slightly different source builds of the system. Thus you might have a driver that works perfectly fine, *except* in some international release.[8] In this case, you will have to load the appropriate international release on your development machine and attempt to debug it. This requires at least two machines, one to show you what the menus say in your everyday language and the other the development machine that you manipulate by finding the corresponding menu position in a script or language you cannot read—all the while hoping the programmer or person who localized the application did not do something like alphabetize the menus or other controls in the native language.

Note that this is yet another reason for needing two machines to test drivers. Given the cost of developing a driver, the cost of a second machine is minimal. Driver development can easily cost a company in excess of $100/hour, whether they do it in-house or go to outside contractors. If a second machine can save only 20 hours in development, it has paid for itself even at the lowest estimate for cost. Be assured that the second machine will pay for itself within the first month.

In addition to the issues of debugging drivers under international versions of NT, you may also be faced with the problem of creating drivers that are intended for an international marketplace. It may even be the case that the driver name and the Registry entries it uses must be in the local language. We do not say much about internationalization in this book (it is already too large), but some key ideas can be gleaned from the excellent book, *Developing International Software for Windows 95 and Windows NT* (see the Further Reading section at the end of the chapter).

Driver Coding

Coding a driver is unlike most coding the normal programmer encounters. Not only must you not use static data of any sort, but you must be conscious of issues such as multithreading, multiprocessing, and parallelism induced by interrupts.

Generally, when coding an *experiment*, something that is attempting to deduce what the device actually does, it is a reasonable practice to do everything as inline code. This is *experimental* code and is intended to be throwaway. After doing the experiments and learning what the device *really* does (as opposed to what its documentation *claims* it does), you want to throw this code away and recode a driver using proper modular programming techniques. But if you apply these techniques too soon in the experimental stage, you will likely do either of two things. You will find that you will forget what a subroutine does and it will do something you didn't expect, thus perturbing your experiment, or you will discover that it needs a simple "tweak" and soon you have subroutines with a dozen Boolean parameters that tailor their behavior to each call site. In this case, you really *didn't* have common code and it should not have been made into a subroutine. Nearly all driver coding falls into the two-phase "experiment" and "production" coding model because devices are not always well-behaved.

---

[8] This actually happened to me; the display driver worked fine except in the Japanese release of Windows. *–end*

One of the guiding principles of software design is the maxim popularized by Fred Brooks, "Plan to throw one away. You will anyway". Unfortunately, everybody remembers this bit of folklore, but nobody seems to have actually read the book. The result is a degree of incredible sloppiness in design and programming based on the premise that there will always be a chance to redo it. This means that a number of really poorly designed pieces of software exist that are badly implemented and virtually unmaintainable. Fred's actual admonition was that you will *have* to throw one away, no matter how good a job you do, because systems, needs, and expectations evolve. He goes on to say, in the book, "Delivering that throwaway to customers buys time, but it does so only at the cost of agony for the user, distraction for the builders while they do the redesign, and a bad reputation for the product that the best redesign will find hard to live down" (page 116 of the 1975 edition). Anyone who can quote the "throwaway" maxim without being able to quote the significant supplement is a hazard to a project. Fred *never* intended this maxim to be justification for poor design or implementation and in fact says quite the opposite. See the Further Reading section at the end of the chapter for the full citation. *–jmn*

Do not, under any circumstances, confuse the experimental code with production code. *Throw away the experimental code.*

Driver Testing

While drivers may be tested "thoroughly", there is nothing like reality to uncover bugs that you never tested for and only barely suspected. This is another reason for maintaining sophisticated and complete Event Logs, at least in a diagnostic mode. You cannot hope to have a client give you the complete set of commands to four concurrently running applications that lead to driver failure after half an hour.

In the best of all possible worlds, of course, your Quality Assurance Department will do extensive testing on all of the international releases of Windows NT (and for WDM drivers, Windows 98 as well), using all of the possible applications across all possible platforms. Unfortunately, this takes not only man-years of time, but also months of calendar time and is almost completely infeasible. In any but the largest companies, it is nearly impossible to test even on a tiny subset of releases, applications, and platforms. Thus it is essential to provide decent tools for field maintenance.

It is, however, essential that a driver be tested on the real-world applications that talk to it. Some display cards (we might call them "Brand D") are notorious for the fact that their drivers work only until the next new application is run, at which point the intrinsic problems caused by shortcuts and "efficiency" hacks crash the system. Such products get a bad reputation. After you get tired of downloading the 11 a.m. version of the driver off the Web, which corrects the bugs of the 10 a.m. version, which corrected the bugs of the 9 a.m. version, you remove this (usually expensive) product from your machine and relegate it to the scrap box or find some charity that accepts donations of computer parts. You *do not* want your product to have such a reputation. Some display cards have drivers that break on software that sells *millions* of copies and is incredibly popular. Their cards are excellent. Their drivers are garbage. You don't want your driver to be like that.

You should at least check out your product on the mainstream applications that will use it. For example, a display driver or printer driver needs to support all of Microsoft Office and similar office suites, key drawing programs including CAD systems, and the top ten current games. This is a *minimal* test before beta release. You'll still likely find a valid application that, when executing valid GDI commands, will cause a failure, in which case you add that application to your test suite.

Of course, a *thorough* test of a display driver or printer driver consists of walking into your local software dealer, looking at the walls of boxes, and saying, "I'll take one of each". But the time required to actually perform such testing is unrealistic.

The short-form test for most drivers, particularly display and printer drivers, is the Microsoft Hardware Compatibility Test (MHCT). This is an excellent test suite, but it is only a small test compared to the size of the application world.

The testing burden is much lower if you are developing specialized hardware that will be used only by your company's application. In this case, it has to work only with one application or a very small suite over which you have control. Nonetheless, you must never "fix" driver problems by telling your application programmers, "Don't do that". This is not an acceptable solution. Between short memories and personnel turnover, this legendary information will be forgotten, and the next generation of your applications may well hit these same bugs and crash the system, or at least malfunction. Fix the drivers. And write *thorough and complete* documentation if there are problems intrinsic to the device that must be dealt with by the applications.

Further Reading

Brooks, Frederick P., Jr., *The Mythical Man-Month: Essays on Software Engineering*, Addison-Wesley, 1975. ISBN 0-201-00650-2.

Brooks, Frederick P., Jr., *The Mythical Man-Month: Essays on Software Engineering, Anniversary Edition*, Addison-Wesley, 1995. ISBN 0-201-83595-9.

Kano, Nadine, *Developing International Software for Windows 95 and Windows NT*, Microsoft Press, 1995. ISBN 1-55615-840-8.

Klein, Mark, Thomas Ralya, Bill Pollak, and Ray Obenza, *Practitioner's Handbook for Real-Time Analysis: Guide to Rate Monotonic Analysis for Real-Time Systems*, Kluwer Academic Publishing, 1993. ISBN 0792393619.

"Windows NT as Real-Time OS?" *Real-Time Magazine, 1997 Quarter 2*. Also available on `http://www.realtime-info.be/encyc/magazine/97q2/winntasrtos.htm`.

"Windows NT Real-Time Extensions: an Overview", *Real-Time Magazine, 1997 Quarter 2*. Also available on `http://www.realtime-info.be/encyc/magazine/97q2/winntext.htm`.

The newsgroup `comp.realtime` FAQ is duplicated at the following sites:

- `www.realtime-info.be/encyc/techno/publi/faq/rtfaq.htm`
- `www.groupipc.com/rtfaq.htm`
- `www.faqs.org/faqs/realtime-computing/faq/`
- `www.cis.ohio-state.edu/hypertext/faq/usenet/realtime-computing/top.html`

Vendors with real-time extensions to NT are at the following sites:

- `http://www.qnx.com/whitepaper/qnxwin32.html`
- `http://www.vci.com`

- `http://www.radisys.com`
- `http://www.nematron.com`
- `http://www.lp-elektronik.com`

We have not used any of the products from these vendors and thus cannot confirm or deny any claims they have made.

Chapter

4 *I/O Hardware: Internal Busses*

Part of what makes writing a Device Driver a complex task is the huge variety of ways in which a computer can interact with its attached devices. Exactly *how* a specific device interacts with the computer is the heart of the situation. Before you can even start coding, you need to answer several questions about the device.

- How do you set or read the status of the device?
- How do you send data to or receive data from the device?
- How does the device notify you of events of interest?
- Does the device use any physical memory?

We cover each of these topics in subsequent sections.

In addition, we distinguish between internal busses and external busses. We do this based on whether the device(s) on the bus connect(s) directly to the processor or there is a single processor interface to a bus controller on which commands are sent. You can plug a SCSI card into an ISA, EISA, or PCI bus. The protocols by which the processor communicates to the card are one level, while the protocols embodied in the data sent or received are a different level. A device on a SCSI bus doesn't know or care who manufactured the SCSI card or whether it is connected to ISA, EISA, or PCI. The software that sends SCSI commands to an I/O port to control an external SCSI device doesn't care if the SCSI device is a disk, tape, or CD-ROM; it deals only with getting commands onto the bus and taking information off of the bus. In a properly layered I/O system, the actual details of controlling a SCSI disk drive are implemented at a level quite different from how those commands get put onto the SCSI bus itself. Thus this chapter is devoted to the internal busses. We discuss the external busses in Chapter 5.

Device Registers

To communicate to a device, the computer must be able to send to it requests for the desired operation (generally called *commands*) and query the state of the device (generally called *status requests*). If the device is one that supplies data to the computer or receives data from the computer, there might be an additional need to supply this data.

Much of this communication takes place via *device registers*. A device register can be represented by a specific address given to an I/O instruction (a *port address*) or by a location in the memory address space (*memory-mapped registers*). Some architectures, such as the PDP-11 Unibus, had no I/O ports or even special I/O instructions at all; the device registers were in the memory address space and responded to ordinary memory read/write instructions. Mostly. Sometimes. For example, most I/O devices would not respond, or would respond incorrectly, if byte, rather than word, instructions were used.

The use of device registers can be quite complex. For example, the VGA chip has a small number of device registers, but the *meaning* of a particular device register address depends on *the last value written to another device address*. Some chips—for example, certain serial I/O chips—interpret the first write to a specific I/O address as meaning one thing and the second write to the same I/O address as meaning another!

Some really horrid devices—for example, the old EGA chip—have the same I/O address mean one thing when written to and something completely different when read from! Some chips have the property that the act of reading from a specific register causes some internal state to be reset, so two consecutive reads of the same I/O register can produce quite different results. Besides making these chips hard to program, this property makes them very difficult to debug because you can't set or read the device registers from the debugger. The "write-only" register, a favorite of many hardware designers (who usually have never programmed anything as complex as a Device Driver), is one of the worst design misfeatures a device will present to you. But you don't have any choice; your job is to get that card to *work*, despite its being unprogrammable! We show several examples of these problems as we look at some real-world Device Drivers in this chapter.

On an Intel *x*86 architecture, there are 65,535 possible I/O registers, accessed by a set of instructions generically called IN and OUT. The complete set of instructions for the 486 is shown in Table 4.1, but they all work pretty much the same as far as the I/O space is concerned. You will normally never write the actual I/O instructions; you'll instead use the HAL equivalents shown.

The use of the I/O space is illustrated in Figure 4.1. This is a somewhat idealized version of what is really going on. In the old IBM PC, only the low-order 9 bits of the I/O address were presented on the address lines, so the vendors of add-on cards decoded only the low-order 9 bits of the address. This means that these cards are "aliased" 64 times in the I/O space! (See the following screened "information" box for some considerations on how to handle this.)

Table 4.1: *Intel x86 I/O Instructions*

Instruction	HAL	Action
IN AL, *port*		Reads an 8-bit byte into the AL register from *port*.
IN AL, DX	READ_PORT_UCHAR	Reads an 8-bit byte into the AL register from the port whose number is in the DX register.
IN AX, *port*		Reads a 16-bit word into the AX register from *port*
IN AX, DX	READ_PORT_USHORT	Reads a 16-bit word into the AX register from the port whose number is in the DX register.
IN EAX, *port*		Reads a 32-bit doubleword into the EAX register from *port*.
IN EAX, DX	READ_PORT_ULONG	Reads a 32-bit doubleword into the EAX register from the port whose number is in the DX register.
INSB		Reads an 8-bit byte from the port whose number is in the DX register and then stores it in the memory location ES:(E)DI. (E)DI is advanced by 1 based on the direction flag setting.
INSW		Reads a 16-bit word from the port whose number is in the DX register and then stores it in the memory location ES:(E)DI. (E)DI is advanced by 2 based on the direction flag setting.
INSD		Reads a 32-bit doubleword from the port whose number is in the DX register and then stores it in the memory location ES:(E)DI. (E)DI is advanced by 4 based on the direction flag setting.

Note: The previous three instructions use ES:DI if the address is 16-bit and ES:EDI if the address is 32-bit. The REP instruction can be used, with the value in CX determining the number of elements read.

Instruction	HAL	Action
OUT *port*, AL		Writes an 8-bit byte from the AL register to *port*.
OUT DX, AL	WRITE_PORT_UCHAR	Writes an 8-bit byte from the AL register to the port whose number is in the DX register.
OUT *port*, AX		Writes a 16-bit word from the AX register to *port*.
OUT DX, AX	WRITE_PORT_USHORT	Writes a 16-bit word from the AX register to the port whose number is in the DX register.
OUT *port*, EAX		Writes a 32-bit doubleword from the EAX register to *port*.
OUT DX, EAX	WRITE_PORT_ULONG	Writes a 32-bit doubleword from the EAX register to the port whose number is in the DX register.
OUTSB		Writes an 8-bit byte taken from the location ES:(E)DI to the port whose number is in the DX register. (E)DI is advanced by 1 based on the direction flag setting.
OUTSW		Writes a 16-bit word taken from the location ES:(E)DI to the port whose number is in the DX register. (E)DI is advanced by 2 based on the direction flag setting.
OUTSD		Writes a 32-bit doubleword taken from the location ES:(E)DI to the port whose number is in the DX register. (E)DI is advanced by 4 based on the direction flag setting.

Note: The previous three instructions use ES:DI if the address is 16-bit and ES:EDI if the address is 32-bit. The REP instruction can be used, with the value in CX determining the number of elements written.

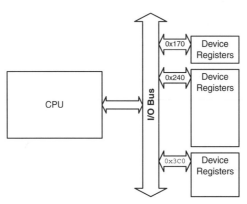

Figure 4.1: *I/O address space.*

The abstract image of the I/O bus is that it is a totally separate set of wires in the machine, as illustrated in Figure 4.1. But this image is a bit of poetic license. On most machines, the address of the IN or OUT instruction is placed on the system address bus, and a special line called the I/O Request Line ($\overline{\text{IOR}}$) is set active to indicate that the address is an I/O address, as opposed to a memory address. The device places its data on, or reads its data from, the system data bus.

 In many cases, the cards that only partially decode the I/O address perform functions that are superseded by more modern cards that decode all 16 bits, and the correct strategy is to discard them in favor of the more modern card. But this is not always an option, particularly for older cards that are both highly specialized (custom A/D data collection cards come to mind) and have not been redesigned to modern standards. Another consideration is the overall cost of replacement. If it is one card, for one machine, it may make sense to buy a replacement. If the company has a thousand cards deployed, the cost of developing a driver may well be justified.

The macros shown in Table 4.1 are shown with their sort-of-equivalent *x*86 instructions primarily to help those who have programmed the *x*86 at the bare metal level to see how the corresponding operations are done in Windows NT. However, this table is an oversimplification. The macros provide a great deal more than a simple simulation of the IN and OUT instructions, and it is *not* correct to assume that you can "optimize" or "simplify" the driver by executing these instructions directly. Not only does doing this render the driver *very* nonportable; it may also render the driver nonfunctional or even erroneous.

In the Alpha, these macros expand into in-line code to perform the operations. On *x*86 machines, they expand to subroutine calls. At least this week.

Memory-Mapped Device Registers

Device registers might also be mapped into the physical address space of the processor. An example of memory-mapped registers is shown in Figure 4.2. It is not coincidental that this figure closely resembles Figure 4.1. The only real difference between I/O ports and memory-mapped device registers is whether the $\overline{\text{IOR}}$ line is activated. If it is not, the address is placed on the system address bus and the device must respond to a full 32-bit address. Typically, a device

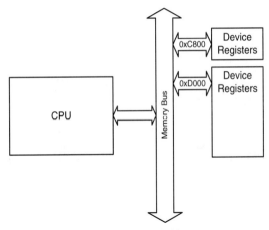

Figure 4.2: *Memory-mapped I/O registers.*

will respond only to certain address ranges. For example, it might choose to require the high-order 12 bits of the address be 0 and provide a variation only of the address bits <12:19> to select the card and <0:11> to select a register. This requires the device's physical memory addresses to exist in the lower 1MB of physical memory. For example, it might require that the device have an address such as 0xD8000. If you've ever programmed a PC-based device, you'll recognize this as being in the gap between the end of the PC's "low" system memory (0x0009FFFF) and the start of system ROM (0x000FFFF0).

Device Memory

For many devices, the notion of having to use DMA to transfer large blocks of data to the computer's main memory is considered a grossly inefficient mechanism. Instead, these devices have some amount of *device memory* that is addressed as normal memory but that really lives on the device. Thus the device directly transfers data to or from the "outside world" using this memory.

A prime example of this that is likely familiar to most readers is the display memory on a display card. Modern cards can have several megabytes of addressable memory into which the processor directly writes the pixel information. The display hardware scans this memory at some rate (50–72 times per second are typical ranges) and thus causes the pixels to appear on a display screen. But this technique is also used by network cards; most of the popular ones have onboard memory. As we move into an era of real-time devices, there are many video and audio interface cards that have directly addressable memory. In some cases, the memory is addressable in its entirety. In others (particularly video cards), only part of it can be seen at one time (see Figure 4.3), in which case there is a *window* into the shared memory. Exactly how shared memory is made visible in the address space of the computer is highly system-specific and often depends on the bus structure of the computer and the kind of card that is plugged in (many computers support two or more external bus structures). The ways in which windows into shared memory are manipulated are also quite specific to the computer architecture and the device.

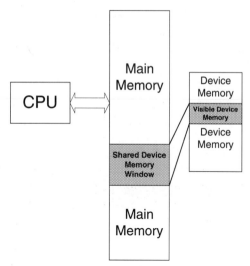

Figure 4.3: *Device memory.*

The dependencies are usually related to the particular *bus structure* of the computer, so next we look at the common bus structures, at least those found in Intel-based platforms, and how they can affect you as a Device Driver writer.

Bus Structures

A number of bus structures are available on Intel-based machines. Many are processor-independent, and a number of other processors have adopted these busses because they make low-cost devices readily available. In the early 1980s, for example, the IBM PC/RT RISC-based processor and the Apollo 68020-based workstation both adopted the 16-bit ISA bus as a standard. Modern processors often have PCI-compatible busses independent of the processor architecture. What do these busses do, and what distinguishes them? We answer those questions in the following sections.

ISA Bus

The ISA bus is the oldest, most venerable, most popular, and least capable of all PC bus architectures. The acronym stands for "Industry Standard Architecture" and is an admission that this bus is the *de facto* standard. This 16-bit bus was introduced by IBM on its 286-based PC/AT to replace the older 8-bit bus of the original IBM PC and IBM PC/XT. Because the IBM PC architecture was so widely copied, both 8-bit and 16-bit cards for a variety of functions are readily available. The 16-bit ISA bus contains the 8-bit PC bus as a proper subset.

The original ISA bus provides for only 24 address lines, so only 16MB of memory can be addressed on an ISA bus. The lower 640K of physical memory (`0x00000000` through `0x0009FFFF`) are usually fully populated in modern machines; addresses `0x0010000` through `0x00FFFFFF` are also usually populated. Because of the addressing restriction, "modern" ISA-bus machines use a completely separate memory bus to allow more than 16MB of memory to be addressed.

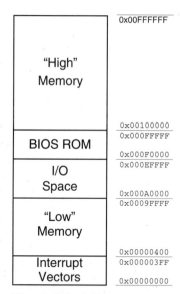

Figure 4.4: *Addresses on an 80x86/Pentium ISA bus.*

The memory layout of an ISA-bus computer is shown in Figure 4.4. While the HAL may protect you from many of the details, you might actually have to configure the device you are programming to live in this physical address space. In most machines, the locations 0xA0000 through 0xBFFFF are reserved for the display card memory, so the only addresses you would typically have available for any device addresses are 0xC0000 through 0xEFFFF.

ISA Machines with > 16MB of Memory

You may actually own a machine that has an ISA bus and much more than 16MB of memory. How is this possible? Simple: The memory *does not live on the ISA bus*. Instead, there is a separate, usually 32-bit address, dedicated memory bus between the processor and the memory (see Figure 4.5). This is important for performance reasons. The ISA bus is limited by its specifica-

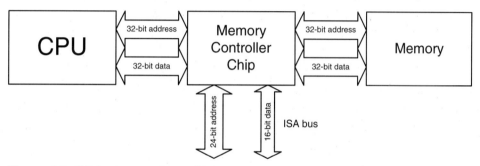

Figure 4.5: *ISA bus/memory bus architecture.*

tion to a maximum clock rate of 8.33MHz, or approximately 120 ns per clock cycle. A 200MHz machine could access memory once every 5 ns. This discrepancy drove hardware designers to provide the second, faster memory path to the processor as far back as the 386 architecture. However, any card that plugs into the ISA bus must respond to addresses in the first 16MB, since the bus itself has only 24 address lines.

So how does an ISA machine determine if it should put an address on the ISA bus or the internal memory bus? Normally, you don't ever see this because it is handled by a programmable memory controller chip. This chip determines if specific addresses are on the ISA bus or the internal memory bus. However, in many machines, the "Advanced BIOS Setup" lets you control which addresses are delivered to the ISA bus and which are sent to the memory bus. It is generally considered a Bad Idea to change any of these parameters, unless you cannot get your card to work in any other way.

I/O Space on ISA Machines

The I/O space on an ISA machine is a 16-bit address space. A properly designed ISA card will decode all 16 bits of the I/O space to determine if it should respond. Older cards, as we indicated earlier in the chapter, respond to only 9 bits of the address space. Despite this shoddy design, many cards continue to have this misfeature.

Direct Memory Access on ISA Machines

The ISA architecture provides for seven DMA channels. Channels 0..3 can do only 8-bit transfers, and channels 5..7 can do only 16-bit transfers. Channel 4 is reserved as a "cascade" channel that connects the two separate DMA controller chips. (In modern practice, these "two chips" are often on the same piece of silicon with many other control functions, but since the original PC/AT used two actual separate chips for DMA, all other compatible machines have to emulate this.) Generally, the HAL layer isolates you from most of these details, but you will need to deal with assigning DMA channels to your device. Other bus architectures allow the individual devices to have their own private DMA controllers, but pure ISA has no such provision.

Perhaps the most significant restriction of the pure ISA architecture is that the DMA controllers on the motherboard can generate only 24-bit addresses. This means that all memory buffers used for DMA must live in the lower 16MB of memory. Fortunately, the HAL layer provides the facilities you need to do this.

Interrupts on ISA Machines

The ISA bus supports 16 interrupt lines. The canonical assignments are shown in Table 4.2. Note that there are only four unassigned interrupt request lines and possibly two others if there is no primary or secondary printer attached to the machine. Because the ISA bus uses *edge-triggered* interrupts, if you have two devices assigned to the same IRQ line you will get a malfunction. Either one device will keep the signal level from changing (hence no edge will be seen) or the first device will mask the second device's signal change, losing the second interrupt entirely. This limits how many additional devices you can add to a machine.

Table 4.2: *ISA Bus IRQ Assignments*

Level	Used For
IRQ0	8253 Timer channel 0
IRQ1	Keyboard
IRQ2	Cascade from IRQ 9
IRQ3	COM2
IRQ4	COM1
IRQ5	LPT2 or available
IRQ6	Floppy disk
IRQ7	LPT1 or available
IRQ8	Real-time clock
IRQ9	Redirected to IRQ2
IRQ10	Available
IRQ11	Available
IRQ12	Available
IRQ13	Math coprocessor
IRQ14	Hard disk controller
IRQ15	Available

The MicroChannel (MCA) Bus

IBM introduced the MicroChannel Architecture (MCA) bus for two major reasons. One was to introduce a bus that was technically superior to the ISA bus—faster negotiations, bus masters, parallel DMA, dynamically assignable interrupts, multiple devices on a single interrupt, self-identifying boards, and software-configurable boards. In this, it succeeded. Another reason was to get a "lock" on the PC marketplace by introducing a patented bus structure. In this, it failed completely.

The second reason was extremely important to IBM. The original PC, PC/XT, and PC/AT had very little that was patentable in their architecture. Thus it was widely copied by clone manufacturers who built functionally identical machines, sold them at a fraction of IBM's price, and paid IBM not one cent in licensing fees. The first 386-based machine was introduced by Compaq[1] while IBM was living in a dream world in which the 286 was the ultimate computing engine. Clone 386 boards soon became widely available. The IBM PS/2, with its faster and technically superior bus structure, was designed to recapture the market and guarantee that IBM had a revenue stream from the clonemakers. Unfortunately, add-on cards for the MCA were much more expensive and far less available than cards for the old ISA, and IBM's licensing requirements meant that virtually no clonemakers licensed the MCA architecture. The marketplace

---

[1] At least one unnameable source at IBM claims that when Compaq released their 386, which became an overnight best-seller, IBM didn't even have a 386 chip in the company because the 286 was "clearly good enough".

responded to the MCA with something between indifference and outright hostility; as a result, the MCA is effectively dead. We have never encountered an MCA machine and have never programmed one, and you probably won't either.

However, the MCA *did* introduce some important concepts, which are still around today. We discuss these further when we look at the EISA, PCI, and USB architectures. These concepts are also critical to the Plug-and-Play software concepts of Windows 95, Windows 98, and Windows 2000.

The key ideas of MCA, which come up again in the other bus architectures, are as follows:

- Self-identifying devices
- Devices that are configured by software, rather than with onboard DIP switches or jumpers; reconfiguration includes both device addresses and interrupt assignments, as well as any device-specific parameters that may need to be set
- Level-triggered interrupts and the ability of multiple devices to share the same interrupt line
- Bus masters
- Distributed DMA control

The EISA Bus

The EISA bus (Extended Industry Standard Architecture bus) was the industry's response to IBM's MCA initiative. The goal was to get many of the features of the MCA in a vendor-neutral, open specification that everyone could build without paying royalties. You will quite likely encounter EISA machines that run NT.

There are several accepted ways of pronouncing the names of the various architectures. For example, "ISA" is often pronounced "eye-sa", while "EISA" is "ee-sa". Unfortunately, there is no universal agreement on these pronunciations; in any case, they are rather local pronunciations. I had a discussion with a German computer professional, and it was about ten minutes into the conversation when I realized (and I should have known better, as I can speak a bit of German) that "ISA" in German is pronounced "ee-sa", whereas "EISA" is pronounced "eye-sa". Since then, I have insisted on spelling them out, e.g., "ISA" is "eye-ess-ay" and "EISA" is "ee-eye-ess-ay".– *jmn*

The EISA bus was designed to contain the ISA bus as a proper subset so that if you have an EISA slot on a machine, you can plug an 8-bit PC-bus card, a 16-bit ISA-bus card, and a 16-bit or 32-bit EISA-bus card into it. At the hardware level, this need for compatibility makes the hardware more complex, but you are unlikely to see this. The physical slot compatibility is achieved by a special 2-level connector. The upper level of the connector is standard ISA, and the lower level, which is too far down for an ISA card to reach, implements the additional EISA signals. Those of you who care about the details, of the signals can read about the EISA bus signals in *The Indispensable PC Hardware Book, Second Edition*, pp. 491–493. As a Device Driver writer, what you need to know is that the EISA bus supports a full 32-bit address and 32-bit data path (or, optionally, a 16-bit data path).

The EISA bus structure is shown in Figure 4.6. Note that there are three busses involved here: the bus that connects the CPU to memory (and possibly caches, not shown) and two logically equivalent but physically separate peripheral busses: the *Motherboard I/O bus* and the

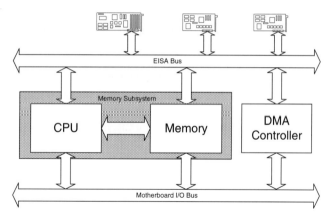

Figure 4.6: *EISA bus architecture.*

EISA bus. The latter two are distinguished by the fact that the EISA bus is implemented as physical slots on the backplane, while the Motherboard I/O bus is connected to the onboard peripherals. These usually include the floppy and hard disk controllers, serial and parallel ports, and, in some systems, even network interfaces (usually 10Base-T networks).

I/O Space on EISA Machines

The EISA I/O address space is also special. Although it is still a 16-bit address space, some very specific assignments of I/O addresses make it possible to address an individual card by its physical position, as shown in Table 4.3. Note that we do not say individual *device*. A card can contain potentially several devices, such as a typical "multifunction disk card", which can contain a pair of serial ports, a parallel port, a game port, a floppy controller, and an IDE controller. These six devices are all addressed via unique device addresses, and they generate potentially unique interrupts. But on an EISA machine, the *card* is the basic unit of management, so for a multifunction disk card the card must contain the descriptions of all six devices (we discuss this in detail shortly).

A properly designed EISA card ignores any I/O address whose high-order 4 bits are 0. If it sees an address whose high-order 4 bits are nonzero, it knows that it now has its slot address. The I/O bus of an EISA slot does *not* resemble that of an ISA slot; in the ISA slot, all of the control signals are run from the processor to all of the boards. For an EISA backplane, I/O addresses determine which slot receives the additional signals for decoding the address. Thus if you do I/O to address `0x7000`, only slot 7 gets the signals that tell the board a valid address is present. It is the responsibility of the motherboard's EISA controller to deal with this.

The BIOS saves additional state information into the CMOS RAM (an EISA machine has a much larger CMOS RAM than an ISA machine does). There are the HAL operations that will give you this information. It is the responsibility of some administrative software, in this case, Windows NT, to deal with configuring EISA cards. Each vendor is required to deliver a file on a floppy that contains the important EISA configuration information. This information is stored in the CMOS RAM. When the system boots, the card information is read for each slot and then the corresponding parameters are read from the CMOS RAM. This is documented in detail in *The*

Table 4.3: *EISA I/O Space*

I/O Address	Meaning
0x0000..0x00FF	ISA motherboard
0x0100..0x03FF	ISA expansion
0x0400..0x04FF	EISA motherboard
0x0800..0x08FF	EISA motherboard
0x0C00..0x0CFF	EISA motherboard
0x1000..0x1FFF	Expansion slot 1
0x2000..0x2FFF	Expansion slot 2
0x3000..0x3FFF	Expansion slot 3
0x4000..0x4FFF	Expansion slot 4
0x5000..0x5FFF	Expansion slot 5
0x6000..0x6FFF	Expansion slot 6
0x7000..0x7FFF	Expansion slot 7
0x8000..0x8FFF	Expansion slot 8
0x9999..0xFFFF	Reserved for additional expansion slots

Indispensable PC Handbook, Second Edition, pp. 485–489. Much of this will be handled for you by the HAL, but you will need to know how to work with other parts of it. We look at this in detail in later chapters.

Direct Memory Access on EISA Machines

A major advance of EISA over ISA is that in an EISA-based machine, a device can become a bus master and can transfer data directly into system memory. To accomplish this, a device contains its own DMA controller, rather than requiring one of the seven DMA channels of the ISA architecture (although, for ISA compatibility, these must be present on an EISA machine). The device's DMA controller can access any memory in the full 32-bit address space; therefore the constraint about buffers being in the first 16MB of physical memory goes away. Because the DMA negotiation is faster, it is possible to have DMA speeds of 5.56MB/sec (using "type A" DMA) and 8.33MB/sec (using "type B" DMA) and bursts at 33MB/sec (using "type C" DMA). We look at what these different DMA types mean when we discuss DMA in Chapter 17.

Unlike with the ISA architecture, each of the seven built-in EISA DMA controller channels can transfer 8-, 16-, or 32-bit data. There are other differences between the two architectures that are largely masked by the HAL. For example, the transfer count register for DMA is (almost) always a byte count in EISA, while in ISA it is a byte count for the 8-bit channels and a word count for the 16-bit channels. (The one exception is that a DMA channel can be programmed to transfer 16-bit data using a word count, for compatibility with ISA.)

Table 4.4: *EISA Bus IRQ Assignments*

Level	Priority	Used For
IRQ0	1	8253 Timer channel 0
IRQ1	2	Keyboard
IRQ2	–	Cascade from IRQ 9
IRQ3	11	COM2
IRQ4	12	COM1
IRQ5	13	LPT2 or available
IRQ6	14	Floppy disk
IRQ7	15	LPT1 or available
IRQ8	3	Real-time clock
IRQ9	4	Redirected to IRQ2
IRQ10	5	Available
IRQ11	6	Available
IRQ12	7	Available
IRQ13	8	Math coprocessor
IRQ14	9	Hard disk controller
IRQ15	10	Available

Interrupts on EISA Machines

EISA supports the same 16 interrupt levels that the ISA bus supports. However, the priorities are programmable (instead of being fixed based on the IRQ number, as with the ISA). The default assignments are shown in Table 4.4. In addition, you can program each IRQ channel as being either edge-triggered or level-triggered. Thus you can assign two or more EISA cards to the same IRQ line without conflict. Furthermore, the bus architecture supports more than one card on the same IRQ line. There are various ways of determining the IRQ level; you will interact with the HAL layer to set these interrupt levels when appropriate. The EISA bus uses "open drain" or "open collector" drivers for the EISA IRQ lines. These are illustrated in Figure 4.10 on page 88 and discussed in more detail when we deal with the PCI Bus.

The PCI Bus

The most serious limitation of the ISA, EISA, and even the MCA busses is the total bus bandwidth. While the MCA bus definitely supports very high bandwidth DMA transfers, it is not particularly impressive in handling single memory transactions, such as might take place, for example, when writing to a display memory. As display resolution increases, the amount of time required to update the display becomes more and more noticeable. For example, a $1600 \times 1200 \times 24$ display requires moving 5.76MB of data to completely redraw the screen. Assuming you could get the full bandwidth of the bus—and you can't even come close—it

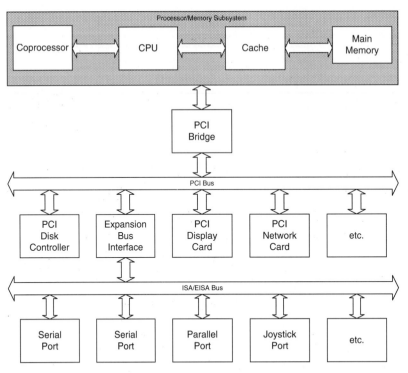

Figure 4.7: *PCI Bus architecture.*

would take about 1 second to redraw the screen. However, with the percentage of bandwidth you can actually get, it might take 2 seconds to redraw the screen, a totally unacceptable value. What was needed was a faster bus, something that worked at close to memory speeds. A PCI Bus can achieve a transfer rate of 266MB/sec.

The industry wanted a vendor-neutral, high-speed bus that everyone could use, similar to the EISA specification. A couple of aborted attempts at developing such a bus were made. Finally, the PCI Bus (Peripheral Component Interconnect Bus), specified by Intel, became the new standard. (One other standard was nearly accepted, until the lawyers for one firm noted that the firm held the patent on the connector. The firm decided it wanted a royalty for every connector sold. The proposal for this standard died virtually overnight. Everyone remembered IBM and MCA.)

PCI has turned out to be not only vendor-independent within the Intel processor vendors; it also is platform-independent and has appeared in other machines. Of particular interest to Device Driver writers is the fact that one of these machines is the Alpha, which runs NT.

Of course, it would be a shame to waste this power on just the display, so disk drives and network cards also use the PCI Bus. As a Device Driver writer, you will find there are many other high-speed devices that will be built for the PCI Bus. We discuss PCI interface issues a lot throughout this book.[2]

The PCI bus structure is much more complex than those for ISA or EISA. Its most important feature is that a PCI machine actually has three separate bus systems: the processor/memory bus, the PCI Bus, and the "expansion" bus, which is either ISA or EISA (note that although EISA has three physically separate busses, two of them are functionally identical). This is shown in Figure 4.7. The PCI Bus multiplexes data and address lines. Multiplexing reduces the total number of signals; however, it also means that one separate clock cycle is required to send the address and another to send the data. For 32-bit transfers, this normally limits the bus transfer rate to 44MB/sec for read accesses and 66MB/sec for write accesses. But in *burst mode*, the address is sent once and is automatically incremented or decremented (as appropriate) for the transfer. Using burst mode, the bus can transfer 133MB/sec for 32-bit transfers and 266MB/sec for 64-bit transfers.

The key to PCI performance is that the PCI Bridge can synthesize burst accesses if it notices that the accesses coming in are sequential. The PCI Bridge also contains buffers that allow the main memory bus and the PCI Bus to work with their disparate speeds. This allows the PCI Bus and processor to operate in parallel during PCI transfers.

Also, a PCI controller allows the addressing of a configuration data area. This area, a section on each PCI card, contains the relevant autoconfiguration data. So a PCI Bridge can access ISA/EISA addresses, PCI addresses, and PCI configuration addresses.

The PCI bus allows for multiple bus masters. In fact, one PCI device can take control of the PCI bus and transfer data directly to another device on the PCI Bus, without any processor intervention at all. This makes it ideal for transferring high-speed video or audio data from a source to a destination without any intermediate stops in the main memory of the system.

The PCI electrical specification is quite complex. For example, the bus is more like an analog device than a digital device, as Tom Shanley explains in *PCI System Architecture* (on page 51). For correct functioning, the bus actually depends on the fact that the reflection of the signal from the end of the bus causes the voltage level to double! We refer those readers who care about this to Shanley's book.

I/O Space in a PCI System

Referring to the EISA I/O address assignments, you will see that there are several "holes" in the I/O space that are not assigned: 0x400..0x4FF, 0x800..0x8FF, and 0xC00..0xCFF. The suggested PCI implementation uses only two I/O addresses, which are in these holes:

1. 0xCF8, in which you place the configuration address, which has a complex format
2. 0xCFC, which holds the data to be stored to the Configuration Memory on an OUT instruction or the data to be read on an IN instruction

[2] With the increase in processor speed and capabilities and the other demands for PCI bandwidth, the PCI bus is now considered slow for use by video adapters. The Advanced Graphics Port (AGP) was developed to provide a higher bandwidth path to display memory. The AGP provides dedicated bandwidth to the display adapter (there is only one AGP slot in a system). The AGP will operate in single or double speed mode. In the future, quad speed mode will also be available. This provides a processor-to-display bandwith of 133 MB/sec (single), 266 MB/sec (double), or 533 MB/sec (quad). The AGP appears to the programmer very much like another PCI bus in the system.

The details don't matter much because you will normally access this data through the HAL layer.

Configuration Memory Space in a PCI System

A PCI Bus system contains a special address space, the *Configuration Memory*. The Configuration Memory is onboard memory that describes each device on the card. A card can contain up to eight devices. Each device is described by a 256-byte block of memory, of which the initial 64 bytes must be in a standard format called the *device header*. You generally won't care how you access this data; you'll do it through the HAL layer. But you will care about what information is in the header. A diagram of the header information is shown in Figure 4.8.

- The vendor ID is a 16-bit value in the range `0x0000..0xFFFE`; the value `0xFFFF` indicates a nonexistent device. Each ID is unique.

- The device ID is assigned by the vendor and identifies the device.

- The status register is a funky register. You can read it, but when you write it, you can clear bits only by setting the bit you write to a 1. Writing a 1-bit to the register sets the corresponding register bit to 0.

- The command register enables various features of the card; we look at these in detail later in the chapter.

31		16	15			0	
Device ID			Vendor ID				0x00
Status			Command				0x04
Class Code					Rev		0x08
BIST	Hdr		Lat		Cache		0x0C
Base Address 0							0x10
Base Address 1							0x14
Base Address 2							0x18
Base Address 3							0x1C
Base Address 4							0x20
Base Address 5							0x24
CardBus CIS Pointer							0x28
Subsystem ID			Subsys Vendor ID				0x2C
Expansion BIOS ROM Addr.							0x30
Reserved							0x34
Reserved							0x38
MaxLat	MinGnt		IntPin		IntLn		0x3C

Figure 4.8: *PCI device configuration header.*

- The Class Code is used to identify the class of the device, and is subdivided into three 8-bit fields: class, subclass, and "Prog I/F", meaning "programming interface". The 8-bit class field defines classes such as display devices, mass storage devices, network controllers, multimedia devices, docking stations, and many other classes of devices. The 8-bit subclass field and the 8-bit Prog I/F field describe particulars of the general device specified by the class field. For details, consult Chapter 17 of the *PCI System Architecture* book cited in Further Reading.

- The revision ID is assigned by the vendor and indicates the revision level of the device.

- The BIST field indicates if the device has a built-in self test. It is optional and is discussed in detail in Chapter 17 of *PCI System Architecture*.

- The header type (Hdr) indicates which revision of the PCI standard was used for this device. The low-order 7 bits value in this field determines how the other fields are interpreted. The PCI header shown in Figure 4.8 is for a Type 0 header, the only type currently defined for nonbridge devices. A PCI-to-PCI Bridge will have a Type 1 header. The high-order bit of this field is 0 for single-function devices and 1 for multifunction devices.

- The latency timer (Lat) is an optional register that may or may not be implemented for a specific device. If present, it is used to control the amount of time the PCI device will own the bus when it is a bus master. For details on this, consult Chapter 17 of *PCI System Architecture*.

- We discuss the cache line size when we talk about the effects of caches on I/O operations in Chapter 6.

- The base address registers (0..5) define the base address of I/O registers or onboard memory for up to six ranges of I/O registers or memory for each device. We discuss how these registers are used in Chapter 21.

- The CardBus CIS register is used when the device is also on the CardBus. It is optional and is discussed in detail in Chapter 17 of *PCI System Architecture*.

- The subsystem ID and the subsystem vendor ID are used when the device is a component of a multifunction PCI device. They are optional and are discussed in detail in Chapter 21.

- We discuss the ROM BIOS extension address in Chapter 21.

- The IntPin value indicates which of the PCI interrupts (if any) are to be used by this device. A zero value means no interrupt; the values 1..4 represent $\overline{INTA}..\overline{INTD}$.

- The MaxLat and MinGnt values are optional and apply only to bus mastering controllers.

- The IntLn register maps the PCI interrupt to an IRQ line; values 0..15 correspond to IRQ0..IRQ15 levels.

Direct Memory Access in a PCI System

There is no central DMA controller chip that manages PCI cards. Each PCI card that does DMA is a bus master. It contains its own control registers and is responsible for any DMA-like transfers. Two PCI devices are always involved in any DMA transfer: the *initiator* and the *target*. The *initiator* is a PCI device that has become a bus master. The *target* is a PCI device that is addressed by the initiator and will send or receive data as requested by the initiator. There is a completely symmetric relationship, that is, any device can be an initiator or a target and they may exchange roles at any time. In Chapter 21, we study, in exquisite detail, how these functions are handled.

Interrupts in a PCI System

Interrupts in PCI work differently than in ISA/EISA systems. PCI busses have four interrupt lines designated $\overline{\text{INTA}}$, $\overline{\text{INTB}}$, $\overline{\text{INTC}}$, and $\overline{\text{INTD}}$. A single-function board must use $\overline{\text{INTA}}$; multi-function boards use $\overline{\text{INTA}}$ as well as $\overline{\text{INTB}}$, $\overline{\text{INTC}}$, and $\overline{\text{INTD}}$. These signals are handled by the PCI Bridge, which maps the interrupt to one of the IRQ levels on the processor board. The PCI Bridge can map the $\overline{\text{INTA}}$ signal from each PCI card (or the $\overline{\text{INTB}}$, $\overline{\text{INTC}}$, and $\overline{\text{INTD}}$ signals) to any IRQ. Thus there is a very flexible IRQ mapping capability. The $\overline{\text{INTA}}$, $\overline{\text{INTB}}$, $\overline{\text{INTC}}$, and $\overline{\text{INTD}}$ are level-triggered, so there is no conflict when several single-function cards all activate $\overline{\text{INTA}}$ or when two different multifunction PCI cards activate $\overline{\text{INTB}}$. In addition, the PCI Bridge can program the priority of each IRQ. Much of this configuration is handled by the HAL layer.

The interrupt lines are referred to as "open drain", the NMOS equivalent of the TTL "open collector". Here, we explain this in terms of TTL because that technology is simpler to understand.

A standard TTL driver is shown in Figure 4.9. In each of Devices 1 and 2, the two transistors, Q1 and Q2, are driven in a complementary fashion. Thus if Q1 is conducting, Q2 is not and the output is nearly at ground level. If Q2 is conducting, Q1 is not and the output is nearly at the +V level (5 volts in TTL, but many computers now run at 3.3 volts, and the voltage is dropping with each generation). Note that if Device 1 has Q1 conducting and Device 2 has Q2 conducting, the results can be undefined. This setup could even blow out one of the two conducting transistors. This is why the ISA bus cannot have multiple interrupts assigned to the same IRQ line.

Figure 4.10 shows the TTL "open collector" technique. Here, the pull-up is a passive resistor, so if any device turns on its transistor Q1, the line will be pulled low. This is why the interrupt lines are active-low on the PCI and EISA busses and the interrupts are all level-triggered. As long as any device holds the signal low, interrupts will continue to occur until all devices are satisfied and the line is allowed to go high. (Of course, a device may be satisfied and release the interrupt signal but then reassert it before the last device on that line is satisfied. This is perfectly acceptable!)

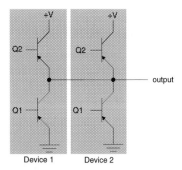

Figure 4.9: *Active pull-up bus drivers.*

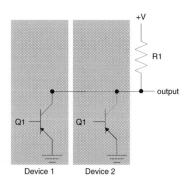

Figure 4.10: *"Open-collector" ("open drain") bus drivers.*

BIOS Extension ROM in a PCI System

The BIOS Extension ROM on a PCI board is a bit more elaborate than one on a normal ISA or EISA card. Normally, a BIOS ROM contains a special "signature". When an Intel *x*86/Pentium system does its Power-On Self-Test (POST), it looks at addresses in the range 0xC000 through 0xE800 at intervals of 0x800. If the signature is found, the POST code calls the entry point of the BIOS ROM that is at a specific offset. In a PCI system, the BIOS ROM has a more elaborate header and the BIOS can contain code for multiple platforms, such as the Intel *x*86 and the Alpha, so one card can be manufactured for multiple machines. You don't need to worry about how this works. The POST code on the specific platform is responsible for figuring out how to find the BIOS code and executing it.

PCI Bridges

A PCI Bus is limited to four slots. This is unrealistic, no matter how many vendors build mother-boards with four PCI slots. Eight is comfortable, and for serious file servers, twelve might be a better number. But the physics of the bus design (capacitance, inductance, loading, and the use of reflection waves from the unterminated ends of the bus to boost the signal) make it impossible to create a bus with more than four slots. (Some vendors have tried. What is amazing is that when an ordinary PCI card fails when plugged into their bus, it is "the customer's fault", not the fault of their engineers who have played fast and loose with the specs.)

The solution is the *PCI-to-PCI Bridge*. The PCI-to-PCI Bridge is an active PCI component (it has its own Configuration Space memory, with its own vendor ID and device ID, for example) and is normally programmed by the BIOS and/or the HAL. Generally, you will find that as a Device Driver writer, you will never notice the effects of a PCI-to-PCI Bridge, except that some devices will have a bus number other than 0 during bus enumeration (see Chapter 21).

As shown in Figure 4.11, the concept of the PCI-to-PCI Bridge is fairly general. A minimal configuration with a PCI-to-PCI Bridge would have only one bridge. The primary bus would be Bus 0, and the one on the other side of the bridge would be Bus 1. But there can be more than one bridge on a single bus, in which case the secondary busses are assigned unique bus numbers by the BIOS or the HAL. This bus number is stored as part of the configuration information for the Bridge. A two-bridge configuration could have two bridges off the primary bus, which would be Bus 0, and the two secondary busses would be Bus 1 and Bus 2. In addition, any secondary bus can have a PCI-to-PCI Bridge. In this case, a tree structure of bridges similar to that of Figure 4.11 can exist. In effect, each PCI Bus is a node in the tree, and it is the responsibility of the BIOS and the HAL to establish a unique "node numbering" for the nodes in the tree, where the "root node" is 0.

A device on the PCI bus must respond within a short period of the address being placed on the bus. This allows access to unimplemented locations to be detected and the access cycle aborted. The time requirement does not allow the bridge to query the lower-level bus before responding. In order to respond within this timing limit, the bridge must know all addresses contained on lower level busses. The bridge may respond to a range larger than the lower-level bus actually uses, but must not respond to addresses that some other device (not accessed through the bridge) recognizes.

An individual PCI card may itself contain a bridge and, within itself, one or more PCI devices. A classic example is a multifunction card. The designer of such a card is free to introduce a PCI-to-PCI Bridge if that is required to maintain the proper operation of the PCI Bus into which it is plugged.

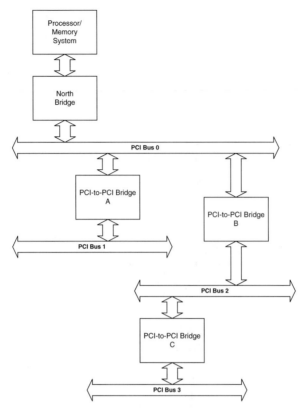

Figure 4.11: *PCI-to-PCI Bridge example.*

We said that "ideally" you would never have to worry about bridges. In the Real World, alas, you not only may have to worry about bridges, you can be seriously done in by them. This is because the bridges partition the I/O space *and* the adapter memory space into disjoint regions. If these regions ever overlap, your device will not work.

When a card is initialized, it establishes that it has a base address and size. Consider the case of a card with 64K of onboard memory. The card claims that the base address of its memory is 0xA0000. If you plug two of these cards into a single PCI Bus, they would not work because the addresses conflict. So the BIOS, which reads the Configuration Memory, determines that it can assign the second card to address 0xB0000. It then rewrites the Configuration Memory to indicate this assignment. All Is Well.

The same thing happens if you have a two-PCI-bus system. One of the cards gets its address reassigned. But the situation is a bit more complex because of the intervening bridge. The bridge acts like a router; the only signals it passes are to memory addresses on the other side of the bridge. The result is that the addresses assigned to devices on the other side are *not* arbitrary addresses. A PCI-to-PCI Bridge has one or two of *base address registers* that define the base address, length, and type of *all* of the addresses on the other side. Each of the register's contents may describe a window in either I/O address space or memory address space. This allows a typical bridge to have one I/O address range and one memory address range.

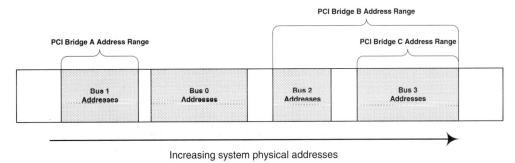

Figure 4.12: *PCI-to-PCI Bridge address partitioning.*

The typical case for a bridge in a PC system is for one base address register to map I/O addresses and the other to map memory addresses. This means that the memory addresses for *all* devices on its other side *must* fall into a single range (the addresses need not be contiguous, but they must fall in that one range). Additionally this means that the I/O addresses for *all* devices on its other side *must* fall into a single range (again, the addresses need not be contiguous, but they must fall in that one range).

If there is another Bridge on that bus, the addresses on that bus must be included in the range of the first bus. We show this in Figure 4.12. Note that the address range of a superior Bridge must include the address range of its contained busses. For the case of single mapping registers, we end up with a tree-like structure as shown in the figure. Note that the ranges do not have to be contiguous. Nor are they necessarily ordered by bus number (for example, here, the Bus 0 addresses are higher than the Bus 1 addresses).

The implications of this are significant. The BIOS must do a treewalk down the (multiway) tree of PCI busses, assigning address ranges. The treewalk must assign all addresses on the deepest busses before it is able to assign addresses to the bus containing the bridge to the less deep bus, since the addresses assigned to the bridge will be needed.

The assigned addresses must be unique across all other busses and programming the higher-level bridges to cover that range. The Windows NT HAL will do some reassignment of the address ranges, both at NT startup and when the device driver for the device starts. In a system with multiple bridges, the reassignments are limited by the ability to move the memory assigned to bridges. There is no facility in NT 4.0 to notify a running device driver that assigned resources have moved due to a forced bus reassignment. So any resources used by a device driver that has already started are not movable.

You can see that with the addition of reassignment of addresses, a simplistic assignment algorithm could well become confused and assign overlapping address ranges or assign a higher-level bus range that does not include all of the addresses found on the busses on the bridge's other side. The result will be a device that is nonresponsive or a system that malfunctions in other ways.

It should now be clear that we face severe problems if we need to make large adjustments to the memory or I/O asssignments of a device after Windows NT has started.[3]

---

[3] This is not a hypothetical case. I believe I am seeing exactly this behavior on at least one combination of machine and device. As this is being written, I am still trying to track down the problem. *–end*

The use of a PCI Bus Monitor, which we describe in Chapter 9, can aid considerably in trying to track down errors of this type. A PCI Bus Monitor can track, at the hardware level, all of the configuration initialization traffic during the BIOS setup. Since a PCI-to-PCI Bridge is itself a PCI device, the setup of this device, including the register assignments, can also be tracked. Careful analysis of the traces is required to ascertain exactly what is happening. It doesn't hurt to have a reasonably complete specification of the particular PCI-to-PCI Bridges that are on the system you are debugging.

Note that the PCI Bus Monitor will see only traffic which passes through the particular bus. That is to say that (referring to Figure 4.11) a PCI Bus Monitor installed in PCI Bus 0 will see all traffic between the North Bridge (and therefore the CPU) and and all devices in all busses. The monitor will not see local traffic within PCI Bus 1, PCI Bus 2, or PCI Bus 3, or intra-traffic between PCI Bus 2 and PCI Bus 3. If instead the monitor were installed into PCI Bus 1, it would see only traffic for devices on PCI Bus 1 and no traffic to devices in PCI Bus 2 or PCI Bus 3.

For more detail on PCI-to-PCI Bridges, we suggest Chapter 19 of *PCI System Architecture*. For additional details of how a PCI BIOS and/or the HAL must operate, see Chapter 20 of the same book. While this latter chapter does not go into as much detail as you will need to debug a faulty bridge setup, it provides information that, when coupled with the actual data sheet for the PCI Bridge, should help you interpret the BIOS setup traces from a trace.

Basic Questions About the Device

When you confront a device you need to program, you need to ask the following questions.

- How can I find the base of the I/O register space?
- How many device registers are there in the I/O register space?
- How many device registers are there, really?
- What device registers are utterly crucial to my driver?
- (Devices with memory attached) How can I find the base address of the memory?
- (Devices with memory attached) How can I find the size of the memory?
- (Devices with ROM attached) How can I find the base address of the ROM?
- (Devices with ROM attached) How can I execute the ROM code?
- (Devices that do Direct Memory Access) Does the device require one or more of the system DMA channels?
- (Devices that do Direct Memory Access) Is the device a bus mastering device?

We show you how we answer all of these questions when we get to Chapter 20 and Chapter 21.

Summary

This chapter has introduced a number of internal busses and discussed how they are accessed. The different I/O architectures were compared. The two most important busses, the ISA bus and the PCI Bus, were covered in some detail. We will look at these busses again, from the NT viewpoint, in Chapter 20 and Chapter 21.

Further Reading

Intel Corporation, *i486 Microprocessor Programmer's Reference Manual*, McGraw-Hill, 1990. ISBN 0-07-881674-2.

Messmer, Hans-Peter, *The Indispensable PC Hardware Book, Second Edition*, Addison-Wesley, 1995. ISBN 0-201-87697-3.

Mindshare, Inc.: Don Anderson and Tom Shanley, *Pentium™ Processor System Architecture, Second Edition*, Addison-Wesley, 1995. ISBN 0-201-40992-5.

Mindshare, Inc.: Tom Shanley and Don Anderson, *PCI System Architecture, Third Edition*, Addison-Wesley, 1995. ISBN 0-201-40993-3.

Chapter

5 *Device Driver Basics*

Drivers are not like application programs. Because drivers live in the kernel, they must follow some very specific rules of behavior. These make a lot of your "common knowledge" about application programs inapplicable. In addition to the fundamental rules, because a driver has so many different contexts in which it executes, there are additional rules that must be followed depending on what the driver is doing. Sometimes, violating these rules results in an immediate Blue Screen, thereby making your point of violation easy to detect. Sometimes, violating these rules results in some other malfunction, far beyond the point where the violation occurred, thereby making the identification of the violation difficult. Sometimes, the violation simply causes some random piece of kernel state to become scrambled, thereby resulting in some component you never heard of malfunctioning hundreds of millions of instructions later. These violations are virtually impossible to identify. And finally, there are the violations that occur only in an obscure, rarely-called case, such as in an error handler or as a consequence of some odd interaction with the application. Trying to recreate the conditions that led to this violation of the rules—particularly if the software has been deployed in the field for weeks or months—is, for most practical purposes, impossible.

NT Device Drivers must follow a strict protocol to work with the Windows NT system. The Device Driver writer must be aware of the environment in which the driver will run and work with that environment in order to achieve a successful result. In many drivers, talking to the device is the *easy* part of writing the Device Driver; talking to NT is the *hard* part. The Device Driver writer must be aware that other devices will be generating interrupts while the Device Driver is executing. Multiprocessor systems further complicate the issues because different parts of the driver could be executing concurrently on separate processors. Before you can address the more sophisticated issues of writing a Device Driver, you must have a fundamental understanding of the basics of how a Device Driver works.

A Taxonomy of Kernel-Mode Drivers

There are several basic types of Windows NT Kernel-mode drivers, each having a slightly different structure but significantly different behavior.

- The *physical (lowest-level) Device Driver* directly controls physical devices. It is sometimes called *lowest-level driver* because it is the lowest layer in a layered structure. The lowest-level driver may be called by another driver or directly by application code.

- The *intermediate driver* is a device-type-specific driver. It does not manipulate devices directly; rather, it calls lower-level drivers to manipulate the device. It is called by higher-level drivers.

- The *highest-level driver* is called in the context of application programs. The programs, in turn, may call lower-level drivers to implement the I/O operation.

- The *File System Driver* is a type of highest-level driver that supports the various file systems such as FAT, NTFS, and CDFS.[1] It depends on lower-level Class Drivers or Physical Device Drivers to access hardware. This type of driver is not covered in this book.

- The *Filter Driver* inserts itself either between the user and a driver or between two layers of drivers to modify the behavior of the underlying driver.

- The *network driver* implements support for network adapters and network protocols. This type of driver is not covered in this book.

Driver Limitations

The only drivers we are concerned about in this book are the drivers that live in the kernel and execute in Kernel mode. There are significant limitations on what a kernel driver can do and how it is coded.

- A Kernel-mode driver cannot call user-level API or C runtime library functions because these functions are not available in the kernel. Instead, NT provides a set of kernel-level functions that provide a subset of the API and C runtime library functions.

- Drivers cannot perform floating-point operations. If a driver running in Kernel mode attempts to perform a floating-point operation, it will crash the system. There is a particularly nasty misfeature of the MMX (Multimedia) architecture: It overlaps the multimedia control registers with the floating-point registers, and you cannot necessarily predict which mode the processor will be in when you process an interrupt.

- A Device Driver cannot manipulate physical memory. However, drivers *can* obtain virtual addresses for physical addresses and manipulate the data by means of the virtual address mapping.

---

[1] Support for HPFS, the OS/2-compatible file system, was removed in NT 4.0.

- A driver, to be portable, must not rely on implementation-defined language features. It should be written in the ANSI-compliant subset of the C language. However, in certain circumstances, a driver must be prepared to handle an *exception*—this requires a Microsoft-defined extension to the C language. Microsoft has licensed this technology to any C compiler vendor who wants it. All of the mainstream non-Microsoft 32-bit C compilers that we know of that can compile for an NT platform have this extension. (Neither Microsoft nor other compiler vendors support writing Device Drivers in other than Microsoft C.)

- You should be careful about data structures used to interface to device-dependent information, whose size or layout (and this includes the packing of structures) can vary by platform. RISC systems in particular may add arbitrary padding to structures to ensure that certain members are aligned on valid hardware boundaries.

- You should never write a function for your Device Driver that maintains internal state in "hidden" variables. The most familiar function at the application level is probably `strtok`, but there are several others. The multithreaded, preemptive nature of NT, combined with the fundamental asynchronous nature of I/O, makes it impossible to guarantee that this state will ever be maintained correctly. All state you manipulate must be maintained in structures that are unique to the task being performed, a task that in some cases can be performed by many different threads.

- The driver must not spend excessive time at elevated IRQL. A basic design criterion for Windows NT was that the total amount of time that the processor would be running at elevated IRQL would be very brief; the current value is approximately 50μs.

- You cannot guarantee the integrity of your driver by turning off interrupts or raising IRQL, techniques that work in many other operating systems. In a multiprocessor system, turning off interrupts or raising the IRQL on one processor has no effect on the other processors.

- If at all possible, a driver should not contain any platform-specific code. If it absolutely must, such code should be under conditional compilation.

- In general, a driver should never try to circumvent the HAL layer. However, as we will show you in this book, efficiency sometimes makes it necessary to violate this guideline.

The Registry

The *Registry* is a tree-structured database that manages information about the hardware, peripheral devices, and drivers. It may be familiar to you because it is also used to maintain and configure application-level packages. In general, you must have Administrator privileges to change any of the system-level features of the Registry. Many entries cannot be changed at all; they are created when the system boots. Incorrectly changing a Registry entry, or creating one that is incorrect, will almost certainly be fatal to the system. This is one of the many reasons you need a second, sacrificial machine for Device Driver development. If you survive corrupting the disk or the file system, you will undoubtedly fall victim to a corrupted Registry. Sometimes, this is caused by simply putting the wrong information into it, successfully. In other cases, because the Registry is cached in memory, your test may correctly update the Registry, but some parts of it may not be successfully written to disk because the driver caused a crash. Then, when you reboot, the information in the Registry is inconsistent. The usual effect of this is that the system will not boot or will crash in the process as it tries to use the incorrect information. You can sometimes use a *recovery disk* to restore the Registry, but all too often, you'll just have to reinstall Windows NT.

The Registry is used by the Configuration Manager and can be manipulated using the Zw-prefix functions provided for that purpose.

Drivers: Always Preemptible, Always Interruptible

Drivers are always preemptible and always interruptible. Many Device Driver writers who have come from other environments will find this aspect of Windows NT a challenge. The key architectural decisions of NT make all drives inherently reentrant. This is because the thread executing in the drive may be preempted at any time. The driver may be executing when the device interrupts. The non-ISR component is suspended and the ISR is entered. If the driver was in a "critical section", say writing the third register in a series of five registers which must be written as a set, the ISR will find the hardware in an inconsistent state. The driver must prevent this by use of the synchronization mechanisms provided by Windows NT.

In general, the system defines an ordered set of IRQLs. Some of these IRQLs are based on actual physical Interrupt Request (IRQ) lines in the hardware; some are software interrupts used by the kernel to dispatch certain threads of control.

Most threads run at IRQL `PASSIVE_LEVEL`. At this level, all interrupts are possible; no interrupts are masked. Some software-defined levels are assigned at a fairly low priority level, one that is higher than `PASSIVE_LEVEL` but lower than the lowest hardware interrupt level. These levels are `APC_LEVEL`, `DISPATCH_LEVEL`, and `WAKE_LEVEL` (the last is used only when debugging). Above these are the hardware IRQ levels. The highest-level interrupts are reserved for the system clock and bus-error or memory-error interrupts.

Some Kernel-mode support routines run at IRQL `PASSIVE_LEVEL`. Kernel-mode components can establish their own threads, and these will want to run at `PASSIVE_LEVEL`. Also, many functions that support Kernel mode are pageable code. If you attempt to call these functions at a level above `APC_LEVEL` and those functions have been paged out, you will crash the system. For any function you call, be sure of the valid IRQL level and from which level you are calling the function.

Most driver routines run at `DISPATCH_LEVEL`.[2] `DISPATCH_LEVEL` routines run at a level higher than `PASSIVE_LEVEL` routines and can be interrupted by any hardware interrupt. The remaining routines run at the DIRQL (Device IRQL).

Because drivers are preemptible and interruptible, they are often executed in the context of whatever thread was running when the interrupt was taken and may resume control at a different level in the context of some other thread. Rarely, if ever, is this thread the same thread that initiated the operation. Thus, while you may have a user-level address in hand, you have no way of actually resolving it to a physical address because you are not in a thread that is actually part of the process that initiated the I/O. Only a thread that is in the process that initiated the I/O has the address context which makes the user-level address meaningful. For this reason, if you need to directly access addresses in the application, you must map user virtual addresses to system-wide virtual addresses while you are still in the thread that initiated the I/O. And then later, use these

---

[2] There is some confusing terminology. The entry routines of a driver are the Dispatch Routines. These routines run at `PASSIVE_LEVEL`. Other routines within the driver run at `DISPATCH_LEVEL`. These routines are *not* Dispatch Routines.

system-wide virtual addresses (which are valid in all threads) so that you can actually modify or read the memory at that location. This is accomplished using MDLs (Memory Descriptor Lists). There are a number of `Mm`-prefix and `Io`-prefix functions that let you manipulate these descriptors. Only the highest-level driver executes in the context of the thread making the I/O request.

Not only are drivers preemptible and interruptible, but they also can be executed in parallel on a multiprocessor system. For example, a disk driver might be executed simultaneously (literally) on two different processors to manipulate the disks. You must ensure not only that you are properly synchronizing data accesses by using locks properly, but also that two processors are not going to "fight" over who controls the disk. A fight results when two processors that alternatively force a seek generate an "infinite loop" in which the disk arm is requested to move here, then there, then here, and then there, but no Read or Write operation can succeed because the disk arm is always in the wrong position. In addition, any ISR can be interrupted by an ISR that is at a higher-priority level. So you cannot depend on any time-sensitive code; between any two instructions in your driver, there may be hundreds of thousands of clock cycles' delay because of higher-priority interrupts being processed. There are no "timing loops" that can be written easily. (There are, however, functions that you can call that have this effect, are automatically recalibrated for each platform, and deal with the problems of interrupts for you.)

To enable you to take interrupts at one level and process them at a lower level, you can use a DPC. Typically, you will enqueue a DPC and exit the ISR, and the DPC will be handled at a lower IRQL level, `DISPATCH_LEVEL`.

Multithreading and Multiprocessor Considerations

You cannot program Windows NT without being aware of multithreading and multiprocessing. While preemptibility and interruptibility are difficult to understand, multithreading, particularly multithreading in a multiprocessor environment, is a completely new and even more complex level of difficulty.

The only way to handle multithreading effectively is to have a set of rules about access management and how it is done. If access management is done correctly, generally no difficulty results when multiprocessing becomes a consideration. But writing "thread-safe" code is not enough; you must take extra care in writing a driver because it must be *multiprocessor-safe*. This means not only that the accesses to data must be done properly at a gross level (for example, preventing two threads from accessing a data structure at the same time), but in some cases you must be concerned with synchronization all the way down to the instruction level! The key point here is that *you cannot ignore multiprocessing*. It is so fundamental to NT that, if ignored, your driver will fail when put on a multiprocessor. Multiprocessor NT machines are readily available and, in many cases, at near-commodity prices. NT incorporates many mechanisms to allow you to write thread-safe, multiprocessor-safe drivers, but it is your responsibility to use these mechanisms correctly. We discuss these topics in great depth throughout this book.

Windows NT is designed to run on multiprocessors, with some constraints that are assumed.

- All CPUs are identical. Either all have coprocessors or none have coprocessors. Either all are MMX-based, or none are.

- All CPUs share memory and have uniform access to memory.

- A multiprocessor configuration can be either *symmetric* or *asymmetric*. In a symmetric multiprocessor (SMP), all processors have uniform access to a shared I/O space and any processor can take an interrupt from the I/O system. In an asymmetric multiprocessor, either only one processor has access to I/O space and takes interrupts or particular processors have distinct I/O spaces and can handle only specific interrupts from specific devices. Windows NT provides multiprocessor support only for SMPs.[3] For a description of the Pentium SMP interrupt support (for the morbidly curious), see Chapter 15 of *Pentium Processor System Architecture*, cited in the Further Reading section at the end of this chapter.

Because multiprocessors are assumed, you must be prepared to lock shared data structures. Whenever possible, lock *data,* not *code.* For example, you might have several disk drives. Locking disk drive code could make parallelism among the drives impossible. Instead, you should lock the per-drive data structures. Doing this preserves the integrity of the individual drive structures while allowing multiprocessors, or even multiple threads on a single processor, to have each physical disk in a different state of activity while sharing the same code.

Generally, you do not have the higher level synchronization primitives, such as Semaphores, Events, and Mutexes, available in a Device Driver. When they are available in a driver, they are also fairly expensive to use. So a much simpler (although if not carefully used, more expensive) technology is used instead: the *Spin Lock*.

You cannot directly access a Spin Lock, as you might expect, because of the considerations of caching, data pipelining, and multiprocessor memory access. Instead, you must use the Ke-prefix functions (summarized in Table 5.1) to manipulate Spin Locks. Spin Locks are multiprocessor-safe. We introduce two special types of Spin Locks later in the book: Spin Locks used to synchronize access to an ISR (ISR Spin Lock) in Chapter 14 and a Spin Lock used to synchronize access to queued requests (the Cancel Spin Lock) in Chapter 22, page 457.

A standard Spin Lock can be acquired only at DISPATCH_LEVEL or below. Below DISPATCH_LEVEL (for example, in any PASSIVE_LEVEL), your old IRQL will be recorded when you acquire the lock and the IRQL will be raised to DISPATCH_LEVEL. When you release the Spin Lock, you must provide the previously saved value.

However, you can use *dispatcher objects* at most of the intermediate-level and top-level drivers. A dispatcher object (also known as a "waitable object") can be a Semaphore, Mutex, Event, timer, or even another thread. However, such objects require that the driver set up a pri-

Table 5.1: *Spin Lock Function Summary*

Function	Effect
KeAcquireSpinLock	Acquires a Spin Lock.
KeAcquireSpinLockAtDpcLevel	Acquires a Spin Lock at DISPATCH_LEVEL.
KeInitializeSpinLock	Initializes a Spin Lock.
KeReleaseSpinLock	Releases a Spin Lock.
KeReleaseSpinLockFromDpcLevel	Releases a Spin Lock acquired at DISPATCH_LEVEL.

---

[3] Windows NT 3.1 did support one asymmetric multiprocessor architecture via a special HAL.

vate thread, which generates a context swap when control is transferred. For efficiency, most Kernel-mode support functions and drivers use Spin Locks for running at IRQL <= DISPATCH_LEVEL. We illustrate the use of Events extensively in Chapter 28 and Chapter 30.

Microsoft recommends having no more than one Spin Lock acquired at a time. This is sound advice if you wish to avoid *deadlock*, in which contention for two resources results in two different threads of execution waiting for each other.[4] This advice, however, is often unrealistic. This is because in order to get maximum throughput with your driver, you might need to have multiple Spin Locks that synchronize nominally independent resources. Only when these resources are shared is there a potential problem. Whenever multiple Spin Locks are needed, you should always *lock* resources in the *same* order and *unlock* them in the *inverse* order. To do otherwise is to invite deadlock, which is difficult to debug, both intellectually and from down in the bits using a debugger.

I/O Request Packets

The IRP (I/O request packet) is the basis of all transactions within the I/O system. It is the way the general I/O system talks to a top-level driver and how a top-level driver talks to a driver below itself. The last place an IRP visits is the actual driver level that talks to the physical device. One IRP at a high level may generate a sequence of IRPs at lower levels. For example, a request to open a file starts with a single IRP to the file system. However, before that IRP can actually open the file, it must read the root directory and each directory along the path until the desired directory is found. It might generate additional IRPs to "prime the pump" by prereading the initial part of the file, if the file system chooses to do this sort of optimization.

Without an IRP, there can be no I/O transaction. Therefore, no device can spontaneously interrupt a running application thread to notify the *application* that the device requires attention. Furthermore, an I/O request will always provide information precisely *once* to the application that called it. Only after you have managed to get an IRP into the system is there the possibility of interrupting the flow of a application thread by an asynchronous callback.

This suggests a discipline regarding how you write a driver: You don't actually enable interrupts on a device until you have an IRP, and you disable them after the IRP is completed. However, some devices may generate interrupts continuously for events that can be handled entirely within the driver. The *effect*, however, is that the device is doing no I/O unless an IRP is present.

IRPs are always allocated out of nonpaged memory. So if you have a pointer to an IRP, you can be sure that it is in memory and accessible. You cannot be as certain about the memory it *references*, but the IRP itself is always accessible.

Figure 5.1 shows a simplified I/O transaction. There, the IRP takes a simple—well, more-or-less simple—path. In reality, layered drivers can add substantial additional complexity. Some of the art of writing a driver is determining exactly what the layering looks like or where your driver fits into existing layers. In the figure and the discussion of it that follows, we've glossed over some critical details (which we look at in much greater depth throughout the book) so we don't confuse the issue with too much detail.

---

[4] For a more detailed discussion of deadlock, see Chapter 11, page 248; Chapter 14, page 294; and Chapter 17, page 350, which includes an example scenario.

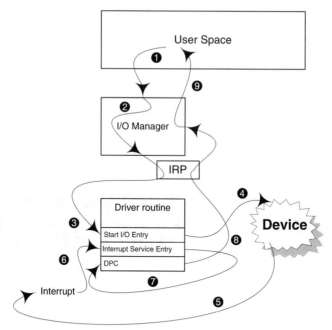

Figure 5.1: *Simplified IRP structure and I/O logic.*

- A call to the I/O system takes place in ❶. This call is routed to the I/O Manager.

- The I/O Manager allocates an IRP, initializes it, verifies the parameters (for example, it verifies that addresses are in the user's virtual address space), and then calls the driver's Dispatch Routine ❷.

- This routine calls the "Start I/O" entry point of the driver ❸.

- The driver initializes the I/O operation and activates the device ❹. At this point, if the I/O operation is a synchronous I/O operation, the user thread that initiated the I/O is suspended.

- Some time later, after the device completes its operation, the device uses an interrupt ❺ to report this situation.

- This interrupt is routed through the HAL and the kernel to the Interrupt Service entry point ❻.

- The Interrupt Service handler uses a DPC activated by the DpcForIsr function ❼ to set the necessary status code in the IRP and return control ❽ to the I/O Manager.

- The I/O Manager frees the IRP and uses the status to return the completion code to the user ❾.

We study all of these transactions in detail in Chapter 14.

Note that within the kernel space, I/O operations are *always* asynchronous, independent of the user-level availability of asynchronous I/O. The synchronicity perceived at the user level is an illusion. You will always program with the awareness of this asynchrony.

A single IRP can be passed from one driver layer to another during the I/O process. Rather than having to allocate a new IRP at every layer, you divide an IRP into two sections: the *fixed part* and a set of *I/O stack locations*. In the fixed part, or *header*, the I/O Manager works with information about the original I/O request as formulated by the user-to-kernel function call. This includes the caller's parameters, the address of the applicable Device Object, and some other state that we will discuss shortly. The fixed part also contains an *I/O status block*, which is used by drivers to report the status of the operation and, depending on the type of operation, the number of bytes transferred.

The highest-level driver has one or more *I/O stack locations* (there is always at least one). This location contains driver-specific parameters, such as a function code indicating the nature of the operation and other information. This is used by the highest-level driver to control its action. Each driver sets up the I/O stack location for the next lower-level driver, except, of course, for the lowest-level driver.

Each level of the driver can access its I/O stack location in the IRP. When an IRP is allocated for a monolithic driver, it has only one I/O stack location. When layered drivers are used (see Chapter 23), a driver can ask the driver it is going to call how many stack locations *it* requires. Then it can allocate an IRP with that value plus 1. The I/O Manager will do this for any IRPs it creates for you.

Once an IRP is allocated, the number of I/O stack locations cannot be changed. There is also no error checking done for bounds-checking, so if you allocate too few I/O stack locations, you will eventually crash the system.

Figure 5.2 illustrates how IRP packets use I/O stacks. It also illustrates some additional kernel subsystem interactions.

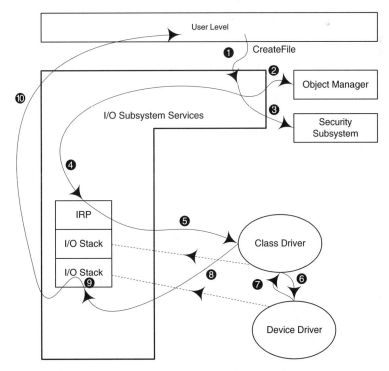

Figure 5.2: CreateFile, *illustrating an IRP and use of I/O stacks.*

- The application performs a `CreateFile` operation ❶.

- The filename (in this case, the device name) is passed to the *Object Manager* ❷. This manager performs the necessary lookup in the Object Manager Namespace and determines which Device Object will be used for the device. If this fails, the `CreateFile` operation will fail.

- Once the device has been located, the I/O subsystem calls the *security subsystem* ❸ to verify that the calling thread has access to the device. Note that we did not say "that the user has access to the device" or "that the process has access to the device". These are orthogonal concepts in NT. A process can create a thread that has different security attributes than the process itself, and while the *process* might have access to the device, a thread might not necessarily have the same privileges.

- If the lookup and security check are successful, the I/O Manager prepares to call the driver and then allocates the IRP ❹. It knows, by using one of the fields in the Device Object structure, how many I/O stack locations are required.

- The I/O Manager then calls the Class Driver ❺, which performs any necessary work required to complete the `CreateFile` operation. This level uses the first I/O stack location, as shown.

- The Class Driver calls the Device Driver ❻, which performs *its* `CreateFile`-related work. Note that it uses, in addition to the fixed part of the IRP, the second I/O stack location. Before calling the Device Driver, however, the Class Driver has to set up the contents of this location for the lower-level driver.

- Finally, the Device Driver returns ❼ to the Class Driver, which may complete any intitialization that may be based on the lower-level driver.

- The Class Driver then returns to the I/O Manager ❽, which deallocates the IRP ❾.

- The I/O Manager finally returns the status to the user ❿. The status is returned by the drive's setting the `Status` field (in the I/O stack location of the IRP). This will eventually cause the I/O Manager to call the kernel's internal equivalent of `SetLastError` before returning to the application. If the return code is other than `STATUS_SUCCESS`, the application gets a `FALSE` return value or some other similar failure indication; for example, `CreateFile` returns `INVALID_HANDLE_VALUE`. The application then calls `GetLastError` to determine the cause of the problem.[5]

Layered Drivers and IRPs

A higher-level driver can safely access only its own I/O stack location and the I/O stack location of its immediately lower driver. As the writer of a higher-level driver, you can make no assumptions about any layer other than the one immediately below your driver's layer. The number of layers can change dynamically (although infrequently); for example, when Filter Drivers are inserted or removed.

The lowest-level driver can safely access only its own I/O stack location and the common IRP fields.

Any driver that is added as a new layer can set its own completion function pointer into the IRP's I/O stack location. This function will be called by a lower-level driver and allows the layer

---

[5] The mapping between internal error codes and user-visible error codes is set out in Appendix B.

that sets it to determine how the I/O operation completes (success, cancelled, or error). This function can also update IRP state, release any resources (usually memory) that were allocated, and perform similar housekeeping tasks. The completion function can reuse an incoming IRP to send another request to the lower-level driver before completing.

Any driver that is added as a new layer can allocate new IRPs, but it cannot create an *Associated IRP* with the `IoMakeAssociatedIrp` function. An Associated IRP is an IRP that has the property that when it completes, the IRP it is associated with is implicitly completed. This saves you from writing the code to handle what is often a very common case. We discuss IRP completion in much greater detail throughout the book. Only a top-level driver can create Associated IRPs.

A driver that is added as a new layer must set up the next-lower driver's I/O stack locations. It should also expect to have its I/O stack location set up by its parent and must recognize that it may have to pass this state downward in the chain. In addition, this driver can pass any incoming IRPs to lower drivers by setting up the next-lower driver's I/O stack location and calling `IoCallDriver`.

Asynchronous I/O

As we mentioned earlier in the chapter, the I/O system is inherently asynchronous. This is independent of whether asynchronous I/O is supported at the user level. Although in theory asynchronous I/O is supposed to provide faster I/O throughput at the user level, measurements contradict this theory (at least for the simple cases). However, there may be other compelling reasons to support asynchronous I/O, including compatibility with other devices. So you need to be aware of the implications of asynchronous I/O on your driver structure, should you choose to support it.

A driver will normally process IRPs in FIFO order. However, if the IRPs are not interdependent, a driver may choose to maximize concurrency by processing as many IRPs concurrently as possible. For example, if an IRP comes in while another IRP is being processed, it might even be possible to process it directly in the Dispatch Routine without requiring any serialization; in such a case, this should be done. Another example of maximizing concurrency is a low-level disk driver, which might choose to process incoming IRPs in a way that tries to minimize response time back to the applications. This includes keeping as many disk channels busy as possible, sorting the requests to minimize seek latency, and the like. This can impact performance of applications that use asynchronous I/O because the various pending asynchronous I/O requests will ideally be satisfied as quickly as possible. And, for that matter, it will also optimize overall system performance if ordinary synchronous I/O is used, although the effect may not be as noticeable for a single application.

Thus one of the most important implications of fully supporting asynchronous I/O is that the I/O requests may not be processed in the same order in which they were sent to the kernel by the user. Since an IRP is only partially processed at any level, it is entirely possible that a later I/O request could make it through before an earlier one. Perhaps the most obvious example of this is the so-called "elevator scheduling" of disk drives, whereby I/O requests are sorted by disk address and thus seek time is minimized by "sweeping" the disk arm in alternate directions. Thus a request for a high-numbered disk address that has not yet been passed on a downward sweep will get into the queue and may well be processed before a low-numbered disk address that came in earlier. Other types of devices may present other examples.

Actions can occur at various levels, and a device may need to maintain device-specific state independent of an I/O request (for our previous example, the direction of the disk head sweep and the current disk address are obvious pieces of state of the lower-level driver). A special provision is made for this in the form of a Device Extension, which we first discussed in Chapter 3. Recall that a Device Extension is a device-specific area associated with a Device Object. Some devices, such as displays and printers, have high-level Device Extensions that are readable and manipulatable by the user using special API functions. These include, for displays, such parameters as the resolution, width and height, and color depth. For printers, these include such features such as the currently selected paper source for a printer or the selection of portrait or landscape mode. But internally, you might also need to record state that is not necessarily available externally.

Object-Oriented Structures

The I/O system is *pseudo-object-oriented*. That is, it is not as cleanly object-oriented as C++, but it implements the basic concepts of object orientation. For example, in C++ *virtual methods* are implemented by a *virtual dispatch table*, or *VTable*. You provide a similar interface from your Device Driver to the I/O Manager by preloading a vector of function addresses. Thus the I/O Manager sees a uniform interface to the lower-level drivers, maintained by its interface via the "virtual" methods of the dispatch table. And while the C++ compiler will automatically "pass through" a request at one level that is handled at a higher level of the class structure, you must implement this explicitly in your Device Driver.

Further Reading

Custer, Helen, *Inside Windows NT*, Microsoft Press, 1993. 1-55615-481-X.

Mindshare, Inc.: Don Anderson and Tom Shanley, *Pentium™ Processor System Architecture, Second Edition,* Addison-Wesley, 1995. ISBN 0-201-40992-5.

Solomon, David A., *Inside Windows NT (Second Edition)*, Microsoft Press, 1998. ISBN 1-57231-677-2.

This book is the revision of the Custer book and is now considered to be the definitive edition.

Chapter

6 *Overview of Kernel Memory: Caching, Paging, and Pipelining*

When you are writing a Device Driver, you must be conscious of such issues as paging, caching, physical addresses, the virtual address space, locked pages, and similar hardware-specific details. The job of an operating system is to protect the user from those details. But a Device Driver is the *implementation* of one of those abstractions. Thus you need to use and understand the concepts of the underlying machine.

The HAL protects you from some of this, as does the kernel. However, interacting with them requires very specific protocols, particularly if you want your driver to be portable across different platforms. The same physical device, plugged into the backplane of two different platforms, such as an Intel platform and an Alpha, might require somewhat different interactions to control it. While these are *mediated* by the HAL, you must actually ask it what is going on; for example, are the device registers in a separate I/O space or are they mapped to physical memory addresses? How you use them depends on the answer to this question. You need to know what the options are so that you can properly code a completely platform-independent driver.

Device Drivers and Memory Management

Memory management for Device Drivers is far more complex than it is for ordinary user applications. In particular, there is nothing that automatically notifies you if a process terminates. If a process terminates and it has the *last* remaining reference to a File Object, your Close handler will be called. You have to know exactly how much memory was allocated, how it was allocated, and where it is—and then free it all up. One thing the system *will* do when a process finally terminates is check the I/O structures for errors such as process pages that are still locked down for an I/O transaction. If such an error occurs, the system will Blue Screen. Device Drivers are assumed to be "trusted subsystems". There are no validity checks for memory addresses that are passed around. If you do something bogus, you have an excellent chance of corrupting the operating system—or a process you never heard of (and which never heard of you, and would rather not have). This is one of the main reasons you need a separate, sacrificial development machine.

The underlying hardware also impacts how you deal with synchrony. It is entirely possible that on a multiprocessor you will see bugs that you would never see on a uniprocessor because you have failed to handle synchronization properly. A serious Device Driver writer should have a multiprocessor machine on which to test the code. Testing for race conditions is nearly impossible, but most of the evident problems can be found quickly. What is more important is that you *must* code your driver with full expectation that it *will* be run on a multiprocessor. This means you must design it from the beginning to be multiprocessor-safe. Device Drivers are hard to write. Retrofitting multiprocessor-safety to *any* application that was not designed for it is difficult or impossible. Trying to do this to an artifact as complex as a Device Driver is unbelievably challenging. So you'll see that every Device Driver in our examples is constructed to be multiprocessor-safe. This complicates the explanations a bit, but this is an area in which you cannot cut corners.

One of the most critical multiprocessor concerns is how memory is managed, so you need to be conscious of this at the memory-management level. Fortunately, NT was designed to be a multiprocessor operating system, and some of the memory primitives are designed to be intrinsically multiprocessor-safe. Allocation in particular is always multiprocessor-safe. Some deallocation is handled by reference counting, so when you unmap some object in one thread you need not be concerned that another thread is, at the same instant, actually using it. But most deallocation requires that you make sure it is safe to deallocate or unmap the memory in question, relative to other potential threads through your driver. Some of these might be intraprocess threads, all working on behalf of the same process but representing different state of the process. But in other cases, system threads or threads from other processes (particularly if the device can be shared simultaneously among several processes) can be interacting.

For example, suppose you are keeping some shared list of objects representing all of the running processes that are using your driver and a process terminates. You must not update this list unless you have protected it by using a synchronization lock. Otherwise, another concurrently executing thread in your driver could run on another processor and therefore could access the list you are in the middle of modifying. This is a certain path to at least a Blue Screen. But also, you quite possibly could corrupt some user process, the File System, the disk, or some other part of NT. Device Drivers are trusted. There is little room for error in the exercise of ultimate power.

In this chapter, we look at the memory-management strategies and structures. You don't necessarily have enough information yet to make use of all of this detail, but we decided it was best to consolidate it all into one reference chapter. So don't worry if you don't fully understand the explanations or details. Read this chapter for a memory-management overview. As we talk about the various driver techniques, we refer back to this chapter for the memory-management functions.

The Virtual Address Space

The layout of the NT virtual address space is shown in Figure 6.1. It is critical to understand that at no time when you are working with a Device Driver do you *ever* work with a physical address. You can work only with virtual addresses. If, for some reason, you need a physical address, there are functions that will map physical memory into the virtual address space and give you a 32-bit virtual address for it. However, you will not actually use the physical address itself for any operations other than the mapping request or to program a DMA Device.

The lower 2GB of virtual memory is the user space; it is available for however the user wants to use it. It is *fully pageable memory.* This means that if you plan to touch it at elevated IRQL (for example, in a DPC Routine), you must either make sure the page has been "wired down" by an earlier action or expect to get an exception because you have tried to touch a page that is not in memory. In general, such an exception will immediately be translated to a BugCheck and crash the system. The user space is private to each process (except when memory-mapped files are involved). Thus you can touch a page based on its address only if your driver is running in the context of the user process. As this is seldom, you rarely use a user address in a Device Driver. Instead, you use a *process-independent translation* of that address.

In the figure, the 2GB block of memory starting at the 2GB boundary is shared among all processes, including kernel contexts. Note that not all addresses in this block are available to a program running in user space, but all addresses in this block are identical when a process

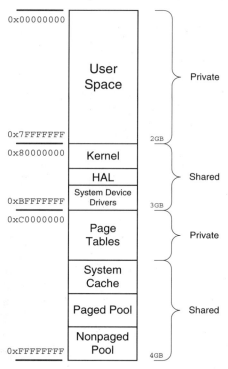

Figure 6.1: *Windows NT virtual address space.*

changes to run in Kernel mode. In this block of memory is the "kernel", which includes the Executive Services, Win32k, and other key modules. Also located here is the HAL code and the System Device Drivers, those drivers that are required to boot the system and get it to the point at which a user can log in.

Starting at the 3GB boundary are two classes of memory: *private* and *shared*. The private space holds process-associated page tables, which are loaded when the process is loaded. This means that the page tables, which can be quite large, are pageable as part of the process context. The private space holds the *system cache*, which is used by the File System to cache portions of files. The cache is a minimum of 64MB of virtual address space and can expand depending on the amount of physical memory available.

With Windows NT 4.0, Microsoft added a boot-time option for the Enterprise Server that will increase the user space to a total of 3GB. Experimentation has suggested that this option works on NT Workstation 4.0 and NT Server 4.0.

Also in the shared space are the two key areas of memory of most interest to Device Driver writers: the *Paged Pool* and the *Nonpaged Pool*. Kernel-mode drivers are loaded into the Non-paged Pool. Drivers can allocate blocks of memory from the Nonpaged Pool for buffers and other purposes. They also can allocate memory from the Paged Pool, as long as they take precautions to make sure that the pages are in memory when they need to use them.

The Physical Memory System

We discussed the various memory bus structures extensively in Chapter 4. There, we were concerned with the interface to the devices and we ignored the memory structure. We can ignore that no longer. The memory system is critical to a Device Driver. So we simplify our I/O system diagram in one dimension while expanding it in more detail in another, as shown in Figure 6.2 and Figure 6.3. In these figures, we show the entire I/O system that we spent so much time on as a single box, but we now look at the cache structure.

There is a problem with running a 200MHz CPU capable of one memory access every clock cycle (5 ns) in a system in which the memory system is running more than an order of magnitude slower (70 ns, typically). The processor would be forced to wait on each memory reference until the memory could supply data to it—this is an unacceptable performance penalty. This problem is addressed by the use of *caches*. The cache can respond to requests for data that is already in the cache in a single clock cycle. A simple cache architecture is illustrated in Figure 6.2.

We start with a simple example in which the cache is empty. During the first fetch of data from memory, the cache is checked to see if that information is already present. It isn't (since

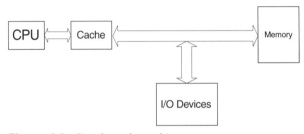

Figure 6.2: *Simple cache architecture.*

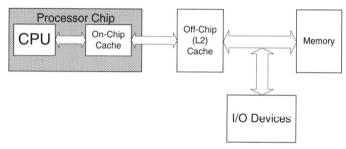

Figure 6.3: *Memory/cache architecture.*

we're starting with an empty cache)—this is a *cache miss*. So the processor must wait the full memory cycle as the signals go out to the memory system and the information is retrieved. The cache is updated to record the address and the data. Now, suppose the next instruction fetches the data from the same address. The cache is checked and the data is present, so the processor gets it immediately—this is a *cache hit*. No memory cycle is involved.

Next, the processor fetches the data 4 bytes past the first fetch. Is this data in the cache? Well, that depends on the *cache line size*. A cache tends to work best when you access nearby data because instead of the memory system's just fetching a single byte or word, it often delivers a larger chunk of data to the cache. Depending on the architecture, this might be 4 bytes, 8 bytes, 16 bytes, 32 bytes, 64 bytes, 128 bytes, or even 256 bytes (supercomputers tend to very wide cache line sizes to deal with the imbalance between the processor and memory). Some caches *prefetch* data, running "hidden" memory cycles in the background. Some memory systems have the property that the *first* bus-width-worth of memory takes a full memory cycle, but subsequent fetches that are part of the same transaction can proceed somewhat faster, often twice as fast. So even if the cache-to-memory bus is 32 bits wide, the cache line might be much wider and take advantage of prefetching. In such a case, a subsequent hit to a cache line that is still being prefetched will wait, although usually not nearly as long as it would have to wait for a full memory cycle.

The cache is much smaller than the main memory. Eventually, every slot in the cache is filled with data that is a copy of the data in memory. The next fetch is to an address whose information is not in the cache; this is another cache miss. But the cache is full! This leads to the notion of *cache line replacement*, whereby one of the existing cache lines is selected and its contents are replaced by the address and data for the most recent fetch.

What strategy is used for cache line replacement? The answer could consume an entire book, and you would get to learn such cool terms as "set-associative cache", "LRU replacement", and "modulo-line replacement". For our purposes here, the answer doesn't matter. All you need to know is that there *is* a replacement algorithm. (In fact, we lied a bit—the cache doesn't have to be full to generate a cache line conflict. For example, a 256K cache might use only the low-order 18 bits of the address to determine the cache line. Thus, even if only one cache line was valid, a cache line conflict might result if you addressed a byte 262,144 bytes from it. We could digress like this for another dozen pages and not cover the whole design space of caches.)

So far we've been looking at Read operations. But what about Write operations? When does the data actually get to memory?

There are two cache strategies to handle writing: the *write-through* cache and the *write-back* cache. In a write-through cache, the data in the cache is changed and a memory cycle is started to write back the changed data. The processor must wait until the write cycle completes. A write-back cache will typically be a *buffered write-through* cache. In this architecture, the write is made to the cache, the processor is released, and the cache undertakes to write the data back to memory asynchronously. Only if another write to the same cache location occurs before the write-back completes will the processor have to wait. Many other levels of sophistication can be used here to improve performance, but we'll stop with this simple write-through model.

In the write-back model, data written to the cache is not immediately written back to memory. Only when a cache line needs to be replaced will the memory be written back. In a write-back cache, each cache line has a "dirty" bit that is set if there is any Write operation to that cache line. The next attempt to load that particular cache line will force the "dirty" data to be written back to memory. In some cases, there is no dirty bit for the whole cache line but a bit for each memory-bus-width section of the entire cache line, so only those units that have been modified need to be written back. When the cache line size is much wider than the memory bus width, this gives a significant performance gain on write-back.

Note that these models have quite different effects on the memory. In the write-through model, changes to memory appear in memory fairly quickly. In the write-back model, depending on the nature of the computations and memory accesses, the data in the cache may not be written back for thousands of clock cycles, perhaps even *seconds*, after the change is made.

An operation supported by most caching systems is the *cache flush operation*. For a write-back cache, this operation will initiate a complete write-back of every "dirty" cache line, which is potentially the entire cache. In addition, the processor is completely "locked out" until the cache flush completes. In the worst case, *all* of the cache lines could be dirty and it would take 256K/bus width memory cycles to complete this operation. This is heavy-duty. It often also means that the cache is completely invalidated, so not only is all of the data written back, but the cache lines are marked as having no data. Thus, subsequent computations require refilling the cache and will exhibit serious performance problems.

In a single-processor system, the difference between write-through and write-back is essentially indistinguishable from the viewpoint of the CPU. There are slight performance differences, but the logic of the computations does not change.

As it turns out, a single cache is insufficient for most modern architectures. For cache memory that is not on the CPU chip, there is a significant cost in performance to get the signals off the chip and across the printed circuit board to the cache. So most modern architectures have at least one cache built onto the same chip as the processor. This is the "Level 1", "L1", or "on-chip" cache. This cache varies in size with the technology, but 64K is common and many chips support larger caches. The former outboard cache is still present. It is much larger than the on-chip cache—256K or 512K are not uncommon sizes on modern PCs. This cache is the "Level 2", "L2", or "off-chip" cache. There is no particular reason to assume that the cache prefetch, association, replacement algorithms, and write-back strategies of the two caches are the same; the L1 cache might do write-back while the L2 cache does write-through, or vice versa. The fine points don't matter too much to Device Driver writers. (Historically, some multiprocessor supercomputers have used as many as *five* levels of caches.)

Life gets a lot more complicated when you have two or more processors. Take a look at a typical multiprocessor architecture, as shown in Figure 6.4. The figure shows two processors, each with its own on-chip cache, L2 cache, and path to memory—this is common. Suppose Processor 1 fetches the value, say 0, from location 0x1000. It takes this value, adds 1 to it, and

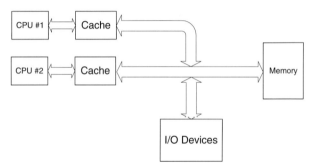

Figure 6.4: *Simple multiprocessor cache architecture.*

writes it back. It then fetches the value again, which comes from its cache, adds 1 to it, and writes it back. This continues for some time before the write-through or write-back makes the value visible in memory again. Now assume that somewhere along the line, Processor 2 fetches the contents of location `0x1000`. It fetches a 0, even though by the time this happens, the value in Processor 1's cache (assume write-back, to make life really miserable) is quite different. It then proceeds to increment it. Finally, Processor 1 performs an operation that forces the cache to be written back. The value in location `0x1000` is now the value from the cache, say 7500. Processor 2 does something else and forces its cached value to be written back. Its value, at the time this happens, is 75. How many times did the loop occur? It occurred 7,575 times between the two processors. But the value in memory could be either 7500 or 75, neither of which is correct.

This is a total disaster if you are trying to synchronize independent threads running on separate processors by using any kind of lock on data. Consider how you might handle this on a uniprocessor. On an Intel machine, you might use the "bit-test-and-set" (BTS) instruction to read the value of a bit in memory and change it. The carry flag tells you the previous value. If the flag was unset, you can proceed because you own the lock. If it was set, someone else already has the lock and you have to wait. But what if the bit that is set is a bit in the copy of the data in the cache? The next processor that does a BTS instruction fetches the value in memory (which is still 0), sets it to 1 (in its own cache), and proceeds to simultaneously access the "locked" information. The complementary problem also exists, where Processor 1 releases the lock (in the cache) and Processor 2 keeps spinning on the set lock. Neither of these is acceptable.

The problem of dealing with values that have been cached, but updated behind the cache, is called the *cache coherency problem*. It is an important problem, and you will encounter it. How? You might say, "I'm not going to write for a multiprocessor!" Well, you don't really have a choice in the matter. You don't know what machine an end user will use for your device. Currently, NT-based systems with two, four, six, or even eight processors are available—and the number of processors is likely to increase in the near future. Since you can't predict the usage of your device, you can't presume to ignore cache coherency.

But the situation is even simpler than that! *Every* PC is a multiprocessor system! It is just that only the CPU, the device you would like to think of as the "processor", executes user-level instructions. The other processors are DMA controllers and bus-mastering I/O devices, which in fact can read or change memory independent of the CPU.

So here's a simple failure scenario. You write a bunch of bytes into a buffer and request an output operation to write these bytes to disk. What bytes are written to the disk? Well, if you didn't deal with the effects of the cache, you might find that the last few bytes, which might be the checksum of the data, are still in the L2 cache at the time the DMA Device transfers the data to the output device. The recipient of this data will see the previous contents of memory in some location, such as the checksum, and report an error. Of course, if the data in the cache was the disk address to write and this information was handled by the disk controller that got the information from a DMA transfer, a disk driver that failed to account for caching effects could corrupt the file system. This is not a Good Thing.

The Intel architecture provides for memory-locked access by providing an operation called the *LOCK prefix*. This 1-byte operation causes the next instruction to perform an interlocked read-modify-write bus cycle. While this is happening, no other bus master (including I/O devices) can get into the memory system. Not all multiprocessor systems support this feature, and it doesn't handle the case just described, in which part of an I/O buffer is still in the cache.

You must also provide for synchronization on shared data. Low-level synchronization is handled by the HAL, but you'll normally use even higher-level locks and Semaphores. There are quite elaborate mechanisms that involve queueing certain kinds of requests when resources are in use by multiple threads or multiple processors.

Some caches watch the memory bus. If they see a cached address go by, they can respond by invalidating the cache line whose data has been written; this is called *cache snooping*. An alternative is to load the new data into the cache—this is called *cache snarfing*. The Pentium architecture supports a snooping mechanism and is described in more detail than you can possibly cope with in Chapter 4 of the book *Pentium Processor System Architecture* (see the Further Reading section at the end of the chapter). The Pentium also supports a means of allowing two L2 caches to communicate in an attempt to maintain cache consistency. The high-end Pentium models provide an elaborate set of signals to allow dual-processor systems to successfully snoop each other's memory accesses. This is described in Chapter 14 of *Pentium Processor System Architecture*.

The problem with cache snooping and snarfing in general is that they require a single system-wide memory bus. Many multiprocessors can have several memory data paths, using techniques similar to memory interleaving, so that the multiple processors can simultaneously access different banks of memory. For small multiprocessor configurations, a *crosspoint switch architecture* works very well. Figure 6.5 shows a simple crosspoint switch multiprocessor architec-

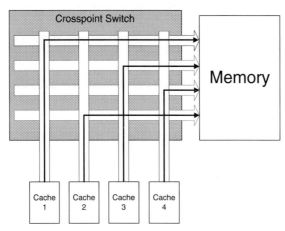

Figure 6.5: *Crosspoint switch memory system.*

ture. In the figure, the four different processors are accessing different banks of memory, and thus, in any given memory cycle, all four processors can be accessing memory.

The ultimate realization of an SMP (symmetric multiprocessor) with a 16×16 crosspoint switch is described in the book *The C.mmp/Hydra Multiprocessor System*; see the Further Reading section at the end of the chapter. The book describes one of several possible strategies to handle conflicts when two or more processors need to access the same memory bank. One of the authors (*jmn*) worked on this system. Tom McWilliams, one of the designers of the S-1 multiprocessor and a graduate of Carnegie Mellon University, where we did C.mmp, used this same design for the 16-processor S-1. He observed that maintaining cache coherency with cache snarfing could require as much as a terabyte per second of intercache bandwidth on that machine. Since you cannot tell what kind of memory architecture an NT multiprocessor system uses, you cannot depend on cache snooping or cache snarfing as a means of maintaining cache consistency. In fact, you can't depend on cache consistency at all. Some extreme cases such as the IBM RISC 6000 have no cache consistency mechanism, and in fact the *multiprocessor* RISC 6000 requires a special 4,096-register shared hardware I/O device to provide the necessary interlocks. The HAL layer worries about this for you.

More-Sophisticated Caching

Many processors implement separate *data caches* and *instruction caches*. The decision to have two different kinds of caches is based on the observation that data caches need complex write-back or write-through circuitry. But in an era in which instructions are treated as read-only, an instruction cache needs no write-back or other logic to deal with Write operations. In fact, in some machines you simply cannot write self-modifying code. Thus, modifying an executable page (for example, by just-in-time, or JIT, compilation strategies) requires special interactions to make the page executable, just so the instruction cache can be kept coherent.

Cache Management on Intel Hardware

The Intel *x86* family (386, 486, Pentium, Pentium Pro, and so on) uses page tables to describe each page in virtual memory. *All* of the addresses used by NT, whether in user space or kernel space, are *virtual addresses*. There is absolutely no way to write a piece of NT code that accesses a physical memory address. If you need to access a physical memory address (which, as you'll see, is quite common when writing a Device Driver), you must first map it to a virtual address. The page table entry (PTE) for the virtual address will be coupled to a specific physical address, but you yourself cannot access a physical address. You can only request that NT give you a virtual address corresponding to the physical address.

A PTE for a 486 machine is shown in Figure 6.6. The high-order 20 bits encode a physical page frame address. When you present a virtual address to the addressing system, it combines

Figure 6.6: *Page table entry.*

these high-order 20 bits with the low-order 12 bits of the virtual address you have presented and generates a 32-bit physical memory address. We skip the details of how a PTE is found, at least for now, and look at the other bits of the PTE.

- Bit 0 is the *present* bit.

  If the value in this bit is 0, an attempt to access the page will generate a page fault. If the value in this position is 1, the page is in memory and the high-order 20 bits are used as just described to form the physical address. When the value is 0, the remaining 31 bits are available for whatever purpose the operating system writer wishes to put them to; for example, holding the disk address of where the page has been moved or an indicator that the page should be allocated and zeroed.

- Bit 1 is the *read/write* bit.

  If this bit is 1, the page is writable as well as readable; if it is 0, the page is only readable. The processor will take an access fault if an instruction attempts to write to a page that has this bit 0 in its PTE.

- Bit 2 is the *user/supervisor* bit.

  Your Device Driver code and data pages have this bit set to 0 (although you won't see this), thereby indicating a Supervisor-mode page. Application program pages have this bit set to 1.

- Bit 3 is the *page write-through* bit.

  When this bit is 1, a page whose data is cached will have that data cached as write-through data. Unfortunately, Windows NT does not provide any way to set this bit because it is not common across all architectures. Setting it affects only hardware that uses write-back caching; it has no effect on write-through caching.

- Bit 4 is the *page cache data* (PCD) bit.

  If this bit is 1, the values read from the page will not be cached. Because they are not cached, data written to the page will be written back directly.

- Bit 5 is the *page accessed* bit.

  This bit is set to 0 by the operating system. If there is any processor Read operation from the page, the paging hardware will set it to 1.

- Bit 6 is the *dirty* bit.

  This bit is set to 0 by the operating system. If there is any processor Write operation to the page, the paging hardware will set it to 1. (Note that if you are doing DMA into a page, you are using physical addresses that do not go through the page table. Thus it is up to the I/O Manager and/or Memory Manager to explicitly mark as "dirty" those pages that could be written by DMA. This is handled transparently for you.)

- Bits 7 and 8 are reserved and must be 0.

- Bits 9 through 11 are available for whatever purpose an operating system wants.

Various memory-management functions in Windows NT allow you to create pages with the PCD bit set, thereby inhibiting the caching of the references. You *must* set this bit for any PTE that represents a memory-mapped device register. Otherwise, you have no guarantee when the data will actually be written to the device. (Remember, not all Intel implementations are identical. Some will use write-through caching, and some will use write-back caching. You can't depend on what type of caching is being used.)

Pipelining: A Form of Caching

Many modern processors implement a feature known as *instruction pipelining*. Pipelining affects how both instructions and data are processed. In older architectures, a significant number of clock cycles were wasted doing what is called *instruction decoding*, that is, setting up the internal logic of the processor to actually execute the instruction. In modern processors, instructions are prefetched into a *pipeline*. As they proceed along the pipeline, they are decoded until they finally hit the execution unit; this occurs when all of the important decoding has already been done. So modern machines such as the Pentium can execute many instructions in exactly one clock cycle. In addition, if you have a very tight loop, the partially decoded instructions remain available. The processor doesn't even have to go out to the cache to get them. This generates a significant performance improvement.

    This performance boost comes at a cost, however. You can't write self-modifying code, even if you do it in noncached pages, because the instruction you are modifying could have been prefetched. (The effects of the pipeline on self-modifying code form the basis of subroutines that determine which kind of processor you are running on. The subroutine modifies the code stream some number of instructions ahead. By detecting whether the modification was seen, the subroutine infers the model of processor by knowing the depth of the various processor instruction pipelines.)

    There is also *data pipelining*. This has some particularly nasty effects for Device Driver writing. Perhaps the most difficult machine to deal with is the Alpha. Let's look at what the Alpha does and see where it gets you into serious trouble. Suppose you have a device with a memory-mapped control register at position 0x000D0000 and you write to this location in memory. *Before the data and address even get to the cache, they are stored in an intermediate pipeline.* As a simple example, we show in Figure 6.7 an Alpha-like pipeline, four deep. Write requests are inserted into the pipeline at the left and flow through to the right. As they flow off the right side, they enter the hardware caching system. The write pipe is used because the Alpha

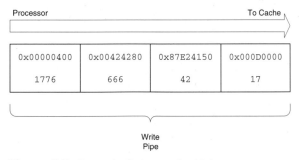

Figure 6.7: *Data pipelining on the Alpha.*

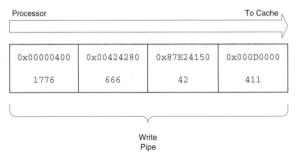

Figure 6.8: *Overly clever data pipelining.*

is so blindingly fast (in excess of 625MHz clock time!) that it would be slowed down even by a fast cache; building a cache that is well-matched to its speed is not considered feasible.

Now this is where the world desperately needs to be protected against clever engineers. Consider the pipeline shown in Figure 6.7. *What would happen if the program wrote again to the address 0x000D0000?* You might think that the new Write operation would be shoved into the pipeline at the left, thereby forcing the existing Write to the address 0x000D0000 to fall off into the caching logic. Since that address is a memory-mapped device address, the write to the address is probably an uncached access, so it would go directly to the device. This would be too easy. Instead, the clever engineer detects that *there is already an instance of address 0x000D0000 in the pipeline* and thus oh-so-cleverly changes the value associated with this address so that the pipeline now looks like the one shown in Figure 6.8. Note that the Write to 0x000D0000 has been changed from 17 to 411. So the first Write operation, which happened to be critical for setting up the device to receive the next Write to that location, is lost. The device misbehaves, and the cause is hard to determine. This sort of insanity makes it difficult to write truly portable Device Drivers.

What is worse, the engineer provided absolutely no efficient, effective way to circumvent this design misfeature. Of course, it isn't a misfeature if you're doing a matrix inversion, but apparently such engineers never actually had to read or write data from the machines they designed. The operation the hardware engineers provided is an instruction to flush the pipes. This is very expensive on the Alpha, since the Alpha will be producing no results as the pipeline fills again.

There is a clever hack that Device Driver writers used to use. They would set up the memory map so that the devices would respond to four different bus addresses. Thus the device address 0x000D0000 could have been aliased to several other physical (and hence virtual) addresses. The trick was that the driver had to keep track of which register it wrote to and write to the next one in sequence. For example, the device might have responded by mapping registers modulo-64 into the address space for some small piece of the address space. The addresses 0x000D0000, 0x000D4000, 0x000D8000, and 0x000DC000 might all map to the same device register. So the device would keep track of which address it wrote to and use the next one in sequence.

This worked fine until the higher-performance Alpha came out, which had a pipeline twice as deep. Suddenly, all over the world, device drivers stopped working when run on the new machine. So a new instruction was introduced that would effectively flush the write pipe without affecting the read pipe (the instruction is a "write block", and the details are somewhat more complex than we need to go into here). This method is slower than the old one. However, one can hope that the faster Alpha's improvement of application code performance will compensate for the loss of performance in driver code.

Some device drivers are conditionally compiled to run on the old EV4 Alpha and will not run properly on the newer EV5 and later Alphas. Or they are compiled to run on the EV5 and later and will not work on the EV4. All of this impacts distribution and support. A driver that checks at runtime what type of system it is on incurs some additional overhead by having to incorporate both styles and constantly be testing which one to use.

One way the caching can be defeated on a single instruction is a trick we discuss in great detail in Chapter 13: the use of a LOCK prefix. The *x*86 architecture includes a LOCK prefix that lets it interlock access to memory. Using this prefix on a single transfer instruction will guarantee an interlocked operation direct to memory. This handles single data transfers efficiently.

Caching Page Table Information

We discussed in previous sections caches for data, caches for instructions, data pipelines, and instruction pipelines. There is one more type of cache, which, fortunately, is managed for you by the kernel. This is the cache of active PTEs. The use of this cache saves the processor from having to look up a virtual address from a physical address each time it accesses memory. The cache has many names, but the most common one in modern usage is the *translation lookaside buffer*, or TLB. TLB architectures have varied over the years with the various processor architectures. In the 386, 486, and Pentium family, it is a 4-way *set associative* architecture, in which the number of entries can differ on each platform. Other platforms, including the Alpha and the Merced, have different specifications; for example, the Alpha uses a *direct-mapped* TLB.

The Intel architecture has eight sets of four registers for a total of 32 TLB registers. The details don't matter too much for our purposes here (you can read about them in, for example, the book *i486 Microprocessor Programmer's Reference Manual* or the MindShare books such as the *Pentium System Architecture*). However, the basic idea is that when a virtual address is presented to the TLB, the TLB will virtually instantly map the virtual address to a physical address, provided the table contains the translation information. If it does not, the system must go through the segment and page decoding logic to look up the PTE in a page table in memory. When this is done, the contents of the PTE are transferred to the TLB so that the next access to any location on that page will be instantly decoded.

If you change a PTE in memory, you must flush its (now obsolete) version from the TLB. The various memory-management functions of the kernel that work with page tables force the TLB to be flushed if they make a change in the PTEs.

Cache-Line Alignment

Because caches store blocks of data, usually multiple words wide, you can sometimes get better performance if you cause certain data to line up on addresses that are multiples of the cache size. In addition, some devices do not properly support cache snooping and snarfing, particularly those that contain onboard memory and in some cases those that perform Bus-Master DMA. These situations may require you to be aware of the general nature of hardware caches. This is because Windows NT runs on a variety of platforms. You can't do something that is platform-specific to an Alpha, a Pentium, a Pentium Pro, or a Pentium II unless you can be sure it will work on other platforms. Even within those families, the different support chip sets can result in detailed differences. A knowledge of the *cache line size* can also be helpful. Windows NT allows you to query the cache line size and has allocation operations for getting blocks of memory that are cache-line aligned.

Memory Management in NT

All of Windows NT is based on *virtual memory*. Even the operating system, except in a couple of very restricted places, uses *only* virtual memory. And those restricted places are set up solely for the purpose of converting a physical memory address to a virtual memory address.

The Windows NT system manages two kinds of memory: *paged*, which can be moved out to backing store to make room for some other process's pages, and *nonpaged*, which, as the name suggests, is never paged.

At the user application level, the magic that maps the 200MB application address space into a 16MB Windows NT machine is completely invisible . . . except for one point. You can't put 200 pounds of sand in a 16-pound sack, no matter how hard you try. Your only choice is to keep moving some of the sand out of the sack to make room for some of the sand that isn't in the sack. You could end up spending a lot of time just removing sand to make room for more sand.

Similarly, in the world of computers, an application that tends to use a lot of pages can spend nearly all of its time waiting for pages to be brought in. We call this *page thrashing*, and it is a serious performance problem on small machines. We discuss page thrashing in more detail shortly. But although the performance suffers, the programmer can naively assume that the magic works and can happily access any word in the 200MB that the application is currently using.

What makes all this work? The architecture—Intel, PowerPC, MIPS, or Alpha, not to mention the dozens of machines that have not hosted NT (and with NT 4.0, only the Intel and Alpha are supported)—supports a concept called *page mapping*. The details don't matter too much and differ a fair amount between the machines. However, we can capture this concept in an abstract model, shown in Figure 6.9. In the model, you can see a number of pages in the "application program" that apparently exist in memory. In fact, if you use a debugger to examine any location in that memory you will get a value. But what really happens when page mapping occurs?

The locations that apparently exist in memory do not really exist in all cases. Instead, an intermediary called the *page map* converts a *virtual address* in the application's memory to a *physical address* in the real memory. Note that real memory is substantially smaller than virtual memory. So only *some* of the pages (those shown in white in the memory map) are actually in memory. The rest are somewhere else, or maybe nowhere else. Yes, really . . . nowhere else.

The pages we show in physical memory that have the crosshatch pattern are pages that are not allocated to the application. They may be free, or reserved for the operating system, or in use by another process. The idea of the model is to show that they do not belong to the application shown.

If you attempt to access one of those pages shown with a textured pattern, the page map indicates that it is "not present". This won't do you a lot of good—it means you can't complete the instruction! Well, that's part of the magic of modern hardware. The instruction is aborted, and any changes it started to make are undone. The processor then interrupts to a *page fault handler*, saving a pointer to the instruction that failed. Some of the state that is available allows the underlying software to determine which page was missing. That software then looks in the PTE for that page, which in NT, as in most operating systems, contains some information about

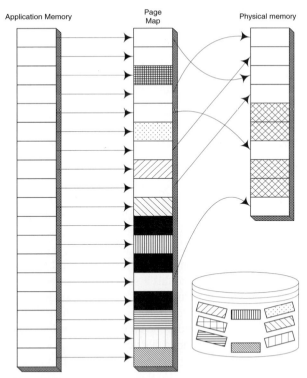

Figure 6.9: *Virtual memory mapping.*

where to find the page on disk. (You can imagine this information as being an index into the disk, but it could be a pointer to a more complex data structure in the kernel that contains the information about where to find the page on disk.) At that point, the operating system finds an unused page in physical memory and starts a read operation to bring the page, which has been temporarily stored on disk, into memory. When this page-in operation is complete, the page map is updated so that the entry that previously said "not present" now says "it's over there". The application program that had been interrupted is then restarted at the failed instruction. The instruction will now succeed because the page it accesses is now in memory. All Is Good.

Well, it isn't quite that simple. For example, what is the processor doing while that page is coming in? Nothing? Not a chance! The processor is off executing some other application whose pages *are* in memory. And what if there are no free pages in physical memory? Well, the processor first has to start a paging operation to page one of those pages *out* before it can page the desired page *in*. And this is just the beginning. What if the page it has started to page out is the one needed by the process to which the context switch is occurring?

Consider a program that manipulates a 100MB array of pixels and does transformations by walking along the pixels in order. It does one page's worth, then has to wait for the next page. It then works on the pixels for that page, then has to wait for the next page following the one it just finished, and so on. By the time it finishes one pass and starts over, the first page is long gone. This means the program spends most of its time waiting for pages, rather than doing useful work—it is page thrashing. This can cause your program to run hundreds or thousands of times slower than it should. We talk about this further in the next section.

Some entries in the page map in the figure are shown in solid black, and they don't appear to have any equivalents on disk. This setup is an optimization; these are pages that the application has declared that it wants but which it has not yet attempted to access. When an access is made, the usual page fault is taken, but when the operating system looks into the page map to see where the page is stored on disk, it discovers that the page is "uncreated". So it finds an empty slot in physical memory (or creates one by paging out some other page) and zeroes it and then maps in the page. Thus eventually all of the pages come to have a real existence.

The Least-Recently-Used Algorithm, Working Set, and Thrashing

There are many problems involved in making a paged virtual memory system work well. For example, if physical memory is completely occupied and a page needs to be written out, which page should be selected? In the mid-to-late 1960s, it was discovered, after much research, that the Least-Recently-Used (LRU) algorithm seemed to work fairly well, better than most alternatives. According to this algorithm, the page chosen to be paged out is the one that is the "oldest" in terms of its most recent access. The presumption (and it is *only* a presumption) is that, because this page hasn't been used in a long time, it probably won't be used in the near future. Data gathered on real systems indicates that this assumption is correct most of the time.

However, Laszlo Belady, while working at IBM's T. J. Watson Research Center, asked, "Is LRU as good as we can do?" So he collected traces of actual system paging behavior from a carefully instrumented research system and came up with an algorithm now known as *Belady's Algorithm*. This algorithm is based on the idea that you have perfect knowledge of the future and thus, instead of paging out the LRU page, you page out the page that is furthest used in the future. This *has* to be as good as you can do. He then compared the results of LRU to those of his algorithm and found that LRU came within 4% of the performance of his algorithm. Since LRU uses knowledge gained from the past, while his algorithm requires perfect knowledge of the future, it was clear that LRU really was "good enough". Any alternative to LRU only has to be measured against Belady's Algorithm to determine how effective it is. Thus far, LRU and minor variants of it have held the lead.

Another concept to consider, introduced by Peter Denning, is the *Working Set*. Consider the following, very real problem. You have an application that is fairly large. It blocks on an I/O operation. While it is blocked (for example, it might be waiting for a network packet and have a full minute of timeout), most of its pages are paged out as they become more and more LRU. Then the packet arrives. The thread that was waiting is restarted (assume for the moment that it is the only thread in the process). The program counter value is loaded, and the processor starts to execute. Oops. The page to which the program counter points is not in memory. That's OK. You start a paging operation to bring it in. It comes in. You restart the instruction. The instruction is now there, and it just happens to be the x86 REP MOVS instruction. So the REP opcode is fetched. It is followed by an instruction that is to be executed, which is the MOVS opcode. But the REP opcode was on the last byte of a page, and the next page, which holds the MOVS opcode, is missing. Fine. You start a paging operation to bring in that byte and restart the REP MOVS instruction. The MOVS tries to fetch the source byte. Oops! That page is missing. You repeat the paging operation and restart the instruction. The REP instruction is present, the MOVS instruction is present, the source byte is present, the destination page is . . . oops! OK, another paging operation. This works well until each of the MOVS pointers crosses a page boundary. Each of these causes a page fault. If you are moving a 64K chunk, you could get as many as 17 + 17 + 2, or *36*, *page faults* on that move. (A 64K chunk, unless it is page-aligned at the start, can span 17 pages and one page fault for the instruction.)

For more details on paging and paging algorithms, check out one of the books on operating systems given in Further Reading at the end of the chapter.

To use the Working Set concept, you need to look to the past some distance and ask, "What is the set of pages that were most recently accessed?" While the code page holding the inner loop of an iteration and that holding the function it calls are fairly recently accessed, the code page holding `main` (or `WinMain`) may not have been accessed in hours. The most recent data pages are the ones most likely to be accessed in the future. Note that some applications have a very small working set, perhaps a dozen pages, while others have a very large one, perhaps hundreds of pages. The key feature here is that overall system performance can be enhanced if you don't use "lazy evaluation" and not bring pages in until they are touched. Instead, you use "eager evaluation" and try to bring in the entire working set before dispatching the process (or in the case of NT, a thread in the process). This works fine, up to a point; see the following warning inset.

I have corrected many Windows NT application programmers who think that they have optimized their application by calling the Win32 function `VirtualLock` on a large buffer (1 to 75MB). The programmer thinks that this function locks the buffer into physical memory and that doing this improves the performance of the application and the system.

The programmer is wrong.

Some of the "better" programmers think that the application performance will improve at the cost of lower system performance.

These programmers are wrong, too.

`VirtualLock` does not lock pages into physical memory. It locks pages into the application's working set. This requires that all pages of the buffer must be resident in physical memory before the application can run. Locking a large buffer in the working set will increase the application's use of physical memory. The increased use of memory means more time spent paging.

Locking pages in the working set will not prevent the pages from being paged out when the application is not the active process. The larger working set for the application means more pages of the application will be paged out when other applications and tasks run. Other tasks that will run include all User mode portions of NT, the file system, updates to the clock in the task bar, as well as other user applications.

When the NT scheduler gives the application a chance to run, the application is not able to start until all pages of the buffer have been paged into main memory. This results in a much longer delay to start execution at the beginning of each execution quantum or completion of I/O. And the result of this is lower application performance.

There will be less memory available for the file cache, so all file I/O will be slower (for all processes). Other tasks, when given a quantum, will also be slower starting, since they will compete for memory and need to be paged in. The increased total paging activity and the delays in starting other tasks result in lower system performance.

So you end up trading lower system performance for lower application performance. – *end*

Use of the working set also tends to reduce page thrashing. Thrashing can be reduced by careful consideration of the paging behavior of the application; however, application design is beyond the scope of this book. (A detailed discussion of the implications of paging on an application is in the Rector/Newcomer book, *Win32 Programming*.) You can also get two or more processes mutually thrashing, particularly in the case described in the inset. Generally, as a Windows NT Driver writer, you will not need to be unduly concerned about this, unless your device tends to induce pathological behavior in an application, such as requiring an application to have 100MB of memory to hold the data from or required by the device. In this case, the techniques we describe in Chapter 19 may help you to get around some of the problems caused by such requirements.

To give you an idea about the impact of using the working set, consider the article "Tips for Improving Time-Critical Code" from the MSDN CD. This article suggests that the cost of missing the L1 cache is 10–20 processor clock cycles (depending on the particular processor architecture, chip set, and processor clock speed). The cost of missing the L2 cache is 20–40 processor clock cycles. A page fault can cost over a *million* lost instructions! Therefore, the article states, "It is in the best interest of program execution to write code that will reduce the number of missed cache hits and page faults". The goal of the Working Set model is to try to manage the page faults to minimize those lost instructions.

Nonpaged Memory

In a now-famous incident early in computer history, Burroughs Corporation (which eventually became, through a series of mergers, Unisys) had a new architecture, the B5500. An architecture unlike nearly anything else seen before or since, it had variable-length descriptors with implicit bounds checking. Any segment could be automatically paged out. This was all wonderfully transparent. In an early test of the operating system, it was discovered that it frequently locked up for no apparent reason. After some serious debugging work, it was discovered that the code segment containing the page-in subroutine had been paged out! This problem required some changes to mark certain segments as requiring permanent residency.

In Windows NT, the operating system requires that certain pieces of code and data remain permanently in memory. There are various reasons for this.

- The obvious reason is that some pieces of code, such as the code to read pages into memory, must always be in memory.

- The hardware itself will, via the interrupt system, transfer control to specific locations in memory. These locations must be present when the interrupts come in.

- The pages of data that are being written to a DMA Device, or into which data is being placed from a DMA Device, cannot change position or be paged out while the DMA Device is active because that device is, in effect, a totally separate processor that just happens to be accessing memory.

The NT architecture itself requires that certain pieces of code and data always be present in memory. This requirement follows from the way in which the IRQL hierarchy is arranged. The level called DISPATCH_LEVEL represents the lowest level at which scheduling and scheduler preemption are locked out. Below this level, the scheduler and preemption are possible. A page fault at levels < DISPATCH_LEVEL can cause a thread to be suspended, another thread to be scheduled for execution, and all of the related actions involved in such a control transfer. A page fault requires that the thread that caused the page fault be suspended and the operating system initiate a page-input operation. These operations *cannot* be performed at levels >= DISPATCH_LEVEL, that is, at DISPATCH_LEVEL or any DIRQL level. Consequently, any code or data that is touched by code running at these elevated levels must not cause a page fault or perform any action that would force a thread context transfer. (It might appear that operations such as marking an IRP as pending would cause a thread to be suspended or that completing an IRP would do this, even from DISPATCH_LEVEL. Not so. They only set state that is later handled at an IRQL < DISPATCH_LEVEL.)

This leads to many considerations you must be aware of as a Device Driver writer. You must ensure that any operation that could cause a page fault is performed only at PASSIVE_LEVEL. Thus, if the application program hands you a pointer to a block of, say, 20 pages, you must take into account that not all of those pages may be resident in memory. There are two methods for handling this. First, because it is such a common thing to need done, it is almost always done for you by the I/O Manager. When your driver gets control in one of its IRP_MJ_ Dispatch Routines, all of the pages you may care about are already "locked down" in physical memory. This means you can safely touch any of them at any level up to and including the DIRQL of your device. You can also initiate a DMA transfer into them, or from them, and know that they will not change position while the DMA operation is active. The second method is to explicitly lock down the application memory. This is the I/O method known as "Neither", which you should avoid until you are comfortable with writing Device Drivers.

In addition to dealing with the application-level memory, you usually need to allocate memory internally in your driver. This can be done directly from the Nonpaged Pool with a variety of allocation calls.

Memory Management for Device Drivers: Overview

The Paged and Nonpaged Pools are areas of memory in which the kernel code (including Device Drivers) can allocate storage. The Nonpaged Pool is created early in the bootstrap process of Windows NT. The size of the Nonpaged Pool is based on the memory size of the computer and on several Registry values. All data needed when running at elevated IRQL levels (above DISPATCH_LEVEL) must be in nonpaged memory. If code running at an IRQL level is above the level of the page fault interrupt and the handler, the system is unable to page in the required memory. Touching a page not in physical memory results in an IRQL_NOT_LESS_OR_EQUAL Blue Screen.

One important factor to consider is that the Nonpaged Pool will be fragmented seriously by the time your driver is loaded. Just because you added physical memory to the system and adjusted the Registry entry, do not expect to find the memory contiguous. One of the authors has helped several clients with projects that have required large DMA buffers (more than 100MB . . . yes, a *contiguous nonpaged* buffer of more than 100MB). There are limitations on the additional nonpaged memory available after physical memory is added to the system; only 80% of the physical memory may be added to the pool. The default allocation will be much less than this. All hardware that requires a large nonpaged buffer should include scatter/gather to eliminate the dependency on the allocation of large contiguous nonpaged memory.

In Chapter 12, we talk about the many memory allocation routines available to a driver.

Recall from Chapter 3 that Memory Descriptor Lists, or MDLs, are the basis of how a Device Driver gets hold of user memory and makes it available in contexts other than the initiating thread. The quick summary here is that either an MDL can be constructed explicitly by you, the Device Driver writer, from within the driver, or one can be constructed for you automatically by the I/O Manager. We discuss these concepts in Chapter 12.

Internal buffer allocation done by (or for) Device Drivers is handled by a sequence of memory manager (Mm-prefix) calls, Executive Services calls, and some general mapping (Zw-prefix) calls. You must be very careful in using these memory allocation primitives. Failure to release memory can cause a Blue Screen, and at the very least will compromise system performance and reliability.

The File Cache

This is not a book about File System Drivers. However, the File System is an important component of NT, and you must be aware of how some of it works so that you do not inadvertently do something that will compromise its performance. The file cache is one of the components you can severely impact if you are not careful.

Most operating systems provide for improved performance of the file system by maintaining a cache of recent file pages in memory and performing the actual I/O operations in the background. Thus a process that "writes a file" does not have to wait for the actual disk I/O to complete; the blocks are written to the in-memory file cache and the process runs at nearly full memory speed. In addition, if the process then "reads a file" to read information it has just "written", the data may not actually be read from the physical device but simply copied out of the page already in memory. Finally, if a file is being read sequentially, front-to-back, the operating system can anticipate what is about to happen and *prefetch* the blocks of the file so that when the process finally needs them, they are already in memory and need only to be copied. The process does not actually have to wait for the I/O. In this sense, the operating system has pipelined the file system access.

How much memory is allocated to the file system cache? There is a certain minimum amount so that the File System will function at all, but beyond that, that system is free to use any unallocated pages it can find. As processes need space to execute, for code, and for data, these pages will be reclaimed from the File System. Thus there is a continuous dynamic balance of the file system cache and the needs of the system.

Further Reading

Belady, Laszlo A., R. A. Nelson, and G. S. Shedler, "An Anomaly in Space-Time Characteristics of Certain Programs Running in a Paging Machine", *Communications of the ACM* 12 (June 1969), pp. 349–353.

Custer, Helen, *Inside Windows NT*, Microsoft Press, 1993. ISBN 155615481X.

Denning, Peter J., "The Working Set Model for Program Behavior", *Communications of the ACM* 11 (1968), pp. 323–333.

———, "Thrashing: Its Causes and Prevention", *Proceedings AFIPS National Computer Conference* (1968), pp. 915–922.

———, "Working Sets, Past and Present", *IEEE Transactions on Software Engineering*, Vol. SE-6 (January 1980), pp. 64–84.

Habermann, A. Nico, *Introduction to Operating System Design*, Science Research Associations, 1976.

Intel Corporation, *i486 Microprocessor Programmer's Reference Manual*, McGraw-Hill, 1990. ISBN 0-07-881674-2.

Microsoft Corporation, *Microsoft Windows NT Device Driver Kit Design Guide*, Microsoft Developer Network (MSDN) CD-ROM.

Mindshare, Inc.: Don Anderson and Tom Shanley, *Pentium™ Processor System Architecture, Second Edition*, Addison-Wesley, 1995. ISBN 0-201-40992-5.

Mindshare, Inc.: Tom Shanley, *Pentium® Pro and Pentium® II System Architecture, Second Edition*, Addison Wesley Longman, 1998. ISBN 0-201-30973-4.

Sites, Richard L., and Richard T. Witek, *Alpha AXP Architecture Reference Manual (Second Edition)*, Digital Press, 1995. ISBN 1-55558-145-5.

Solomon, David A., *Inside Windows NT (Second Edition)*, Microsoft Press, 1998. ISBN 1-57231-677-2.

Tanenbaum, Andrew S., *Operating Systems: Design and Implementation*, Prentice-Hall, 1987. ISBN 0-13-637406-9.

Wulf, William, Roy Levin, and Samuel P. Harbison, *Hydra/C.mmp: An Experimental Computer System*, McGraw-Hill, 1981. ISBN 0-07-072120-3.

Chapter

7 *Driver Data Structures*

For a driver to properly load and execute, a variety of information is required. Some of this information is stored in memory data structures that are created and managed by the various NT services. Some of these services you never see, as they are called only by the I/O Manager, and some you are responsible for calling yourself. Information also is maintained regarding the names of drivers that are active and, in the Registry, that describe the properties of the driver.

To help you understand the structures and information, this chapter starts with an introduction to the overall process of loading a driver. It then discusses in somewhat more detail the Driver Object and Device Object, gives a brief overview of some other objects, and concludes with a somewhat detailed discussion of specific types of IRPs (I/O Request Packets). Subsequent chapters cover all of these objects in detail.

Loading and Starting a Driver

Certain key drivers are loaded during the boot process. Which drivers to load at boot time is determined by information stored in the Registry. The Registry also tells what to do if a boot-time driver fails to load or initialize properly. The mechanisms used at boot time are not quite the same as those used after the boot has successfully completed, but this detail is not visible to you as a Device Driver writer. To simplify the discussion, by ignoring this transient condition during the boot, we consider only the case of starting a driver after the system has completed its boot process.

After the boot process has completed, a Device Driver is started and stopped by the Service Control Manager (SCM). In this chapter, we show what goes on when the SCM starts and stops a driver.

The first question is, how does the SCM locate the driver? To do this, it goes to the Registry to the key HKEY_LOCAL_MACHINE\CurrentControlSet\Services*drivername*. Under that entry are a number of descriptive entries, which we detail in Chapter 9, page 178 and Appendix A, in Table A.16 on page 897. One of those entries is the ImagePath value, which tells the SCM where the executable for the driver is found. This is shown in Figure 7.1. If

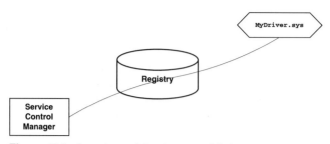

Figure 7.1: *Locating a driver's executable image.*

ImagePath is omitted, a default path, %systemroot%\Drivers*drivername* is used to locate the executable.

A driver is a type of Dynamic Link Library (DLL) module (in fact, it is just a DLL with some specific requirements and the extension .sys instead of .dll). If you are familiar with Windows application-level programming, what is done next is the equivalent of a LoadLibrary call. This call invokes the system loader to bring the executable image into memory. A location is found in which to put it, relocatable addresses are bound, and all of the usual machinations of processing an executable image are performed. Now the SCM must execute the code.

To execute the code, the SCM invokes the kernel-level equivalent of the GetProcAddress API. This is a function which, when given a handle to an executable object and a symbolic name, returns the address to which that symbolic name has been bound. The SCM can now call through this pointer. The name known to the SCM is DriverEntry, which is the first function called by the SCM for any driver.

The ImagePath can specify any location on the local disk. Thus, although there is a default location for storing a driver executable file (which is where the system looks if ImagePath is omitted), the executable can actually be placed anywhere (but only on the local disk, not on a network drive). The driver can also appear under any name in the Registry. The actual name under which the Registry entry is stored is passed into DriverEntry as one of its input parameters. To be able to fully exploit this generality, you might need to take extra care in how you code your driver. The call of DriverEntry is shown in Figure 7.2. The parameters are indicated by the dashed lines.

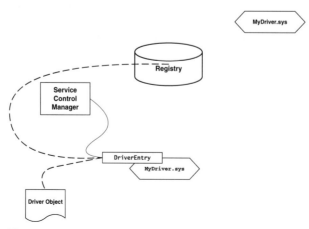

Figure 7.2: *Calling* DriverEntry.

DriverEntry performs several functions. One is to make the rest of the code of the driver accessible to the I/O Manager. The I/O Manager accesses these functions via pointers in the *Driver Object*, the first object you encounter when your driver starts up. It is the responsibility of DriverEntry to set to a non-NULL value a pointer to a *handler* for each of the IRP functions that it supports. These *Dispatch Routines* include operations that will open a device, close a device, read from it, write to it, control it, and so on. (Nearly 30 functions are actually supported, shown in Table 7.1 on page 137.) Starting with NT 5.0 beta releases and Windows 2000, the functions to support power management and Plug-and-Play capabilities are available. A simple driver might specify only the open, close, and unload routines, and (if the device is at all interesting) at least one operation to read from or write to the device. This is shown in Figure 7.3, where the driver has open, close, read, and unload operations but no write operation.

Next, if the device is on a self-identifying bus such as the PCI Bus, DriverEntry performs an operation called "enumerating the bus". On an ISA bus, the driver will skip the enumeration and must obtain the device's I/O and memory addresses (and other resources used by the card) from some persistent storage, preferably by looking in the Registry. We discuss these techniques in much greater detail later in the chapter. For this example, assume the devices are on a PCI Bus. DriverEntry looks at *every* device on the PCI Bus.

For each device the driver recognizes, it creates a Device Object. A Device Object represents a general kind of device. Every device has its own private device-specific information and state that it wants to maintain, so every Device Object has a Device Extension. A Device Extension is a data structure entirely invented by the Device Driver writer (that's you) in which you store all of the information you want that is specific to your device. If the information is of variable length and potentially large, you can, as you might expect, allocate your own structures, such as linked lists, that hang off of the Device Extension. After creating a Device Object, you will initialize not only the Device Object but whatever fields you have defined in your Driver Extension.

A partially enumerated PCI bus is shown in Figure 7.4. This figure shows that the enumeration has found the first device on the bus of type "MyDevice" (the other MyDevice device hasn't been found yet) and has created a Device Object, as well as its Device Extension to represent it. The dashed line between the Device Object and MyDevice indicates that stored in the Device

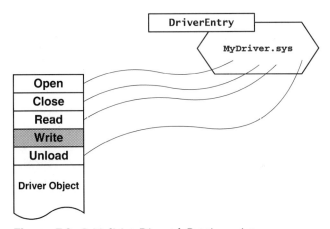

Figure 7.3: *Initializing Dispatch Routine pointers.*

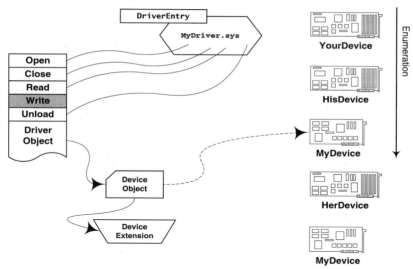

Figure 7.4: *A partially enumerated PCI Bus.*

Object (or Device Extension) is key information, such as which bus and the bus address, that will associate that Device Object with that specific device. DriverEntry ignores any device it does not recognize.

This may seem a bit clumsy, and it is. However, it is the only way to enumerate a bus in Windows NT 4.0. Coming with Windows 2000 is a new Bus Enumerator component; we discuss this in Chapter 28.

A fully enumerated PCI Bus is shown in Figure 7.5. At this point, the driver has looked at all of the devices on the bus, found two instances of MyDevice, and created two Device Objects.

Thus Are Created Device Objects.

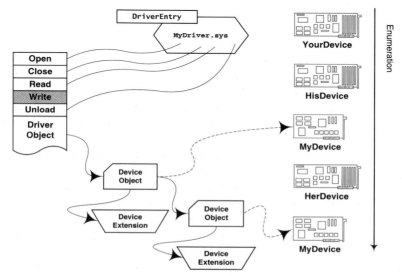

Figure 7.5: *A fully enumerated PCI Bus.*

But how do you name a device in order to open it? By giving a "filename" to the CreateFile operation. But how does this name get mapped to a specific Device Object?

One of the side effects of the IoCreateDevice call, which creates the Device Object, is the creation of an entry in the in-memory symbol table, called the *Object Manager Name Space*. The Object Manager Name Space is a tree-structured, named-node data structure that looks very much like a directory structure. Each device, when it is created, is added to the Object Manager Name Space under the entry \Device. The name is suffixed with a number to distinguish between various devices; for example, the first (or only) instance of MyDevice is named MyDevice0; the second is MyDevice1; and so on. This is shown in Figure 7.6.

But there is more. These names are not the names seen by the CreateFile call! Because of a complex piece of history, the actual device name for a CreateFile call is *not* the name in the \Device entry, but under a different key in the Object Manager Name Space, \DosDevices. To make your device visible to the CreateFile call, you must create a symbolic link between a name in the DosDevices entry and the actual entry under \Device. This is done by a call to create a symbolic link. The result is shown in Figure 7.7.

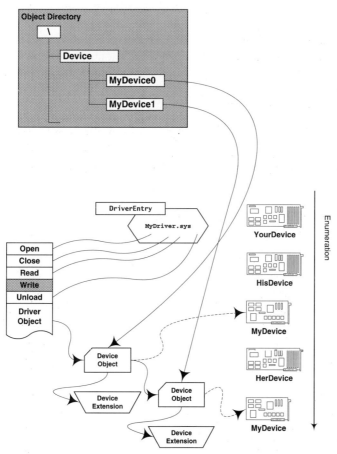

Figure 7.6: *The Object Manager Name Space and Driver data structures.*

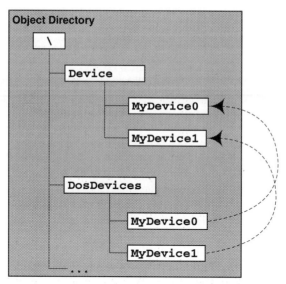

Figure 7.7: *The Object Manager Name Space.*

It would be nice if we could stop here and say, "Yes, that's how it is". But, in fact, the truth is a bit more complex. However, you don't need to see all of it right now because it is largely invisible to you, so we leave it at this level for now and tell you the whole truth in Chapter 23, page 466.

Driver Objects

The Driver Object is the first object you encounter when your driver starts up. The DriverEntry routine is called, with the first parameter, a PDRIVER_OBJECT parameter, being a pointer to a system-created Driver Object. But where did the system get the Driver Object? How did it know to create one?

Driver Loading

A Driver Object is created by the system when a driver is loaded. A non-WDM driver (Windows NT 4.0 and Windows NT 4.0-compatible drivers running on Windows 2000) is loaded either when the system boots up or on demand. A WDM driver (Windows 2000 only, and only for certain kinds of devices) is loaded when the Bus Driver for a bus detects that a device requiring that driver has been connected to that bus.

A driver is loaded at boot time if the Registry entry for the driver has the subkey

```
Start=0x00000000 (SERVICE_BOOT_START)
```

Such devices are usually those that are critical for the boot process. Once the system has loaded, additional drivers may be loaded if they have the subkey

```
Start=0x00000001 (SERVICE_SYSTEM_START)
```

Such drivers are not critical for the boot but are usually considered "necessary" for the system. Additional drivers may have the subkey

```
Start=0x00000002 (SERVICE_AUTO_START)
```

and are started by the Service Control Manager (SCM). Finally, a driver may be loaded explicitly, either as a result of the user's interaction with the Control Panel or by a program's issuing SCM calls. Such drivers have the key

```
Start=0x00000003 (SERVICE_DEMAND_START)
```

Driver Load Order

How do you know in what order a driver loads? And how do you control the order so that when there are layered drivers, you load the lowest driver first followed by the higher level drivers in the correct order? This is all handled by a fairly complex mechanism that involves several Registry keys.

The first determinant of the load order is the Start subkey under the driver name, as discussed in the previous section. The full Registry pathname to a driver is

```
HKEY_LOCAL_MACHINE\System\CurrentControlSet\Services\drivername
```

So the Start subkey is

```
HKEY_LOCAL_MACHINE\System\CurrentControlSet\Services\drivername\Start
```

To simplify the notation for the rest of this chapter, we abbreviate the use of lengthy key names like this by ignoring the common part of the name. For example:

```
HKEY_LOCAL_MACHINE\System\CurrentControlSet\Services
```

We indicate its required presence by ellipses; for example, the notation

```
...\drivername\Start.
```

Within any given load sequence, such as SERVICE_BOOT_START, SERVICE_SYSTEM_START, or SERVICE_AUTO_START, you must first determine with what *group* the driver is associated and in what order the group should be loaded. The group is specified by the Registry key ...\drivername\Group. The group load order is under the key ...\Control\ServiceGroupOrder. Once you begin loading a group, the drivers within a group are loaded in an order specified by their ...\drivername\Tag property.

If the group to which the driver belongs is not found in the ServiceGroupOrder list, it is loaded after all other groups have been loaded. There is no guarantee of the order in which drivers in different unknown groups will be loaded. After all drivers that have groups specified are loaded, all drivers without any Group subkey are loaded.

The use of the ...\drivername\Tag value is also somewhat complex. It is a number that is looked up in an array in the GroupOrderList under the name of the class. The GroupOrderList value is an array of DWORD values. The first value is a DWORD that is the count of the number of tags in the rest of the array. The remaining tags are the load order for drivers within that group. Within a group, all drivers whose Tag value corresponds to the first entry in this array (not the count DWORD) are loaded. Then, all drivers whose Tag value corresponds to the second entry in the array are loaded. When all drivers whose tags are specified in the `Tag` array are loaded, any remaining drivers for that group are loaded.

A typical entry in the Registry has a value like this:

```
SCSI CDROM Class: REG_BINARY: 02 00 00 00 01 00 00 00 02 00 00 00
```

We reformat this typographically so that the value boundaries can be better seen:

```
SCSI CDROM Class: REG_BINARY: | 02 00 00 00 | 01 00 00 00 | 02 00 00 00 |
```

Because of how the byte order is swapped, with the low-order byte on the left and the high-order byte on the right, this is really the equivalent of

```
SCSI CDROM Class: 0x00000002 0x00000001 0x00000002
```

That is, the array has 2 DWORDs, whose values are 1 and 2. The leftmost byte of a DWORD, when a 4-byte array is interpreted as a DWORD, becomes the low-order byte of the DWORD. This entry indicates that within the SCSI CDROM Class, all drivers whose `Tag` field is 1 will be loaded, followed by all drivers whose `Tag` field is 2, followed by any drivers without `Tag` fields. There is no particular reason, other than reader convenience, that the order of elements in the array is in numeric order. A class could just as easily specify that the load order for tags was 7, 3, 1, 2, and 4 (with no specification for 5 or 6), but it is easier to keep everything straight if the load order is also the numeric tag value order.

Adding a Driver

To add a new driver, you make assignments so that the load order is correct. This is particularly important for WDM drivers. You must specify

- a `Start` value,
- a `Group` value (unless you are content with its loading after all named groups),
- a `Tag` value (if you want to control the order within the group), and
- a dependency tag if there is a driver dependency.

If none of the existing groups are suitable, you must create a new group name. If you are content with your group's being loaded last, you can stop there. Otherwise, you must add your group name to the `...\Control\GroupOrderList` key and specify its order by adding an entry to `...\Control\ServiceGroupOrder`. When we discuss the issues of building a redistributable product driver in Chapter 26, we tell you more about how you can accomplish this easily.

Driver Object Structure

A `DRIVER_OBJECT` is a "semi-opaque" data structure. This means that only a few fields are documented *and these are the only fields you can legitimately use*. Microsoft makes no promises if you use an undocumented field, so Microsoft advises that if you don't want a version nightmare (perhaps even a Service Pack nightmare), *don't use the undocumented fields*. Unfortunately, there are some cases in which the exact information you need is contained in an undocumented field. Some of the fields listed as "undocumented" at the ordinary DDK level in fact *are* documented as part of the Installable File System (IFS). So it is often hard to tell what is and is not legitimate to depend on, especially when there sometimes is no other way to discover utterly critical information. The Driver Object structure—at least the documented fields—is shown next.

```
typedef struct {
    PDEVICE_OBJECT DeviceObject;
    PUNICODE_STRING HardwareDatabase;
    PFAST_IO_DISPATCH FastIoDispatch;
    PDRIVER_INITIALIZE DriverInit;
    PDRIVER_STARTIO DriverStartIo;
    PDRIVER_UNLOAD DriverUnload;
    PDRIVER_DISPATCH MajorFunction[IRP_MJ_FUNCTION+1];
    // many other undocumented fields...
} DRIVER_OBJECT, * PDRIVER_OBJECT;
```

When `DriverEntry` is called, it is passed a pointer to this structure and must initialize it. Some of the initialization is done directly and some by calling particular functions. The `DriverInit` field was already set by the I/O system when it loaded the driver. The `HardwareDatabase` field is also initialized by the I/O system and is used by the driver to locate hardware-specific values in the Registry.

The `FastIoDispatch` field is used only by File System Drivers and network drivers. We do not discuss its use for general drivers.

The `DriverEntry` routine initializes the `DriverStartIo`, `DriverUnload`, and, most important, the `MajorFunction` array. We discuss and illustrate these assignments throughout our discussion of `DriverEntry`.

Each `MajorFunction` table entry provides for a dispatch to a driver Dispatch Routine. These are the functions that are called for operations such as Open (`CreateFile`), Close (`CloseHandle`), Read (`ReadFile/ReadFileEx`), Write (`WriteFile/WriteFileEx`), and IoControl (`DeviceIoControl`) and are shown in Table 7.1. (All codes are shown, but the ones not directly related to ordinary Windows NT 4.0 Device Drivers are grayed out. These functions are file-system-oriented, internal to specialized devices, or for Windows 2000, which is covered later.) All Dispatch Routines have this same form:

```
typedef NTSTATUS (*PDRIVER_DISPATCH) (IN PDEVICE_OBJECT DeviceObject, IN PIRP Irp)
```

Table 7.1: `MajorFunction` *Dispatch Codes*

Dispatch Code	Use
IRP_MJ_CREATE	This IRP is sent whenever the application issues a `CreateFile` call. Every driver must support this IRP.
IRP_MJ_CREATE_NAMED_PIPE	
IRP_MJ_CLOSE	This IRP is sent whenever the application issues a `CloseHandle` call that releases the last handle to a device.
IRP_MJ_READ	This IRP is sent whenever the application issues a `ReadFile(Ex)` call.
IRP_MJ_WRITE	This IRP is sent whenever the application issues a `WriteFile(Ex)` call.

Table 7.1: `MajorFunction` *Dispatch Codes (continued)*

Dispatch Code	Use
IRP_MJ_QUERY_INFORMATION	
IRP_MJ_SET_INFORMATION	
IRP_MJ_QUERY_EA	
IRP_MJ_SET_EA	
IRP_MJ_FLUSH_BUFFERS	
IRP_MJ_QUERY_VOLUME_INFORMATION	
IRP_MJ_SET_VOLUME_INFORMATION	
IRP_MJ_DIRECTORY_CONTROL	
IRP_MJ_FILE_SYSTEM_CONTROL	
IRP_MJ_DEVICE_CONTROL	The IRP is sent for a `DeviceIoControl` call issued from the application.
IRP_MJ_INTERNAL_DEVICE_CONTROL	The IRP is sent for an IRP that is generated within the I/O system for internal purposes. These IRPs can never be directly generated by an application. Use of this technique allows for internal IoControl operations that should not be visible at the application level.
IRP_MJ_SHUTDOWN	This IRP is sent whenever the system is shutting down, provided the Device Object has been registered using `IoRegisterShutdownNotification`.
IRP_MJ_LOCK_CONTROL	
IRP_MJ_CLEANUP	If your driver has a Cancel Routine, it must handle Cleanup requests as well. This IRP is sent when the open handle reference count goes to 0 and the File Object reference count is nonzero.
IRP_MJ_CREATE_MAILSLOT	
IRP_MJ_QUERY_SECURITY	
IRP_MJ_SET_SECURITY	
IRP_MJ_POWER	This applies to Windows 2000; see Chapter 28.
IRP_MJ_DEVICE_CHANGE	
IRP_MJ_QUERY_QUOTA	
IRP_MJ_SET_QUOTA	
IRP_MJ_PNP	This applies to Windows 2000; see Chapter 28.
IRP_MJ_MAXIMUM_FUNCTION	This value is the largest legitimate value of a `MajorFunction` index.

Creating Device Objects

One of the first things your driver should do in its `DriverEntry` routine is to create one or more Device Objects, each representing a single device. Note that in Windows NT 4.0, a driver is loaded exactly *once* even if there are multiple devices installed. Thus a dual-port COM board (COM1 and COM2) has only one driver, but that driver has two Device Objects.

How do you know how many Device Objects to create? For a PCI driver, you must enumerate the bus, which we mentioned earlier in the chapter, searching each PCI slot looking for a device you understand how to handle. For each such device, you create a Device Object. We show how to do PCI Bus enumeration in Chapter 21. PCMCIA (PC-Card) enumeration resembles PCI bus enumeration. For the old ISA bus, the task of doing an actual bus enumeration is essentially impossible if you are trying to automatically detect the device because, on the whole, ISA busses have no guarantees about how the cards behave. In this case, you will need to install Registry entries that tell you information about the device. For example, you might store information about the number of devices, the devices' IRQs, and their device addresses. Your DriverEntry routine will then query the Registry to determine these values.

You create a Device Object by calling the IoCreateDevice function, given next.

```
NTSTATUS IoCreateDevice(IN PDRIVER_OBJECT DriverObject,
                        IN ULONG DeviceExtensionSize,
                        IN PUNICODE_STRING DeviceName,
                        IN DEVICE_TYPE DeviceType,
                        IN ULONG DeviceCharacteristics,
                        IN BOOLEAN Exclusive,
                        OUT PDEVICE_OBJECT * DeviceObject);
```

You pass in the pointer to the Driver Object that you got as a parameter to DriverEntry. If your device requires additional storage, you should define a structure that contains this additional information and pass its sizeof value in as *DeviceExtensionSize*. The *DeviceName* must be a full path specification in Unicode, converted to a UNICODE_STRING; for example, L"\\Device*devicename*" is converted using the RtlInitUnicodeString function. *DeviceType* defines the type of the device and is one of the FILE_DEVICE_*xxx* constants.

The *DeviceCharacteristics* parameter applies primarily to File System Drivers and for most other drivers will be 0. If *Exclusive* is TRUE, only one thread at a time can own the device and send it I/O requests; if it is FALSE, then several threads could access the device.

A new Device Object is created and a pointer to it is stored in the location referenced by *DeviceObject*. If the result is STATUS_SUCCESS, the newly created Device Object is added to *DriverObject*. The chain of devices is accessible starting with the DriverObject->DeviceObject field and is traversed using the NextDevice field of the Device Object. An entry is made in the Object Manager Name Space under \Device, using the name as specified by *DeviceName*.

Device Object Structure

A Device Object, like a Driver Object, is semi-opaque. This means that if you look at the C definition, you will find many more fields than we document here. *Only the documented fields are guaranteed to remain compatible across releases*. The use of any undocumented field may cause your driver to be nonportable across platforms and/or broken by new releases or Service Packs. The Device Object structure—at least the documented fields—is shown next.

```
typedef struct _DEVICE_OBJECT {
          PDRIVER_OBJECT DriverObject;
          struct _DEVICE_OBJECT * NextDevice;
```

```
            struct _IRP * CurrentIrp;
            ULONG Flags;
            ULONG Characteristics;
            PVOID DeviceExtension;
            DEVICE_TYPE DeviceType;
            CCHAR StackSize;
            ULONG AlignmentRequirement;
            // ...Many other private fields, not documented
        } DEVICE_OBJECT;
```

When IoCreateDevice returns, the newly created Device Object has several of these fields initialized. The DriverObject field is initialized to point to the Driver Object that was passed into IoCreateDevice. The NextDevice field is also initialized. If there is only one device in the chain, the field will be NULL; if there are multiple devices, it can refer to the next device in the chain. (There is no specified order in which a device is added, whether to the head of the device chain or at the end. Do not do anything that depends on any ordering of this chain.) The Flags field may be initialized to one of several flags (mostly for use by the File System Drivers), and you must initialize the flag indicating the type of I/O you are doing. This must be done by using the bitwise OR operator in C. The bit can be either of DO_BUFFERED_IO or DO_DIRECT_IO, for example:

```
    MyDevice->Flags |= DO_BUFFERED_IO;  // set I/O type
```

IoCreateDevice also initializes the Characteristics field to the parameter passed for device characteristics, which for non-File System Drivers will usually be 0.

The Device Object that is created is of size sizeof(DEVICE_OBJECT) + *DeviceExtensionSize*, but you should not depend on the fact that the Device Object and its Extension are contiguous. There is a direct pointer to the Device Object extension area initialized by IoCreateDevice. This is how you should access the Device Extension. The reason is that if your driver obtains the base of the extension by using sizeof(DEVICE_OBJECT), a later release or service patch that extends the private fields of the Device Object will invalidate your code. The pointer will always be correct. Given a typedef for your Device Extension, you can now access it using the assignment illustrated below.

```
typedef struct { ... } MyExtensions ; // definition of my device extensions
    ...
    MyExtensions * ext = (MyExtensions *)MyDevice->DeviceExtension;
```

The one tricky field you must deal with is StackSize. This is initialized to 1 by IoCreateDevice. Thus if your driver is a lowest-level driver, you do not need to change this value. However, if your driver is layered, you must allow enough stack space for the (in principle, unknown) number of layers below your driver. In fact, the number of drivers under yours might change after a reboot, or even when a new filter driver is started. So you cannot "know" how much stack space is required at compile time.

If you are building some sort of "filter driver" (see Chapter 23), the operations IoAttachDevice or IoAttachDeviceToDeviceStack (used by WDM) will automatically set the StackSize field to a valid value for the number of layers below your driver. It is uncommon to use these calls for ordinary drivers. For other layered drivers, you must first obtain the handle to the Driver Object of the driver you intend to call and then set your StackSize to 1 higher than the `StackSize` of the driver you call. (If you call more than one driver, which would be unusual, it needs to be 1 plus the maximum of all of the `StackSize` fields of the drivers you call.)

Adapter Objects

An Adapter Object is used when the device can do DMA. If the device does DMA using the motherboard DMA channels, the Adapter Object is used to synchronize the use of the DMA channel with other devices that wish to use the same DMA channel. If the device contains its own DMA controller (typical in bus mastering), an Adapter Object is theoretically unnecessary. But in practice there are a number of useful library routines for I/O support that require an Adapter Object, and there is no way to easily do what they do without having one. Consequently, bus mastering devices will usually have an Adapter Object, which you create during `DriverEntry`.

Controller Objects

Some multi-function devices, particularly multimedia devices, provide several independent capabilities but use a set of control registers, data registers, or memory locations on the device that are shared among the various functions. However, from an application viewpoint it makes more sense to represent each of these individual devices with its own Device Object. Because there can be multiple threads trying to access the different (logical) devices, a means must exist to synchronize the use of the one physical device. This is accomplished by using a *Controller Object*, which is normally created during `DriverEntry`, when the several Device Objects are also being created. There is normally one Controller Object shared among all of the Device Objects (although more complex arrangements are possible depending on how the physical device is shared among its logical devices).

Interrupt Objects

Each NT Driver of a physical device that generates interrupts must register an ISR when the driver initializes. The NT kernel defines the *Interrupt Object* type to hold information about each interrupt vector, such as its system-assigned DIRQL and the ISR to be called when the interrupt occurs. The operation `IoConnectInterrupt` creates and returns an Interrupt Object.

Timer Objects

Any NT Driver can set up a Timer Object with `KeInitializeTimer` or `KeInitializeTimerEx` that it can use to time out operations within the driver's other routines or to perform a periodic operation. Such mechanisms are critical for devices that can be shut down or unplugged or that otherwise can block for long periods of time. For example, a printer can run out of paper, but unless there is a timeout, the application might be locked up until the printer is reloaded. A timeout allows the driver to complete the IRP with a timeout error, thus allowing the application to unblock and notify the user that there is a problem.

Other cases occur when you are dealing with devices that exhibit pathological behavior. Back in the Bad Old Days Of Mainframes, it was common for peripherals (notably disk drives) to simply fail to generate interrupts (or, alternatively, for the processor to fail to see them—this got much more exciting when the peripheral was from a vendor other than the mainframe vendor). Adding Timer Objects allows your driver to handle such devices as well. Those of us who "grew up" on mainframes and experimental peripherals know that hardware can be arbitrarily unreliable. If you want a robust driver when the hardware is not, Timer Objects Are Your Friend.

DPC Objects

A driver that uses either a custom DPC (Deferred Procedure Call) from the ISR or uses DPCs from threads must provide space for a DPC Object. This space is typically allocated in the Device Extension, although it can, in principle, be allocated in any form of nonpaged memory. The DPC Object must be initialized by calling `KeInitializeDpc`. A driver that uses the `DpcForIsr` mechanism uses a DPC Object that is preallocated in the Device Object but is not visible (it is in one of those undocumented fields).

File Objects

Normally, you will rarely see a File Object. A File Object is created whenever `CreateFile` is called to create a file handle. The File Object is created with a reference count of 1. Certain operations, such as the API call `DuplicateHandle`, will create a "copy" of the handle. This does not make a copy of the `HANDLE` value (as a program might do), but rather creates a new `HANDLE` value that is unique in the context of the process and different from the original `HANDLE` value. However, this new `HANDLE` value represents the same File Object. A side effect of creating this new `HANDLE` value is to increment the open-handle count for the File Object. In principle, when the last open handle for a File Object is closed, the File Object can be deleted. This is signaled by the Device Driver's receiving an `IRP_MJ_CLEANUP` request. Each time the open-handle count is incremented or decremented, the File Object's reference count is also incremented or decremented.

An example of this is shown in Figure 7.8. Here, Process A opened a handle on the device and consequently has a File Object that represents this handle. Process A then spawns Process B and passes a duplicate of its file handle to Process B. File Object 1 now has two handles. Process B now opens its *own* handle to the device, creating a *second* File Object, which is *not* shared with Process A. Both Process A and Process B can use Handle 1 (original) or Handle 1 (duplicate) to access File Object 1. Process B can use Handle 2 to access File Object 2. Both of them access the same Device Object. If the Device Object needs to maintain separate state for each open File Object, it must do so on its own, with its own data structures (unless it is a File System Driver or File System Filter Driver, in which case the IFS tells what fields of the File Object are available for this purpose).

If Process B closes Handle 1 (duplicate) or Process A closes Handle 1 (original), there is still one outstanding handle to the File Object, and nothing happens. When the second handle is closed (the order doesn't matter), the open-handle count for File Object 1 goes to 0.

However, if there are any outstanding IRPs at the time the last handle is closed, each IRP has also incremented the reference count, and the reference count, decremented as each IRP is

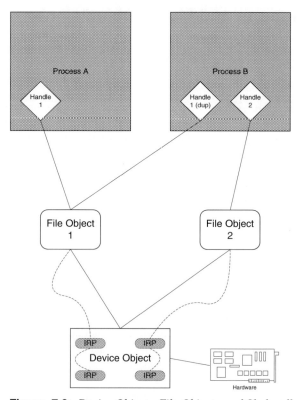

Figure 7.8: *Device Objects, File Objects, and file handles.*

completed, is nonzero. This will cause the device to receive an IRP_MJ_CLEANUP request. All outstanding IRPs must then be cancelled. When the last outstanding IRP is cancelled, the reference count goes to 0 and the IRP_MJ_CLOSE request occurs. Devices that do not support IRP_MJ_CANCEL do not need to support IRP_MJ_CLEANUP; the I/O system will automatically cancel outstanding IRPs for such a device.

The place a File Object appears is in each IRP. The IRP has a FileObject field in its IRP Stack that contains a pointer to the associated File Object. When you need to detect which file an IRP represents, possibly because of an auxiliary state you maintain (particularly for nonexclusive devices), you can use the FileObject field as a value to uniquely identify the associated File Object. You cannot know anything about what is in the File Object (unless you are using the IFS to write your driver), but you *can* distinguish one File Object from another.

This is particularly useful if your Device Driver does any sort of queueing and you have to cancel all of the IRPs for one file; for example, the application may have called CancelIo on outstanding asynchronous requests. To do this, you search your internal IRP queues for IRPs whose FileObject pointer matches the one of the incoming IRP_MJ_CANCEL IRP. We have an example of this in Chapter 28.

Event, Semaphore, and Mutex Objects

Event, Semaphore, and Mutex Objects are used for serialization between threads of one or more drivers. They are described in Chapter 24.

I/O Request Packets

Recall from Chapter 5 that an IRP is the basis of all transactions within the I/O system. It is how any I/O request is communicated to your driver. For every IRP type you wish to process, you must initialize the dispatch vector `MajorFunction` in the Driver Object. We summarize these locations by their `IRP_MJ_` code in Table 7.1.

Each Dispatch Routine is called with the reference to the Device Object and the reference to the current IRP:

```
typedef NTSTATUS (*PDRIVER_DISPATCH) (IN PDEVICE_OBJECT DeviceObject,
                                      IN PIRP Irp)
```

When the I/O Manager sees an operation from the application, such as `CreateFile`, `CloseHandle`, `ReadFile`, `WriteFile`, or `DeviceIoControl`, it creates an IRP and uses the address stored in the `MajorFunction` table to route the IRP to the correct handler. In addition, certain internal events, such as a system shutdown, can generate IRPs. If yours is not a top-level driver, the drivers above it may also generate certain IRPs. For example, a top-level driver will receive a shutdown notification, but it might translate this into a "flush your buffers" operation for its lower-level clients.

When you write each handler, you need to process the request and then mark the IRP as to its status. A simple IRP, for example, `IRP_MJ_CLOSE`, may do nothing more complex than set the I/O Status Block of the IRP to `STATUS_SUCCESS` and return `STATUS_SUCCESS`. Other drivers may create new IRPs, mark the current IRP as still pending, post a completion routine to be called, and return. Still others may partially process the IRP and then mark it as pending, and have to wait until some other event occurs before the IRP can be completed. The most common example is a driver that starts an I/O operation but cannot mark it as completed until the device sends a completion interrupt. The actual techniques for doing this are the heart of driver design, and much of the next few chapters will concentrate on what to do to and with an IRP and how and why to do it. However, we summarize the handlers here so that you have a quick reference to the overall strategy.

Following is the structure of an IRP. Like most of the other driver structures, an IRP is semi-opaque and contains fields that should not be used by a driver. (Some are reserved for File System Drivers. We don't show those here, either.)

```
typedef struct _IRP {
    // ... private fields
    PMDL MdlAddress;
    ULONG Flags;
    union {
            struct _IRP *MasterIrp;
            // ... private fields
            PVOID SystemBuffer;
            } AssociatedIrp;
    IO_STATUS_BLOCK IoStatus;
    KPROCESSOR_MODE RequestorMode;
```

```
        BOOLEAN Cancel;                         // read-only!
        KIRQL CancelIrql;
        PDRIVER_CANCEL CancelRoutine;           // set only with IoSetCancelRoutine!
        PVOID UserBuffer;
        union {
                struct {
                        // ... private fields
                        union {
                                KDEVICE_QUEUE_ENTRY DeviceQueueEntry;
                                struct {
                                        PVOID DriverContext[4];
                                        };
                                };
                        // private fields
                        PETHREAD Thread;
                        LIST_ENTRY ListEntry;
                        } Overlay;
                } Tail;

} IRP, *PIRP;
```

In the sections that follow, we will look at the various common IRPs that you might have to process and what these fields mean for each IRP.

IRP_MJ_CREATE

IRP_MJ_CREATE is a request made when an application performs a CreateFile call. A typical response to IRP_MJ_CREATE is simply to set STATUS_SUCCESS in the IoStatus field of the IRP and complete the creation request. However, some drivers require that additional initialization be performed. For example, a driver that has parts of itself paged out will force the pages to become resident and lock them down. If any additional resources need to be allocated to handle the I/O traffic that will follow, they are allocated in response to this message. If there is a failure in the initialization, the handler should set STATUS_*something* (other than STATUS_SUCCESS) in the IoStatus.Status field and return that same status code as its value. For example, a driver that cannot obtain the resources it needs might return STATUS_INSUFFICIENT_RESOURCES. For some other error, it might return the simple STATUS_UNSUCCESSFUL.

IRP_MJ_READ

IRP_MJ_READ is a request to read data from the device. Microsoft's documentation states that "every device driver that transfers data from its device to the system must handle read requests", with the implication that each Device Driver that does such a transfer must have an IRP_MJ_READ handler. ***This is not true***. This handler is required only if your driver expects to accomplish that data transfer in response to an application's ReadFile(Ex) call (or, if you have layered drivers, some other driver's IRP_MJ_READ request). A driver that uses DeviceIoControl as its sole means of transfer does not require an IRP_MJ_READ handler.

If you support ReadFile(Ex), then you must have a Read handler. The first thing your handler will do is call IoGetCurrentIrpStackLocation to get the IO_STACK_LOCATION descriptor. Once you have the stack location (we use the variable stk for our discussion), you can query its Parameters block to obtain the required information for your transfer. stk->Parameters.Read.Length is the (maximum) number of bytes to transfer in. If the device supports some sort of random access, the `stk->Parameters.Read.Key` field provides this additional information. This field can also be used to sort the IRPs into some internal request order that may be used to optimize performance, although this technique usually applies only to disk-like devices. Some drivers may require the information stored in `stk->Parameters.Read.ByteOffset`, which can indicate a starting offset for the transfer.

If the device uses buffered I/O (the `DO_BUFFERED_IO` flag is set in the `Flags` field of the `DEVICE_OBJECT`), the address of the buffer for a given IRP can be found in its `Irp->AssociatedIrp.SystemBuffer` field. This is a kernel virtual address in the Nonpaged Pool where the data should be stored. If the device is using direct I/O (the `DO_DIRECT_IO` flag is set in the `Flags` field of the `DEVICE_OBJECT`), the MDL (Memory Descriptor List) describing the memory can be found in `Irp->MdlAddress`. We show how to convert a MDL to an address in Chapter 10.

A driver may pass the IRP on to a lower-level driver for additional processing. Your driver would do this when it is not the lowest-level driver in a layered driver hierarchy, such as a Class Driver, a WDM driver, or a Filter Driver. In this case, your driver should also call `IoGetNextIrpStackLocation` to get the `IO_STACK_LOCATION` of the next-lower driver and set up the IRP parameters for that driver. It may also set up a completion routine using `IoSetCompletionRoutine` (this is mandatory if a driver creates one or more new IRPs to send to lower-level drivers). It then should call the lower-level driver using `IoCallDriver`. If the handler *is* a lowest-level handler, it interacts with the device to obtain data and store it in the indicated location. The driver ultimately sets the `Irp->IoStatus.Information` block to the number of bytes actually transferred and completes the IRP.

IRP_MJ_WRITE

`IRP_MJ_WRITE` is a request to write data to the device. Microsoft's documentation states that "every device driver that transfers data from the system to its device must handle write requests", with the implication that each Device Driver that does such a transfer must have an `IRP_MJ_WRITE` handler. ***This is not true***. This handler is required only if your driver expects to accomplish that data transfer in response to an application's `WriteFile(Ex)` call (or, if you have layered drivers, some other driver's `IRP_MJ_WRITE` request). A driver that uses `DeviceIoControl` as its sole means of transfer does not require an `IRP_MJ_WRITE` handler.

If you support `WriteFile(Ex)` either directly at the application level or as a consequence of a higher-level driver wanting to use this function, then you must have a Write handler. The first thing your handler should do is call `IoGetCurrentIrpStackLocation` to get the `IO_STACK_LOCATION` descriptor. Once you have the stack location (we use the variable `stk` for our discussion), you can query its `Parameters` block to obtain the required information for your transfer. `stk->Parameters.Write.Length` is the number of bytes to transfer in. If the device supports some sort of random access, the `stk->Parameters.Write.Key` field provides this additional information. This can also be used to sort the IRPs into some internal request order that may be used to optimize performance, although this technique usually applies only to disk-like devices. Some drivers may require the information stored in `stk->Parameters.Write.ByteOffset`, which can indicate a starting offset for the transfer.

If the device uses buffered I/O (the `DO_BUFFERED_IO` flag is set in the `Flags` field of the `DEVICE_OBJECT`), the address of the buffer for a given IRP can be found in its `Irp->AssociatedIrp.SystemBuffer` field. This is a virtual address in the Nonpaged Pool from which you will read the data you are writing to the device. If the device is using direct I/O (the DO_DIRECT_IO flag is set in the Flags field of the DEVICE_OBJECT), the MDL describing the memory can be found in Irp->MdlAddress. We show how to convert a MDL to an address in Chapter 10.

When this IRP is received, if your handler is not a lowest-level driver it should also call IoGetNextIrpStackLocation to get the IO_STACK_LOCATION of the next-lower driver and set up the parameters for that driver. It may also set up a completion routine using IoSetCompletionRoutine (this is mandatory if a driver creates one or more new IRPs to send to lower-level drivers). It will then call the lower-level driver using IoCallDriver. If the handler *is* a lowest-level handler, it interacts with the device to transfer the data stored in the indicated location. The driver ultimately sets the Irp->IoStatus.Information block to the number of bytes actually transferred and completes the IRP.

IRP_MJ_CLOSE

Every Device Driver you write will be expected to handle CloseHandle operations, which generate an IRP_MJ_CLOSE request. The only drivers that do not handle IRP_MJ_CLOSE are those that are essential for the system's operation (for example, you cannot close the device on which the paging file resides). This request is sent when the File Object that represents the device is being released, that is, the last unclosed handle has been closed. This means that you will *not* receive an IRP_MJ_CLOSE request for every CloseHandle call issued at the application level. You will receive only one, and that will finally result in the File Object's reference count being decremented to 0.

Most devices have a trivial Create handler (sets completion successful and returns). Consequently, they usually have an equally trivial Close handler, which sets the status in the IoStatus field to STATUS_SUCCESS. However, for any driver that has allocated resources during its execution, whether in the Create handler or in some later operation, this is where the allocated resources must be freed.

IRP_MJ_DEVICE_CONTROL

An IRP_MJ_DEVICE_CONTROL message is sent whenever an application program issues a DeviceIoControl call. This is one of the primary messages that most Device Driver writers will want to implement. Not only does this message provide for "device control", but, as we observe in Chapter 2, this is often the primary method of reading data from and writing data to a device for which ordinary ReadFile(Ex) and WriteFile(Ex) are unsuitable.

The first thing your handler should do is call IoGetCurrentIrpStackLocation to get the IO_STACK_LOCATION descriptor. Once you have the stack location (we use the variable stk for our discussion), you can query its Parameters block to obtain the required information for your transfer.

The control code sent by the application as the second parameter of the DeviceIoControl call is found in stk->Parameters.DeviceIoControl.IoControlCode. You will normally dispatch to your specific I/O control handler using this code.

The control code is created using the CTL_CODE macro (see Chapter 2, page 39). One of the parameters to this macro is a code that indicates the method of access, direct or buffered. This causes the I/O Manager to perform the appropriate setup for the IRP.

- If the I/O method is buffered (METHOD_BUFFERED—which is completely independent of the DO_BUFFERED_IO flag in the Device Object), the input data is found in Irp->AssociatedIrp.SystemBuffer and the length of the data is found in stk->Parameters.DeviceIoControl.InputBufferLength. The output data that is to be written back to the application (remember that "input" and "output" mean "input to the DeviceIoControl" and "output from the DeviceIoControl"[1]) must be written back to this same buffer, and the maximum permitted output length is found in stk->Parameters.DeviceIoControl.OutputBufferLength. The size of the system buffer is the maximum of the input and output buffer lengths.

- If the method is direct (METHOD_IN_DIRECT or METHOD_OUT_DIRECT), the input data is found in the area described Irp->AssociatedIrp.SystemBuffer and the length of the input data is found in stk->Parameters.DeviceIoControl.InputBufferLength. The output buffer will be described by a MDL referred to by the location Irp->MdlAddress. The size will be found in stk->Parameters.DeviceIoControl.OutputBufferLength. For METHOD_IN_DIRECT, this buffer will be write-protected and therefore can be in a read-only data segment. For METHOD_OUT_DIRECT, this buffer must be read/write.

- If the method is METHOD_NEITHER (which is defined as code 3), an application address for the input buffer is stored in stk->Parameters.DeviceIoControl.Type3InputBuffer. An application address for the output buffer is stored in the location Irp->UserBuffer. The Irp->AssociatedIrp.SystemBuffer and Irp->MdlAddress fields have no meaning. Since both addresses are application addresses, it is your responsibility to translate them to a form that will be accessible from another thread if the operation requires access to either data in an ISR or DPC.

IRP_MJ_INTERNAL_DEVICE_CONTROL

In some cases, you need to do device control operations as part of a higher-level IRP function. However, these operations are entirely opaque to the upper levels and are strictly internal to your driver. You may not wish to make these functions visible at the application level. This may be to maintain portability across platforms or because an ill-considered sequence of such operations could physically damage the device or compromise safety or security. In these cases, you can limit the visibility of these device control operations by making them possible only from within the driver hierarchy *below* the application interface. This is done by using the IRP_MJ_INTERNAL_DEVICE_CONTROL code. This code works exactly like IRP_MJ_DEVICE_CONTROL, except that either the IRPs are generated by a higher-level driver and sent to you or you generate the IRPs and send them to a lower-level driver. If you are generating IRPs, you must make sure that all of the proper fields are initialized.

---

[1] One instance of documentation—for the SNA interface—refers to the "input" buffer as the "parameter" buffer and the "output" buffer as the "data" buffer, which strikes us as a more sensible notation, but since it is not the standard notation we mention it only in passing.

IRP_MJ_SHUTDOWN

The IRP_MJ_SHUTDOWN request is used to notify a driver that the system is being shut down. A driver will receive a shutdown request if it has registered the Driver Object by calling the function IoRegisterShutdownNotification. Once a device is registered, it will receive a shutdown notification. If, for some reason, a device no longer wishes to have a shutdown notification (for example, it has already quiesced the device and knows it is in a stable, shut-downable state), it can call the function IoUnregisterShutdownNotification to avoid a potentially lengthy, and unnecessary, operation.

 The Microsoft documentation states that drivers for mass-storage devices that have internal caches for data must handle the IRP_MJ_SHUTDOWN request. It is also important that any driver controlling an external device that has external state process this message if the external state must be returned to a known, or in some cases, "safe" value. For example, a system controlling an external robotic arm might use this message to determine that the arm should be returned to a "standby" or "idle" position, and just possibly also to remove any hydraulic pressure or electrical signals from the arm actuators. We find the Microsoft documentation somewhat misleading in that it appears to limit the shutdown IRP to "file systems". In fact, *any* Device Driver can receive a shutdown request, provided it has been registered.

IRP_MJ_CLEANUP

Drivers that have a Cancel routine must support the IRP_MJ_CLEANUP IRP. The receipt of such a request is an indication that the handle of the File Object is being released. The response depends on whether you created the device as an "exclusive" device, limited to a single thread of control, or you allow multiple threads to access it. For exclusive access, this handler completes all pending IRPs by setting their IoStatus field to STATUS_CANCELLED. If the driver is for non-exclusive access, the handler must cancel and complete only those IRPs for the thread that holds the file handle. After the outstanding IRPs are cancelled, this IRP's IoStatus.Status field is set to STATUS_SUCCESS.

IRP_MJ_FLUSH_BUFFERS

A device that maintains an internal cache or internal buffers should be prepared to process the IRP_MJ_FLUSH_BUFFERS IRP. When this IRP is received, the appropriate device-specific action should be taken. This action will vary by device. Some devices, particularly those with pending output, should try to immediately transfer any changed cache information or pending output information to the device. Those with inputs pending may simply flush the cache, may choose to free up the space at that time, and may discard pending input buffers. Each device and application domain will dictate the proper response to this IRP.

Summary

This chapter discusses the key data structures. Succeeding chapters are concerned with how they are put together with code to build a driver.

Chapter

---

8 *Device Driver Structure*

In this chapter, we cover the overall structure of a Device Driver in considerable detail. This includes such basic techniques as how to do debug printouts, initialize a driver, code Dispatch Routines, and compile, install, and run a driver.

As is traditional in any book on programming, we write the "Hello World" program. In our case, it is written as a Device Driver.

The "Hello World" Driver

The "Hello World" driver is one of the simplest drivers that can be written. It doesn't actually control a device. Its purpose is to illustrate key points about the driver structure. It writes trace data to the output debugging port. So before we can actually write the driver, we need to look at the ways that debug printout can be done.

Doing Debug Printout

There are several ways you can do debug printout. Debug printout is sent to the output debug port and can be seen in the debugger when you have an attached debugging computer. However, any condition that generates a debug printout should probably, in a production system, cause an event to be logged in the system log.

Sometimes, you need to be cautious about including debug printouts in a driver. They consume time and change the timing relationships of events. If your device is sufficiently fast, the act of issuing a debug printout may actively interfere with its proper operation. The same constraints apply to event logging. However, event logging is usually done in less time-critical portions of a driver, usually at reduced IRQL, and consequently will interfere with the device less seriously.

The DbgPrint Function

Ultimately, the low-level primitive for doing debug output is DbgPrint. This is a kernel-level function that is equivalent to the C printf function. You cannot do any floating-point formatting in this function because you cannot call floating-point functions in a Device Driver. The DbgPrint function uses *8-bit* characters to define its format string and writes 8-bit characters to the debug port. If you need a Unicode string, you can use the %ls format to cause the Unicode string to be converted to an 8-bit character string before it is printed. Note that this may cause some unexpected transliterations if the original string uses other than the character codes 0x0000 through 0x00FF. You can also call the function RtlUnicodeStringToAnsiString to convert the Unicode string to an 8-bit string.

The DbgPrint function can also be called from an ISR at elevated IRQL. Note, however, that although we recommend that you log debug printout events to the Event Log as well, you cannot call the event logging functions from an ISR.

The KdPrint Macro

A very simple macro, KdPrint, is defined as part of the ntddk.h or wdm.h files. This macro is defined conditionally to be either DbgPrint or nothing, depending on whether the compile-time name DBG is defined. We use the KdPrint macro in our example here.

Other Macros

There are many other approaches for selectively turning debugging on and off. However, one of the most ill-suited methods is one we warn you against right now: the notion of "debug levels", where the levels are based on some notion that a Level 4 debug output should somehow produce all of the output of Level 4, Level 3, Level 2, and Level 1. This pseudo-hierarchical notion is incredibly clumsy to use and generally deluges you with far more information than you may need. Avoid it.

You can encapsulate DbgPrint or KdPrint however you wish. One aspect of selective debugging is that it is one of the very, very, very few instances in which it actually makes sense to have one or more global variables in a Device Driver. (The usual problems *will* apply. For example, if the driver is unloaded and reloaded, the variable will be reset.) You could use a single global variable that would use individual bits to enable selective debug output, thus providing for up to 32 different kinds of debug traces. The only problem with this scheme is that you must keep setting the variable based on the correct bit assignments. This means that you have to keep a listing handy of what all of the values mean. It is sometimes more expedient to use some number of independent Boolean variables to hold this same information. In this way, you can set the Boolean values just by remembering their names. This is much easier than creating hexadecimal constants. (This applies only when you need to set the values from the debugger. If you are setting the values *only* from the Registry, you could use named Boolean values in the Registry and convert them to bits in a single variable in your driver.)

Although the normal paradigm is to set such variables from the debugger, it also is quite sensible to supply an application-level DeviceIoControl option for setting these debug flags. Thus, your application test harness can provide a quite humane interface to allow the program to set these debug flags. In a product version of the driver, you can cause this DeviceIoControl option to return an error code so that the application level can actually query the debug state and determine that the debug version of the driver is not loaded. Note that it is important to have such an interface be able to retrieve, as well as set, such options. This means that the application-level test harness can correctly reflect the actual state of the debug flags, including those that have been set by the debugger itself. This is another example of exploiting the capabilities of Windows to make your job easier.

The ASSERT Macro

An ASSERT macro is defined in `ntddk.h` and `wdm.h` that takes a simple Boolean expression as its argument. If the expression evaluates as TRUE, nothing happens. If the expression evaluates as FALSE, the WinDbg debugger will display the source-code string for the test, the source filename, and the source file line number. You will then be given an option to ignore the assertion, enter the debugger, or terminate the process or thread in which the ASSERT occurred. Note that if you elect to continue, you must have actual executable code that will cause the driver to execute a reasonable recovery. If you don't, execution continues as if the statement wasn't there. If the statement was something like this:

```
ASSERT(somevalue != NULL)
```

it had better be followed by some code that will, for example, reject the IRP with some meaningful return code. Otherwise, continuing from the assertion will probably cause a Blue Screen of Death. Furthermore, you really don't want this bug to show up by crashing the end user's system. So you need code to recover from the error and preferably log the error as an event trace. Following is our recommended style.

```
ASSERT(condition)
if(!condition)
    {
    // log event indicating the nature of the failure
    // prepare to complete the operation with an error code
    // clean up anything that would be left dangling by leaving now
    // exit this level of the operation
    }
```

The ASSERTMSG Macro

The ASSERTMSG macro works exactly like the ASSERT macro, except that it takes an additional parameter, a message that is also displayed along with the usual ASSERT text:

```
ASSERTMSG(message, expression)
```

If *expression* evaluates to FALSE, the string of *message*, as well as the source code file and line number, are displayed:

```
ASSERTMSG("Bogus pointer derived from IRP", ptr != NULL);
// ...
ASSERTMSG("Bogus pointer from MDL", ptr != NULL);
```

Note that *message* is an 8-bit character string. Note, too, that if the ordinary ASSERT macro was used, the only message would be `"ptr != NULL"`. This might be hard to decode, since you would have to remember the source line number in order to distinguish which ASSERT failed. By using ASSERTMSG, you can disambiguate similar ASSERT statements.

Forcing Debug Breakpoints

If you need to force a debug breakpoint, you can call the DbgBreakPoint function. This will cause a breakpoint trap and display the trap in the debugger. Note that you must not leave any of these active in product code, and therefore any calls to DbgBreakPoint must be under a conditional compilation switch, such as DBG. or conditional execution. If a DbgBreakPoint is executed in product code, the system will hang waiting for the debugger to take control. You may also selectively enable these by using additional conditional compilation switches of your own devising, for example, the following.

```
#if defined(DBG) && defined(_MY_DEBUG_OPTION)
#define MyDebugBreak() DbgBreakPoint()
#else
#define MyDebugBreak()
#endif
```

As we have already suggested for the debugging options, it is quite useful to provide a DeviceIoControl function that calls DbgBreakPoint. This would normally be disabled in a product version, but it allows your application test harness to force a breakpoint condition. This is a highly effective programming style. It is also useful to have a DeviceIoControl function that queries if a breakpoint *can* be forced so that the user-level application can enable or disable the option in the menus or elsewhere.

The hello.h *File*

```
#define HELLO_SIZE 4096

#define HELLO_BUSADDRESS        0x1C0010000
#define HELLO_BUSADDRESS_HIGH 0x1C0011FE0
#define HELLO_CSR_BUSADDRESS   0x1C0018000
#define HELLO_PAGESIZE          256

#define HELLO_BUSNUMBER 0x1
```

The bus addresses, device page size, and bus number have no meaning for our "Hello World" driver because it does not touch hardware. For devices that touch hardware, these values may be constants, as shown here. They may have to be read from the Registry in which they were configured during the hardware installation process. Or, they may be discovered dynamically by querying the system. The exact way in which they are determined depends on the nature of the device and the bus. We discuss the techniques in more detail in Chapter 20 and Chapter 21. For now, we pretend these values have some meaning.

The hello.c *File*

In the prologue part of the file shown in the following Listing 8.1, we specify the standard include files, declare some string constants to define our device, and declare the function headers for our functions. There is nothing particularly deep here, except to note that the string constants are declared as Unicode strings by preceding them with L".

Listing 8.1: *"Hello World": Prologue*

```
// Simple driver that demonstrates dynamically loading and unloading

#include "ntddk.h"
#include "hello.h"

#define NT_DEVICE_NAME      L"\\Device\\HELLO"
#define DOS_DEVICE_NAME     L"\\DosDevices\\HELLO"

NTSTATUS HelloOpen(
    IN PDEVICE_OBJECT DeviceObject,
    IN PIRP Irp );

NTSTATUS HelloClose(
    IN PDEVICE_OBJECT DeviceObject,
    IN PIRP Irp );


VOID HelloUnload(
    IN PDRIVER_OBJECT DriverObject );
```

The "Hello World" `DriverEntry` *Routine*

The `DriverEntry` function is called whenever the driver is loaded. Its tasks are as follows:

- Create the device object for this device.
- Initialize the dispatch table for the implemented functions.
- Create a symbolic link to `DosDevices` so that the short "DOS"-name can be used in `CreateFile` calls.

In a "real" Device Driver, we would also have to create Interrupt Objects, establish the ISR, and do many other things, the details of which we cover in later, more elaborate (and more real) examples.

Note that most of the action of this Device Driver is to send debug strings to the output port so that we can see it working.

Listing 8.2: *The "Hello World"* `DriverEntry` *Routine*

```
NTSTATUS DriverEntry(
    IN PDRIVER_OBJECT DriverObject,
    IN PUNICODE_STRING RegistryPath )
{

    PDEVICE_OBJECT deviceObject = NULL;
    NTSTATUS status;
    UNICODE_STRING NtNameString;
    UNICODE_STRING Win32NameString;

    KdPrint( ("HELLO: Entered the HELLO driver!\n") );

    //
    // Create counted string version of our device name.
    //
```

```
        RtlInitUnicodeString( &NtNameString, NT_DEVICE_NAME );

        //
        // Create the device object
        //

        status = IoCreateDevice(
                    DriverObject,
                    0,                      // We don't use a device extension
                    &NtNameString,
                    FILE_DEVICE_UNKNOWN,
                    0,                      // No standard device characteristics
                    FALSE,                  // This isn't an exclusive device
                    &deviceObject
                    );

        if ( NT_SUCCESS(status) )
        {

            //
            // Create dispatch points for create/open, close, unload.
            //

            DriverObject->MajorFunction[IRP_MJ_CREATE] = HelloOpen;
            DriverObject->MajorFunction[IRP_MJ_CLOSE] = HelloClose;

            DriverObject->DriverUnload = HelloUnload;

            KdPrint( ("HELLO: just about ready!\n") );

            //
            // Create counted string version of our Win32 device name.
            //

            RtlInitUnicodeString( &Win32NameString, DOS_DEVICE_NAME );

            //
            // Create a link from our device name to a name in the Win32
            // namespace.
            //

            status = IoCreateSymbolicLink( &Win32NameString, &NtNameString );

            if (!NT_SUCCESS(status))
            {
                KdPrint( ("HELLO: Couldn't create the symbolic link\n") );

                IoDeleteDevice( DriverObject->DeviceObject );
            }
            else
            {
                KdPrint( ("HELLO: All initialized!\n") );
            }
        }
        else
        {
            KdPrint( ("HELLO: Couldn't create the device\n") );
        }
        return status;
}
```

First, the driver creates the UNICODE_STRING from the constant. This value is then passed into IoCreateDevice. Note that the type for the device is FILE_DEVICE_UNKNOWN because this device (as are many devices) is not one of the "common" Windows devices. We do not require any device-specific state to be saved for this device, so there is no Device Extension (we give the length as 0).

This device can be shared, that is, several different threads could open it, so we provide a FALSE parameter for the exclusive-access option. If this creation fails, we return the error code, which will ultimately cause the driver to be unloaded and an error code to be logged by the system. Note that if this driver was marked in the Registry as a bootstrap-load driver (which is essential for starting the system), the boot process will fail.

If the operation was successful, we initialize the various dispatch functions. For example, to handle the CreateFile and CloseHandle operations, we initialize the DriverObject->MajorFunction dispatch table to point to our handler functions. We also initialize the DriverObject->DriverUnload entry to point to our Unload function. Although the unload entry point is nominally optional, any driver will allocate objects and create state that *must* be undone if it is unloaded, and so in practice this dispatch is always required.

We also have to create a symbolic link between the \DosDevices directory and the \Device directory. These are not file directories, but object directories. The name used in CreateFile, for example, "HELLO", cannot be found unless the \DosDevices link is in place. The device can also be opened by specifying the file name "\\\\.\\HELLO" to the CreateFile operation. Observe that we double the \ character because it is an escape character for C strings. It is possible for an application to create such a symbolic link, given the NT name of the device specified by IoCreateDevice, by using the DefineDosDevice call. However, if the user-visible name cannot be registered, we will declare that the driver has failed to initialize. This is a safer assumption based on the expectations of the end-user application programmer.

The important point here is that if this creation of the symbolic link fails, we cannot simply return the error code; we have already allocated a Device Object. Furthermore, this Device Object has pointers to where our code currently is! If the code is unloaded, not only is this Device Object "orphaned", but in more extreme cases there might already be operations, such as interrupt services, that will attempt to dispatch interrupts through that object. These will transfer control to the addresses specified. If the addresses are not in use, a Blue Screen of Death will occur immediately. If they are pointing to memory that has been allocated for other purposes, such as another driver that has loaded successfully, the interrupts will transfer into the other driver. This will almost certainly cause a Blue Screen, but the Blue Screen will mistakenly be attributed to some failure in the other driver. Consequently, you *must* clean up any state you have established before terminating a DriverEntry with an error code. In our sample here, this is quite simple. All we must do is call IoDeleteDeviceObject. In more complete drivers, there would be additional state that we would have to clean up, such as interrupt connections.

The HelloOpen *Function*

HelloOpen is called when the user calls CreateFile specifying the "HELLO" device. Note that the application program may be written as an 8-bit application, but this means it will call the function CreateFileA. This function will expand the filename to Unicode before passing it on to the rest of the system.

Listing 8.3: *The* HelloOpen *Function*

```
NTSTATUS HelloOpen(
    IN PDEVICE_OBJECT DeviceObject,
    IN PIRP Irp )
{
    KdPrint( ("Hello: Opened!!\n") );


    //
    // No need to do anything.
    //

    //
    // Fill these in before calling IoCompleteRequest.
    //
    // DON'T get cute and try to use the status field of
    // the IRP in the return status.  That IRP IS GONE as
    // soon as you call IoCompleteRequest.
    //


    Irp->IoStatus.Status = STATUS_SUCCESS;
    Irp->IoStatus.Information = 0;

    IoCompleteRequest( Irp, IO_NO_INCREMENT );

    return STATUS_SUCCESS;
}
```

HelloOpen is called for a CreateFile operation. In a driver connected to a real device, this would probably initialize any device state required to handle subsequent operations. (You must be cautious if the device is a shared device. For such cases, you may have to store a "device has been initialized" flag in the Device Extension.)

Take particular note of the comment that appears in the listing that precedes the last few lines of the function. You *cannot* return Irp->IoStatus.Status as the return result because, as the comment indicates, the execution of the IoCompleteRequest has made the IRP unavailable. Attempting to use it will almost certainly cause a Blue Screen. It will certainly produce the wrong result. The priority boost of the IoCompleteRequest is set to IO_NO_INCREMENT because this operation is handled entirely within the Open Routine. Since there was no actual I/O operation, and therefore the process was not delayed waiting for I/O, there is no reason to boost the priority of the thread that executed the operation. Microsoft defines a set of symbolic values you can use here. However, they are all device-specific and have very little use if you are not writing a device that conforms to one of those for which Microsoft has defined a symbolic constant.

The HelloClose *Function*

HelloClose is called when the reference count for the File Object associated with the device goes to 0. Each outstanding handle on the File Object increments the reference count, as does each outstanding IRP still in process. But suppose there are no outstanding IRPs (this is the simple case, for this driver) and the last outstanding handle on the File Object is closed, either explicitly via a `CloseHandle` call or implicitly by termination of the process, thereby forcing the operating system to call `CloseHandle` on all the process's handles. In this case, the `IRP_MJ_CLOSE` request will be dispatched to this handler.

Listing 8.4: *The* HelloClose *Function*

```
NTSTATUS HelloClose(
    IN PDEVICE_OBJECT DeviceObject,
    IN PIRP Irp )
{

    KdPrint( ("HELLO: Closed!!\n") );

    //
    // No need to do anything.
    //

    //
    // Fill these in before calling IoCompleteRequest.
    //
    // DON'T get cute and try to use the status field of
    // the irp in the return status.  That IRP IS GONE as
    // soon as you call IoCompleteRequest.
    //

    Irp->IoStatus.Status = STATUS_SUCCESS;
    Irp->IoStatus.Information = 0;


    IoCompleteRequest( Irp, IO_NO_INCREMENT );

    return STATUS_SUCCESS;
}
```

The Close Routine is also quite simple for our device. It marks the IRP as successfully completed and calls `IoCompleteRequest` to terminate the IRP processing. In a real device, it would also have to cancel any pending I/O requests and place the device into its idle state, such as setting a device register to disable interrupts. Note also that because the device might actually have an active DMA transfer going on, a Close operation does not always complete immediately. It may have to wait for the cancellation to complete. Thus a Close function may have to mark itself as pending rather than as being complete.

The HelloUnload *Function*

HelloUnload is called whenever the driver is being unloaded.

Listing 8.5: *The* HelloUnload *Function*

```
 VOID HelloUnload( IN PDRIVER_OBJECT DriverObject)
{
    UNICODE_STRING Win32NameString;
```

```
    //
    // All *THIS* driver needs to do is to delete the device object and the
    // symbolic link between our device name and the Win32 visible name.
    //
    // Almost every other driver would need to do a
    // significant amount of work here deallocating stuff.
    //

    KdPrint( ("HELLO: Unloading!!\n") );

    //
    // Create counted string version of our Win32 device name.
    //

    RtlInitUnicodeString( &Win32NameString, DOS_DEVICE_NAME );

    //
    // Delete the link from our device name to a name in the Win32 namespace.
    //

    IoDeleteSymbolicLink( &Win32NameString );

    //
    // Finally delete our device object
    //

    IoDeleteDevice( DriverObject->DeviceObject );
}
```

It is the responsibility of the Unload routine to clean up whatever state is required before the driver is unloaded. In our simple example, this involves only removing the symbolic link and deleting the Device Object. In a driver connected to a real device, we would also have to disconnect the interrupt mapping to the device, delete the Interrupt Object, and return the device to a clean "device not in use" state, as defined by the device itself.

The Test Program

Having written the driver, we need to write an application program that tests it. This program is very simple. It opens the device and closes it. By watching the output in your debugger, you can see the driver load and the Open and Close functions being called.

Listing 8.6: *"Hello World" Test Program*

```
#include "windows.h"
#include "stdio.h"

HANDLE hTest;

int main(int argc, char **argv)
    {
    hTest = CreateFile(
                    "\\\\.\\HELLO",                  // device name
                    GENERIC_READ | GENERIC_WRITE,    // desired access
                    0,                               // share access
```

```
                  NULL,                            // security attributes
                  OPEN_EXISTING,                   // creation options
                  FILE_ATTRIBUTE_NORMAL,           // attributes
                  NULL);                           // template file handle

      if (hTest != INVALID_HANDLE_VALUE)
        { /* successful open */

        printf("Wow - CreateFile really worked!!!\n");

        //
        // Point proven. Be a nice program and close up shop.
        //

        CloseHandle(hTest);

        } /* successful open */
    else
        { /* open failed */

        printf("Can't get a handle to HELLO device\n");

        } /* open failed */

    return 0;
}
```

This simple test program is a "console mode" application. It has a conventional `main` function, rather than the `WinMain` function of a GUI-based application. So it will work like a conventional DOS or UNIX C program. All it does is open and close the file. The file is opened with the `CreateFile` operation. Next, we look at each of the parameters of `CreateFile`.

The device name is "\\\\.\\HELLO". This is the DOS name for the `HELLO` device on the current system. Unless we were planning to write a network redirector, which is an intimidating task, we will not be able to open this device on another machine on the network.

This device is opened for reading and writing, as specified by GENERIC_READ | GENERIC_WRITE. The modes that are permitted for the device itself are defined when we set the flags in the Device Object when it is created. In addition, the application may not be permitted to open a device because the thread possesses insufficient rights to the device. This is handled for us by the security system, and we never see it.

The share access parameter allows us to control whether other threads can open the device. For a device that is marked as exclusive access, this parameter has no effect—the opening thread always gets exclusive access. However, for sharable devices we can, on an individual Open operation, determine if any other thread will be permitted to open the device for reading or writing. In this case, we have specified 0 as the parameter, meaning we want the default access to the device. Since our device is a shared device, other threads can also open it for reading and writing.

The security attributes parameter can be used to modify the assumed security. For example, a thread can open a device that has lower or different security than the thread itself. We specify this parameter as NULL, meaning that we want the default security attributes of the thread. This parameter is handled by the I/O Manager that calls the security subsystem. Thus we can be guaranteed in our driver that if we are called at all, the caller has the right to open the device. This centralization of security is critical to the proper maintenance of security in NT. No individual

Device Driver ever needs to concern itself with security; thus an ordinary Device Driver cannot compromise security. Of course, a maliciously written Device Driver could take advantage of its Kernel-mode existence to perform actions that compromise security.

We specify that `CreateFile` should `OPEN_EXISTING`, which is the only reasonable mode for a non-File System Device.

We specify `FILE_ATTRIBUTE_NORMAL`, although in practice this parameter is going to be ignored by any non-File System Device. There are other flags we could specify here, such as flags enabling asynchronous (overlapped) I/O.

The last parameter is `NULL` for all but File System calls. This allows the creation of a file whose attributes match some other file. The main purpose of this `NULL` parameter is to create files that immediately have the same security as, say, the input file. For non-File System devices, which is all we are concerned about, it has no meaning. It is also not supported in Windows 95, except for some specific devices such as the serial ports.

We test the success by comparing the value to the special constant `INVALID_HANDLE_VALUE`. If it succeeded, we print out the success message; otherwise, we indicate an error. After a successful open, we close the device by calling `CloseHandle`.

Building the Driver

A driver is always built from the command line. There is no clean interface to the GUI-based Integrated Development Environments (IDEs) for building a driver. This is because the NT project predates the IDE environment on Win32 (in fact, it was initially cross-compiled from Win16 machines). Thus the mechanisms appear a bit arcane, and also a bit dated. However, they are the methods necessary to build a driver.

The Checked and Free Build Environments

Builds come in two flavors:

- The Checked Build is equivalent to the IDE Debug build.
- The Free Build, also called a Retail Build, is equivalent to the IDE Release build.

To perform one of these builds, you must start a command shell and make sure that all necessary environment variables are set to the correct values to produce the desired output. The set of values can change from release to release of the DDK, so in the DDK folder are two entries, one each for "Checked Build Environment" and "Free Build Environment". Selecting one of these causes a command shell to be started with the correct environment variables set. You may have both running simultaneously (although there is a caution related to doing this, which we point out later). The Checked Build defines the compile-time name `DBG` to include conditionally compiled code within the driver.

The BUILD Command

Building a particular release is quite simple. To build a driver, you use the BUILD command. In the command shell, type the command and the Device Driver will be built. All necessary dependencies, both the usual `#include` dependencies and those based on subdirectories, will be accounted for.

For an incremental build, type

```
build
```

This will build only those components that need to be rebuilt.

For a full build, type

```
build -c
```

This deletes all of the object files, thus forcing a complete rebuild.

After the build is completed, you can install it.

For the BUILD command to work properly, there must be two special files in the same directory as the source files: `SOURCES` and `DIRS`. These are the actual filenames; these files have no file extensions.

The **SOURCES** File

The `SOURCES` file structure is shown in Table 8.1. The parameters given are in the order typically found in a `SOURCES` file. Note that for our purposes, some of these fields are constants.

Table 8.1: *Specification of the* SOURCES *File*

Parameter	Meaning
TARGETNAME=drivername	This value specifies the name of the driver, with no extension. This will produce a *drivername*.sys file as output.
TARGETPATH=.\lib	This value specifies the root of the output path. For drivers, use .\lib.
TARGETTYPE=DRIVER	The BUILD mechanism can build many different kinds of objects, but for this book, this is the only type we can build.
INCLUDES=path1;path2;...	This value is optional and, if specified, gives the `#include` search path as a list of semicolon-separated names, which can include relative pathnames.
TARGETLIBS=lib1;lib2;...	This value is optional, and if specified, gives the linker search path for one or more libraries specified as a semicolon-separated list, which can include relative pathnames.
SOURCES=file1.c file2.c ...	This value specifies the actual source filenames to be compiled. The extension must be provided. This is a *space*-separated list of names.

The **DIRS** File

The `DIRS` file specifies a list of subdirectories of the current directory that must be built before the current directory is built. A directory in the BUILD tree may contain *only* a `SOURCES` file, *only* a `DIRS` file, or both.

A directory that contains a `DIRS` file and not a `SOURCES` file indicates that there is nothing in *that* directory to build but that there are *subdirectories* that require building. A directory that contains a `SOURCES` file and *not* a `DIRS` file will be built, but no subdirectories will be built. A directory with both will be built only after all of its subdirectories are built. It is erroneous for a subdirectory listed in a `DIRS` file to have neither a `SOURCES` nor a `DIRS` file.

The contents of a `DIRS` file is the keyword `DIRS=` followed by a space-delimited set of directory names. Line continuation is by a backslash. By convention, a `DIRS` file has one subdirectory name, of the immediate subdirectory per line, indented with a tab. The system does not permit other than a simple subdirectory name (no backslashes, no colons) for each name.

```
DIRS= \
        subdir1 \
        subdir2 \
        subdir3
```

This file would cause all of `subdir1` (and its subdirectories if it contained a `DIRS` file), `subdir2` (likewise), and `subdir3` (likewise) to be built before the current directory is built.

Output from the BUILD Process

The BUILD process creates a large subdirectory tree rooted in the `TARGETPATH` and a separate `OBJECTS` subdirectory under the source directory. These directories in turn contain subdirectories for each of the platform types, as shown in Figure 8.1. For this example, we built only for the Intel architecture, and consequently the only output files are under the `i386` subdirectories. The results shown here were produced by compiling a free build and then switching to the Checked Build Environment command window and doing a `build -c` to get a Checked Build as well.

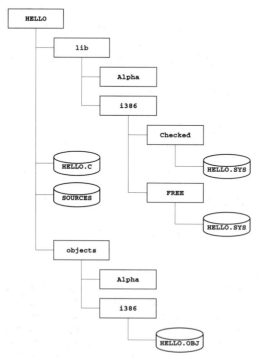

Figure 8.1: *The BUILD directory structure for "Hello World".*

A major difference between the BUILD process and the general IDE compilation process is that in the BUILD process, there is precisely *one* OBJECTS subdirectory for each platform type. This means that both the Checked and the Free Builds build into the same subdirectory. While there are arguments as to why this might be a Good Thing, it means that if you switch from doing a Checked Build to doing a Free Build, you *must* specify the -c option the first time you start a build of the other type. Otherwise, your OBJECTS directory will end up as a mixture of checked and free object files. This is so different from how the ordinary IDE works that it is a potential hazard.

Registry Entries for "Hello World"

The Registry entries for "Hello World" are specified in the file hello.ini:

```
\registry\machine\system\currentcontrolset\services\HELLO
    Type = REG_DWORD 0x00000001
    Start = REG_DWORD 0x00000003
    Group = Extended base
    ErrorControl = REG_DWORD 0x00000001
```

The REGEDIT/REGEDT32 *Programs*

You could add the Registry entries manually using the REGEDIT or REGEDT32 programs. This is possible but awkward. It is described in more detail in Chapter 20 (page 390) and Chapter 21 (page 413). Fortunately, we don't need to use it to run our program.

The REGINI *Program*

To run the RegIni program on the hello.ini file, as described in Chapter 9, page 178, just type

```
ddk\bin\regini hello.ini
```

where *ddk* is the path to the directory in which you installed the DDK. You can do this in the DOS shell in which you just finished the build, since it has a path to the *ddk*\bin directory.

Running the "Hello World" Test Program and Driver

Once you have successfully installed the driver, you can run it. This involves two sets of operations. The first consists of those required to actually start the driver. They load the driver and call its DriverEntry. Once this has completed successfully, you can then test your driver by opening it and closing it. For a real driver, you would also perform I/O operations, but our "Hello World" program supports only Open and Close operations.

Starting the Driver

To start the driver in Windows NT 4.0, we use the Devices applet in the Control Panel. Double-click the icon for this applet, and you will see a screen that presents a list of drivers. Scroll down until you find the Hello driver. If you don't find it, you may need to reboot so that the new Registry entries are seen. Click the Hello driver and then the Start button on the panel. The driver should start. And if you did everything right, it won't crash the system.

Using the Devices applet is one of the options for starting a driver. We explore other methods in later chapters.

Running the Test Program

You run the program `hello_test.exe` from the command prompt. The program should print out that it was successful. If you did everything right, running this program won't crash the system. If you have another machine connected to the serial port, you will even see the famous "Hello World" message printed out. In most cases, though, you need to get the debugging machine set up to listen to this port. That's a whole chapter on its own, and a long one at that. The Good News is that it is the very next chapter, so just turn the page and start right in.

The I/O Explorer

Now that you've seen the simple test program, you can start to experiment with the program we call "I/O Explorer". This program lets you execute a `CreateFile` with all of the reasonable options, then execute a `ReadFile`, a `WriteFile`, and a `DeviceIoControl`, and finally perform a `CloseHandle`, all from the comfort of your chair. No need to write programs of ever-increasing complexity. Some of the details of the I/O Explorer are given in Chapter 27. The rest are found in the rather complete online help file that accompanies the program. We show here, in Figure 8.2, a screen snapshot of the I/O Explorer showing the symbolic links found in the `DosDevices` subtree of the Object Manager Name Space. In the left column we select a name

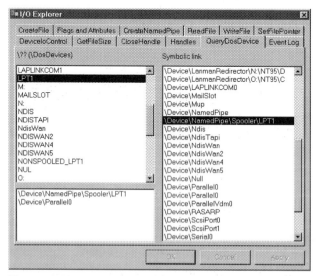

Figure 8.2: *The I/O Explorer showing symbolic links from* `DosDevices`.

that we could open with `CreateFile`. The box below it shows the names associated with the selected name. Only the first name in the list is current; the other names represent prior mappings to the device.

Further Reading

Newcomer, Joseph M., "Debugging Real-Time Systems", *Dr. Dobb's Journal 18, 7* (July 1993). Also on *Dr. Dobb's Journal on CD-ROM.*

Chapter

9 *Debugging a Device Driver*

When you are debugging a Device Driver, you often must debug the application level as well. Each task uses different tools; however, you must be fluent in both. You need to know not only how your driver is behaving, but also how you can determine what the higher-level application code is doing and how it is reacting to your driver. It is generally not optional to ignore the application level. If your Device Driver appears to be behaving erroneously, it may be that it is the application level that is behaving erroneously.

In the following subsections, we briefly discuss some of the available debuggers. We will then cover the WinDbg debugger, from Microsoft, in considerable depth.

Application Level: The IDE Debugger

Most applications are debugged using an application-level debugger. If you are using Microsoft Visual C++, the IDE (Integrated Development Environment) debugger of Microsoft's Visual Studio is an extremely pleasant debugger to use. While not perfect (what software is?), it is certainly one of the best development environments that we have ever used. No, we have not used any of the competing Windows environments, but we have been debugging since the days of lights-and-switches debugging and have covered (and in some cases, written) many debuggers in that history. Since this is a book on debugging Device Drivers, we do not discuss any of the details of the IDE debugger. We recommend any of the variety of books that already cover that topic.

Application Level: Bounds Checker for Windows

A product we consider mandatory for application-level debugging is Bounds Checker Pro for Windows NT, from NuMega Technologies. This debugger supplements and enhances the Visual

C++ IDE Debugger. (If you don't use VC++, it also runs stand-alone, but you lose some of the nice integration to Microsoft's debugger and some compiled-in features.) It provides such useful features as validation of input parameters to system calls and validation of the result of system calls. (In the latter case, yes, you probably should check each and every call for a successful return, but we usually trust that they will complete successfully. Bounds Checker checks *every* call for a valid return.) It also tracks resource utilization and reports if you have any kind of resource leak. We consider it an essential tool in the Quality Assurance (QA) cycle, and would not release a product that has not passed its tests.

Kernel: WinDbg

WinDbg is the Microsoft-supplied debugger. It has a nice GUI interface and is quite humane. Unfortunately, it is not well supported. If you have problems with it, you will get virtually no support from Microsoft. Once, it was "accidentally" broken in the "release candidate 2" version (the final beta) of one version of NT and remained broken for over a year, totally preventing its use for debugging any display driver. In spite of some of its problems, you will almost certainly want to use it for much of your debugging. It has many minor bugs, and its use continues to be an adventure in frustration. WinDbg is distributed as part of the SDK for Windows NT 4.0 and as part of the DDK for Windows NT 5.0.

Kernel: SoftICE

SoftICE, from NuMega Technologies, is fully supported, in contrast to WinDbg. It is perhaps one of the finest debuggers ever written for the NT kernel. In fact, when nothing else will help find your problem, SoftICE will give you capabilities WinDbg never dreamed of. These include the ability to set breakpoints on the read or write of an I/O port and the ability to display the entire Interrupt Descriptor Table. The ability to step into a system service from User mode allows you to understand what is really happening in the kernel.

Its downside is that it was originally developed as an MS-DOS, character-based debugger, and it still looks like one. The user interface is bizarre. The shortcut keys are barely documented, and when they are, they are documented not in terms of their functions, but in terms of the arcane keystrokes they simulate. For the first several years of its life, SoftICE for NT could not display structures or local variables. Fortunately, that was finally fixed in later releases, and this capability exists in all current versions.

SoftICE is also Intel-specific. You cannot use it to debug a driver on the Alpha or any other NT platform.

NuMega also has a bias towards single-machine debugging. We strongly urge you to not once, not ever, try to debug a driver on a machine that does any other form of useful work and *never* debug a driver on your principal development machine. We strongly wish that the company spent the time wasted on supporting single-machine driver debugging on developing a better user interface, preferably a GUI-based one, even if it requires two machines.

Ultimately, the choice is yours: a flaky semi-product with a great interface capable of doing heterogeneous platform debugging, or a great genuine product that is only Intel-compatible with an MS-DOS-compatible character-mode interface. But remember: When WinDbg is hopeless, SoftICE will keep on ticking. A serious driver developer will learn to use both.

Kernel: kd

Microsoft also has another kernel debugger, kd, which is not a source debugger. It is distributed as part of the DDK. We mention it here solely for completeness. Consider it mentioned.

Retail and Checked Builds

Windows NT is distributed in two forms:

1. As a *Retail Build*, which is what you get if you buy the shrink-wrapped version in your local computer store (called a *Free Build* when referring to developers, as discussed in Chapter 8)
2. As a *Checked Build*, which is available only as part of the MSDN subscription

While it is perfectly reasonable to use the Retail Build as a test bed for your development, it is often desirable to have the Checked Build installed as well. The latter is a special version of Windows NT that has additional checking enabled by compile-time options. The system runs more slowly than with the Retail Build, but it tends to detect many errors earlier and give more informative messages as to what is wrong. You can install both versions on the same drive. Note, however, that the two versions must live in separate directories, so each version has its own copy of the Registry. If you install a piece of software, whether your driver or application-level software, in the Retail Build version, its Registry entries will not be set up in the Checked Build version, so you will have to install it a second time. Because this is your debug machine and will require frequent reinstallations of software, you want to minimize the number of applications you actually have to install each time.

Symbol Tables

Debugging symbols are provided for both builds of NT. They are on the CD-ROM. If you install a Service Pack, you will find a set of symbols on the Service Pack distribution, as a self-extracting compressed file. You must download this file, since it is a separate distribution file. We show the locations of the symbols in Table 9.1. Note that in past releases, Microsoft has changed the directory structure under which the symbols are stored, so this may change again in the future. To use the symbols, you must copy the entire Symbols directory tree to some appropriate place on your host (development) machine. Note that if you are going to be using multiple versions of NT, including Checked Build, Service Packs, etc., you must have the correct set of symbols, so you probably want to store these Symbols trees in separate subdirectories.

Table 9.1: *Location of Symbols directory on various distributions*

NT 4.0 for *x86*	Symbol tables for kernel	`\support\debug\i386\Symbols`
	Debugger support DLLs	`\support\debug\i386\*.dll`
	kd	`\support\debug\i386\kd.exe`
NT 4.0 for Alpha	Symbol tables for kernel	`\support\debug\alpha\Symbols`
	Debugger support DLLs	`\support\debug\alpha\*.dll`

Traditionally, Microsoft does not release Service Packs for the Checked Build. However, as we write this, a Service Pack for the NT 4.0 Checked Build has been released.

In addition to Service Packs, there are also Hot Fixes, which are slightly-tested fixes to NT. Hot Fixes are released for the Free Build only. Hot Fixes do not come with symbols, so if you install one, parts of the symbols you have may be incorrect.

You must have the correct set of kernel symbols to effectively debug a Device Driver.

A compilation, using the techniques we have shown in the previous chapter, builds a driver (`.sys`) file that contains the symbol table information. With the newer compilers and the newer version of WinDbg, the symbol table can be a separate Program Database (`.pdb`) file, using the same format as application-level compilations.

Stripping Symbol Tables

The symbol tables delivered by Microsoft are the symbol tables stripped from the kernel files. These are all `.dbg` files. You can create `.dbg` files for your own driver.

You normally build your driver with symbols, making your debugging somewhat simpler. To ship a driver, however, you probably want to strip the symbols out to reduce the size of the driver. This is done by the following procedure:

- Use the program `dumpbin`, contained in the `msdev\bin` subdirectory.

  ```
  dumpbin /headers driver.sys
  ```

- Using the address that you find as the base address, use the `rebase` program, found in the `sdk\bin` directory.

  ```
  rebase -b address -x path driver.sys
  ```

The effect of this is to create a new `.sys` file for the driver, from which all the symbolic information has been stripped. The debugging information is placed in a `.dbg` file, created in the specified path. A sample of the output of `dumpbin` is shown in Figure 9.1, with the important line highlighted. The execution of `rebase` is shown in Figure 9.2. The execution produces an updated `helloworld.sys` file in the directory and creates `helloworld.dbg` in the same directory (using "`.`" as the path). The sample file sizes before and after are summarized in Table 9.2.

Table 9.2: *File sizes for symbol stripping example*

Condition	File	Size
Created by BUILD process	`helloworld.sys`	49,704
Updated by `rebase`	`helloworld.sys`	4,960
Created by `rebase`	`helloworld.dbg`	45,416

```
Microsoft (R) COFF Binary File Dumper Version 4.20.6164
Copyright (C) Microsoft Corp 1992-1996. All rights reserved.
Dump of file helloworld.sys

PE signature found

File Type: EXECUTABLE IMAGE

FILE HEADER VALUES
      14C machine (i386)
        3 number of sections
 36072865 time date stamp Tue Sep 22 00:32:37 1998
     1572 file pointer to symbol table
       6A number of symbols
       E0 size of optional header
      102 characteristics
              Executable
              32 bit word machine

OPTIONAL HEADER VALUES
      10B magic #
     5.00 linker version
      EE0 size of code
      100 size of initialized data
        0 size of uninitialized data
      409 address of entry point
      200 base of code
      F20 base of data
```

...lots more irrelevant output follows, deleted from this figure

Figure 9.1: *Output from the* dumpbin *program.*

```
C:\hello\lib\i386\Checked>rebase -b 1572 -x . helloworld.sys
REBASE: Total Size of mapping 0x00010000
REBASE: Range 0x00001572 -0x00011572
C:\hello\lib\i386\Checked>
```

Figure 9.2: *Execution of* rebase.

Using the Debugging Tools

Any sufficiently advanced technology is indistinguishable from magic.
— *Arthur C. Clarke*

As we discuss the use of the debugging tools and the necessary preparations for their use, bear in mind the amazing fact of the incident of the Sorcerer's Apprentice. It was *not* that he couldn't stop the brooms from carrying water, but instead that he got them to do anything at all! We are about to give you incantations, complete with the equivalent of pentagrams. If you don't follow these steps precisely, you very likely will invoke nothing, rather than having the demon devour you. Of course, we have to plead that these incantations are known to work only on NT 4.0 and on our early beta release of NT 5.0. They *may* work on the product release of Windows 2000, which will not be out until months after this book goes to press. If these incantations don't work in the product, check out our Web sites for updates.

Physical Configuration

You need to have two systems. The first, or primary, system is your development system. On this system are all of your major development tools, your precious source files, and all of the other bits that make your life pleasant. *Do not debug drivers on this system.* When a driver crashes and burns, it all too often takes some part of the disk with it. You must then reinstall NT, and possibly even reformat the disk. You do not want to do this to your precious working environment. Therefore, you will do all of the actual execution on your second, debug target (sacrificial) system.

This second system must have *at least enough* memory, disk space, and peripherals to load and run NT and test your driver. A CD-ROM drive is mandatory, and you may as well leave the NT installation CD-ROM in it all of the time. If you are part of a group, you must have your own copy of the NT CD-ROM even if the group has a site license. The cost of having a frustrated programmer wandering the halls late at night trying to find the one and only NT CD-ROM quickly exceeds the cost of buying, even at retail, a full NT Workstation license and CD-ROM. For that matter, the cost of *not* having a full MSDN subscription for each programmer, calculated over most realistic time schedules for driver development, is very much higher than the cost of buying a full MSDN subscription. This must be, at the least, the level of the subscription that provides for full NT distribution disks, Checked and Retail kernels, the Resource Kit, full Visual C++, and all of the other development environments and many other features we find indispensable. With programmer time (all costs, including benefits and overhead) valued at well over $10,000 per month (nominally 20 workdays, or 160 hours), you don't need many hours saved to add up to two days, or $1,000. This $1,000 is the difference between the base software required for development and a full MSDN subscription.

Your debug machine should be at least a dual-processor machine. This is because if you haven't debugged your driver on a multiprocessor, you haven't debugged your driver. Yes, it is hard to make the case to bean-counters that an expensive dual-processor machine should be devoted to a developer who uses it about 10% of the time, but trust us, you will pay *far* more than the cost of that machine if your customers try to use your driver on *their* multiprocessor machines and find out it doesn't work. If nothing else, ask how much your company's reputation is worth.[1]

Both machines must have a network connecting them. While a network is not "necessary", about the third time you have to do the floppy-copy hack you will realize that *must have* is an appropriate phrase to apply to the presence of a network. Network cards are cheap enough that there is no excuse not to network the two machines. It will cost you *much* more to do otherwise.

---

[1] It is also worth pointing out that the week we drafted this chapter, in October of 1997, each of the authors acquired a dual-processor Pentium-based server, reconditioned, via Internet auction, for under $1,000. Eight months later we upgraded these to quad-processor machines for under $250. A bit of research will go a long way to reduce your costs.

The two machines must be connected via serial ports using a null-modem cable. If you have serial mice, you must have two serial ports. You will need to use your mice and the serial ports at the same time. This interconnect is used by WinDbg.

The Reset button of your debugging machine should be within arm's reach of where you sit. It is astonishing what a barrier the simple act of getting up from your chair to push the Reset button will become. You will push it a *lot*.

 Should you be so unfortunate as to have one of the boxes made by IBM, who, for reasons unfathomable to rational people, insist on *not* putting a Reset button on their boxes, get it replaced by a *real* product that has a Reset button. The hundreds, or thousands, of off-on cycles stress every part of the machine. Using an IBM-manufactured PC while doing driver development, I ruined a perfectly good display because the turn-off caused a "hot spot" in the center of the screen during each shutdown. This hot spot eventually ate an ugly black hole in the phosphor. Boxes without Reset buttons: Just Say No! *–jmn*

One way to deal with the phenomenon of disk corruption on a crash is to buy a disk unit that allows you to exchange drives by switching simple plug-in modules. For example, Kingston makes a unit we use, shown in Figure 9.3. This unit allows us to have multiple drives formatted for NT 4.0, NT 5.0, Windows 95, and Windows 98 and exchange them simply by pulling out one cartridge and installing another. Unfortunately, NT cannot currently boot from a removable-media device like an Iomega Zip® drive or Jaz® drive. However, instead of having multiple different operating systems on your drives, you can have copies of the same NT system loaded onto the drives. Then you can "install" a new NT system in less than a minute by replacing the crashed drive with a preloaded new drive. The "dead" disks can be reloaded at a more leisurely pace, or perhaps even by a paraprofessional or service person. A number of utility programs are available at nominal prices that will restore a disk from a compressed image on another drive. You can also use a backup tape system (we can particularly recommend the Seagate Software Backup Exec with the Intelligent Disaster Recovery add-on). If you are already using multiple systems and have any of the commercially available screen-mouse-keyboard multiplexor boxes already set up to switch between your various machines, buy a second display head, keyboard,

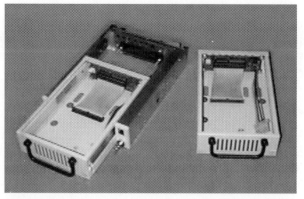

Figure 9.3: *Swappable hard drive caddies and carrier. Left: complete unit. Right: additional carrier. Shown without drives.*

and mouse. It is impossible to debug a Device Driver unless you can see both the debugging screen on your development machine and the screen of the debug system *simultaneously*.

 Although the Kingston hard drive caddies are of exceptionally high quality, they have one problem that can be significant: They are physically taller than a normal "half-height" unit. If your computer is like most we've seen, it has little metal "shelves" that allow you to slide a half-height unit into place. The Kingston units will not fit in this space, and you may be forced to physically modify your case by removing these "shelves". If you decide to do this, you should remove *everything* from your case, *including the power supply*, and then remove the shelf brackets. If your drive bay is a physically separate unit in the main case, you can just remove it. If you have used any method that produces small metal particles, you should vacuum and then *wash* your case or drive bay unit; if you do not, these little particles will haunt you for years. And whatever you do, make sure that if you are using some technique that generates little metal particles, there are *no* backplane connectors or similar connectors anywhere nearby—you may never get them to work again! Little metal particles are insidious.

Kingston sells an external case that *does* hold their drive units. It is quite useful if you have SCSI drives because the drives have an external SCSI coupling mechanism. If your drives are IDE or EIDE, it is a lot less convenient to use the external case because of cable length limitations.

One author (*jmn*) found that a cold chisel (in the guise of a high-quality Vaco screwdriver) worked well on an inexpensive case. But if you plan to hammer on the case, you *must* remove all components with movable parts, especially hard drives, floppy drives, and CD-ROMs.

We hope you get the picture. For driver development, penny-wise is pound-foolish (or, to work up a pun on the British currency system, kiloton-foolish). Writing and debugging drivers is a nontrivial exercise; everything you can do to expedite the process saves money. If a developer must swap drives and reboot to do a test, many tests will not get done. The result will be an inadequately tested product. Employee cost is not fixed. Wasting a programmer's time by short-changing the development environment will ultimately cost far more than the cost of an extra computer, an extra disk drive, an extra prototype board, or anything else we have recommended. Making developers more efficient shows up in products that are better-tested products, out the door sooner, and produced at a lower development cost and a lower maintenance cost than if someone saves $1,500 by not buying a machine or some accessories. Price, delivery, and reputation are important.

It is worth pointing out that we are both self-employed consultants; we don't have a corporate-sized budget to spend. Often, the choices we make impinge on us directly: a new computer or a weekend vacation, a new computer or a new lawn tractor, or whatever. Each of our own computer networks rivals or exceeds that of many medium-sized software companies. We *know* where our time goes, and we strive to optimize it.

Using Autologin

Configure your test machine to perform an autologin. This is done by modifying the Registry. Since this also requires that you put the plaintext (unencrypted) password to that account in the Registry, be aware that this is a potential security compromise. However, the fact that a full NT installation CD-ROM is present is a greater danger to security, since anyone can reinstall NT and become an Administrator.

To modify the Registry for autologin, you can either edit the Registry manually or use the AutoLogon program that is in the Configuration folder of the NT Resource Kit that comes on the

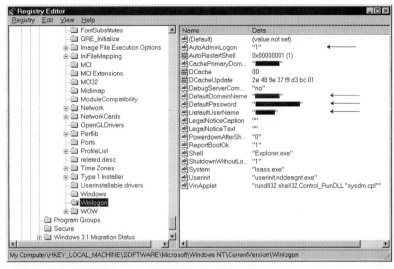

Figure 9.4: *Registry entries to support autologin.*

full MSDN CD-ROM subscription, and is available also from the `sysinternals` Web site. To modify the Registry manually, you need to use the Registry editor to add new values under the path, as follows, adding the keys as shown in Figure 9.4:

`HKEY_LOCAL_MACHINE\SOFTWARE\Microsoft\Windows NT\CurrentVersion\WinLogin`

Note that in the figure, we blacked out the actual values so as to protect *our* security.[2] The keys and their values are summarized in Table 9.3. If you are on a domain, you specify `DefaultDomainName` as being the domain you are in. If you are not on a domain, you use your computer's name as the value.

 If your development machine is part of an NT domain, the Windows kernel debugger, WinDbg, requires Administrator privileges. Run the User Manager application on your development machine, and on your target, and add `domain\yourlogin` as a member of the Administrators group.

Table 9.3: *Keys and Values for Autologin*

Key	Type	Value
`AutoAdminLogin`	REG_SZ	`"1"`
`DefaultDomainName`	REG_SZ	`"your computer/domain name here"`
`DefaultPassword`	REG_SZ	`"your password here"`
`DefaultUserName`	REG_SZ	`"your name here"`

[2] For additional security, we painted the pixels black three times in conformance with DoD security procedures.

Installing Your Driver

At some point in this process, you must actually install your driver on the debug machine.

You should put the driver in a separate subdirectory so that it doesn't generate a conflict with any other driver's executable name. If you do happen to overwrite some other driver's executable with your own, you will probably have to, at some point, figure out where that executable came from, what floppy or CD-ROM it is on, and which version you had loaded so that you can reload it. If the driver you overwrote was a critical driver, you may not even be able to boot without reinstalling NT. (We recommend that you put your company name in the name of the driver file and in the `DisplayName` so that it is clear which driver is being specified.) For testing purposes, the subdirectory in which you install your driver is up to you. You could create a `test` subdirectory under the `system32` subdirectory of your Windows installation directory (for example, `c:\winnt5\system32\test`, if `c:\winnt5` is where your system is loaded). The simplest way to do this is to have two copies of the Windows NT Explorer running, one displaying your target executable directory on your development machine and the other displaying the test directory on the debug machine. Then, to do a copy, you need only make both Explorers visible and drag the icon representing the driver from the development machine to the test subdirectory on the debug machine.

Copying a driver executable to the debug target is *not* installing it. The act of "installing" a driver means creating the necessary Registry entries to allow it to be found. While there are many alternative ways of doing this, the simplest one is to create the Registry entry as a file and cause that file to be processed in a way that creates the Registry entries.

The `RegIni` Program

An easy way to install a driver is to create a Registry initialization file and use the `RegIni` program that comes as part of the DDK support. You can use any text editor to create a text file that describes your driver. A typical example is shown in Figure 9.5. For all of the details of what these entries mean, see Chapter 18.

The Registry does not handle symbolic constants, so you must look them up and encode them as the actual numbers required. We specified here an entry for a Device Driver (`Type=1`, SERVICE_KERNEL_DRIVER), which is to be loaded on demand (`Start=3`, SERVICE_DEMAND_START). It has no dependencies on other drivers and no drivers depend on it,

```
\registry\machine\system\currentcontrolset\services\drivername
    ImagePath=c:\winnt5\system32\test\drivername.sys
    DisplayName = Your Driver description
    Type = REG_DWORD 0x00000001
    Start = REG_DWORD 0x00000003
    Group = Extended base
    ErrorControl = REG_DWORD 0x00000001
\registry\machine\system\currentcontrolset\services\drivername\Parameters
    BreakOnEntry = REG_DWORD 0x1;
    DebugMask = REG_DWORD 0x0;
    LogEvents = 0x0
```

Figure 9.5: *Registry initialization file* `TEST.INI`.

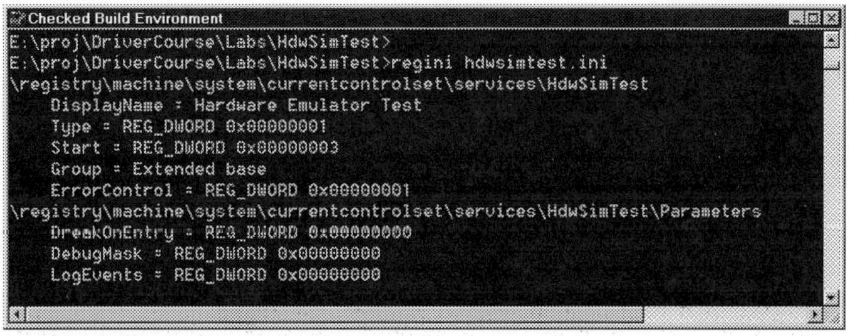

Figure 9.6: *Sample execution of* RegIni.

and if it were changed to automatically load, it would be among the last few drivers loaded
(Group=Extended base). If it cannot be found or it fails to load (DriverEntry returned
FALSE), the system will log the error in the Event Log and continue execution
(ErrorControl=1, SERVICE_ERROR_NORMAL). The remaining three entries are interpreted by
our driver as follows.

- BreakOnEntry indicates whether we should take our initial programmed hard-coded breakpoint.
- DebugMask can be used to enable various debugging options of our choosing.
- LogEvents indicates if internal events should be logged to the Event Log.

We cover these in detail in Chapter 26.

The RegIni program can be used to write these values in the Registry. It will also display
which values were changed. If we want to change a value (for example, the BreakOnEntry,
DebugMask, or LogEvents entries), we need only to edit the file and rerun RegIni. It will
tell us which options we have changed. A sample of a run is shown in Figure 9.6.

After running RegIni, you must reboot the debug machine before the Devices applet can
see the new Registry entries. You can avoid this reboot by using the SCM (Service Control Manager). However, saving one reboot in the development of a driver is not a major saving.

Modifying the BOOT.INI File

You must also modify the BOOT.INI file on the test machine. This requires several discrete
steps.

First, locate the BOOT.INI file in the Explorer. An example of this file is shown in
Figure 9.7. Then use the right mouse button or the menu to select the Properties display. The
result is a display that resembles Figure 9.8. Note that the "Read-Only" attribute is checked.
This is the default that is set when the file is created. Remove this check mark. You may now edit
the BOOT.INI file using your favorite text editor. NotePad works well.

The next step is to edit the file. A typical BOOT.INI file, appearing as it does before any
modifications have been made, is shown in Figure 9.9. The BOOT.INI file has two sections.

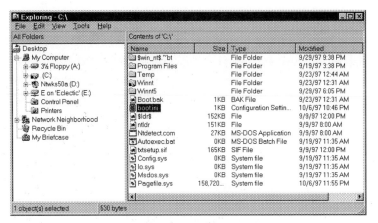

Figure 9.7: *Locating the* BOOT.INI *file.*

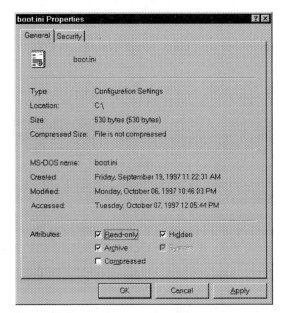

Figure 9.8: *Displaying and modifying* BOOT.INI
properties.

```
[boot loader]
timeout=30
default=multi(0)disk(0)rdisk(0)partition(1)\WINNT5
[operating systems]
multi(0)disk(0)rdisk(0)partition(1)\WINNT5="Windows Workstation Version 5.0"
multi(0)disk(0)rdisk(0)partition(1)\WINNT5="Windows Workstation Version 5.0
[VGA]" /basevideo
```

Figure 9.9: *A* BOOT.INI *file before modifications.*

1. [boot loader] specifies the timeout interval and the default configuration to be used. The timeout interval is the amount of time the configuration options are displayed, thereby allowing the user to choose which configuration to boot. If the timeout interval is set to 0, the system will boot without delay and the default configuration cannot be changed. If the timeout interval is set to −1, the system will wait indefinitely for you to select the desired boot configuration.
2. [operating systems] specifies which operating systems are bootable. You may have any number of Windows NT operating systems, in any number of versions, on any disks, but only at most one non-NT (usually Windows 95 or 98) operating system. Only the first ten entries will be displayed at boot time.

The way to interpret the boot line is shown in Table 9.4. Because you may have any number of NT configurations installed, on one or more drives or partitions, you may have both a Retail Build of NT installed in a WINNT directory and a Checked Build installed in the WINCHECKED directory. You must decide which one is to be loaded at boot time. The options for the BOOT.INI file are shown in Table 9.5. This is the only place we know of where all of these options are documented in one table. You will want to create one or more lines with the appropriate boot options set and add them to the list. We show a simple modification of BOOT.INI in Figure 9.10.

To determine which is the default configuration, we use the *first* configuration that matches the default specification. Thus, the order in which you specify the remaining configurations is important. We want our default configuration to be the one we normally boot with, so we place it first in the list. We also change the delay time to be only one second so as to expedite our rebooting efforts.

Table 9.4: *Interpretation of a* BOOT.INI *Configuration*

Option	Specification	Meaning
[boot loader]		
Timeout	timeout=n	The number of seconds the boot display will remain up until the default configuration is booted. If this value is set to 0, the default configuration cannot be changed. If the value is set to −1, there is no timeout and you must always explicitly tell the boot process to continue.
Default configuration	default=	A specification of the controller, drive, unit, partition, and path that constitute the default configuration. The *first* operating system configuration found that matches this specification is the one that is the default configuration. The description and options are not part of this specification.
[operating systems]		
Disk controller	multi(n)	A SCSI drive with a SCSI BIOS or a non-SCSI (usually IDE) controller. The controller number *n* is the controller number if more than one controller is installed. This value is 0-based. Normally, there is only one controller, so the typical value is 0.
	scsi(n)	The SCSI controller when no SCSI BIOS is used. This number is 0-based and represents the number of the SCSI controller card. For a system with a single controller card, this value is 0.

Table 9.4: *Interpretation of a* BOOT.INI *Configuration (continued)*

Option	Specification	Meaning
Disk number	disk(n)	For IDE, the disk number on the controller. It is 0-based. Typically, this value is 0 for the first IDE master drive.
		The SCSI unit number on a selected SCSI controller, whether multi or scsi.
Unit number	rdisk(n)	For IDE, must be 0.
		For SCSI, the Logical Unit Number (LUN) of the drive. If you are not using LUNs in your SCSI hardware, this should be 0.
Partition number	partition(n)	Indicates the partition on the drive in which the operating system is stored. *CAUTION:* This number is 1-based, so the first partition is number 1!
Path	*pathname*	The directory in which the desired operating system is stored. Note that only the directory name is supplied.
Description	="*text*"	A description that informs the user about the properties of the configuration. This is what is displayed at boot time.
Options	(see Table 9.5)	A set of options that enable or disable features during the boot or in the loaded system.

Table 9.5: BOOT.INI *option switches*

Option	Meaning
/3gb	Increases the user partition from 2GB to 3GB (thus reducing the kernel from 2GB to 1GB). It requires NT 4.0 Service Pack 3 or higher.
/basevideo	Bypasses all special video display drivers and loads a VGA-compatible display driver.
/baudrate=*value*	Sets the baud rate for the debug port. The *value* may be any standard baud rate, but for most purposes, 115,200 is a good selection. If /baudrate is specified, /debug is assumed.
/burnmemory=*value*	Reduces the total amount of memory available by removing the indicated number of megabytes from the available memory. This is an option similar to the /maxmem option, except /maxmem sets an absolute limit and this subtracts a relative value from the total amount of memory available. Note that to artificially limit memory on an Alpha, /maxmem does not work, and /burnmemory must be used instead.
/crashdebug	Enables the debugger as the system crashes. It is not used very often.
/debug	Enables the kernel debugger as the system boots.
/debugport=COM*n*	Used to specify which port to use. The default debug port is COM2.

Table 9.5: BOOT.INI *option switches (continued)*

Option	Meaning
/hal=*filename*	Specifies a particular executable file for the HAL to be loaded. While of primary interest to HAL debuggers, this also allows a Device Driver Writer to check out a driver using a variety of HALs (all of which must be valid on the test machine).
/kernel=*filename*	Specifies a particular executable file for the kernel to be loaded.
/maxmem=*n*	Specifies the desired memory size in megabytes. It is useful for testing your driver on a "small" machine without having to actually go in and change the memory chips. This does not work on the Alpha (see /burnmemory).
/nodebug	(Default) Disables the kernel debugger.
/noserialmice= /noserialmice=COM*n*	Normally, when NT boots it "probes" each of the serial ports to determine if a mouse is connected and if so, what kind. In some cases, a nonmouse device will react to these probes in a highly unfriendly fashion. Specified without an argument, this switch inhibits all testing for a serial mouse. Specified with an argument, it inhibits serial mouse testing on the indicated COM port.
/numproc=*n*	Enables the first *n* processors of a multiprocessor system. The order in which physical chips are numbered is platform-dependent.
/onecpu	Limits a multiprocessor system to run with only one processor. It is very useful for determining if your crashes are caused by intrinsic problems or by a failure to deal with a multiprocessor system. It is the same as /numproc=1.
/pcilock	Disables the reassignment of PCI resources. When this switch is specified, the HAL leaves the I/O port and memory addresses as assigned by the BIOS (provided there is no conflict). This option is used when you discover that adding a new PCI device causes the machine to lock up, usually on boot.
/sos	Provides a "verbose" system boot. It is very useful for watching various modules load, especially if the system is crashing on boot.

```
[boot loader]
timeout=1
default=multi(0)disk(0)rdisk(0)partition(1)\WINNT5
[operating systems]
multi(0)disk(0)rdisk(0)partition(1)\WINNT5="Debug 5.0" /sos /debug /baudrate=115200
multi(0)disk(0)rdisk(0)partition(1)\WINNT5="Windows Workstation Version 5.0"
multi(0)disk(0)rdisk(0)partition(1)\WINNT5="Windows Workstation Version 5.0 [VGA]"
/basevideo
```

Figure 9.10: *A modified* BOOT.INI *file for driver debugging.*

At first, you might be tempted to use the /hal and /kernel switches to get a "debug kernel" without having to do a full install of the Checked Build. Unfortunately, this is *exactly* what you get: a checked kernel and a checked HAL. This is unlike the full Checked Build install, in which you get a number of checked DLLs, checked Device Drivers, and many other checked components. This technique has been floating around for a while, but we discourage this.

Setting Parameters on the Alpha

The Alpha does not use a BOOT.INI file. Instead, the parameters are stored as part of the ARC configuration information. These appear as the OSLOADOPTIONS in the setup information. To set these, consult the documentation for your particular model of the Alpha.

Configuring WinDbg

WinDbg is a powerful debugger that even allows you to do cross-platform debugging. You can run WinDbg on an Intel platform and debug a program on an Alpha. For now, we assume that you are debugging an Intel-based driver from an Intel-based development machine.

The version of WinDbg described here is the version of WinDbg that is distributed with the Windows NT 4.0 SDK, for use the Visual C++ version 4.2 compiler. Newer versions of WinDbg have a slightly different set of screens and appearance.

You will have to do some initial configuration of WinDbg, typically only once. After that, you will have to make two additional configuration changes: platform-specific and project-specific. We look at each of these in turn next.

Initial Configuration

The initial configuration is set up using the **Options | Kernel Debugging...** menu item. This brings up the dialog shown in Figure 9.11. All of these options except the Platform are usually set only once. The Baud Rate and Port are obvious. The Cache Size should be set to "not too small, not too large". WinDbg caches the values that you examine, either explicitly or via a preset watch, in this cache so that it doesn't have to query the debug target each time it needs to update the display. A single-step or Go command invalidates the cache, thereby forcing it to be reloaded. If your cache is too large, your debugging performance will suffer as the massive

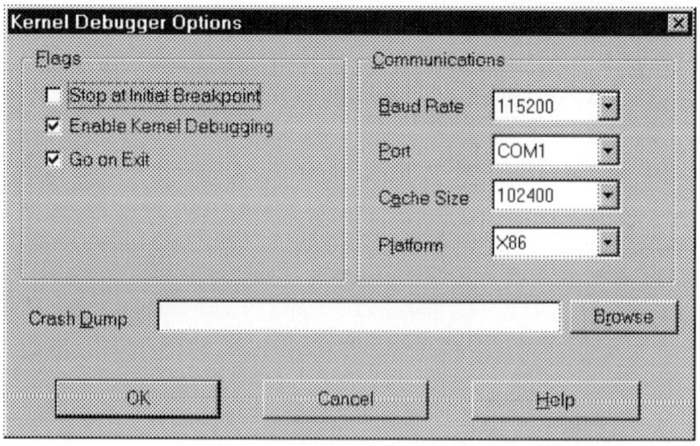

Figure 9.11: *WinDbg: Kernel Debugger Options.*

cache is reloaded each time the program stops. If it is too small, your debugging performance will suffer as each variable is reloaded each time from the debug target. In our debugger, we used the default value of 102,400 bytes. If you need to examine DMA buffers or other variables, such as memory-mapped device registers, because these can change after the debugger has cached them, you must set the cache size to 0. The cache size can be changed at any time using the .cache command to WinDbg and specifying the desired cache size.

The Platform option is discussed in the next subsection.

The flag options on the left of the dialog box establish the basic configuration for debugging. Normally, you want to check Enable Kernel Debugging, since that is what you are doing. Also select Go on Exit so that if you exit the debugger while it is stopped at a breakpoint, the debuggee will be automatically continued (otherwise, there is no way to get it to continue). Finally, there is an initial breakpoint set internally in NT. Selecting the option Stop at Initial Breakpoint allows you to take an initial breakpoint.

The Crash Dump option is used for reading crash dumps symbolically. We discuss that under the section "Reading a Crash Dump" on page 205.

Platform Configuration

There are two kinds of platform configuration you need to do. The first deals with choosing the platform type (Intel, Alpha) and the second deals with choosing the particular variant of NT you are running.

The platform type is set in the Kernel Debugger Options dialog box, as shown in Figure 9.11. The platform selected here is X86, since we are currently developing an Intel-based driver.

You need also to select the **Options | Debugger DLLs** menu item. This brings up a dialog box that resembles Figure 9.12. Here, you select options about the type of symbol table being used (Symbol Handler), the type of remote platform (Expression Evaluator), and the type of CPU chip (Execution Model). These should all be obvious. Not obvious is the highlighted option: the Transport Layer. You might think that for remote debugging, you would want to select the option for using remote debugging via COM1 (although the selection says at 300 baud, this is untrue; the speed is not that restricted). In fact, you do not. Surprisingly, you want to select the incredibly counterintuitive option of "Local—Debugging on same machine". Why? We don't know. But if you don't choose this option, debugging won't work.

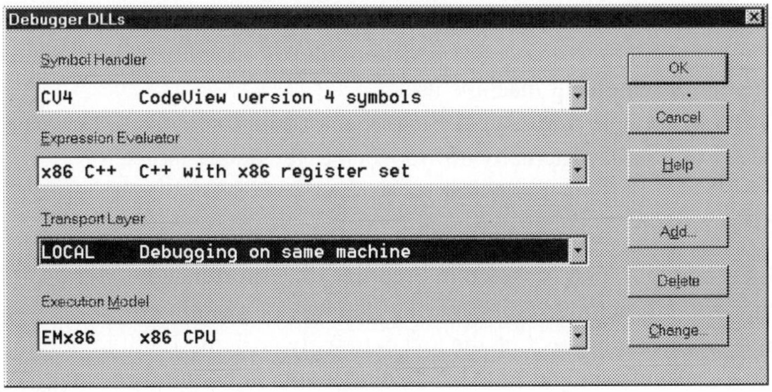

Figure 9.12: *WinDbg options Debugger DLLs dialog box.*

NT is characterized by its version number (for example, 4.0 and 5.0) and by its Service Pack number (Service Pack 1, 2, 3, and so on). Each variant of NT has its own set of debug files associated with it. A Service Pack will have both the Retail, or Free, Build and the Checked Build updates. You may wish to check out your driver under each of the Service Packs as well as on the base operating system in order to ensure you have not relied on some undocumented feature or idiosyncrasy that has been changed, or "fixed", in a Service Pack (of course, a Service Pack would *never* actually introduce a bug).

To debug a version of NT, you must have, on your development machine, the symbol table information for the correct base version and Service Pack of the operating system. You must tell WinDbg where to find this. Typically, you will have a directory path with a `Symbols` subdirectory. When you get a Service Pack or install a Checked Build, you should copy the entire `Symbols` subdirectory. Thus you may have directories of these forms:

```
c:\winnt4\symbols
c:\winnt4\sp2\symbols
c:\winnt5\symbols
```

Each `Symbols` directory will have subdirectories such as `\dll`, `\exe`, and `\sys`. These contain the appropriate debugging information for WinDbg; it knows which subdirectory to use for each of its needs. Note that these directories are *not* directories created by the installation procedure; they are directories that you have explicitly created. Also, there is one directory optionally created by the SDK installation procedure: `%SystemRoot%\symbols`. This procedure installs the set of symbols for the *local* machine's installation of NT. This is not generally useful for driver work because for a driver, you need the set of symbols for the *target* machine, and you need them on your development machine. In addition, you could update your development machine without updating your target machine, or vice versa. Having the symbols in a directory not explicitly identified by the target operating system version is an error waiting to happen.

You specify the path to the symbols using the **Options | User DLLs...** menu item. This brings up the screen shown in Figure 9.13. In the Symbol Search Path field, specify both the platform symbols path and the project symbols path(s). We discuss the project symbol paths in the next section. For now, you need to specify, usually as the first entry, the path to the symbols for the kernel modules. This is shown in the figure as

```
%SystemRoot%\symbols
```

We do this in this way because we happened to be debugging the exact same target configuration. This is not generally recommended because you will likely be debugging a different configuration than your development machine uses.

Use the Browse button to find your test driver and add it to the list. Be certain that you are referring to the driver you have actually downloaded to the debug target.

Project Configuration

Part of the project configuration is shown in Figure 9.13. Unfortunately, Microsoft has fallen in love with the horizontally scrolled edit control as the way of handling the configuration. This makes adding, deleting, and inspecting the text extremely difficult. (Hint to developers: This is possibly the most user-*un*friendly way to handle this. Avoid it in your own code!) What you can't see is the path component entry we have given for one of our applications, which actually reads

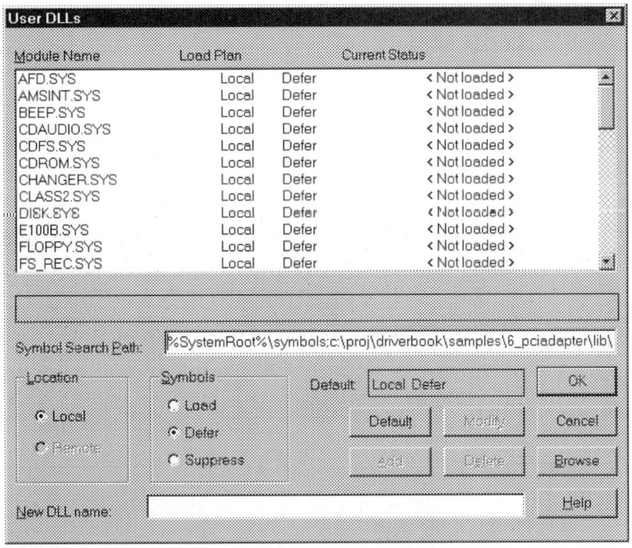

Figure 9.13: *WinDbg: User DLLs settings.*

```
c:\proj\driverbook\samples\6_pciadapter\lib\i386\checked
```

Individual path elements are separated by semicolons. If you're wondering what all those subdirectories are for, go back and read about the BUILD process on page 162.

Also check the **Options | Debug...** settings to ensure you have suitable settings. A typical setup is shown in Figure 9.14. In particular, you should make sure that under Debugger, the

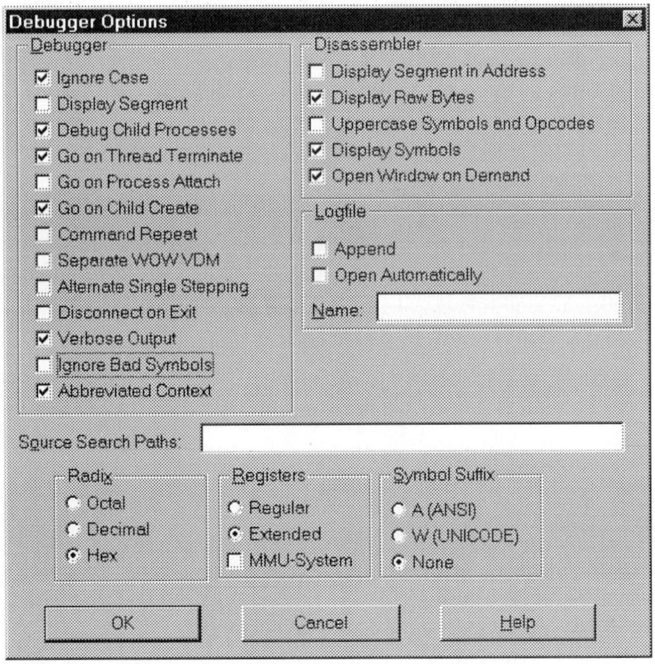

Figure 9.14: *WinDbg Debugger Options dialog.*

Alternate Single Stepping and Ignore Bad Symbols options are unchecked and under Disassembler, Open Window on Demand is checked.

Starting a Debug Session

Starting a debug session is a carefully choreographed dance. If you get out of step, you probably won't get a successful start-up of the debug session.

First, start WinDbg on the development machine. If it was already running, it may have to be restarted, particularly if the last debugging session ended in a Blue Screen. Once WinDbg is loaded, you must tell it to start the debug session. You can do this by using the **Run | Go** menu item, pressing the **F5** function key, or clicking the "play" or "Go" icon (▶) on the toolbar, shown in Figure 9.15. You should see a message saying WinDbg is now waiting to connect to the target system, similar to that shown in Figure 9.16.

Figure 9.15: *WinDbg Go and Stop icons.*

WARNING: If you start an NT system as your debug target and you have not started WinDbg in advance and you then execute any hardcoded breakpoint (such as our suggested `BreakOnEntry` technique), the NT debug target system will hang. This is because it is waiting for the debugger to signal that it can continue, but no debugger was found at boot time!

Note that starting WinDbg before booting the debug target is no guarantee that the debugger will actually be found, unless you have actual *communication* between your development machine and your debug target. If you see this behavior and believe that you have correctly started WinDbg in advance, there may be a communication error between WinDbg and the debug target. Check for all of the usual failure modes: loose cable, incompatible data rates, incorrect COM port assignment, and the like. If it is your first time debugging, make sure the cable is a full null-modem cable. If you have a switch box between the two machines, ensure it is switched properly and that it switches all of the signals. Run a terminal emulation program on both the development machine and the debug target to ensure that the complete hardware path is functioning. (For example, a situation in which a user complained that a piece of software would

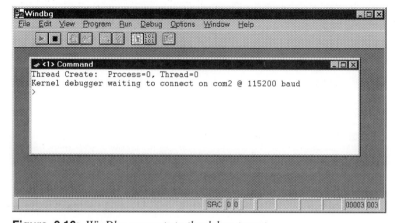

Figure 9.16: *WinDbg connects to the debug target.*

```
                        CD     DSR  CTS
Kernel Debugger Using: COM1 (Port 0x3f8, Baud Rate 115200)
Microsoft (R) Windows NT (TM) Version 4.0 (Build 1381: Service Pack 1).
2 System Processors [144 MB Memory] Multiprocessor Kernel
```

Figure 9.17: *NT load screen for the debuggee.*

not work on COM2 was resolved when, after careful inspection of the innards of the machine, we explained to the user that the *presence* of a COM2 port on the back of the machine does not imply there is an actual chip plugged into the appropriate socket to make COM2 work!)

The second step is to boot the debug system. We assume that you either select the debug configuration or have it set as your default configuration. During the boot process, the initial boot screen will resemble Figure 9.17.[3] The symbols along the topmost line and to the right—CD DSR CTS—are a brief display of the state of the serial connection between the debug system and the WinDbg host. If you see these changing a lot, you can be assured that WinDbg is probably successfully talking to the debug target. Otherwise, you may have a connection problem, either in the hardware or in a bad configuration of the software, such as incompatible line speeds set between the host and the target.

This will become much more apparent momentarily, as the system begins a serious boot cycle. Your WinDbg window will display the list of DLLs being loaded and other boot event notifications (provided you included the /sos switch in BOOT.INI as we recommended in Figure 9.10). This is shown in Figure 9.18.

You are now ready to start debugging your driver.

Loading the Driver

It is generally best if you configure your driver as a manual-start driver. You can then perform other tasks on the debug target without worrying about the driver's crashing the system before it comes up. If you make it an auto-start driver and it crashes coming up, you may still be able to recover by using the Last Known Good Configuration technique. We describe this technique later in the chapter.

You can start a driver either from the Drivers applet of the Control Panel or from a command line. From a command line, type

```
net start drivername
```

To stop a driver, type

```
net stop drivername
```

which will call the Unload routine in your driver. Note that you specify the *driver* name. The executable path is derived either from the ImagePath in the Registry or, if no ImagePath is

---

[3] Regarding what type of machine to use, note that one machine we use that is reserved for debugging drivers is a 144MB dual-processor Pentium. Its speed is 133MHz, although that doesn't show here. This is a fairly adequate minimal debugging system for a serious Device Driver writer. Next to it, also reserved for driver debugging, sits a quad-processor Pentium 100 with 128MB of memory.

Figure 9.18: *WinDbg sample boot sequence.*

specified, from the `Drivers` subdirectory of your Windows directory, specifically, a *drivername.*`SYS` file.

Figure 9.19: *Control Panel Devices icon.*

You use the Control Panel Devices applet (whose icon is shown in Figure 9.19) to cause the Driver applet to load. An example of this applet is shown in Figure 9.20. From there, select the driver whose description you supplied in the Registry, and click Start. To stop the driver, click Stop. If you have set your `BreakOnEntry` flag to 1, your programmed breakpoint will be executed. The "Stop" icon will gray out, and the "Go" icon will un-gray. At this point, you can use the single-step icon twice, and you will see the current line of code highlighted in yellow. At this point, your WinDbg screen will show you that the breakpoint has been taken. You may now proceed with your debugging.

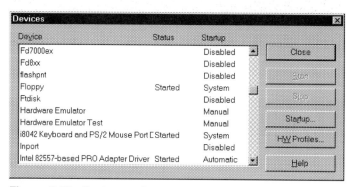

Figure 9.20: *Devices applet.*

You can set additional breakpoints or perform any other operations. You then start execution by pressing the **F5** key and selecting the **Debug | Go** menu item or by clicking the "Go" toolbar icon (▶). Alternatively, you can use either of the single-step options to carefully walk through your code. If this is the first time your driver has been tested, you will almost certainly see your debug target come up with the infamous Blue Screen of Death. Now you can get down to work.

It Crashed. Now What?

For your initial debugging, most of your bugs are going to be relatively simple, silly errors. You will be able to find them quickly by single-stepping through the source code. Many of the errors will show up quickly as you debug the DriverEntry routine, and the rest will start to show up as the driver begins to run. The techniques you use for finding these errors are not particularly different from those for finding ordinary bugs in user code—there is nothing magical going on. But once you get the driver up and starting seriously to run, a whole new set of driver-specific bugs will begin to emerge.

Let's take a look at a sample Blue Screen of Death dump. Unfortunately, you can't do a "print screen" to capture this, so we've simply retyped the contents of a screen, as shown in Figure 9.21. [4]

```
***STOP 0x0000001E (0xC0000005 0xF71D0495 0x00000001 0x00000038
KMODE_EXCEPTION_NOT_HANDLED

CPUID: Genuine intel 5.2.c  irql: 1f  SYSVER: F0000565

Dll base DateStmp - Name                Dll base DateStmp - Name
80100000 3202c07e - ntoskrnl.exe         80010000 31ee6c52 - hal.dll
80001000 31ed06b4 - atapi.sys            80006000 31ec6c74 - SCSIPORT.SYS
802c6000 31ed06bf - aic78xx.sys          802cd000 31ed2c7c - Disk.sys
802d1000 31ec6c7a - CLASS2.SYS           8037c000 31eed0a7 - Ntfs.sys
fc698000 31ec6c7d - Floppy.SYS           fc6a8000 31ec6ca1 - cdrom.sys
fc98a000 31ec6df7 - Fs_Rec.sYS           fc9c9000 31ec6c99 - Null.sys
fc864000 31ed868b - KSecDD.SYS           fc9ca000 31ec6c78 - Beep.sys
fc6d8000 31ec6c90 - i8042prt.sys         fc86c000 31ec6c97 - mouclass.sys
fc874000 31ec6c94 - kbdclass sys         fc6f0000 31f50722 - VIDEOPORT.SYS
feffa000 31ec6c62 - mga_mil.sys          fc890000 31ec6c6d - vga.sys
fc708000 31ec6ccb - Msfs.SYS             fc4b0000 31ec6cc7 - Npfs.SYS
fefbc000 31eed262 - NDIS.SYS             a0000000 31f954f7 - win32k.sys
fefa4000 31f91a51 - mga.dll              fec31000 31eedd07 - Fastfat.SYS
feb8c000 31ec6c6d - TDI.SYS              fefa0000 31ed0754 - nbf.sys
feacf000 31f130A7 - tcpip.sys            feab3000 31f50a65 - netbt.sys
fc550000 31601a30 - e159x.sys            fe560000 31f8f864 - afd.sys
fc710000 31ec6e7a - netbios.sys          fcf58000 31ec6c9b - Parport.sys
fc870000 31ec6c9b - Parallel.sys         fc954000 31ec6c9d - ParVdm.SYS
fc5b0000 31ec6b61 - Serial.sys           fea4c000 31f5003b - rdr.sys
fea3b000 31f7a1ba - mup.sys              fe9da000 32031abe - srv.sys

Address DWORD dump     [Build 1381]                      - Name
fec32d84 80143e00 80143e00 80144000 ffdff000 00070b02    - Npfs.sys
801471c8 80144000 80144000 ffdff000 c03000b0 00000001    - ntoskrnl.exe
801471dc 80122000 f0003f00 f830eee0 e133c4b4 e133c4d0    - ntoskrnl.exe
80147384 80302cf0 0000023c 00000034 00000000 00000000    - ntoskrnl.exe

Restart and set the recovery options in the system control panel
or the /CRASHDEBUG system start option. If this message reappears,
contact your system administrator or technical support group
```

Figure 9.21: *Sample Blue Screen of Death.*

---

[4] After we wrote this chapter, the folks at wininternals (the commercial arm of sysinternals) released a product that saves the Blue Screen data to a disk file. A trial version of this is on the sysinternals Web site.

Much of this screen is not terribly useful unless you are a seriously hard-core kernel debugger and have the kernel sources handy. However, a few key parts are very useful to a Device Driver writer and, consequently, essential for you to understand.

The first and most important part is the top line, which contains the BugCheck code. This is a text string that attempts to explain why the system crashed. It may be followed by four additional values that provide BugCheck-specific information. The complete set of BugCheck messages appears in Table 9.6. Note that not all of the numeric values appear in the table; some are

(text continues on page 203)

Table 9.6: *BugCheck Error Codes*

Code	Name	Meaning
0x00000001	APC_INDEX_MISMATCH	
0x00000002	DEVICE_QUEUE_NOT_BUSY	
0x00000003	INVALID_AFFINITY_SET	
0x00000004	INVALID_DATA_ACCESS_TRAP	
0x00000005	INVALID_PROCESS_ATTACH_ATTEMPT	
0x0000006	INVALID_PROCESS_DETACH_ATTEMPT	
0x00000007	INVALID_SOFTWARE_INTERRUPT	
0x00000008	IRQL_NOT_DISPATCH_LEVEL	You called a function that was valid only at IRQL == DISPATCH_LEVELfrom a higher IRQL, such as a DIRQL.
0x00000009	IRQL_NOT_GREATER_OR_EQUAL	You called a function that was valid only at IRQL >= current level from a lower IRQL.
0x0000000A	IRQL_NOT_LESS_OR_EQUAL	You called a function that was valid only at IRQL <= current level from a higher IRQL, such as a DIRQL, and it has touched a page that was paged out. 1. The address that was referenced (this is an address in paged memory) 2. The IRQL value that was active at the time of the reference 3. The type of access: 0 for read, 1 for write 4. The address of the instruction that was executing when the error occurred
0x0000000B	NO_EXCEPTION_HANDLING_SUPPORT	

Table 9.6: *BugCheck Error Codes (continued)*

Code	Name	Meaning
0x0000000C	MAXIMUM_WAIT_OBJECTS_EXCEEDED	You called `KeWaitForMultipleObjects` with a count of more than `THREAD_WAIT_OBJECTS` but you have not allocated your own `KWAIT_BLOCK` array.
0x0000000D	MUTEX_LEVEL_NUMBER_VIOLATION	An attempt was made to acquire a Mutex that has the wrong level number. 1. The current thread's Mutex level 2. The Mutex level attempting to acquire
0x0000000E	NO_USER_MODE_CONTEXT	
0x0000000F	SPIN_LOCK_ALREADY_OWNED	
0x00000010	SPIN_LOCK_NOT_OWNED	A thread attempted to release a Spin Lock it did not set.
0x00000011	THREAD_NOT_MUTEX_OWNER	An attempt has been made to release a Mutex that was set by some other thread.
0x00000012	TRAP_CAUSE_UNKNOWN	
0x00000013	EMPTY_THREAD_REAPER_LIST	
0x00000014	CREATE_DELETE_LOCK_NOT_LOCKED	
0x00000015	LAST_CHANCE_CALL_FROM_KMODE	
0x00000016	CID HANDLE CREATION	
0x00000017	CID_HANDLE_DELETION	
0x00000018	REFERENCE_BY_POINTER	
0x00000019	BAD_POOL_HEADER	The header for the storage pool was corrupted, or the reference was not to a storage pool.
0x0000001A	MEMORY_MANAGEMENT	The heap was corrupted.
0x0000001B	PFN_SHARE_COUNT	
0x0000001C	PFN_REFERENCE_COUNT	
0x0000001D	NO_SPIN_LOCK_AVAILABLE	

Table 9.6: *BugCheck Error Codes (continued)*

Code	Name	Meaning
0x0000001E	KMODE_EXCEPTION_NOT_HANDLED	An exception occurred in the kernel. 1. The exception code; the usual exception code values apply, as defined by winerror.h. (see also Table 9.7) 2. The address of the instruction that caused exception 3. The first parameter of the exception 4. The second parameter of the exception
0x0000001F	SHARED_RESOURCE_CONV_ERROR	
0x00000020	KERNEL_APC_PENDING_DURING_EXIT	
0x00000021	QUOTA_UNDERFLOW	
0x00000022	FILE_SYSTEM	
0x00000023	FAT_FILE_SYSTEM	
0x00000024	NTFS_FILE_SYSTEM	
0x00000025	NPFS_FILE_SYSTEM	
0x00000026	CDFS_FILE_SYSTEM	
0x00000027	RDR_FILE_SYSTEM	
0x00000028	CORRUPT_ACCESS_TOKEN	
0x00000029	SECURITY_SYSTEM	
0x0000002A	INCONSISTENT_IRP	The IRP contains two or more members that conflict. This is most likely caused by mistakenly using the IRP pointer for another kind of access. 1. The address of the IRP
0x0000002B	PANIC_STACK_SWITCH	Kernel-mode stack overflow. This can be caused by large arrays or objects being allocated on the stack and/or too much (or infinite) recursion.
0x0000002C	PORT_DRIVER_INTERNAL	
0x0000002D	SCSI_DISK_DRIVER_INTERNAL	

Table 9.6: *BugCheck Error Codes (continued)*

Code	Name	Meaning
0x0000002E	DATA_BUS_ERROR	This error is normally caused by a parity error in system memory. It can also be caused by a driver that is accessing an address in the range 0x8xxxxxxx that does not exist. 1. The virtual address that caused the fault 2. The physical address that caused the fault 3. Processor Status Register (PSR) 4. Faulting Instruction Register (FIR)
0x0000002F	INSTRUCTION_BUS_ERROR	
0x00000030	SET_OF_INVALID_CONTEXT	
0x00000031	PHASE0_INITIALIZATION_FAILED	
0x00000032	PHASE1_INITIALIZATION_FAILED	
0x00000033	UNEXPECTED_INITIALIZATION_CALL	
0x00000034	CACHE_MANAGER	
0x00000035	NO_MORE_IRP_STACK_LOCATIONS	You created an IRP that does not have enough stack locations for the layers of drivers it is being processed by. Make sure you have allocated the correct stack size. 1. The address of the IRP
0x00000036	DEVICE_REFERENCE_COUNT_NOT_ZERO	IoDeleteDevice has detected that the Device Object has a non-zero reference count. 1. The address of the Device Object
0x00000037	FLOPPY_INTERNAL_ERROR	
0x00000038	SERIAL_DRIVER_INTERNAL	
0x00000039	SYSTEM_EXIT_OWNED_MUTEX	
0x0000003A	SYSTEM_UNWIND_PREVIOUS_USER	
0x0000003B	SYSTEM_SERVICE_EXCEPTION	
0x0000003C	INTERRUPT_UNWIND_ATTEMPTED	

Table 9.6: *BugCheck Error Codes (continued)*

Code	Name	Meaning
0x0000003D	INTERRUPT_EXCEPTION_NOT_HANDLED	
0x0000003E	MULTIPROCESSOR_CONFIGURATION_NOT_SUPPORTED	The processor chips of a multi-processor are not identical. Processor chips cannot be mixed.
0x0000003F	NO_MORE_SYSTEM_PTES	The system page table is full. The most likely cause is a driver that has not properly released pages. It may also be due to a page table that is too small. A technique for increasing the number of PTEs is discussed in Chapter 12 on page 274.
0x00000040	TARGET_MDL_TOO_SMALL	IoBuildPartialMdl has been passed a target MDL that is too small for the range of addresses required.
0x00000041	MUST_SUCCEED_POOL_EMPTY	You did an allocation from the must-succeed pool, and there are so many outstanding allocations that there is no space left. Make certain you have released any must-succeed allocations you have made. 1. The size of the request that failed 2. The number of pages in use in the Nonpaged Pool 3. The number of too-large PAGE_SIZE requests from the Nonpaged Pool 4. The number of pages available
0x00000042	ATDISK_DRIVER_INTERNAL	
0x00000043	NO_SUCH_PARTITION	
0x00000044	MULTIPLE_IRP_COMPLETE_REQUESTS	The IRP received a second IoCompleteRequest call. 1. Address of the IRP

Table 9.6: *BugCheck Error Codes (continued)*

Code	Name	Meaning
0x00000045	INSUFFICIENT_MAP_REGS	
0x00000046	DEREF_UNKNOWN_LOGON_SESSION	
0x00000047	REF_UNKNOWN_LOGON_SESSION	
0x00000048	CANCEL_STATE_IN_COMPLETED_IRP	IoCompleteRequest was called for an IRP that has an outstanding Cancel function. 1. Address of the IRP
0x00000049	PAGE_FAULT_WITH_INTERRUPTS_OFF	An attempt was made to a nonresident or nonexistent page at a very high IRQL. This error is often caused by an access from within a Spin-Lock-protected area.
0x0000004A	IRQL_GT_ZERO_AT_SYSTEM_SERVICE	
0x0000004B	STREAMS_INTERNAL_ERROR	
0x0000004C	FATAL_UNHANDLED_HARD_ERROR	

0x0000004D	NO_PAGES_AVAILABLE	There are no more free pages left in the system. If WinDbg is active, typing the following commands will give more-useful information.
		
		`!process 0 7`
		`!vm`
		`dd mmpagingfiles`
		`dd @$p`
		
		1. The number of dirty pages
		
		2. The number of physical pages in machine
		
		3. The extended commit value, in pages
		
		4. The total commit value, in pages

Table 9.6: *BugCheck Error Codes (continued)*

Code	Name	Meaning
0x0000004E	PFN_LIST_CORRUPT	The most likely cause is that a MDL was trashed. 1. The constant 1 2. The ListHead that was corrupted 3. The number of pages available 4. The constant 0 or 1. The constant 2 2. Entry in list being removed 3. Highest physical page number 4. Reference count of entry being removed
0x0000004F	NDIS_INTERNAL_ERROR	
0x00000050	PAGE_FAULT_IN_NONPAGED_AREA	
0x00000051	REGISTRY_ERROR	The most likely cause is that the Registry was corrupted by an earlier crash. You will probably have to reinstall NT.
0x00000052	MAILSLOT_FILE_SYSTEM	
0x00000053	NO_BOOT_DEVICE	
0x00000054	LM_SERVER_INTERNAL_ERROR	
0x00000055	DATA_COHERENCY_EXCEPTION	
0x00000056	INSTRUCTION_COHERENCY_EXCEPTION	
0x00000057	XNS_INTERNAL_ERROR	
0x00000058	FTDISK_INTERNAL_ERROR	The system was booted from a revived primary partition, so the hives say the mirror is all right, when in fact it is not. The real images of the hives are on the shadow. You must boot from the shadow.
0x00000059	PINBALL_FILE_SYSTEM	
0x0000005A	CRITICAL_SERVICE_FAILED	
0x0000005B	SET_ENV_VAR_FAILED	

Table 9.6: *BugCheck Error Codes (continued)*

Code	Name	Meaning
0x0000005C	HAL_INITIALIZATION_FAILED	
0x0000005D	UNSUPPORTED_PROCESSOR	
0x0000005E	OBJECT_INITIALIZATION_FAILED	
0x0000005F	SECURITY_INITIALIZATION_FAILED	
0x00000060	PROCESS_INITIALIZATION_FAILED	
0x00000061	HAL1_INITIALIZATION_FAILED	
0x00000062	OBJECT1_INITIALIZATION_FAILED	
0x00000063	SECURITY1_INITIALIZATION_FAILED	
0x00000064	SYMBOLIC_INITIALIZATION_FAILED	
0x00000065	MEMORY1_INITIALIZATION_FAILED	
0x00000066	CACHE_INITIALIZATION_FAILED	
0x00000067	CONFIG_INITIALIZATION_FAILED	
0x00000068	FILE_INITIALIZATION_FAILED	
0x00000069	IO1_INITIALIZATION_FAILED	
0x0000006A	LPC_INITIALIZATION_FAILED	
0x0000006B	PROCESS1_INITIALIZATION_FAILED	
0x0000006C	REFMON_INITIALIZATION_FAILED	
0x0000006D	SESSION1_INITIALIZATION_FAILED	
0x0000006E	SESSION2_INITIALIZATION_FAILED	
0x0000006F	SESSION3_INITIALIZATION_FAILED	
0x00000070	SESSION4_INITIALIZATION_FAILED	
0x00000071	SESSION5_INITIALIZATION_FAILED	
0x00000072	ASSIGN_DRIVE_LETTER_FAILED	
0x00000073	CONFIG_LIST_FAILED	
0x00000074	BAD_SYSTEM_CONFIG_INFO	
0x00000075	CANNOT_WRITE_CONFIGURATION	

Table 9.6: *BugCheck Error Codes (continued)*

Code	Name	Meaning
0x00000076	PROCESS_HAS_LOCKED_PAGES	A process is terminating, but it still has locked pages. This is usually due to a failure to unlock pages in the Unload or Shutdown handlers. 1. The process address 2. The number of locked pages 3. The number of private pages 4. The constant 0
0x00000077	KERNEL_STACK_INPAGE_ERROR	I/O error occurred while reading a page of the Kernel-mode stack.
0x00000078	PHASE0_EXCEPTION	
0x00000079	MISMATCHED_HAL	The kernel and the HAL images are not consistent. This inconsistency can result from improper use of the /kernel and /hal switches in BOOT.INI. See Knowledge Base article Q103059 for a more detailed explanation.
0x0000007A	KERNEL_DATA_INPAGE_ERROR	I/O error occurred while reading pageable kernel data. 1. The lock type that was held (value is 1, 2, 3, or the PTE address) 2. The error status (normally an I/O status code) 3. The current process (virtual address for lock type 3 or the PTE) 4. The virtual address that could not be paged in

Table 9.6: *BugCheck Error Codes (continued)*

Code	Name	Meaning
0x0000007B	INACCESSIBLE_BOOT_DEVICE	During the initialization of the I/O system, the driver for the boot device may have failed to initialize the device that the system is attempting to boot from, or the file system that is supposed to read that device may have either failed its initialization or simply not recognized the data on the boot device as a file system structure. In the former case, the first argument is the address of a Unicode string data structure that is the ARC name of the device from which the boot was being attempted. In the latter case, the first argument is the address of the Device Object that could not be mounted. This error can also be caused by certain configurations of devices that are incompatible, software that is incompatible with NT, a boot-sector virus, or by removing or reconfiguring an ATAPI CD-ROM drive. See also Knowledge Base articles Q103069, Q105026, Q115339, Q120744, Q124307, Q126423, Q131337, Q131712, Q136074, Q137860, Q153296, Q156168, and Q161960.
0x0000007D	INSTALL_MORE_MEMORY	Insufficient memory is available to boot the system. This could be caused by specifying the BOOT.INI /maxmem switch with too small a value. Or you could really have too little memory. 1. The number of physical pages found 2. The lowest physical page 3. The highest physical page 4. The constant 0
0x0000007F	UNEXPECTED_KERNEL_MODE_TRAP	(Intel platforms only) The hardware generated a trap that cannot be handled. 1. The trap code
0x00000080	NMI_HARDWARE_FAILURE	

Table 9.6: *BugCheck Error Codes (continued)*

Code	Name	Meaning
0x00000081	SPIN_LOCK_INIT_FAILURE	The Spin Lock could not be initialized. The conditions that cause this are not well-defined, but they always represent a programming error.
0x00000082	DFS_FILE_SYSTEM	
0x00000083	OFS_FILE_SYSTEM	
0x00000084	RECOM_DRIVER	
0x00000085	SETUP_FAILURE	
0x00000086	AUDIT_FAILURE	
0x0000008A	THREAD_TERMINATE_HELD_MUTEX	
0x0000008B	MBR_CHECKSUM_MISMATCH	This message occurs during the boot process when the Master Boot Record (MBR) checksum the system calculates does not match the checksum passed in by the loader. This is usually an indication of a virus. There are many forms of viruses, and not all can be detected. The newer ones usually can be detected only by a virus scanner that has recently been upgraded. Boot a write-protected disk containing a virus scanner and attempt to clean out the infection. 1. The disk signature from the MBR 2. The MBR checksum computed by the OS Loader 3. The MBR checksum calculated by the system
0x0000008F	PP0_INITIALIZATION_FAILED	
0x00000090	PP1_INITIALIZATION_FAILED	
0x00000091	WIN32K_INIT_OR_RIT_FAILURE	
0x00000092	UP_DRIVER_ON_MP_SYSTEM	
0x00000093	INVALID_KERNEL_HANDLE	
0x00000094	KERNEL_STACK_LOCKED_AT_EXIT	
0x00000095	PNP_INTERNAL_ERROR	
0x00000096	INVALID_WORK_QUEUE_ITEM	

Table 9.6: *BugCheck Error Codes (continued)*

Code	Name	Meaning
0x00000097	BOUND_IMAGE_UNSUPPORTED	
0x00000098	END_OF_NT_EVALUATION_PERIOD	
0x00000099	INVALID_REGION_OR_SEGMENT	
0x0000009A	SYSTEM_LICENSE_VIOLATION	
0x0000009B	UDFS_FILE_SYSTEM	
0x0000009C	MACHINE_CHECK_EXCEPTION	

codes for system messages that do not represent BugCheck codes. There are a few very common causes for system crashes that are easy to induce. These are highlighted in the table. Following each description, if any of the four additional values are meaningful, their (numbered) descriptions follow the description of the error. Some of these conditions are very unusual and have long explanations of their causes or the interpretations of their parameters; we refer you to the Knowledge Base article Q103059.

One very common error is BugCheck 0x1E, KMODE_EXCEPTION_NOT_HANDLED—this is what is shown in Figure 9.21. In the case of some errors, there will be up to four useful values following the stop code on the first line. (Actually, there are either no extra parameters or four, and of the four, not all may be useful.)

- 0xC0000005, which indicates the nature of the unhandled exception.
- The address of the instruction that caused the error.
- The first parameter of the exception (not meaningful for 0xC0000005).
- The second parameter of the exception (not meaningful for 0xC0000005).

This particular error is usually caused by a bad pointer and either accessing memory that does not exist or attempting to write a write-protected page. It can also occur by an accidental overwriting of the return address on the stack due to an erroneous write access to a local array or structure. Note that because the kernel runs using mapped addresses, it is possible to protect pages against writing simply by making their map entries read-only. Unlike most operating systems, the NT kernel does not have unlimited and unrestricted access to every single hardware resource. (Of course, it could change a page table entry to make the page writable, but it can't *accidentally* write to a protected page.) The causes of this error in the kernel are the same as in any user application: uninitialized local variables or pointers in allocated memory, dangling pointers, and writing an incorrect access. For additional KMODE_EXCEPTION_NOT_HANDLED codes, see the include file `winnt.h`. We have summarized the most frequent errors in Table 9.7 on page 204.

The large table of addresses, date stamps, and module names shown in Table 9.6 is intended to help you locate the source of the error if it is in one of the "known" modules. The addresses are the virtual memory addresses in which the module was loaded and are almost always (but not guaranteed to be) the same on every system boot for a given system. In general, if you have an error in one of these modules, it was almost certainly caused by your either passing in a bad

Table 9.7: *Frequently Seen Exception Codes for* KMODE_EXCEPTION_NOT_HANDLED

Exception Code	Meaning
0x80000003	An attempt was made to execute a hard-coded breakpoint in a kernel that was booted without the /debug switch.
0xC0000005	Indicates an access violation: a bad pointer or an attempt to write to a read-only page.
0xC000001D	Indicates an illegal instruction. Either there was an indirect call via a bad pointer or the return address on the stack was clobbered by an out-of-bounds write to a stack array.
0xC0000094	Indicates integer divide by zero.
0xC00000FD	Indicates a stack overflow; usually an infinite recursion.

pointer to a kernel function or corrupting some memory that wasn't yours and thus killing an innocent bystander. Most invalid access errors will come from your own code, at least during initial debugging.

The small stack dump at the bottom of Figure 9.21 is almost but not quite totally useless.

Restarting After an Error

When you crash in a Blue Screen and have the debugger attached, you will not get the complete dump shown in Figure 9.21. Only the first two lines will display on the debug target, and your debugger will get control. This allows you some limited poking and prodding to try to determine the cause of the error. Not all errors will give control to the debugger. In particular, you may have really trashed things to the point where the debugger interface code in the debug target fails. In this case, you will have to restart the system and try for a better insight on what caused the bug.

Usually, you must reset the debug target to get it to reboot. If it doesn't reboot, don't panic yet. Sometimes, particularly with new devices and new drivers, you might have left the hardware in a state in which the device actively interferes with the boot process. Or your error might have caused some other device to enter a state that causes problems. Not all such states are cleared by pressing the Reset button. As one last try, turn off the machine, wait a few seconds, and turn it back on. If it successfully boots, all is well. If it doesn't boot, there is one more recovery technique you can use, the "Last known good" configuration.

The Last Known Good Configuration Recovery Technique

Normally, when NT boots successfully (displays the login box or begins an autologin), it copies the CurrentConfiguration information to a backup configuration. If it fails to boot, that is, it crashes during the boot process, the copy is not made. When the boot process starts, you see a message to strike the spacebar to load the "Last known good" configuration. If the crash occurred because of a change in configuration that caused the boot process to fail before completion, the "Last known good" configuration is the configuration that worked before the change. If, however, the previous boot process actually completed, the boot configuration it used is considered "good" and it becomes the "Last known good" configuration. In this case, you may have to reinstall NT to get around the problem.

The Last Known Good Configuration technique can fail for a couple of reasons, as follows.

- If the crash is caused by a new version of a driver that is started at boot time, the same driver name was started in the "Last known good" configuration (only the driver image has changed), so you are out of luck.

- If the driver loads successfully, the system reaches the login stage, and *then* the driver crashes or hangs, the current configuration has already been copied, and it is too late.

If it doesn't boot after all this, welcome to the Reinstall of the Day Club.[5]

When you reboot, you may find that WinDbg doesn't see the reboot. In this case, you must shut down WinDbg, restart it, and then reboot the debug target yet again.

Do *not* use the `.reboot` command in the 4.0 SDK version of WinDbg. Although this nominally is supposed to do a "warm reboot" of the debug target, in fact either it fails to reset the breakpoints or it somehow loses track of them, in either event because you will not take another breakpoint until you have done a "real" reboot. This appears to be fixed in later versions.

Reading a Crash Dump

System

Figure 9.22:
System applet icon.

You can configure NT to perform a crash dump to disk whenever there is a failure. This works by having NT write the crash dump to the paging file and then, after the system has restarted, copying the crash dump from the paging file to the desired file. You configure this option by using the System applet of the Control Panel, shown in Figure 9.22. Clicking it brings up the System applet. In the System applet, click the **Startup/Shutdown** tab, shown in Figure 9.23. Check the item labeled "Write debugging information to"; if you do not like the default filename provided, `%systemroot%\MEMORY.DMP`, create one of your own. You

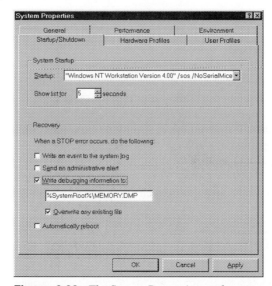

Figure 9.23: *The System Properties applet.*

---

[5] There some workarounds; see our footnote regarding the NTRecover program in Chapter 1 on page 19.

will normally want the crash dump to overwrite an earlier dump. For this to work properly, you must have a paging file *on the boot device* that is large enough to hold an entire snapshot of physical memory. For example, if your debug target has 144MB of memory, you will need a minimum of 144MB of paging file allocated on the boot device.

Once you have done this, any Blue Screen crash will indicate that a dump has taken place. You can then examine this crash dump by using WinDbg. Normally, you should have configured WinDbg to run on your development system, with it pointing to all of the right symbols for the debug target. Thus reading the crash dump is easy. You simply open the crash dump file by running WinDbg on your development machine and use the network to bring over the actual crash dump from the debug target.

Unhandled Exceptions

The BugCheck code KMODE_EXCEPTION_NOT_HANDLED requires you to determine what caused the exception. The most common cause is touching memory that is not locked down or is not in the virtual address space of the thread in which the driver is executing. The result of this exception is the 0xC0000005 exception code, which appears as the first value of the four BugCheck codes summarized in Table 9.7. In some cases, a stack trace may not be possible, perhaps due to corruption of the stack itself that led to the error. If, however, you see the function NT!PspUnhandledExceptionInSystemThread on the stack, you can use the kb command (described in the next section) to display the parameters in the stack trace. The first parameter is a pointer to an exception structure. Using the dd command will display the contents of this exception structure. The first value of the exception structure is a pointer to an *exception record*, which can be displayed using the !exr command. The second value of the exception structure is a pointer to a *context record*, which can be displayed using the !cxr command. This will give you the necessary information for the !kb command, which will give a stack backtrace from the site of the exception.

WinDbg Reference

One problem when reading the WinDbg documentation is to determine which commands are most useful to a Device Driver writer. We summarize the most popular debugger commands in Table 9.8. (A couple of these commands are not useful, but we include them to point out their problems.) Note that many of the commands specify *physical* addresses. These are addresses that are represented by the actual hardware on the target machine, without any memory mapping. If an address is a *virtual* address, it will be specified as other than a physical address. The argument notation is described in Table 9.9 on page 209. This table summarizes both the built-in commands and the *extension* commands (which start with an exclamation point, !).

The extension commands are implemented in a set of .dll files which are specific to the build of NT. The Checked or Free Build each has its own set of DLLs, which are in the \support\debug*platform* (for *platform* either i386 or alpha). Just to make life easy for the developer, you are required to *copy* all of the DLLs from the appropriate version to the directory that contains WinDbg.exe. By default, after installing the SDK and DDK, the directory will contain the Free Build version. As you switch between running the Checked Build and the Free Build, you have to remember to perform this copy operation. Are We Having Fun Yet?

Table 9.8: *WinDbg Commands*

Command	Explanation
*	Starts a comment line.
|	Displays the process status.
~	Displays the thread status.
# *pattern*	Searches for the disassembly pattern.
%	Changes the context.
.ATTACH	Attaches to a process.
.cache [*size*]	Sets the cache size in the host. This cache holds various values from the target machine and is invalidated on each single step or Go command. To enable an examination of memory addresses of memory-mapped devices, the cache size should be set to 0. This command changes the default cache size configured in the debugger options (Figure 9.11).
!cxr *address*	Displays a context record (from an exception).
db [*address* [*range*]]	Displays hexadecimal and ASCII representations starting at the specified virtual address. If *address* is omitted, the dump is done of the 128 bytes following the last db command. If *range* is omitted, 128 bytes are displayed.
!db [*physicaladdress*]	Displays hexadecimal and ASCII representations of 128 bytes starting from the specified physical memory address on the target machine. If *physicaladdress* is omitted, the dump is done of the 128 bytes following the last !db command.
dd [*address* [*range*]]	Displays a hexadecimal dump of 32 ULONG values from the specified virtual memory address on the target machine. If *address* is omitted, the dump is done of the 32 ULONGs following the last dd command.
!dd [*physicaladdress*]	Displays a hexadecimal dump of 32 ULONG values from the specified physical memory address on the target machine. If *physicaladdress* is omitted, the dump is done of the 32 ULONGs following the last !dd command.
!devobj *address*	Displays a list containing information about a specified Device Object. The *address* argument is a pointer to that object. The command displays the device name, the current IRP status, and any pending IRPs in the device's queue.
!drvobj *address*	Displays a list of all Device Objects created by the Driver Object referenced by *address*. This value is usually obtained from examining the DriverEntry parameters after a breakpoint has been set.
!drivers	Displays information about all loaded drivers.

Table 9.8: *WinDbg Commands (continued)*

Command	Explanation
du [*address* [*range*]]	Displays the memory contents at the specified virtual address as a Unicode string. If *address* is omitted, the next 64 memory locations following the last du command are displayed.
!ed *physicaladdress ulong0* [*ulong1 ulong2 ...*]	Writes one or more ULONG values to the physical memory address on the target machine.
!errlog	Displays information about any pending events in the I/O system's Error Log. These are events that have been queued via IoWriteErrorLogEntry but that have not yet been written out. This command can be used after a crash to see any unwritten Event Log messages.
!exr *address*	Displays the formatted contents of the EXCEPTION_RECORD referenced by *address*.
f *thread*	Freezes the thread. The thread will not be schedulable until it is unfrozen using the z command.
!frag [*flags*]	Displays information about fragmentation in the Nonpaged Pool. The two low-order bits of the *flags* argument specify the level of detail displayed.
g	Signifies "go". Execution resumes and will not stop until the next breakpoint, an explicit halt command, or a crash.
!handle [*handle* [*flags* [*process*]]]	
!heap [*address* [*flags* [*process*]]]	Dumps the heap for a process.
!irp *address*	Displays formatted information about the IRP specified by *address*. Does not verify that *address* actually points to an IRP.
k	Displays the stack backtrace.
!kb	Displays a stack trace from the last frame dumped by !cxr or !trap.
!locks [-v] [*address*]	Displays information about a Kernel-mode resource lock at *address*. If *address* is omitted, it dumps information about all Kernel-mode resource locks. Specify -v for verbose mode.
!memusage	Displays summary statistics on physical memory usage, collected from the page frame database.
!object *address*	Displays information about the object at *address*.
!pool	Dumps the kernel heap.
.reboot	Reboots the target machine. After this type of reboot, breakpoints are no longer functional. You must use the Reset button to successfully reboot the debug target.

Table 9.8: *WinDbg Commands (continued)*

Command	Explanation
`.reload`	Reloads symbols. This is usually done after the load states of various DLLs are modified.
`!time`	Displays the `PerformanceCounterRate` and `TimerDifference` values.
`!trap address`	Dumps the machine state that was in effect when the trap occurred. The address is that of the trap frame. On x86 platforms, a trap frame is generated for an interrupt or system call. The kv command allows you to find the trap frame address.
`!vm`	Displays summary statistics about virtual memory usage.
`z thread`	Unfreezes the thread.

Table 9.9: *Command Argument Syntax*

Argument	Explanation	
`physicaladdress`	An expression that evaluates to a physical address on the target machine.	
`address`	An expression that evaluates to a virtual address in the current context on the target machine.	
`range`	Specifies a range of addresses for an operation. Can be one of the forms below:	
	`address`	A second address expression. The operation takes place between the two addresses.
	`L count`	The number of bytes involved in the range.
	`I count`	For the DC and U commands, the number of instructions to display.
`process`	Designates a process ID. Can be one of the specifications below:	
	`|.`	The current process.
	`|number`	The process *number*.
	`|*`	All processes.
`thread`	Designates a thread ID. Can be one of the specifications below:	
	`~.`	The current thread.
	`~number`	Thread *number*.
	`~*`	All threads.
`[anything]`	An optional argument. The square brackets do not appear in the command. They are metasyntactic symbols.	

If in Doubt, Get Hardware Debug Assistance

When all else fails—and inevitably, it will, for some device—you're in deep trouble. You are convinced your driver is correct, but the device doesn't work, and no matter what you do, you can't get the problem to appear when the debugger is loaded and you've got breakpoints set. Now what?

Now is when you have to figure out if the hardware itself is actually correct. Is there a "sneak path" in your driver? Is some other driver you never heard of writing to your device's register? Is the hardware itself faulty? At this point, you get really "down and dirty" and start looking at what is going on.

The levels at which you debug can vary. We discuss hardware debuggers from the simplest to the most complex. These are, in order, a PCI Bus Monitor, a logic analyzer, an in-circuit emulator (ICE), and an oscilloscope. If you're a serious hardware jock, you will ultimately want to *look* at those signals on the bus. But unless you understand what you are looking at, an oscilloscope is mostly decorative. To use these diagnostic tools, it is often necessary to make the card you are working on physically accessible. Trying to couple a few dozen probes to the signal paths of a card inserted in a tight space can be incredibly difficult, and has the additional hazard that a slight twitch of the fingers while making a connection to a live card (powered up) has the potential for shorting something out and destroying the card. To make a card more readily accessible, you use an *extender card*.

Extender Cards

Depending on the hardware and the environment, it may not be possible to actually probe the hardware in place. For some of the techniques we describe, you will need to plug an extender card into the motherboard, and plug the card you are debugging into the extender card, to raise it above the motherboard. The problem is that the extender card can induce failures [that you won't see if the extender card isn't there.] Even the best cards can cause problems if the device is already "at the margins" for timing, drive capacity, or sensitivity. The worst extender cards will fail even for properly implemented devices. It is very important that your extender card not change the behavior of the device being debugged, particularly if you suspect a hardware problem.

One aspect we hesitate to mention is the "gross shipping weight" criterion, which we remap to computer components and their cost.[6] That is, the more expensive card is almost always the better card. Of course, any vendors of marginal ethics reading this will immediately quadruple the price of their low-end cards so that they look better, hence our hesitation to establish the criterion. However, our experience has been fairly consistent.

For example, Figure 9.24 shows a fairly ordinary-looking ISA extender card that can be bought in a common bargain developer parts catalog. Such a card is no bargain, however. What

---

[6] This is also known as the "Mashburn Criterion". It is based on the criterion a mutual friend of ours uses in evaluating tools. When all the specs in the catalog look otherwise identical, compare gross shipping weights. The heavier tool is the better tool, simply because it has more mass to resist wear, provide stability, and resist deformation (particularly important for lathes and vertical mills). In addition to the tool weight, there is the weight of the shipping packaging. The heavier-weight packaging will protect the tool better than lighter-weight packaging will (particularly important for micrometers and vernier calipers).

Figure 9.24: *An ISA extender card.*

doesn't show up on the photo is that it has no ground plane between the front and back. The capacitive and inductive effect of putting this card in, even into an ordinary 8.33MHz ISA backplane, is that not only will the card plugged into this extender fail, but other cards on the backplane will also fail. The failures will be random and impossible to diagnose—you will be pulling out your hair attempting to diagnose your real bugs when random failures are mixed in. (Don't try to read the vendor name from the photo; we smudged it out.) But if you hold a card up to the light and can see through it, it probably won't work.

PCI extender cards are even more difficult to deal with. A PCI Bus has very careful capacitive and inductive loading rules. Adding six inches to its length will cause the entire bus to fail. Instead, a PCI extender card such as that shown in Figure 9.25 must be used. This particular one (model PCIEXT-64, made by NewBus Corporation and sold by VMetro) has not only active components to provide proper loading to each end of the bus, but also a large header onto which logic analyzers can be easily connected. The power applied to the card under test is limited to

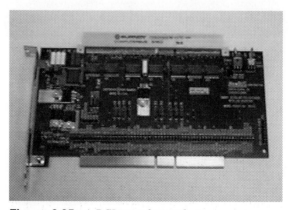

Figure 9.25: *A PCI extender card.*

10W, 15W, or 25W, selected by a small switch. The limit on power can limit the damage done by a short circuit on the card.[7] This card provides a power switch for the power lines to the slot, thereby allowing the card under test to be removed without the system's first being powered down. The switch is not at all useful with NT 4.0 (it is unknown if Windows 2000 will make it useful by providing a mechanism to trigger a PCI Bus re-enumeration).

A PCI extender card might also contain a *PCI Bridge*, thus placing your device on another PCI Bus. A card like this is very handy to have around because it lets you check out your bus enumeration code. You really want to make sure that you can find your device when it *isn't* on PCI Bus 0. A good example of this kind of extender card is produced by Digital Equipment Corporation (DEC 4 Slot PCI Extender with Bridge ZAC-10 94V-01). (As this is being written, it is not known if Compaq, which recently acquired Digital Equipment Corporation, will keep this card in production.) This extender card offers four slots in which you can plug cards: two on the front, one on the top, and one on the back. Note that you must use something to physically support the card (a block of foam or an empty cardboard box works).

We've been told that Catalyst Enterprises is a good source for ISA extender cards. We can only pass on this information; we have not used these extenders.

Expect to spend between $300 and $500 for an extender card; more for a card with a bridge.

The PCI Bus Monitor

The simplest of the hardware tools is the PCI Bus Monitor. It looks remarkably like a PCI card or a PCI Bus extender card; it is a very definitely an active card. The one we've used is shown in Figure 9.26. Basically, a PCI Bus Monitor triggers the bus clock. At each bus clock tick, it stores

Figure 9.26: *The VMetro PCI Analyzer.*

---

[7] One theory is that electronic parts stop working when the internal magic smoke is allowed to escape.

all of the bus signal state appropriate for that tick. Most bus monitors have a significant amount of onboard RAM to hold this information. You can later extract this information using a program that formats it in a human-readable form, such as a state trace or a waveform diagram.

An advanced form of the PCI Bus Monitor allows you to tweak the operating parameters. For example, you can run right at the end of the timing margins or the signal margins to see how reliably the card actually performs. The PCI Bus Specification has fairly stringent specifications of the timing, but within those specifications there is still some wiggle room. Some vendors wiggle more than others. Thus your driver, which works perfectly in Brand A machine, may fail utterly in Brand B machine because the Brand B machine is more sensitive to the specifications. Does this mean the device is out of spec? No; maybe the Brand B machine has misinterpreted the specs and is applying tighter or looser specifications to the interpretation of the signals and simply can't handle the card that meets the specs. Or the card could be out of spec and the Brand A machine will accept more sloppiness than the PCI Bus Specification permits. Only when you can test at the margins can you determine where the fault really lies.

The PCI Bus Analyzer can be used to diagnose hardware or software problems. The use will vary somewhat. To diagnose hardware problems, the hardware engineer will be interested in the data on the bus during each PCI clock cycle. The programmer, however, will be interested in the data only during the clock cycles in which the data is valid.

It is important to keep in mind what the bus analyzer can and cannot do. The analyzer will see, and capture, only what is on the PCI Bus. If there is a PCI Bridge, it will see only the data on one PCI Bus segment. This means that if the source and target of the interesting cycles are on a bridged bus and the analyzer is on another segment, the analyzer will not see the data.

The VMetro PCI Analyzer

The VMetro PBT-315 PCI Analyzer is shown in Figure 9.26. It plugs into the PCI Bus, and the device under test plugs into it. This particular card does not have a PCI Bridge in it, so it leaves your device on the same PCI Bus that it was in when it was plugged directly into the backplane.

The device connects to the host machine via a serial cable. Two forms of display are available:

- A character-oriented display that is sort of clunky
- A GUI interface that is quite nice

The character-oriented display is compatible with several popular "dumb terminals", so you don't really need a separate computer. This setup does assume you know some place that actually sells "dumb terminals" or you have access to a convenient landfill. Character-mode software requires a terminal program that emulates the ANSI cursor control operations. We were unable to get this software to work on Windows NT or Windows 95, but it does work on an old laptop with DOS 3.1 and ANSI.SYS installed. The old laptop was used with the PBT-315 for debugging the most complex of these problems.

The GUI offered a better user interface but could use an update to today's Windows User Interface standards. The version of the Windows software provided with the PBT-315 we used does not execute correctly on a dual-processor Windows NT system, but it does work well on uniprocessor Windows NT 4.0 and beta 5.0 systems.

The trigger signal may be a simple logical combination of signals or a sequence of simple signal combinations. The result of the trigger condition's being satisfied may be either that cycle being captured or every cycle being captured after the trigger (until the memory fills).

Up to eight external inputs can be used. They can be used for trigger expressions and/or stored for display. The external signals are very useful for the signals on the PCI bus that are unique to each card ($\overline{\text{REQ}}$ and $\overline{\text{GNT}}$) or for the signals that may be unique to each card ($\overline{\text{INTA}}$, $\overline{\text{INTB}}$).

A trigger signal may be generated from the PBT-315 and used to trigger an oscilloscope. This trigger signal may represent a simple trigger or the result of a sequence of simple triggers.

Options provide a PCI Bus Anomaly Trigger and a Timing Analyzer. The PCI Bus Anomaly Trigger can detect PCI protocol violations. The Timing Analyzer can capture events on the PCI Bus as short as 5-ns check. Both can be helpful for detecting hardware and compatibility problems.

A particularly useful technique is to capture PCI configuration cycles. Doing this shows the configuration of the devices on the PCI Bus by the PCI BIOS on startup and by the NT HAL when the routine `HalAssignSlotResources` is called.

I've used the VMETRO PBT-315 PCI analyzer to diagnose several difficult problems, problems I would not have found without hardware assistance.

I highly recommend it. *–end*

One time, a bug caused a system crash with a totally black screen. The system was running a very complex product that included several proprietary boards and drivers. One board included a display chip, and the display driver had been modified to work with enhanced hardware.

The modified display driver was the first suspect in the crash. The PCI Bus Analyzer was used to capture the PCI Bus cycles that were writing to the display chip. The display was given the operation code to return it to VGA mode using the ROM BIOS.

There is only one place in NT that returns the display to VGA mode: the Video Miniport function `HwVidResetHw`, a function in the display driver miniport. This function is called when NT crashes and when NT is being shut down in preparation for a soft reboot. For crashes, it is called to allow the Blue Screen of Death to be printed out in a video-adapter-independent way via a call to the VGA ROM BIOS. The standard video driver requires that a large fraction of NT run correctly in order to display a new window.

The cause of the crash was traced to one of the drivers in the system. This was done by noting the PCI accesses to hardware before the crash and then tracing using WinDbg. The cause was initialization code in the `DriverEntry` routine of this driver. *The interrupt in this driver was connected before the data structures used by the interrupt service were available.* This did not cause a problem on the developer's other computers. On these computers, the driver for this device was loaded before any other devices sharing the interrupt were loaded. No interrupts were passed to the ISR of the driver in the timing window between the time of connecting the interrupt and that of initializing the data structure. On the computer that failed, the Ethernet card shared an interrupt and was active in this period. The Ethernet interrupt was passed to this driver first. The driver was expected to look at its hardware, determine if its hardware was the source of the interrupt, and return, indicating that the interrupt was not generated by that hardware. The I/O Manager was then to call the next driver connected to the particular interrupt. The failure was produced by the driver's accessing a data structure in the ISR that had not been initialized yet. The programmer of the failing driver had not considered it a problem when he was coding. He knew his device was not capable of generating an interrupt yet, so he thought it unimportant that the data had not been initialized. (Don't connect an interrupt until your data structures are sufficiently initialized to handle an interrupt on the next memory cycle.)

The Blue Screen of Death was not printed due to another bug. The PCI card was incompatible with the HAL and the PCI BIOS on this particular computer. The ROM address in PCI Configuration Space was not set, the VGA BIOS could not be mapped into memory, and therefore the VGA BIOS calls to print the Blue Screen could not work. *–end*

The Logic Analyzer

A logic analyzer works at a level lower than a PCI Bus Analyzer. With a logic analyzer, you're looking at the raw signals. You then combine these signals into a *trigger signal*, a pattern that is used to start the logic analyzer running. The logic analyzer can then be programmed to store the next *n* clock cycles worth of data. For example, if you're looking for a Write operation to register 0xFA8, you must combine the Write signal, the I/O space signal, and the low-order 12 bits of the data line and then use this combination as a trigger signal. You can next record the data that goes by. In this way, you can tell what data is written to 0xFA8, albeit in a form much harder to interpret than what is provided by the PCI Bus Analyzer.

Sometimes, however, you may have to drop down to this level, especially when the signals you need to analyze are not all on the PCI Bus itself. For example, you might have an incoming signal to your card that is supposed to trigger an interrupt. You might use this external signal as a trigger and start watching the bus traffic that goes by. A PCI Bus Analyzer cannot readily synchronize to multiple external signals (or even on-card, internal signals) that have no representation on the PCI Bus. Modern logic analyzers may be programmed to present data in a formatted manner similar to that of a PCI Bus Analyzer or even an ICE. A bus analyzer, connected to the CPU bus, might even be programmed to disassemble instructions as the processor executes them. (Such a disassembler is a program purchased from the logic analyzer manufacturer, not something coded in one's spare time.)

Yes, there really is a need to monitor bus signals and analyze I/O port write sequences at a level below what a PCI Bus Monitor can do. For one device, it appeared that some of the registers were being written incorrectly. There was nothing to indicate what was causing this. Was it a bug in the driver? Another driver misbehaving? A combination of logic analyzer and PCI Bus Analyzer demonstrated conclusively that there were absolutely *no* write operations going to that register address after the operation was started. However, it *was* correlated with a sequence of write operations to *other* registers. Other register modifications were then found; the damage was happening to random registers. In some cases, the damage had no effect (the registers were not used for the operations on this board). In others, the damage was not noticed.

Once the problem was identified, additional hardware testing by the designer revealed that the problem concerned the ground plane. Currents induced in the ground plane were coupling to signal lines and causing bogus write operations. A board redesign was required to fix the problem. But without the evidence from the hardware diagnostic devices, there was no way to suggest that this was an actual problem in the hardware.

Debugging this device would have been easier if the board (which contained a bridge) had a connector (of any type) for the bridged PCI Bus. This connector and a suitable adapter would have allowed the use of a bus analyzer in place of the logic analyzer. In this case, the board had no space available for such a connector. *–end*

The Oscilloscope

You're desperate, you're a hardware jock, and you *really* have read the PCI Bus Specification. Those cute little "ideal" signal diagrams are OK, but you suspect that the card has a design problem, or possibly even has damage (static electricity is deadly to a PCI card, even at the bus connector level, because the bus transmitter/receivers are CMOS). You need to see if the waveform that is specified is the waveform that is actually there, in the right form, and at *precisely* the right time. Remember that a 66MHz PCI Bus has only a 15-ns clock cycle. That's not much time. (And, contrary to popular legend, the speed of light is *not* 1 foot/ns; it is more like 6 inches/ns, because it is traveling not in a vacuum, but in copper wire. So, depending on the capacitive loading and impedances involved, Your Mileage May Vary.) This means that a long trace on the board can induce a delay that is a significant percentage of the total clock time. Is this what happened? An oscilloscope will tell you, if you know how to ask the right question.

A really sophisticated oscilloscope can even trigger on complex digital signals coming in from a logic-analyzer-like connection, and some logic analyzers (and PCI Bus Analyzers) provide a "trigger" output you can use to trigger an oscilloscope. Even with the slow-decay phosphor, however, you really must watch closely if you want to see what just went by. High-end digital oscilloscopes don't actually display the waveform; they display the reconstructed image that has been sampled from the incoming analog signal and stored digitally. If your company doesn't own an oscilloscope, you might have to rent one.

But if the PCI Bus Analyzer and Logic Analyzer have failed to find the problem, it just might be bad waveforms or signals that are delayed too long or arrive too soon. You can detect this by setting the oscilloscope to "trigger" on one signal while displaying another. This will show the relative timings of the two signals. A sophisticated oscilloscope like the one shown in Figure 9.27 can even use its logic analyzer capability to trigger the display of a waveform so that you can see the actual timing of the signal relative to a complex combination of other signals.

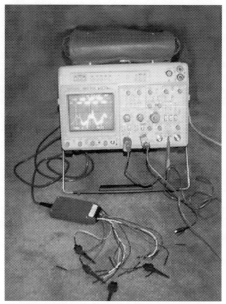

Figure 9.27: *A "fully loaded" Tektronix 4625 oscilloscope showing the logic analyzer pod.*

If Still in Doubt, Rent an ICE–It's Expensive, but So Are You

Debugging Device Drivers is among the most difficult of the Black Arts of Programming. The real-time, nonreproducible nature of a problem makes it extremely intractable.

Consider, for example, the case in which you are trying to debug a new Device Driver for a new piece of hardware. There is no guarantee that the hardware actually *works* or works under "full-load" conditions. It makes no difference how many diagnostics the chips claim to have passed. As with any real piece of hardware, the final "diagnostic" is, "Will it work in the environment it was designed to work in?"

Sometimes the answer is no. Sometimes the answer is, "Well, maybe, if you do these things in this order...". While there are many useful techniques for debugging real-time systems,[8] they may not reveal the actual problem. In this case, there is one last resort. Buy or rent a full-fledged hardware, in-circuit emulator (ICE) system. Based on the oft-quoted number of programmer hours being worth well over $10,000 per month, you can *buy* some ICE systems for the cost of two programmer-months or rent one for three months for the cost of one programmer-month. So what are all those application programmers going to do while they're waiting for the Device Driver? A dozen programmers delayed for a month represent a *very* large expense. And while programmer time is expensive, missing a marketing window is even more so. Either the competition is about to come out with a similar product, or it is the "Christmas shopping season", or you've already rented a booth at COMDEX to show it,[9] or any number of other seriously "hard" deadlines. Weigh the *total* cost of missing a deadline against the cost of renting or buying an ICE ($30,000 to $100,000, fully configured), and you will quickly determine that this is a highly cost-effective solution.

An ICE generally monitors all of the output pins of a processor and gathers the data in real time. Like the PCI Bus Monitor, it stores this information in a fairly large RAM and provides interfaces—either built-in or via a connected PC—to analyze the information in a more readable form. The ICE also allows you to take complete control of the processor, allowing you to stop or start the processor or single-step it at the instruction or even clock cycle level. If your device has an onboard processor, you might need the ICE (or *another* ICE) to watch *its* performance. An ICE can give you essentially line-by-line correlation of the machine code (or assembly code) representation of the program and external information. Is your device timing-sensitive? Is your *driver* timing-sensitive? What *really* happens if two interrupt events occur within 1 ms? Sometimes an ICE is the only way to find out. One powerful feature of an ICE is its ability to display

---

[8] For a few of my favorites, see "Debugging Real-Time Systems", cited in the Further Reading section at the end of the chapter. *–jmn*

[9] Yes, it really happens. We were once given a non-working prototype Printer Driver (and associated printer) three weeks before COMDEX. The client had scheduled a "technology demonstration" for the COMDEX trade show floor and it was necessary for us to produce a "working" driver. We assembled a small team, divided the work, and actually had a "functioning" printer on the trade show floor. We delivered to the client a list of operations to avoid, and operations to emphasize (naturally, this list was ignored). The promised host machine failed to materialize, and as a substitute, a pre-prototype of a third party's new workstation was used. No one had ever used the printer port on this machine before, and after much pain and finger-pointing it was discovered that the printer port was defective. One of the bits of the printer port was stuck "high". There is no atmosphere quite like a pavilion at COMDEX, midnight the Sunday before COMDEX opens. You can smell the frenzy in the air, *especially* if your demo isn't working! (There *are* some good side effects, at least for consultants who bill by the hour. Result: for one of us, a new laptop, and for the other, a new 21" display.) – *end & jmn*

the instructions that occurred *before* the failure, allowing you to step backwards through the instructions to determine the cause. For some ICEs, the more you pay, the bigger instruction backtrace buffer you get.

An ICE is fairly complex to learn and use, so you might be better off renting an ICE, as well as an ICE expert to go with it. The trade-offs depend on all of the considerations we just gave: development cost for months of delays, time-to-market, competitive positioning, and marketing window. So *don't* rule out an ICE based on raw cost.

An ICE has a downside: It is designed for one, and only one, processor implementation. Not one processor family or one processor architecture, if you think of "architecture" as being "the instruction set". An ICE, to function properly, must understand the L1 cache, instruction pipelining, and many other features "hidden" inside that processor "chip" package. (We place quotation marks around "chip" because the package can contain several chips or, in the case of the "Slot 1" design of Pentium Pro machines, there can even be several packages that the ICE must properly understand in order to work correctly.) An ICE has a limited product lifetime. But during that lifetime, it can save your company.

Summary

Debugging a driver is *hard*. What we've covered here is the details of how to set up the basic debugging tool, WinDbg, and recommendations about other debugging techniques and tools you should become familiar with. But don't expect that debugging a driver is like debugging and application, particularly if you are working with new silicon. The more familiar you are with the tools, and the more tools you have readily available, ideally the more productive you will be in the debugging process. Good judgment is required to know which tool to use, and when. But always remember the saying, "Good judgment is the result of experience. Experience is the result of bad judgment".

Product List

SoftICE and Bounds Checker for Windows are available from:
> NuMega Technologies
> 9 Townsend West
> Nashua, NH 03063 USA
> +(603) 578-8400
> +(800) 468-6342
> Web: `http://www.numega.com`

PCI extender cards and the PCI analyzer cards are both available from:
> VMetro, Inc.
> 1880 Dairy Ashford, Suite #535
> Houston, TX 77077 USA
> Phone: +(281) 584-0728
> Fax: +(281) 584-9034
> E-mail: `info@vmetro.com`
> Web: `http://www.vmetro.com`

ISA extender cards are available from:
> Catalyst Enterprises, Inc.
> 1439 Torrington Court
> San Jose, CA 95120 USA
> Tel: +(408) 268-4145
> Fax: +(408) 268-8280
> E-mail: `info@catalyst-ent.com`
> Web: `http://www.catalyst-ent.com`

ICEs are available from a variety of vendors. One we know of is:
> American Arium
> 14281 Chambers Road
> Tustin, CA 92780 USA
> Voice: +(714) 731-1661
> Fax: +(714) 731-6344
> E-mail: `info@arium.com`
> Web: `http://arium.com`[10]

Further Reading

Newcomer, Joseph M., "Debugging Real-Time Systems", *Dr. Dobb's Journal 18, 7* (July 1993). Also on the *Dr. Dobb's Journal on CD-ROM*.

---

[10] Yes, really, there is no www in front of this address!

10 *Approaching Reality: Moving Data*

In this chapter, we cover the `MajorFunction` codes that actually perform I/O, specifically,

- `IRP_MJ_READ`,
- `IRP_MJ_WRITE`,
- `IRP_MJ_DEVICE_CONTROL`, and,
- by implication, `IRP_MJ_INTERNAL_DEVICE_CONTROL`.

The points we emphasize here are how to access data that is passed in. We don't yet tell you what to do with it once you have it, but we can guarantee that you can't do anything with it until you know how to get hold of it. And that's what this chapter is all about.

IRP_MJ_DEVICE_CONTROL and IRP_MJ_INTERNAL_DEVICE_CONTROL

For most drivers other than File System Drivers, most of the work is usually done with the `IRP_MJ_DEVICE_CONTROL` function, which supports the application-level `DeviceIoControl` function. `IRP_MJ_DEVICE_CONTROL` is easier to discuss than are `IRP_MJ_READ` and `IRP_MJ_WRITE`, so we begin here. We also cover the `IRP_MJ_INTERNAL_DEVICE_CONTROL` request.

Just a reminder about how the `DeviceIoControl` function is specified: The *input* parameter is input *to* the `DeviceIoControl` operation, and the *output* parameter is output *from* the `DeviceIoControl` operation. That is, for a bidirectional device for which this is supplying data for I/O, the *input* buffer holds the *output data* to the device and the *output* buffer receives the *input data* from the device. This is a bit confusing, but it is how the operation is designated. It becomes even more complicated when you realize that the "output" buffer can actually be used to provide data *to* the device. In one obscure Microsoft document, we have seen the `DeviceIoControl` input parameter called the "parameters" value and the output parameter called the "data" value, which makes a great deal more sense, but that is not the standard way to refer to them.

`IRP_MJ_DEVICE_CONTROL` and `IRP_MJ_INTERNAL_DEVICE_CONTROL` are essentially identical. They differ in that the latter is issued only by a higher-level Device Driver to a lower-level Device Driver. Thus, the lower-level driver is told that it can be "more trusting" of the information that is being passed down. A Device Driver will frequently skip time-consuming parameter checks for calls from other Device Drivers. The other driver is assumed to have fully checked the parameters before passing them. This optimization can result in a significant increase in system performance. If your driver uses this optimization, be sure to insert parameter-checking code, but omit it for production builds by using conditional compilation.

Buffers for Device Control

The *input* buffer to `DeviceIoControl` will always be *buffered*, independent of the setting of the `TransferType` parameter of the `CTL_CODE` macro. `TransferType` affects only how the *output* buffer is handled.

The transfer method to be used for the output buffer is declared as Buffered or Direct in the `CTL_CODE` macro that defines the IOCTL number. `TransferType` can be defined as one of the four values, `METHOD_BUFFERED`, `METHOD_IN_DIRECT`, `METHOD_OUT_DIRECT`, or `METHOD_NEITHER`, but only one per `CTL_CODE`, e.g., `CTL_CODE(... , METHOD_BUFFERED, ...)` defines `TransferType` as `METHOD_BUFFERED`. However, a macro `CTL_CODE(... , METHOD_IN_DIRECT, ...)` defines `TransferType` as `METHOD_IN_DIRECT`.

These are discrete values and must not be ORed together.

An IOCTL Using Buffered I/O

Buffered operations copy data passing between the system and user address spaces. The application calling a buffered operation passes a pointer to a user buffer. Buffered Output operations specify that the I/O Manager is to copy data from the user buffer to an I/O Manager-allocated system buffer before transferring control to the driver, passing to it the pointer to the system buffer. Buffered Input operations specify that the I/O Manager is to allocate a system buffer, and a pointer to this buffer is to be passed to the Device Driver. The I/O Manager will regain control after the driver completes and copy the data to the user's buffer.

For buffered operation, the `IRP_MJ_[INTERNAL_]DEVICE_CONTROL` Dispatch Routine is passed a single pointer to a buffer that is the maximum of the size of the input and output buffers. The buffered data is addressed by the pointer `Irp->AssociatedIrp.SystemBuffer`. The length of the input buffer, that is, the data sent *to* the driver, is set in the current IRP stack location, `stack->Parameters.DeviceIoControl.InputBufferLength`. The maximum number of bytes that can be written back to the application is specified in `stack->Parameters.DeviceIoControl.OutputBufferLength`. This is shown in Figure 10.1. Note that the only pointer available to the driver is the one to the IRP. Within the

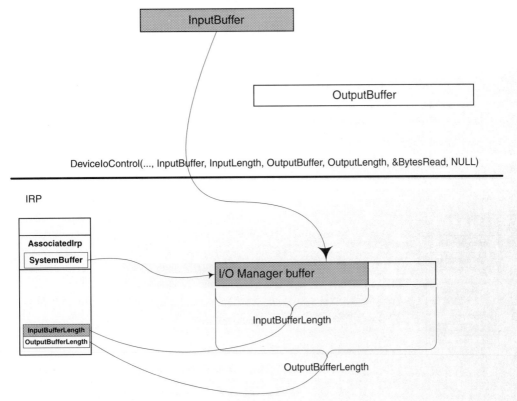

Figure 10.1: *Buffered IOCTL: Calling the driver.*

IRP, it uses the union `AssociatedIrp`. The `AssociatedIrp.SystemBuffer` field contains a pointer to the buffer allocated by the I/O Manager. That buffer is as long as the longest of the input and output buffers. In this example, the output buffer is longer than the input buffer—this longer length dictates the length of the system buffer. When you process the IRP, you can read only the specified number of bytes. The bytes beyond the specified `InputBufferLength` are undefined.

When you have completed reading the input data, you can start writing the output data back to the application. You can write up to the number of bytes specified by the `OutputBufferLength`. *You must not write more than this*. To do so will corrupt some other data structure. However, you can write *fewer* bytes. The number of bytes you actually return to the application is indicated by setting the `Irp->IoStatus.Information` field. This field's value is copied back out to the application as the number of bytes written *and determines how many bytes are copied back*. This is shown in Figure 10.2. Here, the driver has overwritten the input data. (Note that it wrote more bytes than the input buffer length, but that is fine because the buffer is large enough to hold the number of bytes that can be written.) The driver does not have to write *all* of the bytes of the buffer. It then sets the *actual* number of bytes written in the `Information` field. Doing this causes that number of bytes to be copied back to the application-level output buffer and then sets this value in the `BytesWritten` location supplied by the caller. If you fail to set the `Information` field properly, the wrong number of bytes (for example, none, if you set it to 0) will be copied back.

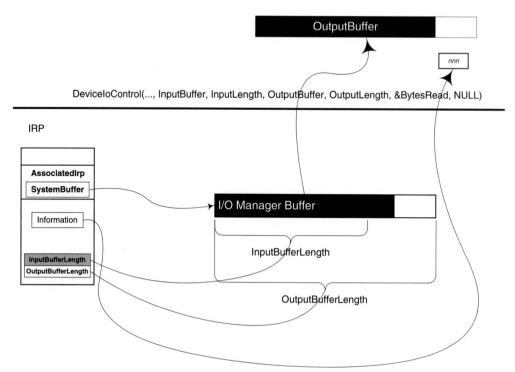

Figure 10.2: *Buffered IOCTL: Returning from the driver.*

If you have an error and set the `Irp->IoStatus.Status` field to other than `STATUS_SUCCESS` before completing the IRP, you must set the `Irp->IoStatus.Information` value to 0.

The driver must complete its read (and possibly copy the data to a temporary location) before any output data is written, since the output data will overwrite the input data.

An IOCTL Using Direct I/O

The `METHOD_IN_DIRECT` is used if the underlying Device Driver will read data from the device. If the underlying Device Driver will write data to the device, `METHOD_OUT_DIRECT` is used. The difference is that for `METHOD_IN_DIRECT`, the user address must point to read/write memory, but for `METHOD_OUT_DIRECT`, it can point to read-only memory.

With Direct transfer, the I/O Manager creates a Memory Descriptor List (MDL) to represent the data buffer, which is the *output* parameter to `DeviceIoControl`. Recall that the MDL is a description of the memory region. The I/O Manager calls a `MmProbeAndLockPages` routine on this MDL. This routine locks the pages of the data buffer into physical memory, paging them in from the paging file if necessary. The MDL contains a list of the physical addresses and sizes of

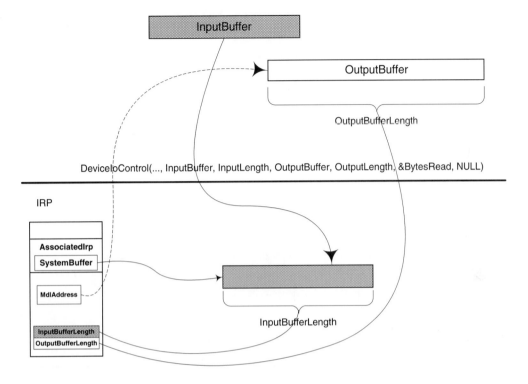

Figure 10.3: *IOCTL using Direct I/O.*

each contiguous chunk of physical address space of the buffer. The driver is passed the MDL in the `Irp->MdlAddress`. It may call `MmGetSystemAddressForMdl(Irp->MdlAddress)` to get the system address for the data buffer for access within the driver. (Alternatively, the driver may use the MDL to set up a DMA transfer.) Remember that the *input* buffer is still buffered, so you will have something like the structure shown in Figure 10.3. The buffered input is still available via the `Irp->AssociatedIrp.SystemBuffer`. The output buffer, however, is accessed directly. Figure 10.3 shows a dotted line from the `Irp->MdlAddress` because the address has not yet been resolved and all of the pages of the output buffer might not be in memory.

Mapped Memory with Direct I/O

An example of the memory setup at the time the I/O Manager is called is illustrated in Figure 10.4. In this case, two of the pages are not even in memory. Note also that although we show links between the MDL and the pages, the MDL is an opaque structure and how this information is represented is not really known. From the application's viewpoint, as shown by the application memory map, these pages are contiguous within the application address space and represent the number of pages that cover the output buffer from its starting address for its length.

Before calling your driver, the I/O Manager calls the `MmProbeAndLockPages` function. This function verifies that the pages are all suitable for the operation. The pages for a buffer that is to

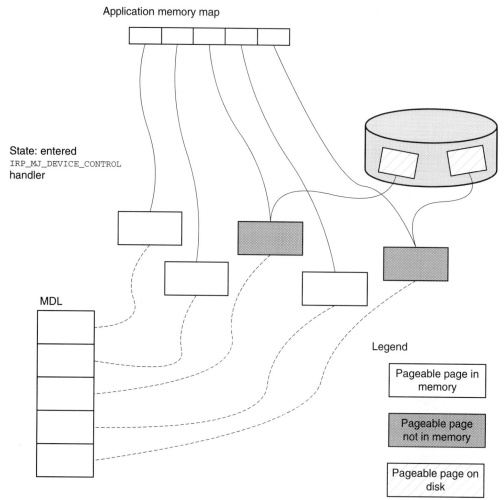

Figure 10.4: *Example of memory configuration for Direct IOCTL.*

receive data must all exist in the application virtual memory and must be writable. The pages for a buffer that is used to send data must all exist in the application virtual memory, but they can be read-only. The MmProbeAndLockPages function then *locks down the pages*. That is, it informs the paging system that these pages must not be removed from memory. It does this by setting appropriate status bits in the appropriate data structures. At the time your driver is called, the configuration is as shown in Figure 10.5. The pages that were on the disk are now in memory and will not be paged out until they are explicitly released by the I/O Manager. The pages, however, are not necessarily in contiguous physical memory; this is illustrated by their random placement in the figure. This doesn't matter, though, because you don't currently have a pointer to them (except the "secret" pointers of the MDL or whatever it uses to represent the pages).

There are many things you can do with these locked pages. For example, you can use a function called IoMapTransfer as part of the setup to do a DMA transfer. However, suppose

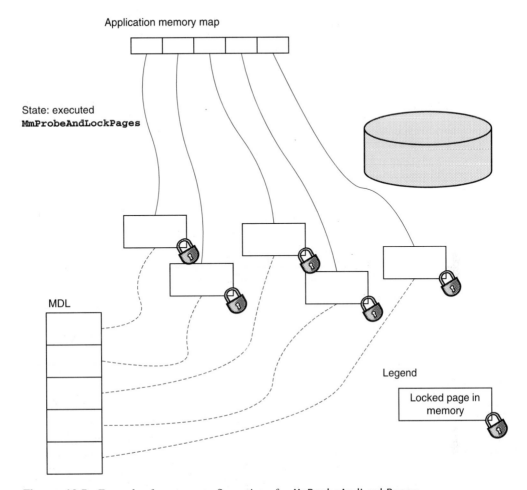

Application memory map

State: executed
MmProbeAndLockPages

MDL

Legend

Locked page in memory

Figure 10.5: *Example of memory configuration after* MmProbeAndLockPages.

you want to do programmed I/O and have the driver write data to the buffer. This presents some problems. You don't actually have an *address* to this data. So the pages are locked, but you need a way of writing to them. To do this, you need a *system virtual address*, which represents the same information about the pages as the application page map but does not depend on which thread is running. (Actually, you have a *user address* of the buffer, but you can't use it in a DPC because you aren't in the context of the process that supplied the address.)

However, after you perform the MmGetSystemAddressForMdl call you do have a system virtual address. This address is, in effect, an address represented by a contiguous sequence of mapping registers. Thus the *mapped* address appears to be to five contiguous pages of virtual memory (in our example). This is an illusion, and if you were going to do DMA, life would get a lot more complicated (exactly *how* complicated is the topic of an entire chapter, Chapter 17). But for non-DMA drivers, you can copy data to these pages without worrying about the physical layout in memory. Note that the system virtual address uses a different set of mapping registers than the application uses because the application map is available only when the application thread is running. The system virtual address map is available at any time any thread is executing any component of the driver. This is shown in Figure 10.6. You can store this address in your Device Extension and can use it in the ISR, the DPC, or, of course, in the Dispatch Routine itself.

An example of the result of copying data is shown in a highly representative fashion in Figure 10.7. In this "scale model", we use five letters to represent 4,096 bytes of actual data copied (this is obviously an *x*86 system, since an Alpha has 8K pages). In the Device Driver, the data `"SAMPLE DATA FROM DEVICE"` was copied to the system virtual address obtained from `MmGetSystemAddressForMdl`. As soon as this was copied to the physical page, it was also visible from the application memory map.

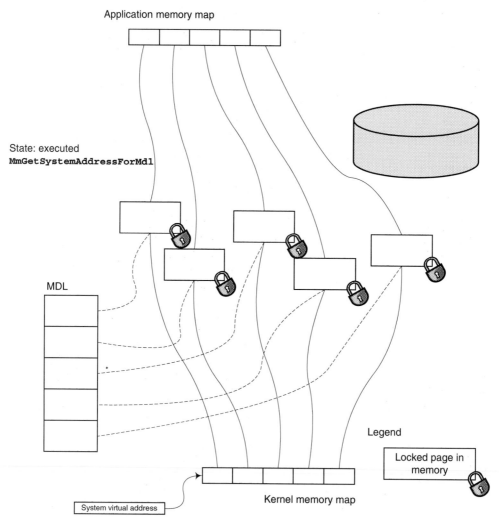

Figure 10.6: *Direct IOCTL with system virtual address.*

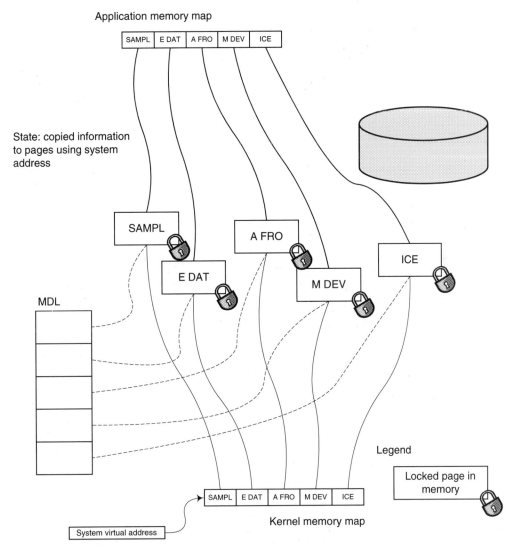

Figure 10.7: *Effect of copying data to the system virtual address.*

After you complete the IRP, the I/O Manager will unlock all of the pages that it locked down with `MmProbeAndLockPages`. To do this, the I/O Manager calls `MmUnlockPages`. The result is shown in Figure 10.8. At the moment this drawing was made, all of the pages were still in memory, but shortly thereafter a couple of them were paged out. Since we were done with the driver, we didn't bother to illustrate this last condition.

A performance problem can arise for Direct I/O if you map the pages into system space. Because, as shown in Figure 10.7, there are *two* page map entries for a given page (called *doubly mapped pages*), a problem with cache coherency can arise. A page that is changed from the driver has a different address than the same page changed from the application. Consequently, the I/O Manager guarantees that the application will see the new data that has been written by the driver by forcing all processors in the system to flush their caches so that future references to

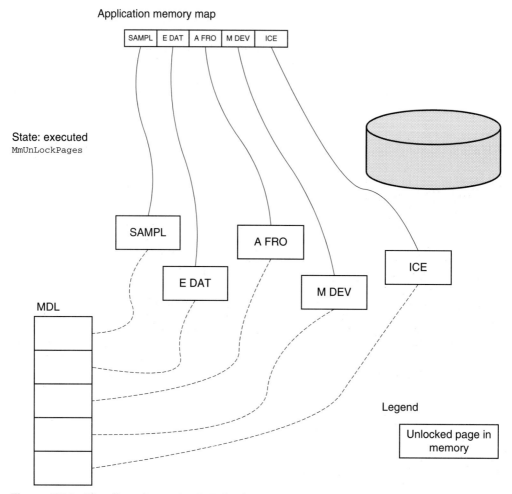

Application memory map

State: executed
`MmUnLockPages`

MDL

Legend

Unlocked page in memory

Figure 10.8: *The effect of executing* `MmUnlockPages`.

the data will force the cache to be reloaded. Devices that do Direct I/O operations extremely often may impact overall system performance.

The Neither Method

The final method, `METHOD_NEITHER`, may be used only if the code which accesses the buffers will execute in the context of the calling thread. The driver can handle such a request only while it is running in the context of the thread that originates the I/O Control request. This means that the driver must either be a top-level driver or be guaranteed that the request will come only from the Dispatch Routine of a top-level driver (or by transitive closure of all drivers in the chain leading to it). Alternatively, you must create your own MDLs "by hand", duplicating all of the work that Direct mode does for you already. This includes doing the `MmProbeAndLockPages` call and the `MmUnlockPages` call that the I/O Manager normally does for you. This is risky. If you leave pages mapped accidentally and the process that owned the pages terminates, the system will Blue Screen.

Method Summary

Buffered transfers are ideal for operations that transfer a small amount of data. The overhead of copying the small buffer will cost less than the cost of creating the MDL and mapping the buffer to system space.

Direct transfers are favored for larger buffers and whenever the I/O may be performed with a DMA transfer with the device.

The Neither method is uncommon because of the additional effort required.

Completion of the Request

The Device Control Routine may either completely process the request and complete the IRP or mark the IRP pending and return control. If the routine is marked pending, the IRP must be completed in a DPC such as one invoked from an interrupt or by a timer.

To complete the IRP, you must set the `Irp->IoStatus.Information` field to the size of the buffer transferred by the driver. For Buffered output, the field will be the number of bytes the I/O Manager is to copy back to the user buffer. The `Irp->IoStatus.Status` field must be set to the return code (STATUS_SUCCESS for successful operations) and `IoCompleteRequest` be called. The Dispatch Routine will usually return with the same status code stored in the `IoStatus` structure. If `Irp->IoStatus.Status` is set to *other* than STATUS_SUCCESS and the IRP is completed (as opposed to being left pending), you should set the `Irp->IoStatus.Information` field to 0. A successful completion of an IOCTL is shown in Figure 10.2.

Example: Buffered IOCTL

This example is taken from our hardware simulator, which is included in its entirety as part of the software that accompanies this book. This simulator, for purposes of considering this code, reads the contents of six internal state register locations and then writes into up to six of those same locations (as determined by a bit mask that accompanies the operation). It can also force an interrupt to occur on a selected IRQ line. The IRQ level that is set can be read or written. For more details of this simulator, see Chapter 27. Here, we look only at the `DeviceIoControl` handler.

Declarations and Interface

As usual, we start with a specification of what the `DeviceIoControl` operation looks like. The operations we chose for the simulator are shown in Table 10.1.

We define the data structures used in a header file that can be shared between the driver and the application that uses it. Note that we do *not* define anything in this header file that is *not* relevant to the application writer (minimizing header files is seldom a useful exercise!).

We include here the excerpts from the header file. We needed to assign a device type that is in the range 32768..65535. After a few coin tosses, we ended up with the value 43000. (It is not clear what the significance of this value is, since presumably you will never send an IOCTL destined for one device to a different device, but this adds a bit of extra protection.) The IOCTL code is likewise chosen, in this case to be in the "user-defined" range of 2048..4095.

Table 10.1: *Simulator* `DeviceIoControl` *Operations*

IOCTL	Input	Output	Meaning
`IOCTL_HDW_SIM_SET_INTR`	Interrupt number structure	NULL	Sets the interrupt vector to be called.
`IOCTL_HDW_SIM_GEN_INTR`	NULL	NULL	Generates an interrupt on the selected line.
`IOCTL_HDW_SIM_REGS`	Pointer to the structure to be written to simulated registers	Pointer to the structure to a receive copy of simulated registers	Reads the current copy of registers and then writes a new copy of the registers.
`IOCTL_HDW_SIM_GET_TRACE`	NULL	Pointer to location that gets debug mask	Reads a copy of the debug mask.
`IOCTL_HDW_SIM_SET_TRACE`	Pointer to the location that contains the debug mask	NULL	Sets the debug mask.

When you create a header file for the IOCTLs, be certain that it contains *only* the declarations an application writer would need. Do not clutter it up with various constants and macros you use to write your driver. These driver-related definitions belong in a separate header file, one used only by the driver source. The driver source and the application source will share the IOCTL definitions.

Listing 10.1: *IOCTL Declarations for Sample Program*

```
#define HDW_SIM_TYPE (ULONG)43000      // 32768..65535 "User defined" range
#define HDW_SIM_IOCTL_BASE (USHORT)2833 // 2048..4095 "User defined" range

enum
    {
    HDW_SIM_IOCTL_INITIALIZE  = HDW_SIM_IOCTL_BASE,
    HDW_SIM_IOCTL_SET_INTR,
    HDW_SIM_IOCTL_GEN_INTR,
    HDW_SIM_IOCTL_REGS,
    HDW_SIM_IOCTL_SET_TRACE,
    HDW_SIM_IOCTL_GET_TRACE
    };

/*************************************************************************
*                       IOCTL_HDW_SIM_SET_INTR
* Inputs:
*       InBuffer: LPHDW_SIM_SET_INTR
*       InBufferSize: sizeof(HDW_SIM_SET_INTR)
*       OutBuffer: NULL
*       OutBufferSize: 0
* Result: BOOL
*
* Effect:
*       Sets the IRQ line to be used for generating IRQs
*************************************************************************/
```

```
#define IOCTL_HDW_SIM_SET_INTR \
    CTL_CODE(HDW_SIM_TYPE,  HDW_SIM_IOCTL_SET_INTR, METHOD_BUFFERED, \
                                      FILE_WRITE_DATA)


/**************************************************************************
*                        IOCTL_HDW_SIM_GEN_INTR
* Inputs:
*        InBuffer: NULL
*        InBufferSize: 0
*        OutBuffer: NULL
*        OutBufferSize: 0
* Result: BOOL
*
* Effect:
*        Generates an IRQ request on the previously-established IRQ line
***************************************************************************/
#define IOCTL_HDW_SIM_GEN_INTR \
    CTL_CODE(HDW_SIM_TYPE,  HDW_SIM_IOCTL_GEN_INTR, METHOD_BUFFERED, \
                                      FILE_WRITE_DATA)


/**************************************************************************
*                        IOCTL_HDW_SIM_REGS
* Inputs:
*        InBuffer: LPHDW_SIM_REGS: Pointer to register structure which has
*                              a valid write bitmap (may be 0)
*        InBufferSize: sizeof(HDW_SIM_REGS)
*        OutBuffer: LPHDW_SIM_REGS: Pointer to a place to put new register
*                              values
*        OutBufferSize: sizeof(HDW_SIM_REGS)
* Result: BOOL
*
* Effect:
*        Reads all current register values into the OutBuffer, then writes
*        the selected register values from the InBuffer
***************************************************************************/

#define IOCTL_HDW_SIM_REGS  \
    CTL_CODE(HDW_SIM_TYPE,  HDW_SIM_IOCTL_REGS, METHOD_BUFFERED, \
                                  FILE_WRITE_DATA | FILE_READ_DATA)


/**************************************************************************
*                        IOCTL_HDW_SIM_GET_TRACE
* Inputs:
*        Input: unused, can be NULL
*        Output: at least sizeof(HDW_SIM_DEBUGMASK)
* Result: BOOL
*
* Effect:
*        Retrieves the current state of the debug mask
***************************************************************************/
#define IOCTL_HDW_SIM_GET_TRACE  \
    CTL_CODE(HDW_SIM_TYPE,  HDW_SIM_IOCTL_GET_TRACE, METHOD_BUFFERED, \
                                          FILE_READ_DATA)
```

```
/****************************************************************************
*                          IOCTL_HDW_SIM_SET_TRACE
* Inputs:
*        Input: at least sizeof(HDW_SIM_DEBUGMASK)
*        Output: unused, can be NULL
* Result: BOOL
*
* Effect:
*        Sets a new state of the debug mask
****************************************************************************/
#define IOCTL_HDW_SIM_SET_TRACE   \
    CTL_CODE(HDW_SIM_TYPE,  HDW_SIM_IOCTL_SET_TRACE, METHOD_BUFFERED, \
                                                     FILE_WRITE_DATA)
```

These are the data structures that we pass in. For convenience we also define a data
structure that is the union of all of the component data structures.

```
typedef struct _HDW_SIM_REGS
    {
    UCHAR writeBitmap;             // used on write, ignored on read
    UCHAR registers[6];            // actual register image
    ULONG interrupt_IDT;           // ignored on write, filled in on read
    ULONG interrupt_Line;          // ignored on write, filled in on read
    } HDW_SIM_REGS, * LPHDW_SIM_REGS, *PHDW_SIM_REGS;

// This macro is used to set the bit in the bitmap based on the
// register index
#define WRITE_BITMAP(r) (1 << (r))

typedef struct _HDW_SIM_SET_INTR
    {
    ULONG interrupt_Line;
    } HDW_SIM_SET_INTR, * LPHDW_SIM_SET_INTR, *PHDW_SIM_SET_INTR;
typedef struct _HDW_SIM_DEBUGMASK
    {
    ULONG value;
    } HDW_SIM_DEBUGMASK, * LPHDW_SIM_DEBUGMASK, * PHDW_SIM_DEBUGMASK;
// DebugMask bits
#define DEBUGMASK_TRACE_REGISTERS 0x00000002 //
#define DEBUGMASK_TRACE_IOCTLS    0x00000004 //

typedef union _HDW_SIM_DATA_OUTPUT
    {
    HDW_SIM_REGS registers;
    HDW_SIM_DEBUGMASK mask;
    } HDW_SIM_DATA_OUTPUT, * LPHDW_SIM_DATA_OUTPUT, *PHDW_SIM_DATA_OUTPUT;

typedef union _HDW_SIM_DATA_INPUT
    {
    HDW_SIM_REGS registers;
    HDW_SIM_SET_INTR setInterrupt;
    HDW_SIM_DEBUGMASK mask;
    } HDW_SIM_DATA_INPUT, * LPHDW_SIM_DATA_INPUT, *PHDW_SIM_DATA_INPUT;
```

Sample Usage: Application Level

To demonstrate how this simulator is used, we show you some excerpts from an application program, the Hardware Simulator Driver (whose source code is included with the software for this
book). Listing 10.2 shows a `DeviceIoControl` that only reads the registers. It has a dummy

"write block" that is essentially ignored because its `writeBitMap` field is set to 0. However, the interface specification requires that the input parameter be present.

Listing 10.2: *Using* `DeviceIoControl` *to Call a Driver*

```
DWORD BytesRead = 0;
HDW_SIM_REGS nothing;

nothing.writeBitmap = 0;                            // Nothing to write
BOOL result = DeviceIoControl(
                  simulator,                        // Simulator device
                  IOCTL_HDW_SIM_REGS,
                  &nothing,                         // Empty register write set
                  sizeof(nothing),
                  &SimulatedRegisters,              // Place to put result
                  sizeof(SimulatedRegisters),       // Size
                  &BytesRead,                       // How many read
                  NULL);                            // Not overlapped
```

Listing 10.3: `IRP_MJ_DEVICE_CONTROL` *for a Sample Driver*

```
NTSTATUS HdwSimDeviceControl(
                            IN PDEVICE_OBJECT DeviceObject,
                            IN PIRP Irp )
{
    NTSTATUS ret = STATUS_SUCCESS; // assume success unless changed
    PIO_STACK_LOCATION stack;
    HDW_SIM_DATA_OUTPUT * pOutBuffer;
    HDW_SIM_DATA_INPUT  * pInBuffer;
    PHDW_SIM_DEVICE_EXTENSION extension;
    NTSTATUS status;
    extension = DeviceObject->DeviceExtension;
```

The following code illustrates how to use the debug mask to conditionally trace events within the driver. We have also added an IOCTL code that allows us to set this mask dynamically.

```
if(extension->debugMask & (DEBUGMASK_TRACE_IOCTLS |
                           DEBUGMASK_TRACE_REGISTERS))
    { /* trace */
      KdPrint( ("HdwSim: Device Control!!\n") );
    } /* trace */
```

The pointers to the buffers are found in the IRP stack. We are using buffered IOCTL codes, so there is actually a single buffer that is used for both input and output. We use it to copy the input data to the device; we can use the same buffer to create the output data. The size of the buffer is the maximum of the specified input buffer size and output buffer size specified to the `DeviceIoControl` *operation. Note that if we have to generate the output data before we have read the input data, we will have to make our own copy of the input data. Consequently, our two pointers,* `pInBuffer` *and* `pOutBuffer`, *actually point to the same area and are used essentially as additional documentation of what is going on.*

```
stack = IoGetCurrentIrpStackLocation(Irp);
pInBuffer = (HDW_SIM_DATA_INPUT *)Irp->AssociatedIrp.SystemBuffer;
pOutBuffer = (HDW_SIM_DATA_OUTPUT *)Irp->AssociatedIrp.SystemBuffer;
```

Next, we actually dispatch on the IoControlCode. *Note that we dispatch on the entire 32 bits of the code:*

```
switch(stack->Parameters.DeviceIoControl.IoControlCode)
   { /* IoControlCode */
```

These two cases allow the Hardware Simulator Driver application to read and set the trace flag. (We have omitted all conditional trace code from these cases to reduce space on the page. The actual Hardware Simulator Driver contains conditional trace statements for each case.)

```
case IOCTL_HDW_SIM_SET_TRACE:
            extension->debugMask = pInBuffer->mask.value;
            Irp->IoStatus.Information = 0;
            break;
case IOCTL_HDW_SIM_GET_TRACE:
            pOutBuffer->mask.value = extension->debugMask;
            Irp->IoStatus.Information = sizeof(HDW_SIM_DEBUGMASK);
            break;
```

This IOCTL code allows us to change the IRQ level at which the Hardware Simulator Driver will generate interrupts. Furthermore, this value is updated in the Registry so that the next time the driver starts up, it will use the latest setting.

```
case IOCTL_HDW_SIM_SET_INTR:
            extension->interrupt_Line =
                            pInBuffer->setInterrupt.interrupt_Line;

            extension->Level  = extension->interrupt_Line;
            extension->Vector = extension->interrupt_Line;
```

Since we have now established a new interrupt line, we need to call HalGetInterruptVector. *This is because the mapped system vector is what we need to generate the simulated interrupt. This call returns no data, so we set the* Information *field to 0.*

```
            extension->mappedSysVect = HalGetInterruptVector(
                    Isa,
                    0,                      // BusNumber,
                    extension->Level,       // Level
                    extension->Vector,      // Vector,
                    &extension->irql,       // IRQL
                    &extension->Affinity);  // Affinity mask
//
// Save mapping in registry
//
```

```
        ret = saveConfig(
             extension->ephemeralRegistryPath.Buffer,
             extension->interrupt_Line,
             extension->interrupt_IDT,
             (VOID *)extension->pSimulatedRegisterLogicalAddress,
             extension->pSimulatedRegisterPhysicalAddress
                          );
   Irp->IoStatus.Information = 0;
   break;
```

This is the most complex of the cases. This call will read the register values that are current in the simulator and then write new values to the simulated registers. Only some of the register values may be stored because there is a bit mask that indicates which registers to update. Because we want to write back the old contents of the simulated register set before we modify them, we actually must make a copy of the buffer contents. We then copy the current simulated register set to the buffer and use the copy we made to modify those simulated registers.

```
case IOCTL_HDW_SIM_REGS:
        {
        HDW_SIM_REGS inBuf = pInBuffer->registers;    // COPY

        pOutBuffer->registers.registers[INDEX_inCommand] =
               extension->simulatedRegister[INDEX_inCommand] ;
        pOutBuffer->registers.registers[INDEX_inStatus] =
               extension->simulatedRegister[INDEX_inStatus] ;
        pOutBuffer->registers.registers[INDEX_inData] =
               extension->simulatedRegister[INDEX_inData] ;
        pOutBuffer->registers.registers[INDEX_outCommand] =
               extension->simulatedRegister[INDEX_outCommand] ;
        pOutBuffer->registers.registers[INDEX_outStatus] =
               extension->simulatedRegister[INDEX_outStatus] ;
        pOutBuffer->registers.registers[INDEX_outData] =
               extension->simulatedRegister[INDEX_outData] ;
        pOutBuffer->registers.interrupt_Line =
               extension->interrupt_Line;
        pOutBuffer->registers.interrupt_IDT =
               extension->interrupt_IDT;

        if (writeBitmap_inCommand & inBuf.writeBitmap)
            {
            extension->simulatedRegister[ INDEX_inCommand] =
                inBuf.registers[INDEX_inCommand];
            }
        if (writeBitmap_inStatus & inBuf.writeBitmap)
            {
             extension->simulatedRegister[ INDEX_inStatus] =
                 inBuf.registers[INDEX_inStatus];
            }
        if (writeBitmap_inData & inBuf.writeBitmap)
            {
             extension->simulatedRegister[ INDEX_inData] =
                 inBuf.registers[INDEX_inData];
            }
        if (writeBitmap_outCommand & inBuf.writeBitmap)
            {
             extension->simulatedRegister[ INDEX_outCommand] =
```

```
                              inBuf.registers[INDEX_outCommand];
                     }
            if (writeBitmap_outStatus & inBuf.writeBitmap)
                     {
                       extension->simulatedRegister[ INDEX_outStatus] =
                              inBuf.registers[INDEX_outStatus];
                     }
            if (writeBitmap_outData & inBuf.writeBitmap)
                     {
                       extension->simulatedRegister[ INDEX_outData] =
                              inBuf.registers[INDEX_outData];
                     }

            Irp->IoStatus.Information = sizeof(HDW_SIM_REGS);
            }
         break;
```

This IOCTL generates an interrupt that the driver talking to this simulated hardware device will then process.

```
       case IOCTL_HDW_SIM_GEN_INTR:
               generateInterrupt((UCHAR)extension->interrupt_IDT);
               break;
```

It is always a good idea to make sure you have covered all of the cases, including the ones in which you have no interest. This code will return an error code that will eventually be returned to the user as a failure code. The GetLastError *function will return an error code based on this value.*

```
       default:
               ret = STATUS_UNSUCCESSFUL;
   } /* IoControlCode */

   Irp->IoStatus.Status = ret;
   IoCompleteRequest( Irp, IO_NO_INCREMENT );
   return ret;
}
```

IRP_MJ_READ and IRP_MJ_WRITE

The Read and Write Dispatch Routines are called to implement the user ReadFile(Ex) and WriteFile(Ex) operations. These operations are frequently implemented by a single function within the driver, since the processing is similar or identical, in that the request is merely queued up for later processing. The driver may complete processing within the Dispatch Routine or later in a DPC triggered by an interrupt or a timer.

Disk drivers often will use the routine implementing the Read function to implement the Verify Device Control.

Buffers for Read and Write

The transfer method for input or output buffers used in the IRP_MJ_READ and IRP_MJ_WRITE functions is controlled by the Device Object Flags field. After the driver creates the Device

Object, it initializes the `Flags` field. This field can have several flag values ORed together. If the initialization of the `Flags` field includes `DO_BUFFERED_IO` or `DO_DIRECT_IO` flags, the transfer method will be Buffered or Direct. If the `Flags` field is not initialized, the transfer method is Neither.

The same transfer method will be used for both Read and Write operations. You cannot specify a device that does Buffered I/O in one direction and Direct I/O in the other.

Buffered Mode for `IRP_MJ_READ` and `IRP_MJ_WRITE`

Buffered operation copies data passing between the system and user address spaces. The application calling a Buffered operation passes a pointer to a user buffer. Buffered Output operations specify that the I/O Manager is to copy data from the user buffer to an I/O Manager-allocated system buffer before transferring control to the driver, passing it the pointer to the system buffer. Buffered Input operations specify that the I/O Manager is to allocate a system buffer and that a pointer to this buffer is to be passed to the Device Driver. The I/O Manager will regain control after the driver completes and copy the data to the user's buffer.

In Buffered mode, the Read or Write Dispatch Routine is passed a pointer to a buffer that is the size of the input or output buffer. The buffered data is addressed by the pointer `Irp->AssociatedIrp.SystemBuffer`. The length of a read buffer for an `IRP_MJ_READ` operation is `stack->Parameters.Read.Length` and is stored in the IRP stack. The length of a write buffer for an `IRP_MJ_WRITE` operation is also stored in the IRP stack, at `stack->Parameters.Write.Length`. This is shown in Figure 10.9. These lengths are stored in the IRP stack because the IRP could be modified as it descends through a set of layers. For example, an IRP to create a file starts life as an `IRP_MJ_CREATE` IRP, but as it descends the driver chain, it can become (by changing the stack location for the lower-level driver) a Read operation to read the directory or a Write operation to update the directory. An `IRP_MJ_READ` operation might become an `IRP_MJ_WRITE` to update the date-last-read. Thus the I/O buffers are always local to the current IRP stack location.

Direct input is used if the underlying Device Driver will read data from the device. If the underlying Device Driver will write data to the device, `METHOD_OUT_DIRECT` is used.

Direct I/O Mode for `IRP_MJ_READ` and `IRP_MJ_WRITE`

With Direct transfer, the I/O Manager creates an MDL to represent the data buffer. The I/O Manager calls a `MmProbeAndLockPages` routine on this MDL that locks the pages of the buffer into physical memory, paging them in from the paging file if necessary. The MDL will contain a list of the physical addresses and sizes of each contiguous chunk of physical address space of the buffer. The driver is passed the MDL in the `Irp->MdlAddress`. The driver may call `MmGetSystemAddressForMdl(Irp->MdlAddress)` to get the system address for the buffer for access within the driver. (Alternatively, the driver may use the MDL to set up a DMA transfer.) The use of the MDL for `IRP_MJ_READ` or `IRP_MJ_WRITE` is exactly like the use for `IRP_MJ_DEVICE_CONTROL`, as shown in Figure 10.4 through Figure 10.8. You can follow the logic we show there to see how the MDL is handled. The only difference will be the access checking: For `IRP_MJ_READ`, the buffer must be writable.

Neither Mode for `IRP_MJ_READ` and `IRP_MJ_WRITE`

The final method, `METHOD_NEITHER`, may be used only if the Dispatch Routine will execute in the context of the calling thread. The driver can handle such a request only while it is running in

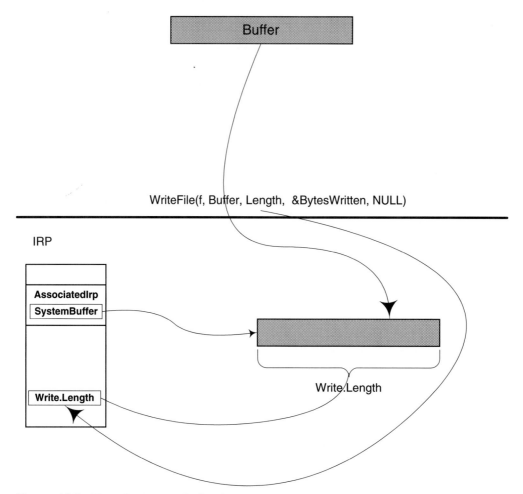

Figure 10.9: `IRP_MJ_WRITE` *in buffered (*`DO_BUFFERED_IO`*) mode.*

the context of the thread that originates the I/O control request. This means that the driver must either be a top-level driver or be guaranteed that the request will come only from the Dispatch Routine of a top-level driver (or by transitive closure of all drivers in the chain leading to it).

Buffered transfers are ideal for operations that transfer a small amount of data. The overhead of copying the small buffer will cost less than the cost of creating the MDL and mapping the buffer to system space.

Direct transfers are favored for larger buffers and for whenever the I/O may be performed with a DMA transfer with the device.

Completion of the Request

The Dispatch Routine can either completely process the request and complete the IRP or mark the IRP pending and return control. In the latter case, the IRP must be completed in a DPC that results from an interrupt or a timer.

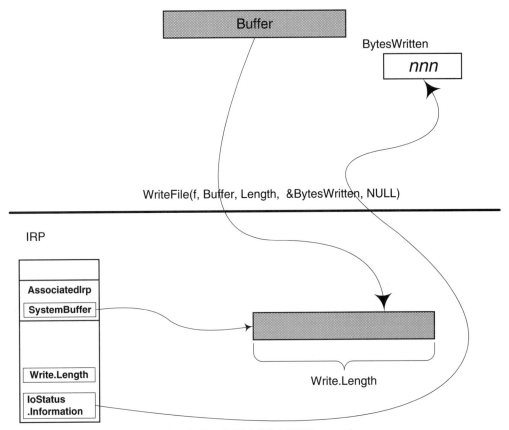

Figure 10.10: *Completion of the (buffered)* IRP_MJ_WRITE *operation.*

To complete the IRP, you must set the Irp->IoStatus.Information field to the size of the buffer transferred by the driver. For buffered IRP_MJ_READ, the field will be the number of bytes the I/O Manager is to copy back to the user buffer. For any form of IRP_MJ_WRITE or IRP_MJ_READ, this value is returned as the value stored for the *BytesWritten* or *BytesRead* parameter to WriteFile(Ex) or ReadFile(Ex) (the fourth parameter, the LPDWORD value). The Irp->IoStatus.Status field must be set to the return code (STATUS_SUCCESS for successful operations), and IoCompleteRequest is called. The Dispatch Routine will usually return with the same status code stored in the IoStatus structure.

When the I/O Manager completes the IRP, it copies the contents of the IoStatus.Status field, as shown in Figure 10.10.

Example: Buffered IRP_MJ_READ *and* IRP_MJ_WRITE Completed in Dispatch

Here, we discuss an example of a very simple driver that simulates a storage device, shown in Listing 10.4 and Listing 10.5. It has two operations, Read and Write, that write a block of data to the "device". Any such operation can be only of the one, fixed "block size" this device supports. A WriteFile(Ex) operation writes a block of data by calling the driver with IRP_MJ_WRITE;

the ReadFile(Ex) operation reads that block of data back by calling the driver with
IRP_MJ_READ. Since the device contains only one block of storage, any ReadFile reads back
that one block and any WriteFile operation overwrites it. This action enforces the block size by
refusing to process any I/O request that has an incorrect block size, that is, one that differs from
the only one it supports. This allows us to demonstrate parameter validation.

Listing 10.4: *The* DriverEntry *Routine for Buffered I/O*

```
NTSTATUS DriverEntry(PDRIVER_OBJECT DriverObject, PUNICODE_STRING registry)
{
    ...
    ntStatus = IoCreateDevice(
                DriverObject,           // Our Driver Object
                sizeof( THE_EXTENSION ), // Size of state information
                &ntUnicodeString,       // Device name "\Device\The"
                FILE_DEVICE_UNKNOWN,    // Device type
                0,                      // Device characteristics
                FALSE,                  // Exclusive device
                &deviceObject );        // Returned ptr to Device Object
    if ( !NT_SUCCESS( ntStatus ) )
        {
         // process error creating device object
        }

    deviceObject->Flags |= DO_BUFFERED_IO;
    DriverObject->MajorFunction[IRP_MJ_READ] = TheReadWrite;
    DriverObject->MajorFunction[IRP_MJ_WRITE] = TheReadWrite;

    ...
}
```

Listing 10.5: *The Read/Write Handler for Buffered I/O*

```
NTSTATUS TheReadWrite(
    IN PDEVICE_OBJECT DeviceObject,
    IN PIRP Irp
    )
{
```

*This routine is called to handle both read and write because there is very little differ-
ence between what read and write actually do. Inside this function, we split out the two
cases where it matters. This function returns* STATUS_SUCCESS *if there is no problem
and* STATUS_INVALID_PARAMETER *if there is a parameter error. We could have chosen
the more obvious implementation of two separate routines, but we chose this route as
an opportunity to demonstrate a fairly common driver technique.*

```
    //
    // Set up necessary object and extension pointers.
    //
    PTHE_EXTENSION  theExtension = DeviceObject->DeviceExtension;
    PIO_STACK_LOCATION  stack  = IoGetCurrentIrpStackLocation( Irp );
```

This variable holds a pointer to the buffer that has been provided for reading or writing. This buffer has already been checked to ensure the correct access is supported and, because this is Buffered I/O, is known to be in nonpaged system storage.

```
PUCHAR TheSystemAddress = Irp->AssociatedIrp.SystemBuffer;
```

This device returns a fixed amount of information for each Read operation. Thus the number of bytes to be copied back to user space is known and is (supposedly) the same number as that the user actually asked to read. We set that value in the `Irp->IoStatus.Information` *field. If the user has called this function with the incorrect length, we will detect that condition later and fail the operation.*

```
Irp->IoStatus.Information = stack->Parameters.Read.Length;
```

We now distinguish between the read and write functions.

```
switch (stack->MajorFunction)
    { /* MajorFunction */
    case IRP_MJ_READ:
     //
     // Check for invalid parameters. The buffer must be the proper length
     //
        if (stack->Parameters.Read.Length != THE_BUFFER_LENGTH)
            { /* bad read length */
             Irp->IoStatus.Status = STATUS_INVALID_PARAMETER;
             Irp->IoStatus.Information = 0; // Set to 0 on error
             IoCompleteRequest( Irp, IO_NO_INCREMENT );
             return STATUS_INVALID_PARAMETER;
            } /* bad read length */
```

Next, we copy the data to the system buffer. A driver that did not return a fixed-length packet of data would copy however many bytes it needed to, up to the maximum specified in `stack->Parameters.Read.Length`, *and then set the* `Irp->IoStatus.Information` *field to the actual number of bytes copied.*

```
        RtlMoveMemory(
                      TheSystemAddress,
                      diskExtension->Image,
                      stack->Parameters.Read.Length);
    break;
    case IRP_MJ_DEVICE_CONTROL:
        //
        // Add device control here
        //
        break;
    case IRP_MJ_WRITE:
        if (stack->Parameters.Write.Length != THE_BUFFER_LENGTH)
            { /* bad write length */
             Irp->IoStatus.Status = STATUS_INVALID_PARAMETER;
             IoCompleteRequest( Irp, IO_NO_INCREMENT );
             return STATUS_INVALID_PARAMETER;
            } /* bad write length */
```

```
                    RtlMoveMemory(
                                    diskExtension->Image,
                                    TheSystemAddress,
                                    stack->Parameters.Read.Length);
                    break;
            default:
                    Irp->IoStatus.Information = 0;
                    break;
            }
        Irp->IoStatus.Status = STATUS_SUCCESS;
        IoCompleteRequest( Irp, IO_NO_INCREMENT );
        return STATUS_SUCCESS;
}
```

Example: Direct I/O `IRP_MJ_READ`and `IRP_MJ_WRITE` Completed in Dispatch

This example has the same specifications as the previous example. The difference is that in the implementation, this driver uses Direct I/O, not Buffered I/O. Listing 10.6 and Listing 10.7 show the `DriverEntry` routine and Read/Write handler for Direct I/O.

Listing 10.6: *The* `DriverEntry` *Routine for Direct I/O*

```
NTSTATUS DriverEntry(PDRIVER_OBJECT DriverObject, PUNICODE_STRING registry)
{
    ...
    ntStatus = IoCreateDevice(
                    DriverObject,               // Our Driver Object
                    sizeof( THE_EXTENSION ),    // Size of state information
                    &ntUnicodeString,           // Device name "\Device\The"
                    FILE_DEVICE_UNKNOWN,        // Device type
                    0,                          // Device characteristics
                    FALSE,                      // Exclusive device
                    &deviceObject );            // Returned ptr to Device Object
    if ( !NT_SUCCESS( ntStatus ) )
        {
         // Process error creating device object
        }

    deviceObject->Flags |= DO_DIRECT_IO;
    DriverObject->MajorFunction[IRP_MJ_READ] = TheReadWrite;
    DriverObject->MajorFunction[IRP_MJ_WRITE] = TheReadWrite;

    ...
}
```

Listing 10.7: *The Read/Write Handler for Direct I/O*

```
NTSTATUS TheReadWrite(
    IN PDEVICE_OBJECT DeviceObject,
    IN PIRP Irp
    )
{
    PTHE_EXTENSION  theExtension = DeviceObject->DeviceExtension;
    PIO_STACK_LOCATION  stack  = IoGetCurrentIrpStackLocation( Irp );
    PUCHAR TheSystemAddress;
```

If the length is invalid, fail the IRP.

```
if (stack->Parameters.Read.Length != THE_BUFFER_LENGTH)
  { /* bad read length */
    Irp->IoStatus.Status = STATUS_INVALID_PARAMETER;
    IoCompleteRequest( Irp, IO_NO_INCREMENT );
    return STATUS_INVALID_PARAMETER;
  } /* bad read length */
```

We are doing Direct I/O. This means that we need to get a system-space pointer to the user's buffer. In general, we may not be running in the context of the calling thread when we need to copy data in or out, so we have to map the address into system space so that it is available to all possible contexts for the driver.

```
TheSystemAddress = MmGetSystemAddressForMdl( Irp->MdlAddress );
 Irp->IoStatus.Information = stack->Parameters.Read.Length;
 switch (stack->MajorFunction)
     { /* MajorFunction */
     case IRP_MJ_READ:
         RtlMoveMemory(
                       TheSystemAddress,
                       diskExtension->Image,
                       stack->Parameters.Read.Length);
         break;
     case IRP_MJ_DEVICE_CONTROL:
         //
         // Add device control here
         //
         break;
     case IRP_MJ_WRITE:
         if (stack->Parameters.Read.Length != THE_BUFFER_LENGTH)
             { /* bad write length */
               Irp->IoStatus.Status = STATUS_INVALID_PARAMETER;
               Irp->IoStatus.Information = 0;
               IoCompleteRequest( Irp, IO_NO_INCREMENT );
               return STATUS_INVALID_PARAMETER;
             } /* bad write length */
         RtlMoveMemory(
                       diskExtension->Image,
                       TheSystemAddress,
                       stack->Parameters.Read.Length);
         break;
     default:
         Irp->IoStatus.Information = 0;
         break;
     } /* MajorFunction */
 Irp->IoStatus.Status = STATUS_SUCCESS;
 IoCompleteRequest( Irp, IO_NO_INCREMENT );
 return STATUS_SUCCESS;
}
```

Summary

This chapter has examined in detail the way in which Buffered and Direct I/O can be used for `DeviceIoControl`, `ReadFile(Ex)`, and `WriteFile(Ex)`.

11 *Approaching Reality: Synchronization*

In this chapter, we address the problems of synchronization that a multitasking, multithreaded, preemptive multiprocessor system tends to induce, particularly with the architecture of NT. The NT architecture tends to take advantage of those characteristics to optimize overall I/O performance.

Synchronization is essential in all but the most trivial drivers—and even there, it is important. Some synchronization is implicit in how the I/O Manager and application interact, and some is implicit in how the driver and the hardware interact. For nontrivial drivers, synchronization problems are "in your face" all of the time. Although we devote an entire chapter (Chapter 22) to synchronization, we introduce the core functions here because they are needed in a number of subsequent examples. We discuss all of the key synchronization primitives except Event Objects here. Event Objects are discussed in Chapter 24.

Spin Locks

The simplest form of lock is the *Spin Lock*. This is discussed in detail in Chapter 5, and the Spin Lock functions are summarized in Table 5.1 on page 100. A Spin Lock forms the basis of *all* other synchronization primitives. For example, resource locking operations, such as Adapter Control functions, Controller Control functions, and other topics we discuss in Chapter 17 all use Spin Locks as part of their underlying synchronization mechanisms, even if the sole purpose is to enqueue a function for later execution.

A Spin Lock is always multiprocessor-safe. It does whatever magic is required to assure that it is properly set even if two processors are trying to access it at exactly the same nanosecond; only one will get it. The operation that acquires a Spin Lock will first raise the IRQL to

DISPATCH_LEVEL and then obtain the lock. If it fails to obtain the lock, the code will poll the lock until it can obtain it. While waiting for the lock, the Spin Lock is "spinning" at DISPATCH_LEVEL, thereby preventing any lower IRQL code from running. In operation, the Spin Lock will be interruptible by any thread running at an IRQL above DISPATCH_LEVEL. The Spin Lock and the code it protects will not be preemptible; excluding interrupts, it will run to completion. Because there is no preemption at DISPATCH_LEVEL, a thread running within a lock, or waiting for a lock, will block out all other work that can be done at or below that level, including DPCs. On a multiprocessor system, this means that several processors could be waiting at DISPATCH_LEVEL, unable to do anything else. This is why the code executed within control of a Spin Lock is required to be very fast.

A Spin Lock has two forms:

- The ordinary Spin Lock just described

- The *interrupt synchronization Spin Lock*

An ordinary Spin Lock can be acquired at IRQL <= DISPATCH_LEVEL, and an interrupt synchronization Spin Lock can be acquired at IRQL > DISPATCH_LEVEL and less than or equal to the highest DIRQL associated with the device. When an ordinary Spin Lock is acquired, the thread is raised to DISPATCH_LEVEL (there is a special, more efficient call to acquire a Spin Lock if the thread is known to be running *at* DISPATCH_LEVEL). When an interrupt synchronization Spin Lock is acquired, the thread is raised to a DIRQL level to lock out interrupts at that level and below. The interrupt synchronization code is run as the SynchCritSection routine described on page 261.

Microsoft actually documents a third form of Spin Lock, the *Cancel Spin Lock*, which we mentioned in Chapter 6. It is actually just a special case of an ordinary Spin Lock.

The problem with a Spin Lock is captured in its name. If the lock cannot be captured, the processor sits at an elevated IRQL level, testing the value repeatedly until the lock is free. At that point, it will probably get the lock; then it can continue. But only probably. If other processors try to access the same lock, they are *all* spinning on the lock; only one of them will get through. There is *no* priority, FIFO queueing, or any other mechanism that controls which of several contending processors will next get the lock.

Deadlock is possible if Spin Locks are not used carefully. Suppose two threads use Spin Locks A, B, and C:

Thread 1 acquires A, followed by C.

Thread 2 acquires C, followed by B, followed by A.

If these threads happen to start at the same time on two processors, the system will deadlock. Thread 1 will have Spin Lock A and be spinning, waiting for Spin Lock C. Thread 2 will have Spin Lock C and be spinning, waiting for Spin Lock A. Unlike some other operating systems, NT provides no mechanism to break out of deadlock conditions. Depending on how the threads affect the system, the only way to get out of this might be to reset (or fully power-cycle) the system. This always opens the risk of other data structures being corrupted because caches have not been flushed. Deadlock is not merely an inconvenience. It threatens the fundamental integrity of the system.

You must avoid deadlock. There are two simple ways to do this:

1. The simplest is the technique Microsoft advises: Never acquire more than one Spin Lock at a time.

Although this technique works, it requires that all of the driver data structures be locked with the same Spin Lock. Often, however, it is desirable to divide the locking up so that the driver's data might be partially locked.

2. *Always* acquire Spin Locks in exactly the same order and release them *in the reverse order.*

The locking order would have been A, B, C in both routines in the previous example, with the order of the unlocking being C, B, A. This would prevent the two threads from ever deadlocking on these Spin Locks. The threads acquire all of the Spin Locks in the sequence, including the Resource B, which only Thread 2 needs. So there is no time when these two threads or another thread can attempt to get a lock that stops processing.

The code protected by the Spin Lock will run at DISPATCH_LEVEL. It must not access any pageable memory.

A Spin Lock should be used carefully and only to protect a data object that has a very small section of code that works on it.

In the following subsections, we briefly discuss each of the operations that work on Spin Locks.

KeInitializeSpinLock

```
VOID KeInitializeSpinLock(IN PKSPIN_LOCK SpinLock);
```

The KeInitializeSpinLock function must be called before a Spin Lock may be used. The spin lock is in nonpaged memory.

KeAcquireSpinLock

```
VOID KeAcquireSpinLock(IN PKSPIN_LOCK SpinLock, OUT PKIRQL OldIrql);
```

The KeAcquireSpinLock function acquires a Spin Lock. It saves the IRQL (which must be <= DISPATCH_LEVEL) in the variable whose reference is passed in and raises the IRQL to DISPATCH_LEVEL. You need this old IRQL when you release the Spin Lock.

KeReleaseSpinLock

```
VOID KeReleaseSpinLock(IN PKSPIN_LOCK SpinLock, IN KIRQL NewIrql);
```

The KeReleaseSpinLock function releases a Spin Lock and restores the original IRQL. The *NewIrql* value must be the value that was saved by KeAcquireSpinLock.

KeAcquireSpinLockAtDpcLevel

```
VOID KeAcquireSpinLockAtDpcLevel(IN PKSPIN_LOCK SpinLock);
```

The KeAcquireSpinLockAtDpcLevel function is an optimization called when the thread is already running at DISPATCH_LEVEL. Otherwise, it works the same as KeAcquireSpinLock. If you use this function, you must release the Spin Lock with the `KeReleaseSpinLockFromDpcLevel` function.

KeReleaseSpinLockFromDpcLevel

VOID KeReleaseSpinLockFromDpcLevel(IN PKSPIN_LOCK *SpinLock*);

The `KeReleaseSpinLockFromDpcLevel` function releases a Spin Lock. It is called to release Spin Locks acquired with `KeAcquireSpinLockAtDpcLevel`.

Example Use of KeReleaseSpinLockFromDpcLevel

```
... DriverEntry(...)
{
  KIRQL OldIrql;
  ....
   KeInitializeSpinLock(&extension->spinlock);
}

MyReadWriteDispatch(....)
{
    ....
    KeAcquireSpinLock(&extension->spinlock, &OldIrql);
    //
    // do something here - protected by the spinlock
    //
    KeReleaseSpinLock(&extension->spinlock, OldIrql);
....
}
```

Mutexes and Fast Mutexes

A *Mutex* is the high-level equivalent of a Spin Lock. It is a synchronization object that operates at the thread level; thus, you cannot block on a Mutex unless you are at a schedulable level. A call on the function that waits on a Mutex, `KeWaitForMutexObject`, can be performed only at IRQLs *lower* than DISPATCH_LEVEL (usually at PASSIVE_LEVEL). You can use the *nonblocking* form of this function, in which you specify a timeout interval of 0, at or below DISPATCH_LEVEL. Generally, Mutexes have little application in most monolithic Device Drivers. However, they can have application in some Filter Drivers and File System Drivers and are often used for layered drivers such as WDM drivers in Windows 2000 (see Chapter 30). If you block on a Mutex, the thread that blocks will not be rescheduled until the Mutex is released. This means that it should not be used unless you *know* you are in the context of a *driver* thread. If you are in the context of a *user* thread, some application you never heard of (and which would rather not have heard of you) will be blocked until the Mutex is released.

Windows NT provides two forms of Mutexes: the plain vanilla Mutex and the Fast Mutex. A Fast Mutex is a more restricted form of Mutex. It may not be entered recursively, and it offers no assistance in deadlock prevention. However, as its name implies, if you can live with the restrictions you will get significantly better performance if you use this Mutex.

Mutex objects are more complex than Fast Mutexes. The Mutex may be acquired "recursively" by a single thread.[1] Also, a *level* may be associated with a Mutex. This level is used when you acquire several Mutexes. The level's value corresponds to the location in the list of Mutex objects to be acquired. When a Mutex is acquired, the kernel compares the level of this Mutex and the level of a current Mutex (if any). All previously acquired Mutexes must have a level less than that of the current Mutex. There is a special case, however, in which the recursive acquisition of a Mutex is acquired. Note that if you acquire the same Mutex more than once, you must release it once for each time you have acquired it. A Mutex can be released only by the thread that has acquired it, and a Signaled Mutex cannot be released at all. Violation of either of these constraints will cause a BugCheck.

Once a Fast Mutex has been acquired, APCs to the thread are blocked. If there is no need to worry about APCs, the even more efficient ExAcquireFastMutexUnsafe can be used. However, because a thread can pass a Mutex it owns, this call is quite dangerous. This is because the Fast Mutex can't protect a data structure shared with an APC handler operating in the same thread.

The following sections define the Mutex-specific and Fast Mutex-specific operations.

Fast Mutex Operations

The following operations can only be performed on Fast Mutex objects. You cannot pass a Mutex Object in to these as a parameter. Note that a Fast Mutex is not a waitable object, and cannot be used with KeWaitForSingleObject or KeWaitForMultipleObjects.

ExAcquireFastMutex

```
VOID ExAcquireFastMutex(IN PFAST_MUTEX FastMutex);
```

The ExAcquireFastMutex function acquires an initialized Fast Mutex, possibly after putting the caller into a wait state until it is acquired, and gives the calling thread ownership with Asynchronous Procedure Calls (APCs) disabled.

ExTryToAcquireFastMutex

```
BOOLEAN ExTryToAcquireFastMutex(IN PFAST_MUTEX FastMutex);
```

The ExTryToAcquireFastMutex function either acquires the given Fast Mutex immediately for the caller, with APCs disabled, and returns TRUE, or fails to acquire the Fast Mutex and returns FALSE.

ExReleaseFastMutex

```
VOID ExReleaseFastMutex(IN PFAST_MUTEX FastMutex);
```

---

[1] Actually, Mutexes are acquired serially. We conjecture that the term "recursive" came about either to represent acquisition-within-acquisition of a single Mutex or because this behavior allows you to write recursive routines (for example, to walk a tree structure) that can repeatedly lock the same base controlling structure without blocking.

The ExReleaseFastMutex function releases ownership of a Fast Mutex that was acquired with ExAcquireFastMutex or ExTryToAcquireFastMutex.

ExAcquireFastMutexUnsafe

VOID ExAcquireFastMutexUnsafe(IN PFAST_MUTEX *FastMutex*);

The ExAcquireFastMutexUnsafe function acquires an initialized Fast Mutex, possibly after putting the caller into a wait state until it is acquired. It can be called only if there will be no APCs delivered to the thread while the thread is waiting on this Mutex. Because it avoids the extra work required to handle APCs safely, it is the fastest form of Mutex.

ExReleaseFastMutexUnsafe

VOID ExReleaseFastMutexUnsafe(IN PFAST_MUTEX *FastMutex*);

The ExReleaseFastMutexUnsafe function releases ownership of a Fast Mutex that was acquired with ExAcquireFastMutexUnsafe.

Mutex Operations

The following operations apply to a Mutex Object. They cannot be applied to a Fast Mutex Object. A Mutex is also a waitable object and thus can be used with KeWaitForSingleObject and KeWaitForMultipleObjects.

KeReleaseMutex

LONG KeReleaseMutex(IN PKMUTEX *Mutex*, IN BOOLEAN *Wait*);

The KeReleaseMutex function releases a given Mutex object, specifying whether the caller will call one of the KeWait*Xxx* routines as soon as KeReleaseMutex returns. Returns the previous value of the Mutex state (0 for Signaled; otherwise, Not-Signaled).

KeReadStateMutex

LONG KeReadStateMutex(IN PKMUTEX *Mutex*);

The KeReadStateMutex function returns the current state (1 for Signaled or any other value for Not-Signaled) of a given Mutex object. Note that this is, at best, a heuristic because whatever state it returns can change before you get control back from the call.

KeWaitForMutexObject

NTSTATUS KeWaitForMutexObject(IN PKMUTEX *Mutex*,
                              IN KWAIT_REASON *WaitReason*,
                              IN KPROCESSOR_MODE *WaitMode*,
                              IN BOOLEAN *Alertable*,
                              IN PLARGE_INTEGER *Timeout* OPTIONAL);

The KeWaitForMutexObject function puts the current thread into an alertable or nonalertable wait state until a given Mutex is set to the Signaled state or (optionally) until the wait times out.

Semaphores

A *Semaphore* is another high-level locking mechanism. It is a synchronization object that operates at the thread level; thus you cannot block on a Semaphore unless you are at a schedulable level.

A Semaphore is initialized with a *count*, the number of concurrent entries into the Semaphore. The driver can use the Semaphore to permit a controlled level of concurrency. Generally, Semaphores are used to synchronize producer/consumer and multiserver queuing systems by remaining Signaled as long as there is something in the queue to do and becoming Not-Signaled when the queue is empty. One or more queue servers can wait on the Semaphore. Note that the queue still requires protection against simultaneous access, which is usually provided by a Mutex, Fast Mutex, or Spin Lock.

An example of a classic "Producer-Consumer" multiserver queueing system is shown in Figure 11.1. Note carefully that the order in which the Producer and Consumer are started and their relative timings are irrelevant. One of them will create the Mutex, and the other will open it. Similarly for the Semaphore. The Semaphore Object is initialized to a count of 0 because the

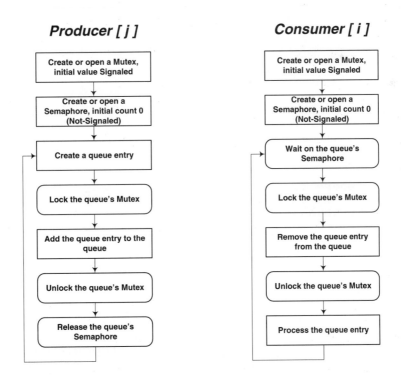

Figure 11.1: *Classic Producer-Consumer algorithms.*

queue is empty. When the Consumer waits for the Semaphore Object, it blocks. When the Producer adds an element to the queue, it releases the Semaphore Object, thus allowing the Consumer to begin to run. Note also that there can be several Consumer threads, or several Producer threads, running concurrently, and the code will still operate correctly.[2] Depending on your needs, you can imagine many clients (Producers) and a single server (Consumer), one client but many servers, or many clients and many servers. Furthermore, the correctness is not compromised (at least as far as the queue is concerned) by increasing the number of Producers or Consumers.

A call on the function that waits on a Semaphore, `KeWaitForSingleObject` or `KeWaitForMultipleObjects`, can be performed only at IRQLs *lower* than `DISPATCH_LEVEL` (usually at `PASSIVE_LEVEL`). Generally, Semaphores have little application in most Device Drivers, but they are used in drivers with dedicated threads, Filter Drivers, and File System Drivers. If you block waiting for access to a Semaphore, the thread that blocks will not be rescheduled until the Semaphore is released. This means that it should not be used unless you *know* you are in the context of a driver thread. If you are in the context of a user thread, some application you never heard of will be blocked until the Semaphore is released.

Semaphore Operations

The following operations can be used to manipulate Semaphore Objects. A Sempahore is also a waitable object and thus can be used with `KeWaitForSingleObject` and `KeWaitForMultipleObjects`.

KeInitializeSemaphore

```
VOID KeInitializeSemaphore(IN PKSEMAPHORE Semaphore,
                           IN LONG Count,
                           IN LONG Limit);
```

The `KeInitializeSemaphore` function initializes a Semaphore for which you have provided the storage (whose size is `sizeof(KSEMAPHORE)`). It provides both the initial count and a maximum limit. If the initial count is 0, the Semaphore is initialized as Not-Signaled; otherwise, it is initialized as Signaled.

KeReleaseSemaphore

```
LONG KeReleaseSemaphore(IN PKSEMAPHORE Semaphore,
                        IN KPRIORITY Increment,    // Amount to increment Semaphore
                        IN LONG Adjustment,        // Priority boost
                        IN BOOLEAN Wait);          // TRUE if KeWaitxxx will follow
```

---

[2] These basic mechanisms were first presented in the late 1960s by Edsgar Dijkstra, who called the operations "P" (the Wait operation, an abbreviation for the Dutch word for "decrement") and "V" (the Release operation, an abbreviation for the Dutch word for "increment"). Computer science literature of the 1970s is rife with instances and variations on synchronization problems, such as the deadlock problem, solutions to the starvation problem (a thread never gets to run because other threads always get to run ahead of it), and rigorous mathematical proofs of the correctness of various algorithms. For a good bibliography, any book on basic operating systems principles will give you more than you need. Some of the more important papers are summarized at the end of Chapter 6 in this book.

The `KeReleaseSemaphore` function releases a given Semaphore object. It supplies a (run-time) priority boost for waiting threads if the release sets the Semaphore to the Signaled state, augments the Semaphore count by the *Increment* value, and specifies whether the caller will call one of the `KeWaitXxx` routines as soon as `KeReleaseSemaphore` returns. The *Semaphore* and *Increment* parameters are fundamental, and the *Adjustment* and *Wait* parameters are there to provide for better performance.

KeReadStateSemaphore

`LONG KeReadStateSemaphore(IN PKSEMAPHORE` *Semaphore*`);`

The `KeReadStateSemaphore` function returns the current state (0 for Not-Signaled or a positive value for Signaled) of a given Semaphore object. It is, at best, a heuristic because the state can change between the time it is read and the time this function returns.

The Executive Resource

The Executive Resource is a variant of the Mutex. Like all the high-level synchronization primitives, it can be called only at levels < `DISPATCH_LEVEL`, usually `PASSIVE_LEVEL`. It allows two forms of locking:

- *shared*, which allows multiple users to request nonexclusive access to the Resource
- *exclusive*, which prevents any concurrent access

Consider the problem of serialization. A thread that wishes to inspect a shared data structure must synchronize on a lock of some sort. While it is inside the code protected by the lock on that structure, it is guaranteed to have exclusive access to the information protected by that lock, provided all of the other users of that information have *also* obeyed the locking protocol. However, this means that if a shared data structure is heavily used, the locked access to that structure becomes a performance bottleneck in the system.

Not locking the data structure, however, can be unacceptable for reasons of correctness. Should one of the threads have to modify the data, uncontrolled access could even be fatal to the system. With the normal locking primitives, you are restricted to an all-or-nothing choice. And when correctness dictates *all* and performance dictates *nothing*, you lose performance. (Remember, it *never* matters how fast something is if it is incorrect!)

The Executive Resource Objects provide a more powerful way to handle this. A Resource can have "multiple readers", threads that are reading information protected by the Resource but that do not need to modify it. When a thread requires write access, it can request *exclusive* access. Such a thread is queued until all existing readers have released the Resource. Generally, Read accesses that queue after a Write request will be processed in FIFO order; that is, they will be forced to wait until the Write (exclusive) transaction has completed. However, it is possible (although not necessarily a good idea) to force read-only, shared requests to have a priority higher than the pending exclusive request and thus be placed in the queue ahead of the exclusive request.

This maps well to the single writer or multiple reader semantics used within File Systems, which are the major users of the Executive Resource. A thread that has acquired shared access should treat the information controlled by the Executive Resource as read-only. A thread that wishes to modify the information (other than using thread-safe primitive operations such as `InterlockedIncrement`) must acquire the Executive Resource as exclusive access.

Under normal queueing, the thread that wishes to write, and has requested exclusive access, is eventually granted exclusive access to the Resource. Readers, as well as other potential writers, are blocked out during this access. Thus there is much less serialization of access to read-mostly data structures; performance is not compromised by the need to synchronize, and correctness is not compromised by the use of uncontrolled access. This dictates that the readers not enter into any lengthy computations or block while they have the shared access because this can cause unacceptable performance blocking of the exclusive (write) request. Similarly, the forced-priority shared access requests should not be used indiscriminately because they can result in complete starvation of the thread requesting the exclusive access.

There are even operations that can convert a nonexclusive acquisition to an exclusive acquisition without requiring the reader to release the Resource and then reacquire it in exclusive mode. There also is a way to convert an exclusive access to a nonexclusive access once a write operation has completed.

According to Microsoft documentation, this function can be called *only* at IRQL < DISPATCH_LEVEL (even though some of the calls have a non-blocking form).

 The term "resource" has a particular meaning to a GUI programmer; specifically, it is those pieces of information stored in the Resource Segment of an executable file. However, this has nothing to do with the "Executive Resource" of the kernel, specifically, the ERESOURCE data type. Kernel "resources" and GUI "resources" share only the same name. This can be confusing.

Executive Resource Operations

Several routines are provided to acquire Executive Resources. The choice of routine determines the priority of the request compared to pending shared and exclusive access requests for the resource.

The following sections describe the operations on Executive Resources.

ExInitializeResourceLite

```
NTSTATUS ExInitializeResourceLite(IN PERESOURCE Resource);
```

The `ExInitializeResourceLite` function initializes an Executive Resource for which the caller provides the storage. It is used for synchronization by a set of threads (shared readers, exclusive writers).

ExAcquireResourceExclusiveLite

```
BOOLEAN ExAcquireResourceExclusiveLite(IN PERESOURCE Resource, IN BOOLEAN Wait);
```

The `ExAcquireResourceExclusiveLite` function acquires an initialized Executive Resource for exclusive access. Optionally, it waits for the Resource to be acquired. It returns TRUE if the *Resource* is acquired and FALSE if *Wait* was FALSE and the resource could not be acquired. The *Resource* cannot be acquired if any other thread has already acquired it for exclusive access or if one or more threads have acquired it for shared access. When all current threads release the *Resource*, it can be acquired. If the attempt to acquire the *Resource* blocks, other requests for exclusive or shared access that come in after this request are usually handled in FIFO order. This order can be defeated by certain other functions described later in this section.

ExTryToAcquireResourceExclusiveLite

```
BOOLEAN ExTryToAcquireResourceExclusiveLite(IN PERESOURCE Resource);
```

The ExTryToAcquireResourceExclusiveLite function either acquires a given Executive Resource for exclusive access immediately or returns FALSE. It is slightly faster than ExAcquireResourceExclusiveLite with *Wait* set to FALSE. If any other thread has exclusive access or any threads have shared access, this function will return FALSE.

ExAcquireResourceSharedLite

```
BOOLEAN ExAcquireResourceSharedLite(IN PERESOURCE Resource,
                                    IN BOOLEAN Wait);
```

The ExAcquireResourceSharedLite function acquires an initialized Executive Resource for shared access. Optionally, it waits for the Resource to be acquired. If the *Wait* parameter is FALSE, the function will return FALSE immediately without waiting. A Resource cannot be acquired for shared access if any other thread has acquired it for exclusive access.

ExAcquireSharedStarveExclusive

```
BOOLEAN ExAcquireSharedStarveExclusive(IN PERESOURCE Resource,
                                       IN BOOLEAN Wait);
```

The ExAcquireSharedStarveExclusive function acquires a given Executive Resource for shared access without queuing up behind any pending attempts to acquire exclusive access to the same Resource. In effect, this request is moved ahead of any pending exclusive requests that are already waiting in the queue. If the Executive Resource cannot be acquired because there is already an exclusive access active and the *Wait* parameter is FALSE, the function immediately returns with a FALSE result.

ExAcquireSharedWaitForExclusive

```
BOOLEAN ExAcquireSharedWaitForExclusive(IN PERESOURCE Resource,
                                        IN BOOLEAN Wait);
```

The ExAcquireSharedWaitForExclusive function acquires a given Executive Resource for shared access. Optionally, it queues up behind any pending exclusive waiters to acquire and release the Resource first. If the Executive Resource cannot be acquired because there is already an access active and the *Wait* parameter is FALSE, the function immediately returns with a FALSE result.

ExReleaseResourceForThreadLite

```
VOID ExReleaseResourceForThreadLite(IN PERESOURCE Resource,
                                    IN ERESOURCE_THREAD ResourceThreadId);
```

The ExReleaseResourceForThreadLite function releases a given Executive Resource that was acquired by the specified thread. The thread reference can be obtained by using ExGetCurrentResourceThread.

ExReinitializeResourceLite

VOID ExReinitializeResourceLite(IN PERESOURCE *Resource*)

The ExReinitializeResourceLite function reinitializes an existing Executive Resource.

ExIsResourceAcquiredExclusiveLite

BOOLEAN ExIsResourceAcquiredExclusiveLite(IN PERESOURCE *Resource*);

The ExIsResourceAcquiredExclusiveLite function returns whether the calling thread has exclusive access to a given Executive Resource.[3]

ExIsResourceAcquiredSharedLite

USHORT ExIsResourceAcquiredSharedLite(IN PERESOURCE *Resource*);

The ExIsResourceAcquiredSharedLite function returns how many times the calling thread has acquired shared access to a given Executive Resource.

ExGetExclusiveWaiterCount

ULONG ExGetExclusiveWaiterCount(IN PERESOURCE *Resource*);

The ExGetExclusiveWaiterCount function returns the number of threads currently waiting to acquire a given Executive Resource for exclusive access.

ExGetSharedWaiterCount

ULONG ExGetSharedWaiterCount(IN PERESOURCE *Resource*);

The ExGetSharedWaiterCount function returns the number of threads currently waiting to acquire a given Executive Resource for shared access.

ExConvertExclusiveToSharedLite

VOID ExConvertExclusiveToSharedLite(IN PERESOURCE *Resource*);

The ExConvertExclusiveToSharedLite function converts a given Executive Resource from "acquired for exclusive access" to "acquired for shared access". Any pending requests for shared access that had been blocked are now permitted to acquire the Resource for shared access.

---

[3] If this was named symmetrically with other operations, it would be something like ExReadStateResource, which would return three possible values: released, exclusive, and shared. But it seems to be a naming anomaly among the synchronization primitives. Instead, there are two separate functions that return BOOLEAN or USHORT values.

ExGetCurrentResourceThread

`ERESOURCE_THREAD ExGetCurrentResourceThread();`

The `ExGetCurrentResourceThread` function returns the thread ID of the current thread.

ExReleaseResourceForThreadLite

```
VOID ExReleaseResourceForThreadLite(IN PERESOURCE Resource,
                                    IN ERESOURCE_THREAD ResourceThreadId);
```

The `ExReleaseResourceForThreadLite` function releases a given Executive Resource that was acquired by the specified thread.

ExDeleteResourceLite

`NTSTATUS ExDeleteResourceLite(IN PERESOURCE Resource);`

The `ExDeleteResourceLite` function deletes a caller-initialized Executive Resource from the system's resource list. It does not free the storage. The storage must be freed after this function returns successfully.

Wait Routines

Objects such as Semaphores, Mutexes, and Events are *dispatcher objects* (or "waitable objects"). You can use these with a generic set of *wait routines*. In particular, `KeWaitForMultipleObjects` let you wait

- until *any one* of a set of dispatcher objects becomes Signaled or a timeout occurs, or
- until *all* of a set of dispatcher objects become Signaled or a timeout occurs.

A wait function is used in a driver most commonly to wait for a single object (usually an Event), so there is a special-case wait function, `KeWaitForSingleObject`, for waiting for just one object.

The wait functions can be called *only* at IRQL < DISPATCH_LEVEL, unless the *Timeout* parameter is a non-NULL pointer to a 0 value, indicating that the call should return immediately instead of waiting. If the wait time is specified as 0, these routines can be called at IRQL <= DISPATCH_LEVEL.

The *WaitReason* parameter is the value Executive if the thread is waiting in the kernel for kernel purposes, and UserRequest if it is waiting in the initiating thread on behalf of the application. The *WaitMode* parameter is similar; it specifies whether the caller waits in KernelMode or UserMode. Lowest-level and intermediate drivers should specify KernelMode. If one of the objects is a Mutex, the caller *must* specify KernelMode.

The *Alertable* parameter specifies whether the thread can be alerted in the wait state. If the value of this parameter is TRUE and the thread is alerted for a mode that is equal to or more privileged than the given *WaitMode*, the thread's wait will be satisfied with a completion status of STATUS_ALERTED. For most drivers, you will set this value to FALSE.

The *Timeout* parameter to these functions must be either NULL or a pointer to a LARGE_INTEGER whose value is the time at which the function times out. A positive value is an absolute time; a negative value is a relative time, expressed in 100ns units. For no timeout, the value of the LARGE_INTEGER must be 0. A *parameter* value of 0 is interpreted as a NULL pointer, meaning "infinite wait".

KeWaitForMultipleObjects

```
NTSTATUS KeWaitForMultipleObjects(IN ULONG Count,
                                  IN PVOID Objects [ ],
                                  IN WAIT_TYPE WaitType,
                                  IN KWAIT_REASON WaitReason,
                                  IN KPROCESSOR_MODE WaitMode,
                                  IN BOOLEAN Alertable,
                                  IN PLARGE_INTEGER Timeout OPTIONAL,
                                  IN PKWAIT_BLOCK WaitBlockArray OPTIONAL);
```

The KeWaitForMultipleObjects function puts the current thread into a wait state until any one or all of a number of dispatcher objects are set to the Signaled state or (optionally) until the wait times out.

If the *WaitType* parameter is specified as WaitAll, then all objects must (simultaneously) be in the Signaled state to allow the wait to complete. If *WaitType* is WaitAny, any one object becoming Signaled will allow the wait to complete. This function will return—in addition to the return values indicating various failures, APC notifications, and timeouts—a value in the range of 0..MAXIMUM_WAIT_OBJECTS (for any given call, the range 0..(*Count* -1)) that is the index of the lowest-numbered signaled object that satisfied the wait. The other generally interesting value is STATUS_TIMEOUT, which can occur only occur if a non-NULL *Timeout* parameter is specified.

If more than one object can be signaled by the time the wait completes, and you want to know how many objects are signaled, you must poll their state explicitly. Only the lowest-indexed object is known to actually be signaled. You must be very careful here. If the object is one that can have a side effect invoked by passing a Wait operation, you must poll it with a KeWaitForSingleObject with a timeout value of 0. This means the *Timeout* parameter must be a pointer to a LARGE_INTEGER whose value is 0. A parameter value of 0 is interpreted as a NULL pointer, meaning "infinite wait".

If the *Count* parameter is less than or equal to THREAD_WAIT_OBJECTS, the wait will use the KWAIT_BLOCK array that is preallocated in the thread. If *Count* exceeds THREAD_WAIT_OBJECTS, you must explicitly allocate storage of size *Count* * sizeof(KWAIT_BLOCK) bytes to hold the temporary information required by the wait request and deallocate it at some later time before the thread exits. If you don't allocate the storage and use more wait objects than the default thread area supports, the system will Blue Screen with the BugCheck code MAXIMUM_WAIT_OBJECTS_EXCEEDED. *Count* must not exceed MAXIMUM_WAIT_OBJECTS, or the same Blue Screen will occur.

KeWaitForSingleObject

```
NTSTATUS KeWaitForSingleObject(IN PVOID Object,
                               IN KWAIT_REASON WaitReason,
                               IN KPROCESSOR_MODE WaitMode,
                               IN BOOLEAN Alertable,
                               IN PLARGE_INTEGER Timeout OPTIONAL);
```

The KeWaitForSingleObject function puts the current thread into a wait state until a given dispatcher object is set to the Signaled state or (optionally) until the wait times out. This completes with STATUS_SUCCESS if the object becomes signaled and STATUS_TIMEOUT if a timeout occurs.

SynchCritSection Routine

The *synchronization routine* is a routine called at a specified hardware interrupt synchronization priority. It is generally referred to as a *SynchCritSection routine*. It is used to synchronize access to hardware registers and data structures used in the ISR (Interrupt Service Routine). Since hardware registers are accessed in the ISR, we must synchronize other potential access when the access would conflict. (In Chapter 14, we discuss the fact that hardware registers are accessed in the ISR and a little about how this is done.) A device that requires a multistep process to access them will require this technique.

Here's an example. A device is initialized by performing a reset operation and then writing the assorted parameter values of 20 1-byte registers in 20 1-byte writes. If an interrupt occurs while you are in the middle of the sequence, either the ISR might fail because it is expecting a different starting state of the hardware or the setup might fail if the state is not restored on return. These multibyte Write operations are usually done at PASSIVE_LEVEL (within a dispatch routine or driver thread) or DISPATCH_LEVEL (within a DPC or StartIo handler), so they could be interrupted.

The solution is to use a *synchronization routine.* Before this routine executes, the system first raises the IRQL to the same level as the interrupt. Then, the reset and the 20 1-byte writes to the chip are performed at DIRQL level; they cannot be interrupted. This prevents the ISR from interrupting while you're in the "critical section". When the routine completes, the IRQL is restored to its state before the synchronization routine was called.

The synchronization routine uses the second form of Spin Lock: the *interrupt synchronization Spin Lock.* We discuss the use of this lock in the next section and in Chapter 14.

Device Consistency: KeSynchronizeExecution

One problem with code that runs at an IRQL less than the Device IRQL is that if the device registers are shared, for example, on some multifunction devices or most multimedia devices, the lower IRQL code cannot safely manipulate device registers without doing some sort of interlock. This is because the device might be active (imagine, for example, a device that interrupts at fixed periodic intervals) even when an I/O transfer is being prepared. Interrupting the lower IRQL code in the middle of setting up a set of I/O registers or writing to device memory might result in data corruption, or even a system crash. Consequently, you must protect against this possibility by interlocking accesses between the ISR and lower IRQL code. However, you cannot call a Spin Lock at Device IRQL level because if it should interlock (on a uniprocessor system), it will have preempted the processor that can release the lock. A classic deadlock situation results. But the need to do the interlock has not gone away, even if the simple mechanism won't work. So, for those devices for which such an interlock is required, the kernel supports the KeSynchronizeExecution function. This function provides a safe, deadlock-free interlock between the ISR and lower IRQL code. For simple devices that cannot interrupt unless an I/O transaction is actually underway, this synchronization is unnecessary.

```
BOOLEAN KeSynchronizeExecution(IN PKINTERRUPT Interrupt,
                               IN PKSYNCHRONIZE_ROUTINE SynchronizeRoutine,
                               IN PVOID SynchronizeContext);
```

The *Interrupt* parameter is a pointer to the Interrupt Object that was returned by
`IoConnectInterrupt`. It is usually stored in the Device Extension. The *SynchronizeRoutine*
parameter is a pointer to a function that is called when the interlock is passed. The
SynchronizeContext parameter is an arbitrary pointer that will be passed to
SynchronizeRoutine when it is called. *SynchronizeRoutine* has this form:

```
BOOLEAN (*PKSYNCHRONIZE_ROUTINE) (IN PVOID SynchronizeContext);
```

Note that *SynchronizeContext* is the *only* parameter passed in. To access the Device
Object, IRP, or other values, you must arrange to pass in the appropriate pointer. Typically, you
will pass in a pointer to the Device Object, from which the Device Extension and current IRP
can be derived. When `KeSynchronizeExecution` is called, it first raises the IRQL level to the
value of *SynchronizeIRQL* specified for `IoConnectInterrupt`. This value is usually equal to
the highest IRQL level at which the device can interrupt. Because of how the IRQL is assigned,
particularly for PCI Busses and other shareable-interrupt busses, you almost certainly have to
store this value during your `DriverEntry` setup. If you have more than one IRQL, this value
will be the maximum of the values returned from `IoConnectInterrupt`.

Next, `KeSynchronizeExecution` attempts to obtain the Spin Lock in the Interrupt Object.
Because the processor is now running at an elevated IRQL, the deadlock problem cannot arise.
When the Spin Lock is acquired, *SynchronizeRoutine* is called with *SynchronizeContext*.
It can assume that its manipulations of the registers constitute an atomic action that will not be
interrupted. When *SynchronizeRoutine* returns, the Spin Lock is released and the IRQL is
restored to the original IRQL that had been active when `KeSynchronizeExecution` was called.

Because `KeSynchronizeExecution` raises the IRQL to a DIRQL level before attempting
to acquire the Spin Lock, any interrupt that could not interrupt the thread once it has the Spin
Lock cannot interrupt the thread while it is *waiting* for the Spin Lock. This means that several
processors in a multiprocessor system could be forced to spin at elevated DIRQL as they all try
to acquire the same Spin Lock. This could happen when an ISR is active, a DPC is active, and
one or more processors need to access the device from `StartIo`. This means that the response
latency to all other same or lower DIRQL devices could be extended beyond the latency limit.
We discuss more about how to use the `KeSynchronizeExecution` routine in Chapter 14 (page
307).

The Cancel Spin Lock

As mentioned earlier in the chapter, a special type of Spin Lock is the *Cancel Spin Lock*. This
lock is used by drivers that use system queueing to control access to the system IRP queue. We
discuss this lock in Chapter 22 (page 455).

Summary

Synchronization is essential in the NT environment. This chapter has discussed various forms of
synchronization and the synchronization primitives. Spin Locks are used to synchronize low-

level, very fast critical sections. Mutexes, Semaphores, Events, and Executive Resources are used to synchronize multithreaded drivers. Two special synchronization mechanisms are used to synchronize key driver operations. `KeSynchronizeExecution` is used to synchronize an ISR with lower levels such as dispatch routines and DPCs. The Cancel Spin Lock is used to synchronize access to the internal queues in a driver.

Further Reading

The literature of synchronization techniques dates back over three decades. There is a body of work by Edsgar Dijkstra, C.A.R. Hoare, Niklaus Wirth, and many others (a good bibliography on synchronization problems would run twenty or thirty pages). A bibliography of synchronization mechanisms can be found in nearly any book on operating systems. Two classics are cited below, but there are many others.

Habermann, A. Nico, *Introduction to Operating System Design*, Science Research Associations, 1976.

Tanenbaum, Andrew S., *Operating Systems: Design and Implementation*, Prentice-Hall, 1987. ISBN 0-13-637406-9.

12 *Achieving Reality: Memory Management*

In this chapter, we discuss memory management within the driver. Any complex system allows for dynamic allocation and deallocation of memory. For a driver, there are many different ways to manage memory, depending on considerations such as the purpose the memory will be used for and the desired performance. But drivers add a new kind of complexity to memory management in the form of other *kinds* of memory to manage, specifically, *application-level memory* and *device memory.*

Both types must be handled carefully. Unlike in ordinary application programming, where the operating system manages your memory and protects you, or more correctly, the rest of the system (including other processes) from your blunders, down at the driver level you have no such protections—or the ones that are there tend to do the "wrong thing".

Generally, there is no protection against such trivial bugs as uninitialized pointers, array bounds errors, and similar blunders. But what happens is even worse. You can corrupt the entire system or totally destroy the integrity of the information on disk (including directories and basic File System structures). Almost invariably, such blunders will Blue Screen the system. In this case, the file blocks that are not yet written out can be lost, thereby contributing to the damage suffered.

Failure to manage user memory correctly might not Blue Screen, but it *can* corrupt a process you've never heard of—usually the one that just happened to be executing when your device took an interrupt. Further, mismanaging memory can lead to poor system performance or erratic behavior. For example, badly fragmenting memory might mean that some application cannot be started, and the error message given will *not* say, "Application cannot run because kernel memory is badly fragmented".[1]

---

[1] Running a large application may require that several contiguous kernel pages be available, for example, for page table information. If the contiguous pages cannot be allocated, the attempt to launch the application will fail.

Memory Allocation/Management Operations

Kernel memory is managed by different strategies. There is simple, "raw" allocation, in which memory is allocated from the global memory area. There also are special variants of this basic allocation for specific kinds of memory. For kernel code that does frequent allocations and deallocations of identically sized objects, there is the *lookaside list*, which replaced the form of allocation you might encounter in older drivers called *zone allocation*, now considered obsolete. (We do not spend any time on this obsolete form of allocation.)

Basic Kernel Memory Allocation Operations

Kernel memory can be allocated directly using the ExAllocatePool function and related functions. This is a *raw allocation*, in which all of the available memory is treated as a uniform pool of memory. The available memory is divided by its use: paged or nonpaged memory. In addition, there is a special reserved pool for critical memory allocation. There also are special allocators for allocating noncached memory and blocks of physically contiguous memory. Many of these functions are discussed in the following sections.

ExAllocatePool

```
PVOID ExAllocatePool(IN POOL_TYPE PoolType,
                     IN ULONG NumberOfBytes);
```

The ExAllocatePool function is one of the most popular calls for allocating memory. It can be used to allocate memory from any of a variety of storage pools, the most common being PagedPool (often used for scratch buffers needed at various points during driver setup) and NonPagedPool (for data areas that must be available at DISPATCH_LEVEL or above).

PoolType is one of the values from Table 12.1. Normally, it would be PagedPool or NonPagedPool. If the memory is from a Nonpaged Pool, the call can be from DISPATCH_LEVEL or below. If it is from the Paged Pool, the call must be from a level < DISPATCH_LEVEL.

Table 12.1: ExAllocatePool POOL_TYPEs

Pool Type	Description
Nonpaged Pool Allocations	
NonPagedPool	The normal allocation used for allocating from the Nonpaged Pool.
NonPagedPoolCacheAligned	Allocation will be aligned to a cache line.
Must-Succeed Allocations	
NonPagedPoolMustSucceed	Used only for special cases in drivers that are required for system boot.
NonPagedPoolCacheAlignedMustS	
Paged Pool Allocations	
PagedPool	The normal allocation used for allocating from the Paged Pool.
PagedPoolCacheAligned	Allocation will be aligned to a cache line.

Often, when you allocate from `PagedPool`, you are allocating some temporary work area that is being used during the execution of `DriverEntry` or some other function at `PASSIVE_LEVEL`. Such allocations almost always have a duration entirely within one function and are freed before that function exits. It is very rare to need cache-aligned Paged Pool memory. You cannot use memory you have allocated in the Paged Pool in any routine executing at IRQL >= `DISPATCH_LEVEL` without going through a *lot* of extra work. It is easier to allocate nonpaged memory for such uses.

For some devices, if the storage allocated is not aligned on a cache-line boundary, either you get poorer performance or the device will not work correctly. In such cases, you can use the `NonPagedPoolCacheAligned` option. Very rarely will you need cache-aligned buffers from the Paged Pool.

The Nonpaged Pool is a limited resource. Possibly, a driver that requires truly massive buffers might be loaded early in order to get the large buffers before significant memory fragmentation occurs. However, this might interfere with a later driver that must be loaded in order for the boot process to complete. If you are coding one of these critical drivers, you typically should call `ExAllocatePool` using one of the usual Nonpaged Pool options, such as `NonPagedPool`. However, if this call fails, the system will fail to complete the boot process. Thus, instead of taking the simple failure path that you might normally code, you instead try to allocate again, this time using the corresponding "must-succeed" allocation. This type of allocation has the property that when it returns, it will *always* return a valid pointer, in which case you need not check that it succeeded. However, if it fails, it will generate a Blue Screen. The cause of the Blue Screen will be that the must-succeed pool has been used up (BugCheck code `MUST_SUCCEED_POOL_EMPTY`). Thus, technical support people can locate the problem by looking for a driver that is consuming all available memory.

You must use the must-succeed options carefully. They use an even scarcer resource than the ordinary Nonpaged Pool: the must-succeed pool. You should not use the must-succeed pool except for drivers critical to the boot process. However, judicious use of that pool can enhance the robustness of your driver.

You free memory you have allocated with `ExAllocatePool` by using `ExFreePool`.

Here's one strategy for dealing with the failure of a device to allocate massive amounts of memory utterly critical to its running correctly: Allow it to load "successfully". That is, it will return the appropriate `STATUS_SUCCESS` code even if it *couldn't* get the memory it needs. The boot process is not aborted, but the driver won't work. You must set a status flag (usually in the Device Extension) that causes it to later fail all I/O operations with an "insufficient resources" error. Thus you do not compromise the integrity of the system. Delivering a driver that renders your users' machines unbootable and requires them to reinstall NT is not viewed as customer-friendly. Depending on your device and the requirements of the application, you may be able to provide a degraded performance mode when such problems arise.

ExAllocatePoolWithTag

```
PVOID ExAllocatePoolWithTag(IN POOL_TYPE PoolType,
                            IN ULONG NumberOfBytes,
                            IN ULONG Tag);
```

The `ExAllocatePoolWithTag` function is identical to `ExAllocatePool`, except that it has the *Tag* parameter. *Tag* is used to provide some more useful information during a memory dump, diagnostic dump (see the commands in WinDbg), or other diagnostic procedure. It is a

string of up to four characters, expressed as a "character value", in reverse order. You might
think it would make more sense to program the dump code to transpose the bytes instead of the
Device Driver writer's having to do so, but this seems to have been some historical accident.
Thus, an area called Temp would have a tag value of 'pmeT'. Note that this value is in 8-bit characters, not Unicode.

You free storage that is allocated with ExAllocatePoolWithTag by using ExFreePool.

ExFreePool

```
VOID ExFreePool(IN PVOID address);
```

The ExFreePool function frees a block of memory allocated by ExAllocatePool
(WithTag). The *address* passed in *must* be an address of storage that was returned from an
ExAllocatePool (WithTag) call.

MmAllocateNonCachedMemory

```
PVOID MmAllocateNonCachedMemory(IN ULONG NumberOfBytes);
```

The MmAllocateNonCachedMemory function allocates the specified *NumberOfBytes* of
noncached memory. If the memory cannot be allocated, the return value is NULL. The memory is
normally allocated during DriverEntry and freed at unload time. Because of memory fragmentation, it might be difficult to get noncached memory after the system has been operating for a
while, so it is best to allocate this storage, when needed, only during DriverEntry. This call is
used to allocate memory that will not be cached. The use of such memory might be critical for
devices that do not support, or cannot work well with, normal cache snooping techniques. This
storage is freed using MmFreeNonCachedMemory.

MmFreeNonCachedMemory

```
VOID MmFreeNonCachedMemory(IN PVOID BaseAddress,
                           IN ULONG NumberOfBytes);
```

The MmFreeNonCachedMemory function frees a block of noncached memory allocated by
MmAllocateNonCachedMemory. The *BaseAddress* and *NumberOfBytes* parameters must be
the value returned by MmAllocateNonCachedMemory.

MmAllocateContiguousMemory

```
PVOID MmAllocateContiguousMemory(IN ULONG NumberOfBytes,
                                 IN PHYSICAL_ADDRESS HighestAcceptableAddress);
```

The MmAllocateContiguousMemory function attempts to allocate contiguous physical
memory of the indicated size. If there is a restriction within the physical address space as to
where the space can be allocated, the limit can be specified in the *HighestAcceptableAddress*
parameter. This is a PHYSICAL_ADDRESS. The values shown in Table 12.2 are the values in
.LowPart of the address; .HighPart is set to 0 for the values shown. The return value is a system logical address where the memory has been allocated. If the request cannot be satisfied, the
pointer returned is NULL. The memory allocated with this function should be freed using
MmFreeContiguousMemory when it is no longer required. Often the memory is allocated in
DriverEntry and freed in the Unload handler.

Table 12.2: *Memory Limits*

Limit	Value
< 1MB	0x000FFFFF
< 16MB	0x00FFFFFF
< 4GB	0xFFFFFFFF

For some devices, performance can be enhanced and the driver simplified if there is a single, contiguous buffer allocated in memory. However, this memory is allocated from the Nonpaged Pool and counts against the system usage of the Nonpaged Pool. It is a design decision as to whether the memory should instead be provided in the application and handled by scatter/gather (ideally by scatter/gather implemented in hardware, but if necessary by a software simulation of scatter/gather hardware—see page 340).

MmFreeContiguousMemory

VOID MmFreeContiguousMemory(IN PVOID *BaseAddress*);

The MmFreeContiguousMemory function frees any memory allocated by MmAllocateContiguousMemory. The *BaseAddress* parameter must be the value returned from MmAllocateContiguousMemory. This function is usually called in the Unload handler.

Lookaside Lists

In many cases, a driver will tend to allocate and deallocate temporary storage frequently. Rather than suffer the performance penalties involved in a full-blown call to the memory allocator each time, a *lookaside list* can be used to gain significant performance improvement. A lookaside list is a list of preallocated blocks of storage (all of the same size) that allows for faster allocation and deallocation.

A lookaside list is constructed dynamically. Initially, no storage is allocated to it; only a small amount of storage is allocated for the lookaside header. Then, on each allocation, the lookaside list is checked for an existing block of storage. If there is no lookaside memory available (as will be true in the initial state), a block of memory is allocated from the selected Paged or Nonpaged Pool using normal allocation techniques.

A lookaside list has a "high-water mark" that is established when it is created. When a block of memory is freed to the lookaside list, the behavior that ensues depends on whether the current lookaside list allocation is above or below this high-water mark.

- If the usage is less than or equal to the mark, the storage is not returned to the selected Paged or Nonpaged Pool but instead is retained on the list. Thus, on the next allocation request, this freed block will be immediately available for use. This strategy of keeping a cache of recently used blocks avoids having to go through the complete pool allocation mechanism.

- If the usage is above the high-water mark, the storage will be freed directly back to the storage pool from which it came.

Thus the lookaside list is of benefit primarily when a predictable number (usually an average number) of elements can be determined. Therefore, the lookaside behavior can be optimized for the typical case.

There are two kinds of lookaside lists: those that manage nonpaged memory and those that manage paged memory. The operations on each are identical, except for the names of the functions; see the following list. The nonpaged lookaside functions can be called at IRQL <= DISPATCH_LEVEL, while the paged lookaside functions can be called only at IRQL < DISPATCH_LEVEL. Calling a paged-lookaside-list function at DISPATCH_LEVEL will cause the system to Blue Screen.

ExInitializeNPagedLookasideList (or ExInitializePagedLookasideList)

```
VOID ExInitializeNPagedLookasideList(IN PNPAGED_LOOKASIDE_LIST Lookaside,
                             IN PALLOCATE_FUNCTION Allocate OPTIONAL,
                             IN PFREE_FUNCTION Free OPTIONAL,
                             IN ULONG Flags,
                             IN ULONG Size,
                             IN ULONG Tag,
                             IN USHORT Depth );

VOID ExInitializePagedLookasideList( IN PPAGED_LOOKASIDE_LIST Lookaside,
                             IN PALLOCATE_FUNCTION Allocate OPTIONAL,
                             IN PFREE_FUNCTION Free OPTIONAL,
                             IN ULONG Flags,
                             IN ULONG Size,
                             IN ULONG Tag,
                             IN USHORT Depth );
```

Initializes a lookaside list in nonpaged (or paged) memory that will cache a maximum of *Depth* entries of the indicated *Size*. In addition to the basic functionality, this function allows you to specify a pair of functions to allocate and free memory. If the *Allocate* function pointer is NULL, ExAllocatePoolWithTag will be used to allocate from the desired (Paged or Nonpaged) Pool. If the *Free* function pointer is NULL, ExFreePool will be used to deallocate as needed. The only values permitted for Flags are 0 and the value POOL_RAISE_IF_ALLOCATION_FAILURE; the latter value indicates that an exception should be raised if the allocation fails. The *Lookaside* parameter must be in nonpaged memory even for a lookaside list that manages paged memory.

ExAllocateFromNPagedLookasideList (or ExAllocateFromPagedLookasideList)

```
PVOID ExAllocateFromNPagedLookasideList(IN PNPAGED_LOOKASIDE_LIST Lookaside);

PVOID ExAllocateFromPagedLookasideList(IN PPAGED_LOOKASIDE_LIST Lookaside);
```

Allocates an entry from the specified lookaside list. If the list is empty, allocates memory if necessary by calling the allocation routine specified when the lookaside list was created (or ExAllocatePoolWithTag if no allocation routine was specified). Returns a pointer to the allocated memory. If the allocation failed, returns a NULL pointer or raises an exception, as requested when the lookaside list was initialized.

ExFreeToNPagedLookasideList (or ExFreeToPagedLookasideList)

```
VOID ExFreeToNPagedLookasideList(IN PNPAGED_LOOKASIDE_LIST Lookaside,
                                 IN PVOID Entry);

VOID ExFreeToPagedLookasideList( IN PPAGED_LOOKASIDE_LIST Lookaside,
                                 IN PVOID Entry);
```

Frees an entry back to the specified lookaside list. If the lookaside list already contains the maximum number of entries specified when it was created, the entry is freed by calling the deallocation routine specified when the lookaside list was created (or `ExFreePool` if no deallocation routine was specified).

ExDeleteNPagedLookasideList (or ExDeletePagedLookasideList)

```
VOID ExDeleteNPagedLookasideList(IN PNPAGED_LOOKASIDE_LIST Lookaside);

VOID ExDeletePagedLookasideList(IN PPAGED_LOOKASIDE_LIST Lookaside);
```

Deletes a nonpaged (or paged) lookaside list. Any entries left in the list are freed back to their original source by calling the deallocation routine specified when the lookaside list was created (or `ExFreePool`). The lookaside list header itself is *not* deallocated.

Zone Buffers

Zone buffers are now obsolete. They were replaced by Lookaside Lists. We mention them only to tell you to not use them in any new driver.

Mapping Device Memory and I/O Space

Many devices provide for *device memory*. This is memory that is physically on the device but is defined as existing on the memory bus. In principle, it is designed to be read and written exactly like ordinary system memory. In practice, this cannot be done in NT unless the device memory is *mapped* into the system logical memory address space, or even into user space. This memory starts out as *bus-relative* memory, that is, memory that has a physical address on a particular bus. If you have programmed MS-DOS, Windows 3.*x*, or Windows 9*x* device drivers, you might be familiar with concepts such as the video memory being at location `A000:0000` or Ethernet memory being at location `D800:0000`. In NT, the address must be represented as a physical address because concepts such as segments have no applicability in Windows NT. If your documentation refers to memory using the segmented address notation, you must convert the segmented address to a physical address. Do this by taking the segment value, multiplying by `0x10`, and adding the offset to the resulting value; thus the segmented address `D800:0123` is the physical address `D8123`. But even then, physical addresses have no meaning on Windows NT, since the operating system cannot refer to them. So you must set up address registers that map these physical addresses to system virtual addresses.

For PCI devices, we say more about how to get the bus-relative physical addresses in Chapter 21, starting on page 417, where we give a detailed example.

The mapping is done in two steps:

1. Map a bus-relative address (such as D8000) to a system-wide physical address using `HalTranslateBusAddress`.
2. Map this system-wide physical address to a system logical address using `MmMapIoSpace`.

Once you have the system logical address, you can access the memory on the adapter directly.

Functions to Manage Device Memory

The following functions are used to manage memory that is on a device.

HalTranslateBusAddress

```
BOOLEAN HalTranslateBusAddress(IN INTERFACE_TYPE InterfaceType,
                               IN ULONG BusNumber,
                               IN PHYSICAL_ADDRESS BusAddress,
                               IN OUT PULONG AddressSpace,
                               OUT PPHYSICAL_ADDRESS TranslatedAddress);
```

The `HalTranslateBusAddress` function translates a bus-relative physical address to a system-wide physical address. This system-wide physical address can then be used as the input to `MmMapIoSpace` to obtain a system virtual address.

The *InterfaceType* parameter will be one of several constants that describe the bus type. For most current machines, it will be a value such as `IsaBus` or `PCIBus` (although this function can apply to many other bus types). The *BusNumber* parameter is the physical bus number of the specified bus in the machine. The *BusAddress* parameter is the 64-bit bus-relative address that is to be mapped to system physical memory. For example, if you know the value is D8000 (in the bus-relative physical address space), then you would copy the value 0x000D8000 into the low-order (.LowPart) 32 bits of a PHYSICAL_ADDRESS variable, which is what you pass in for *BusAddress*.

The *AddressSpace* parameter is available for cross-platform drivers. In some machines, I/O registers are mapped into physical memory and hence into system logical memory. In others, the I/O registers remain in a separate I/O register space. Proper use of macros generally hides these differences, but this value will be set to indicate which type of translation was done. A value of 0 indicates that the address is a memory address, and a value of 1 indicates that the address is an I/O address. For adapter memory, this will be a memory address because that is how the adapter memory is specified. For a port address, you still must do the translation because a *bus-relative* port address is not a *system-relative* port address. Note that we have observed that on most *x86*-based machines, if the documentation tells you that your ISA device has a port address of 0xFA8, then the translated port address is *also* 0xFA8. Don't be fooled by this. That is one HAL's opinion of the correct translation. It might not be true for a different HAL, even for the "trivial" ISA case.

You cannot use the *AddressSpace* value to *change* how a device's memory or data are accessed. If you have a port, you must access it as a port; it is up to the HAL to implement this as an access to memory. However, the HAL is free to translate an address specified as an I/O port

(*AddressSpace* set to 1 before the call) to an address specified as physical memory (*AddressSpace* will be changed to 0 after the function returns).

The *TranslatedAddress* parameter points to a location where the *system* physical address will be placed. This value will be valid if the function returns TRUE. If the function returns FALSE, you must handle this as a problem, typically by refusing to load the driver and by releasing any resources already allocated. To have a completely portable driver, you must, among other things, test the *AddressSpace* value on return. If the result is 1, then .LowPart of *TranslatedAddress* is the system port number. If the result is 0, *TranslatedAddress* is a memory address and you will have to use MmMapIoSpace to translate it to a useful value. You must specify the correct *AddressSpace* type on input; it is not an option for you to change the type. The HAL might choose to change an I/O port to a physical memory address, but it will never change a memory address to a port.

MmMapIoSpace

```
PVOID MmMapIoSpace(IN PHYSICAL_ADDRESS PhysicalAddress,
                   IN ULONG NumberOfBytes,
                   IN BOOLEAN CacheEnable);
```

The MmMapIoSpace function takes a *system physical address* and a length and maps the address to an address in nonpaged memory. This newly mapped address can then be used to access information, in this context the onboard memory of the device. For a PCI device, the *NumberOfBytes* value can be obtained by using the example shown in Listing 21.3 on page 402. For other busses that can be queried, similar techniques can be used. Generally, for an ISA bus device, you will obtain this information from the Registry. In addition, the *CacheEnable* value must be set for the device. Note that devices such as network adapters that can change the contents of their onboard memory might not implement the necessary lines to support proper cache snooping, and thus they are noncacheable. You are responsible for determining, either from dynamic configuration data or from the printed specification of the device, if the device memory is cacheable, and you must pass this information on to the system via this function.

MmMapIoSpace will return either the address in nonpaged memory or NULL if there is insufficient space available to perform the mapping.

MmUnmapIoSpace

```
VOID MmUnmapIoSpace(IN PVOID BaseAddress,
                    IN ULONG NumberOfBytes);
```

The MmUnmapIoSpace function is the inverse operation of MmMapIoSpace. Once you have mapped adapter memory into your address space, you must take responsibility for mapping it out. This is usually done in the Unload handler.

The *BaseAddress* parameter is the value returned from MmMapIoSpace. The *NumberOfBytes* parameter must be the same value that was passed into MmMapIoSpace.

There is a limitation on the amount of memory that can be mapped. This limitation is the amount of space allocated for PTEs (page table entries) by the kernel. Each PTE represents a platform-specific amount of information (4K on x86 systems and 8K on Alpha systems). For a mapping operation to succeed, there must be enough PTEs to map the requested space. At boot time, NT scans the main memory and allocates sufficient page table space to map the physical memory and allow some extra space to map the expected adapter memories. A problem arises when more adapter memory is required than the "expected" amount. In such a case, you must tell the system how many PTEs are necessary.

The amount of space allocated for PTEs is under the key
\HKEY_LOCAL_MACHINE\SYSTEM\CurrentControlSet\Control\Session Manager\Memory Management
   The value of the SystemPages entry under this key is a REG_DWORD value that specifies the number of entries required. For driver debugging, a reasonable value to set this to is 65535. A value this large will do no harm, but it will eliminate problems that a smaller value will generate. In NT 4.0, the sum of all onboard memory on all cards that can be concurrently mapped is limited to 300MB. This was a reasonable limit at the time NT was created, but with declining memory prices, current devices are approaching, and in some cases exceeding, this limit.
   To modify the amount of space reserved for PTEs, you must use the Registry Editor program RegEdt32 and then reboot. For a product shipment, you should consider supplying an end-user-friendly way to set this value.

The location of the key used to specify the number of PTEs has been documented, incorrectly, as being under
\HKEY_LOCAL_MACHINE\SYSTEM\CurrentControlSet\Control\Session Manager\SubSystems
   The correct location is under
\HKEY_LOCAL_MACHINE\SYSTEM\CurrentControlSet\Control\Session Manager\Memory Management

Managing User Memory

Generally, the operations required to access user memory are done for you by the I/O Manager. It is uncommon to perform any operation other that MmGetSystemAddressForMdl, unless you are using the Neither transfer method. The I/O Manager performs the MmProbeAndLockPages before transferring control to your driver and performs the MmUnlockPages when the operation has completed.

Functions to Manage User Memory

The functions for mapping user memory are shown below.

MmProbeAndLockPages

```
VOID MmProbeAndLockPages(IN OUT PMDL Mdl,
                         IN KPROCESSOR_MODE AccessMode,
                         IN LOCK_OPERATION Operation);
```

   The MmProbeAndLockPages function causes all of the pages associated with the MDL Mdl to be brought into memory (if they were pageable) and locks the physical pages into memory. This is particularly important for doing DMA transfers because the various DMA controllers require physical memory addresses to operate. It also is used to lock in application space pages prior to initiating a sequence of programmed I/O operations. This is usually done at the dispatch level of the highest-level driver that works with the pages. It is needed only when you specify that I/O is to be *Direct*, that is, by setting the DO_DIRECT_IO flag in the Device Object or by using METHOD_IN_DIRECT or METHOD_OUT_DIRECT specifications on a DeviceIoControl operation, or when you use the Neither mode. Normally, this is done for you by the I/O Manager and you have no need to execute this call yourself. However, if you have selected the Neither mode and are constructing your own MDLs, this is essential.

Note that the return value of this function is VOID. If this function fails—in particular, if it cannot access a page or if the locking of these pages would exceed the process's locked-page quota—it will raise an exception. Therefore, you should call this function using a structured exception handler around the call. A lower-level driver must not attempt to pass such an exception on to a higher-level driver. It cannot assume anything about a higher-level driver's exception-handling capabilities. In particular, the driver cannot call ExRaiseStatus to pass on such an exception.

The *AccessMode* parameter tells if the I/O operation is to work on kernel data pages or user pages. If *AccessMode* is UserMode, then this function will check the pages as if it was the application that is subject to the application page map. If the *AccessMode* is KernelMode, these additional tests are bypassed. Do not use KernelMode if you are checking on an application-level MDL.

The nature of the *Operation* parameter indicates the type of access desired. If it is IoReadAccess, the pages do not need to be writable; this is particularly significant if Access is UserMode. There is a subtle distinction between IoWriteAccess and IoModifyAccess. Both permit the driver to write to the buffer. They differ in that IoWriteAccess assumes that the entire contents of the buffer will be rewritten and does not guarantee that the contents of the buffers are left intact. IoModifyAccess guarantees that the contents of the buffers are intact. This subtlety applies primarily when the pages are pageable. IoWriteAccess does not necessarily page the previous contents of the page back into memory when doing the mapping and locking; it might just map the page frame to the physical page. IoModifyAccess forces the page contents to be reloaded if the pages have been swapped out. If the entire buffer contents are to be rewritten, IoWriteAccess is clearly more efficient.

In Listing 12.1, we show how an exception frame can be used to detect that an IRP has asked the I/O system to transfer data into a read-only area. This usage represents an error on the part of the application programmer, but unless we properly check the access, the kernel can quite happily overwrite the nominally "write-protected" user data with a DMA transfer. This is because DMA transfer does not go through the page map and therefore is not subject to the write protection provided by the page map.

Listing 12.1: MmProbeAndLockPages *and Exception Handler*

```
__try {
      MmProbeAndLockPages(Mdl, UserMode, IoModifyAccess);
      }
__except(EXCEPTION_EXECUTE_HANDLER)
      {
      Irp->IoStatus.Status = STATUS_ACCESS_VIOLATION;
      Irp->IoStatus.Information = 0;
      IoCompleteRequest(Irp, IO_NO_INCREMENT);
      return;
      }
// if we get here, we can continue with the DMA setup
```

When an exception handler is established, the code within the `__try` block is executed. If there are no exceptions raised, execution continues just past the `__except` block, that is, the code in the `__except` block is ignored. If, however, an exception is raised, the code within the `__except` block is executed, provided the conditional attached to the `__except` clause evaluates to the value `EXCEPTION_EXECUTE_HANDLER`. In this case, you always want to execute the handler. Failure to put an exception handler around an `MmProbeAndLockPages` means any exception to be raised, including the simple case of an application's handing down a bogus address, *will crash the entire operating system.*

Once `MmProbeAndLockPages` is called, it doesn't matter if another thread that has a MDL to the same pages is terminated. Since the physical pages are locked down by this IRP, they will remain intact.

There are two types of MDLs.
1. Those associated with an IRP, and consequently with a process via the IRP.
2. Those owned by the driver and not associated with any process.

A process has a quota for the number of pages it can have locked concurrently. An attempt to lock more pages than the process's quota permits will generate an insufficient resource exception, `STATUS_INSUFFICIENT_RESOURCES`.

Once a process locks pages in a MDL, it must make sure it unlocks them using the `MmUnlockPages` function. If it fails to do so, then when the process is being cleaned up the system will crash with a `PFN_SHARE_CHECK` (0x1B) BugCheck. Therefore, you must keep track of all MDLs you have explicitly allocated (not including the one implicitly allocated by the I/O system, if you've chosen that method) so that you can unlock them.

MmGetSystemAddressForMdl

```
PVOID MmGetSystemAddressForMdl(IN PMDL Mdl)
```

The `MmGetSystemAddressForMdl` function returns a pointer to nonpaged system memory for the *Mdl* specified as the argument. This address can be stored for later use by an ISR or a DPC. The pages must have already been locked down by using `MmProbeAndLockPages`. Normally, if you specify Direct I/O (either by setting `DO_DIRECT_IO` for the Device Object or by specifying a Direct I/O method in an IOCTL code used for `DeviceIoControl`), the I/O Manager will have already performed the `MmProbeAndLockPages` operation when it created the MDL.

MmUnlockPages

```
VOID MmUnlockPages(IN PMDL mdl);
```

The `MmUnlockPages` function unlocks any pages that have been locked by `MmProbeAndLockPages`. Note that if you do not properly unlock all of the pages associated with a process, then when the process terminates the system will be shut down with a BugCheck `PFN_SHARE_COUNT`.

IoAllocateMDL

```
PMDL IoAllocateMdl(IN PVOID VirtualAddress,
                   IN ULONG Length,
                   IN BOOLEAN SecondaryBuffer,
                   IN BOOLEAN ChargeQuota,
                   IN OUT PIRP Irp);
```

The IoAllocateMdl function is usually called only if you choose to do all of the memory mapping yourself (for example, using the Neither method for DeviceIoControl). It takes a specification of a virtual memory address and a length and creates a MDL that will allow the buffer represented by the user virtual memory address to be mapped. It can optionally associate the MDL with an IRP.

This function allocates and returns a MDL for the specified virtual address and length. The *SecondaryBuffer* flag indicates whether this MDL is the primary (FALSE) or secondary (TRUE) buffer of the associated IRP; if the *Irp* parameter is NULL, this value of the *SecondaryBuffer* parameter must be FALSE. The *ChargeQuota* flag indicates how the space should be charged. In a layered driver hierarchy, this must be FALSE except for the top-level driver called in the context of the application thread. If *Irp* is non-NULL, the MDL is added to the MDL list of the IRP as either a primary or secondary buffer, as determined by the *SecondaryBuffer* parameter.

MmPrepareMdlForReuse

```
VOID MmPrepareMdlForReuse(IN PMDL Mdl);
```

The MmPrepareMdlForReuse function is used for those very few drivers that allocate their own MDLs and need to do so repeatedly. It prepares the MDL for reinitialization for MmInitializeMdl. Because it is so rarely used, we mention it only in passing here and refer you to the DDK documentation should you actually need to use the function.

IoFreeMdl

```
VOID IoFreeMdl(IN PMDL Mdl);
```

The IoFreeMdl function must be called to free any MDL you have explicitly allocated.

Summary

This chapter has covered the key functions you need for memory management within a driver. We will see some of these functions used in the examples that appear throughout the remainder of the book. In the simple cases, such as using Direct I/O for a Device Driver (either by specifying DO_DIRECT_IO in the Device Object or by using the METHOD_IN_DIRECT or METHOD_OUT_DIRECT specification for an IOCTL), many of these functions are already performed on your behalf by the I/O Manager, and you will not need to call them yourself.

13 *Achieving Reality: Touching the Hardware*

Ultimately, you *must* touch the hardware. That's the whole point of learning to write a Device Driver. It's amazing that we have barely discussed it until 279 pages into the book, before getting to a chapter that explains what is apparently the fundamental mechanism of a Device Driver. But until you've done all of the necessary setup, built the frameworks, done the synchronization, and dispatched the IRPs *and* you are sitting (usually) in your `StartIo` handler or Adapter or Controller callback (which we discuss in Chapter 17), you haven't even been *ready* to touch the hardware.

It might surprise you, but it is uncommon in NT 4.0 to need to touch real hardware during `DriverEntry`, except for querying PCI configuration data. Similarly, it is uncommon to touch hardware during `IRP_MJ_CREATE` processing. You might even be surprised to discover, in Chapter 28, that in Windows 2000, you *can't* touch the hardware at `DriverEntry` time because it might not even be there! But now we're going to show you that you *are* ready. It is time to Go For It.

Exactly how do you Go For It? Not, as it turns out, by writing `IN` and `OUT` instructions. That would be too simple. And not portable. And it probably wouldn't work anyway. We explore exactly why not as we plunge into the details of access macros in this chapter.

Accessing memory on the device differs some from accessing the port of the device. A key feature to be aware of is that if the device *says* it has a port, then you *use* that as a port. You might "know" that on an Alpha the port doesn't really exist, and you "know" that the "port" is really a memory address out there in system logical memory. But, in fact, if you follow the Windows NT Device Driver rules, you will still access it as if it was a port, and it is up to the HAL to work the magic to map this apparent port access to a memory access. This detail is transparent to you, the Device Driver writer.

Accessing Ports

Most simple devices have only I/O ports. If you were programming these on a bare *x*86, you would write directly to these ports using IN and OUT instructions. You do it almost the same way on Windows NT, using these macros:

```
READ_PORT_UCHAR
READ_PORT_USHORT
READ_PORT_ULONG
WRITE_PORT_UCHAR
WRITE_PORT_USHORT
WRITE_PORT_ULONG
```

There are two subtle tricks you must be aware of when using these macros. One is directly visible to you: how you obtain the port number you use for these operations. We discuss this next. The other trick is magic that deals with architecture-specific hardware optimizations that can change the meaning of your driver's execution. This is handled by the HAL. We examine this magic in more detail later.

Mapping Ports

We start with the fact that you have a "port number" into which to write. You might have obtained this from the device documentation, from the Registry, or, in the case of a PCI Bus or other queryable bus, from the device's Configuration Space information. In the case of the PCI Bus, you can find out from the device whether an address is a port address or a memory address. We assume at this point that you've already done that step (which is described in great detail in Chapter 21) and that you now have a variable that holds the nominal port address. However, this port address is what is called a *bus-relative* port address; it is not useful to you in that form. Before you can use it, you need to convert it to a *system-relative port address*.

Following is a simple code fragment that converts a bus-relative port address to a system-relative port address. The PortAddress variable is the 32-bit, bus-relative port address. This example is for an ISA bus, whose bus number is 0. It could also be for a PCI Bus, which might have a different bus number. (A machine with a single PCI Bus will often have the devices on PCI Bus number 0, but you cannot depend on your device's being on PCI Bus 0. Details about this are in Chapter 21.)

```
PHYSICAL_ADDRESS busPort;
PHYSICAL_ADDRESS systemPort;
ULONG AddressSpace = 1; // it is a port address

busPort.LowPart = PortAddress;
busPort.HighPart = 0;
if(!HalTranslateBusAddress(Isa, 0, &busPort, &AddressSpace, &systemPort))
    { /* handle failure */
    // ...
    } /* handle failure */

// See what type of value was returned
```

Life is a little more complex on some platforms. For example, on the Alpha a "port" is actually memory-mapped. So, for such platforms, HalTranslateBusAddress returns a *physical* memory address for the port and sets the `AddressSpace` value to 0 (FALSE). If `AddressSpace` is still 1 after `HalTranslateBusAddress` returns, the value returned is a system port address in the port address space. All you need to do is store and use that address. But if the `AddressSpace` value was changed to 0, then the HAL has chosen to remap the address into system *memory* space. So this value is not useful to you. You need also to map this physical address into system logical memory using `MmMapIoSpace` (which we discuss in detail in the next section). Having done this, you still use the `PORT` macros to read and write this address.

```
if(AddressSpace)
    extension->myPort = systemPort.LowPart; // it is still a port
else
    { /* remapped */
     extension->myPort = MmMapIoSpace(systemPort, Length, FALSE);
     if(extensions->myPort == NULL)
         { /* mapping failed */
         //... handle failure here
         } /* mapping failed */
    } /* remapped */
```

Reading and Writing Ports

Once you have successfully computed the value of `myPort`, which you typically store in your Device Extension, you have a value that can be used to access the device's ports. The following sections show how this value can be used to read values from or write values to a device's ports.

Reading and Writing Single Values

Registers on a device usually come in contiguous *blocks*. That is, if the reference documentation tells you the following:

```
0xFA8: Command Register
0xFA9: Status Register
0xFAA: Data Register
```

then you can safely say this:

```
extension->myPort: Command Register
extension->myPort+1: Status Register
extension->myPort+2: Data Register
```

The `myPort` variable would be of type `ULONG`. In addition, you would probably want to define macros that gave symbolic names to these values, such as these:

```
#define CommandRegister (extension->myPort)
#define StatusRegister (extension->myPort+1)
#define DataRegister (extension->myPort+2)
```

For this discussion, we assume certain kinds of (fairly typical) behavior of the device. To initiate an I/O operation on this device, we put the byte to be written in the data register and set the low-order (GO) bit in the command register. To enable the device to interrupt, we set the

Interrupt Enable (IE) bit in the command register. Here's the code, along with the two definitions of the bits, as derived from reading the device manufacturer's documentation:

```
#define CMD_GO 0x01
#define CMD_IE 0x04

WRITE_PORT_UCHAR( CommandRegister, CMD_GO | CMD_IE);
```

In your debugger, you might display the value of `extension->myPort`. You might see that it is `0xFA8`. Or, it might be `0x80000FA8`. It might even be `0xC0000A42`. The point is that once you have converted the physical port address to a system port address, you don't need to worry about what that value is.

Reading and Writing Multiple Values

The following operations can read a block of data from a port or write a block of data to a port.

```
void READ_PORT_BUFFER_UCHAR(IN PUCHAR Register,
                            IN PUCHAR Buffer,
                            IN ULONG Count)

void READ_PORT_BUFFER_USHORT(IN PUSHORT Register,
                             IN PUCHAR Buffer,
                             IN ULONG Count)

void READ_PORT_BUFFER_ULONG(IN PULONG Register,
                            IN PULONG Buffer,
                            IN ULONG Count)

void WRITE_PORT_BUFFER_UCHAR(IN PUCHAR Register,
                             IN PUCHAR Buffer,
                             IN ULONG Count)

void WRITE_PORT_BUFFER_USHORT(IN PUSHORT Register,
                              IN PUCHAR Buffer,
                              IN ULONG Count)

void WRITE_PORT_BUFFER_ULONG(IN PULONG Register,
                             IN PULONG Buffer,
                             IN ULONG Count)
```

It is very important to understand what these functions do. They read a block of data from or write a block of data to a *single port address*. This is in contrast with the `WRITE_REGISTER_BUFFER...` operations that are defined for device memory. Thus, for a particular value of a port, the operation

```
WRITE_PORT_BUFFER_UCHAR(port, myData, 1024);
```

is the same as

```
for(i = 0; i < 1024; i++)
    WRITE_PORT_UCHAR(port, ((PUCHAR)myData)+i);
```

and is *not* the same as

```
for(i = 0; i < 1024; i++)
    WRITE_PORT_UCHAR(port+i, ((PUCHAR)myData)+i)); // NOT this!
```

Contrast this with the similar equivalent shown for WRITE_REGISTER_UCHAR, shown on page 288.

Accessing Device Memory

Using adapter memory is a bit trickier. Aside from the magic mentioned earlier in the chapter, several other pieces of magic, both overt and covert, are involved when you use adapter memory.

The key piece of overt magic is that after you have done the HalTranslateBusAddress (with *AddressSpace* set to 0, meaning it is a memory address), you have a *system physical address*. You have now done half of the translation process. Unlike with a port address, for which you directly use the value returned from HalTranslateBusAddress, for a memory address you need to go through one more step: map the system physical address to system logical address space. You do this with MmMapIoSpace.

In the following example, the variable MemoryAddress is a 32-bit memory address, such as we might have gotten from a PCI Bus (details for the PCI Bus start on page 417). Length is the length of the memory to map; it might be, for example, 16384, or 65536, or 4096, or 48 (but memory on devices usually comes in multiples of 4096 bytes). But once you have the length (from whatever source you find it out), you just pass it in to MmMapIoSpace. The result of MmMapIoSpace is stored in a pointer variable in the Device Extension (the pointer value might be, for example, a PVOID, but any pointer type will work).

```
PHYSICAL_ADDRESS busPhysical;
PHYSICAL_ADDRESS systemPhysical;
ULONG AddressSpace = 0; // it is a memory address

busPhysical.LowPart = MemoryAddress;
busPhysical.HighPart = 0;

if(!HalTranslateBusAddress(Isa, 0, &busPhysical, &AddressSpace,
                                  &systemPhysical))
    { /* handle failure */
    // ...
    } /* handle failure */

extension->myMemory = MmMapIoSpace(systemPhysical, Length, FALSE);

if(extension->myMemory == NULL)
    { /* handle map failure */
    // ...
    } /* handle map failure */
```

Once you have the translated address, you can use it. But usually not quite like a "plain" memory address. Device memory introduces some additional complexities, which we discuss in the next section.

Reading and Writing Device Memory

Device memory is written by using the rather badly named WRITE_REGISTER_... series of operations, summarized in Table 4.1 on page 73. The terminology is somewhat confusing for those who think of device "registers" as the concept that NT calls "ports". The WRITE_REGISTER_... operations are used to write device *memory*. There is a corresponding set of READ_REGISTER_... operations that read device memory.

Why do you need a special operation to read and write *memory?* After all, it is just memory! The explanation is a consequence of how I/O devices work. How I/O devices work is even more complex if you use the value TRUE to MmMapIoSpace, meaning you are allowing caching. (This is in opposition to what we did in the previous example.)

Consider the case in which the computer is caching the data in the L1 and L2 caches. If the device has memory addresses that actually cause actions to take place when information is written to them, the order in which the data is written is *not* the order in which you issued the memory write instructions. Rather, it is the order in which the data is flushed from the cache back to the "memory". This order is controlled by the cache implementation and the access patterns of the instructions executed after your writes. If control returns to the application level or even to the I/O Manager fairly immediately, the access patterns are completely outside your control. Suppose there *are* no "ports", simply three "memory locations" for the command, status, and data values. You write the data to memory, and then you write the command register. But the cache flushes the command register first, so the I/O transaction starts, using whatever data was already in the device. This is not what was intended.

For the simple case, in which you use only the WRITE_REGISTER... operations, a function such as WRITE_REGISTER_UCHAR will actually force the hardware to do the Right Thing. The first WRITE_REGISTER..., which writes to the Data Register, is guaranteed to have its data written to the adapter memory *before* the WRITE_REGISTER... that writes the command register.

It is worth looking at how this is done because the implications of the implementation are significant. This is the covert magic we referred to; you rarely need to be concerned with it, and it is largely hidden from you. We look at them so that you'll be better able to make some engineering trade-offs and make them with the full knowledge of all of the second-order effects with which you will have to deal (it is always dangerous to play with magic you *don't* understand).

We show in Listing 13.1 the code for WRITE_REGISTER_ULONG; it is identical for all WRITE_REGISTER... operations, except for the data length. The operation is defined as
void __stdcall WRITE_REGISTER_ULONG(IN PULONG dest, IN ULONG value);

This code is implemented in assembler, not C, and is an example of the few thousand lines of system-specific and performance-critical assembly code that are in the HAL. We added the comments.

Listing 13.1: WRITE_REGISTER_ULONG: *The Assembly Code*

```
location      instruction  symbolic
NT!_WRITE_REGISTER_ULONG@8:
0x8015edc0    8b542404     mov   edx, dword ptr[esp+04]      ; load dest
0x8015edc4    8b442408     mov   eax, dword ptr[esp+08]      ; load value
0x8015edc8    8902         mov   dword ptr[edx], eax         ; [dest] = value
0x8015edca    f009542404   lock or dword ptr[esp+04], edx    ; magic!
0x8015edcf    c20800       retn  0008                        ; _stdcall: pop and return
```

- The first instruction in this sequence loads the pointer to the destination, which is 4 bytes above the current stack pointer (`esp`), into the `edx` register.

- The second instruction loads the value, which is 8 bytes above the current stack pointer, into the `eax` register.

- The third instruction stores the contents of the `eax` register in the location referenced by the `edx` register.

Thus far, there is nothing particularly unexpected happening here. But the heart of this function is in the next instruction.

- The fourth instruction ORs the pointer we loaded into `edx` back into the location it came from.

This instruction appears to be remarkably useless in what it does (we ignore the `lock` prefix for the moment). It makes no change in any data value. A sillier instruction in this context you could not imagine. It is the `lock` prefix that makes this instruction important.

Most modern machines, in particular those in the Pentium family, have processors that are *vastly* faster than the memory systems to which they are connected. Anything beyond the L1 cache is far away. So if you must have your processor wait until simple operations such as a write to memory complete, *even a write to the L2 cache*, you are hitting a performance bottleneck. So modern machines have a *write pipe*, an internal hardware queue that handles some of this performance disparity by queueing up the memory write operations and allowing them to proceed asynchronously with the processor. Because programs, statistically, do more reads than writes and can execute several instructions between writes (remember, this is *average* data), the reality is that a write pipe can significantly improve total processor throughput.

The Intel P6 processor (Pentium Pro) and later versions have an additional feature. That is, if you write to a location and then read back from that location, the read can be satisfied from the write pipe. Here's what this means. Suppose you write to a device register that has the property that it can modify the data you've written, and then you read back what you wrote. You might get the value you just wrote! But the value you wrote hasn't even gotten to the device yet!

For ordinary memory, which is side-effect-free, this is harmless. The Intel processors carefully preserve the sequential semantics of the compiled code while doing whatever internal reordering that can make the instruction stream run faster. Because it is true in an ordinary program that writing a value to memory will mean that the same value will be read from memory, the readback from the write pipe is an important optimization. But while reading back from the write pipe is an optimization for ordinary memory, for device memory it could lead to incorrect driver behavior.

The `lock` prefix has the property that it causes all data in the write pipe to be *written back to memory*. So through the execution of the otherwise useless OR instruction, which is a sophisticated sort of NOP instruction (but which contains a memory write request), the write pipe is flushed and the data you just wrote to the device memory goes back to memory. This also means that on the higher-level Pentium processors, if you issue an immediate read request from your driver, the data *can't* be read back from the write pipe; it has already been flushed back to memory. So the only recourse is to go back out to memory and read the data. If you have indicated that the data should not be cached, an actual memory read from the memory itself will be necessary, and you will get completely honest data.

You pay a penalty for this, however. First, you've disabled caching of any of the data from the device memory. This means that every memory read operation is going to have to wait for the device, which is, by the comparison of processor and memory speeds, very, very, very far away. If you write a lot of data to the device, the use of the `lock` technique will cause your driver to again slow down to be in lockstep with the memory.

It is problems like this that give Device Driver writers gray hair.

There are *all kinds* of solutions to these problems. We talk about some of them here, but the design space is very large, and the variety of devices and the patterns of their use vary greatly. Perhaps even the same device, used for different purposes, would find one solution very acceptable and another horrible for one purpose, and the reverse situation for another purpose.

For many devices, there are both ports and memory. Typically, you act on the ports and then retrieve lots of data from memory, or you put lots of data in memory and act on the ports. For some devices, such as displays, you act on the registers infrequently after device initialization, but bash the memory ferociously. These all suggest different scenarios of use.

We consider here the "typical" device, as might be found on a modern PCI card. (We chose PCI because it is the common bus supported on both *x*86 and Alpha platforms and on the forthcoming Merced architecture, Intel's 64-bit platform.) It has a small number of ports and a moderate amount of onboard memory. Just to give a concrete number, we give it 16384 bytes of onboard memory.

If you know the performance trade-offs, and in particular the cost of doing the `WRITE_REGISTER...` operations, you can make some engineering trade-offs. For example, you don't really have to use `WRITE_REGISTER...` if you are simply transferring a block of data to uncached device memory. All you must do is a standard `RtlCopyMemory` call (the NT kernel equivalent of `memcpy`). While this is slow because of the lack of caching, it is still faster than the unit-by-unit transfer of `WRITE_REGISTER...` operations. You would not want to do this if the write pipe could affect the semantics of your transfer.

Or, you could enable caching when you did the `MmMapIoSpace` call. This is particularly useful if the device memory retains what you write in it, as opposed to changing it spontaneously underneath you (for example, a data acquisition card with values changing all of the time would be a poor candidate for caching). This would give you a significant performance improvement if you had to frequently read the data from the device. But remember that for a cache to work properly, it needs to know when the data has changed, either by doing snooping and snarfing or by explicit request on the part of the programmer. Because most onboard device memory is being changed by a processor that has never heard of your bus, let alone caching (for example, the onboard processor that is reading data from some external source), standard snooping/snarfing doesn't work because the signals that change the device memory are simply not presented to the system memory bus. But if you enable caching and you do a lot of write operations without using the `WRITE_REGISTER...` calls, you eventually end up with a fair discrepancy between the *logical* contents of the memory (the contents you have written from your driver) and the *physical* contents of the memory (the contents that are actually present and not pending somewhere in a cache or write pipe). Somehow, you must make these pictures match, for example, just before you tweak the ports to initiate the actual output operation. In the case of our sample device, you could even imagine all 16K of its data still floating around in caches somewhere. What to do?

You can call `KeFlushIoBuffers`, which you can do from any IRQL <= DISPATCH_LEVEL. This means it can be called in the Dispatch Routines (which run lower than DISPATCH_LEVEL, an admitted confusion of names, but that's how it is). Or, it can be called in a DPC, APC, `StartIo`, or a Controller or Adapter callback. Using `KeFlushIoBuffers` is sometimes like using a 20-pound sledgehammer to kill a fruit fly. This is because it can force the *complete* flushing of *all* caches on *all* processors. (While you pass in a description of the memory to be flushed, some architectures do not support selective flushing of cache lines—they just flush everything back.) If you are about to do a write operation, you can flush only the dirty cache lines while not invalidating the cache contents. If you are about to do a read operation, you need to flush *and invalidate* the cache lines. Otherwise, a read of the device memory will give you what was last in the cache, even though it is now invalid relative to the actual contents of the device memory. But doing this might still give you better overall performance than using uncached data. It depends on what kind of usage patterns you need to support to the device memory.

Note that you can call `KeFlushIoBuffers` only from IRQL <= DISPATCH_LEVEL; this is a further discouragement from doing too much in the ISR. You would think that you would want to move out all of the data during the ISR—if you followed traditional "device driver" style, that is. But NT is *not* traditional, and doing something like that in the ISR will make your Device Driver a "bad citizen". You can't actually do this because the key function you need to execute can be done only at DISPATCH_LEVEL; it is harder to set everything up so that you can safely do a massive copy in the ISR. It is easier to follow the NT design model and do this all at the DPC level.

You also need to look carefully at your device. The decision about whether to cache cannot be made unless you understand the overall trade-offs. We said the example device has 16K of onboard memory. You must balance the overall system impact of flushing all caches on all processors against the cost of moving such a small amount of data. On the other hand, we could have given it 16MB of memory. In this case, the trade-offs for moving this large amount of memory would be quite different.

Several operations are available to move blocks of information from a device. These are similar to the READ_PORT_BUFFER_... functions discussed earlier in the chapter. The move functions include READ_REGISTER_BUFFER_UCHAR, READ_REGISTER_BUFFER_USHORT, and READ_REGISTER_BUFFER_ULONG, and their corresponding WRITE operations. They have the following forms.

```
void READ_REGISTER_BUFFER_UCHAR(IN PUCHAR Register,
                                IN PUCHAR Buffer,
                                IN ULONG Count)

void READ_REGISTER_BUFFER_USHORT(IN PUSHORT Register,
                                 IN PUCHAR Buffer,
                                 IN ULONG Count)

void READ_REGISTER_BUFFER_ULONG(IN PULONG Register,
                                IN PULONG Buffer,
                                IN ULONG Count)

void WRITE_REGISTER_BUFFER_UCHAR(IN PUCHAR Register,
                                 IN PUCHAR Buffer,
                                 IN ULONG Count)

void WRITE_REGISTER_BUFFER_USHORT(IN PUSHORT Register,
                                  IN PUCHAR Buffer,
                                  IN ULONG Count)

void WRITE_REGISTER_BUFFER_ULONG(IN PULONG Register,
                                 IN PULONG Buffer,
                                 IN ULONG Count)
```

These all take a pointer to device memory (*Register*), a pointer to a memory buffer (*Buffer*), and a *Count* of the number of items to transfer (that is, how many UCHARs, USHORTs, or ULONGs). The READ_ operations transfer data from the device to the memory; the WRITE_ operations transfer data from memory to the device.

These composite operations are semantically equivalent to a *sequence* of WRITE_REGISTER_... or READ_REGISTER_... operations. For example, writing

```
WRITE_REGISTER_BUFFER_UCHAR(deviceMemory, myData, 1024)
```

is semantically equivalent to writing

```
for(i = 0; i < 1024; i++)
    WRITE_REGISTER_UCHAR(((PUCHAR)deviceMemory)+i, ((PUCHAR)myData)+i);
```

Contrast this operation, which increments both the destination and source, with the corresponding WRITE_PORT_BUFFER_... operations (see page 282), which increment only the memory pointer while holding the port value constant.

The Joy of Hardware

If you're new at this, we want to warn you in this section about some of the really weird things you might see when you touch Real Hardware. If you are an experienced device driver writer for other systems, you probably already know everything we tell you in this section. Feel free to skip it.

- *Write-only registers*: These are registers that can be written, but when they are read back, the results are not the data that was written and might even be some specific value such as 0x00 or 0xFF. This was a classic problem of the EGA controller.

- *Register aliasing*: When you write data to a register, it performs some function, but when you read from it, you read some state other than the register you wrote. Essentially, there are two internal registers in the device accessed from the same physical address. Which one is accessed depends on whether the operation is a read or write. This is a special case of the write-only register. The CGA and EGA controllers had this problem.

- *Autoreset bits*: When you write a bit to the register, writing a 1 initiates some action, but the bit automatically resets to 0. This is often the case in many devices, where the bit that initiates the action resets to 0.

- *Indexed registers*: One register is used to read and write data, but another register selects which "real" register of the device it will access. You load the index of the "logical" register you want to access in one register and then write to or read from the desired register through another address. The base VGA controller works this way.

- *Unrecoverable state*: The device has some state, but you can't discover what state it is in because not only is the critical information not available for read-back, but selecting what state you are going *to* depends on knowing what state you are *in*. We have encountered far too many devices like this, but the nondisclosure agreements we signed some years ago are still in effect, so we can't say.[1]

- *Autoreset-on-read*: You can read a register, but doing so resets its value so that the next read produces a different result, often `0x00`.

- *8/16- or 16/32-bit problems*: Some devices have 16-bit registers that *must* be read or written as 16-bit values, not as two 8-bit values. Some have 32-bit registers that must be read or written as 32-bit values, not as four 8-bit or two 16-bit values. These limitations are particularly hazardous if you are circumventing the `READ_REGISTER_...` or `WRITE_REGISTER_...` operations for performance reasons; you must make sure your compiled code accesses the registers using the correct width.

Note that all of these oddities are for hardware that is working according to the specifications they were designed to meet. We have encountered even more problems in devices because of bugs in the preproduction silicon or of flaws in the fundamental design. In the past, we have had to deal with devices that failed to complete an operation (and thus never interrupted) and devices that completed the operation and failed to interrupt in spite of the fact that they were set to interrupt. In one infamous case, one production device simply returned garbage in its status flags every few thousand operations. (Fortunately, the flags were *not* autoreset flags, so the solution was to read a flag's value three times to see if all three reads produced the same result. If a difference was found, the reads were repeated until three consecutive reads produced the same result.) Particularly with new silicon, be prepared to write "defensive" code.

If you find a device that has autoreset registers (virtually unheard of today, but common a few years ago), walk away from the project. It is doomed. Modern architectures will do *speculative reads* in an attempt to maximize the processor throughput by doing instruction lookahead, often along both possible paths of control following an as-yet-unexecuted branch instruction. The results of the speculative read may be discarded if it is later discovered the instruction lookahead fetched an instruction that will not be executed because the branch took a different path. A speculative read would reset the autoreset register without actually doing anything with the value it read.

There are even odd interactions you can get on specific platforms or with certain variant HALs. PCI cards that are designed on the margins work only on some machines. Also, all too common are PCI Busses that stretch the interpretation of the standards or misinterpret the standards for signals or misinterpret or fail to meet the standards for the configuration cycles (and thus confuse the HAL). Not unheard of are cards that will work with one speed processor but not a higher-speed or lower-speed processor (even though, nominally, the busses are running at the same speed). You might need to write diagnostic code that tries to do the simplest things just to see if the hardware is working at all! And, as we have discussed, this code might have to be

---

[1] One of these was an interesting device I wish I could talk about in detail, but it is still covered by a nondisclosure agreement. It turns out that the vendor's software driver—which was useless for my client's purposes and which we had to replace with one of our own—expected that the hardware would start out in its power-up-reset state. But suppose the hardware was left in any other state, say, from a "soft reboot" that did not include a power on/off or reset (for example, the Shutdown-and-restart menu option exercised after the application program crashed due to a driver error). Then there was no way to easily discover in what state it *was*, and returning it programmatically to the "power-up" state depended on knowing that. After three days of experimenting, I found a sequence of operations that would eventually lead to a known state. From the known state, I could set it to the power-up-reset state. *Do not assume your hardware is in some power-up-reset state. –jmn*

coupled with your use of hardware debugging aids to validate that the failures are in the silicon and not in your software.

It is worthwhile to consider adding "diagnostic" features to your driver that are invoked by otherwise undocumented IOCTLs (unless the customer has signed an appropriate nondisclosure agreement). You can then deliver, or make available (for example, over the Web), your own diagnostic software. Sometimes, the purpose of this software is to verify that the driver is the correct version for the hardware, so IOCTLs that return the driver version number and the configuration data (including the hardware version number) for the device are very useful to add. Techniques like this can seriously reduce field maintenance costs. Forget the notion that a driver has to be "small". A driver has to be *useful*, *robust*, and, above all, *reliable*. Code added to meet these goals is critical.[2]

Summary

In many ways, touching hardware is the easiest part of writing a driver. But if performance is an issue, you may have to move "outside the box" of what is simple and incur additional complexities. And while the conceptual model of accessing hardware is simple, the realities of platform dependencies, idiosyncrasies of the hardware itself, and, in some cases, problems in early silicon or in bus implementations can all affect how complex your task actually becomes.

---

[2] An interesting failure mode exists between the Toshiba Desk Station V and the Intel EtherExpress 10/100. After I spent hours on the telephone with technical support for Intel and Toshiba (and many more hours on hold), neither could explain why the EtherExpress card would not work on the Desk Station (with a Tecra laptop). For years, I blamed the device driver and assumed that the problem was the shared interrupt. The Desk Station allows exactly *one* IRQ line, IRQ11, for its PCI expansion slots. If your driver gets exclusive use of IRQ11, no other driver can operate on that bus, including drivers that know how to share interrupts! Recently, from the Tecra Internet mailing list, I learned that the Desk Station does not allow bus mastering devices in its PCI slots—a violation of the expected behavior. Make sure you instrument your drivers and provide information to your support staff so that you will not be blamed for problems not in your driver. This is *not* a hypothetical, what-if problem. It exists right now. Don't make it worse, and try to avoid being a victim of it. *–end*

14 *Achieving Reality: Interrupts and the Driver*

This chapter discusses how a low-level driver works. The low-level driver is the driver that, in a stack of layered drivers, actually interacts with the hardware. If you are writing a monolithic driver, this chapter discusses what the driver actually does in implementing the interface to interrupts and the rest of the driver. In this chapter we cover the nature of an interrupt, the ISR, the DPC, and how they are all related.

Role of the Low-Level Driver

The low-level Device Driver is where "the rubber meets the road". This is where the abstractions stop and reality intervenes. This is where you write data to and read data from a device's control registers, manipulate any mapped memory that belongs to the device, and field the actual interrupts. The interface between the lowest-level Device Driver and the device is specific to the device and system architecture. Although IRPs come into this driver, it has no lower-level driver to which it sends them.

When we discuss the WDM (Win32 Driver Model) in Chapter 30, we show you that in many cases the lowest-level interrupt driver is already written for you. Further, what you will think of as your "low-level" driver is actually quite high in the driver food chain. But this chapter concentrates on the low-level driver—the "bottom feeder" (see Figure 14.1)—and how it works. If you are writing a simple monolithic driver, it is the one and only layer in the driver hierarchy.

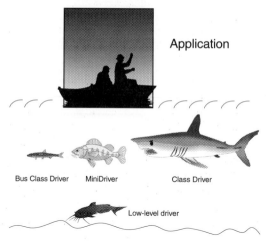

Application

Bus Class Driver   MiniDriver   Class Driver

Low-level driver

Figure 14.1: *Driver hierarchy.*

Interrupt Processing

In Windows NT, processing an interrupt is a multistep process. It involves two key components of a Device Driver: the ISR (Interrupt Service Routine) and the DPC (Deferred Procedure Call) routine.

- The hardware triggers an interrupt.
- The ISR does the most time-critical processing and clears the interrupt. A DPC is scheduled.
- The DPC Routine continues processing and completes the request (or sets up the hardware and starts the processing of the next portion of a multistage I/O operation).

What Is an Interrupt?

In this section, we review how hardware interrupts work and how they fit into the NT architecture.

Most devices generate an interrupt to notify the host computer that they have finished their task. The sole responsibility of the device is to pull the signal line low, knowing that this will invoke whatever magic is necessary to respond to the condition that it is reporting. What happens after that is a consequence of the implementation of the bus, the chip set, the processor, and the operating system. You get to write some of the magic for the operating system.

Interrupts come in two styles:

- *Sharable:* An interrupt that can be assigned concurrently to two or more devices. The PCI Bus allows many PCI devices to share the same interrupt line. A properly written driver will be able to handle this sharing of interrupts, but it requires your cooperation to make it happen.

- *Nonsharable:* An interrupt unique to one device on the system. No other device can use the same interrupt line. This is very limiting. The ISA Bus suffers badly from this (mis)feature, and configuring a device to coexist with other devices on the bus can be a nightmare.

Interrupt Levels

Interrupts are usually split into *levels*. The levels of interrupt as viewed by NT are the DIRQLs, or Device Interrupt Request Levels. An interrupt line is mapped from its identity as a physical line to an IRQ level. In the *x*86 hardware, this is done by a chip, either a *Programmable Interrupt Controller* (PIC) or *Advanced Programmable Interrupt Controller* (APIC). This chip maps the interrupt to an IRQ, which, in turn, is associated with a position in the *Interrupt Dispatch Table* (IDT). A PIC and APIC differ in that a PIC can report an interrupt by routing it to one of 16 different locations in the IDT. The priority of an interrupt is based on the input line on which the interrupt occurred. An APIC can report an interrupt by routing it to one of 256 different locations in the IDT, and the priority of each interrupt is programmable independent of the line on which it occurs.

When a device yanks its IRQ line low, the (A)PIC maps it to an IRQ. We assume the simple case that the processor is running an ordinary user application at the time this interrupt occurs (we show more-complex cases shortly). The processor proceeds to process the interrupt according to the following steps (although not necessarily in the order given here; each platform may differ slightly in how this is done).

- The processor pushes the current processor state (flags register and program counter) onto the active stack.
- The processor requests an interrupt number from the (A)PIC.
- The processor loads a new program counter value from the IDT, indexed by the interrupt number. This is a pointer to the kernel, and execution begins in Kernel mode.
- The processor raises its DIRQL level of the processor to the assigned DIRQL for the interrupt. This locks out further interrupts at this and lower levels.

The interrupt code dispatches through some code in the Interrupt Object and eventually gets to an NT kernel component called `KiInterruptDispatch` (a function you will not otherwise see, as hinted at by the `Ki` prefix). This can raise the IRQL to an even higher DIRQL level (we discuss why on page 294). This code then acquires, in the Interrupt Object, a Spin Lock that protects the ISR from being called multiple times before it completes. It then calls the code that is the ISR itself. When this code returns, `KiInterruptDispatch` releases the Spin Lock, drops the IRQL to the value it had when `KiInterruptDispatch` was entered, and returns. The processor will eventually execute, on an *x*86 machine, an `IRET` (Interrupt Return) instruction, which restores the program counter and flags register that had been stored on the stack. Execution then resumes in the application program, which has been oblivious to this whole sequence of events.

ISR Synchronization: the ISR Spin Lock

Some of this might seem a bit unusual, especially if you are accustomed to other types of Device Drivers. Why a Spin Lock? Why raise the IRQL?

You must remember, at all times, that NT is intrinsically a *multiprocessor* system. In an ordinary uniprocessor system, once the ISR has been entered, the IRQL of the processor is raised to the IRQL of the interrupt, and no other interrupt can come in at that level until that IRQL is lowered. But in a multiprocessor system, only *one* processor has its IRQL raised. All other processors in the system are independent. If another IRQ comes in, even though it is blocked on one processor, another processor can take it and attempt to call the ISR. Having two processors executing the same ISR simultaneously for the same device can be very hazardous. This is because the ISR services one device, and consequently two processors could be accessing the same device registers concurrently. This is where the Spin Lock comes in. On a uniprocessor, use of a Spin Lock introduces virtually no additional overhead, even though it is redundant. On a multiprocessor, it protects the ISR against pathological behavior.

The ISR Spin Lock is also essential for synchronizing hardware register access throughout the driver. You will manipulate hardware registers from various routines in the driver: the `StartIo` or Dispatch Routine, the ISR, and the DPC. A device might interrupt periodically after I/O operations have been started on the adapter. You should view as an atomic operation the sequence of commands you issue to the hardware to process the interrupt, as well as the sequence you issue in the `StartIo` and DPC. If you cannot guarantee that these manipulations of the adapter will not occur concurrently (for example, a device with a single functional unit and IRP queueing to allow only a single in-progress IRP), you must provide explicit synchronization.

To synchronize access, you can call a `KeSynchronizeExecution` routine, which raises the IRQL to the *Synchronization IRQL* of the Interrupt Object and acquires the Spin Lock. The Synchronization IRQL will be the IRQL of the hardware interrupt or higher. When the driver generates several interrupts, the Synchronization IRQL allows you to force all of the ISRs for this device to run at the same IRQL while also preventing them from interrupting each other. This IRQL must be at least the highest possible IRQL at which the device can interrupt. While in the synchronization routine, execution cannot be interrupted by the hardware on any processor. You therefore can be certain that your code will run to completion.

You cannot make any assumption about how long it takes to execute an ISR, a DPC, or a synchronization routine. An ISR can be interrupted by any device whose DIRQL is higher than its own. A DPC can be interrupted by any device. A synchronization routine can be interrupted by any device whose DIRQL is higher than the Synchronization IRQL. All of these interrupts can change the amount of time it takes to complete one of these routines. However, the *total* time spent at elevated IRQL is the sum of the time spent in the routine itself and the time spent in all routines that might have executed at higher levels because of interrupts coming in.

Deadlock Hazards

Some very complex devices embody several functions with shared registers. Sometimes, these devices share the same ISR but interrupt at different levels. This can have a serious effect when the Spin Lock is the only mechanism used for protecting the ISR. Consider the following scenario. A device interrupts at level 5. The interrupt code successfully acquires the Spin Lock and calls the driver's ISR. While in the ISR, the device generates another interrupt at level 7. The processor now tries to acquire the Spin Lock, but it is already acquired, so the processor starts spinning on the lock, waiting for it to release. *But the lock won't be released until the ISR completes, and the ISR can't complete because the machine is locked up at level 7.* Deadlock. Checkmate. To solve this, first the `KiInterruptDispatch` function raises the processor level to the highest possible IRQL necessary so as to block *any* additional calls to the ISR. *Then* the processor tries to acquire the Spin Lock. If the higher-level interrupt comes in at any time up to the raising of the level, it will be taken, and no harm will be done. If it comes in after the level is raised, it will be blocked by the hardware until the ISR completes and the IRQL is dropped.

ISR Levels and Device Priority

On many older architectures, such as the PDP-11 and any ISA-based PC, the importance of a device (for example, an assertion about how quickly it needs service after generating an interrupt) was literally hardwired, in the wiring of the card, to a specific interrupt level. A device that was wired to IRQ11 was clearly more important than a device wired to IRQ7. The problem with this on the ISA bus was that there were more devices than interrupts, and you really needed to be able to reassign the interrupt levels. Today, there is little, if any, correlation between an interrupt level of a device and its "importance". Interrupt levels are dynamically assigned on the PCI Bus during system initialization and/or when a driver is loaded. Furthermore, if your system has an APIC, an interrupt's *priority* might differ considerably from its assigned IRQ line.[1] The priorities assigned to devices might differ from system to system, even for systems that superficially appear to be identically configured. And even on the same system, there is the chance that after a reboot the devices could have different IRQLs assigned (especially if the reboot was required after the installation of a new device!). Generally, you can assume there is no correlation between IRQLs and importance. If you must have a correlation, you might have to program it yourself, as we describe in Chapter 21.

Overview of an ISR

You don't actually manipulate the interrupt vectors in memory;[2] this is handled by the HAL. The HAL also calls your ISR entry point when the interrupt occurs.

There are some fairly stringent restrictions you should adhere to when writing an ISR. The key one is performance. When an interrupt occurs, you should do the absolute minimum required to service the interrupt at the device level. For example, you might read the contents of a small number of I/O registers, write some information to a small number of I/O registers to indicate that the interrupt has been handled, prepare the device for the next transaction, and get out. Anything more sophisticated than this is discouraged. This is because the ISR executes at an elevated IRQL, a level at which no interrupts for lower-priority devices can be serviced. Extended execution at elevated IRQL will potentially "starve" lower IRQL devices, thereby causing I/O transactions to fail. For example, a high-speed 56K modem might want to interrupt each time its FIFO is nearly full. If a new character arrives every 174µs, a 16-byte FIFO would generate an interrupt every 2.7 ms. Thus, keeping an interrupt at elevated IRQL for much more than 2 ms would probably result in characters being dropped.

---

[1] The APIC remains compatible with the PIC until software enables its advanced features. The MPS (multiprocessor) HAL will enable advanced APIC mode on system start-up. The Standard PC HAL will not.

[2] If you ever wrote any device support code for MS-DOS, for example, you know that you simply plugged a pointer to your ISR into the low-numbered memory locations that held the interrupt vectors. You can't do this in NT.

The ISR Prototype

An ISR is defined by this generic prototype:

```
BOOLEAN (*PKSERVICE_ROUTINE) (IN PKINTERRUPT Interrupt,
                              IN PVOID ServiceContext);
```

This function has a BOOLEAN result. If the function determines that the interrupt was not from its device, it must return FALSE. If the function either knows the interrupt *must* be from its device (*never* a safe assumption if the device is on the PCI Bus!) or determines that it *is* from its device, it must return TRUE after it has done its processing. Note that for modern busses, such as PCI (see Chapter 21), several different devices can share the same IRQL. In this case, they are *chained* by the I/O system. In effect, each driver is "queried" through its ISR as to whether it can process the interrupt on that DIRQL. If it can't because the interrupt wasn't for that ISR, it returns FALSE and the interrupt handling code then calls the next ISR in the chain. The first ISR that returns TRUE terminates the routing of that interrupt.

Interrupt Service Routine Requirements

An ISR is run at the DIRQL, in particular at the *SynchronizeIrql* level that was specified when the Device Driver registered its ISR with IoConnectInterrupt. When an NT Device Driver's ISR runs, every interrupt with an equivalent or lower IRQL value is masked off on the current processor. Note that the processor is implicitly raised to the device's DIRQL when the interrupt occurs. But the IRQL could be raised by KiInterruptDispatch to an even higher level, which is the *SynchronizeIrql*.

Note, however, that some other device whose DIRQL is *higher* than the ISR's can cause an interrupt. Thus *an ISR is interruptible*. The elevated IRQL also limits the functions that can be called. Many functions have a specification similar to this: "The thread that calls this function must be running at IRQL <= *something*". Calling a low-IRQL function from a high-IRQL thread will cause anything from erratic behavior to system crashes to corruption of disk data. *Heed the warnings of the specification!*

In many traditional operating systems, the rules were that you did as much as you could in the ISR because that was where the work was done most efficiently. Hefty ISRs would do as much I/O handling as possible, including data copying to the application space, perhaps parsing and processing the input stream, and so on. Windows NT is quite different from such operating systems. NT Device Drivers actually get better performance if their ISRs return control as quickly as possible, rather than attempting to retain control of a CPU and doing as much I/O processing as possible. Performance improvements are particularly noticeable in SMP (Symmetric Multiprocessor) machines, where the machine handling the ISR might be operating in parallel to another machine doing the upper-level processing.

A typical NT ISR will first check to see that the interrupt is from its device, and immediately return FALSE if the interrupt is not. It should next do whatever it takes to clear the interrupt condition. It also should save any necessary state information about or context for the operation that caused the interrupt in memory in the Nonpaged Pool. Usually, this information is stored in the Device Extension. Then, the ISR should queue a request to continue processing at a lower IRQL by calling the driver's DpcForIsr routine or a CustomDpc routine. The ISR then returns. The processing then completes at a lower IRQL, DISPATCH_LEVEL.

Every NT driver that has an ISR also must have a DPC. It can use the DpcForIsr or, alternatively, a CustomDpc routine. At the Device Driver writer's discretion, any NT Device Driver can have additional CustomDpc routines that are used to complete particular kinds of interrupt-driven I/O operations.

If any driver routine shares data, device registers, or context information with the driver's ISR, that driver usually requires one or more SynchCritSection routines. These are covered on page 307.

Note that in a Windows NT uniprocessor machine, the ISR must return before the DpcForIsr or a CustomDpc routine can execute. This is because the DPC Routines, in order to execute, require that the processor IRQL be lower than all DIRQLs. Also, by default, the DPC is queued to run on the same machine on which the IoRequestDpc (for the DpcForIsr) or KeInsertQueueDpc (for a CustomDpc) routine was called. However, it is worth noting that under Windows 2000, it is possible to specify *which* processor in an SMP will execute a DPC (using the SetTargetProcessorDpc call, which has no effect on a uniprocessor). This means that it is possible for the ISR and DpcForIsr (or a CustomDpc) to run *concurrently* in an SMP machine under Windows 2000 (unless the processor that queued the request is the same as the assigned DPC processor). Once you have used the SetTargetProcessorDpc call and queued a DPC request, if the specified processor's IRQL is lower than all of the DIRQLs, it can start executing the DPC request immediately. You must do nothing that could modify data that the lower-IRQL service routine uses—or depend on data that the lower-IRQL service routine might modify—unless proper synchronization is done with the synchronization primitives. The simplest way to handle this is to do nothing after queueing the DPC. If you construct your NT 4.0 driver in this fashion, you will not have a lurking catastrophe if you later want to optimize it for Windows 2000.

Registering the ISR

An NT Device Driver's DriverEntry routine must register the driver's ISR(s) by calling IoConnectInterrupt when the driver is loaded. It must provide resident storage for at least one Interrupt Object pointer if it has an ISR. Usually, this pointer is stored in the Device Extension of the Device Object that represents the physical device that generates interrupts. The Interrupt Object pointer can be stored in a controller extension if the driver creates a Controller Object, or it can be stored in other Nonpaged Pool memory allocated by the driver.

If an NT driver has a single ISR that handles interrupts for more than one device on different vectors or has more than one ISR, it must provide storage for an ISR Spin Lock to be associated with every set of Interrupt Objects for all of its devices. Its ISR Spin Lock must be initialized with KeInitializeSpinLock before the driver registers its ISR(s) by calling IoConnectInterrupt. Such a driver also must provide storage for as many Interrupt Object pointers as the IRQs it handles.

Processing the Interrupt

On entry, an ISR is given pointers to the driver's Interrupt Object and a *ServiceContext* pointer, which is a copy of the pointer registered by the DriverEntry routine setup when it called IoConnectInterrupt. Most Device Drivers set the *ServiceContext* pointer to their Device Objects that represent physical devices that generate interrupts or to such a Device Object's Device Extension. Such a driver uses the Device Extension to set up state information for the driver's `DpcForIsr` routine, which usually does almost all of the I/O processing to satisfy each request that caused the device to interrupt.

In general, an ISR does no actual I/O processing to satisfy an IRP. Instead, it stops the device from interrupting, sets up necessary state information, and queues the driver's `DpcForIsr` or `CustomDpc` to do whatever I/O processing is necessary to satisfy the current request that caused the device to interrupt. In fact, the `IoCompleteRequest` call that signals that the IRP has been handled *cannot* be issued from the ISR level; it *must* be issued from `DISPATCH_LEVEL` (or lower). For many devices, the act of reading in the data from the device is usually done at the lower IRQL. In addition, the lower-IRQL level must initiate the necessary processing to start the next I/O operation, such as actually telling the device that the data has been successfully read. Devices in which the act of clearing the interrupt signals the device that I/O has been handled by the host (and thus the next I/O transfer can start) are particularly driver-hostile in an NT environment and require that proper state saving be done in the ISR.

It is sometimes possible to improve interrupt latency by doing a bit more work in the ISR than the NT philosophy suggests. This should be done only after careful consideration of the effects. *Do not preoptimize your code by "cheating"*. You should apply these techniques only *after* it has been determined that the traditional NT methods are not satisfactory. Otherwise, you might be introducing a driver that has a serious overall system impact without producing a noticeable improvement in the overall performance of the driver itself. NT is a system that can be globally pessimized without achieving local optimization!

Here is a high-level sketch of an ISR.

- Determine whether the interrupt is intended for your driver. If not, return `FALSE` immediately so that the next ISR in the chain will be called promptly. Otherwise, continue interrupt processing.

- Stop the device from interrupting. Note that this is not quite the same as "acknowledging the interrupt". For many devices, acknowledging the interrupt is the signal that all of the necessary state information has been retrieved and the device can initiate the next input operation. The method for "stopping the device from interrupting" will differ by device and by bus. Note that the "IACK" operation, which notifies the interrupt controller that the interrupt has been processed, is handled by the HAL.

- Gather whatever context information the `DpcForIsr` (or `CustomDpc`) routine will need to complete I/O processing for the current operation. This is generally whatever state that might change by the time the DPC Routine is executed. For some devices, there is no context information that must be saved in the ISR. This is very device-dependent.

- If any information has been read that is needed for later processing (and which cannot be read later), store this context in an area accessible to the `DpcForIsr` or `CustomDpc` routine, usually in the Device Extension of the target Device Object for which processing the current I/O request caused the interrupt.

- If the driver has a `DpcForIsr` routine, call `IoRequestDpc` with pointers to the current IRP, the target Device Object, and the saved context. `IoRequestDpc` queues the `DpcForIsr` routine to be run as soon as the IRQL falls to `DISPATCH_LEVEL` or lower on a processor. (Note the careful wording: "on *a* processor". In an SMP environment, *any* processor might execute this routine and might start doing so immediately if it is at a suitable IRQL.)

- If the driver has a `CustomDpc` routine, call `KeInsertQueueDpc` with a pointer to the DPC Object (associated with the `CustomDpc` routine) and pointer(s) to any saved context that the `CustomDpc` routine will need to complete the operation. Usually, the ISR also passes pointers to the current IRP and target Device Object. The `CustomDpc` routine is run as soon as the IRQL falls below `DISPATCH_LEVEL` on *a* processor. (See the previous note about the wording of this last phrase!)

- Return `TRUE` to indicate that the ISR's device generated the interrupt and it has been handled.

Deferred Procedure Call Overview

The DPC is the technique used to provide enhanced priority for interrupt driver processing without keeping the processor at device IRQL. This keeps your processing from blocking other interrupts.

When you enter a DPC, the IRQL is set to `DISPATCH_LEVEL`. This is a lower level than all device interrupt processing but higher than all application code. The DPC might be interrupted by any hardware interrupt, but it is not subject to preemptive scheduling. Only code running below `DISPATCH_LEVEL` can be preempted by the NT scheduler. So while you have no guarantee that a DPC will run to completion without being interrupted by hardware, you know that it will not be preempted by exhausting a time slice. Furthermore, because there is no scheduling, on a uniprocessor you can be sure that all DPCs queued up after it, for any other reasons, will not run until it completes (there are no such guarantees on a multiprocessor). A simplistic view is that DPCs are always handled in FIFO order, but the truth is much more complex. The second-level truth is that (a) DPCs are handled in *queue order* and (b) in an SMP, each processor has its own DPC queue. Generally, you will not have to worry about either of these more detailed truths.

The next level of truth is even more complex, as follows.

- A DPC is inserted in the queue of the processor that calls `IoRequestDpc` or `KeInsertQueueDpc`. It does not run until that processor drops below `DISPATCH_LEVEL`.

- The `SetTargetProcessorDpc` call can be used to assign a DPC to a specific processor's DPC queue. Once entered in that processor's DPC queue, it will be executed in queue order.

- The FIFO order within a queue can be modified by using the `KeSetImportanceDpc` call. This changes the priority of the DPC *at the time it is queued*. Once the DPC is queued, its importance cannot be changed. Once a DPC is in the queue, the *queue* is handled in the order that the DPCs appear.

The `KeSetImportanceDpc` call is specified in Chapter 28 as a Windows 2000 addition. This is not strictly true. It actually exists in NT 4.0, *but it is undocumented*. While we do not generally encourage the use of undocumented features, the fact that this *is* documented for Windows 2000 indicates it is now a fully supported call.

Within a DPC, a driver is interruptible by its own device (as well as any other device in the system). If there is any chance its own device could produce another interrupt while a DPC is being processed, and the DPC must read or modify the hardware state, you must use a `SynchCritSection` handler to synchronize the DPC with the ISR. This is described on page 307.

We consider three forms of DPC Routines:

- The DPC for ISR
- Custom DPCs
- Timer DPCs (covered in Chapter 15)

DPC for ISR versus Custom DPC

The `DpcForIsr` is a facility provided by the I/O Manager. The I/O Manager calls for the `DpcForIsr` are wrappers for the kernel routines that actually deal with DPCs. The storage for the DPC Object used for the `DpcForIsr` is provided as part of the Device Object. A pointer to the Device Object is passed to the I/O Manager routines. There is only one `DpcForIsr` for each Device Object. The parameters of the `DpcForIsr` are fixed and are a special case of the custom DPC parameters. The `DpcForIsr` routine is requested by calling `IoRequestDpc`.

The `CustomDpc` is created and queued by calling the kernel calls directly, instead of using the higher-level `IoRequestDpc` routine. The driver must explicitly allocate storage for the DPC Object. The DPC Routines called are passed a pointer to the DPC Object. A driver can implement as many `CustomDpc` routines as needed. The Custom DPC allows for three parameters to be passed to the DPC Routine: *DeferredContext*, set when the DPC is initialized, and two that are specified when the DPC is queued.

Multiple DPC Routines

For some devices, having just one DPC handler might not make sense. An example is a multifunction device (perhaps a multimedia device) that has several distinct functions sharing a common interrupt line. Rather than a single DPC that must decide how to behave for each device dynamically, it is often easier, for such devices, to have distinct per-function DPCs that are not cluttered by irrelevant code. It might even be the case that you don't have *any* `DpcForIsr` handler, but *only* custom DPC handlers. Alternatively, you could use the `DpcForIsr` for one subfunction and custom DPCs for the other functions. Just because the `DpcForIsr` mechanism exists, you should not feel compelled to use it. It is merely a convenience that handles most, but not quite all, drivers.

The techniques for using custom DPCs are quite similar to those for using `DpcForIsr`. However, instead of calling `IoInitializeDpcRequest`, you call `KeInitializeDpc`. Also, you must allocate nonpageable space (typically in the Device Extension) to hold the DPC Object. And instead of calling `IoRequestDpc`, you call `KeInsertQueueDpc`. Otherwise, these DPCs work just like the `DpcForIsr` invoked by the `IoRequestDpc` call. (In fact, because `IoRequestDpc` is just a wrapper on the core kernel routines, it could even be more efficient to use the Ke-based calls explicitly.)

NT assumes that an ISR will enqueue at most one DPC request for a DPC Object. If it enqueues multiple requests for the same DPC Object, the requested DPC Routine will run only once when the IRQL is lowered.

In a multiprocessor environment, the DPC Routine can potentially run concurrent with the ISR. In particular, once the ISR queues the DPC Routine, the DPC Routine can start running as soon as the processor it is queued on drops to at least `DISPATCH_LEVEL`. In addition, while the DPC Routine is running on one processor, another processor can take another interrupt for the same device. Even on a uniprocessor system, the DPC might be interrupted by the same device. Thus the use of locks and other DPC-to-ISR synchronization techniques is critical.

DpcForIsr

The following functions are used to support the DpcForIsr mechanism.

The DPC Routine

The DPC Routine points to the driver-supplied DpcForIsr routine, which is declared as follows:

```
VOID (*PIO_DPC_ROUTINE)(IN PKDPC Dpc,
                        IN PDEVICE_OBJECT DeviceObject,
                        IN PIRP Irp,
                        IN PVOID Context);
```

The parameters for DpcForIsr are the DPC Object pointer, the Device Object pointer, the IRP pointer, and a context pointer. The context is specified when the DPC is queued.

IoRequestDpc

```
VOID IoRequestDpc(IN PDEVICE_OBJECT DeviceObject,
                  IN PIRP Irp,
                  IN PVOID Context );
```

The IoRequestDpc routine queues a driver-supplied DpcForIsr routine from the ISR to complete interrupt-driven I/O processing at a lower IRQL.

The *DeviceObject* parameter points to the Device Object for which the request that caused the interrupt is being processed. The *Irp* parameter points to the current IRP for the specified device. An optional *Context* parameter points to a driver-determined context to be passed to the DPC Routine. The DPC must have already been established in the Device Object by using IoInitializeDpcRequest. The storage referenced by *Context* must be valid at the time the DPC executes. It is normally resident memory, typically from the Nonpaged Pool. If you do not need additional information, you can use NULL for this value. How the value is interpreted when the DPC finally executes is entirely up to you.

Because IoRequestDpc is called from the Device Driver's ISR, the IRQL is the *SynchronizeIrql* value that was specified when the driver called IoConnectInterrupt and is one of the DIRQLs. However, it is actually possible to queue a DPC at any IRQL >= DISPATCH_LEVEL using the Ke..Dpc routines.

IoInitializeDpcRequest

```
VOID IoInitializeDpcRequest(IN PDEVICE_OBJECT DeviceObject,
                            IN PIO_DPC_ROUTINE DpcRoutine);
```

The IoInitializeDpcRequest function registers a driver-supplied DpcForIsr routine. This is the routine called as a consequence of calling IoRequestDpc. It is normally registered when a Device Driver initializes.

Custom DPC Routines

The following functions support the use of Custom DPC Routines.

The Custom DPC Routine

The Custom DPC Routine is defined as follows.

```
VOID (*PKDEFERRED_ROUTINE)(IN PKDPC Dpc,
                           IN PVOID DeferredContext,
                           IN PVOID SystemArgument1,
                           IN PVOID SystemArgument2);
```

The parameters specify the DPC Object, plus three values provided by the driver, each of which usually contains a pointer. The first, *DeferredContext*, is specified when the DPC Object is initialized. The second and third are specified when the DPC is queued.

KeInitializeDpc

```
VOID KeInitializeDpc(IN PKDPC Dpc,
                     IN PKDEFERRED_ROUTINE DeferredRoutine,
                     IN PVOID DeferredContext);
```

The KeInitializeDpc function initializes a DPC Object, setting up a deferred procedure that can be called. When the function is called, it is passed the specified *DeferredContext* as one of its parameters. This value must be a reference to storage that is valid at the time the DPC is called. Because the DPC can execute in an arbitrary thread context, you can't pass a user-level address here. The storage must also be resident when the DPC executes.

The *DeferredRoutine* parameter specifies the entry point for a routine to be called when the DPC Object is removed from the DPC queue. *DeferredRoutine* is declared as follows.

```
VOID (*PKDEFERRED_ROUTINE)(IN PKDPC Dpc,
                           IN PVOID DeferredContext,
                           IN PVOID SystemArgument1,
                           IN PVOID SystemArgument2);
```

The *DeferredContext* parameter of KeInitializeDpc points to a caller-supplied context to be passed to *DeferredRoutine* as its *DeferredContext* parameter when *DeferredRoutine* is called. The value passed, if interpreted as an address, must represent valid storage at the time the DPC is executed. The values of the *SystemArgument* parameters to the deferred routine are supplied when the DPC is queued.

The caller can queue an initialized DPC with KeInsertQueueDpc. It also can set up a Timer Object associated with the initialized DPC Object and queue the DPC with KeSetTimer.

Storage for the DPC Object must be resident, either in the Device Extension of a driver-created Device Object, in the Controller Extension of a driver-created Controller Object, or in the Nonpaged Pool allocated by the caller.

KeInsertQueueDpc

```
BOOLEAN KeInsertQueueDpc(IN PKDPC Dpc,
                         IN PVOID SystemArgument1,
                         IN PVOID SystemArgument2);
```

The `KeInsertQueueDpc` function queues a DPC for execution when the IRQL of a processor drops below `DISPATCH_LEVEL`.

The *SystemArgument1* and *SystemArgument2* parameters point to untyped data. These pointers are passed into the DPC Routine. If they are used as addresses, they must reference resident storage and be valid when the DPC is executed.

If the specified DPC Object is not currently in the queue, `KeInsertQueueDpc` queues the DPC and returns TRUE. If the specified DPC Object is already in the DPC queue, no operation is performed and FALSE is returned.

Note that a given DPC Object and the function it represents can each be queued for execution only once at any given moment.

KeRemoveQueueDpc

```
BOOLEAN KeRemoveQueueDpc(IN PKDPC Dpc);
```

The `KeRemoveQueueDpc` function removes a given DPC Object from the system DPC queue. It returns TRUE if the DPC Object is in the DPC queue. If the given DPC Object is not currently in the DPC queue, no operation is performed and FALSE is returned.

Writing an ISR

An ISR has many restrictions on what it can do. It cannot cause a page fault, for example, so it can touch only nonpaged memory. The memory it touches must be "locked down". That is, the memory must either be allocated from the Nonpaged Pool or be paged memory that is locked by an explicit call to the Memory Manager. The ISR cannot call any of the mapping functions to convert application addresses to system logical addresses, so any required address mapping must be done long before the interrupt occurs. Most runtime functions and nearly all other functions are unavailable.

If you fail to follow these limitations, you'll likely get a Blue Screen. Or the machine might just hang. In the worst case, parts of the operating system might become corrupted. This might lead to the ultimate form of failure: complete, unrecoverable loss of the contents of the hard drive. You must be very, very careful what you ask for in an ISR. The "ideal" ISR is very, very short and does practically nothing. In general, this is sufficient for all but very high-performance devices with severe latency constraints.

A Prototypical ISR

Listing 14.1 shows an interrupt handler for an ISA device, our Hardware Simulator. (We describe this more fully in Chapter 27. The complete working function appears on page 632.) Because it is an ISA device, it does not need to check for sharability of interrupts. However, it is worth pointing out that some ISA devices (for example, the COM ports) have a notorious reputation for generating *spurious* interrupts. It is always good to test that the interrupt came from your device, even on an ISA bus! How a driver checks to see if the interrupt is for itself is very device-dependent. For example, it might check a status register to see if a interrupt status bit is set. The way in which this check is performed will depend on the nature of the device. Note that other than in a few places where we suggest where to test or poke the device registers, this ISR only queues up the DPC request.

When we registered the ISR using IoConnectInterrupt, we specified as the *Context* parameter a pointer to the Device Extension. Therefore, we know that our *Context* parameter here is a pointer to the Device Extension.

Listing 14.1: *A Prototypical ISR*

```
BOOLEAN Lab5InterruptServiceRoutine(
    IN PKINTERRUPT Interrupt,
    IN OUT PVOID Context)
  {
    PLAB5_DEVICE_EXTENSION deviceExtension = Context;
    PDEVICE_OBJECT deviceObject = deviceExtension->DeviceObject;

    // Note that the use of DbgPrint should only be done during initial testing
    // This will keep the IRQL elevated until the entire message has printed!
    // This is here only for the first rough-cut debugging!

    DbgPrint("%s  InterruptServiceRoutine - Got one!",  DBG_MSG_HDR);

    /*
    * Look at our Interrupt Status Register...
    */

    // ...do whatever is appropriate here

    /*
    * Clear the Interrupt ASAP, or get out if it isn't us...
    */

    // ... as appropriate for the device

    //
    // Note: the CurrentIrp field of the Device Object gets filled in
    // by IoStartPacket or IoStartNextPacket (which eventually leads
    // calling the drivers StartIo routine, which should lead to the
    // interrupt).
    //
    // If this interrupt was not the result of driver-initiated I/O
    // then this field would not be a correct IRP pointer, and perhaps
    // not even a valid IRP pointer.
    //
    IoRequestDpc(deviceObject,
                 deviceObject->CurrentIrp,
                 NULL);
    return TRUE;
}
```

ISRs and Shared Interrupts

You might wonder about the "correctness" of an ISR when multiple devices share a single IRQL. For example, suppose Device A generates an interrupt, which it happens to generate while the ISR for some higher-level IRQL is running. Thus it cannot be taken right away. While this interrupt is pending, Device B generates an interrupt on the same IRQ line as Device A.

Finally, the processor IRQL lowers to where the IRQ can be taken. During the ISR dispatch, it just happens that the ISR for Device B is asked *first*, "Is this your interrupt?" The Device B ISR looks at the status register and says, "Indeed, yes!" and happily goes off to process the interrupt, returning TRUE. At this point, the interrupt dispatcher realizes the interrupt has been processed and doesn't even bother to call Device A's ISR. Did we fail to handle the interrupt for Device A?

If it weren't for the production problems, we'd print the answer to this question upside-down. If you think the answer is "Yes", think a bit more about it before you read the next paragraph.

The only way you can get multiple devices interrupting on the same IRQL is if the interrupt line is shared, which means that the interrupt must be a *level-triggered* interrupt. If you are lost at this point, check out Chapter 21, where we discuss PCI interrupts. Here's what happens. When you "clear the interrupt" on Device B, that device is no longer holding down the IRQL line for an interrupt. *But Device A still is holding down the line*. There is *still* an interrupt pending on that IRQL, and, as soon as the processor IRQL is lowered, that interrupt will be taken. This will actually happen as soon as the ISR completes and the stacked return to whatever code was interrupted is performed. What you might expect is that the DPC would be dispatched. In fact, the pending interrupt is taken and the whole interrupt-dispatch operation starts over. The first ISR called is that for Device B. The ISR looks at the status register for Device B, but since the pending interrupt condition was cleared, it sees no pending interrupt on the device and returns FALSE, meaning, "I See No Interrupt Here". So the interrupt-dispatch code passes the interrupt event to the next ISR in its chain, the ISR for Device A, which looks at its associated status register and says, "Mine! Mine!" It then goes on about its ISR-handling duties, happy and confident that it is Doing Its Thing. While the interrupts are not processed in FIFO order, they all will be handled, unless there is some "nasty device" or "nasty driver". A nasty device is a device that keeps interrupting at a ferocious rate, so the next time the ISR dispatch is executed the device has another interrupt pending. Other interrupts sharing the interrupt line may experience excessive latency. A nasty driver is a driver that fails to properly clear the interrupt condition for the device in its ISR. The interrupt will be processed again as soon as the driver returns from the interrupt. If the driver never clears the interrupt, the system will hang because it spends all of its time in the ISR. If the driver clears the interrupt intermittently, the latency of other interrupts and system overhead will be excessive.

> Note the implication of how the device chain works. The ISR for Device B must clear the status it uses to determine that Device B was the interrupting device, or you'll end up with an infinite loop! If the interrupt status is not cleared, as soon as the ISR returns, the interrupt will occur again because Device B will still be reporting the interrupt condition. Device B's ISR would erroneously think that its device had generated a new interrupt, so it would redundantly attempt to queue up a DPC (which would be ignored) and would return TRUE. Device A would keep holding the IRQ request line low, but its ISR would never be called because the ISR for Device B would erroneously continue to return TRUE. A power-cycle or reset is required to get out of this! Always test a shared-interrupt driver in a condition under which some other device shares the interrupt. Arrange the load order so that you can test the drivers in two different orders!

The Deferred Procedure Call

The DPC routine is the heart of the interrupt handler; the ISR is merely a gateway to this function. Because this function executes at a lower IRQL, it can be interrupted by any other device (including its own, a problem we discuss in much more detail starting on page 307). This means that trying the usual "count instruction cycles" technique in an attempt to figure out "how fast" it is won't work. (Actually, because of cache and pipelining this technique has been obsolete for years.) The full text of a working instance of a DPC is given on page 633. A key point here is that you *must*, before leaving this function, perform *one* of the following actions:

- Complete the IRP with a success code and perform whatever action is required to initiate the next IRP, in case there is one pending.

- Complete the IRP with an error code and perform whatever action is required to initiate the next IRP, in case there is one pending.

- Do nothing to the IRP and perform whatever action is required to initiate additional I/O activity on the device, leading to the eventual completion of the IRP.

If you fail to do just one of these, then even if the action requested by the IRP has completed, no other IRP pending for the device can be processed. The current IRP will remain pending forever because the driver is no longer doing anything to advance the completion of the IRP. This will give the appearance that the device is hung.

We do not discuss here what is meant by "initiate the next IRP". There are several mechanisms that could be used, and they take an entire chapter (Chapter 22) to describe. For now, just accept that this must be done. For the simplest form of queueing, the `IoStartNextPacket` function is the one that is used. An example of a DPC, including `IoStartNextPacket` usage, is shown in Listing 14.2.

Listing 14.2: *A DPC Example*

```
VOID Lab5DpcRoutine(
    IN PKDPC Dpc,
    PDEVICE_OBJECT deviceObject,
    IN PVOID SystemArgument1,
    IN PVOID SystemArgument2
    )
{
    PLAB5_DEVICE_EXTENSION deviceExtension;
    PIRP Irp;

    Irp = deviceObject->CurrentIrp;
    deviceExtension = deviceObject->DeviceExtension;
    deviceExtension->InterruptCount++;
    DbgPrint("    DPCRoutine - Got one!\n");
    if (Irp != NULL)
        {

        // (see page 633)

        // Here's how to complete an IRP successfully...

        //
        // need to fill in the Information field to the length of the data in
        // order to get the I/O manager to copy the data back to user address
        // space (this is a device which uses DO_BUFFERED_IO mode, as
        // established in DriverEntry)
        //
        Irp->IoStatus.Information = 0; // use something other than 0 to get copy!

        Irp->IoStatus.Status = STATUS_SUCCESS;
        IoCompleteRequest(Irp, IO_NO_INCREMENT);
```

```
        // The IRP is now complete. Start the next IRP, if there is one

        IoStartNextPacket(deviceObject, FALSE);
    }
    return;
}
```

ISRs and the Unload Routine

Once you have connected an interrupt, you must disconnect it. Leaving an interrupt connected after a driver has unloaded is almost certain to generate a Blue Screen—if you're lucky. (If you aren't, it will merely cause parts of the operating system to be corrupted and lead to more insidious damage.) To disconnect an interrupt, you call `IoDisconnectInterrupt`. But here's a serious warning: If you have not connected the interrupt, do not call `IoDisconnectInterrupt` to disconnect it. This will crash the system. (In general, attempting to free any kernel resource twice will crash the system.)

In Listing 14.3, we know there is only one Device Object attached to this driver, so we do not iterate down the list freeing up all possible Device Objects.

Listing 14.3: *An Unload Routine for a Driver with Interrupts*

```
VOID Lab5Unload( IN PDRIVER_OBJECT driverObject)
{
    UNICODE_STRING uniDosNameString;
    PLAB5_DEVICE_EXTENSION extension;
    BOOLEAN GotResources;
    extension = driverObject->DeviceObject->DeviceExtension;

    KdPrint( ("%s: Unloading!!\n",   DBG_MSG_HDR) );

    //
    // Disconnect the interrupt
    //
    IoDisconnectInterrupt(extension->InterruptObject);

    //
    // Delete the link from our device name to a name in the Win32 namespace.
    //

    RtlInitUnicodeString( &uniDosNameString, DOS_DEVICE_NAME );
    IoDeleteSymbolicLink( &uniDosNameString );

    //
    // Finally delete our Device Object
    //
    IoDeleteDevice( driverObject->DeviceObject );
}
```

The SynchCritSection Routine

The `SynchCritSection` routine is a routine called at hardware interrupt synchronization priority. It is used to synchronize access to hardware registers (we discuss this also in Chapter 11 on page 261). Since hardware registers are accessed in the ISR (see page 295), you must synchronize other potential access when the access would conflict. Devices that require a multistep access to device registers in order to complete an I/O transaction will require this technique. An example is a device that is initialized by writing a reset command to a register and then writing 20 register values in 20 1-byte writes. If an interrupt occurs in the middle of the sequence, the ISR may fail because it expected a different state of the hardware, or the nonintegrated code may fail if the state is not properly restored on return from the interrupt. For some devices, it simply might not be possible to interrupt the multistep sequence reliably. The solution is to use a synchronization routine to raise the IRQL to the same level as the interrupt to perform the 21 writes to the device. This prevents the interrupt service from interrupting while the code is in a "critical section".

The synchronization routine uses the second form of Spin Lock, the *interrupt synchronization Spin Lock*.

The routine passed to `KeSynchronizeExecution` is called at the IRQL of the `SynchronizeIrql` entry of the Interrupt Object. The Spin Lock was specified when the `IoConnectInterrupt` call was executed to create the Interrupt Object and must be in the resident storage that you supply (usually in the Device Extension). In the following `IoConnectInterrupt` call, we know the device interrupts at only one DIRQL, so we can set `SynchronizeIrql` to be the same as the interrupt's IRQL. For some multifunction devices, the IRQL of the interrupt might be lower than `SynchronizeIrql`, which is the *highest* IRQL at which the device can interrupt.

KeSynchronizeExecution

The *Interrupt* parameter points to the Interrupt Object established by `IoConnectInterrupt`. You typically put this in your Device Extension. The *SynchronizeRoutine* is the routine that is called to execute the critical section code; for a given Interrupt Object, this function guarantees that no more than one *SynchronizeRoutine* execute at a time, even on a multiprocessor. When the *SynchronizeRoutine* is called, it is passed the *SynchronizeContext* value as its parameter. A *SynchronizeRoutine* is always executed at an elevated IRQL, the *SynchronizeIrql* specified in the call to *IoConnectInterrupt*.

An example of how to use `KeSynchronizeExecution`, including an example of a *SynchronizeRoutine*, is shown in Listing 14.5. The setup necessary for its use is shown in Listing 14.4.

```
BOOLEAN KeSynchronizeExecution(IN PKINTERRUPT Interrupt,
                               IN PKSYNCHRONIZE_ROUTINE SynchronizeRoutine,
                               IN PVOID SynchronizeContext);
```

Listing 14.4: *A* DriverEntry *Routine for a Driver with a* SynchCritSection *Routine*

```
... DriverEntry(...)
{
    ....

    //
    // Initialize the spinlock
    //
    KeInitializeSpinLock( &deviceExtension->ISRSpinLock);
    //
    // connect the Device Driver to the IRQ
    //
```

```
    ioConnectStatus = IoConnectInterrupt(&deviceExtension->InterruptObject,
                                HdwSimTestInterruptServiceRoutine,
                                deviceExtension,
                                &deviceExtension->ISRSpinLock,
                                MappedSysVect,
                        Irql,            // Device Interrupt IRQL
                        Irql,            // Synchronization IRQL
                        Latched,
                        FALSE,
                        deviceExtension->Affinity,
                        FALSE);    // Save Floating Point stack
                                   // on interrupt

    if ( !NT_SUCCESS (ioConnectStatus) )
            {
                //  Error action here
            }
    ....
}
```

Listing 14.5: *The* SynchCritSection *Routine and Its Use*

```
BOOLEAN mySynchronizeWrite( IN PVOID SynchronizeContext );
{
    MY_REGISTER_CONTEXT *localRegisters =
                    (MY_REGISTER_CONTEXT *)SynchronizeContext;

    ....

    //
    // Access device registers here -- will not be interrupted by ISR
    //
    *HardwarePointer->register1 = localRegisters->register1;


    ....
}

NTSTATUS wantToAccessHardware(VOID)
{
    MY_REGISTER_CONTEXT theLocalRegisters;
    .....
    KeSynchronizeExecution(
            &deviceExtension->InterruptObject,  // the interrupt object
            &mySynchronizeWrite,                // routine to be called
            (PVOID)&theLocalRegisters);         // address of the context
                                                // structure

}
```

Resource Allocation Interlocks

Certain resources of hardware can be represented by Controller Objects and Adapter Objects.
These objects require synchronization at DISPATCH_LEVEL, but at intervals far longer than a
Spin Lock is suitable. Thus Mutexes are unsuitable because they can block only at IRQLs lower
than DISPATCH_LEVEL. These resources are interlocked by using features of the I/O Manager
that allow blocking at DISPATCH_LEVEL. The Controller and Adapter Objects maintain queues
that allow the scheduling of the resources. An implication of this is that the function that is

called when the resource becomes free is not necessarily executing in the thread context that was executing when the request was queued.

We discuss these objects in detail in Chapter 17.

Summary

This chapter has covered the key ideas of the ISR and DPC routines. The key idea is that very little processing is done at interrupt level; most of the work is done in the DPC, which is interruptible. The nature of NT requires careful synchronization between levels to avoid conflict in accessing the device's registers. Shared IRQ lines require cooperation of the driver for proper handling.

Chapter

15 *Achieving Reality: Timers*

An NT driver often must depend on the passage of time. A driver might have to wait for a predetermined interval between operations or perform an operation at a specific time. To measure performance, a driver might wish to determine the amount of time spent performing some operation. NT provides support for all of these time-specific operations. This chapter covers the various types of timers you can have in NT, and how to use them.

Hardware Timers

NT timers on the *x*86 are based on two sources for time information: the motherboard *interval timer* and the CPU (the Pentium cycle counter register and the execution time of instructions). The motherboard interval timer is set to interrupt the CPU at a regular interval. NT uses this regular interrupt to increment the system tick count and check its work list for scheduled work. The tick count is the basis for the NT time-of-day values.

The default interval depends on the processor and the HAL. Typical values are 10 ms for a standard (uniprocessor) *x*86 system, 15 ms for a dual processor *x*86 system, and 7.5 ms for an Alpha system. These intervals can be reduced if a User-mode program has used the multimedia timer API. The User-mode API call `timeGetDevCaps` returns the minimum and maximum values for the time interval acceptable on the system. The User-mode API call `timeBeginPeriod` sets the system timer to at most the specified higher resolution. It indicates that the time interval can be restored to the default value. Several User-mode programs might have called `timeBeginPeriod`; in this case, the time interval will be the minimum of the specified values.

Time Delay

The resolution of the timers capable of restarting the driver's thread defaults to 10 ms on the Standard PC HAL and 15 ms on the Multiprocessor *x*86 (MPS) HAL. This resolution is determined by the interval used to increment the system interval timer. This interval can be changed by applications using the multimedia timer functions. NT 4.0 does not export a function to allow drivers to modify the resolution. As this is written, there are reports that functions will be added to Windows 2000 that allow drivers to manipulate the counter increment, but no formal announcement has been made. The kernel routine KeQueryTimeIncrement can be called within a driver to determine the current value of the clock increment.

Following are the descriptions of the key timer functions you can use in your driver.

Performance Measurement

It is often useful to be able to instrument your driver to determine if it is spending an undue amount of time somewhere. The key function for this purpose is KeQueryPerformanceCounter.

KeQueryPerformanceCounter

```
LARGE_INTEGER KeQueryPerformanceCounter(
                    IN PLARGE_INTEGER PerformanceFrequency OPTIONAL);
```

The KeQueryPerformanceCounter function obtains "high-resolution" timing. The definition of "high-resolution" depends on the platform and the HAL and, for some combinations, is not what you might think of as "high" resolution. For some platforms, this call has sufficient overhead that its use can actually distort the performance being measured. KeQueryPerformanceCounter returns a time value that is a large integer and that represents a number of "ticks". You can call this function once at the start of a block of code whose time is to be measured and once at the end and then compute the difference. This value can be converted to time by knowing how many ticks per second occur, which is the value optionally returned in the location specified by the input parameter.

The *PerformanceFrequency* parameter is a pointer to a LARGE_INTEGER to be set to the value of the tick rate. If it is NULL, the tick rate will not be returned. The return value is the value of the count.

The effects of this routine are HAL-dependent. The Microsoft documentation contains a warning about high overhead for this function, since all interrupts are disabled during its execution. This warning applies only if the system is running the Standard PC HAL. The MPS HAL version does not disable interrupts.

With the Standard PC HAL, KeQueryPerformanceCounter uses the countdown register in the motherboard clock timer chip, which counts at 1,193,180Hz. Used here, this routine is expensive, costing 5 to 10µs per call. With the MPS HAL (MPS single or multiprocessor HAL), this routine uses the Pentium RDTSC instruction to read the processor tick count. It returns the count of ticks of the Pentium clock. Here, the cost to execute this routine is about 8 instructions per call. On multiprocessor systems, processor clocks are not perfectly synchronized. There might be 10–20 ticks of skew between processors.

NT (with the MPS HAL) provides high-resolution time measurement, but it does not provide a high-resolution time-based wake-up of driver code.

If you want to do minimally invasive instrumentation and can sacrifice portability, you can also use the _asm directive to insert the Pentium RDTSC instruction directly inline in your driver. This limits your driver, at least if the instruction is actually executed, to running *only* on Intel platforms. Intel-"compatible" processors from other vendors do not currently implement this instruction.

Time Delays

Sometimes you need to insert a time delay in a driver. For very short delays, less than 50µs, you can delay the thread itself with a calibrated busy loop. For longer delays, you must use a separate thread. Threads are covered in detail in Chapter 24. The sections below describe the time delay operations available to drivers.

KeStallExecutionProcessor

```
VOID KeStallExecutionProcessor(IN ULONG MicroSeconds);
```

The KeStallExecutionProcessor function is used to delay for very brief periods of time. Its use must be limited to very short delays because when the processor is executing this function, the processor is unavailable for any other use. Microsoft strongly suggests that such periods be less than 50µs in duration. KeStallExecutionProcessor is the simplest of the delay functions.

The input parameter is the number of microseconds to wait. The routine will stall at least as long as specified. It executes a calibrated instruction loop, spinning until the specified time has elapsed. In a multiprocessor system, other processors are still free to execute.

The actual interval may be much longer. KeStallExecutionProcessor does not raise IRQL and might be interrupted.

KeDelayExecutionThread

```
NTSTATUS KeDelayExecutionThread(IN KPROCESSOR_MODE WaitMode,
                                IN BOOLEAN Alertable,
                                IN PLARGE_INTEGER Interval);
```

The KeDelayExecutionThread function provides a longer delay than KeStallExecutionProcessor does. It operates by putting the current thread into a wait state for at least the specified interval. The actual delay will not be less than the specified time. However, it could be longer, for several reasons, as follows.

- The interval will be rounded up to the nearest integer multiple of the system clock time.[1]

- The thread will have to wait while higher-priority threads run and will not actually be scheduled until all higher-priority threads have completed. Within its priority class, the thread, once the time expires, might have to wait for a currently running thread to complete.

- Any code running at any DIRQL or at DISPATCH_LEVEL can extend the times by preempting the processor.[2]

KeDelayExecutionThread must not be used for long delays in an arbitrary thread context. If a wait is executed in the DPC, whatever thread was current when the DPC started will be

---

[1] Currently, this is 10 ms on the uniprocessor *x*86 HAL, 15 ms on the multiprocessor *x*86 HAL, and 7.5 ms on the Alpha.

[2] If any Device Driver is "badly behaved", the system might spend more time than Microsoft suggests at elevated IRQL (the IDE disk driver is an example of one such driver—a condition forced on it by the need to deal with some older-style IDE devices. The IDE CD-ROM driver has the reputation of tying up the processor at elevated IRQL for as long as 1½ seconds).

unable to run until this timer expires. This call can be used freely in a dedicated driver thread or in the Dispatch Routine of a highest-level driver.

The *WaitMode* parameter specifies the processor mode in which the caller is waiting. This is KernelMode for a driver. The *Alertable* parameter specifies whether the wait state is alertable. For drivers, specify FALSE.

The *Interval* parameter is the absolute or relative time of the delay, specified in 100-ns units. A negative value indicates relative time. Absolute expiration times track any changes in system time; relative expiration times are not affected by system time changes.

Note that while the time is specified in 100-ns units, the clock operates in terms of timer ticks. The delay will last for the number of timer ticks with a delay equal to or greater than the specified time.

Timeout Routines

In some situations, you need not a delay, but a timeout: that is, a way to start a timer, and to detect if the timer has expired before some other event, such as an interrupt or completion of an IRP, has occurred. In such cases you usually want to take some remedial action to recover from what is apparently a failure of some sort. This could represent a hardware failure, or the failure of some remote software to respond (such as a failure to receive an ACK packet in response to a message transmittal).

IoTimer Routines

The IoTimer function provides a simple mechanism to implement a fixed 1-second timer. It is used primarily for a driver-implemented timeout. A DPC Routine provided by the driver is executed each time the timer fires. There is one and only one IoTimer associated with each Device Object. To use IoTimer, the driver calls the IoInitializeTimer routine to specify the timer routine and a context parameter. The context parameter is a pointer to a driver-determined data structure that will be passed to the timer routine in addition to the pointer to the Device Object. Unlike with the Custom DPC (discussed in Chapter 14), only one parameter may be passed to the timer DPC Routine.

The *TimerRoutine* parameter to IoInitializeTimer points to the driver-supplied IoTimer routine. The routine called by the timer is as follows.

```
VOID (*PIO_TIMER_ROUTINE) (IN PDEVICE_OBJECT DeviceObject,
                           IN PVOID Context);
```

There are three IoTimer functions.

1. The driver must first call IoInitializeTimer.
2. Then the driver might call IoStartTimer.
3. When the timer is no longer needed, the driver can call IoStopTimer to stop the timer.

The I/O Manager routines used to implement the IoTimer object call the kernel timer functions to manipulate kernel Timer Objects.

The timer is started in the DriverEntry routine. You need to define a flag in the Device Extension indicating that no I/O is active. In the StartIo routine (or Dispatch Routine, if there is no `StartIo`), you set another Device Extension variable to the timeout count desired and the flag to indicate that I/O is active. The value set is the desired length of the timeout in seconds plus 1 second to allow for the partial second in progress when the interval starts. The timer DPC checks the I/O active flag. If the flag indicates no I/O is outstanding, it returns. If the flag indicates that there is I/O outstanding, the count value is decremented by 1 and tested. If the counter reaches 0, the appropriate device-specific action necessary to recover from the error condition should be initiated. Note that this can involve queueing up another DPC or creating one or more IRPs, among the many options available.

If your driver permits multiple concurrent I/O operations, the driver must maintain one counter for each pending I/O transfer. This might require keeping an array or linked list of pending timeout counters. Which you do depends on how you design your driver and what restrictions you choose to impose on the total number of outstanding I/O transfers.

IoInitializeTimer

```
NTSTATUS IoInitializeTimer(IN PDEVICE_OBJECT DeviceObject,
                           IN PIO_TIMER_ROUTINE TimerRoutine,
                           IN PVOID Context);
```

Initializes the `IoTimer` for the specified Device Object. The timer must be started using `IoStartTimer`. After the timer is started, once a second, the specified `TimerRoutine` will be called, and the value `Context` will be passed into it as a parameter. If this is used to represent an address, it must be an address in nonpaged memory, and it must be valid each time the `TimerRoutine` is called.

IoStartTimer

```
VOID IoStartTimer(IN PDEVICE_OBJECT DeviceObject);
```

Starts the `IoTimer`. It will call the `TimerRoutine` specified by `IoInitializeTimer` once a second until it is stopped. Note that it is uncommon to start and stop the `IoTimer`; normally, a flag in the Device Extension is used to signal whether the timer expiration is meaningful or not.

IoStopTimer

```
VOID IoStopTimer(IN PDEVICE_OBJECT DeviceObject);
```

Stops the `IoTimer`. Normally this is done in the Unload routine.

Example: Using a Custom Timer

In this example, three IOCTL codes are implemented, one each to start, stop, and read the count. In Listing 15.1, we show the actual routine that is called once per second. In Listing 15.2, we show how to initialize the `IoTimer`, and in Listing 15.3 we show the IOCTL handlers that allow an application to start and stop the timer and query the timer count.

Listing 15.1: *An* `IoTimer` *Routine*

```
VOID calledOncePerSecond(IN PDEVICE_OBJECT DeviceObject,
                         IN PVOID Context)
```

```
{
    PMY_EXTENSION extension;
    extension = DeviceObject->extension;

    extension->count++;       // Count the number of seconds
                              // This timer has been active
}
```

Listing 15.2: *The* DriverEntry *Routine for a Driver Using* IoTimer

```
... DriverEntry(...)
{
    ....
    status = IoInitializeTimer(DeviceObject,
                        calledOncePerSecond,    // The routine to be called
                               extension->Context;// A pointer to be passed
    if (STATUS_SUCCESS != status)
        {
            // Process error here
        }
    ....
}
```

Listing 15.3: DeviceIoControl *Handler for Timer*

```
NTSTATUS myDeviceControl(IN PDEVICE_OBJECT DeviceObject, IN PIRP Irp)
{
    NTSTATUS ret = STATUS_SUCCESS;
    PIO_STACK_LOCATION stack = IoGetCurrentIrpStackLocation(Irp);

    PMY_DEVICE_EXTENSION extension = DeviceObject->DeviceExtension;
    MY_OUTPUT * pOutBuffer = (MY_INITIALIZE_OUTPUT *)Irp->UserBuffer

    switch(stack->Parameters.DeviceIoControl.IoControlCode)
        { /* IOCTL */
        case   IOCTL_MY_START_COUNT:
                IoStartTimer(DeviceObject);
                Irp->IoStatus.Information = 0;
                break;

        case   IOCTL_MY_STOP_COUNT:
                IoStopTimer(DeviceObject);
                Irp->IoStatus.Information = 0;
                break;

        case   IOCTL_MY_GET_COUNT:
                *pOutBuffer = extension->count;
                Irp->IoStatus.Information = sizeof(extension->count);
                break;
        default:
                ret = STATUS_UNSUCCESSFUL;
        } /* IOCTL */

    Irp->IoStatus.Status = ret;
    IoCompleteRequest(Irp, IO_NO_INCREMENT);

    return ret;
}
```

Custom Timer Routines

When more flexibility is needed than `IoTimer` can provide, the custom (kernel) timer might be used. This timer routine requires that the driver allocate nonpaged storage for a KTIMER object. To use a custom timer, you first must initialize the timer structure and then tell the system to use it, as follows.

- Initialize the kernel Timer Object by calling `KeInitializeTimer`.
- Set the time with `KeSetTimer` or `KeSetTimerEx`. This puts the Timer Object in the system timer queue.

You can choose one or more of the following methods to determine when the timer interval has expired.

- You can set up a timer DPC Routine that will be called at `DISPATCH_LEVEL` shortly after the timer expires. This DPC Routine is set up using `KeInitializeDpc`, which can specify a *Context* parameter value to be passed to the DPC.
- You can poll the Timer Object to see if it has expired. This is done by waiting for the Timer Object with a timeout value of 0 (which can be done at any IRLQ <= `DISPATCH_LEVEL`).
- You can wait for the Timer Object (at any IRQL < `DISPATCH_LEVEL`).

Waiting on a Custom Timer Object

The `KeWaitforSingleObject` routine accepts a Timer Object reference as a waitable object. For the `KeWaitForMultipleObjects` routine, one or more Timer Objects can be among the waitable objects. When the timer expires, the Timer Object enters the Signaled state.

Polling a Custom Timer Object

You can read the current state of the timer (expired or not expired) by using `KeReadStateTimer` or the `KeWait...` calls with a timeout value of 0 (note, this is *not* the same as passing a NULL pointer for the timeout value—that means "infinite wait").

The `CustomTimerDpc` Routine

The `CustomTimerDpc` routine is defined by the kernel as follows.

```
VOID (*PKDEFERRED_ROUTINE)(IN PKDPC Dpc,
                          IN PVOID DeferredContext,
                          IN PVOID SystemArgument1,   // Reserved
                          IN PVOID SystemArgument2 ); // Reserved
```

The *DeferredContext* parameter passed to the custom timer DPC is the *Context* pointer specified when `KeInitializeDpc` was called. The routine also has two unused parameters: *SystemArgument1* and *SystemArgument2*. For a custom timer DPC, these parameters are specified when `KeInsertQueueDpc` is called. The `KeSetTimer` and `KeSetTimerEx` routines, although they use the DPC mechanism, provide no mechanism to set these values, so the timer DPC is called with these values undefined.

Notification Timers and Synchronization Timers

There are two types of timers: *Notification* and *Synchronization*. They are distinguished by how threads waiting on the Timer Object are handled when the timer interval expires. For a Notification Timer, all waiting threads are released and the timer remains in the Signaled state until explicitly reset, for example, by calling KeSetTimer or KeSetTimerEx. For a Synchronization Timer, exactly one thread is released and the timer automatically resets.

Functions for Custom Timers

The following functions are used to handle general kernel timers.

KeInitializeTimer

```
VOID KeInitializeTimer(IN PKTIMER Timer);
```

The KeInitializeTimer function initializes a Timer Object. The *Timer* parameter points to a Timer Object, for which the caller provides the storage. The Timer Object is initialized in the Not-Signaled state. Storage for a Timer Object must be resident, either in the Device Extension of a driver-created Device Object, in the Controller Extension of a driver-created Controller Object, or in a Nonpaged Pool allocated by the caller.

KeInitializeTimer can initialize only Notification Timers. KeInitializeTimerEx can initialize both Notification Timers and Synchronization Timers.

KeInitializeTimerEx

```
VOID KeInitializeTimerEx(IN PKTIMER Timer, IN TIMER_TYPE Type);
```

The KeInitializeTimerEx function initializes a Timer Object. The Timer Object can be initialized as a Notification Timer (all threads released, manual reset) by specifying NotificationTimer or as a Synchronization Timer (one thread released, automatically reset) by specifying SynchronizationTimer.

KeSetTimer

```
BOOLEAN KeSetTimer(IN PKTIMER Timer,
                   IN LARGE_INTEGER DueTime,
                   IN PKDPC Dpc OPTIONAL);
```

The KeSetTimer function sets the absolute or relative interval at which a Timer Object is to be set to the Signaled state and, optionally, supplies a CustomTimerDpc routine to be executed when that interval expires.

The *DueTime* parameter specifies the absolute or relative time at which the timer is to expire. If the value of *DueTime* is negative, the expiration time is relative to the current system time. Otherwise, the expiration time is absolute. The expiration time is expressed in system time units (100-ns units). Absolute expiration times track any changes in the system time; relative expiration times are not affected by system time changes. The optional *Dpc* parameter points to a

DPC Object that was initialized by `KeInitializeDpc`. If the Timer Object was already in the system timer queue, it is implicitly cancelled before being set to the new expiration time, and `KeSetTimer` returns TRUE. If the Timer Object was not already in the queue, it is entered and `KeSetTimer` returns FALSE. A call to `KeSetTimer` before the previously specified *DueTime* has expired cancels both the timer and the call to the DPC, if any, associated with the previous call.

When the timer expires, the Timer Object is removed from the system timer queue and its state is set to Signaled. If a DPC Object was associated with the timer when it was set, that object is inserted in the system DPC queue, to be executed as soon as conditions permit after the timer interval expires.

Callers of `KeSetTimer` specify a timer that times out once. To set a recurring timer, use `KeSetTimerEx`.

KeSetTimerEx

```
BOOLEAN KeSetTimerEx(IN PKTIMER Timer,
                     IN LARGE_INTEGER DueTime,
                     IN LONG Period OPTIONAL,
                     IN PKDPC Dpc OPTIONAL);
```

The `KeSetTimerEx` function sets the absolute or relative interval at which a Timer Object is to be set to the Signaled state. It also optionally supplies a custom timer DPC Routine to be executed when that interval expires, as well as a recurring interval for the timer. The Timer Object is entered in the system timer queue.

The *DueTime* parameter specifies the absolute or relative time at which the timer is to expire. If the value of *DueTime* is negative, the expiration time is relative to the current system time. Otherwise, the expiration time is absolute. The *Period* parameter specifies an optional period for the timer in milliseconds. The *Dpc* parameter points to an initialized DPC Object. If the Timer Object was already in the system timer queue, it is implicitly cancelled before being set to the new expiration time. A call to `KeSetTimerEx` before the previously specified *DueTime* has expired cancels both the timer and the call to the DPC, if any, associated with the previous call.

When the timer expires, the Timer Object is removed from the system timer queue, unless it is a recurring timer. In the latter case, the expiration time is computed by adding the *Period* value and the Timer Object's state is set to Signaled. If a DPC Object was associated with the timer when it was set, that object is inserted in the system DPC queue, to be executed as soon as conditions permit after the timer interval expires.

A DPC Routine cannot deallocate a periodic timer but can deallocate a nonperiodic timer.

KeCancelTimer

```
BOOLEAN KeCancelTimer(IN PKTIMER Timer);
```

The `KeCancelTimer` function dequeues a Timer Object before the timer interval, if any was set, expires. If the specified Timer Object was in the system timer queue, `KeCancelTimer` returns TRUE. If it is currently in the queue, it is removed from the queue. If a DPC Object is associated with the timer, it too is cancelled. Otherwise, no operation is performed.

KeReadStateTimer

```
BOOLEAN KeReadStateTimer(IN PKTIMER Timer);
```

The KeReadStateTimer function reads the current state of a given Timer Object. The *Timer* parameter points to an initialized Timer Object, for which the caller provides the storage. If the current state of the Timer Object is Signaled, TRUE is returned.

Example: Setting an IoTimer *Routine*

The setup for handling a custom timer is shown in Listing 15.4. If the function completes before the timer expires, it simply cancels the timer. If the function does not complete before the timer expires, a timeout routine established by KeInitializeDpc will be called. The timeout routine will then cancel the IRP. In Listing 15.5, we show a timeout routine that simply cancels the active IRP. The IRP was established by the KeInitializeDpc call in Listing 15.4. For this example cancellation, there is no need to touch the device's hardware and consequently no need for a SynchCritSection routine. If cancelling the IRP requires resetting the hardware, you will have to use KeSynchronizeExecution to safely synchronize this with the ISR. We show this in Listing 15.6.

Listing 15.4: *Setting Up a Custom Timer*

```
{
    LARGE_INTEGER dueTime;
    KeInitializeTimer(&extension->TheTimer);
    KeInitializeDpc(&extension->TimerDpc,
                    timerDPC,
                    irp);
    dueTime.QuadPart = -10000 * TIMEVALUE; // Negative time for relative value
    KeSetTimer(&extension->TheTimer,
               dueTime,
               &extension->TimerDpc);

    //
    // Timer is active
    //


    //
    // Do whatever here
    //

    //
    // Stop the timer
    //
    KeCancelTimer(&extension->TheTimer);
}
```

Listing 15.5: *A* CustomTimerDpc *Routine without a* SynchCritSection

```
VOID timerDPC(IN PKDPC Dpc,
              IN PVOID DeferredContext,
              IN PVOID SystemArgument1,
              IN PVOID SystemArgument2)
```

```
{
    PIRP Irp = (PIRP)DeferredContext;
    BOOLEAN cancelled;
    //
    // Do timed action
    cancelled =  IoCancelIrp(Irp);
    ASSERT(cancelled == TRUE);

}
```

Listing 15.6: *A* CustomTimerDpc *Routine with a* SynchCritSection

If the timer DPC Routine will touch hardware, one more step is needed: a SynchCritSection routine. This routine synchronizes access with the ISR.

```
VOID timerDPC(IN PKDPC Dpc,
              IN PVOID DeferredContext,
              IN PVOID SystemArgument1,
              IN PVOID SystemArgument2)
{
    PIRP irp;
    BOOLEAN status;
    //

    KeSynchronizeExecution(extension->InterruptObject,
                           timeSynch,
                           extension);

// Do timed action
    status =  IoCancelIrp(irp);
    ASSERT(status == TRUE);
}


BOOLEAN timeSynch(IN OUT PVOID Context)
{
    MY_DEVICE_EXTENSION extension;
    extension = (PSTAT_DEVICE_EXTENSION) Context;

    //
    //   Access hardware here at Device IRQL
    //
}
```

Time-of-Day Functions

While it is uncommon to use actual time-of-day functions in drivers, they are available. A system time is represented by a 64-bit value expressing the number of 100-ns ticks since January 1, 1601, which is the epoch date for Windows NT times.[3] This value can be converted to a more useful form that splits out the year, month, day, hour, minute, second, and millisecond. A date or time expressed in a conventional form can be converted to a 64-bit system time.

---

[3] Unlike the Y2K problem, the TOPS-10 date rollover back in 1975, or the upcoming UNIX/VMS crisis of 32-bit time rollover sometime in 2038, the NT date crisis will occur sometime in the year 30,848 (there are actually only 63 bits of time in the signed LARGE_INTEGER value).

Reading the Time of Day

The following functions are used to query the time-of-day information.

KeQuerySystemTime

```
VOID KeQuerySystemTime(OUT PLARGE_INTEGER CurrentTime);
```

The KeQuerySystemTime function returns the time represented as a count of 100-ns ticks since January 1, 1601. The time can be converted to a useful format using the RtlTimeFieldsToTime function.

KeQueryTickCount

```
VOID KeQueryTickCount(OUT PLARGE_INTEGER TickCount);
```

The KeQueryTickCount function maintains a count of the interval timer interrupts that have occurred since the system was booted. The *TickCount* parameter is a pointer that will be set to the value of the system tick count. Its value is incremented by 1 at each interval timer interrupt while the system is running.

The use of KeQueryTickCount is the preferred method for determining elapsed time, for measuring relative timing, and for time stamps.

KeQueryTimeIncrement

```
ULONG KeQueryTimeIncrement();
```

The KeQueryTimeIncrement function returns the number of 100-ns units that are added to the system time each time the interval clock interrupts.

Time-of-Day Conversion Functions

The following functions are used to convert the LARGE_INTEGER time-of-day value to a more meaningful value in traditional Western calendar units, or convert a value from calendar units to a LARGE_INTEGER time-of-day value.

RtlTimeToTimeFields

```
VOID RtlTimeToTimeFields(IN PLARGE_INTEGER Time, IN PTIME_FIELDS TimeFields);
```

The RtlTimeToTimeFields function takes a value returned by KeQuerySystemTime and converts it to a more useful form for formatting or other purposes for which conventional time-of-day representation is more appropriate. Note that this conversion loses some precision, because its resolution is only to milliseconds. The milliseconds can have no better resolution than the system timer.

The *Time* parameter is the value in the same format returned by KeQuerySystemTime. The *TimeFields* parameter is a pointer to a TIME_FIELDS structure, defined as follows.

```
typedef struct _TIME_FIELDS {
    CSHORT Year;         // Range [1601...]
    CSHORT Month;        // Range [1..12]
    CSHORT Day;          // Range [1..31]
    CSHORT Hour;         // Range [0..23]
    CSHORT Minute;       // Range [0..59]
    CSHORT Second;       // Range [0..59]
    CSHORT Milliseconds;// Range [0..999]
    CSHORT Weekday;      // Range [0..6] == [Sunday..Saturday]
} TIME_FIELDS, * PTIME_FIELDS;
```

The time is converted from an epoch value in 100-ns units to a fielded representation in which the year, month, day, hour, minute, second, and millisecond values are easily manipulated. After manipulation, the TIME_FIELDS value could be converted back to a 64-bit system time value using RtlTimeFieldsToTime.

RtlTimeFieldsToTime

```
VOID RtlTimeFieldsToTime(IN PTIME_FIELDS TimeFields, IN PLARGE_INTEGER Time);
```

The RtlTimeFieldsToTime function takes a TIME_FIELDS structure and converts it to the time representation that is compatible with a time returned by KeQuerySystemTime.

The *TimeFields* parameter is a pointer to a TIME_FIELDS structure, as defined in the previous section. The *Time* parameter is a pointer to a place to which to return the value.

Summary

This chapter covered the functions for using timers, measuring time, and reporting time. In addition to the mechanisms described here, certain Wait operations have an optional timeout after which they will terminate the wait. These are described in Chapter 11 on page 259.

Chapter

16 *Achieving Reality: Driver Initialization*

Windows NT 4.0 has two important event times for a driver: driver initialization, which is done in `DriverEntry`, and driver finalization, which is done in the Unload routine. Driver initialization and finalization will be more complex in Windows 2000 (at least, it will if you want to take full advantage of all of the neat new Windows 2000 features). In Windows 2000, there are several stages of initialization and finalization, although the functions that are called for these purposes are largely the same as those in earlier versions of NT. They are simply called at different places than in an NT 4.0 driver.

Initialization Functions

The functions listed in Table 16.1 are useful in driver initialization.

Table 16.1: *Driver Initialization Function Summary*

Function	Page	Description
HalAssignSlotResources	891	Like IoAssignResources, takes an input list of preferred and alternative hardware resources and claims available hardware resources in the Registry ResourceMap tree, returning information about the resources it claimed to the caller. However, this routine claims hardware resources only for drivers of devices on any given type of dynamically configurable I/O bus that has a published standard interface.
HalGetAdapter	892	Returns a pointer to the Adapter Object that represents the DMA channel to which the driver's device is connected or to the driver's bus master adapter and also the maximum number of map registers that the driver can specify for each DMA transfer, given the input device description. The value returned is either a pointer to a shared System DMA Controller Adapter Object or a new Adapter Object that is created for a bus-mastering device.

Table 16.1: *Driver Initialization Function Summary (continued)*

Function	Page	Description
HalGetBusData	893	Given a bus type, a system-assigned bus number, and a slot number, returns the bus-relative configuration information for any dynamically configurable I/O bus in a driver-supplied buffer. For the PCI bus, this buffer contains the PCI_COMMON_CONFIG information. Returns the number of bytes actually written to the buffer.
HalGetBusDataByOffset	893	Like HalGetBusData, returns bus-relative configuration information for a given type of dynamically configurable I/O bus to a driver-supplied buffer. However, this routine returns configuration information starting at the given offset in the bus-type-specific configuration data structure.
HalGetInterruptVector	894	Returns a mapped system interrupt vector, DIRQL, and processor-affinity mask that a driver can use to set up its ISR. It does this when given the type of bus on which the driver's device is connected, the system-assigned bus number, and the bus's interrupt vector and IRQL.
HalSetBusData	894	Sets I/O bus configuration data for a given slot or address on a particular bus.
HalSetBusDataByOffset	894	Sets I/O bus configuration data for a given slot or address on a particular bus, starting at the given offset in the bus-type-specific configuration structure.
HalTranslateBusAddress	895	Returns the corresponding physical address in system memory for a given bus-specific address.
IoAssignResources	903	Takes an input list of preferred and alternative, or required, hardware resources needed for a driver or device. It inspects the Registry for available hardware resources, claims hardware resources in the Registry ResourceMap tree, and returns configuration information about the hardware resources it claimed for the caller.
IoConnectInterrupt	909	Tells the kernel how to map an interrupt event to a call on an ISR handler function.
IoGetConfigurationInformation	918	Returns a pointer to the I/O Manager's configuration information structure. This structure indicates the number of disk, floppy, CD-ROM, tape, SCSI HBAs, serial, and parallel Device Objects that have already been named by previously loaded drivers. It also tells whether certain address ranges have been claimed by "AT" disk-type drivers.
IoQueryDeviceDescription		Supplies to a driver-supplied configuration-callback routine basic hardware information about one or more of (1) the given bus type and bus number, (2) the controller type and controller number, and/or (3) the peripheral type and peripheral number from the Registry. As an alternative, device drivers can call HalGetBusData or HalGetBusDataByOffset.

Table 16.1: *Driver Initialization Function Summary (continued)*

Function	Page	Description
IoReportResourceUsage		Claims hardware resources, such as ports in I/O space, device registers in memory space, an interrupt vector, or a particular DMA controller channel, in the Registry so that a subsequently loaded driver cannot attempt to use the same resources. To claim most types of resources, calling IoAssignResources or HalAssignSlotResources is preferred.
KeGetDcacheFillSize	939	Returns the processor's data cache-line boundary.

Driver Initialization Prototype

In this section, we present a complete DriverEntry example, Listing 16.1. This is a typical initialization routine for a simple interrupt-driven device. The naming convention of names, such as "LAB5", comes from the fact that this is the fifth lab exercise in our course on NT drivers.

Listing 16.1: *Prototype* DriverEntry *Routine*

```
NTSTATUS DriverEntry(
    IN PDRIVER_OBJECT driverObject,
    IN PUNICODE_STRING RegistryPath )
{
```

We start out with the usual long list of declarations. The one significant advantage of C++ over C (ignoring the whole class mechanism) is that these declarations can appear anywhere. But we're working in C, so they all end up here.

```
    PDEVICE_OBJECT deviceObject = NULL;
    NTSTATUS status;
    UNICODE_STRING NtNameString;
    UNICODE_STRING DosNameString;
    NTSTATUS retReg;
    BOOLEAN GotResources;
    //
    //   Registry values
    //
    ULONG debugMask;
    ULONG eventLog;
    ULONG shouldBreak;
    ULONG interruptLine;
    ULONG interruptIDT;
    PLAB5_DEVICE_EXTENSION extension;
    VOID            *registerAddress;
    PHYSICAL_ADDRESS  registerPhysicalAddress;
    unsigned int      vgaBaseReg;
    unsigned int      baseReg = 0;
    ULONG             baseAddressReg1;
    ULONG             lengthToMap;
    unsigned int      i;
```

This is some boilerplate, much of which we've already explained in earlier chapters. However, we have not yet discussed how to read the Registry. The readRegistry *routine reads parameters such as the debug mask, Event Log flag, and initial breakpoint flag from the Registry variables. An example of this function is in Listing 18.1.*

```
KdPrint( ("%s: Entered the Lab5 driver!\n", DBG_MSG_HDR) );
//
// Read the Registry for our parameters
//
retReg = readRegistry(driverObject, RegistryPath,
                         &debugMask,
                         &eventLog,
                         &shouldBreak );
```

This is a driver for a simulated hardware device. The "registers" for this device are established by another driver and stored in the Registry. We use another subroutine to read these values.

```
//
// Read the Registry for the "address" of the hardware simulator
//
retReg = hardwareSimReadRegistry(driverObject, RegistryPath,
                                   &interruptLine,
                                   &interruptIDT,
                                   &registerAddress,
                                   &registerPhysicalAddress );
KdPrint( ("%s: returned from readRegistry!\n",   DBG_MSG_HDR) );
```

If we have set the initial break flag in the Registry, now is the time to take it. Note that this will hang the system if WinDbg is not active!

```
if (shouldBreak)
    {
      DbgBreakPoint();
    }
```

We need to create a Unicode string that is the name of this device.

```
//
// Create counted string version of our device name
//
RtlInitUnicodeString( &NtNameString, NT_DEVICE_NAME );
```

Next, we create the Device Object itself, using its associated Device Extension.

```
status = IoCreateDevice(
            driverObject,
            sizeof(LAB5_DEVICE_EXTENSION),        // Device Extension
            &NtNameString,
            FILE_DEVICE_UNKNOWN,
            0,                        // No standard device characteristics
            FALSE,                    // This isn't an exclusive device
            &deviceObject
            );

if ( !NT_SUCCESS(status) )
    {
```

```
        KdPrint(("%s could not create device\n",    DBG_MSG_HDR));
        status = STATUS_NO_SUCH_DEVICE;
        return status;
    }
```

We now store some key information in the Device Extension. For example, we store a pointer back to the Device Object itself. We also store the information about interruptLine, interruptIDT, *and the register addresses (which we have obtained from the Registry). Note that because there is no bus iteration, this driver greatly resembles the driver for an ISA device.*

```
extension = deviceObject->DeviceExtension;
extension->DeviceObject = deviceObject;
//
// Save information from Registry in Device Extension
//

extension->registerAddress          = registerAddress;
extension->registerPhysicalAddress  = registerPhysicalAddress;
extension->interruptLine             = interruptLine;
extension->interruptIDT              = interruptIDT;
extension->debugMask                 = debugMask;
extension->eventLog                  = eventLog;
extension->shouldBreak               = shouldBreak;
```

The next step is to initialize the MajorFunction *table for the operations we support. For this device, we support* CreateFile, CloseHandle, *and* DeviceIoControl, *so we fill in those slots. We also fill in the pointer to the Unload function.*

```
//
// Create dispatch points for create/open, close, unload
//
driverObject->MajorFunction[IRP_MJ_CREATE]         = Lab5Open;
driverObject->MajorFunction[IRP_MJ_CLOSE]          = Lab5Close;
driverObject->MajorFunction[IRP_MJ_DEVICE_CONTROL] = Lab5DeviceControl;
driverObject->DriverUnload = Lab5Unload;
//
// Other possible dispatch entries
//
// DriverObject->MajorFunction[IRP_MJ_READ] =
// DriverObject->MajorFunction[IRP_MJ_WRITE] =
// DriverObject->MajorFunction[IRP_MJ_INTERNAL_DEVICE_CONTROL]  =
//                              For calls from other drivers
// DriverObject->MajorFunction[IRP_MJ_SHUTDOWN] =
//              Note driver MUST call IoRegisterShutdownNotification()
// DriverObject->MajorFunction[IRP_MJ_QUERY_INFORMATION] =
// DriverObject->MajorFunction[IRP_MJ_SET_INFORMATION] =
// DriverObject->MajorFunction[IRP_MJ_CLEANUP] =
// DriverObject->MajorFunction[IRP_MJ_FLUSH_BUFFERS]     =
// DriverObject->MajorFunction[IRP_MJ_SET_VOLUME_INFORMATION]   =
// DriverObject->MajorFunction[IRP_MJ_QUERY_VOLUME_INFORMATION] =
// DriverObject->MajorFunction[IRP_MJ_DIRECTORY_CONTROL] =
// DriverObject->MajorFunction[IRP_MJ_FILE_SYSTEM_CONTROL] =
// DriverObject->MajorFunction[IRP_MJ_LOCK_CONTROL] =
// DriverObject->MajorFunction[IRP_MJ_QUERY_EA] =
// DriverObject->MajorFunction[IRP_MJ_SET_EA] =
// DriverObject->MajorFunction[IRP_MJ_SCSI] =
```

```
KdPrint( ("%s: just about ready!\n",   DBG_MSG_HDR) );
```

The following code, which is conditionally compiled in for this driver, tests to see if the assignments that have been made are feasible and don't conflict with any existing assignments. For our example driver, since we do not actually allocate any resources, we have nothing to report. We discuss this problem in Chapter 21 on page 408.

```
//
// Do Buffered I/O. A nop Read and Write are not supported by this driver
//
 deviceObject->Flags |= DO_BUFFERED_IO;
```

We are far enough along that we can safely create the symbolic link from the "DOS Device Name".

```
   //
   // Create counted string version of our Win32 device name
   //
   RtlInitUnicodeString( &DosNameString, DOS_DEVICE_NAME );
   //
   // Create a link from our device name to a name in the Win32 namespace
   //
   status = IoCreateSymbolicLink( &DosNameString, &NtNameString );
   if (!NT_SUCCESS(status))
      {
      KdPrint( ("%s: Couldn't create the symbolic link\n",   DBG_MSG_HDR) );
       IoDeleteDevice( driverObject->DeviceObject );
       return status;
      }
```

Here's the key to an interrupt handler: We connect to an interrupt line. For PCI devices, we can use HalAssignSlotResources *or* IoAssignResources *to determine the interrupt line value that we should use. For ISA devices, such as our simulated ISA device, we can (and should) store the value in the Registry. The subroutine, which is shown as follows, will store a pointer to the Interrupt Object.*

```
   //
   //  Connect an ISR for our device
   //
   status = Lab5SetupISR( deviceObject, interruptLine );
   if(status != STATUS_SUCCESS)
      {
      // Assume any error printout was done in Lab5SetupISR
      IoDeleteSymbolicLink( &DosNameString);
      IoDeleteDevice(driverObject->DeviceObject);
      return status;
      }
   KdPrint( ("%s: All initialized\n",   DBG_MSG_HDR) );
   return status;
   }
```

Setting Up the ISR

In the function shown in Listing 16.2, we actually do all of the work to establish the ISR.

Listing 16.2: *Setting Up an ISR:* `HalGetInterruptVector`

```
static NTSTATUS Lab5SetupISR(
        PDEVICE_OBJECT deviceObject,
        ULONG interruptLine )
   {
     PLAB5_DEVICE_EXTENSION deviceExtension;
     NTSTATUS               ioConnectStatus;
     KIRQL                  Irql;
     ULONG                  MappedSysVect;

     deviceExtension = deviceObject->DeviceExtension;
     KdPrint(("%s  Lab5SetupISR - Started\n", DBG_MSG_HDR));
```

Because calling a single DPC handler is the most common action of an ISR, this special case is simplified by providing functions to handle that easily. The first one registers a DPC handler to be called by the ISR, `IoInitializeDpcRequest`.

```
     IoInitializeDpcRequest(deviceObject, Lab5DpcRoutine);
     KdPrint(("%s  Lab5SetupISR - Initialize DPC Request\n", DBG_MSG_HDR));
```

Now we have to establish the interrupt line that will be used. We know the IRQ we want to use, which we got from the Registry. We store this information in the Device Extension in variables we have created for that purpose. We then call `HalGetInterruptVector` *to obtain an actual IRQL and a processor affinity mask. The* `HalGetInterruptVector` *function maps a bus-relative IRQ value to a system IRQ value.*

```
     deviceExtension->Vector  = interruptLine;
     deviceExtension->Level   = interruptLine;
     MappedSysVect = HalGetInterruptVector(
                             Isa,
                             0,                       // BusNumber,
                             deviceExtension->Level,  // Level
                             deviceExtension->Vector, // Vector,
                             &Irql,                   // IRQL
                             &deviceExtension->Affinity);
                                                      // Affinity mask
```

The following code just prints out some debugging information. Note that you should use `KdPrint` *here if you want the debug output to disappear in a production version of the code.*

```
DbgPrint("%s Lab5SetupISR - Vector       = 0x%08x\n",
                             DBG_MSG_HDR, deviceExtension->Vector);
DbgPrint("%s Lab5SetupISR - Level        = 0x%08x\n\n",
                             DBG_MSG_HDR, deviceExtension->Level);
DbgPrint("%s Lab5SetupISR - MappedSysVect = 0x%08x\n",
                             DBG_MSG_HDR, MappedSysVect);
DbgPrint("%s Lab5SetupISR - IRQL         = 0x%08x\n", DBG_MSG_HDR, Irql);
DbgPrint("%s Lab5SetupISR - Affinity     = 0x%08x\n",
                             DBG_MSG_HDR, deviceExtension->Affinity);
```

To connect the interrupt to the ISR, we must provide a Spin Lock, which must be initialized before we call `IoConnectInterrupt`.

```
//
// Initialize the Spin Lock
//
KeInitializeSpinLock( &deviceExtension->ISRSpinLock);
```

Now we can actually connect the interrupt (the system interrupt line) to the ISR.

```
//
// Connect the Device Driver to the IRQ
//
ioConnectStatus = IoConnectInterrupt(
                        &deviceExtension->InterruptObject,
                        Lab5InterruptServiceRoutine,
                        deviceExtension,
                        &deviceExtension->ISRSpinLock,
                        MappedSysVect,
                        Irql,
                        Irql,
                        Latched,   // Not LevelSensitive,
                        FALSE,     // Interrupt vector is sharable
                        deviceExtension->Affinity,
                        FALSE            // Save Floating Point
                                         // Stack on interrupt
                        );
    if ( !NT_SUCCESS (ioConnectStatus) )
        {
        KdPrint(("%s  Lab5SetupISR - IoConnectInterrupt Failed (0x%08x)\n",
                                DBG_MSG_HDR, ioConnectStatus));
        }
    else
        {
         KdPrint(("%s  Lab5SetupISR - IoConnectInterrupt Passed\n",
                                DBG_MSG_HDR));
        }
    return ioConnectStatus;
}
```

Functions Used by Initialization

The following functions are the ones most commonly needed for managing the interrupt connections for a driver.

IoInitializeDpcRequest

```
VOID IoInitializeDpcRequest(IN PDEVICE_OBJECT DeviceObject,
                            IN PIO_DPC_ROUTINE DpcRoutine);
```

The `IoInitializeDpcRequest` function establishes the `DpcForIsr` handler. The *DeviceObject* parameter is the Device Object, and the *DpcRoutine* parameter is the pointer to the `DpcForIsr` handler routine, which is defined as follows.

```
VOID (*PIO_DPC_ROUTINE)(IN PKDPC Dpc,
                        IN PDEVICE_OBJECT DeviceObject,
                        IN PIRP Irp,
                        IN PVOID Context);
```

The *DpcRoutine* will be called when the DPC is dispatched. It receives the Device Object, the current IRP, a pointer to the KDPC object, and a pointer to a "context" that is passed in from the ISR. The pointer could be NULL if there is no specific context information available from the Device Object (and Device Extension) and the IRP. Note that any information referenced by the *Context* parameter *must* be in nonpaged memory. A pointer to an ISR stack parameter will be meaningless because that stack will be long gone before the DPC is executed. Since an ISR cannot allocate memory, the memory must be preallocated at a lower IRQL level. However, there is rarely any need to do this because most times the space can be preallocated as part of the Device Extension. So, for most DPC routines, the *Context* pointer will be NULL. Some drivers may use pointers to buffers or pointers into the Device Extension as this value.

HalGetInterruptVector

```
ULONG HalGetInterruptVector(IN INTERFACE_TYPE InterfaceType,
                            IN ULONG BusNumber,
                            IN ULONG BusInterruptLevel,
                            IN ULONG BusInterruptVector,
                            OUT PKIRQL Irql,
                            OUT PKAFFINITY Affinity);
```

The HalGetInterruptVector function maps a bus-specific interrupt level and interrupt vector to a *system* IRQL. It handles the case in which multiple devices on multiple busses may be dynamically mapped to different DIRQLs. Only the mapped DIRQL is useful; the "DIRQL" specified by the device isn't really a DIRQL. It is a suggestion of what the DIRQL might be, but it is up to the HAL to determine the actual DIRQL that is used.

The *InterfaceType* parameter describes the bus type. Most typically, it will be one of the constants Isa or PCIBus, but many other bus types are possible and the list is open-ended. The *BusNumber* parameter is the system-assigned, zero-based bus number. For most ISA busses, this value will be 0; for a PCI Bus, it is the value returned by the PCI Enumerator function you use to locate the device you are programming.

The *BusInterruptLevel* and *BusInterruptVector* parameters are usually the same number for any kind of device. This is the value obtained from such operations as HalGetBusData, HalAssignSlotResources, and IoAssignResources. For ISA devices, it is either some default value or a value obtained from the Registry.

HalGetInterruptVector maps the bus-specific interrupt level and interrupt vector to a *system* IRQL. The return value is the mapped system vector (for those of you who have looked at the hardware architecture, this is the IDT Table Index). A machine with an APIC (Advanced Programmable Interrupt Controller; see Chapter 14, page 295) can remap interrupt lines to IRQLs in the range 0..255. You get back, in the location referenced by the *Irql* parameter, a DIRQL level that is assigned to this device, along with a *processor affinity mask* that indicates which processors can handle the interrupts. This mask is important for some multiprocessor systems that might not be able to process interrupts symmetrically. You will use these returned values in IoConnectInterrupt.

IoConnectInterrupt

```
NTSTATUS IoConnectInterrupt(OUT PKINTERRUPT * InterruptObject,
                            IN PKSERVICE_ROUTINE ServiceRoutine,
                            IN PVOID ServiceContext,
                            IN PKSPIN_LOCK SpinLock OPTIONAL,
                            IN ULONG Vector,
                            IN KIRQL Irql,
                            IN KIRQL SynchronizeIrql,
                            IN KINTERRUPT_MODE InterruptMode,
                            IN BOOLEAN ShareVector,
                            IN KAFFINITY ProcessorEnableMask,
                            IN BOOLEAN FloatingSave);
```

The IoConnectInterrupt function maps the interrupt to the ISR. It takes a pointer to the ISR, *ServiceRoutine*. It also takes a pointer to a user-defined *ServiceContext* that will be passed into the ISR each time (this is usually a pointer to the Device Object or Device Extension) and the results of the HalGetInterruptVector operation, which are the values of *Vector*, *Irql*, and *ProcessorEnableMask* (affinity mask). These are all pretty straightforward.

This function also requires a pointer to an *initialized* Spin Lock that is used for synchronization. This Spin Lock is almost always an object you must place in the Device Extension. It is required only if the device can interrupt on more than one level or if there is more than one driver associated with the device (for example, separate functional units with shared register state). If the device is simple and has no need of a Spin Lock, this parameter can be NULL.

SynchronizeIrql is the IRQL level used when KeSynchronizeExecution is used, and, for most devices, it is the same value as *Irql*. If the ISR handles more than one interrupt level from the device, *SynchronizeIrql* would be the *highest* level IRQL that could be requested by the device. The ISR is always called with the IRQL equal to the *SynchronizeIrql* value. The *InterruptMode* parameter describes whether the interrupt is LevelSensitive (for example, the PCI Bus) or Latched (for example, the ISA bus). The *FloatingSave* parameter is always FALSE for *x*86 compatible systems, but for other platforms, it might require a different value. It indicates whether the state of the floating-point hardware needs to be saved on interrupt entry.

The *ShareVector* parameter tells whether you have programmed your driver to allow it to share interrupts. For an ISA-based driver, this is FALSE. For PCI drivers, it really, really ought to be TRUE. A PCI driver (or a driver for any other kind of shared-interrupt bus) has little, if any, excuse for not being aware of interrupt sharing. We will go so far as to say that a PCI driver that does not set this parameter to TRUE is an Erroneous Driver. If you do not allow interrupt sharing and there is no IRQ that can be assigned to guarantee that you have exclusive use of it, IoConnectInterrupt will fail. Furthermore, depending on the load order, even if you *do* get an exclusive interrupt, you have now consumed a scarce resource. Thus, some other driver you've never heard of (and which may actually be a correct driver, but on a bus that has only one available interrupt[1]) may not be able to get an exclusive vector. The end user, who couldn't care less about such details, knows only that after installing *your* driver, some other driver—which is important to that end user—no longer functions. So it will be *your* fault, which will be screamed

---

[1] An example is the Toshiba Desk Station V, which has exactly *one* IRQ line available for its PCI expansion slots! If your driver gets IRQ11 with exclusive access, no other driver can operate on that bus, including drivers that know how to share interrupts! For your driver to work correctly in all environments, you *must* assume that PCI interrupts will be shared!

in no uncertain terms to your Product Support people. Make your life easy. Write handlers that can share interrupts.

If the interrupt was connected, the return value will be STATUS_SUCCESS. The other return values are (at least) STATUS_INVALID_PARAMETER and STATUS_INSUFFICIENT_RESOURCES. The latter can mean that the connection could not be made to the IRQL, either because your driver cannot share it or because the only IRQL is already allocated.

 Somewhere during the execution of IoConnectInterrupt, the connection between the selected IRQ and your driver is established. At this point, *your ISR can start to see interrupts*. This can happen even before IoConnectInterrupt returns. Although it is possible the interrupts could be from your device, it is more likely that they are from some other device that is sharing the IRQ, and the query just happens to be directed to your ISR because it is now ahead of the intended ISR. This means that before you call IoConnectInterrupt, you must be certain that you have set up everything required for your ISR to execute properly, if only to reject the interrupt. This may be as simple as a flag in the Device Extension that you can test in the ISR and that indicates if the driver is fully initialized, or you can delay calling IoConnectInterrupt until the driver is fully ready to handle interrupts.

The Unload Routine

Once you have connected an interrupt, you must disconnect it. Leaving an interrupt connected after a driver has unloaded is almost certain to generate a Blue Screen—if you're lucky. (If you aren't, it will merely cause parts of the operating system to be corrupted and lead to more insidious damage.) To disconnect an interrupt, you call IoDisconnectInterrupt. If you have not connected the interrupt, do not call IoDisconnectInterrupt to disconnect it. This will crash the system.

Note also that if you fail DriverEntry after calling IoConnectInterrupt, you *must* call IoDisconnectInterrupt before returning the error status from DriverEntry.

In Listing 16.3, we know there is only one Device Object attached to this driver, so we do not iterate down the list freeing up all possible Device Objects.

Listing 16.3: *A Prototype Unload Routine*

```
VOID Lab5Unload( IN PDRIVER_OBJECT driverObject)
{
    UNICODE_STRING uniDosNameString;
    PLAB5_DEVICE_EXTENSION extension;
    BOOLEAN GotResources;
    extension = driverObject->DeviceObject->DeviceExtension;

    KdPrint( ("%s: Unloading!!\n",   DBG_MSG_HDR) );

    //
    // Disconnect the interrupt
    //
    IoDisconnectInterrupt(extension->InterruptObject);

    //
    // Delete the link from our device name to a name in the Win32 namespace
    //
```

```
    RtlInitUnicodeString( &uniDosNameString, DOS_DEVICE_NAME );
    IoDeleteSymbolicLink( &uniDosNameString );

    //
    // Finally, delete our one-and-only Device Object
    //
    IoDeleteDevice( driverObject->DeviceObject );
}
```

Summary

This chapter covered some more of the details of driver initialization. Details about PCI initialization can be found in Chapter 21.

Now that you have successfully initialized your driver, you can start to worry about what to do next. That's where the next few chapters are going.

Chapter

17 *Achieving Reality: Direct Memory Access*

Direct Memory Access (DMA) is a method by which a device can transfer its data to or from memory without requiring the intervention of the CPU. In this chapter, we discuss how you access a DMA Controller using the facilities of NT.

How Is DMA Done at the Hardware Level?

DMA is done by a *DMA Controller*, which is a hardware component that handles the details of a transfer. Depending on the device, there may be a single DMA Controller for a card, a DMA Controller for each device on the card, or no DMA Controller at all (only for legacy ISA bus cards that use a DMA Controller built into the motherboard).

To initiate a DMA transfer, the DMA Controller is programmed (by you) to know the address to transfer information from or to, and the amount of information to transfer. The device is then told to perform the transfer. When the device wishes to transfer information to or from the main memory, it uses the information programmed into the DMA Controller. The DMA Controller initiates a *bus request* to gain access to the bus, which is normally under control of either the processor or a bus controller. When the processor or controller *grants* the bus, the DMA Controller transfers one or more units of information (a unit can be a single byte, or as much as the bus width—which can mean up to 128 bits for some busses). The DMA Controller then releases the bus, making it available to the processor or other DMA Controllers. Other than a slight change in timing because the bus is being snatched away occasionally, the code running on the processor is completely oblivious to the DMA activity. At the programming level, once the DMA is started, no instructions need to be executed to support it until it has completed.

When the DMA operation completes, the usual action is that the device interrupts the processor. At that point, the driver once again participates in the transfer operation by calling the ISR. The ISR and DPC do whatever is necessary to respond to the completion of the actual transfer.

We should point out that it is not *necessary* to use the NT facilities to access a DMA device; you can program the device directly without using these facilities. But it is somewhat more difficult to do so and requires greater care. The NT facilities described in this chapter are those you would use to handle the most common cases of DMA easily.

Direct Memory Access Operations

The NT DMA system provides the user with support to write a "nearly portable" DMA driver. The problem with writing a "portable" (cross-platform, identical source) driver is that unless you are already an expert on each platform, you cannot possibly hope to get all of the platform-specific conditions correctly coded. However, there are things you can do that will make the port easy—and things you can do that make it difficult. You want to avoid the latter. Thus, you should follow many of the specified conventions even if you discover that the function you just called consists of a single "return" instruction (if HAL-dependent) or a macro that compiles into nothing (if architecture-dependent). It might not be this simple on a platform you have not yet seen— a multiprocessor system or a RISC system—but you don't know that. There also are tricks you might need to use (such as using "write blocks" that are required on the Alpha) that are both platform-dependent and even model-dependent. DMA is an area that has many platform dependencies. If you follow the specifications, you'll get most of them right.

Use of DMA

The hardware on the system that provides for DMA capabilities can vary. The greatest distinction at the moment is the difference between System DMA, which uses the System DMA Controller, and Bus Master DMA, which uses a controller on the device itself and does not require the use of the System DMA Controller. System DMA is slow relative to Bus Master DMA. It also is slow relative to programmed I/O. Often, a device that allows both System DMA and programmed I/O will be supported using programmed I/O simply because it is faster.

Almost any driver that communicates with a DMA device will use Direct mode for buffering. That is, it will transfer the information directly into the application's address space. This can reduce the need to copy the data to or from a system buffer and significantly reduces the overhead in performing the I/O operation.

Most DMA devices require contiguous *physical* memory. This is because DMA devices (whether Bus Master DMA or System DMA) must be programmed using physical addresses; the transfers do not use any of the page mapping hardware of the host platform. For some high-data-rate devices, this results in a significant problem in getting (for example) 100MB of contiguous physical memory. (No, that number is *not* an exaggeration! Nondisclosure agreements do not allow us to say anything more about such devices, but they do exist!)

There is a "hidden" feature of the I/O Manager that can seriously impact performance. Because most DMA devices require contiguous physical memory, the system somehow has to assure that a large data block actually resides in contiguous physical memory. Unfortunately, the

I/O Manager does not have any access to the paging system to reshuffle the pages in memory so that they are contiguous (and this would be a bad idea anyway, from a performance viewpoint). So, it fakes this. This leads to a concept called *Mapping Registers.*

A Mapping Register, as a hardware entity, is (at least in current versions of NT on the current platforms it runs on) a fictitious invention of the HAL. A device is assigned a number of Mapping Registers that "map" the DMA requests to a contiguous memory. In some historical architectures, DMA actually was handled using some sort of virtual memory mapping and you would program the DMA device with a logical address. If the address spanned several physical pages, the I/O mapping hardware would handle it by allocating contiguous logical pages for the I/O map. Alas, modern machines are not as sophisticated and do not have Mapping Registers for I/O (although the fiction is maintained in case, someday, an NT-capable platform actually gets them!). So the HAL simulates them. It does this by copying output data from physically discontiguous application pages to physically contiguous pages before initiating the output or by allocating contiguous pages for input and copying the input data from them to the physically discontiguous input pages of the application. This results in a hidden overhead.

The function `IoMapTransfer` "remaps" the I/O operation so that the pages reside in physical memory. It then returns the physical address where the pages may be found.

```
PHYSICAL_ADDRESS IoMapTransfer(IN PADAPTER_OBJECT AdapterObject,
                               IN PMDL Mdl,
                               IN PVOID MapRegisterBase,
                               IN PVOID CurrentVa,
                               IN OUT PULONG Length,
                               IN BOOLEAN WriteToDevice);
```

This operation takes a set of parameters specifying the nature of the transaction and returns a 64-bit physical address that can be used to program the DMA device. The *AdapterObject* is required only for the System DMA Controller. It is the Adapter Object obtained by `HalGetAdapter`, and it must have its channel allocated by `IoAllocateAdapterChannel`. For bus mastering I/O, *AdapterObject* must be NULL. *Mdl* is a pointer to the MDL (Memory Descriptor List) that came from the IRP or has otherwise been created. *MapRegisterBase* is a value that has been returned by `IoAllocateAdapterChannel`. *CurrentVa* describes the system logical address that represents the start of the transfer. *Length* is the length of the data to be transferred. Note that this last parameter is actually an IN OUT parameter, but until we talk about scatter/gather (in the next section), you can assume that the output result is the same as the input result. *WriteToDevice* tells if this is a Write operation (TRUE) or a Read operation (FALSE). The PHYSICAL_ADDRESS value that is returned is valid only if the DMA device is a Bus Master DMA device. It is not valid for System DMA Controller transfers.

Once you have made this call, you have the physical address and length that you can program into a Bus Master DMA Controller. Also, you are now guaranteed that all of the data is contiguous starting at that physical address (for non-scatter/gather devices, see the next section). Thus the DMA, once started, will be able to access all of the data sequentially.

For this to occur, `IoMapTransfer` might have had to allocate a new buffer, copy the discontiguous portions of the output data to it, and return the pointer to the new buffer. For reading, it will allocate a contiguous buffer large enough to satisfy the *Length* request; the data will be read into that buffer. For input requests, the data will not be copied out of this intermediate buffer back to the application space until you call `IoFlushAdapterBuffers`. If this copy is required, the physical address returned is the physical address of the buffer that holds the copy, not the physical address of the *CurrentVa*.

Scatter/Gather

One solution to the problem of not enough contiguous physical memory is a technique called *scatter/gather*. A DMA device that supports this technique scatters incoming data to a collection of physically disjoint memory blocks or gathers outgoing data from a similar collection. If you are involved in the design of DMA devices, be aware that a device that requires very large input or output buffers but does not support scatter/gather might be unsupportable in a real operating environment. This is because either it might simply be impossible to obtain a single contiguous large buffer or doing so might require adding truly massive amounts of physical memory. In some cases, the driver might work only on some machines but not on other physically identical machines because the operating systems might go through slightly different startup sequences depending on the order in which other drivers were installed. For example, if a driver is loaded that causes some memory fragmentation of the Nonpaged Pool, loading a driver that needs a massive contiguous physical memory buffer might be impossible. This can often be handled by forcing a driver that requires a large contiguous buffer to load early in the NT boot sequence. This gives it the opportunity to allocate the buffer in `DriverEntry` at a time before the Non-paged Pool becomes badly fragmented. This technique is not without risk. Once this device gets into the field, the technique is sensitive to each installation's drivers and their load order. Some boot-critical devices could have to precede your driver and they could fragment memory. Because this problem becomes installation-specific, it can lead to a situation in which customer support costs skyrocket and customer satisfaction plummets. The additional cost of scatter/gather hardware can pay for itself in reduced driver development costs and reduced support costs.

Scatter/gather can be done in hardware, by the I/O System, or explicitly by the programmer of the Device Driver (that means you).

Scatter/gather hardware usually falls into two distinct subtypes:

- Those that support a fixed number of blocks of memory
- Those that support a very large or unlimited number of blocks of memory

The former usually have a fixed number of address/length registers on the device. The latter usually use a pointer to a list or array—located in memory—of address/length pairs. You can compute these address/length pairs using `IoMapTransfer` in the same way that we describe for its use for a software simulation on page 341.

The bus on which the device lives will usually dictate where in physical memory the buffers may be placed. An ISA bus has a limit of 16MB (24-bit address) of addressable memory. A PCI Bus usually allows the buffers to be anywhere in a 32-bit address space, while newer PCI64-compliant cards will allow placement anywhere in a maximum of 64 bits of physical address space. The native 64-bit version of NT already exists and may even be released (at least in Beta) by the time you read this.

Microsoft documentation refers to a concept of Map Register whereby Map Registers are used to map DMA I/O requests. These registers do not exist on current hardware that we know of. They are entirely a fiction of the HAL. Each Map Register maps one page (whose size you do not know and cannot assume; you must use the constant PAGE_SIZE). A Map Register maps addresses supplied by the adapter to physical addresses of the buffer(s). Suppose a device has constraints on the physical addresses it can map (an ISA DMA device in a 32-bit system or a 32-bit bus mastering device in a 64-bit system). Then the NT system will actually copy the information between the target pages and the pages accessible to the adapter.

This implicit copying introduces a hidden overhead. You might think you are performing Direct I/O to the user's pages, but in fact a copy operation is going on, either to system buffers for output or from system buffers for input. Unless you actually instrument your driver, you may not even see this performance hit.

Address mapping is not the only time when this implicit copying is done. It is also implicitly done by the I/O system to implement scatter/gather on a device that does not support scatter/gather. For example, assume that the application wants to write 64K of data to a device and it is running on an *x86* platform (page size 4K). The 16 application-level pages are almost certainly *not* physically contiguous, even though they form a contiguous 64K block in application-mapped memory. If the device is known to support scatter/gather, you will get a MDL with 16 entries, which you can tear apart into the device-specific scatter/gather list using IoMapTransfer and then hand off to the device. However, if the device is known to *not* support scatter/gather, the I/O Manager will allocate a 64K buffer in contiguous physical memory, then copy each of the 16 pages to this buffer, and then initiate the DMA I/O. This massive copying defeats the advantages of doing DMA and introduces a lot of gratuitous overhead. How can you avoid it? Well, one solution is to apply Newcomer's First Law Of Getting What You Want From Your Computer:

"If your computer doesn't do what you want, *lie to it.*"

In this case, you can lie and tell the I/O Manager that your device *does* support scatter/gather. Now the I/O Manager will pass on the MDL and *not* do the coalesce/copy. This Is Good. The problem is that the device *doesn't* do scatter/gather, so now you must back up your bluff and simulate it.

We assume for this discussion that you actually know how to initiate a single DMA operation and now want to initiate multiple DMA operations. Here's how you back up your bluff. While this introduces some complexity to the driver, it reduces the need to have the I/O system simulate the scatter/gather by copying. For large DMA transfers, the additional cost of the computations and the overhead of the additional interrupts will still be faster than requiring the I/O system to allocate new buffers, copying massive amounts of data, and then freeing the buffers.

The trick is to use a feature of IoMapTransfer that we hinted at on page 339: calling IoMapTransfer with a NULL pointer to *AdapterObject*. (Actually, you can use this same technique to create scatter/gather lists for hardware scatter/gather. The difference is that you will do this all at once in the Dispatch Routines, rather than incrementally as we describe here.) You set the *Length*, on the first call, to be the entire length to be transferred. You get back a new *Length*, which is the length of the largest contiguous segment that can be transferred in a single operation, and the physical address of the start of that segment. You use these to program the DMA Controller for the first transfer. Normally, we would store these values in the Device Extension, along with the original length less the new length. Thus, we could keep a running total of the size of the remaining transfer. Here, though, we do something different.

Note that IoMapTransfer can be called at any level ≤ DISPATCH_LEVEL, which means it can be called in the DPC Routine. So in the DPC Routine, we add the previous *Length* to the previous start address to come up with a new *CurrentVa* value for IoMapTransfer. The

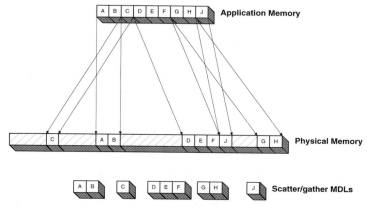

Figure 17.1: *Software simulation of scatter/gather.*

Length in this case is the remaining length of the transfer, and we get back a new physical address and an updated *Length*. We then initiate a DMA transfer on this new segment of the buffer. We repeat this, adding the *Length* to the *CurrentVa* start address and subtracting it from the bytes remaining, until we have no more bytes to transfer. Thus we have simulated in software the scatter/gather capability that the hardware does not have. And no copying will be done (as long as you lie and say that the hardware has scatter/gather when you create the Adapter Object!). This is illustrated in Figure 17.1.

Using Adapter Objects to Represent DMA Adapters

Any device that does DMA should use an Adapter Object that represents the DMA adapter. (Although doing this is not always necessary, if you try to build a DMA-based driver without one you lose a lot of the built-in functionality that NT provides.[1]) For devices that use the System DMA Controller, there is one Adapter Object for the System DMA that handles the sharing of this limited resource. For PCI, EISA, and other bus mastering controllers, there is one Adapter Object for each bus master controller. Note that some multifunction PCI cards may have one DMA Controller for each functional unit, whereas others (such as sound cards) may have a single DMA Controller shared among many functional units. The Adapter Control represents a DMA channel.

To obtain an Adapter Object, use the HalGetAdapter function.

```
PADAPTER_OBJECT HalGetAdapter(IN PDEVICE_DESCRIPTION DeviceDescription,
                    IN OUT PULONG NumberOfMapRegisters);
```

This function takes an elaborate description of the device (shown in Figure 17.2) and a specification of the desired number of map registers. It returns an Adapter Object (or NULL if

---

[1] You are not compelled to always tell the truth to NT. Just remember the saying about tangled webs. You must make sure the lies are all in agreement. Sometimes this is easy, and sometimes it is more work than using the built-in mechanisms. But when you are down in the kernel working at the privileged level, all things are possible, although not all are desirable.

```
typedef struct _DEVICE_DESCRIPTION {
    ULONG Version;
        //Currently, DEVICE_DESCRIPTION_VERSION or
        //DEVICE_DESCRIPTION_VERSION1 to use IgnoreCount
    BOOLEAN Master;
        //TRUE = busmaster adapter
        //FALSE = slave DMA device (System DMA)
    BOOLEAN ScatterGather;
        //Device supports scatter/gather
    BOOLEAN DemandMode;
        //Uses system DMA controller's demand mode
    BOOLEAN AutoInitialize;
        //Uses system DMA controller's autoinit mode
    BOOLEAN Dma32BitAddresses;
    BOOLEAN IgnoreCount;
        //DMA controller in this platform does not maintain
        //an accurate transfer counter, so requires workaround,
        //and Version must be DEVICE_DESCRIPTION_VERSION1
    BOOLEAN Reserved1;
    BOOLEAN Reserved2;
        //Preceding Reserved members must be FALSE, and
        //version must be DEVICE_DESCRIPTION_VERSION1
    ULONG BusNumber;
        //System-assigned value for I/O bus
    ULONG DmaChannel;
        //Slave device attached to this number channel
    INTERFACE_TYPE InterfaceType;
    DMA_WIDTH DmaWidth;    // 8-bit, 16-bit, etc.
    DMA_SPEED DmaSpeed;
    ULONG MaximumLength;
        //Maximum number of bytes device can handle per DMA operation
    ULONG DmaPort;
        //MicroChannel-type bus port number
  } DEVICE_DESCRIPTION, *PDEVICE_DESCRIPTION;
```

Figure 17.2: *The* DEVICE_DESCRIPTION *structure.*

there was an error) and the maximum number of Map Registers that can be used by this device. The pointer to the returned Adapter Object is typically stored in the Device Extension. The input parameter *NumberOfMapRegisters* is initially set to at most the value of the MaximumLength field of the DEVICE_DESCRIPTION divided by the (PAGE_SIZE + 1). The value returned may be less than this initial value. This value also should be stored someplace useful, such as in the Device Extension.

Some typical values are shown in Table 17.1. These are typical settings; for some of the values such as speed or width, Your Mileage May Vary.

Adapter Control Routine

The Adapter Control Routine controls the DMA adapter. Typically, the IRP will be queued to the Adapter Control Routine from the StartIo routine. System DMA will use one of the Adapter Objects created at system startup for each system DMA channel. A device that supports Bus

Table 17.1: *Typical Values for the* DEVICE_DESCRIPTION *Structure*

Field	ISA	PCI
Version	DEVICE_DESCRIPTION_VERSION	DEVICE_DESCRIPTION_VERSION
Master	FALSE (with a few exceptions)	TRUE
ScatterGather	(See text, page 341.)	
DemandMode	TRUE/FALSE	FALSE
AutoInitialize	TRUE/FALSE	FALSE
Dma32BitAddresses	FALSE	TRUE
IgnoreCount	FALSE	FALSE
Reserved1 Reserved2	FALSE	FALSE
BusNumber	0 (almost always)	PCI Bus Number
DmaChannel	(System DMA channel number)	0 (not used)
InterfaceType	Isa	PciBus
DmaWidth	Width8Bits Width16Bits Width32Bits	Width32Bits (almost always)
DmaSpeed	Compatible TypeA	Compatible TypeA
MaximumLength	(From device spec)	
DmaPort	0 (not applicable)	

Master DMA will create, in `DriverEntry`, an Adapter Object for the device. The
`HalGetAdapter` call determines whether the caller gets a reference to an existing System DMA
Controller Adapter Object or gets a newly created one.

The I/O Manager prepares a MDL structure that describes the buffer passed in to the I/O
Manager from the application. It does this only if the access type is `DO_DIRECT_IO`, the most
common mode of operation for a DMA driver. The physical pages described by the MDL are
locked in physical memory by the time the Dispatch Routines are called. If you create your own
MDLs, you must ensure that any pages referenced are locked down by the time the Adapter
Control Routine is called. The physical addresses may be passed to the adapter, and the driver
may obtain a system address for the pages (using `MmGetSystemAddressForMDL`). (Generally,
you have no reason to actually look at the contents of the pages. Thus, using
`MmGetSystemAddressForMdl` is a call that would serve no useful purpose. Rather, it introduces
"double-mapping" of the pages. Unnecessary double-mappings should be avoided, as they
impose some performance penalties at other levels of the operating system.)

Depending on the capabilities of the device, the physical address derived from
`IoMapTransfer` might be the address either of the user-supplied buffer or of a contiguous copy
of that buffer. Which it is depends on the scatter/gather capability specified in the
`HalGetAdapter` initialization and is based on the capabilities of the driver/adapter pair. Copying
the buffer into a new, contiguous buffer is a slow operation. For a very large buffer, it results not

only in a performance problem but also in the problem stated previously, that of not being able to obtain a large block of physically contiguous memory. One workaround to this is to simulate scatter/gather by splitting the single user-based request into a sequence of smaller requests handled as independent operations. However, if there are a lot of small fragments, this, too, might introduce a performance problem. It might also require careful consideration in the programming to decide when to coalesce many small requests into one large one (simulating scatter/gather by copying) and when to split one large request into many smaller ones (simulating scatter/gather with multiple requests).

Overview of DMA Processing

How you program a DMA transaction is largely bus-independent. Thus the techniques for performing ISA DMA or PCI DMA are identical, except for the details of actually programming the device. We present in this section an overview of how DMA is conducted.

Some or most of the synchronization techniques we describe here may be omitted, depending on the complexity of the hardware and the desired degree of parallelism (for example, whether to allow simultaneous reads and writes to the same device, at least from the application program's viewpoint). We summarize these synchronization techniques at the end of the section.

DriverEntry Setup

One of the first things you must do is establish the Adapter Object in `DriverEntry`, as we have already discussed. Once you have the Adapter Object, you can initiate a DMA operation using it.

Dispatch Routine Processing

In the normal course of an operation that is going to be DMA, the initial processing in the Dispatch Routine is fairly straightforward. You must establish the addressibility of the data to be transferred and ensure the pages are locked down. Normally, this is done for you by the I/O Manager. However, you might need to construct additional MDLs for your own purposes (for example, if you are implementing a `DeviceIoControl` function that passes in a list of addresses that represent blocks of memory to be read or written). If you are doing software scatter/gather (see page 341), you might also need to map the pages into System Logical Address Space. At this point, you are unable to continue with any processing, so you must mark the IRP as pending. You then call `IoStartPacket` to initiate the queueing and return to the caller. Since the I/O is still pending, the I/O Manager will either mark the thread that initiated it as pending completion and suspend it, or (if asynchronous I/O is used) return to the user with a `STATUS_IO_PENDING` value. At this point, you no longer have to worry about the application thread; this is handled completely by the I/O Manager.

StartIo Processing

The pending packet is eventually dequeued, and the `StartIo` handler is called for the IRP. The `StartIo` handler can't do much because it doesn't have a DMA channel assigned to it; however, it does prepare for proper DMA execution by calling `KeFlushIoBuffers`. This guarantees that any cached information is written back to memory so that the DMA will be accessing the correct values.[2] On a multiprocessor, this will guarantee that all the appropriate cached data on all the processors is written back. On some machines, this function actually does nothing, but *can you be sure?* Of course not. So call it, even if you "know" it doesn't do anything on the platform you are currently programming. Your driver might have to run on machines that have not yet been designed. If you call this function, the NT kernel will, on those machines, Do The Right Thing. Note also that depending on the cache architecture, this may simply flush all dirty cache lines, flush and invalidate the entire cache, or flush any dirty lines defined by the range specified in the parameters of the call. The choice of what is done is platform-specific.

Having flushed the buffers, `StartIo` calls `IoAllocateAdapterChannel` to get an adapter channel. `IoAllocateAdapterChannel` might have to wait for a previously active I/O operation that is using the DMA channel represented by its Adapter Object. Thus this function maintains a queue of requests that wish to use the DMA channel. As soon as the channel is free, the next request is dequeued. This request now owns the DMA channel and is dispatched to an `AdapterControl` routine that has been specified.

The `AdapterControl` routine performs an `IoMapTransfer` function to allocate as many Map Registers as necessary (up to the limit available for the device) in order to complete the DMA transaction (or, for software scatter/gather, the next pending block of the scatter/gather operation).

KeSynchronizeExecution

At this point, you might think that you could actually initiate the DMA operation via the appropriate poking and prodding of registers. Alas, it is not yet that simple.

The complexity exists because the act of initiating the DMA requires poking and prodding at registers that the ISR might actually be using, even possibly be in the midst of changing. On a multiprocessor, any other driver level can be executing concurrent with an ISR. On either a uniprocessor system or multiprocessor system, another level can have control wrested from it, in the middle of a sequence of modifications, by the ISR. So, you need to protect these registers against simultaneous (or interleaved) access by the ISR and any other level (in this case, the `AdapterControl` routine). In some cases, it could be that poking at one register could start an interrupt sequence that would actually dispatch immediately, before a second or third register could have its value loaded. Thus, what appears to be a sequence of Load A, Load B, Load C could suddenly become Load A, process interrupt, modify A, modify B, modify C, Load B, Load C—and the Load B, Load C would be working on incorrect device state. Imagine a device that, if an error situation is pending, would interrupt as soon as device Register A was set, thereby causing the sequence just stated. The consequences are too horrible to contemplate.

So the `AdapterControl` routine uses a `KeSynchronizeExecution` call, which will first raise the IRQL to that of the device synchronization IRQL. It will then attempt to acquire the interrupt synchronization Spin Lock (waiting if necessary). `KeSynchronizeExecution` then calls the synchronized code, and, when the synchronized code returns, lowers the IRQL to the original level and releases the ISR Spin Lock.

---

[2] One question we have been asked is, "Why do you need to flush the cache before a *read* operation? After all, the buffer contents will be replaced!" The answer is that if you don't flush the cache before a read, then at some time after the data has been read in, the data in the cache may be written back, corrupting the information that has just been read in. Such bugs are, for all practical purposes, impossible to find.

Once the `KeSynchronizeExecution` function can pass the ISR Spin Lock, it calls a `SynchCritSection` function. It is in this function that you actually write to the device registers to initiate the device-specific actions to start a DMA transfer. This routine is executed at elevated IRQL (in fact, at the Device IRQL), so it should be as small and fast as possible. Any complex computations that need to be done should be done in preceding functions or subsequent lower-IRQL functions.

Once control returns from the `AdapterControl` function, nothing else will be dispatched until the device interrupt is taken and the ISR is invoked.

ISR Processing

The ISR is fairly simple and follows the model already presented in this chapter. It first determines if the interrupt that has been dispatched to it actually is from its device. (Remember, for shared IRQs, each ISR assigned to that IRQ will be called, in turn, until one acknowledges that it has processed the interrupt by returning `TRUE`.) As usual, ***DO NOT ASSUME THAT BECAUSE YOUR ISR IS CALLED, THE INTERRUPT IS FOR YOUR DEVICE***.[3] Check your device status registers to see if the device actually interrupted. If it did, you may then proceed; otherwise, return `FALSE`.

Having determined properly that the interrupt is for your device, you must then quiesce the interrupt condition. You do this by performing whatever magic the device specification reveals to you, storing whatever state is required for the future processing of the completed I/O request, queuing a DPC request using the `IoRequestDpc` function, and returning `TRUE`.

DPC Processing

In the DPC Routine, you should call `IoFlushAdapterBuffers` to ensure that any caching that was done in the adapter itself is properly flushed back to memory (at least for input functions). If you are using software-simulated scatter/gather, you check to see if you have processed all of the MDLs necessary for the operation. If you have not (and there was no error from the last transfer), you can then initiate the next MDL transfer by directly calling the `AdapterControl` routine to start this next transfer. If the transfer completes, or an error has occurred that should cause the operation to abort, you must release the DMA channel so that other requests that are pending on it will have access to it. You do this by calling `IoFreeAdapterChannel`. You can then call `IoStartNextPacket` to tell the I/O system that this packet has completed and that any pending packets can now start through. Then you call `IoCompleteRequest` to indicate that the request is complete (either successfully or with an error).

Optimizations and Simplifications

Now, what can be omitted? Suppose that there is exactly one Bus Master DMA channel on the device and only a single IRQ and also that the device does not contain any functional units that share the DMA channel. In this case, an Adapter Object might not be necessary. If only one I/O

---

[3] We wanted to put this in fluorescent red 72-point type, but our publisher told us this would cause production problems, so we had to settle for all capitals in boldface italic.

operation can be pending at a time, there might be no need to handle the
KeSynchronizeExecution operation. If the device does not have interrupts and all operations
can be completed in the Dispatch Routines, there is no need for StartIo. (There is another case
in which you will not use StartIo. That is when you provide your own queueing mechanism.
However, that case is not quite the same as the one here. Here, we are actually referring to the
general case of not needing any queueing mechanism.)

Maintaining Cache Consistency

DMA requires that all of the data to be written is actually in physical memory. Because DMA
uses physical addresses, it might or might not be subject to cache snooping, depending on the
platform. To "level the playing field", Microsoft provides two cache-management calls used during DMA setup and completion: KeFlushIoBuffers and IoFlushAdapterBuffers. The first
call guarantees that all data in the processor caches is flushed to the physical memory. The second handles the caching that might be done to handle scatter/gather operations when they are not
supported by the hardware or driver.

```
VOID KeFlushIoBuffers(IN PMDL Mdl,
                      IN BOOLEAN ReadOperation,
                      IN BOOLEAN DmaOperation);
```

The KeFlushIoBuffer function guarantees that all data specified by the MDL will be
flushed from all caches in all processors. The implementation is platform-specific and can span
the range from flushing *all* data in all processor caches to doing nothing at all because some
hardware magic will handle the problem. You should always call it before initiating a DMA
transfer.

```
BOOLEAN IoFlushAdapterBuffers(IN PADAPTER_OBJECT AdapterObject,
                              IN PMDL Mdl,
                              IN PVOID MapRegisterBase,
                              IN PVOID CurrentVa,
                              IN ULONG Length,
                              IN BOOLEAN WriteToDevice);
```

The IoFlushAdapterBuffers function is called upon completion of a DMA operation.
AdapterObject, Mdl, MapRegisterBase, CurrentVa, and Length all describe the area of the
transfer and are the same parameters that were passed to IoMapTransfer. The Boolean
WriteToDevice is set to TRUE for a Write operation and FALSE for a Read operation. This function handles not only cache consistency, but also the issues involved when the system has allocated private DMA buffers "behind your back".

DMA Channel Allocation

An adapter channel can be a shared resource. For ISA devices, there are a limited number of System DMA Controllers that can be shared among all of the ISA devices that require DMA. For
other busses, such as PCI, each card that requires DMA can have a Bus Master DMA controller.
However, for some multifunction cards, such as multimedia cards, a single Bus Master DMA
controller can be shared among several devices on the card. To handle such cases, you will typically create an Adapter Object that provides a central synchronization point for the DMA channel
allocation. To handle this synchronization, you call the IoAllocateAdapterChannel function.

```
NTSTATUS IoAllocateAdapterChannel(IN PADAPTER_OBJECT AdapterObject,
                                  IN PDEVICE_OBJECT DeviceObject,
                                  IN ULONG NumberOfMapRegisters,
                                  IN PDRIVER_CONTROL ExecutionRoutine,
                                  IN PVOID Context);
```

To use this pointer, you must pass in a pointer to the Adapter Object and a Device Object and state the number of Map Registers that will be required. The function queues a request for a DMA channel with the Adapter Object and returns STATUS_SUCCESS. If the request could not be queued because the *NumberOfMapRegisters* value exceeded the value returned by HalGetAdapter, it returns STATUS_INSUFFICIENT_RESOURCES. The request is queued until a channel and the requisite number of Map Registers become available. When these conditions are satisfied, *ExecutionRoutine*, whose prototype is given below, will be called.

```
IO_ALLOCATION_ACTION (*PDRIVER_CONTROL)(IN PDEVICE_OBJECT DeviceObject,
                                        IN PIRP Irp,
                                        IN PVOID MapRegisterBase,
                                        IN PVOID Context);
```

The driver should do nothing to the device itself until the *ExecutionRoutine* is called. This is because it does not (in general) know if the device is in use for some other purpose by another driver performing DMA. Its taking any action could corrupt that device's DMA transfer.

When the *ExecutionRoutine* is called, there is no guarantee regarding in what context it is executing. In particular, you cannot assume that the application virtual address space is the same as in the Dispatch Routine. Similar to an ISR or DPC, you can be in any process context when *ExecutionRoutine* is called. When this function is called, the DMA channel is known to be available. You can then perform operations such as IoMapTransfer on the Adapter Object. At this point, you can initiate the DMA operation. If synchronization is needed with the ISR or DPC (or other levels), you should call KeSynchronizeExecution (as described in the previous section) to be certain that you are not going to get into trouble with other device activities. Some devices require no such synchronization. In that case, you can just initiate the DMA transfer and return.

ExecutionRoutine must return one of the following values:

- DeallocateObjectKeepRegisters for a Bus Master DMA device
- KeepObject for a System DMA Controller device

When you have completed your DMA transfer, you must free the DMA channel for subsequent usage. This is done by calling the IoFreeAdapterChannel function.

```
VOID IoFreeAdapterChannel(IN PADAPTER_OBJECT AdapterObject);
```

IoFreeAdapterChannel is typically called in the DPC handler when it is determined that the I/O transaction has been completed (usually sometime just before IoCompleteRequest is called). It has an important side effect in any driver that does not support scatter/gather either in the hardware or by software simulation. That is, it frees up the Map Register and, in the process, copies the data from the kernel-allocated buffer to the user space. This is important to recognize because until you have freed the Adapter Object, the data is not available to the application. If you needed to examine the data for some reason, you would have to examine it in the kernel buffer whose pointer you had, not by examining the application memory you might have mapped into System Logical Address Space.

Controller Objects

A *Controller Object* is very much like an Adapter Object. The Controller Object is used not for DMA, but rather when there is any shared resource between two Device Objects whose use must be synchronized. For example, on a multimedia card the MIDI (Musical Instrument Digital Interface) port and wavetable upload port might both use a particular status register to record the completion of the successful programmed I/O operation. In this case, it would be a Bad Idea to try to do wavetable upload at the same time as doing MIDI output. But MIDI output is relatively "slow" (a note or six every musical beat), so wavetable upload could take place during the idle MIDI time. To do this, you would use a Controller Object to synchronize the use of the single status register. (There are other performance considerations that creep in here, but they're *your* problem as a Device Driver writer. If you decide to interleave the operations on the MIDI Device Object and the Wavetable Device Object, the Controller Object can be there to help you.)

If the device does DMA and the DMA shares state with other functional units on the card, you might need *both* an Adapter Object and a Controller Object.

Multiple Synchronization Objects and Deadlock

You must know what resources are shared in the set of devices you are managing. Thus, only you can create the necessary Controller Objects to manage them. If you have multiple functional units with a complex sharing of state, you may want to create more than one Controller Object. While having multiple synchronization objects can increase throughput by allowing a maximum amount of parallelism, this also introduces the possibility of *deadlock* caused by having different operations wait for each other to complete.

Consider the following scenario. We have a complex device that has some shared logic. During `DriverEntry`, we create three Device Objects that represent the three functional units on the device. In addition, we create two Controller Objects to handle the shared state on the board. In this case, the state is the state that can be used by more than one functional unit on the board. (These units include shared status registers and shared I/O addresses, but not DMA. If it was DMA, we'd also have an Adapter Object, and this is a discussion of Controller Objects.) Each device has its own dispatch handler, its own ISR, and its own DPC.

The device is now active, and the application is using them concurrently. It doesn't know (or necessarily care) that Device A, Device B, and Device C are all on one board. So we need to synchronize the use of the shared resources. Thus we specify that Device A wants Resource P. It tries to acquire Resource P using whatever locking mechanism is appropriate (in this case, we assume that a Controller Object represents resource P, which might be a status register). Device B, meanwhile, wants Resource Q, which it obtains using another Controller Object. Everything is copacetic: The driver is happy, the user is happy, and I/O is proceeding as expected. Now Device B wants Resource P. It tries to acquire it by using the shared Controller Object, but it can't get it because Device A already has it. This is OK; Device B simply blocks on the lock, waiting for Device A to release the resource. But now Device A wants Resource Q. Resource Q has already been acquired by Device B, but Device A doesn't know this, so it happily blocks on the lock, waiting for Resource Q to come free.

So what do we have? Device A has Resource P and is waiting for Resource Q. Device B has Resource Q and is waiting for Resource P. Device B won't release Resource Q until it gets Resource P, but Device A won't release Resource P until it gets Resource Q. Deadlock. At this point, both Device A and Device B have gone catatonic, the I/O ceases, and the application program is nonresponsive (unless it was doing asynchronous I/O, in which case it is merely waiting indefinitely for the operation to complete). The end user is Very Unhappy.

There is one, and *only one*, method for assuring deadlock-free operation in such a case. The resources must be arranged in a hierarchy and *always* locked in the same order dictated by that hierarchy. You can do this either by creating a list of such resources and locking them in the order specified by the list or by simply knowing the order and never violating it. But whatever method you use, you *must* do the locking in the specified order and unlock in the inverse order. The existence of multiple Controller Objects is an invitation to deadlock, so if you create more than one, you must have a plan for deadlock avoidance.

This situation is not unique to Controller Objects. If you have an Adapter Object, it would be just one more resource in the locking hierarchy. If you have your own Spin Locks or use any other synchronization mechanism up to and including Mutexes and Semaphores, you have the potential for deadlock.

Note that since Adapter Objects are used only in *some* transactions (DMA), but Controller Objects will be used in all transactions that share state, if an Adapter Object shares state with other functions, you must acquire the Controller Object *first*, or you have a potential deadlock situation.

Creating and Managing Controller Objects

Whenever you create Device Objects in your `DriverEntry` routine that require synchronization, you will probably allocate a `PCONTROLLER_OBJECT` pointer in their Device Extensions. For each Device Object that shares the resource represented by the Controller Object, you will point a pointer to the Controller Object that controls that resource into the corresponding Device Extension. Note that you can have as many Controller Objects as you have shared resources or as few as one that represents all shared resources, depending on how you have designed your driver. (You can also ignore Controller Objects entirely and do your own synchronization and queueing, but life is often easier if you take advantage of the built-in mechanisms.)

A Controller Object, like a Device Object, is a largely opaque structure. If you have any information that is specific to the controller, you can add a Controller Extension Object of your own devising, as follows.

```
PCONTROLLER_OBJECT IoCreateController(IN ULONG Size);
```

The `IoCreateController` function is called in `DriverEntry` and returns a pointer to a `CONTROLLER_OBJECT` structure. If this pointer is `NULL`, the driver cannot load and should free up any resources it has allocated. Although a `CONTROLLER_OBJECT` has many internal fields, only one is documented: the `ControllerExtension` field. This field contains a pointer to a Controller Extension of the specified `Size` allocated by `IoCreateController`, or `NULL` if that value was 0.

```
typedef struct _CONTROLLER_OBJECT {
    // ... Opaque fields
    PVOID ControllerExtension;
    // ... Opaque fields
    } CONTROLLER_OBJECT, *PCONTROLLER_OBJECT;
```

To queue a request on the Controller Object, call the `IoAllocateController` function, given as follows.

```
VOID IoAllocateController(IN PCONTROLLER_OBJECT ControllerObject,
                          IN PDEVICE_OBJECT DeviceObject,
                          IN PDRIVER_CONTROL ExecutionRoutine,
                          IN PVOID Context);
```

Here, *ExecutionRoutine* is queued for later execution when *ControllerObject* can be acquired. When *ControllerObject* is acquired, the pending *ExecutionRoutine* is called and is passed the `Context` pointer.

ExecutionRoutine has the following definition.

```
IO_ALLOCATION_ACTION (*PDRIVER_CONTROL)(IN PDEVICE_OBJECT DeviceObject,
                                        IN PIRP Irp,
                                        IN PVOID MapRegisterBase,
                                        IN PVOID Context);
```

This is the same prototype for a Driver Control function that is used by `IoAllocateAdapterChannel`. *MapRegisterBase* has meaning for `IoAllocateAdapter`, but for `IoAllocateController` this value is designated as system-reserved, and as far as any documentation that we can find shows, it has no meaning for Controller Objects.

The Controller Object remains acquired until the `IoFreeController` function is called.

```
VOID IoFreeController(IN PCONTROLLER_OBJECT ControllerObject);
```

`IoFreeController` releases the Controller Object. This is usually done in the DPC Routine after the transaction that required the Controller Object has completed. However, it also can be done in *ExecutionRoutine* when the only requirement is to change a register value or a set of values that do not result in generating an interrupt.

To delete a Controller Object in the Unload routine, call the `IoDeleteController` function.

```
VOID IoDeleteController(IN PCONTROLLER_OBJECT ControllerObject);
```

Any resources you have allocated in the Controller Extension must be freed before you call `IoDeleteController`. Note also that you usually have several pointers to a Controller Object, one in each Device Object that uses the Controller Object. You must free the Controller Object exactly *once*. It is your responsibility to see that this is done correctly.

Summary

In this chapter we have covered the key concepts involved in using the NT support for handling DMA. In addition to the DMA support, we have shown how to program your own software scatter/gather mechanism. We have discussed how to synchronize access to shared hardware resources such as DMA channels (using Adapter Objects) and shared hardware state (using Controller Objects).

Chapter

---

18 *Achieving Reality: The Rest of the Details*

We're nearly there. The driver is nearly complete. We have a few remaining details to cover, but once we've done that, you'll have the core of what you need to know to write a driver. The key topics we cover in this chapter are how to write the Unload function and how to use the Registry to get driver-specific parameters.

In subsequent chapters, we cover many other interesting topics that are needed when building many types of drivers:

- How to map device memory to user space (Chapter 19)

- The ISA bus (Chapter 20) and the PCI Bus (Chapter 21)

- Serialization and queuing within the driver (Chapter 22)

- Layered drivers (Chapter 23)

- Driver threads (Chapter 24)

- Some interesting driver techniques (Chapter 26)

The Unload Function

We showed you a simple example of an Unload function, in Chapter 14 and Chapter 16, that simply deletes the symbolic link(s) and the Device Object. However, for more complex drivers, you must totally undo any state set up by the `DriverEntry` routine and free up all resources that have been claimed by the driver. This affects not only the immediate operating system state (allocated memory and the like), but also more persistent state, such as the resources the driver might have (should have) claimed in the Registry. A summary of the deallocations required is shown in Table 18.1.

353

Table 18.1: Unload *Requirements*

Resource or State	Unload Must Call	Notes
If DriverEntry Called		
IoConnectInterrupt	IoDisconnectInterrupt	Must be called before the Interrupt Object is freed. Must *not* be called if IoConnectInterrupt was not called.
IoCreateSymbolicLink	IoDeleteSymbolicLink	
IoCreateController	IoDeleteController	
IoAssignArcName	IoDeassignArcName	
ExAllocatePool	ExFreePool	All other allocations performed must also be cleaned up.
MmMapIoSpace	MmUnmapIoSpace	
MmAllocateNonCachedMemory	MmFreeNonCachedMemory	
MmAllocateContiguousMemory	MmFreeContiguousMemory	
HalAllocateCommonBuffer	HalFreeCommonBuffer	
IoAssignResources HalAssignSlotResources	IoAssignResources	Call with a NULL pointer to the resource request. This removes the claimed resources from the Registry.
IoReportResourceUsage	IoReportResourceUsage	
KeRegisterBugCheckCallback	KeUnregisterBugCheckCallback	
Other State To Be Cleaned Up		
IoTimer routine is enabled.	IoStopTimer	
KeSetTimer(Ex) was called.	KeCancelTimer	
A call was queued to the CustomDpc handler.	KeRemoveQueueDpc	
Threads are waiting on a dispatcher object.		Must cause the threads to proceed so that the dispatcher object can be deleted.
IoGetDeviceObjectPointer called for a lower-level driver.	ObDereferenceObject	Must be called by the higher-level driver. The lower-level driver must not be unloaded until this has been called.
IoAttachDevice called for a lower-level driver.	IoDetachDevice	
PsCreateSystemThread has been called.	(See the notes.)	The Unload routine must cause the thread to run so that the thread itself can call PsTerminateSystemThread.

Parameterizing a Driver: The Registry

Many drivers require some system-specific parameters. These are usually established by the `DriverEntry` routine long before the driver is capable of processing an IRP. These are not parameters that can be compiled into the driver using `#define` because we want to distribute the same binary to many different sites, and the values of these parameters may be site-specific.

The best source of parameters to a driver is the Registry. In our example, we are providing some rather simple parameters. However, some drivers, particularly those for configurable ISA cards, might need to know the IRQ, DMA channel, I/O register addresses, and/or mapped memory addresses of the card. For these cases, you would allow your installation program to set these values. You also would provide a utility program that would change these values. We show examples of this in Chapter 20.

The parameters for a Device Driver that are stored in the Registry are shown in Table 18.2. The attributes are shown in two groupings:

1. Those required to load the driver, as specified by the NT standards
2. Those that are driver-specific

We make this split for presentational reasons. The contents of Table 18.2 that are not shaded are actually the contents of the *driverName*.Ini file that we show in Chapter 8 (page 165) and which forms part of the installation procedure.

Table 18.2: *Registry Entries for Typical Drivers*

Entry Type	Contents	Explanation
\registry\machine\system\currentcontrolset\services*drivername*		
Specified by the Registry requirements for a Device Driver in NT (see page 896).	Type = REG_DWORD 0x00000001	Kernel driver (SERVICE_KERNEL_DRIVER)
	Start = REG_DWORD 0x00000003	Demand start (SERVICE_DEMAND_START)
	Group = Extended base	Group
		No tag (this driver will be loaded after all tagged drivers in its group)
	ErrorControl REG_DWORD 0x00000001	Error option (log and continue to boot) (SERVICE_ERROR_NORMAL)
\registry\machine\system\currentcontrolset\services*drivername*\Parameters		
Driver-specific entries designed by the implementor.	BreakOnEntry REG_DWORD 0x0	DriverEntry break (do not break on entry)
	DebugMask REG_DWORD 0x0	Bitmask of debugging options (no debugging bits are set)
	LogEvents = 0x0	Bitmask of logging options (logging is disabled)

The minimum boilerplate required for every driver is shown in the table.

- The `Type` is 1, the actual value of the symbol `SERVICE_KERNEL_DRIVER`.

- The `Start` code is 3, the code for `SERVICE_DEMAND_START`. This means that after the system boots, the user will have to go to the Control Panel, select the Driver icon, and explicitly start the driver. Alternatively, the user will have to go to a command window and use the command "`net start drivername`" to start the driver.

- The group code is `Extended base`. This group controls when an automatically loaded driver is started; the code has no meaning for demand-loaded drivers. The `Extended base` is the last group to be loaded.

- `ErrorControl` is 1, the actual value for the symbol `SERVICE_ERROR_NORMAL`, indicating that any load error should not affect the boot process but that the failure will be logged in the Event Log.

Note that there is no `Tag` field. This means the driver will be loaded after all tagged drivers within the `Extended base` group. It has no other load dependencies.

Reading the Registry

Reading the Registry in the kernel differs somewhat from how the Registry is read in an application program. The function `RtlQueryRegistryValues` obtains the values. It takes a table of keys, default values, and locations (as well as several other required and optional values). It then proceeds to look up the value in the Registry for each key given in the table. If it finds the value, it sets the corresponding location to hold that value.   A static table cannot be used, so we create the table on the stack, initialize its entries, and call `RtlQueryRegistryValues`. It is very important to note that if there is an error for some reason, you should still set the required values to some hardwired default, rather than leave the variables uninitialized. Doing this makes your driver far more robust and less likely to crash or, worse, to corrupt the system if the Registry is not correctly initialized.

`RtlQueryRegistryValues` is a convenient wrapper around the lower-level Zw-prefix operations that manipulate the Registry.

Listing 18.1 illustrates a special-purpose Registry read routine we did for the example in Listing 18.2. It reads the Registry variables given in Table 18.2.

Listing 18.1: *Reading Values from the Registry*

```
NTSTATUS readRegistry(
    IN PDRIVER_OBJECT DriverObject,    // Driver Object
    IN PUNICODE_STRING RegistryPath,   // Base path to keys
    OUT PULONG debugMask,              // 32-bit binary debug mask
    OUT PULONG eventLog,               // Boolean: do we log events?
    OUT PULONG shouldBreak,            // Boolean: break in DriverEntry?
    )
{
    //
    // We use this to query into the Registry to get initialization and
    // debug information for our driver
    //
    RTL_QUERY_REGISTRY_TABLE paramTable[4];   // Parameter table
    ULONG zero = 0;                           // Default value 0
```

```
PWCHAR path;                                  // The Registry path
NTSTATUS status = STATUS_UNSUCCESSFUL;        // Assume failure
UNICODE_STRING parms;                         // Temporary string variable
ULONG pathLength;                             // Length to allocate for path

RtlInitUnicodeString(&parms, L"\\Parameters");

// We want a path that will hold the base path plus the parameters key
// plus NUL
pathLength = RegistryPath->Length  + parms->Length + sizeof(WCHAR);

// We set these values to their defaults in case there are any failures
*debugMask = 0;
*shouldBreak = 0;
//
// Since the Registry path parameter is a "counted" UNICODE string, it
// might not be NUL-terminated. For a very short time, allocate memory
// to hold the Registry path NUL-terminated so that we can use it to
// delve into the Registry
//

path = ExAllocatePool(PagedPool, pathLength);
if (path != NULL)
    { /* got path */
    KdPrint( ("readReg: Pool allocated\n") );

    RtlZeroMemory(paramTable, sizeof(paramTable)); // Mandatory

    // Create the path name

    RtlZeroMemory(path, pathLength);
    RtlMoveMemory(path, RegistryPath->Buffer, RegistryPath->Length);
    RtlAppendUnicodeStringToString(&path, &parms);

    paramTable[0].Flags = RTL_QUERY_REGISTRY_DIRECT;
    paramTable[0].Name = L"BreakOnEntry";
    paramTable[0].EntryContext = shouldBreak;
    paramTable[0].DefaultType = REG_DWORD;
    paramTable[0].DefaultData = &zero;
    paramTable[0].DefaultLength = sizeof(ULONG);

    paramTable[1].Flags = RTL_QUERY_REGISTRY_DIRECT;
    paramTable[1].Name = L"DebugMask";
    paramTable[1].EntryContext = debugMask;
    paramTable[1].DefaultType = REG_DWORD;
    paramTable[1].DefaultData = &zero;
    paramTable[1].DefaultLength = sizeof(ULONG);

    paramTable[2].Flags = RTL_QUERY_REGISTRY_DIRECT;
    paramTable[2].Name = L"LogEvents";
    paramTable[2].EntryContext = eventLog;
    paramTable[2].DefaultType = REG_DWORD;
    paramTable[2].DefaultData = &zero;
    paramTable[2].DefaultLength = sizeof(ULONG);
```

```
              if (!NT_SUCCESS(
                      RtlQueryRegistryValues(
                          RTL_REGISTRY_ABSOLUTE | RTL_REGISTRY_OPTIONAL,
                          path,
                          &paramTable[0],
                          NULL,
                          NULL)))
              { /* failed */
                 // If it failed, it may have partially updated the variables
                 // The query function quits on the first error
                 // To ensure that everything is consistent, we reset the values
                 KdPrint( ("readReg: Failed return unsuccessful\n") );
                 *shouldBreak = 0;
                 *debugMask = 0;
                   status = STATUS_UNSUCCESSFUL;
              } /* failed */
          else
              { /* ok */
                 status = STATUS_SUCCESS;
              } /* ok */

      //
      // We don't need the path anymore
      //
      ExFreePool(path);
   } /* got path */
 }
 return status;
}
```

Using the Registry Values

Having supplied a function to read the Registry, we next show you how to use it. The example in
Listing 18.2 consists of some additions to the `Hello.c` source codes of Chapter 8, so we don't
explain the features of this driver that are already present in `Hello.c`. We show the new sections of code in a bold font.

Listing 18.2: *A* `DriverEntry` *Routine Using Registry Values*

```
#include "ntddk.h"
#include "readreg.h"

// ... Assorted grubby detail omitted here

/*************************************************************************
            DriverEntry
*************************************************************************/
NTSTATUS DriverEntry(
    IN PDRIVER_OBJECT DriverObject,
    IN PUNICODE_STRING RegistryPath )
    {
    PDEVICE_OBJECT deviceObject = NULL;
    NTSTATUS status;
    UNICODE_STRING NtNameString;
    UNICODE_STRING Win32NameString;
```

```
        PdriverName_DEVICE_EXTENSION extension;
        ULONG   ret = 0;
        //
        // Store these values in the Device Extension after it is created
        //
        ULONG debugMask;
        ULONG eventLog;
        ULONG shouldBreak;
        KdPrint( ("driverName: Entered DriverEntry!\n") );
        KdPrint( ("driverName: about to call readRegistry!\n") );
        readRegistry( DriverObject, RegistryPath,
                      &debugMask, &eventLog, &shouldBreak );

        // If we have indicated a desired debugger break, do it now
        if(shouldBreak)
            DbgBreakPoint( );  // Requires that the debugger be active

        KdPrint( ("mapMem: returned from readRegistry!\n") );
```

In this example is an important use of a breakpoint that makes the example more than gratuitous. It turns out that in order to set a breakpoint somewhere else in the code, you need to have the debugger active and the symbol tables for your code loaded. But the symbol tables cannot be loaded before the driver starts, and the `DriverEntry` routine might be the routine you want to debug! In any case, you will find it hard to set breakpoints in a location for which the executable code has not been loaded. So this initial breakpoint is of great use to a developer. Since it can be activated at any time (simply by setting the Registry variable), this also is a very useful field maintenance technique.

Having read the Registry variables, we continue with the rest of our example.

Initializing the Driver Object

We initialize the `UNICODE_STRING`, which we need for the `IoCreateDevice` call. Unlike in our original "Hello World" example, this `IoCreateDevice` call creates a Device Extension. The format of the Device Extension is defined in the file `MapMem.h`. We show the relevant section of that header file here.

Listing 18.3: `MapMem.h` *(excerpt)*

```
//...
#define MAX_NUM_CHUNKS       100
#define MAX_CONCURRENT_OPENS   5

typedef struct _driverName_DEVICE_EXTENSION {
    ULONG   debugMask;            // Set from Registry
    ULONG   shouldBreak;          // Set from Registry
} driverName_DEVICE_EXTENSION, *PdriverName_DEVICE_EXTENSION;
//...
```

We get our Device Extension by supplying, to the `IoCreateDevice` *call, the desired length,* `sizeof(driverName_DEVICE_EXTENSION)`. *We also allow this device to be shared.*

```
//
// Create counted string version of our device name
//
RtlInitUnicodeString( &NtNameString, NT_DEVICE_NAME );
//
// Create the Device Object
//
status = IoCreateDevice(
            DriverObject,
            sizeof(driverName_DEVICE_EXTENSION),
            &NtNameString,
            FILE_DEVICE_UNKNOWN,
            0,                      // No standard device characteristics
            FALSE,                  // This isn't an exclusive device
            &deviceObject
            );
```

If we fail to create a Device Object, we simply set an error status and return. If we succeed in getting it, we can proceed to do some initialization. We can defer the initialization of the Driver Object fields to this point, since there was little reason to initialize them earlier (if we fail, the Driver Object will be deleted). You need to specify whether the device will be doing Buffered I/O or Direct I/O. In this example, we show doing Direct I/O (DO_DIRECT_IO). This affects only the ReadFile and WriteFile operations. You also need to establish whether your driver is exclusive or nonexclusive, that is, whether it will allow only one open at a time, or can it allow multiple concurrent opens.

```
if ( NT_SUCCESS(status) )
    { /* have device object */
    //
    // Create dispatch points for create/open, close, unload
    //
    DriverObject->MajorFunction[IRP_MJ_CREATE] = driverNameOpen;
    DriverObject->MajorFunction[IRP_MJ_CLOSE] = driverNameClose;
    DriverObject->MajorFunction[IRP_MJ_DEVICE_CONTROL] =
                                             driverNameDeviceControl;
    DriverObject->DriverUnload = driverNameUnload;
    KdPrint( ("driverName: just about ready!\n") );

    //
    // Do direct I/O.  That is, the I/O system will provide pointers
    // to/from user data from/to the user buffer
    //
    deviceObject->Flags |= DO_DIRECT_IO;
```

Now comes an important part of the initialization. Because we have a Device Extension part, we should initialize it here. For robustness, we clear it to zeroes first. This guarantees that if we add additional fields and forget to initialize them, they will be zero, often the most harmless value you can supply. Here, we do most of the initialization, including allocating any memory required by the driver.

```
    //
    // Fill in the Device Extension
    //
    extension =
        (PdriverName_DEVICE_EXTENSION) deviceObject->DeviceExtension;
```

```
        RtlZeroMemory(extension, sizeof(driverName_DEVICE_EXTENSION)));
        extension->debugMask = debugMask;
        extension->shouldBreak = shouldBreak;
```

We have now initialized both the "fixed" part of our Device Extension and the part whose initialization depends on the values we obtained from the Registry. Except for the names printed out, the remainder of the code is pretty much like Hello.c. *We create the application-level name for the device. Also, if there is failure, we delete the Device Object. First, however, we must free up all memory chunks that were allocated; otherwise, we have a storage leak. Since this memory is allocated out of the Nonpaged Pool, this would be a serious error. So it is best to "leave gates as you find them" (as defined by all books on how to be a polite hiker/hunter) and clean up any memory that is allocated.*

```
        //
        // Create counted string version of our Win32 device name
        //
        RtlInitUnicodeString( &Win32NameString, DOS_DEVICE_NAME );
        //
        //
        // Create a link from our device name to a name in the Win32
        // namespace
        //
        status = IoCreateSymbolicLink( &Win32NameString, &NtNameString );
        if (!NT_SUCCESS(status))
            {
            KdPrint( ("driverName: Couldn't create the symbolic link\n") );
            // Free up any resources you may have allocated in the
            // Device Extension
            IoDeleteDevice( DriverObject->DeviceObject );
            }
        else
            {
            KdPrint( ("driverName: DriverEntry success!\n") );
            }
        } /* have Device Object */
    else
        {
        KdPrint( ("driverName: Couldn't create the device\n") );
        }
    return status;
}
```

The Unload Handler

The Unload handler is very much like the one shown for the hello driver. However, in Listing 18.3 we show how to iterate down the device list to free multiple instances of devices.

Listing 18.4: *An Unload Handler for Multiple Device Objects*

```
/**********************************************************************
                          driverNameUnload
**********************************************************************/
```

```
VOID driverNameUnload( IN PDRIVER_OBJECT DriverObject)
{
    UNICODE_STRING Win32NameString;
    PDEVICE_OBJECT device;
    PDEVICE_OBJECT next;
    //
    // This driver needs to free up any resources allocated to each
    // device and delete the Device Object(s) and the symbolic link between
    // our device name and the Win32 visible name
    //
    KdPrint( ("driverName: Unloading!!\n") );
    //
    // Create counted string version of our Win32 device name
    //
    RtlInitUnicodeString( &Win32NameString, DOS_DEVICE_NAME );
    //
    // Delete the link from our device name to a name in the Win32 namespace
    //
    IoDeleteSymbolicLink( &Win32NameString );
    //
    // Finally delete the Device Object(s)
    //
    for(device = DriverObject->DeviceObject; device != NULL; device = next)
        { /* delete each */
          next = device->NextDevice; // Save before we delete the object
          // Free up any resources the device has assigned
          IoDeleteDevice( device );
        } /* delete each */
}
```

Summary

Reality Has Been Achieved. Any Remaining Problems Are Your Own.[1]

---

[1] With apologies to Douglas Adams.

Chapter

19 *Mapping Kernel and Device Memory to User Space*

In earlier chapters, we discussed that devices can have their own onboard memory. Normally, this memory is managed entirely by the Device Driver. However, for some devices, it is reasonable, possible, or even necessary to map this memory directly into the application address space. In this chapter, we cover, down to the code level and with a completely worked-out example, how you map kernel and device memory into user space.

Mapping Nonpaged Pool to User Space

The first reaction to the subject of mapping the Nonpaged Pool to user space is usually *why?* Why would you ever want to make memory in the Nonpaged Pool accessible to the user? This is dangerous. Unless the memory is in page-sized chunks and page-aligned, a user program that accessed memory outside of the bounds could damage arbitrary and unknown system data, thereby causing horrendous crashes and/or corrupted disks. This is a genuine danger. So why would you ever want to make memory in the Nonpaged Pool accessible to the user?

Reality has several ways of rearing its nasty head. An example is the simple case of an attached coprocessor that needs to communicate to the host memory. To do this, the coprocessor needs physical addresses in the host. The problem is that the programs that are loaded into this coprocessor are loaded from the host, and only the host will know the locations of the physical memory. However, the program for the coprocessor is constructed and loaded from an application. The application will need the physical memory addresses to give to the coprocessor. It also will need a virtual address that *it* can use to read or modify the data that is seen by the coprocessor.

Another case is when the "application" is really a User-mode Device Driver. In this case, the work of doing the setup and interpretation of the data is not something that should be running in

Ring 0 space. Nor should it be running with kernel-level priority. But the application is required to program the DMA chips, for which it needs actual physical addresses.

Yet another case is created by some of the very high-speed I/O devices that are available. For example, to keep some of the new ATM hardware working at full speed, internal buffers of a hundred megabytes or more are required. You certainly don't want to *copy* this huge amount of data to user-space buffers. Often, the best approach is to have the application and kernel share the buffer space in the device memory. Other devices, such as high-resolution color video cameras or displays working on full-motion video problems, often require pools of massive frame buffers. The best performance for these can be obtained by sharing those buffers with the application.

The driver we develop here, `MapMem`, might seem a bit contrived, but it is based on real drivers that have been written to solve real problems. It is clearly an artifice, designed to illustrate the different system calls and techniques required to do the memory mapping. The calls you are about to see are real. Only the driver structure has been changed to protect the innocent.

An Overview of the `MapMem` Driver

The `MapMem` driver is fairly simple, but it introduces a surprising amount of additional mechanism for what appears to be a simple task. Its purpose is to allow a number of concurrent threads to "open" the device and request one or more chunks of memory. This memory is in the Nonpaged Pool. Each thread that requests a block is given both a physical address of the block (which it presumably will hand off to its magical device that needs a physical address) and a virtual address in its own memory map that allows it to access the memory.

In this implementation of `MapMem`, we simplify the task of building the driver by requiring that the application programs all agree on the unique integer that each program will use to identify itself. It is also possible to have the Device Driver provide a unique integer to each application; we discuss how this could be done in Chapter 22 on page 454.

The driver keeps three internal maps of its chunks of memory:

- A map indexed by chunk number that is an array of the associated system virtual memory addresses

- A map indexed by chunk number that is the corresponding physical memory address

- A map that is a fixed-size, two-dimensional array

The third map's columns are indexed by chunk numbers, and its rows are indexed by the application code identifier, which calls a "session number". This map gives, for each session number, the session-relative application-level virtual addresses for each chunk.

We allocate the memory at `DriverEntry` so that we can grab chunks of memory before the Nonpaged Pool becomes fragmented.

Whenever an application sends a request to the `MapMem` device, it specifies a session number. It receives back the vector that gives the virtual addresses in its virtual memory where all of the chunks can be found. There is nothing to keep any set of applications from using any chunk and thus either establishing a sharing relationship (cooperative use) or producing a disaster (conflicting use). Since the purpose of this exercise is to illustrate only a slightly more complex driver than "Hello World", we make no attempt to provide a more elegant solution. We will sketch how this is done once we have explained how to build a "proper" allocator.

The Registry Entry

The Registry entry is almost identical to the general form of a Registry entry, which is shown in Table 18.2, with the exception of the two new entries specific to the `MapMem` driver. The complete `MapMem.Ini` file is shown next. We highlight the differences between `MapMem` and the earlier drivers by using a bold font.

```
\registry\machine\system\currentcontrolset\services\MapMem
    Type = REG_DWORD 0x00000001
    Start = REG_DWORD 0x00000003
    Group = Extended base
    ErrorControl REG_DWORD 0x00000001
\registry\machine\system\currentcontrolset\services\MapMem\Parameters
    BreakOnEntry REG_DWORD 0x0
    DebugMask REG_DWORD 0x0
    ReservedMemorySize REG_DWORD 0x4000
    ReservedMemoryChunk = 0x1
    LogEvents = 0x0
```

Reading the Registry

To read the Registry, we use code quite similar to that shown in Listing 18.1, except that we add entries to read the two items specific to the `MapMem` driver. The enhancements are shown in bold font.

```
NTSTATUS readRegistry(
    IN PDRIVER_OBJECT DriverObject,       // Driver Object
    IN PUNICODE_STRING RegistryPath,      // Base path to keys
    OUT PULONG debugMask,                 // 32-bit binary debug mask
    OUT PULONG eventLog,                  // Boolean: do we log events?
    OUT PULONG shouldBreak,               // Boolean: break in DriverEntry?
    OUT PULONG reservedMemorySize,        // ULONG: Size of each memory chunk
    OUT PULONG reservedMemoryChunks       // ULONG: Number of memory chunks
    )
{
    //
    // We use this to query into the Registry as to get initialization and
    // debug information for our driver
    //
    RTL_QUERY_REGISTRY_TABLE paramTable[6];  // Parameter table
    ULONG zero = 0;                          // Default value 0
    ULONG one = 1;                           // Default value 1
    ULONG sixteenK = 16 * 1024;              // Default value for 16K
    ULONG notConfigurable = 0;
    ULONG model30 = 0;
    PWCHAR path;                             // The Registry path
    NTSTATUS status = STATUS_UNSUCCESSFUL;   // Assume failure
    //... Code identical to Listing 18.1

    // We set these values to their defaults in case there are any failures
    *debugMask = 0;
    *shouldBreak = 0;
    *reservedMemorySize = sixteenK;
    *reservedMemoryChunks = 1;

    //... Code identical to Listing 18.1
```

```
paramTable[3].Flags = RTL_QUERY_REGISTRY_DIRECT;
paramTable[3].Name = L"ReservedMemorySize";
paramTable[3].EntryContext = reservedMemorySize;
paramTable[3].DefaultType = REG_DWORD;
paramTable[3].DefaultData = &sixteenK;
paramTable[3].DefaultLength = sizeof(ULONG);

paramTable[4].Flags = RTL_QUERY_REGISTRY_DIRECT;
paramTable[4].Name = L"ReservedMemoryChunks";
paramTable[4].EntryContext = reservedMemoryChunks;
paramTable[4].DefaultType = REG_DWORD;
paramTable[4].DefaultData = &one;
paramTable[4].DefaultLength = sizeof(ULONG);

//... Code identical to Listing 18.1
//... except that in case of failure, be sure to set default values
//... for the new parameters
}
```

Using the Registry Values

Having supplied a function to read the Registry, we next show how to use it. Listing 19.1 consists of some additions to our `Hello.c` driver of Chapter 8, so we don't explain the features of this driver that are already present in `Hello.c`. We show the new sections of code in a bold font.

Listing 19.1: `DriverEntry` *Routine for* `MapMem`*: Part 1*

```
#include "ntddk.h"
#include "MapMem.h"
#include "readreg.h"

// ... Assorted grubby detail omitted here

/*************************************************************************
            DriverEntry
*************************************************************************/
NTSTATUS DriverEntry(
    IN PDRIVER_OBJECT DriverObject,
    IN PUNICODE_STRING RegistryPath )
    {
    //... Code identical to Listing 18.1

    PMAPMEM_DEVICE_EXTENSION extension;
    ULONG MappedVector;
    BOOLEAN GotResources;
    //
    // Store these values in the Device Extension after it is created
    //
    //... Code identical to Listing 18.1

    ULONG reservedMemorySize;
    ULONG reservedMemoryChunks;
    KdPrint( ("mapMem: Entered the MapMem driver!\n") );
    KdPrint( ("mapMem: about to call readRegistry!\n") );
```

```
readRegistry( DriverObject, RegistryPath,
              &debugMask, &eventLog, &shouldBreak,
              &reservedMemorySize, &reservedMemoryChunks );

// Make sure that the Registry value does not exceed our
//compile-time limits
if(reservedMemoryChunks > MAX_NUM_CHUNKS)
    { /* too big */
      KdPrint( ("mapMem: Registry value %d exceeds limit of %d\n",
                    reservedMemoryChunks, MAX_NUM_CHUNKS) );
      reservedMemoryChunks = MAX_NUM_CHUNKS;
    } /* too big */
```

Initializing the Driver Object

Next, we initialize the UNICODE_STRING, which we need for the IoCreateDevice call. Unlike in our original "Hello World" example, this IoCreateDevice call creates a Device Extension. The format of the Device Extension is defined in the file MapMem.h. We show the relevant section of that header file in Listing 19.2.

Listing 19.2: MapMem.h *file*

```
//...
#define MAX_NUM_CHUNKS       100
#define MAX_CONCURRENT_OPENS   5

typedef struct _MAPMEM_DEVICE_EXTENSION {
    ULONG   debugMask;             // Set from Registry
    ULONG   shouldBreak;           // Set from Registry
    ULONG   reservedMemorySize;    // Set from Registry
    ULONG   reservedMemoryChunks;  // Set from Registry
    ULONG   currentOpens;
    KSPIN_LOCK ControlLock;        // Protects currentOpens;
    PVOID   DMABufferSystemVirtualAddr[MAX_NUM_CHUNKS];
                                   // System address of shared memory
    PHYSICAL_ADDRESS  DMABufferSystemPhysicalAddr[MAX_NUM_CHUNKS];
    PVOID   DMABufferUserVirtualAddr[MAX_NUM_CHUNKS]
                                   [MAX_CONCURRENT_OPENS];

    PUCHAR testbuffer;
} MAPMEM_DEVICE_EXTENSION;
typedef MAPMEM_DEVICE_EXTENSION *PMAPMEM_DEVICE_EXTENSION;
```

Listing 19.3: DriverEntry *Routine for* MapMem: *Part 2*

```
//...
```

We get our Device Extension by supplying the desired length,
sizeof(MAPMEM_DEVICE_EXTENSION), *to the* IoCreateDevice *call. We also allow this device to be shared.*

```
status = IoCreateDevice(
            DriverObject,
            sizeof(MAPMEM_DEVICE_EXTENSION),
```

```
                    &NtNameString,
                    FILE_DEVICE_UNKNOWN,
                    0,                        // No standard device characteristics
                    FALSE,                    // This isn't an exclusive device
                    &deviceObject
                    );
    if ( NT_SUCCESS(status) )
       { /* have device object */
       //
       // Create dispatch points for create/open, close, unload
       //
       DriverObject->MajorFunction[IRP_MJ_CREATE] = mapMemOpen;
       DriverObject->MajorFunction[IRP_MJ_CLOSE] = mapMemClose;
       DriverObject->MajorFunction[IRP_MJ_DEVICE_CONTROL] = mapMemDeviceControl;
       DriverObject->DriverUnload = mapMemUnload;
       KeInitializeSpinLock(&extension->ControlLock);
       KdPrint( ("mapMem: just about ready!\n") );

       //
       // Do direct I/O. That is, the I/O system will provide pointers
       // from/to the user buffer
       //
       deviceObject->Flags |= DO_DIRECT_IO;

       //... Code similar to Listing 18.1, but stores the additional
       //... values in the Device Extension

       { /* initialize blocks */
        unsigned int x;
        PHYSICAL_ADDRESS HighLimit;
        HighLimit.QuadPart = 0xFFFFFFFFFFFFFFFF;
        // The highest valid physical address the driver can use.
        // For example, if a device can only reference physical memory
        // in the lower 16MB, this value would be set to 0x00000000FFFFFF

        for (x=0;  x < extension->reservedMemoryChunks; x++)
           { /* initialize each */
            extension->DMABufferSystemVirtualAddr[x] =
                            MmAllocateContiguousMemory
                                  (extension->reservedMemorySize, HighLimit);
            extension->DMABufferSystemPhysicalAddr[x] =
                            MmGetPhysicalAddress
                                  (extension->DMABufferSystemVirtualAddr[x] );
            KdPrint(
               ("mapMem: extension->DMABufferSystemVirtualAddr[x] = %x"
               "    extension->DMABufferSystemPhysicalAddr[x] = %x %x\n",
               extension->DMABufferSystemVirtualAddr[x],
               extension->DMABufferSystemPhysicalAddr[x].HighPart,
               extension->DMABufferSystemPhysicalAddr[x].LowPart ) );
           } /* initialize each */
       } /* initialize blocks */
       //... Code identical to Listing 18.1, except that in the case of
       //... failure, we must free the memory we just allocated

       memMapFreeMemory(DeviceObject);
```

The `MapMem` IRP_MJ_CREATE *Handler*

Whenever the application calls `CreateFile`, we must initialize any state required by the opening of a new handle to this device. In this case, we need do nothing because all of the significant initialization was done in the `DriverEntry` routine. This is a shared driver, which means it can be opened simultaneously by multiple threads, so we might want to maintain per-handle state, which we would initialize here. We also keep track of the number of concurrent opens so that we do not exceed the maximum permitted count. All of this must be properly synchronized, since this driver could be opened on several processors of a multiprocessor at the same time. Otherwise, this handler, except for the print string, is the same as the `Hello.c` handler.

Listing 19.4: IRP_MJ_OPEN *Handler for* MapMem

```
/********************************************************************
             mapMemOpen
 ********************************************************************/
NTSTATUS mapMemOpen(
    IN PDEVICE_OBJECT DeviceObject,
    IN PIRP Irp )
{
    PMAPMEM_DEVICE_EXTENSION extension = DeviceObject->DeviceExtension;
    KIRQL OldIrql; // Holds IRQL during Spin Lock

    KeAcquireSpinLock(&extension->ControlLock, &OldIrql);
    if(extension->currentOpens >= MAX_CONCURRENT_OPENS)
        { /* too many opens */
         Irp->IoStatus.Status = STATUS_INSUFFICIENT_RESOURCES;
         Irp->IoStatus.Information = 0;
        } /* too many opens */
    else
        { /* successful open */
         extension->currentOpens++;
         Irp->IoStatus.Status = STATUS_SUCCESS;
         Irp->IoStatus.Information = 0;
        } /* successful open */
    KeReleaseSpinLock(&extension->ControlLock, OldIrql);
```

The IRP_MJ_CLOSE *Handler*

This handler has only one responsibility: to decrement the count of current open sessions. It must protect this operation with a Spin Lock to avoid multithread and multiprocessor conflicts.

Listing 19.5: IRP_MJ_CLOSE *Handler for* MapMem

```
/********************************************************************
             mapMemClose
 ********************************************************************/
NTSTATUS mapMemClose(
    IN PDEVICE_OBJECT DeviceObject,
    IN PIRP Irp )
{
    PMAPMEM_DEVICE_EXTENSION extension = DeviceObject->DeviceExtension;
    KIRQL OldIrql;
```

```
KeAcquireSpinLock(&extension->ControlLock, &OldIrql);
extension->currentOpens--;
KeReleaseSpinLock(&extension->ControlLock, OldIrql);

//... Code identical to hello.c
```

The MJ_IRP_DEVICE_CONTROL Handler

The DeviceIoControl operation is very useful for many Device Drivers, particularly those for which operations such as ReadFile and WriteFile might either make no sense or require quite contrived patterns of usage in order to make sense. Packaging the set of operations into a DeviceIoControl call allows you to specify an arbitrary set of parameters to the operation (the input parameters) as well as input data. It also allows you to specify an arbitrary set of parameters to read *from* the device. Using ReadFile, you have, at best, one 64-bit value (nominally the file position pointer) as your supplied parameter.

For a quick refresher, here is the DeviceIoControl call.

```
BOOL DeviceIoControl(HANDLE Device, DWORD IoControlCode,
                     LPVOID InBuffer, DWORD IBufferSize,
                     LPVOID OutBuffer, DWORD nOutBufferSize,
                     LPDWORD BytesReturned,
                     LPOVERLAPPED Overlapped);
```

For our example, This Is Where The Action Is. We provide for two user-level IOCTL codes. One obtains the virtual and physical addresses of one of the allocated chunks. The other performs an important housekeeping task that must be done, but we defer discussion of that for a bit while we handle the first case.

The IOCTL code IOCTL_MAPMEM_INITIALIZE and its data structures are defined in MapMemIoctl.h; we show an excerpt of that file here. The DeviceIoControl operation points to two blocks of storage. The input parameter references a block of structure MAPMEM_INITIALIZE_INPUT, and the output parameter references a block of structure MAPMEM_INITIALIZE_OUTPUT. The IOCTL codes indicate that these use buffered I/O, so we use buffers within the kernel space to read and store values. These buffers are created by the I/O Manager. The I/O Manager copies the contents of the input pointer to the input buffer before calling us and, upon completion, copies the contents of the output buffer to the area specified by the output pointer of the DeviceIoControl operation.

Listing 19.6: MapMemIoctl.h *(excerpt)*

```
typedef LARGE_INTEGER PHYSICAL_ADDRESS, * PPHYSICAL_ADDRESS;
typedef struct
  {
    PVOID DMABufferVirtualAddress[MAX_NUM_CHUNKS];
    PHYSICAL_ADDRESS DMABufferPhysicalAddress[MAX_NUM_CHUNKS];
  } MAPMEM_INITIALIZE_OUTPUT;

typedef struct
  {
    unsigned int  sessionNumber;
  } MAPMEM_INITIALIZE_INPUT;

// The IOCTL function codes from 0x800 to 0xFFF are for customer use.
#define IOCTL_MAPMEM_INITIALIZE \
```

```
        CTL_CODE(MAPMEM_TYPE,   0x0B10, METHOD_BUFFERED, \
                                        FILE_WRITE_DATA | FILE_READ_DATA)
#define IOCTL_MAPMEM_FLUSH_PROC_CACHE \
        CTL_CODE(MAPMEM_TYPE,   0x0B11, METHOD_BUFFERED, \
                                        FILE_WRITE_DATA | FILE_READ_DATA)
```

Listing 19.7: *Calling the* MapMem *Driver*

A typical call from the application looks something like the following.

```
        MAPMEM_INITIALIZE_INPUT  InBuffer;
        MAPMEM_INITIALIZE_OUTPUT OutBuffer;
        BOOL IoctlResult;
        HANDLE hTest;
        int ReturnedLength;

        hTest = CreateFile("\\\\.\\MapMemDev",
                        GENERIC_READ | GENERIC_WRITE,
                        0,
                        NULL,
                        OPEN_EXISTING,
                        FILE_ATTRIBUTE_NORMAL,
                        NULL);

        if(hTest != INVALID_HANDLE_VALUE)
            { /* open succeeded */
            // Initialize the board
            InBuffer.sessionNumber = 1;
            IoctlResult = DeviceIoControl(
                            hTest,               // Handle to device
                            IOCTL_MAPMEM_INITIALIZE, //
                            &InBuffer,           // Buffer to driver
                            sizeof(InBuffer),    // Length of buffer in bytes
                            &OutBuffer,          // Buffer from driver
                            sizeof(OutBuffer),   // Length of buffer in bytes
                            &ReturnedLength,     // Bytes placed in OutBuffer
                            NULL      // NULL means wait until op. completes
                            );
            // ... Use the values that were returned
```

This call must then be interpreted by the driver, in its IRP_MJ_DEVICE_CONTROL handler. Since the IOCTL used specifies METHOD_BUFFERED, we know that both the input and the output are buffered. (If the method specified Direct I/O, the output would still be buffered because that's how DeviceIoControl works.)

Listing 19.8: IRP_MJ_DEVICE_CONTROL *Handler for* MapMem

```
/*********************************************************************
            mapMemDeviceControl
*********************************************************************/
NTSTATUS mapMemDeviceControl(
    IN PDEVICE_OBJECT DeviceObject,
    IN PIRP Irp )
{
    NTSTATUS  ret = STATUS_SUCCESS;
    DWORD len = 0;
    PIO_STACK_LOCATION irpStack;
```

```
MAPMEM_INITIALIZE_OUTPUT  *pOutBuffer;
MAPMEM_INITIALIZE_INPUT   *pInBuffer;
PMAPMEM_DEVICE_EXTENSION extension;
ULONG msInExposure, halfMsInExposure;
PVOID pIo_port_base;
PVOID pShared_memory;
PHYSICAL_MEMORY_INFO InBuffer;
NTSTATUS the_NTSTATUS;

KdPrint( ("mapMem: => Device Control!!\n") );
extension = DeviceObject->DeviceExtension;
irpStack = IoGetCurrentIrpStackLocation(Irp);
```

The references to the buffers are stored in the IRP. The value in the UserBuffer *field is
a pointer to the buffer area for the output; the pointer to the input area is found in the*
AssociatedIrp.SystemBuffer *field. We cast these values to our structures to make
the code easier to write. The* mapSystemLogicalMemory *function takes an address in
system logical memory and obtains both the physical memory address and the application virtual address for it, storing them in our array. Since each process can have a separate virtual address, we store the process's virtual address in an array indexed by the
small integer (session number) representing the process.*

*Note the careful check for the size of the output buffer. You are responsible for
checking that there is sufficient space to handle your output. Otherwise, you may overwrite information beyond the end of the kernel-assigned buffer, corrupting some random part of the kernel space. In this example, we fail the IRP with the error code*
STATUS_BUFFER_TOO_SMALL, *which is returned to the caller (via* GetLastError*) as*
ERROR_INSUFFICIENT_BUFFER.

*Note that this requires that each application call this driver with a unique "session
number". We discuss File Objects in Chapter 22. By using the File Object pointer
found in the IRP as a token that identifies a unique session, you can build a table that
maps File Object pointers to the appropriate session number. Then the application-
supplied session number is no longer required, since it can be deduced from the File
Object itself. Two separate applications using a driver that distinguishes IRPs by using
their File Object pointers cannot accidentally overwrite each other's allocation.*

```
pInBuffer = (MAPMEM_INITIALIZE_INPUT *)Irp->AssociatedIrp.SystemBuffer;
                                            // Buffered I/O
pOutBuffer = (MAPMEM_INITIALIZE_OUTPUT *)Irp->UserBuffer;
                                            // Buffered I/O

switch(irpStack->Parameters.DeviceIoControl.IoControlCode)
     { /* ioctl */
       case  IOCTL_MAPMEM_INITIALIZE:
           { /* MAPMEM_INITIALIZE */
             unsigned int x;
             KdPrint( ("mapMem: => IOCTL(MAPMEM_INITIALIZE)\n") );
             UINT sno = pInBuffer->sessionNumber;

             if(irpStack->Parameters.DeviceIoControl.OutputBufferLength
                             < sizeof(MAPMEM_INITIALIZE_OUTPUT))
                 { /* too small */
                 ret = STATUS_BUFFER_TOO_SMALL;
                 break;
```

```
                            } /* too small */

                for (x=0;  x < extension->reservedMemoryChunks; x++)
                    { /* map each */
                    // Map the memory
                    KdPrint(("mapMem: =>mapSystemLogicalMemory[%d[%d]]\n",
                                                             x, sno));

                    ULONG result =
                         mapSystemLogicalMemory(
                               DeviceObject,
                               extension->DMABufferSystemVirtualAddr[x],
                               extension->reservedMemorySize,
                               &extension->DMABufferUserVirtualAddr[x][sno]
                                                         );

                    if (STATUS_SUCCESS != result)
                      { /* failed */
                      KdPrint(("mapMem: failed mapSystemLogicalMemory\n"));
                      ret = result;
                      break;
                      } /* failed */

                    KdPrint(("mapMem: <= mapSystemLogicalMemory\n") );
                    pOutBuffer->DMABufferVirtualAddress[x] =
                               extension->DMABufferUserVirtualAddr[x][sno];
                    pOutBuffer->DMABufferPhysicalAddress[x] =
                               extension->DMABufferSystemPhysicalAddr[x];
                    KdPrint(
                        ("mapMem: DMABuffer Physical = %x %x "
                         "DMABuffer User Virtual = %x\n",
                         pOutBuffer->DMABufferPhysicalAddress[x].HighPart,
                         pOutBuffer->DMABufferPhysicalAddress[x].LowPart,
                         pOutBuffer->DMABufferVirtualAddress[x] ) );
                    } /* map each */

                len = sizeof(MAPMEM_INITIALIZE_OUTPUT);

                KdPrint( ("mapMem: <= IOCTL(MAPMEM_INITIALIZE)\n") );
                } /* MAPMEM_INITIALIZE */
            break;
```

*One problem we are likely to encounter whenever we have two processors sharing
memory (such as our NT machine and the attached coprocessor we are postulating) is
the fact that the NT machine is likely to have L1 and L2 caches. This means that after
we've written something "to memory", we have no guarantee that it is in memory. At
best, we know only that it is on its way to memory. However, if our goal is to set up
some data for our attached coprocessor and then signal it to begin computations, it
would be nice to be certain that the data it is working on actually is the data we think it
is working on.*

    *Thus we must ensure that the caches are flushed back to memory. Fortunately, the
HAL gives us a simple way of doing this. But because our application program is the
one writing the data, the underlying system has no idea when to flush the caches. The
same would be true if we were about to initiate a DMA operation; we'd want to make
sure that the data written via the DMA channel is actually the data we think was there.*

To accomplish this, we "expose" the low-level cache-flushing operation via another IOCTL code. The handler for this is shown next.

```
case IOCTL_MAPMEM_FLUSH_PROC_CACHE:
    { /* IOCTL_MAPMEM_FLUSH_PROC_CACHE */
    PMDL PMdl;
    PVOID  Base;
    ULONG  Length;
    unsigned int x;
    ULONG sno = pInBuffer->sessionNumber;

    KdPrint( ("mapMem: => enter IOCTL(Flush)\n") );
    Length = extension->reservedMemorySize

    for (x=0;  x < extension->reservedMemoryChunks; x++)
        { /* each chunk */
        Base = extension->DMABufferUserVirtualAddr[x][sno];
        if (x == 0)
          { /* first time */
          PMdl = MmCreateMdl( NULL, Base, Length );
          } /* first time */
        else
          { /* second or higher */
          MmPrepareMdlForReuse( PMdl );
          MmInitializeMdl( PMdl,  Base,  Length );
          } /* second or higher */

        KeFlushIoBuffers( PMdl, FALSE,  TRUE );
        } /* each chunk */
      IoFreeMdl( PMdl );
      }/* IOCTL_MAPMEM_FLUSH_PROC_CACHE */
    break;
```

If we do not recognize the IOCTL code, we set the status to an error status and fall out of the switch. *When we exit the* switch, *we fill in the status code of the IRP, complete it, and return to the I/O Manager. The I/O Manager copies the output buffer back to the location specified in the* DeviceIoControl *call and returns* TRUE *or* FALSE *depending on the completion code. If the result is not* STATUS_SUCCESS, *it also will set an error code so that* GetLastError *can provide the application with additional information about the failure.*

```
    default:
            ret = STATUS_UNSUCCESSFUL;
            break;
    } /* ioctl */

KdPrint( ("mapMem: <= Device Control\n") );
//
// Fill these in before calling IoCompleteRequest
//
Irp->IoStatus.Status = ret;
Irp->IoStatus.Information = len;
IoCompleteRequest( Irp, IO_NO_INCREMENT );

return ret;
}
```

The `MapMem` *Unload Handler*

The Unload handler is very much like the one we gave for `hello.c`. The only difference is that it calls `mapMemFreeMemory` to release the resources.

Listing 19.9: `IRP_MJ_CLOSE` *Handler for* `MapMem`

```
/*******************************************************************************
                        mapMemUnload
*******************************************************************/
VOID mapMemUnload( IN PDRIVER_OBJECT DriverObject)
{
 //...Just like hello.c

     for(device = DriverObject->DeviceObject; device != NULL; device = next)
        { /* delete each */
         next = device->NextDevice; // Save before we delete object
         mapMemFreeMemory(device)
         IoDeleteDevice( device );
        } /* delete each */
}
```

The *mapSystemLogicalMemory Function*

The `mapSystemLogicalMemory` function maps the system logical memory to the user logical memory address space. Be warned: This is a complex and subtle routine and contains certified Black Magic. The Black Magic is really, truly magic. Nothing in the documentation will lead you to exercise it; the documentation that explains what it does is sparse and vague. But if you don't add Eye of Newt and/or Toe of Frog, the code won't work. We make no pretensions. We aren't actually sure what is going on here, but we know that if we don't do this, it won't work.

Listing 19.10: *The* `mapSystemLogicalMemory` *Function, Part 1*

```
/*******************************************************************************
             mapSystemLogicalMemory
*******************************************************/
NTSTATUS mapSystemLogicalMemory(
  IN PDEVICE_OBJECT DeviceObject,    // The Device Object
  IN PVOID          LogicalAddress,  // The logical address to be translated
                                     // (for device memory see page 381)
  IN ULONG          LengthToMap,     // The length of the area to map
  OUT PVOID *       OutBuffer        // A pointer to the output buffer
  )
/*******************************************************************
Routine Description:
    Given a system logical address, maps this address into a user mode
    process's address space

    Assume the logical address passed to this routine points to a contiguous
    buffer large enough to contain the buffer requested

Return Value:
    STATUS_SUCCESS if successful, otherwise
    STATUS_UNSUCCESSFUL,
```

```
      STATUS_INSUFFICIENT_RESOURCES,
      (other STATUS_* as returned by kernel APIs)
***********************************************************************/
{
    PHYSICAL_ADDRESS    physicalAddress;
    ULONG               length;
    UNICODE_STRING      physicalMemoryUnicodeString;
    OBJECT_ATTRIBUTES   objectAttributes;
    HANDLE              physicalMemoryHandle  = NULL;
    PVOID               PhysicalMemorySection = NULL;
    NTSTATUS            ntStatus;
    PHYSICAL_ADDRESS    viewBase;
    PVOID               virtualAddress;

    //
    // Mapping kernel memory: Get a pointer to physical memory...
    // Mapping device memory: We would have passed in a physical address
    // (see page 381)
    //

    physicalAddress = MmGetPhysicalAddress(LogicalAddress);
    // see also page 381

    KdPrint( ("mapMem: mapSystemLogicalMemory  physicalAddress = %x %x\n",
                    physicalAddress.HighPart, physicalAddress.LowPart ));
```

At this point, we might think we're done; after all, we have the physical address. But it isn't that simple. We have a physical address, but we don't have the ability to actually access it! We need to obtain one or more slots in our virtual address map that grant us access to the memory. This is only a kernel map. Later, when the application needs the address, we will additionally map it into the user's memory map, but for now, we just need to get access.

To get the desired access, we must call the ZwOpenSection function. This will give us a handle to the physical memory, one step along the way. We'll concentrate on that step for the moment. To obtain a handle to physical memory, we need to call ZwOpenSection on a particular device, the one called \Device\PhysicalMemory. We need two steps to get to this. First, we convert an ordinary PWSTR to a PUNICODE_STRING, which we do with RtlInitUnicodeString. Then we use this PUNICODE_STRING to InitializeObjectAttributes on an OBJECT_ATTRIBUTES structure.

We use this OBJECT_ATTRIBUTES structure to call ZwOpenSection to obtain a handle to the physical memory object. This gives us a handle to all of physical memory. We can't do anything with it yet, because it isn't in our address space, but we can at least talk about it to the system.

```
    RtlInitUnicodeString (&physicalMemoryUnicodeString,
                    L"\\Device\\PhysicalMemory");
    InitializeObjectAttributes (&objectAttributes,
                        &physicalMemoryUnicodeString,
                        OBJ_CASE_INSENSITIVE,
                        (HANDLE) NULL,
                        (PSECURITY_DESCRIPTOR) NULL);
```

```
ntStatus = ZwOpenSection (&physicalMemoryHandle,
                          SECTION_ALL_ACCESS,
                          &objectAttributes);
if (!NT_SUCCESS(ntStatus))
{
    KdPrint (("mapMem.SYS: ZwOpenSection failed\n"));
    goto done;
}
```

Whew! Did you follow all that? Well, here comes the Black Magic. We have to create an object reference to the physical memory section. Given the physical memory handle, we obtain a "pointer to the object". That's what ObReferenceObjectByHandle *does. We don't really care about the actual value for this reference. However, it is important for the other side effect of* ObReferenceObjectByHandle *to increment that reference count of this object, thereby ensuring the object won't go away, taking our memory map with it.*

```
ntStatus = ObReferenceObjectByHandle (
                          physicalMemoryHandle,
                          SECTION_ALL_ACCESS,
                          (POBJECT_TYPE) NULL,
                          KernelMode,
                          &PhysicalMemorySection, // Never used
                          (POBJECT_HANDLE_INFORMATION) NULL);
if (!NT_SUCCESS(ntStatus))
{
    KdPrint (("mapMem.SYS: ObReferenceObjectByHandle failed\n"));
    goto close_handle;
}
```
// (continued on page 379)

Next, we finally map this memory into the user space. We have our kernel virtual address that was passed in as the parameter and that started all this. The problem with real hardware is that we cannot map an arbitrary physical location to a virtual page. We can only map physical pages to virtual pages. This imposes some limitations and, in this case, opens some dangers. For example, if we need only to map a single DWORD, we get an entire page (4,096 bytes on Intel; 8,192 bytes on Alpha). The DWORD might even be in the middle of a page of the Nonpaged Pool because of how the kernel allocator gave it to us. Unless we can guarantee that we are mapping only page-aligned, multiple-of-page-size chunks, there is absolutely nothing to prevent the application program from writing anywhere in the page or reading anywhere in the page. This compromises both security and reliability. Consequently, if you are concerned about these issues you yourself must undertake to ensure that the memory mapped into the user space is *exclusively* used by the user. If you are getting your memory using ExAllocatePool or any of its variants, you are guaranteed that allocating a chunk of memory >= PAGE_SIZE will allocate a page-aligned address and an integral number of pages. If you are using any other allocation strategy, the only way we know how to do this is a bit grotesque, but if your allocation strategy does not support page alignment there is no other mechanism supported to manage this. Note the implication on device memory that is mapped; it must be mapped on page-aligned boundaries. This has implications on hardware design that must not be ignored.

What we do is allocate a chunk of memory that contains at least as many paged-aligned pages as we need. To accomplish this, we need to over-allocate memory to guarantee that there is a sufficiently large amount of memory contained within the allocation. For example, if we wish to allocate *n* pages (and no matter what the user asks for, we will round it up to the next multiple of n pages), then we allocate a block of storage whose size is *n* + 1 pages and map into the user space an *n*-page, page-aligned chunk out of the middle of that allocated space. If the requested allocation is actually delivered page-aligned, we have wasted one page of Nonpaged Pool, a bit wasteful unless the physical memory is large. If the allocation is not page-aligned, we still lose a page's worth of space because we can't free up the unused head or tail of the allocation, but there is nothing that can be done about this. The loss of a page's worth of space is the price we pay for increased robustness and security. This technique is illustrated in Figure 19.1. In this figure, we show how allocating n + 1 pages can produce a result that is not page-aligned. However, we can extract and map an *n*-paged-sized region, illustrated in gray in the figure. The code of this example does not implement this algorithm, because it uses ExAllocatePool.

The ZwMapViewOfSection function is defined as:

```
NTSTATUS ZwMapViewOfSection(
                    IN HANDLE SectionHandle,
                    IN HANDLE ProcessHandle,
                    IN OUT PVOID * BaseAddress,
                    IN ULONG ZeroBits,
                    IN ULONG CommitSize,
                    IN OUT PLARGE_INTEGER SectionOffset OPTIONAL,
                    IN OUT PULONG ViewSize,
                    IN SECTION_INHERIT InheritDisposition,
                    IN ULONG AllocationType,
                    IN ULONG Protect);
```

The first two parameters we pass to ZwMapViewOfSection are simple; we pass in the physical memory handle we got from ZwOpenSection and the handle of a process into which to map the memory. Since we are doing this within the IOCTL handler, the current process is the one we wish to do the mapping for, so we can simply use the special constant –1 to indicate "current

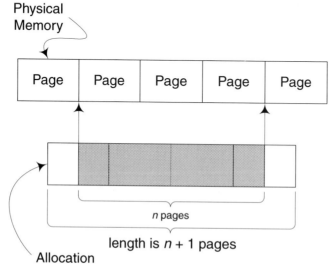

Figure 19.1: *Allocating page-aligned memory within a large block.*

process". If we were doing this from an interrupt routine or deferred processing routine (such as a DPC), there is no guarantee that we would be in the same process that initiated the operation, and we would have to do something more complex to identify the process.

We initialize the `virtualAddress` variable to NULL. This allows the mapping function the freedom to map the memory anywhere it can find room in the process address space. Otherwise, we might specify a (application-space, process-relative) virtual address that has a page already existing either at it or beyond it at an address our mapping request requires. In this case, the mapping request will fail. So rather than our trying to figure out where the right place is, we let `ZwMapViewOfSection` figure it out for us. The *ZeroBits* parameter is used to force some number of high-order bits to be zero and represents the *minimum* number of zero bits required. It must be less than or equal to 32 – log_2(PAGE_SIZE), that is, on an *x86* with 4096-byte pages, less than or equal to 21 (otherwise, we would be allocating partial pages). In this example, we don't care how many high-order zero bits are in the address, so we set this parameter to 0.

In preparing this example, we carefully read some of the DDK examples. What we found odd was that those examples did not conform to the specifications of the call as documented. We figured there must be something mysterious here, or perhaps this is just a harmless error in the DDK examples. We really don't like to perpetuate an error, but we're not sure that this is not what actually works and that it's the documentation that is in error. Such are the joys of reverse-engineering when you have evidence that the documentation is sometimes wrong. The particular error here is that the *CommitSize* parameter is documented as being nonzero if the storage is backed up by the paging file (that is, allocated from the Paged Pool) and zero if the storage is not backed by the paging file (as we would expect from the Nonpaged Pool). Nonetheless, the actual DDK example uses a nonzero value here. This may be additional Black Magic, or it could be a harmless parameter that is ignored for nonpaged memory anyway. We don't know.

The *ViewSize* parameter is an in/out parameter. It is initialized to the desired size of the view we wish. Upon successful return, it is changed to represent the view size we actually have. This means the value will be rounded up to the next highest multiple of the page size.

The *InheritDisposition* parameter is another mystery. The official documentation says that it is a value that specifies whether the view can be inherited by a child process and recommends that drivers set this value to 0. However, in the examples we found, it was set to the constant `ViewShare`, meaning a child process *would* inherit the view. Go figure.

The *AllocationType* parameter is specified by the documentation as "A set of flags that describes the type of allocation to be performed for the specified region of pages". However, nothing we have been able to locate by simple searches in the documentation even hints at what those values might be. The examples we have found set the value to 0, so that's what we did.

The *Protect* parameter indicates the type of protection we wish to grant. It is recommended that drivers grant the privileges PAGE_READWRITE. We have also supplied the flag PAGE_NOCACHE, which inhibits the caching of data in the L2 cache. Note that our operation to flush caches also guarantees that the data is flushed from the L1 cache.

Listing 19.11: *The* mapSystemLogicalMemory *Function, Part 2*

```
// (continued from page 377)
//
// Initialize view base that will receive the physical mapped
// address after the ZwMapViewOfSection call
//
viewBase = physicalAddress;
//
```

```
        // Let ZwMapViewOfSection pick an address
        //
        virtualAddress = NULL;
        //
        // Map the section
        //
        ntStatus = ZwMapViewOfSection (physicalMemoryHandle, // Physical memory handle
                                (HANDLE) -1,      // -1 means current process
                                &virtualAddress,  // In/out parameter
                                0L,               //
                                LengthToMap,      // Page file CommitSize
                                &viewBase,        // In/out offset into memory
                                &length,          // In: desired size
                                                  // Out: actual size
                                ViewShare,        // Allow sharing with child
                                0,                // AllocationType
                                PAGE_READWRITE | PAGE_NOCACHE);
        if (!NT_SUCCESS(ntStatus))
            {
            KdPrint (("mapMem.SYS: ZwMapViewOfSection failed\n"));
            goto close_handle;
            }
```

Are we there? Almost! It turns out that one feature of the mapping is that the section maps only on 64K boundaries. So the virtual address we get for the result, virtualAddress, *is rounded down to a 64K boundary and the* viewBase *variable is updated to indicate the offset into the mapped memory. There is no guarantee that any of the pages between that address and the desired page exist, and in any case, we want to return to the user a virtual address that is actually in the page in which the data resides. So we now compute the difference between the physical address and the virtual address and use that offset to increment the virtual address to the value we want. Finally, we use the* OutBuffer *pointer to store this address and return, eventually completing the processing of our* IRP_MJ_DEVICECONTROL *operation.*

```
        //
        // Mapping the previous section rounded the physical address down to the
        // nearest 64K boundary. Now return a virtual address that sits where
        // we want by adding in the offset from the beginning of the section
        //
        (ULONG) virtualAddress += (ULONG)physicalAddress.LowPart -
                                  (ULONG)viewBase.LowPart;

        *OutBuffer = virtualAddress;         // Return VM address

        KdPrint( ("mapMem: mapSystemLogicalMemory() returning virtualAddress = %x\n",
                                                        virtualAddress));
        ntStatus = STATUS_SUCCESS;

close_handle:
        ZwClose (physicalMemoryHandle);

done:
        return ntStatus;
    }
```

We have gone to a great deal of effort to accomplish an apparently simple task. Yet, in the writing of actual Device Drivers, the need to map memory into the user space, whether it is non-paged memory, adapter memory, or other special memory, is entirely too common a problem. One reason for presenting this example is to show you the (literally) mysterious methods that have to be used to do this. Somewhere, once, someone at Microsoft figured out (probably from reading the NT sources) what had to be done and wrote some DDK examples to do it. We try, as best we can, to explain them. But when working code conflicts with the documentation, we close our eyes, cross our fingers, and follow the working code. Such is the life of the Device Driver writer.

Mapping Device Memory

Mapping onboard device memory is not substantially different from what we did in Listing 19.10 and Listing 19.11. There are a few minor differences. Instead of passing in a logical address to be mapped to the user space, we would pass in a system physical address, so the parameters shown in Listing 19.10 would be

```
NTSTATUS mapSystemLogicalMemory(
    IN PDEVICE_OBJECT    DeviceObject,
    IN PHYSICAL_ADDRESS PhysicalAddress, // instead of PVOID LogicalAddress
    IN ULONG             LengthToMap,
    OUT PVOID *          OutBuffer)
```

Consequently, we would not have to issue the `MmGetPhysicalAddress` call to map the logical address to a physical address, since we already have a physical address in hand. We would typically get the physical address for the device memory using `HalTranslateBusAddress`. Otherwise, there is no difference between how we map arbitrary kernel memory and how we map device memory.

Summary

This shows a technique for mapping an arbitrary space in the kernel address space (which can include onboard memory on a device) into application space. This technique is not without significant risk. Depending on the nature of the device, an application that writes random information into its memory can potentially compromise the integrity of the entire NT system. If you are working with someone who *requires* full C2 security compliance, the existence of a device which uses this technique will generally be grounds for denial of C2 certification. Nonetheless, for some devices this may be the ideal solution for obtaining the necessary I/O bandwidth. Just be aware that this is a very risky technique, and certainly not approved by Microsoft.

20 *I/O Hardware: The ISA Bus*

The ISA bus is a dinosaur. It is too big, too slow, and remarkably ill-suited to the modern ecological systems that form the PC we now know. In fact, the asteroid has already struck, and as with the Chixulub event that appears to have been the death knell of the dinosaurs, it will take a few million years before the ISA bus completely dies out. The "PC98" standard that Microsoft has published suggests that it is a bad idea to provide any ISA bus slots. The "PC99" standard states that no ISA slots are to be provided on a PC99-compliant system.

So why do we worry about it? In fact, the "few million years" it will take this dinosaur to die, expressed in computer-generation years, is about three to five years of real-time. Meanwhile, however, you might have to provide support for legacy ISA devices.

Problems with the ISA Bus

ISA has a number of "advantages", if your sole criterion is absolute bottom-line development and manufacturing cost. The infinitesimal advantages of low-cost design and manufacture are offset, however, by the numerous disadvantages of the ISA bus, including the following:

- Hardwired, nonsharable[1] IRQ lines, limited to no more than 16 IRQ levels, most of which are already preallocated

- An existing base of poorly designed cards that decode only part of the I/O address space, replicating the same device multiple times throughout the I/O address space

- Abysmal I/O bandwidth suitable only for the slowest possible devices, by current standards

- Poor-to-nonexistent Plug-and-Play support

---

[1] The exception is COM1/COM3, COM2/COM4 interrupt sharing, which sort of works some times, if you are lucky, and don't need to use all four COM ports concurrently.

- Support for only a 24-bit address space, thereby limiting DMA I/O to the lower 16MB of memory and complicating the operating system

- Poor or idiosyncratic support for any form of bus mastering,[2] and the need to share the "system DMA" chip, with its peculiar set of programming and performance limitations

- Significantly higher cost of support because of the problems of integrating an ISA bus device into a system. These problems are a consequence of the potential an ISA device has for IRQ conflicts, memory conflicts, and device register conflicts with other devices

But the worst point is the overall impact on system performance. A machine with an ISA bus has uniformly poorer performance than one that is otherwise identically configured but has no ISA bus, because the entire system has to absorb the ISA limitations (particularly for cache management).

Despite all of these problems, there are still many tens of millions of ISA machines capable of running Windows NT, as well as tens of millions of ISA-compatible peripheral devices, many of which are highly specialized controllers of some sort for which there is no current motivation to redesign to modern interface specifications.

History of the ISA Bus

The ISA bus is the natural evolutionary outgrowth of the 8-bit bus used on the original IBM PC. The original ISA bus supported up to 20 bits of address (addressing a whopping megabyte of memory) and 8 bits of data transfer. The ISA bus most of us know was introduced with the 80286-based PC/AT, which could support 24 bits of address (addressing an unbelievably large 16MB of memory) and with 16 bits of data transfer. The PC/AT bus defined a *de facto* standard whose boundary conditions were largely undefined; many of those conditions became apparent only after use.[3] The bus is "officially" limited to 8.33MHz, although many systems could be "tweaked" to run it at about 12MHz.[4]

---

[2] Not all ISA bus masters work with all processor support chip sets. Therefore there is no guarantee that if you have a bus master ISA card, it will work on any particular motherboard. If you really want to use an ISA bus master, then instead of buying a computer and plugging in your desired ISA bus mastering peripheral, you call the peripheral vendor, find out with what systems its card is certified to work, and find a system that matches its description. Better still, buy the PCI version of the vendor's card. For more details on ISA bus mastering, see the MindShare book *ISA System Architecture*, Chapter 20. ISA bus mastering is not a pretty sight.

[3] For example, it is not possible to plug in an 8-bit monochrome card and a 16-bit VGA card while leaving the 16-bit VGA card operational in 16-bit mode. This is due to a misdesign of how the address and data line signals decode. The VGA card can be used only in 8-bit mode! What made this particularly annoying was that the effect of plugging in the VGA card was the loss of all video; the trick to get this to work was to remove the 8-bit monochrome card, run the VGA setup software to reconfigure the VGA for 8-bit mode, and then reinstall the monochrome card. This procedure could not be discovered without talking to the actual engineers (not product support, who were clueless) at the VGA card company. The buffers for the monochrome card and VGA card were both contained within some boundary of the bus that triggered this behavior. (Note that some VGA cards detected the presence of a monochrome card and configured themselves to 8-bit mode automatically.)

[4] I did this regularly, using a divide-by-3 on my 33MHz processor clock to get a faster ISA bus. Only some of the oldest devices failed to work at the higher clock rate. *–jmn*

It became clear that the ISA bus, which originally was the memory interface (all of the memory plugged into the ISA bus), was not going to be suitable for the next generation of machines. Most 386-based systems used a separate memory bus so that memory access was not limited by the slow bus. A number of 386-based systems used proprietary memory cards that plugged into the ISA bus but in fact had special connectors to get 32 bits of data transferred or to provide a "back door" bus cycle not limited by the ISA speed constraints.

Many alternatives were proposed. The ill-fated MicroChannel Architecture (MCA) bus was one. The MCA bus allowed for higher bus bandwidth, bus mastering, autoconfiguration, and many other nice features. But it was IBM's attempt to recapture the PC market. IBM patented the MCA bus, and the bus died because it was a proprietary bus that could not be freely used by other manufacturers, most of which did not have the resources, or interest, to meet IBM's licensing conditions. Ultimately, it would not have been suitable for today's high-performance processors, and it quietly disappeared except in some tiny niche markets for workstations. We don't even talk about it in this book.

Another alternative was the VL-Bus. This bus started as an industry initiative to come up with a high-speed, nonproprietary bus, primarily for video interfaces, but it died for a variety of technical and political reasons. The most serious problem of the VL-Bus was that it had to be redesigned for each new generation of processors, an unacceptable constraint in a world in which new processors seem to be an annual event.

A third alternative was the EISA bus. It was an attempt to preserve the legacy ISA peripherals, while allowing for new, modern devices. It, too, has become irrelevant.

The modern contender is the PCI Bus, which we discuss in detail in the next chapter. The PCI Bus also hosts a number of "external" busses such as the USB, IEEE-1394, SCSI, and IDE busses.

Overview of the ISA Architecture

The "traditional" ISA architecture is shown in Figure 20.1. In the original PC/AT, the memory was also on the ISA bus. In later versions of systems, such as the 386, it was put on a separate processor/memory bus, as shown in the figure.

Modern machines, including the Pentium, implement a much more complex structure, shown in Figure 20.2. This structure makes the ISA bus programmatically look like the system shown in Figure 20.1. A program that would execute on an old 386 system, touching the device registers, enabling interrupts, processing interrupts, and the like, will execute correctly on the Pentium. The PCI Bridge that connects the processor/memory subsystem to the PCI Bus, traditionally drawn, as shown, as the upper bridge, is often referred to as the *North Bridge*. The bridge from the PCI subsystem to the ISA bus and X-bus is called the *South Bridge*. We have greatly simplified the relationships of the processor, North Bridge, and memory and have not illustrated details such as the L2 cache. This is detail that you do not need to worry about at this level.

The "X-bus" is an ISA-compatible bus for the low-speed peripherals and is the bus on the motherboard. No connector is provided to install additional X-bus devices. The "ISA" bus shown is the bus into which the familiar external ISA devices are plugged. The "North Bridge" handles the issues of cache coherency. The need to do this with the ISA bus is one of the sources of performance degradation.

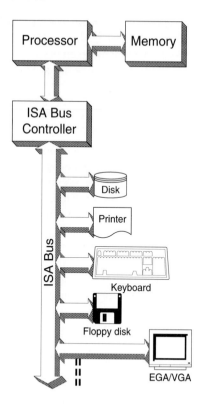

Figure 20.1: *Traditional ISA bus architecture.*

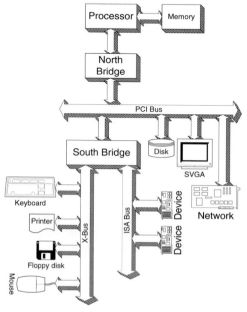

Figure 20.2: *Modern ISA bus architecture.*

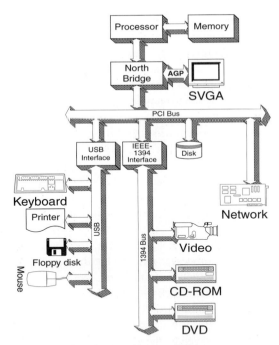

Figure 20.3: *The (non)future of ISA.*

A serious problem is that a program that writes to the ISA bus can queue up multiple writes in the North Bridge. These will be delayed until the South Bridge can process them. This can result in the entire system's synchronizing down to the speed of the ISA bus transfers.

We have said that the ISA bus is effectively dead. However, at least one view of a possible future for it is shown in Figure 20.3. Note that in this future design (a natural follow-on to the PC99 specification), the South Bridge is entirely gone, as is the X-bus and ISA bus. The low-speed peripherals are connected via the USB (Universal Serial Bus), and the high-speed peripherals are connected via the IEEE-1394 bus.

More about ISA Bus Problems

The most notorious of the ISA bus problems is the consequence of a rather naive assumption that no more than five devices would ever need to be added to a PC. (This assumption, alas, is still with us in a more insidious form, which we address in the PCI chapter, Chapter 21.) Thus the fact that the original IBM PC could handle only 8 interrupt levels was not a serious restriction. Two serial ports, a parallel port, a floppy disk controller, a keyboard, the system timer. . . lots of room. There could be no reason to share the interrupts; this would only complicate the software.

So the bus was designed so that the interrupts had to be unique to each device. If two devices on the ISA bus are assigned the same IRQ level, the result is usually a malfunction (in extreme cases, one or more of the boards sharing the IRQ level can be destroyed). This means that even with the expanded ability to handle up to 15 IRQ levels (for obscure historical reasons, IRQ 9 cascades through the second interrupt controller chip to IRQ 2 of the primary interrupt controller chip[5]), there are never enough interrupts. In fact, some "entry-level" consumer systems with a full multimedia peripheral load have *no* spare IRQs!

Not only is there a bandwidth limitation. The problem is worse than a simple throughput restriction. The ISA bus imposes serious latency limits on modern machines and can tie up the processor for a very large number of wait states (during which it can be doing nothing else) while it waits for an ISA bus transaction to complete. By contrast, the PCI Bus can allow several operations to be queued.

When an ISA bus is used in a system with a PCI Bus, many potential performance pitfalls result. One of the most serious is the nature of the PCI Bus versus the nature of the ISA bus. The PCI Bus is a positive-acknowledgment bus. That is, if a device is addressed, it must assert an "I am responding" signal before the PCI Bus transaction can complete. The ISA bus has no such positive acknowledgment. On the ISA bus, you can put out a memory or I/O address and at the appropriate time read back the results. But if there is no memory or device out there to respond, you will read rubbish (usually 0xFF for each byte read). If you write data, it will fall into the mythical Bit Bucket without having any effect—and you won't even know it was lost. To properly simulate the ISA bus from the processor's viewpoint, the South Bridge must wait four PCI clock cycles. If no PCI device has responded in that time, the South Bridge asserts the "I am here" signal between the fifth and sixth clock cycles and passes the address down to the ISA/X-bus for all addresses that could be on the ISA/X-bus. This means that access to the ISA bus is slowed significantly while the PCI Bus is waiting for a (nonexistent) ISA device to respond. Furthermore, the overall response is delayed by the need to impose a significant number of wait states to allow for the "slow" ISA peripheral response. All in all, this makes the ISA bus even less effective in a PCI-based system than it was stand-alone.

Bus mastering DMA is slower on an ISA bus than a PCI bus. Consult the MindShare book *ISA System Architecture*, Chapter 20, for the horrid details, including the impact of a bus mastering device on DRAM refresh. You will begin to appreciate why ISA is not particularly system-friendly.

If you plan to write a Device Driver for an ISA bus, you must be aware that it will, at best, be a stopgap and possibly be obsolete by the new millennium. Companies working on ISA devices need to seriously consider PCI, IEEE-1394, USB, or other interfaces that are likely to be supported for the next decade.

Having said all this, you may still be confronted with the problem of how to write an ISA Device Driver. So let's see what has to be done.

ISA Interrupt Structure

There are 15 levels of interrupts that can be used on the ISA bus. Most are preallocated, as shown in Table 20.1. Obviously, for those devices that are not installed, the IRQs specified for that device are available. We show in the shaded entries the available, or typically available, IRQ values. Note that for many modern machines, the presence of a network card, sound card, and the like rapidly consume the remaining interrupts. One or more of the shaded IRQs will be used by the PCI Bus if one is present.

---

[5] See *The Undocumented PC*, Chapter 7, for more details. See the full citation in "Further Reading".

Table 20.1: *ISA IRQs*

IRQ	Interrupt	Typical Use
0	0x08	Timer
1	0x09	Keyboard
2	0x71	Cascade from IRQ 9
3	0x0B	COM2
4	0x0C	COM1
5	0x0D	LPT2
6	0x0E	Floppy disk
7	0x0F	LPT1
8	0x70	Real-time clock
9	0x71	Available, cascaded to IRQ 2
10	0x72	Available
11	0x73	Available
12	0x74	Mouse port
13	0x75	Numeric coprocessor
14	0x76	Hard disk
15	0x77	Available

The interrupts cannot be shared. They are edge-triggered interrupts and use active drivers (no three-state or open-collector/drain styles of circuits) so that exactly one card on the bus is permitted to be assigned to a particular IRQ level. We show in the next chapter that PCI makes this limitation disappear.

ISA cards use one of three different methods to assign the IRQ level.

1. *The IRQ is hardwired as part of the circuitry.*

   Thus if you have any other card installed that uses the same IRQ, you simply cannot install the new card. In the early days of PCs, the BBS systems abounded with techniques regarding (a) how to use an X-Acto knife and 28-gauge wire to redirect an interrupt and (b) which locations of the applications and/or drivers needed to be patched to recognize the reassignment. This is not usually done today. This is not User Friendly.

2. *The IRQ is set by moving a physical jumper on the card.*

   On 8-bit cards and poorly designed 16-bit cards, you get choices based on the old 8-bit bus, usually 2, 3, 4, 5, and 7 (and if you have COM1, COM2, or LPT1, your choices are constrained to 2 and 5). On modern cards, you usually get the "high" IRQs available, typically 9, 10, 11, 12, and 15. You must not only configure the card, but also tell the software which IRQ you selected.

3. *The IRQ is set by software.*

A fairly large number of "modern" ISA cards use this method. During Device Driver initialization, the Registry is used to determine the I/O address(es) of the card and the IRQ level that is desired, and then the IRQ level is set by writing to the port. In some cards, the IRQ level is stored in nonvolatile RAM on the card and does not need to be reprogrammed each time.[6]

ISA Plug-and-Play

Plug-and-Play is difficult or impossible on the ISA bus. In general, you should not even try.[7] The risks are much too high. For example, you would need to configure the I/O address(es) because any default might conflict with some other card that might be in the system. So you would usually have a jumper for this purpose. On a completely jumperless card, it might be impossible to write the configuration information to the card to reconfigure the register address because the address in question is already in use. If you can reconfigure the card by a jumper, you might still want the user to not have to know the details. In this case, you would then write a driver that poked at location `0x280`, then `0x300`, then `0x320`, then `0x340`, and so on. You also would have to hope and pray that writing to a location would not activate some undesirable side effect in some "innocent bystander" card, for example by causing a low-level disk format operation, or by turning on the speakers to full volume, or by resetting a video display register and burning out the display (yes, it can be done!) None of these are likely to make your product popular with its end users. So you must at least put in the Registry the desired address(es) to use. Think of the Registry as "soft jumpers" for such cards; do *not* attempt to do Plug-and-Play. The risks are higher than any notional gains. If you really want Plug-and-Play, use a USB, IEEE-1394, or PCI interface. Note that most of the ISA Plug-and-Play devices are those traditional devices with well-defined behavior, such as COM1, COM2, LPT1, and two or three brands of sound cards and their clones, all of which have well-defined device addresses.

Claiming Resources

A properly designed driver will claim whatever resources it uses by registering its claims. This registration will allow dynamic resource assignment to work properly for non-ISA devices. Using the Registry Editor, you can examine this structure, as illustrated in Figure 20.4. To do this, you must use the "older" Registry Editor, `RegEdt32`, not the newer, slicker `RegEdit`. The older `RegEdt32` program knows about the NT structures. The newer one was written originally for Windows 95, and as of Windows NT 4.0 has still not been updated to understand Windows NT entries (we don't know about Windows 2000 yet).

Note that if you fail to register your ISA device properly, then PCI devices that rely on operations such as `HalAssignSlotResources` or `IoAssignResources` might not be usable. This is

---

[6] An example of such a card is the Intel EtherExpress ISA card. You can set the IRQ, the I/O addresses, and the memory addresses via either a setup utility or a Device Driver that knows how to set this card. It is an example of one of the best software-configurable ISA cards.

[7] One major PC maker's manual for a desktop system recommended that only the "most experienced" users attempt to use Plug-and-Play.

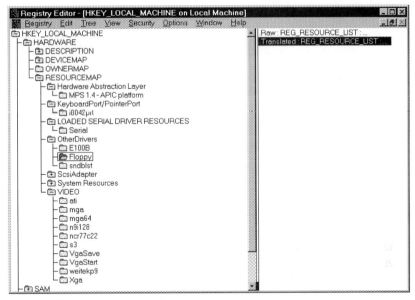

Figure 20.4: *Registry view of resources.*

because the automatic assignment of resources can allocate a memory range, I/O register range, or IRQ value that conflicts with your unregistered ISA device. Given how hard it is for an end user to discover that this is the problem (since the card that fails is manufactured by someone else), the end user can become *very* unhappy if the problem is traced to your driver. Be A Good Bus Citizen.

Under the key `HKEY_LOCAL_MACHINE` is the `HARDWARE` key and below that, `RESOURCEMAP`. Under `RESOURCEMAP` are the allocations under the set of subkeys, such as for the HAL, video adapters, and `OtherDrivers`, as shown in Figure 20.4.

You can select a particular driver and open it. Figure 20.4 shows we opened the floppy driver. Under it are two values (shown in the right-hand column), `Raw:` and `Translated:`. Double-clicking `Translated:` results in the screen shown in Figure 20.5. That figure shows that the floppy drive is allocated on ISA Bus 0.

The tree shown in the last two figures is the same database that `HalAssignSlotResources` and `IoAssignResources` use. Once your driver claims a resource, that claim remains until the system is rebooted (all resource claims are ephemeral Registry entries). An implication of this is that after a reboot, your driver might have a different set of IRQ, I/O addresses, and/or memory addresses assigned, depending on when it was started in the boot sequence or in what order it was manually started. Even an ISA card can use `IoAssignResources` to allocate its resources, provided it is software-programmable (it is up to you, of course, to actually *do* the

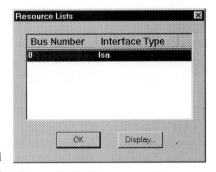

Figure 20.5: *The resource list.*

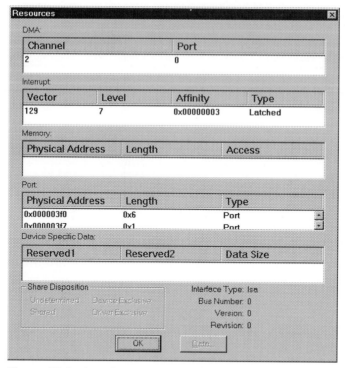

Figure 20.6: *Actual resources assigned to an ISA device.*

programming). `IoAssignResources` simply creates the Registry entries after verifying that no other device has created conflicting Registry entries. If you use `IoAssignResources` properly, you cannot depend on the assignments being the same across invocations of your driver. You cannot use `HalAssignSlotResources` to program an ISA card. This is because there is no standard for programming an ISA card, and `HalAssignSlotResources` depends on knowing how to reprogram the card. We show in the next chapter that `HalAssignSlotResources` is the simplest way to allocate and reprogram a PCI Bus card. But we must emphasize that if you do *not* register your ISA card's claims, PCI cards in the same system will conflict with your card and thus may malfunction.

Double-clicking the entry shown highlighted in Figure 20.5 expands the view to that shown in Figure 20.6. In Figure 20.6. are the details of the assignments, such as the DMA channel, the IRQ level, and the processor affinity (this snapshot was taken on a dual-processor system and the affinity is to either processor, hence the mask `0x00000003`). Observe that the interrupt type is "Latched", meaning edge-triggered. Also, the I/O ports are shown.

It is important that when your driver is unloaded, it *deallocate* any resources it has registered. This is done by calling `IoAssignResources` with a `NULL` pointer.

ISA DMA

Doing DMA for an ISA card is painful. Some of this pain is due to the need to synchronize through a single shared Adapter Object that represents the highly idiosyncratic System DMA Controller (except for the bus mastering ISA cards that are available). Part of this pain is because

ISA DMA using the System DMA Controller is actually *slower* than doing programmed I/O. Alas, some vendors (particularly of some sound cards) provided for I/O *only* via DMA, based on the (erroneous) premise that DMA *must* be faster than programmed I/O. Therefore you have no choice, even though you *know* you are burning processor and memory bandwidth unnecessarily. The overall impact of ISA DMA on total system throughput is also serious because the DMA forces the entire system, including the PCI Bus, to slow down in order to handle each ISA DMA cycle. Finally, because ISA DMA is limited to the lower 16MB of memory, it will almost always be the case that NT will construct buffers in the lower 16MB and copy data to or from them, thereby adding yet one more performance problem to the system. By now you might have a very full appreciation of Why ISA Must Die.[8]

There are no important differences in how ISA DMA is done from an NT driver, other than your having to declare the adapter information properly, including the feature that the System DMA Controller might lose track of the actual transaction (see the `IgnoreCount` feature discussed on page 343). You could even use the scatter/gather simulation techniques discussed in Chapter 17 (page 340) for an ISA bus. But given the amount of copying required because of the 24-bit address space limitation, this likely would actually reduce the overall performance of an ISA DMA transfer.

Summary

This chapter has introduced the details of the ISA bus. With any luck, you will not need this knowledge. Or you may be fortunate enough to be able to use it to successfully talk someone out of building yet another ISA device.

Further Reading

MindShare, Inc.: Tom Shanley and Don Anderson, *ISA System Architecture*, *Third Edition*, Addison-Wesley, 1995. ISBN 0-201-40996-8.

Like the other books in the MindShare series, this book is an indispensable companion. We highly recommend it for anyone having the misfortune to have to write an ISA driver. While much of the technical detail is too low-level for a lot of what you would code, when the device doesn't work (and it is rare that a new device works perfectly), the information in this book will help you debug your ISA problems at the Logic Analyzer level. We rate this book a Must Have.

(There is one caveat with the MindShare series: There is *no* redundancy in it. This means, for example, that you might have to research four or five volumes to find information about a key topic, such as cache management, because each volume assumes you know everything in the previous volume, which has assumed you knew everything in *its* predecessor. We find this to be an unpleasant feature of an otherwise excellent series.)

van Gilluwe, Frank, *The Undocumented PC*, Addison-Wesley, 1993. ISBN 0-201-62277-7.

---

[8] The ISA bus is sometimes referred to as "The bus whose design is so horrible that if it didn't exist, no one would be so tasteless as to invent it."

21 *I/O Hardware: The PCI Bus*

The *Peripheral Component Interface* (PCI) Bus was proposed by Intel in 1992 as the desired bus for long-term growth. It fixed most of the errors and deficiencies of the old ISA bus, as well as the problems of the largely obsolete Local Bus (or VL-Bus), MicroChannel Architecture (MCA) bus, and the various proprietary busses.

Chapter 4 gives an overview of PCI Busses (starting on page 83), and explains what you must do in a Device Driver to actually program a device on the PCI Bus. In this chapter, we take the discussion further and include a PCI enumerator function, as well as an example of using it in a utility program we developed, the PCI Explorer.

The PCI Bus Hardware

The PCI Bus was designed to be *processor-independent*. Unlike the VL-Bus and other proprietary local bus implementations that were tied to one particular model of a processor, the PCI Bus can work with 386, 486, Pentium, Pentium II, Pentium Pro, and future *x*86 processors. It can also work with competing *x*86-compatible processors. But not only is it processor-independent; it is actually *architecture-independent*. That is, it works with NT on the Alpha as well as on high-end UNIX-based workstations and PowerPC platforms. The 64-bit PCI supports 64-bit addressing for the forthcoming 64-bit platforms and the 64-bit native version of NT for the Alpha and these new platforms.

A given PCI Bus is limited to a small number of sockets due to its electrical properties (which are integral to its design). However, a given card can contain many separate PCI *functional devices*, and a single PCI Bus can support up to 256 functional devices. A platform could have as many as 256 PCI Busses. A single add-in card or on-board PCI unit can have as many as eight functional devices—more if the card has an internal bridge and an internal PCI Bus.

The PCI Bus by default supports a full 32-bit address space, thereby eliminating the old 24-bit restriction of the ISA bus. In addition, the PCI Bus is specified as being capable of supporting a 64-bit address space, thus making its extension to the Alpha and other 64-bit processors quite natural. All transfers read or write a 32-bit value and in addition can selectively read or write individual bytes within that 32-bit value.

All PCI transfers use *burst mode* transfers. The device that wishes to transfer (the *initiator*, more commonly referred to as a "bus master") negotiates with the device to which it wishes to transfer (the *target*) and sends the information in a long burst, thus eliminating lengthy bus-access protocols on a per-unit transfer. Using burst mode, a PCI Bus can transfer up to 66Mbytes/sec (or 133Mbytes/sec for a PCI 2.1-compliant bus). When there are multiple busses, a transfer between two devices on the same PCI Bus can take place concurrent with transfers between devices on other, disjoint, PCI Busses on the same machine. Furthermore, while two PCI devices are transferring information, arbitration for the next transfer can take place, thus "hiding" the bus arbitration in the ongoing transfer.

A PCI Bus device can also do burst mode transfers even when the device itself is not aware of the burst mode capability. The PCI controller chip will queue up individual requests and schedule a burst transfer.

Interrupts can be shared among many PCI devices. The I/O and memory spaces that a device supports can be dynamically assigned, thus eliminating the traditional ISA conflicts of IRQ levels, I/O addresses, and mapped memory. This is all handled via the PCI Configuration Space, which allows each PCI card to be uniquely addressed. The major contribution of the PCI Configuration Space is that it provides, for *every* PCI peripheral, a completely *uniform* way of determining that device's resource requirements. The PCI parameters can be set by the BIOS during the preboot phase and later by the operating system itself. The Configuration Space also allows PCI to participate in Plug-and-Play. Although there is no "hot insert" capability currently supported for PCI, you can power the machine down, plug or unplug a PCI card, reboot, and a Plug-and-Play-aware operating system can detect the removal, insertion, or replacement of a PCI device.

One of the more fascinating features, at least to us, is the fact that the PCI Bus is essentially an "analog" rather than a "digital" bus. It critically depends on the signal on the bus being reflected off of the ends of the bus and this reflected wave's being added into the original wave to produce a specific logic level. For those who find this equally fascinating, we suggest you read Chapter 4 of the excellent book, *PCI System Architecture*, which we cite in the Further Reading section at the end of this chapter.

PCI Transactions

All PCI transactions consist of two phases: an initial *address phase* during which an address is placed on the bus and a *data phase* in which data is placed on the bus. The PCI Bus uses the same physical lines to carry both address and data (thus reducing pin counts) at the cost of requiring these two separate phases.

An address phase is either one PCI clock cycle (for 32-bit addresses) or two PCI clock cycles (for 64-bit addresses). The data phase consists of as many PCI clock cycles as required to transfer the data. This includes any wait states that may have to be inserted; each wait state is one PCI clock in duration.

During the address phase, the address of the target is placed on the bus by the initiator, along with a specification of the nature of the transfer. At the end of the address phase, each potential PCI target must have latched the address for decoding and then decodes the address. The target that is selected asserts the $\overline{\text{DEVSEL}}$ signal line. If no target asserts the $\overline{\text{DEVSEL}}$ line within a time-out period, the initiator aborts the transfer. Needless to say, only one PCI target is permitted to assert $\overline{\text{DEVSEL}}$ in response to an address. Unlike ISA, PCI always knows if there is a device that can respond and will not simply transfer data to nonexistent space.

We do not discuss the full PCI transaction protocol here. Instead, we refer you to *PCI System Architecture*.

During the data phase, some number of bytes are transferred. Although the best performance is achieved when multiples of bytes on aligned boundaries are transferred, individual bytes, too, can be transferred. However, one of the powerful features of the PCI architecture is that the PCI Controller/Bridge between the processor and the PCI Bus can actually store transfer requests and convert a series of individual transfers that are pending into a burst request. For example, if the processor generates a series of Write requests to bytes X, X + 2, and X + 3, these will be handled as a 4-byte burst transfer to X, X + 1, X + 2, and X + 3. However, a signal will be asserted to inhibit the Write operation for address X + 1.

The address specified is the *start address* for the transaction. The selected target must not only latch this, but also must increment it appropriately for each unit of information transferred (for example, for 32-bit transfers the address would be incremented by 4).

When a PCI transaction has completed, the processor can be notified via an interrupt. Each PCI device can interrupt on any of four PCI interrupt lines, designated $\overline{\text{INTA}}$, $\overline{\text{INTB}}$, $\overline{\text{INTC}}$, and $\overline{\text{INTD}}$. A single-function PCI package can interrupt only on $\overline{\text{INTA}}$. If a PCI package has additional functions, the first function (arbitrarily selected by the BIOS or operating system) must interrupt on $\overline{\text{INTA}}$, while the second can use $\overline{\text{INTB}}$. If a third function is present, it can use $\overline{\text{INTC}}$; a fourth can use $\overline{\text{INTD}}$. Note, however, that there is nothing in the PCI specification that forbids all functions from using the $\overline{\text{INTA}}$ line if doing so is satisfactory. Since a single PCI device can have up to eight functional units, it is implicit that if all eight were implemented and capable of interrupting, then some sharing of the $\overline{\text{INT}x}$ lines would be necessary.

Note that a PCI device *must* generate parity information for the data on the address/data/command lines of the bus. It is *strongly* recommended that a PCI card check the parity and report an error if it is incorrect. In addition, a PCI card can issue a system error signal that will trigger some serious error response in the processor. For example, in most *x*86 architectures this signal will trigger an NMI (Nonmaskable Interrupt), which the operating system usually treats as a nonrecoverable (Blue Screen of Death) condition.

Once an $\overline{\text{INT}x}$ condition is established, the processor must be interrupted. This action is complex only because it is platform-dependent; two apparently equivalent motherboards might route the $\overline{\text{INT}x}$ signals quite differently. It is up to the BIOS software and the HAL to know what this method is. An in-depth discussion of this problem can be found in Chapter 11 of *PCI System Architecture*. From your viewpoint as a Device Driver writer, what matters is that the BIOS and HAL will determine a mapping between a PCI functional device $\overline{\text{INT}x}$ line and an IRQ level. The IRQ level might not be unique so that other devices on the PCI Bus can share it. The preferred interrupt solution is shown in Figure 21.1 and involves a *programmable interrupt router*, such as the Intel APIC (Advanced Programmable Interrupt Controller) to handle the mapping. This is only a suggested, representative sample of the most general case; any given vendor is free to implement any of a large number of variants, some of which are illustrated in *PCI System Architecture*. As it turns out, most modern PCI-based architectures use the style shown in Figure 21.1, where each $\overline{\text{INT}x}$ line goes separately into the APIC. Within the APIC, multiple devices can be remapped to a single interrupt level. The implication of this is that you cannot be certain that an interrupt is not shared, so you must explicitly program your ISR to determine if the interrupt is for your device.

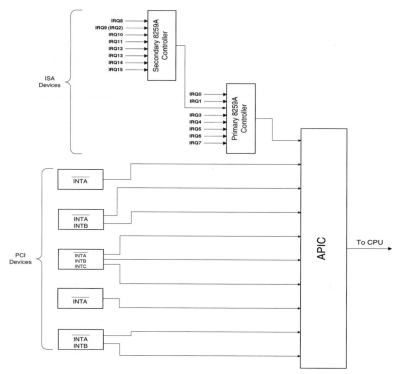

Figure 21.1: *PCI interrupt structure.*

Note that in a system with an APIC, the APIC comes up in a "PIC-compatible" mode, meaning only interrupts IRQ0..IRQ15 are available. An APIC, however, allows interrupts to be in the range IRQ0..IRQ255 with the lower 20 IRQs reserved. To take full advantage of the APIC, your machine must be configured to boot using an APIC-aware HAL (usually any MPS-compatible configuration).

The North Bridge

The North Bridge, the bridge between the processor/memory system and the PCI Bus, is a very complex entity. It must handle the requests to the PCI Bus, and in most modern systems, it actually manages the L2 cache and memory components as well. It must arbitrate between the contending PCI initiators to grant bus mastership. Each PCI device has a pair of signals called "Request" ($\overline{\text{REQ}}$) and "Grant" ($\overline{\text{GNT}}$). These are routed from the device to the component called the *PCI Arbiter*, which is almost always simply integrated into the North Bridge. A device that wants bus mastership (or, in the PCI terminology, wants to become an initiator) asserts its $\overline{\text{REQ}}$ line. The arbiter chooses which of the PCI devices asserting $\overline{\text{REQ}}$ will next get bus mastership and asserts the $\overline{\text{GNT}}$ line for the selected device. Generally, the devices will have no fixed priorities because the arbiter is required to implement a "fairness" algorithm that will prevent any one device from being indefinitely deferred. Precisely how this algorithm is implemented is left up to the designer of the arbiter; the PCI specification only states some criteria of what constitutes fairness.

The North Bridge also queues up requests from the processor so that burst transmissions can be implemented. Because this often intimately ties in to how cache write-back is managed, the North Bridge usually handles the L2 cache so that it can schedule reads and writes properly. It has the right to reorder both to maximize throughput, as long as the serial access semantics are preserved (for example, it cannot schedule a read to precede an already-pending write to the same location). The North Bridge almost always handles the bus snooping required to maintain cache consistency, either directly in its role as the L2 cache manager or as an intermediary forwarding the information to the L2 cache manager.

Windows NT Support of the PCI Bus

Windows NT 4.0 supports the PCI Bus, while Windows 95, Windows 98, and Windows 2000 support PCI Plug-and-Play.

PCI Device Enumeration

In Windows NT 4.0, the Device Driver must explicitly enumerate the entire PCI Bus system. The driver enumerates each PCI Bus and, for each, must enumerate all of the devices. For each device found that the driver recognizes, it enumerates the functional devices. For each functional device that it supports, it creates a Device Object to represent it. This means that a driver must know how to identify all of the devices it can handle and must ignore all devices it is not handling.

Fortunately, this is easy.

You can always determine if a card is a card you understand. This is because the PCI Configuration Space provides an absolutely uniform way of identifying the card and its key resources, and one of the values stored in that Configuration Space is the (read-only) vendor ID and another is the (read-only) device ID. It is even possible to examine a version number. So for each card the enumeration gives you, you can decide by vendor ID, device ID, and even revision ID if it is a card with which you want to deal.

In Windows 2000 and beyond, the PCI Bus is enumerated by the underlying operating system; the driver will be called only for those devices for which it is registered. However, for upward compatibility the technique of enumerating devices used in NT 4.0 will continue to be valid in Windows 2000. The use of the built-in PCI Enumerator in Windows 2000 requires several additional changes and some reorganization of the Device Driver code, since the driver must be cognizant of other Windows 2000 features to take advantage of the Enumerator (see Chapter 29).

Note that some optimizations are, of course, possible. If you know that your device contains only one functional device, you do not need to enumerate the functional devices if they are completely disjoint (for example, a "combo-card" with a serial interface, a parallel interface, and a game port). Your serial driver can just recognize that the second functional device is what it concerns itself with and that it can safely ignore all of the others. If, however, the various devices share registers (as is the case in most multimedia cards), you will have to create all of the Device Objects in your driver, as well as a Controller Object to represent their shared state.

PCI Configuration Space

PCI Configuration Space Header is shown in Figure 21.2. The PCI Configuration Space consists of a mandatory 64-byte header followed by up to 192 additional bytes of information to a maximum size of 256 bytes. The interpretation of the bytes after the header is entirely up to the device vendor. Only the highlighted fields are required in the header. The other fields, if not used, will return specified values such as all zeroes or all ones.

Note that this configuration block uses 32-bit addresses. A configuration block for a 64-bit PCI card uses 64-bit addresses, but it also has a different header type. The configuration block shown here is a Type 0.

The Interrupt Pin field contains a read-only constant in the range 0..4, where 0 indicates that the device uses no interrupts and 1..4 represent $\overline{\text{INTA}}..\overline{\text{INTD}}$. The Interrupt Line field specifies which of the IRQ levels (0..254, with 255 meaning "unassigned") have been assigned to the device. The maximum latency (Max_Lat) and minimum grant (Min_Gnt) values are intended to be used by programmable PCI Arbiters to implement the "fairness" algorithm that still satisfies the constraints of the device (insofar as possible). Thus they have no meaning to the Device Driver writer; they are handled entirely (if at all) by the BIOS and HAL.

Byte			
3	2	1	0

Device ID		Vendor ID		00
Status Register		Command Register		01
Class Code			Revision ID	02
BIST	Header Type	Latency Timer	Cache Line Size	03
Base Address 0				04
Base Address 1				05
Base Address 2				06
Base Address 3				07
Base Address 4				08
Base Address 5				09
CardBus CIS Pointer				10
Subsystem ID		Subsystem Vendor ID		11
Expansion ROM Base Address				12
Reserved				13
Reserved				14
Max_Lat	Min_Gnt	Interrupt Pin	Interrupt Line	15

Figure 21.2: *PCI Configuration Space.*

Other key fields of interest are

- the Vendor ID and Device ID fields, which must be used to determine that a device is handled by your Device Driver
- the Status Register and Command Register fields, which allow you to program the device
- the Class Code field, which can influence how your driver operates (ideally this can help support "rev levels" of the device, if handled properly by the vendor)
- the Base Addresses, which specify the I/O registers and mapped memory that may be present for the card
- the Subsystem ID and Subsystem Vendor ID, which can be used to further determine if the device is one controlled by your driver (see the discussion starting on page 405)

In NT 4.0, you must enumerate the PCI Bus yourself. This means that you must take the following steps.

1. Do a triply nested loop, with the outer loop enumerating all of the PCI Busses (you must plan on up to 256 busses).
2. Within each bus, enumerate up to 255 PCI devices.
3. Within each device, enumerate its functions using a third loop.
4. Create a Device Object for each function that your driver supports.

In Windows 2000, this style is still supported, but you can also register your driver in such a way that your driver will be called only for those devices for which it is registered, and you don't need to do the explicit enumeration yourself. To take advantage of this, you must recode parts of your driver to conform to the Windows 2000 style.

The data structure that supports the PCI Configuration Space is the `PCI_COMMON_CONFIG` structure, shown in Figure 21.3. The structure itself in the header file `ntddk.h` defines these fields. The structure is intended to be expandable to support 64-bit PCI descriptions, so the current 32-bit descriptions are contained in a `union` under the selection `type0`.

A sample PCI Bus enumeration routine is shown in Listing 21.1. This function can be called by a `DriverEntry` routine to locate all of the devices for that driver. It is called with an initial state indicator (`First == TRUE`), a vendor ID, and a device ID. It returns `TRUE` when it finds a matching device, having updated the slot number, bus number, and configuration data area. On subsequent calls (indicated by `First == FALSE`), it uses the previously established bus number and slot number as the initial conditions and returns `TRUE` with the *next* matching device information set or `FALSE` with the other values being undefined.

This enumerator is quite general and allows you to enumerate *all* of the devices on the bus; this may be used for diagnostic purposes. Note that this enumerator does not pay attention to the Subsystem ID or Subsystem Vendor ID; if you are concerned about these, you can either use additional parameters or check the information when the call returns.

```
    typedef struct _PCI_COMMON_CONFIG {
        USHORT VendorID;
        USHORT DeviceID;
        USHORT Command;
        USHORT Status;
        UCHAR RevisionID;
        UCHAR ProgIf;              // Part of Class Code
        UCHAR SubClass;            // Part of Class Code
        UCHAR BaseClass;           // Part of Class Code
        UCHAR CacheLineSize;
        UCHAR LatencyTimer;
        UCHAR HeaderType;
        UCHAR BIST;
        union {
            struct _PCI_HEADER_TYPE_0 {
                ULONG  BaseAddresses[PCI_TYPE0_ADDRESSES];
                ULONG  CIS;
                USHORT SubVendorID;
                USHORT SubSystemID;
                ULONG  ROMBaseAddress;
                ULONG  Reserved2[2];
                UCHAR  InterruptLine;
                UCHAR  InterruptPin;
                UCHAR  MinimumGrant;
                UCHAR  MaximumLatency;
            } type0;
        } u;
        UCHAR DeviceSpecific[192];
    } PCI_COMMON_CONFIG, *PPCI_COMMON_CONFIG;
```

Figure 21.3: PCI_COMMON_CONFIG *structure.*

Listing 21.1: *A PCI Enumerator Function*

```
/***********************************************************************************
Routine Description:
    This function is called by the driver to find the next PCI device and
    initialize the adapter's configuration.
Arguments:
    IN BOOLEAN First                       - TRUE if scan is to start with
                                                 first device
                                           FALSE to start with last iteration
                                                 value returned
    IN unsigned int pciVendorId            - Specified vendor ID or
                                             0xFFFF for all vendors
    IN unsigned int pciDeviceId            - Specified device ID or 0xFFFF
                                             for all devices
    IN OUT  PCI_SLOT_NUMBER *returnSlotData - Slotdata for found device
                                             (starting point for first == FALSE)
    IN OUT  unsigned int *returnBusNumber  - Bus number for found card
Return Value:
    BOOLEAN                                - TRUE if successful
                                           - FALSE if no more devices found

    ***********************************************************************************/
```

```
BOOLEAN pciUtilIteratePCI( IN BOOLEAN First, IN unsigned int pciVendorId,
                           IN unsigned int pciDeviceId,
                           IN OUT PCI_SLOT_NUMBER * returnSlotData,
                           IN OUT PCI_COMMON_CONFIG * returnPciData,
                           IN OUT unsigned int * returnBusNumber   )


{
     PUCHAR                 ioSpace;
     ULONG                  i,j;
     ULONG                  irq;
     ULONG                  portBase;
     ULONG                  retryCount;
     PCI_SLOT_NUMBER        slotData;
     PCI_COMMON_CONFIG      pciData;
     UCHAR                  statusByte;
     BOOLEAN                preConfig = FALSE;
     BOOLEAN                Found = FALSE;
     unsigned int           busNumber = 1;

     KdPrint( ("pciUtil: FindPCI \n") );
     //
     // Iterate over all PCI slots
     //
     slotData.u.AsULONG = 0;
     //
     // Iterate over all busses looking for devices
     //
     // Although it may appear to make sense to limit the bus number to a value
     // smaller than 256, be aware that this is very risky, since you do not know
     // how many busses exist on machines you've never seen that might want to run
     // this driver
     //
     for ( busNumber = First ? 0 : *returnBusNumber;
           busNumber < 256;
           busNumber++)
     { /* Bus Enumeration */
      //
      // Iterate over all devices
      //
      for (slotData.u.bits.DeviceNumber = First
                                       ? 0
                                       : returnSlotData->u.bits.DeviceNumber;
           slotData.u.bits.DeviceNumber < PCI_MAX_DEVICES - 1  ;
           slotData.u.bits.DeviceNumber++)
       { /* Device Enumeration */
        //
        // Iterate over all functions
        //
        for ( slotData.u.bits.FunctionNumber =
                         First ? 0
                             :(returnSlotData->u.bits.FunctionNumber++);
             slotData.u.bits.FunctionNumber < PCI_MAX_FUNCTION - 1  ;
             slotData.u.bits.FunctionNumber++)
         { /* Function Enumeration */
          KdPrint( ("pciUtil: FindPCI - call HalGetBusData  DeviceNumber= %x,"
                    "Function = %x, busNumber = %x     %x ",
                       slotData.u.bits.DeviceNumber,
                       slotData.u.bits.FunctionNumber,
                       busNumber,
                       slotData.u.AsULONG) );
```

```
                    if (HalGetBusData( PCIConfiguration,
                                       busNumber,
                                       slotData.u.AsULONG,
                                       &pciData,
                                       sizeof(PCI_COMMON_CONFIG)))
                      { /* Function Exists */
                        if ( ((0xFFFF == pciVendorId) ||
                              ( pciData.VendorID == pciVendorId )) &&
                             ((0xFFFF == pciDeviceId) ||
                              (pciData.DeviceID == pciDeviceId))
                           )
                          { /* Return This Function */
                            // Found it. This is the next instance of this card type
                            // dumpPciConfig( pciData );
                            KdPrint( ("\n\n") );
                            *returnSlotData = slotData;
                            *returnPciData =  pciData;
                            *returnBusNumber =  busNumber;
                            Found = TRUE;
                            break;
                          } /* Return This Function */
                        else
                          { /* Skip This Function */
                            KdPrint( (" - no match    pciData.VendorID = %x    %x\n",
                                      pciData.VendorID, slotData.u.AsULONG) );
                          } /* Skip This Function */
                      } /* Function Exists */
                    else
                      { /* HalGetBusData failed */
                        KdPrint( (" -  HalGetBusData  returned FALSE   %x \n",
                                  slotData.u.AsULONG ) );
                      } /* HalGetBusData failed */
                  } /* Function Enumeration */
                  if (Found)
                    {
                      break;
                    }
              } /* Device Enumeration */
          if (Found)
            {
                break;
            }
      } /* Bus Enumeration */

    if (!Found)
      {
          return(FALSE);
      }

    KdPrint( ("pciUtil: exiting Find routine\n") );
    return (TRUE);
} // End pciUtilFindPCI()
```

It is very important that you enumerate *all* of the PCI Busses. Even if you *think* that there is only one bus, you could be mistaken, since you might not know how your motherboard is implemented. The PCI slots might actually already be on Bus 1, with Bus 0 being the onboard PCI controllers! As PCI becomes more important, manufacturers are producing motherboards with six or eight PCI slots—this could mean at least three PCI Busses (the onboard controllers, the first four slots, and the last two or four slots). If you are trying to debug the device and have to use a PCI extender card, many PCI extender cards actually contain bridges and thus introduce one more level of bus. You might wish to assume fewer than 16 busses, but the safest method is to follow the PCI specification and assume the maximum. Note that PCI bus numbers are always assigned starting at 0, with no gaps, so you can stop the first time you get an error that the bus does not exist.

A Potential Problem in Bus Enumeration

As PCI devices become more complex, the simplistic bus enumeration we have shown here is not sufficient. To explain why, we show a not-atypical multifunction device. To add some concreteness to this example, we have invented a hypothetical multifunction card, the GeeWillikers G800 Game Card.[1] This card consists of a 3D video chip, a 3D-sound processor, and a fancy-playing console interface. GeeWillikers, Inc., does not make any of these chips. It builds a card that contains these three packages, which are complete PCI devices in their own right and thus have their own PCI Configuration Spaces. The fancy playing console interface is some general-purpose multi-input digital interface and a couple multiplexed analog interfaces. It couples up to the GeeWillikers PlayEverything™ Console. Because of bus loading considerations, this card actually contains a PCI-to-PCI Bridge. (This shows that you *can't* depend on any assumptions about the nature of the motherboard and its PCI Busses. This bridge introduces the $n + 1^{st}$ PCI Bus in the system.We show this card in Figure 21.4.)

The problem is that we want to load the GeeWillikers PlayEverything driver. But when we do the bus enumeration, we see four discrete devices, *none* of which is a GeeWillikers device!

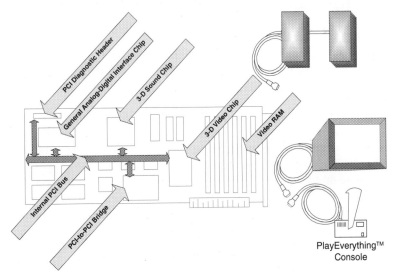

Figure 21.4: *A fictitious multi-PCI device card.*

---

[1] This is another of those cases in which this is not just a neat idea. Right now, there are PCI subsystems being built that look exactly like the card we are describing. Nondisclosure agreements prevent us from identifying the nature of the cards, so we invented something with all of the properties of these real cards, but otherwise completely unrelated to what the cards do.

We see a Chips'R'Us PCI-to-PCI Bridge (since we don't know this exists, we will simply ignore it when it is found on Bus 0). On bus 1, we see a VideoMagic 3-D chip, a Sounds Cool sound chip, and a General Thingies Analog-Digital Interface chip. To say that this makes our job a nightmare is to understate the situation, particularly because the VideoMagic 3-D chip is sold by three other vendors in their (simple 3-D video only) cards and the General Thingies Analog-Digital chip is sold in various laboratory data collection boards. So the Boys In The Lab want to install the game board to play games when management isn't watching, but all they can get is the driver for their Heterogeneous-Products 87411A Gas Analyzer, which also uses that chip. This Is Not What Was Intended.

One approach that has been taken is to check during the enumeration to see if the combination of a bridge of one particular vendor followed by the discovery of three chips by other specific vendors means that this card is a GeeWillikers Game Card and the GeeWillikers driver will take over. But this doesn't help! Suppose the GeeWillikers driver is loaded later. Because it does its own PCI enumeration, it finds the General Thingies A/D chip and decides it wants to process those interrupts. But is the device/function the enumerator found *really* the one on the GeeWillikers Game Card? And has the Heterogeneous Products Gas Analyzer already been loaded, in which case we are going to be snatching away its interrupt? If the Gas Analyzer driver is loaded, it can't tell a General Thingies device enumerated on the GeeWillikers internal PCI Bus from a General Thingies device enumerated on the main or some secondary PCI Bus. Will we have two ISRs called on every interrupt? Will playing the game produce bogus gas analyses? And what if next year, the GeeWillikers folks get a better deal from CloneChips Unlimited for a pin-compatible 3-D video chip and they add it to a new board revision. This chip identifies itself as a Clone-Chips (VendorID) 3-D video chip (DeviceID 0x0666), and this card is *supposed* to be absolutely identical to the previous "rev" level. But the old driver won't work. This Is Not a Good Thing.

Fortunately, there is a solution.

Every PCI card should program the SubVendorID and SubSystemID fields in the board firmware. So even though the VendorID and DeviceID fields will return the discrete information that identify the unique chips, *each* chip should also include a SubVendorID that is the ID assigned to GeeWillikers, Inc., and a SubSystemID that identifies the card as the G800 Game Card. This is easy to do. One simple implementation is to store the information on an SROM (a serially accessed ROM), a tiny little (and very cheap) device. Depending on the nature of the card, there can be only one SROM or there can be one SROM per PCI chip. The net effect, however, is that when the PCI Configuration is read, each of these chips will have either programmed the configuration or returned for that configuration address the correct information to identify the conglomerate of chips as the GeeWillikers G800 Game Card. Thus these fields, which are typically ignored in most PCI enumeration algorithms today, will become essential in the future. Based on prerelease information on Windows 2000 that we have seen, it seems unbelievably difficult to do what the operating system claims to be able to do *without* having the SubSystemID and SubVendorID fields actually implemented on cards.

HalGetBusData in More Detail

Once a PCI device is found, its Configuration Space can be read, and perhaps written, so as to assign IRQ levels, I/O addresses, and mapped memory addresses. It is unusual, but not unheard of, for a Device Driver to actually do this. In principle, it is unnecessary, but reality sometimes has a nasty way of making itself known. Normally, a special function,

`HalAssignSlotResources`, is called. This call allows the HAL to manage the assignment of the I/O device parameters to provide for overall system integrity.

Since `HalGetBusData` is a reasonably important function, we look at it in some detail. Note that this function applies to any kind of queryable bus, not just PCI Busses (excluding the ISA bus, which is not queryable), but we look only at the PCI-related features here.

```
ULONG HalGetBusData(IN BUS_DATA_TYPE BusDataType, IN ULONG BusNumber,
                    IN ULONG SlotNumber, IN PVOID Buffer, IN ULONG Length);
```

The first parameter, *BusDataType*, is the constant `PCIConfiguration`, indicating that we are querying about a PCI Bus. The *BusNumber* parameter is any value in the range 0..255. The *SlotNumber* parameter is any value in the range 0..255; for this parameter, we use the `PCI_SLOT_NUMBER` structure's `u.AsULONG` member. The last two parameters indicate the destination of the bus data information and, for a PCI Bus, are a pointer to a `PCI_COMMON_CONFIG` data structure and the `sizeof(PCI_COMMON_CONFIG)`.

In principle, the PCI BIOS has already gotten the configuration data and assigned it so that the memory, IRQ, and I/O addresses are nonconflicting across all PCI devices. The PCI BIOS makes a good guess, but that guess might not be suitable for all cards in the system once they are enabled. Furthermore, there might be performance reasons for reassigning the IRQ line (such as reducing interrupt latency by not sharing interrupts or assigning a higher-priority interrupt). Finally, there is the situation in which the BIOS's best guess is simply unsuitable for reasons beyond its ability to guess, and the device simply will not work as assigned.

Assigning Resources

The set of resources claimed by the various devices is, by convention, stored in the Registry. Nothing compels a driver to actually do this (although emerging certification standards for Device Drivers will certainly make this mandatory). If you want your Device Driver to be a "good citizen", you must make sure that you maintain this database properly. There are several functions that will do this easily for you.

The easiest function to use is `HalAssignSlotResources`. It is a composite function that

- reads the existing Registry database;
- comes up with an assignment of memory, IRQ, and I/O addresses that do not conflict with any properly registered Device Driver;
- reprograms the device to use these values; and
- writes the current set of values to the Registry to make certain that the current driver is properly registered.

Note that the otherwise apparently similar function, `IoAssignResources`, does not reprogram the device. If you use this function, you must explicitly call `HalSetBusData` to reprogram the device itself.

A well-designed PCI Device Driver not only will allow for the default assignments, but also will allow the user to override the memory, I/O, and IRQ assignments explicitly, thereby giving you the maximum amount of freedom. It also reduces customer support calls and saves your tech support people from having to say, "We're sorry, that card cannot be made to work in your machine. We will transfer you to Customer Support so that you can send it back for a refund". People who buy products do not want refunds; they want working products. A little extra effort in the Device Driver code can save a lot of customer dissatisfaction. It is important to realize that there are still drivers out there that do *not* properly register their claims on resources, and in a given target system, you might have to manually assign some resources simply because the HAL cannot detect a conflict with unregistered devices.

With the enumeration function in Listing 21.1, each time we get a TRUE return from the function we create a Device Object to represent the device. We can then call HalAssignSlotResources to obtain the necessary information about where the I/O registers, mapped memory, and IRQs are set. We will need this information in subsequent operations. A driver might also explicitly call IoAssignResources to more directly manipulate the values. Note that if HalAssignSlotResources or IoAssignResources fails, you must clean up any resources (such as Device Objects) that have been allocated by the DriverEntry routine and terminate with an error, thus indicating that the driver cannot be loaded. It is usually considered good practice at this point to log an event in the Event Log so that the user can determine what has gone wrong. Be certain you log enough information so that your tech support people have enough information to help the end user understand what is going on. And remember . . . the problem is likely to come back to you, and the more information you have the better chance you have of understanding what went wrong.

Using HalAssignSlotResources

```
NTSTATUS HalAssignSlotResources(
                IN PUNICODE_STRING RegistryPath,
                IN PUNICODE_STRING DriverClassName,
                IN PDRIVER_OBJECT DriverObject,
                IN PDEVICE_OBJECT DeviceObject,
                IN INTERFACE_TYPE BusType,
                IN ULONG BusNumber,
                IN ULONG SlotNumber,
                IN OUT PCM_RESOURCE_LIST * AllocatedResources);
```

HalAssignSlotResources lets you obtain the necessary information about where the I/O registers, mapped memory, and IRQs are set. The *RegistryPath* parameter is important. It allows HalAssignSlotResources to access the Parameters subkey of the driver. Its value is the one passed in to the DriverEntry function. If the device is a multifunction adapter and must claim several sets of resources, you are responsible for creating the appropriate keys for the additional devices. The keys are of the form

\Registry\Machine\System\CurrentControlSet\Services*DriverName*

The *DriverClassName* parameter is optional and may be NULL. It specifies the class name under which driver-specific information is stored in the Registry. If its value is NULL, the string OtherDrivers will be used. This key is used to record, as ephemeral Registry information, the resources claimed by the device at the given bus and slot number.

The *DriverObject* parameter is the Driver Object that was passed in to the DriverEntry routine. The *DeviceObject* parameter is the Device Object created to represent the device. Note that during an enumeration, a new Device Object will be created for each device that matches.

The *BusType* parameter for PCI Busses is the defined constant PCIBus. The *BusNumber* and *SlotNumber* parameters are the values returned from the enumeration function. Note that the *SlotNumber* value will usually be the u.AsULONG member of a PCI_SLOT_NUMBER structure.

AllocatedResources is a pointer to an uninitialized pointer. Upon successful return, the pointer that is referenced is modified to have a PCM_RESOURCE_LIST pointer. It is the responsibility of the caller in this case to call ExFreePool to free up the block of storage that was allocated by HalAssignSlotResources.

The PCM_RESOURCE_LIST structure contains key information about what was allocated for the device. This information might differ from what an earlier HalGetBusData might have originally returned because HalAssignSlotResources is free to perform new assignments.

```
typedef struct _CM_RESOURCE_LIST {
    ULONG Count;
    CM_FULL_RESOURCE_DESCRIPTOR List[1];
} CM_RESOURCE_LIST, *PCM_RESOURCE_LIST;
```

CM_RESOURCE_LIST is a fairly complex structure. It consists of a number of variable-length substructures and is illustrated in all its glory in Figure 21.5 (this figure is intended to be representative and show all of the substructure; Your Mileage May Vary). This is the information stored in the Registry \ResourceMap entry and represents this driver's claim on resources. Once the Registry \ResourceMap entry is created, normal allocation policies will not create any resource allocations that conflict with any of the existing resource allocations defined in \ResourceMap.

```
typedef struct _CM_FULL_RESOURCE_DESCRIPTOR {
    INTERFACE_TYPE InterfaceType;
    ULONG BusNumber;
    CM_PARTIAL_RESOURCE_LIST PartialResourceList;
} CM_FULL_RESOURCE_DESCRIPTOR, * PCM_FULL_RESOURCE_DESCRIPTOR;
```

This intermediate descriptor does not contain a lot of information in its first two fields; it simply states the interface type (PCIBus) and the bus number as supplied to

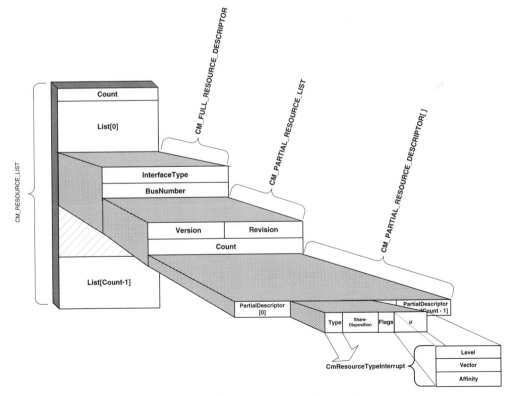

Figure 21.5: CM_RESOURCE_LIST *and its substructures, showing the* CmResourceTypeInterrupt *values.*

`HalAssignSlotResources`. What we are really concerned about is its `PartialResourceList`. Within it, we find a number of resource types. We are particularly concerned with the interrupt vector, which is a resource descriptor of type `CmResourceTypeInterrupt`. The code fragment shown in Listing 21.2 is an example of how we scan this list. We then store the results in our Device Extension in the fields indicated, which we, of course, added to the Device Extension declaration.

The Partial Resource Descriptor contained in the `PartialResourceList` is a complex union of information; we are concerned here only with the interrupt type. Once we find this, we are finished with what we need. The structure of a Partial Resource Descriptor is shown in Figure 21.6.

```
typedef struct _CM_PARTIAL_RESOURCE_LIST {
    USHORT Version;
    USHORT Revision;
    ULONG Count;
    CM_PARTIAL_RESOURCE_DESCRIPTOR PartialDescriptors[1];
} CM_PARTIAL_RESOURCE_LIST, *PCM_PARTIAL_RESOURCE_LIST;

typedef struct _CM_PARTIAL_RESOURCE_DESCRIPTOR {
    UCHAR Type;
    UCHAR ShareDisposition;
    USHORT Flags;
    union {
        // CmResourceTypePort
        struct {
            PHYSICAL_ADDRESS Start;     // 8-byte physical address
            ULONG Length;
        } Port;

        // CmResourceTypeInterrupt
        struct {
            ULONG Level;
            ULONG Vector;
            ULONG Affinity;
        } Interrupt;

        // CmResourceTypeMemory
        struct {
            PHYSICAL_ADDRESS Start;     // 8-byte physical addresses
            ULONG Length;
        } Memory;

        //CmResourceTypeDma
        struct {
            ULONG Channel;
            ULONG Port;
            ULONG Reserved1;
        } Dma;

        // CmResourceTypeDeviceSpecific
        struct {
            // ...
                } DeviceSpecificData;
    } u;
} CM_PARTIAL_RESOURCE_DESCRIPTOR, *PCM_PARTIAL_RESOURCE_DESCRIPTOR;
```

Figure 21.6: CM_PARTIAL_RESOURCE_LIST *and* CM_PARTIAL_RESOURCE_DESCRIPTOR.

Listing 21.2: *Finding Key Results from* `HalAssignSlotResources`

```
// Add to the Device Extension structure
//     IRQL - the IRQ level at which we interrupt
//     Vector - the IRQ vector we need to assign the Interrupt Object
//     Affinity - the processor affinity mask

PCM_RESOURCE_LIST resources = NULL;
int i;
int j;

// ...

status = HalAssignSlotResources(RegistryPath,
                                NULL,          // DriverName
                                DriverObject,
                                DeviceObject,
                                PCIBus,        // Must be this for PCI
                                BusNumber,
                                SlotData.u.bits.DeviceNumber,
                                &resources);

for( j = 0; j < resources->Count; j++)
    { /* Scan resource list */
     for(i = 0; i < resources->List[j].PartialResourceList.Count; i++)
        { /* Scan partial resource list */
         if(resources->List[j].PartialResouceList.PartialDescriptors[i].Type
             == CmResourceTypeInterrupt)
          { /* Found interrupt */

            extension->IRQL = resources->List[j].PartialResourceList
                                        .PartialDescriptors[i]
                                        .u.Interrupt.Level;
            extension->Vector = resources->List[j].PartialResourceList
                                        .PartialDescriptors[i]
                                        .u.Interrupt.Vector;
            extension->Affinity = resources->List[j].PartialResourceList
                                        .PartialDescriptors[i]
                                        .u.Interrupt.Affinity;
           break;
          } /* Found interrupt */
        } /* Scan partial resource list */
    } /* Scan resource list */

ExFreePool(resources);
```

Now that we have established the basic interrupt parameters, we need to locate the I/O register addresses and the memory addresses. Note that although the PCI Configuration Header specifies the *start* address of each block of I/O registers or memory, it does not specify a length. Nor, in fact, is there any apparent way to tell if the address represents I/O or memory space. Both of these pieces of information, however, can be derived from the PCI Configuration Header information (although obtaining the length requires a special trick).

Because `HalAssignSlotResources` might have reprogrammed the device, you must do a `HalGetBusData` to get the latest information from the device.

When the `HalGetBusData` operation returns the Configuration Header, the value in the `u.type0.BaseAddresses[i]` tells the meaning of the ith address. If the low-order bit is 1, then

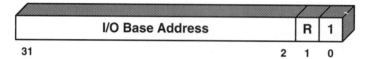

Figure 21.7: `BaseAddresses[i]` *format for I/O address register.*

the address is in I/O space and bits 31..2 are the base address. Bit 1 is reserved. This is illustrated in Figure 21.7. A PCI device that uses I/O registers cannot, by the PCI specification, use more than 256 registers designated by any one `BaseAddress` location. The base address is always a multiple of 4 and can be obtained by simply masking off the low-order 2 bits of the value.

For memory addresses, the low-order bit of the I/O base address is 0. Additional bits indicate constraints on the memory address and whether accesses to it are cacheable (you must specify the cacheability when you map the memory). This is shown in Figure 21.8. The type bits indicate if the address can be anywhere in the 32-bit address space (full 32-bit addressing), anywhere in the 64-bit address space (only for PCI 64), or, for PCI devices with legacy support issues, whether the device memory must be mapped in the lower 1MB (MS-DOS) memory space. The actual address is obtained by masking off the low-order 4 bits.

For mapping the memory, you must also know the length of the memory block. You further might need to discover the length of the register space so that you know how much to reserve if you are assigning resources yourself instead of using `HalAssignSlotResources`. The PCI specification requires that a device support a special "hack" that allows you to determine the range of addresses to allocate. If you write `0xFFFFFFFF` (all ones) into a register block and then read back the value, the value you read back will be the *highest valid assignable address*, that is, the complement of the size minus 1. For example, if the mapped memory block must be 4K and you write `0xFFFFFFFF`, you will read back `0xFFFFF000`. Negate[2] this and you get 4,096, the size of the block. A code fragment that does this is shown in Listing 21.3. Note that this fragment reads the data, then determines the sizes, and finally restores the original data. If you write any value in the registers *other* than `0xFFFFFFFF`, then that value will be stored. Note that this code is greatly simplified in that it does not actually perform any error checks. Also, it is assumed to be for a 32-bit system, in which the address size and the `int` size are both 32 bits. It simply stores the sizes in the Device Extension for later use.

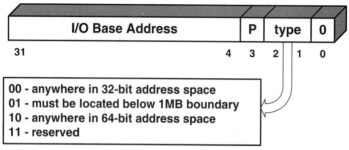

Figure 21.8: `BaseAddresses[i]` *format for memory address.*

---

[2] Two's complement. Negating is the same as complementing and adding 1.

Listing 21.3: *Determining Register Lengths*

```
PCI_COMMON_CONFIG registers;
PCI_COMMON_CONFIG lengths;

HalGetBusData(PCIConfiguration, bus, slot, &registers,
              sizeof(PCI_COMMON_CONFIG));
lengths = registers;
for(i = 0; i < 6; i++)
    lengths.u.type0.BaseAddresses[i] = 0xFFFFFFFF;

HalSetBusData(PCIConfiguration, bus, slot, &lengths,
              sizeof(PCI_COMMON_CONFIG));
HalGetBusData(PCIConfiguration, bus, slot, &lengths,
              sizeof(PCI_COMMON_CONFIG));

// Restore the original values

HalSetBusData(PCIConfiguration, bus, slot, &registers,
              sizeof(PCI_COMMON_CONFIG));

for(i = 0; i < 6; i++)
    extension->size[i] = -(int)lengths.u.type0.BaseAddresses[i];
```

Note, however, that the address returned is a physical address. Addresses that are memory addresses will have to be mapped to a *logical* address using `HalTranslateBusAddress`. This is discussed in the section "Mapping Memory" on page 417.

Claiming Resources

A properly designed driver will claim whatever resources it uses by registering its claims. This registration allows `HalAssignSlotResources` to work properly. Using the Registry Editor, you can examine this structure, such as is shown in Figure 21.9. To do this, you must use the older

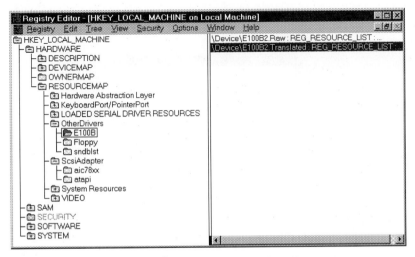

Figure 21.9: *The tree view of resources.*

Registry Editor, `RegEdt32`, not the newer, slicker `RegEdit`. The older `RegEdt32` program knows about the NT structures. The newer one was written originally for Windows 95 and, at least as of Windows NT 4.0, has still not been updated to understand Windows NT entries (we don't know yet about Windows 2000).

Under the key `HKEY_LOCAL_MACHINE` is the `HARDWARE` key, and under `HARDWARE` is the `RESOURCEMAP`.Under this last key is the allocations under the set of subkeys; such as for the HAL, video adapters, and `OtherDrivers`.

We can select a particular driver and open it. Figure 21.9 shows the Intel Ethernet 10/100 (rev B) driver. Under it are two values: `Raw:` and `Translated:`. Double-clicking the `Translated:` entry produces the screen shown in Figure 21.10. This shows that the Ethernet card is allocated on PCI Bus 0. Double-clicking this entry expands the Resources display shown in Figure 21.11. Here are contained the details of the assignments, such as

- the DMA channel
- the IRQ level
- the processor affinity (this snapshot was taken on a dual-processor system, and the affinity is to either processor, hence the mask `0x00000003`)

Also shown are the interrupt type Level Sensitive and the I/O ports and memory mappings.

This tree is the same database that `HalAssignSlotResources` and `IoAssignResources` use. Once your driver claims a resource, that claim remains until the system is rebooted (all resource claims are ephemeral Registry entries). This implies that after a reboot, your driver might have a different set of IRQ, I/O addresses, and/or memory addresses assigned, depending on when it was started in the boot sequence or in what order it was manually started. If you use `HalAssignSlotResources` or `IoAssignResources` properly, you cannot depend on the assignments being the same across invocations of your driver.

It is also important that your driver, when it is unloaded, deallocate any resources it has registered. This is done by calling `IoAssignResources` with a `NULL` pointer.

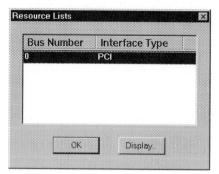

Figure 21.10: *The resource list.*

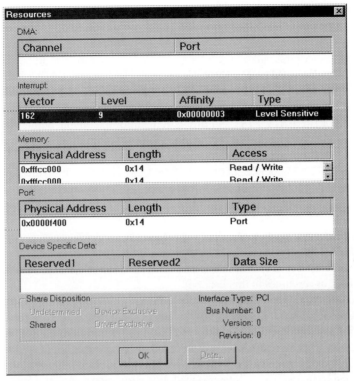

Figure 21.11: *PCI resource assignments.*

Using *IoAssignResources*

For a queryable bus, such as PCI, you can call `HalAssignSlotResources`. As an alternative, you can do the allocations yourself using `IoAssignResources`; for nonqueryable busses, in particular ISA, this is the only way to register resources.

```
NTSTATUS IoAssignResources(
          IN PUNICODE_STRING RegistryPath,
          IN PUNICODE_STRING DriverClassName,
          IN PDRIVER_OBJECT DriverObject,
          IN PDEVICE_OBJECT DeviceObject OPTIONAL,
          IN PIO_RESOURCE_REQUIREMENTS_LIST RequestedResources,
          IN OUT PCM_RESOURCE_LIST * AllocatedResources);
```

`IoAssignResources` implements part of the functionality of `HalAssignSlotResources` (and in fact is called by `HalAssignSlotResources`). Unlike `HalAssignSlotResources`, however, it does *not* reprogram the device; it merely allocates resources from the Registry. It is typically used when you must do something more complex than `HalAssignSlotResources` permits.

Its parameters are similar to those of `HalAssignSlotResources`. *RegistryPath* is the Registry path passed into `DriverEntry`. *DriverClassName* is the name under which the resources are listed in the Registry and may be NULL, meaning `OtherDrivers`.

DriverObject is the Driver Object passed into `DriverEntry`. *DeviceObject* is the Device Object that was created for this device. This Device Object may be NULL. *AllocatedResources* is also the same as for `HalAssignSlotResources` and points to an uninitialized pointer. Upon successful completion of this call, the pointer is updated to point to a CM_RESOURCE_LIST, which is handled as described on page 408.

The major difference is how information is passed in. You are responsible for allocating a block of memory (which, because this is done in `DriverEntry`, could be in the Paged Pool) for IO_RESOURCE_REQUIREMENTS_LIST and filling in the information that defines the resources that are required. This information can be obtained via `HalGetBusData` or from the Registry or even hardcoded into the driver if that is appropriate.

The structure of IO_RESOURCE_REQUIREMENTS_LIST is shown in Figure 21.12. Note that because the array at the end is a placeholder for accessing a longer array, the structure is actually variable-length. Consequently, you must know how long this array will have to be before allocating the space.

The `List` array contains a set of values for the allocation of resources. Note that `ListSize` is the size of this list in bytes because the list contains embedded variable-length items. The format of IO_RESOURCE_LIST is shown in Figure 21.13. `Version` and `Revision` must be set to 1. `Count` is the count of resources in this list.

As with `HalAssignSlotResources`, if this function fails, you cannot actually start the driver with the proposed set of resources or with any of the possible alternatives. In this case, you must free up any resources already allocated (such as Device Objects) and leave `DriverEntry` with a FALSE return, thereby indicating that the driver could not be started.

If `IoAssignResources` is called with the *RequestedResources* pointer NULL, then any resources that had been assigned will be released. It is very important that if you unload the driver or are forced to abort the `DriverEntry` routine, you release all of the assigned resources.

```
typedef struct _IO_RESOURCE_REQUIREMENTS_LIST {
    ULONG ListSize;                    // In bytes
    INTERFACE_TYPE InterfaceType;      // For PCI, the constant PCIBus
    ULONG BusNumber;                   // Zero-based number of this bus
    ULONG SlotNumber;                  // Logical slot or location on the bus
                                       // of the device
    ULONG Reserved[3];                 // For system use
    ULONG AlternativeLists;            // Count of alternative IO_RESOURCE_LIST
                                       // Elements with IO_RESOURCE_DESCRIPTORs
    IO_RESOURCE_LIST List[1];          // First of a variable-sized array
} IO_RESOURCE_REQUIREMENTS_LIST, *PIO_RESOURCE_REQUIREMENTS_LIST
```

Figure 21.12: *The* IO_RESOURCE_REQUIREMENTS_LIST *structure.*

```
typedef struct _IO_RESOURCE_LIST {
    USHORT Version;                    // Of this structure, currently 1
    USHORT Revision;                   // Of this structure, currently 1
    ULONG Count;                       // Of IO_RESOURCE_DESCRIPTORs in array
    IO_RESOURCE_DESCRIPTOR Descriptors[1];
} IO_RESOURCE_LIST, *PIO_RESOURCE_LIST;
```

Figure 21.13: *The* IO_RESOURCE_LIST *structure.*

Otherwise, the next time the driver is loaded it will not be able to reuse the resources it had, since they will appear to be already claimed by some other driver.

Setting up the IO_RESOURCE_REQUIREMENTS_LIST structure is fairly complex because the structure contains variable-length embedded structures.

Overriding Assignments

A driver constructed for maximum robustness will want to allow the user to override any implicit assignments that would be made by IoAssignResources or HalAssignSlotResources. This allows a device to function in an environment in which poorly written drivers that have not registered their resource requirements end up fooling IoAssignResources or HalAssignSlotResources into making an assignment that conflicts with existing hardware.

There are no standards for how this overriding information should be stored; each driver is free to use its own convention. However, we suggest that such parameters be stored as either values or subkeys in the Parameters subkey, that is, under
HKEY_LOCAL_MACHINE\System\CurrentControlSet\Set\Services*drivername*\Parameters

Mapping Memory

Once a memory address is determined by using HalGetBusData, it must be made available for use. The addresses returned from the PCI card are all *bus-relative physical addresses*, which NT cannot address directly. So you must perform a two-step translation, first to a system-wide physical address and then to a system logical address. A PCI card can have an address in, for example, the range 0..1M, independent of which PCI Bus it is plugged into. However, the system might, via the PCI bridges, remap each PCI Bus so that the busses have disjoint system physical addresses. The first step of this translation is done by HalTranslateBusAddress.

```
BOOLEAN HalTranslateBusAddress(IN INTERFACE_TYPE InterfaceType,
                               IN ULONG BusNumber,
                               IN PHYSICAL_ADDRESS BusAddress,
                               IN OUT PULONG AddressSpace,
                               OUT PHYSICAL_ADDRESS TranslatedAddress);
```

The *InterfaceType* parameter will be, for a PCI Bus, the constant PCIBus (although this function can apply to many other bus types, including ISA). The *BusNumber* parameter is the physical bus number of the specified bus in the machine.

The *BusAddress* parameter is the 64-bit bus-relative address that is to be mapped to system physical memory. Note that since the HalGetBusData information supplies only a 32-bit address for Type 0 headers, this value must be copied into a temporary variable as the low-order 32 bits so that it can be passed to this call. You cannot reference it directly in the type0 variant of the PCI_COMMON_CONFIG structure directly.

You must also mask off the low-order bits of the address and pass the information encoded about whether the address is a memory address or port address in the *AddressSpace* parameter. *AddressSpace* is available for cross-platform drivers. In some machines, I/O registers are mapped into physical memory and hence into system logical memory; in others, the I/O registers remain in a separate I/O register space. You examine the address that you have obtained from the PCI configuration data and determine, based on its low-order bit, whether it is a port address or a memory address. Then you set this value accordingly.

The *TranslatedAddress* parameter points to a location where the system physical address will be placed. This value will be valid if the function returns TRUE. If *AddressSpace* is 0, this address must then be passed to the MmMapIoSpace function. However, the HAL might translate a port address (*AddressSpace* set to 1 on input) to a memory address (*AddressSpace* set to 0 on output).

If the address was originally established as a memory address, you can deal with it directly. Or you can read or write the memory address determined by MmMapIoSpace by using the appropriate HAL operations such as WRITE_REGISTER_*xxx*. If the *AddressSpace* value was originally 1, you must deal with it using the appropriate HAL operations WRITE_PORT_*xxx*. *You must do this even if the value returned was set to 0 to indicate the translation had mapped to physical memory and you have used MmMapIoSpace to get a system logical address.* For all of the details regarding this, see Chapter 12, starting on page 273.

In the following listing, we know, from the specification of the card we are programming, that its second address is the address of its memory.

Listing 21.4: *Mapping PCI Adapter Memory to System Logical Memory*

```
PHYSICAL_ADDRESS addr;
PCI_COMMON_CONFIG config;
ULONG MemOrIO;
PHYSICAL_ADDRESS translated;

HalGetBusData(PCIConfiguration, bus, slot.u.AsULong, &config, sizeof(config));

addr.LowPart = config.u.type0.BusAddresses[1] & ~0xF;
                            // Our hypothetical card uses [1]
                            // We mask off the low order 4 bits
                            // (See Figure 21.8)

addr.HighPart = 0; // we are on a 32-bit machine

if(!HalTranslateBusAddress(  PCIBus,           // Bus type
                             bus,              // Bus number
                             addr,             // Address to translate
                             &MemOrIO,         // Tell how translated
                             &translated) )
    { /* deal with failure */
    // ... As appropriate
    } /* deal with failure */
```

Having translated the bus-relative physical address to system physical memory before we can use it, we need to map it into nonpaged system logical memory. This is done with MmMapIoSpace.

```
PVOID MmMapIoSpace(IN PHYSICAL_ADDRESS PhysicalAddress,
                   IN ULONG NumberOfBytes,
                   IN BOOLEAN CacheEnable);
```

MmMapIoSpace takes a system physical address and a length and maps the address to an address in nonpaged memory. This address can now be used to access the information, which in this context is the onboard memory of the device. For a PCI device, the *NumberOfBytes* parameter can be obtained by using the example shown in Listing 21.3 on page 413. In addition, the

CacheEnable parameter value must be set for the device. Note that devices such as network adapters that can change the contents of their onboard memory might not implement the necessary lines to support proper cache snooping and thus are noncacheable. The cacheability of such memory is encoded in `BaseAddresses` of the `PCI_COMMON_CONFIG` structure, as shown in Figure 21.8, and you are responsible for passing this information on to the system. Further, if you plan to defer the mapping, you must at this point store the cacheability information for the later mapping.

`MmMapIoSpace` returns the address in nonpaged memory, or, if there is insufficient space available to perform the mapping, returns NULL.

Having mapped the memory, you are responsible, typically in the Unload routine, for unmapping it using `MmUnmapIoSpace`.

The PCI Explorer

The "PCI Explorer" is a little application we wrote that allows you to see which PCI devices you have in your system. It consists of two components: an application and a PCI Enumerator that is a Device Driver. A sample of the output is shown in Figure 21.14. The first page of the display is the index; it names the vendors whose devices are found in the machine. Within each vendor are the devices. The ordering is based on how the devices are found on the PCI Bus. The decoding in this program has been greatly aided by the file `pcicode.h`, maintained by Jim Boemler (`jboemler@halcyon.com`), and is available at `www.halcyon.com/scripts/jboemler/pci/pcicode`.

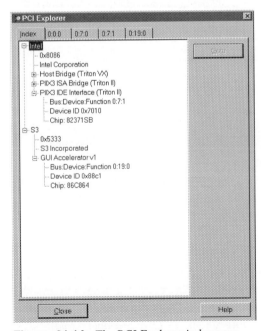

Figure 21.14: *The PCI Explorer index page.*

`pcicode.h` contains a mapping from PCI vendor IDs to printable names and is the list of vendors maintained by the PCI central authority. Jim also tracked down the assorted device IDs (which are *not* administered by any central authority) and a table of vendor ID/device ID pairs to chip IDs and descriptions. If you discover, using our program, a PCI device for which there is no displayed device description and you know what the device is, we are sure he would be happy to hear from you. If you are involved in developing a device, it would be nice to pass the information on to him as soon as legally permissible. Before deciding that our program doesn't know about the device, you might want to download the latest copy of his file and recompile our program with it (full source is available with the code that accompanies this book).

This program exhibits many useful techniques. For example, the application installs, starts, stops, and uninstalls the driver, a topic we discuss in some detail in Chapter 26. If it can't find the driver immediately, it prompts you to tell it where the driver, `pciscan.sys`, is located. You need to do this only once; the program will remember where the driver last was by making an entry in the Registry.

The driver supports two operations, "Get First PCI Device" and "Get Next PCI Device", implemented as `DeviceIoControl` IOCTLs.

You can view the PCI information by clicking one of the tabs or by selecting any device in the tree view (or select any subitem of any device) and clicking the **Goto** button. The information is displayed so as to appear similar to the standard PCI pictures, for example Figure 21.2. In addition, the bus, device, and function codes are displayed. You have a choice of seeing the data displayed in hexadecimal or decimal. The vendor-specific data can be displayed in a variety of formats including byte, word, and doubleword, in decimal or hexadecimal, as characters, or as Unicode characters. A sample of the output is shown in Figure 21.15.

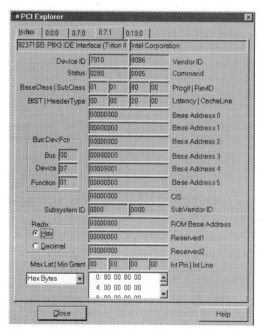

Figure 21.15: *PCI Explorer data display.*

The PCISCAN *Driver*

Much of the PCISCAN driver is a simple variation on our core driver example, so we do not include this code in print; it is available as part of the code that accompanies this book. The interesting parts are the DeviceIoControl handler and the function it calls.

The **pciscan.h** Header File

DeviceIoControl passes in a pointer to a structure that returns not only the PCI_COMMON_CONFIG information but also other key PCI information. Note the use of the "u" suffix on the PCI_SCAN_TYPE. If you don't indicate that this value is unsigned, you will get compiler warnings about signed/unsigned conversions when you call DeviceIoControl (and if you don't get these warnings, you've got your warning level set too low!).

Listing 21.5: *The* pciscan.h *Header File*

```
// Device type           -- in the "User Defined" range.
#define PCISCAN_TYPE 42000u

// The IOCTL function codes from 0x800 to 0xFFF are for customer use.
/***********************************************************************
*                         IOCTL_PCISCAN_GET_FIRST
*
*---------------------------------------------------------------------
* BOOL DeviceIoControl(h, IOCTL_PCISCAN_GET_FIRST,
*                      InputBuffer, InputBufferLength,
*                      OutputBuffer, OutputBufferLength,
*                      BytesWritten, NULL);
*---------------------------------------------------------------------
* Inputs:
*       InputBuffer: NULL
*       InputBufferLength: 0
*       OutputBuffer: PPCISCAN_OUTPUT
*       OutputBufferLength: sizeof(PPCISCAN_OUTPUT)
* Return: BOOL
*       TRUE - a valid PCI device has been found and the PCISCAN_OUTPUT data
*                is valid
*       FALSE - no PCI device has been found, and PCISCAN_OUTPUT data is
*                undefined
* Effect:
*       The internal position pointers are set to point to the lowest-numbered
*       PCI Bus:device:function, 0:0:0. The driver then iterates until it
*       either finds a valid bus:device:function code or exhausts the
*       PCI limits.
***********************************************************************/
#define IOCTL_PCISCAN_GET_FIRST \
    CTL_CODE(PCISCAN_TYPE,  0x0B11, METHOD_BUFFERED, \
                                 FILE_WRITE_DATA | FILE_READ_DATA)
/***********************************************************************
*                         IOCTL_PCISCAN_GET_NEXT
*
*---------------------------------------------------------------------
* BOOL DeviceIoControl(h, IOCTL_PCISCAN_GET_NEXT,
*                      InputBuffer, InputBufferLength,
*                      OutputBuffer, OutputBufferLength,
*                      BytesWritten, NULL);
*---------------------------------------------------------------------
```

```
*  Inputs:
*        InputBuffer: NULL
*        InputBufferLength: 0
*        OutputBuffer: PPCISCAN_OUTPUT
*        OutputBufferLength: sizeof(PPCISCAN_OUTPUT)
*  Return: BOOL
*        TRUE - a valid PCI device has been found and the PCISCAN_OUTPUT data
*                 is valid
*        FALSE - no PCI device has been found, and PCISCAN_OUTPUT data is
*                 undefined
*  Effect:
*        The internal position pointers are incremented until the driver
*        either finds a valid bus:device:function code or exhausts the
*        PCI limits.
*************************************************************************/
#define IOCTL_PCISCAN_GET_NEXT \
    CTL_CODE(PCISCAN_TYPE,  0x0B12, METHOD_BUFFERED, \
                                    FILE_WRITE_DATA | FILE_READ_DATA)


typedef struct _PCISCAN_OUTPUT {
                PCI_SLOT_NUMBER   SlotData;
                PCI_COMMON_CONFIG PciData;
                unsigned int      BusNumber;
                          } PCISCAN_OUTPUT, * PPCISCAN_OUTPUT;
```

PCISCAN DeviceIoControl Handler

This handler follows the model of an IRP_MJ_DEVICE_CONTROL handler in a very straightforward fashion. The IOCTL specifies that the Buffered I/O method be used. This means that the
Irp->UserBuffer pointer holds a pointer to the kernel's internal buffer that will be copied back
to the application space when the I/O Manager handles the return. The two cases are virtually
identical. They differ only in that they call the pciScanIteratePCI function with a different
initial argument.

Listing 21.6: *The* pciScanDeviceControl *Function*

```
NTSTATUS pciScanDeviceControl(
                            IN PDEVICE_OBJECT DeviceObject,
                            IN PIRP Irp )
   {
   NTSTATUS  ret = STATUS_SUCCESS;
   PIO_STACK_LOCATION irpStack;
   PCISCAN_OUTPUT * pOutBuffer;
   PCISCAN_DEVICE_EXTENSION * extension;
   PCI_SLOT_NUMBER returnSlotData;
   PCI_COMMON_CONFIG returnPciData;
   unsigned int returnBusNumber;

   extension =
       (PCISCAN_DEVICE_EXTENSION *) DeviceObject->DeviceExtension;
   irpStack = IoGetCurrentIrpStackLocation(Irp);
   pOutBuffer = (PCISCAN_OUTPUT *)Irp->UserBuffer; // For Buffered I/O
   switch(irpStack->Parameters.DeviceIoControl.IoControlCode)
       { /* IOCTL */
       case  IOCTL_PCISCAN_GET_FIRST:
              if (pciScanIteratePCI( TRUE, 0xffff, 0xffff,
                                      &extension->returnSlotData,
                                      &extension->returnPciData,
                                      &extension->returnBusNumber   ))
```

```
                  { /* got first */
                  pOutBuffer->SlotData = extension->returnSlotData;
                  pOutBuffer->PciData =  extension->returnPciData;
                  pOutBuffer->BusNumber = extension->returnBusNumber;
                  ret = STATUS_SUCCESS;
                  break;
                  } /* got first */
              else
                  { /* failed first */
                  ret = STATUS_UNSUCCESSFUL;
                  break;
                  } /* failed first */
              break;
      case  IOCTL_PCISCAN_GET_NEXT:
              if (pciScanIteratePCI( FALSE, 0xffff, 0xffff,
                                    &extension->returnSlotData,
                                    &extension->returnPciData,
                                    &extension->returnBusNumber))
                  { /* got next */
                  pOutBuffer->SlotData = extension->returnSlotData;
                  pOutBuffer->PciData =  extension->returnPciData;
                  pOutBuffer->BusNumber = extension->returnBusNumber;
                  ret = STATUS_SUCCESS;
                  break;
                  } /* got next */
              else
                  { /* no more */
                  ret = STATUS_UNSUCCESSFUL;
                  break;
                  } /* no more */
              break;
      default:
              ret = STATUS_UNSUCCESSFUL;
      } /* IOCTL */
//
// Fill these in before calling IoCompleteRequest
//
Irp->IoStatus.Status = ret;
Irp->IoStatus.Information = 0;
IoCompleteRequest( Irp, IO_NO_INCREMENT );
return ret;
}
```

The PCI Iterator Function

The PCI Iterator function is a fairly complex function, so we annotate it in some detail. The "obvious" technique of using three nested loops doesn't quite work, for reasons we explain as we annotate the code. The nature of this function is either to initialize the bus:device:function information in the Device Extension (First is TRUE) and then find the first device or to start with the previous value and then continue to find the following device. When it finds a device, it returns TRUE. If it does not find a device, it returns FALSE.

This iteration function is actually a bit more general-purpose than our PCISCAN driver requires. However, we base it on the more general iterator so that you have an example of what you can use when your specific PCI device is searching for a VendorID/DeviceID combination in your driver. When you call this, you can specify 0xFFFF either for the VendorID, meaning "all vendors", or for the DeviceID, meaning "all devices for the matching vendors". As is customary for most of our examples, we removed the assorted debug output statements, so you will often see empty blocks. We left these as placeholders so that you could insert appropriate code for your own purposes.

Listing 21.7: *The* `pciScanIteratePCI` *Function*

```
/*++
Routine Description:
    This function is called by the driver to find the next PCI card and
    initialize the adapter's configuration.
Arguments:
    IN BOOLEAN First                        - TRUE if scan is to start with
                                              first device
                                              FALSE to increment to the
                                              next device

    IN unsigned int pciVendorId             - Specified vender ID,
                                              or 0xFFFF for all vendors

    IN unsigned int pciDeviceId             - Specified device ID,
                                              or 0xFFFF for all devices

    IN OUT  PCI_SLOT_NUMBER *returnSlotData - Slotdata for found device
                                              (starting point for
                                              first == FALSE)

     IN OUT  unsigned int *returnBusNumber  - Bus number for found card
Return Value:
    ULONG
--*/

BOOLEAN pciScanIteratePCI( IN BOOLEAN First, IN unsigned int pciVendorId,
                    IN unsigned int pciDeviceId,
                    IN OUT  PCI_SLOT_NUMBER * returnSlotData,
                    IN OUT  PCI_COMMON_CONFIG * returnPciData,
                    IN OUT  unsigned int * returnBusNumber   )
{
    PCI_SLOT_NUMBER    slotData;
    PCI_COMMON_CONFIG pciData;
    BOOLEAN nextBus = FALSE;
    ULONG   busNumber = 1;
    ULONG   bytesReturned;
    BOOLEAN firstFunction;
    BOOLEAN firstDevice;
    //
    // Iterate over all PCI slots
    //
    firstFunction = First;
    firstDevice = First;
```

This assignment is a bit of a cheat because it uses the union in `PCI_SLOT_NUMBER` *to clear the device number and function number as well as the reserved bits.*

```
    slotData.u.AsULONG = 0;
```

If we are doing the Next operation, we want to point to the last device we found, plus one. This means that we must increment the function number, and if it overflows, we must increment the device number and reset the function number to 0. If the device number overflows, we reset the device number to 0 and increment the bus number. We do all of these operations to the values referenced by the parameters, which are the values that we store in the Device Extension.

```
if (!First)
  { /* continuation */
    //
    // If not the first, we want to point after the last device we found
    //
    returnSlotData->u.bits.FunctionNumber++;
    if (PCI_MAX_FUNCTION <= returnSlotData->u.bits.FunctionNumber)
      { /* next device */
        returnSlotData->u.bits.FunctionNumber = 0;
        returnSlotData->u.bits.DeviceNumber++;
        if (PCI_MAX_DEVICES <= returnSlotData->u.bits.DeviceNumber)
          { /* next bus */
            returnSlotData->u.bits.DeviceNumber = 0;
            *returnBusNumber++;
          } /* next bus */
      } /* next device */
  } /* continuation */
```

Following are the core nested loops. The PCI specification states that there can be no more than 256 busses in a system, but Microsoft seems to provide no symbolic constant for this value (at least not one that we could find in the NT 4.0 DDK). Note that we reset firstDevice *to* TRUE *each time we increment the bus number.*

```
for ( busNumber = (First ? 0 : *returnBusNumber);
      busNumber < 256;
      busNumber++, firstDevice = TRUE)
      { /* busses loop */
        unsigned int DeviceNumber;
        nextBus = FALSE;
```

The next loop in iterates over all devices. Note that we set firstFunction *to* TRUE *each time we increment the device number. If this is not the first iteration on a new bus, we start with the* DeviceNumber *that is stored in the* PCI_SLOT_NUMBER *information referenced by the parameter. There is a defined constant for the maximum number of devices on a PCI Bus.*

```
      for(DeviceNumber = firstDevice
                          ? 0
                          : returnSlotData->u.bits.DeviceNumber;
          DeviceNumber < PCI_MAX_DEVICES ;
          DeviceNumber++, firstFunction = TRUE )
          { /* devices loop */
            unsigned int FunctionNumber;
            slotData.u.bits.DeviceNumber = DeviceNumber;
```

The innermost loop iterates over all of the possible functions. Like the devices loop, it determines if it should start at 0 or the most recent function number used.

```
for(FunctionNumber =
            firstFunction
                  ? 0
                  : returnSlotData->u.bits.FunctionNumber;
      FunctionNumber < PCI_MAX_FUNCTION ;
      FunctionNumber++)
    { /* functions loop */
     slotData.u.bits.FunctionNumber = FunctionNumber;
     bytesReturned = HalGetBusData(
                          PCIConfiguration,
                          busNumber,
                          slotData.u.AsULONG,
                          &pciData,
                          sizeof(PCI_COMMON_CONFIG));
```

The following code is worth noting. HalGetBusData, *on successful return, returns the number of bytes it wrote into* PCI_COMMON_CONFIG. *Because there is a large block of vendor-defined data that could be returned, the actual number of bytes will range from the minimum size of the configuration data to the maximum size. There has been in the past an error in the Microsoft documentation, which stated that* HalGetBusData *would return 0 if a bus did not exist and 4 if a device/function pair did not exist on the bus. This is incorrect and has been documented as a correction in the Knowledge Base article Q126428, "Incorrect Return Value for* HalGetBusData *(PCI)". The correct documentation is that* HalGetBusData *will return 2 if the device/function pair does not exist. While this error was corrected in the formal documentation as early as Windows NT 3.51, we have found both that the error remains in code written years ago, based on the earlier incorrect documentation, and that the error has entered the folklore as developers clone older drivers to get newer drivers.*

If the device/function pair does not exist, we do not need to do anything; devices and functions are not required to have contiguous numbers. Even functions within a single device can have noncontiguous function IDs. In case you're wondering why this might make sense, consider a family of chips that have a span of features from the low-end bargain chip to the high-end superchip.[3] You could use a single driver to control the entire family. It would just ignore those devices or functions that were not defined for the particular chip that was installed.

```
if (2 == bytesReturned)   // Device/function pair does
                          // not exist
    { /* no device/function */
    // Ignore missing device
    } /* no device/function */
else
if (0 == bytesReturned)   // Bus does not exist
    { /* no bus */
```

---

[3] The old distinction was "consumer", "commercial", and "high-performance", but the reality is that most consumer computers require the high-end chips for audio, video, 3-D graphics, and gaming, while "commercial" workstations (those found in most offices) actually require less power. As I am a high-end developer, the areas in which I need serious power are almost, but not entirely, completely disjoint from the gaming market, so I can, on the whole, use less expensive devices. *–jmn*

```
            //
            // We can skip to next bus,
            //    set flag to break out of device loop,
            //    and break out of function loop
            //
            nextBus = TRUE;
            break;
        } /* no bus */
```

If the VendorID *field is* 0xFFFF, *the device did not respond correctly. This value indicates an invalid vendor ID.*

```
        else
        if (0xffff == pciData.VendorID)
            { /* invalid vendor ID */
            } /* invalid vendor ID */
```

Here's a relatively complex test, but what it boils down to is that we can accept the device we just found if (a) we passed in 0xFFFF, *thus indicating "all vendors", or (b) the vendor IDs match and we passed in* 0xFFFF, *thus indicating "all devices" or (c) the vendor IDs match and the device IDs match.*

```
        else
        if (   ((0xFFFF == pciVendorId)
                || ( pciData.VendorID == pciVendorId )) &&
                  ((0xFFFF == pciDeviceId)
                     || ( pciData.DeviceID == pciDeviceId)))
            { /* found next */
            // Found it. This is the next instance of
            // this card type
            *returnSlotData = slotData;
            *returnPciData  = pciData;
            *returnBusNumber =  busNumber;
            return TRUE;
            } /* found next */
        else
            { /* does not match */
            } /* does not match */
    } /* functions loop */
```

Breaking out of the functions loop with nextBus *set* TRUE *means we are trying to look at a nonexistent bus (remember that we don't know if a bus is defined until the innermost call of the inner loop). Therefore there is no need to iterate over all of the devices of the bus, since the bus doesn't exist. The* nextBus *flag forces us to terminate the devices loop and move on to the next bus.*

```
        if (nextBus)
            break;     // Break to next bus
    } /* devices loop */
  } /* busses loop */
```

Each time we find a valid bus:device:function value, we return TRUE *internally. Falling off the end of the triply nested loop means we have exhausted all of the values and there are no more devices to find.*

```
  return FALSE;
} // End pciScanFindPCI()
```

The PCI Explorer Source

The PCI Explorer is written in C++ using the MFC (Microsoft Foundation Classes) libraries. A detailed discussion of the code would be more suited for a book on application-level programming, but there are some key ideas about the interface that are worth noting.

The most serious problem we had was that we returned a data structure from the kernel that contains `PCI_SLOT_NUMBER` and `PCI_COMMON_CONFIG` structures. The obviously correct way to get these definitions is to include the header file that contains them, which turns out to be `...\ddk\inc\miniport.h`. Unfortunately, this file, for reasons that are fundamentally incomprehensible to us, defines two data types, `LARGE_INTEGER` and `ULARGE_INTEGER`. We would have thought that fundamental definitions like this would be more reasonably found in a header file defining core data types. Alas, they are not, and these definitions conflict with the user-level definitions declared when `windows.h` is included. *There is no way to avoid this.* What we had to do was unbelievably ugly, but necessary: We copied the definitions from `miniport.h` and created our own header file. This should not have been necessary.

This application needs to load the driver. Rather than placing this burden on the user, we use the SCM (Service Control Manager) to load it. The actual sequence of operations, whose progress we display to the user (see Figure 21.16), is as follows.

1. Open the SCM.
2. Add the `PCISCAN` driver to the system.
3. Start the `PCISCAN` driver.
4. Open the `PCISCAN` device.
5. Perform a series of `DeviceIoControl` operations to locate all of the PCI devices.
6. Close the `PCISCAN` device.
7. Stop the `PCISCAN` driver.
8. Remove the `PCISCAN` driver from the system.
9. Close the SCM.

For the details of how to add, start, stop, and remove a driver programmatically, using the SCM, see Chapter 26.

The first time you run this application, it probably will not be able to find the `PCISCAN.sys` file that is the driver executable. You'll get a file-open dialog box, and you'll need to locate the `PCISCAN.sys` file. The program will save this name in a Registry entry of its own. On subsequent executions, the program will use this Registry entry to locate the driver and will not bother you unless it has an error finding the file. If there are any errors during the process, an error message will be displayed in the status region (the large white box at the bottom of the illustration in Figure 21.16). After successful execution of the program, the Exit button will terminate execution.

Opening the Driver

The application is written in C++, so it is considered good practice to specify the correct global scope for most API functions. This means that `CreateFile` is written as `::CreateFile`. The value `PCISCAN` is a macro that is used to define the device name (so it needs to be defined only in one place). In C (and C++), the effect of using the syntax of two string constants written without

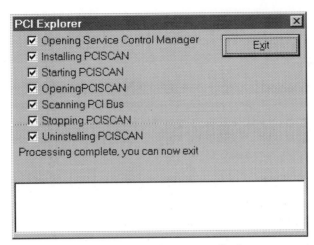

Figure 21.16: *The PCI Explorer status display.*

an intervening comma is that the compiler will concatenate them into a single string, so the device name string used as the first parameter to `CreateFile` is "\\\\.\\PCISCAN".

```
pci = ::CreateFile(_T("\\\\.\\") PCISCAN,
                        GENERIC_READ,
                        0,
                        NULL,
                        OPEN_EXISTING,
                        FILE_ATTRIBUTE_NORMAL,
                        NULL);
if(pci == INVALID_HANDLE_VALUE)
    { /* failed */
     err = ::GetLastError();
     // ... Error-handling code
    } /* failed */
```

Calling the Driver

The following fragment drops a lot of detail found in the actual application code, such as the Finite State Machine model that walks through the installation and the starting, use, shutting down, and unloading of the driver. This fragment is from one of the states that performs the scanning of the bus.

```
result =  ::DeviceIoControl( pci,
                        IOCTL_PCISCAN_GET_FIRST,
                        NULL, 0, // No input
                        &pciBuffer,
                        sizeof(pciBuffer),
                        &length,
                        NULL);
if(!result)
    { /* failed */
     // ... Handle failure condition: no PCI Bus or no devices in it
    } /* failed */
```

The PCIData *class is a C++ class that represents Type 0 PCI devices (the only kind the application currently supports). We use the C++* new *operator to create a* new *instance of this class for each device found. Then we call a function called* AddPage *that adds a new PCI object to the display.*

```
PCIData * data;
while(TRUE)
  { /* scan PCI */
  PCISCAN_OUTPUT pciBuffer;
  CString s;
  s.Format(_T("%d:%d:%d"),
                    pciBuffer.BusNumber,
                    pciBuffer.SlotData.u.bits.DeviceNumber,
                    pciBuffer.SlotData.u.bits.FunctionNumber);
  data = new PCIData(s);
  data->data = pciBuffer;
  dlg.AddPage(data);
```

Having successfully added the PCI device to the display, we next iterate through the devices using the IOCTL_PCISCAN_GET_NEXT *request, until there are no more devices.*

```
ZeroMemory(pciBuffer.PciData.DeviceSpecific,
            sizeof(pciBuffer.PciData.DeviceSpecific));
result = ::DeviceIoControl(pci,
                            IOCTL_PCISCAN_GET_NEXT,
                            NULL,
                            0,
                            &pciBuffer,
                            sizeof(pciBuffer),
                            &length,
                            NULL);
if(!result)
      break; // Stops at end
} /* scan PCI */
```

Summary

This chapter has covered the details of how to use the PCI Bus from the viewpoint of programming an NT Device Driver. In addition to the basic principles of accessing the PCI parameters, we have shown the importance of some of the lesser-used PCI features (such as Subsystem ID and Subsystem Vendor ID), particularly as they will impact newer features such as Plug-and-Play. Finally, we have presented fragments of actual working enumeration code. The full working code is available from our Web sites.

Further Reading

MindShare, Inc.: Tom Shanley and Don Anderson, *PCI System Architecture, Third Edition,* Addison-Wesley, 1995. ISBN 0-201-40993-3.

Like the other books in the MindShare series, this book is an indispensable companion. We highly recommend it for anyone writing a PCI Device Driver. While much of the technical detail is too low-level for a lot of what you would code, when the device doesn't work (and it is rare that a new device works perfectly), the information in this book will help you debug your PCI problems at the PCI Bus Analyzer or Logic Analyzer level. We rate this book a Must Have.

Chapter

---

22 *Serialization within the Driver*

One key principle that governs most of driver architecture is that you can do only one thing at a time. We showed in Chapter 17 how to use Adapter Objects (page 342) and Controller Objects (page 350) to avoid using certain critical resources concurrently. But there are many other reasons for avoiding conflicts. The process of keeping various transactions in proper sequence is called *serialization*. In this chapter, we discuss the basic issues of serialization and the facilities provided in Windows NT for managing serialization.

Introduction to Serialization

Serialization takes many forms. Some of it is required by the intrinsic nature of NT as a multi-threaded, multiprocessor system, where some thread executions might change context due to hardware interrupts. Some of it is required to maximize the throughput for an I/O device by managing queueing. And some of it is due to the nature of interrupts. In this case, the fundamental effects of interrupts already require certain levels of serialization, but their effects and potential problems are exacerbated by the interrupt protocols (particularly the use of the DPC) and the multiprocessor nature of Windows NT.

A driver can be called with I/O requests from several programs and several threads within each application program. A nonexclusive device can be opened concurrently by several applications programs, each of which might be doing I/O through your driver to a single device. You want each I/O operation to be started as soon as possible, yet not before the previous operation is out of the way. If the device is simple and exclusive and all processing is done in the Dispatch Routines, there is no problem and no further serialization is needed.

A typical driver will initiate some action and rely on the ISRs and DPC Routines to complete the I/O. If the second I/O happens in this window, the I/O operations will conflict. The second I/O request could change hardware settings before the first has been completed by the hardware. Serialization of the I/O requests ensures that only one I/O request is touching hardware at any time.

We discuss two serialization techniques:

- The `StartIo` routine, a simple mechanism built into NT that is suitable for most drivers
- The Queuing primitives, which allow a driver to manage queues in more complex ways

We also present an example that requires the latter method: a device that can have two I/O operations pending at any time.

Device Control operations can be processed in the Dispatch Routine or passed a queue, depending on the operation. If the Device Control operation involves hardware access, it should be handled through some sort of queueing mechanism. If it is reasonable to process an I/O request in the Dispatch Routine, it is best to do so.

Each driver that queues IRPs needs a Cancel Routine to remove IRPs queued for processing.

Serializing the processing of IRPs does *not* synchronize the access to hardware between the ISR, the DPC, and the IRP dispatch. If the hardware has multiple concurrent operations and there is hardware shared by the access paths, you need to enclose the access within a Critical Section. When the `StartIo` or DPC Routine will access the device, it should enter a `KeSynchronizeExecution` handler (see Chapter 14, page 293) to ensure that there is no interference between these stages of processing.

Basic Serialization: `StartIo`

A very high percentage of the drivers written use highly stylized methods of queuing I/O transactions. The `StartIo` mechanism simplifies the writing of most drivers.

A new entry, traditionally called `StartIo`, is made to a driver. The usual naming convention is to write a function called *drivername*`StartIo`. This simplifies the setting of breakpoints at it with the debugger. However, all documentation simply refers to it as the `StartIo` function, so that is what we call it here. The entry to the `StartIo` routine is established in the `DriverEntry` routine. It is part of the Driver Object, so it applies to all instances of the devices.

The WinDbg debugger sometimes becomes confused and unhappy if it has symbols for multiple routines that have the same name. One of the pieces of folklore is to avoid duplicate names in different drivers.

```
NTSTATUS DriverEntry(
    IN PDRIVER_OBJECT DriverObject,
    IN PUNICODE_STRING RegistryPath)
{
    // Pretty much like all other examples...
    DriverObject->DriverStartIo = myDriverStartIo;
    // ... More stuff here
}
```

In the Dispatch Routine, you check your parameters, copy any information in pageable memory to a nonpaged buffer, or cause the pageable memory to be locked down (become temporarily unpageable). You then enqueue a request to process the IRP. First, you indicate that the

IRP has not been completed by calling `IoMarkIrpPending` and `IoStartPacket`, passing in the IRP pointer. This will queue the IRP for the `StartIo` routine. If this routine is not already "busy", the I/O system dequeues the IRP from the `StartIo` queue and calls `StartIo` at IRQL level `DISPATCH_LEVEL`.

`StartIo` usually accesses hardware and initiates the actions needed to satisfy this I/O request. If the request is simple, `StartIo` might actually complete the operation entirely within itself, without causing or handling an interrupt. In this case, `StartIo` can complete the IRP by calling `IoCompleteRequest`, and the I/O transaction is finished. An example of this is on page 438.

It is not always possible to actually initiate the I/O transaction in the `StartIo` handler. All that the `IoStartNext Packet` call on the `StartIo` handler *really* means is that "the last IRP processed for this device is complete and another one can be processed". However, not all of the resources needed to *do* the desired I/O operation might be available. You might have to synchronize on an Adapter Object, if the device uses DMA with any kind of shared DMA unit, either the System DMA Controller or a Bus Master DMA. Or you might have to synchronize on a Controller Object, if the device shares any registers with some other device that it might be part of. The strategies for doing DMA are discussed in detail in Chapter 17, starting on page 343. Controller Objects are discussed in Chapter 17 starting on page 350.

The `StartIo` routine is called at `DISPATCH_LEVEL`. At this level, you must not do anything that can cause a page fault, so you must have already made certain that any pageable buffers are already locked into nonpaged memory. This will be done automatically with parameter passing by the I/O system for the I/O buffers specified for `ReadFile`, `WriteFile`, or `DeviceIoControl` operations. This passing is either

- Buffered, that is, `DO_BUFFERED_IO` established in `DriverEntry` or `METHOD_BUFFERED` IOCTLs, or

- Direct, that is, `DO_DIRECT_IO` established in `DriverEntry`, `METHOD_IN_DIRECT`, or `METHOD_OUT_DIRECT` IOCTLs.

When Neither mode parameter passing is used (when either none of the `DO_...._IO` flags are set in `DriverEntry` or `METHOD_NEITHER` is specified for an IOCTL), the application buffers must be handled in the Dispatch Routine before `IoStartPacket` is called.

When the request is completed, whether in the `StartIo` function or the DPC Routine, the `IoStartNextPacket` routine is called. This routine causes the I/O Manager to look for the next IRP queued to `StartIo` and to call `StartIo` with this IRP. If no other packets are queued, the `StartIo` will be marked "not busy".

IRPs in the queue need not be processed in FIFO order, although that is the most common method. They may be sorted by key and dequeued using `IoStartNextPacketByKey`.

Note that the `StartIo` mechanism serializes the processing of IRPs. It does *not* synchronize the access to hardware between the ISR, the DPC, and `StartIo`. If your hardware has multiple concurrent operations and there is hardware shared by the access paths, you need to enclose the access within a Critical Section. When the `StartIo` and DPC Routines will access the device, it should enter a `SynchCritSection` to ensure that there is no interference between these stages of processing. This is usually done using `KeSynchronizeExecution`, as described in Chapter 14, on page 308.

The `StartIo` function has the following prototype.

```
typedef VOID (*PDRIVER_STARTIO) (IN PDEVICE_OBJECT DeviceObject,
                                 IN PIRP Irp);
```

Thus your `StartIo` routine has a pointer to the *DeviceObject* (and hence your Device Extension) and the IRP that has been dequeued. It then can do whatever it needs in order to complete the request.

- Set a value in a device register to establish some device condition that generates no interrupts.

- Initiate an I/O transfer that will later interrupt.

- Do a complete DMA setup and start it.

The `StartIo` handler was established in the `DriverEntry` routine by storing a pointer to it in the Driver Object:

```
DriverObject->DriverStartIo = myDriverStartIo;
```

A typical Dispatch handler might look like that in Listing 22.1. This handler is for the `IRP_MJ_DEVICE_CONTROL` operation. For the case shown here, the requirement is to write to one of the device control registers and wait for an interrupt. When you queue a packet, you must return `STATUS_PENDING` to indicate that the I/O operation has not yet completed.

Listing 22.1: `IRP_MJ_DEVICE_CONTROL` *Using* `IoStartPacket`

```
NTSTATUS myDriverDeviceControl (IN PDEVICE_OBJECT DeviceObject, IN PIRP Irp)
    {
        PIO_STACK_LOCATION stack = IoGetCurrentIrpStackLocation(Irp);
        PMYDRIVER_DEVICE_EXTENSION extension = DeviceObject->DeviceExtension;
        NTSTATUS status = STATUS_SUCCESS; // Assume success unless changed

        switch(stack->Parameters.DeviceIoControl.IoControlCode)
            { /* IoControlCode */
            case MY_IOCTL_DO_SOMETHING:
                    // This particular operation requires initiating an I/O
                    // transfer that will eventually generate an interrupt
                    IoMarkIrpPending(Irp);
                    IoStartPacket(DeviceObject, Irp, NULL, NULL);
                    status = STATUS_PENDING;
                    break
            case ...:
                    // ...
            default:
                    status = STATUS_UNSUCCESSFUL;
                    Irp->IoStatus.Status = STATUS_UNSUCCESSFUL;
                    Irp->IoStatus.Information = 0;
                    IoCompleteRequest(Irp, IO_NO_INCREMENT);
                    break;
            } /* IoControlCode */
        // Return either the default status or an updated status value
        return status;
    }
}
```

The Dispatch Routine that wants to enqueue a request for the `StartIo` queue calls `IoStartPacket`.

```
VOID IoStartPacket(IN PDEVICE_OBJECT DeviceObject,
                   IN PIRP Irp,
                   IN PULONG Key,
                   IN PDRIVER_CANCEL CancelFunction);
```

`IoStartPacket` enters an IRP into the queue. The obvious parameters are *DeviceObject* and *Irp*. The *Key* value is optional. It is used only if you plan to use `IoStartNextPacketByKey`; otherwise, specify *Key* as NULL. If it is non-NULL, it points to a value that determines where the IRP is entered in the `StartIo` queue. This positions the new entry in the Device Queue *after* any entries in the queue that have *Key* values less than or equal to its *Key* value and preceding any entries with *Key* values that are greater. This seems to suggest that the order is FIFO within equal sort keys, but this is not explicitly stated. The documentation of `IoStartPacket` doesn't actually state this, but it uses `KeInsertByKeyDeviceQueue`, which *does* state this behavior. If this value is NULL, the entry is added to the end of the current queue. You can also specify a *CancelFunction* parameter to be called if this IRP is cancelled. This function will be set as the Cancel function for the IRP and will be called if the IRP is cancelled. It is responsible for handling any cleanup that might be required. If you don't need a Cancel Routine (we discuss why you would want one shortly), you can use the value NULL for this parameter.

The `StartIo` routine is shown in Listing 22.2. A `StartIo` routine is always executed at DISPATCH_LEVEL. You must be careful not to call any functions that require PASSIVE_LEVEL for their execution. An interesting factoid here is that *all* of the queued requests, no matter which Dispatch Routine originally queued them, end up here. This means that the IRP_MJ_READ, IRP_MJ_WRITE, IRP_MJ_DEVICE_CONTROL, and all of the other IRP_MJ_ functions that have queued their packets lose their identity. You can handle this in several ways. One common way is that all of the IRP_MJ_ functions that are going to enqueue their actions all go to the same Dispatch handler. This handler doesn't care exactly what the IRP is going to do; it is going to queue it anyway. You can then do a `switch` statement in the `StartIo` handler very much as we've shown in Listing 22.2.

Listing 22.2: *A* `StartIo` *Routine*

```
void myDriverStartIo(PDEVICE_OBJECT DeviceObject, PIRP Irp)
   {
   PIO_STACK_LOCATION stack = IOGetCurrentIrpStackLocation(Irp);
   switch(stack->MajorFunction)
       { /* type */
       case IRP_MJ_READ:
               myDriverStartRead(DeviceObject, Irp);
               return;
       case IRP_MJ_WRITE:
               myDriverStartWrite(DeviceObject, Irp);
               return;
       case IRP_MJ_DEVICE_CONTROL:
               myDriverStartDeviceControl(DeviceObject, Irp);
               return;
```

```
        default:
                Irp->IoStatus.Status = STATUS_UNSUCCESSFUL;
                                        // Why are we here?
                Irp->IoStatus.Information = 0; // Be safe, make it 0
                IoCompleteRequest(Irp, IO_NO_INCREMENT);
                IoStartNextPacket(DeviceObject, FALSE);
        } /* type */
    }
```

A very important feature of the code in the listing is the fact that it checks for *all* possible cases, and if it finds one it is not prepared for, it still acts on it. It rejects it, which is a Good Thing. Even more important, it calls `IoStartNextPacket` to dequeue the next packet. If it did not do this (for example, the default case was omitted), then a programming error somewhere else in the driver would not only cause the *current* packet to be lost; it would simply pause the driver until the next `IoStartPacket` was done at the dispatch level. But for most I/O transactions, the application program is stopped, waiting for the current operation to complete. Thus there won't be another I/O operation started and therefore no `IoStartPacket`, and consequently, the whole device driver is now locked up. Shutting down the program and restarting it might help, but that won't get you the User Friendly Device Driver Award.

All paths through `StartIo` must at some point execute `IoStartNextPacket`. In the previous listing, this would normally be done in the various `myDriverStart...` routines. But if you fail to start the next packet, the device is essentially dead.

```
VOID IoStartNextPacket(IN PDEVICE_OBJECT DeviceObject,
                       IN BOOLEAN Cancelable);
```

`IoStartNextPacket` starts the next packet in the queue. If there is no next packet pending, the device becomes "idle". The second parameter to `IoStartNextPacket` tells if the IRPs in the Device Queue are cancellable, that is, whether your driver has a Cancel handler. This tells the `IoStartNextPacket` function whether it needs to synchronize the removal of an IRP using the general cancel mechanism.

Normally, the queue is handled in a FIFO fashion. This is generally required in order to preserve application-level semantics, which are expected to occur in the order in which they are executed by the application.[1] However, in some cases you might have operations that for priority reasons must execute out of sequence. For these, you can assign a *key value* to the IRP and execute the function `IoStartNextPacketByKey`.

```
VOID IoStartNextPacketByKey(IN PDEVICE_OBJECT DeviceObject,
                            IN BOOLEAN Cancelable,
                            IN ULONG Key);
```

---

[1] It is amazing how often this requirement is overlooked. Some years ago, a certain printer driver from a well-known vendor of a page description language took it upon itself to "optimize" the printing by sending all bitmaps out *first*. This meant that if you used a common application such as PowerPoint to create, say, a border using a standard clipart insert and then put in lots of bitmaps, what printed was a blank border. This was because the border (and its enclosing whitespace) was printed *on top of* all of the bitmaps that had been "optimized". The older driver, which did no "optimization", did it right. What made this driver very odd was that (a) it was allowed to pass an internal design review, (b) the vendor assured me that it was a correct decision to reorder the output, and (c) it took something like a year to get it replaced. Be *very* careful about how you decide to redefine the application semantics! Or *you* might end up as a footnote in somebody's book. *–jmn*

IoStartNextPacketByKey is like IoStartNextPacket, with the addition of the *Key* parameter. When this function is used, the queue entry that matches *Key* will be dispatched, even though the matching entry might not be the first entry in the queue. The *Key* value is the value that was assigned to the IRP when IoStartPacket was called. Although the documentation is not explicit on this, it seems that if in the queue there are multiple entries with identical keys, the first one found will be dispatched. What is *not* stated anywhere that we can find is what happens if *no* entry matching the specified *Key* is found. In this case, we suggest that the behavior might revert to IoStartNextPacket, that is, the first entry is taken off the queue. However, we have not done any experiments to verify this.

You might think that using IoStartNextPacketByKey would be a cool way to implement multiple "threads" of requests, for example for I/O or other purposes. This is not a good idea. There are more general ways of handling this. We look at one in the next section.

Driver-Managed Queues

Instead of using the StartIo queueing mechanism, you can do your own queue management, using either the low-level queue management functions or the higher-level Device Queue primitives.

Low-Level Primitives

Several low-level queue-management operations are used. When these are used for IRP queues, you can use one of the built-in queue element in the IRP. You must establish a variable that is a list header of a doubly linked list and initialize it. You then can perform a number of operations on the queue represented by this list header. These operations and the operations on the list header are summarized in Table 22.1.

Table 22.1: *Queue Operations for Doubly Linked Lists*

Operation	Function
ExInterlockedInsertHeadList	Inserts an entry at the head of a list in a multiprocessor-safe manner.
ExInterlockedInsertTailList	Inserts an entry at the tail of a list in a multiprocessor-safe manner.
ExInterlockedRemoveHeadList	Removes an entry from the head of a list in a multiprocessor-safe manner.
InitializeListHead	Initializes storage that is used for a list head.
InsertHeadList	Inserts an entry at the head of the list.
InsertTailList	Inserts an entry at the tail of the list.
IsListEmpty	TRUE if the list is empty; FALSE if it is not.
RemoveEntryList	Removes an entry from an arbitrary location in the list.
RemoveHeadList	Removes an entry from the head of the list.
RemoveTailList	Removes an entry from the tail of the list.

A low-level device-managed queue is most often implemented by allocating a list header, usually by declaring it in the Device Extension, initializing it with `InitializeListHead`, and then adding to the tail and retrieving from the head. (Or, if you like symmetry, you could add to the head and retrieve from the tail.)

Doubly linked lists are general-purpose and could be used for a variety of purposes, but the most common use is to provide an alternative to the `StartIo` queue.

All of these operations work on `LIST_ENTRY` values. A `LIST_ENTRY` value should normally be allocated in nonpaged memory. (However, you could think of a list header as a local variable on the stack, if it is used only within one function; this usage is rare. There is almost no way to manage list entries within the list that would be allocated on the stack.)

```
typedef struct _LIST_ENTRY {
    struct _LIST_ENTRY * volatile Flink;
    struct _LIST_ENTRY * volatile Blink;
} LIST_ENTRY, *PLIST_ENTRY;
```

You can traverse the list by following its `Flink` or `Blink` pointers. You could, of course, add, remove, or otherwise manipulate these pointers directly, but it is a great deal more convenient to use the built-in functions. For example, you could add the following declaration to your Device Extension:

```
LIST_ENTRY listHead;
```

You can then initialize it by calling

```
InitializeListHead(&extension->listHead);
```

At this point, you can now freely add or remove entries in the list.

Freely? Not quite. Nothing is free (and if you think it is, the system will eat your lunch). In fact, you have several synchronization problems. If you are trying to add a list element in the Dispatch Routine while the device is active, the device will quite possibly take an interrupt and the DPC Routine will try to dequeue an element to start the next I/O operation. Now, the ISR operates at DIRQL level and the DPC operates at `DISPATCH_LEVEL`, but the Dispatch *Routines* operate at `PASSIVE_LEVEL`. Thus the list insertion can be preempted in the middle of changing the list, and then another operation will complete before the first one resumes. Oops! And don't forget that the thread running at `PASSIVE_LEVEL` might be on Processor 2 while the DPC is executing on Processor 3. We cannot emphasize often enough that *every driver must be multiprocessor-safe*.

The solution is obvious and absolutely necessary. You can't cheat on this. You *must* protect the list with a Spin Lock. If the list can be accessed from the ISR (not a common case, but not inconceivable), it must be protected by `KeSynchronizeExecution`. Before you do any operation that modifies the list or depends on its integrity (such as traversing it), you must lock the list. There should be one lock for every list. (You should not use one lock to protect multiple lists unless you are commonly transferring things between the two lists. Otherwise, you serialize access that does not need to be serialized—this hurts performance.)

Because it is very common to add elements to or remove them from the list at `PASSIVE_LEVEL` and `DISPATCH_LEVEL`, special functions exist to do this in a multiprocessor-safe fashion. There is a slight performance advantage to using these. They require that you have created and initialized a Spin Lock to control the list. Thus your declaration of a queue should almost always be accompanied by a declaration of a Spin Lock to accompany it. Note that the use of a Spin Lock means that these functions may not be called at any IRQL > DISPATCH_LEVEL.

```
LIST_ENTRY listHead;
KSPIN_LOCK listLock;
```

In your DriverEntry routine, you would then call

```
InitializeListHead(&extension->listHead);
KeInitializeSpinLock(&extension->listLock);
```

You can now use the ExInterlocked...List functions, which take both a list head and a Spin Lock. The insertion or removal is an atomic operation, fully multiprocessor-safe.

```
PLIST_ENTRY newListEntry = ...; // Creates a new entry
LIST_ENTRY oldhead = ExInterlockedInsertTailList(&extension->listHead,
                                                 newListEntry,
                                                 &extension->listLock);
// ...
LIST_ENTRY next = ExInterlockedRemoveHeadList(&extension->listHead,
                                              &extension->listLock);
```

These two functions are defined as follows.

```
PLIST_ENTRY ExInterlockedInsertHeadList(IN PLIST_ENTRY ListHead,
                                        IN PLIST_ENTRY ListEntry,
                                        IN PKSPIN_LOCK Lock);

PLIST_ENTRY ExInterlockedInsertTailList(IN PLIST_ENTRY ListHead,
                                        IN PLIST_ENTRY ListEntry,
                                        IN PKSPIN_LOCK Lock);
```

These functions insert *ListEntry* at the head or tail of the list defined by the *ListHead* parameter. They use the specified *Lock* for synchronization. The return value is the previous list head or tail. This value is NULL if the list was empty. The return value is important when you are using this to maintain your own driver queues, as we will show, because it allows you to determine if you need to initiate the first I/O action to start the device operating. If there is active I/O going on, the enqueued entry will be dequeued by the DPC or other place where the operation currently being performed is completed.

There is only one function for removing items from an interlocked list, as follows.

```
PLIST_ENTRY ExInterlockedRemoveHeadList(IN PLIST_ENTRY ListHead,
                                        IN PKSPIN_LOCK Lock);
```

This function removes the head entry from the specified *ListHead*, using *Lock* for synchronization. If the list is empty, this function returns NULL.

Now you may observe that a LIST_ENTRY is actually a pretty boring structure. It has a forward pointer and a backward pointer, and, well, nothing else. This makes it not terribly interesting because it contains no information (and for that matter, no place to put any!). A common way to use a LIST_ENTRY structure is to include it as the first element of some other structure.

```
typedef struct _moreInteresting {
    LIST_ENTRY list;
    ULONG stuff;
    ULONG moreStuff;
    // ...
    } moreInteresting, * PmoreInteresting;
```

Because of how C allocates structures, you can now cast any `PmoreInteresting` pointer to a `PLIST_ENTRY` and add it to a list of your choice. When you remove it from the list, you recast it to a `PmoreInteresting` structure. Thus we can rewrite our earlier example to be more interesting, as follows.

```
PmoreInteresting newListEntry = ...; // Creates a new entry
PmoreInteresting oldhead =
            (PmoreInteresting) ExInterlockedInsertTailList(
                                        &extension->listHead,
                                        (PLIST_ENTRY)newListEntry,
                                        &extension->listLock);
// ...
PmoreInteresting next =
            (PmoreInteresting)ExInterlockedRemoveHeadList(
                                        &extension->listHead,
                                        &extension->listLock);
```

For queueing IRPs, a `LIST_ENTRY` field is defined as part of the public part of the IRP structure, as `Tail.Overlay.ListEntry`, and you can access it by writing something like the following.

```
PLIST_ENTRY result = ExInterlockedInsertTailList(&extension->listHead,
                                        &Irp->Tail.Overlay.ListEntry,
                                        &extension->listLock);
```

The sort of structure that is created by linking IRPs is shown in Figure 22.1. Note the oddity that the `LIST_ENTRY` field in the IRP is *not* at the beginning, as we suggested in our earlier example. So given a pointer to a `LIST_ENTRY`, how do you derive the actual IRP address from it?

Microsoft solves this by providing a macro called `CONTAINING_RECORD`. This macro takes a pointer, the name of the structure, and the description of the field and returns the address of the actual start of the record. The definition is

```
#define CONTAINING_RECORD(address, type, field)
```

where *address* is the pointer to the `LIST_ENTRY`, *type* is the type of the structure, and *field* is the description of the field. The result is a *type* * value. For an IRP, the `LIST_ENTRY` within an IRP is the field `Tail.Overlay.ListEntry`, and that is what you provide for this argument.

```
PIRP Irp = CONTAINING_RECORD(
            listEntry,
            IRP,
            Tail.Overlay.ListEntry);
```

The use of this macro is also illustrated in Figure 22.1.

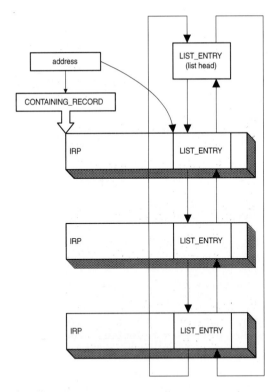

Figure 22.1: *A Driver-Managed Queue of IRPs.*

The Device Queue

Another type of queue is the Device Queue. There are higher-level operations available for the Device Queue than those of Table 22.1. With a Device Queue, the IRPs might be added to the queue with a sort key (much like the `StartIo` queue) that can be used to manage priorities within each dequeueing operation. These operations are summarized in Table 22.2. These are the operations that are used to implement the `StartIo` queue.

Table 22.2: *Device Queue Operations*

Function	Use
KeInitializeDeviceQueue	Initializes a Device Queue head, including its Spin Lock and busy state.
KeInsertDeviceQueue	Inserts a queue entry at the tail of a busy Device Queue.
KeInsertByKeyDeviceQueue	Inserts a queue entry in the Device Queue at a position determined by a sort key.
KeRemoveDeviceQueue	Removes a queue entry from the head of the Device Queue.
KeRemoveByKeyDeviceQueue	Removes a queue entry from within the Device Queue.
KeRemoveEntryDeviceQueue	Removes an arbitrary entry from within the Device Queue.

The insertion and deletion of entries in Device Queues is controlled by a Spin Lock that is part of the KDEVICE_QUEUE structure. When you are using a Device Queue to implement IRP queues, there is a special field inside the IRP that is used to represent a KDEVICE_QUEUE_ENTRY.

To use a Device Queue, you must declare storage for a DEVICE_QUEUE object, which is the header for the structure. This object also contains a Spin Lock and some additional state:

```
VOID KeInitializeDeviceQueue(IN PKDEVICE_QUEUE DeviceQueue)
```

For most Device Queues you will manage, you will declare this in the Device Extension:

```
KDEVICE_QUEUE myQueue;
```

and initialize it as follows:

```
KeInitializeDeviceQueue(&extension->myQueue);
```

An entry, usually an IRP, is added to the queue by calling KeInsertDeviceQueue or KeInsertByKeyDeviceQueue.

```
BOOLEAN KeInsertDeviceQueue(IN PKDEVICE_QUEUE DeviceQueue,
                            IN PKDEVICE_QUEUE_ENTRY DeviceQueueEntry);

BOOLEAN KeInsertByKeyDeviceQueue(IN PKDEVICE_QUEUE DeviceQueue,
                                 IN PKDEVICE_QUEUE_ENTRY DeviceQueueEntry,
                                 IN ULONG SortKey);
```

These two functions behave in an identical, apparently idiosyncratic, but in fact quite useful fashion, with the exception of the *SortKey* in the second one. KeInsertDeviceQueue queues the entry to the tail of the Device Queue. KeInsertByKeyDeviceQueue positions the new entry in the Device Queue *after* any entries in the queue with *SortKey* values less than or equal to its *SortKey* value and preceding any entries with *SortKey* values that are greater. This seems to suggest that the order is FIFO within equal sort keys, but this is not explicitly stated.

The apparent oddity of these functions is *if the queue is empty and not in the busy state, the entry is not inserted and the function returns* FALSE. This seems at first sight to be rather strange (especially because we haven't yet said what "busy state" means—but keep reading!). But in fact it is *exactly* the behavior you want. If there is nothing in the queue, you can initiate the I/O operation yourself by calling your equivalent of StartIo. You don't have to wait for the dequeueing, and in fact there is no mechanism that would do the dequeueing. However, the attempt to insert an entry into an empty queue *also* sets an internal state flag to the busy state. If you attempt to remove a queue entry from a "busy" queue and the queue is empty, the operation returns a NULL pointer and the queue is set to a nonbusy state. Note that this notion of "busy" refers to a *state of the queue* and not to the state of the Spin Lock that controls access to the queue.

The way you use this is as follows. The first time you attempt to queue an entry on an empty queue, the operation fails because the queue is empty. The queue becomes "busy". So you call your equivalent of StartIo to start the I/O transaction. While the I/O transaction is underway— for example, the device is waiting for the actual data transfer to complete—another call is made to one of your Dispatch Routines. This time, when you attempt to queue the operation, the queue is in its "busy" state, so the operation succeeds and the queueing operation returns TRUE. At this point, you do *not* attempt to call your StartIo equivalent; rather, you simply return from your Dispatch Routine.

When you are using the Device Queue to handle IRPs, the following field within the IRP can be used:

```
KeInsertDeviceQueue(myDeviceQueue, &Irp->Tail.Overlay.DeviceQueueEntry);
```

You dequeue a Device Queue entry using one of the dequeueing functions. Suppose, for example, you are using these functions to manage an IRP queue. When your device has interrupted, dispatched to its DPC Routine, and completed processing of the current IRP, it calls one of the following dequeueing functions.

```
PKDEVICE_QUEUE_ENTRY KeRemoveDeviceQueue(
                    IN PKDEVICE_QUEUE DeviceQueue);
PKDEVICE_QUEUE_ENTRY KeRemoveByKeyDeviceQueue(
                    IN PKDEVICE_QUEUE DeviceQueue,
                    IN ULONG SortKey);

BOOLEAN KeRemoveEntryDeviceQueue(
                    IN PKDEVICE_QUEUE DeviceQueue,
                    IN PKDEVICE_QUEUE_ENTRY DeviceQueueEntry);
```

These three functions perform quite similar tasks.

- KeRemoveDeviceQueue

    This function removes a queue entry from the head of the queue. If the queue is busy but empty, the function returns NULL. The documentation states that it is "an error" to call KeRemoveDeviceQueue if the queue is empty but not busy. However, it does not hint or suggest what happens in this case. Does it simply return NULL? Does it crash in some strange way? Does it generate its own specific Blue Screen of Death? Inquiring Readers Need To Know, but all we get is "no comment" from the documentation. If the queue is busy but empty, the function also sets the state of the queue to "not-busy". This function must run at IRQL == DISPATCH_LEVEL.

- KeRemoveByKeyDeviceQueue

    This function behaves just like KeRemoveDeviceQueue regarding the side effects of dequeueing (including the statement that it is an error to operate on an empty, not-busy queue). However, the queue entry that is returned is "the position in the *DeviceQueue* from which the entry is to be removed". Exactly what happens if there *is* no matching queue entry is left to the imagination. This function must run at IRQL == DISPATCH_LEVEL.

- KeRemoveEntryDeviceQueue

    This function differs a bit in behavior from the previous two. It takes a pointer to a specific *DeviceQueueEntry* and simply removes it from the queue that contains it. If this happens to make the queue empty, no changes are made to the busy state. Furthermore, this function can be executed at any IRQL <= DISPATCH_LEVEL. If the level is lower than DISPATCH_LEVEL, it is raised to DISPATCH_LEVEL, the Spin Lock is acquired, the removal takes place, and the IRQL is returned to its original value. If the *DeviceQueueEntry* is *not* in the specified *DeviceQueue*, it is not removed and the function returns FALSE; otherwise, it is removed and the function returns TRUE. This function is particularly useful when you have to implement a Cancel Routine that removes entries from the queue (or removes *some* entries from the queue). Cancel functions often do their processing at PASSIVE_LEVEL; hence you need to raise the IRQL to DISPATCH_LEVEL to avoid preemption by the scheduler.

These functions are the primitives out of which the `StartIo` queueing is built. We show in the example starting on page 458 that we can use these functions (in particular, `KeRemoveEntryDeviceQueue`) to remove an IRP from the `StartIo` queue. When used by `StartIo`, or if you use them yourself directly, there is a `KDEVICE_QUEUE_ENTRY` in the IRP that is used to build the IRP queue.

A Substitute for `StartIo`

There are times the simple `StartIo` technique for queuing is insufficient, for example if you have a *full-duplex* driver. The driver must perform I/O operations concurrently, if both input and output operations have been queued. If you used `StartIo` and completed an operation, the `StartIo` model would give you the next IRP to start. This IRP might be either an input or an output operation. So you need to get the next input operation when you finish an input operation and an output operation when you finish an output operation, keeping both the input and output portions of your device busy. You have no way to do this with `StartIo`.

However, you can do this with one of the Driver-Managed Queue techniques, either your own queueing using the operations of Table 22.1 or the Device Queue operations of Table 22.2. Since the driver controls the queuing, it can maintain two (or even more) queues of IRPs. For a full-duplex driver, there would be two queues: one containing the input operations and the other containing the output operations. The Dispatch Routine will inspect each IRP and queue it to the appropriate queue. The queuing is less automatic. The Dispatch Routine must look at the queuing operation, and if the queue was empty before you inserted a packet, the Dispatch Routine must start the output operation. By this, we mean the Dispatch Routine will directly call the I/O function if the queue was empty. The I/O function is the equivalent of the `StartIo` routine in a driver using `StartIo` queuing.

In the DPC Routine, the driver must dequeue the next IRP from the appropriate queue and start the I/O Routine. Again, this means that the driver will call your output function directly.

A Multiqueue Device

The classic example of the need for a multiqueue device is the full-duplex device, such as a serial port or sound card, that needs to support independent input and output streams on a single device. However, the multiqueue technique is not limited to full-duplex devices, and we have deliberately chosen an example that is *not* a full-duplex device.

For purposes of this example, we postulate a device that has two *output* streams that it manages. One output stream delivers short packets to one of the device channels, and the other delivers very large packets to the other device channel. There is no interdependency between these two channels and hence no need to maintain a FIFO order of short and long packets. There are two ways for selecting to which channel the output goes.

1. Use separate IOCTLs to send requests to each output channel.
2. Use the packet size as a discriminant.

Exactly which way is chosen depends on the needs of the application and the device. In this case, the old version 1.0 board had only one channel. This led to performance problems because the packets were handled only in FIFO order, thus delaying the short packets unduly when long packets were being transmitted. The version 2.0 board has two channels, but we postulate an application that isn't supposed to know this. Therefore the application code works only with a single IOCTL ("Write Data"), while the new, version 2.0 driver needs to support the older applications. So we choose the second alternative and discriminate on packet size.

In this driver, we use two device-managed queues and we do not use StartIo at all.

In the following examples, much of the code is the conventional boilerplate that we've shown many times elsewhere in the book. So we include only those parts that are significant for the example.

To simplify the discussion, we assume that the two channels use disjoint register sets in the hardware and thus that modifying the registers for one channel will not cause problems for the other channel. This is particularly important if the ISR could be modifying registers in response to the "long buffer" channel when a request for the "short buffer" channel was dequeued. If we don't make this assumption, we must create a Controller Object to do the necessary synchronization between the two channels using the same hardware. Likewise, we assume that a SynchCritSection is not required to synchronize between the start functions and the ISR. Both of these additional features might be required in an actual driver, but they would only lend undue complications and mask the point this example is trying to make.

The Device Extension has the queue-management structures for the two queues. These are defined as type QUEUE_INFO and contain the list head for the queue, the lock to synchronize access, a Boolean value indicating if any I/O is active, and a pointer to the current IRP if one is active. In addition, a Boolean value, isLong, is used to indicate which of the two queues this entry represents. Because we can't pass an arbitrary context into a Cancel Routine, we store a pointer to the appropriate short-queue or long-queue Cancel Routine as shown in Listing 22.3.

Listing 22.3: *The Device Extension for the Multiqueue Device*

```
typedef struct _QUEUE_INFO {
    LIST_ENTRY ListHead;
    KSPIN_LOCK Lock;
    BOOLEAN IoActive;
    PIRP CurrentIrp;
    BOOLEAN isLong;
    PDRIVER_CANCEL CancelRoutine;
} QUEUE_INFO, * PQUEUE_INFO;

typedef struct _DBLQ_EXTENSION {
    PDEVICE_OBJECT DeviceObject;
    // ... Other common information
    QUEUE_INFO longQueue;
    QUEUE_INFO shortQueue;
} DBLQ_EXTENSION, * PDBLQ_EXTENSION;
```

Listing 22.4: DriverEntry *for a Multiqueue Device*

```
NTSTATUS DriverEntry(...)
{
    PDEVICE_OBJECT deviceObject;
    NTSTATUS status;
    ...
    ...
    status = IoCreateDevice( ..., &deviceObject);
    ...
```

```
        DriverObject->MajorFunction[IRP_MJ_DEVICE_CONTROL] =
                                        dblQDeviceControl; // Page 448

        ntStatus = IoConnectInterrupt(&extension->InterruptObject,
                                dblQInterruptService, // Page 452
                                deviceObject,         // ISR Context
                                NULL,
                                extension->Vector,
                                extension->Irql,
                                extension->Irql,
                                extension->InterruptMode,
                                extension->SharableVector,
                                extension->ProcessorMask,
                                extension->SaveFloatState);

        IoInitializeDpcRequest(deviceObject, dblQDPC); // Page 453

        InitializeListHead(&extension->longQueue.ListHead);
        KeInitializeSpinLock(&extension->longQueue.Lock);
        extension->longQueue.IoActive = FALSE;
        extension->longQueue.isLong = TRUE;
        extension->longQueue.CancelRoutine = dblQCancelLong;  // Page 450

        InitializeListHead(&extension->shortQueue.ListHead);
        KeInitializeSpinLock(&extension->shortQueue.Lock);
        extension->shortQueue.IoActive = FALSE;
        extension->shortQueue.isLong = FALSE;
        extension->shortQueue.CancelRoutine = dblQCancelShort; // Page 450

        ...
        return status;
    }
```

We initialize the MajorFunction pointer for DeviceIoControl (the other
MajorFunction initializations are not shown), connect the interrupt, and initialize the queue-
management blocks for the "short item" and "long item" queues.

Listing 22.5: IRP_MJ_DEVICE_CONTROL *Handler for Multiqueue Device*

```
NTSTATUS dblQDeviceControl(IN PDEVICE_OBJECT DeviceObject,
                        IN PIRP Irp)
{
    NTSTATUS status = STATUS_SUCCESS;
    PIO_STACK_LOCATION stack = IoGetCurrentIrpStackLocation(Irp);
    UCHAR * pBuffer  = (UCHAR *)Irp->AssociatedIrp.SystemBuffer;
                // Buffered I/O
    ULONG outBufferLength =
            stack->Parameters.DeviceIoControl.OutputBufferLength;
    ULONG inBufferLength =
            stack->Parameters.DeviceIoControl.InputBufferLength;
```

This is all fairly standard for an IRP_MJ_DEVICE_CONTROL *handler. Next, we declare
some variables that are specific to this handler.*

```
    BOOLEAN previousActive;
    PLIST_ENTRY resultList;
    PQUEUE_INFO queue;
```

```
        .
        .
    switch(stack->Parameters.DeviceIoControl.IoControlCode)
        { /* ioControlCode */
          case IOCTL_DBLQ_INITIALIZE:
                  // ...

                  break;
          case IOCTL_DBLQ_OUTPUT:
```

We cannot complete the IRP in this handler, so the first thing we do here is mark it as pending. Then we look at the output buffer length and determine if this is a short-message item or a long-message item. Depending on the buffer length, we enqueue it in one of our two queues. We also establish a Cancel Routine so that if the IRP is cancelled, we can remove it from its queue. If the queue is empty when we perform the insertion, `ExInterlockedInsertTailList` *will return* NULL. *In this case, either the device is idle, in which case we need to start the first packet, or the device is in the midst of processing a previous IRP that has been already removed from the queue, in which case we can't start a new one. To determine the state of processing, we set a flag. Now we have a problem: We can't test the flag and set it as an atomic operation unless we somehow lock out other processors in a multiprocessor system. To handle this, we use the* `InterlockedExchange` *function, which sets the variable to a specific value and returns its previous setting.*

```
                IoMarkIrpPending(Irp);
                if ( outBufferLength <= SHORT_QUEUE_SIZE_LIMIT)
                   queue = &extension->shortQueue;
                else
                   queue = &extension->longQueue;

                IoSetCancelRoutine(Irp, queue->CancelRoutine)
                resultList = ExInterlockedInsertTailList(
                                        &queue->ListHead,
                                        &Irp->Tail.Overlay.ListEntry,
                                        &queue->Lock);

                if (NULL == resultList)
                    { * list empty */
                    // List was empty -- if not active, start I/O
                    // operation here
                    previousActive =  InterlockedExchange(&queue->IoActive,
                                                          (LONG)TRUE);

                    if (!previousActive)
                        dblQStartNext(deviceObject, queue);
                    } /* list empty */
                status = STATUS_PENDING;
                break;
          case ...

          default:
                  status = STATUS_UNSUCCESSFUL;
                  break;
        } /* ioControlCode */
        .
        .
        .
    return status;
}
```

Listing 22.6: *Cancel Support for Multiqueue Driver*

```
//-------------------------------
void dblQCancelShort(IN PDEVICE_OBJECT DeviceObject, IN PIRP Irp)
    {
     dblQCancel( DeviceObject, Irp, &DeviceObject->Extension->shortQueue);
    }
//-------------------------------
void dblQCancelLong(IN PMYDEVICE_OBJECT DeviceObject, IN PIRP Irp)
    {
     dblQCancel( DeviceObject, Irp, &DeviceObject->Extension->longQueue);
    }
//-------------------------------
void dblQCancel(IN PDEVICE_OBJECT DeviceObject,
                IN PIRP Irp,
                PQUEUE_INFO queue)
  {
  KIRQL previousIRQL;
  PDBLQ_EXTENSION extension = DeviceObject->DeviceExtension;
  PIRP thisIRP;
  BOOLEAN  irpFound;
```

Because we are using Device-Managed Queueing, we do not need the global Cancel Spin Lock. We must release this lock when we are done using it, and consequently, because we never need it, we can release it here. The CancelIrql *field holds the necessary IRQL for the release.*

```
IoReleaseCancelSpinLock(Irp->CancelIrql);
```

Having released the global Cancel Spin Lock (and thereby allowing other cancels to proceed), we still must synchronize the access to our private queues. To do this, we lock the queue we are cancelling.

```
KeAcquireSpinLock(&queue->Lock, &previousIRQL);
```

If the IRP is the current IRP for its channel, the IRP is in the middle of being processed. Cancelling an IRP that is in the middle of being processed is risky, so we simply skip the Cancel request for the active IRP. Note that the cancel flag is set in the IRP, a condition we can test for in later processing.

```
if (Irp == queue->CurrentIrp)
   { /* current IRP */
    KeReleaseSpinLock( &queue->Lock, previousIRQL);
    return;
   } /* current IRP */
```

*The IRP is not current, so we can cancel it. To do so, we search the queue to find the entry that represents it. We walk the list following its forward link (*Flink*), continuing until either we find the matching list entry or we end up back at the list head. If the loop terminates, we set the* irpFound *flag to indicate the cause of the termination.*

```
{ /* find entry */
 PLIST_ENTRY thisOne = queue->listHead->Flink;
 while ((thisOne != &Irp->Tail.Overlay.ListEntry)
         && (thisOne != &queue->listHead))
    { /* scan list */
      thisOne = thisOne->Flink;
    } /* scan list */
    irpFound =  (thisOne != &Irp->Tail.Overlay.ListEntry);

} /* find entry */
```

*If we find the list entry, we remove it from the queue. Then, we must clear the Cancel
Routine by calling* IoSetCancelRoutine *with a* NULL *parameter (otherwise, we can
get into serious trouble). We set the* IoStatus.Status *flag to indicate that the request
has been cancelled. We then mark the IRP as being completed.*

```
if (irpFound)
   { /* cancel it */
     RemoveEntryList(thisOne);
     IoSetCancelRoutine (Irp, NULL);

     Irp->IoStatus.Status = STATUS_CANCELLED;
     Irp->IoStatus.Information = 0;
     IoCompleteRequest(Irp, IO_NO_INCREMENT);
   } /* cancel it */
 KeReleaseSpinLock(&queue->Lock, previousIRQL);
}
```

Listing 22.7: *Device Start Routines for Multiqueue Driver*

```
void dblQStartNext(PDEVICE_OBJECT DeviceObject,
                   PQUEUE_INFO queue)
  {
   BOOLEAN previousActive;
   PLIST_ENTRY currentEntry;
   PDBLQ_EXTENSION extension =
              (PDBLQ_EXTENSION)DeviceObject->DeviceExtension;
   Irp = NULL;
```

*We can now remove the element from the head of the queue. We try to do so. If the list
is empty, we set the queue's* IoActive *flag to* FALSE *to indicate that there is no more
activity on this channel. Otherwise, we set the* IoActive *flag to* TRUE *and initiate the
processing of the IRP.*

```
   currentEntry = ExInterlockedRemoveHeadList( &queue->ListHead,
                                               &queue->Lock);

 if (NULL != currentEntry)
    { /* dequeued IRP */
      previousActive = InterlockedExchange( &queue->IoActive, (LONG)TRUE);
      currentIrp =
          CONTAINING_RECORD(currentEntry, IRP, Tail.Overlay.ListEntry);
    } /* dequeued IRP */
 else
    { /* list now empty */
```

```
      previousActive = InterlockedExchange( &queue->IoActive, (LONG)FALSE);
      return;
   } /* list now empty */
```

We now have the IRP. We have marked the channel as being active. At this point, we can do whatever is required to initiate the IRP on the channel; typically we tweak various hardware registers. Recall that we have made the assumption that the registers for the two channels are disjoint. Otherwise, we would have to use a Controller Object to synchronize the access to the device registers.

```
queue->CurrentIrp = Irp;

if (Irp->Cancel)
   {
      Irp->IoStatus.Status = STATUS_CANCELLED;
      Irp->IoStatus.Information = 0;
      IoCompleteRequest( Irp, IO_NO_INCREMENT );
      Irp = NULL;
   }
else
   {
      IoSetCancelRoutine(Irp, NULL);
      //
      // Start the operation on the hardware
      //
      ...
      ...
      ...

   }
}
```

Listing 22.8: *ISR for Multiqueue Driver*

```
BOOLEAN dblQInterruptService(IN PKINTERRUPT Interrupt,
                             IN PVOID Context )
   {
      PDEVICE_OBJECT deviceObject = (PDEVICE_OBJECT) Context;
      PDBLQ_EXTENSION extension = deviceObject->DeviceExtension;
```

In the following conditional, we perform whatever test will tell us whether the interrupt is ours. If this test fails, we immediately return FALSE so that the interrupt can be passed on to other devices on the DIRQL chain.

```
   if (!whatever)
      { /* not from this device */
       return FALSE
      } /* not from this device */
```

Having determined that the interrupt is indeed from our device, we must clear the condition that caused the interrupt. (Otherwise, we'll end up either in an infinite loop or doing something disastrous that will crash the hardware, the driver, or the entire machine.)

```
.... // Clear interrupt condition
```

We are now prepared to queue the DPC to handle this interrupt. Both the short-packet channel and the long-packet channel interrupt on the same DIRQL, so we have to sort out which one actually caused the interrupt. Having done that, we queue up the DPC with either a TRUE (long packet) or FALSE (short packet) parameter. This demonstrates the use of the user-supplied parameters for the DPC. Alternatively, we could have chosen not to use the DpcForIsr *and explicitly queued up either of two DPCs to handle the request. Because the request handing is virtually identical, we use the* DpcForIsr *mechanism.*

```
if ( ...interrupt from long-packet channel... )
    { /* long */
      IoRequestDpc(deviceObject,
                   extension->longQueue.CurrentIrp,
                   &extension->longQueue);
    } /* long */
else
    { /* short */
      IoRequestDpc(deviceObject,
                   extension->shortQueue.CurrentIrp,
                   &extension->shortQueue);
    } /* short */
```

Since we have actually handled this interrupt, we return TRUE *to tell the interrupt dispatch code that it does not need to call other handlers that follow in the chain.*

```
 return TRUE;
}
```

Listing 22.9: *DPC Handler for Multiqueue Driver*

```
VOID dblQDPC(IN PKDPC Dpc,
             IN PDEVICE_OBJECT DeviceObject,
             IN PIRP Irp,
             IN PVOID Context)
 {
  PQUEUE_INFO queue = (PQUEUE_INFO)Context;
  NTSTATUS status = STATUS_SUCCESS;
```

At this point, we do whatever processing is required to handle the IRP, such as copying data back to its result buffer or determining what status code is to be set for completion. This might involve reading information from the device. Note that if any of the device registers are shared between the long-packet and short-packet channels, we would have to use KeSynchronizeExecution *to guarantee that the DPC could complete for one channel without interfering with, or being interfered with by, the ISR for the other channel. Since we use a common processing routine, we use the* Context *parameter, which is a pointer to the appropriate queue entry information in the extension, to determine which type of packet we need to process.*

```
if (queue->isLong)
   {
     // Long packet interrupt

     // Handle hardware for long packet
     ...
     ...
   }
else
   {
     // Short packet interrupt

     // Handle hardware for low packet
     ...
     ...
   }

//
// Complete the interrupting packet
//
Irp->IoStatus.Status = status;
Irp->IoStatus.Information = ...  ;   // Size of data
                                     // returned to application
IoCompleteRequest( Irp, IO_NO_INCREMENT );
queue->CurrentIrp = NULL;
```

We have completed this IRP and now need to initiate the next IRP. Since this is a Device-Managed Queue, we do not use IoStartNextPacket. *Instead, we call our own queue-management handler. Since the address of the queue info block has been passed in, and that is what is required to start the next entry, we simply pass it on to our own Start Routine.*

```
   dblQStartNext(DeviceObject, queue); // Page 451
}
```

Nonexclusive Devices

With a nonexclusive device, you have an additional type of concurrency. Each IRP might refer to a different file handle, and each file handle might be opened by different applications. In such cases, you might have to maintain additional state on a per-handle basis. This is handled by creating your own data structure to represent each file handle's state. One of the elements (usually the first element, for convenience) of this structure is a LIST_ENTRY structure so that it can be chained onto a list. In your Device Extension, you allocate a LIST_ENTRY that is the head of this list and initialize it during DriverEntry. We call this the *Open Handle List*.

On a CreateFile operation, you create, in your IRP_MJ_CREATE handler, a new instance of this per-handle structure and enqueue it on the Open Handle List. On a CloseHandle operation that deletes the last instance of that handle (and thus calls your IRP_MJ_CLOSE routine), you find this entry and remove it. You determine the file handle that is associated with the IRP by looking in the current IRP stack entry for the FileObject pointer. This pointer is assigned by the I/O Manager when a file is created. It is established before the IRP_MJ_CREATE routine is called and remains valid and unique until the File Manager regains control after the IRP_MJ_CLOSE routine. When you create your per-handle context structure, you store the FileObject pointer in it. To locate the appropriate structure for a given IRP, you obtain the FileObject pointer and walk down the list you have constructed until you find the entry whose stored `FileObject` pointer matches. Remember that you will have to provide a Spin Lock so that you can safely access this list of devices. This is because operations (including `CreateFile` and `CloseHandle`) can be taking place on concurrent processors in a multiprocessor environment.

Cancelling an I/O Request

Any time there are operations happening asynchronously, pending operations must be cancelled. If the application program is using asynchronous I/O, it is fairly easy to have many outstanding I/O requests pending, and the application may at any time call the `CancelIo` API function. Alternatively, when the application process is terminated, the I/O rundown will cause the I/O Manager to generate a series of Cancel requests for any pending I/O operations. For each IRP that is cancelled, the I/O Manager may call a Cancel function, if one has been established. The pointer to the Cancel function is stored in a field of the IRP. The driver sets this field (with `IoSetCancelRoutine`) to the routine to be called to cancel this IRP. Generally, you will want to remove the IRP from the queue it is in and complete it with an appropriate error indication (`STATUS_CANCELLED`, in fact). We can set a different Cancel Routine for each phase of operation within the driver, since the current phase of operation of the IRP will determine what we must do to cancel the IRP.

Before an IRP is completed, the Cancel Routine must be set to `NULL` using `IoSetCancelRoutine`.

Generally, there is one exception to cancelling an IRP. The *current* IRP is seldom cancelled because it is assumed that the I/O operation will be completed in a "short" time. Typically, once an IRP is dequeued for processing, its Cancel Routine is set to `NULL`. The reason is that the IRP, being current, is already into execution. Thus it has already modified the device registers in some important way to initiate the I/O transaction. DMA could be underway. Hydraulic arms could be moving. In almost all real devices, it is easier to let the pending I/O operation complete normally than to try to stop it in the middle. If you *do* have a device for which this is desirable, make sure that it is *possible*. Not all devices react well to having their state changed abruptly in the middle of a transaction. And if you are in any way responsible for the design or feedback to the designers of a device that requires the cancelling of the current I/O operation, be certain the device has well-specified ways to cleanly terminate.[2]

When the I/O operation will involve a long delay in processing, you should enable the operation to allow the system to terminate even the current operation. The system will cancel the I/O operation when the thread is terminated. If the user kills the thread or shuts down the system, the thread termination cannot complete until the I/O completes. If the I/O operation will take more than a few seconds, consider providing a Cancel Routine to terminate the operation. This might involve complex synchronization with the IRP processing for the IRP that is currently being processed. We show a simple example of this in Chapter 24, in Listing 24.11.

---

[2] Over the years, I've known a lot of robotics people. One infamous hydraulic arm I was told about had the property that the "terminate" command, for "safety" reasons, released all hydraulic pressure. This sounded to the engineers like a Good Idea. Unfortunately, the arm was very heavy and when all pressure was released, it fell downwards, smashing itself on the floor and damaging its "hand". It turns out that the engineers assumed that this command would be given only when the arm was properly "docked". Think *very* carefully about such designs and their implications. And as a Device Driver writer, try to find out what the designer *really* meant. *–jmn*

Some devices, particularly those that require long intervals to complete IRPs, might require that you be able to cancel an IRP that is being actively processed. In this case, you can do one of two things.

- Set up special Cancel Routines that reflect the proper cancellation actions required at each step of the processing.

- Leave the Cancel Routine set to NULL and at various points in the (lengthy) processing, check to see if `Irp->Cancel` is TRUE, and if so, take the appropriate action for the device.

Generally, an IRP that is being processed will complete within a few milliseconds, or tens of milliseconds. Thus cancelling it involves a lot of work and complexity for very little gain. For devices for which this is not true, the gain might justify the complexity.

The Cancel Spin Lock is a lock on the system queue of pending IRPs. You must hold the lock whenever you change the Cancel Routine assigned to an IRP. This is to prevent the I/O Manager from dequeueing an IRP we are in the process of modifying.

The Cancel Routine first will confirm that the IRP can be cancelled and is owned by the driver.

- If the IRP cannot be cancelled or is not owned by the driver, the driver should release the Cancel Spin Lock and return.

- If the IRP can be cancelled, the driver should do the following.

  •Remove the IRP from any internal queues.

  •Terminate any processing of the IRP.

  •Set the Cancel Routine to NULL (by calling `IoSetCancelRoutine`).

  •Release the Cancel Spin Lock.

  •Set the `Irp->IoStatus.Information` field to 0 and the `.Status` field to STATUS_CANCELLED.

  •Call `IoCompleteRequest` to complete the IRP.

Cancel and Layered Drivers

When a layered driver calls a lower-level driver and passes an IRP to it, the upper-level driver no longer "owns" the IRP and must have set the IRP's Cancel routine to NULL before it calls `IoCallDriver`. The upper-level driver can request that notification of the cancellation of IRPs be sent to lower-level drivers. It does this by calling the `IoSetCompletionRoutine` function with the *InvokeOnCancel* parameter set to TRUE before it calls `IoCallDriver` to pass the IRP to lower-level drivers.

An upper-level driver can cancel IRPs it has allocated by calling `IoCancelIrp`. This should be called only with IRPs allocated by the caller.

The Cancel Routine

The driver's Cancel routines will have the following form.

```
VOID (*PDRIVER_CANCEL) (IN PDEVICE_OBJECT DeviceObject,
                        IN PIRP Irp);
```

A Cancel routine is called with the Cancel Spin Lock held and at IRQL == DISPATCH_LEVEL. The Cancel Routine must release the Cancel Spin Lock before it returns control.

Cancel Routine and Cancel Spin Lock

The following functions are used to manage the Cancel Routine and the Cancel Spin Lock.

IoSetCancelRoutine

```
PDRIVER_CANCEL IoSetCancelRoutine(IN PIRP Irp,
                                  IN PDRIVER_CANCEL CancelRoutine);
```

The IoSetCancelRoutine function sets up or disables a driver-supplied Cancel Routine, which will be called if a given IRP is cancelled. If the driver uses system IRP queuing, the driver must hold the Cancel Spin Lock when calling this routine.

IoAcquireCancelSpinLock

```
VOID IoAcquireCancelSpinLock(OUT PKIRQL Irql);
```

The IoAcquireCancelSpinLock function acquires the Cancel Spin Lock.

IoReleaseCancelSpinLock

```
VOID IoReleaseCancelSpinLock(IN KIRQL Irql);
```

The IoReleaseCancelSpinLock function releases the Cancel Spin Lock. You must call this function as quickly as possible after your Cancel routine is called. You must not call it before you have completed operations on the StartIo queue. You should call it immediately if you are managing your own queues and do not need the StartIo queue synchronization.

IoCancelIrp

```
BOOLEAN IoCancelIrp(IN PIRP Irp);
```

The IoCancelIrp function sets the *cancel bit* in a given IRP and calls the Cancel Routine for the IRP if there is one. It returns TRUE if the IRP was cancelled and FALSE if the IRP's cancel bit was set but the IRP was not cancellable.

Cancelling IRPs Managed by StartIo

The Cancel Routine in Listing 22.10 assumes that the desired action of cancelling the *current* IRP is to simply let it complete, but it cancels the IRP it is handed as long as that IRP isn't the current one. This cancels all IRPs on the StartIo queue. It is assumed that there is some other mechanism to cancel IRPs that have not yet entered the StartIo queue. We discuss this code in more detail after the listing. When you use a StartIo-managed queue, there is a field in the Device Object, CurrentIrp, that is set by the IoStartPacket or IoStartNextPacket operation to point to the current IRP.

Listing 22.10: *A Cancel Routine for* `StartIo`-*Managed Queue*

```
void myDriverCancelRequest(PDEVICE_OBJECT DeviceObject, PIRP Irp)
    {
    // Is this IRP the current IRP?
    if(Irp == DeviceObject->CurrentIrp)
        { /* current IRP */
        IoReleaseCancelSpinLock(Irp->CancelIrql);
        } /* current IRP */
    else
        { /* not current */
        KeRemoveEntryDeviceQueue(
                            &DeviceObject->DeviceQueue,
                            &Irp->Tail.Overlay.DeviceQueueEntry);
        Irp->IoStatus.Status = STATUS_CANCELLED;
        Irp->IoStatus.Information = 0;

        IoReleaseCancelSpinLock(Irp->CancelIrql);

        IoCompleteRequest(Irp, IO_NO_INCREMENT);
        } /* not current */
    }
```

Cancelling is a rare but perilous action. Consequently, *all* Cancel operations are serialized through a *single, system-wide Spin Lock*. Since the system does not know what style of queueing you are using, the Cancel Spin Lock is *always* set when the Cancel Routine is called. If you are doing your own queueing with interlocked queues, you still must release it.

The following example uses the `StartIo` queue, which is managed by the lower-level `Ke...DeviceQueue` functions. (These functions are lower-level that the `IoStartPacket`/`IoStartNextPacket` but still higher level than the queue-management functions summarized in Table 22.1.) So we leave the Spin Lock in place until we have finished.

The first thing we do is check to see if the IRP that is passed in is the same as the `CurrentIrp` of the device. If it is, the IRP is active and we choose to let it complete. So we *don't* want to complete it. However, we *must* release that global Spin Lock. As with releasing most Spin Locks, we need to restore the IRQL that was active before the Spin Lock was set. Conveniently, the IRP that is being cancelled has been loaded with this value, in its `Irp->CancelIrql` field. So we call the function `IoReleaseCancelSpinLock` to release the global Spin Lock, passing in the IRQL value.

To remove the IRP from the `StartIo` queue, we call `KeRemoveEntryDeviceQueue` using the field `Tail.Overlay.DeviceQueueEntry`.

We have only two things left to do now: Release the Spin Lock, and complete the IRP. The order in which we do this is important, given how we have written the code. Since `IoReleaseCancelSpinLock` uses the `Irp->CancelIrql` field, the IRP must be valid at the time it is executed. However, once `IoCompleteRequest` is executed there is no guarantee that the IRP pointer is still value. So unless you copy this value to a temporary variable, you must release the Spin Lock before you complete the IRP.

Completing the IRP follows the standard model. That is, we set the status field to the appropriate status, in this case, `STATUS_CANCELLED`. Then we set the `Information` field to 0 to prevent anything being copied back to the application and call `IoCompleteRequest`, as shown in Listing 22.10.

Cancelling Device-Managed IRPs

A driver that maintains its own queueing of IRPs should provide a technique to remove a pending IRP in response to the driver's Cancel Routine being called.

Listing 22.11: *Cancel Routine for a Device-Managed Queue*

```
VOID CancelQueued(IN PDEVICE_OBJECT DeviceObject, IN PIRP Irp)
    //
    //  The Cancel Routine. Will remove the IRP from the queue and will
    //  complete it
    //  The Cancel Spin Lock is already acquired when this routine is called
    //
{
    KIRQL oldIrql ;

    //
    // Set the Cancel Routine pointer to NULL
    //
    IoSetCancelRoutine(Irp, NULL);
    IoReleaseCancelSpinLock(Irp->CancelIrql);

    //
    // Get the queue Spin Lock, remove the list entry, release the
    // Spin Lock
    //
    KeAcquireSpinLock(&extension->QueueLock, &oldIrql) ;

    RemoveEntryList(&Irp->Tail.Overlay.ListEntry);

    KeReleaseSpinLock (&extension->QueueLock, oldIrql) ;

    //
    // Set the return status
    //
    Irp->IoStatus.Status = STATUS_CANCELLED;
    Irp->IoStatus.Information = 0;

    IoCompleteRequest(Irp, IO_NO_INCREMENT);
    return;
}
```

Summary

This chapter has covered the key ideas of serialization within the driver, including the `StartIo` queue and Device-Managed Queues. We covered the ideas of how to create, enqueue, and dequeue requests from these queues. Note that not all drivers will do queueing using these techniques; some drivers manage their queues by using *Driver Threads*, the topic of Chapter 24. We also covered the basic ideas involved in cancelling a request. Cancelling a request that is being processed requires additional, device-specific care.

23 *Layered Drivers*

NT supports a notion of drivers that fits into a functional hierarchy. Some drivers have as their sole purpose in life the sending of data to a device and the receiving of data from that same device. Exactly what the data is, what it means, or how it affects the device are inconsequential to it. Other drivers worry greatly about the nature of the data and what it means but couldn't care less about how the data is actually read and written. NT has supported this delegation of labor since its inception, using a concept called *layered drivers*.

In Windows NT 4.0, layered drivers are a Good Idea. You can greatly simplify your life by taking advantage of either existing layered drivers or creating a set of layered drivers for your own device. Well, perhaps not simplify it in the short term, but certainly in the long term. Layered drivers are important not only because of their abstraction mechanism. You also can insert new layers in the hierarchy of layered drivers to create new and interesting effects. The most common example of this is the notion of introducing an encryption layer in a File System driver stack. But there are many other reasons to use layered drivers.

In Windows 2000, layered drivers are more than a Good Idea: They're The Law. Most drivers in 2000 are intrinsically layered drivers, even those we would think of as "monolithic drivers" in NT 4.0. A "monolithic" native 2000 driver would almost invariably talk to the application level at one end and to a suitably well-defined driver at the other end, in addition to talking to the hardware directly.

This chapter covers the key concepts and functions required to write a layered driver.

Layered Driver Architecture

A Device Driver can call other Device Drivers to complete an IRP. In the NT driver model, a Device Driver is passed an IRP specifying the I/O operation to be performed. The driver can complete the processing of the I/O request and pass the result back to the caller, or it can call a lower-level Device Driver to perform some of the work to complete the I/O request.

You can use this in your driver design to gain modularity and reusability in your driver code. In Windows NT, the File System is implemented as a higher-level driver. It calls lower-level drivers to do I/O to mass storage devices. In this case, there will be additional levels of drivers. An example is an I/O operation directed to a SCSI disk that will invoke the SCSI Disk Class

Driver, which in turn will call the SCSI Port Driver, which then invokes the SCSI Miniport Driver for the SCSI adapter.

You might want to divide the work supporting your device among several drivers. You can define a general interface for a class of devices and refine the interface with lower-level drivers to support specific hardware.

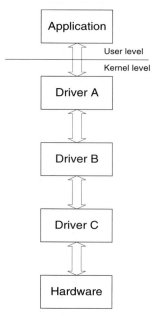

Figure 23.1: *Classic layered drivers.*

The use of driver layering is essential in Windows 2000 with the introduction of the WDM (Win32 Driver Model). A layered driver understands that it is part of a driver hierarchy. It knows which IRPs it can use to talk to its lower-level driver, and it specifies a set of IRPs it will accept from its higher-level driver or the application. An important distinction about a lower-level driver is that it *cannot* assume that it is being called in the thread context of the user-level code. A classic example of layered drivers is shown in Figure 23.1. Each driver defines the IRPs it will process, and the driver above it communicates to it using those IRPs. An intermediate-level or lowest-level driver may process IRP_MJ_INTERNAL_DEVICE_CONTROL IRPs. The IRP_MJ_DEVICE_CONTROL IRP can be sent by either the application or a higher-level driver.

Filter Drivers

A special form of layered driver is the *Filter Driver*. The Filter Driver is a driver that can be inserted into the driver hierarchy ahead of a preexisting driver. IRPs directed to the preexisting driver will be sent instead to the Filter Driver. It controls the processing of the IRP and can call other drivers as needed. It can process the IRP itself, returning the completed IRP directly to the caller, or it can pass the IRP to a lower-level driver, such as the original driver to which it was attached. It also might allow a lower-level driver to complete the IRP, returning to the caller, or set a Completion Routine to allow for further processing within it.

A classic illustration of a Filter Driver is shown in Figure 23.2.

A Filter Driver can perform any function, including the following.

- Do simple transformations of the data flowing through it. For example, a software encryption Filter Driver could be used to guarantee that no plaintext appeared on the physical drive.

- Do much more complex transformations, even calling other drivers to accomplish something not previously anticipated by the author of the original driver. For example, an encryption Filter Driver that calls another driver that interfaces to a hardware encryption device.

- Compensate for idiosyncratic or even defective hardware by performing operations that meet the higher-level specification while still conforming to whatever silliness the hardware has imposed.

- Correct for the different behavior of particular devices, adding commands to a sequence of commands or changing the commands.

- Monitor the activity of drivers and devices. The NT Disk Activity monitor is implemented by the use of a Filter Driver. This driver receives each IRP, notes the time it received it, and sets a completion routine. Within the completion routine, the elapsed time for each call is computed and passed to the performance monitor utility.

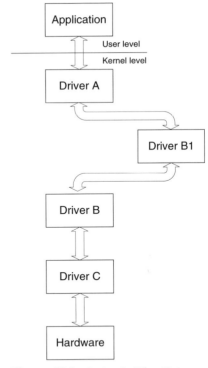

Figure 23.2: *A classic Filter Driver.*

The NT CdAudio driver is an example of the kind of Filter Driver that compensates for hardware differences. There are some differences between different models of CD-ROM drives in the processing of the audio operations. The driver checks each CD-ROM drive, determining if that drive requires special processing. If it does, the I/O operations are modified to accommodate the drive.

Another use of Filter Drivers is to perform I/O redirection.

A Filter Driver can be used for a device that has real-time constraints but that also talks to an existing interface, such as a serial port. In the Bad Old Days of MS-DOS, the application itself often managed the device, intercepting the interrupts and responding to the device. In NT, it might not be possible, due to preemptive multitasking, to guarantee that an application gets scheduled within the real-time window required by the device. (The responses in NT in such cases have been measured as being typically on the order of hundreds of milliseconds, 300 ms–500 ms, depending on processor speed, but occasionally extending to multiple seconds.) You can write a Filter Driver that opens the serial port to which the device is assigned (for example, by checking the Registry). The driver, having established a completion routine to be called when the IRP is completed, then sends an IRP_MJ_READ to the serial port driver. When data comes in on the serial port, the completion routine executes at elevated IRQL. This is because the completion routine will execute at the IRQL of the lower-level driver, and the serial driver will be completing its request in a DPC. If there is an IRP_MJ_READ pending from an application, the Filter Driver might choose to complete it. If not, the Filter Driver will have to figure out what it should do. For example, it can ignore the request, but meanwhile it can respond directly to the device to let it know someone cares (some devices can become very lonely and shut down unless they are reminded that someone cares).

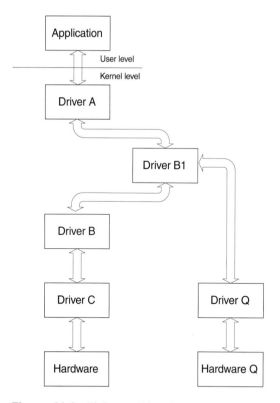

Figure 23.3: *Elaborate Filter Driver.*

The key technique for writing a Filter Driver is that the driver should appear to its caller as if it is the driver it is trying to imitate. Thus in Figure 23.2, the Filter Driver B1 should look exactly like Driver B. That is, it must implement all of the functionality of Driver B; otherwise, Driver A might malfunction in unexpected ways. Of course, one interesting idea of a Filter Driver is a driver that injects errors so that you can test the error recovery of the higher-level driver! But otherwise, you want a Filter Driver to emulate the lower-level driver. The calling driver won't know (or even suspect!) that it is calling not the driver it expects to call, but rather a Filter Driver that has interposed itself in the driver call hierarchy.

A Filter Driver is not restricted to working within the driver hierarchy. A more complex version is shown in Figure 23.3. In this driver, some requests might be passed down to Driver B, but others might be routed over to Driver Q, which talks to some entirely different piece of hardware. For example, a driver that implements some sort of elaborate encryption scheme might talk to a serial port that is linked to a key generator or other security-related device.

If you have ever done "interrupt chaining" in some other operating system (most notably, MS-DOS), you will find that this trick has been replaced in NT by the more systematic and elegant Filter Driver concept. It is true that interrupts are "chained" in NT, but that is for the purpose of distributing shared-IRQ interrupts to the drivers that might need to process them. Interrupt chaining was used in MS-DOS to provide for the insertion of Filter Drivers, usually in the form of a TSR (Terminate-and-Stay Resident) program.

You attach multiple Filter Drivers by requesting the same base driver. Thus, as shown in Figure 23.4, Driver B1 attaches itself to Driver B, but Driver B2 *also* attaches itself to Driver B, *not* to Driver B1! NT took care of chaining the Filter Drivers. A new Filter Driver will always be attached to the head of the chain of Filter Drivers that are attached to a base driver. Thus a Filter Driver does not need to know if there is already another Filter Driver attached to the base driver. Of course, there could be Bad Interactions between such drivers; the Filter Driver mechanism doesn't do anything to prevent that. But if the order in which the drivers are attached is critical, then when multiple Filter Drivers are attached to the same base driver, you can use the Driver Load Order in the Registry to control which Filter Driver loads ahead of which other Filter Driver.

The writer of a Filter Driver can never be sure of the complete list of IRPs and Device Control operations supported by a driver. Even if all operations are known when the driver is first implemented, things change. The lower-level driver might be enhanced by the original vendor and thus have a new interface. If the Filter Driver does not support the new operations, an application that was depending on the enhanced features to which the driver that it thinks it is interfacing might think the driver is failing, when in fact it is the Filter Driver that is failing. If the lower-level driver is vendor-specific and supports some private Device Control operations that are unique to that vendor and not supported by other vendors, replacing the first lower-level driver by the second will not be transparent if the Filter Driver only passed down the original set of operations. A Filter Driver written solely to the specification of one vendor's driver will likewise make it appear that the second vendor's driver is "failing", when it is merely a failure of the Filter Driver. The correct solution to this is that the Filter Driver must pass all operations that it is not otherwise handling down to the lower level transparently.

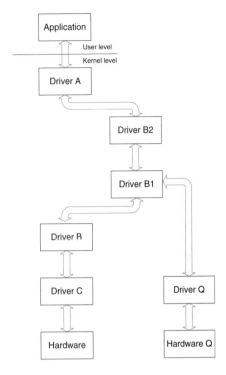

Figure 23.4: *Multiple Filter Drivers.*

One exception to this rule is a Filter Driver intended to compensate for problems with a device that is attached at a low level in the driver stack. An example is a CD-ROM drive that requires an extra SCSI command before the first Read command. The vendor of this device might choose to implement a Filter Driver that slips in just above the standard CD-ROM driver. Then when that Filter Driver sees a Read command coming down, before passing it to the lower-level (standard CD-ROM) driver, it first passes down the command or sequence of commands required by that particular CD-ROM.

The general Filter Driver should pass all IRPs and Device Control operations it does not modify down to the lower-level driver unchanged. It therefore must fill all entries in the driver function dispatch table with an entry within the driver. This is unlike the normal driver, which could pick and choose only the Dispatch Routines that the driver implementor needed to support.

Listing 23.1: DriverEntry *for a Filter Driver*

```
NTSTATUS DriverEntry(...)
{
....
    //
    // Send everything down unless specifically handled
    //
    for (i = 0; i <= IRP_MJ_MAXIMUM_FUNCTION; i++) {
        DriverObject->MajorFunction[i] = xxxSendToNextDriver;
    }
    DriverObject->MajorFunction[IRP_MJ_CREATE]        = xxxCreate;
```

```
DriverObject->MajorFunction[IRP_MJ_READ]            = xxxReadWrite;
DriverObject->MajorFunction[IRP_MJ_WRITE]           = xxxReadWrite;
DriverObject->MajorFunction[IRP_MJ_DEVICE_CONTROL]  = xxxDeviceControl;
DriverObject->MajorFunction[IRP_MJ_PNP]             = xxxPnp;
DriverObject->MajorFunction[IRP_MJ_POWER]           = xxxPower;
DriverObject->DriverExtension->AddDevice            = xxxAddDevice;
DriverObject->DriverUnload                          = xxxUnload;
....
}
```

Object Manager

Layered drivers are one of the places in which you must also be aware of the existence and functionality of the *Object Manager*. Proper use of the Object Manager is critical to the correct functioning of a layered driver.

The Object Manager is the NT component that exports data objects to Device Drivers, other Kernel-mode components of Windows NT, and User-mode applications. It also exports data structures encapsulated in NT Objects. You might have noticed that you cannot create key Device Driver objects directly; instead, you call specific functions to create them. This is because "under the floor", the I/O Manager works with the Object Manager to create these objects. The NT Object Structure adds opaque header fields to the data structures defined by the various executive components (we are interested only in the I/O Manager, but other components of the NT system use objects, also). Specific operations are defined and exported by the module defining the object.

The Object Manager performs the following functions.

- Provides a common mechanism for the management of all objects.
- Provides a uniform naming hierarchy for objects within a single NT system.
- Processes all Open and Close requests.

Other capabilities of the Object Manager are beyond the scope of this book, including the following:

- Security
- Quota management
- Dynamic creation of new object types
- Association of operations with an object type (Open, Close, Delete, Parse)

In general, Kernel-mode components of Windows NT refer to objects by pointers, while User-mode components refer to kernel objects by handles. In a driver that is issuing IRP_MJ_READ I/O requests, reading from a lower-level driver, is a *pointer* to the Device Object of the lower-level driver. In an application program reading from the same device is a *handle* to the device. The Object Manager can translate handles to object pointers. In a few cases, you might want to refer to Kernel Objects by both handle and pointer. In these cases, you use the Object Manager function for the transformation. An example of this is the thread handle. When you create a thread, you are given the thread handle as a return code. For some operations, such as waiting for the thread to complete with KeWaitForSingleObject or

`KeWaitForMultipleObjects`, you need the thread object pointer. An example of this is in Chapter 24, on page 504.

Reference Counts

The Object Manager maintains the Object Manager Name Space and a *reference count* on each object. Object Manager Routines increment and decrement the reference count. If the reference count is decremented to 0, the object is deleted. Thus it is critical that you maintain the reference count properly.

For most of what we've shown you up to this point, the reference count is implicitly managed by the I/O Manager functions that have been used. For example, `IoCreateDevice` sets the reference count to 1, while `IoDeleteDevice` decrements the reference count from 1 to 0, thus actually deleting the Device Object. However, now that you are concerned with layered drivers, you will discover that a Device Object is now shared with another driver and that proper reference count maintenance is critical.

Two routines are provided to increment the reference count: `ObReferenceObjectByHandle` and `ObReferenceObjectByPointer`.

ObReferenceObjectByHandle

`ObReferenceObjectByHandle` is called when the caller has a handle to the object, and wishes to obtain a pointer (as well as increment the reference count).

```
NTSTATUS ObReferenceObjectByHandle(
           IN HANDLE Handle,
           IN ACCESS_MASK DesiredAccess,
           IN POBJECT_TYPE ObjectType OPTIONAL,
           IN KPROCESSOR_MODE AccessMode,
           OUT PVOID * Object,
           OUT POBJECT_HANDLE_INFORMATION HandleInformation OPTIONAL);
```

The reference count of the object designated by the handle is incremented. This routine also returns a pointer to the object, the handle attributes, and the granted access rights. The *DesiredAccess* parameter indicates which types of access are desired. For Kernel-mode accesses, this is always a mask of the form *typename*_ALL_ACCESS. A parameter to the call specifies the access mode of the request. If the *AccessMode* parameter is `KernelMode`, the access is always granted; if it is `UserMode`, the access rights to the object are checked. Access is determined by the NT security system.

The *HandleInformation* parameter can be NULL, in which case no handle information will be returned.

The *ObjectType* pointer references an OBJECT_TYPE structure and, if non-NULL, will cause the information about the object type to be returned in this structure.

ObReferenceObjectByPointer

`ObReferenceObjectByPointer` is a simpler function than `ObReferenceObjectByHandle`, called with a pointer to the object. This is the method you will most commonly use in a Device Driver. The *ObjectType* pointer will almost always be NULL. The reference count is incremented.

```
NTSTATUS ObReferenceObjectByPointer(IN PVOID Object,
                                    IN ACCESS_MASK DesiredAccess,
                                    IN POBJECT_TYPE ObjectType,
                                    IN KPROCESSOR_MODE AccessMode);
```

NT defines a number of Object Manager Object types, including:

- Object Directory
- Symbolic Link
- Timer
- Mutex
- Event
- Process
- Thread
- Section
- File
- Access Token

ObDereferenceObject

One routine, ObDereferenceObject, decrements the reference count:

```
VOID ObDereferenceObject(IN PVOID Object);
```

If the reference count goes to 0, the object is deleted.

Object Manager Name Space

The Object Manager Name Space is a tree-structured hierarchical name space. Like the File System Name Space, the root node is named "\". The File System Name Space and the Object Manager Name Space are distinct; however, the former is rooted at a node within the Object Manager Name Space.

There are three distinct tree-structured name spaces within NT. One is the Object Manager Name Space, which we are about to describe. This structure lives entirely in memory. The Registry lives in a collection of files known as *hives*, whose actual details are semi-opaque. (Consult the *Windows NT Resource Kit* documentation for more details). The remaining name space is the file system name space, which is maintained on the physical disk drives or CD-ROMs. This name space is *rooted* in the Object Manager Name Space, but is distinct once the disk drive itself becomes involved. Note that both the Object Manager Name Space and the Registry can have *symbolic links* from one (apparent) leaf level to another level in their respective trees.

The second level of the name hierarchy is shown in Table 23.1.

The ?? name replaces DosDevices name used prior to NT 4.0. This is an optimization. The node is frequently accessed, and the question mark sorts alphabetically to the beginning of the alphabet. The old name DosDevices is now a symbolic link to ?? for compatibility.

Table 23.1: *Second-Level Names in the Object Manager Name Space*

Name	Meaning
??	The directory of all named devices available for `CreateFile`. The object directory formerly known as "`DosDevices`"
arcname	Used only on RISC-based machines
BaseNamedObjects	Mutexes, Semaphores, Events, Waitable Timers, Section Objects
Device	Device names
DosDevices	A symbolic link to "`??`"
Driver	Driver names
FileSystem	File System types
KnownDlls	Section names and paths for "known DLLs"; the DLLs mapped by the system at startup time
nls	Section names for mapped national language support tables
ObjectTypes	Names of types of objects
RPC Control	Port objects used by Remote Procedure Calls
Security	Names of objects used by the Security Subsystem
windows	Win32 Subsystem Ports and Window Stations

When an NT component attempts to open an object, the Object Manager is called to look up the object name supplied. The manager parses the name left-to-right, one token at a time. Each token is matched to the corresponding object in the Object Manager Name Space until an object has an associated parsing routine. This parsing routine will be called with the remainder of the path.

NT uses a simple naming scheme for NT devices. Any Device Object that can be the target of an I/O request or can be connected to by a higher-level NT driver has a name of the form `\Device\<GenericDeviceType><Digits>` where `<GenericDeviceType>` indicates the kind of device, such as `Harddisk`, `Serial`, `Tape`, and so on, and the `<Digits>` suffix indicates the zero-based number of this device, where the numbers depends on how many other devices of the same type have already been named. Thus names might be `HardDisk0`, `HardDisk1`, `Serial0`, `Serial1`, `Serial2`, and so on.

Some NT drivers, which divide a simple device into lower-level devices, might create the `\Device\<GenericDeviceType><Digits>` entry as an Object Manager directory and the lower-level objects as

`\Device\<GenericDeviceType><Digits>\<deviceSubType><Digits>`

The routine `ZwCreateDirectoryObject` makes a directory in Object Manager Name Space. This routine can be used by a driver that establishes its own device hierarchy to create a Directory Object in the Object Manager Name Space.

An example of this naming convention is the hard drive, in which the first hard disk partition is named

`\Device\Harddisk0\Partition0`

The name space supports *symbolic links*. The name
`\Device\Harddisk0\Partition1` might be the partition linked to `\??\C:`. A representation of the split between the Object Name Space and the File System Name Space and the use of symbolic links is shown in Figure 23.5.

If a user process tries to open the file `c:\projects\driver`, the sequence of operations is as follows.

- The Win32 subsystem translates `C:` to `\??\C:`.

- `\??\C:\projects\driver` is sent to the Object Manager.

- The Object Manager follows the symbolic link `\??\C:` to
  `\Device\Harddisk0\Partition1`.

- `\Device\Harddisk0\Partition1\projects\driver` is parsed by the
  Object Manager.

- When the parse reaches the `Partition1` object, a type-specific parsing routine is
  found.

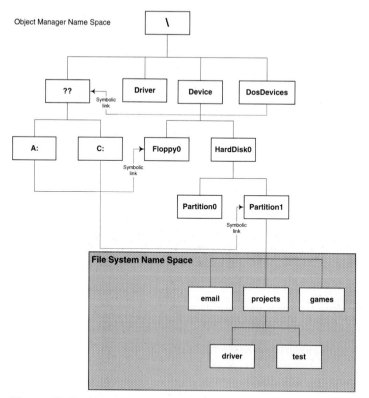

Figure 23.5: *Object Manager Name Space.*

- The `Partition1` parsing routine is called with `\projects\driver`.

- The parse continues with the On-Disk directory using the parse routine for the File System on this disk.

- A reference to the `\projects\driver` directory is returned.

Note that each `GenericDeviceType` guarantees that all Device Objects representing a particular type of device have the same name, so NT higher-level drivers can readily find Device Objects representing the set of underlying physical devices over which such a higher-level driver can layer itself. Note also that the `Digits` suffix guarantees that each Device Object of that type has a unique name in every Windows NT machine.

The SDK program `DDKdirectory\mssdk\bin\winnt\winobj.exe` allows you to explore the Object Manager Namespace (where `DDKdirectory` is where you installed the DDK on your machine).

Object Manager Functions

Although the Object Manager is a quite important component of Windows NT, it has surprisingly few functions that directly support it. The only three Ob-prefix functions are shown next.

- `ObReferenceObjectByHandle`

  Given the handle to an object and the object type, this routine returns the pointer to the object and increases the object reference count by 1.

- `ObReferenceObjectByPointer`

  Given a pointer to an object, this routine increments the reference count of that object.

- `ObDereferenceObject`

  This routine decrements the reference count of an object (by 1). If the count reaches 0, the object is deleted.

Creating Object Manager Entries

Hard drives and partitions are structured in the Object Manager Name Space. Each hard drive is represented by a Object Directory `\Device\Harddiskn` (where *n* is a disk count), which is the parent for the Device Objects for each partition contained on that hard drive.

Other hardware has a logical structure than can be encoded in the object structure. For example, a machining center (a metalworking system) might have a number of spindles. You could encode this by creating a `\Device\MachCenter\Spindle0`.

The following listing illustrates how the SCSI disk Class Driver creates the structured name space. We modified it for use here to show the more general NT driver calls used in place of the SCSI port calls used in this example. See Chapter 25 for more on SCSI drivers.

Listing 23.2: *Managing a Structured Object Manager Name Space*

```
{
  CCHAR          ntNameBuffer[MAXIMUM_FILENAME_LENGTH];
  STRING         ntNameString;
  UNICODE_STRING ntUnicodeString;
```

```
OBJECT_ATTRIBUTES objectAttributes;
HANDLE          handle;
NTSTATUS        status;
PDEVICE_OBJECT deviceObject = NULL;
//
// Set up an Object Directory to contain the objects for this
// device and all its partitions
//
// The variable "DeviceCount" is a pointer to a counter that tells
// which <Digits> to suffix to our device name //

// The variable "PartitionCount" is a pointer to a counter that tells
// which <Digits> to suffix to our partition name

sprintf(ntNameBuffer,  "\\Device\\Harddisk%d",  *DeviceCount);
RtlInitString(&ntNameString, ntNameBuffer);
status = RtlAnsiStringToUnicodeString(&ntUnicodeString, &ntNameString, TRUE);

if (!NT_SUCCESS(status))
    return status;

// Initialize the object; the object name will be case-insensitive and the
// object will persist across system boots


InitializeObjectAttributes(&objectAttributes,
                           &ntUnicodeString,
                           OBJ_CASE_INSENSITIVE | OBJ_PERMANENT,
                           NULL,
                           NULL);

status = ZwCreateDirectoryObject(&handle,
                                 DIRECTORY_ALL_ACCESS,
                                 &objectAttributes);

RtlFreeUnicodeString(&ntUnicodeString);

if (!NT_SUCCESS(status))
{
    DebugPrint((1,
                "CreateDiskDeviceObjects: Could not create directory %s\n",
                ntNameBuffer));

    return status;
}

For( partition=0; PartitionCount > partition ; Partition ++)
{
    //
    // Create a Device Object for this device. Each physical disk will
    // have at least one Device Object. The required Device Object
    // describes the entire device. Its directory path is
    // \Device\HarddiskN\Partition0, where N = device number.
    //
    // If your device is not a disk device, you will have to do something
    // appropriate to name your device here

    sprintf(ntNameBuffer,
            "\\Device\\Harddisk%d\\Partition%d",
            *DeviceCount, PartitionCount);
```

```
//
//  This section creates an object for the physical device specified
//  and sets up the Device Extension's function pointers for each entry
//  point in the device-specific driver
//
  {


    OPTIONAL PDEVICE_OBJECT PhysicalDeviceObject - NULL;
    DeviceObject = NULL;
    DebugPrint((2,
            "ScsiClassCreateDeviceObject: Create Device Object %s\n",
            ntNameBuffer));
    RtlInitString(&ntNameString, ntNameBuffer);
    status = RtlAnsiStringToUnicodeString(&ntUnicodeString,
                                          &ntNameString,
                                          TRUE);
    if (!NT_SUCCESS(status))
    {
      DebugPrint((1,
              "CreateDiskDeviceObjects: Cannot convert string %s\n",
              ntNameBuffer));
      return status;
    }

    status = IoCreateDevice(DriverObject,
                        InitData->DeviceExtensionSize,
                        &ntUnicodeString,
                        InitData->DeviceType,
                        InitData->DeviceCharacteristics,
                        FALSE,
                        &DeviceObject);
    if (!NT_SUCCESS(status))
    {
        DebugPrint((1,
            "CreateDiskDeviceObjects: Cannot create Device Object %s\n",
              ntNameBuffer));
        return   status;

    }
    else
    {
      PDEVICE_EXTENSION deviceExtension = deviceObject->DeviceExtension;

        //
        // Fill in the Device Object
        //
    }

    RtlFreeUnicodeString(&ntUnicodeString);
    //
    // Indicate that ntUnicodeString is free
    //
    ntUnicodeString.Buffer = NULL;

  }
  }
        return STATUS_SUCCESS ;
} // End of creation of named subdevice
```

Objects and Waiting

You can use the Object Manager to get a pointer to an object, when given a handle to the object, and to wait on the object. In this example, we use a Thread Object. The wait on this object will implement a wait until the thread exits.

Listing 23.3: *Getting a Pointer from a Handle*

```
//
// Start the thread and capture the thread handle into the extension
//

status = PsCreateSystemThread(
                &threadHandle,
                THREAD_ALL_ACCESS,
                NULL,
                NULL,
                NULL,
                ParallelThread,
                Extension);

if (!NT_ERROR(status))
   { /* success */

   //
   // We've got the thread; now get a pointer to it
   //

   status = ObReferenceObjectByHandle(
                   threadHandle,
                   THREAD_ALL_ACCESS,
                   NULL,
                   KernelMode,
                   &Extension->ThreadObjectPointer,
                   NULL);

   if (NT_ERROR(status))
      { ... }
   else
      {

      //
      // Now that we have a reference to the thread
      // we can simply close the handle
      //

      ZwClose(threadHandle);
   } /* success */


   .
   .
   .


//
// Wait on the Thread Object; when the wait is satisfied, the
// thread has gone away
//
```

```
statusOfWait = KeWaitForSingleObject(extension->ThreadObjectPointer,
                                UserRequest, KernelMode, FALSE, NULL);
//
// The thread is gone; status is successful for the close
// Decrement the reference count on the pointer to the Thread Object
//

ObDereferenceObject(extension->ThreadObjectPointer);
extension->ThreadObjectPointer = NULL;
```

Implementation of Layered Drivers

Of the two types of Device Drivers that can be layered, there are drivers that represent logical layers in the structure and drivers that are used as Filter Drivers. Each uses slightly different protocols for how they link into the driver hierarchy. This section describes how a general layered driver links itself into the driver chain, while the next section describes how a Filter Driver links itself into the driver chain.

The most popular functions for implementing a general layered driver are shown in Table 23.2.

Table 23.2: *Useful Functions for Implementing Layered Drivers*

Function	Use
IoGetDeviceObjectPointer	Returns a pointer to a named Device Object and corresponding File Object if the requested access to the objects can be granted.
IoCallDriver	Sends an IRP to the next lower-level driver after the caller has set up the I/O Stack location in the IRP for that driver. Call IoSetCancelRoutine to set the Cancel Routine of an IRP to NULL before queueing it to a lower-level driver.
IoSetCompletionRoutine	Registers an IoCompletion routine to be called when the next lower-level driver has completed the requested operation for the given IRP.
IoCancelIrp	Sets the cancel flag in a given IRP, and calls the Cancel Routine for the IRP if there is one.

DriverEntry

The DriverEntry routine for a layered driver differs in some ways from a DriverEntry routine for other drivers. For example, it performs the following operations.

- Creates a Device Object for the "Layered Device". The device may be unnamed.
- Calls IoGetDeviceObjectPointer to get a pointer to the lower-level driver Device Object, given the driver name. This call also increments the reference count for the File Object that references this Device Object (this is the File Object for the device name, \\.*drivername*).
- Set its own StackSize to be the lower-level driver's Device Object Stacksize, plus 1. Note that if a layered driver can call several different lower-level drivers, its StackSize must be the maximum of all of the lower-level stack sizes, plus 1. This applies only if the layered driver will pass an IRP it receives directly to the lower-level

driver. If it never does this (for example, it creates its own IRPs to pass down), it can leave its StackSize as 1.

- May allocate one or more IRPs for future use. (This saves having to allocate and deallocate them on demand. Thus you create them when you have time, rather than having their creation occur in the critical path of I/O performance.)
- May send an IRP to the lower-level driver with an IRP_MJ_CREATE function. This is necessary if the IRP_MJ_CREATE will not be passed down directly.
- May call IoCreateSymbolicLink to create a symbolic link.

Unload Routine

The Unload routine for a layered driver must gracefully remove itself from the driver hierarchy. This involves several steps.

- It deletes the symbolic link (if one was created) by calling IoDeleteSymbolicLink.
- It calls the lower-level driver to cancel any pending I/O.
- If it opened the lower-level driver with IRP_MJ_CREATE, it closes the lower-level driver by sending an IRP_MJ_CLOSE.
- It decrements the Device Object file pointer by calling ObDereferenceObject for the File Object returned by IoGetDeviceObjectPointer. Recall that the File Object reference count was implicitly incremented by IoGetDeviceObjectPointer done in the DriverEntry routine. There is no corresponding implicit decrement, so you must do it explicitly.

Implementation of Filter Drivers

A Filter Driver inserts itself into the driver hierarchy in a fashion slightly different from the way in which a general layered driver inserts itself. For example, it must insert itself transparently for those operations it does not modify. This section describes how a Filter Driver performs this operation.

The most popular functions for implementing a general layered driver are shown in Table 23.3.

Table 23.3: *Functions Useful for Writing a Filter Driver*

Function	Use
IoGetDeviceObjectPointer	Returns a pointer to a named Device Object and corresponding File Object if the requested access to the objects can be granted.
IoAttachDevice	Attaches the caller's Device Object to a named target Device Object so that I/O requests bound for the target device are routed first to the caller.
IoAttachDeviceToDeviceStack	Attaches the caller's Device Object to the highest Device Object in the chain and returns a pointer to the previous highest Device Object. I/O requests bound for the target device are routed first to the caller.
IoDetachDevice	Releases an attachment between the caller's Device Object and a lower-level driver's Device Object.

DriverEntry

The `DriverEntry` routine for a Filter Driver also differs some from those of an ordinary driver and of a general layered driver.

- It calls `IoGetDeviceObjectPointer` for the lower-level driver to get its Device Object, given its name. This call also increments the reference count for the File Object that references this Device Object (this is the File Object for the device name, `\\.\drivername`).
- From the returned Device Object, it gets the lower-level Driver Object.
  - It checks the function table and assures that every function supported by the target driver will be supported by the Filter Driver. You must support all of the functions, even if all you do is pass the `IRP_MJ_` requests to the lower-level driver.
- For each Device Object linked to the target Driver Object to be filtered, it does the following (iterate on the `NextDevice` field of the Device Object).
  - It calls `IoCreateDevice` to create a Filter Device Object for each Device Object of the target Driver Object to be filtered. Note that not all Device Objects will necessarily be filtered (for example, if you want to attach a special device to COM1, you don't need to filter COM2..COM*n*).
  - It calls `IoAttachDevice` to attach the Filter Device Object to the target Device Object.
  - It copies the target Device Object `DeviceType`, `Characteristics`, and `AlignmentRequirement` to the Filter Device Object. The Filter Device Object `Stacksize` must be set to the lower-level driver `StackSize`, plus 1.

Unload Routine

The Unload routine for a Filter Driver is slightly different than the Unload routine for an ordinary driver. To handle the Unload for a Filter Driver, you must do the following steps:

- Dereferences the File Object pointer (returned by `IoGetDeviceObjectPointer`) by calling `ObDereferenceObject`.
- Iterates over the Filter Device Objects, and for each such object, it calls `IoDetachDevice` and `IoDeleteDevice`.

Implementation Techniques

The implementation techniques for layered drivers and Filter Drivers are remarkably the same. The key technique of all layered drivers is to use `IoCallDriver` to send IRPs down to the lower-level. In addition, the incoming IRP can itself be passed down if the IRP Stack is properly created and used.

The IRP Stack

There are four ways in which a layered driver can respond to an incoming IRP.

- It can process the IRP completely itself.

- It can pass the original IRP to the lower-level driver, one or more times.

- It can pass allocated IRPs to the lower-level driver. These can be either created as needed or preallocated at `DriverEntry` for efficiency (or some mix of these techniques).

- It can pass *Associated IRPs* to the lower-level driver.

A key to making this all work is the *IRP Stack*. The IRP Stack is a block of locations allocated in an IRP that are used in a stack-like fashion. A given driver can access its own stack location and the stack location that will be used by its lower-level driver. We've already shown that the IRP Stack contains many interesting parameters, such as pointers to input and output buffers. However, we have not yet addressed the whys and wherefores of the IRP Stack itself, other than giving you some canned techniques for use by simple monolithic drivers. Table 23.4 lists the management functions of the IRP Stack.

Table 23.4: *IRP Stack Management Functions*

Function	Use
IoGetCurrentIrpStackLocation	Returns a pointer to the caller's stack location in the given IRP.
IoGetNextIrpStackLocation	Gives a higher-level driver access to the next lower-level driver's I/O Stack location in an IRP so that the caller can set it up for the lower-level driver.
IoSetNextIrpStackLocation	Sets the IRP Stack location in a driver-allocated IRP to that of the caller.

IRP Processing

A higher-level driver passes IRPs to lower-level drivers in such a way that it is immaterial to the lower-level driver if a request comes from a highest-level driver, an intermediate-level driver, or an application program. This gives the programmer of a higher- or intermediate-level driver freedom in the handling of IRPs. An incoming IRP might be handled in any of the several ways we discussed earlier in the chapter.

A layered driver can set up to receive notification when an IRP is completed by establishing an `IoCompletion` handler for the IRP. When the lower-level driver calls `IoCompleteRequest`, the IRP that is completed will first be passed to the `IoCompletion` routine established for the IRP.

You can use the following techniques when working with IRPs in a layered driver:

- Process the IRP completely in the upper-level driver.

  The IRP can be processed by the layered driver and completed. Completing the IRP might involve hardware controlled by the Driver, and the Driver might process interrupts in the IRP's operation. Some devices and operations might require multiple interrupts in order to complete the I/O operation.

The driver calls `IoCompleteRequest` to complete the IRP. It does not necessarily know what is going to happen when that request completes.

- Pass the original IRP to the lower-level driver one or more times.

  By using the IRP Stack, you can pass the original IRP to a lower-level driver. This requires that you use `IoGetNextIrpStackLocation` to the IRP Stack location that will be used by the lower-level driver and initialize various fields of that stack location to specify the operation to be done by the lower-level driver.

- Pass allocated IRPs to the lower-level driver.

  There are two reasons for using IRPs allocated by your driver. One is that it can be more efficient: By keeping your own cache of IRPs, you need not constantly allocate and deallocate memory during I/O transactions. Second, allocated IRPs allow for concurrent lower-level operations. This is clearly a desirable optimization for a class of higher-level drivers.

A layered driver can also create an IRP that becomes an Associated IRP. This IRP is associated with another IRP, usually the IRP that came in to the driver. This particular kind of IRP processing is described in the following section.

NT provides a number of support routines for the allocation and initialization of IRPs. Some of these can be used only at IRQL == PASSIVE_LEVEL, and some can be used at any IRQL <= DISPATCH_LEVEL. These are summarized in Table 23.5.

Table 23.5: *IRP Management Functions*

Function	IRQL	Use
`IoAllocateIrp`	`<= DISPATCH_LEVEL`	Allocates an IRP, given the number of I/O Stack locations for each driver layered under the caller and, optionally, for the caller. The IRP must be then initialized with `IoInitializeIrp`.
`IoBuildAsynchronousFsdRequest`	`<= DISPATCH_LEVEL`	Allocates and initializes an IRP for an asynchronous request (not necessarily for the File System!).
`IoBuildDeviceIoControlRequest`	`== PASSIVE_LEVEL`	Allocates and initializes an IRP for a synchronous function, either `IRP_MJ_DEVICE_CONTROL` or `IRP_MJ_INTERNAL_DEVICE_CONTROL`.
`IoBuildSynchronousFsdRequest`	`== PASSIVE_LEVEL`	Allocates and initializes an IRP for a synchronous request (not necessarily for the File System!).
`IoMakeAssociatedIrp`	`<= DISPATCH_LEVEL`	Allocates and initializes an IRP to be associated with a master IRP sent to a highest-level driver, thereby allowing the caller to split the original request and send associated IRPs on to lower-level drivers.

Table 23.5: *IRP Management Functions (continued)*

Function	IRQL	Use
`IoInitializeIrp`	`<= DISPATCH_LEVEL`	Initializes a block of storage allocated by any valid means.
`IoFreeIrp`	`<= DISPATCH_LEVEL`	Frees an allocated IRP allocated by one of the previous functions in this table.
`IoSizeOfIrp`	`<= DISPATCH_LEVEL`	Determines the size in bytes for an IRP, given the number of stack locations in the IRP.

The Dispatch Routine must set up the next lower-level driver's I/O Stack location in the newly allocated IRP, usually by copying (possibly modified) information from its own stack location in the original IRP. If a higher-level driver allocates an I/O Stack location of its own in such an IRP, the Dispatch Routine can set up per-request context information there for the `IoCompletion` routine to use.

`IoAllocateIrp` allows the caller to allocate an I/O Stack location for itself in the IRP and initializes all I/O Stack locations in the IRP with zeros.

`IoBuildAsynchronousFsdRequest` sets up the next-lower driver's I/O Stack location for the caller according to caller-specified parameters. Higher-level drivers can call this routine to allocate IRPs for `IRP_MJ_READ`, `IRP_MJ_WRITE`, `IRP_MJ_FLUSH_BUFFERS`, and `IRP_MJ_SHUTDOWN` requests. Although the name suggests, by the inclusion of "Fsd" in the name, that this is used only by File System Drivers, in fact it is a general-purpose function for constructing an IRP which has a callback.

When an `IoCompletion` routine is called with such an IRP, it can check the I/O status block. If necessary (or possible), it can again set up the next lower-level driver's I/O Stack location in the IRP and retry the request or reuse it. However, the `IoCompletion` routine has no local context storage for itself in such an IRP, so the driver must maintain context about the original request elsewhere in resident memory.

A driver can use some convenience functions to allocate an IRP. `IoBuildDeviceIoControlRequest` or `IoBuildSynchronousFsdRequest` can be called only at IRQL == PASSIVE_LEVEL. The other functions that allocate IRPs are available at IRQL <= DISPATCH_LEVEL. If you need to create IRPs at IRQL <= DISPATCH_LEVEL, you can use `IoAllocateIrp` and fill in all of the details yourself. Or you can call `IoBuildAsynchronousFsdRequest` or use any allocated block of nonpaged memory that is at least `IoSizeOfIrp` bytes long and that has been initialized with `IoInitializeIrp`.

Passing Associated IRP(s) to the Lower-Level Driver

Associated IRPs are a special form of IRP for highest-level drivers. The highest-level driver can create a number of Associated IRPs and pass them to lower-level drivers. Each Associated IRP references an IRP called the *Master IRP*, which is usually the original IRP passed into the driver. When the last Associated IRP completes, the Master IRP is completed by the I/O Manager (unless a completion routine had been declared for it).

The highest-level driver can create Associated IRPs by calling `IoMakeAssociatedIrp` to create the new IRP.

The highest-level driver that uses Associated IRPs can return control to the I/O Manager after calling `IoCallDriver` for each of its Associated IRPs and calling `IoMarkIrpPending` with the original IRP. If such a highest-level driver calls `IoSetCompletionRoutine` for an Associated IRP it creates, the I/O Manager does not complete the Master IRP. In these cases, the driver's `IoCompletion` routine must explicitly complete the Master IRP by using `IoCompleteRequest`.

Calling Lower-Level Drivers

The normal way a driver "calls" a lower-level driver is by sending it an IRP. (There is another, highly specialized technique of doing direct calls, discussed on page 486, but it is unusual, complex, and dangerous.)

The `IoCallDriver` function is used to pass an IRP to a lower-level driver.

```
NTSTATUS IoCallDriver(IN PDEVICE_OBJECT DeviceObject,
                      IN OUT PIRP Irp);
```

To use `IoCallDriver`, you must first get the IRP Stack location that the lower-level driver will use and initialize it. Once you pass an IRP to a lower-level driver, it becomes inaccessible. Unless you have set up an `IoCompletion` routine, you will never see it again. Of course, if the IRP is one that you have allocated, you *must* have the `IoCompletion` routine set up. Otherwise, you'll have something between a memory leak and a corrupt system. We discuss `IoCompletion` routines shortly.

Passing Buffers to Lower-Level Drivers

A request received in your layered driver might contain a pointer to a buffer, such as `IRP_MJ_READ`, `IRP_MJ_WRITE`, `IRP_MJ_DEVICE_CONTROL`, or `IRP_MJ_INTERNAL_DEVICE_CONTROL`. What you do with this buffer is entirely your decision. You have three options.

- Pass the original buffer to the lower-level driver.
- Pass a portion of the original buffer to the lower-level driver. (This might be done if, on each transaction, the lower-level driver can deliver data only in smaller sizes than the entire buffer.)
- Allocate your own buffer and pass it down, or use a buffer you have preallocated—it doesn't matter which.

Completion Routines

The `IoSetCompletionRoutine` function is called to establish with the I/O Manager that the current driver requires control after a lower-level driver finishes processing the specified IRP. The completion routine will be called in whatever IRQL the lower-level driver was running when it completes the IRP.

```
VOID IoSetCompletionRoutine(IN PIRP Irp,
                            IN PIO_COMPLETION_ROUTINE CompletionRoutine,
                            IN PVOID Context,
                            IN BOOLEAN InvokeOnSuccess,
                            IN BOOLEAN InvokeOnError,
                            IN BOOLEAN InvokeOnCancel);
```

Boolean parameters control whether the completion routine is called if the IRP is completed successfully, completed with an error, or was cancelled. A *Context* parameter is passed that allows the driver to pass additional information about the processing of the IRP.

The completion routine has the following form.

```
NTSTATUS (*PIO_COMPLETION_ROUTINE)(IN PDEVICE_OBJECT DeviceObject,
                                   IN PIRP Irp,
                                   IN PVOID Context);
```

You *must* set a completion routine if you have done any allocation of IRPs. If you are using your own preallocated IRPs and completion implies that you are now done with them, you can take this opportunity to do whatever you need to do to reclaim the IRP for later use. For IRPs that you have allocated with `IoAllocateIrp` or `IoBuildAsynchronousFsdRequest` to be disposed of, the `IoCompletion` routine must call `IoFreeIrp`, or return the IRP to your private IRP cache.

You can also use the completion routine for sequencing operations or for error recovery, as follows.

- You can reuse an incoming IRP to request that lower-level drivers complete some number of operations, such as partial transfers, until the original request can be satisfied and completed. When all of these "subfunctions" have been completed, the `IoCompletion` routine can complete the incoming request.

- You can check to see that the operation completed successfully. Then, if the device permits it—and it makes sense—your `IoCompletion` routine can retry a request that a lower-level driver completed with an error. It is up to you to establish limits on the number of retries in this case. Highest-level NT drivers, such as File System Drivers, are more likely to have `IoCompletion` routines that attempt to retry requests for which lower-level drivers have returned an error status than are intermediate-level drivers, except possibly Class Drivers layered above a closely coupled Port Driver. Nevertheless, any NT intermediate-level driver can retry requests from its `IoCompletion` routine(s) at your discretion.

In other words, a highest-level or intermediate-level driver's Dispatch Routine (for Read, Write, or Device Control) usually determines whether a given IRP requires the driver to set up an `IoCompletion` routine. At your discretion, other Dispatch Routine(s) also can set up an `IoCompletion` routine for any given IRP that is passed on to lower-level drivers.

For driver-allocated and reused IRPs, the Dispatch Routine must call `IoSetCompletionRoutine` with the following Boolean parameters:

- *InvokeOnSuccess* set to TRUE

- *InvokeOnError* set to TRUE

- *InvokeOnCancel* set to TRUE if any lower-level driver in the chain might handle cancellable IRPs

Usually, the *InvokeOnCancel* parameter is set to TRUE to ensure that the IoCompletion routine frees each driver-allocated IRP or checks the completion status of each reuse of an IRP. This occurs regardless of whether an IRP might be returned with STATUS_CANCELLED.

Consider the following implementation guidelines for calling IoSetCompletionRoutine in the Dispatch Routines of higher-level drivers.

- Any Dispatch Routine that allocates IRPs for lower-level drivers by using IoAllocateIrp or IoBuildAsynchronousFsdRequest must set an IoCompletion routine in each driver-allocated IRP.

- The Dispatch Routine must set up state about the original IRP and the IRP(s) it allocated for the IoCompletion routine to use. At a minimum, the IoCompletion routine needs access to the original IRP and a count of how many additional IRPs were allocated.

- If the Dispatch Routine allocates an I/O Stack location of its own in an IRP, it must call IoSetNextIrpStackLocation before it calls IoGetCurrentIrpStackLocation to set up context in its own I/O Stack location for the IoCompletion routine.

- The Dispatch Routine must call IoMarkIrpPending with the original IRP. However, it must not do so with any driver-allocated IRPs because the IoCompletion routine will free them.

- The Dispatch Routine must return STATUS_PENDING after it has sent all driver-allocated IRPs on to lower-level drivers. The driver's IoCompletion routine should free all driver-allocated IRPs with IoFreeIrp before it calls IoCompleteRequest with the original IRP. When it completes the original IRP, the IoCompletion routine must free all driver-allocated IRPs before it returns control.

- The Dispatch Routine must set up state about the original IRP for the IoCompletion routine to use. For example, a Dispatch Routine for read or write must save the relevant transfer parameters of an input IRP for the IoCompletion routine before the Dispatch Routine for read or write sets up a partial transfer for the next lower-level driver in that IRP. This must be done particularly if the Dispatch Routine modifies any parameters that the IoCompletion routine needs in order to determine when the original request has been satisfied. If the IoCompletion routine can retry the request, the Dispatch Routine must set up a driver-determined upper limit on how many retries its IoCompletion routine should attempt before it completes the original IRP with an error.

- Any Dispatch Routine that allocates per-IRP resources for a type of request that it passes on to lower-level drivers must call IoSetCompletionRoutine with any IRP of that type. For example, if the Dispatch Routine allocates a MDL with IoAllocateMdl and calls IoBuildPartialMdl for a partial-transfer IRP that it allocates, the IoCompletion routine must release the MDL by using IoFreeMdl. If it allocates resources to maintain state about the original IRP, it must free those resources, preferably before it calls IoCompleteRequest with the original IRP and definitely before it returns control. In general, an IoCompletion routine should free any per-IRP resources such a Dispatch Routine allocated before the corresponding IRP is freed or completed. Otherwise, the driver must maintain state about the resources to be freed before its IoCompletion routine returns control from completing the original request.

Required Functionality of a Completion Routine

On entry, an `IoCompletion` routine is called with *DeviceObject*, *Irp*, and *Context* pointers, as shown by the declaration. The Dispatch Routine that called `IoSetCompletionRoutine` can pass a *Context* pointer to whatever driver-determined context it set up for the `IoCompletion` routine to use in processing the given IRP. Note that such a context area cannot be pageable because the `IoCompletion` routine can be called at IRQL == `DISPATCH_LEVEL`.

When it is called, an `IoCompletion` routine is responsible for doing whatever additional IRP processing the Device Driver writer chooses and any necessary cleanup operations for the request, as determined by how the Dispatch Routine set up the request.

Here are some implementation guidelines for `IoCompletion` routines.

- If the input IRP was allocated by the Dispatch Routine with `IoAllocateIrp` or `IoBuildAsynchronousFsdRequest`, the `IoCompletion` routine must call `IoFreeIrp` to release that IRP, preferably before it completes the original IRP.

- If the input IRP was allocated out of a private cache of preallocated IRPs, it must be returned to that private cache.

- The `IoCompletion` routine must release any per-IRP resources that the Dispatch Routine allocated for such a driver-allocated IRP, preferably before it frees the corresponding IRP.

  For example, if the Dispatch Routine allocated a MDL for a partial-transfer IRP that the `IoCompletion` routine is processing, the `IoCompletion` routine must call `IoFreeMdl` to free that MDL before it returns control after completing the original request.

- If the `IoCompletion` routine cannot complete the original IRP with `STATUS_SUCCESS`, it must set the I/O status block in the original IRP to the value returned in the driver-allocated IRP that caused the `IoCompletion` routine to fail the original request.

- If the `IoCompletion` routine will complete the original request with `STATUS_PENDING`, it must call `IoMarkIrpPending` with the original IRP before it calls `IoCompleteRequest`.

- When the `IoCompletion` routine has processed such a driver-allocated IRP and freed it, it must return control with `STATUS_MORE_PROCESSING_REQUIRED`. Returning `STATUS_MORE_PROCESSING_REQUIRED` from the `IoCompletion` routine forestalls the I/O Manager's completion processing for a driver-allocated and freed IRP.

- If the `IoCompletion` routine reuses an incoming IRP to send one or more requests to lower-level drivers, it should update whatever context the `IoCompletion` routine maintains about each reuse (or retry) of the IRP before it sets up the next lower-level driver's I/O Stack location again, calls `IoSetCompletionRoutine` with its own entry point, and calls `IoCallDriver` with the IRP.

- The `IoCompletion` routine should *not* call `IoMarkIrpPending` at each reuse or retry of the IRP. The Dispatch Routine has already marked the original IRP as pending. Until all drivers in the chain complete the original IRP with `IoCompleteRequest`, it remains pending.

If any still-higher-level driver has set its `IoCompletion` routine in the original IRP, that driver's `IoCompletion` routine is not called until all lower-level drivers have called `IoCompleteRequest` with the original IRP.

Use of *IoMarkIrpPending*

One piece of functionality in the previous list is *extremely important*. Omitting this from a driver that calls a lower-level driver will lead to certain disaster. The `IoCompletion` handler *must* contain the following `if` statement:

```
if(Irp->PendingReturned)
    IoMarkIrpPending(Irp);
```

This `if` statement must be present in any completion routine called in a driver that calls lower-level drivers. It has the added charm that if you put it into a driver that does *not* call a lower-level driver, *no harm is done*. Thus it should be placed in every completion routine.

Assume your driver has already called `IoMarkIrpPending` for the IRP, before it passed the IRP down to a lower level. When you initially called `IoMarkIrpPending`, it set an internal bit in the current IRP Stack frame (`SL_PENDING_RETURNED` in the `Control` field). The I/O Manager scanned the IRP Stack when the IRP was completed by the lower-level driver. For each IRP Stack entry with this bit set, the `PendingReturned` flag is set and the completion routine is called. The `Irp->PendingReturned` value indicates that a lower-level driver called `IoMarkIrpPending` to mark this IRP as pending and returned `STATUS_MORE_PROCESSING_REQUIRED`.

The `IoMarkIrpPending` routine is called to propagate the pending status to the current IRP Stack frame. Without this statement, there is the chance that drivers layered above this driver will either process this IRP incorrectly or hang. It is required because of an optimization in the I/O Manager.

When the I/O Manager completes an I/O request to an application program, it must do some of the final completion processing in the thread of the caller. The I/O Manager can queue a Kernel-mode APC (Asynchronous Procedure Call) to the thread to force the thread context to switch to the caller's thread. This is an expensive operation. The I/O Manager uses two conditions as a heuristic to determine that the original thread is still the current thread:

- The state of the `PendingReturned` flag
- Knowing whether the original application call was a synchronous call or an asynchronous call

To skip the APC, the I/O operation must have been synchronous and the IRP must not have been completed asynchronously (that is, the `PendingReturned` value must be `FALSE`). If the driver is the second (or lower) driver in a chain of drivers (with either a higher-level driver or a Filter Driver layered above it), the higher-level driver must be informed if there was any asynchronous activity in the lower-level driver. To accomplish this, when the lower-level driver completes, your driver must include the statements shown previously; otherwise, the `PendingReturned` flag state will be lost. Since the I/O Manager will never not see the `PendingReturned` flag set to `TRUE`, it will assume that there was no asynchronous operation involved in the processing of the IRP and that the caller's thread is the thread that is still executing. The I/O Manager will do the completion processing in whatever thread happens to be current. In so doing, it will do some unknowable damage (the thread might be a kernel thread), and the thread that issued the I/O operation will never wake up.

Direct Calls from Driver to Driver

Direct calls to routines in other drivers is a last resort for very tightly coupled drivers and done only if absolutely needed. It should not be considered a general-purpose technique. NT uses it for fast calls into File System Drivers.

The technique is simply to pass procedure pointers and context for routines that are within the first driver to a second driver. The second driver can then directly call routines within the first driver.

The second driver does not know the state of the first driver, so any time the second driver is capable of making the call, the first driver must allow the call. The calls can be concurrent on a multiprocessor system. The second driver must be passed sufficient context for the call to make sense. As a minimum, a pointer to a Device Object, Device Extension, or Driver Object for the calling driver will be provided.

Layered Driver Examples

This section illustrates two of the common techniques for passing control downward in a driver hierarchy. The first technique is to allocate an IRP and pass it down synchronously. When the IRP completes, it is deallocated. The second technique is to pass the incoming IRP downwards in the driver hierarchy, but also set a completion routine to receive a notification of when it has completed. These are just two of the many possible ways to work with a driver hierarchy.

Passing an Allocated IRP to a Lower-Level Driver

This example is adapted from the DDK example of passing a `DeviceIoControl` request to a lower-level driver by using an allocated packet. The input parameter is a pointer to the Device Extension of the lower-level driver. There are some interesting features to this code, as well as a few features that indicate its origins but otherwise have no meaning. For example, this code is obviously running at `PASSIVE_LEVEL` because it is able to do a `KeWaitForSingleObject` call. It is calling a CD-ROM driver to perform some operation that is understood by the lower-level driver, `IOCTL_CDROM_READ_Q_CHANNEL`.

Listing 23.4: *Passing an Allocated IRP to a Lower-Level Driver*

```
BOOLEAN CdRomIsPlayActive( IN PDEVICE_OBJECT DeviceObject)
    {
    PDEVICE_EXTENSION  deviceExtension = DeviceObject->DeviceExtension;
    PIRP irp;
    IO_STATUS_BLOCK ioStatus;
    KEVENT event;
    NTSTATUS status;
    PSUB_Q_CURRENT_POSITION currentBuffer;
```

```
    // The SUB_Q_CURRENT_POSITION structure is something this driver uses
    // for dealing with CD-ROM drives

    currentBuffer = ExAllocatePool(NonPagedPoolCacheAligned,
                                        sizeof(SUB_Q_CURRENT_POSITION));
    if (currentBuffer == NULL)
        return FALSE;


    //
    // Create a notification event object to be used to signal the
    // request completion
    //
    KeInitializeEvent(&event, NotificationEvent, FALSE);

    //
    // Build the synchronous request to be sent to the Port Driver
    // to perform the request
    //
    irp = IoBuildDeviceIoControlRequest(IOCTL_CDROM_READ_Q_CHANNEL,
                                        deviceExtension->DeviceObject,
                                        currentBuffer,
                                        sizeof(CDROM_SUB_Q_DATA_FORMAT),
                                        currentBuffer,
                                        sizeof(SUB_Q_CURRENT_POSITION),
                                        FALSE,
                                        &event,
                                        &ioStatus);

    // If the IRP allocation failed, we must free up the buffer we allocated

    if (irp == NULL)
        {
         ExFreePool(currentBuffer);
         return FALSE;
        }

    //
    // Pass the request to the Port Driver, and wait for request to complete
    //

    status = IoCallDriver(deviceExtension->DeviceObject, irp);

    if (status == STATUS_PENDING)
        {
         KeWaitForSingleObject(&event, Suspended, KernelMode, FALSE, NULL);
         status = ioStatus.Status;
        }

    ExFreePool(currentBuffer);
}
```

Passing the IRP to a Lower-Level Driver By Using a Completion Routine

This is an example of a Filter Driver that collects performance statistics. It uses the completion routine to determine when the operation has completed and thus how long it took.

Routine Description

This is the driver entry point for Read and Write requests to disks to which the `diskperf` driver has attached. This driver collects statistics and then sets a completion routine so that it can collect additional information when the request completes. Then it calls the next lower-level driver.

Listing 23.5: *Using an* IoCompletion *Routine*

```
NTSTATUS DiskPerfReadWrite(IN PDEVICE_OBJECT DeviceObject,
                           IN PIRP Irp)
{
    PDEVICE_EXTENSION  deviceExtension = DeviceObject->DeviceExtension;
    PDEVICE_EXTENSION  physicalDisk =
                            deviceExtension->PhysicalDevice->DeviceExtension;
    PIO_STACK_LOCATION currentIrpStack = IoGetCurrentIrpStackLocation(Irp);
    PIO_STACK_LOCATION nextIrpStack = IoGetNextIrpStackLocation(Irp);

    //
    // Increment queue depth counter
    //

    InterlockedIncrement(&deviceExtension->DiskCounters.QueueDepth);

    if (deviceExtension != physicalDisk) {

        //
        // Now get the physical disk counters and increment queue depth
        //
        InterlockedIncrement(&physicalDisk->DiskCounters.QueueDepth);
    }

    //
    // Copy current stack to next stack
    //
    *nextIrpStack = *currentIrpStack;

    //
    // Time stamp current request start
    //
    currentIrpStack->Parameters.Read.ByteOffset =
                                KeQueryPerformanceCounter((PVOID)NULL);

    //
    // Set completion routine callback
    //
    IoSetCompletionRoutine(Irp,
                    DiskPerfIoCompletion, // function to call
                    DeviceObject,
                    TRUE,
                    TRUE,
                    TRUE);

    //
    // Return the results of the call to the disk driver
    //
```

```
        return IoCallDriver(deviceExtension->TargetDeviceObject, Irp);

} // End DiskPerfReadWrite()

NTSTATUS DiskPerfIoCompletion( IN PDEVICE_OBJECT DeviceObject,
                               IN PIRP           Irp,
                               IN PVOID          Context)
{
    PDEVICE_EXTENSION deviceExtension    = DeviceObject->DeviceExtension;
    //
    // Time stamp current request complete
    //

    timeStampComplete = KeQueryPerformanceCounter((PVOID)NULL);

    //
    // Decrement the queue depth counters for the volume and physical disk.
    // This is done without the Spin Lock's using the Interlocked functions.
    // This is the only legal way to do this.
    //
    InterlockedDecrement(&partitionCounters->QueueDepth);

    if (deviceExtension != physicalDisk) {
        InterlockedDecrement(&diskCounters->QueueDepth);
    }

     if (Irp->PendingReturned)
        IoMarkIrpPending(Irp);

    return STATUS_SUCCESS;

} // DiskPerfIoCompletion
```

Summary

This chapter has introduced the key primitives for dealing with layered drivers, including the specialized layered driver known as the Filter Driver. In addition, the rules for handling IRPs, including the use of completion routines, have been given. A large number of drivers for Windows 2000 will be layered drivers, and the technique is used extensively for many of the built-in devices for NT 4.0 (and earlier).

Chapter

24 *Driver Threads*

To support certain devices, a driver might have to perform operations involving a long delay (more than 50 μs) or might need to wait for one or more operations to complete. If a device cannot generate interrupts, it requires the driver to poll for completion periodically until the operation is finally finished. If either or both of these statements describe your device, it will require special handling in the Device Driver. Supporting the device will require a *Driver Thread*.

This chapter explores the issues of how to use Driver Threads and the key functions required to use them effectively. Driver Threads almost always demand using one or more of the forms of serialization discussed in Chapter 22.

The Need for Driver Threads

A highest-level driver might wait for events within the Dispatch Routine. These events can be either a timer event or some other event. The cost of this waiting is that the calling thread will be delayed. However, if the driver is not in the Dispatch Routine, but running at elevated IRQL, it will be operating in a random thread context, and that thread could be any thread in the system. It is not acceptable to delay the execution of that random thread. So you can't wait for events in any ISR, DPC Routine, or StartIo routine. You should wait in only Dispatch Routines for the highest-level drivers and not any driver that might be called from another driver. Since a Filter Driver can actually be inserted above what you think is a top-level routine, you should not even assume that your "top-level" routine can safely wait!

Furthermore, the nature of the device and the application might dictate that the application *cannot* be delayed while waiting for a device action. Consider a system that requires a long wait for a device to achieve a desired state (for example, "Turn on hydraulic pump and wait for pressure to come up"). You would end up "locking up" the application thread during this period. Unless the application programmer has used asynchronous I/O or a separate thread, the entire application is locked until this I/O request completes. This could dismay the user, who, after a few seconds, might want to manually cancel the I/O request. So waiting in the Dispatch Routine for an event might not even be an acceptable option. By waiting in a Dispatch Routine, you violate the expectations of an application programmer who is using any of the forms of Asynchronous I/O.

If you wait in a DPC Routine, you are waiting in the context of an arbitrary thread. Consequently, you are very unlikely to be delaying the thread that initiated the I/O request. Instead, you are delaying for arbitrary periods of time a thread that never heard of your driver, and probably doesn't care to. Imposing arbitrarily long, unpredictable delays in threads that are selected at random is almost certainly a bad policy. The File System, for example, depends on threads that run at a priority lower than the DPC's. Thus if you wait in the DPC Routine, you could be delaying the File System itself—this will have a very visible effect on the performance. Doing this on a device connected to a File Server would be a disaster.

Finally, there are times when you *must* operate at PASSIVE_LEVEL, and all driver threads operate at PASSIVE_LEVEL. For example, imagine a device with loadable code that reports back "my code has become corrupted, please reload it". You can't do this at DISPATCH_LEVEL because the operations that open, read, and close files are available only at PASSIVE_LEVEL. Spawning a driver thread to handle this situation is the only way to deal with it.

Threads that run at PASSIVE_LEVEL are preemptible and are subject to scheduler priorities. Thus you can assign a thread priority to your thread that reflects its importance. In most cases, you'll assign a value such as LOW_REALTIME_PRIORITY. This value means the thread is of higher priority than all normal application threads and will have preferential access to the CPU resource, so it will normally run to completion quickly by preempting all lower-priority threads. (Remember, the NT scheduler is round-robin within priority class. Thus, if your LOW_REALTIME_PRIORITY thread reaches the end of its timeslice, it will end up being the most important thread to be scheduled again, competing under most conditions only with other LOW_REALTIME_PRIORITY driver threads.)

However, you can set the priority higher, up to the value HIGH_PRIORITY, if you have a really time-critical device that requires servicing quickly. Note that most of the File System Worker Threads operate at a priority lower than this. So if you do use this priority and your device requires a lot of thread activity at this level, you will seriously impact File System performance. The priority values for NT 4.0 are summarized in Table 24.1. The application-level values have no visible names in the DDK header files, but they represent the currently documented values for application threads. An application can use an API call to boost its priority up to two levels above the base process priority; for example, a fully boosted GUI thread running in the foreground can be as high as priority 11. The same call can be used to lower a thread's priority up to two levels below the base process priority. Thus a fully lowered GUI thread running in the background can be running as low as priority 5.

Table 24.1: *Priority Values*

Name	Use	Value
LOW_PRIORITY	Idle thread (reserved for system use)	0
	Low priority GUI thread	5
	Background GUI thread	7
	Foreground GUI thread	9
	High-priority GUI thread	11
LOW_REALTIME_PRIORITY	Most kernel Worker Threads	16
HIGH_PRIORITY	Really, really, really time-critical threads	31

A driver might create a *driver-dedicated thread* or queue a WorkItem, which runs a subroutine, to a *System Worker Thread*. The driver-dedicated thread provides a thread dedicated to execution within your driver. NT creates a few System Worker Threads when the system is started. You can queue a routine to execute within one of those preallocated Worker Threads.

System Worker Thread WorkItems

A System Worker Thread *WorkItem* describes a driver-supplied subroutine that must run to completion in a "short" time. System Worker Threads are used primarily by File System Drivers. For example, consider the case of the optimization of a sequential file read. Such an optimization uses a "read-ahead" operation, which loads the cache manager with the next blocks of a file in anticipation that they will be read by the application that has opened the file handle. There are several work queues maintained by NT.[1] This read-ahead is implemented by queueing a WorkItem to the *Critical Work Queue*.

The number of System Worker Threads is fixed. Excessive time delaying in a single Worker Thread may delay the execution of other drivers' WorkItems. You should not use System Worker Threads if you can have several requests pending, particularly if the requests can take potentially a very long time (relative to the computer's notion of "very long", that is, in excess of a few hundred milliseconds).

Two routines are used to queue a routine for processing under a System Worker Thread: `ExInitializeWorkItem` and `ExQueueWorkItem`. `ExInitializeWorkItem` initializes a WorkItem with a caller-supplied context and callback routine to be queued for execution. When a System Worker Thread is given control, this callback routine is called to actually handle the request. `ExQueueWorkItem` inserts a given WorkItem into a queue. A System Worker Thread removes the item and gives control to the routine specified by the call to `ExInitializeWorkItem`. The callback routine must call `ExFreePool` to reclaim the storage allocated for the WorkItem.

```
VOID ExInitializeWorkItem(IN PWORK_QUEUE_ITEM Item,
                          IN PWORKER_THREAD_ROUTINE Routine,
                          IN PVOID Context);

VOID ExQueueWorkItem(IN PWORK_QUEUE_ITEM WorkItem,
                     IN WORK_QUEUE_TYPE QueueType);
```

The parameter *QueueType* to `ExQueueWorkItem` controls the characteristics of the thread that will execute the WorkItem. The DDK documents two values for the parameter: `CriticalWorkQueue` and `DelayedWorkQueue`. A thread used for the `CriticalWorkQueue` will run the WorkItem in a system thread with a real-time priority. A thread used for the `DelayedWorkQueue` will run the WorkItem in a system thread with a variable priority.

---

[1] Most WorkItems are queued by the File System. The whole System Worker Queue mechanism is actually implemented by the File System. If you are interested in how this is done and have the IFS development kit, which is separately licensed (see the Further Reading section as the end of the chapter), you can check out the module *ddk\src\filesys\rdr2\supplied\rxce\rxworkq.c*.

Sources in the Microsoft Installable File System (IFS) kit show that a third value exists: `HyperCriticalWorkQueue`. The hypercritical queue is used for high-priority WorkItems that never block. A hypercritical WorkItem must not wait for any object.[2]

Note that the called routine is responsible for discarding the queue item. Typically, this means that a device that will have only one pending worker queue item at a time can store a pointer to the queue item in the Device Extension. A driver that can have multiple worker queue items pending will have to make provision for its Thread handler to know for which item it was called. One way to do this is to allocate an additional data structure that contains a pointer to the WorkItem and a pointer to the Device Object or Device Extension and then pass *this* item in as the `Context` parameter. The thread routine then must delete not only the WorkItem, but also the object referenced by its `Context` parameter.

Driver-Dedicated Threads

A driver-dedicated thread operates at IRQL `PASSIVE_LEVEL` and may have any priority in the `NORMAL` or `REALTIME` priority classes. To set thread priority, use `KeSetPriorityThread` from within the thread or call `KeSetInformationThread` from the driver. By default, the thread will have a priority in the `NORMAL` priority class.

You will customarily set the thread priority to `LOW_REALTIME_PRIORITY` by using this statement:

```
KeSetPriorityThread(KeGetCurrentThread(), LOW_REALTIME_PRIORITY);
```

These calls will also change the priority class as well as the priority within the class, so the thread might have a `Normal` priority at some times and a `REALTIME` priority at others. If a `REALTIME` priority is used, you must take care to avoid the starvation of critical system threads. NT will not tolerate a compute-bound `REALTIME` thread!

For synchronization, a driver and its dedicated thread(s) can share interlocked queues, Events, Semaphores, Mutexes, Fast Mutexes, and Executive Resources. These are covered in detail in Chapter 11.

To create a system thread, a driver calls `PsCreateSystemThread`. This routine returns the handle of the thread. Its parameters specify the routine to be executed in the thread context and the context pointer to be passed to this thread routine on startup. When a thread is finished and is being terminated, it will call `PsTerminateSystemThread`. A thread exit status code is passed to this routine, but it is not used anywhere at the kernel level.

The thread and the driver must have some method of communication. Usually, this is something as simple as a shared Boolean value (in the Device Extension), which is tested as part of the thread's loop. The driver Unload routine must tell the thread to call `PsTerminateSystemThread` and exit. It must not itself call `PsTerminateSystemThread` because it cannot know in what context the system thread is. Consequently, it could corrupt critical data structures by terminating a thread that has allocated resources, is in the middle of a synchronization section and is holding a synchronization primitive, or is in the midst of an operation whose completion is essential for system integrity.

---

[2] Presumably, a hypercritical WorkItem that claims it will not block, and then does, is a hypocritical WorkItem. *–jmn*

A driver will execute the following statement at PASSIVE_LEVEL to create a thread running ThreadRoutine. In this example, assume that the place where the handle is stored is in the Device Extension and that the context pointer is a pointer to the Device Extension (from which a pointer to the Device Object is obtained).

```
{
NTSTATUS ntstatus;
extension->running = TRUE;
ntstatus = PsCreateSystemThread(
                &extension->ThreadHandle, // Result
                THREAD_ALL_ACCESS,        // All operations
                NULL,                     // Object attrs
                NULL,                     // Process handle
                NULL,                     // Client ID
                ThreadRoutine,            // Thread function
                extension);               // Context
}
```

Here, the supplied routine has the following form.

```
VOID ThreadRoutine(IN PVOID Context)
    {
    NTSTATUS ntstatus;
    MY_EXTENSION * extension = (MY_EXTENSION *)context;

    // Perform any thread initialization here

    while (extension->threadRunning)
      {/* worker loop */
      //
      // Do the work of the thread
      //
      } /* worker loop */

    // Clean up anything that was allocated or whose state must be restored

    ntstatus = PsTerminateSystemThread(STATUS_SUCCESS);
    }
```

It then loops until it is no longer needed, as indicated by setting the threadRunning Boolean to FALSE. At that point, the loop terminates and the function calls PsTerminateThread and terminates itself. The *StartContext* parameter is passed into the thread function when it is called. Note that if the thread is blocked on a wait of any sort, you may need to force it out of the wait (in our example below, by doing a KeSetEvent on the Event Object) and immediately test the threadRunning flag as shown, so the "normal" event and the "stop" event can be distinguished:

```
        while(extension->threadRunning)
            { /* worker loop */
            KeWaitForSingleObject(extension->event, ..., NULL);
            if(!extension->threadRunning)
              break;
            // ...
            } /* worker loop */
```

You can also consider using a timed wait, when this is possible, and polling to see if the flag is set:

```
LARGE_INTEGER time = 10000; // 1 second (1000000 ns)
while(extension->threadRunning)
    { /* worker loop */
     NTSTATUS reason;
     reason = KeWaitForSingleObject(extension->event, ..., &time);
     if(reason == STATUS_TIMEOUT)
        if(extension->threadRunning)
            continue;
      else
          break;
    // ...
    } /* worker loop */
```

Yet another solution is to use a multiple-wait, where one of the events is the signal to stop the loop. This avoids the need to wake up at all, even on a timeout.

Note the difference between the service routine used by a System Worker Thread and the routine defined by `PsCreateSystemThread`. The service routine for the System Worker Thread is called by the System Worker Thread loop. When it returns, that thread usually blocks until there is something else in its queue to do. A dedicated device thread enters an infinite loop and executes until the loop exits. At this point, it must clean up or otherwise restore any state that has been associated with the thread and then call `PsTerminateThread`, which terminates itself. Within that loop, you typically block until some interesting condition occurs, such as a completion of an I/O operation (usually signaled by an Event), expiration of a timer, or release of a Mutex, Semaphore, or other synchronization object. Consequently, you also must have a way to release the thread so that it can detect that it is being shut down; this condition causes it to exit its loop. The Unload routine must not delete any objects referenced by this thread until the thread is shut down.

Multiprocessor Systems and Threads

The Driver Thread can execute on any processor in the system. That is, by default the processor affinity of the system thread will allow the execution of the thread on any processor in the system. The routine `ZwSetInformationThread` can be used to reset the affinity and restrict the thread to a subset of the available processors. However, this will impact performance because if that processor is otherwise occupied, the thread will have to wait until it comes available. It is generally better not to limit the processor affinity unless you have very good reasons to do so (for example, the Device Driver has been badly written and cannot execute correctly on a multi-processor system).

The routine `KeGetCurrentProcessorNumber` returns the processor number of the executing processor. The number of processors in the system can be obtained from a global variable `KeNumberProcessors`:

```
extern PCCHAR KeNumberProcessors;
```

This is an example of one of the few instances of an actual global variable in the system. However, this variable is never modified and thus is logically a constant. To get the number of processors, you dereference the global.

```
CCHAR count = *KeNumberProcessors;
```

As an example of when the driver needs to know the number of a processor, consider the Pentium, which contains a number of processor-specific performance counters you might want to read. However, those counters are local to each processor. It is important to control the execution processor (for example, the affinity) in order to read the intended counter. With a single thread, you'll need to set the affinity multiple times to enable you to read the processor counters for each CPU. Alternatively, you could create one thread per CPU with an affinity that restricts the execution of each thread to the corresponding CPU.

Are the high-level mechanisms—events, Semaphores, Mutexes, Fast Mutexes, and Resources—multiprocessor-safe? The answer is yes. They are all implemented using the core low-level synchronization primitives such as Spin Locks and atomic increment/decrement.

Waits

Most of the synchronization techniques we talk about will put the current thread into the wait state until the synchronization condition is satisfied. This frees the processor to run other threads until the waiting thread is able to run.

The exception is the Spin Lock. The Spin Lock will execute unless interrupted by a higher IRQL thread, but no scheduling can take place while it is waiting. It consumes all of the processor time during its execution, except that time spent in ISRs as interrupts come in. Normal Spin Locks always execute at DISPATCH_LEVEL, locking out the scheduler. (A few, such as the ISR Spin Lock, execute at even higher priority.)

Alertable and Nonalertable Waits

A wait state may be *alertable* or *nonalertable*. A thread in an alertable wait state will wake up for the delivery of an alert for the wait mode or a more privileged mode. The wait will also be associated with a *WaitMode*. The wait mode will either be UserMode or KernelMode. A User-mode alert will be generated for the delivery of a User-mode APC.

If an alertable wait is terminated for an alert, the status returned is STATUS_ALERTED. Alertable wait states are used by the File System and are outside the scope of this book.

Asynchronous Procedure Call

An APC (Asynchronous Procedure Call) is a procedure that is queued to a particular thread for execution asynchronously.

Windows NT has three kinds of APCs:

- The User APC
- The Kernel APC
- The Special Kernel APC

A User APC provides an asynchronous notification to the User-mode program that some event has happened. Unlike with the APCs of other operating systems (VMS comes to mind), the Windows NT APC will not be delivered to the User-mode thread until the thread is in an alertable wait state. This ensures that the APC routine will be called only at well-defined points within the program. User APCs are used for timers and user-specified I/O completion routines.

A Kernel APC is much like a User APC, except that it is executable by default. The thread need not be in the alertable wait state. That is, a Kernel APC is enabled except when the thread is already executing a Kernel APC. A Special Kernel APC will always preempts a Kernel APC.

A Special Kernel APC can't be blocked except by running at a raised IRQL. It is executed at APC_LEVEL IRQL, in Kernel mode. Special Kernel APCs are used by the system to force a thread to execute a procedure in the thread's context. An example of this is I/O completion. In this case, the I/O Manager needs to get back into the context of the original requestor of the I/O operation so that it can copy buffers and so on. To do this, the manager must be able to access the virtual address space of the thread/process. The most efficient way to complete the operation is to be in the calling thread's context.

The Wait Routines

The wait routines treat certain objects specially. A Wait operation that passes a Mutex gives the thread exclusive ownership of that Mutex. A Wait operation that passes a Synchronization Event resets the event so that any other waiting threads are blocked. A Wait operation that passes a Semaphore decrements the Semaphore count. In the case of KeWaitForMultipleObjects, if the wait is inclusive (all objects must be signaled to proceed) the special actions are taken on all objects that can accept them.

Note that you cannot wait on certain kinds of objects with these operations. You cannot use them, for example, to wait on a Spin Lock, a Fast Mutex, or an Executive Resource. You can use them as arguments to these operations only on *dispatcher objects*, which include Mutex Objects, Semaphore Objects, and Event Objects, as well as Timer Objects and Thread Objects. Next, we discuss each of these objects, as well as the specialized objects and their specialized wait routines.

KeWaitForSingleObject

```
NTSTATUS KeWaitForSingleObject(IN PVOID Object,
                               IN KWAIT_REASON WaitReason,
                               IN KPROCESSOR_MODE WaitMode,
                               IN BOOLEAN Alertable,
                               IN PLARGE_INTEGER Timeout);
```

The KeWaitForSingleObject function puts the current thread into a wait state until a given dispatcher object is set to the Signaled state or (optionally) until the wait times out.

KeWaitForMultipleObjects

```
NTSTATUS KeWaitForMultipleObjects(IN ULONG Count,
                                  IN PVOID Object[],
                                  IN WAIT_TYPE WaitType,
                                  IN KWAIT_REASON WaitReason,
                                  IN KPROCESSOR_MODE WaitMode,
                                  IN BOOLEAN Alertable,
                                  IN PLARGE_INTEGER Timeout,
                                  IN PKWAIT_BLOCK WaitBlockArray);
```

The KeWaitForMultipleObjects function puts the current thread into a wait state until any one or all of a number of dispatcher objects are set to the Signaled state or (optionally) until the wait times out. It is discussed in detail in Chapter 11 on page 260.

Event Objects

There are two kinds of *Event Objects* provided by Windows NT: *Synchronization Events* and *Notification Events.*

Both Notification Events and Synchronization Events are used to coordinate execution. Each Event has the state of *Signaled* or *Not-Signaled*. The operations performed on the Event Objects are the same, setting the state to either Signaled or Not-Signaled.

Signaling an Event has a side effect of satisfying a *Wait request*. The effect differs depending on whether the Event is a Synchronization Event or a Notification Event.

When a Synchronization Event is set to the Signaled state, a single thread of execution that was waiting on the Event is released and the Synchronization Event is reset to the Not-Signaled state. This is the equivalent of the user-level *autoreset Event*.

Unlike a Synchronization Event, a Notification Event is not autoresetting. Once a Notification Event is in the Signaled state, it remains in that state until it is explicitly reset. It can be reset (set to the Not-Signaled state) with a call to `KeResetEvent` or `KeClearEvent`. `KeResetEvent` clears the state to Not-Signaled and returns the previous state. If the driver will not use the previous state value, the driver can use `KeClearEvent`, which is more efficient, since it does return the previous state.

Sharing Events with Applications

A Windows NT Kernel-mode driver can share an Event with an application program in either of two ways. This allows the driver (or a driver thread) to signal an Event to a Win32 application.

Following is the first method.

- The application creates an Event Object using the Win32 routine `CreateEvent`.
- The application passes the Event handle to the driver in an IOCTL.
- The driver is running in the application's thread context during the IOCTL so there is a valid User-mode handle at that time.
- The driver calls the Object Manager to get a system pointer to the object from the User mode. To do this, the routine `ObReferenceObjectByHandle` is called to get the kernel Event Object
  `ObReferenceObjectByHandle(Event handle, SYNCHRONIZE, NULL, KernelMode, &pDeviceExtension->hEvent, NULL);`
- The driver signals the Event via `KeSetEvent(pDeviceExtension->hEvent, …)`. The driver may call `KeSetEvent` at IRQL <= DISPATCH_LEVEL.
- The driver must dereference the Event with `ObDereferenceObject` before returning from the Unload routine.

The second method is to create a named Event in the driver via `IoCreateNotificationEvent`, set the Access Control List (ACL) to permit the application to access the Event, and then open the Event by name in the application.

This Event-sharing technique should not be confused with the use of the event available to an application for use with the `OVERLAPPED` structure when the device is opened with `FILE_FLAG_OVERLAPPED`. When an application does asynchronous I/O (Read, Write, or Device Control) with the `OVERLAPPED` structure, the I/O Manager signals the Event to indicate that the Device Driver has completed the processing of the IRP and has called `IoCompleteRequest`.

Table 24.2: *Event Management Functions*

Function	Purpose
Creation/Destruction	
KeInitializeEvent	Initializes an Event Object as a Synchronization Event (single waiter) or a Notification Event and sets its initial state to Signaled or Not-Signaled.
IoCreateNotificationEvent	Creates or opens a *named* Notification Event used to notify one or more threads of execution that an Event has occurred. When a Notification Event is set to the Signaled state, it remains in that state until it is explicitly cleared.
IoCreateSynchronizationEvent	Creates or opens a *named* Synchronization Event for use in the serialization of access to hardware between two otherwise unrelated drivers. When a Synchronization Event is set to the Signaled state, it is reset by the first Wait function that passes it.
ZwClose	Closes the handle to a named Event. When all outstanding handles to the named Event have been closed, that Event will be deleted by the system.
Status Change/Inspection	
KeClearEvent	Sets the given Event to the Not-Signaled state. It is slightly faster than KeResetEvent.
KeResetEvent	Sets the state of a specified Event Object to Not-Signaled and returns the previous state of that Event Object.
KeSetEvent	Sets the state of an Event Object to Signaled if the Event was not already Signaled and returns the previous state of the Event Object.
KeReadStateEvent	Returns the current state, either Signaled or Not-Signaled.
Synchronization	
KeWaitForSingleObject	Puts the current thread into an alertable or nonalertable wait state either until the given dispatcher object is set to the Signaled state or (optionally) until the wait times out.
KeWaitForMultipleObjects	Puts the current thread into an alertable or nonalertable wait state either until any or all of a number of dispatcher objects are set to the Signaled state or (optionally) until the wait times out.

A thread that blocks on an Event must not block at an elevated IRQL. The Wait functions may be executed only when the thread is at an IRQL <= DISPATCH_LEVEL. Table 24.2 gives the Event management functions.

Semaphore Objects

The Semaphore Object maintains a count. The semaphore is Signaled if the count is nonzero. The count is incremented by releasing the Semaphore Object by calling KeReleaseSemaphore. The count is decremented by satisfying a wait on the Semaphore. If the count goes to 0, the Semaphore becomes Not-Signaled. The Semaphore Object is more general

Table 24.3: *Semaphore Management Functions*

Function	Purpose
Creation/Destruction	
KeInitializeSemaphore	Initializes a Semaphore Object with a given count and specifies an upper limit that the count can attain.
Status Change/Inspection	
KeReleaseSemaphore	Releases a given Semaphore Object. This routine supplies a runtime priority boost for waiting threads. If this call sets the Semaphore to the Signaled state, the Semaphore count is augmented by the given value.
KeReadStateSemaphore	Returns the current state, Signaled or Not-Signaled.
Synchronization	
KeWaitForSingleObject	Puts the current thread into an alertable or nonalertable wait state either until the given dispatcher object is set to the Signaled state or (optionally) until the wait times out.
KeWaitForMultipleObjects	Puts the current thread into an alertable or nonalertable wait state either until any or all of a number of dispatcher objects are set to the Signaled state or (optionally) until the wait times out.

than a Mutex or a Spin Lock; many threads can pass a Semaphore whose count is greater than 1. For a complete discussion of Semaphores, see Chapter 11, page 253.

Generally, Semaphores are used for blocking on a queue; as long as there is information in the queue, the Semaphore count is greater than 0 and the Semaphore remains Signaled. However, if the queue becomes empty, the count goes to 0 and any and all threads that service the queue block until the queue becomes nonempty.

As with an Event, a thread must not block on a Semaphore at an elevated IRQL. A thread that calls a Wait function must be running at IRQL <= DISPATCH_LEVEL. Table 24.3 gives the management functions of Semaphores.

Mutexes

A *Mutex* is a specialized form of Semaphore. It is almost, but not quite, like a Semaphore whose maximum count is 1. The difference is that a Mutex, once acquired by a thread, allows the thread to pass it multiple times. The only requirement is that the same number of Release operations must be performed as Wait operations. Table 24.4 gives the management functions of Mutexes.

Fast Mutexes

A *Fast Mutex* is a restricted form of the Mutex that may not be recursively requested. It does not need to maintain the addition reference count of the number of times a thread has passed it, and thus it is slightly more efficient. A Fast Mutex cannot participate in a KeWaitForSingleObject or KeWaitForMultipleObjects call. Instead, a special, and slightly more efficient, function is used, ExAcquireFastMutex.

Table 24.4: *Mutex Management Functions*

Function	Purpose
Creation/Destruction	
KeInitializeMutex	Initializes a Mutex Object and sets it in a Signaled state.
Status Change/Inspection	
KeReleaseMutex	Releases a given Mutex Object.
KeReadStateMutex	Returns the current state, Signaled or Not-Signaled.
Synchronization	
KeWaitForMutex	Represents a macro that expands to KeWaitForSingleObject but that can be more convenient to use when a Mutex is involved.
KeWaitForSingleObject	Puts the current thread into an alertable or nonalertable wait state either until the given dispatcher object is set to the Signaled state or (optionally) until the wait times out.
KeWaitForMultipleObjects	Puts the current thread into an alertable or nonalertable wait state either until any or all of a number of dispatcher objects are set to the Signaled state or (optionally) until the wait times out.

A Fast Mutex cannot be shared with user-level code. Table 24.5 gives the management functions of Fast Mutexes.

Table 24.5: *Fast Mutex Management Functions*

Function	Purpose
Creation/Destruction	
ExInitializeFastMutex	Initializes a Fast Mutex Object and sets it in a Signaled state.
Status Change/Inspection	
ExReleaseFastMutex	Releases a given Mutex Object.
Synchronization	
ExAcquireFastMutex	Acquires a Fast Mutex. If the Mutex is already owned, this will block. APCs to the current thread are blocked until the Mutex is released.
ExAcquireFastMutexUnsafe	Acquires a Fast Mutex. If the Mutex is already owned, this will block. APCs to the current thread are not blocked.
ExTryToAcquireFastMutex	Attempts to acquire a Fast Mutex. If it succeeds, the return value is TRUE; if it does not succeed, the return value is FALSE.

Resources

An *Executive Resource* is a particularly powerful synchronization object. It is, by consequence, also extremely dangerous. However, it has high payoff for certain kinds of synchronization. These are discussed in detail in Chapter 11, on page 255.

Table 24.6 lists the management functions of Executive Resources.

Table 24.6: *Executive Resource Management Functions*

Function	Purpose
Creation/Destruction	
`ExInitializeResource`	An obsolete entry point provided to support existing driver binaries. Use `KeInitializeResourceLite`.
`ExInitializeResourceLite`	Initializes a Resource Object, and sets it in a Signaled state.
`ExDeleteResourceLite`	Deletes the Resource Object.
Status Change/Inspection	
`ExReleaseResourceForThreadLite`	Releases a given Mutex Object.
`ExIsResourceAcquiredExclusiveLite`	Returns TRUE if the Resource is currently acquired in an exclusive mode; returns FALSE if not.
`ExGetExclusiveWaiterCount`	Returns a count of the number of threads waiting for exclusive access. This can be used, for example, by a thread that already has shared access to decide to release that access and let pending writes have control.
`ExGetSharedWaiterCount`	Returns a count of the number of threads waiting for shared access. This can be used, for example, by a thread that has exclusive access to decide when to release that access and let pending shared requests proceed.
`ExConvertExclusiveToSharedLite`	Called by a thread that has exclusive access. When this operation completes, the thread has shared access, and pending shared-access requests from other threads are permitted to proceed.
Synchronization	
`ExAcquireResourceExclusiveLite`	Acquires a Resource that has exclusive access. A *Wait* parameter determines if the thread will block until the Resource is available.
`ExAcquireResourceSharedLite`	Acquires a Resource that has nonexclusive access. This request is guaranteed to be queued behind any pending exclusive access request.
`ExAcquireSharedStarveExclusive`	Acquires a Resource that has nonexclusive access. This request is placed in the queue ahead of any pending exclusive access request. Overuse of this call can starve threads waiting for exclusive access.
`ExAcquireSharedWaitForExclusive`	Acquires a Resource that has nonexclusive access. This request will be granted immediately if shared access can be granted, but it will fail (either wait or return FALSE) if there is a pending exclusive request.
`ExTryToAcquireResourceExclusiveLite`	Attempts to acquire a Resource exclusively. This function is slightly more efficient than calling `ExAcquireResourceExclusiveLite` with its *Wait* parameter set to FALSE.

Synchronizing on Thread Objects

You can wait for a thread to exit by executing a wait on the Thread Object. When you create a thread, you are given a Thread *handle*. You can use the Object Manager to get an *Thread Object pointer*. Then you just wait on the Thread Object pointer, which will wait until the thread exits.

Listing 24.1: *Synchronizing on Thread Objects: Creating the Thread*

```
{
    //
    // Create a thread
    //
    nt_status = PsCreateSystemThread(&extenson->thread_handle,
                                     (ACCESS_MASK) 0,
                                     (POBJECT_ATTRIBUTES) NULL,
                                     (HANDLE) 0,
                                     (PCLIENT_ID) NULL,
                                     (PKSTART_ROUTINE) myThreadFunction,
                                     (PVOID) extension->myThreadContext );
    if ( !NT_SUCCESS( nt_status ) )
        {
         // Failed -- do something here
         return ????;
        }
}
```

Listing 24.2: *Synchronizing on Thread Objects: Waiting for the Thread*

```
{
    NTSTATUS nt_status;
    // We can wait for the thread to exit
    //
    //  When we created the thread, we saved the Thread handle
    //
    //  We need a pointer to the Thread Object, so we call the Object Manager
    //
    nt_status = ObReferenceObjectByHandle(extension->thread_handle,
                                          THREAD_ALL_ACCESS,
                                          NULL,
                                          KernelMode,
                                          (PVOID *) &thread_object_ptr,
                                          NULL );
    if ( !NT_SUCCESS( nt_status ) )
        {
         // Error
         return ???;
        }

    // The Thread Object will be signalled when it dies.
    nt_status = KeWaitForSingleObject((PVOID) thread_object_ptr,
                                      Suspended,
                                      KernelMode,
                                      FALSE,
                                      (PLARGE_INTEGER) NULL );
    ASSERT( nt_status == STATUS_SUCCESS );
```

```
    //
    // Dereference the Thread Object pointer
    //
    ObDereferenceObject( thread_object_ptr );
}
```

A Multiple Queue Example Using Threads

The multiqueue driver of this example is very much akin to that given in Chapter 22. However, this driver maintains two queues for low-priority actions and high-priority actions. Both sets of requests are handled by driver threads created for that purpose. Some requests can require very long times to complete stages of their processing, such as requiring a minimum delay, when processing a single IRP, between phase 1 and phase 2 and another minimum delay between phase 2 and phase 3. Here's a concrete example. Imagine a hydraulic robotic arm, with operations such as "turn on hydraulic pump", "check hydraulic pressure", "open actuator number n", and "wait for motion to start". Failure modes include failure to come up to pressure and failure to move (possibly indicating an obstruction of the arm or a leak in the hydraulic system for that actuator).

For the example in this section, we show only two queues; by induction you can generalize this to n queues. For our purposes here, the two queues represent high-priority and low-priority requests, but you can apply whatever criteria are appropriate for your device.

The basic queue structure is interlocked by the usual Spin Locks. However, the threads themselves wait on Semaphores. The Semaphore count is a count of the number of items in the queue. When the queue is empty, the Semaphore count is 0 and the Semaphore is Not-Signaled. The Wait operation on the Semaphore will block. Each time an item is placed in the queue, the Semaphore is incremented. The first increment frees the wait, which decrements the Semaphore count. If more items are queued while the first one is being processed, the next time the Wait operation is executed, the count is still greater than 0, so the wait passes. This is the classic "Producer/Consumer" queueing model discussed earlier in the chapter.

One of the major differences between this driver and the example in Chapter 22, and for that matter most other drivers, is there is no start routine to handle the packets, that is, there is no call to a conventional start routine from the DPC. The use of the thread for this purpose eliminates the need for a start routine. Note that for other drivers, a mixture of threads and conventional start routines might be appropriate. For this device, however, there is no other method of doing I/O except through the threads, so no start routine is required.

Listing 24.3: *The* `DriverEntry` *Routine for the Multiqueue, Multithread Driver*

```
NTSTATUS DriverEntry(...)
    {
      PDEVICE_OBJECT deviceObject;

    // ... Usual DriverEntry stuff...

      KeInitializeSpinlock( &extension->lowSpinLock);
      KeInitializeSpinlock( &extension->highSpinLock);
      KeInitializeSemaphore( &extension->lowRequestSemaphore, 0, MAXLONG);
      KeInitializeSemaphore( &extension->highRequestSemaphore, 0, MAXLONG);

      KeInitializeTimer(extension->DelayTimer1  );
      KeInitializeTimer(extension->DelayTimer2  );
```

```
          // Create the threads
        status = PsCreateSystemThread(&extension->lowThreadHandle,
                                      (ACCESS_MASK) 0L,
                                      NULL,
                                      (HANDLE) 0L,
                                      NULL,
                                      LowThread,  // Page 509
                                      DeviceObject);

        status = PsCreateSystemThread(&extension->highThreadHandle,
                                      (ACCESS_MASK) 0L,
                                      NULL,
                                      (HANDLE) 0L,
                                      NULL,
                                      HighThread, // Page 512
                                      DeviceObject);

    IoInitializeDpcRequest(DeviceObject, DBLQThreadDPC); // Page 516

    ntStatus = IoConnectInterrupt( &extension->InterruptObject,
                                   dblQInterruptService, // Page 515
                                   deviceObject,
                                   NULL,
                                   extension->Vector,
                                   extension->Irql,
                                   extension->Irql,
                                   extension->InterruptMode,
                                   extension->SharableVector,
                                   extension->ProcessorMask,
                                   extension->SaveFloatState);

    extension->ExitFlag = FALSE;
                          // Allow threads to run -- set to TRUE in unload

    // ...
  }
```

Listing 24.4: IRP_MJ_DEVICE_CONTROL *Handler for Multiqueue, Multithread Driver*

```
NTSTATUS DblQDeviceControl(
    IN PDEVICE_OBJECT DeviceObject,
    IN PIRP Irp)
{
    NTSTATUS status = STATUS_SUCCESS;
    PIO_STACK_LOCATION stack = IoGetCurrentIrpStackLocation(Irp);
    UCHAR * pBuffer = (UCHAR *)Irp->AssociatedIrp.SystemBuffer;
          // Buffered I/O
    ULONG outBufferLength =
          stack->Parameters.DeviceIoControl.OutputBufferLength;

    ULONG inBufferLength  =
          stack->Parameters.DeviceIoControl.InputBufferLength;
    PLIST_ENTRY  resultList;
    .
    .
    .
    switch(stack->Parameters.DeviceIoControl.IoControlCode)
      { /* ioControlCode */
```

```
        case  IOCTL_DBLQ_INITIALIZE:
            ....

            break;
        case IOCTL_DBLQ_OUTPUT_LOW: // Handler on page 510
            IoMarkIrpPending(Irp);
            status = STATUS_PENDING;
            IoSetCancelRoutine(Irp, cancelLowQueuedIrp)
            resultList = ExInterlockedInsertTailList(
                                &extension->lowListHead,
                                &Irp->Tail.Overlay.ListEntry,
                                &extension->lowSpinLock);

            KeReleaseSemaphore( &extension->lowRequestSemaphore,
                                (KPRIORITY) 0,
                                1,
                                FALSE );
            break;
        case IOCTL_DBLQ_OUTPUT_HIGH: // Handler on page 513
            IoMarkIrpPending(Irp);
            status = STATUS_PENDING;
            IoSetCancelRoutine(Irp, cancelHighQueuedIrp);
            status = STATUS_PENDING;
            resultList = ExInterlockedInsertTailList(
                                &extension->highListHead,
                                &Irp->Tail.Overlay.ListEntry,
                                &extension->highSpinLock);
            KeReleaseSemaphore(  &extension->lowRequestSemaphore,
                                (KPRIORITY) 0,
                                1,
                                FALSE );
            break;
        case ...:
            ...
            ...
            ...
        default:
            status = STATUS_UNSUCCESSFUL;
            Irp->IoStatus.Status = status;
            Irp->IoStatus.Information = 0;
            IoCompleteRequest(Irp, IO_NO_INCREMENT);
            break;
        } /* ioControlCode */

    return status;
}
```

Listing 24.5: *Cancel Routines for Multiqueue, Multithread Driver*

Cancelling an IRP on a device that uses threads can potentially be more complex than using the simple, and familiar, Cancel Routines. In conventional Cancel Routines, you should never try to cancel the current IRP because "it will finish soon, anyway". Often a device that is using Driver Threads uses them because the delays and timeouts are potentially *very* long. For example, imagine a device that is in a power-down state and requires 30 seconds or 2 minutes to come up to speed, or pressure, or whatever. The application might need to cancel the IRP that is being processed, but the code that follows will not cancel the current IRP. In this case, you need to do a much more sophisticated type of cancellation. We talk about this and related issues when we talk on page 518 about using *Finite State Machine* (FSM) models for drivers, a technique particularly well-suited for driver threads.

```
void cancelLowQueuedIrp(IN PDEVICE_OBJECT DeviceObject, IN PIRP Irp)
{
    PDBLQTHREAD_EXTENSION extension = DeviceObject->DeviceExtension;
    cancelQueuedIrp( DeviceObject, Irp,
                    &extension->lowSpinLock,
                    &extension->currentLowIRP,
                    &extension->lowListHead );
}

void cancelHighQueuedIrp(IN PDEVICE_OBJECT DeviceObject, IN PIRP Irp)
{
    PDBLQTHREAD_EXTENSION extension = DeviceObject->DeviceExtension;
    cancelQueuedIrp( DeviceObject, Irp,
                    &extension->highSpinLock,
                    &extension->currentHighIRP,
                    &extension->highListHead );
}

void cancelQueuedIrp(IN PDEVICE_OBJECT DeviceObject, IN PIRP Irp,
                    PKSPIN_LOCK spinLock, PIRP currentIrp,
                    PLIST_ENTRY listHead)
    {
    KIRQL previousIRQL;
    PDBLQTHREAD_DEVICE_EXTENSION extension = DeviceObject->DeviceExtension;

    PIRP thisIRP;
    BOOLEAN irpFound;

    IoReleaseCancelSpinLock(Irp->CancelIrql);
    KeAcquireSpinLock(spinLock, &previousIRQL);
```

Here is where we skip cancelling the current IRP. However, as we note in the introductory paragraph to this listing, this might not be appropriate for all situations, particularly those that involve long timeouts. For simplicity, we simply refuse to cancel the current IRP here.

```
    if (Irp == currentIRP)
      { /* ignore current */
        KeReleaseSpinLock( spinLock, previousIRQL);
        return;
      } /* ignore current */
    //
    // Find the IRP in the queue
    //
    {
      PLIST_ENTRY thisOne = listHead->Flink;
      while ((thisOne != &Irp->Tail.Overlay.ListEntry)
            && (thisOne != listHead))
        {
          thisOne = thisOne->Flink;
        }
      irpFound =  (thisOne != &Irp->Tail.Overlay.ListEntry);
    }
```

```
//
// If found, dequeue
//
if (irpFound)
    {
      RemoveEntryList(thisOne);
      IoSetCancelRoutine (Irp, NULL);

      Irp->IoStatus.Status - STATUS_CANCELLED;
      Irp->IoStatus.Information = 0;
      IoCompleteRequest(Irp, IO_NO_INCREMENT);
    }
  KeReleaseSpinLock( spinLock, previousIRQL);
}
```

Listing 24.6: *Low-Priority Thread Routine for Multiqueue, Multithread Driver*

```
VOID LowThread( PVOID Context  )
{
    PDEVICE_OBJECT DeviceObject = (PDEVICE_OBJECT) Context;
    PDBLQTHREAD_EXTENSION extension = DeviceObject->DeviceExtension;

    PIRP Irp;
    PIO_STACK_LOCATION stack;
    PLIST_ENTRY request;
    NTSTATUS status;
    NTSTATUS waitStatus;
    LARGE_INTEGER queueWait;
```

We choose a priority at which this thread will execute. We can choose any priority we wish. If the device requires a very fast response, we might choose a high priority. As it is, we chose to set this thread at the "low real-time priority", meaning it has higher priority than all normal applications, but it is well down on the priority compared to real-time threads.

```
    KeSetPriorityThread(KeGetCurrentThread(), LOW_REALTIME_PRIORITY);
```

```
#define uToMs 10000  // Units-to-Ms conversion constant
```

By setting a timeout value, we are able to "poll" the shutdown flag that will cause this thread to terminate. The Unload routine will set this flag to indicate that the driver is going to be unloaded. However, the unload cannot complete until the threads are terminated. We show how this is done in the Unload handler. The choice of 3 seconds is completely arbitrary (we tossed coins to determine this was the best compromise between gratuitous wakeups and shutdown delays). Note that the value assigned is negative, *indicating a relative wait time. A positive value would indicate an absolute ("date-and-time-of-day") wait time. The* uToMs *constant is convenient because it allows us to convert a value in milliseconds to a value in 100-ns units just by multiplying by it.*

```
    queueWait.QuadPart = -(3 * 1000 * uToMs);
```

This loop is the heart of the thread; it waits for the Semaphore. It will proceed from this wait if either an item is in the queue or the timeout interval is exceeded. If it is a timeout, there might be a need to reset the device to a known state, so there are comments placed to this effect. The other thing it does is to force the continuation flag to be polled because the continue *will check the loop condition. If the Unload handler has set the exit flag to* TRUE, *the loop will terminate.*

```
do {
    //
    // Wait for a request from the Dispatch Routines
    // KeWaitForSingleObject won't return error here - this thread
    // Isn't alertable and won't take APCs
    //
    waitStatus = KeWaitForSingleObject(
                            (PVOID) &extension->lowRequestSemaphore,
                            Executive,
                            KernelMode,
                            FALSE,
                            &queueWait );
    if (waitStatus == STATUS_IO_TIMEOUT)
        { /* timeout */
        // Reset device if needed -- we must have a timeout so
        // that our thread will wake up occasionally and check the
        // exit flag
        ...
        continue;
        } /* timeout */
    else
        { /* queue release */
        request = ExInterlockedRemoveHeadList( &extension->ListEntry,
                                    &extension->ListSpinLock);
      Irp = CONTAINING_RECORD( request, IRP, Tail.Overlay.ListEntry );
        stack = IoGetCurrentIrpStackLocation( Irp );

    switch ( stack->MajorFunction )
            { /* MajorFunction */
            case IRP_MJ_READ:
            case IRP_MJ_WRITE:
                {
                //
                // Do low-priority read/write
                //

                break;
                }
            case IRP_MJ_DEVICE_CONTROL:

                switch
                  ( stack->Parameters.DeviceIoControl.IoControlCode )
                    { /* IOControlCode *
                    case IOCTL_DBLQ_OUTPUT_LOW:

                            // Start  low-priority DBLQ_OUTPUT I/O here

                            ...
                            ...
                            ...
                            ...
```

```
                // Wait for hardware to generate a completion
                waitStatus = KeWaitForSingleObject(
                        (PVOID)&extension->InterruptLowEvent,
                        Executive,
                        KernelMode,
                        FALSE,
                        &queueWait );
                //
                //  Complete processing and return data
                //
                status = ...;
                break;
            case ...:
                ...        // Start other device controls here
                ...
                ...
        } /* IoControlCode */
        break;
    default:
        status = STATUS_NOT_IMPLEMENTED;
}  /* MajorFunction */
```

We complete the request almost in the usual way. Note that we do not use the
IO_NO_INCREMENT *constant here; instead, we specify a priority boost. There are symbolic values defined for this argument, but they are all device-specific for the devices Microsoft already supports. If you happen to have a device that shares these characteristics and type, you can use one of these symbolic constants. Otherwise, you specify the amount by which the priority should be boosted. This is typically a small increment. It boosts the priority of the thread that is release as a consequence of this operation by the indicated amount. It does not change the priority of the thread that calls*
IoCompleteRequest.

    A normal GUI program executes at priority 9 when it is in the foreground and at priority 7 when it is not. A program is in the foreground when one of its windows "has the focus", that is, it can accept input from the mouse or keyboard. If you choose a priority boost of 2, a background program that is waiting will now compete directly with a foreground GUI program. A foreground program will have the waiting thread boosted; this can affect how the thread competes with other threads in the same process for the CPU resource. Generally, you will not use values much larger than 3 here unless you are boosting kernel threads for time-sensitive devices or have special needs dictated by the application. For example, a mouse device completion boosts its application by
IO_MOUSE_INCREMENT, *a value defined as 6, and an audio device completion boosts its waiting application by* IO_AUDIO_INCREMENT, *which is defined as 8. These reflect the need of the application to be highly responsive to these I/O events. Note that a GUI application running in foreground and processing audio data will request a boost to priority $9 + 8 = 17$. This would move it out of the normal priority class and into the realtime priority class, and thus the priority will be capped at priority 15. This large boost reflects the critical timing requirements of audio. The priority boost is ignored for threads that are running in the realtime priority class.*

```
            Irp->IoStatus.Status = status;
            IoCompleteRequest( Irp, 1 );
        } /* queue release */
```

```
        } while ( !extension->ExitFlag );   // Loop until exit flag set
}
```

Listing 24.7: *High-Priority Thread Routine for Multiqueue, Multithread Driver*

```
VOID HighThread( PVOID Context )
{
    PDEVICE_OBJECT DeviceObject = (PDEVICE_OBJECT) Context;
    PDBLQTHREAD_EXTENSION extension = DeviceObject->DeviceExtension;

    PIRP Irp;
    PIO_STACK_LOCATION stack;
    PLIST_ENTRY request;
    NTSTATUS status;
    NTSTATUS waitStatus;
    LARGE_INTEGER queueWait;
    LARGE_INTEGER DueTime1;
    LARGE_INTEGER ISRWait;
```

This device has two time values that are of interest: a half-second delay and a tenth-second delay. We initialize the time values here, along with the same 3-second timeout that is used to poll for termination. We have also decided that if the ISR does not interrupt within an arbitrarily chosen value (which for this device we have decided is 2 seconds), there is most likely a problem.

```
    DueTime1.QuadPart = -(5 * 100 * uToMs); //  1/2 second delay (uToMs: page 509)
    DueTime2.QuadPart = -(1 * 100 * uToMs); //  1/10 second delay
    queueWait.QuadPart = -(3 * 1000 * uToMs); // uToMs: page 509
    ISRWait.QuadPart = -(2 * 1000 * uToMs); // 2-second ISR timeout
```

This is a higher-priority thread than the low-priority thread (after all, that's what this example is all about: two independent threads of differing priority!). So we want it to run even if the low-priority thread could be running. To do this, we have to set its priority to be higher than that of the low-priority thread. The only constants we have in ntddk.h *define the limits (*LOW_REALTIME_PRIORITY *is the lowest real-time priority, and* HIGH_PRIORITY *is the highest real-time priority). We have arbitrarily chosen to set the priority only one notch higher than the lowest real-time priority.*

```
    KeSetPriorityThread(KeGetCurrentThread(), LOW_REALTIME_PRIORITY + 1);
```

The first part of this loop is identical to the low-priority loop described on page 510, so we do not duplicate that information here.

```
    do { /* thread loop */
        //
        // Wait for a request from the Dispatch Routines
        // KeWaitForSingleObject won't return error here - this thread
        // isn't alertable and won't take APCs
        //
        waitStatus = KeWaitForSingleObject(
                            (PVOID) &extension->highRequestSemaphore,
                            Executive,
                            KernelMode,
                            FALSE,
                            &queueWait );
```

```
      if (waitStatus == STATUS_IO_TIMEOUT)
         { /* timeout */
          // Reset device if needed --
          // We must have a timeout so that our thread will wake up
          // occasionally and check the exit flag
          ...
          continue;
         } /* timeout */
      else
         { /* dequeued request */
          request = ExInterlockedRemoveHeadList(
                                        &extension->ListEntry,
                                        &extension->ListSpinLock);
          Irp = CONTAINING_RECORD( request, IRP, Tail.Overlay.ListEntry );
          stack = IoGetCurrentIrpStackLocation( Irp );
          switch ( stack->MajorFunction )
             { /* MajorFunction */
              case IRP_MJ_READ:
              case IRP_MJ_WRITE:
                 {
                  //
                  // Do high read/write
                  //

                  break;
                 }
              case IRP_MJ_DEVICE_CONTROL:
                 {
                  switch
                     ( stack->Parameters.DeviceIoControl.IoControlCode )
                     { /* IoControlCode */
                      case IOCTL_DBLQ_OUTPUT_HIGH:

                       // Start high-priority output I/O here

                       ...
                       ...
                       ...
```

Here is the first phase of processing. We have just set some values in the hardware registers, and we expect to get an interrupt within a time specified by ISRWait. *We wait on the Event Object. Either this will be set by the ISR to indicate that the interrupt has been handled or we will time out. If we time out, there is something wrong and we complete the IRP with an error status.*

```
               // Wait for hardware to generate a completion
               // interrupt
               waitStatus = KeWaitForSingleObject(
                           (PVOID) &extension->InterruptHighEvent,
                           Executive,
                           KernelMode,
                           FALSE,
                           &ISRWait );
```

If we time out, the device is malfunctioning. We might need to restore it to a known state, so we have left comments to indicate where this is to be done. Life becomes very complex if this restoration could generate an interrupt, but that is just a Small Matter

Of Programming. Using the FSM model is very appropriate in the case in which we have very complex transitions.

```
if(waitStatus == STATUS_TIMEOUT)
    { /* initial transaction timeout */
    // ... Restore device to known state if
    // necessary...
    Irp->IoStatus.Status = STATUS_IO_TIMEOUT;
    Irp->IoStatus.Information = 0;
    IoCompleteRequest(Irp, IO_NO_INCREMENT);
    continue;
    } /* initial transaction timeout */
```

We have received the interrupt. We naively assume that the device has not actually returned an error code, so we wait the necessary half-second specified by the hardware before initiating the next I/O operation. (Error detection and recovery are left as the traditional Exercise For The Reader.) Note that when we call KeSetTimer *here, we do not supply a DPC because we are going to wait on the Timer Object itself.*

```
KeSetTimer(extension->HighDelayTimer,
           DueTime1,
           (PRKDPC) NULL);
```

Here, we wait for the timer. We do not supply a timeout value for this Wait operation because we are waiting on a time!

```
waitStatus = KeWaitForSingleObject(
             (PVOID) &extension->HighDelayTimer,
             Executive,
             KernelMode,
             FALSE,
             NULL);
```

Next, we perform whatever hardware tweaks are required, setting appropriate values in the registers, and then wait again for an interrupt. Note that although we use the same ISRWait *time interval, each Wait could have its own operation-specific timeout.*

```
waitStatus = KeWaitForSingleObject(
             (PVOID) &extension->InterruptHighEvent,
             Executive,
             KernelMode,
             FALSE,
             &ISRWait );
```

Next, we test the status returned from the Wait operation to see if the interrupt came in or we timed out. If we timed out, we perform the appropriate recovery action.

```
if(waitStatus == STATUS_TIMEOUT)
    { /* timeout */
    // ... Restore device to known state if
    // necessary...
    Irp->IoStatus.Status = STATUS_IO_TIMEOUT;
    Irp->IoStatus.Information = 0;
    IoCompleteRequest(Irp, IO_NO_INCREMENT);
    continue;
    } /* timeout */
```

```
                         //
                         //   Output next commands to hardware
                         //
                         //
                         // Wait for 1/10 second
                         //
                         KeSetTimer(extension->HighDelayTimer, DueTime2,
                                     ( PRKDPC) NULL );
                         //
                         //   Output next commands to hardware

                         //  ... Pretty much duplicates the code just above

                         Irp->IoStatus.Status = STATUS_SUCCESS;
                         Irp->IoStatus.Information = ...; // Whatever...
                         IoCompleteRequest(Irp, 1);        // Priority boost
                                                           // completion

                         continue;
                         break;
                    case ...:
                         ...             // Start other device controls here
                         ...
                         ...
                    } /* IRP_MJ_DEVICE_CONTROL */
                    break;
                }
            default:
                status = STATUS_NOT_IMPLEMENTED;
            }  /* MajorFunction */
        //
        // Copy status to the IRP, and then complete the operation.
        //
        Irp->IoStatus.Status = status;
        IoCompleteRequest( Irp, IO_DISK_INCREMENT );
        } /* dequeued request */
    } /* thread loop */
    while ( !Dextension->ExitFlag );     // Loop until exit flag is set
}
```

Listing 24.8: *ISR for Multiqueue, Multithread Driver*

```
BOOLEAN dblQInterruptService(IN PKINTERRUPT Interrupt,
                             IN PVOID Context)
{
    PDEVICE_OBJECT deviceObject = (PDEVICE_OBJECT) Context;
    PDBLQTHREAD_EXTENSION extension = DeviceObject->DeviceExtension;
    //
    // CONFIRM INTERRUPT WAS FROM THIS DEVICE
    //
    if ( ...Interrupt not from this device... )
    {
        Return FALSE
    }
    //
    // Clear interrupt and disable hardware interrupts from our device
    //

    ....
```

What we want to do is release the Worker Thread. The limitation is that an ISR cannot set requests because it is running at high IRQL. So it queues a request for the DPC, whose sole purpose is to execute at DISPATCH_LEVEL, thus enabling it to release the Worker Thread that is waiting. Note that the parameter we pass to the DPC, although nominally PVOID, can actually be any value, whose meaning is interpreted by the DPC. In this case, we pass a BOOLEAN indicating whether it is a high-priority queue request or a low-priority queue request. You could pass an integer indicating which of several queues was involved.

```
    if ( ...interrupt from high priority... )
        IoRequestDpc(currentDeviceObject,
                    extension->CurrentHighIrp, (PVOID)TRUE);
    else
        IoRequestDpc(currentDeviceObject,
                    extension->CurrentLowIrp, (PVOID)FALSE);
    return TRUE;
}
```

Listing 24.9: *DPC Handler for Multiqueue, Multithread Driver*

```
VOID DBLQThreadDPC(IN PKDPC Dpc,
                   IN PDEVICE_OBJECT DeviceObject,
                   IN PIRP Irp,
                   IN PVOID Context)  // Context BOOLEAN TRUE if high-priority op
{
    PDEVICE_OBJECT deviceObject = (PDEVICE_OBJECT) DeferredContext;
    PDBLQTHREAD_EXTENSION extension = deviceObject->DeviceExtension;
```

This is the major difference between this driver and all of the others we've discussed thus far. This driver does no hardware-related work in the DPC; instead, it simply releases the appropriate Worker Thread. Note that for some interrupts, we might actually want to use ordinary StartIo-style or device-managed queueing in the DPC, but we have defined this particular device to use only Worker Threads as the means of processing I/O transactions. It is the responsibility of the ISR and/or DPC to leave whatever information is required by the thread in a useful place (usually within the Device Extension), where it can be found. For most devices, no information needs to be stored by the ISR or DPC. The necessary information, such as device state, can be read by the thread.

```
    if ( (BOOLEAN) Context)
      {
      KeSetEvent( &extension->InterruptHighEvent,  (KPRIORITY) 0,  FALSE );
      }
    else
      {
      KeSetEvent( &extension->InterruptLowEvent,  (KPRIORITY) 0,  FALSE );
      }

}
}
```

Listing 24.10: *Unload Handler for Multiqueue, Multithread Driver*

```
void DBLQUnload(PDRIVER_OBJECT DriverObject)
    {
    // We may have either a single Device Object or be iterating
    // on a list of Device Objects hanging off the Driver Object
    // For each Device Object, we must shut down its Worker Threads

        {
        PDEVICE_OBJECT DeviceObject = ...;
        PDBLQTHREAD_EXTENSION extension = DeviceObject->DeviceExtension;
        PVOID Objects[2];
```

We shut down the threads by setting the ExitFlag value to TRUE. *The next time the*
Wait *in the thread runs, the loop will terminate. We then wait for the threads to com-*
plete. However, there is a problem. PsCreateSystemThread *has created a thread han-*
dle, which is useless as a waitable object in the kernel. What we need is a Thread
Object. To do this, we use ObReferenceObjectByHandle, *which takes an object han-*
dle (in this case a thread handle) and returns an object pointer. We can then use this ob-
ject pointer in a WaitForMultipleObjects *call. When the call completes, we must*
call ObDereferenceObject *to reduce the reference count that*
ObReferenceObjectByHandle *incremented.*

```
        //... Shut down threads

        ObReferenceObjectByHandle(extension->lowThreadHandle,
                                  THREAD_ALL_ACCESS,
                                  NULL,
                                  KernelMode,
                                  &Objects[0],
                                  NULL);
        ObReferenceObjectByHandle(extension->highThreadHandle,
                                  THREAD_ALL_ACCESS,
                                  NULL,
                                  KernelMode,
                                  &Objects[1],
                                  NULL);

        extension->ExitFlag = TRUE;

        KeWaitForMultipleObjects(
                    2, // Number of objects to wait for
                    Objects,
                    WaitAll,     // All threads must terminate
                    Executive,
                    KernelMode,
                    FALSE,       // Not alertable
                    NULL,        // No timeout
                    NULL);       // No wait block array

        ObDereferenceObject(Objects[0]);
        ObDereferenceObject(Objects[1]);
    }
```

Finite State Machines and Drivers

We present in Listing 24.7 a fairly simplistic model of a Thread handler (or any other handler, for that matter). The flow is essentially straight-line; all the cases succeed, and there is no need for error recovery. You will rarely see a device that looks like this in Real Life. A real device will have properties more properly displayed by Figure 24.1. The various state transitions may involve interrupts. Furthermore, this diagram illustrates only *one* of the many operations the device is capable of performing. Writing code to handle this sort of control flow can become immensely complex. Given the limitations of the control structures of C, it can also become laden with goto statements, which have been recognized for decades as contributing to unmaintainable and incomprehensible software.[3]

The diagram shown in Figure 24.1 is an FSM diagram. FSMs have several characteristics. First, they can't count arbitrary amounts, only fixed amounts. Second, they cannot handle any task that requires a stack to represent state. They are best characterized by a switch statement. A sample handler for the machine described in Figure 24.1 is shown in Listing 24.11. In that listing, we use READ_PORT_UCHAR to represent any sequence of operations that lead to reading device registers and WRITE_PORT_UCHAR to represent any sequence of operations that lead to writing device registers. Think of these as representing atomic sequences of actual reads and writes to get information. Analogously, the devStatus, bytesToRead, and data variables are used to represent intermediate locations that hold information. Real devices can be much more complex than this. This device uses Programmed I/O to do data transfers.

You may notice a transition in the example that is not directly related to the hardware states. That is, the STATE_CANCELLED is a software state we added to handle the case in which the IRP is cancelled while it is the current IRP. The Cancel Routine either will return without completing the IRP or might never be called because it was set to NULL in the IRP, but the Cancel flag will still be set by the I/O Manager. When we come out of the wait, we check this flag to see if the IRP should be cancelled. If so, we transition to a state that resets the hardware to an initial condition (if necessary) and returns. Note, however, that we can't cancel the IRP until the startup interval completes. We discuss this problem after the listing.

Listing 24.11: *Code to Implement an FSM*

```
NTSTATUS ImplementFigure(PDEVICE_OBJECT DeviceObject, PIRP Irp)
    {
    enum {STATE_IDLE=0,          // Initial state
          STATE_START,           // Device is starting
          STATE_ERR1,            // No interrupt on startup
          STATE_ERR3,            // Exhausted retries
          STATE_ERR4,            // Not ready at startup
          STATE_ERR5,            // Read timed out
          STATE_READY,           // Ready to read data
          STATE_READ,            // Active read of data
          STATE_RETRY,           // Data error on read
```

---

[3] Both authors have been proficient in the BLISS language, a language developed at Carnegie Mellon University and later adopted by Digital Equipment Corporation. The first compiler began turning over in 1969, and one author (*jmn*) was the first user of the language outside the development group, in 1970. This language was notable for the fact that it had no goto statement. Nearly three decades of this style of programming tends to ingrain certain programming habits.

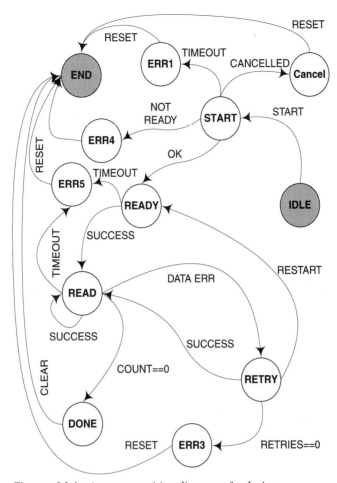

Figure 24.1: *A state-transition diagram of a device.*

```
        STATE_DONE,              // Completed I/O successfully
        STATE_CANCELLED,         // Cancelled while waiting for start
        STATE_COMPLETED          // All roads lead here, completes IRP
    };
ULONG state = STATE_IDLE;
PDBLQTHREAD_EXTENSION extension = DeviceObject->DeviceExtension;
NTSTATUS waitStatus;
LARGE_INTEGER ISRWait = ...;
LARGE_INTEGER StartupWait = ...;
UCHAR devStatus;
UCHAR data;
UCHAR bytesToRead;
UCHAR count;
UINT  retries = MY_RETRY_COUNT;
UINT  boost = IO_NO_INCREMENT;

while(TRUE)
    { /* state loop */
     switch(state)
```

```
        { /* state */
         case STATE_IDLE:
            // ... Start device
            WRITE_PORT_UCHAR(...);
            state = STATE_START;
            continue;

         case STATE_START:
            waitStatus = KeWaitForSingleObject(
                           (PVOID) &extension->InterruptHighEvent,
                           Executive,
                           KernelMode,
                           FALSE,
                           &StartupWait );
            if(waitStatus == STATUS_TIMEOUT)
               { /* timeout */
                state = STATE_ERR1;
                continue;
               } /* timeout */

            if(Irp->Cancel)
               { /* cancelled while waiting */
                state = STATE_CANCELLED;
                continue;
               } /* cancelled while waiting */

            devStatus = READ_PORT_UCHAR(...);

            if(devStatus & DEV_STATUS_OFFLINE)
               { /* device offline */
                state = STATE_ERR4;
                continue;
               } /* device offline */

            state = STATE_READY;
            continue;

         case STATE_CANCELLED: // Cancelled during startup wait
            WRITE_PORT_UCHAR(...); // Return device to idle state
            Irp->IoStatus.Status = STATUS_CANCELLED;
            Irp->IoStatus.Information = 0;
            state = STATE_COMPLETED;
            continue;

         case STATE_READY:
            // Device is ready to start read transfer
            WRITE_PORT_UCHAR(...); // Request data from device
            waitStatus = KeWaitForSingleObject(
                           (PVOID) &extension->InterruptHighEvent,
                           ...,
                           &ISRWait);
            if(waitStatus == STATUS_TIMEOUT)
               { /* timeout */
                state = STATE_ERR5;
                continue;
               } /* timeout */
            bytesToRead = READ_PORT_UCHAR(...); // Up to 255 bytes
            count = bytesToRead;
            state = STATE_READ;
            continue;
```

```
case STATE_READ:
    devStatus = READ_PORT_UCHAR(...);
    if(devStatus & DEV_STATUS_ERROR)
        { /* device had read error */
          state = STATE_DATA_ERROR;
          continue;
        } /* device had read error */
    data = READ_PORT_UCHAR(...);
    // ... Store data value in appropriate buffer for
    // I/O request
    count--;
    if(count == 0)
        state = STATE_COMPLETED;
    continue;

case STATE_ERR1: // Interrupt timed out on startup
    Irp->IoStatus.Status = STATUS_IO_TIMEOUT;
    Irp->IoStatus.Information = 0;
    state = STATE_COMPLETED;
    continue;

// STATE_ERR2 (device has teleported to Redmond) not defined
// for this type of transaction
// (see IOCTL_DBLQ_BEAM_ME_DOWN)

case STATE_ERR3: // Retry count exhausted
    WRITE_PORT_UCHAR(...); // Reset device and clear error
    Irp->IoStatus.Status = STATUS_IO_DEVICE_ERROR;
    Irp->IoStatus.Information = 0;
    state = STATE_COMPLETED;
    continue;

case STATE_ERR4: // Device not ready
    Irp->IoStatus.Status = STATUS_DEVICE_OFF_LINE;
    Irp->IoStatus.Information = 0;
    state = STATE_COMPLETED;
    continue;

case STATE_ERR5: // Interrupt timed out on read initiation
    WRITE_PORT_UCHAR(...); // Send reset operation to device
    Irp->IoStatus.Status = STATUS_IO_TIMEOUT;
    Irp->IoStatus.Information = 0;
    state = STATE_COMPLETED;
    continue;

case STATE_DONE:
    WRITE_PORT_UCHAR(...); // Tell device we've read it all
    Irp.IoStatus.Status = STATUS_SUCCESS;
    Irp.IoStatus.Information = bytesToRead;
    boost = 1; // complete and boost
    state = STATE_COMPLETED;
    continue;

case STATE_RETRY:   // Initiate retry sequence
    retries--;
    if(retries == 0)
        { /* no more retries */
          state = STATE_ERR3;
          continue;
        } /* no more retries */
```

```
                        state = STATE_READY;
                        WRITE_PORT_UCHAR(...); // Reinitialize for I/O retry
                        continue;

                    case STATE_COMPLETED:
                        status = Irp.IoStatus.Status;
                        IoCompleteRequest(Irp, boost);
                        return status;
                } /* state */
            } /* state loop */
        }
```

There are several features of note about this programming style, as follows.

* No one case is very long. In fact, if a case gets too long, you might want to add another state.

* There are *no* nested ifs! All tests are quite simple.

* The code is easy to read.

* The code is easy to debug.

* Adding error recovery at any point is very easy—just add error recovery states. Error recovery that is very complex and that can generate interrupts is easy to add because the code is so easy to write.

* If necessary, you can record a log of all of the state transitions by putting the code in one place, at the top of the loop (see "Debugging Real-Time Systems" in the Further Reading section at the end of the chapter).

* Changing the behavior is easy, by adding or splitting states.

* Complex waits and retries look no more difficult than simple straight-line code.

This is a style that, if you are not familiar with it already, is worth studying.

Cancelling the Active IRP

In this section, we discuss a case in which we want to be able to cancel the active IRP. The Cancel Routine, if called, simply returns without cancelling. If the Cancel Routine is set to NULL, the Cancel flag is still set. However, the way we have coded this dictates that we must wait for the StartupWait time to complete before we can cancel it. If this was a device with a very long StartupWait, perhaps in tens of seconds, we could do this in a slightly different way. We could choose a much shorter pollTime and poll a number of times. This can be implemented by having a number of additional states to represent the waiting-for-startup, cancelled-before-completed, and the like. Again, each state should be fairly short and simple.

When the active IRP is cancelled, it is important that you return your device to its idle state. This might be implicit in how the device works, or it might require more complexity. For example, if the IRP is cancelled before the wait completes, the device could still interrupt, even though there is no IRP waiting. In this case, you would need to enter a sequence of states that still waited for the Event to be signaled. However, because the IRP would be completed in the cancel state, the states that recognized timeout or success would then proceed to set the device to an appropriate idle state. What you do is going to be very device-specific, but you can easily trace what is happening by using the state model and a state-trace buffer. Having an IOCTL that retrieves the contents of the state-trace buffer and a simple application that displays the states in a helpful form is a very useful addition to the driver. *The cost of writing good diagnostic tools is usually much lower than the cost of not having them.*

Further Reading

Microsoft Corporation, "Windows NT IFS Kit", on www.microsoft.com\hwdev\ntifskit\default.htm.

The IFS kit is a separately licensed developer product. At the time we went to press, it required a separate licensing fee, but what Microsoft is doing by the time you read this book is, of course, unknowable. So check out the Web site for current information.

Newcomer, Joseph M., "Debugging Real-Time Systems", in *Dr. Dobb's Journal 18, 7* (July 1993). Also on *Dr. Dobb's Journal on CD-ROM.*

25 *Specialized Drivers in NT: An Overview*

Windows NT has many different kinds of drivers. So far, we have concentrated on what can be thought of as "generic" Device Drivers for unspecified but novel devices. However, NT itself relies heavily on some very specialized drivers: Graphics Drivers, such as Display Drivers and Printer Drivers, Network Drivers, and many others. These drivers have very specialized interfaces and often do not strictly follow the generic Device Driver model. The entire File System, for example, is a collection of very tightly coupled Device Drivers that share information and control according to very strict, if perhaps ill-defined, protocols (that is, you might not be able to find out the right way, but the wrong way will definitely cause you problems).

Each of these specialized drivers is worth a book in its own right.[1] So we can't do much more than give you a brief overview of some of these types of drivers. Our introduction will give you some of the concepts and vocabulary you need for studying the Microsoft DDK documentation and the sample DDK sources.

Graphics Drivers

Windows NT has two types of *Graphics Drivers*: the *Display Driver* and the *Printer Driver*. Each of these drivers has one purpose: to cause images to be generated on the output device (the monitor or a piece of paper). The Windows NT system allows a device-specific driver to do as much of the rasterization process in a device-specific manner, presumably via a hardware-accelerated technique. The GDI, the Windows NT Graphics component, calls the driver to display or draw an image. The operation being specified might be very high-level (for example, Realize Brush) or very low-level (for example, draw a single pixel at a given position).

---

[1] Actually, this has already been done in at least one case. See the citation to *Windows NT File System Internals* in the Further Reading section at the end of this chapter.

The minimal generic graphics driver supports a very simple set of drawing operations. Higher-performance drivers for the same hardware support higher-level functions in hardware.

An NT Graphics Driver provides entry points to the GDI for pixel operations and, optionally, high-level graphics operations. For most graphics operations, these high-level operations are *required* to achieve reasonable performance![2]

For the following discussions, we assume that you are familiar with the GDI interface and understand some or most of the following operations and concepts: Display Contexts (DCs), client area, client coordinates, `SelectObject`, `MoveToEx`, `LineTo`, `Rectangle`, `Ellipse`, `TextOut`, `DrawText`, `ExtTextOut`, `GetTextExtent`, `BeginPath`, `EndPath`, `StrokePath`, `FillPath`, `StrokeAndFillPath`, `SetClipRgn`, clipping in general, regions in general, pens, brushes, cosmetic pens, fonts, and `WM_PAINT`. There are a lot more operations, but these will get you started. If you need to understand these and all of the others, you might check out the chapters on drawing and GDI in *Win32 Programming*.[3]

There are several major differences between Display Drivers and Printer Drivers. These differences are derived from the characteristics of the devices. We discuss both drivers in more detail later in the chapter. For now, briefly, the Display Driver can write directly to the frame buffer in adapter memory[4] and control the properties of the device, such as resolution (800 × 600, 1024 × 768, and so on), color depth (8-, 15-, 16-, or 24-bit, typically), refresh frequency, and similar parameters.

The graphics adapter will always have sufficient frame buffer memory to display the current page. However, depending on the mode, it might not have sufficient off-screen memory to use some optimization techniques. For example, one way to get flicker-free animation is to have a driver that first creates the bitmap in off-screen device memory and then use the fast BitBlt hardware of the card to transfer the off-screen bitmap to the on-screen bitmap.

The calls to the Display Driver will be queued by the GDI. The driver for coprocessor-based graphics adapters might start an operation and return to the GDI, which provides a queuing and synchronization mechanism for this type of adapter.

The Printer Driver does not talk to printer hardware. It prepares a *metafile* of information that will be sent to the printer later. Therefore the driver has no direct control of the printer hardware. The metafile can be a high-level file format such as PCL or PostScript or as simple as a bitmap of the page.

The speed of a Printer Driver is related to the level of the Printer Driver's output. While a Display Driver is judged by its speed of display while running typical Windows programs, a Printer Driver has two components of performance: the creation of the metafile and the print speed. The effective speed will be limited by either the slower of the two or the sum of the two,

---

[2] For example, filling a circular area by computing the necessary pixel positions and drawing each pixel would give incredibly poor performance. An only slightly smart graphics card would typically have a "draw line to" operation, and instead of computing fill pixels, the GDI would compute the start and end points of each horizontal line that, when drawn, would fill the circle. Compare this to a modern SVGA chip set, which has primitive operations such as "fill the polygon defined by this set of points using a texture map" (an operation that has no user-visible manifestation in the GDI!). All the application programmer sees is a "fill" operation. GDI translates that operation to whatever is required to get maximum performance from the card. For printers, a PostScript Level 2 printer can accept compressed bitmap images, thus speeding up the transfer of data to the printer.

[3] Admittedly, one of us has a distinct bias about this book. *–jmn*

[4] ISA SuperVGA cards used a bank-switching technique to fit into the memory space available.

depending on how your system is configured.[5] The speed of creation of the metafile is also not, strictly speaking, a correct measure. This is because the *size* of the metafile will directly relate to the time needed to transmit the file from the computer to the printer and, for some printers, might also influence how quickly the print engine can render the image.[6] A smaller metafile will result in a much faster transmission. Ultimately determining the "printer speed" is the rasterization speed, the rate the metafile information is converted to the input of the print engine, the transmission speed, and/or the raw print engine speed. A PostScript Level 3 printer implemented with a RISC chip and sitting at the end of a 100-BaseT connection is going to end up on the high end of performance, almost independent of what the driver and metafile do. Of course, a driver that creates a massive metafile will not perform as well as one that creates a small metafile. The creation of an optimized metafile is an art. For PostScript, some of the tricks are well-documented. See the reference to Glenn Reid's book, *PostScript Language Program Design*, in the Further Reading section at the end of the chapter.

Display Drivers

The overall display architecture is shown in Figure 25.1. A Display Driver consists of two components:

- The DDI Driver (Display Driver Interface Driver, usually called just the "Display Driver"), shown to the left of the GDI in the figure
- The *Miniport Driver*, shown at the bottom of the video Port Driver.

Both components are typically written in C, with critical subroutines of the Display Driver possibly recoded in assembly language. Both components are interruptible and fully preemptible. The Display Driver operates at IRQL PASSIVE_LEVEL and therefore should be made pageable. The Miniport Driver optionally can have an interrupt handler and SynchCritSection, which operates at elevated IRQL. Many display cards are completely incapable of generating an interrupt.

The DDI Driver contains the code to draw GDI requests (the *DDI interface*) and may also have code to support the Mini Client Driver (MCD) OpenGL, the DirectDraw, and the Direct3D interfaces. The latter three interfaces are alternatives to the Windows GDI. OpenGL is a programming interface originally designed for, and available only on, Silicon Graphics (SGI) machines. SGI has licensed it for wider implementation. DirectDraw and Direct3D are part of the DirectX family of functions. These were implemented because Microsoft realized that the GDI was completely unsuitable for high-performance, animation-type graphics. Programmers doing graphics needed something "closer to the hardware", but this would have defeated the entire abstraction mechanism that GDI provided. DirectDraw and Direct3D give a higher-performance and more "direct" access to the rendering engine without compromising portability.

---

[5] You can set up printing so that it starts as soon as the first page of the metafile is created, and then either the printer must wait for at most the next page to be created or you force it to wait until the entire metafile is created.

[6] For example, an image rendered to my PostScript Level 1 printer (which requires all the bits be sent and uses a 68000 processor) takes 10 minutes to send to the printer and be rendered. That same image sent to my PostScript Level 2 printer, which supports bitmap compression and uses a RISC chip, is sent and rendered in about 20 seconds. Both are directly connected to a 10-BaseT network. But the 68000-based printer prints *text* at 22 ppm, while the RISC-based printer prints text at only 16 ppm. (But it prints *everything* at 16 ppm, while the former has, as indicated, a *very* wide variance.) *–jmn*

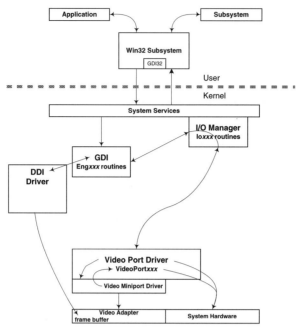

Figure 25.1: *Display Driver architecture.*

The largest part of the DDI Driver code is the code that implements the drawing operations needed by the GDI using whatever acceleration the graphics adapter can provide. The drawing operations are the heart of the Display Driver. When the driver is created, the largest part of the implementation process will be to write and optimize the drawing routines. Clipping, that is, restricting each drawing to the appropriate portion of the screen or page, makes the implementation of each drawing routine more difficult.

The breakdown for a typical NT 4.0 driver with DirectDraw and MCD support (and without Direct3D support) is shown in Table 25.1. The table shows that there is nearly five times as much code in the DDI Driver to provide DDI and MCD command sets as there is in the Miniport Driver.

Table 25.1: *Graphics Driver File Sizes*

Component		Size
Miniport		476K
	`.c` files	364K
	`.h` files	112K
DDI Driver		2.201K
	`.c` files	1.740MB
	`.h` files	266K
	`.asm` files	152K
	`.inc` files	43K

The Miniport Driver

The *Miniport Driver* can be thought of as a DLL that contains coroutines called from the display Port Driver. The Port Driver is provided by Microsoft and provides exports of all system routines that the Miniport Driver is allowed to access.

The Miniport Driver for a Display Driver is similar to an NT Kernel-mode driver. It does the following, in order.

1. Searches for a supported device by enumerating the devices on the bus.
2. Does the required hardware initialization.
3. Maps the frame buffer and adapter registers into system address space (and therefore makes them accessible to the Display Driver and the GDI). This allows the Display Driver (and the GDI) to write directly to the frame buffer. The Display Driver can directly access memory or I/O memory-mapped registers.
4. Sets up the basic graphics chip mode.
5. Sets the initial control parameters (resolution, color depth, refresh rate, and so on).

The Miniport Driver handles the time-critical and interrupt-based operations for the Display Driver. Interrupts (if any) must be handled in the Miniport Driver. Any operation that must be synchronized with the interrupt must also be done in that driver.

On older ISA adapters, the Miniport Driver handles mapping pages of video memory into the "memory window". With the PCI and AGP busses, this technique is now obsolete.

Miniport Driver functions should be located in a section declared as pageable, with the exception of the following:

- The interrupt handler, `HwVidInterrupt`
- The `SynchCritSection` handler, `HwVidSynchronizeExecutionCallback` (a pointer to this callback that is passed in calls to `VideoPortSynchronizeExecution`)
- The hardware reset function, `HwVidResetHw`
- `HwVidBankedMemoryCallback` for those ISA devices that require memory windowing

In general, Miniport Driver functions should be called infrequently.

The Display Driver will call the Miniport Driver via the `EngDeviceIoControl` routine, passing an operation code generated with the `CTL_CODE` macro. The video Port Driver is called and builds a `VIDEO_REQUEST_PACKET` (VRP) with the operations specified by the IRP. The Port Driver then calls the `StartIo` routine of the Miniport Driver. The Miniport Driver `StartIo` routine is called with the VRP. This resembles how the `DeviceIoControl` routine in a Kernel-mode driver is called with an IRP.

The Port Driver serializes the requests for processing by the Miniport Driver(s). Only one Miniport Driver `StartIo` routine may be executing at any time. If a VRP is being processed by a Miniport Driver and another I/O request occurs, the Port Driver queues the operation until the preceding call to the Miniport Driver is complete.

Requests (IOCTLs) to the Miniport Driver are passed in a `VIDEO_REQUEST_PACKET`.

```
typedef struct _VIDEO_REQUEST_PACKET {
    ULONG IoControlCode;
    PSTATUS_BLOCK StatusBlock;
    PVOID InputBuffer;
    ULONG InputBufferLength;
    PVOID OutputBuffer;
    ULONG OutputBufferLength;
} VIDEO_REQUEST_PACKET, *PVIDEO_REQUEST_PACKET;
```

Miniport Driver Entry Points

The video Miniport Driver must have the system-defined functions shown in Table 25.2.

Table 25.2: *Miniport Driver Entry Points for Display Drivers*

Miniport Driver Entry Point	Description
DriverEntry	Initializes the Miniport Driver.
HwVidFindAdapter	Detects if one or more driver-supported video adapter(s) is in the machine. Claims hardware resources for supported video adapter(s) in the Registry. Sets up communication with the adapter(s).
HwVidInitialize	Called in response to a request to open the adapter. Performs one-time initialization of the adapter for the corresponding Display Driver.
HwVidStartIO	Starts processing for each incoming VRP.
HwVidResetHw	Resets the adapter to VGA BIOS-controlled character mode. This function is used by the HAL to put the adapter in VGA mode so that the HAL can display the Blue Screen of Death. This routine is required unless the adapter's registers can be reset by an INT 10.
Other Functions That May Be Implemented in a Driver	
HwVidQueryDeviceCallback and/or HwVidQueryNamedValueCallback	Processes configuration information stored in the Registry. This is optional if the Miniport Driver's HwVidFindAdapter function uses I/O bus-type-specific configuration information or driver-supplied defaults.
HwVidInterrupt	Handles adapter-generated interrupts. This function is required if the Miniport Driver's adapter generates interrupts.
HwVidSynchronizeExecutionCallback	Used to synchronize access for critical sections of code. The critical section is executed at higher than normal IRQL. This disables lower IRQL interrupts. This function is required if other Miniport Driver functions share state with a HwVidInterrupt function.
HwVidTimer	Called periodically at approximately 1-second intervals by the Port Driver. This function is optional.

Table 25.2: *Miniport Driver Entry Points for Display Drivers (continued)*

Miniport Driver Entry Point	Description
SvgaHwIoPortXxx	Supplied by VGA-compatible SVGA Miniport Drivers to validate accesses to I/O ports by full-screen MS-DOS applications. Ordinarily the trap handler will intercept any IN or OUT instructions and return an exception to the User-mode application.
	DOS applications are a special case. A DOS application expects the ability to access the hardware registers, including the VGA registers. A VGA-compatible Miniport Driver will allow DOS programs running in a full-screen command window (a.k.a. MS-DOS shell) to directly or indirectly access the VGA register set by using the IN and OUT instructions. If the indirect access is used when the full-screen DOS application executes IN or OUT instructions, the instructions are trapped by NT and these routines are called for each access. If direct access is allowed, the IN and OUT instructions will be trapped and the trap handler will execute the IN or OUT instruction for the DOS application.
	This function is implemented only for *x*86-based machines.

The only routine with a required name is DriverEntry. The others are called via a function vector initialized in DriverEntry. The suggested name is *xxx*_name, where *xxx* is the driver name and name is the name from this section.

DDI (Display) Driver

The DDI Driver is logically a support DLL for the GDI. It contains coroutines called by the GDI. They, in turn, call GDI functions exported for use by this module. It is intended that the driver call only functions exported by the GDI. These functions have names beginning with Eng.

On startup, the driver notifies the GDI of support routines implemented in the driver. The driver must implement simple drawing functions, while more-complex functions can be implemented by the driver or the GDI.

Drawing operations are called with the drawing parameters and a *Clip List*. The Clip List is a list of rectangles of the logical drawing surface that can be drawn. The driver may not draw into other screen areas that are occluded by other windows. It is the driver's responsibility to interpret the Clip List properly.

The driver can optimize the Clip List computations by making some special-case analysis and reducing the number of tests required on a per-request basis, including the following.

- The Clip List has one rectangle that is the entire screen.
- The Clip List has one rectangle.
- The Clip List has multiple rectangles.

The driver also can examine the drawing request and compute a *bounding box* for the request. It then can further optimize the computations relative to the Clip List by determining which of the following cases apply.

- The bounding box is outside the one (and only) clipping rectangle.

- The bounding box is entirely inside the one (and only) clipping rectangle.

- The bounding box overlaps the one (and only) clipping rectangle.

- The bounding box is outside all clipping rectangles.

- The bounding box is entirely inside one of the clipping rectangles.

- The bounding box overlaps exactly one of the clipping rectangles.

- The bounding box overlaps more than one of the clipping rectangles.

The Clip List is in physical device coordinates. However, the *Clipping Region* seen by the application programmer is always in *client coordinates*. The GDI must transform the client coordinates to physical device coordinates before passing the list to the driver. Note also that the GDI may itself perform some of the optimizations suggested and not even call the driver if a request would clearly be rejected (such as drawing a filled rectangle that is completely outside the client area of a window). The Clip List for the driver is built by the GDI based on the placement of windows on the screen and may be additionally modified by clipping regions specified by the application.

Historical Perspective

Understanding how the DDI Driver evolved can help you to understand the division between the Miniport Driver and the DDI Driver.

Before NT 4.0, the DDI Driver was a *User-mode* component of the GDI (which also operated in User mode). The Miniport Driver was the Kernel-mode component of the Port Driver. An application program calling a GDI function caused a context switch to the CRSS process. The CRSS process contained the GDI, which executed and called the DDI Driver. If any I/O space access was needed, the Miniport Driver would be called. Memory such as the frame buffer would be "double-mapped" to both the User-mode CRSS process and the Miniport Driver (in system space).

The problem with this design was performance. A context switch is a relatively expensive operation. As Windows applications became more graphics-intensive, the fact that it took four context swaps to implement a single GDI call became one of the major performance bottlenecks in the system. An attempt to improve this performance somewhat was the addition of a mechanism to *queue* GDI requests within the application context by the GDI DLL. The queue would accumulate GDI operations until either the queue filled or a watchdog timer expired. The timer would be reset on each GDI operation. A GDI call was provided to set the size of the queue. The effect of this was to bunch GDI requests that occurred close to the same time for execution. However, performance was still impacted by the eventual need for context switches and the fact that some GDI operations required "positive acknowledgment" that would force the queue to be flushed so that the operation could be performed and a meaningful value could be returned to the application.

In NT 4.0, the GDI was moved to Kernel mode. The division of functionality between the DDI Driver and the Miniport Driver was preserved with minor changes. (For example, I/O operations can now be done directly in the DDI Driver in the same way that memory-mapped register access has always been done.)

Originally, it was thought that this change meant that the GDI queue was no longer necessary. After some additional performance measurement in NT 4.0 beta, GDI queueing was restored in the product release.

The driver can use any of three methods to communicate with the hardware.

- Queue an IOCTL to the Miniport Driver.

  This should be done infrequently and reserved for special operations. It will be used when the operation must be synchronized to an interrupt. It also is used to enable and disable a hardware cursor if one is supported in the hardware. Miniport IOCTL operations include device reset; video mode setting (screen size, resolution, and refresh rate); query-supported modes; mapping of display memory to a system virtual address; power management; setting of the RAMDAC color palette; and font management.

- Directly manipulate the frame buffer memory.

  This is used any time the DDI Driver needs to draw pixels, which it draws directly into the frame buffer.

- Directly manipulate the adapter registers.

  This is used by the DDI Driver for any commands, which it sends to the graphics accelerator. Examples are setting the endpoints of a line and initiating a line-draw operation or setting the top-left and bottom-right corners for a filled rectangle and initiating a fill-rectangle operation.

Surfaces

GDI operations are directed to a *surface*. The surface is a digital representation for the sheet of paper being printed or the display screen that is the ultimate target for the drawing operation. It is a data structure that will contain the representation for the pixels on the target device.

Two kinds of surfaces are provided to the GDI: *Engine-Managed* and *Device-Managed*.

Engine-Managed Surfaces. An Engine-Managed Surface must be a *Device-Independent Bitmap* (DIB). A DIB is a standard-format windows bitmap used at the application level as well as in Display Drivers. It has a single-plane, packed-pixel format representation. Each scan line of the bitmap is aligned on a 4-byte boundary. Depending on the color depth, it might use 1 bit per pixel (a monochrome DIB) or 8 bits, 16 bits, or 32 bits per pixel. (For efficiency, 24-bit color is represented as the low-order 24 bits of a 32-bit value.)

DIBs are created by the GDI (the engine) when the DDI Driver calls the GDI function `EngCreateBitmap`. The driver can create a DIB as its primary surface and let the GDI render directly to this DIB. Then, the GDI can directly write to the frame buffer of the display device.

A driver for a frame buffer-type display adapter will create an Engine-Managed Surface as its primary surface in its `DrvEnableSurface` entry.

Device-Managed Surfaces. A Device-Managed Surface is controlled by the driver. The driver may use any data structure (DIB or non-DIB) to represent the surface. The GDI calls the driver for all rendering operations. A device with a device-managed DIB surface allows its driver to call back to the GDI to have it draw on the surface. With a non-DIB representation, the driver will actually do all of the rendering, while with a DIB representation, the driver may decide to punt the request back to the GDI.

To create a DIB representation of a Device-Managed Surface, the driver can call `EngCreateBitmap`. It gives a handle to the DIB and passes this handle to

`EngCreateDeviceSurface` to create the surface. The GDI calls the driver for all rendering operations, some of which may be punted back to the GDI for processing. The device-managed DIB technique is used to support banked frame buffer Display Drivers. Banked frame buffers are used in ISA SVGA display adapters because the window in address space is insufficient to map the entire frame buffer.

To create a Device-Managed Surface that is a non-DIB, a DDI Driver can call `EngCreateDeviceSurface`. The GDI then will create the surface and return a handle to it. However, it cannot access pixels in the frame buffer. It instead calls the driver to access, to draw to, and to read from the surface.

A *Device Dependent Bitmap* (DDB) is a type of non-DIB Device-Managed Surface. The DDB is supported to allow drivers, such as the VGA, to implement faster bitmap-to-screen block transfers. The DDB also allows drivers to draw to bitmaps in off-screen display memory.

The driver can implement `DrvCreateDeviceBitmap` to create a device format bitmap. This routine will call `EngCreateDeviceBitmap` to have the engine return a handle to the bitmap.

Hooks

When an Engine-Managed Surface is associated with a device (by calling `EngAssociateSurface`), specific operations may be *hooked* by the driver. The hooked operations will be passed to the Display Driver without the GDI simulation. The driver may do specialized processing for the function or punt the request back to the GDI.

Operations that can be hooked are given in Table 25.3.

Table 25.3: *Hookable DDI/GDI Operations*

BITBLT	LINETO	STROKEANDFILLPATH	SYNCHRONIZEACCESS
COPYBITS	PAINT	STROKEPATH	TEXTOUT
FILLPATH	STRETCHBLT	SYNCHRONIZE	

DDI Driver Startup Sequence

The DDI Driver startup sequence is shown in Figure 25.2.

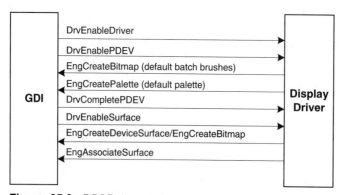

Figure 25.2: *DDI Driver startup sequence.*

1. When the GDI is called to create the first Device Context (DC) for the video hardware, the GDI calls the Display Driver function `DrvEnableDriver`.

2. `DrvEnableDriver` returns to the GDI with a `DRVENABLEDATA` structure. This structure holds both the driver version number and the entry points of all functions that the driver chooses to support.

3. The GDI then typically asks for a physical device to be created by a call to the Display Driver function `DrvEnablePDEV`.

4. The call uses the GDI `DEVMODEW` structure to identify the exact device and mode that the GDI wants to access.

5. The Display Driver initializes the hardware to a known state by sending requests to the video port/Miniport Driver pair.

6. If the GDI requests a mode that the Display Driver or underlying Miniport Driver does not support, the Display Driver must fail this call.

7. The Display Driver represents a logical device controlled by the GDI. A single logical device can manage several physical devices, each characterized by type of hardware, logical address, and surfaces supported.

8. The Display Driver allocates the memory to support the device it creates. The driver can manage more than a single display defined as a `PDEV`. It copies device information to a `PDEV` structure that represents the display and its current operating state. `DrvEnablePDEV` can be called more than once by the GDI, with each call creating another `PDEV` that is used with a different surface. If a driver is to support more than one `PDEV`, it must not use global variables.

9. The GDI calls `DrvEnableSurface`. An actual surface is not supported until the GDI does this.

10. When installation of the physical device is complete, the GDI calls the Display Driver `DrvCompletePDEV` function. This function provides the driver with a physical device handle to be used when requesting GDI functions for the device.

11. As the final stage of initialization, a surface is created for the video hardware by a GDI call to `DrvEnableSurface`, which enables graphics output to the hardware. Depending on the device and the environment, the Display Driver enables a surface in one of two ways, as follows.

    - The driver manages its own surface by calling the GDI function `EngCreateDeviceSurface` to obtain a handle for the surface. The Device-Managed Surface method is required for hardware that does not support a standard-format bitmap and is optional for hardware that does.

    - The GDI manages the surface completely as an Engine-Managed Surface if the hardware device has a surface organized as a standard-format bitmap. Even in this case, when it calls `EngAssociateSurface`, the driver can still hook any drawing functions that it can more efficiently handle.

The Display Driver can obtain a bitmap handle for a surface by calling `EngCreateBitmap` with a pointer to the device pixels. The GDI collects the graphics directly in a bitmap. The Display Driver then calls `EngCreateBitmap`, thereby allowing the GDI to allocate space for the pixels.

Any existing GDI bitmap handle is a valid surface handle. Before the Display Driver returns a surface, it must associate the surface with the PDEV, using a call to `EngAssociateSurface`, in which it specifies which functions it wishes to hook for drawing to the surface. If the surface is engine-managed, the GDI can handle any or all drawing operations. If the surface is device-managed, the driver must, at a minimum, handle `DrvTextOut`, `DrvStrokePath`, and `DrvCopyBits`.

Sequence of Events: GDI Operation

In this section, we show you the sequence of events when an application calls the GDI to draw in a window. Note that from the application's perspective, "the GDI does the drawing"—the interactions of the GDI, the DDI, the Miniport Driver, and so on are essentially hidden from the application. The application can query the GDI to see if the device will support certain operations. If it can't, the application might have to use an alternative implementation of the operation. However, the common graphics operations are supported on all devices. (However, rendering a bitmap on a 6-pen plotter is probably not supported by the plotter driver. This might change how the application renders bitmaps. Usually this is not an issue.)

The simplistic mode goes as follows.

1. The application calls GDI32 for a drawing request.
2. The GDI32 calls the kernel GDI to complete the request.
3. The GDI calls the Display Driver.
4. The Display Driver communicates via frame buffer memory and chip registers to start the drawing operation.
5. The Display Driver waits for the drawing operation to complete. Once it does, the driver returns.

The truth is more complex. For example, the GDI might enqueue the operation and not actually call the Display Driver until the queue is flushed. Often the flushing is implicit in some other operation, and it is *that* operation that actually must wait for the Display Driver to complete the drawing of all queued requests before it can complete and return. Unless the application programmer is single-stepping through source code to do debugging, the queueing in the GDI is invisible to the programmer. A general technique for debugging is to set the queue size to 1 while debugging the application. This guarantees that each GDI operation will complete before it returns, thereby allowing the programmer to see each drawing operation take place. (Setting the queue size to 0 means "set it to the system default size". To get no queueing, set it to 1.)

An actual operation will include, in addition to the queueing, processing of the Clip List, as already described, and might include callbacks to the GDI.

It is worth noting that when the GDI was rewritten to be in Kernel mode, the concept of the GDI queue was removed—all GDI operations worked directly. After some testing, performance problems were still seen, so between the final Beta of Windows NT 4.0 and the product release, the GDI queue was reinstated.

Mandatory DDI Driver Entry Points

All Graphics Drivers must support the entry points that the GDI calls to enable and disable the driver, the PDEV, and the surface associated with each PDEV. Table 25.4 lists the needed functions in the order in which they are typically called.

Table 25.4: *Mandatory DDI Driver Entry Points*

Entry Point	Description
DrvEnableDriver	As the initial driver entry point, provides the GDI with the driver version number and entry points of optional functions supported.
DrvGetModes	Lists the modes supported by a specified video hardware device. This function is required only for Display Drivers.
DrvEnablePDEV	Enables a PDEV.
DrvCompletePDEV	Informs the driver of completion of device installation.
DrvEnableSurface	Creates a surface for a specified hardware device.
DrvDisableSurface	Informs the driver that the surface created for the current device is no longer needed.
DrvDisablePDEV	When the hardware is no longer needed, frees the memory and resources used by the device, as well as any surface created but not yet deleted.
DrvDisableDriver	Frees all allocated resources for the driver, and returns the device to its state when initially loaded.
DrvAssertMode	Resets the video mode for a specified hardware device. This function is required only for Display Drivers.

Conditionally Required DDI Driver Entry Points

Depending on how a driver is implemented, other functions, such as those listed in Table 25.5, are required. If the driver manages its own surface (using EngCreateDeviceSurface to get a handle to the surface), the driver must also support several drawing functions. Drivers writing to standard-format DIBs usually allow the GDI to manage most or all of these operations. Displays that support settable palettes must also support DrvSetPalette.

It is more common for a Printer Driver than a Display Driver to define or draw fonts. A Display Driver is not required to handle fonts unless it must be able to draw its own fonts or those of the video hardware on a Device-Managed Surface. If the hardware has a resident font, the driver must supply information to the GDI about this font. This information includes font metrics, mappings from Unicode to individual glyph identities, individual glyph attributes, and kerning tables.

Table 25.5: *Conditionally Required DDI Driver Entry Points*

Entry Point	When Required	Description
DrvCopyBits	Device-Managed Surfaces	Translates between a device-managed raster surface and a GDI standard-format bitmap.
DrvStrokePath	Device-Managed Surfaces	Renders a path on the display.
DrvTextOut	Device-Managed Surfaces or drivers that define fonts	Renders a set of character components (glyphs) at specified positions.
DrvSetPalette	Displays that support settable palettes	Realizes the palette for a specified device.
DrvPaint	Device-Managed Surfaces	Fills ("paints") a specified region.
DrvDescribePixelFormat	Displays that support windows with different pixel formats on a single surface	Describes a PDEV's pixel format.
DrvSetPixelFormat	Displays that support windows with different pixel formats on a single surface	Sets a window's pixel format.
DrvSwapBuffers	Drivers that support a pixel format with double-buffering	Displays contents of a surface's hidden buffer.
DrvResetPDEV	Devices that allow mode changes in documents	Transfers driver state from old PDEV to new PDEV.
DrvQueryFont	Drivers that draw fonts	Retrieves a GDI structure for a given font.
DrvQueryFontData	Drivers that draw fonts	Retrieves information about a realized font.
DrvQueryFontTree	Drivers that draw fonts	Queries a tree structure defining one of three types of font mapping.
DrvLoadFontFile	Font drivers	Specifies the file to use for font realizations.
DrvUnloadFontFile	Font drivers	Informs the driver that a font file is not needed.
DrvQueryFontCaps	Font drivers	Asks the driver for font driver capabilities.
DrvQueryFontFile	Font drivers	Asks the driver for font file information.
DrvQueryTrueTypeTable	TrueType font drivers	Gives the GDI access to TrueType font files.
DrvQueryTrueTypeOutline	TrueType font drivers	Returns TrueType glyph handles to the GDI.
DrvGetTrueTypeFile	TrueType font drivers	Gives the GDI access to memory-mapped TrueType font files.

Optional DDI Driver Entry Points

In the interests of reducing driver size, drivers usually add only those optional functions that are well-supported in hardware. If a driver is written for hardware that supports these specialized functions, the appropriate functions in Table 25.6 can be included.

Table 25.6: *Optional DDI Driver Entry Points*

Entry Point	Description
DrvCreateDeviceBitmap	Creates and manages a bitmap with a driver-defined format.
DrvDeleteDeviceBitmap	Deletes a device-managed bitmap.
DrvDitherColor	Requests a device to create a brush dithered against a device palette.
DrvFillPath	Paints a closed path for a Device-Managed Surface.
DrvMovePointer	Moves a pointer to a new position, and redraws it.
DrvBitBlt	Executes general bit block transfers to and from surfaces.
DrvRealizeBrush	Realizes a specified brush for a defined surface.
DrvSaveScreenBits	Saves or restores a specified rectangle of the screen only for Display Drivers.
DrvSetPointerShape	Removes the pointer from the screen, if the driver has drawn it, and then sets a new pointer shape.
DrvStretchBlt	Allows stretching block transfers among Device-Managed Surfaces and GDI-managed surfaces.
DrvStrokeAndFillPath	Simultaneously fills and strokes a path.
DrvSynchronize	Coordinates drawing operations between the GDI and a Display Driver-supported coprocessor device; for Engine-Managed Surfaces only.
DrvFree	Frees font storage associated with an indicated data structure.
DrvDestroyFont	Notifies the driver that a font realization is no longer needed. The driver can free allocated data structures.
DrvEscape	Queries information from a device not available in a device-independent DDI.
DrvDrawEscape	Implements draw-type escape functions.
DrvEndDoc	Sends end-of-document information; only for Printer Drivers.
DrvGetGlyphMode	Returns type of font information to be stored for a particular font; only for Printer Drivers.
DrvSendPage	Sends raw bits from a surface to the printer; only for Printer Drivers.
DrvStartDoc	Sends start-of-document control information; only for Printer Drivers.
DrvStartPage	Sends start-of-page control information; only for Printer Drivers.
DrvFontManagement	Allows access to printer functionality not directly available through the GDI; only for Printer Drivers.
DrvQueryAdvanceWidths	Supplies character advance widths for a specified set of glyphs (font driver).

Table 25.6: *Optional DDI Driver Entry Points (continued)*

Entry Point	Description
`DrvLineTo`	Draws a single, solid, integer-only cosmetic line.
`DrvNextBand`	Realizes the contents of a surface's just-drawn band.
`DrvStartBanding`	Prepares the driver for banding.

OpenGL

The driver may provide hardware acceleration support for OpenGL 3D drawing operations. OpenGL is an API and technique for 3D drawing. It provides a standard interface between application programs and (accelerated and unaccelerated) hardware for the display of 3D images from within programs. The API offers the programmer a high-level set of operations in the API to minimize the effort involved in developing programs. OpenGL was initially developed by Silicon Graphics and is now controlled by an eight-company Architectural Review Board.

The OpenGL runtime has been a part of Windows NT since version 3.5. These operations work with the runtime to provide an efficient yet simple method to draw 3D objects. A driver can choose to support OpenGL in any of three ways: no driver support, the MCD support, and the Installable Client Driver (ICD) support.

Because the OpenGL operations are higher-level than GDI operations, it is easier to directly map an OpenGL operation to 3D accelerator hardware. In fact, some modern 3D cards implement OpenGL primitives directly in hardware, so the mapping from the application to the hardware is very efficient.

Implementation of OpenGL

There are three strategies for supporting OpenGL, depending on the amount of money the user has spent. A "low-end" system usually has a "stock" SVGA card installed. A midrange system usually has a fairly sophisticated SVGA accelerator card installed, and a "high-end" system has an OpenGL-based or similar sophisticated accelerator card installed. Following are the three strategies.

- For low-end systems, the GDI supports OpenGL by simulation.

  The simplest thing for a Device Driver writer to do is nothing. If the Display Driver provides no support for OpenGL, the GDI will simulate all OpenGL operations and call the driver with standard drawing operations. This technique offers no hardware acceleration and is the lowest performance technique.

  This technique is suitable for low-end video systems.

- For midrange systems, an MCD Interface supports OpenGL.

  The MCD interface is a simplified interface to allow hardware acceleration for OpenGL functions. This interface allows acceleration of only a portion of the OpenGL functionality, the part that will have the greatest result for the work. Development sources and documents for the MCD are in the Windows NT DDK.

Microsoft has announced that the MCD interface will continue to be supported, but the interface will not be expanded to accelerate new capabilities on Windows NT.

- For high-end systems, an ICD supports OpenGL.

  The ICD interface is a full interface for hardware acceleration. It allows all OpenGL functions to be accelerated. Today, the development sources and resources to develop an ICD driver requires licenses from both Microsoft and Silicon Graphics. Microsoft promises to produce a special DDK for the ICD interface under Windows 2000. This DDK will contain the required components and documentation. It *will* require a license from Microsoft, and in some cases, the license will require that the vendor also support DirectDraw and Direct3D.

  With the freeze in functionality for the MCD interface, the ICD will, over time, move into midrange systems as well as high-end systems.

Direct3D and DirectDraw

The DirectDraw interface allows an application program access to the frame buffer. Direct3D provides equivalent support for 3D graphics cards.

Direct3D Overview

Essentially, Direct3D is a drawing interface for 3D hardware. In its Immediate mode, Direct3D allows developers to port games and other high-performance multimedia applications onto Windows. Its features include switchable z-buffering, hardware independence, and support for the Intel MMX architecture. Direct3D Immediate mode also supports drawing primitives without the use of "execute buffers".

Direct3D's Retained mode lets developers create high-quality 3D applications without wading through low-level object structures. It simplifies the building and animation of 3D worlds with two new features:

- Animation interpolators, which enable the blending of colors, smooth movement of objects, and many other transformations
- Progressive meshes, which allow the increasing refinement of a coarse mesh over time, thereby helping with progressive downloads from remote locations

DirectDraw Overview

DirectDraw is a memory manager for graphics and video surfaces. It provides the foundation for high-performance multimedia on Windows platforms. It bypasses the traditional layers associated with Windows-based graphics, thereby allowing direct access to display memory and hardware features while maintaining compatibility with Windows-based applications.

DirectDraw works with a wide variety of display hardware, from simple monitors to advanced hardware implementations. Operating at the graphics surface level, it provides the base for high-level graphics APIs. Its graphics acceleration capability assesses the video hardware's capabilities, making use of special features whenever possible and emulating features not implemented in the hardware.

Printer Drivers

The role of a Printer Driver is to maintain device independence across a wide variety of printing devices. Thus it converts the GDI level requests to whatever insane representation the printer requires. Printers can be roughly partitioned into three categories:

- PCL-compatible
- PostScript-compatible
- Other

Within the first two categories are different levels: PCL4, PCL5, PostScript Level 1, Post-Script Level 2, and PostScript Level 3. Color versus monochrome is a separate dimension.

The architecture of a Printer Driver is shown in Figure 25.3. Note that it shares the GDI with the Display Driver. Note, too, the addition of the Spooler, which ultimately handles the communication to the physical device by working through the I/O Manager. A typical arrangement is shown in the figure, whereby a serial or parallel interface is used to talk to the device. The GDI sends information to the Spooler via the WinSpool component of the Win32 Subsystem.

How the driver does the rendering can vary, even within a single type of device. For example, a PCL printer will accept a TIFF (a graphics file format) file with a small header prepended. The GDI is then told to rasterize everything and pass the TIFF file to the driver. A Printer Driver that supports a PCL printer with this simple technique will be a major failure in today's market because the amount of data to be sent to the printer for each page will be maximized, thus slowing printing. Enhancements in the printer to maximize the print quality of fonts will never be used.

A realistic Printer Driver will download fonts to the printer and use the font painting capabilities of the printer, as well as other higher-level drawing operations supported by the print engine. For example, PCL and PostScript both directly support operations such as MoveTo and

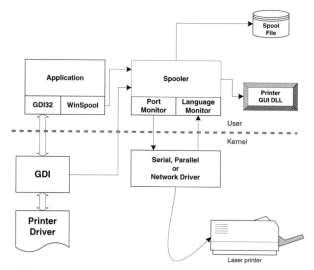

Figure 25.3: *Printer Driver architecture.*

`LineTo`. In addition, PostScript supports such operations as `StrokePath`, `FillPath`, and `StrokeAndFillPath`.[7]

A printer might not have sufficient memory to rasterize an entire page before starting to print the page. In this case, the driver must divide the page into "bands" and structure the meta-file to describe the bands in the order in which the print engine will need the rasterized data. The printer then processes the data band-by-band while feeding the rasterized data to the print engine. This is especially true for large-format, high-resolution printers. But it can also be true for printers such as low-resolution ink-jet printers that print a band of pixels in one sweep of the print head across the page and then advance the paper and sweep the head the opposite direction. It is a choice of the Device Driver writer as to whether such a device is handled by banding or by creating the bitmap for the entire page and sending it.

The Printer Driver also has a User Interface component. This interface is the dialog box(es) that allows the user to set the printer mode and control its behavior. The User Interface is executed in User mode in the context of the Spooler.

A printer vendor may elect to provide two other components: a Port Monitor and a Language Monitor. The Port Monitor, a User-mode driver, controls the communication with a printer. It is called by the Spooler to send metafile data to the printer. If the printer is connected via an unusual technique or protocol, a Port Monitor will implement the communication technique. The Language Monitor, the last component, is used with bidirectional printers that report status information. A single module may implement both a Port Monitor and a Language Monitor.

Sequence of Events: Printer Driver

The Printer Driver uses the same GDI primitives as a Display Driver does to draw onto the printer surface. However, the sequence of operations is somewhat different than for a Display Driver because the Spooler is involved.

1. The Application calls the GDI32 for a drawing request.
2. GDI32 calls the kernel GDI to complete the request.
3. The GDI calls the Printer Driver to convert the drawing request to a printer-specific set of commands.
4. The GDI calls the Spooler to write the commands to a disk file.
5. Eventually, the Spooler will retrieve the commands to send to the printer.
6. The Port Monitor sends the commands to the target printer.
7. The Language Monitor receives the status from the printer (if the printer is bi-directional).

---

[7] Actually, PCL might support these as well. I spent nearly a decade developing PostScript applications and have ignored PCL, so I simply plead total ignorance of PCL as my excuse for not knowing for sure. *–jmn*

The SCSI Bus

The SCSI Bus is an *external* bus, one of several that includes IDE, USB, and P1394 ("FireWire").[8] SCSI is both a *bus* and a *protocol*. For example, there are a number of implementations of SCSI commands on *serial* busses, such as Fibre Channel (FC) and Serial Standard Architecture (SSA). Thus, while the SCSI Bus might slowly be replaced by physical layers such as Fibre Channel, Serial Standard Architecture, or P1394, the SCSI *protocols* will remain relatively transport-layer-independent. For readers interested in the details of SCSI programming, we recommend Brian Sawert's *The Programmer's Guide to SCSI* (see the Further Reading section at the end of the chapter).

The SCSI Physical Bus

The SCSI Bus is a specification of electrical and physical connectors. The original SCSI specification, now known as SCSI-1, used a 50-pin connector. (Generally, it is called a "Centronics-style" connector because it is the same style as the 36-pin connector first used by the first PC printer manufacturer.) Newer SCSI standards use a 68-pin "subminiature-D connector".

The SCSI-1 physical bus limited transfers to 8-bit-wide transfers at a maximum of 5MB/sec. Most modern SCSI Busses are SCSI-2, which encompasses options such as *wide SCSI* (16-bit transfers), *fast SCSI* (10MB/sec for 8-bit transfers), and *fast wide SCSI* (20MB/sec for 16-bit transfers). The 32-bit SCSI controllers can double the transfer rate, but as we discuss shortly, there are no physical busses that can transfer 32 bits in parallel. SCSI-3 provides for up to 80MB/sec. Most SCSI devices are *single-ended*, meaning that there are two voltage levels: nominally ground and +5V. SCSI also allows for *differential SCSI*, which uses balanced line signals. (Balanced lines use two opposing voltages to represent a bit. This makes them insensitive to certain kinds of electrical noise and makes the detection of definite 0/1 states easier. RS-232 is an example of a differential transmission line.) This allows the cables to be longer and to run at higher data rates reliably. The new SCSI-3 specification for *Ultra2-SCSI*, specified at 40MB/sec, and *wide Ultra2-SCSI*, specified at 80MB/sec, require a new voltage level called *Low Voltage Differential* (LVD). The names and transfer rates are summarized in Table 25.7.

Because of the problems of cabling, there appear to be no 32-bit-wide SCSI implementations on parallel SCSI Busses. Because most physical busses require two wires for each signal (either a ground wire between each signal wire, or two signal wires for differential SCSI), a 32-bit-wide SCSI Bus would require 64 wires for data signals alone, not counting any of the control signals (each of which also requires two wires). If the physical diameter of the wires is reduced, the resistance goes up and the cable length over which transfer is feasible decreases. However, using the 32-bit *protocol* over a high-speed serial line would be quite feasible. Thus we move from the realm of physical connectivity to the realm of protocols.

---

[8] There are different interpretations of the meanings of "internal" and "external". Microsoft, for example, thinks of IDE as an "internal" bus because there is no "external" connector for it. We think of "internal" as those busses that are directly on the processor, such as ISA and PCI, and "external" as anything plugged into something that is accessed via an internal bus.

Table 25.7: *SCSI Transfer Rates*

Name	Data Rate	Transfer Width
Synchronous SCSI (SCSI-1)	5MB/sec	8 bits
Fast SCSI	10MB/sec	8 bits
Wide SCSI (Wide-16)	10MB/sec	16 bits
Wide SCSI (Wide-32)	20MB/sec	32 bits
Fast Wide SCSI (Wide-16)	20MB/sec	16 bits
Fast Wide SCSI (Wide-32)	40MB/sec	32 bits
Ultra SCSI (Fast-20)	20MB/sec	8 bits
Ultra2 SCSI (Fast-40)	40MB/sec	8 bits
Wide Ultra SCSI	40MB/sec	16 bits
Wide Ultra2 SCSI	80MB/sec	16 bits

The SCSI Command Set

The SCSI *protocol* is actually independent of the physical transfer means. The SCSI Command Set, which has been more precisely specified in each of the SCSI standards, provides a transport-level-independent specification of what a device should respond to and how it should respond. The command set is shown in Table 25.8. Some commands of the SCSI set are mandatory, such as those used to query device characteristics. Others are optional, but if present, must conform to the standard. The ones labeled "Device-specific" are those required only for certain kinds of devices; if present, they must conform to the standards. And, as usual with most standards, there are vendor-defined commands that are usually unique to each device. Each SCSI device can act, usually interchangeably, as either a bus master or a slave, known respectively as the *initiator* and the *target*. It is perfectly permissible for two "smart" SCSI devices to communicate independently of the processor.

A SCSI command is a sequence of bytes called a *Command Descriptor Block* (CDB). Currently these CDBs are one of a selected set of lengths: 6 bytes, 10 bytes, or 12 bytes. The first byte is always the SCSI Operation Code and determines, by the type of operation, how many bytes are in the CDB. In addition, a CDB may be followed by some number of *parameter values*. For the details of this, we suggest Chapter 5 of *The Programmer's Guide to SCSI*.

SCSI commands that use multibyte data values provide a somewhat jarring discontinuity with the classic PC platforms. The SCSI protocol is set up for "big-endian" transfers, that is, the most significant byte first. PCs all use "little-endian" representations, that is, the least significant byte is first in sequential addressing order. It is the responsibility of the Device Driver to convert multibyte values in the SCSI command blocks from little-endian to big-endian and vice versa while dealing with the transfers. Note that it is your responsibility, or the responsibility of the application, to deal with data transformations if the device requires its *data* to be endian-specific. This requirement might be because of how the device interprets the data or how the data will be used. For example, a tape that will be read by a big-endian mainframe might be written with its bytes in big-endian order. When talking to SCSI from NT, you will generally create a

Table 25.8: *SCSI Command Set*

Opcode	Type	Command Name
0x00	Mandatory	Test Unit Ready
0x03	Mandatory	Request Sense
0x12	Mandatory	Inquiry
0x15	Device-specific	Mode Select (6-byte)
0x18	Optional	Copy
0x1a	Device-specific	Mode Sense (6-byte)
0x1c	Optional	Receive Diagnostic Results
0x1d	Mandatory	Send Diagnostic
0x39	Optional	Compare
0x3a	Optional	Copy and Verify
0x3b	Optional	Write Buffer
0x3c	Optional	Read Buffer
0x40	Optional	Change Definition
0x4c	Optional	Log Alert
0x4d	Optional	Log Sense
0x55	Device-specific	Mode Select (10-byte)
0x5a	Device-specific	Mode Sense (10-byte)

SCSI Request Block (SRB) and pass it down to the SCSI Port Driver. At the lowest level, the conversion of the command values from little-endian to big-endian will be automatically done for you by the Miniport Driver. We discuss this in detail in the next section. Thus you will not need to worry about this unless, of course, *you* are the one writing a Miniport Driver.

Because the SCSI Command Set has little or nothing to do with the actual physical means of transfer of the commands and data, the set does *not* require a SCSI physical bus in order to implement the transfer. Thus there are already implementations of SCSI-3 disk servers connected via a P1394 serial bus. The P1394 bus has data rates of 100Mb/sec, 200Mb/sec, 400Mb/sec, and, on the horizon, 1Gb/sec. Thus these implementations could provide for data transfer rates in excess of 100MB/sec. As a Device Driver writer, you will see the SCSI Command Set as an abstraction (unless you are writing the lowest-level Miniport Driver to one of these high-speed busses!).

SCSI Drivers

The SCSI Driver system in Windows NT consists of at least three types of drivers:

- One or more *Class Drivers*
- A *Port Driver*

 • One or more SCSI *Miniport Drivers*

These are shown in Figure 25.4. NT also includes a Tape Device Class Driver that requires a Miniport Driver for each type of tape device to be supported.

The Class Driver

The Class Driver implements support for a type of SCSI device, such as a hard drive, CD-ROM, or scanner. If the SCSI Command Set is standardized, the Class Driver will operate for the entire SCSI class of devices. For example, the SCSI CD-ROM Driver will work for all brands of SCSI CD-ROM drives that use a standard command set (you can use Filter Drivers to handle individual brand idiosyncrasies).

The Class Driver supports the IRPs needed for an application or higher-level driver. If the device is a SCSI version of a preexisting device type, the same IRPs (IRP_MJ_*xxx* codes) must be supported. The Class Driver translates each IRP to an SRB and passes the SRB to the SCSI Port Driver.

A typical Class Driver will support at least IRP_MJ_CREATE, IRP_MJ_CLOSE, IRP_MJ_DEVICE_CONTROL, IRP_MJ_READ, IRP_MJ_WRITE, and IRP_MJ_SHUTDOWN.

The SCSI Class Driver does the following.

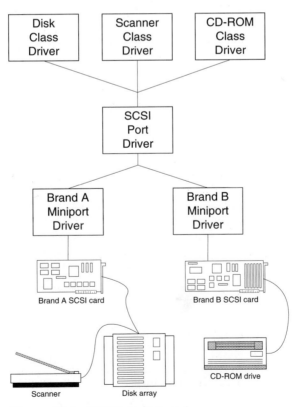

Figure 25.4: *SCSI Driver hierarchy.*

1. Initializes and then opens the Port Driver in order to pass SRBs.
2. Enumerates the SCSI Bus, scanning it for the supported device(s).
3. Creates one or more Device Objects for each supported device found on the SCSI Bus.
4. Initializes the supported hardware as needed.

For each IRP, it will do the following.

- Translate IRPs into SRBs as necessary (note, some IRPs might be satisfied internally).

- Possibly split the I/O request. The IRP might specify a data transfer larger than the hardware is capable of processing.

- Handle device errors for the supported device. You should log and report these errors as appropriate. Error processing might include resubmitting operations. Errors include time-outs and hardware detected faults.

The Port Driver

The SCSI Port Driver provides the common support for SCSI operations. It is a DLL of routines called by the SCSI Miniport Driver to allow the SCSI system to function with the supported adapter. There is only one SCSI Port Driver, and it is provided by Microsoft.

The Miniport Driver

The SCSI Miniport Driver communicates with a SCSI Device Adapter. One Miniport Driver is required for each type of adapter. The Miniport Driver is a restricted form of Device Driver—it can call only the NT Kernel-mode support routines exported by the SCSI Port Driver for use by Miniport Drivers. The Miniport Driver entry points are shown in Table 25.9.

Table 25.9: *SCSI Miniport Driver Entry Points*

Entry Point	Description
Required Entries	
DriverEntry	Initializes the driver (the name DriverEntry is required).
HwScsiFindAdapter	Enumerates the SCSI Bus and scans for supported adapters.
HwScsiInitialize	Initializes supported SCSI adapters.
HwScsiStartIo	Starts pending operations on the SCSI adapter.
HwScsiResetBus	Handles SCSI Bus-reset requests.
Optional Entries	
HwScsiInterrupt	Handles adapter-generated interrupts. This function is required if the adapter generates interrupts. Only a low-performance adapter will operate in a polled mode (without interrupts).
HwScsiDisableInterruptsCallback	Handles deferred I/O processing if interrupt-driven I/O operations take a long time.
HwScsiEnableInterruptsCallback	

Table 25.9: *SCSI Miniport Driver Entry Points (continued)*

Entry Point	Description
HwScsiTimer	Handles timer calls to the driver.
HwScsiDmaStarted	Required if the adapter uses a system DMA controller.
HwScsiAdapterState	An NT-only entry. Used only if the adapter has no BIOS.

Properly written SCSI Miniport Drivers are portable between Windows NT and Windows 9x. This portability is lost if the Miniport Driver calls any routine not exported by the SCSI Port Driver (that is, a name in the form ScsiPort*Xxx*).

Advanced SCSI Programming Interface

The Advanced SCSI Programming Interface (ASPI) is an API layered on top of the SCSI driver hierarchy. It is designed for application compatibility with the DOS and Windows 9x ASPI implementations and ease of development.

In the early days of MS-DOS (and PC-DOS), after SCSI hard drives were introduced to the PC, the SCSI vendor would provide a SCSI hard drive driver. The driver would be monolithic, claiming exclusive control of the SCSI adapter and bus, as well as of the drive(s). As other SCSI peripherals became available, there was market resistance to adding a new adapter card for each peripheral. With the monolithic driver, the disk driver "owned" the adapter card and no other driver could share it.

SCSI device vendors wanted a protocol that would allow them to easily add their device to a system and have it coexist with other SCSI devices. The SCSI adapter vendors came up with protocols to provide layered support. In the UNIX world, it was the *Common Access Method* (CAM). In the PC world, it was the ASPI, which was supported by Adaptec and, in fact, was initially called the *Adaptec* SCSI Programming Interface. However, the vendors realized it was to their advantage to publish an open specification. Eventually, the ASPI standard became a multi-vendor standard. With ASPI, the adapter card support could be shared by several SCSI Device Drivers. A single SCSI Bus and adapter could be used with disk, tape, scanner, CD-ROM, and other SCSI devices.

Adaptec distributes a version of ASPI for NT (ASPI for Win32, also compatible with Windows 95 and Windows 98). The drivers are available on its Web site (www.adaptec.com), and it sells an ASPI Developer's Kit at a nominal price.

The NT device model allows Class Drivers to be added for each new SCSI device type. However, ASPI still has a place. The ASPI device support operates in User mode. A program that uses ASPI support can be debugged in the same way as any other application. The ASPI device support and its relationship to the rest of the NT system is shown in Figure 25.5.

ASPI is a very attractive way to support a SCSI device under development. Changing an ASPI application program can be much easier than changing a Class Driver. ASPI also can be very attractive as a way to support a low-speed, low-production SCSI device. Its use can significantly reduce both time-to-market and cost-of-development. The resulting application is then portable across Windows NT, Windows 2000, Windows 98, and Windows 95, thus further reducing development costs.

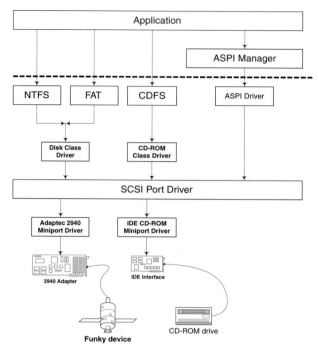

Figure 25.5: *ASPI driver architecture.*

ASPI is good for "generic" SCSI devices. A high-speed device or a device with unusual SCSI requirements will present problems for ASPI and will require that you write your own Class Driver. If you have input to the hardware developers and it looks like ASPI will do the job, it is worthwhile to make sure that the developers don't impose gratuitous hardware requirements that would make ASPI unusable for the device. Of course, there can be fundamental require-ments of the device that would make this equally impossible. You need to distinguish with which of the two cases you are dealing.

Because ASPI is user-level, it is also possible to build an ASPI-emulator that allows soft-ware developers to start work long before working silicon is available.[9]

The application program prepares a SCSI request structure for each command to be sent to the device. (To add to the confusion, it is called a SCSI Request Block, which is also abbreviated SRB. But it is almost, but not quite totally, unlike the NT SCSI Port Driver's SRB structure.) The application can use one of three techniques to determine when the operation is done: a callback, a wait on an Event, and polling. The callback can post a message to the application's main win-dow, and the Event can be used to activate another thread that is waiting for the Event.

The application programmer will need the same low-level knowledge of the SCSI device that is needed for a Class Driver.

The documentation states that the Adaptec ASPI for Win32 requires an Adaptec adapter. It is possible that the ASPI implementation is restricted to using nonstandard device control entry

---

[9] You might gather that I tend to favor simulators, emulators, and other means of expediting development. *–jmn*

points. However, this restriction might simply be a response to the support problem mentioned earlier in the section (and a desire to not provide free consulting to support competitor's boards—not an unreasonable position).

For more information, visit the Adaptec developer's page at
`http://www.adaptec.com/adaptec/developers`

Our experience has been that this site is very confusing and has much obsolete and contradictory material. To find the ASPI information, which is extensive, start at `www.adaptec.com` and search for the string "ASPI". The content clearly has been badly neglected. For example, it often cites calling the Adaptec BBS, and it doesn't mention Web-accessible sources of information. Also, there are far too few hyperlinks, although all of the information actually does appear on their Web site, if you click around a bit. The search within the site does not work. Current pages and obsolete versions of the same pages exist at different points in the hierarchy.

A few other useful links within the Adaptec site are the following.

- Specifications for ASPI for Win32 for the PostScript version may be downloaded from
  `ftp://ftp.adaptec.com/pub/BBS/adaptec/aspi_w32.ps`.

- Specifications for ASPI for Win32 for the text version may be downloaded from
  `ftp://ftp.adaptec.com/pub/BBS/adaptec/aspi_w32.txt`.

However, we got the best version of ASPI documentation by writing to `acap@corp.adaptec.com` and requesting the ASPI for Win32 specifications. We got a response by e-mail, with a Zip file attachment that contained a `pdf` file (Adobe Acrobat format) of the ASPI specification dated January 2, 1997 (more recent than any we found on the Web site) and a sample program.

Adaptec also has a FAQ for ASPI programming at
`http://www.adaptec.com/adaptec/developers/aspi1.html`.
The ASPI runtime is at
`ftp://ftp.adaptec.com/pub/BBS/winnt/aspi32.exe`.

Summary

This chapter has presented a quick overview of several specialized drivers in NT. The Display Driver and Printer Driver were covered in slight depth. We also covered SCSI Drivers and the particular variant of a SCSI Driver, the ASPI driver.

Further Reading

Nagar, Rajeev, *Windows NT File System Internals*, O'Reilly & Associates, 1997. ISBN 1-56592-249-2.

Rector, Brent E., and Joseph M. Newcomer, *Win32 Programming*, Addison Wesley Longman, 1997. ISBN 0-201-63492-9.

Reid, Glenn C., *PostScript Language Program Design*, Addison-Wesley, 1988. ISBN 0-201-14396-8.

Sawert, Brian, *The Programmer's Guide to SCSI*, Addison Wesley Longman, 1998. ISBN 0-201-18538-5.

This is an excellent reference book and contains, besides numerous Win32 code samples, an extensive bibliography of current and even out-of-print SCSI information, interesting Web sites for SCSI programmers, and extensive sample code and documents on a CD-ROM, including browsable pages and the draft SCSI-3 specification. It includes examples of UNIX/Linux drivers as well.

Chapter

---

26 *Useful Driver Techniques*

Every book has a discussion about miscellaneous techniques, and ours is no exception. In this chapter, you'll find the odd little factoids and useful techniques that didn't quite fit anywhere else or that perhaps would have logically, but whose discussion would have been an unnecessary and complicated digression from the mainstream of the presentation. So we gathered these techniques into this eclectic chapter.[1]

The techniques we discuss in this chapter include

- Using the general DPC mechanism (below)
- Multiphase driver initialization (page 558)
- Using the Registry (page 559)
- Using the Event Log (page 565)
- Creating, intercepting, and responding to a system crash (page 577)
- Reading and writing files from within a driver (page 580)
- Creating a pageable driver (page 590)
- NT 4.0-specific product installation techniques (page 595)
- Handling the Alpha write pipe (page 602)

Deferred Procedure Calls

A Deferred Procedure Call (DPC) can be used for purposes other than responding to an interrupt. In the case of an ISR, a DPC is used to lower the IRQL so that the processor is interruptible (but not preemptible) during extended processing of the I/O event. DPCs also can be used to

---

[1] Eclectic chapters are certainly a specialty of one of the authors, as I am founder and president of Eclectic Engineering. *–end*

raise the IRQL, for example, if the routines that must be called to perform the service must be called at IRQL >= DISPATCH_LEVEL. If called at a lower IRQL, the service could deadlock or even crash the system.[2]

Of course, you can simply raise the IRQL temporarily in a thread by calling `KeRaiseIrql` and `KeLowerIrql`, although this has some drawbacks from the viewpoint of coding style. In this case, you must maintain the previous IRQL and, upon completion of your code, lower the IRQL to that value. This introduces the potential for adding a `return` statement and forgetting to reset the IRQL, thus leaving the system in a permanently raised state—not a healthy situation. Often it is cleaner to enqueue a DPC request that can be serviced. Note that on a multiprocessor system, *each* processor can be executing a DPC Routine on behalf of a driver, perhaps even the *same* DPC Routine. Raising the IRQL on one processor has absolutely no effect on the other processors.

There is nothing special about setting up for a DPC from a System Worker Thread or dedicated Driver Thread, and almost nothing special about using it. We discussed those techniques in Chapter 24. There is one serious precaution, however, which we discuss in the next section.

Threads and DPC Queueing: A Fatal Problem

There is an assumption hidden in the design of NT that a given DPC will be queued by one, and exactly one, thread. The code that queues DPCs for execution later is *not* multiprocessor-safe! If the same DPC is queued simultaneously on two processors, the system will crash.

If you queue a DPC from more than one thread on a multiprocessor machine without doing explicit locking, NT *will* eventually execute the queuing operation simultaneously and crash. Remember that *all* drivers must be multiprocessor-safe. The crash occurs because the DPC Object itself is not protected; rather, the DPC *queues* on each of the processors are each individually protected. So if you have a driver that occasionally crashes a multiprocessor system, uses threads, and uses DPCs, this queueing without explicit locking is the most likely place you will want to look for a problem.

To work around this, you need to create a Spin Lock for *queueing* your DPC Routine, acquire it before you call `KeInsertQueueDpc` or `IoRequestDpc`, and release it after the function returns. Thus you are providing external locking for the shared DPC queue structure. Because DPC queueing is normally done from the ISR, there was no perceived need to provide this synchronization from within NT itself.

Example: DPC Queueing Failure

In this example, we show a small driver posted to the following newsgroup by Jim McCollum and included here with his permission: `comp.os.ms-windows.programmer.nt.kernel-mode`. Jim wrote this driver, which has Spin Locking in conditional compilation. When compiled with the Spin Locks in the driver, there is no problem. Without the Spin Locks, the system will crash.

Remember, to try this yourself you will need a multiprocessor system so that the crash can happen. This code will not crash on a uniprocessor (another reason that you need to always test your driver on a multiprocessor!).

---

[2] An analogous method for *lowering* the IRQL is available by using Driver Threads, a topic discussed in Chapter 24.

Listing 26.1: *Causing a DPC Queueing Failure on a Multiprocessor*

```c
//++
//
//   MODULE: dpccrash.c
//
//   DESCRIPTION:
//
//       This driver starts up a group of passive system threads that wake up
//       periodically and queue a DPC; the goal is to reproduce the NT 4.0 SMP
//       problem in which a DPC's link fields are trashed by KeInsertQueueDpc
//
//   AUTHOR:
//
//       Jim McCollum
//
//   CREATION DATE:
//
//       December 16, 1997
//
#include <ntddk.h>
//
// If DPC_CRASH_WORKAROUND is defined, the workaround for the crash is
// compiled in
//
// #define DPC_CRASH_WORKAROUND 1
#define NUMBER_OF_THREADS 15        // Number of thread to create
#define THREAD_WAIT_MSEC 50         // Msec for thread to wait between calls
                                    //   to KeInsertQueueDpc
KDPC dummyDpcObject;                // DPC object, shared by all threads
ULONG dummyDpcRuns;                 // Number of times the DPC has run
#ifdef DPC_CRASH_WORKAROUND
KSPIN_LOCK queueDpcSpinLock;        // DPC Spin Lock for workaround
#endif
//
//
//   STATIC FUNCTION PROTOTYPES
//
//
VOID QueueDpcThread (IN PVOID pthreadContext);
VOID DummyDpc ( IN PKDPC pdummyDpcObject,
                IN PVOID pdeferredContext,
                IN PVOID psystemArgument1,
                IN PVOID psystemArgument2);


//*******************************************************************************
//                          DriverEntry
//*******************************************************************************
//       This function is invoked by the NT driver when it is loaded
//       explicitly
//       It starts NUMBER_OF_THREADS system threads, which wake up periodically
//       and queue a DPC
//
//   RETURN VALUE:
//
//       STATUS_SUCCESS          Successfully initialized
//       STATUS_UNSUCCESSFUL     Initialization failure
```

```
NTSTATUS DriverEntry(
    IN PDRIVER_OBJECT DriverObject,
    IN PUNICODE_STRING RegistryPath)
{
    ULONG idx;                        // Loop index
    HANDLE newThreadHandle;           // Thread handle
    DbgPrint ("DPCCRASH: in DpcCrash.sys DriverEntry.\n");
    //
    // Initialize the DPC Object and Spin Lock
    //
    KeInitializeDpc (&dummyDpcObject, DummyDpc, NULL);

#ifdef DPC_CRASH_WORKAROUND
    KeInitializeSpinLock (&queueDpcSpinLock);
#endif

    //
    // Try to start the threads; return STATUS_UNSUCCESSFUL on error
    //
    for (idx = 1; idx <= NUMBER_OF_THREADS; idx++)
    {
        //
        // Try to start a new thread
        //
        if (PsCreateSystemThread (
                    &newThreadHandle,
                    THREAD_ALL_ACCESS,
                    NULL, NULL, NULL,
                    QueueDpcThread,
                    (PVOID) idx) != STATUS_SUCCESS)
        {
            //
            // Print an error message and exit DriverEntry with error status
            //
            DbgPrint ("DPCCRASH: Failed to create thread %d in StartThreads!\n", idx);
            return STATUS_UNSUCCESSFUL;
        }
        DbgPrint ("DPCCRASH: Successfully created thread %d in StartThreads.\n", idx);
        //
        // Release the thread handle
        //
        ZwClose (newThreadHandle);
    }
    //
    // Threads are started; return success
    //
    return STATUS_SUCCESS;
}

//******************************************************************************
//      QueueDpcThread
//******************************************************************************
//
//      This routine runs as a thread started by the previous routine during
//      DriverEntry; this thread sleeps for THREAD_WAIT_MSEC milliseconds,
//      wakes up, queues a dummy DPC, and goes back to sleep
//
```

```
//   FORMAL PARAMETERS:
//
//        startContext          Thread ID
//

VOID QueueDpcThread (IN PVOID startContext)
{
    ULONG threadId = (ULONG) startContext;
    LARGE_INTEGER waitTime;
    KIRQL savedIrql;
    //
    // Calculate relative wait time
    //
    waitTime = RtlConvertLongToLargeInteger
                          ((LONG) -(10*1000*THREAD_WAIT_MSEC));
    while (TRUE)
        {
         KeDelayExecutionThread (KernelMode, FALSE, &waitTime);

#ifdef DPC_CRASH_WORKAROUND
         KeAcquireSpinLock (&queueDpcSpinLock, &savedIrql);
#endif

         KeInsertQueueDpc (&dummyDpcObject, NULL, NULL);

#ifdef DPC_CRASH_WORKAROUND
         KeReleaseSpinLock(&queueDpcSpinLock, savedIrql);
#endif

        }
    DbgPrint ("DPCCRASH: Worker thread %d terminating abnormally!\n", threadId);
    PsTerminateSystemThread(STATUS_UNSUCCESSFUL);
    return;
}

//****************************************************************************
//                            DummyDpc
//****************************************************************************
//
//      This routine runs as DPC; it doesn't do anything-it just returns and
//      the DPC terminates
//
//   FORMAL PARAMETERS:
//
//      pdummyDpcObject          Pointer to the DPC object
//      pdeferredContext         Not used
//      psystemArgument1         Not used
//      psystemArgument2         Not used
//
VOID DummyDpc (
    IN PKDPC pdummyDpcObject,
    IN PVOID pdeferredContext,
    IN PVOID psystemArgument1,
    IN PVOID psystemArgument2)
{
```

```
//
// Nothing to do here but bump a counter and return to the caller
//
dummyDpcRuns++;
return;
}
```

Deferred and Multiphase Driver Initialization

We can control the driver load order to specify when our driver will load. This is described at a high level in Chapter 7, and covered in extensive detail in the Microsoft documentation. Sometimes the load order is insufficient to handle complex cases, and we have conflicts. The driver may need to load early in the boot sequence to allocate a large block of contiguous non-paged memory, yet needs to establish communications with lower-level drivers that are loaded much later.

NT provides a mechanism to handle this: the *Reinitialize Routine*. The Reinitialize Routine is a callback function within the driver which is called after all the other drivers have completed their `DriverEntry` routine processing.

This is frequently used by higher level drivers to allow all lower level drivers to load. The higher level driver then has a chance to access all lower level drivers of a particular type. The Fault Tolerant File System driver is an example of such a driver.

To request a reinitialization callback, the driver must call `IoRegisterDriverReinitialization` in its `DriverEntry`.

```
VOID IoRegisterDriverReinitialization(
                IN PDRIVER_OBJECT DriverObject,
                IN PDRIVER_REINITIALIZE DriverReinitializationRoutine,
                IN PVOID Context);
```

The `Context` block must be set up by the `DriverEntry` routine to pass whatever information is needed by the Reinitialize Routine to process the request. For example, if the Registry will be accessed by the driver, the `DriverEntry` must make its `RegistryPath` parameter available to the Reinitialize Routine (alternatively, if all that is needed is a few simple entries, the `DriverEntry` may retrieve them and pass the entries in the `Context` block). The `Context` value, if interpreted as a pointer, must be available at the time the Reinitialization Routine is called. It may be a reference to paged memory.

The Reinitialize Routine has the form:

```
VOID(*PDRIVER_REINITIALIZE)(IN PDRIVER_OBJECT DriverObject,
                IN PVOID Context,
                IN ULONG Count);
```

The Reinitialize Routine is called at PASSIVE_LEVEL in a system thread. The Reinitialize Routine must either complete any remaining startup processing or, if it needs to defer yet again, call `IoRegisterDriverReinitialization` once more. This will allow any other drivers to complete processing Reinitialize Routines. Each time the `IoRegisterDriverReinitialization` routine is called, the callback is queued at the end of the reinitialization queue. The `Count` parameter to the Reinitialize Routine is the number of times the reinitialize routine has been called for this driver.

The Registry

We've shown you many examples of using the Registry to hold information. The Registry is a very powerful mechanism for organizing the various small bits of information needed to customize a piece of code. This piece of code can be a driver, or it can be an application, including ordinary GUI-based applications, system service applications, and even console applications. The Registry is a way of preserving customization settings. It is *not* especially well-suited for storing massive amounts of information about an application. If you need to store large amounts of information about the application, you would be better off creating an application-specific configuration file and storing a *reference* to that file in the Registry. Always bear in mind that NT is potentially a *multiuser* system as well, that is, a particular workstation can be logged onto by a variety of users. With the "Hydra" multiuser support, it can even support multiple users concurrently. Thus, if you do any per-user customization, you need to store the information under the HKEY_CURRENT_USER root in the Registry. If you have private customization files, you must arrange them so that they are separate for separate users. Otherwise, you have an Erroneous System.

A driver likely never has any per-user parameters, so such considerations are moot for most drivers. However, drivers usually have *per-system* parameterizations. The obvious ones are IRQ levels, memory mapping, and I/O port assignment. But we have shown that there are many other interesting parameters, such as debug masks, error logging options, and breakpoint options, that most drivers will want to support. For example, say you want to tune your driver for different kinds of performance trade-offs. An example of this is a file driver that would prefetch but have a small working cache based on sequential access or that does no prefetch but has a large working cache based on random access. You should not establish these by parameters in the Registry. Rather, you should provide for customization on a per-application basis, for example, by using flags on CreateFile or by having DeviceIoControl operations that provide for such tuning. The only Registry parameters you add should be those that are universally applicable to any application running on the platform.

Registry manipulation falls into two categories: that done to the driver's own key and that which uses the Registry in a more general fashion. The string to access a driver's key is passed into the DriverEntry routine. The driver may request access to other keys by specifying explicit pathnames. How it computes these explicit pathnames is up to you. However, we strongly recommend that such keys be based on information derivable from the Registry itself, rather than having absolute hardwired paths in the driver code. One caution you must always bear in mind is that during boot time, the entire Registry is not available; only the HKEY_LOCAL_MACHINE\Hardware key is available. If your driver expects other parts of the Registry to be available, it must make sure that it is not being incorrectly loaded at boot time and it must be prepared to fail gracefully if it is incorrectly configured as a boot-time driver.

Because it is common to want to manipulate the keys under the root HKEY_CURRENT_MACHINE, this key is implicitly open at the kernel level. This allows you to use composite functions such as RtlQueryRegistryValues (which we used in all of our previous examples) to access the Registry.

```
NTSTATUS RtlQueryRegistryValues(IN ULONG RelativeTo,
                                IN PWSTR Path,
                                IN PRTL_QUERY_REGISTRY_TABLE QueryTable,
                                IN PVOID Context,
                                IN PVOID Environment);
```

Table 26.1: `RtlQueryRegistryValues`: *RelativeTo Parameter Values*

RelativeTo	**Meaning**
RTL_REGISTRY_ABSOLUTE	Path is an absolute Registry path.
RTL_REGISTRY_SERVICES	Path is relative to `\Registry\Machine\System\CurrentControlSet\Services`.
RTL_REGISTRY_CONTROL	Path is relative to `\Registry\Machine\System\CurrentControlSet\Control`.
RTL_REGISTRY_WINDOWS_NT	Path is relative to `\Registry\Machine\Software\Microsoft\Windows NT\CurrentVersion`.
RTL_REGISTRY_DEVICEMAP	Path is relative to `\Registry\Machine\Hardware\DeviceMap`.
RTL_REGISTRY_USER	Path is relative to `\Registry\User\CurrentUser`.
RTL_REGISTRY_OPTIONAL	Specifies that the key referenced by this parameter and the *Path* parameter are optional.
RTL_REGISTRY_HANDLE	Specifies that the *Path* parameter is actually a Registry handle to use. This value is optional.

The `RtlQueryRegistryValues` function takes a pointer to a *QueryTable*; this allows you to specify the value to be retrieved, its type, and its size. It also takes a pointer to where the result should be placed, the size of the result, and a default value to be used if the specified value is not found in the Registry itself. Note that this table is of an unspecified length; the end is determined by an entry that is entirely zeroes. Thus you must allocate one more entry than you need and make sure to zero memory for the whole table before assigning any values to it.

The *RelativeTo* parameter allows you to choose one of many different default paths to which your *Path* is interpreted as being relative (including the special value RTL_REGISTRY_ABSOLUTE, which means that the path is an absolute path). These are summarized in Table 26.1.

The most common form you will likely use is RTL_REGISTRY_ABSOLUTE, using the *Path* parameter passed into the `DriverEntry` routine. There is an important caution here. The input parameter passed to `DriverEntry` is a PUNICODE_STRING, a *counted* Unicode string. *There is no guarantee that it is NUL-terminated!* However, the `RtlQueryRegistryValues` function wants a PWSTR, a pointer to a NUL-terminated Unicode string. Therefore you must actually copy the string into a temporary working buffer and put at the end a NUL character (note we did *not* say "NUL byte"). You could also specify, instead of a PWSTR, a HANDLE to an open key, cast to a PWSTR. This is a less common usage for this function.

We show shortly that a query to the Registry can be accompanied by a call to a function. The *Context* parameter of `RtlQueryRegistryValues` represents information that will be passed to this function. It is unusual to have a callback function when doing this from a Device Driver, so this parameter is most commonly NULL.

Generally, when a Registry entry is queried, the value desired is stored in the Registry entry itself. However, some values can be specified as REG_EXPAND_SZ type. This means the string is an *expandable string*. You've seen these; they have forms such as

`%system32%\MyStuff\Whatever`

What does that '%system32%" mean? Because this string is stored as an *expandable* string, a macro substitution will be made. The environment will be searched for a value of the form

```
system32=c:\winnt\system32
```

and the value %system32% will be replaced with its environment value. Thus, when you get the value back, it will actually say

```
c:\winnt\system32\MyStuff\Whatever
```

If you have expandable string values in your Registry entries, you must provide an environment in which these values can be looked up. This is the *Environment* parameter of the call. Since it is uncommon to have expandable strings in a driver environment, this parameter is usually NULL. If you want expandable parameters, you must provide an environment of the form

$$L"keyword_1=value_1\backslash 0 keyword_2=value_2\backslash 0 ... keyword_n=value_n\backslash 0"$$

Since each entry is terminated with a NUL character, the entire environment is terminated by the implicit NUL that is always included in a string. Thus there is a sequence of two NUL characters terminating the entire environment. You can find the user's environment in the Registry, or you can set up an environment string in the Registry that you retrieve yourself.

RtlQueryRegistryValues is easy to use partly because there is an implicit HKEY_CURRENT_MACHINE key that is always open and readily available for its use. If, however, you need some key value that is *not* part of your device's path or you want to create a key not already in your device's Registry entry, you must drop down to a lower level and open or create a key.

The code shown in Listing 26.2 shows the function we use to create a "volatile subkey", or ephemeral Registry entry, for a driver (actually, for our Hardware Simulator Driver, which we describe in detail in Chapter 27. The example in this listing uses the ZwOpenKey function to open an existing key and creates the desired ephemeral Registry entry as a subkey under it. It then returns the handle to this subkey via an OUT parameter.

Listing 26.2: *Creating a Volatile Key*

This code follows the documentation but does not in fact create an ephemeral key! Our research has shown that apparently no one else knows how to do this either. The DDK contains no examples. We have seen unanswered questions on this problem in the online forum archives. Since this example actually works *except for the ephemeral property*, we had to decide whether to remove it or include it. We decided to include it, along with this warning, because it shows how to create a key, a generally useful technique.

If you know how to do this, please send us a note. We'll post the information on our Web sites, and the first one to send us a working example will get a nice acknowledgment in the next edition of this book.

```
NTSTATUS openDevicesKey(IN   PWSTR RegistryPathName,
                        OUT PHANDLE DevicesKey)
{
    HANDLE hKey;
    OBJECT_ATTRIBUTES oa;
    NTSTATUS Status;
    UNICODE_STRING uStr;

    RtlInitUnicodeString(&uStr, RegistryPathName);
    //
    //   First try opening this key
    //
    InitializeObjectAttributes(&oa,
                               &uStr,
                               OBJ_CASE_INSENSITIVE,
                               NULL,
                               (PSECURITY_DESCRIPTOR)NULL);
    Status = ZwOpenKey(&hKey,
                       KEY_CREATE_SUB_KEY,
                       &oa);
    if (!NT_SUCCESS(Status))
        return Status;
```

At this point we have, in hKey, *a handle to the key for our device driver. We can now use this to create a new key whose option is* REG_OPTION_VOLATILE. *Note that the handle is returned directly to the handle location provided by our caller.*

```
    RtlInitUnicodeString(&uStr, DEVICES_SUBKEY);
    InitializeObjectAttributes(&oa,
                               &uStr,
                               OBJ_CASE_INSENSITIVE,
                               hKey,
                               (PSECURITY_DESCRIPTOR)NULL);

    Status = ZwCreateKey(DevicesKey,
                         KEY_ALL_ACCESS,
                         &oa,
                         0,
                         NULL,
                         REG_OPTION_VOLATILE,
                         NULL);
    ZwClose(hKey);
    return Status;
}
```

Registry Access Functions

The following functions are the low-level functions used to access the Registry from a Device Driver. In addition, there are a number of Rtl-prefix functions that work on the Registry.

InitializeObjectAttributes

The Registry actually is a *securable object database*. Thus, to create or look up a key, you must provide an OBJECT_ATTRIBUTES structure that specifies such details as the name of the object, whether the name should be interpreted as case-sensitive, and either your purported level of security (to open) or the level of security to use (on creation). Why "purported level"? Because you are in the kernel, and you can do *anything*. However, you might not wish to do something on behalf of a user that results in a violation of the established security. Thus you must execute such a call in the same security context as the application-level code that called you. You need to obtain a security descriptor for the calling application and provide it, or, if you are not enforcing security, you can use a NULL pointer to the security descriptor. Generally, a driver, during its initialization, does not wish to limit itself to the security of the running application (for example, the administrator might have set up the devices subtree so that ordinary users can't change it), so you will almost always use a NULL pointer here.

Similarly, when you create a key, you can restrict who can access it by providing an appropriately restricted security descriptor. Note, however, that if you are creating a subkey in the devices tree and the administrator has already protected the higher level of the tree, no one can access your key except through that level of protection. Thus you can be reasonably assured that using a NULL key will not compromise security. We are *not* going to talk about security here. There are books thicker than ours that treat this topic in great detail, from the sysadmin level down to the programming details. You might consider getting one of those if you are truly concerned about security.[3]

```
VOID InitializeObjectAttributes(
                OUT POBJECT_ATTRIBUTES InitializedAttributes,
                IN PUNICODE_STRING ObjectName,
                IN ULONG Attributes,
                IN HANDLE RootDirectory,
                IN PSECURITY_DESCRIPTOR SecurityDescriptor);
```

The InitializeObjectAttributes function simply initializes the data structure *InitializedAttributes* in the proper way. It takes

- a pointer to a counted Unicode string for the name,
- a set of flags that specify the object attributes,
- a handle for the "root directory", which is really the handle of the object tree under which the *ObjectName* parameter will be found (for open) or created, and
- the security descriptor, which is almost always NULL, as we just explained.

If *ObjectName* is a fully qualified pathname, the *RootDirectory* parameter can be NULL. *ObjectName* is always interpreted relative to the \Registry root; if *RootDirectory* is NULL, *ObjectName* must *start* with the \Registry path.

Many *Attributes* values are possible for this function because it initializes all sorts of object descriptors. For Registry descriptors, as far as we can tell from the documentation, only OBJ_CASE_INSENSITIVE seems to be valid (that is, according to the documentation, "the validity of these values depends upon the object type").

---

[3] Actually, by using NULL in both places, we place all of the burden of security on the sysadmin, which is where it belongs anyway. The folks at OSR tell the story that in most of their classes, they ask, "Does anybody care about security?" A whole room of people in T-shirts say, "Huh?", but one fellow, in the back, wearing a dark suit and tie, says, "I care." As long as you don't do anything that *breaks* security, all of it is really handled at a much higher level than you'll see, in the I/O Manager, which negotiates with the Security Manager.

ZwOpenKey

```
NTSTATUS ZwOpenKey(OUT PHANDLE KeyHandle,
                   IN ACCESS_MASK DesiredAccess,
                   IN POBJECT_ATTRIBUTES ObjectAttributes);
```

The ZwOpenKey function opens an existing key whose name, root path, and security are specified by the *ObjectAttributes* parameter. The *DesiredAccess* parameter specifies what kind of access is desired. This access is then mediated by the security descriptor in *ObjectAttributes* to decide if the function can gain that specified access. Since we are working generally with driver properties during initialization, the security descriptor will be NULL and *DesiredAccess* will be either KEY_READ or KEY_ALL_ACCESS.

ZwCreateKey

```
NTSTATUS ZwCreateKey(OUT PHANDLE KeyHandle,
                     IN ACCESS_MASK DesiredAccess,
                     IN POBJECT_ATTRIBUTES ObjectAttributes,
                     IN ULONG TitleIndex,
                     IN PUNICODE_STRING Class,
                     IN ULONG CreateOptions,
                     OUT PULONG Disposition OPTIONAL)
```

The ZwCreateKey function creates a key under a specific subkey. The key name and the subkey, along with the desired security, are specified by the *ObjectAttributes* parameter. If the function is successful, the key to the newly created subkey is placed in the location specified by the *KeyHandle* parameter. The access is specified by the *DesiredAccess* parameter, which for most drivers is KEY_ALL_ACCESS. (This is because most drivers require read/write access, since, after all, the key is just being created and undoubtedly needs to be filled in.)

The *TitleIndex* parameter is not used by drivers and must be 0. Likewise, the *Class* parameter is irrelevant and so is set to NULL. Of the various *CreateOptions*, the ones relevant to a Device Driver writer creating a Registry key are REG_OPTION_NON_VOLATILE, which creates an ordinary key, and REG_OPTION_VOLATILE, which creates a key that will not survive a reboot. For our example in Listing 26.2, we wanted to create a volatile key, so we specified the latter.

The *Disposition* parameter can be NULL, or it can point to a ULONG that receives a value that says what ZwCreateKey actually did. If it is non-NULL, it is set to one of two values: REG_CREATED_NEW_KEY, which means the key did not already exist and has been created, or REG_OPENED_EXISTING_KEY, which means the key already existed and has just been opened. In our example, it didn't matter whether the key was newly created or it already existed, so we passed in a NULL.

While you can create keys for a driver, you must be careful about trying to create keys in other than HKEY_LOCAL_MACHINE in a driver. If the driver can be loaded at boot time, only some of the Registry is available. In particular, the "software hive" is not available. Thus you cannot create keys for other than your device.

The Windows NT Event Log

The NT *Event Log* is a facility that allows the logging of events of interest using a uniform facility. Events can be logged by application programs, System Services, Device Drivers, and any other component of NT that wishes to log a piece of interesting information. While it is uncommon for GUI-based applications to log to the Event Log (after all, they are generally talking directly to the user), non-GUI components such as System Services and Device Drivers have no place to write. The Event Log is the modern analog of the "system console" of the days of massive timesharing systems.

Consequently, there are only two areas of interest in using the Event Log:

- Writing events into the Event Log
- Reading events from the Event Log.

Both of these require specific effort on your part.

The Event Viewer Utility

Windows NT comes with an application called the *Event Viewer* that allows the user to view an Event Log. A system administrator with sufficient privileges can view the Event Log of any machine on the network. The intelligibility and usefulness of a message depends on your providing some key information to the Event Log, both when you write a specific event and when you allow the Event Viewer to interpret the record you have written. An example of the Event Log display is shown in Figure 26.1. The output from our sample driver (Listing 26.2) is shown in the lines whose source is labeled LogIt.

Double-clicking a selected entry presents you with a more detailed display of the information. Each event can have event-specific information, called the *Dump Data*, associated with it. This is always displayed in hexadecimal and is intended to be reported to someone's Technical Support group. You can often make your Tech Support people's lives, and ultimately your own life, easier if you can put useful information into the Dump Data area rather than issue a "generic" message that does not convey much more information than "it broke".

You also can attach a description that contains certain formatting text parameters. The annotated result of this is shown in Figure 26.2, where we double-clicked the entry for LogIt, whose event ID was 1.

There is nothing magic about the Event Viewer utility. It uses ordinary API functions to read and display the Event Log contents. Thus you can build your own facilities to examine the Event Log. We know of at least one product that will send a text message to the sysadmin's pager, displaying the latest error-level message from the Event Log of an NT Server.

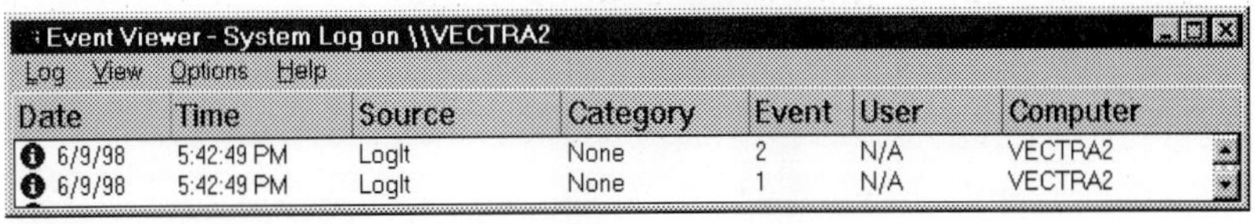

Figure 26.1: *The Event Viewer display.*

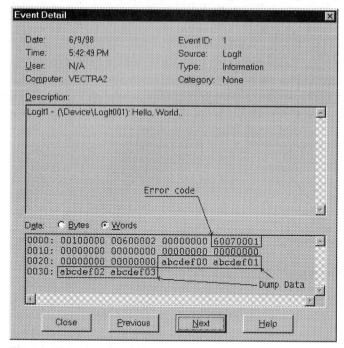

Figure 26.2: *Expanded Event Log entry.*

The Message Table

To use the Event Log facility, you must create a *Message Table*. The information in the Message Table is used to create the display of the information in the Event Viewer. The Message Table is stored as a *Resource* in the *Resource Segment* of the driver executable[4] or in a separate DLL. The actual file in which the Message Table is stored is given by an entry in the Registry. This allows you to distribute a driver with multiple languages supported and have the events given in the local language. (We don't go into this much in this book. For internationalization issues, we suggest Nadine Kano's *Writing International Applications for Windows 95 and Windows NT,* cited in the Further Reading section at the end of the chapter.)

Message Table Format

A Message Table is defined by a text file you create and that has the extension mc, for "Message Compiler". This file defines which languages you are supporting, the event code you will use, and the symbolic name you wish to assign to that event code. (Or it can assign the numbers for you, if you like to live dangerously.) You can assign a severity level (success, informational, warning, or error), a language, and some message text. The Message Table is actually a quite

---

[4] Not to be confused with the "Executive Resource", a facility that shares only its name with the kind of resources represented by a Message Table.

general facility that can be used by applications, System Services, and other programs for their own purposes. For more details on how this is done, we recommend *Win32 Programming*, cited in the Further Reading section at the end of the chapter.

Listing 26.3 is a sample Message Table file for our LogIt driver. We eliminated a number of extensive comments from the original file in the interest of a compact display here.

Listing 26.3: *A sample Message Table file*

In the first declaration, we define the data type that the values will have. For a driver, this is NTSTATUS.

```
MessageIdTypedef=NTSTATUS
```

Next, we can add any languages other than English that we want to support. The following declaration declares the name of a language that we can use later in the file. It also associates that language with a code (usually the value defined by Windows for the language; for example, Japanese is assigned the integer value 0x411*). Finally, it defines the name of the output file to be used for that language. The following declaration causes all Japanese messages to be written to an output file whose filename part is* MSG000002.

```
LanguageNames=(Japanese=0x411:MSG00002)
```

You can also use the three-letter ISO abbreviation as part of the name, for example MSGENG *for English messages, since ENG is the three-letter name used for English, and* MSGJPN *for Japanese. This allows an international installation program to query the language of the machine on which the driver is being installed. It then can form the correct filename using the three-letter value. It obtains this value from the* GetLocaleInfo *API call (a call available at the application level, not the driver level) by using the* LOCALE_SABBREVLANGNAME *option (for the short abbreviation of the language name).*

Next, we assign names to the severity code value, the high-order 2 bits of the 32-bit code value.

```
SeverityNames=(Success=0x0:STATUS_SEVERITY_SUCCESS
              Informational=0x1:STATUS_SEVERITY_INFORMATIONAL
              Warning=0x2:STATUS_SEVERITY_WARNING
              Error=0x3:STATUS_SEVERITY_ERROR
              )
```

Then, we assign some facility parameters that define that this is a device driver.

```
FacilityNames=(System=0x0
              RpcRuntime=0x2:FACILITY_RPC_RUNTIME
              RpcStubs=0x3:FACILITY_RPC_STUBS
              Io=0x4:FACILITY_IO_ERROR_CODE
              LogIt=0x7:FACILITY_LogIt_ERROR_CODE
              )
```

The declaration of the facility allows us to create messages for a variety of facilities with which we may interact. In this case, the DDK template predefined System, RpcRuntime, RpcStubs, *and* Io *as names already known. You do not need to include these names in your driver if you are not going to log messages from these facilities. We chose to add our* `LogIt` *facility as facility number 7 because the DDK example used 7—there appears to be no documented rationale for the assignment of these values. We also set the Customer bit, thereby indicating that the code we are using is not a Microsoft code. However, this is done when we run the* `mc` *compiler rather than being part of the declaration of the messages.*

```
MessageId=0x0001 Facility=LogIt
Severity=Informational
SymbolicName=LOGIT_INFORMATION
Language=English
LogIt1 -  (%1): %2.
.
Language=Japanese
LogIt1 -  (%1): %2.
```

Each message entry resembles this one. You define the basic event ID properties by specifying the `MessageId` *value, facility, severity, and symbolic name to be used. The Microsoft/User bit will be set by the command line to the* `mc` *compiler. Following the* `MessageId` *line, you must have one message entry for each declared language. This consists of a declaration of which language is to follow, then one or more lines of message text terminated by a line that begins with a period, followed by the next language message (since we do not know Japanese, we left in English text).*

If you do not include the same declarations in the following message, it inherits the declarations of the most recent message that had them. For example, for the second message we do not need to provide the facility or severity specifications because these are the same as the previous message's. Generally, you will group messages of different classes (for example, a severe error 2 is a different message than an informational message 2), so this reduces your typing. Note also that the syntax is keyword-based, so the keywords can appear either on separate lines or on one line, in any order.

```
MessageId=0x0002 SymbolicName=LOGIT_INFORMATION2
Language=English
LogIt 2 - (%1): %2.%n
LogIt 2 blah blah blah ..... more more %n
LogIt 2 %2        %3
note which line this comes out on
.
Language=Japanese
LogIt 2 - (%1): %2.%n
LogIt 2 blah blah blah ..... more more %n
LogIt 2 %2   %3
note which line this comes out on
this is really unusual kanji  -- looks a lot like english
```

Message Table Strings

In the previous example, we showed you the use of % flags to format the information. Unlike `sprintf`, however, these use funny formatting codes like %1 and %2. What do these mean?

A message from a Message Table is usually formatted with the `FormatMessage` API call. This call takes a variable-length array of parameters to be substituted, but unlike `sprintf`, does not require that the parameters be positionally correlated with the format strings. Instead, each

Table 26.2: *Event Log* **%** *Format Codes*

Code	Meaning
%0	This forces the formatted text to not end with a newline. This is not required for Event Log messages.
%1	This substitutes the driver name in the message.
%2 ... %9	The $(n-1)^{\text{th}}$ parameter string is substituted for this formatting code. The strings are treated as numbered 1, 2, ...
%%	A % is placed in the result string.
%n	A hard line break is placed in the formatted text. Otherwise, line breaks are added as needed and those in the string itself are treated as equivalent to spaces.
%space	A % followed by a space places a space in the formatted output.
%.	A single period is placed in the formatted output. This is useful if a period would otherwise have to appear as the first character of a text line.
%!	An exclamation point is placed in the formatted output.
%n!format!	As far as we can tell, this formatting option of FormatMessage is not supported for Event Log entries.

parameter is assigned a numeric index starting at 1, so %1 will be replaced with the first parameter, %2 with the second, and so on. This can be important for internationalization, where the word order in a sentence might not be the same as in English.

For an Event Log entry, you can provide one or more additional strings that will be substituted. The DDK documentation we have states, "The I/O Manager assumes that the initial insertion string, if any, is either the name of the driver or of the device on which the error occurred". As far as we can tell, this is not true; the first string seems to be implicitly supplied by the I/O Manager, and the first string *we* supply is substituted for the %2 item.

The amount of data you can include is limited. The total Event Log packet, including the packet itself, any binary Dump Data, and any strings, must not exceed ERROR_LOG_MAXIMUM_SIZE (currently 152 bytes).

The values that can be used for % substitution are given in Table 26.2.

Compiling and Linking the Message Table

To compile a Message Table as part of constructing the Device Driver, you must add some lines to the various control files for the BUILD.

- Add the following lines to the Makefile.INC file:

```
LogIt.h LogIt.rc msg00001.bin: LogIt.mc
    mc -v -c LogIt.mc
```

The -v switch tells mc to operate in "verbose" mode (producing some additional output during the compilation process), and the -c switch sets the Customer bit, thereby indicating that this is a non-Microsoft facility.

- In the SOURCES file, add to the SOURCES list the .rc filename:

  SOURCES=*existing files* LogIt.rc

  This will cause the resource compiler to be invoked and the linker to recognize the .res file.

- You must also add to the SOURCES file this line:

  NTTARGETFILE0=LogIt.h

  This line causes the BUILD facility to read the Makefile.INC to discover how to build LogIt.h.

The name you choose for your .mc file must not conflict with any existing .h or .rc file you might already have. This is because the mc program will create .h and .rc files with the same name as your .mc file and thereby will overwrite any existing files of the same name. So if you call your driver MyDriver and you have a MyDriver.h file (which probably contains the Device Extension structure), you don't want to call its Message Table file MyDriver.mc— the first time you compile it, your carefully crafted Device Extension file will disappear.

Using the Message Table

To make the message file available to the Event Viewer at runtime, you must create a Registry entry, as follows.

```
\registry\machine\system\CurrentControlSet\Services\EventLog\System\filename
    EventMessageFile = REG_EXPAND_SZ %SystemRoot%\DriverLocation
    TypesSupported = REG_DWORD 0x00000007
```

So for our LogIt driver, which we installed in the Windows\System32\Drivers area and which contains its Message Table as part of the .sys file, we added this Registry entry:

```
\registry\machine\system\CurrentControlSet\Services\EventLog\System\LogIt
    EventMessageFile = REG_EXPAND_SZ %SystemRoot%\System32\Drivers\LogIt.sys
    TypesSupported = REG_DWORD 0x00000007
```

If you create separate language-specific DLLs, your EventMessageFile entry will refer to the appropriate DLL. This late binding also allows an international distributor you never heard of when you wrote the program to create a locale-specific Message Table as a separate DLL and distribute it to customers who don't speak your language. Thus you could take a driver written for a language you don't know, find a translator to convert the strings to your own language, and then install a different message file from your own mc compilation and DLL build, as follows.

```
\registry\machine\system\CurrentControlSet\Services\EventLog\System\LogIt
    EventMessageFile = REG_EXPAND_SZ %SystemRoot%\System32\Drivers\Esperanto.dll
    TypesSupported = REG_DWORD 0x00000007
```

And without having to modify the driver at all!

This process is summarized in Figure 26.3. This figure shows that the only files you create are the source files for your driver (the box labeled ".c files") and the Message Table source file

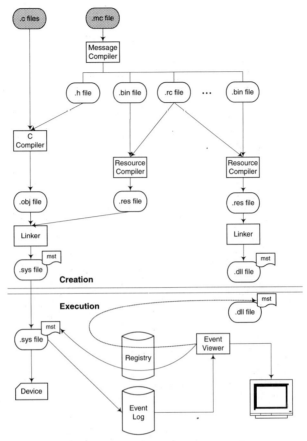

Figure 26.3: *Message Table construction and use.*

("`.mc` file"). The other files are generated for you. The "mainstream" single-language path is shown with solid lines from the `.bin` file, while the alternative path (which can replace the "mainstream" path, as well as supplement it) is shown with dotted lines. We show the explicit Message Table (abbreviated "mst") as an appendage to the `.sys` file or the DLL.

Creating Driver Events

Now that you have a Message Table, and its corresponding header file, you can use the table when your Device Driver logs an event using the Event Log mechanism. To do this, you create an Event Log entry that contains one of the error codes specified in your Message Table.

The Driver Code

To create an event, you must first create an *Event Packet* by allocating some storage to hold the event information and then initializing that storage. Then, you call the Event Log function that writes this Event Packet to the Event Log.

Historically, the Event Log was seen as a place to log errors, so most of the functions have the name "Error" in them. Don't be misled by this; the Event Log is for logging all sorts of events. (Of course, if you abuse it, it will grow to massive size, thus making your users, and their sysadmins, very unhappy.) You can also use it to help you debug, as an alternative to debug printouts. This can be useful during Beta testing when you can't depend on your end users' having a full, two-machine, WinDbg environment for testing.

Listing 26.4 is a trivial example, a simple variant of our "Hello World" driver. It logs two "Hello World" events to the Event Log. We first present the code in its entirety in the listing, and then we examine a few key lines of it.

Listing 26.4: *Writing an Event Log Entry*

```
#define NUMBER_DUMP_DATA_ENTRIES 4

NTSTATUS DriverEntry(
    IN PDRIVER_OBJECT DriverObject,
    IN PUNICODE_STRING RegistryPath
    )
{
    PDEVICE_OBJECT deviceObject = NULL;
    NTSTATUS status;
    UNICODE_STRING DeviceName;

    UNICODE_STRING ErrorString ;
    UNICODE_STRING ErrorString2 ;

    PWCHAR insertionString ;
    PIO_ERROR_LOG_PACKET errorLogEntry ;
    int i ;

    KdPrint(("LogIt: DriverEntry.\n"));
    //
    // Form the name for the first device
    //
    RtlInitUnicodeString( &DeviceName, L"\\Device\\LogIt001");
    //
    // Create the Device Object
    //
    status = IoCreateDevice(DriverObject,
                            0,
                            &DeviceName,
                            FILE_DEVICE_UNKNOWN,
                            0,
                            FALSE,
                            &deviceObject
                            );
    if (!NT_SUCCESS(status))
        {
        KdPrint(("LogIt: failed creating device object! Status: %X\n", status));
        return status ;
        }
    // Note that we do not have a Device Object, but we could issue an Event Log
    // entry for the DriverObject; we do not do this because we are simply re-using
    // our example code, so logging this error is left as an exercise for the reader
```

```
//
// Fill in the Dispatch Routine addresses; we don't do anything, so just the
// unload routine is specified
//
DriverObject->DriverUnload = LogItUnload;
status = STATUS_SUCCESS ;
//
// We will do an Error Log here to show how it is done
// Note that for international applications, you would not actually put
// native-language strings here
//
RtlInitUnicodeString (&ErrorString, L"Hello, World.") ;
//
// Remember, the insertion string should be NUL-terminated. So we allocate
// the extra space for one WCHAR.
//
// The first parameter to IoAllocateErrorLogEntry can be either the Driver
// Object or the Device Object. If it is given a Device Object, the name
// of the device (used in IoCreateDevice) will show up in the place of %1
// in the message; see the message file (.mc) for more details
//
// The size is the size of the core Error Log packet, plus the number of
// ULONGs we need for the dump data (NUMBER_DUMP_DATA_ENTRIES), plus the
// length of the string, in bytes, plus space for one Unicode NUL character
// Since the structure already has one Dump Data slot allocated, we only need
// to allocate the additional Dump Data slots

errorLogEntry = IoAllocateErrorLogEntry (deviceObject,
                (UCHAR) (sizeof (IO_ERROR_LOG_PACKET)
                        + (NUMBER_DUMP_DATA_ENTRIES - 1) * sizeof (ULONG)
                        + ErrorString.Length
                        + sizeof (WCHAR))) ;
KdPrint (("LogIt:eventlogentry length: %d    MAX: %d\n",
            sizeof (IO_ERROR_LOG_PACKET)
              + (NUMBER_DUMP_DATA_ENTRIES - 1) * sizeof (ULONG)
              + ErrorString.Length + sizeof (WCHAR),
            ERROR_LOG_MAXIMUM_SIZE  )) ;

if (errorLogEntry == NULL)
   { /* failed */
   KdPrint (("LogIt: Can not allocate error log entry.\n")) ;
   } /* failed */
else
   { /* allocated */
   KdPrint (("LogIt: Going to log an error entry.\n")) ;

   errorLogEntry->ErrorCode = LOGIT_INFORMATION; // see page 568
   errorLogEntry->SequenceNumber = 0;
   errorLogEntry->MajorFunctionCode = 0 ;
   errorLogEntry->RetryCount = 0;
   errorLogEntry->UniqueErrorValue = 0;
   errorLogEntry->FinalStatus = STATUS_SUCCESS ;
   errorLogEntry->DumpDataSize = NUMBER_DUMP_DATA_ENTRIES * sizeof (ULONG);
   errorLogEntry->StringOffset = sizeof (IO_ERROR_LOG_PACKET)
                              + (NUMBER_DUMP_DATA_ENTRIES - 1) * sizeof (ULONG) ;
   errorLogEntry->NumberOfStrings = 1 ;
```

```
                // Fill in the Dump Data; for our example, we use the synthetic values
                // 0xabcdef00 plus a simple increment

                for (i = 0 ; i < NUMBER_DUMP_DATA_ENTRIES ; i++)
                   { /* dummy dump data */
                     errorLogEntry->DumpData[i] = 0xABCDEF00L + i ;
                   } /* dummy dump data */

                // Append the one parameter string just past the end of the Dump Data
                insertionString = (PWSTR)((PCHAR)(errorLogEntry)
                                              + errorLogEntry->StringOffset) ;
                RtlMoveMemory (insertionString, ErrorString.Buffer, ErrorString.Length) ;
                *(PWSTR)((PCHAR)insertionString + ErrorString.Length) = L'\0' ;
                IoWriteErrorLogEntry (errorLogEntry) ;
           } /* allocated */
      return STATUS_SUCCESS;
}
```

The data structure that is filled in is the IO_ERROR_LOG_PACKET, shown in Figure 26.4. This packet *must* be dynamically allocated using IoAllocateErrorLogEntry. It represents information that is queued for later writing. The Event Log mechanism will take care of deallocating the storage after the packet has been successfully written to the Event Log.

Note that we do not fill in all of the fields. Our sample structure is as shown in Figure 26.5. We show only a subset of the fields we initialize.

The key value is the ErrorCode value, which must be filled in because this is the value reported in the Event Log. We use the value LOGIT_INFORMATION, which is the name we declared in the Message Table (see the declaration on page 568). Values such as SequenceNumber, MajorFunctionCode, RetryCount UniqueErrorValue, and FinalStatus are there so that operations can provide additional information. For example, the IRP_MJ_ code for an IRP should be stored in the MajorFunctionCode field. The number of times the I/O transaction has been retried can be stored in the RetryCount field. The IoControlCode field is set to the IOCTL code for IRP_MJ_DEVICE_CONTROL or IRP_MJ_INTERNAL_DEVICE_CONTROL, or 0 for other IRP values or general events.

```
typedef struct _IO_ERROR_LOG_PACKET {
                              UCHAR MajorFunctionCode;
                              UCHAR RetryCount;
                              USHORT DumpDataSize;
                              USHORT NumberOfStrings;
                              USHORT StringOffset;
                              USHORT EventCategory;
                              NTSTATUS ErrorCode;
                              ULONG UniqueErrorValue;
                              NTSTATUS FinalStatus;
                              ULONG SequenceNumber;
                              ULONG IoControlCode;
                              LARGE_INTEGER DeviceOffset;
                              ULONG DumpData[1];
             } IO_ERROR_LOG_PACKET, *PIO_ERROR_LOG_PACKET;
```

Figure 26.4: *The IO_ERROR_LOG_PACKET structure.*

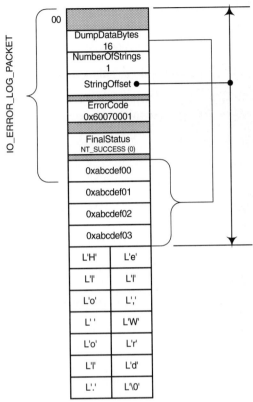

Figure 26.5: *An* IO_ERROR_LOG_PACKET *in memory.*

The DumpDataSize allows you to specify how many bytes of Dump Data will be provided. This value should be an integral multiple of sizeof(ULONG). Because the structure already contains one DumpData slot, you will need to allocate space for additional DumpData words. For example, to compute the additional space required for our dump data we use the computation (NUMBER_DUMP_DATA_ENTRIES - 1) * sizeof(ULONG).

We need to compute the StringOffset value to be the offset from the base of the structure to the first parameter string. The number of parameter strings is determined by NumberOfStrings. Each string is a NUL-terminated Unicode string. Note that a UNICODE_STRING is *not* guaranteed to be NUL-terminated, so we must explicitly store a NUL character following the actual text. For our current event notification, we have exactly one string, as shown in Figure 26.5.

The total length of an Error Packet, including the DumpData and the parameter strings, cannot exceed ERROR_LOG_MAXIMUM_SIZE (currently 152 bytes).

Finally, we call IoWriteErrorLogEntry to write the event. We do not deallocate the entry; IoWriteErrorLogEntry queues the event for writing. Note the implication here. That is, if the system Blue Screens, there is no guarantee that the most recent Event Log entries were committed to disk. Consequently, you cannot depend on the contents of the Event Log after a crash.

A more complex example is shown in Listing 26.5. We show only the key differences. Here, we have two parameter strings, and the formatting string specifies a %n formatting code to force a newline break in the output.

Listing 26.5: *Multiple Parameter Strings for* IO_ERROR_LOG_PACKET

```
RtlInitUnicodeString (&ErrorString1, L" String1.") ;
RtlInitUnicodeString (&ErrorString2, L"  String2.") ;

errorLogEntry = IoAllocateErrorLogEntry(deviceObject,
                         (UCHAR) (sizeof (IO_ERROR_LOG_PACKET)
                         + (NUMBER_DUMP_DATA_ENTRIES - 1) * sizeof (ULONG)
                         + ErrorString1.Length + sizeof (WCHAR)
                         + ErrorString2.Length + sizeof (WCHAR))
                                  ) ;
if (!errorLogEntry)
   { /* failure */
    KdPrint (("LogIt: Can not allocate error log entry.\n")) ;
   } /* failure */
else
   { /* allocated */
    KdPrint (("LogIt: Going to log an error entry.\n")) ;
    errorLogEntry->ErrorCode = LOGIT_INFORMATION2;
    errorLogEntry->SequenceNumber = 0;
    errorLogEntry->MajorFunctionCode = 0 ;
    errorLogEntry->RetryCount = 0;
    errorLogEntry->UniqueErrorValue = 0;
    errorLogEntry->FinalStatus = STATUS_SUCCESS ;
    errorLogEntry->DumpDataSize = NUMBER_DUMP_DATA_ENTRIES * sizeof (ULONG);
    errorLogEntry->StringOffset = sizeof (IO_ERROR_LOG_PACKET) +
                  (NUMBER_DUMP_DATA_ENTRIES - 1) * sizeof (ULONG) ;
    errorLogEntry->NumberOfStrings = 2 ;
    for (i = 0 ; i < NUMBER_DUMP_DATA_ENTRIES ; i++)
       {
        errorLogEntry->DumpData[i] = 0xABCDEF00L + i ;
       }
    insertionString = (PWSTR)((PCHAR)(errorLogEntry)
                            + errorLogEntry->StringOffset) ;

    RtlMoveMemory (insertionString, ErrorString1.Buffer,
                            ErrorString1.Length) ;
    insertionString[ErrorString.Length / sizeof(WCHAR) ] = L'\0' ;

    insertionString =
        &insertionString[ErrorString1.Length / sizeof(WCHAR) + 1] ;

    RtlMoveMemory (insertionString, ErrorString2.Buffer,
                            ErrorString2.Length) ;
    insertionString[ErrorString2.Length / sizeof(WCHAR)] = L'\0' ;

    IoWriteErrorLogEntry (errorLogEntry) ;
   } /* allocated */
```

Given this specification of the message:

```
MessageId=0x0002
SymbolicName=LOGIT_INFORMATION2
Language=English
LogIt 2 - (%1): %2.%n
LogIt 2 blah blah blah ..... more more %n
LogIt 2 %2        %3
note which line this comes out on
```

we show in Figure 26.6 the output that this produces. Observe that the %n forces the second and third lines to come out as separate lines. But also observe that the line that is separate in the input file, "note which line this comes out on", comes out as part of the third output line because there is nothing to force it as a separate line.

The data structure is shown in Figure 26.7.

BugCheck!

A BugCheck, otherwise known as the Blue Screen of Death, is a serious problem. Generally, you get one only as a consequence of doing something improperly. You will rarely code a BugCheck into a driver, unless you have a driver that, when it detects an error, knows that if it lets the system keep running, serious damage to system integrity will follow. Often, you will write very careful checking code into your driver that you will use during debugging. You might also embed BugCheck calls in this code. But normally, you will have this code under the DBG conditional and have it excluded in nondebug builds (and you should use this mechanism, rather than actually removing the code; if you needed it once, you will need it again!).

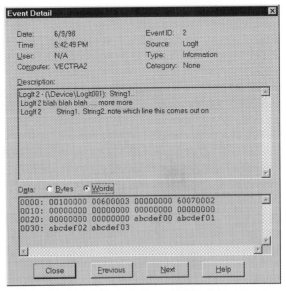

Figure 26.6: *Multistring Event Log entry (with %n).*

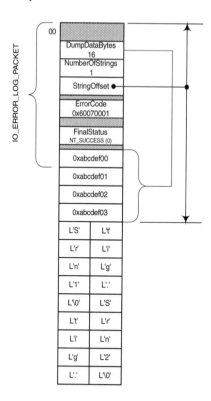

Figure 26.7: IO_ERROR_LOG_PACKET
with multiple strings.

You are not writing an application program. It was seldom correct to write "exit(0)" in a program (although it was frequently done), and it is *never* correct to write it in a subroutine library that is used in ways you can't predict. But in a device driver, most things that go wrong should be reflected back to the application space as error codes. You *don't* want to shut down the entire system because your driver ran out of some resource it needs. Instead, the correct action is to fail the IRP with STATUS_INSUFFICIENT_RESOURCES and let the application or the user decide what to do. You must *not* shut down the system. Only if you have determined that peculiar, unrecoverable damage has occurred should you even *think* of this as an option. And this damage must have the implication that it will damage the entire system. If your driver structures become corrupted, you could well set an internal flag that says "this driver is dead" and that will fail all future IRPs, if that can be safely done. Failing the entire system is an absolute, positive, last resort. An operating system is not an application program. *It must not fail.* Shutting down is a *major* failure mode. It is entirely reasonable to log an error to the Error Log as the action taken on an internal error. You can even "fail" your driver, such as by setting the flag we just posed. But *do not fail the system.*

Invoking a Blue Screen of Death

Having said all that, we add that you still might have to shut down the system. There are two functions you can use to do this.

```
VOID KeBugCheck(IN ULONG BugCheckCode);

VOID KeBugCheckEx(IN ULONG BugCheckCode,
                  IN ULONG BugCheckParameter1,
                  IN ULONG BugCheckParameter2,
                  IN ULONG BugCheckParameter3,
                  IN ULONG BugCheckParameter4);
```

These have identical behavior in terms of shutting down the system, but the second one displays four additional 32-bit values to aid in diagnosing the problem. What these values are is entirely up to you.

These functions result in the infamous Blue Screen of Death and lead you into debugging, a topic we discussed in detail in Chapter 9. The next section deals extensively with the Blue Screen of Death.

Surviving a Blue Screen of Death

The problem with getting a BugCheck is that the system really, truly shuts down. If your device is a robotic arm that has had some action initiated on it, you might really, really want to shut it down before the system terminates. In fact, you really, really want to shut it down *for any BugCheck caused for any reason by any component*. Failure to do so could cause serious damage or, in the extreme, death. If you are doing some sort of medical application, then before the system crashes the last thing you might want to do is cause an alarm to sound to bring people running. Or, you might simply want to save some state for the debug log.

Handling of BugChecks is addressed by the KeRegisterBugCheckCallBack function.

```
BOOLEAN KeRegisterBugCheckCallback(
                  IN PKBUGCHECK_CALLBACK_RECORD CallbackRecord,
                  IN PKBUGCHECK_CALLBACK_ROUTINE CallbackRoutine,
                  IN PVOID Buffer,
                  IN ULONG Length,
                  IN PUCHAR Component);
```

This function, normally called in the DriverEntry function, registers a function to be called when the system is shutting down as a consequence of a BugCheck. The BugCheck can be caused by any component of the system.

The *CallbackRecord* parameter must be allocated in nonpaged memory (it's not unreasonable to declare a KBUGCHECK_CALLBACK_RECORD in your Device Extension). Before calling this function, you must initialize this record with KeInitializeCallbackRecord.

In the Device Extension:

```
KBUGCHECK_CALLBACK_RECORD callback;
UCHAR registers[6]; // Place to store six status registers
```

In the `DeviceEntry` *function*:

```
// ...
KeInitializeCallbackRecord(&extension->callback);
KeRegisterBugCheckCallback(&extension->callback, myDriverBugCheck,
                           &extension->registers,
                           sizeof(extension->registers),
                           "myDriver");
```

In the Unload function:

```
KeDeregisterBugCheckCallback(&extension->callback);
```

In the callback function:

```
// We can't actually show any code here because what your callback
// function does is very device-dependent.
```

When the callback routine is called, there is a very limited number of things it can do. It cannot touch paged memory or do anything that would require changing the IRQL. It may not attempt to acquire a Spin Lock. It executes effectively at an IRQL *above* every DIRQL in the system. (What really happens is that it is called with all interrupts masked off!) It can call `READ_PORT` and `READ_REGISTER` functions. It could do `WRITE_PORT` or `WRITE_REGISTER` calls if necessary to do a shutdown or otherwise quiesce the device (bear in mind that these calls must essentially "complete" without the opportunity to interrupt). Because it cannot acquire Spin Locks, you cannot attempt to synchronize with Adapter Objects or Controller Objects. You can't "fail" the current IRP. (It wouldn't matter if you did. The IRP would never get back to the application anyway because the system is shutting down—this would like washing the windshield of a burning automobile.) Microsoft does not specify what happens if you cause an access error or otherwise try to do anything that would cause a BugCheck while you are in this handler. But we suspect it's nothing that can be described in a family publication.

The Microsoft documentation *does* state, however, that you can call any `Ke-` or `Hal-` function that will not touch paged memory or attempt to use any synchronization.

A BugCheck callback is handled on a "best-effort" basis. Even though you have registered it, there is absolutely no guarantee that it will actually *be* called successfully. The system may be far too sick to get to your handler. It is best to make any external device which needs to be quiesced on a system shutdown designed to be rendered "harmless" should the system shut down abruptly.

Reading and Writing Files

What's the Big Deal about reading or writing a file? Isn't that what a Device Driver is *supposed* to do? Well, not quite. A *file system driver* will handle reading and writing of files based on application program requests. But what about a driver that needs to read a file, for example, to read the binary code required to load the microcontroller on a sophisticated board? Many multiport serial boards have onboard chips that handle the bulk of the I/O traffic. (Figure out the interrupt rate that NT would have to withstand to support 64 serial lines running at a mere 9600 baud, a nearly obsolete speed because it is so slow by modern standards.) Instead, many of these boards have massive onboard buffer memory that can be accessed directly by the NT-based driver and a programmable chip (such as an Intel 960 or a 386SX). The code for the chip is *not* stored in nonvolatile RAM for some of these. Instead, it must be explicitly loaded when the driver is loaded.

As for writing files, we covered the use of the Event Log. However, the Log is not always the most appropriate mechanism for logging information, particularly for massive diagnostic dumps. Consider a driver that is keeping track of its complex internal state using any of various techniques.[5] When the driver locks up or otherwise misbehaves, it would be nice to snapshot this information. There are many ways to do this. One that springs to mind is to have an IOCTL that can be sent to the device (possibly by another application or another thread in the single application) that can cause this diagnostic information to be written to a file.

It is important to realize that none of the file operations can be called at other than PASSIVE_LEVEL. You cannot write data to a file from an ISR, or even a DPC. Any data written must be done from the Dispatch Routines (such as IRP_MJ_DEVICE_CONTROL) that take place at PASSIVE_LEVEL, and even then, only for the highest-level driver. To handle file I/O from DISPATCH_LEVEL or DIRQL level, you can use a Driver Thread and your own queue. Alternatively, you can use a System WorkItem to execute your subroutine in a System Worker Thread. See Chapter 24.

Functions for Reading and Writing Files

The following sections detail the operations for reading and writing files from a Device Driver.

ZwCreateFile

```
NTSTATUS ZwCreateFile(OUT PHANDLE FileHandle,
                      IN ACCESS_MASK DesiredAccess,
                      IN POBJECT_ATTRIBUTES ObjectAttributes,
                      OUT PIO_STATUS_BLOCK IoStatusBlock,
                      IN PLARGE_INTEGER AllocationSize OPTIONAL,
                      IN ULONG FileAttributes,
                      IN ULONG ShareAccess,
                      IN ULONG CreateDisposition,
                      IN ULONG CreateOptions,
                      IN PVOID EaBuffer OPTIONAL,
                      IN ULONG EaLength);
```

The ZwCreateFile function appears to be much more intimidating than the user-level CreateFile call, so we'll look at it in some detail. Like CreateFile, it returns a handle, but not as the result of the function. Instead, a pointer to a variable of type HANDLE is provided as the first argument.

The *DesiredAccess* parameter is a bit more powerful than GENERIC_READ and GENERIC_WRITE of the user-level call. The attributes that can be supplied are summarized in Table 26.3. However, for our purposes here, the only flags to be concerned about are FILE_READ_DATA and FILE_WRITE_DATA, and possibly FILE_APPEND_DATA. The GENERIC_READ flag of the user level translates directly into STANDARD_RIGHTS_READ for ZwCreateFile, and the GENERIC_WRITE flag of the user level translates directly into STANDARD_RIGHTS_WRITE.

[5] See, for example, my article on real-time debugging techniques, cited in the Further Reading section at the end of the chapter. *–jmn*

Table 26.3: *Some of the* `DesiredAccess` *Flags for* `ZwCreateFile`

`DesiredAccess` **Flag**	**Meaning**
DELETE	The file can be deleted.
FILE_READ_DATA	Data can be read from the file.
FILE_READ_ATTRIBUTES	`FileAttributes` flags, described later in the chapter, can be read.
FILE_READ_EA	Extended attributes associated with the file can be read. This flag is irrelevant to device and intermediate drivers.
FILE_WRITE_DATA	Data can be written to the file.
FILE_WRITE_ATTRIBUTES	`FileAttributes` flags can be written.
FILE_WRITE_EA	Extended attributes (EAs) associated with the file can be written. This flag is irrelevant to device and intermediate drivers.
FILE_APPEND_DATA	Data can be appended to the file.
SYNCHRONIZE	The returned `FileHandle` can be waited on to synchronize with the completion of an I/O operation.
STANDARD_RIGHTS_READ	FILE_READ_DATA | FILE_READ_ATTRIBUTES | FILE_READ_EA
STANDARD_RIGHTS_WRITE	FILE_WRITE_DATA | FILE_WRITE_ATTRIBUTES | FILE_WRITE_EA | FILE_APPEND_DATA

Casual inspection of the call shows that there is no place to specify a filename! The filename is actually specified as part of the OBJECT_ATTRIBUTES structure, which is shown in Figure 26.8.

The `Length` field must be set to `sizeof(OBJECT_ATTRIBUTES)`. The `RootDirectory` value is optional. If it is NULL, the `ObjectName` field must specify a full path for the file to be opened. If it is non-NULL, it is a handle to a directory obtained by an earlier call to `ZwCreateFile`, and `ObjectName` is a name interpreted relative to that path. Generally, you will set this value to NULL and use the Registry to obtain the full pathname for the file, which you will place in `ObjectName`.

The `Attributes` field should be set to OBJ_CASE_INSENSITIVE to make your request compatible with the standard NT file system conventions. Since we have carefully avoided all discussions of security, and your driver is a trusted component, we suggest that you set both `SecurityDescriptor` and `SecurityQualityOfService` to NULL.

```
typedef struct _OBJECT_ATTRIBUTES {
        ULONG Length;
        HANDLE RootDirectory; // Optional
        PUNICODE_STRING ObjectName;
        ULONG Attributes; // 0 or OBJ_CASE_INSENSITIVE
        PSECURITY_DESCRIPTOR SecurityDescriptor; // Optional
        PSECURITY_QUALITY_OF_SERVICE SecurityQualityOfService; // Optional
} OBJECT_ATTRIBUTES, * POBJECT_ATTRIBUTES;
```

Figure 26.8: *The* OBJECT_ATTRIBUTES *structure.*

Table 26.4: `Information` *Field Values from* `ZwCreateFile`

`FILE_CREATED`
`FILE_OPENED`
`FILE_OVERWRITTEN`
`FILE_SUPERSEDED`
`FILE_EXISTS`
`FILE_DOES_NOT_EXIST`

The next parameter that is specified is a pointer to an `IO_STATUS_BLOCK`. Upon completion of the operation, the `Information` field of this block will contain one of the values shown in Table 26.4. These should be self-explanatory.

The `AllocationSize` parameter can be used to specify an initial file allocation. This has no effect on an existing file that is being opened for reading. Offhand, we can think of no reason to specify other than 0 here.

Next is a set of file attribute flags. These are the same as the user-level flags, but for our purposes `FILE_ATTRIBUTE_NORMAL` suffices. They are summarized in Table 26.5.

Table 26.5: `FileAttribute` *Flags for* `ZwCreateFile`

`FileAttribute` **Flag**	**Meaning**
`FILE_ATTRIBUTE_NORMAL`	A file with standard attributes should be created.
`FILE_ATTRIBUTE_READONLY`	A read-only file should be created.
`FILE_ATTRIBUTE_HIDDEN`	A hidden file should be created.
`FILE_ATTRIBUTE_SYSTEM`	A system file should be created.
`FILE_ATTRIBUTE_ARCHIVE`	The file should be marked so that it will be archived.
`FILE_ATTRIBUTE_TEMPORARY`	A temporary file should be created.

The `ShareMode` parameter is identical to that of the user level and uses the same names. Generally, you will specify 0 for this flag, thereby giving your driver exclusive access to the file as long as it is open. `ShareMode` flags are summarized in Table 26.6.

Table 26.6: `ShareMode` *Values for* `ZwCreateFile`

`ShareMode` **Flag**	**Meaning**
`0`	The file cannot be accessed by any other thread until it is closed.
`FILE_SHARE_READ`	The file can be opened for read access by the calls of other threads to `ZwCreateFile`.
`FILE_SHARE_WRITE`	The file can be opened for write access by the calls of other threads to `ZwCreateFile`.
`FILE_SHARE_DELETE`	The file can be opened for delete access by the calls of other threads to `ZwCreateFile`.

The *CreateDisposition* parameter tells how to handle the case of the file's already existing, or not existing, for this call. Normally, for reading data you want to load to the device, you will use the FILE_OPEN flag. This flag fails if the file is not found. To write data, you will typically use FILE_OPEN_IF (to append data) or FILE_OVERWRITE_IF (to completely replace the contents if it already exists). *CreateDisposition* values are summarized in Table 26.7.

Table 26.7: *CreateDisposition Values for* ZwCreateFile

CreateDisposition Flag	If File Exists	If File Does Not Exist
FILE_SUPERSEDE	Replace it.	Create it.
FILE_CREATE	Fail.	Create it.
FILE_OPEN	Open it.	Fail.
FILE_OPEN_IF	Open it.	Create it.
FILE_OVERWRITE	Open it, and overwrite it.	Fail.
FILE_OVERWRITE_IF	Open it, and overwrite it.	Create it.

The difference between "replace" and "overwrite" depends on the settings of the other flags and whether the file has already been opened by another thread. We assume here a simple case of exactly one reader or exactly one writer and no need to deal with concurrent access. So we punt these complex discussions to the Microsoft DDK documentation.

CreateOptions flags, some of which are shown in Table 26.8, generally deal with how NT will handle the file internally. Most of these deal with fairly sophisticated File System features of little or no interest unless you are writing a File System Driver. However, for loading information to a device, FILE_SEQUENTIAL_ONLY allows the File System to prefetch data from the file. For files used to log diagnostic data, you might want to include flags such as FILE_WRITE_THROUGH or FILE_NO_INTERMEDIATE_BUFFERING to guarantee that all of the data makes it out to disk before the system crashes. Note that while you might be tempted to call KeRegisterBugCheckCallback to register a function that calls ZwClose on the file, *this probably won't work.* ZwClose can be called only at PASSIVE_LEVEL, and there is no guarantee that the callback will be at PASSIVE_LEVEL.

Table 26.8: *Some of the CreateOptions Flags for* ZwCreateFile

CreateOptions Flag	Meaning
FILE_NON_DIRECTORY_FILE	The file being opened must not be a directory file, or this call will fail. The File Object being opened can represent a data file; a logical, virtual, or physical device; or a volume.
FILE_WRITE_THROUGH	System Services, FSDs, and Device Drivers that write data to the file must actually transfer the data into the file before any requested Write operation is considered complete. This flag is automatically set if the *CreateOptions* flag FILE_NO_INTERMEDIATE_BUFFERING is set.
FILE_SEQUENTIAL_ONLY	All accesses to the file will be sequential.

Table 26.8: *Some of the* `CreateOptions` *Flags for* `ZwCreateFile` *(continued)*

`CreateOptions` Flag	Meaning
FILE_RANDOM_ACCESS	Accesses to the file can be random, so no sequential read-ahead operations should be performed on the file by FSDs or the system.
FILE_NO_INTERMEDIATE_BUFFERING	The file cannot be cached or buffered in a driver's internal buffers. This flag is incompatible with the *DesiredAccess* FILE_APPEND_DATA flag.
FILE_SYNCHRONOUS_IO_ALERT	All operations on the file are performed synchronously. Any wait on behalf of the caller is subject to premature termination from alerts. This flag also causes the I/O system to maintain the file position context. If this flag is set, the *DesiredAccess* SYNCHRONIZE flag also must be set.
FILE_SYNCHRONOUS_IO_NONALERT	All operations on the file are performed synchronously. Waits in the system to synchronize I/O queueing and completion are not subject to alerts. This flag also causes the I/O system to maintain the file position context. If this flag is set, the *DesiredAccess* SYNCHRONIZE flag also must be set.
FILE_DELETE_ON_CLOSE	The file can be deleted when the last handle to it is passed to ZwClose.
FILE_OPEN_BY_FILE_ID	The filename contains the name of a device and a 64-bit ID to be used to open the file. This flag is irrelevant to device and intermediate drivers.
FILE_OPEN_FOR_BACKUP_INTENT	The file is being opened for backup intent. Thus the system should check for certain access rights and grant the caller the appropriate accesses to the file before checking the input *DesiredAccess* against the file's security descriptor. This flag is irrelevant to device and intermediate drivers.

We're almost there! *EaBuffer* and *EaLength* are used if you want to get the extended attributes (EAs) back from the ZwCreateFile. Microsoft states that you should set these to NULL (0).

Example: Opening a File for Reading

So what would a typical File Open call look like? Listing 26.6 shows a simple example. This is the sort of code you might write to open a file of binary data that is to be loaded to the controller. This would typically be done in the DriverEntry routine in NT 4.0 or in NT 5.0 at the point where the Device Object was created. ZwCreateFile can be called *only* at PASSIVE_LEVEL.

Listing 26.6: *Using* ZwCreateFile *to Open a File for Reading*

```
NTSTATUS openForRead(OUT PHANDLE handle, IN PUNICODE_STRING filename)
    {
    OBJECT_ATTRIBUTES attrs;
    NTSTATUS status;
    IO_STATUS_BLOCK IoStatus;

    RtlZeroMemory(attrs, sizeof(attrs));
```

```
attrs.Length = sizeof(attrs);
attrs.ObjectName = filename;
status = ZwCreateFile(
            handle,
            STANDARD_RIGHTS_READ,
            &attrs,
            &IoStatus,
            0,
            FILE_ATTRIBUTE_NORMAL,
            0,              // exclusive access
            FILE_OPEN,    // Must exist
            FILE_SYNCHRONOUS_IO_NONALERT |  // No asynch alerts
            FILE_NON_DIRECTORY_FILE |       // Must not be dir
            FILE_SEQUENTIAL_ONLY,           // Optimize read
            NULL,
            0);

if(status == STATUS_SUCCESS)
    return STATUS_SUCCESS;
// If you want to, either directly return the status value or look
// in IoStatus.Information to determine the cause of the error

status = STATUS_NO_SUCH_FILE;  // Typical sort of error to return

return status;
}
```

We noted that in a similar example, the Microsoft code failed to specify the FILE_NON_DIRECTORY_FILE flag. Consider what this could lead to if, for some reason, the user managed to create a directory file of the same name as the expected data file. If you don't have this flag, ZwCreateFile would happily open the directory file, thinking it was valid data, *and load the contents of the directory file to the device*. Even worse, imagine what can happen to a poor defenseless system if your driver opens some sort of logging file for output, and it successfully opens a directory file. This is what gives Technical Support Managers nightmares.

Be aware that if you manage to fulfill their worst nightmare, they could become *your* worst nightmare. Be conservative. Be very conservative. Unless your driver can accept a directory, make sure you include this flag. Note that this call can still open a logical device, a virtual device, a physical device, or a volume. You could actually open one of these if the user has incorrectly edited the Registry, but we have been unable to find any call that, given a handle, could tell us if we have other than a data file. We are hoping that FILE_ATTRIBUTE_NORMAL will limit this operation to files only, but we are not certain and can find no confirming documentation.

ZwQueryInformationFile

```
NTSTATUS ZwQueryInformationFile(
                        IN HANDLE FileHandle,
                        OUT PIO_STATUS_BLOCK IoStatusBlock,
                        OUT PVOID FileInformation,
                        IN ULONG Length,
                        IN FILE_INFORMATION_CLASS FileInformationClass);
```

The ZwQueryInformationFile function returns various information about the file. Its most common use when you are reading a file is to obtain the file length. You then can allocate a block of memory of that size and do a single ZwReadFile to read the file contents into that memory.

The *FileHandle* parameter references the file handle returned from ZwCreateFile. The *IoStatusBlock* parameter is used to receive the completion status of the operation. The desired information about the file is placed in the *FileInformationBlock* parameter, which must be of a suitable length for the type of information returned. The *Length* parameter specifies the length of *FileInformationBlock*. The type of information that is returned is determined by the *FileInformationClass* parameter, whose value must be one of those given in Table 26.9.

Table 26.9: *FileInformationClass Values for* ZwQueryInformationFile

FileInformationClass	*FileInformation* **Type**	**Meaning**
FileBasicInformation	FILE_BASIC_INFORMATION	The caller must have opened the file with the *DesiredAccess* FILE_READ_ATTRIBUTES flag set.
FileStandardInformation	FILE_STANDARD_INFORMATION	The caller can query this information as long as the file is open, without any particular requirements for *DesiredAccess*.
FilePositionInformation	FILE_POSITION_INFORMATION	The caller must have opened the file with the *DesiredAccess* FILE_READ_DATA or FILE_WRITE_DATA flag set and with either of the *CreateOptions* flags, FILE_SYNCHRONOUS_IO_ALERT or FILE_SYNCHRONOUS_IO_NONALERT.
FileAlignmentInformation	FILE_ALIGNMENT_INFORMATION	The caller can query this information as long as the file is open, without any particular requirements for *DesiredAccess*. This information is useful if the file was opened with the *CreateOptions* FILE_NO_INTERMEDIATE_BUFFERING flag set.

FILE_STANDARD_INFORMATION

```
typedef struct _FILE_STANDARD_INFORMATION {
    LARGE_INTEGER AllocationSize;
    LARGE_INTEGER EndOfFile;
    ULONG NumberOfLinks;
    BOOLEAN DeletePending;
    BOOLEAN Directory;
} FILE_STANDARD_INFORMATION, * PFILE_STANDARD_INFORMATION;
```

The FILE_STANDARD_INFORMATION structure is filled in by ZwQueryInformationFile when the *FileInformationClass* parameter is FileStandardInformation. The AllocationSize value is the actual size allocated to the file and is usually a multiple of the block size of the device. It is rarely interesting. The EndOfFile value is the actual number of valid data bytes in the file, as established by the Write operations that created the file. This is the most useful value. The NumberOfLinks value indicates the number of hard links to the file, suggestive of more sophistication that we currently are aware of the File System supporting. The DeletePending flag indicates that the file has been deleted, but because there are open handles, the deletion has not yet completed. The Directory flag indicates that the handle is to a directory rather than to a data file.

Example: Reading the File Size

Listing 26.7: *Using* ZwQueryInformationFile *to Determine the File Size*

```
NTSTATUS getFileSize(HANDLE handle, PLARGE_INTEGER size)
    {
    IO_STATUS_BLOCK IoStatus;
    NTSTATUS status;
    FILE_STANDARD_INFORMATION info;

    status = ZwQueryInformationFile(handle,    // File handle
                                    &IoStatus, // Status return
                                    &info,
                                    sizeof(info),
                                    FileStandardInformation);
    if(!NT_SUCCESS(status))
        return status; // Error
    *size = info.EndOfFile;
    return STATUS_SUCCESS;
    }
```

ZwReadFile

```
NTSTATUS ZwReadFile(IN HANDLE FileHandle,
                    IN HANDLE Event OPTIONAL,
                    IN PIO_APC_ROUTINE ApcRoutine OPTIONAL,
                    IN PVOID ApcContext OPTIONAL,
                    OUT PIO_STATUS_BLOCK IoStatusBlock,
                    OUT PVOID Buffer,
                    IN ULONG Length,
                    IN PLARGE_INTEGER ByteOffset OPTIONAL,
                    IN PULONG Key OPTIONAL);
```

The ZwReadFile function reads a block of data from a file that has been opened by ZwCreateFile. The *FileHandle* parameter designates the file to read. The *Event*, *ApcRoutine*, and *ApcContext* parameters should all be set to NULL. The *IoStatusBlock* parameter is used to receive the detailed information about the completion of the Read operation. The number of bytes actually read can be found in the Information field.

The *Buffer* parameter is a pointer to the place to put the information, and the *Length* parameter is the maximum number of bytes that can be read into *Buffer*. For the examples we are using, of a single reader with exclusive access, the File System can maintain the position internally, so the *ByteOffset* parameter can be NULL. The *Key* parameter should be set to NULL.

This function can be called only at PASSIVE_LEVEL. Therefore the *Buffer* can point to paged memory.

ZwWriteFile

```
NTSTATUS ZwWriteFile(IN HANDLE FileHandle,
                     IN HANDLE Event OPTIONAL,
                     IN PIO_APC_ROUTINE ApcRoutine OPTIONAL,
                     IN PVOID ApcContext OPTIONAL,
                     OUT PIO_STATUS_BLOCK IoStatusBlock,
                     IN PVOID Buffer,
                     IN ULONG Length,
                     IN PLARGE_INTEGER ByteOffset OPTIONAL,
                     IN PULONG Key OPTIONAL);
```

The `ZwWriteFile` function writes a block of data to a file that has been opened by `ZwCreateFile`. The *FileHandle* parameter designates the file to write. The *Event*, *ApcRoutine*, and *ApcContext* parameters should all be set to NULL. The *IoStatusBlock* parameter is used to receive the detailed information about the completion of the Write operation. The number of bytes actually written can be found in the `Information` field.

The *Buffer* parameter is a pointer to the place to put the information, and the *Length* parameter is the maximum number of bytes to write from *Buffer*. For the examples we are using, of a single reader with exclusive access, the File System can maintain the position internally, so the *ByteOffset* parameter can be NULL. The *Key* parameter should be set to NULL.

This function can be called only at PASSIVE_LEVEL.

ZwClose

```
NTSTATUS ZwClose(IN HANDLE Handle);
```

The `ZwClose` function closes a file handle that was opened by `ZwCreateFile`. It can be called only at PASSIVE_LEVEL.

Rebooting: Avoid When Possible

There are few things in the world more frustrating than the annoying message, "You must reboot your system for this change to take effect". This is based on the old single-user, single-task MS-DOS model of the world, in which the premise is that rebooting the computer won't cost the user anything but a brief (very brief) delay. *This does not work today.* It is not only a severe annoyance to reboot your machine, forcing you to shut down your word processor, compiler environment, e-mail, and everything else have open (we rarely have fewer than a dozen programs running concurrently on our main machines). It also is a cardinal sin to require a file server to be shut down. Furthermore, the shutdown and startup times seem to be getting longer and longer with each release and with the added richness of the environments we install. Requiring a reboot is an unnecessary imposition on the user. *Whatever you can do to avoid reboots, DO IT!* We wish Microsoft would heed this advice (for example, have you ever made a change in your network configuration?).

A properly operating computer should *never* need to be shut down, even for hardware upgrades. (Our file servers have hot-swap disk bays. Also, in the USB/IEEE-1394 world, hot-pluggable Plug-and-Play is about to become the normal mode of existence.) While we will admit that for the short term, you must shut down to change internal hardware and make changes on the external SCSI chain, as far as we can tell, most other reboots are entirely gratuitous and could be avoided if more work was put into developing the drivers. Thus, if your device has loadable code or other information, *provide an IOCTL that does this on the fly*, that is, that quiesces the device properly, loads the new code, and properly restarts it. Plug-and-Play makes this easy, but a smooth configuration is by no means impossible (or in many cases even difficult) in the ordinary driver world. For Windows 2000, you won't have the option of doing reconfiguration badly. According to a recent poll,[6] users will become quite vocal about inadequate Plug-and-Play support. Good drivers don't just happen; they are the result of careful design and coding.

---

[6] This survey was conducted on the authors of this book. One hundred percent of users polled said they would complain about inadequate Plug-and-Play support. None were undecided or would not complain.

Pageable Drivers

Normally, pageable drivers is a topic you won't need to worry about. There usually is very little need to make drivers pageable and very little advantage in doing so. Most drivers are intrinsically very small, relative to applications. But once in a great while, you will encounter a situation in which a pageable driver makes perfect sense, so we very briefly discuss here some of the issues concerning them and the functions that you would use. The functions are summarized in Table 26.10.

Table 26.10: *Functions for Pageable Drivers*

Function	Description
MmLockPagableCodeSection	Locks pageable driver routines into system space, sometimes during driver initialization but usually in a driver's IRP_MJ_CREATE routine.
MmLockPagableDataSection	Locks pageable data into system space when that data is accessed infrequently, predictably, and at an IRQL < DISPATCH_LEVEL.
MmLockPagableSectionByHandle	Locks a pageable section into system memory using a handle returned from either MmLockPagableCodeSection or MmLockPagableDataSection.
MmUnlockPagableImageSection	Releases a section that was previously locked into system space when the driver is no longer processing IRPs or when the content of the section is no longer required.
MmPageEntireDriver	Allows a driver to page out all of its code and data regardless of the attributes of the various sections in the driver's image.
MmResetDriverPaging	Resets a driver's pageable status to that specified by the sections that make up the driver's image.

Any component of a driver that executes solely at PASSIVE_LEVEL can be pageable. Any component that executes at DISPATCH_LEVEL or above *must not* be pageable at the time it can be executed. Note carefully how that was stated. A driver that is completely inactive can even have its ISR and DPC paged out, *provided you have disconnected the interrupt*. Once you disconnect the interrupt, neither the ISR nor the DPC can be executed, so they could be removed. If any component of the driver is pageable and is paged out when it is called from an IRQL >= DISPATCH_LEVEL, the result will be a Blue Screen *and* an Unhappy User.

A driver can have both pageable and nonpageable components concurrently. As long as the components called at or above DISPATCH_LEVEL are nonpageable, the driver will work perfectly well.

Why a Pageable Driver?

Why a Pageable Driver? That's a good question. We give a few examples here.

One example is a driver that has large amounts of PASSIVE_LEVEL code or data. It can live more comfortably in a system if that massive code or data is pageable. Because this driver is executing at PASSIVE_LEVEL, if needed it will automatically be paged in using the standard page fault handling, even though it is executing in the kernel (much of the kernel is pageable already).

A large driver that is used infrequently might take advantage of this to reduce its nonpaged memory footprint. Typical examples of these kinds of drivers are drivers that have complex processing to do under stringent real-time requirements. Although NT is not by nature a system for real-time programming, depending on your definition of "real-time" it might be adequate if you do all of the time-critical computations entirely within the driver. As with most algorithms, there is usually a time/space trade-off. That is, to get the best performance you might choose to use truly massive tables (in some cases, complex algorithms can be reduced to "constant time" if your table is big enough). You might do this in the DPC, or you might use a separate Driver Thread to do it. You can either depend on the working set to keep the pages you need in memory or force the pages to be made resident while the driver is active.

Another example of a need for a pageable driver is a driver that has several large, optional components. Microsoft's example is a disk driver that supports disk mirroring, stripe sets, and volume sets. Those features of the disk driver that are not used are left as pageable components, and because they are never called, they are never brought into memory. Be aware, however, that if you do per-component pageability for multiple components, you are pushing the envelope of what the NT BUILD process supports when used in its "black box" mode. This is beyond the scope of anything we cover here.

You can also cause the *entire* driver to be paged out—ISR, DPC, and everything. Doing this usually has very little to recommend it because the critical functions of the ISR and DPC are often quite small anyway. However, a driver that performs complex processing in the DPC that involves lookups in a massive table (usually to get performance) might well want that DPC data pageable when the driver is not actually active.

Creating a Pageable Driver

No special programming action needs to be taken to make a driver pageable if you are working only with passive-level code. The pageability is determined by how you specify certain directives to the compiler using #pragma directives in the source code. To expedite development, these are often placed inside a conditional compilation so that the driver can be compiled either as fully resident or as pageable. The advantage of compiling a driver as fully resident is that you get to debug it in a slightly more friendly environment (nonpaged), while verifying that the parts you thought you could page are in fact pageable. You can, however, execute various kernel calls to lock down parts of a pageable driver and make them nonpageable, if there is reason to do so.

Pageable Code

To compile a driver with pageable segments, you must force the code and data into link sections with known names (the names were arbitrarily chosen by the creators of the BUILD process). This allocation is handled at the function level for code. To force a specific function into a specific code section, use the alloc_text pragma.

```
#ifdef ALLOC_PRAGMA
#pragma alloc_text("INIT", DriverEntry)
#pragma alloc_text("PAGE", MyDriverRead)
#pragma alloc_text("PAGE", MyDriverWrite)
#pragma alloc_text("PAGE", MyDriverIoControl)
#pragma alloc_text("PAGE", MyDriverClose)
#endif
```

592 Chapter 26 Useful Driver Techniques

To use this pragma, you first must declare the function (as a forward reference). Then you place the pragma and define the function. Typically, you would declare all of the functions as forward references, include a block of pragmas similar to the one just shown, and then declare the functions. If you fail to declare the functions first, the use of the pragma will generate a compilation error.

An alternative, which is either substantially uglier or much easier to maintain, depending on your aesthetics,[7] is the following style.

```
NTSTATUS MyDriverClose(IN PDEVICE_OBJECT DeviceObject, IN PIRP Irp);

#ifdef ALLOC_PRAGMA
#pragma alloc_text("PAGE", MyDriverClose)
#endif

NTSTATUS MyDriverClose(IN PDEVICE_OBJECT DeviceObject, IN PIRP Irp)
    {
     NTSTATUS status;
     // ... More decls

     status = STATUS_SUCCESS;
     PAGED_CODE();
     ...
     return status;
    }
```

In this example, `DriverEntry` is declared to be in the `INIT` segment and the `IRP_MJ_` handlers to be in the `PAGED` section. The BUILD process has linker commands that say "if there are any segments of this name, mark them pageable". For maximum pageability, you should also put into the pageable segment(s) all of the functions that are called only from pageable functions. You must not put into the pageable segment(s) the ISR, any DPC routine, and any functions that are called from the ISR or any DPC. (A function called from both pageable and nonpageable code *must* be in the nonpageable set.)

If you compile without the conditional value defined, which is true for the debug build, you will get an ordinary, fully resident driver. When you compile the release build, the `ALLOC_PRAGMA` symbol will be defined, and the functions you have declared will be in the pageable segments of the driver.

For pageable *data*, use the declaration

```
#pragma data_seg("PAGE")
```

before any declarations of data that are to go into the paged segment.
Follow these declarations with

```
#pragma data_seg()
```

---

[7] Because this puts the #pragma near the code, it means you can easily see that the code is declared pageable, particularly if you use my style, which is to obsessively put one function per physical page. If I ever did a pageable driver, I suspect I'd adopt this style because I believe it minimizes the chance of errors during maintenance. Code should have as one of its major criteria of goodness "robust under maintenance". *–jmn*

Note that all variables that are declared between these two pragmas *must* be initialized or they will not go into the specified segment.

```
#pragma data_seg("PAGE")
const MY_BIG_TABLE neatData[] = {
    { 0, 17, ... }
    { 411, 2048, ... }
    ...
};
#pragma data_seg( )
```

Unless you take special actions, this data cannot be accessed from the ISR or the DPC or any other elevated IRQL.

Validating Pageability

If you declare a function as pageable and it is called from elevated IRQL, there is an excellent chance the system will crash. (If the page just happens to be resident, the system will not fail. If it happens to be paged out at the time it is called . . . Blue Screen!) The problem is that this might or might not happen right away. It might run perfectly well on your lightly loaded development machine and yet crash in the field on a heavily loaded server.

To validate that all of your functions that are in the pageable segment are called only from PASSIVE_LEVEL, you should add the following statement near the beginning of each function you have marked as pageable:

```
PAGED_CODE();
```

This is a debugging aid. In the debug version of your driver, this statement compiles into an ASSERT that checks that the current IRQL is lower than DISPATCH_LEVEL. If the function is ever called at elevated IRQL, this statement will generate a diagnostic message on the debug output port. If you get such a diagnostic message, it identifies the file and line on which the PAGED_CODE call appears. In this case, go back into the file and remove the PAGED_CODE call and the pragma for the function that contained it.

Locking Down Data

You can call the MmLockPageableDataSection function, passing it a parameter that is any address within the pageable data segment. Then the entire pageable data segment will be locked down and remain so until you explicitly unlock it. When you lock it down, you get a handle to the section that you must store somewhere (usually in the Device Extension) so that you can use it later to unlock the data segment.

Of course, the driver must be multiprocessor-safe, hence the use of the Interlocked... functions for updating the reference count you supply in the Device Extension (and set to 0 in DriverEntry).

Listing 26.8: *Example of Dynamically Locking and Unlocking Data for a Pageable Driver*

```
NTSTATUS MyCreate(IN PDEVICE_OBJECT DeviceObject, IN PIRP Irp)
    {
    PMY_EXTENSION extension = (PMY_EXTENSION)DeviceObject->DeviceExtension;
    int ref;
    NTSTATUS status = STATUS_SUCCESS;

    ...

    ref = InterlockedIncrement(&extension->ActiveOpens);
    if(ref == 1)
        { /* no previous opens */
          extension->DataSection = MmLockPageableDataSection(&neatData);
        } /* no previous opens */
    ...
    return status;
    }

NTSTATUS MyClose(IN PDEVICE_OBJECT DeviceObject, IN PIRP Irp)
    {
    PMY_EXTENSION extension = (PMYEXTENSION)DeviceObject->DeviceExtension;
    int ref;
    NTSTATUS status = STATUS_SUCCESS;

    ...

    ref = InterlockedDecrement(&MyExtension->ActiveOpens);
    if(ref == 0)
        { /* no longer needed */
          MmUnlockPageableImageSection(extension->DataSection);
        } /* no longer needed */
    ...
    return status;
    }
```

Improving Performance by Locking Down Code

You might want a driver to be nonresident much of the time but want to take advantage of the performance improvement of having all of the service routines resident. This could be very important if your device needs to quickly receive a request or control function. Consider what may happen if you send an IOCTL to a device that has a paged driver. If the system is heavily loaded and the IOCTL is rare, it might be that the page holding the IRP_MJ_DEVICE_CONTROL handler is paged out. Also, the system might not have a free page frame. In such a case, the IOCTL will be delayed until a page can be successfully moved out of memory and the handler page moved in. This could be tens to hundreds of milliseconds, and the effects of this delay could be somewhere between inconvenient and serious. You can make a driver temporarily non-paged while it has open file handles and make it fully paged when all file handles are closed, or at any other time that suits your needs and the performance/space trade-offs.

The techniques for doing this are identical to the techniques for locking down data. The function that is called is MmLockPageableCodeSection. It unlocks either a code or data section. We can take our IRP_MJ_CREATE handler from the previous example and add one line to lock down the code section. This code assumes that the handler itself is in the paged code section and therefore uses its address as the address to lock down the code (the function locks down all of the code in the section that contains the address passed as a parameter).

Listing 26.9: *Example of Dynamically Locking and Unlocking Code for a Pageable Driver*

```
NTSTATUS MyCreate(IN PDEVICE_OBJECT DeviceObject, IN PIRP Irp)
    {
    PMY_EXTENSION extension = (PMY_EXTENSION)DeviceObject->DeviceExtension;
    int ref;
    NTSTATUS status = STATUS_SUCCESS;

    PAGED_CODE();
    ...

    ref = InterlockedIncrement(&extension->ActiveOpens);
    if(ref == 1)
       { /* no previous opens */
         extension->DataSection = MmLockPageableDataSection(&neatData);
         extension->CodeSection = MmLockPageableCodeSection(MyCreate);
       } /* no previous opens */
    ...
    return status;
    }

// The corresponding Unlock operation should be done in the Close handler
```

Paging Entire Drivers

As indicated earlier in the chapter, paging entire drivers is very rarely done. The MmPageEntireDriver function marks *all* pages in the driver as pageable, even if they were declared as nonpageable. The ISR, the DPC, and everything else become pageable. MmPageEntireDriver returns no value. To reset to the original settings, and thus force the non-pageable pages back into memory and lock them down (while leaving the pageable parts of the driver still pageable), you call MmResetDriverPaging. The addresses supplied to these two functions can be *any* address within the driver, such as DriverEntry.

Be sure you disconnect the interrupts before setting the entire driver to be pageable. Also, be aware that some devices are notorious for generating spurious interrupts, so it might not be sufficient to say, "But I don't have any active I/O, and I turned off the Interrupt Enable bit!" In fact, the interrupt might not have even come from your device! It might have come from a device that is sharing that interrupt line (this would require calling your ISR, even if your device is *totally quiescent*). Or it might have come from a device that has erroneously generated an interrupt on the line you thought you had exclusive access to (we've seen this happen far too often!).

Product Driver Installation

Installing a product driver is a Black Art in many ways. For many of the standard subsystem drivers (video drivers, network drivers, or printer drivers), you must install them using the Control Panel applets, and these require a .inf file to control the installation. The format of this file is, for all practical purposes, undocumented; the documentation in the DDK is sparse, confusing, and almost totally incomprehensible. If you are writing a standard driver, you should budget a lot of time to explore the intricacies of the file. We had hoped to say something more about the file formats than is said in the DDK, but we concluded that we are no more expert at this than anyone else who hasn't done it. The construction of a valid `.inf` file is not improved by the fact that there is virtually no support for debugging such files.

Fortunately, a large class of specialty drivers does not require the use of `.inf` files. Many of these drivers are packaged as part of an application-with-hardware package, and you can install them along with the application. Thus your setup program can install the application and its drivers, and you never need to have any contact with the `.inf` file.

At the moment, the product vendor still has the option of writing a setup program, either from scratch (a fairly challenging task, as it turns out) or by using one of the prepackaged setup generators. Depending on your needs and the complexity of your installation, one of these setup generators might be adequate. (However, our experience is that these generators either have a very simplistic world view, as well as all of the limitations *that* brings along, or are fully general with a scripting language—and often bug-ridden, poorly documented, and needlessly complex for doing the just-beyond-simplest setups.)

Some of these setup generators allow you to provide your own DLL for handling the "extensions" to the core setup. Whether you write a setup program yourself or take advantage of the extension DLL, you will need to know something about how Device Drivers are installed.

The Service Control Manager

Device Drivers are controlled by the NT component called the SCM (Service Control Manager). The SCM can be invoked from the Control Panel by either of two applets: one for System Services and one for Devices. The truth is that there is only one SCM, but it has two GUI interfaces, since both of these applets call the SCM API functions. The only difference in using them is that some operations make sense only for System Services and some make sense only for Device Drivers. The two GUIs keep these separate.

You can also use the SCM to start and stop an application-specific driver, independent of the Control Panel applets. Your application can call the SCM to start the service when the application comes up and to shut it down as the application terminates. A driver does *not* need to load at boot time to be useful.

The Registry

You will need to write Registry entries for your driver. You can do this by invoking the `regini` program from your setup program or by using the Registry API functions. In addition to the core Registry entries required to specify a driver, you can add your own entries for your own purposes.

Programming the SCM

Access to the SCM is only from the application level. There is no defined interface for calling it from the kernel. The following sections describe how an application program calls the SCM. The steps are as follows.

- Obtain a handle to the SCM.
- Obtain a handle for the service (create a new service or open an existing service).
- Perform the desired operation (start, stop, delete).
- Close the handle to the service.
- Close the handle to the SCM.

The details of these operations are discussed in the following sections.

OpenSCManager

```
SC_HANDLE OpenSCManager(
                  LPCTSTR machine,
                  LPCTSTR database,
                  DWORD desiredAccess);
```

To communicate to the SCM, you need to open a connection to the manager. To do this, you call the OpenSCManager API function, which returns a handle to the SCM. You then use this handle in subsequent SCM calls.

To get a handle on the local machine, for the default database, you make the first two parameters NULL. You will want all of the access rights, so you specify, for the third parameter, SC_MANAGER_ALL_ACCESS. Note that for a nonprivileged user in a properly administered network, this means that the user might not be able to install the driver due to insufficient privileges. This, however, is not your problem. Your typical call will be

```
SC_HANDLE scm = OpenSCManager(NULL, NULL, SC_MANAGER_ALL_ACCESS);
```

CreateService

```
SC_HANDLE CreateService(
          SC_HANDLE hSCManager,      // handle to service control manager
          LPCTSTR lpServiceName,     // pointer to name of service to start
          LPCTSTR lpDisplayName,     // pointer to display name
          DWORD   dwDesiredAccess,   // type of access to service
          DWORD   dwServiceType,     // type of service
          DWORD   dwStartType,       // when to start service
          DWORD   dwErrorControl,    // severity if service fails to start
          LPCTSTR lpBinaryPathName,// pointer to name of binary file
          LPCTSTR lpLoadOrderGroup,// pointer to name of load ordering
                                     // group
          LPDWORD lpdwTagId,         // pointer to variable to get tag id
          LPCTSTR lpDependencies,    // pointer to array of dependency names
          LPCTSTR lpServiceStartName,
                                     // pointer to account name of service
          LPCTSTR lpPassword);       // pointer to password for service
                                     // account
```

Once you have opened an SCM handle, you can create one (or more) services, that is, Device Driver entries. When you create a driver, you specify an internal name, a display name, and an executable name. The internal name, *lpServiceName*, is the name of the driver; it is used for subsequent calls to the SCM. This is the name of the Registry entry that CreateService will create for the driver. The display name, *lpDisplayName*, is the name that is shown in the Drivers applet. The executable name, *lpBinaryPathName*, is the path to the executable code. The load order group, tag, and dependencies are the same values we describe in Chapter 7, starting on page 135. The *lpServiceStartName* and *lpPassword* are always NULL.

For example, you might use a service name such as "ADM32", but a display name such as "Analog/Digital Converter 32-channel" and an executable name of %systemroot%\ drivers\ADM32V1.sys. The CreateService call returns either NULL or a service handle (type SC_HANDLE). When you are done with this handle, you must close it by using CloseServiceHandle. The *dwServiceType* is SERVICE_KERNEL_DRIVER, the *dwStartType*

Table 26.11: *Service Start options for* `CreateService`

Value	Meaning
`SERVICE_BOOT_START`	Specifies a device driver started by the system loader. This value is valid only for driver services.
`SERVICE_SYSTEM_START`	Specifies a device driver started by the IoInitSystem function. This value is valid only for driver services.
`SERVICE_AUTO_START`	Specifies a service to be started automatically by the service control manager during system startup.
`SERVICE_DEMAND_START`	Specifies a service to be started by the service control manager when a process calls the `StartService` function.

Table 26.12: *Error control options for* `CreateService`

Value	Meaning
`SERVICE_ERROR_IGNORE`	The startup program logs the error but continues the startup operation.
`SERVICE_ERROR_NORMAL`	The startup program logs the error and puts up a message box pop-up but continues the startup operation.
`SERVICE_ERROR_SEVERE`	The startup program logs the error. If the last-known-good configuration is being started, the startup operation continues. Otherwise, the system is restarted with the last-known good configuration.
`SERVICE_ERROR_CRITICAL`	The startup program logs the error, if possible. If the last-known-good configuration is being started, the startup operation fails. Otherwise, the system is restarted with the last-known good configuration.

is one of the start types from Table 26.11, such as `SERVICE_DEMAND_START`, and the `dwErrorControl` indicates the response to a failure of the *DriverEntry* routine, one of the values from Table 26.12, such as `SERVICE_ERROR_NORMAL`.

For our Hardware Simulator Driver, we show the Devices applet in Figure 26.9 and the corresponding Registry entries in Figure 26.10. Note that the start type is Manual, and because the Start button is highlighted, this driver is not actually running yet.

A simple installation routine is shown in Listing 26.12.

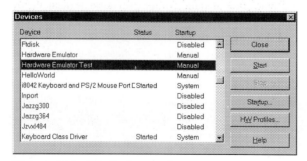

Figure 26.9: *The Devices applet.*

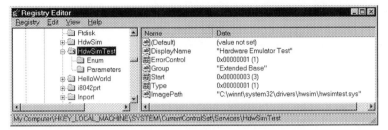

Figure 26.10: *Registry entries created by* `CreateService`.

One way to get the strings is to use the `VERSIONINFO` structure to provide them. This means that you can write a single, general-purpose installer for a variety of drivers without having to actually hardwire the strings in the installer program. The use of the `VERSIONINFO` structure is exhibited in the code that accompanies *Win32 Programming* and is well beyond the scope of this book.

OpenService

```
SC_HANDLE OpenService(SC_HANDLE scm,
                      LPCTSTR DriverName,
                      DWORD DesiredAccess);
```

Given an SCM handle, you can obtain a handle to a service by using `OpenService`. The name you give is the service name provided as the second parameter to `CreateService`. This is the name that appears in the Registry for the service. Typically, you will specify the *DesiredAccess* as `SERVICE_ALL_ACCESS`. If you need lesser access, you can specify only the flags you need.

StartService

```
BOOL StartService(SC_HANDLE service, DWORD argcount, LPTSTR * args);
```

The `StartService` function takes a reference to a service and causes it to start. The *argcount* value and its corresponding *args* pointer are used only for System Services and then to construct the command line to the System Service. Device Drivers do not use these parameters. Thus they will be 0 for *argcount* and `NULL` for *args*. The `SC_HANDLE` is a handle to the service obtained from `OpenService`.

Listing 26.10: *Starting a Driver Programmatically*

```
BOOL StartDriver(IN SC_HANDLE scm, IN LPCTSTR DriverName)
    {
     SC_HANDLE service = OpenService(scm, DriverName, SERVICE_START);
     BOOL result;

     if(service == NULL)
         { /* error */
          // .. Handle the error
          // .. See Listing 26.12 for an example of how to use FormatMessage
          return FALSE;
         } /* error */
```

```
    result = StartService(service, 0, NULL);
    if(!result)
        { /* start failed */
        // ... Report error
        CloseServiceHandle(service);
        return FALSE;
        } /* start failed */
    CloseServiceHandle(service);
    return TRUE;
    }
```

ControlService

```
BOOL ControlService(SC_HANDLE service,
                    DWORD flags,
                    LPSERVICE_STATUS status);
```

The ControlService function is used for both System Services and Device Drivers. Consequently, this function offers a large number of options that you will never use. A System Service can be paused, continued, and queried; these operations have no meaning for a Device Driver.

The only valid *flags* option for a Device Driver is SERVICE_CONTROL_STOP.

An example of how to shut down a driver is shown in Listing 26.11.

Listing 26.11: *Stopping a Driver Programmatically*

```
BOOL StopDriver(IN SC_HANDLE scm, IN LPCTSTR DriverName)
    {
    SC_HANDLE service;
    SERVICE_STATUS status;
    BOOL result;

    service = OpenService(scm, DriverName, SERVICE_STOP);
    if(service == NULL)
        { /* report error */
        // .. Take whatever action is needed to report an error
        // .. See Listing 26.12 for an example of FormatMessage
        return FALSE;
        } /* report error */

    result = ControlService(service, SERVICE_CONTROL_STOP, &status);
    if(!result)
        { /* error */
        // .. Report error
        CloseServiceHandle(service);
        return FALSE;
        } /* error */

    CloseServiceHandle(service);
    return TRUE;
    }
```

DeleteService

```
BOOL DeleteService(SC_HANDLE service);
```

The `DeleteService` parameter takes the handle to a service and deletes the service. You can get the service handle from either `CreateService` (if there was an error in the installation and you have to "back out" the installation) or from `OpenService`.

CloseServiceHandle

```
BOOL CloseServiceHandle(SC_HANDLE service);
```

The `CloseServiceHandle` parameter can be applied to any `SC_HANDLE` handle. It closes the handle and releases any internal resources that were consumed by having the handle open.

We show an example of how to install a driver using the SCM in Listing 26.12.

Listing 26.12: InstallDriver

```
BOOL InstallDriver(IN SC_HANDLE scm,
                   IN LPCTSTR DriverName,
                   IN LPCTSTR DisplayName,
                   IN LPCTSTR ExecutableName)
  {
  SC_HANDLE service;

  service = CreateService(scm,      // Handle to SCM database
                          DriverName,
                          DisplayName,
                          SERVICE_ALL_ACCESS,
                          SERVICE_KERNEL_DRIVER, // Service type
                          SERVICE_DEMAND_START,  // Type of start
                          SERVICE_ERROR_NORMAL,  // Error control type
                          ExecutableName,        // Executable
                          NULL,             // No load ordering group
                          NULL,             // No load tag identifier
                          NULL,             // no load dependencies
                          NULL,             // Use "LocalSystem" account
                          NULL);            // No password
    if(service == NULL)
       { /* failed */
         DWORD err = GetLastError();
         LPTSTR msg;

         if(err == ERROR_SERVICE_EXISTS)
            { /* replace */
             // Ask user if current service should be replaced
             // If response is 'Yes', delete the existing service and
             // replace it
             // ...
            } /* replace */
         // If response is 'No' or the error was not ERROR_SERVICE_EXISTS,
         // issue the error message
         if(FormatMessage(FORMAT_MESSAGE_ALLOCATE_BUFFER |
                          FORMAT_MESSAGE_FROM_SYSTEM,
                          NULL,
                          err,
                          0, // Default language
                          (LPSTR)&msg,
                          0, // No length restriction
                          NULL) != 0)
             { /* issue message */
```

```
                // Issue a dialog box with the contents of the string
                // referenced by 'msg'
                // ...
                LocalFree(msg);
            } /* issue message */
        else
            { /* error converting message */
            TCHAR text[50];
            wsprintf(text, "%08x", err);
            // Issue a dialog box with the hex error number
            } /* error converting message */
        return FALSE;
        } /* failed */

    CloseServiceHandle(service);

    return TRUE;
}
```

The Alpha Memory Barrier

Chapter 6 (page 117) discussed the Alpha architecture and the issue of the Alpha write pipe. In the case of the Alpha write pipe, you must *force* anything in the write pipe to be purged before you write new data to the same location. Otherwise, the problem we described in which the write pipe "optimizes" the two sequential writes will almost certainly cause your device to malfunction.

The memory barrier is an instruction you must force into the instruction stream. There are two forms of the memory barrier: the general "memory barrier" instruction available on all Alpha platforms, and the somewhat better-performing "write memory barrier" instruction available on the EV5 and later Alpha processors. Earlier versions must use the memory barrier. The memory barrier, according to the Alpha documentation, stalls *all* memory-referencing instructions until the write buffer is flushed. The write memory barrier stalls only subsequent memory write instructions to the same location until the pending write operations complete.

If you use the WRITE_REGISTER_*type* and WRITE_PORT_*type* functions, presumably (we infer this based on the stated semantics of the WRITE_ operations) you will get the best memory barrier for the platform, based on the HAL implementation. This means you will get either the straight memory barrier, which gives you totally abysmal performance, or the much better write memory barrier, which gives you merely horrible performance.

Consequently, if you need to transfer large amounts of data to your device, you may choose to bypass the HAL. In this case, you are responsible for putting the appropriate write barriers in place.

To force the contents of the write pipe to be flushed, and consequently to be written to the device register, you insert a *memory barrier* in your code in such a way as to guarantee the serialization of writes to memory. Thus your code will resemble the following sort of sequence:

```
    *location1 = value1;
    // insert memory barrier here
    *location1 = value2;
```

You must be very careful; if you are writing to the same location, just make certain that you have placed the memory barrier before the next write to that location. If you can't be sure you are writing to the same location, you must definitely insert the memory barrier, because the code *might* malfunction. For this you pay a potentially high performance penalty. Generally, a Device Driver writes to a specific set of locations in a specific order, so you always know the exact locations and order. Note that if you are doing a block copy to device memory, because the address is always incrementing you don't need a memory barrier between each write. In such a case, you may simply put the memory barrier after the last write to guarantee everything is written back:

```
for(; count > 0; count--)
    *location++ = *source++;
// put memory barrier here
```

You must not "optimize" your use of the memory barrier by "knowing" the size of the write pipe. Instead, assume you don't know the size of the write pipe (or assume it is fantastically large) and put the memory barriers in as needed for correctness.

These are not predefined for you. Define a memory barrier with the following macro:

```
#ifdef _ALPHA_
#define MEMORY_BARRIER() (void)asm("mb")
#else
#define MEMORY_BARRIER() // does nothing
#endif
```

The write memory barrier is defined as:

```
#ifdef _ALPHA_
#define WRITE_MEMORY_BARRIER() (void)asm("wmb")
#else
#define WRITE_MEMORY_BARRIER() // does nothing
#endif
```

Although Visual C++ version 5.0 and later RISC editions support an intrinsic function –mb, it does not appear to support the write memory barrier.

Summary

This chapter has described a number of useful techniques. These included using the Registry, using the Event Log, creating, intercepting, and responding to a system crash, reading and writing files, and creating a pageable driver, as well as advanced DPC techniques, an Alpha-specific technique, and some NT 4.0-specific product installation techniques.

Further Reading

Kano, Nadine, *Developing International Software for Windows 95 and Windows NT*, Microsoft Press. ISBN 1-55615-840-8.

Newcomer, Joseph M., "Debugging Real-Time Systems", in *Dr. Dobb's Journal 18, 7* (July 1993). Also on the *Dr. Dobb's Journal on CD-ROM*.

Rector, Brent E., and Joseph M. Newcomer, *Win32 Programming*, Addison Wesley Longman, 1997. ISBN 0-201-63492-9.

Chapter

27 *A Hardware Simulator*

In this chapter, we describe how we built a software simulator for a representative hardware device that allows students to experiment with writing a Device Driver without needing special hardware on the machine. This simulator, because it is done in software, will run on any NT 4.0 system. And while we tried to maintain a transparent approach, there are just enough idiosyncrasies to this "device" (some deliberately added to Make The Problem Interesting and some just artifacts of its software nature) that using it will give you a real-world flavor of what it is like to write a real Device Driver.

Why a Simulator?

The flippant response to the heading is, to paraphrase Groucho Marx, "Why *not* a simulator?" There are many valid reasons for providing a simulator. Our original goal was to provide a device that students could program whose behavior was uniform, well-defined, and, as it turned out, just a little bit idiosyncratic, a device developed in conjunction with the course we developed for Technology Exchange Company. We had some interesting logistics. Technology Exchange teaches a large number of hands-on courses and consequently has a large inventory of teaching computers. These go in and out as the needs of the courses dictate: six here, a dozen there, week after week. If we required that a special hardware device be installed, they would have to purchase a number of such devices, install them in the machines going out for teaching our course, and remove them when the machines were returned. We realized that this would be a nightmare. In addition, the instructor setting up the class would have to make sure that a machine "with" was paired with a machine "without" and that the students understood which was the "development platform" and which was the "test platform". It would be inevitable that some of the machines with the special boards would be out for an ordinary MFC course, thereby causing a shortage for the Device Driver course. Finding an inexpensive board that had desirable student characteristics turned out to be harder than we thought.

Finally, we hit on the idea of *simulating* a device. This had many benefits.

- It would involve no special hardware; hence there would be no inventory problem.
- It would involve no added hardware expense.
- We could produce a "device" of uniform characteristics.
- It could be run at "any speed from DC to light"—or at least it could be simulated at a speed consistent with a student using a debugger (for example, no interrupt would occur until the student *wanted* it to occur!).
- It could have "manual" and "automatic" modes of operation, one in which the student would have complete control of the device properties and the other in which the simulator would try to behave like real hardware.
- It would allow us to do error injection, selectively or randomly, to allow the students to test their error recovery code (just try to force *real* hardware to have an error so that you can test the code).

Given how useful the simulator turned out to be for us, we thought you might find it useful also. This applies particularly to someone designing new hardware, where the actual silicon might be in short supply. A simulator can provide for a lot of development to be done in advance of receiving even the first silicon and, with appropriate customization, can even allow application developers to test parts of their code.

Basic Design of a Simulator

The challenge was to build a software simulator that mimicked hardware. We had to design three major components:

- The Hardware Simulator Driver, which is a special Device Driver that provides the necessary kernel-level control
- The Hardware Simulator "control panel"—a bit of a misnomer, since this is where most of the actual simulation is done
- The interface between the student Device Driver and our "device"

Although not critical to the design, we also designed a "dummy load" application, the *I/O Explorer*.[1]

The relationships of these components to each other is shown in Figure 27.1. On the left-hand side, the Device Driver and/or application writer work. Here, our application is shown as the I/O Explorer, but any other application would suffice. This application talks to its Device Driver by the API specified by the driver designer: CreateFile, CloseHandle, and one or more of ReadFile, WriteFile, the asynchronous functions ReadFileEx and WriteFileEx, or

---

[1] The Explorers are a concept I introduced in the book *Win32 Programming*. They are convenient GUIs to underlying APIs that allow you to poke at the API and see the results in a human-readable form. A collection of such Explorers for the GUI level, which cover such concepts as the Device Context, GDI, and a host of controls (sometimes called "widgets" in other windowing systems), is on the CD-ROM that accompanies that book. The complete source for everything described here for the I/O Explorer accompany this book.

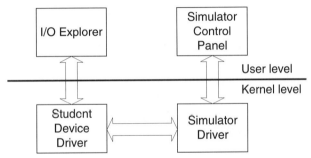

Figure 27.1: *Simulator architecture.*

`DeviceIoControl`. Ideally, the synthetic load has no idea that it is talking to a driver that is talking to a simulated device.

The Device Driver itself will probably know that it is talking to simulated hardware only because there are many details that a simulator cannot accurately model. An example is the exact timing of the real device; because of some of the timing delays, there can be some failures in state transitions of the simulator. We discuss these in great detail in the following sections. The driver also has to kludge in some "windows" where the scheduler can actually allow the Hardware Simulator Control Panel to run. However, these can all be placed under the control of an `#ifdef` (or even tested dynamically). These perturbations, for our simple device, were quite minor and did not materially affect the actual internal structure of the Device Driver itself.

On the right-hand side of Figure 27.1 is the actual Deep Magic. The Hardware Simulator Driver is the deepest of the Deep Magic—it needs to actually generate interrupts that the Device Driver sees as real interrupts. It took us a while to discover exactly how this is done, but in practice it is quite simple. The Hardware Simulator Driver also presents to the Device Driver a set of "I/O ports", which just happen to be memory addresses, into which the driver writes information and from which it reads information.

The device has six 8-bit registers that define its behavior. There are three input registers and three output registers, shown in Figure 27.2. Each side has an 8-bit data register. (Input data is

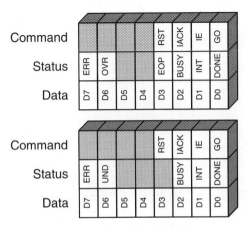

Figure 27.2: *Simulated device registers.*

register offset 2; output data is register offset 5.) For input, the input character is read from this register after an Input operation completes; for output, the character to be written is put in this register before the Output operation is initiated.

The Command registers for both sides are the same. That for input is at register offset 0, and that for output is at register offset 3. Setting the GO bit to 1 initiates the operation. The GO bit is automatically cleared. The IE (Interrupt Enable) bit is set to permit the device to interrupt upon completion of the operation. Note that input and output interrupt on the same IRQ line; it is up to the driver to determine if the interrupt was for completed input or completed output (or both!). If an interrupt is taken, it must be cleared by setting the IACK bit. The IACK bit is automatically cleared when the interrupt state is cleared. If an error occurred, the error state is cleared by setting the RESET (RST) bit. This bit is automatically cleared when the error state is cleared. Note that of the Command register bits, only the IE bit is persistent and can be set and cleared by the driver. It is never changed by the device. (However, our Hardware Simulator Control Panel will let the tester clear the IE bit as a debugging aid. The real device can't do this.)

The Status registers for both sides are nearly the same. That for the input side is at register offset 1, and that for the output side is at register offset 4. Each side has a BUSY bit. Once the GO bit is set, the device enters the BUSY state, as indicated by clearing the GO bit and setting the BUSY bit. When the transaction completes, with or without an error, the DONE bit is set to indicate the completion. If the transaction completed successfully and the IE bit is set, this will also cause the device to interrupt. This is indicated by setting the INT status bit. The INT status is cleared by setting the IACK bit. If an error occurs, the ERR bit will be set and the DONE bit will be set, and if the IE bit is set, the INT bit will be set and an interrupt will occur. The interrupt is cleared with IACK, but the device remains in the error state until it is cleared by setting the RST bit. Note that setting RST will clear the INT bit if it was set. However, when writing a Device Driver, you will typically IACK in your ISR but you can't analyze the device for success or failure until your DPC Routine runs. Clearing INT does not reset ERR.

A state transition diagram for all of these states is shown in Figure 27.6.

For an input device, one specific kind of error is the *data overrun*. This means the device is sending data to the computer faster than the computer can respond. The result is that when the next datum arrives, the previous one has not yet been removed from the device register. There is no place to put the incoming datum. It falls on the floor. The device signals the computer that it should have gotten off its lazy rear end[2] and met the timing constraints. This is done by having the overrun (OVR) bit set along with the ERR bit. (There may be other, generic errors that the ERR bit indicates, but the combination of ERR and OVR indicates an overrun.)

For an output device, the corresponding condition is the *data underrun*. This means that the device requires data at a specific minimum rate, but the processor was unable to deliver it. Audio output devices are particularly prone to this. If the audio data is not there when it is needed, an annoying "click" is usually heard (the human perceptual system can easily detect a 1-ms loss of signal!). This is signaled by telling the processor it has failed to meet the real-time window by using the underrun (UND) bit. Like the OVR bit, the UND bit is always signaled with ERR, but ERR can be signaled without UND.

To simplify some of the coding and to make other coding a bit more complex, we decided to send input data in as *packets*. This is really just to let the application be able to "read a line" of data. Packets are of variable length. The device decides when the end of a packet is connected.

---

[2] This applies to all machines except *front*-end processors. Sorry, I couldn't resist. *–jmn*

(Actually, this is done by the Hardware Simulator Control Panel module when it sends the last character of an input string.) When the last character is put in the input register and DONE is signaled for that character, the End Of Packet (EOP) bit is also set. It is the responsibility of the Device Driver writer for this device to detect the EOP bit and use this as the basis for deciding when to call `IoCompleteRequest` to indicate a successful packet transfer.

The Hardware Simulator Control Panel is where all the real work happens. It has the GUI that lets the Device Driver writer "touch" each of the hardware bits, setting status, forcing actions, and even generating interrupts. It interfaces to the Hardware Simulator Driver via a `DeviceIoControl` interface. There are operations to read the registers, write the registers, generate an interrupt, set the interrupt vector that is being used, and even enable and disable internal tracing in the Hardware Simulator Driver itself (after all, *we* had to debug it). The Hardware Simulator Driver, being a real "device" from the viewpoint of NT, has its own device name, which we can use on a `CreateFile` operation.

The Hardware Simulator Control Panel presents an appearance much like that shown in Figure 27.3. (If the one you see in the real code differs in minor details, don't be surprised— we're improving it all the time.) As you can see from the figure, there is a set of check boxes for the Status and Control register bits. The simulated device is a full-duplex device with both input and output sides. (We wanted to provide the students with a number of design options, and full-duplex devices add interesting complexity.) This device can accept a stream of text characters, so there are buttons to generate random text strings (or the student can type in a text string to send) and send the text. There are options to run in Manual mode, in which nearly all of the state changes are handled by having the student click the Control registers, or Free-Running mode, in which the simulator really tries to act like a "live" device (except for the timing). Note the section labeled Error Injection. This allows the student to inject errors into the stream, manually or, when free-running, randomly. Other dialogs allow the error types and frequencies to be set. Spurious interrupts can be introduced, as well as simulated lost interrupts. At the bottom is a trace panel that lets the student see exactly what state transitions have occurred. This leads to the interesting button on the left labeled Comment. This button allows the trace to be commented—

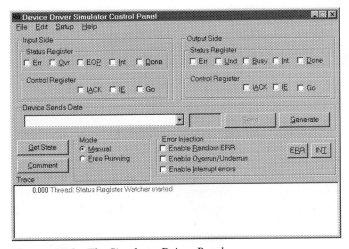

Figure 27.3: *The Simulator Driver Panel.*

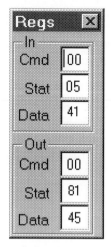

Figure 27.4:
Register display.

this is essential for debugging. The student can set up an "experiment": Insert a comment line stating what is about to occur, and then watch to see if the correct events transpire. The contents of the trace log can be saved to a file and later printed or examined using any sort of text editor (even Notepad).

In addition to the symbolic display shown with the check boxes, a straight hexadecimal display of registers can be popped up as a floating window. This is shown in Figure 27.4.

The Hardware Simulator Driver

The Hardware Simulator Driver is loaded as a Device Driver. Usually, it is a "manual start" style of driver. You will have to start the Hardware Simulator Driver before starting any driver that uses it, and it must not be stopped until the driver(s) that uses it have been stopped.

The code for the Hardware Simulator Driver, located in hdwsim.sys, must be in the \windows\system32\drivers directory, and the driver must be registered. The hdwsim.reg file, shown in Figure 27.5, needs to be processed once to establish the proper registration. To process this, simply locate the file in the Windows NT Explorer and double-click on the file. The Registry Editor will read this file and load the values into the Registry. (Note the syntax of this file is slightly different from the hdwsim.ini file used with the regini program).

```
REGEDIT4
[HKEY_LOCAL_MACHINE\SYSTEM\CurrentControlSet\Services\HdwSim]
"Type"=dword:00000001
"Start"=dword:00000003
"Group"="Extended Base"
"ErrorControl"=dword:00000001
[HKEY_LOCAL_MACHINE\SYSTEM\CurrentControlSet\Services\HdwSim\Parameters]
"BreakOnEntry"=dword:00000000
"DebugMask"=dword:00000006
"LogEvents"=dword:00000000
"DefaultInterruptLine"=dword:00000007
```

Figure 27.5: *The* hdwsim.reg *file.*

Hardware Simulator Driver Source Code

The complete source accompanies this book. What we show here are the interesting fragments that make this driver different from the classic "Hello World" driver. In most of the examples, we dropped all of the debug output statements (except where they illustrate how we log HdwSim-specific information). We indicated other sites where we have dropped code by using "/...". We do not include the utility subroutines that have nothing simulator-specific to say. There is little point in reproducing all of the stock code in a listing in the book when it is all available as part of the code distribution that accompanies this book.

Listing 27.1: *Hardware Simulator* `DriverEntry` *Routine*

```
NTSTATUS DriverEntry(
    IN PDRIVER_OBJECT DriverObject,
    IN PUNICODE_STRING RegistryPath)
{
    PDEVICE_OBJECT deviceObject = NULL;
    NTSTATUS status;
    UNICODE_STRING NtNameString;
    UNICODE_STRING DosNameString;
    NTSTATUS retReg;
    //
    //   Registry values
    //
    ULONG debugMask;
    ULONG eventLog;
    ULONG shouldBreak;
    PHDW_SIM_DEVICE_EXTENSION extension;
    PHYSICAL_ADDRESS    physicalAddressBase1;
    ULONG               lengthToMap;
    unsigned int        i;
    ULONG interrupt_Line;
    UNICODE_STRING ephemeralRegistryPath;
    UNICODE_STRING parameterRegistryPath;
    UNICODE_STRING registryPathName;

    status = initDevicePath(DriverObject, RegistryPath,
                                    &ephemeralRegistryPath,
                                    &parameterRegistryPath,
                                    &registryPathName);
    retReg = readRegistry(DriverObject, &parameterRegistryPath,
                                    &debugMask,
                                    &eventLog,
                                    &shouldBreak,
                                    &interrupt_Line);
    if (shouldBreak)
        DbgBreakPoint();

    // ... Unicode string setup
    status = IoCreateDevice(
                DriverObject,
                sizeof(HDW_SIM_DEVICE_EXTENSION),          // Device Extension
                &NtNameString,
                FILE_DEVICE_UNKNOWN,
                0,                       // No standard device characteristics
                FALSE,                   // This isn't an exclusive device
                &deviceObject
                );

    if ( !NT_SUCCESS(status) )
        return status;

    extension = deviceObject->DeviceExtension;
    extension->DeviceObject = deviceObject;
    extension->debugMask = debugMask;
    extension->ephemeralRegistryPath = ephemeralRegistryPath ;
    extension->parameterRegistryPath = parameterRegistryPath;
    extension->registryPathName = registryPathName;
```

```
extension->pSimulatedRegisterLogicalAddress =
                        &extension->simulatedRegister[0];
extension->pSimulatedRegisterPhysicalAddress =
        MmGetPhysicalAddress(extension->pSimulatedRegisterLogicalAddress);
KeInitializeSpinLock(&extension->registerLock);

//... Create dispatch points for create/open, close, unload

// Do Buffered I/O; a nop Read and Write are not supported by this driver
//
deviceObject->Flags |= DO_BUFFERED_IO;

// ... Register device name, and create symbolic link

// Save the address in the Device Extension
//
extension->interrupt_Line = interrupt_Line;
extension->Level  = extension->interrupt_Line;
extension->Vector =  extension->interrupt_Line;

extension->interrupt_IDT = HalGetInterruptVector(Isa,
                                (ULONG)0,              // BusNumber,
                                extension->Level,      // Level
                                extension->Vector,     // Vector,
                                &extension->irql,      // IRQL
                                &extension->Affinity); // Affinity mask

status = saveConfig( extension->ephemeralRegistryPath.Buffer,
                    extension->interrupt_Line,
                    extension->interrupt_IDT,
                    (VOID *)extension->pSimulatedRegisterLogicalAddress,
                    extension->pSimulatedRegisterPhysicalAddress
                    );

KdPrint(("%s  DriverEntry - interruptLine   = 0x%08x\n",
                DBG_MSG_HDR,    extension->interrupt_Line ));
KdPrint(("%s  DriverEntry - interruptIDT    = 0x%08x\n",
                DBG_MSG_HDR,    extension->interrupt_IDT ));
KdPrint(("%s  DriverEntry - registerAddress = 0x%08x\n",
                DBG_MSG_HDR,
                (ULONG)extension->pSimulatedRegisterLogicalAddress));
KdPrint(("%s  DriverEntry - PhysicalAddress= 0x%08x 0x%08x\n",
                DBG_MSG_HDR,
                extension->pSimulatedRegisterPhysicalAddress.HighPart,
                extension->pSimulatedRegisterPhysicalAddress.LowPart));
return status;
}
```

One of the new features is the notion of the *ephemeral* Registry path. As discussed in Chapter 26, some Registry entries are "ephemeral", meaning they do not survive the reboot process.[3] The Hardware Simulator Driver is a driver that does *not* want to inherit the state from a previous incarnation of itself for some of the values. We store these values in an ephemeral Reg-

---

[3] Although this is true in principle, we have found it impossible to create an ephemeral entry, in spite of following the documented procedures for doing so. See our example in Chapter 26, on page 561.

istry entry. This means that after each reboot, only the default values coded in the driver itself will be assigned. Following are the values we store in the ephemeral Registry entries:

- The physical address of the simulated register block
- The system virtual address of the simulated register block
- The interrupt line used
- The interrupt hardware IDT (Interrupt Descriptor Table) entry

Note that we store the Registry path values in the Device Extension. Because these are UNICODE_STRING values—a structure that contains a pointer to a buffer containing the actual characters—a copy of the structure made by the assignment will create a new *pointer* to the buffer, not a new *copy* of the buffer. Changes to the buffer will affect both UNICODE_STRING values.

In the Device Extension, we allocate a block of storage for the simulated registers. We store a pointer to this block in the Device Extension as well, but in order to share this value with the target Device Driver being tested, we need a *physical address*. To get this, we use MmGetPhysicalAddress. The Device Driver will eventually obtain this physical address from the ephemeral Registry entry and map the address into the System Logical Address Space for its own use.

We are treating this as an ISA device without shared interrupts, so the Interrupt Line and Interrupt Level values will be the same. We store the Interrupt Line value we obtained from the (permanent) Registry entry.

Having assigned an interrupt line in the Registry, we call HalGetInterruptVector to perform the appropriate mapping. The result of HalGetInterruptVector is "the mapped interrupt vector". What this translates to is the IDT index of the interrupt. This is what we need when we actually use a software INT instruction to generate the interrupt to the desired driver. We store this in the Device Extension.

Finally, we call a function, saveConfig, in our driver. This function stores the various parameters in the permanent and ephemeral Registry entries, prints out some useful debug information, and returns. Code that shows how the ephemeral Registry entry is supposed to be created appears in Listing 26.2 on page 561.

Open and Close Functions

The Open and Close functions are identical to those in the "Hello World" driver. Nothing special needs to be done.

DeviceIoControl

Surprisingly, we have already shown the code for DeviceIoControl. We used it as the example for how to do a DeviceIoControl handler. You can find it in Listing 10.3 on page 235.

generateInterrupt

generateInterrupt is an amazingly boring routine. We call it with the IDT value for which we wish to generate an interrupt, and it interrupts. The tedium is that there is no way to easily generate an INT instruction using a dynamically computed interrupt value. This is a limitation of the *x*86 architecture.

We took a very simple-minded approach, one that is guaranteed not to be done in by caching and pipelining, as writing self-modifying code might be. This is shown in the following listing. Consider the case in which you might store the interrupt value in the byte of the next instruction and then cause that instruction to be executed with the assigned value. This requires having write privileges to the code page (which is easily achieved), but note that on any machine of 386 or higher power, such a modification of code to the next instruction would be too late! Because of instruction pipelining, the instruction has already been fetched and partially decoded! And unlike with caching, there is no "pipeline snooping" going on (code is assumed to be read-only), so what will execute is the INT instruction with the value it had at the time it was prefetched, *not* with its updated value. Of course, you could put some number of instructions ahead of it to force the pipeline to wait, but that works only on one instance of the architecture. Thus what might work on a 386 will not work on a 486, while what worked on the 486 won't work on a Pentium. (And we were two generations beyond that at the time this code was written!) Not a good idea. Tedious though the following code looks, it is easy to get working and it is completely architecture-independent for any of the *x*86 architectures. (We did not do an Alpha version of this code, largely due to lack of time.) We use the Microsoft _asm directive to insert a machine instruction directly inline.

Listing 27.2: *Generating a Software Interrupt*

```
void generateInterrupt(UCHAR interrupt_IDT)
{
    switch ( interrupt_IDT )
    {
      case 0x00:    _asm { int 0x00 }
                    break;
      case 0x01:    _asm { int 0x01 }
                    break;
      case 0x02:    _asm { int 0x02 }
                    break;
      case 0x03:    _asm { int 0x03 }
                    break;

      // ... You get the idea by now...

      case 0xfe:    _asm { int 0xfe }
                    break;
      case 0xff:    _asm { int 0xff }
                    break;
    }
}
```

The Unload Routine

The Unload routine is little different from the stock Unload function we've shown you many times in this book. All that significantly differs is that we must delete the ephemeral Registry entries. While these are (supposed to be) deleted on a reboot, once the driver is unloaded the physical address of the register block has no meaning and so must be removed; otherwise, the test driver will obtain it and try to write to it. This can result in anything from a memory access error to massive—or, even worse, *subtle*—system damage, since the space formerly occupied by the register block might now be occupied by some other data structure entirely.

Listing 27.3: *The Hardware Simulator Unload Routine*

```
VOID HdwSimUnload( IN PDRIVER_OBJECT DriverObject)
{
    UNICODE_STRING DosNameString;
    PHDW_SIM_DEVICE_EXTENSION extension;
    NTSTATUS status;

    extension = DriverObject->DeviceObject->DeviceExtension;
    //
    // Free ephemeral Registry entries
    //
    if (extension->ephemeralRegistryPath.Buffer)
        {
        HANDLE hKey;
        //
        //  Free devices key
        //
        if (NT_SUCCESS(
                    openDevicesKey(
                    extension->ephemeralRegistryPath.Buffer,
                    &hKey)))
            {
             // Delete the open key from the Registry

             ZwDeleteKey(hKey);

             ZwClose(hKey);
            }
         else
            {
                KdPrint( ("HdwSim: can't open ephemeral key\n") );
            }
        }
    //
    // We don't need the path anymore
    //

    ExFreePool(extension->parameterRegistryPath.Buffer);
    ExFreePool(extension->registryPathName.Buffer);

    // ... Delete symbolic link

    IoDeleteDevice( DriverObject->DeviceObject );
}
```

The Hardware Simulator Control Panel

The Hardware Simulator Control Panel application implements not only the control panel but also the entire simulation logic code.

Hardware Simulator State Diagram

The state transition diagrams for input and output are quite similar. The output state diagram is shown in Figure 27.6. The device starts out in the IDLE state. The driver can cause it to leave

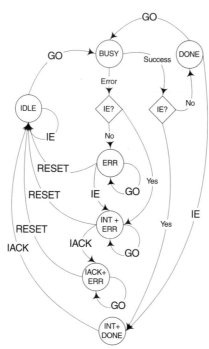

Figure 27.6: *Simulated device: output side state diagram.*

this state by setting the GO bit in the device's Output Command register. At this point, the device enters the BUSY state; this is signaled by clearing the GO bit and setting the BUSY bit in the Output Status register. The device leaves the BUSY state by either completing the output transfer successfully or taking an error. When the device leaves the BUSY state, the BUSY bit is cleared.

If the Output operation completes successfully, the next state is determined by whether the IE bit is set.

- If the IE bit is set, the device enters the INT+DONE state, signaled by setting the DONE bit and the INT bit. Entry to this state also causes an interrupt to be generated. The device is returned to the IDLE state by setting the IACK bit; when the device returns to the IDLE state, the IACK bit is cleared.

- If the IE bit is not set, the device then enters a state called DONE, which is almost like IDLE, except the DONE bit is set (in IDLE mode the DONE bit is cleared).

  - If in the DONE state the IE bit is set, an interrupt will be generated and the device will transition to the INT+DONE state, setting the INT bit.

  - If in the DONE state the IE bit is not set, a new transaction can be initiated by loading the Output Data register and setting the GO bit in the Output Command register.

Note that if the IE bit is set in the IDLE state, the device remains in the IDLE state.

If there is an error, the action again depends on whether the IE bit is set.

- If the IE bit is not set, the device enters the ERR state. This is signaled by setting at least the ERR bit and the DONE bit, as well as possibly additional status bits to indicate a more specific error (such as UND for output or OVR for input).

- If the IE bit is set, the device enters the INT+ERR state. This is signaled by setting at least the ERR bit, the DONE bit, and the INT bit, as well as possibly additional status bits to indicate a more specific error. Entry into the INT+ERR state also causes an interrupt to be generated.

- If the IE bit is set while the device is in the ERR state, it will enter the INT+ERR state and cause an interrupt. Once the device is in the ERR or INT+ERR state, setting the GO bit has no effect until the RST bit is set to clear the device's error condition. If the device is in the INT+ERR state and IACK is set, the INT condition is cleared and the device enters a new state, designated IACK+ERR. The ERR (and OVR or UND) bits remain set, as does DONE. As with the previous error states, GO has no effect until the error is cleared with RST.

From the Hardware Simulator Control Panel, you can force these various state transitions. You can even force a few state transitions that are not actually possible for a "live" device but that are convenient for testing situations such as the response of the driver to weird states. The control panel also allows you to force a condition that was not properly set by the driver but that must be so for the driver to complete its operation. For example, if you are waiting for an interrupt but notice that the driver forgot to set the IE bit, you can force the IE bit on (and take an interrupt) just by clicking it. In Manual mode, the Hardware Simulator also acts as a diagnostic tool on your driver. In Free-Running mode, these situations do not arise, except for the error injection mechanisms, which can lose interrupts, cause spurious interrupts, or generate ERR, ERR+OVR (input), or ERR+UND (output) conditions.

Using the Hardware Simulator Controller

To debug a driver using the simulator, you should follow these steps:

1. If the HdwSim driver is not started, start it.
2. If the Hardware Simulator Control Panel is not started, start it.
3. You can now start your driver.
4. Start the test application to exercise your driver.

Before the Simulator Controller can be run, the HdwSim driver must be started. If you attempt to start the Simulator Controller before you have started the HdwSim driver, it will fail to open the driver and will enter a mode in which its internals can be debugged but which has no effect on the driver. If you then start the HdwSim driver, you will have to restart the Hardware Simulator Control Panel.

Your Device Driver will have to locate the HdwSim driver during its DriverEntry processing. If you have not started the HdwSim driver, your driver should terminate with an error return.

The Hardware Simulator setup should be performed at least once. The Setup dialog is shown in Figure 27.7. The primary purpose here is to establish an IRQ that is used by the Hardware Simulator Driver. This must be a nonshared IRQ. If you attempt to choose an IRQ that is in use, you will get a warning.

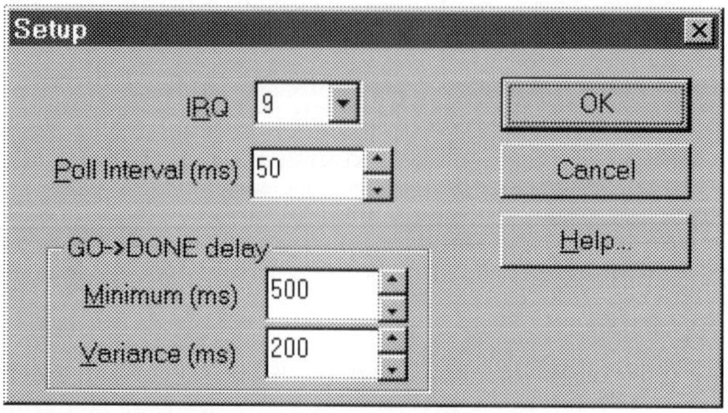

Figure 27.7: *Hardware Simulator's Setup dialog box.*

The Simulator Controller works by *polling* the status. When the Hardware Simulator is running in Manual mode, you must explicitly poll the status of the driver by clicking the **Get State** button. You can then set the various status bits, which will immediately reflect back to the HdwSim driver. In Free-Running mode, the Simulator Controller polls at regular intervals (subject, of course, to the vagaries of the NT scheduler). The polling interval is established in the Setup dialog.

When in Free-Running mode, the Hardware Simulator provides a statistical behavior by introducing a random time between when it detects the GO command and when it establishes a DONE state. This is parameterized by two values that are set in the Setup dialog: the *minimum* time, which is fixed, and the *variance*, which is chosen to be in a uniform random distribution in the range of 0 to the selected setting. Thus the values shown in Figure 27.7 mean the response time will vary from 500 ms (500 + 0) to 700 ms (500 + 200). This is a very slow setting designed to allow easy watching of the simulated I/O traffic. It can be speeded up considerably, but the traffic will be harder to watch. To get a completely steady delay, set the variance to 0.

A real benefit of the Hardware Simulator is the ability to inject errors. In Manual mode, this can be done by setting either the ERR bit in the appropriate Status register or by setting UND/OVR, which will implicitly set ERR. Doing this also will trigger DONE and, if interrupts are enabled, INT as well.

In Free-Running mode, the error can be injected automatically and randomly. This is controlled by two sets of parameterizations. The first set is on the main control panel and is a set of check boxes, as shown in Figure 27.8. Simple ERR states or OVR/UND states can be injected randomly. Interrupt errors include spurious interrupts and dropped interrupts (particularly important if you are writing a driver that must recover from a device that drops interrupts). In addition, you can click the ERR button to inject an error at the next opportunity (usually

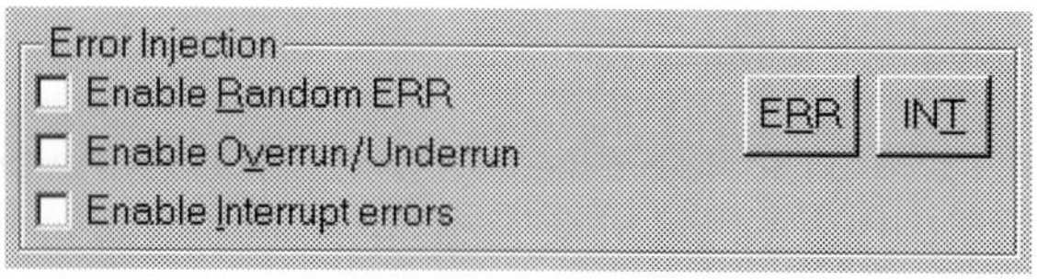

Figure 27.8: *Hardware Simulator Error Injection control.*

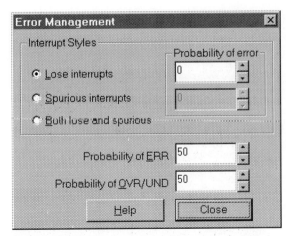

Figure 27.9: *Simulator Error Management dialog.*

responding to the next GO request) or the INT button to generate a spurious interrupt as quickly as possible.

The "random" behavior of the error injection is controlled by an Error Management dialog shown in Figure 27.9. This parameterizes the ERR injection by two values:

- The Probability of ERR, which determines the chances that an ERR will occur on any given transaction. In the figure, this is shown as 50%. This means that, on average, half of the transactions will fail (this is obviously configured to test the error recovery!).
- The Probability of OVR/UND, which determines that a certain percentage of these ERR states will be OVR/UND errors. This is also configured as shown as 50%. This means that the distribution is, on average, 50% success, 25% ERR only, and 25% ERR+UND or ERR+OVR.

Interrupt failure modes are configured in the Interrupt Styles section, which offers three options:

- Lose interrupts
- Spurious interrupts
- Both lose and spurious

The probabilities apply to an INT Event. Thus if Lose interrupts is configured to 20%, then, on average, 20% of the INT events will be lost. If Spurious interrupts is chosen, the probability is the probability that any given polling event will generate an interrupt. Thus if the spurious probability is set to 20% and the Polling Interval is set to 100 ms, there will be 10 polling events per second and, on average, two spurious interrupts per second.

The I/O Explorer

One of the annoyances of testing a new driver is the need to test all of the interesting combinations of state. For example, what happens if a particular `DeviceIoControl` is executed after the

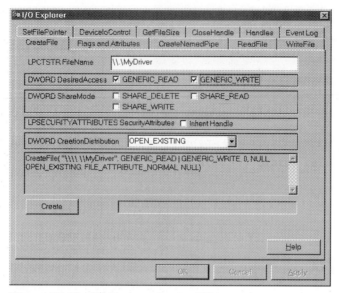

Figure 27.10: *I/O Explorer* CreateFile *panel.*

first ReadFile instead of before? How does the driver respond to this request? Does it work correctly if apparently independent requests appear in any sequence? Setting up all of the difference scenarios in a test program can be very tedious, especially if they need to be tested only once. An additional problem is that in many cases, you test it by setting a debug breakpoint, looking at the results of GetLastError, and then looking up the numeric value in a table. Very tedious.

The I/O Explorer is an outgrowth of the Explorer technology developed for *Win32 Programming*. It allows you to configure an operation such as CreateFile with any of its possible configurations and then click a button and see the result. You can execute ReadFile, WriteFile, DeviceIoControl, and the other operations and study their effects. A sample I/O Explorer screen is shown in Figure 27.10. This figure shows just one of the many pages available, the one for CreateFile. In this example, the driver named \\.\MyDriver is about to be opened in Read/Write mode. Clicking one of the tabs along the top allows other operations to be performed. The actual call that is executed is shown in the display box below all of the parameters. This allows you to see how the call would be written in C code.

Sample Device Drivers

The driver we develop next has a simple interface. Although it has CreateFile (IRP_MJ_CREATE) and CloseHandle (IRP_MJ_CLOSE) handlers, these are as trivial as the ones for the simple "Hello World" drivers. The driver does not handle ReadFile and WriteFile operations, just to simplify its construction. The specification is that DeviceIoControl performs the I/O operations. The two IOCTLs defined are IOCTL_LAB2_READ and IOCTL_LAB2_WRITE.

Listing 27.4: *A Driver for the Hardware Simulator*

```
#define LAB2_TYPE 43000
#define LAB2_IOCTL_BASE 2833
enum
{
    LAB2_IOCTL_READ = LAB2_IOCTL_BASE,
    LAB2_IOCTL_WRITE
};

#define IOCTL_LAB2_READ \
    CTL_CODE(LAB2_TYPE, LAB2_IOCTL_READ, METHOD_BUFFERED, FILE_READ_DATA)
#define IOCTL_LAB2_WRITE \
            CTL_CODE(LAB2_TYPE, LAB2_IOCTL_WRITE, METHOD_BUFFERED, FILE_WRITE_DATA)
```

Thus a Read operation is performed by an application doing the following.

```
DeviceIoControl(
                hTest,             // Handle to device
                (unsigned long)IOCTL_LAB2_INITIALIZE, // IO Control code for Read
                &InBuffer,         // Buffer to driver
                sizeof(InBuffer),  // Length of buffer in bytes
                NULL,              // Buffer from driver
                0,                 // Length of buffer in bytes
                &ReturnedLength,   // Bytes placed in DataBuffer
                NULL               // NULL means wait till op. completes
                    );
```

And a Write operation is performed by the following.

```
DeviceIoControl(
                hTest,             // Handle to device
                (unsigned long)IOCTL_LAB2_INITIALIZE, // IO Control code for Read
                NULL,              // Buffer to driver
                0,                 // Length of buffer in bytes
                &OutBuffer,        // Buffer from driver
                sizeof(OutBuffer), // Length of buffer in bytes
                &ReturnedLength,   // Bytes placed in DataBuffer
                NULL               // NULL means wait till op. completes
                );
```

Testing State: Macros, Bitmaps, and Offsets

Rather than constantly be writing code of the form

```
if((READ_REGISTER_UCHAR(deviceExtension->registers[IN_STATUS])
    & IN_STATUS_BUSY))
```

we simplify our coding considerably by defining a few macros that represent state checks. Thus we can rewrite the previous line as the much simpler, and much more readable,

```
if(IN_BUSY_STATE)
```

Register Offsets

```
#define IN_COMMAND      (0)
#define IN_STATUS       (1)
#define IN_DATA         (2)
#define OUT_COMMAND     (3)
#define OUT_STATUS      (4)
#define OUT_DATA        (5)
```

Register Bit Definitions

```
// INPUT STATUS BITS
#define IN_STATUS_DONE     0x01
#define IN_STATUS_INT      0x02
#define IN_STATUS_BUSY     0x04
#define IN_STATUS_EOP      0x08
#define IN_STATUS_OVR      0x40
#define IN_STATUS_ERR      0x80

// INPUT COMMAND BITS
#define IN_COMMAND_GO      0x01
#define IN_COMMAND_IE      0x02
#define IN_COMMAND_IACK    0x04
#define IN_COMMAND_RESET   0x08

// OUTPUT STATUS BITS
#define OUT_STATUS_DONE    0x01
#define OUT_STATUS_INT     0x02
#define OUT_STATUS_BUSY    0x04
#define OUT_STATUS_UND     0x40
#define OUT_STATUS_ERR     0x80

// OUTPUT COMMAND BITS
#define OUT_COMMAND_GO     0x01
#define OUT_COMMAND_IE     0x02
#define OUT_COMMAND_IACK   0x04
#define OUT_COMMAND_RESET  0x08
```

State Test Macros

The following macros are used to test state. We show some of the definitions, but since the definitions are quite symmetrically patterned, we save space (and boring you) by showing the later ones with just a comment indicating what the body would be.

```
#define IN_ERROR_STATE \
        (READ_REGISTER_UCHAR(&extension->registerAddress[IN_STATUS]) & \
         IN_STATUS_ERR)
#define IN_OVERRUN_STATE \
        (IN_ERROR_STATE && \
         (READ_REGISTER_UCHAR(&extension->registerAddress[IN_STATUS]) & \
          IN_STATUS_OVR))
#define IN_END_OF_PACKET_STATE \
        (READ_REGISTER_UCHAR(&extension->registerAddress[IN_STATUS]) & \
         IN_STATUS_EOP)
#define IN_INTERRUPT_STATE  // ... Tests IN_STATUS_INT bit
#define IN_DONE_STATE       // ... Tests IN_STATUS_DONE bit
#define OUT_ERROR_STATE     // ... Tests OUT_STATUS_ERR bit
```

```
#define OUT_UNDERRUN_STATE \
        (OUT_ERROR_STATE &&
        (READ_REGISTER_UCHAR(&extension->registerAddress[OUT_STATUS]) & \
         OUT_STATUS_UND))
#define OUT_BUSY_STATE      // ... Tests OUT_STATUS_BUSY bit
#define OUT_INTERRUPT_STATE // ... Tests OUT_STATUS_INT bit
#define OUT_DONE_STATE      // ... Tests OUT_STATUS_DONE bit
```

A Polled Device Driver

The first student assignment we give using the Hardware Simulator is to write a polled Device Driver. We present this here because it shows how to pick up the configuration parameters for the Hardware Simulator, as well as a couple of the tricks required to talk to the Hardware Simulator itself. You might choose to compile these conditionally.

DriverEntry

The DriverEntry routine does not differ significantly from those we've given previously, so in the following example we show only the highlights. Note that we use a common routine to read the Registry that is shared with later labs in our course. Thus, although we read the interrupt vector and IDT lines, we ignore them for this version.

Listing 27.5: DriverEntry *for a Driver for the Hardware Simulator*

```
NTSTATUS DriverEntry(IN PDRIVER_OBJECT driverObject,
                     IN PUNICODE_STRING RegistryPath )
{
    PDEVICE_OBJECT deviceObject = NULL;
    NTSTATUS status;
    UNICODE_STRING NTNameString;
    UNICODE_STRING DosNameString;
    NTSTATUS retReg;
    BOOLEAN GotResources;
    //
    //  Registry values
    //
    ULONG debugMask;
    ULONG eventLog;
    ULONG shouldBreak;
    ULONG interruptLine;
    ULONG interruptIDT;
    unsigned int busNumber = 0;
    PLAB2_DEVICE_EXTENSION extension;
    VOID           *registerAddress;
    PHYSICAL_ADDRESS  registerPhysicalAddress;

    // ... Read usual Registry parameters
    //
    // Read the Registry for the "address" of the hardware simulator
    //
    retReg = hardwareSimReadRegistry(driverObject, RegistryPath,
                          &interruptLine, &interruptIDT,
                          &registerAddress, &registerPhysicalAddress);
    if (shouldBreak)
        DbgBreakPoint();
```

```
// ... Create Device Object

extension = deviceObject->DeviceExtension;
extension->DeviceObject = deviceObject;
extension->BusNumber = busNumber;
//
// Save information from Registry in Device Extension
//

extension->registerAddress          = registerAddress;
extension->registerPhysicalAddress  = registerPhysicalAddress;
extension->interruptLine             = interruptLine;
extension->interruptIDT              = interruptIDT;
extension->debugMask                 = debugMask;
extension->eventLog                  = eventLog;
extension->shouldBreak               = shouldBreak;

// ... Create dispatch points for create/open, close, unload, symbolic
// ... links, and the usual stuff
  return status;
}
```

Open and Close Functions

The Open and Close functions are no different than those in the simple "Hello World" driver. They simply complete the request and return success.

Lab2DeviceIoControl

The `Lab2DeviceIoControl` function uses `DeviceIoControl` operations to read and write data to the Hardware Simulator Driver. The IOCTLs are dispatched to functions that handle the Hardware Simulator I/O operations.

Listing 27.6: IRP_MJ_DEVICE_CONTROL *Handler for a Driver for the Hardware Simulator*

```
NTSTATUS Lab2DeviceControl(IN PDEVICE_OBJECT DeviceObject,
                           IN PIRP Irp )
{
    NTSTATUS  ret = STATUS_SUCCESS;
    PIO_STACK_LOCATION stack;
    UCHAR *pBuffer;
    ULONG outBufferLength;
    ULONG inBufferLength;
    ULONG charCount = 0;
    PLAB2_DEVICE_EXTENSION extension;
    NTSTATUS status;

    extension = DeviceObject->DeviceExtension;
    stack = IoGetCurrentIrpStackLocation(Irp);
    pBuffer = (UCHAR *)Irp->AssociatedIrp.SystemBuffer;  // Buffered I/O
    inBufferLength = stack->Parameters.DeviceIoControl.InputBufferLength;
    outBufferLength = stack->Parameters.DeviceIoControl.OutputBufferLength;

    switch(stack->Parameters.DeviceIoControl.IoControlCode)
        { /* ioControlCode */
          case IOCTL_LAB2_READ:
```

```
                        status = Lab2GetPacket(
                                        DeviceObject,
                                        pBuffer,
                                        outBufferLength,
                                        inBufferLength,
                                        &charCount);      // RETURN transfer SIZE
                        break;
                case IOCTL_LAB2_WRITE:
                        status = Lab2PutPacket(
                                        DeviceObject,
                                        pBuffer,
                                        outBufferLength,
                                        inBufferLength,
                                        &charCount);      // RETURN transfer SIZE
                        break;
                default:
                        ret = STATUS_UNSUCCESSFUL;
            } /* ioControlCode */

    //
    // Fill these in before calling IoCompleteRequest
    //
    Irp->IoStatus.Status = ret;
    Irp->IoStatus.Information = charCount;
    IoCompleteRequest( Irp, IO_NO_INCREMENT );
    return ret;
}
```

Listing 27.7: GetPacket *Function for the Driver for the Hardware Simulator*

```
NTSTATUS Lab2GetPacket(IN PDEVICE_OBJECT deviceObject,
                        IN OUT UCHAR    *pBuffer,
                        IN ULONG    outBufferLength,
                        IN ULONG    inBufferLength,
                        OUT ULONG   * charCount)
{
    PLAB2_DEVICE_EXTENSION extension = deviceObject->DeviceExtension;
    UCHAR *inBuf = pBuffer;
    ULONG count = 0;
    ULONG status;

    // If we were left in an error state, reset the device

    if(IN_ERROR_STATE)
        WRITE_REGISTER_UCHAR(&extension->registerAddress[IN_COMMAND],
                        IN_COMMAND_RESET);

    // Loop until error or EOP
    do { /* character loop */
        //
        // If buffer too small
        //
        if (count >= outBufferLength)
            {
             *charCount =  count;
             return STATUS_BUFFER_OVERFLOW;
            }
```

```
        //
        // Set GO bit
        //
        WRITE_REGISTER_UCHAR(&extension->registerAddress[IN_COMMAND],
                             IN_COMMAND_GO);

     // This is required because the Hardware Simulator does not clear
     // the DONE bit instantly; we have to wait for the BUSY bit to set
     // before we can start polling for the DONE bit's being set
      do
         {
           LARGE_INTEGER delay;    // Wait 20 ms
           delay = RtlConvertLongToLargeInteger ((LONG) -(10 * 1000 * 20));
           status = KeDelayExecutionThread( KernelMode, FALSE, &delay);
         } while ((!IN_BUSY_SET) && (STATUS_SUCCESS == status ));
        //
        // Wait for character ready
        //
        do
         {
           LARGE_INTEGER delay; // Wait 20 ms
           delay = RtlConvertLongToLargeInteger ((LONG) -(10 * 1000 * 20));
           status = KeDelayExecutionThread( KernelMode, FALSE, &delay);
         } while ((!IN_DONE_STATE) && (STATUS_SUCCESS == status ));

        //
        // Buffer the new character
        //
        count++;
        *inBuf++ = READ_REGISTER_UCHAR(&extension->registerAddress[IN_DATA]);

        if (IN_OVERRUN_STATE)
           {
           // Overrun
           *charCount =  --count;                  // Last char bogus
           return STATUS_DATA_OVERRUN;
           }
        if (IN_ERROR_STATE)
           {
           // Error other than overflow
           *charCount =  --count;                  // Last char bogus
           return STATUS_UNSUCCESSFUL;
           }

        if (IN_END_OF_PACKET_STATE)
           {
           *charCount =  count;
           return STATUS_SUCCESS;
          }

        //
    }   /* character loop */
     while (TRUE);
}
```

Most of this code is fairly obvious, given the discussion of the device and the protocols. If
we find the device in an error state, we reset it. We test the count versus buffer length at the start
of the loop just in case the buffer length passed in was 0; this will fail immediately because
count is equal to the buffer size. Otherwise, it will fail on the first iteration following the filling
of the buffer.

We signal our desire to read a character by setting the GO bit. If a character is present in the device, this will immediately generate a completion situation; if one is not present, the device will wait until a character arrives.

The next section of code is specific to talking to the Hardware Simulator. We need to wait for the BUSY state to be set so that we can poll for DONE. In real hardware, this will happen so quickly that this delay would not be required. So we poll for BUSY.

However, this is not quite as simple as you might expect. If we sat in a loop just testing the BUSY bit, it would take a long time to see that it is set! Why? Because this is a Device Driver and it is operating at an ordinary schedulable level. It will have to exhaust its time slice before any other thread in the system can run. So the Hardware Simulator Control Panel, which is running at the user level, will have to wait until the end of the time slice! Thus we must add one more trick to our driver: We call `KeDelayExecutionThread`, which forces the current thread to relinquish its time slice and allows some other thread to execute.

```
NTSTATUS KeDelayExecutionThread(IN KPROCESSOR_MODE WaitMode,
                                IN BOOLEAN Alertable,
                                IN PLARGE_INTEGER Interval);
```

The `KeDelayExecutionThread` function delays the execution by a specified interval, which is expressed in 100-ns units. A delay of 200 units is 20,000 ns, or 20 ms. For drivers, we specify the *WaitMode* parameter as `KernelMode` and the *Alertable* parameter as FALSE. This function can be called only when we are working at IRQL < DISPATCH_LEVEL. Since we are in the IRP_MJ_DEVICE_CONTROL handler, we are at PASSIVE_LEVEL.

Listing 27.8: *The* `PutPacket` *Routine for the Driver for the Hardware Simulator*

This routine is, not surprisingly, almost identical to the `Lab2GetPacket` routine.

```
NTSTATUS Lab2PutPacket(PDEVICE_OBJECT deviceObject,
                       UCHAR    * pBuffer,
                       ULONG    outBufferLength,
                       ULONG    inBufferLength,
                       ULONG    * charCount)
{
    PLAB2_DEVICE_EXTENSION extension = deviceObject->DeviceExtension;
    UCHAR *buf = pBuffer;
    ULONG count = 0;
    ULONG status;
    if (OUT_ERROR_STATE)
        WRITE_REGISTER_UCHAR(&extension->registerAddress[OUT_COMMAND],
                        OUT_COMMAND_RESET);

    do { /* character loop */

        //
        // Put character from buffer to port
        //
        count++;
        WRITE_REGISTER_UCHAR(&extension->registerAddress[OUT_DATA], *buf++);

        //
        // Set GO bit
        //
```

```
        WRITE_REGISTER_UCHAR(&extension->registerAddress[OUT_COMMAND],
                              OUT_COMMAND_GO);
        //------------------------------------------------------------------
        // This is required because the Hardware Simulator does not clear
        // the DONE bit instantly; we have to wait for the GO bit to reset
        // before we can start polling for the DONE bit being set
        do
          {
          LARGE_INTEGER delay;
          delay = RtlConvertLongToLargeInteger ((LONG) -(10 * 1000 * 20));
          status = KeDelayExecutionThread( KernelMode, FALSE, &delay);
          } while ((OUT_GO_SET) && (STATUS_SUCCESS == status ));
        //------------------------------------------------------------------
        //
        // Wait for character complete
        //
        do
          {
          LARGE_INTEGER delay;
          delay = RtlConvertLongToLargeInteger ((LONG) -(10 * 1000 * 20));
          status = KeDelayExecutionThread( KernelMode, FALSE, &delay);
          } while ((! OUT_DONE_STATE) && (STATUS_SUCCESS == status ));


        if (OUT_UNDERRUN_STATE)
            {
            // Underrun
            *charCount = count;
            return STATUS_DATA_OVERRUN;
            }
        if (OUT_ERROR_STATE)
            {
            // Error other than underrun
             *charCount = count;
            return STATUS_UNSUCCESSFUL;
            }

        if (count == outBufferLength)
            {
            *charCount = count;
            return STATUS_SUCCESS;
            }

    } /* character loop */
    while (STATUS_SUCCESS == status);
  *charCount = count;
  return STATUS_UNSUCCESSFUL ;
}
```

A Simple Interrupt-Driven Device Driver

The second student assignment we give for the Hardware Simulator is to write an interrupt-driven Device Driver. The bulk of this code is identical to the code for the simple polled driver. For example, the only difference in DriverEntry is to actually connect the interrupt to the device. However, the actual processing of DeviceIoControl is substantially different, since the operations must remain pending until the last character has been transmitted.

In addition, to avoid the problems of multiple queueing for input and output, we limit the task to an input-only or output-only device, ignoring the other side for this exercise. In the example shown here, we are implementing only the input side of the device. A discussion of multiple queueing, along with example code, is shown in Chapter 22 on page 446, and a more sophisticated example is given in Chapter 24 on page 505.

Listing 27.9: *The* DriverEntry *Routine for the Interrupt Driver for the Hardware Simulator*

```
NTSTATUS DriverEntry(IN PDRIVER_OBJECT driverObject,
                     IN PUNICODE_STRING RegistryPath )
{
    // ... Identical to the DriverEntry for Lab2 (see page 623) except at
    // the end

    // ... Create dispatch points for create/open, close, unload, symbolic
    // ... links, and the usual stuff

    MappedSysVect = HalGetInterruptVector(
                        Isa,
                        0,                        // BusNumber,
                        deviceExtension->Level,   // Level
                        deviceExtension->Vector,  // Vector,
                        &Irql,                    // IRQL
                        &deviceExtension->Affinity);
                                                  // Affinity mask

    IoInitializeDpcRequest(deviceObject, Lab5DpcRoutine);
    DriverObject->DriverStartIo = Lab5StartIo;

    KeInitializeSpinLock(&deviceExtension->ISRSpinLock);

    status = IoConnectInterrupt(
                        &deviceExtension->InterruptObject,
                        Lab5InterruptServiceRoutine,
                        deviceExtension,
                        &deviceExtension->ISRSpinLock,
                        MappedSysVect,
                        Irql,
                        Irql,
                        Latched,    // Interrupt not LevelSensitive
                        FALSE,      // Interrupt vector not sharable
                        deviceExtension->Affinity,
                        FALSE       // Do not save floating-point state
                        );
    if ( !NT_SUCCESS (status) )
        {
        // ... Report error
        // ... Free up resources that have been allocated
        }
    return status;
}
```

At the end, we attempt to connect the device's interrupt. If we succeed, STATUS_SUCCESS is returned and the driver is successfully loaded. If we fail, we can either print a failure message on the debug console, log a failure to the Event Log, or do anything else we want to do to report the error. We must then, as in all other DriverEntry examples, free up any resources we have allocated, such as freeing storage, deleting the Device Object, and removing any symbolic links.

Because we are going to use StartIo queueing, we must set a StartIo handler. This is set in the Driver Object and thus applies to all devices associated with that driver (of which we have exactly one).

Note that our Device Extension has also some new fields, whose usages we show here. Included is an INTERRUPT_OBJECT used to route the interrupt to our ISR and a Spin Lock that it uses to lock out multiple concurrent uses of the same ISR (see Chapter 14, page 293). Note that the Spin Lock had to be previously initialized, which we show right before IoConnectInterrupt. The fact that we have connected an interrupt requires some additional code in our Unload function.

Unload Function

```
VOID Lab5Unload( IN PDRIVER_OBJECT driverObject)
{
    // ... Much like the stock Unload routine except for...
      IoDisconnectInterrupt(extension->InterruptObject);
}
```

DeviceIoControl

This is a nonexclusive device, so in the DeviceIoControl handler we queue up the request. Even if it were an exclusive device, we could not be certain, even though it was opened only by one thread, that there could not be multiple threads in the same process using that same handle to generate requests, since handles are process-wide entities.

Listing 27.10: IRP_MJ_DEVICE_CONTROL *for an Interrupt Driver for the Hardware Simulator*

```
NTSTATUS Lab5DeviceControl(
    IN PDEVICE_OBJECT DeviceObject,
    IN PIRP Irp)
{
    NTSTATUS ret = STATUS_SUCCESS;
    PIO_STACK_LOCATION stack;
    PLAB5_DEVICE_EXTENSION extension;
    NTSTATUS status;

    extension = DeviceObject->DeviceExtension;
    stack = IoGetCurrentIrpStackLocation(Irp);

    switch(stack->Parameters.DeviceIoControl.IoControlCode)
        { /* ioControlCode */
        case IOCTL_LAB5_READ:
                IoMarkIrpPending(Irp);
                IoStartPacket(DeviceObject, Irp, NULL, NULL);
                return STATUS_PENDING;
        default:
                Irp->IoStatus.Status = STATUS_UNSUCCESSFUL;
                Irp->IoStatus.Information = 0;
                IoCompleteRequest( Irp, IO_NO_INCREMENT );
                return STATUS_UNSUCCESSFUL;
        } /* ioControlCode */

}
```

Listing 27.11: *The* `StartIo` *Handler for the Driver for the Hardware Simulator*

```
void Lab5StartIo(PDEVICE_OBJECT DeviceObject, PIRP Irp)
    {
    switch(Irp->Type)
        { /* type */
        case IRP_MJ_DEVICE_CONTROL:
                Lab5StartDeviceControl(DeviceObject, Irp);
                return;
        default:
                Irp->IoStatus.Status = STATUS_UNSUCCESSFUL;
                // Why are we here?
                Irp->IoStatus.Information = 0; // Be safe; make it 0
                IoCompleteRequest(Irp, IO_NO_INCREMENT);
                IoStartNextPacket(DeviceObject, FALSE);
        } /* type */
    }
```

Note that although in principle it is impossible to send *other* than
`IRP_MJ_DEVICE_CONTROL` to this routine, we added the additional protective code at the end.
This makes our handler robust against future maintenance and enhancement. If someone adds a
new case (perhaps a power-down response) and fails to finish coding it, this handler *will* fail
without *failing* (catch the difference?).

StartDeviceControl

Consistent with our style of not-too-much-inline, we broke out the handling of `StartIo` into a
series of separate functions; for this example, there is only one. This function establishes in the
Device Extension a count that is the buffer size (if this ever goes to 0, we have filled the buffer)
and a pointer to the next position in the buffer. Contrast this with how we handled the polled I/O
case. For polled I/O, we could keep this state in local variables on the stack. We have no such
ability here, however, because each character is handled in the DPC, which can execute in a different thread context on each interrupt. Thus any state that we must maintain must be in some
external storage area. For a simple, unidirectional device like this one, it is sufficient to add this
state to the Device Extension.

Listing 27.12: `StartDeviceControl`

```
VOID Lab5StartDeviceControl(PDEVICE_OBJECT DeviceObject, PIRP Irp)
    {
    PIO_STACK_LOCATION stack;
    UCHAR *pBuffer;
    ULONG outBufferLength;
    ULONG inBufferLength;
    ULONG charCount = 0;
    PLAB5_DEVICE_EXTENSION extension;
    NTSTATUS status;

    extension = DeviceObject->DeviceExtension;
    stack = IoGetCurrentIrpStackLocation(Irp);
    extension->pBuffer  = (UCHAR *)Irp->AssociatedIrp.SystemBuffer;
    extension->BufferLength =
                    stack->Parameters.DeviceIoControl.InputBufferLength;
    extension->count = 0;
```

```
    // We initiate an input operation by setting the GO+IE bits
    WRITE_REGISTER_UCHAR(&extension->registerAddress[IN_COMMAND],
                              IN_COMMAND_GO | IN_COMMAND_IE);
}
```

The ISR

This assignment requires implementing only one side of the I/O device; in this example, we have
implemented only the input side. Note that to clear the interrupt, we must write into the Input
Command register a nonzero IACK bit. However, if we *just* write the IACK bit, we would clear
the IE bit—this would then cause the device to fail. So we first read the register to get the current
IE status and then write back the IACK, plus the current IE status. Note that the DPC Routine
could have cleared the IE bit just as an interrupt came in. An example might be that the interrupt
occurred just as the bit was being written in a Cancel Routine, so at the end of the instruction
that cleared the IE bit, the interrupt was finally accepted. Thus we *must* read the IE bit state and
not just assume it.

Listing 27.13: *An ISR for the Driver for the Hardware Simulator*

```
BOOLEAN Lab5InterruptServiceRoutine(
    IN PKINTERRUPT Interrupt,
    IN OUT PVOID Context
    )
  {
    PLAB5_DEVICE_EXTENSION extension = Context;
    PDEVICE_OBJECT deviceObject = deviceExtension->DeviceObject;
    UCHAR cmd;

    // 1. If it is not our interrupt, get out

    if(!IN_INT_STATE)
        return FALSE;   // Not our interrupt

    // 2. Clear the interrupting condition

    cmd = READ_REGISTER_UCHAR(&extension->registerAddress[IN_COMMAND]);
    cmd &= IN_COMMAND_IE;

    WRITE_REGISTER_UCHAR(&extension->registerAddress[IN_COMMAND],
                              IN_COMMAND_IACK  | cmd);

    // 3. Save any necessary device state

    // (this device has no state that must be saved in the ISR)

    // 4. Dispatch the DPC

    IoRequestDpc(deviceObject,
                deviceObject->CurrentIrp,
                NULL);

    // 5. Return TRUE indicating we have processed the interrupt

    return TRUE;
}
```

The DPC

The DPC is where all of the hard work gets done.

- If we have not received an EOP signal by the time we exhaust the buffer size, we fail the IRP with a Data Overrun error.
- If any device error occurred, we discard the character we just read (it was bogus) and fail the IRP appropriately.
- If we have an EOP signal, we complete the IRP successfully.
- Otherwise, we signal the device that we are ready for the next character, return, and wait for the next interrupt.

Listing 27.14: *The DPC for the Driver for the Hardware Simulator*

```
VOID Lab5DpcRoutine(
    IN PKDPC Dpc,
    PDEVICE_OBJECT  deviceObject,
    IN PVOID SystemArgument1,
    IN PVOID SystemArgument2)
{
    PLAB5_DEVICE_EXTENSION extension;
    PIRP Irp;
    UINT byteCount;

    Irp = deviceObject->CurrentIrp;
    extension = deviceObject->DeviceExtension;

    if (Irp != NULL)
        {
         if (extension->count >= extension->BufferCount)
             { /* buffer overflow */
              Lab5CompleteIrp(deviceObject, Irp,
                            extension->BufferCount,
                            STATUS_BUFFER_OVERFLOW);
              return;
             } /* buffer overflow */

        // Read the character in the data register

        *extension->pBuffer++ =
                READ_REGISTER_UCHAR(&extension->registerAddress[IN_DATA]);
        extension->count++;

        if (IN_OVERRUN_STATE)
             {
              // Overrun
              extension->count--;                     // Last char bogus
              Lab5CompleteIrp(deviceObject, Irp,
                            extension->count,
                            STATUS_DATA_OVERRUN);
              return;
             }
```

```
        if (IN_ERROR_STATE)
            {
            // Error other than overflow
            extension->count--;              // Last char bogus
            Lab5CompleteIrp(deviceObject, Irp,
                            extension->count,
                            STATUS_UNSUCCESSFUL);
            return;
            }

        if (IN_END_OF_PACKET_STATE)
            {
            Lab5CompleteIrp(deviceObject, Irp,
                            extension->count,
                            STATUS_SUCCESS);
            return;
            }
        }
    // The interrupt was for a non-EOP character; initiate the transfer of
    // the next character

    WRITE_REGISTER_UCHAR(&extension->registerAddress[IN_COMMAND],
                         IN_COMMAND_GO | IN_COMMAND_IE);
    return;
}
```

Lab5CompleteIrp

This function is used to complete the IRP. It is quite simple. Note that the number of bytes trans-ferred is set in the `Irp->IoStatus.Information` field.

Listing 27.15: *The Completion Handler for the Driver for the Hardware Simulator*

```
VOID Lab5CompleteIrp(IN PDEVICE_OBJECT deviceObject,
                     IN PIRP Irp,
                     IN ULONG count,
                     IN NTSTATUS status)
{
 Irp->IoStatus.Information = count;
 Irp->IoStatus.Status = status;
 IoCompleteRequest(Irp, IO_NO_INCREMENT);
 IoStartNextPacket(deviceObject, FALSE);
}
```

Summary

In this chapter we have presented a software simulator for a virtual hardware device. While we use this technology in a teaching context, it has wider applicability. In addition to showing the design of the simulator, we show two "real" Device Drivers. The source code for all of these components is available as part of the software distribution for this book.

28 *Windows 2000 Preview*

"I have a feeling we're not in Kansas anymore . . ."
—Dorothy, from The Wizard of Oz

As we wrote this chapter, we were working from the documentation provided with the preliminary Windows NT 5.0 Beta 1 release. Days before the last possible chance to make modifications to the book, Microsoft renamed the product release "Windows 2000". This chapter is intended to be a preview of NT 5.0/Windows 2000 Device Drivers.

The DDK is downloadable from Microsoft, from the Web site

`http://www.microsoft.com/ddk`

Here you will find the NT 4.0 DDK, for as long as it is available, and the Windows 2000 DDK. Prior to product release, it may still be referred to as the "NT 5.0 Beta" version.

We know that the NT 5.0 Beta 1 documentation on which we based this chapter is not yet complete, and we know that some aspects of it will change significantly by the product release. What we don't know is *what* is going to change. Some of the changes will simply be documentation changes and corrections, and some will be functional. In this chapter, we give you a high-level overview of what a Windows 2000 driver will look like. As with any software, many of the details might change by the time the product is released.

Windows 2000 Enhancements

You can build a Device Driver using the information in the preceding chapters, and it will (assuming it is correct) operate under both Windows NT 4.0 and Windows 2000. However, a Device Driver written specifically for Windows 2000 can take advantage of the many new features supported for Windows 2000. These include the following:

- New driver support routines
- New DMA programming interface

- Power management
- Plug-and-Play (PnP)
- The Win32 Driver Model (WDM)
- The Hardware Installer Wizard

We look at each of these in turn.

The Good News is that Windows 2000 drivers are conceptually easier to write, are more flexible, integrate better into the system, and provide capabilities that are utterly necessary for the new machines and bus structures that are emerging. The Bad News is that "conceptually easier" does *not* mean "easier in all of the details". Some of the details are remarkably complex when you first see them. Only after you have worked with them for a while do they appear to be natural.

You can't really write a Windows 2000 driver "from scratch". There is just too much going on. You will have to do what we did—start with one of the many sample drivers that Microsoft wrote for the DDK and apply the "carve an elephant" approach. (How do you carve an elephant from a block of marble? Start with a block of marble, and take away everything that doesn't look like an elephant.) The nice thing about the samples is that they leave a lot of hooks for you to write your own code. We found a couple potential bugs and many erroneous comments, which we have tried to clean up. The examples we show in this chapter are based directly on Microsoft's DDK examples, and we present them heavily annotated. Any differences between these examples and those in the DDK are entirely our responsibility. Be aware that some of these DDK examples have changed from beta release to beta release, and they likely will change again by the time the product is released.

New Driver Support Routines

A large number of new routines have been added to the Windows 2000 DDK. This list of them, shown in Table 28.1, was prepared long before Windows 2000 was finalized and cannot be considered complete.

Table 28.1: *New Support Functions for Windows 2000*

Function	Description
ExInterlockedCompareExchange64	Compares one integer variable to another, and, if they are equal, resets the first variable to a caller-supplied ULONGLONG-type value as an atomic operation.
IoAllocateDriverObjectExtension	Allocates a per-driver context area with a given unique identifier.
IoCopyCurrentIrpStackLocationToNext	Prepares the IRP Stack for the next lower-level driver by copying the current IRP Stack location to the next IRP Stack location. Allows a completion routine to be set.
IoGetAttachedDeviceReference	Returns a pointer to the highest-level Device Object in a driver stack and increments the reference count on that object.

Table 28.1: *New Support Functions for Windows 2000 (continued)*

Function	Description
IoGetDriverObjectExtension	Retrieves a previously allocated per-driver context area.
IoGetRemainingStackSize	Returns the number of bytes available on the processor stack of the current thread. Called by a driver to help the driver decide if processing is to be done in this thread or queued to a system thread. Especially useful for recursive algorithms that use a large amount of stack space.
IoGetStackLimits	Returns the upper and lower bounds of the current thread's stack frame.
IoIsWdmVersionAvailable	Checks to see if a given WDM version is supported by the operating system.
IoSetThreadHardErrorMode	Enables or disables error reporting for the current thread using IoRaiseHardError or IoRaiseInformationalHardError.
IoSkipCurrentIrpStackLocation	Prepares the IRP Stack for the next lower-level driver by copying the current IRP Stack location to the next IRP Stack location. Does not allow a completion routine to be set.
KeGetCurrentThread	Returns a pointer to the opaque thread object that represents the current thread.
KeQueryInterruptTime	Returns the current value of the system interrupt-time count in 100 ns units.
KeQueryPriorityThread	Returns the current priority of a given thread.
KeRaiseIrqlToDpcLevel	Raises the hardware priority to IRQL DISPATCH_LEVEL, thereby masking off interrupts of equivalent or lower IRQL on the current processor.
KeRestoreFloatingPointState	Restores the previous, nonvolatile, floating-point context that was saved with KeSaveFloatingPointState.
KeSaveFloatingPointState	Saves the current thread's nonvolatile floating-point context so that the caller can carry out floating-point operations of its own.
KeSetImportanceDpc	Controls how a particular DPC is queued and, to some degree, how soon the DPC Routine is run.
KeSetTargetProcessorDpc	Controls on which processor a particular DPC subsequently will be queued.
ObGetObjectSecurity	Returns a buffered security descriptor for a given object.
ObReleaseObjectSecurity	Releases the security descriptor returned by ObGetObjectSecurity.
PsGetCurrentProcessId	Returns the system-assigned identifier of the current process.
PsGetCurrentThreadId	Returns the system-assigned identifier of the current thread.

Table 28.1: *New Support Functions for Windows 2000 (continued)*

Function	Description
PsGetVersion	Returns whether the driver is running on a Free or Checked Build of Windows NT, along with caller-selected operating system version information.
PsSetCreateProcessNotifyRoutine	Registers a highest-level driver's callback that is subsequently notified whenever a new process is created or an existing process is deleted.
PsSetCreateThreadNotifyRoutine	Registers a highest-level driver's callback that is subsequently notified whenever a new thread is created or an existing thread is deleted.
PsSetLoadImageNotifyRoutine	Registers a highest-level system-profiling driver's callback that is subsequently notified whenever a new image is loaded for execution.
SeValidSecurityDescriptor	Returns whether a given security descriptor is structurally valid.

Obsolete Driver Support Routines

The routines listed in Table 28.2 are obsolete and should not be used for new drivers written for Windows 2000. They continue to be in the system and available for existing drivers.

Table 28.2: *Obsolete NT 4.0 Functions and Suggested Replacements*

Obsolete Function	Windows 2000 Replacement
USBD_ParseConfigurationDescriptor	USBD_ParseConfigurationDescriptorEx[†]
USBD_CreateConfigurationRequest	USBD_CreateConfigurationRequestEx[†]
LARGE_INTEGER functions	Use compiler 64-bit support.
MmIsNonPagedSystemAddressValid	
KeGetDcacheFillSize	GetDmaAlignment[*]
IoMapTransfer	MapTransfer[*]
IoFreeMapRegisters	FreeMapRegisters[*]
IoFreeAdapterChannel	FreeAdapterChannel[*]
IoFlushAdapterBuffers	FlushAdapterBuffers[*]
IoAttachDeviceByPointer	IoAttachDeviceToDeviceStack
IoAllocateAdapterChannel	AllocateAdapterChannel[*]
HalReadDmaCounter	ReadDmaCounter[*]
HalGetDmaAlignmentRequirement	GetDmaAlignment[*]
HalGetAdapter	IoGetDmaAdapter[*]

Table 28.2: *Obsolete NT 4.0 Functions and Suggested Replacements (continued)*

Obsolete Function	Windows 2000 Replacement
HalFreeCommonBuffer	FreeCommonBuffer*
HalAllocateCommonBuffer	AllocateCommonBuffer*
ExReleaseResourceForThread	ExReleaseResourceForThreadLite
ExReleaseResource	ExReleaseResourceForThreadLite
Zone Buffer functions	Use other memory allocation functions; the lookaside list functions are often the best replacements.
ExInterlockedIncrementLong	InterlockedIncrement
ExInterlockedExchangeUlong	InterlockedExchange
ExInterlockedDecrementLong	InterlockedDecrement
ExInitializeResource	ExInitializeResourceLite
ExDeleteResourceuse	ExDeleteResourceLite
ExAcquireResourceExclusive	ExAcquireResourceExclusiveLite

[†]These functions did not exist in NT 4.0, but are obsolete Windows 98 and NT 5.0 early-Beta-release functions.
*These functions do not exist by name; instead, these names represent the values stored as pointers in a DMA_OPERATIONS structure.

New DMA Programming Techniques

Microsoft has replaced the interface routines used to program a DMA adapter. The old routines remain in the DDK for existing drivers, but new drivers should be written using the new interface functions. The DMA functions added in Windows 2000 are shown in Table 28.3. Those that are obsolete are listed in Table 28.4. The names specified for the new functions are not actual function names. Instead, they are names of pointers in a DMA_OPERATIONS structure. This allows for much greater flexibility in how DMA operations are implemented.

This is preliminary documentation and subject to change.

Table 28.3: *New DMA Functions and Functions in the* DMA_OPERATIONS *Structure in Windows 2000*

Function	Description
IoGetDmaAdapter	Returns a pointer to the Adapter Object representing the DMA channel to which the driver's device is connected or representing the driver's bus master adapter, together with the maximum number of map registers the driver can specify for each DMA transfer, given the input device description.
AllocateAdapterChannel	"Connects" a Device Object to an Adapter Object and calls a driver-supplied AdapterControl routine to carry out an I/O operation through the system DMA controller or a bus master adapter as soon as the appropriate DMA channel is available and/or any necessary map registers are available. (This routine reserves exclusive access to a DMA channel and/or map registers for the specified device.)

Table 28.3: *New DMA Functions and Functions in the* `DMA_OPERATIONS` *Structure in Windows 2000 (continued)*

Function	Description
`FlushAdapterBuffers`	Forces any data remaining in a bus master adapter's internal buffers or the system DMA controller's internal buffers to be written into memory or to the device if the caller currently "owns" the Adapter Object. Terminates a transfer in progress if the driver detects a time-out or other error condition.
`FreeAdapterChannel`	Releases an Adapter Object, representing a system DMA channel, and optionally releases map registers, if any were allocated.
`FreeMapRegisters`	Releases a set of map registers, saved from a call to `AllocateAdapterChannel`, after the registers have been used in one or more calls to `MapTransfer` and the bus master DMA transfer is complete.
`GetDmaAlignment`	Returns the buffer alignment requirements for a given DMA controller or device.
`MapTransfer`	Sets up map registers (up to the maximum returned by `IoGetDmaAdapter`) for the given Adapter Object (already allocated by a call to `AllocateAdapterChannel`) to map a transfer from a locked-down buffer specified by a MDL, starting address, and length. Returns the logical address of the mapped region and, for bus master devices that support scatter/gather, the number of bytes mapped.
`ReadDmaCounter`	Returns how many bytes remain to be transferred during the current system DMA operation (autoinitialize mode), given a pointer to the Adapter Object.

Table 28.4: *DMA Functions Obsolete in Windows 2000*

Function	Description
`HalGetAdapter`	Returns a pointer to the Adapter Object representing the DMA channel to which the driver's device is connected or representing the driver's bus master adapter, together with the maximum number of map registers the driver can specify for each DMA transfer, given the input device description.
`IoAllocateAdapterChannel`	"Connects" a Device Object to an Adapter Object and calls a driver-supplied `AdapterControl` routine to carry out an I/O operation through the system DMA controller or a bus master adapter as soon as the appropriate DMA channel is available and/or any necessary map registers are available. (This routine reserves exclusive access to a DMA channel and/or map registers for the specified device.)
`IoMapTransfer`	Sets up map registers (up to the maximum returned by `HalGetAdapter`) for the given Adapter Object (already allocated by a call to `IoAllocateAdapterChannel`) to map a transfer from a locked-down buffer specified by a MDL, starting address, and length. Returns the logical address of the mapped region and, for bus master devices that support scatter/gather, the number of bytes mapped.
`IoFlushAdapterBuffers`	Forces any data remaining in a bus master adapter's or the system DMA controller's internal buffers to be written into memory or to the device, if the caller currently "owns" the Adapter Object. Terminates a transfer in progress if the driver detects a time-out or other error condition.

Table 28.4: *DMA Functions Obsolete in Windows 2000 (continued)*

Function	Description
KeFlushIoBuffers	Flushes the memory region described by a given MDL from all processors' caches into memory.
IoFreeAdapterChannel	Releases an Adapter Object, representing a system DMA channel, and optionally releases map registers, if any were allocated.
IoFreeMapRegisters	Releases a set of map registers, saved from a call to IoAllocateAdapterChannel, after the registers have been used in one or more calls to IoMapTransfer and the bus master DMA transfer is complete.
HalReadDmaCounter	Returns how many bytes remain to be transferred during the current system DMA operation (autoinitialize mode), given a pointer to the Adapter Object.
KeGetDcacheFillSize	Returns the processor's data cache-line boundary in bytes. Useful for allocating buffers and sizing transfers to prevent cache tearing during DMA transfers.
IoGetDmaAdapter	Returns a pointer to the Adapter Object representing the DMA channel to which the driver's device is connected or representing the driver's bus master adapter, together with the maximum number of map registers that the driver can specify for each DMA transfer, given the input device description.

Power Management

Power management is utterly critical for computers running on self-contained power. Currently, laptop computers are the dominant type of computer in this set, but palmtops, handhelds, and ever-and-ever smaller configurations are appearing (it seems, almost daily!). The key to power management is the ability to "power down" a peripheral that is not being actively "used".

You are probably familiar with the simple power management implemented by Windows 95 running on a laptop. That is, if you haven't used your hard drive in a while, it powers down; if you haven't typed anything in a while, the screen powers down. After some longer interval (usually something you've configured via the Control Panel), if you have done nothing, the computer enters its "hibernation" mode, writes a snapshot of its memory out to disk, and shuts down completely.

Power management is important for the desktop as well. Energy management is now a requirement for all computers purchased by the federal government and the State of California.

The EPA has shown that a significant amount of energy is used by office desktop computers that are running when not used. By their estimate, 5% of all office electrical use is by unused computers, usually left on overnight and over weekends. This works out to approximately $105/year per workstation in direct electrical costs, not counting the cost of the air-conditioning required to remove the heat that is generated.

In a non-Energy-Star-compliant machine, 30% of the power that is consumed is used by the display; much of the rest is consumed by the disk drives.

Since the excuse for leaving machines on, exclusive of servers, is that the cost of restarting them (in terms of time) is so high that nobody wants to turn them off, Microsoft's power initiative promotes a concept of "instant on", which they call OnNow, where a machine can go from a minimum-power state to full-on in a small number of seconds.

Windows 98 and Windows 2000 formalize this whole mechanism. *Any* driver can power down its peripherals. A driver written to meet the Windows 2000 standard *must* respond to the power-down request if it comes in (although it may simply respond that it is unable to comply).

In addition to the notion that a peripheral can be powered down or up, power management introduces *four* levels of power control, shown in Table 28.5. The idea is that for some devices, there might be intermediate, *lower*-powered stages that reduce power consumption at the expense of a slight startup delay. Anyone with an Energy-Star-compliant monitor knows that after the monitor has shut down, there is a period of a few seconds while it warms up before it can be used. Since this is seen as being an infrequent condition, it is a better power state than full-on; it is also a more responsive state than full-off. A device that is power-managed must implement both the D3 (off) and D0 (on) states, but it does not have to implement the intermediate states. The performance numbers given in Table 28.5 are for devices on the USB (Universal Serial Bus). Other devices will have comparable specifications, but the factors might differ considerably. There is no formal specification for disk drives. However, as an example, a disk drive in D1 state might consume less than 1 watt of power versus the nearly 4 watts consumed in D0 state.[1]

Table 28.5: *Power-Management States*

State	Description	Explanation
D3	Off	Unit consumes no power; power-up time is device-specific.
D2	Deep Sleep	Indicates minimum power consumption; typically $< 100\mu A$; power-up less than 30 seconds.
D1	Sleeping	Indicates a compromise between power and full-on speed; power typically < 5 mA; power-up less than 5 seconds.
D0	On	Unit is fully operational.

Table 28.6: IRP_MJ_POWER *Minor Functions*

Function	Meaning
IRP_MN_POWER_SEQUENCE	A request sent by drivers to the next lower-level driver to determine if a device actually entered a specific power state.
IRP_MN_QUERY_POWER	An IRP sent by a Power Policy Manager to determine if it can change the system or device power state to power it down.
IRP_MN_SET_POWER	Sent by the System Policy Manager to set system power state. Sent by a Device Power Policy Manager to set the device's power state.
IRP_MN_WAIT_WAKE	Notifies a PDO that it should enable its device to awaken itself and/or the system.

---

[1] These are representative specifications from
http://www.quantum.com/src/whitepapers/green1.html.

Power management is handled by the `IRP_MJ_POWER` request. This uses the `MinorFunction` field of the IRP to encode which particular power function is desired. The power functions are summarized in Table 28.6.

System power can be represented by several states. These are summarized in Table 28.7. The states shown in Table 28.5 are given the symbolic names `PowerDeviceD0`, `PowerDeviceD1`, `PowerDeviceD2`, and `PowerDeviceD3`.

Table 28.7: *System Power States*

`PowerSystemWorking`
`PowerSystemSleeping1`
`PowerSystemSleeping2`
`PowerSystemSleeping3`
`PowerSystemHibernate`
`PowerSystemShutdown`

The `IRP_MN_SET_POWER` request is sent to change the system power state or device power state. These IRPs add a new variant to the IRP Stack information `Parameters` block, the `Power` member. This addition to the Windows 2000 `IO_STACK_LOCATION` is shown as follows, in the context of the `IO_STACK_LOCATION` definition.

```
typedef struct _IO_STACK_LOCATION {
    UCHAR MajorFunction;
    UCHAR MinorFunction;
    UCHAR Flags;
    UCHAR Control;
    union {
           .
           .
        struct {
            ULONG SystemContext;      // Reserved
            POWER_STATE_TYPE Type;
            POWER_STATE State;
        } Power;
    } Parameters;
     PDEVICE_OBJECT DeviceObject;
     PFILE_OBJECT FileObject;
     .
     .
} IO_STACK_LOCATION, *PIO_STACK_LOCATION;
```

The `Parameters.Power.Type` indicates what type of request is being made. It can be one of the two symbolic values, `SystemPowerState` or `DevicePowerState`. The value of `Parameters.Power.State` depends on the value of `Parameters.Power.Type`.

The `IRP_MN_QUERY_POWER` request is used to determine if power state can be safely changed. Its control parameters are the same as for `IRP_MN_SET_POWER`, but power is not actually changed.

Most of these messages are handed down from one driver level to another. Each driver level above the Physical Device Object level (see the discussion starting on page 646) might need to know what state the device is in so that it can make decisions about how to handle IRPs. We show a handler for `IRP_MJ_POWER` on page 676.

A driver might fail an `IRP_MN_QUERY_POWER` request, indicating that it desires to keep power up on the device. This might be determined by several things:

- The nature of the application. (If the application has opened the device, which is only ever used by that application, it may be important to never power the device down while the application is active. Only the application/device requirements determine if this is important.)

- The number of outstanding IRPs. Note that for some devices the presence of an outstanding IRP may indicate that the device cannot be powered down; for other devices, the IRP might have to be completed with a power-down notification, and for yet other devices the IRP might be left pending even though the device is not actually active. The application/device requirements determine what the proper action should be.

- The state of the device. Some devices may not be powered down while in certain states (for example, a robotic arm that is extended).

- Knowledge of what the device does (just because the doctor has not moved the mouse in an hour, it would be a Bad Idea to shut down the heart monitoring device).

- Whatever other criteria you, the Device Driver writer, care to apply.

However, a driver may *not* fail an `IRP_MN_SET_POWER` request because seeing this IRP might mean the system itself will shortly enter some new power state, and the device had better do so first, cleanly. Note that an `IRP_MN_SET_POWER` may *not* be preceded by an `IRP_MN_QUERY_POWER`. You might not be given the option of refusing to change the power setting, and consequently, you must be prepared to change the power setting on demand.

Plug-and-Play

The Plug-and-Play facility is something that was long overdue twenty years ago (anyone who ever had to configure a Unibus peripheral on the PDP-11 understands this deeply), and it is finally becoming real. Part of what makes it feasible is the scale of modern peripherals; a 3D video accelerator card is far more complex than the mainframes of twenty years ago, let alone the minicomputers or peripherals. The core idea of Plug-and-Play is that the operating system will detect when a new device is installed (or an existing device is removed) and intelligently and correctly reconfigure itself to accommodate this change, and even notify the applications using the device so they can also adapt. Users do not have to understand jumpers, configuration switches, or, ideally, even installation options; they just plug in the new device, and it runs.

This does not come at zero cost. A peripheral, to be fully Plug-and-Play-compatible, must contain enough information to identify it and its properties to the system. It must also contain facilities that allow the system to modify its behavior so that it becomes a "good citizen". Devices such as PCI cards, CardBus (the revised PCMCIA[2]), and peripherals on the USB and the IEEE-1394 serial bus already do this. Some very few ISA cards can do it, but the ISA bus is slowly but surely becoming irrelevant.

In addition to the boot-time "Plug-and-Play" that applies to keyboards, mice, disk drives, and the like, Windows 2000 and Windows 98 support "dynamic" Plug-and-Play for devices that can be "hot-plugged", such as the CardBus, USB, and IEEE-1394 serial bus. For these peripher-

---

[2] This name was a true marketing blunder; anything this hard to remember and say has an uphill battle for acceptance. The only way I can remember the acronym is that "People Can't Manage Computer Industry Acronyms". *–jmn*

als, the instantaneous configuration can change from moment to moment, and the system must be prepared to track it without flinching (and without a reboot). The Windows 2000 drivers can be written to permit this.

The Win32 Driver Model

The Win32 Driver Model (WDM) is an integration of the drivers for Windows 98 and Windows 2000. In Windows 95, there was one way to write drivers (using the VxD) and in Windows NT there was another. Just about the only similarity between these two driver methods was that the results were both called "Device Drivers". This meant that a vendor who wished to support a device on Windows 95 and Windows NT 4.0 (and lower) had to have two complete drivers written. A lot of worthwhile devices never got support under Windows NT because the vendors saw "no market" there (of course, those who *did* see a market often captured the market from those who chose to ignore it). Microsoft's response to this was the WDM, a single model that allows the same driver binary to be executed as a driver on Windows 2000 and Windows 98.[3]

A WDM driver can use only a subset of the full interface available on Windows NT. Not all of the I/O Manager, Executive Services, or memory-management functions are available to a WDM driver. This is because there is a special component for Windows 95 and Windows 98 that *emulates* these functions in the Windows 9x environment, and it does not try to emulate all of the NT Executive Services. As a Device Driver writer, you don't have to worry about this. If you include the header file `wdm.h` instead of the header file `ntddk.h`, you will have the proper definitions of the symbols and functions you need to use. (A WDM driver should *never* include `ntddk.h`, since that would allow it to call non-WDM-compatible functions.)

In addition to the subsetting, a WDM driver has available a number of calls and techniques that are not generally useful to other drivers. These are not defined in `ntddk.h` but are defined in `wdm.h`.

The heart of the WDM, and Windows 2000 drivers in general, is the concept of *layered drivers*. While we treat this topic for Windows NT 4.0 as an advanced topic (in Chapter 23), for WDM it is a *fundamental* concept. You cannot write a WDM driver without being aware of layering.

We discuss the WDM in much greater depth in Chapter 30.

The Hardware Installer Wizard

In the past, it was possible to manually install a driver or write a little installation program that did it for you. We discussed how to do the latter in Windows NT 4.0 in Chapter 26. Because of the dynamic nature of Plug-and-Play, Microsoft has chosen to handle device installation in Windows 2000 with the Hardware Installer Wizard.

To properly install a program, you must provide a `.inf` file that describes the components of the driver and how they are to be installed. For Windows 2000, the Plug-and-Play system makes the use of the `.inf` file mandatory. In particular, the Registry *references* the `.inf` file, rather than its being included "by value", so it must be present for a Plug-and-Play system to work properly.

---

[3] A subset of the WDM functionality is actually implemented on Windows 95 OSR (OEM Service Release) 2.1 and above to support the USB (and only the USB). WDM support, however, did not materialize until Windows 98.

Other Changes

To make all of this work, Windows 2000 has made a number of changes in how devices are handled. For example, how the Registry is handled differs for Windows 2000. However, to maintain compatibility with Windows NT 4.0 drivers and installation programs, Windows 2000 treats the existing Registry entries as "legacy data" and copies their contents over, at boot time, to a new Registry area. Thus installing an NT 4.0-compliant driver on Windows 2000, using the techniques we describe in this book, will still work.

The `DriverEntry` routine in Windows 2000 is both simpler and more complex. It is simpler in that it does less. It is more complex in that what an NT 4.0 `DriverEntry` routine used to do is now found in *three* functions, of which `DriverEntry` is the least interesting. We look at this in considerable detail shortly.

The Windows 2000 `DriverEntry` (and Friends)

A Windows 2000 Device Driver in "steady state" has data structures that look like those in Figure 28.1. Contrast this with the overview of a Windows NT 4.0 Driver we gave in Figure 7.5 (page 132).

Note first that the Driver Object does not have "Device Objects" hanging from it; it has *Functional Device Objects* (FDOs) hanging from it. These FDOs incorporate *some* of the device state formerly put in the Device Object. Each has its own extension storage, which you use just like the Device Extension of a Windows NT 4.0 Device Driver. An FDO is exactly what we all think of as a Device Object, but the change in terminology represents its role in the layered drivers of Windows 2000.

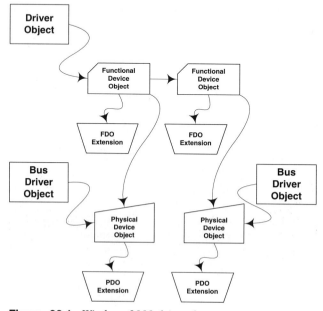

Figure 28.1: *Windows 2000 driver data structures.*

Unlike with Windows NT 4.0, even a simple Windows 2000 "native" driver lives one level up from the lowest-level driver. The lowest-level driver in Windows 2000 is a *Bus Driver*, which you will seldom write. Most Bus Drivers are supplied by Microsoft. A Bus Driver actually manages the physical bus. It is responsible for performing the bus enumeration (you no longer do this explicitly as is done in NT 4.0). A Bus Driver creates a *Physical Device Object* (PDO) for every device it finds on its bus. A PDO can also have a PDO Extension. However, unless you are writing a Bus Driver yourself, you will never actually see this detail; Device Extensions in any layer are private to that layer and are not seen by higher or lower levels directly. Your driver attaches itself to the lower-level PDO managed by the Bus Driver. Figure 28.1 shows something a bit more complex than the trivial case. In the figure, although your driver manages two FDOs, which look uniform to the driver, each FDO attaches to a PDO at the next lower level that is managed by a different Bus Driver. Thus you can have an FDO that looks like a single device as you write it but that can be implemented on two different physical busses, for example, USB and serial port, or SCSI and EPP, or whatever. Note that this means your driver doesn't have to worry about how to enumerate the bus, nor about how the bus is implemented.

The distinction of various Device Object types reflects only their usage. As a Device Driver writer, you see the ordinary DEVICE_OBJECT, just like NT 4.0.

The Windows 2000 `DriverEntry` routine is still called when the driver is loaded. Typically, all it will do is initialize the *driver* state, for example, the IRP_MJ_ dispatch pointers and the Unload pointer, and possibly allocate memory. It does not create the Device Object, and it does not touch hardware. Why? Because the fact that the driver is loaded does not necessarily prove that there is a device for it to control! So it can't take any actions that require that a Device Object be present. Tasks such as creating the Device Object come later.

The AddDevice routine is the next component that is called. It is called by the system when a device is actually found. It gets the name of the device specified in the .inf file for this device, looks up a pointer to the Driver Object, and to the PDO passed by the Bus Driver. The PDO was created by the Bus Driver when it detected the device. Detecting a device does not necessarily guarantee that the device is willing or capable of communication. The AddDevice routine first calls IoCreateDevice to create the FDO. Once it has this, it calls IoAttachDeviceToDeviceStack. The return value of this function is a pointer to the next lower-level device in the device stack. This pointer should be saved in your Device Extension. AddDevice also clears a special flag, DO_DEVICE_INITIALIZING, which had been set in the Flags field when the FDO was created. This latter action is required for compatibility between NT 4.0 drivers running in Windows 2000 and native Windows 2000 drivers. Under NT 4.0, this bit was automatically cleared when DriverEntry returned; however, it had to be cleared explicitly for Device Objects created outside DriverEntry. For Windows 2000, because the Device Objects *are* created outside the DriverEntry routine, this flag must be explicitly cleared.

Now that the device is properly registered, an application could, in principle, actually open it and start performing operations on it. But that would be premature; we have not yet established that the hardware is *ready* to talk to! So we have a "race condition". If processing an IRP (including IRP_MJ_CREATE (CreateFile)) requires touching the hardware, you must queue the IRP and wait for the hardware to come available. What we find unusual is that several examples in the DDK sample code *fail* the IRPs until the IRP_MJ_PNP.IRP_MN_START_DEVICE function completes, thus violating the specified behavior.

In Windows 2000, you must set a flag, typically in your Device Extension, that indicates the state of the device; that is, are you in the AddDevice-completed state or the Ready-To-Roll state? Or the No Longer Ready-To-Roll state? The system does not automatically provide anything to implement this for you.

How *do* you know when the device is finally ready? Now things become even more complex. The simple answer is that you can determine that the device is fully ready when the request to start it has completed. But by *completed*, we mean not only *your* Device Driver has handled it, but all of the Device Drivers *below* yours have successfully processed it! You cannot touch any hardware until the levels below yours have completed the start request. This requires that you use a completion routine. And while completion routines were another "advanced" topic under Windows NT 4.0, they are inescapable under Windows 2000.

The system will send your Device Driver a Plug-and-Play message, IRP_MJ_PNP. This IRP contains not only the *major* function code (MJ), but also has a *minor* function code (MN), IRP_MN_START_DEVICE. You can process this (remember, you can't touch hardware yet), but you *must* hand this down to the PDO (or, in general, the next lower-level layer). Before sending it down, you set its completion routine using IoSetCompletionRoutine. The lower layer in turn does whatever it wants to do and eventually completes the IRP. At this point, when the lower layer calls IoCompleteRequest, your completion routine is invoked. You examine the status. If the operation completed successfully at the lower level, you perform whatever remaining operations you need to perform to make your driver, and possibly the device, ready to process IRPs. You also mark the state of your device as ready and, if you have chosen to queue up IRPs, initiate the dequeueing of the pending IRPs. Your driver is now ready to perform actual I/O operations on the device. Once you get the successful completion from the lower level, you can now actually touch hardware.

To send an IRP downward in the chain, you use the Device Object pointer that was returned by the IoAttachDeviceToDeviceStack function. To do this, you copy the current IRP Stack location to the next IRP Stack location by calling IoCopyCurrentIrpStackLocationToNext. Typically, you will make no changes to this information. Next, you call IoSetCompletionRoutine to reference your completion routine. Finally, you use IoCallDriver to call the next lower-level driver.

Supporting Plug-and-Play is more than just A Nice Idea. A driver that is not Plug-and-Play can limit, or even completely inhibit, the Plug-and-Play ability of the entire system. This is because a Plug-and-Play driver receives a notification when the device is removed, which allows it to free up the resources that device used (particularly, memory addresses, I/O addresses, IRQLs, and the like). An "ordinary" NT 4.0 Device Driver will not know how to process this notification and will leave the resources allocated. If a new device is plugged in that requires some of those same resources, its driver will be unable to allocate those resources (because they are "already in use"), and the new driver will have to fail the installation.

A more significant example is the notion of *reconfigurable devices*. Consider a PCMCIA bus configured as shown in Figure 28.2. In this case we have a two-slot PCMCIA bus which is managed via a bridge. The bridge is configured to have a window of a certain size when the system initially powers up. We now remove Device B from one of the slots and replace it with Device D, which requires a larger address space than will fit in the space allocated to the bridge window. Note that as shown in Figure 28.2, the attempt to utilize the address range required by Device D, and remain within the assigned window, would overlap the address space currently occupied by Device A. Using Plug-and-Play, this is easy. If Device A supports Plug-and-Play, it is only necessary for the system to stop Device A, reconfigure it, reprogram the bridge, reconfigure (or install) Device D, and restart Device A. This is shown in Figure 28.3.

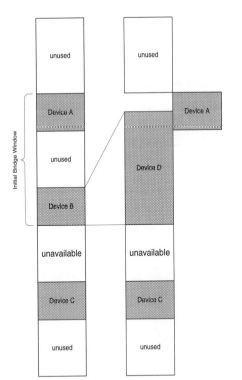

Figure 28.2: *PCMCIA reconfiguration without Plug-and-Play support.*

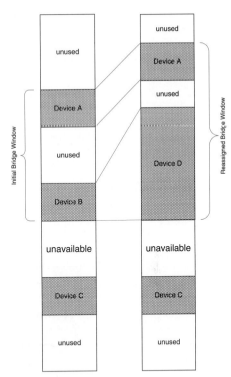

Figure 28.3: *PCMCIA reconfiguration with Plug-and-Play.*

SCSI hardware is already hot-pluggable (although Windows 2000 currently has no support for this), and the technology that is used for hot-swap disk bays could easily be extended to other SCSI devices. There often are rumors of hot-swap PCI Busses being available Real Soon Now (there is a PCI 2.2 specification on how they are supposed to work).

Handling IRP_MJ_POWER

Now that we have shown the driver chain, we can explain more about how to handle IRP_MJ_POWER, at least as it is currently revealed in the available documentation. Normally, the Power Manager will send a system power IRP downward in the chain for each top-level device driver. Each such driver will pass the system power request downward in its stack. Eventually, the request gets to a Power Policy Manager for the device. The device then requests a *device* power IRP. This is shown in Figure 28.4. (Strictly speaking, this figure glosses over many details of how the device power IRP gets routed to the PDO. The path is somewhat more complex than shown. However, the details don't matter here, and we understand that there are changes coming. This figure is based on the latest available DDK documentation.)

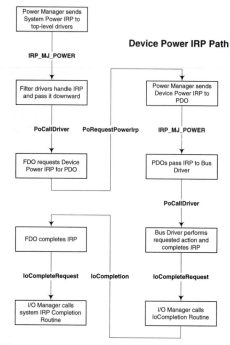

Figure 28.4: *Handling a system power* `IRP_MJ_POWER` *request.*

There are some details of handling power management that go beyond simple "on/off" considerations. The Device Object has flags that a Bus Driver sets when it creates its Device Object:

```
DO_POWER_INRUSH
DO_POWER_PAGABLE⁴
DO_POWER_NOOP
```

The `DO_POWER_INRUSH` indicates if the device has "inrush" current; that is, does turning the device on require, for some brief period, significantly more power than steady-state does. For example, spinning a disk motor up to speed might require a great deal more power than it takes to maintain the rotation speed (in fact, anything with a high inductive or capacitive load is likely to have an inrush current). The Power Manager makes sure that it does not try to power up two devices with inrush current at the same time. A driver that handles inrush current is always called at IRQL == `DISPATCH_LEVEL` and thus cannot be pageable. Any driver that is not associated with a paging device and which does not require inrush current handling should be marked as `DO_POWER_PAGABLE`.

---

⁴ Microsoft would do well to have someone who could spell to approve some of these names. You have to keep remembering that in this instance, "pagable" is incorrect spelling.

A pageable driver must set the DO_POWER_PAGABLE flag. This tells the Power Manager that it cannot call this driver at IRQL == DISPATCH_LEVEL; it must always call the driver at IRQL == PASSIVE_LEVEL.

A driver that does not support devices—for example, the status test driver that we describe in Appendix B—can set the DO_POWER_NOOP flag to indicate nonparticipation in power management.

The DEVICE_CAPABILITIES *Structure*

The DEVICE_CAPABILITIES structure, although nominally for Plug-and-Play support, also contains some key fields used by power management. These are shown next.

```
typedef struct _DEVICE_CAPABILITIES {
      // .. Mostly PnP definitions
      DEVICE_POWER_STATE DeviceState[PowerSystemMaximum];
      SYSTEM_POWER_STATE SystemWake;
      DEVICE_POWER_STATE DeviceWake;
      ULONG D1Latency;
      ULONG D2Latency;
      ULONG D3Latency;
} DEVICE_CAPABILITIES, * PDEVICE_CAPABILITIES;
```

This structure, which is normally placed in the Device Extension of a Device Object, encodes information about the device. This is normally initialized by a Bus Driver, although other drivers might need the information. The information can be obtained from a lower-level driver by sending down an IRP_MJ_PNP request and specifying the minor function code, IRP_MN_QUERY_CAPABILITIES.

DeviceState is an array of values, indexed by SYSTEM_POWER_STATE values. According to the documentation available to us, this array is used when a system power request comes in to determine which device state corresponds to the equivalent system power state. The entry in the table gives the *highest*-powered state the device can support for the corresponding system power state. Consider two examples: a device that has only off/on capability (D3/D0 states) and one that has a "sleep" state. The entries described in the publicly available Beta documentation are shown in Table 28.8.

The SystemWake state specifies the lowest-level system power state from which the device can signal a wake event. Thus you might not wish to power down a device below this level if you want it to be able to wake up the system. A value of PowerSystemUndefined means the device

Table 28.8: DEVICE_CAPABILITIES DeviceState *Sample Entries*

DeviceState Entry	Simple On/Off Device		Sleepable Device	
DeviceState[PowerSystemWorking]	PowerDeviceD0	On	PowerDeviceD0	On
DeviceState[PowerSystemSleeping1]	PowerDeviceD3	Off	PowerDeviceD2	Sleeping
DeviceState[PowerSystemSleeping2]	PowerDeviceD3	Off	PowerDeviceD2	Sleeping
DeviceState[PowerSystemSleeping3]	PowerDeviceD3	Off	PowerDeviceD2	Sleeping
DeviceState[PowerSystemHibernate]	PowerDeviceD3	Off	PowerDeviceD3	Off

cannot wake up the system. Examples would be having a modem wake up a machine when the phone rings and a server that is not awakened unless there are requests for it coming in over the network. The documentation states that a device might receive information about this state from its parent driver.

A corresponding state—DeviceWake—indicates the lowest-level device power state that can signal a wake event. A value of PowerDeviceUndefined for this value means the device cannot wake up the system.

The latency values indicate the approximate time required, in worst case, to returning to the full-on (D0) state from the corresponding powered-down state. The values are in 100µs units. These values might be derived from the vendor's documentation or measured empirically. Or they might be computed the first time such a transition takes place and stored in the Registry (and updated as needed; note that updating the Registry, however, does not change the state of the Device Object, which must remain constant during the life of the Device Object).

The PoCallDriver *Function*

When passing down power IRPs, a driver must use PoCallDriver, rather than IoCallDriver. Semantically, these are the same and they produce a similar result: the lower-level driver is called. PoCallDriver, however, allows the system to synchronize the power IRPs and limit the number of IRPs that may be active at any one time.

- No more than one system power IRP, either IRP_MN_SET_POWER or IRP_MN_QUERY_POWER, can be active at any one time.

- No more than one request to set device power, IRP_MN_SET_POWER, can be active for each physical device at one time.

- No more than one power IRP that requires an inrush of current (DO_POWER_INRUSH) can be active anywhere in the system at any one time.

Because of the limitation on inrush IRPs, other power IRPs can block while waiting for an inrush IRP to complete. Microsoft's documentation carefully states, and we echo, "driver writers should be aware of this behavior while debugging".

The PoSetPowerState*Function*

You must also notify the Power Manager about your response to the power request. To do this, you call the PoPowerState function just after you have increased the power state or just before you decrease the power state. This tells the Power Manager what state your device has actually entered.

The PoRegisterDeviceForIdleDetection*Function*

If your device can power down after some period of idle state, you can call the PoRegisterDeviceForIdleDetection function to specify the time intervals.

```
PULONG PoRegisterDeviceForIdleDetection (IN PDEVICE_OBJECT DeviceObject,
                                         IN ULONG ConservationIdleTime,
                                         IN ULONG PerformanceIdleTime,
                                         IN DEVICE_POWER_STATE State);
```

The *DeviceObject* parameter must be a PDO reference (not an FDO reference!). The *ConservationIdleTime* parameter is the timeout used when the system is trying to conserve power (for example, a laptop running on battery), expressed in seconds. The *PerformanceIdleTime* parameter is the timeout used when the system is not in battery-conservation mode, for example when a laptop is running on an external power source. The *State* parameter is the power level to be set and is a value such as PowerDeviceD3. The value returned is the pointer to the idle counter, which the Power Manager updates once each second. When it reaches one of the specified timeout values, where the value depends on which condition is prevailing (battery or AC power), the new power state is entered. To avoid a power-down, that is, to indicate that your device is active, set this value to 0.

The IRP_MJ_WMI *Message*

The Windows Management Interface, at the moment unspecified, interacts with the power-management system. Details of how this interaction occurs, however, are not available at the time we write this. The only specification we have is that the IRP_MJ_WMI message "must be handled" in order for power management to work correctly.

The IRP_MJ_PNP *Message*

The minor function code IRP_MN_START_DEVICE is one of the many minor function codes supported for Plug-and-Play. Some of these minor functions are first handled by your driver and then passed on; others are first passed on and then handled. Some messages are required, some are optional, and some are not required at all. For the Plug-and-Play messages, the relationship to the Bus Driver is very important. We summarize this relationship in Table 28.9, which shows all of the IRP_MN_ functions documented in the Beta release. Some of these are not yet documented.

Table 28.9: IRP_MN *Functions for* IRP_MJ_PNP

Function	Description
IRP_MN_START_DEVICE	Requests that the device be started.
IRP_MN_STOP_DEVICE	Requests that the device be stopped.
IRP_MN_QUERY_STOP_DEVICE	Queries whether the device can be stopped.
IRP_MN_CANCEL_STOP_DEVICE	Cancels a stop request.
IRP_MN_QUERY_REMOVE_DEVICE	Queries whether the device can be removed.
IRP_MN_REMOVE_DEVICE	Removes the device from the driver.
IRP_MN_CANCEL_REMOVE_DEVICE	Cancels a request to remove the device.
IRP_MN_QUERY_CAPABILITIES	Fills in a DEVICE_CAPABILITIES structure.
IRP_MN_QUERY_PNP_DEVICE_STATE	Sets the Irp->IoStatus.Status field to a bitmap value representing PNP_DEVICE_STATE.

Table 28.9: IRP_MN *Functions for* IRP_MJ_PNP *(continued)*

Function	Description
IRP_MN_FILTER_RESOURCE_REQUIREMENTS	Allows a driver in a stack of drivers to modify (filter) an incoming resource requirements list and potentially generate a new resource requirements list.
IRP_MN_QUERY_RESOURCES	Used by the Plug-and-Play Manager to get a device's boot configuration resources. Functions and Filter Drivers do not handle this IRP. They pass it to the next lower-level driver with no changes to Irp->IoStatus and do not set an IoCompletion routine.
IRP_MN_QUERY_RESOURCE_REQUIREMENTS	A message sent during enumeration to determine the resource requirements and can be sent subsequently if a driver reports that the resource requirements have changed.
IRP_MN_QUERY_DEVICE_TEXT	
DeviceTextDescription	Returns information about the device description.
DeviceTextLocationInformation	Returns information about the device location.
IRP_MN_QUERY_BUS_INFORMATION	Returns a bus information structure, which includes a globally unique ID (GUID) representing the bus type.
IRP_MN_QUERY_INTERFACE	Sent to a lower-level driver to get pointers to functions that can be called directly by the higher-level driver.
IRP_MN_READ_CONFIG	Handled by devices that support configuration space. Provides functionality similar to that provided by HalGetBusData in NT 4.0.
IRP_MN_WRITE_CONFIG	Handled by devices that support configuration space. Provides functionality similar to that provided by HalSetBusData in NT 4.0.
IRP_MN_EJECT	Requests that a device perform an eject operation (typically, ejecting its media).
IRP_MN_SET_LOCK	Locks a device against ejection requests (depending on the device, this might include manual ejection requests made by the user at the device itself), or unlocks the device, thereby allowing ejections.
IRP_MN_QUERY_DEVICE_RELATIONS	Queries a device for its relationship with other devices. The queried device, if it has relations with another device, will return a pointer to all of the devices with which it has a relationship.
BusRelations	Prompts a Bus Driver to provide a list of all devices on the bus.
EjectionRelations	Causes the action of ejecting a device to have the side effect of ejecting some other device (typical case: undocking a laptop).
PowerRelations	Indicates that changing the power state of this device will change the power state of some other device.

Table 28.9: `IRP_MN` *Functions for* `IRP_MJ_PNP` *(continued)*

Function	Description
`RemovalRelations`	Indicates that removing this device will also remove some other device.
`TargetDeviceRelation`	Returns a reference to the underlying PDO.
`IRP_MN_QUERY_ID`	
`BusQueryDeviceID`	Returns a single string representing the device ID.
`BusQueryHardwareID`	Returns a `MULTI_SZ` string representing the hardware IDs.
`BusQueryCompatibleIDs`	Returns a `MULTI_SZ` string representing the compatible IDs.
`BusQueryInstanceID`	Returns a single string representing the instance ID.
`IRP_MN_DEVICE_USAGE_NOTIFICATION`	Notifies drivers that a "special file" has been created on the device. A "special file" may be a paging file, a crash dump file, or a hibernation file.
`IRP_MN_SURPRISE_REMOVAL`	Notifies drivers that the device has been unexpectedly removed and is no longer available (for example, imagine that a USB device has just been unplugged).

A "Simple" Windows 2000 Driver

The "simple" Windows 2000 driver presented here is similar to the "Hello World" driver we described for Windows NT 4.0. It is somewhat simpler in that it does not *actually* say "Hello World" when it runs. It is more complex in that it is a Windows 2000 layered driver. As you will see, this complexity is considerable. Our driver example here is called the "Sample Driver", hence the use of the `SD_` prefix to designate various functions. It is a Filter Driver, so it will not register a name or create a symbolic link.

A Filter Driver is a somewhat better example for Windows 2000 than is a top-level driver. This is because many drivers you write will actually be MiniDrivers and live at intermediate levels in the driver chain.

The example here is adapted from the example that accompanies the Microsoft DDK for Windows 2000. It was surprising to us because in many ways it differs from the requirements of the documentation. We present the example as it was but point out where we see discrepancies.

This example does not handle some of the Plug-and-Play cases such as "surprise removal". This is apparently because the IRP for surprise removal was not defined when this example was created.

We have done minor reformatting of the code but have made no functional changes.

Publishing Books and Software Releases

Software is a moving target. A book which is published at any point in time is merely a snapshot, a single frame from a motion picture. It is not the complete truth. It is even a little blurry. This chapter was originally written using information from the Beta 1 release of Windows NT

5.0. About the time the book went into copy-edit, Microsoft released Beta 2 of Windows NT 5.0. We compared our example code to the example code in the Windows 98 product DDK and the Windows NT 5.0 Beta 2 DDK. The Beta 1 code and Windows 98 code were identical. There were two lines of trivial changes between the Beta 1 code and the Beta 2 code, which we incorporated into the book at the last minute.

We thought we were set, but as this book went into final composition we got last-minute word from Microsoft that the primary example in this chapter, which is drawn from the Beta 2 docs, contained a number of errors, some as yet unspecified. We have attempted to highlight these with "bug" icons and incorporate changes where possible.

 Note that what appears here is the DDK example *as distributed on the Beta 2 DDK source samples*, and indications are that it is incorrect. Ideally, this example, the PnPPower[5] example, will be corrected by the time the Windows 2000 product DDK is released. Fortunately, our publisher was able to accommodate the last-minute changes in the material.

As we find more information, we will attempt to produce more-current versions of this material on our Web sites. You can check them for updates. Our Web addresses appear in the preface.

The DriverEntry*Handler*

A Windows 2000 DriverEntry is simpler than an NT 4.0 DriverEntry routine. This example illustrates those differences.

Listing 28.1: *The Windows 2000* DriverEntry *Routine*

```
NTSTATUS DriverEntry(PDRIVER_OBJECT DriverObject,
                     IN PUNICODE_STRING RegistryPath)
   {
    NTSTATUS status = STATUS_SUCCESS;
    ULONG index;
    PDRIVER_DISPATCH * dispatch;
```

Thus far there is nothing surprising—there is an ordinary DriverEntry *with a couple variables declared. But this is a layered driver. Unlike an ordinary driver, which leaves its* MajorFunction *pointers set to* NULL *for any function it does not handle, this driver doesn't know if some lower-level driver has to process the message, even if this driver couldn't care less. Consequently, before initializing the* MajorFunction *pointers, it first sets every* MajorFunction *pointer to point to a function that, in this example, is called* SD_Pass *(which you must write). This function, which we show on page 674, simply passes the IRP downward in the chain.*

```
      for(index = 0, dispatch = DriverObject->MajorFunction;
          index <= IRP_MJ_MAXIMUM_FUNCTION;
          index++, dispatch++)
          {/* pass all */
           *dispatch = SD_Pass;   // See page 674
          } /* pass all */
```

---

[5] We chose this example because it was obviously intended to represent the Microsoft-approved correct way to handle Plug-and-Play and power management.

Now we can initialize the IRP_MJ_ *dispatches we really want. Note that for even a simple Windows 2000 driver, we need a lot more of these than we do for an NT 4.0 driver.*

```
DriverObject->MajorFunction[IRP_MJ_PNP] = SD_DispatchPnp;       // Page 659
DriverObject->MajorFunction[IRP_MJ_POWER] =
                                 SD_DispatchPower;              // Page 676
DriverObject->MajorFunction[IRP_MJ_CREATE] =
                                 SD_DispatchCreateClose; // Page 669
DriverObject->MajorFunction[IRP_MJ_SHUTDOWN] =
                                 SD_DispatchCreateClose; // Page 669
DriverObject->MajorFunction[IRP_MJ_CLOSE] =
                                 SD_DispatchCreateClose; // Page 669
DriverObject->MajorFunction[IRP_MJ_CLEANUP] = SD_Cleanup;       // Page 669
DriverObject->DriverExtension->AddDevice = SD_AddDevice;        // Page 657
DriverObject->DriverUnload = SD_Unload;                         // Page 681

return status;
}
```

That's it! A Windows 2000 `DriverEntry` in its entirety! Note the use of the Driver Object's Driver Extension. This is the first time we've shown the use of a Driver Extension. The standard Driver Extension has a field that holds a pointer to the `AddDevice` routine.

The `AddDevice` *Handler*

However, we don't really have a device yet. The driver will not be called to add a device until the Plug-and-Play Manager discovers there is an instance of a device associated with this driver. During bus enumeration, the Bus Driver will find a device on the bus. Then it constructs a PDO to represent this device and hands it off to the Plug-and-Play facility, which goes to the Registry and locates the appropriate driver. If the driver has not yet been loaded, the driver will be loaded for the first such device, and its `DriverEntry` routine will be called. Once the driver is loaded and initialized, for the first or each subsequent device, the `AddDevice` function is called. Note the significance of this. Unlike a Windows NT 4.0 driver, which must enumerate the bus and locate each of its devices, a Windows 2000 driver has its `AddDevice` handler called each time a device is found. No explicit enumeration is performed. This is a step forward. It is particularly important in Windows 2000 because the driver can now be independent of the bus itself.

Listing 28.2: *The Windows 2000* `AddDevice` *Function*

```
NTSTATUS SD_AddDevice(IN PRDIVER_OBJECT DriverObject, IN PDEVICE_OBJECT pdo)
    {
      NTSTATUS status = STATUS_SUCCESS;
      PDEVICE_OBJECT fdo = NULL;
      PSD_FDO_EXTENSION fdoExtension;

      status = IoCreateDevice(DriverObject,
                            sizeof(SD_FDO_EXTENSION),
                            NULL, // No name!
                            FILE_DEVICE_UNKNOWN,
                            0,
                            FALSE,
                            &fdo);
```

The AddDevice *routine calls* IoCreateDevice *to create an FDO. In WDM, all drivers except the PDO are nameless, and hence the device name is specified as* NULL. *In our example, we chose to make the device type* FILE_DEVICE_UNKNOWN, *much as we did for any device we wrote for NT 4.0.*

```
if(!NT_SUCCESS(status))
    return status;
```

If we fail at this point, the rest of the device stack will fail to function. However, because we were unable to create a device, it is likely that the rest of the device stack will also fail to create devices, so we lose nothing at this point by simply returning the error. Next, we initialize the fields of the Device Extension. These fields are all fields we invented and for which we provided such features as queueing IRPs, creating an Event Object that handles the queueing, and setting various flags for our internal use. As this example develops, we show how each of these is used.

```
fdoExtension = (PSD_FDO_EXTENSION)fdo->DeviceExtension;

fdoExtension->IsStarted = FALSE;    // Not yet started
fdoExtension->IsRemoved = FALSE;    // Not removed

// Ignore all requests until started
fdoExtension->HoldNewRequests = FALSE;
```

 This assignment, to hold new requests FALSE, is almost certainly wrong. The idea here is that any incoming IRP that is not a PnP or Power IRP should be completed with a failure code as long as this flag is FALSE. This violates Microsoft's own specification that requests should be held and not failed; normally, we would expect to see this flag set to TRUE and not set to FALSE until a shutdown sequence is initiated. We do not know why this example from the DDK works this way instead of according to the specification.

```
fdoExtension->DeviceObject = fdo;
fdoExtension->PDO = pdo;
fdoExtension->NextLowerDriver = NULL;

// Initialize a queue for holding pending requests
IntializeListHead(&fdoExtension->NewRequestsQueue);
KeInitializeSpinLock(&fdoExtension->QueueLock);
```

To synchronize device stopping and device removal, we add two events. These are set to Signaled when their associated actions are feasible and Not-Signaled when the actions are inhibited.

```
// Initialize the Remove Event to Not-Signaled

KeInitializeEvent(&fdoExtension->RemoveEvent,
                SynchronizationEvent, FALSE);

// Initialize the Stop Event to Signaled

KeInitializeEvent(&fdoExtension->StopEvent,
                SynchronizationEvent, TRUE);
```

We maintain a reference count of outstanding IRPs. This count is 1-biased, meaning that zero outstanding IRPs is represented by the value 1. We use the value 0 under the special condition of removing the device. Think of it as a reference count where every IRP maintains a reference and the driver itself maintains a reference. An attempt to shut down the driver will decrement the reference count by one for the "live driver" reference, but if there are any outstanding IRPs, the driver shutdown is inhibited until the last IRP is completed. There are special functions that increment and decrement this reference count and as a side effect signal or unsignal the above-created Event Objects.

```
fdoExtension->OutstandingIO = 1;      // Outstanding-IRP ref count

// Clear the DO_DEVICE_INITIALIZING flag

fdo->Flags &= ~DO_DEVICE_INITIALIZING;

// Attach this driver to the driver stack

fdoExtension->NextLowerDriver = IoAttachDeviceToDeviceStack(fdo, pdo);

// The attach must succeed; if it fails, the Plug-and-Play system is
// seriously broken; issue an error message

ASSERT(NULL != fdoExtension->NextLowerDriver);

if(NULL != fdoExtension->NextLowerDriver)
    return STATUS_SUCCESS;
else
    return STATUS_INSUFFICIENT_RESOURCES;
}
```

At this point, the Device Object is fully initialized. We do not yet have hardware, but we do have a Device Object to represent it when it finally appears.

This is also where we find one of the discrepancies between the documentation and this code. The state the extension has been left in will cause all incoming IRPs to be rejected until the next phase. This contradicts the documented specifications.

The `IRP_MJ_PNP` *Handler*

The `IRP_MJ_PNP` handler is astonishingly long and complex. We show the skeleton of it here and then fill in the details in subsequent sections.

Listing 28.3: *The* `IRP_MJ_PNP` *Handler*

```
NTSTATUS SD_DispatchPnp(IN PDEVICE_OBJECT DeviceObject, IN PIRP Irp)
    {
    PSD_FDO_EXTENSION fdoExtension;
    PIO_STACK_LOCATION stack;
    NTSTATUS status;
    PDEVICE_CAPABILITIES deviceCapabilities;
    KEVENT WaitLowerDrivers;

    fdoExtension = (PSD_FDO_EXTENSION)DeviceObject->DeviceExtension;
    stack = IoGetCurentIrpStackLocation(Irp);
```

If the device has been removed, we simply fail the IRP. We return the status STATUS_DELETE_PENDING.

```
if(fdoExtension->IsRemoved)
    { /* fail request */
    Irp->IoStatus.Information = 0;
    Irp->IoStatus.Status = STATUS_DELETE_PENDING;
    IoCompleteRequest(Irp, IO_NO_INCREMENT);
    return STATUS_DELETE_PENDING);
    } /* fail request */
```

We maintain a reference count of the number of outstanding IRPs for this device. This keeps us from deleting the device while there are IRPs pending at lower levels.

```
SD_IoIncrement(fdoExtension); // Page 672
```

Next, we dispatch on the minor function code. Each function designated by an ellipsis will be expanded in subsequent sections. After the important minor function codes are handled, we catch all of the rest and handle them just like the "default" case. However, your driver might need to handle these, in which case you will need to fill in the details. For any minor function code we don't understand, we pass the IRP down to the next lower-level driver using IoCallDriver. *At this point, we are finished with whatever processing this level is doing, and we can decrement the reference count to the device.*

```
switch(stack->MinorFunction)
    { /* minorFunction */
    case IRP_MN_START_DEVICE:
        // ... Page 661
        break;
    case IRP_MN_QUERY_STOP_DEVICE:
        // ... Page 662
        break;
    case IRP_MN_CANCEL_STOP_DEVICE:
        // ... Page 664
        break;
    case IRP_MN_STOP_DEVICE:
        // ... Page 665
        break;
    case IRP_MN_QUERY_REMOVE_DEVICE:
        // ... Page 665
        break;
    case IRP_MN_CANCEL_REMOVE_DEVICE:
        // ... Page 666
        break;
    case IRP_MN_REMOVE_DEVICE:
        // ... Page 667
        break;
    case IRP_MN_SURPRISE_REMOVAL:
    case IRP_MN_QUERY_DEVICE_RELATIONS:
    case IRP_MN_QUERY_INTERFACE:
    case IRP_MN_QUERY_RESOURCES:
    case IRP_MN_QUERY_RESOURCE_REQUIREMENTS:
    case IRP_MN_QUERY_CAPABILITIES:
    case IRP_MN_READ_CONFIG:
    case IRP_MN_WRITE_CONFIG:
    case IRP_MN_EJECT:
```

```
        case IRP_MN_SET_LOCK:
        case IRP_MN_QUERY_ID:
        case IRP_MN_QUERY_PNP_DEVICE_STATE:
        default:
                IoSkipCurrentIrpStackLocation(Irp);
                status = IoCallDriver(fdoExtension->NextLowerDriver, Irp);
                break;
        } /* minorFunction */

    SD_IoDecrement(fdoExtension); // Page 672
    return status;
}
```

This function uses a new Windows 2000 call, `IoSkipCurrentIrpStackLocation`. This call copies the contents of the current IRP Stack location to the location for the next lower-level driver and does not allow a completion routine to be set. It is one of two similar calls added in Windows 2000 to simplify IRP Stack handling. The other call, which we also use in this example, is `IoCopyCurrentIrpStackLocationToNext`. This call copies the contents of the current stack location to the location for the next lower-level driver, but it *does* allow a completion routine to be set.

The `IRP_MN_START_DEVICE` Handler

The first notification the driver receives that the device is available is the `IRP_MJ_PNP` request with the `IRP_MN_START_DEVICE` minor function. We cannot actually touch the hardware until all of the lower drivers in the device chain have successfully processed this message. Since we are about to actually start the device, however, we make a note that we can enqueue any further IRPs that come in. While not quite what the documentation suggests, this driver is apparently borderline acceptable in this behavior. A driver that met the specification would be queueing IRPs as soon as the `AddDevice` completed.

Listing 28.4: *The* `IRP_MN_START_DEVICE` *Fragment*

```
case IRP_MN_START_DEVICE:
    fdoExtension->HoldNewRequests = TRUE;
```

This is actually incorrect because it means that the device will reject incoming IRPs until it receives the `IRP_MN_START_DEVICE` *request. This violates the specification of how Microsoft wants a Windows 2000 driver to act. The correct place to have done this was in the* `AddDevice` *routine. (We did say that we are presenting this driver as it is in the DDK, including what appear to be bugs.)*
To discover that the lower levels have completed the processing, we need to set an `IoCompletion` *routine. The current thread will not be permitted to continue until the completion routine has finished. To implement this, we create an Event Object on the stack and use it to synchronize with the completion routine.*

```
KeInitializeEvent(&WaitLowerDrivers, SynchronizationEvent, FALSE);
```

Next, we initialize the next IRP Stack location, establish the completion routine, and call the lower-level driver.

```
IoCopyCurentIrpStackLocation(Irp);
IoSetCompletionRoutine(Irp,
                        SD_DispatchPnpComplete,  // Page 668
                        &WaitLowerDrivers,       // Context pointer
                        TRUE,                    // Invoke on success
                        TRUE,                    // Invoke on error
                        TRUE);                   // Invoke on cancel
status = IoCallDriver(fdoExtension->NextLowerDriver, Irp);
```

The result of calling IoCallDriver *is that the IRP might be completed immediately, or fail immediately, or be queued for later processing. For either of the first two cases, we can just return; for the case in which it is queued, we block this thread and wait for the completion. When we get the completion event, we use the Event Object referenced by the context pointer to release the wait.*

```
if(STATUS_PENDING == status)
    { /* pending, wait */
      KeWaitForSingleObject(&WaitLowerDrivers,
                            Executive,   // Waiting for reason of a driver
                            KernelMode,  // Kernel-mode wait
                            FALSE,       // Not alertable
                            NULL);       // No timeout

      status = Irp->IoStatus.Status;    // Status is result of lower driver
    } /* pending, wait */
```

When we get to this point in the code, either status *is directly the result of the* IoCallDriver *call or it is the result copied from the IRP when the lower-level driver completed it. This status will be either a success or failure code. If it is success, we continue with starting our device. We then complete the request, either with the error status or the result of the start attempt. Note that this example ends with a* break, *meaning that we will fall out of the* switch *and decrement the reference count of outstanding IRPs.*

```
if(NT_SUCCESS(status))
    { /* start it */
      status = SD_StartDevice(fdoExtension, Irp);  // Page 671
    } /* start it */

Irp->IoStatus.Status = status;
Irp->IoStatus.Information = 0;
IoCompleteRequest(Irp, IO_NO_INCREMENT);
break;
```

The IRP_MN_QUERY_STOP_DEVICE Handler

A Plug-and-Play device can be stopped and started many times. Once a device is stopped, the hardware is unavailable for further use until another IRP_MN_START_DEVICE comes in. In Windows NT 4.0, we had only the ability to start and stop a *driver*. When a driver was stopped, it was unloaded, thereby making *all* of the devices it controlled unavailable. In Windows 2000, this ability is available for individual devices. A device is usually stopped only to reconfigure I/O addresses or other information that requires shutting down the device for a brief period. It is not always advisable (or even safe!) to simply stop a device. A device stopped in the middle of a transaction might end up leaving the data on the device in an undefined state. For example, a hydraulic arm carrying a heavy object might drop the object when the stop code removes hydraulic pressure and shuts off the pumps. Therefore every device supports the IRP_MN_QUERY_STOP_DEVICE minor function, which allows the device to deny stopping if necessary.

The first thing we do is test to see if the device is already stopped. If it is, we don't need to do anything at our level, although we do need to pass the request down to the lower levels. Note that after we do this, we simply decrement the outstanding IRP reference count and return.

Listing 28.5: *The* IRP_MN_QUERY_STOP_DEVICE *Fragment*

```
case IRP_MN_QUERY_STOP_DEVICE:
    if(!fdoExtension->IsStarted)
        { /* already stopped */
         IoSkipCurrentIrpStackLocation(Irp);
         status = IoCallDriver(fdoExtension->NextLowerDriver, Irp);
         SD_IoDecrement(fdoExtension); // Page 672
         return status;
        } /* already stopped */
```

At this point, we know the device has not been stopped. We call a device-specific function that does whatever tests we need to do to determine if the device can be stopped. This returns either STATUS_SUCCESS *or some other code. A return of* STATUS_SUCCESS *means that the stopping can proceed. Note that a device on which there are outstanding open file handles can be stopped, as long as such stopping does not compromise the data or integrity of the device. There is an assumption that stopping is a temporary phenomenon and that the device will soon be restarted.*

If the stopping can proceed, we must set the flag indicating that any future requests (or perhaps only those requests that actually require the presence of the hardware) should be held pending. This is so that when the device is restarted, it can continue processing the requests that have come in. Thus stopping a device is potentially invisible to the application level, which will simply wait for the completion of the requests. Of course, if the application level uses asynchronous I/O, it could implement timeouts and use CancelIo *to abort pending I/O requests, but that happens at a level different than the one we are working at here.*

Once we have marked the device to queue future requests, we decrement the reference count and wait for the completion of the actual stopping of the device.

```
        status = pSD_CanStopDevice(DeviceObject, Irp); // Page 671
        Irp->IoStatus.Status = status;
        Irp->IoStatus.Information = 0;
        if(NT_SUCCESS(status))
            { /* device is stopped */
             fdoExtension->HoldNewRequests = TRUE;
             SD_IoDecrement(fdoExtension); // Page 672

             KeWaitForSingleObject(&fdoExtension->StopEvent,
                                   Executive,
                                   KernelMode,
                                   FALSE, // Not alertable
                                   NULL); // No timeout
```

```
            IoSkipCurrentIrpStackLocation(Irp);
            status = IoCallDriver(fdoExtension->NextLowerDriver, Irp);
            return status;
        } /* device is stopped */
    else
        { /* device can't stop */
        IoCompleteRequest(Irp, IO_NO_INCREMENT);
        } /* device can't stop */
    break;
```

The IRP_MN_CANCEL_STOP_DEVICE Handler

A stop request has been made, but before the IRP_MN_STOP_DEVICE request comes in, the stop is cancelled.

Listing 28.6: *The* IRP_MN_CANCEL_STOP_DEVICE *Fragment*

```
case IRP_MN_CANCEL_STOP_DEVICE:
    if(!fdoExtension->IsStarted)
        { /* not started */
        IoSkipCurrentIrpStackLocation(Irp);
        status = IoCallDriver(fdoExtension->NextLowerDriver, Irp);
        SD_IoDecrement(fdoExtesion); // Page 672
        return status;
        } /* not started */

    IoCopyCurrentIrpStackLocationToNext(Irp);

    KeIntitializeEvent(&WaitLowerDrivers, SynchronizeEvent, FALSE);
    IoSetCompletionRoutine(Irp,
                        SD_DispatchPnpComplete, // See page 668
                        &WaitLowerDrivers,      // Context
                        TRUE,                   // Complete on success
                        TRUE,                   // Complete on errors
                        TRUE);                  // Complete on cancels

    status = IoCallDriver(fdoExtension->NextLowerDriver, Irp);

    if(STATUS_PENDING == status)
        { /* wait for completion */
        KeWaitForSingleObject(&WaitLowerDrivers,
                            Executive,
                            KernelMode,
                            FALSE,
                            NULL);
        status = Irp->IoStatus.Status;
        } /* wait for completion */

    fdoExtension->HoldNewRequests = FALSE; // Allow requests again
    pSD_ProcessQueuedRequests(fdoExtension); // Page 673

    Irp->IoStatus.Status = status;
    Irp->IoStatus.Information = 0;
    IoCompleteRequest(Irp, IO_NO_INCREMENT);
    break;
```

The `IRP_MN_STOP_DEVICE` Handler

The processing of the stop request is very simple. We pass the IRP downward in the device stack. Note that we have already set the `HoldNewRequests` flag to TRUE, so passing the IRP doesn't actually change any behavior of the device at this level.

Listing 28.7: *The* `IRP_MN_STOP_DEVICE` *Fragment*

```
case IRP_MN_STOP_DEVICE:
    fdoExtension->IsStarted = FALSE;
    IoSkipCurrentIrpStackLocation(Irp);
    status = IoCallDriver(fdoExtension->NextLowerDriver, Irp);
    break;
```

The `IRP_MN_QUERY_REMOVE_DEVICE` Handler

The removal of a device is quite similar to the stopping of a device. The difference is that a device that is being removed is not expected to be restarted. Consequently, we try to process all queued requests before we allow the device to be removed.

There is no implicit coordination about the order of various IRPs. Thus other IRPs might arrive during the time the device removal is occurring, and you might well get a device removal IRP while in the midst of processing some data transfer or other IRP that is actually using the device. It is up to you to deal with these issues. You might need to queue a removal request until the pending I/O completes, or you might need to cancel the active I/O in order to allow the removal to be processed. You need to make sure that during the removal, all arriving IRPs are properly handled—either rejected or queued until a suitable response can be made.

The first thing we do is check to see if the device has already been started. If it has not, we need only pass the IRP downward to the next lower-level driver, decrement the pending-IRP reference count, and return.

Listing 28.8: *The* `IRP_MN_QUERY_REMOVE_DEVICE` *Fragment*

```
case IRP_MN_QUERY_REMOVE_DEVICE:
    if(!fdoExtension->IsStarted)
        { /* not started */
        IoSkipCurrentIrpStackLocation(Irp);
        status = IoCallDriver(fdoExtension->NextLowerDriver, Irp);
        SD_IoDecrement(fdoExtension); // Page 672
        return status;
        } /* not started */
```

Next, we call a device-specific function that determines if the device can be unloaded. What this function does depends on the characteristics of your device and your design decisions as to what will constitute a valid removal. If it returns STATUS_SUCCESS, *the device can be removed; otherwise, we just complete the request with the returned status. For example, a device with open handles or pending IRPs should not be removed.*

```
    status = pSD_CanRemoveDevice(DeviceObject, Irp);  // Page 672
    Irp->IoStatus.Status = status;
    Irp->IoStatus.Information = 0;
    if(!NT_SUCCESS(status))
```

```
        { /* can't remove */
         IoCompleteRequest(Irp, IO_NO_INCREMENT);
         SD_IoDecrement(fdoExtension); // Page 672
         return status;
        } /* can't remove */

    pSD_ProcessQueuedRequests(fdoExtension); // Page 673
```

Now we have begun the removal sequence. We might think that we can start failing incoming requests. However, this removal could yet be cancelled. In this case, failing the requests would be erroneous. Instead, we mark the device as requiring queueing. When the device is finally removed, we can fail these requests; if the device is not removed, they will be processed.

```
    fdoExtension->HoldNewRequests = TRUE;

    SD_IoDecrement(fdoExtension); // Page 672
    KeWaitForSingleObject(&fdoExtension->StopEvent,
                          Executive,
                          KernelMode,
                          FALSE,
                          NULL);
    IoSkipCurrentIrpStackLocation(Irp);
    status = IoCallDriver(fdoExtension->NextLowerDriver, Irp);
    return status;
```

The IRP_MN_CANCEL_REMOVE_DEVICE Handler

The IRP_MN_CANCEL_REMOVE_DEVICE request can come in after a removal has started but before it is completed. It might also come in spontaneously, even if a removal had not been started, due to some condition that is supposed to cancel any pending removals, should there be any.

The first thing we do is check to see that the device is started. If it is not, we simply pass the request down to the lower-level driver.

Listing 28.9: *The IRP_MN_CANCEL_REMOVE_DEVICE Fragment*

```
case IRP_MN_CANCEL_REMOVE_DEVICE:
    if(!fdoExtension->IsStarted)
        { /* not started */
         IoSkipCurrentIrpStackLocation(Irp);
         status = IoCallDriver(fdoExtension->NextLowerDriver, Irp);
         SD_IoDecrement(fdoExtension); // Page 672
         return status;
        } /* not started */

    KeInitializeEvent(&WaitLowerDrivers, SynchronizationEvent, FALSE);
    IoSetCompletionRoutine(Irp,
                    SD_DispatchPnpComplete, // Page 668
                    &WaitLowerDrivers,      // Context
                    TRUE,                   // Complete on success
                    TRUE,                   // Complete on errors
                    TRUE);                  // Complete on cancels

    status = IoCallDriver(fdoExtension->NextLowerDriver, Irp);
```

If the IRP requires additional processing, the completion routine will eventually be called. The completion routine will release the WaitLowerDrivers *Event, thereby allowing the code to proceed.*

```
if(STATUS_PENDING == status)
    { /* pending */
     KeWaitForSingleObject(&WaitLowerDrivers,
                           Executive,
                           KernelMode,
                           FALSE,
                           NULL);
      status = Irp->IoStatus.Status;
    } /* pending */
```

When we get here, the IRP has been completed by the lower-level driver, and the wait has completed. We observe that this code never checks to see if it completed successfully; it simply presumes successful completion and enables the processing of future requests. It then forces the queued requests to be processed and completes the remove-cancel IRP.

```
fdoExtension->HoldNewRequests =
                        FALSE; // Allow new requests to be processed
pSD_ProcessQueuedRequests(fdoExtension); // Page 673
Irp->IoStatus.Status = status;
Irp->IoStatus.Information = 0
IoCompleteRequest(Irp, IO_NO_INCREMENT);
break;
```

The IRP_MN_REMOVE_DEVICE Handler

When the IRP_MN_REMOVE_DEVICE request comes in, the Plug-and-Play system determines that the device should be removed. For some busses, such as the USB, there might be no warning at all that the user is about to yank the cord out of the device. If we have any pending requests in the queue, we will attempt to complete them, but more likely, we will fail them.

Listing 28.10: *The* IRP_MN_REMOVE_DEVICE *Fragment*

```
case IRP_MN_REMOVE_DEVICE:
    fdoExtension->HoldNewRequests = FALSE; // Fail incoming requests
    fdoExtension->IsStarted = FALSE;
    fdoExtension->IsRemoved = TRUE;

    pSD_ProcessQueuedRequests(fdoExtension); // Page 673

    IoSkipCurrentIrpStacLocation(Irp);
    status = IoCallDriver(fdoExtension->NextLowerDriver);
```

Note that we actually decrement the reference count twice here. The first time is for the increment that happens in SD_PnpDispatch. *The other is for the 1-biased value of* OutstandingIO.

```
SD_IoDecrement(fdoExtension); // Page 672

SD_IoDecrement(fdoExtension); // Page 672
```

```
KeWaitForSingleObject(&fdoExtension->RemoveEvent,
                      Extension,
                      KernelMode,
                      FALSE,
                      NULL);
```

Now that we are about to delete the device, we first detach it from the lower-level driver.

```
IoDetachDevice(fdoExtension->NextLowerDriver);
```

Then we delete the Device Object. This is one of the major differences between an NT 4.0 driver and a Windows 2000 driver. In an NT 4.0 driver, we would delete the Device Object in the Unload routine.

```
IoDeleteDevice(fdoExtension->DeviceObject);
return STATUS_SUCCESS;
```

Listing 28.11: *The Plug-and-Play Dispatch-Complete Handler*

```
NTSTATUS SD_DispatchPnpComplete(IN PDEVICE_OBJECT DeviceObject
                                IN PIRP Irp,
                                IN PVOID context)
  {
  PIO_STACK_LOCATION stack;
  PKEVENT event = (PKEVENT)context;
  NTSTATUS status = STATUS_SUCCESS;
```

The SD_DispatchPnpComplete *function knows that the* context *parameter is a pointer to an event that is to become Signaled when the completion routine is finished.*

```
stack = IoGetCurentIrpStackLocation(Irp);

if(Irp->PendingReturned)
   IoMarkIrpPending(Irp);
```

This if *statement must be present in any completion routine called in a driver that calls lower-level drivers. It is necessary because the asynchronous completion state must be explicitly propagated upwards in the layered driver stack. For the details regarding why this is necessary, consult the detailed discussion in Chapter 23 on page 485. Although it is possible, and almost certainly desirable, to have separate completion routines, Microsoft chose for this example to use a common completion handler for both* IRP_MJ_PNP *and* IRP_MJ_POWER. *Therefore, we have to distinguish which of these IRPs was just completed.*

```
switch(stack->MajorFunction)
   { /* MajorFunction */
    case IRP_MJ_PNP:
        switch(stack->MinorFunction)
            { /* MinorFunction */
             case IRP_MN_START_DEVICE:
             case IRP_MN_CANCEL_STOP_DEVICE:
             case IRP_MN_CANCEL_REMOVE_DEVICE:
                 KeSetEvent(event, 0, FALSE);
                 return STATUS_MORE_PROCESSING_REQUIRED;
```

```
          default:
               break;
     } /* MinorFunction */
```

The previous code handles all of the `IRP_MJ_PNP` *special cases. For now, the indicated* `IRP_MN_` *cases are the only ones we have that pass in an event on which they are waiting. We call* `KeSetEvent` *to release the event. Because we need the IRP back where we initiated the call that led to the completion routine, we return the code* `STATUS_MORE_PROCESSING_REQUIRED`. *Thus the I/O Manager will not release the IRP. The Dispatch Routine that was waiting on the event will still have a valid IRP pointer when control returns, but it is responsible for calling* `IoCompleteRequest` *to finish the processing.*

```
      case IRP_MJ_POWER:
           // Add Power Manager support here
      default:
           break;
    } /* MajorFunction */
  return status;
  }
```

Listing 28.12: *The Create-Close Handler*

The create-close handler is a special handler for those IRPs that should not be queued, even if the device is stopped. Also, if there is a surprise removal, they should not be completed with `STATUS_DELETE_PENDING`.

```
NTSTATUS SD_DispatchCreateClose(IN PDEVICE_OBJECT DeviceObject, IN PIRP Irp)
    {
    PSD_FDO_EXTENSION fdoExtension;
    NTSTATUS status;
    fdoExtension = (PSD_FDO_EXTENSION)DeviceObject->DeviceExtension;
    SD_IoIncrement(fdoExtension); // Page 672
    IoSkipCurrentIrpStackLocation(Irp);
    status = IoCallDriver(fdoExtension->NextLowerDriver(Irp));
    SD_IoDecrement(fdoExtension); // Page 672
    return status;
    }
```

 We have been questioned as to why we are passing Create/Close operations downward. All we can say is "that's what the example does". It does seem to us to be the correct way to handle a layered driver since the lower-level drivers *must* see the Create/Close IRPs. Check the latest example code to see if this has changed from the code we are working with.

Listing 28.13: *The Cleanup Handler*

```
NTSTATUS SD_Cleanup(IN PDEVICE_OBJECT DeviceObject, IN PIRP Irp)
    {
    PIRP currentIrp;
    PIRP requeueIrp;
    PIO_STACK_LOCATION cleanupStack;
    PIO_STACK_LOCATION currentStack;
```

```
    LIST_ENTRY cancelList;
    LIST_ENTRY requeueList;
    PLIST_ENTRY headOfList;
    PFDO_EXTENSION fdoExtension;

    fdoExtension = (PFDO_EXTENSION)DeviceObject->DeviceExtension;
    SD_IOIncremnt(fdoExtension);
    cleanupStack = IoGetCurrentIrpStackLocation(Irp);
```

*We walk through the queued IRP lists and decide what to do with each IRP. The options
are to either cancel it or requeue it. If the IRP represents the same File Object as the
cleanup request, it should be cancelled; otherwise, it should be requeued. For a device
that allows nonexclusive access, there can be IRPs for several active file handles (each
represented by a unique File Object). Only those IRPs whose file handles match the one
of the* IRP_MJ_CLEANUP *request should be cancelled. So we iterate through the queue,
splitting the requests out into two other lists. Then we requeue the requests that are for
other File Objects.*

```
    InitializeListHead(&cancelList);
    InitializeListHead(&requeueList);

    while ((headOfList = ExInterlockedRemoveHeadList(
                                &fdoExtension->NewRequestQueue,
                                &fdoExtension->QueueLock)) != NULL)
        { /* scan queued entries */
         currentIrp = CONTAINING_RECORD(headOfList, IRP,
                                    Tail.Overlay.ListEntry);
         currentStack = IoGetCurrentIrpStackLocation(currentIrp);
         if(currentStack->FileObject == cleanupStack->FileObject)
            { /* cancel it */
             currentIrp->Cancel = TRUE;
             IoSetCancelRoutine(curentIrp, NULL);
         InsertTailList(&cancelList, &currentIrp->Tail.Overlay.ListEntry);
            } /* cancel it */
         else
            { /* requeue it */
             InsertTailList(&requeueList,
                         &currentIrp->Tail.Overlay.ListEntry);
            } /* requeue it */
        } /* scan queued entries */
```

*Now that the entries have been split into two lists, we requeue the IRPs for files other
than the one that is being cleaned up.*

```
    while(!IsListEmpty(&requeueList))
        { /* requeue */
         headOfList = RemoveHeadList(&requeueList);
         currentIrp = CONTAINING_RECORD(headOfList, IRP,
                                    Tail.Overlay.ListEntry);
         ExInterlockedInsertTailList(&fdoExtension->NewRequestsQueue,
                                    &currentIrp->Tail.Overlay.ListEntry,
                                    &fdoExtension->QueueLock);
        } /* requeue */
```

Now we actually cancel all of the requests that need to be cancelled.

```
    while(!IsListEmpty(&cancelList))
        { /* cancel */
          headOfList = RemoveHeadList(&cancelList);
    currentIrp = CONTAINING_RECORD(headOfList, IRP, Tail.Overlay.ListEntry);
          currentIrp->IoStatus.Status = STATUS_CANCELLED;
          currentIrp->IoStatus.Information = 0;
          IoCompleteRequest(currentIrp, IO_NO_INCREMENT);
        } /* cancel */
```

*Next, since all outstanding requests have been cancelled, we can complete the cleanup
IRP. We decrement the outstanding IRP reference count.*

```
    Irp->IoStatus.Status = STATUS_SUCCESS;
    Irp->IoStatus.Information = 0;
    IoCompleteRequest(Irp, IO_NO_INCREMENT);

    SD_IoDecrement(fdoExtension); // Page 672

    return STATUS_SUCCESS;
  }
```

Listing 28.14: *The* StartDevice *Function*

```
NTSTATUS SD_StartDevice(IN PSD_FDO_EXTENSION fdoExtension, IN PIRP Irp)
    {
    NTSTATUS status = STATUS_SUCCESS;
    if(fdoExtension->IsRemoved)
        { /* can't start */
          return STATUS_DELETE_PENDING;
        } /* can't start */

    fdoExtension->IsStarted = TRUE;
    fdoExtension->HoldNewRequests = FALSE;
```

*The device state is set, so now we can perform any necessary operations required to
initialize the device. These include, but are not limited to, gathering information about
the device, manipulating the device registers, and updating the Registry. Note that by
the time this function is called, the lower-level drivers have all completed the IRP. If
there are any pending IRPs, they can be processed now.*

```
    pSD_ProcessQueuedRequests(fdoExtension); // Page 673
    return status;
  }
```

Listing 28.15: *The* CanStopDevice *Function*

The CanStopDevice function is called to determine if the device can be stopped, returning
STATUS_SUCCESS if it can be. For our example, this is a trivial function that always indicates that
removal is possible.

```
NTSTATUS pSD_CanStopDevice(IN PDEVICE_OBJECT DeviceObject, IN PIRP Irp)
    {
    return STATUS_SUCCESS;
  }
```

Listing 28.16: *The* `CanRemoveDevice` *Function*

`CanRemoveDevice` is a function that is called to determine if the device can be removed. It returns `STATUS_SUCCESS` if the device can be removed; if the device cannot be removed, it returns some other status code to indicate why. The reasons are specific to your device, so the routine shown here is the simplest possible one—it always approves the removal request.

```
NTSTATUS pSD_CanRemoveDevice(IN PDEVICE_OBJECT DeviceObject, IN PIRP Irp)
    {
      return STATUS_SUCCESS;
    }
```

Reference Count Increment/Decrement

The Device Object maintains a reference count indicating the number of IRPs that are pending. It also maintains two Event Objects: `StopEvent`, which is signaled when a stop can occur, and `RemoveEvent`, which is signaled when a removal can occur. A function that wants to stop the device is expected to wait on the `StopEvent`, and one that wants to remove the device is expected to wait on the `RemoveEvent`. Normally, the system can be stopped if the reference count is 1, meaning it is idle. It cannot be stopped if the reference count is 2 or greater. Thus the increment-reference-count function will clear `StopEvent` if the reference count goes greater than 1. `RemoveEvent` will be set only if the reference count goes to 0, which can happen only when the `IRP_MN_REMOVE_DEVICE` function performs an extra decrement operation. Thus, any thread that wishes to perform a stop or removal will be blocked until the corresponding Event is again set to Signaled.

Listing 28.17: *Reference Count Management*

```
LONG SD_IoIncrement(IN OUT PSD_FDO_EXTENSION fdoExtension)
    {
     LONG result = InterlockedIncrement(&fdoExtension->OutstandingIO);
     if(result == 2)
        { /* clear event */
          KeClearEvent(&fdoExtension->StopEvent);
        } /* clear event */
     return result;
    }
LONG SD_IoDecrement(IN OUT PSD_FDO_EXTENSION fdoExtension)
    {
     LONG result = InterlockedDecrement(&fdoExtension->OutstandingIO);
     if(result == 1)
        { /* set event */
          KeSetEvent(&fdoExtension->StopEvent, IO_NO_INCREMENT, FALSE);
        } /* set event */
     if(result == 0)
        { /* remove happened */
          KeSetEvent(&fdoExtension->RemoveEvent, IO_NO_INCREMENT, FALSE);
        } /* remove happened */
     return result;
    }
```

Queueing Requests

The pSD_QueueRequest function queues a request that is being held pending having the device started. Because the IRP may be in the queue some arbitrarily long time, it is subject to being cancelled. You need to handle this. Because in this example we are using our own private queue, we don't need to use the Cancel Spin Lock. However, we have to supply our own queue interlock; in this example it is fdoExtension->QueueLock.

Listing 28.18: *Queuing Pending Requests*

```
NTSTATUS pSD_QueueRequest(
                IN OUT PSD_FDO_EXTENSION fdoExtension, IN PIRP Irp)
   {
   PIO_STACK_LOCATION stack;

   stack = IoGetCurrentIrpStackLocation(Irp);
```

If the IRP is already cancelled, we simply set its status to STATUS_CANCELLED *and complete it.*

```
   if(Irp->Cancel)
      { /* already cancelled */
      Irp->IoStatus.Status = STATUS_CANCELLED;
      Irp->IoStatus.Information = 0;
      IoCompleteRequest(Irp, IO_NO_INCREMENT);
      return STATUS_CANCELLED;
      } /* already cancelled */
```

If the request was not cancelled, we need to queue it. We do this in the same way we queue a request in Windows NT 4.0, and we enter it in our own private queue.

```
   Irp->IoStatus.Status = STATUS_PENDING;
   IoMarkIrpPending(Irp);
   ExInterlockedInsertTailList(&fdoExtesion->NewRequestsQueue,
                               &Irp->Tail.Overlay.ListEntry,
                               &fdoExtension->QueueLock);
   IoSetCancelRoutine(Irp, SD_CancelQueued); // Page 674
   }
```

Listing 28.19: *Processing Queued Requests*

The pSD_ProcessQueuedRequests function processes the entries in the pending queue. If the routine is called for any purpose other than removing the device, the requests are passed down to the next lower-level driver. If the routine is called for IRP_MN_REMOVE_DEVICE, which is indicated by the IsRemoved flag being set, the IRPs are completed with STATUS_DELETE_PENDING.

```
VOID pSD_ProcessQueuedRequests(IN OUT PSD_FDO_EXTENSION)
   {
   PLIST_ENTRY headOfList;
   PIRP currentIrp;
   PIO_STACK_LOCATION stack;

   while((headOfList =
          ExInterlockedRemoveHeadList(&fdoExtension->NewRequestsQueue,
                              &fdoExtension->QueueLock)) != NULL)
      { /* dequeue it */
```

The first thing we must do here is clear out the Cancel Routine in case some lower level that doesn't need a Cancel Routine should queue this request. If this routine got cancelled from the lower queue, it would be called again because the Cancel Routine would still be set. We increment the reference count of outstanding IRPs.

```
currentIrp = CONTAINING_RECORD(headOfist, IRP, Tail.Overlay.ListEntry);
IoSetCancelRoutine(currentIrp, NULL);
stack = IoGetCurrentIrpStackLocation(currentIrp);
SD_IoIncrement(fdoExtension); // Page 672
```

If the device is being removed, we complete the IRP with STATUS_DELETE_PENDING.

```
if(fdoExtension->IsRemoved)
   { /* device is being removed */
    currentIrp->IoStatus.Information = 0;
    currentIrp->IoStatus.Status = STATUS_DELETE_PENDING;
    IoCompleteRequest(currentIrp, IO_NO_INCREMENT);
   } /* device is being removed */
 else
```

If we are not removing the device, we pass the queued IRP downward. Finally, we decrement the outstanding-IRP reference count.

```
   { /* pass it down */
    IoSkipCurrentIrpStackLocation(currentIrp);
    IoCallDriver(fdoExtension->NextLowerDriver, currentIrp);
   } /* pass it down */
  SD_IoDecrement(fdoExtension); // Page 672
 } /* dequeue it */
}
```

Listing 28.20: *The Cancel Handler*

The Cancel handler is very straightforward. We complete the IRP with STATUS_CANCELLED. Because this is a Cancel Routine, we must release the global Cancel Spin Lock.

```
VOID SD_CancelQueued(IN PDEVICE_OBJECT DeviceObject, IN PIRP Irp)
   {
    IoSetCancelRoutine(Irp, NULL);

    Irp->IoStatus.Status = STATUS_CANCELLED;
    Irp->IoStatus.Information = 0;
    RemoveEntryList(&Irp->Tail.Overlay.ListEntry);
    IoReleaseCancelSpinLock(Irp->CancelIrql);
    IoCompleteRequest(Irp, IO_NO_INCREMENT);
   }
```

The Pass-Thru Handler

There is this little detail about layered drivers: They are fundamentally implementations of "derived objects", in the object-oriented-programming sense of the phrase. Each layer of the driver chain is a "derived driver" of the layer below it. The IRP_MJ_ functions must be thought of as "virtual functions", which means that if the function is not defined in the current class, it must be handled by the superclass. In the world of drivers, this means that if your driver doesn't know how to implement a particular IRP_MJ_ function code, it must pass it downward in the stack to the next lower-level driver. To fail to do so can result in a system that is erroneous. Back in the `DriverEntry` routine, we initialized all of the `IRP_MJ_` pointers to first point to a function called `SD_Pass`. Then we overrode those assignments with specific handlers for our device. Here, we finally define the `SD_Pass` function.

Listing 28.21: *The Pass-Thru Handler*

```
NTSTATUS SD_Pass(IN PDEVICE_OBJECT DeviceObject, IN PIRP Irp)
    {
      PSD_FDO_EXTENSION fdoExtension;
      NTSTATUS status;
      PIO_STACK_LOCATION stack;

      fdoExtension = (PSD_FDO_EXTENSION)DeviceObject->DeviceExtension;
      stack = IoGetCurrentIrpStackLocation(Irp);
```

Any request that comes in before the device is fully initialized will be queued. There are some constraints on this function. For example, because it does not pay attention to what kind of request it is passing on, it cannot know if the request is being handled at an elevated IRQL. Thus, even if most of the driver is pageable, this function cannot be in pageable code.

For our driver, we will pass all of the non-Plug-and-Play IRPs downward in the stack. We hold any requests that come in while the device is stopped or not yet started.

```
      if(fdoExtension->HoldNewRequests)
          { /* queue it */
           ASSERT(!fdoExtension->IsRemoved);
           status = pSD_QueueRequest(fdoExtension, Irp);   // Page 673
           if(NT_SUCCESS(status))
              status = STATUS_PENDING;
           return status;
          } /* queue it */
```

If we are not holding the request, we simply pass it on to the lower level. We must maintain a "reference count" for the number of outstanding active references to our Device Object. Otherwise, we will have serious problems if we try to shut it down or remove it while there are active references.

```
      SD_IoIncrement(fdoExtension);   // Page 672
```

There are some potential race conditions, and we must be prepared to handle them here. For example, the device might have received a removal request, but the application (or a higher-level driver) was in the midst of generating a new request. So the request comes in after the device is removed. Or, the request came in before the device was started. In either case, we simply fail the request. If the device was removed, we return the special status code, `STATUS_DELETE_PENDING`.

What startled us reading this definitive Microsoft code example was its fundamental conflict with the definitive Microsoft documentation. The Microsoft documentation explicitly states that once the Device Object is created, all IRPs should be queued, pending the starting of the device. Yet this pass-thru code clearly fails all IRPs if the device is not started!

```
        if(fdoExtension->IsRemoved || !fdoExtension->IsStarted)
           { /* fail the request */
            if(fdoExtension->IsRemoved)
               status = STATUS_DELETE_PENDING;
            else
               status = STATUS_UNSUCCESSFUL;
            Irp->IoStatus.Information = 0;
            Irp->IoStatus.Status = status;
            IoCompleteRequest(Irp, IO_NO_INCREMENT);
           } /* fail the request */
        else
           { /* forward the request */
            IoSkipCurrentIrpStackLocation(Irp);
            status = IoCallDriver(fdoExtension->NextLowerDriver, Irp);
           } /* forward the request */
```

*At this point, we are done processing the IRP, at least as far as this driver is concerned.
Either it has been handed off to the lower-level driver, or it has been completed with a
failure code. We can now decrement the reference count and return.*

```
        SD_IoDecrement(fdoExtension); // Page 672
        return status;
    }
```

The `IRP_MJ_POWER` *Handler*

Power IRPs are never queued. They are always sent to the next lower-level driver, unless the
device is being removed.

Listing 28.22: *The* `IRP_MJ_POWER` *Handler*

```
NTSTATUS SD_DispatchPower(IN PDEVICE_OBJECT DeviceObject, IN PIRP Irp)
    {
     PIO_STACK_LOCATION stack;
     PSD_FDO_EXTENSION fdoExtension;
     NTSTATUS status;

     stack = IoGetCurrentIrpStackLocation(Irp);
     fdoExtension = (PSD_FDO_EXTENSION)DeviceObject->DeviceExtension;
```

If the device is marked as being removed, we simply fail the IRP with the
`STATUS_DELETE_PENDING` *code. We then call the* `PoStartNextPowerIrp` *function to
start the next power-related IRP.*

```
     if(fdoExtension->IsRemoved)
        { /* removed */
         status = STATUS_DELETE_PENDING;
         PoStartNextPowerIrp(Irp);
         Irp->IoStatus.Information = 0;
         Irp->IoStatus.Status = status;
         IoCompleteRequest(Irp, IO_NO_INCREMENT);
         return status;
        } /* removed */
```

```
    SD_IoIncrement(fdoExtension); // Page 672
    switch(stack->MinorFunction)
        { /* MinorFunction */
          case IRP_MN_WAIT_WAKE:
          case IRP_MN_POWER_SEQUENCE:
                status =
                 SD_PassDownToNextPowerDriver(DeviceObject, Irp); // Page 677
                break;
          case IRP_MN_QUERY_POWER:
                status = SD_QueryPowerState(DeviceObject, Irp); // Page 678
                break;
          case IRP_MN_SET_POWER:
                status = SD_SetPowerState(DeviceObject, Irp); // Page 678
                break;
          default:
                status =
                 SD_PassDownToNextPowerDriver(DeviceObject, Irp); // Page 677
                break;
        } /* MinorFunction */
    SD_IoDecrement(fdoExtension); // Page 672
    return status;
}
```

The `PassDownToNextPowerDriver` Function

The purpose of the `PassDownToNextPowerDriver` function is to hand the IRP down to the next lower-level driver. To pass it down, we call the `PoCallDriver` function, which is used to call a driver for power management. You must *not* use `IoCallDriver` to pass a power IRP downward in the hierarchy. However, we also must ensure that any pending power-management requests will be processed. To do this, we call `PoStartNextPowerIrp`. The order in which we do this is critical. The `PoStartNextPowerIrp` function must be called for the IRP in its current state. This requires that this function be called *before* you call `PoCallDriver`.

Listing 28.23: *The* `PassDownToNextPowerDriver` *Function*

```
NTSTATUS SD_PassDownToNextPowerDriver(IN PDEVICE_OBJECT DeviceObject,
                                      IN OUT PIRP Irp)
    {
    NTSTATUS status;
    PSD_FDO_EXTESION fdoExtension;

    IoCopyCurrentIrpStackLocationToNext(Irp);

    PoStartNextPowerIrp(Irp);

    fdoExtension = (PSD_FDO_EXTENSION)DeviceObject->DeviceExtension;

    status = PoCallDriver(fdoExtension->NextLowerDriver, Irp);

    return status;

    }
```

Listing 28.24: *The* QueryPowerState *Function*

```
NTSTATUS SD_QueryPowerState(IN PDEVICE_OBJECT DeviceObject,
                            IN OUT PIRP Irp)
    {
      Irp->IoStatus.Status = STATUS_SUCCESS;
      PoStartNextPowerIrp(Irp);
      IoCompleteRequest(Irp, IO_NO_INCREMENT);

      return STATUS_SUCCESS;
    }
```

Listing 28.25: *The* SetPowerState *Function*

Setting the power state is a somewhat complex operation. Power state can be set either for a device or for the entire system. Because power state information must be processed entirely by the lower level drivers before the current level can act on them, the key state information must be maintained for the completion routine. To do this, we define the following structure.

```
typedef struct _FDO_POWER_CONTEXT {
        PowerStateType newPowerType;
        PowerState newPowerState;
} FDO_POWER_CONTEXT, * PFDO_POWER_CONTEXT;
```

We use this structure to pass the information to the completion routine.

```
NTSTATUS SD_SetPowerState(IN PDEVICE_OBJECT DeviceObject,
                          IN OUT PIRP Irp)
    {
      NTSTATUS status = STATUS_SUCCESS;
      PSD_FDO_EXTENSION fdoExtension;
      PIO_STACK_LOCATION stack;
      PFDO_POWER_CONTEXT context;
      BOOLEAN passItDown;

      fdoExtension; = (PSD_FDO_EXTENSION)DeviceObject->DeviceExtension;
      stack = IoGetCurrentIrpStackLoation(Irp);

      context = ExAllocatePool(NonPagedPool, sizeof(FDO_POWER_CONTEXT));

      if(context == NULL)
         { /* failed */
           status = STATUS_NO_MEMORY;
         } /* failed */
       else
         { /* got memory */
```

Having successfully initialized the assorted variables, we can now process the power-management request. We first zero the data structure we pass as the context *parameter, which we conveniently call* context *in this function as well. Then we assign the power type and power state parameters from the IRP. This data structure will be used in the completion routine. Since we did an* ExAllocatePool *to get the storage, we know the pointer will be valid when it is needed.*

```
RtlZeroMemory(context, sizeof(FDO_POWER_CONTEXT));
stack = IoGetCurrentIrpStackLocation(Irp);

context->newPowerType = stack->Parameters.Power.Type;
context->newPowerState = stack->Parameters.Power.State;
passItDown = TRUE;
```

We next dispatch based on the power type. This code recognizes the two defined power type requests: a request for a system power state change and a request for a device power state change.

```
switch(stack->Parameters.Power.Type)
   { /* power type */
    case SystemPowerState:
       if(fdoExtension->SystemPowerState ==
                   stack->Parameters.Power.State.SystemState)
          { /* no system state change */
           passItDown = FALSE;
          } /* no system state change */
       break;
```

If the request is for a system power state, all we do is pass the request down to the lower level. If the current system state, as established by the last power request, is the same as for the request that just came in, there is no need to pass the request downward. So in this case, we set passItDown *to* FALSE.

```
    case DevicePowerState:
       if(fdoExtension->DevicePowerState !=
                   stack->Parameters.Power.State.DeviceState)
          { /* device state change */
           if(fdoExtension->DevicePowerState == PowerDeviceD0)
              { /* leaving D0 */
               PoSetPowerState(DeviceObject, DevicePowerState,
                            stack->Parameters.Power.State);
              } /* leaving D0 */
          } /* device state change */
       else
          { /* no state change */
           passItDown = FALSE;
          } /* no state change */
       break;
```

The handling for the device power state change is to check to see if there is a state change. If it is not a state change, it is not passed down. If it is a state change—the special case of a transition to power state D0, that is, fully powered on—you must call PoSetPowerState. *Doing this calls any notification routines that have previously been registered by* PoRegisterDeviceNotify. *A handler must call* PoSetPowerState *before it calls* PoStartNextPowerIrp.

If the power state is not one of the previous two states, it is an error and the IRP is failed with STATUS_NOT_IMPLEMENTED.

```
    default:
       ASSERT(FALSE);
       status = STATUS_NOT_IMPLEMENTED;
       break;
   } /* power type */
} /* got memory */
```

If we have succeeded and the passItDown *flag is* TRUE, *we want to pass down to the lower-level driver. Since we must continue our processing after this returns, we set the completion routine and its context and then call* PoCallDriver *to pass the IRP downward.*

```
if(NTSUCCESS(status) && passItDown)
    { /* pass it down */
     IoCopyCurrentIrpStackLocationToNext(Irp);
     IoSetCompletionRoutine(Irp,
                            SD_PowerCompletionRoutine, // Page 680
                            context,   // Context
                            TRUE,      // Complete on success
                            TRUE,      // Complete on error
                            TRUE);     // Complete on cancel
     return PoCallDriver(fdoExtension->NextLowerDriver, Irp);
    } /* pass it down */
}
```

If we do not need to pass it down or there was an error, we complete the IRP at this level. Note that before we complete the request, we call PoStartNextPowerIrp. *This is because once* IoCompleteRequest *is called, the* Irp *pointer, required by* PoStartNextPowerIrp, *is no longer valid. Finally, if we had successfully allocated the context for the completion routine, we delete it because it is no longer needed.*

```
else
    { /* complete it */
     Irp->IoStatus.Information = 0;
     Irp->IoStatus.Status = status;
     PoStartNextPowerIrp(Irp);
     IoCompleteRequest(Irp, IO_NO_INCREMENT);

     if(context != NULL)
        ExFreePool(context);
    } /* complete it */

}
```

Listing 28.26: *The Set-Power Completion Routine*

```
NTSTATUS SD_PowerCompletionRoutine(IN PDEVICE_OBJECT DeviceObject,
                                   IN PIRP Irp,
                                   IN PVOID context)
    {
    PFDO_POWER_CONTEXT powerContext = context;
    PFDO_EXTENSION fdoExtension = DeviceObject->DeviceExtension;
    BOOL setState;

    if(NTSUCCESS(Irp->IoStatus.Status))
        { /* successful completion */
         setState = TRUE;
         switch(powerContext->newPowerType)
             { /* power type */
              case SystemPowerState:
                 fdoExtension->SystemPowerState =
                                 powerContext->newPowerState.SystemState;
             break;
```

```
            case DevicePowerState:
                if(fdoExtension->DevicePowerState == PowerDeviceD0)
                    { /* in D0 */
                      setPowerState = FALSE;
                    } /* in D0 */
                fdoExtension->DevicePowerState =
                            powerContext->newPowerState.DeviceState;
            break;
        } /* power type */
    if(setPowerState)
        PoSetPowerState(DeviceObject,
                        powerContext->newPowerType,
                        powerContext->newPowerState);
    } /* successful completion */
```

Now that we have completed the processing of this Power IRP, we tell the Power Management system that it can start the next Power IRP.

```
    PoStartNextPowerIrp(Irp);
```

Now that we are done with the context block, we must delete it. Otherwise, we would have a storage leak. Note that any operation which has an asynchronous completion and for which some kernel resource was allocated must have a completion routine established to release the kernel resource. The most common kernel resource that you will deal with this way is memory, which can be allocated in a variety of ways such as driver-allocated IRPs, driver-allocated MDLs, and so on, in addition to the type of raw allocation that we illustrate here.

```
    ExFreePool(context);

    return Irp->IoStatus.Status;
    }
```

The Unload Handler

A Windows 2000 Unload handler is vastly simpler than its NT 4.0 counterpart. For example, a Windows 2000 Unload handler does not need to iterate down the chain of Device Objects and delete each object. It is not even called until all of the Device Objects have been removed. In Windows 2000, the Device Objects are removed by the IRP_MJ_PNP handler for the IRP_MN_REMOVE_DEVICE code; see page 667. A Windows 2000 Unload handler is shown in its entirety as follows.

```
void SD_Unload(IN PDRIVER_OBJECT DriverObject)
    {
    }
```

Summary

This chapter has presented, as best we can tell with the available information, the general principles and key details of writing a Windows 2000 Device Driver. The repartitioning of the task introduces new complexities, but buys significant power and flexibility. This is the Future of Device Drivers.

29 *I/O Hardware: The Universal Serial Bus*

The Universal Serial Bus (USB) is an important technology, supported in Windows 98 and Windows 2000. This chapter covers the basic concepts of the USB and goes into some depth about the protocols. This is a distillation of the information covered far more extensively in the Mind-Share book *Universal Serial Bus System Architecture,* which hereafter we refer to as "USBSA", cited in the Further Reading section at the end of the chapter. We elided much of the detailed information that is normally hidden from the programmer by the lower-level USB drivers, such as Hub Management.

Overview of External Busses

An *external bus* is a bus that is interconnected via one of the internal busses, such as ISA, EISA, or PCI. External busses include IDE, SCSI, USB, and IEEE-1394. The distinction among them becomes a bit confusing because some of them can overlap. For example, some memory devices attached to IEEE-1394, such as hard drives or CD-ROMs, can use SCSI commands sent on the IEEE-1394 bus. In this sense, an external bus such as SCSI might appear in another context as a protocol within the protocol of a different bus.

Need for the Universal Serial Bus

The Universal Serial Bus (USB) came about for several reasons.

- There aren't enough low-speed ports on a standard PC.

- Those that exist have serious limitations, for example the limit of two serial ports on most machines (some machines that claim to support four ports, can't). While there are many multiport serial boards around, they are expensive and sometimes hard to deal with because of the *ad hoc* nature of their interfaces.

- The myriad different devices, their different drivers, their different connections, and their different protocols is a nightmare to manage. While Plug-and-Play is making inroads into this complexity, it isn't there yet and might not be for years. This is because a plethora of legacy devices are not really Plug-and-Play-compatible, while the USB- or IEEE-1394-based alternatives are not even being considered by many vendors.

- Adding or removing a device is a complex procedure that requires a power-down of the machine, physical disassembly of the case, removal of the card (with the attendant hazards of physical and static electricity damage to the motherboard), and reassembly of the case. This is not reasonable for the casual, nontechnical user.

The outgrowth of all of this is the USB standard. Together with other emerging standards, this standard effectively reduces to nearly zero the need to open the case to add a device. Many types of low-bandwidth devices can be added to a USB machine simply by plugging them into a suitable outlet, including modems, ISDN connections, keyboards, and MIDI (music synthesizer protocol) ports, as well as mice, joysticks, and other pointing devices. Further, these outlets can be tiered. One of the design goals of the USB was that any device had to be *hot-pluggable*, that is, it can be added to or removed from a running machine without requiring a power-down operation. This requirement comes in part from careful electrical specifications so that adding or removing a device, or even a lot of devices, doesn't cause "spikes" on the signal lines that can destroy the electronics of other devices. However, it comes largely from the existence of very sophisticated Device Drivers that can detect that a device has been removed and then can deal with that event and, particularly, understand that the device's removal might be temporary and that when the device is plugged in again, it should be made functional without disrupting any programs that depend on it.

Table 29.1: *The USB at a Glance*

Bandwidth	Full-speed: 12Mb/sec (1.5MB/sec). Low-speed: 1.5Mb/sec (187.5KB/sec).
Topology	Tiered-star. Host-centric.
Power distribution	Devices can be powered from the USB cable or can be self-powered.
Power management	Individual devices, entire subtrees, or the entire USB can be put in a power-down state.
Plug-and-Play	Devices are self-identifying. Bus detects and reports connect and disconnect events.
Transactions	Input, output, control, and isochronous transactions.
Cable/electrical	Simple 4-wire cable with power distribution and differential signal; unique connectors make loops impossible.

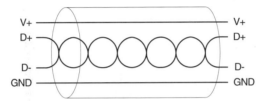

Figure 29.1: *USB cable.*

USB Implementation

Physically, a USB is a 4-wire serial connector that handles its data via serial transmission. Data rates are specified at 1.5Mb/sec and 12Mb/sec. The lower speed allows interfacing to slower, lower-cost peripherals, while the higher speed allows support of such devices as ISDN. For those devices that need more bandwidth, the IEEE-1394 "FireWire" bus provides for speeds up to a current specification of 1.2Gb/sec. A key to the design of the USB was the low number of gates (1,500–2,000) required to implement the USB interface on peripherals. The USB connectors are asymmetric, so a source and a sink cannot be connected in such a way as to form a loop. The cable, depicted in Figure 29.1, uses a differential voltage transmission along a twisted-pair to gain reliability, particularly noise immunity. The icon shown in Figure 29.2 is used to identify USB cable connections.

Figure 29.2: *USB connection icon.*

Logically, the USB is actually a cascadable network that includes the ability to have any device built to act as a "hub" and split the signal in a tree-like fashion. In any configuration, there can be up to 127 USB devices on a bus, with the actual number depending on the power requirements. Simple USB devices (such as mice) can be powered directly from the USB cable, and a hub port can supply from 100 mA to 500 mA to its devices. Generally, but not always, devices that will act as hubs are those that have significant power requirements that cannot be supplied by the bus (for example, a USB flatbed scanner or a USB printer). Such devices can supply additional power to USB devices that are plugged into them. According to the USB specification, a powered hub port is required to support no more than four unpowered devices.

Most of the good ideas from MCA, EISA, and PCI come to maturity in the USB. Devices are self-identifying, with generic headers for key device parameters and with device-specific extensions for each device that are handled by its specific driver. Although the target to which the USB is connected is not specified, at least one vendor is currently producing a PCI-to-USB interface card. In the abstract, a USB card gets to specify its interrupt level and priority, and these specifications can be modified by the software that is doing overall system configuration management. As with PCI or EISA, it is possible to have several USB devices interrupting at the same IRQ level.

For those of you who want to see the USB in exquisite detail, we suggest the *USBSA* (actually, we feel this book is an essential companion for a USB programmer and is *not* optional). The full USB specification can be found in the *Universal Serial Bus Specification, Version 1.0*, also cited in the Further Reading section at the end of the chapter. This document also is essential if you are going to program the USB. We highlight only parts of the USB standard in this book.

USB Architecture

A sample USB configuration is shown in Figure 29.3. It is important to realize that this is just one of many ways the user might have chosen to plug together these components. This might be the configuration on Tuesday at 3:00 p.m., but the 3:30 p.m. configuration might be quite different. And the machine did not have to be powered down to replug to the new configuration!

A USB host controller card typically presents two USB *ports* (the basic specification suggests two). In the figure, the keyboard is plugged into one port and the laser printer into the other. The keyboard also has two ports and acts as a hub. Into one side of the keyboard (the one on the left in the drawing), a mouse and a joystick have been plugged in. On the other side of the keyboard, a display has been connected. The display also acts as a hub; into it, two speakers have been connected. USB bandwidth is too low for the actual display data, but the display *control*, such as centering, height, width, brightness, contrast, and other parameters, can be controlled over the bus, thus removing all of those (actually expensive) controls from the monitor itself.

From the other USB port is the laser printer, which also acts as a two-port hub. Only one of its ports is used; a flatbed scanner is connected to it. A modem is then connected to one of the scanner's ports.

Note that we have illustrated tree-based hub connections (the keyboard to the joystick, mouse, and monitor) and serial chaining (laser printer to scanner to modem). All of these are permissible, up to a total of 127 devices on the USB bus. The overall topology of a USB is what is known as a *tiered star*, where hubs provide connections for multiple devices.

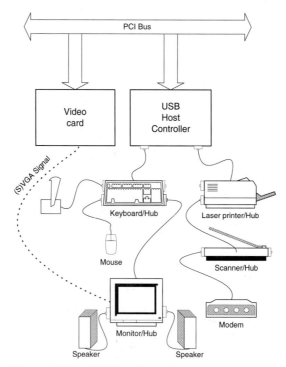

Figure 29.3: *A USB configuration.*

In addition to devices that act as hubs, there are freestanding hubs whose sole purpose is to provide fanout on the bus. These hubs contain no devices or endpoints other than those that support the hub itself.

The Root Hub

The root of the USB tree is the *root hub*, which is part of the USB controller. The USB Device Driver controls the root hub. It is responsible for initiating USB *transactions*. A transaction will specify the USB address of the device, the type of transfer, the direction of transfer, and the address of the associated memory buffer.

Once a transaction has been placed on the USB, the appropriate device detects it based on the device address in the transaction. The device responds, and its response is routed back to the root hub, which transfers the response to the appropriate application program via the Device Drivers.

The root hub supports not only data but also such operations as powering its ports on or off, enabling or disabling its ports, recognizing the devices on each of its ports, and reporting port status.

The root hub sends out a new *frame* every 1 ms. Note that this imposes some fundamental bandwidth limitations on interactions; this is why the USB is primarily intended for low-bandwidth human-interaction devices. High-bandwidth human-interaction devices, such as eye trackers, some kinds of hand transducers (such as gloves), and body motion transducers will probably not work well on the USB. The 1-ms frame time is too long.

Endpoints

The devices at the nodes and leaves of the bus topology are called *endpoints*. A particular physical object plugged into the bus might present several different endpoints, that is, it might be a multifunction device. For example, a combination fax/printer/copier/modem device might present four or more endpoints. Every USB device has at least one endpoint, endpoint 0, which is used for configuration and basic control.

Low-speed functions can have at most two optional endpoints beyond endpoint 0. High-speed functions can have up to 16 input endpoints and 16 output endpoints.

An endpoint cannot be used until it is configured.

Pipes

A USB *pipe* is a logical connection established between the host and an endpoint. The USB specification requires that the host software establish and maintain these pipes. From the viewpoint of the Device Driver writer, you will normally establish a pipe by the existence of a Device Object in the I/O system.

Each pipe will support one of two mutually exclusive pipe communication modes:

- A stream pipe, which moves data with no USB-defined structure
- A message pipe, which moves data with a USB-defined structure

Pipes also have several associated properties:

- A claim on bus access and bandwidth
- A transfer type
- Endpoint characteristics, including such parameters as the direction (input or output) and maximum data payload size, which are determined when the pipe is established as part of the configuration transaction

Endpoint 0 always exists, and therefore there is always a pipe to endpoint 0 of a device. This is called the *default pipe*. The default pipe is normally used for operations such as device identification and configuration transactions. After the device is configured, the default pipe can be used for other device interactions.

Transfer Types

Each USB function (a device could contain many functions) has a set of registers. These registers define the endpoints used by the software driver to access the function. Each endpoint has a particular set of transfer types that it supports. The most important types are

- isochronous
- interrupt
- control
- bulk

Isochronous Transfers

This type of transfer is the one that will be most unfamiliar to most programmers. Isochronous (literally, "uniform time") transfers are primarily required by real-time devices, such as speakers,[1] digital sound synthesizers, and even MIDI devices. Isochronous data is much like a datagram packet sent at high priority on a token-ring network, if that analogy helps you. Isochronous transfers do not guarantee the delivery of data, or the delivery of valid data, but they *do* guarantee *regular* delivery.[2]

---

[1] A data dropout of 1 ms is a noticeably ugly discontinuity in digital sound. This suggests that "speakers" on a USB are not pure digital-to-analog converters. Rather, they would probably have some amount of buffering required to match the isochronous packet rate of the USB with the need to deliver continuous sound. If the CD sampling rate is used, then 44,100 16-bit samples, or just over 700Kb/sec, are required for each channel. This is well within even the low-speed USB data rates, even when other devices are operating on the bus.

[2] In an experiment done around 1990 at Carnegie-Mellon University (CMU), it was observed that every level of the network protocol stack performed a checksum on the data, *even though the hardware at the lowest level generated checksums on output and validated checksums on reception*. Researchers built a video delivery system that could run three channels of full-motion, 24-bit NTSC-resolution video on a 16Mb token ring. Through the elimination of *all* software checksum computations, the observed error rate was nearly zero. The only glitches occurred when a machine in the token ring was powered up or down. Although there is a temptation to be mistrustful of "external" networks such as the USB, they are, in the words of the principal researcher in the CMU work, "as reliable as an internal circuit wire".

There are three methods that an isochronous device can use to match its data rate to the system.

- Asynchronous matching, in which endpoints send or receive data based on either an external clock or a free-running local clock. Synchronization is not relative to the 1-ms frame time of the USB. This is most commonly used for audio data.

- Synchronous matching, which is a negotiation between the device and its driver. A device might synchronize to the 1-ms USB frame interval, or it might require that its driver modify the 1-ms interval to an interval to which it wishes to synchronize. On a USB, one (and only one) device can become a "bus master clock" and force start-of-frame synchronization timing.

- Adaptive matching, in which a device has the freedom to synchronize to the start-of-frame timing, even if it is being adjusted by some other device acting as a synchronous bus master clock.

Isochronous transfer takes place during each (nominally 1 ms) frame time. An isochronous data packet is limited to 1,023 bytes (this gives a maximum of about 1MB/sec, enough to support "CD-quality", 16-bit audio on one channel, with some considerable slack). Isochronous transfers apply only to high-speed USB channels. Table 29.2, reproduced from the *Universal Serial Bus Specification, Version 1.0*, shows the isochronous transfer bandwidth limits. A given endpoint has a maximum data payload that it can accommodate. For an isochronous pipe, either

Table 29.2: *Isochronous Transaction Limits*

Data Payload	Maximum Bandwidth	Frame Bandwidth per Transaction	Maximum Transactions	Bytes Remaining	Bytes per Frame of Useful Data
1	150,000	1%	150	0	150
2	272,000	1%	136	4	272
4	460,000	1%	115	5	460
8	704,000	1%	88	4	704
16	960,000	2%	60	0	960
32	1,152,000	3%	36	24	1,152
64	1,280,000	5%	20	40	1,280
128	1,280,000	9%	10	130	1,280
256	1,280,000	18%	5	175	1,280
512	1,024,000	35%	2	458	1,024
1,023	1,023,000	69%	1	468	1,023
Max	1,500,000				1,500

Packet overhead: 9 bytes (2 sync, 2 pids, 2 EP+CRC, 2 CRC, 1 interpacket).

Excerpted from *Universal Serial Bus Specification, Version 1.0*, January 1996.

this must be met with the available bus bandwidth or the pipe cannot be established. Thus, there is a limit on the total number of isochronous devices that can be supported in a given USB configuration; the sum of the required bandwidth cannot exceed the available bus bandwidth. Note that a given transaction can be *less* than the maximum packet size, but the maximum packet size must be assumed in the computation of bus bandwidth usage. Note that packet sizes of 64..256 actually deliver maximum bandwidth.

Because of the synchronization requirement, there is usually no opportunity to retransmit a packet. It arrives either intact or damaged. If it is damaged, there is no way for the device to request a retry. Consider the implications of keeping sound synchronized with video; retransmitting a packet will accumulate an error between the audio and video until "lip synch" is lost. Retransmitting a sound packet will also cause an audio glitch. If only one bit is corrupted in the message, there might be a 23-microsecond "glitch", which will probably not be noticeable. But a 1-ms "stutter" will definitely be audible! It is the responsibility of the implementor of an isochronous endpoint to determine how the endpoint will deal with a missing or corrupted packet.

Audio is the most sensitive perceptual system we have. An untrained listener can detect a 30-ms error in a supposedly "regular" sequence of beats, such as a drum beat. A drummer or other trained listener can detect a 10-ms error in a rhythmic sequence. If two sounds are supposed to occur at the same time (a wood block and a drum, for example), an untrained listener can detect a 1-ms error in synchronization. For stereo perception, an untrained listener can detect a phase differential of 17 μs between left and right ear perception. By comparison, visually, a video can regularly drop an entire frame (substituting the previous frame), a 33-ms dropout, and it is hard for a viewer to see this unless it happens very often within a short interval. The aural perception system also has a wider dynamic range of volume than the visual system has of brightness and can recover from overload much faster. Audio is the most unforgiving medium as far as user perception of errors goes.

Interrupt Transfers

USB devices do not generate interrupts in the controller. If a device requires attention, it waits until it is polled to report the status. It is the responsibility of the Device Driver to poll each USB device at a selected interval to see if it has anything that requires attention. If a USB device requires attention, it returns a data packet containing its status, an *interrupt transaction*. While a USB root hub might generate hardware interrupts, these are specific to the USB root hub and do not represent any device status on the bus. However, a notice that a device requires service will eventually be routed, via the root hub software, to the appropriate driver for the USB device. This delivery completes the interrupt transfer. Eventually, the root hub driver software will cause this event to call the appropriate driver for the USB device. However, you, as the Device Driver writer, can't really tell if the interrupt was a "real" hardware interrupt or was generated by an interrupt transaction. Table 29.3 shows the maximum interrupt transaction limits for full-speed (12Mb/sec) devices, and Table 29.4 shows the maximum interrupt transaction limits for low-speed (1.5Mb/sec) devices.

A high-speed USB device can be polled as often as once every frame or as infrequently as once every 255th frame. A low-speed USB device can be polled as often as once every 10 ms or as infrequently as once every 255 ms. Failure to poll a USB device "often enough" can result in data loss as the device's internal buffers overflow. The exact polling interval is specified as part of the *ENDPOINT descriptor*, the property information contained in the device.

Table 29.3: *Full-Speed Interrupt Transaction Limits*

Data Payload	Maximum Bandwidth (bytes/sec)	Frame Bandwidth per Transaction	Maximum Transactions	Bytes Remaining	Bytes per Frame of Useful Data
1	107,000	1%	107	2	107
2	200,000	1%	100	0	200
4	352,000	1%	88	4	352
8	568,000	1%	71	9	568
16	816,000	2%	51	21	816
32	1,056,000	3%	33	15	1,056
64	1,216,000	5%	19	37	1,216
Max	1,500,000				1,500
Packet overhead: 13 bytes (3 sync, 3 pids, 2 EP+CRC, 2 CRC, 3 interpacket).					
Excerpted from *Universal Serial Bus Specification, Version 1.0*, January 1996.					

Table 29.4: *Low-Speed Interrupt Transaction Limits*

Data Payload	Maximum Bandwidth (bytes/sec)	Frame Bandwidth per Transaction	Maximum Transactions	Bytes Remaining	Bytes per Frame of Useful Data
1	13,000	7%	13	5	13
2	24,000	8%	12	7	24
4	352,000	9%	11	0	44
8	568,000	11%	8	19	64
Max	187,500				187
Packet overhead: 13 bytes (3 sync, 3 pids, 2 EP+CRC, 2 CRC, 3 interpacket).					
Excerpted from *Universal Serial Bus Specification, Version 1.0*, January 1996.					

Unlike isochronous transfers, interrupt transfers are error checked and can be retransmitted if received incorrectly. An interrupt transfer that needs to be retransmitted will be retransmitted at the next service interval for the device.

Control Transfers

A *control transfer* is used to set up, query, or modify the state of USB devices. Each USB device is required to support a default control endpoint, endpoint 0, which is used for configuring the device and for basic device control. This endpoint always responds to certain USB control transfers. It is typically used to deal with the situation in which a device is detected and its state must be queried, such as what device it is. This allows the software to respond to the insertion of a device and load the appropriate drivers for it.

A control transfer can have as many as three stages:

- The setup stage, during which information is transferred to the device that defines the nature of the request
- The optional data stage, which is needed only for those transfers that require data (read or write); the data stage is limited to a 64-byte "data payload" (excluding assorted header and trailer bytes)
- The status stage, which reports the result of the operation

Control transfers can be error-checked and can be retransmitted if received incorrectly.

Bulk Transfers

A *bulk transfer* is used for time *in*sensitive devices. A printer, modem output, some scanners, some tape drives, and the like might not require precise delivery on time. Bulk transfers are available only for full-speed USB devices. The limits on bulk transfer transactions are shown in Table 29.5.

The bandwidth requirements of the USB are that 90% of the available bandwidth is allocated for isochronous transfers and interrupt transfers and 10% is allocated for control transfers. This doesn't leave much bandwidth for bulk transfers. Actually, the specification is that these percentages must be guaranteed to those transfers *if needed*. If there are no isochronous transfers or if the full bandwidth is not required, then whatever bandwidth is left over in a frame is available for bulk transfers. Thus, in the presence of high isochronous and interrupt traffic, it is possible for a bulk transfer to be delayed by arbitrary amounts of time. The USB specification does not guarantee either bandwidth or minimum latency for bulk transfers.

Table 29.5: *Bulk Transfer Transaction Limits*

Data Payload	Maximum Bandwidth	Frame Bandwidth per Transaction	Maximum Transactions	Bytes Remaining	Bytes per Frame of Useful Data
1	107,000	1%	107	2	107
2	200,000	1%	100	0	200
4	352,000	1%	88	4	352
8	568,000	1%	71	9	568
16	816,000	2%	51	21	816
32	1,056,000	3%	33	15	1,056
64	1,216,000	5%	19	37	1,216
Max	1,500,000				1,500
Packet overhead: 13 bytes (3 sync, 3 pids, 2 EP+CRC, 2 CRC, 3 interpacket).					
Excerpted from *Universal Serial Bus Specification, Version 1.0*, January 1996.					

Bulk transfers take place in packet sizes of 8, 16, 32, or 64 bytes. Each device specifies its maximum packet size, which must be one of the values given. When bulk transfers are done, all data packets except the last must be the maximum packet size or the operation will be terminated with an error condition.

Bulk transfers can be error-checked and retransmitted if received incorrectly.

Packet Bandwidth

Whenever a new pipe is created for a USB device, the host must calculate how much bus bandwidth is required to support a given transaction. The bus time required is based on

- the maximum packet size for an endpoint
- the protocol overhead for the specific request
- the overhead imposed by the need to do bit-stuffing[3]
- interpacket delay times required by the protocol
- intertransaction timings

The formulae shown in Table 29.6 give the bus transaction times in nanoseconds. These are from Chapter 5 of the *Universal Serial Bus Specification, Version 1.0*.

Table 29.6: *Bus Transaction Times*

Definition of Variables	
N	Byte count of data payload.
D_{host}	Host delay. Time required for the host to prepare for or recover from the transmission. For example, interrupt latency will be a component of D_{host}. D_{host} is implementation-specific to the host.
D_{LSHub}	Time allowed by the host controller for a hub to enable a low-speed port. This is measured as the delay from the end of PRE PID to the start of low-speed SYNC. It is by definition limited to a maximum of four full-speed bit times.
BitStuff(N)	The theoretical additional time required due to bit-stuffing in the signaling for a packet of size N. The worst case is $1.1668 \times 8 \times N$
Full-Speed Input	
	Nonisochronous transfer, handshake included:
	$9107 + (83.54 \times \lfloor 3.167 + BitStuff(N) \rfloor) + D_{host}$
	Isochronous transfer, no handshake included:
	$7268 + (83.54 \times \lfloor 3.167 + BitStuff(N) \rfloor) + D_{host}$

[3] Bit-stuffing is an artifact of certain kinds of encodings, such as the Non-Return-to-Zero (NRZI encoding used on the USB). In bit-stuffing, entirely gratuitous bits are inserted in the bit stream to force a transition. This helps keep the signals in sync or enable more-accurate clock recovery from the data stream. This function is handled automatically by the USB transmitting hardware; the USB receiving hardware recognizes stuffed bits and discards them. The Good News is that you basically don't need to worry about this. The Bad News is that bit-stuffing does impact total bandwidth, so as you push the limits you *do* need to worry about this.

Table 29.6: *Bus Transaction Times (continued)*

Full-Speed Output		
	Nonisochronous transfer, handshake included:	
	$9107 \pm (83.54 \times \lfloor 3.167 + BitStuff(N) \rfloor) + D_{host}$	
	Isochronous transfer, no handshake included:	
	$6265 + (83.54 \times \lfloor 3.167 + BitStuff(N) \rfloor) + D_{host}$	
Low-Speed Input		
	$64,060 + (676.67 \times \lfloor 3.167 + BitStuff(N) \rfloor) + D_{host}$	
Low-Speed Output		
	$64,107 + (667.0 \times \lfloor 3.167 + BitStuff(N) \rfloor) + D_{host}$	

USB Packet Protocols

Each USB *transaction* consists of several phases, shown in Figure 29.4. All transactions are defined by three phases:

- The *token phase*, which is a header that specifies the nature of the transaction and, for those transactions directed to a specific device, contains the device address
- The *data packet phase*, which is used when the transaction requires data to be transmitted
- The *handshake packet phase*, which is used for transactions that can be error-checked and retried (all but isochronous transactions); this phase contains the additional hand-shaking information

Transactions are contained in *packets*. Most of the details of what a packet looks like are invisible to you, but for completeness, we show them in Figure 29.5. Packets are described in much more detail in Chapter 7 of *USBSA*.

The *Synchronization (Sync)* sequence is used to allow the hardware to recognize that a packet is coming and to lock in on it. It also lets the device determine if a low-speed or high-

Figure 29.4: *USB transaction structure.*

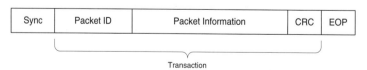

Figure 29.5: *USB packet format.*

speed packet is being transmitted. This is a hardware function and is handled automatically by the hardware.

The *Packet ID* defines the nature of the packet. Following are the major types of packets:

- Token packets, which indicate the beginning of a transaction
- Data packets, which transfer data to or from a USB device
- Handshake packets, which are used to report success or failure of a checked transaction
- Special packets, which are used for purposes other than the previous ones (currently, the only defined special packet is a packet that is used to enable low-speed ports)

After the actual *Packet Information* is a *Cyclic Redundancy Check* (*CRC*). Data packets use a 16-bit CRC; all other packets have a 5-bit CRC. The CRC applies only to the packet information. (A separate check sequence applies to the Packet ID, which is described in detail in *USBSA*.) Finally, there is a hardware-generated *EOP (End-Of-Packet)* sequence that indicates the end of the USB packet.

The various packet types and their uses are given in the following sections. Packets form the basis of the transfer protocols, which are discussed starting on page 700.

SOF Packet

Unless you are writing an actual USB Adapter Device Driver, you will probably never need to worry about a Start-Of-Frame (SOF) packet. The format of this packet includes a frame number and 5-bit CRC and is discussed in *USBSA*. A SOF packet is sent every 1 ms, independent of the bus clock timing. The bus clock timing can be changed to support a particular isochronous endpoint.

IN Packet

The IN packet notifies a USB device that the system wishes to read information from the device. IN transactions can be used for any transfer type: interrupt, bulk, isochronous, and the data phase of control transfers. An IN transaction starts with an IN packet sent by the root hub to the device. The IN packet has a Packet ID, the USB target device and endpoint ID, and a 5-bit CRC. The USB device responds by sending a data packet back to the root. For a checked transaction, the root hub sends a handshake packet back to the device.

OUT Packet

The OUT packet notifies a USB device that the system wishes to send it information. OUT transactions are used for bulk transfers, the data phase of control transfers, and isochronous transfers. An OUT packet has a Packet ID, the USB target device and endpoint ID, and a 5-bit CRC. An OUT packet is followed immediately by a data packet and, for bulk transfers, a handshake packet.

SETUP Packet

This packet is used only during the setup stage of a control transfer. A control transfer starts with a SETUP packet, is followed immediately by a DATA0 packet, and then by an acknowledge packet. A number of standard setup transactions are defined for USB devices. A SETUP transaction can be followed by IN or OUT transactions and optionally by a status stage in which a data packet is transferred from the USB device back to the root hub.

DATA0 and DATA1 Packets

The DATA0 and DATA1 packets handle transfers of up to 1,023 bytes between the device and the host. For some devices, particularly isochronous devices, if there is sufficient bandwidth, a transmitter of data might be able to detect that the data has not been received correctly and so retransmit the data packet. (While the USB specification does not provide for or require any handshaking on isochronous packets, an implementor is free to add additional mechanisms using interrupt or control transfers to provide device-specific validation.) In some cases, this can be expedited by the use of *data toggles*, in which alternating packets are sent as either DATA0 or DATA1 packets. Thus a retransmission of a packet will have the same toggle as the previously sent packet, and the receiver can use this information to discard the redundant packet. There are certain operations, such as configuring the endpoint, that will reset the data toggle to DATA0. The driver software must be aware of these effects and, if one of these operations is performed, reset its internal state to send a DATA0 packet as the next packet, even if a DATA1 packet would otherwise have been the next one sent. For an endpoint that does not support data toggles, only DATA0 packets should be sent.

The handling of data toggle, especially in the case of error, can be quite complex. For the details, we refer you to Chapter 8 of the *USBSA*.

Handshake Packets: ACK, NAK, and STALL

USB devices use handshake packets to provide the status for a transaction. For a checked transaction (that is, anything other than an isochronous transaction), the receiver of a data packet must send a handshake packet to the sender.

- An ACK packet acknowledges that the data has been successfully received.

- A NAK packet reports to the root hub that the device cannot accept or send data, thereby indicating that this is a temporary condition. A NAK is also used during interrupt transactions to indicate that there is no pending interrupt request from the device.

- A STALL packet indicates a permanent condition. If the device finds itself in a state in which it requires serious intervention by the host to recover, it uses the STALL packet. For example, a modem whose output buffer is still full will respond to an OUT packet with a NAK, but a modem that might have a wrong transmission speed set or that has lost a connection will probably respond with a STALL packet. It is suggested by the USB specification that any device that delivers a STALL packet for a request should cause the request to be returned to the user with an error return.

PRE Packets

A special *preamble* (PRE) packet can be issued by the host. It is used to enable bus traffic to downstream low-speed devices.

Transaction Details

In this section, we discuss the types of *transactions* that can take place. A transaction, according to the USB specification, consists of a *token packet*, an optional *data packet*, and an optional *handshake packet*. Depending on the nature of the transaction, specific packets are allowed, or required. The following sections describe each of the transaction types and the packets that are used to form a transaction under various conditions. For example, there are five distinct forms of IN transactions and OUT transactions.

IN Transactions

The way a function responds to an IN packet is shown in Table 29.7.

- If the token is received corrupted, the function does nothing. Eventually, the requestor will timeout and reissue the command.
- If the endpoint is stalled, it can issue a STALL packet in return, informing the host that the endpoint is stalled. The host, in turn, will return the input request to the application with an error code. The application can then decide what to do about the situation.
- If the function has no data to transmit (either it is not ready or there is some internal, recoverable error that will be handled by the endpoint), a NAK packet is sent. Otherwise, the function will send the requested data.

Table 29.7: *Function Responses to an IN Transaction*

Token Received Corrupted	Function Tx Endpoint Stalled	Function Can Transmit Data	Action Taken
Yes	Don't care	Don't care	Returns no response.
No	Yes	Don't care	Issues a STALL handshake.
No	No	No	Issues a NAK handshake.
No	No	Yes	Issues a data packet.

The host response is simpler. If the data packet is corrupted or the host has some internal error that keeps it from accepting the packet (such as buffer overflow), it merely discards the packet. It does not issue a NAK or otherwise handshake. It is up to the function to detect that an ACK has not been received within the timeout period and, if not, to request a retransmission. These actions are summarized in Table 29.8. See Chapter 8 of *USBSA* for a detailed discussion of how to handle timeouts.

Table 29.8: *Host Responses to an IN Transaction*

Data Packet Corrupted	Host Can Accept Data	Action Taken
Yes	Don't care	Discards data; no response.
No	No	Discards data; no response.
No	Yes	Accepts data, issues ACK

OUT Transactions

The way a function responds to an OUT packet is shown in Table 29.9.

- If the token is received corrupted, the function does nothing. Eventually, the requestor will time out and reissue the command.

- If the endpoint is stalled, it can issue a STALL packet in return, informing the host that the endpoint is stalled. The host, in turn, will return the output request to the application with an error code. The application can then decide what to do about the situation.

- If the function is maintaining sequence bits and there is a mismatch, the function returns an ACK but discards the packet.

- If the function cannot receive data (either it is not ready or there is some internal, recoverable error that will be handled by the endpoint), a NAK packet is sent. Otherwise, the function will accept the requested data.

See Chapter 8 of *USBSA* for a detailed discussion of how to handle error recovery and timeouts.

Table 29.9: *Function Responses to an OUT Transaction*

Data Packet Corrupted	Receiver Stalled	Sequence Bits Mismatch	Function Can Accept Data	Handshake Returned
Yes	Don't care	Don't care	Don't care	None
No	Yes	Don't care	Don't care	STALL
No	No	Yes	Don't care	ACK
No	No	No	Yes	ACK
No	No	No	No	NAK

SETUP Transactions

A SETUP transaction is a specialized host-to-function transaction that permits the host to initialize the endpoint's synchronization bits. When a function receives a SETUP transaction, it *must* accept the data; a SETUP transaction cannot generate a STALL or NAK response. A SETUP transaction can be accepted only by a control endpoint; for example, endpoint 0 (although a function might have other control endpoints to which a SETUP can be sent). If a noncontrol endpoint receives a SETUP, it must ignore it and return no response.

IN Transactions

The packet protocols for each of the possible input transactions on the USB are shown in Table 29.10. If you are writing a USB driver, you will need to understand each of these transactions. Also, if you have a USB monitor (the hardware type that plugs into the USB) or are using one of the software USB diagnostic tools available from the USB Developers Forum, you'll likely find it useful to know the general shape of these transactions and how the various packets flow.

Table 29.10: *IN Transactions*

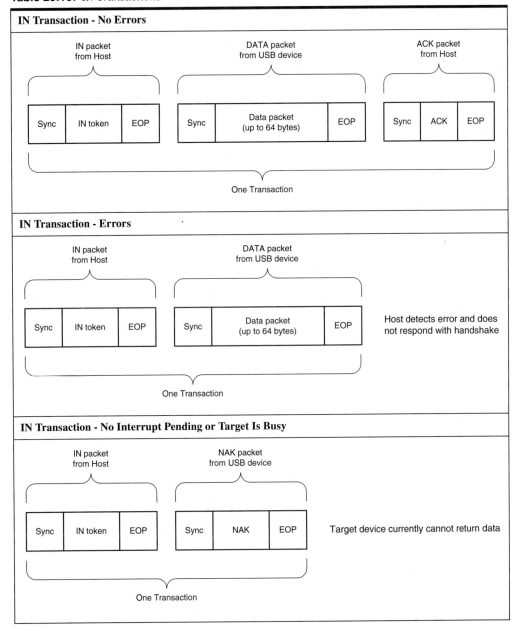

Table 29.10: *IN Transactions (continued)*

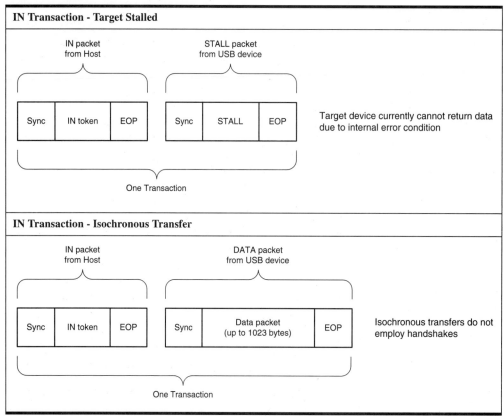

OUT Transactions

The packet protocols for each of the possible output transactions on the USB are shown in Table 29.11. As with the IN transactions in the previous section, if you are writing a USB driver, you will need to understand each of these transactions. Also, if you have a USB monitor (the hardware type that plugs into the USB) or are using one of the software USB diagnostic tools available from the USB Developers Forum, you'll likely find it useful to know the general shape of these transactions and how the various packets flow.

SETUP Transactions and Control Transfers

A control transfer is always initiated by the host. It has either two stages or three. All control transfers start with a SETUP packet, called the *setup stage*. The data phase of a SETUP transaction contains 8 bytes of information that defines the device request to be performed.

In a two-stage control transfer, the second stage is the *status stage*. In this type of transfer, the status stage transfers data from the device to the host.

A three-stage control transfer has a third stage in addition to setup and status: *data*. This type of transfer starts with a setup stage. It then is followed by a *data stage*. In the data stage, either a *read transfer* occurs, involving one or more IN (read transfer) transactions, or a *write transfer* occurs, involving one or more OUT (write transfer) transactions. The third stage, the

Table 29.11: *OUT Transactions*

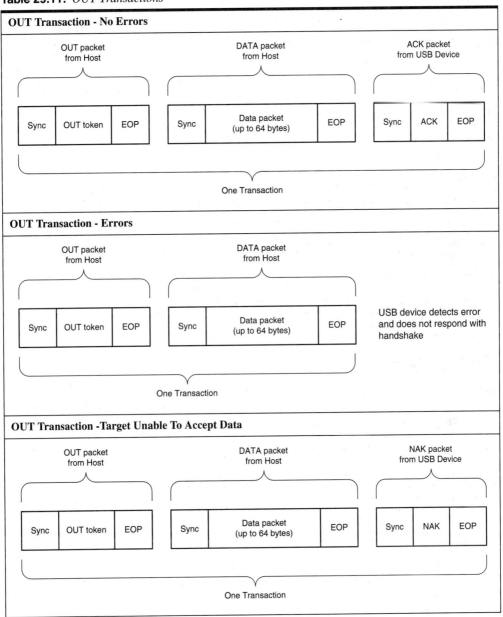

Table 29.11: *OUT Transactions (continued)*

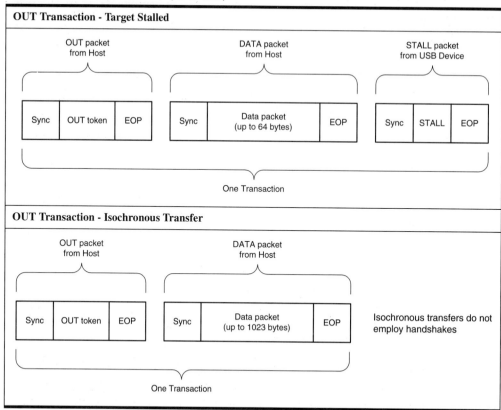

OUT Transaction - Target Stalled

OUT Transaction - Isochronous Transfer

status stage, consists of the complementary transaction to the transfer in the data stage—it transfers data in the opposite direction of the data stage. That is, it is an OUT (for a read transfer) or IN (for a write transfer). The packet length of the status transactions is 0.

These transfers are illustrated in Table 29.12.

Table 29.12: *SETUP Transactions/Control Transfers*

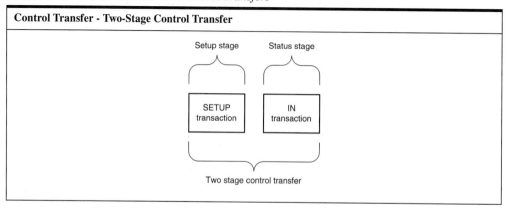

Control Transfer - Two-Stage Control Transfer

Table 29.12: *SETUP Transactions/Control Transfers (continued)*

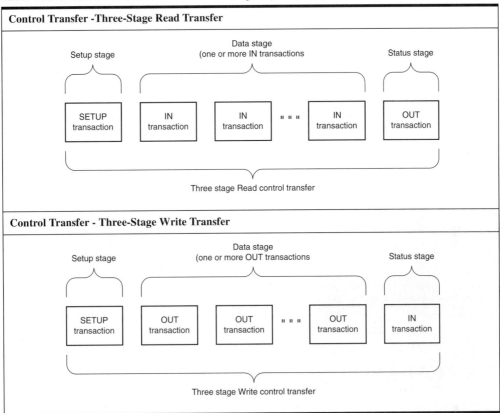

Plug-and-Play Hardware

The differential transmission mode of a USB bus allows the host to detect when a new USB peripheral is plugged into a hub. For all of the details of how this is done, you should read the *Universal Serial Bus Specification, Version 1.0*, Chapter 7. However, here we quickly summarize the electrical techniques to help you understand what is going on and why it works.

The USB uses differential transmission signaling, using a twisted-pair labeled "D+" and "D-". A USB "1" bit is indicated by D+ being 200 mv higher than D-, and a USB "0" is indicated by D- being 200 mv higher than D+. These are also referred to as the "J" state for a USB "1" and the "K" state for the USB "0" (see Figure 29.8).

The power supply is *single-ended*, that is, unlike some differential signaling such as RS-232 that uses positive and negative voltages, the USB uses only positive voltages. The "crossover point" for USB signals is recommended by the specification to be between 1.3 and 2.0 V. A USB driver has two 15KΩ pulldown resistors on D+ and D-. A full-speed hub or function has a 1.5KΩ pullup resistor on D+, and a low-speed function has a 1.5KΩ pullup resistor on D-. The full-speed cabling and drivers are shown in Figure 29.6, and the low-speed cabling and drivers are shown in Figure 29.7. The effect of these resistor arrangements is that it is possible to detect when a new device is plugged in, or when it is unplugged, and whether it is a low-speed or full-speed USB device.

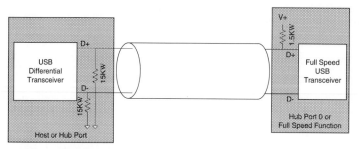

Figure 29.6: *Full-speed USB drivers and cabling.*

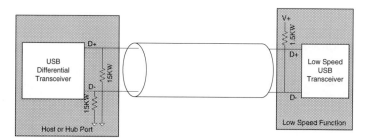

Figure 29.7: *Low-speed USB drivers and cabling.*

If nothing is plugged into a *downstream port*, that is, a host port or hub port, both D+ and D-are pulled down below the normal "low threshold" signal level. So not only is there no 200-mv signal differential, but both signals are held "low". This is called, in USB terminology, a *Single-Ended Zero* (SE0) state (see Figure 29.8). This state is induced for two full-speed bit times to indicate an EOP condition. If a port enters the SE0 state for more than 2.5μs (30 full-speed bit times), then a *disconnect condition* is reported. Disconnect signaling applies only in the "upstream" direction, that is, a USB peripheral cannot detect that it has been disconnected by looking at signal levels.

If SE0 is removed for more than 2.5μs, a *connect condition* is reported. The data line that goes high (because of the pullup resistor) tells the port which type of peripheral—low-speed or full-speed—has been plugged in.

An EOP state is signaled by asserting an SE0 condition on the line for two bit times. This is a distinguishable condition that allows the USB peripheral or the USB host to clearly detect the EOP, thus avoiding some of the ambiguities implicit in a Non-Return-to-Zero (NRZI) encoding, which is what the USB actually uses for sending data. A discussion and illustration of NRZI encoding is given in Section 7.1.5 of the *Universal Serial Bus Specification, Version 1.0*.

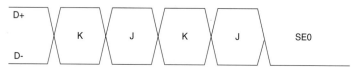

Figure 29.8: *USB signal states.*

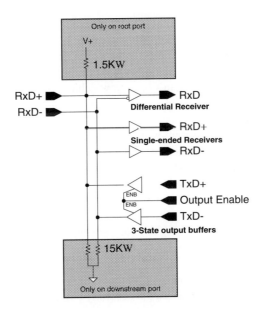

Figure 29.9: *USB hub I/O port drivers.*

A bus reset is signaled by the host or hub asserting an SE0 condition for at least 10 ms. Resets are only transmitted in a downstream direction. A peripheral device recognizes a reset condition when SE0 is asserted for 2.5μs, and it *must* recognize a reset after 5.5μs. A reset propagates through all enabled downstream hubs and ports. After a reset, all functions are in their reset state; they have their default USB address and are unconfigured. It is the responsibility of the host software to properly configure a USB device after it has been reset. A device must be reconfigured within 10 ms after a reset signal is removed.

Part of the key to this is that every hub port transceiver contains *three* receiver circuits, as shown in Figure 29.9. The first circuit is a differential receiver whose output is a 0 bit for the K state and a 1 bit for the J state. The other two receivers are single-ended receivers; one monitors the D+ line and indicates whether it is high or low, and the other monitors the D- line and indicates whether it is high or low. Thus in every clock time, the USB firmware reads *3* bits representing the states of the lines and can easily detect if an SE0 signal is present. The output transmitters are *three-state devices*, in which the outputs can be driven high or low or can be left off so that the output bus drivers do not interfere with signals on the line. Note that because the D+ line has the pullup resistor, the port tells its upstream source that it is a full-speed USB device.

Power Management

The need for power management is becoming critical. This is in part because of a need to reduce overall power consumption of desktop systems, which spend most of their time in an idle state, while still allowing them to "wake up" for administrative tasks such as central configuration or backup. The use of power management has an additional feature beyond reducing power consumption, and that is to allow a desktop system to go almost instantly from the idle low-power state to a fully operational state, hence Microsoft's name for power management, "OnNow Power Management". This eliminates the need for the lengthy boot process. But the most critical need for power management is in laptop and other portable systems. This is because the USB might be supplying power from the system's battery, which is a quite limited resource. Being able to "turn off" unused or idle peripherals can have a significant impact on total battery life.

Microsoft has a new power-management initiative called Advanced Configuration and Power Interface (ACPI), which is a system-wide power-management strategy. ACPI is used to implement the OnNow power-management strategy. For example, a CPU might have its clock speed reduced, thus conserving power. Then it might go to a low-power idle state in which it can still respond to external stimuli to "reawaken" virtually instantly. Finally, it might go into a full-power-down state that requires a reload of disk-saved state to become active again. USB power management allows the USB host software to put selected peripherals, or the entire bus, into various power-down states. Some states allow "remote activation". For example, an idle mouse, when moved, might send a "wake up" signal on the bus, while other states are fully powered down.

A USB device can be in several suspended states, as defined by the ACPI specification. Each device is supposed to support at least two states: fully powered up and fully powered down. The powered-down state is not required to maintain any state information; thus it might be necessary for the host, after reconfiguring the device after a power-up, to reset any internal state required. Intermediate power-down states may retain state in the device. A device can place itself in the suspend state when it stops seeing SOF packets. A suspended device will draw no more than 500µA from the USB.

A device may be awakened from its suspended state by detecting normal bus activity, by detecting a bus reset, or by switching the bus to a resume state. Setting a resume state requires that a resume signal be sent on the bus for at least 20 ms, followed by the EOP's being signaled on the bus (an SE0 state two high-speed clocks in length). The host must then start sending SOF packets within 3 ms to keep the device awake.

All of this is discussed in much more detail in Chapter 7 of the *Universal Serial Bus Specification, Version 1.0*. Further details and illustrations also appear in Chapter 10 of *USBSA*. Further information is available from the Microsoft publication, *OnNow Power Management and USB*. Much of this detail is irrelevant for the Device Driver writer, since you'll make power-down requests via IRPs, and thus much of the detail of USB power management is handled for you. In particular, global power-down is usually a system function, and you will simply receive a notification that you are to power down your device.

As a Device Driver writer, you have the option of implementing power-down states for your USB peripherals. As we showed in Chapter 28 (page 676), each driver has a Power Manager entry point (its IRP_MJ_POWER handler) by which it is notified of various power-management requests.

USB Device States

We have already discussed the USB states. Figure 29.10, taken from the *Universal Serial Bus Specification, Version 1.0*, Chapter 9, shows the state transition diagram for the USB states as a Device Driver writer would perceive them. Note that a device can enter the powered state at any

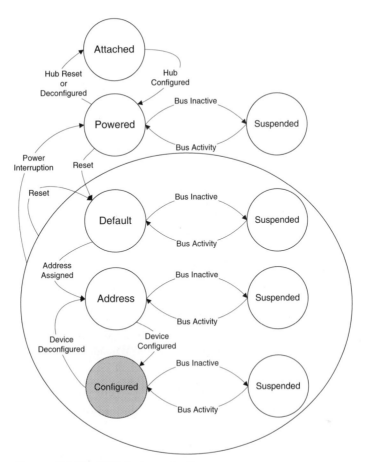

Figure 29.10: *USB device state diagram.*

time, even if it is already configured and active. This is because it can be unplugged and thus have its power interrupted.

It is the responsibility of the USB software to enumerate the devices on the bus. Unlike some busses, such as SCSI, that are enumerated at power-up boot time, a USB bus may be enumerated an arbitrary number of times, and essentially with "no warning" to the devices being enumerated. A device that has been powered down by power-management software action may later be powered up. Then, because it might be an entire hub that is powered up, the system will have to re-enumerate the bus. A device that has been *suspended* by its own power-management software having detected an inactive bus may be reactivated at any time and returned to the state in which it was.

To simplify the diagram, the USB specification includes a large pseudo-"state" around six of the states and implies that a power interruption or reset condition will return a device to the indicated state, independent of in which state the device was. This is merely a notation convenience that the specification writers chose in order to reduce the clutter of arrows that would otherwise be required. The states are explained in Table 29.13. Note that the *configured* state, shown shaded in Figure 29.10, is the only state that actually permits the host to use the device.

Table 29.13: *Interpretation of USB Device States*

State	Meaning
(None)	Device is not attached to the USB.
Attached	Device is attached but is not powered up.
Powered	Device is attached to the USB and is powered but has not been reset.
Default	Device is attached to the USB, is powered, and is reset but has not been assigned a unique address. Device responds to the default address.
Address	Device is attached to the USB, is powered, is reset, and has a unique address but has not been configured.
Configured	Device is attached to the USB, is powered, is reset, has a unique address, and has been configured. The host can now use the device.
Suspended	The device can be in the state of being powered or being reset or can have an address assigned or can be configured. However, it cannot be used by the host.

Bus Enumeration

On a USB bus, not only is each device an active object that can be detected by the bus, but each *hub* also is an active object. Each hub acts as a USB device and can notify the host whenever a device is plugged into or unplugged from one of its ports. When a USB device is attached, the following events take place.

1. The hub into which the device has been plugged notifies the host of the event. It does this by sending a reply on its *status change pipe*. The device is placed in the *attached* state, and the port to which it is attached is disabled.
2. The host determines the nature of the status change by querying the hub.
3. The host learns the port to which the new device is attached and then issues a *port enable* command to the hub and a *reset* command to that port.
4. The hub issues the reset signal and holds it for the required minimum of 10 ms.
5. When the reset is released, the hub enables power to the device (maximum of 100 ma for a bus-powered device). The USB device is now in the *powered* state. All of its internal registers are reset. The default address is the only address to which it will respond.
6. The host reads the *device descriptor* via the default pipe to determine the parameters, such as the maximum payload size used by this device's default pipe and the desired peak power required from the USB.
7. The host uses the default pipe to assign a unique address to the USB device. The device is now in the *address* state.
8. The host reads the *configuration information* from the device by reading each configuration starting with 0 and going to the maximum configuration number determined from the device descriptor. This transaction can take several USB frames to complete.
9. Based on the configuration information, the host assigns a *configuration value* to the device. The device is now in the *configured* state and all of the endpoints of the device are available. The USB device is now permitted to draw the amount of bus power specified by its configuration descriptor, up to 500 ma. (The host might be keeping track of the hub's power budget and might terminate after reading the device descriptor.)

When a device is unplugged from the USB hub, the hub sends a notification of the event to the host via its status change pipe. This causes the host to issue a command to disable the port. The host then updates its internal data structures to indicate the new bus topology.

There is one minor problem with the USB: Devices do not have a unique identity. That is, if you unplug a USB device from one hub and plug it into another hub, it is not seen as the same device, but rather as a completely new device. This has implications for devices such as network printers, for which there is a desired networkwide public name. There is no straightforward way for a computer to tell that the printer that has just been plugged into one USB port is the same printer that had just been unplugged from a different (or actually, even the same!) USB port. Thus there is some trickiness required in higher levels of software to deal with this problem. For example, after establishing the connection to the printer, higher-level software may ask the printer for its network name. This is outside the scope of the USB transactions.

USB Device Requests

A USB device responds to device requests sent from the host on the default pipe. A device request is a control transfer. The request and its parameters are sent to the device in the packet. The host must establish the values passed. A SETUP packet is 8 bytes long and is illustrated in Figure 29.11.

The first byte, bmRequestType, is a bit-mapped field that identifies characteristics of the device. The high-order bit indicates the direction of the data transfer in the second stage, the data stage, of the control transfer. This bit is ignored if the wLength field is 0. The USB specification defines a basic collection of device requests that every device must support. A "device class" (in the USB sense, not the WDM sense) can define additional requests, and a specific vendor may extend the set with vendor-specific requests. When you are writing a Device Driver, you must carefully choose how you support vendor extensions. If you critically depend on them, you will have a vendor-specific driver, which is not consistent with the WDM philosophy.

A request may be directed to the device, to an *interface* on the device, or to a specific *endpoint* on the device. When the recipient subfield specifies an interface or endpoint, the wIndex field identifies which interface or endpoint is selected.

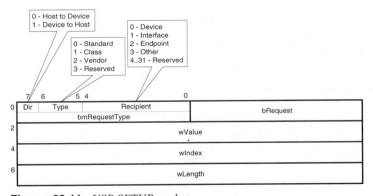

Figure 29.11: *USB SETUP packet.*

The fields of a request are as follows:

- The request type, in the bRequest field, specifies the nature of the request.
- The meaning of the wValue field depends on the request type. See Table 29.14.
- The meaning of the wIndex field depends on the request type. For a request that is sent to an interface or endpoint, the wIndex field encodes the selection of the interface or endpoint. For other messages, the meaning depends on the request type.
- The wLength field specifies the length of the data to be transferred during the second stage, the data stage, of the control transfer. If this field is 0, no data is transferred.

Table 29.14: *USB Standard Device Requests*

bmRequestType	bRequest	wValue	wIndex	wLength	Data
0000 0000 0000 0001 0000 0010	CLEAR_FEATURE	Feature selector	Zero Interface Endpoint	0	None
1000 0000	GET_CONFIGURATION	0	0	1	Configuration value
1000 0000	GET_DESCRIPTOR	Descriptor type and index	0 or language ID	Descriptor length	Descriptor
1000 0001	GET_INTERFACE	0	Interface	1	Alternative interface
1000 0000 1000 0001 1000 0010	GET_STATUS	0	Zero Interface Endpoint	2	Device, interface, or endpoint status
0000 0000	SET_ADDRESS	Device address	0	0	None
0000 0000	SET_CONFIGURATION	Configuration value	0	0	None
0000 0000	SET_DESCRIPTOR	Descriptor type and index	Zero Interface Endpoint	Descriptor length	Descriptor
0000 0000 0000 0001 0000 0010	SET_FEATURE	Feature selector	Zero Interface Endpoint	0	None
0000 0001	SET_INTERFACE	Alternate setting	Interface	0	Nonc
1000 0010	SYNCH_FRAME	0	Endpoint	2	Frame number

Standard Device Requests

The standard device request codes are shown in Table 29.15. Each of these has specific types of parameters, as described in Table 29.14. The following sections illustrate each of these request types.

Table 29.15: *Standard Request Codes*

bRequest	Value
GET_STATUS	0
CLEAR_FEATURE	1
Reserved	2
SET_FEATURE	3
Reserved	4
SET_ADDRESS	5
GET_DESCRIPTOR	6
SET_DESCRIPTOR	7
GET_CONFIGURATION	8
SET_CONFIGURATION	9
GET_INTERFACE	10
SET_INTERFACE	11
SYNCH_FRAME	12

CLEAR_FEATURE

bmRequestType	bRequest	wValue	wIndex	wLength	Data
0000 0000 0000 0001 0000 0010	CLEAR_FEATURE	Feature selector	Zero Interface Endpoint	0	None

CLEAR_FEATURE clears a feature of a device, interface, or endpoint. The wValue field specifies which feature is to be cleared. The value must be device-specific, interface-specific, or endpoint-specific, as specified by the device. An attempt to clear a feature that does not exist will generate a STALL response.

Normally, you issue CLEAR_FEATURE requests in your driver during device initialization. However, the user may select features to be disabled by specific I/O control calls. Such feature requests typically are abstracted from a specific device, and you will have to map the user request to the device-specific feature selector.

The feature selector codes are shown in Table 29.16. The ENDPOINT_STALL feature causes the stall state to be cleared, provided the condition on the remote hardware that caused the stall has been corrected. It also clears a software-induced stall state set by SET_FEATURE. The DEVICE_REMOTE_WAKEUP feature disables the ability of a device to perform a *remote wakeup* on the host system. The remaining feature codes, shown shaded, are not defined by the core USB specification, but are defined by the extension described in the Microsoft document *OnNow Power Management and USB*.

Table 29.16: *Feature Selector Codes*

Feature Selector	Recipient	Value
ENDPOINT_STALL	Endpoint	0
DEVICE_REMOTE_WAKEUP	Device	1
DEVICE_POWER_D0	Device	2
DEVICE_POWER_D1	Device	3
DEVICE_POWER_D2	Device	4
DEVICE_POWER_D3	Device	5
INTERFACE_REMOTE_WAKEUP	Interface	1
INTERFACE_POWER_D0	Interface	2
INTERFACE_POWER_D1	Interface	3
INTERFACE_POWER_D2	Interface	4
INTERFACE_POWER_D3	Interface	5

If the device returns the POWER descriptor *before* any INTERFACE descriptors, then the host transmits DEVICE_POWER_D*x* feature selectors to the device. If the device returns the POWER descriptor *after* the INTERFACE descriptors, the host transmits INTERFACE_POWER_D*x* feature selectors to the interface(s).

The DEVICE_REMOTE_WAKEUP feature causes all interfaces in the device to be enabled or disabled for remote wakeup. Otherwise, selected interfaces can have their remote wakeup state set by the INTERFACE_REMOTE_WAKEUP feature selection.

GET_CONFIGURATION

bmRequestType	bRequest	wValue	wIndex	wLength	Data
1000 0000	GET_CONFIGURATION	0	0	1	Configuration value

GET_CONFIGURATION returns a data packet containing the single byte that represents the current device configuration. If the returned value is 0, the device is not configured.

GET_DESCRIPTOR

bmRequestType	bRequest	wValue	wIndex	wLength	Data
1000 0000	GET_DESCRIPTOR	Descriptor type and index	0 or language ID	Descriptor length	Descriptor

GET_DESCRIPTOR retrieves information from the USB device. The wValue field specifies the descriptor *type* in the high-order byte and the descriptor *index* in the low-order byte. The wIndex field specifies the language ID for STRING descriptors and is set to 0 for other descriptors. The wLength field specifies the number of bytes to return; if the descriptor is longer than wLength bytes, only the first wLength bytes are returned. If the descriptor is shorter than wLength, the device will return either a short data packet or, when further information is requested, a NULL data packet.

The descriptor type for a standard request may be DEVICE, CONFIGURATION, or STRING. (See Table 29.17 for the complete set. INTERFACE and ENDPOINT descriptors cannot be requested by GET_DESCRIPTOR.) A request for a *CONFIGURATION descriptor* returns the CONFIGURATION descriptor, all of the INTERFACE descriptors, and all of the ENDPOINT descriptors for all of

Table 29.17: *Descriptor Types*

Descriptor Type	Value
DEVICE	1
CONFIGURATION	2
STRING	3
INTERFACE	4
ENDPOINT	5
PDC	6

The PDC descriptor is for power management. It is not defined by the core USB specification. However, it is described in the Microsoft document *OnNow Power Management and the USB.*

the interfaces. The resulting packet may be parsed using the Microsoft-provided PARSE.DLL subroutine library that is available to Device Driver writers at the kernel level. (If you pass the packets back to an application, there is a user-level parser called TPARSE.DLL.) Using one of these libraries simplifies the work and allows you to avoid much of the tedium of handling the parsing of standard replies. When a complete CONFIGURATION descriptor is returned, the first INTERFACE descriptor immediately follows the CONFIGURATION descriptor and the ENDPOINT descriptors of the first INTERFACE descriptor follow the first INTERFACE descriptor. For additional interfaces, the INTERFACE descriptor and ENDPOINT descriptors follow in a similar fashion.

The USB specification requires that all devices must provide a device descriptor and at least one CONFIGURATION descriptor. An attempt to request a descriptor that does not exist will generate a STALL response. If the first byte of the buffer returned is nonzero, the buffer contains a valid descriptor.

STRING descriptors are returned in Unicode 16-bit characters. Note that in some cases, you might have to request that a string be converted to ASCII in order to return it to the caller, depending on the nature of the interface. All internal device-driver support should use Unicode, but for some interfaces visible to the application, ASCII might be a necessary option to support.

The language ID is a 16-bit value as described in *Developing International Software for Windows 95 and Windows NT*, which is listed in the Further Reading section at the end of the chapter.

GET_INTERFACE

bmRequestType	bRequest	wValue	wIndex	wLength	Data
1000 0001	GET_INTERFACE	0	Interface	1	Alternate interface

GET_INTERFACE returns the selected alternate interface setting for the specified interface. Some USB devices might have configurations with interfaces that have mutually exclusive settings. GET_INTERFACE allows the host to determine the currently selected alternate setting. A familiar example is a printer that can accept either PostScript or HPCL documents (although most modern printers are adaptive and can recognize which kind of document has been sent and change their configuration on the fly to respond properly). Another example is a scanner that can scan either color or gray scale. Such interface queries might be made visible at the user interface. Again, the user might have used a quite different set of constants, and you will have to map the returned interface code to the appropriate user-visible code. (For example, some printers might encode their mode as 0==PostScript, 1==HPCL, while others might encode their mode as 1==PostScript, 2==HPCL. Your responsibility as a Device Driver writer is to specify the *user* interface to such information and then do whatever it takes to map the internal codes of the device to the visible user interface.)

GET_STATUS

bmRequestType	bRequest	wValue	wIndex	wLength	Data
1000 0000 1000 0001 1000 0010	GET_STATUS	0	Zero Interface Endpoint	2	Device, interface, or endpoint status

GET_STATUS returns the status for a specified endpoint. The status is returned as 2 bytes. The GET_STATUS report for a device is shown in Figure 29.12 and explained as follows.

D7	D6	D5	D4	D3	D2	D1	D0
Reserved; must be 0				Power state		Remote wakeup	Self-powered
D15	D14	D13	D12	D11	D10	D9	D8
Reserved; must be 0							

Figure 29.12: GET_STATUS *return values for a device.*

- If bit D0 is set to 0, the device is bus-powered; if D0 is set to 1, the device is self-powered. This status bit cannot be changed by SET_FEATURE or CLEAR_FEATURE requests.
- Bit D1 indicates whether the device is capable of performing a *remote wakeup*. (For example, a mouse movement or a keyboard keystroke might be wakeup events. These will cause a machine in a power-management environment to leave its suspended state.) If D1 is 0, the device is not enabled for remote wakeup; if D1 is 1, the device is enabled for remote wakeup. The remote wakeup status can be modified by the SET_FEATURE or CLEAR_FEATURE requests by using the DEVICE_REMOTE_WAKEUP feature selector.
- Bits D2 and D3, shown shaded, are not specified by the core USB specification but are by the Microsoft document *OnNow Power Management and USB*. They encode the device power state.

The GET_STATUS report for an interface is shown in Figure 29.13 and explained as follows.

D7	D6	D5	D4	D3	D2	D1	D0
Reserved; must be 0.				Power state		Remote wakeup	Reserved; must be 0.
D15	D14	D13	D12	D11	D10	D9	D8
Reserved; must be 0.							

Figure 29.13: GET_STATUS *return values for an interface.*

- Bit D1 encodes the interface remote wakeup state. If it is 0, the interface cannot perform remote wakeup or the feature has been disabled with CLEAR_FEATURE. If it is 1, the interface can perform remote wakeup and the feature has been enabled with SET_FEATURE.
- Bits D3 and D2, shown shaded, are not specified by the core USB specification but are by the Microsoft document *OnNow Power Management and USB*. They encode the device power state.

The GET_STATUS report for an endpoint is shown in Figure 29.14. If the endpoint is currently stalled, the D0 bit is set to 1; otherwise, it is set to 0. The stall state can be changed by using the SET_FEATURE or CLEAR_FEATURE requests with the ENDPOINT_STALL feature selector.

D7	D6	D5	D4	D3	D2	D1	D0
Reserved, must be 0.							Stall
D15	D14	D13	D12	D11	D10	D9	D8
Reserved, must be 0.							

Figure 29.14: GET_STATUS *return values for an endpoint.*

This allows the host software to set a stall state that is indistinguishable from one caused by a hardware-detected fault of the device.

For those endpoints that use data toggle, clearing a stalled endpoint resets the data toggle to DATA0. The stall state is set to 0 after either a SET_CONFIGURATION request or a SET_INTERFACE request.

SET_ADDRESS

bmRequestType	bRequest	wValue	wIndex	wLength	Data
0000 0000	SET_ADDRESS	Device address	0	0	None

SET_ADDRESS sets the device address that will be used for all subsequent accesses. The device address must be in the range 1..255. The wValue field specifies the device address.

This request does not work like other requests, and the difference is important. Because a request is a control transfer, it takes place in two or three stages: setup, data transfer (optional), and status. The direction of transfer depends on whether the host is sending data to the device or vice versa. The status stage transfers data in the opposite direction of the data transfer stage. If there is no data stage, the status stage transfers data from the device to the host.

Stages after the initial SETUP packet assume the same device address as the SETUP packet. Therefore the USB device will not change its device address until after the status stage of this request completes successfully. Thus the completion of this operation is deferred until after the status stage. For all other requests, the operation must complete *before* the status stage.

SET_CONFIGURATION

bmRequestType	bRequest	wValue	wIndex	wLength	Data
0000 0000	SET_CONFIGURATION	Configuration value	0	0	None

SET_CONFIGURATION sets the desired configuration. The wValue field either must be 0 or must match a configuration value from one of the configuration descriptors of the device. If it is 0, the device is placed in the unconfigured state.

SET_DESCRIPTOR

bmRequestType	bRequest	wValue	wIndex	wLength	Data
0000 0000	SET_DESCRIPTOR	Descriptor type and index	Zero Interface Endpoint	Descriptor length	Descriptor

SET_DESCRIPTOR can be used to modify existing descriptors or add new descriptors. A USB device is not required to support this request.

The wValue specifies the descriptor type (Table 29.17, page 713) in the high-order byte and the descriptor index in the low-order byte. The wIndex field specifies the language ID for STRING descriptors and should be 0 for non-STRING descriptors. The wLength field specifies the number of bytes to transfer to the device.

SET_FEATURE

bmRequestType	bRequest	wValue	wIndex	wLength	Data
0000 0000 0000 0001 0000 0010	SET_FEATURE	Feature selector	Zero Interface Endpoint	0	None

SET_FEATURE sets a feature of a device, interface, or endpoint. The wValue field specifies which feature is set. The value must be device-specific, interface-specific, or endpoint-specific, as specified by the device. An attempt to set a feature that does not exist will generate a STALL response.

Normally, you issue SET_FEATURE requests in your driver during device initialization. However, the user may select features to be disabled by specific I/O control calls. Usually, such feature requests will be abstracted from a specific device, and you will have to map the user request to the device-specific feature selector.

The predefined feature codes are shown in Table 29.16 on page 712. The ENDPOINT_STALL feature causes the stall state to be set, simulating a stall state caused by a hardware fault. The DEVICE_REMOTE_WAKEUP feature enables a device that can support the option to perform a *remote wakeup* on the host system.

SET_INTERFACE

bmRequestType	bRequest	wValue	wIndex	wLength	Data
0000 0001	SET_INTERFACE	Alternate setting	Interface	0	None

SET_INTERFACE allows the host to select an alternate setting to the interface specified by wIndex. The alternate setting must be one of the valid alternate settings for the interface.

A familiar example, which we cited under GET_INTERFACE, is a USB printer that accepts either PostScript or HPCL documents. The selection could be accomplished by using SET_INTERFACE to select which interface is desired.

SYNCH_FRAME

bmRequestType	bRequest	wValue	wIndex	wLength	Data
1000 0010	SYNCH_FRAME	0	Endpoint	2	Frame number

SYNCH_FRAME sets, and then reports, an endpoint's synchronization frame.

A problem in doing isochronous transfers is that the data that must be sent, so as to meet the overall isochronous data rate, might not fit exactly into the nominal 1-ms frame time window. For example, it might be necessary to send n packets in one frame and $n + 1$ packets in the next, or send n packets for three frames and $n - 1$ packets in the fourth. Exactly how this is determined depends on the host software, the endpoint, and the necessary bandwidth. (The bandwidth might vary. An audio device might accept different sampling rates, and the actual packaging will also depend on the sampling rate currently selected.) When this is the case, the host and the endpoint must synchronize to agree on which frame the repeating pattern begins. Once this request is sent, the endpoint will being monitoring the SOF frame number in order to track the position of a frame within this specified pattern. The number of the frame in which the pattern began is returned to the host by this request.

This request is used only for isochronous data transfers using implicit pattern synchronization. If the endpoint is not an isochronous endpoint or does not use implicit pattern synchronization, this request will return a STALL handshake.

The starting frame number is set to 0 by a device reset or by configuring the endpoint or its interface.

USB Descriptors

USB *descriptors* define the properties of a USB device. A descriptor is a binary data structure with a very specific format. Each descriptor begins with a 1-byte field that contains the total number of bytes in the descriptor (limiting descriptors to 255 bytes). This is followed by a 1-byte field that contains the *descriptor type*. The various descriptors form a hierarchy, as shown in Figure 29.15.

The USB specification says that a configuration "may reuse descriptors or portions of descriptors from other configurations that have the same characteristics". From the viewpoint of the Device Driver writer, this is irrelevant; you don't know how a particular descriptor is obtained. This sentence applies to the writers of USB devices and allows them to optimize the storage (often a small ROM) used for descriptors. You will not be able to tell exactly how a descriptor is determined from this internal storage; you will see only the abstract hierarchy of descriptors. The codes that are associated with descriptors are shown in Table 29.17 on page 713.

A descriptor may contain a reference to a *STRING descriptor* that provides a human-readable string. This string, if present, may be in a variety of languages. If a STRING descriptor is not present, its reference field in the descriptor must be set to 0; the field may not be omitted.

A descriptor that returns a number of bytes less than the defined length is invalid. If the descriptor returns a number of bytes greater than the defined length, the additional bytes are ignored, but they must be taken into consideration when computing the location of the next descriptor.

Class-specific and vendor-specific descriptors that are related to a standard descriptor are returned in the same data buffer as the standard descriptors and immediately following the standard descriptor. Class-specific and vendor-specific descriptors that are *not* related to a standard descriptor must be returned using class-specific or vendor-specific requests.

Microsoft provides a parser for descriptors so that you don't have to handle them yourself. In fact, they provide two parsers: one used in the kernel by drivers (PARSE.DLL) and another available for User-mode applications (TPARSE.DLL). Both are created from the same common

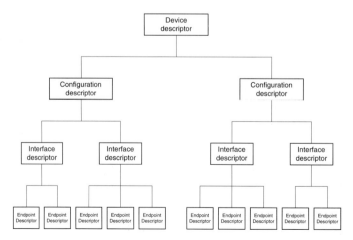

Figure 29.15: *USB descriptor hierarchy.*

source code, but the details of the interfaces vary and some of the capabilities are slightly different. The USB driver also provides for ways to get descriptors so that you don't need to worry about many of the low-level details.

Although Microsoft provides the parsers, it is important that you know what is actually being parsed so that you can make sense of what comes back from them. Next, we examine the USB descriptor definitions in some detail.

DEVICE *Descriptor*

A USB *device* has a single DEVICE descriptor, one of those shown in Table 29.18.

The bLength field gives the length of the descriptor, in bytes. Although only 18 bytes are specified in Table 29.18, the descriptor itself may include several STRING descriptors that will be returned as part of the descriptor request. It appears that the bLength field includes these STRING descriptor lengths as well.

The bDescriptorType field contains the constant for a DEVICE descriptor. This distinguishes this descriptor from other types of descriptors such as ENDPOINT or INTERFACE descriptors.

Table 29.18: DEVICE *Descriptor Fields*

Offset	Field	Size	Value	Description
0	bLength	1	Number	Size of descriptor, in bytes
1	bDescriptorType	1	Constant	DEVICE
2	bcdUSB	2	BCD	The USB Specification Release Number, in BCD format
4	bDeviceClass	1	Number	Class code, assigned by the USB authority
5	bDeviceSubclass	1	Number	Subclass code, assigned by the USB authority
6	bDeviceProtocol	1	Number	Protocol code, assigned by the USB authority
7	bMaxPacketSize0	1	Number	Maximum packet size for endpoint 0
8	idVendor	2	Number	Vendor ID, assigned by the USB authority
10	idProduct	2	Number	Product ID, assigned by the USB authority
12	bcdDevice	2	BCD	Device release number, in BCD
14	iManufacturer	1	Index	Index of the STRING descriptor describing the manufacturer, or 0
15	iProduct	1	Index	Index of the STRING descriptor describing the product, or 0
16	iSerialNumber	1	Index	Index of the STRING descriptor describing the product serial number, or 0
17	bNumConfigurations	1	Number	Number of possible configurations

The bcdUSB field contains the USB specification release number for which this device is valid. This can be used either to modify the behavior of the various levels of drivers or possibly to reject the device as being incompatible, in this case, due to either a too-old release or one that is too new to be supported by the software. This number is expressed in Binary Coded Decimal (BCD) format and a two-digit minor release is assumed. That is, release 2.1 is encoded as release 2.10 and is encoded as 0x210.

If your driver is written for an earlier release of the specification, you might not be able to access all of the device's features, descriptors, and so on. Ideally, the evolution of the specification will maintain upward compatibility, but you must be sensitive to changes that might not be upward-compatible. Thus a driver that is expecting version 2.00-compliant devices might find a version 1.00-compliant device plugged into the USB. In this case, the driver must be aware of what features, descriptors, and other capabilities it cannot access (because they are different in 2.00). It must be prepared to handle the fact that these are absent, or it must reject the device as obsolete. Similarly, if a version 3.00 device is plugged in, the driver can probably safely assume that all version 2.00 capabilities are present. (But this assumption might not be valid, either because of incompatible evolution of the specification or a failure on the part of the manufacturer to adhere to the compatibility requirements or because the version 2.00 specification simply wasn't adequate to support the needs of the device.) A Class Driver should almost always allow the application code to obtain the DEVICE descriptor information so that the application, if it gets an error, can report the necessary diagnostic information to the user. This helps the Technical Support staff provide adequate support (for example, "You have a version 2.00 driver and a version 3.00 device. Please download our latest driver from the Web").

The bDeviceClass field is a class code assigned by a central USB authority. This establishes the basic USB class. This value can also be set to 0, in which case each interface within the configuration specifies its own class information. For example, a combination device might support several distinct USB interfaces, such as a keyboard-and-joystick combination. If this field is set to a value between 1 and 0xFE, the device supports different class specifications on different interfaces, and the interfaces might not operate independently. An example of this might be a telephone connection device that can support a data modem interface, a fax modem interface, and a digital telephony interface—all of which will often be mutually exclusive interfaces. However, the device *might* support "voice over data", thereby allowing both data and digital voice transmission concurrently, but the two interfaces might require interactive cooperation. If the bDeviceClass field is set to 0xFF, the device class is vendor-specific.

The bDeviceSubClass field is a subclass code assigned by a central USB authority. If it is set to 0, the bDeviceSubClass field must be set to 0. If it is not set to 0xFF, the values in the bDeviceSubClass field are administered by the central authority.

The bDeviceProtocol field contains a *protocol code* administered by a central authority. The value is always interpreted based on the bDeviceClass and bDeviceSubClass fields. If bDeviceProtocol is set to 0, the device does not use class-specific protocols for the device, but individual interfaces might specify individual class-specific protocols. If it is set to 0xFF, the device uses vendor-specific protocols.

The bMaxPacketSize0 field specifies the maximum packet size for endpoint 0. The only value permitted here is 8, 16, 32, or 64.

The idVendor field is a vendor ID, which is administered by a central authority. The idProduct field is a product ID, which is assigned by the vendor.

The bcdDevice field is the device release number in BCD. The same discussion we gave for the bcdUSB field applies here. The coding is assumed to be four BCD digits with a two-digit minor version number. For example, device release 1.75 is encoded as `0x175` and device release 10.8 is encoded as `0x1080`. This value should be made available to the application-level code so that it can be displayed, thereby aiding Technical Support people.

The `iManufacturer`, `iProduct`, and `iSerialNumber` fields are indexes to `STRING` descriptors. They define the manufacturer, product, and serial number. These need not be present; if there is no `STRING` descriptor, these should be set to 0. The `iSerialNumber` field, in particular, is optional. High-end devices might include the serial number (which might be used for any purpose such as warranty, technical support, or coupling software to hardware for licensing purposes). Low-end devices that are mass-manufactured and cost-sensitive (such as mice) will probably not have a unique serial number for a device based on simple cost constraints. As a Device Driver writer, you should provide ways for the application program to obtain these strings, if present, particularly if there are a number of vendors of the same product. It might be useful to have these strings for technical support purposes.

In Figure 29.16, we illustrate the presence of an `iManufacturer` string. This string immediately follows the `DEVICE` descriptor in this example, and thus the index `iManufacturer` will be 18. The length of the manufacturer string is shown as the field called $bLength_{STRING}$. The total length of the `DEVICE` descriptor, `bLength`, will be 18 (the length of a `DEVICE` descriptor) plus $bLength_{STRING}$. The string is a Unicode string.

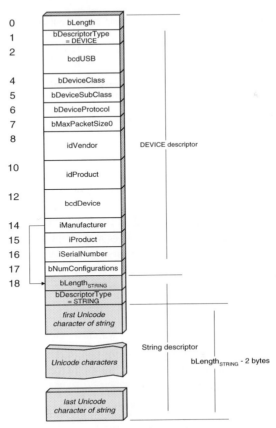

Figure 29.16: *USB* DEVICE *descriptor.*

The bNumConfigurations field defines the number of possible configurations that are present.

CONFIGURATION *Descriptor*

A USB *configuration* has a single CONFIGURATION descriptor, one of those shown in Table 29.19.

Table 29.19: CONFIGURATION *Descriptor Fields*

Offset	Field	Size	Value	Description
0	bLength	1	Number	Size of descriptor, in bytes
1	bDescriptorType	1	Constant	CONFIGURATION
2	wTotalLength	2	Number	The total length of data returned
4	bNumInterfaces	1	Number	Number of interfaces supported by the configuration
5	bConfigurationValue	1	Number	Value used to SET_CONFIGURATION
6	iConfiguration	1	Index	Index of the STRING descriptor for configuration
7	bmAttributes	1	Bitmap	Configuration characteristics: D7 Bus-powered D6 Self-powered D5 Remote wakeup D4..D0 Reserved (set to 0)
8	MaxPower	1	Number	Maximum power consumed by a bus-powered USB device, in 2-ma units

The bLength field is the size of this configuration, in bytes. If the iConfiguration field is nonzero, this appears to include the length of the STRING descriptor referenced by the iConfiguration field.

The bDescriptorType field contains the constant value indicating that this is a CONFIGURATION descriptor.

The wTotalLength field is the total length of the data returned for this configuration, which includes all of the descriptors that are returned. These descriptors include the configuration descriptor itself, the INTERFACE and ENDPOINT descriptors, and any class- or vendor-specific descriptors that are included, as well as all STRING descriptors that form a part of these descriptors. This is illustrated in Figure 29.17, where we show

- the CONFIGURATION descriptor,
- followed by an INTERFACE descriptor, which we call INTERFACE(0),
- followed by the ENDPOINT descriptors for that interface, which we call ENDPOINT(0.1) and ENDPOINT(0.2), for the two endpoints beyond endpoint 0 that INTERFACE(0) supports.

In a similar fashion, INTERFACE(1) has one additional endpoint, INTERFACE(2) has no endpoints other than endpoint 0, and INTERFACE(3) has two endpoints. We do not show any

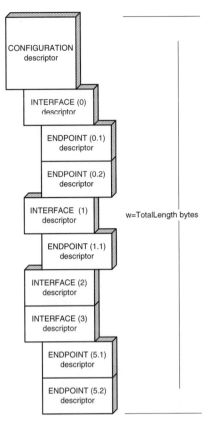

Figure 29.17: CONFIGURATION *data return.*

class or vendor descriptors in this illustration. Nor do we show explicitly any STRING descriptors. We have indented the descriptors to show the "ownership" relationship of the configuration, interfaces, and endpoints.

The bNumInterfaces field is the number of interfaces supported by this configuration. It will be at least 1 but could be larger.

The bConfigurationValue is a value that can be used when SET_CONFIGURATION is used to select a configuration. There is no constraint that this start at 0 or that sequential configurations are one larger than the previous configuration. (This allows a vendor to create a suite of products. For example, one product supports configurations 0, 1, 2, 3, and 4; another supports configurations 2 and 4; and a third supports configurations 0 and 17.)

The iConfiguration field is the index of a STRING descriptor for the configuration. It is the offset of the start of the STRING descriptor relative to the start of this descriptor.

The bmAttributes field specifies which characteristics are possible for the device. For example, a device that is exclusively bus-powered will have D7 = 1 and D6 = 0, and a device that is self-powered (for example, a laser printer) will have D7 = 0 and D6 = 1. However, some devices might be either bus-powered or self-powered, in which case D7 = 1 and D6 = 1. When external power is applied or removed, the device is required to notify the host of the change. Typical examples might be devices designed for laptop use. These might be bus-powered on an airplane but self-powered in a hotel room, where there is an outlet for the power supply. From the viewpoint of a Device Driver writer, you might have to be aware of the fact that some features may not be available when the device is bus-powered, and you might have to notify or be prepared to inform the user-level application of the status of these features. Furthermore, because self-power can be applied or removed at any time, your Device Driver must be prepared to cope with changes in power status that affect device functionality, even in the middle of processing a request.

The D5 bit of `bmAttributes` indicates whether the device can support a remote-wakeup mechanism.

The `MaxPower` field specifies the maximum power consumption that the device will require from the USB bus. The value is expressed in 2-ma units. A device that is self-powered is limited to the amount of power specified in this field if power is removed. Thus a USB laser printer might draw just a few milliamperes if it is unplugged, just enough so that it can, in effect, say to the USB, "I'm a printer that has no power; please turn me on". Other devices might, as we indicated in the previous discussion under `bmAttributes`, limit the device capabilities if they are not self-powered. Note that this field specifies the *maximum* power required. A laptop printer that is not moving paper or printing could require vastly less power than its allowed maximum, but when it has motors active, it could require the maximum.

INTERFACE *Descriptor*

A USB *interface* has a single `INTERFACE` descriptor, one of those shown in Table 29.20.

The `INTERFACE` descriptor describes a specific interface provided by a configuration. Each configuration provides one or more interfaces, and each interface may have zero or more `ENDPOINT` descriptors. When a configuration supports more than one interface, the endpoints for each interface immediately follow the interface, as shown in Figure 29.17 on page 723. The only way to get an `INTERFACE` descriptor is to use `GET_CONFIGURATION`; it cannot be retrieved by a `GET_DESCRIPTOR` request.

Table 29.20: `INTERFACE` *Descriptor Fields*

Offset	Field	Size	Value	Description
0	bLength	1	Number	Size of descriptor, in bytes
1	bDescriptorType	1	Constant	INTERFACE
2	bInterfaceNumber	1	Number	The number of the interface
3	bAlternateSetting	1	Number	The value used to identify an alternate setting of the interface
4	bNumEndpoints	1	Number	Number of endpoints used by this interface, excluding endpoint 0
5	bInterfaceClass	1	Number	Class code (assigned by the USB authority)
6	bInterfaceSubclass	1	Number	Subclass code (assigned by the USB authority)
7	bInterfaceProtocol	1	Number	Protocol code (assigned by the USB authority)
8	iInterface	1	Index	Index of the STRING descriptor for this interface

An interface can include alternate settings. By default, an interface always starts out with alternate setting 0, and the SET_INTERFACE request can select an alternate setting. The GET_INTERFACE request will return the current alternate setting.

An INTERFACE descriptor is followed by zero or more ENDPOINT descriptors. An interface that supports only endpoint 0 has no additional ENDPOINT descriptors. An interface that supports more than endpoint 0 is followed by the ENDPOINT descriptors for all but endpoint 0.

The bLength field is the length of the INTERFACE descriptor. If the iInterface field is nonzero, the bLength field includes the length of the STRING descriptor referenced by iInterface.

The bDescriptorType field is set to the constant representing an INTERFACE descriptor.

The bInterfaceNumber field is the interface number. It is zero-based and is an index into an array of interfaces that are supported by the configuration. The bAlternateSetting selects an alternate to the interface specified in bInterfaceNumber.

The bNumEndpoints field gives the number of endpoints supported by this interface beyond endpoint 0. If only endpoint 0 is supported, this value will be 0.

The bInterfaceClass field is a value assigned by a central authority. If this field is set to 0, the interface does not belong to any USB-specified device class. If it is 0xFF, the interface class is vendor-specific. All other values are reserved for assignment by a central authority.

The bInterfaceSubClass field is a value assigned by a central authority. If bInterfaceClass is 0, this field must be 0. If this value is not 0xFF, it is a value reserved for assignment by a central authority.

The bInterfaceProtocol field is a protocol code assigned by a central authority. If this field is 0, the device does not use a class-specific protocol. If it is 0xFF, the device uses a vendor-specific protocol.

The iInterface field is an index relative to the start of the INTERFACE descriptor that is the STRING descriptor describing this interface.

ENDPOINT *Descriptor*

A USB *endpoint* has a single ENDPOINT descriptor, one of those shown in Table 29.21. Ultimately, the endpoint is where "all the action is"; the device, configuration, and interface descriptions are just ways to arrive at the endpoint. The endpoint represents the *logical* device to which your user's applications will want to talk; from their viewpoint, configurations, devices, and interfaces don't really exist. So the endpoint is the most important component from the user's viewpoint. As a Device Driver writer, you are ultimately providing endpoint support.

An ENDPOINT descriptor is always returned as part of a configuration descriptor; it cannot be directly accessed with a GET_DESCRIPTOR request. There is never an ENDPOINT descriptor for endpoint 0.

The bLength field is the size of the descriptor, in bytes.

The bDescriptorType field contains the constant indicating this is an ENDPOINT descriptor.

The bEndpointAddress field encodes the direction of the endpoint and the endpoint number. Note that the size of this field limits a device to 16 endpoints per interface—actually quite a generous amount.

The bmAttributes field encodes the endpoint attributes as the endpoint is perceived within a configuration (bConfigurationValue is in the Configuration descriptor). We have been

Table 29.21: ENDPOINT *Descriptor Fields*

Offset	Field	Size	Value	Description
0	bLength	1	Number	Size of descriptor, in bytes
1	bDescriptorType	1	Constant	ENDPOINT
2	bEndpointAddress	1	Number	The address of the endpoint on the USB device described by this descriptor. The address is encoded as follows: D0..D3 The endpoint number D4..D6 Reserved; must be 0 D7 Direction; ignored for control endpoints 0 OUT endpoint 1 IN endpoint
3	bmAttributes	1	Bitmap	The endpoint attributes when it is configured by using the bConfigurationValue: D0..D1 00 Control 01 Isochronous 10 Bulk 11 Interrupt All other bits are reserved.
4	wMaxPacketSize	2	Number	Maximum packet size this endpoint will send and receive
6	bInterval	1	Number	Interval for polling endpoint for data or transfers, in milliseconds

unable to determine if the order in which the bits are presented corresponds to the heading shown (it is shown this way in the USB specification) or are read in the traditional way, that is, is a Bulk transfer indicated by the value 2 (as you might believe from how it appears in the table) or the value 1 (if the leftmost bit is D0 as suggested by the heading "D0..D1")?

STRING *Descriptor*

A USB *string* has a single STRING descriptor, one of those shown in Table 29.22.

The bLength field is the length of the entire descriptor, in bytes.

The bDescriptorType field is the constant indicating a STRING descriptor.

The bString field is the string, expressed in Unicode characters. The string has no NUL terminator character, so you must use the length to make a copy of the string or otherwise manipulate it.

Table 29.22: STRING *Descriptor Fields*

Offset	Field	Size	Value	Description
0	bLength	1	Number	Size of descriptor, in bytes
1	bDescriptorType	1	Constant	STRING
2	bString	bLength - 2	Characters	The Unicode character string

For a full description of Unicode, refer to *The Unicode Standard: Worldwide Character Encoding, Version 1.0*. The number of characters in the Unicode string is (bLength - 2) / 2. However, the simplest explanation of Unicode is that it is a 16-bit (rather than 8-bit) character set. Unicode contains ASCII as a subset. If the high-order byte of the character is 0, the low-order 7 bits are ASCII, or the low-order 8 bits are ISO-Latin-1, also known as ISO-8859-1. When programming in ANSI C, you get "wide" characters (Unicode) by prefixing a string or character constant with L; for example, L"Unicode" is a Unicode character string 8 characters, or 16 bytes, in length (7 characters and a terminating NUL character). The character L'A' is the single 16-bit character **A**, 0x0041. Note that a NUL in Unicode is a 16-bit value, 0x0000.

The ANSI C standard defines the reserved word wchar_t ("wide character type") to declare any "wide" (that is, 16-bit) character. Microsoft provides several macros or typedefs for using Unicode. They are shown in Table 29.23.

Table 29.23: *Unicode Declarations*

Declaration	Definition	Explanation
WCHAR	wchar_t	Wide character
PWSTR	wchar_t *	Pointer to wide character string
PCWSTR	const wchar_t *	Pointer to constant wide character string
PUNICODE_STRING	typedef struct {...}	Pointer to a *counted* wide character string

POWER *Descriptor*

A USB *string* has a single POWER (PDC) descriptor, shown in Table 29.24. This descriptor is not part of the core USB specification, but it is described in the Microsoft document *OnNow Power Management and USB*. We discussed power management in more detail in Chapter 28.

Table 29.24: POWER *Descriptor Fields*

Offset	Field	Size	Value	Description
0	bLength	1	Number	Size of descriptor, in bytes
1	bDescriptorType	1	Constant	PDC
2	bCapabilitiesFlags	1	Bitmap	See the description following this table, and Table 29.25
3	EventNotificationSupport	2	Number	Power Device Class Flow ID; 0 means no event notification support
5	D1LatencyTime	2	Number	Time to transfer from D1 to D0 state, in milliseconds; must be 0 if D1 state is not supported
7	D2LatencyTime	2	Number	Time to transfer from D2 to D0 state, in milliseconds; must be 0 if D2 state is not supported

Table 29.24: POWER *Descriptor Fields (continued)*

Offset	Field	Size	Value	Description
9	D3LatencyTime	2	Number	Time to transfer from D3 to D0 state, in milliseconds
11	PowerUnit	1	Number	Power multiplier
12	D0PowerConsumption	2	Number	Power consumption in D0 in units of $10^{PowerUnit}$ μW; 0 means unknown
14	D1PowerConsumption	2	Number	Power consumption in D1 in units of $10^{PowerUnit}$ μW; 0 means unknown
16	D2PowerConsumption	2	Number	Power consumption in D2 in units of $10^{PowerUnit}$ μW; 0 means unknown

The bLength field is the length of the entire descriptor, in bytes.

The bDescriptorType field is the constant indicating a PDC descriptor.

The bCapabilitiesFlags field defines the set of Set Node D*x* Power State commands sent from the host that this node can receive and the wakeup capability of the node from the D1 and D2 power states. These are shown in Table 29.25. If the device does not have a POWER (PDC) descriptor, the host software should act as if it did with a bCapabilities flag of 0.

Table 29.25: bCapabilities *Flags of a* POWER (PDC) *Descriptor*

Bit	7	6	5	4	3	2	1	0
Defines	Reserved	Reserved	Wake up from D2?	Wake up from D1?	Can enter D3?	Can enter D2?	Can enter D1?	Can enter D0?
0	0	0	No	No	No	No	No	No
1			Yes	Yes	Yes	Yes	Yes	Yes

The EventNotificationSupport field defines the *Power Class Flow ID*. If this field is 0, there is no event notification support. Event notifications include such events as power-source changes (bus-powered-to-self-powered or AC-powered-to-battery-powered, and their inverses).

The following latency times indicate the amount of time the device requires to recover from a power state transition. The host is obliged to honor these times and delay sending any traffic to the device until the transition delay has completed.

- The D1LatencyTime field is the number of milliseconds required to transition from the D1 state to the D0 state.
- The D2LatencyTime field is the number of milliseconds required to transition from the D2 state to the D0 state.
- The D1LatencyTime or D2LatencyTime values must be 0 if the corresponding state is not supported. They may also be 0 if either the transition is instantaneous, the transition can occur entirely in response to RESUME signaling (which we don't discuss; see Chapter 11 of the *Universal Serial Bus Specification, Version 1.0*), or the device is not designed to respond to notifications to select the D0 power state.

- The D3LatencyTime field is the number of milliseconds required to transition from the D3 state to the D0 state. Note that a 0 value is not allowed unless the transition is faster than 1 ms. If a PDC descriptor is present, it implies that the device supports at least the D0 and D3 states.

The PowerUnit is the exponent used for the power multiplier. It affects the interpretation of the D0PowerConsumption, D1PowerConsumption, and D2PowerConsumption fields. The value 0 indicates 10^0, and therefore the DxPowerConsumption fields are in units of 1µW. The value 1 indicates 10^1, and therefore DxPowerConsumption fields are in units of 10µW.

The D0PowerConsumption, D1PowerConsumption, and D2PowerConsumption fields express the power consumption in the specified states. This power consumption is expressed in $10^{PowerUnit}$µW. A value of 0 means the power consumption is unknown or the state is not supported. Note that the descriptor specifies power consumption in ma, requiring translation between these two units. The nominal supply voltage is assumed to be 5V, and the power formula is $W = I \times E$, where W is the power in watts, I is the current in amps, and E is the voltage.

If an older device is encountered that does not have a PDC descriptor, the one shown in Table 29.26 should be assumed.

Table 29.26: *Default* POWER *Descriptors*

Offset	Field	Size	Value	Default
0	bLength	1	Number	18
1	bDescriptorType	1	Constant	6
2	bCapabilitiesFlag	1	Bitmap	0
3	EventStatusNotificationSupport	2	Number	0
5	D1LatencyTime	2	Number	0
7	D2LatencyTime	2	Number	0
9	D3LatencyTime	2	Number	0
11	PowerUnit	1	Number	0
12	D0PowerConsumption	2	Number	0
14	D1PowerConsumption	2	Number	0
16	D2PowerConsumption	2	Number	0

Device Communication

The logical communication defined by the USB standard is shown in Figure 29.18. However, this is a simplification. In Win32, the communication defined by the "client" is actually represented at several levels, which we show in Figure 29.19.

In Figure 29.18, we show the USB specification model. In this model, the host side has a client that communicates to the device; the logical interconnect is shown as the horizontal gray arrow. However, this communication is realized via the black-arrow path. In this model, the cli-

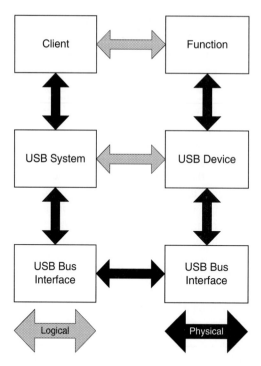

Figure 29.18: *USB Interlayer Communication Model.*

ent communicates to a USB system. This system knows the USB topology and such details as the actual USB address for the device. It also knows if the USB is powered down and must be reactivated, as well as other data about the device. The USB system then sends messages out through the root hub by manipulating the USB bus interface.

The WDM model, shown in Figure 29.19, expands on this model. In this model, the "client" is broken into three levels:

- The MiniDriver, which works with a specific device.

- The Class Driver, which might work with a variety of devices with similar functionality and which might in fact be on a variety of busses. (According to WDM, you could have a Class Driver that talked to, say, four different devices of similar abstract properties. One could be on the ISA bus, one on the PCI Bus, one on the USB, and one on an IEEE-1394 bus!)

- The application level, which works by performing API operations such as `CreateFile`, `ReadFile`, `WriteFile`, and `DeviceIoControl`. This level has no idea that the device is necessarily on the USB. Instead, it works with a much more abstract view of the operations. These operations are communicated to the Class Driver using the API functions.

The Class Driver converts these requests to one or more IRPs and passes those IRPs to the appropriate MiniDriver. Note that a Class Driver can concurrently support several different MiniDrivers. The scenario shown here is an application that works with two different data col-

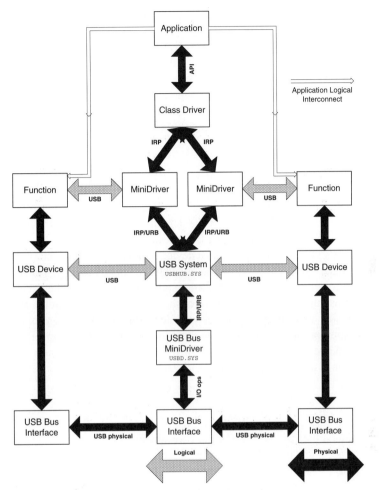

Figure 29.19: *WDM interlayer connectivity for USB.*

lection (analog-digital conversion) devices. Both devices look the same to the application, so it simply does a CreateFile on "ADC0" and another on "ADC1". However, internally these two devices are somewhat (or possibly entirely) different, so each has its own MiniDriver. When the application asks to "Read a sample", the device handle will cause the I/O system to direct the operation to the appropriate MiniDriver.

The MiniDriver forms the appropriate function-oriented request and sends one or more IRPs to the USB system. The IRP contains the information necessary to locate the actual USB logical device and other operations encoded as a USB Request Block (URB). A URB is contained within an IRP. IRPs containing URBs continue down the chain. The USB system directs the packet to the proper USB address. However, the USB system has no idea how to actually send information on the USB. This is because there are many vendors of USB chips and cards. The USB might be a plug-in card on the PCI Bus or integrated onto the motherboard, and a USB interface card might have different I/O space addresses and protocols for its use. These differences are handled by the USB Bus Driver. In Figure 29.19, we show only one such physical interface. But, in fact, you could have two USB cards plugged into a PCI Bus, in which case the IRP would be directed to the appropriate Bus Driver. This driver communicates to the USB Bus Interface using I/O instructions (or, more precisely, using the HAL operations, such as READ_...._UCHAR and WRITE_...._UCHAR). Once the USB packet is on the USB, the communication at the devices proceeds as described for Figure 29.18. (Actually, we simplified Figure 29.19 somewhat by eliminating some of the details below the USB Bus Driver.)

The "logical" connection is shown by the white arrows running from the application to the device. This logical connectivity is actually independent of the bus structure used below the MiniDriver.

USB Device Configuration

Before a USB device can be used, it must be configured. As the writer of a MiniDriver, you will have to configure your device. Initially, only the default endpoint, endpoint 0, is configured, and that endpoint is owned by the underlying USB software.

By the time your MiniDriver is called, the device will have been enabled, its unique address assigned, and the necessary USB-level resources (including power management) guaranteed. At this point, you get to determine which of the alternate configurations of the device is to be used (you can change this later, but you need to establish at least one of them at the start). Exactly *how* you decide which configuration to use is your decision. For example, you might read, for a USB printer, the appropriate Registry keys for the printer to determine if the HPCL or PostScript configuration should be selected. Although we will illustrate some techniques for determining which configuration is desired, this is a design decision that is up to you.

Device Classes

One very important parameter of a USB is its *device class*. The USB uses the word "class" in a quite different fashion than the WDM. For the USB, the class of a device determines exactly how the device is accessed and influences what components of the I/O system will be used to service it. The USB classes are shown in Table 29.27. Note that some of the devices stress the USB bandwidth; for example, it is unlikely the USB could support two full-motion image streams or even support one and do much of anything else. But as we write this, such devices are commercially available. Also, audio and image are consolidated into a more general *stream class*.

Table 29.27: *USB Classes*

Class	Devices
HID	Human Interface Devices: keyboards, mice, joysticks, game controls, monitors, and so on
Communication	Modems, ISDN, ATM, telephones. and other communication devices
Mass storage	Any external storage device such as disks, CD-ROMs, or tapes
Audio	Real-time audio samples: microphones and speakers
Streams	Still images, scanners, full-motion cameras, and DVD (Digital Video Disk)

A WDM class defines a class of *devices*, which might or might not be on the USB; that's a detail that exists below the WDM *Class Driver*. For example, WDM thinks of all scanners as being in the same WDM class, whether their interconnect to the machine is via the parallel port, a SCSI port, the USB, IEEE-1394, or PC Card. But only the USB connection will have a scanner in the *USB* image/stream class, which will be shared with a USB still camera and a USB video camera. But there will be a separate WDM moving-image-Class Driver that will handle both USB cameras and IEEE-1394 cameras. The use of the same word "class" leads to incredible confusion. We do our best to be as clear and precise as we can be about how we are using this word.

We show this in Figure 29.20. In this illustration are two video cameras attached to a machine. One is a very expensive IEEE-1394 camera with every bell and whistle feature, and the other is an inexpensive USB camera with fixed focus, low frame rate, and lower resolution. From the viewpoint of WDM, these are both members of the "camera class". Also attached are two scanners. One is an old SCSI scanner that we had lying around the office that does 2400 dpi interpolated, full-color, and the other is an inexpensive USB scanner that does 600 dpi black-and-white. From the viewpoint of WDM, these are both members of the "scanner class". But

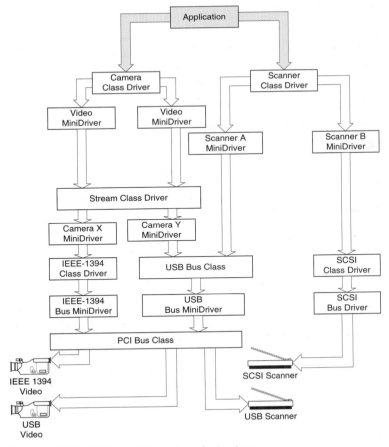

Figure 29.20: *WDM and USB class distinctions.*

let's look at USB's view. The USB sees the USB scanner and the USB camera as instances of the USB "stream" class. What we don't show in this drawing, which is already very dense, is that the SCSI Class Driver is also handling a CD-ROM and tape backup unit, the USB driver is handling a mouse and keyboard, and the IEEE-1394 is handling the DVD (Digital Video Disk) input and the overhead video projector output. If we tried to show all of this, the picture would be too complex to show on one page, and we only wanted to make the point about the USB/WDM class distinction.

Isochronous Transfers

An *isochronous* endpoint will either transmit or receive a time-sensitive stream of information. Typical isochronous applications include video, audio, and high-speed analog-to-digital sampling (input) or digital-to-analog control (output). Isochronous transfers have no error-checking or retransmission capability. Thus the endpoint or the host must know how to deal with lost or corrupted packets.

Isochrony places many limitations on both the host and the device. Data must be delivered in a timely fashion and must be received and processed in a timely fashion. Once an isochronous mode is entered, neither side should allow the concept of "buffer overflow" for receipt or "buffer underflow" for transmission.

Normally, an isochronous endpoint uses the SOF signal as the basis of synchronization. This occurs nominally at 1-ms intervals. The endpoint then packages data for transmission based on this 1-ms interval.

But life is more complicated. It turns out that the USB clock rate is not suitable for some applications. Therefore, one USB device might be designated as the "master clock" device and establish the frequency of the bus clock by negotiating with the root hub. Note that on any one USB, only one such device can exist. Consequently, all other devices must be prepared to deal with this new clock interval. No matter what the bit rate is, the SOF still occurs every 1 ms. The USB specification says that this adjustment in clock rate might not occur at less than 6-ms intervals.

The specification states that there are three possible types of synchronization for an endpoint:

1. Synchronize the clock exactly to the USB clock.
2. Adjust the bus clock.
3. Synchronize with the host by adjusting the data flow.

If an endpoint cannot adjust its synchronization by using method (1), synchronizing to the USB clock, then it must implement *both* methods (2) and (3). The reason for this limitation is that since only one USB device can be the clock master, there is no guarantee that any specific device will be the clock master. This means that the endpoint might not be able to use method (2), and consequently, since it cannot use method (1), if it is to remain a viable USB device, it must be able to use method (3).

USB Hubs

USB hubs are responsible for the distribution of USB signals in the tiered-star USB topology. A hub is also responsible for detecting device connection and disconnection to support Plug-and-

Play capabilities in the host. It provides for selective disabling of devices or subtrees of the USB itself by allowing individual ports to be disabled and handles the presence of low-speed devices on the USB.

Hubs are, consequently, very sophisticated components. A hub may exist as a simple stand-alone hub or be incorporated into some other device (creating what is called a *compound device*). For example, a keyboard might provide one or more ports into which mice, joysticks, game controls, or the like would most likely be connected. A monitor might provide ports into which speakers likely would be connected. (Of course, USB devices are fully interchangeable. It is perfectly legitimate to plug speakers into a keyboard or mice into a monitor, as the end user desires.) In fact, a hub is a full USB device that responds to all USB commands such as being configured, having an address set, and retrieving its configuration information. In addition to the standard USB commands, a hub supports a set of hub-specific requests to perform operations such as the enabling or disabling of its output ports. It will return hub-specific device status, such as notifications to the host of connection status changes. A hub is always a full-speed USB device; a low-speed USB device cannot act as a hub.

The hub architecture is shown in Figure 29.21. The *hub repeater* component manages the routing of messages and the downstream port-management functions. The *hub controller* processes the packets directed to the hub itself and handles all of the details of hub management. The port connected to the host hub or to another hub is the *root port*, and the remaining ports are the *downstream ports*. There is no specified limit on the number of downstream ports on a hub. For a bus-powered hub, the hub cannot take more than 500 ma and must supply a minimum of 100 ma to each downstream port. This limits a bus-powered hub to no more than four downstream ports, although it appears that safety requirements place a practical upper bound at seven. (This upper bound might be due to the fact that a 16-port powered hub would have to supply 8 amps of downstream current to comply with the spec, and that's a hefty amount of power to have floating about, particularly in a consumer electronics environment. Remember also that the USB cable has fairly small-gauge wire, so a high current combined with high wire resistance can be a potential fire hazard. A practical limit chosen for the specification limits a bus-powered hub or compound device to have no more than four downstream ports. Even a seven-port hub requires, for safety conformance, current-limiting circuitry on the downstream ports.)

We discuss hubs briefly here so that you get a sense of what a hub can do and how hubs fit into the overall USB picture. The details of hub behavior, including such complex tasks as clock

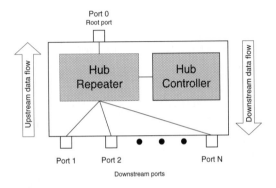

Figure 29.21: *USB hub architecture.*

skew management, are beyond what a Device Driver writer normally needs to know. So, for all of the hub details, we refer you to Chapter 11 of the *Universal Serial Bus Specification, Version 1.0*, or Chapters 11 through 13 of the *USBSA*. Also, although you, as a Device Driver writer, need to know about events such as connection status changes, and you might need to know about disabling of downstream ports of a hub as part of your handling of ACPI (power-management) events, knowing the actual details are not necessary. The USB driver, which is part of the WDM software hierarchy, actually handles all of these details for you. Your driver, whether it is a Class Driver or MiniDriver, will receive notifications of events via its entry points and will send requests to the USB driver via IRPs. For example, if you ask to disable the port to which your device is connected, the USB driver will determine which hub and port actually support that device and direct the disabling request appropriately. Thus we do not cover the details of hub configuration, hub requests, or any other hub-specific material beyond this simple overview.

The *root hub*, which is at the host, is no different than any other hub. It responds to the same commands and performs the same functions as any other hub.

When a hub receives a transmission at its root port, it simply broadcasts it to all of its downstream ports. Thus it is truly a "hub" in the network sense, not a "router"; it does not know or care about the addresses of the devices accessible from the downstream ports. All of the enabled downstream ports receive the message. We show this in Figure 29.22. The third downstream hub from the left is disabled, either because nothing is plugged into it or because it has been explicitly disabled by the host as part of a power-management strategy. The hub repeater also handles low-speed devices on the downstream ports, changing the rate at which data is clocked to the low-speed ports and converting low-speed upstream communication to full-speed upstream communication.

When a hub receives a transmission at one of its downstream ports, it routes it to its root port. Transmission from all other downstream ports is blocked until the EOP is received from the active downstream port; this avoids the need to handle collisions. This is shown in Figure 29.23. Normally, an event at one downstream port causes no additional traffic on any other downstream port. There is an exception to this, dealing with a RESUME message, but we need not be concerned with that here. If you are curious about the details, check Chapter 11 of the *Universal Serial Bus Specification, Version 1.0*.

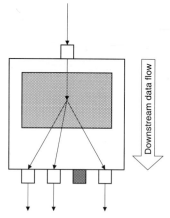

Figure 29.22: *USB hub downstream connectivity.*

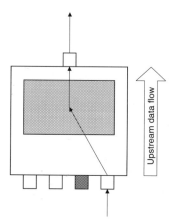

Figure 29.23: *USB hub upstream connectivity.*

The configuration of hubs is normally handled for you by the underlying USB software. So we do not discuss any of the details of hub configuration. In addition to the reference to Chapter 11 of the *Universal Serial Bus Specification, Version 1.0*, we also recommend Chapters 11 through 13 of *USBSA*.

The Hub and Initialization

The role of the hub is critical to the initialization of a USB. For example, if all devices have the same default address, how does the USB keep multiple devices from responding to an initial message? The answer is, with the hubs. When the system first powers up, the root hub powers up with its downstream ports disabled. Thus there is only one device, the root hub, that can respond to the messages. The standard protocol locates the device and then assigns it a unique address. Once the address is assigned, the device will no longer respond to the default address.

Next, each port of the hub is checked, in turn, to see if anything is plugged into it. If there is something connected to the hub, that downstream port is enabled. If what is plugged into the hub is a device, then it is configured with a unique device address, and initialization proceeds to the next port. If what is plugged into the port is a hub or compound device, the hub is initialized, and initialization proceeds in a depth-first treewalk of the tiered-star hierarchy. At no time is more than one device enabled that can respond to the default device address, so there is no conflict.

This same method is followed any time a new device or hub is plugged into any port. The hub into which the connection is made notifies the host via its interrupt pipe that a connection has been made, and the treewalk just described is started at that port, initializing each device and port in the subtree just plugged in (including the "subtree" of a single device).

Further Reading

Compaq, Digital Equipment, IBM, Intel, Microsoft, NEC, Northern Telecom, *Universal Serial Bus Specification, Revision 1.0*, January, 1996

Available from a variety of sources. We downloaded our copy from `http://www.teleport.com/~usb/download.htm`, which you have to get into via `http://www.usb.org`. Then ask for technical document downloads.

This publication is an essential companion to our book. While some of what it contains, such as detailed electrical specifications and detailed drawings of the connectors, is irrelevant to the USB programmer, we have not in any way tried to reproduce the details of the specification in this book. Between this publication and *Universal Serial Bus System Architecture*, if we really attempted to include everything they discuss we would have over 500 pages of USB-only material in this book.

Intel Corporation, *i486 Microprocessor Programmer's Reference Manual*, McGraw-Hill, 1990. ISBN 0-07-881674-2

Kano, Nadine, *Developing International Software for Windows 95 and Windows NT*, Microsoft Press, 1995. ISBN 1-55615-840-8

Messmer, Hans-Peter, *The Indispensable PC Hardware Book, Second Edition*, Addison-Wesley, 1995. ISBN 0-201-87697-3

Microsoft Corporation, *OnNow Power Management and USB*. We found our copy on `http://www.microsoft.com/hwdev/pcfuture/usbdpm.htm`.

MindShare, Inc.: Don Anderson, *Universal Serial Bus System Architecture*, Addison Wesley Longman, 1997. ISBN 0-201-46137-4

We consider this book an essential companion if you are doing USB programming. It contains over 300 pages of incredible detail, much of which explains and clarifies information from the *Universal Serial Bus Specification, Version 1.0*. You should not even consider serious USB programming without this book. While we have summarized much of the basic descriptions, it is simply infeasible for us to discuss USB in the depth that this book does.

Shanley, Tom, *PCI System Architecture*, Mindshare Press, 1993. ISBN 1-881609-01-4

The Unicode Consortium, *The Unicode Standard: Worldwide Character Encoding, Version 1.0, Volume 1 & 2*, Addison-Wesley, 1990. ISBN 0-201-56788-1

Chapter

30 *The Win32 Driver Model*

In this chapter, we present a snapshot of the Win32 Driver Model. The information provided here is based on the Beta release information from Microsoft. While this information will be substantially correct in general, we know that many of the fine details will change by the time of the product release.

How the WDM Extends the Basic Driver Model

The Win32 Driver Model (WDM) offers two major features over the basic NT driver model. First, a uniform binary interface is supported between the two major operating systems, Windows 98 and Windows 2000. Thus, unlike with the support for Windows 95 and Windows NT 4.0 (and earlier), there is no need to write two different Device Drivers in two completely different styles. Second, the WDM allows you to abstract functionality into *layers* so that common code can be shared.

In Windows 98, a substantial amount of code has been added to allow a WDM driver to interface to the Windows 98 system. In Windows NT, very little code has been added; most of the existing code is core functionality. A WDM-conforming driver will not use any facilities other than those defined by the header file wdm.h, which defines the subset of the NT interface that is supported on both platforms. This is shown in Figure 30.1. In the figure, we also show that the Windows 98 extensions to support the WDM are more extensive than the Windows 2000 extensions.

The Driver Hierarchy

At the simplest level, the WDM abstracts *class functionality* (operations common to a set of devices) from *bus interfaces*. Thus a simplistic model would include a *Class Driver*, which handled all of the higher-level interface issues (operations such as opening, reading from, writing to,

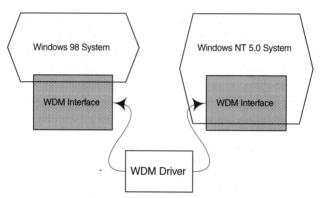

Figure 30.1: *The WDM binary sharable between Windows 98 and Windows 2000.*

and controlling the device)—from the mechanics of how the device is physically interfaced to the computer, such as the I/O address space, the device register functionality, and interrupts.

However, the hierarchy is not actually that simple. There is not really enough abstraction in the two-level split to make it workable. This is because, ideally, there will be standard application interfaces to *classes* of devices, such as scanners, cameras, mice, joysticks, and keyboards. But how the application wants to see the device might not be how the actual device works. For example, the device might need sequences of commands sent to it in particular orders so as to effect the device functionality. A device from a different manufacturer might require a *different* set of commands or commands in a different order to achieve the same functionality. Thus, in the slightly more honest form of the hierarchy, there is an additional layer interposed, the *Mini-Driver*.

The MiniDriver embodies the device-specific features and maps between the class operations and the device operations that implement the class operations. But the MiniDriver does not need to know exactly how this communication to the device takes place. That is handled by a *Bus Driver*. Thus it is perfectly reasonable to have a Class Driver that allows an application to talk to any of a USB-based scanner, an IEEE-1394-based scanner, a SCSI-based scanner, a scanner connected (most likely to a laptop) via a PC-Card port, or a scanner connected via a parallel port. The scanner can be built by vendor A, B, or C. The bus variation is handled by the Bus Driver, the vendor variation is handled by the MiniDriver, and the application interface is handled by the Class Driver. This is illustrated in Figure 30.2, which shows four different scanners connected to a file server. (Why aren't all of these USB scanners? The server already had two scanners, one a very expensive, high-quality 30-bit color scanner with a sheet feeder and a SCSI interface. Legacy devices will need support.)

But Figure 30.2, too, is a lie. In fact, there are many more layers in the picture, which we discuss in subsequent sections. But the figure does give you an idea of what is intended. An illustration somewhat closer to the Real Truth, but simplified to fit in a small illustration, is shown in Figure 30.3. We thought of producing a multipage foldout that was a rendering of what is really going on but realized this would cause production problems with the book.

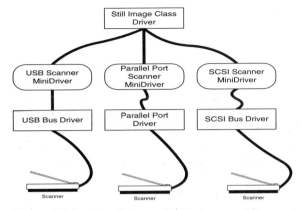

Figure 30.2: *Class Drivers, MiniDrivers, and Bus Drivers.*

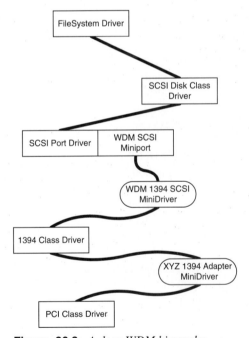

Figure 30.3: *A deep WDM hierarchy.*

The WDM Classes

Microsoft has defined a number of classes. Before you decide to implement a new Class Driver, you should check the list of existing Class Drivers to see if one of them is suitable for your device. If there is, you will have to write only a MiniDriver, a much simpler task.

Following are the most important of the WDM classes.

- The Human Input Device Class
- The Streams Class
- The Audio Class
- The Video Class
- The Still Image Class

The HID Class

The Human Input Device (HID) Class is used to access low-speed devices for user interaction. These devices include keyboards, mice, joysticks, trackballs, and graphics tablets.

Before the USB, the HID devices each connected to a dedicated port on the computer. There is no standard provision for more than one keyboard, one mouse, or one joystick (frequently split for two reduced-functionality joysticks). The desk of an advanced game player is amazing. The game player uses a joystick with many switches and buttons, far more than the joystick interface can accommodate. Next to it is a throttle quadrant and possibly, on the floor, a set of rudder pedals. To allow the game program to read from all of this hardware, the usual hack is to wire each of these in series with the keyboard and mouse. Each device adds characters to the data stream to indicate that it is moving or that a switch has changed state. In some cases, mouse movement will be simulated. These are characters that will not echo on the screen or interfere with the text commands the player is entering via the keyboard in the current game. If the controls are moved while the computer is used for other programs, the characters generated will be interpreted in strange and interesting ways.

This complexity is not limited to game playing. It is not uncommon to have both a graphics tablet (absolute positioning) and a mouse (relative positioning) for design and drawing. The limitation on input devices means that having both devices coexisting on one machine requires complex interfaces. A modern software configuration might require a mouse, a tablet, and a 3-D resolver, depending on the application being used.

There must be a way to clean up this interface and allow multiple input devices. The WDM HID Class provides a way to do this.

One step toward a cleaner version is to use USB peripherals. In this case, each device has a single lightweight cable running from the device to a hub (which may be built into a device). The HID Class receives all input from the HID devices and passes the input to application programs. Note that the HID Class can emulate the legacy chained interface for application compatibility. Software can see the change in position of the rudder pedals as a stream of characters. Existing applications software (even games) will not be broken. However, no longer are the keyboard and mouse chained off a long string of devices; the tangle of cords has been dramatically improved. This arrangement also allows a far larger number of devices to be plugged in—the USB can handle 254 devices at the same time. Thus the opportunity exists to create multiuser programs, with each user controlling a joystick or mouse. New applications can use a more rational interface than keyboard input for these devices.

The HID Class controls the legacy hardware as well as the new USB versions of the hardware.

The Streams Class

The Streams Class provides a mechanism for "streaming" data between devices. The initial applications are video and audio. The Streams drivers allow *filters*[1] to be applied to the data. A filter is a transformation or processing of the data that has some number of input pins and some number of output pins, where *pin* is the name given to a data sink or source.

Without streams, the application sets up the flow of data through the filters in user space. The data is read by user-level code and passed from filter to filter. If a filter has a hardware component, the Device Driver associated with the filter must be called. The stream of data is passed to the driver, and the transformed stream is passed back to User mode. With several filters with driver components, a large amount of time can be spent transferring data between User and Kernel modes. This is illustrated in Figure 30.4.

With the Streams Class, a mechanism is provided for a User-mode component (the application or a common application framework) to set up a chain of filters that execute in Kernel mode. The user program controls the connection of filter input and output pins. The data passing between filters is not passed to the User-mode component. This structure is shown in Figure 30.5.

A filter can have more than one input pin and one output pin. The setup of a series of filters can be thought of as drawing a *filter graph*.

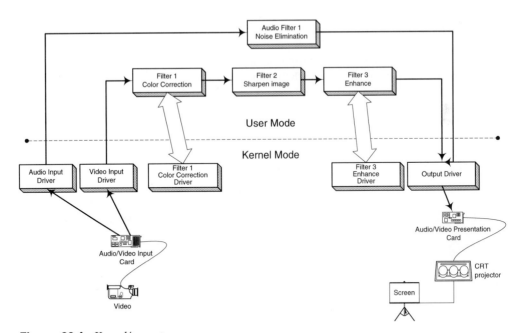

Figure 30.4: *Kernel/user streams.*

---

[1] For a stream, the term *filter* is used in the engineering sense when applied to an analog circuit placed in-line in a signal path. The term *filter* used in the sense of a Filter Driver is slightly different. However, philosophically both provide for the transformation of information. A Filter Driver transforms IRPs; a Streams filter transforms the actual data.

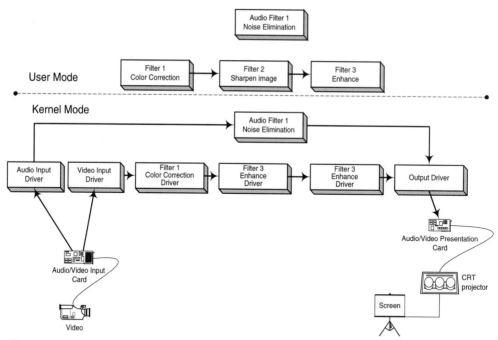

Figure 30.5: *Kernel streams.*

In Figure 30.6, we show a TV signal-processing filter graph. The TV signal is selected with the Tuner filter, which communicates with the tuner hardware to select a TV station. The input pins of the Tuner are the antenna and cable inputs and a control pin. This does not mean that the antenna or cable signal is digitized and fed into the filter; rather, the logical inputs to the Tuner

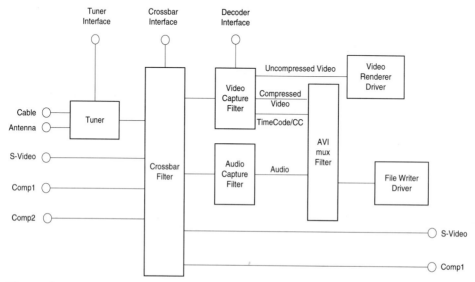

Figure 30.6: *A filter graph.*

component are the RF signals. The Crossbar filter provides switching between the Tuner output and alternate video input. The Video Capture filter compresses video and might append or process timecode. The AVI mux filter synchronizes audio and video. The Video Renderer filter displays the video.

The Audio Class

The Audio Class controls audio input and output devices. The output devices include the USB integrated speaker/amplifier. The input devices can include CD-compatible data streams, telephony connections, or digitized input from an analog microphone. Unlike the "traditional" sound card, which converts the digital data to an analog signal and amplifies on the adapter card, the analog signal is sent to the speaker. The USB system will send digital data to the integrated speaker/amplifier, which will convert the signal, amplify it, and play it.

The Video Class

Full-motion video hardware, such as cameras and video editing consoles, process full-motion video using the Streams Class for routing the video stream through software filters and hardware device drivers while maintaining synchronization with audio.

The Still Image Class

The Still Image Class supports still cameras and scanners. Facilities are provided to read images from the device.

Loading the WDM Drivers

WDM drivers are loaded based on the device identification returned to the Bus Driver as a result of a device interrogation. When the Bus Driver enumerates a bus and finds a device, it passes the hardware identification to the Plug-and-Play Manager. That manager then looks at the string using a combination of information in the Registry and information in a collection of configuration files known as `.inf` files. This information tells the manager if the driver is (1) known but not started, (2) started, or (3) unknown.

- If the driver is known but not started, it is started and called at its `DriverEntry` routine. Processing will continue.
- If the driver is started, it is called at its `AddDevice` entry with the PDO for the new device. The `AddDevice` routine creates the FDO and initializes the data structures. A `IRP_MJ_PNP` message with a minor type `IRP_MN_START_DEVICE` is then sent by the Plug-and-Play Manager to the driver (see Chapter 28). Additional messages will be sent for power management.
- If the Registry indicates that the driver for this device has not been copied to the system disk, a message box appears, asking for the NT distribution CD (or manufacturer's media) to install the driver.
- If the driver is unknown—that is, no reference is found in the Registry—a dialog box is displayed, asking for a driver.

A Monolithic WDM Driver

The term *monolithic driver* takes on a slightly different meaning in the WDM. Normally, when we talk about a monolithic driver, we are talking about a driver whose Driver Object, on one end, interfaces directly to the I/O Manager to process application-level calls and, at the other end, talks to a physical device via its device registers or memory interface.

In the WDM world, a monolithic driver is logically equivalent to an NT monolithic driver, but instead of talking to hardware at the bottom level, it talks to a Bus Driver. If the monolithic driver is for a bus with direct connections like the PCI Bus, the monolithic driver will use the bus driver for enumeration and access its adapter card directly, using the addresses provided by the bus driver. A monolithic driver for an external bus will use the bus driver for all access to the peripheral. A USB monolithic driver, for example, talks to the USB Bus Driver via URBs (USB Request Blocks). These URBs specify all communications with the USB peripheral. The driver we present here is based on one that Microsoft distributes in the DDK.

Important Differences Between Drivers

There are several important differences between a WDM-based monolithic driver and an ordinary NT driver. Because of the availability of reasonably priced USB components, we cast much of this discussion in terms of the USB interfaces. However, the styles will be similar for the IEEE-1394 interface.

We've already stated one of the major differences: The driver doesn't actually talk to physical hardware. The USB interface as specified by the URBs is the "hardware interface". But there are many other important differences that are part of the WDM.

For example, the `DriverEntry` routine no longer creates a Device Object for the device(s). Instead, it initializes three new fields in the Driver Object. There are two entry points in the `MajorFunction` table that need to be initialized:

- The entry for `IRP_MJ_PNP`, for "Plug-and-Play" support
- The entry for `IRP_MJ_POWER`, for power management

In addition, there is a special field in the Driver Object called the `AddDevice` dispatch entry, which is called to actually add devices to the Driver Object.

Because the low-level transactions are asynchronous (at least as far as the WDM driver is concerned), we need to wait for their completion. But since we are not talking to the bare hardware, we don't have an ISR to program or a DPC to handle the transaction. Instead, as is more common, we have the high-level driver wait on an *Event* and have that Event set by a completion routine established before the lower-level driver is called. This means that the higher-level driver may need to use a dedicated driver thread (Chapter 24) to do the work.

Design of a Monolithic USB Driver

The following sample monolithic driver is a test exercise in USB driver construction. It allows an application to send and receive Bulk Transfers and Interrupt Transfers from a USB device and to use the `DeviceIoControl` function to establish a data transfer. The interface is actually very "low level" in that once a "pipe" is established to a USB endpoint, the application can initiate a transaction with any pipe by specifying the pipe number as part of the `DeviceIoControl` parameter information.

A WDM/USB `DriverEntry` Function

Listing 30.1: *A* `DriverEntry` *for the WDM/USB*

```
NTSTATUS DriverEntry(IN PDRIVER_OBJECT DriverObject,
                     IN PUNICODE_STRING RegistryPath)
   {
    NTSTATUS status = STATUS_SUCCESS;

    DriverObject->MajorFunction[IRP_MJ_CREATE] = sampleCreate;
    DriverObject->MajorFunction[IRP_MJ_CLOSE] = sampleClose;
    DriverObject->DriverUnload = sampleUnload;
    DriverObject->MajorFunction[IRP_MF_DEVICE_CONTROL] =
                                      sampleDeviceControl;
```

Thus far, there is nothing here we haven't shown before. This looks just like any other `DriverEntry` *routine we've written, except we add some new, WDM-specific code.*

```
    DriverObject->MajorFunction[IRP_MJ_PNP] = sampleWDMhandler;
    DriverObject->MajorFunction[IRP_MJ_POWER] = sampleWDMhandler;
    DriverObject->AddDevice = pnpAddDevice;
```

These three lines are unique to a WDM driver. Note that we set up both of the major functions to dispatch to the same driver. This is because much of the code and process-ing is identical, so we will simply separate out the few special cases as needed. The `pnpAddDevice` *function will be used to add new Device Objects to the Driver Object. That's important because, unlike with our previous* `DriverEntry` *routines, this is all we do.*

```
    return status;
   }
```

A WDM/USB `AddDevice` Function

Whenever a new device is plugged into the USB, the Driver Object is used to route a call to the `AddDevice` handler, which here is called `pnpAddDevice`. We are passed the Driver Object and a pointer to a PDO, which is the next lower level in the driver hierarchy. This Device Object is cre-ated by the USB Bus Driver. Much of the work of this function is done in the `createDeviceObject` routine.

Listing 30.2: `AddDevice` *for the WDM/USB*

```
NTSTATUS pnpAddDevice(IN PDRIVER_OBJECT DriverObject,
                      IN PDEVICE_OBJECT PhysicalDeviceObject)
   {
    NTSTATUS status = STATUS_SUCCESS;
    PDEVICE_OBJECT deviceObject = NULL;
    PDEVICE_EXTENSION extension;  // WDM state and device-specific state
    status = createDeviceObject(DriverObject, &deviceObject, 0);
```

```
if(NT_STATUS(status))
  { /* successful creation */
    extension = deviceObject->DeviceExtension;
    deviceObject->Flags &= ~DO_DEVICE_INITIALIZING;
```

We have to clear the DO_DEVICE_INITIALIZING *flag because the flag has been set as part of the creation process, which has now successfully completed. At this point, we also set any other* Flags *fields that would be appropriate to the device. For example, if the device supports* ReadFile(Ex) *and* WriteFile(Ex)*, we would set the* DO_DIRECT_IO *or the* DO_BUFFERED_IO *flags. In our Device Extension, we need to supply a field that holds the PDO, and we store there the reference we were passed in.*

```
    extension->PhysicalDeviceObject = PhysicalDeviceObject;
```

Now comes one of the important WDM operations: We attach our Device Object to the PDO so that we can send IRPs and URBs down the stack.

```
    extension->StackDeviceObject =
            IoAttachDeviceToDeviceStack(deviceObject, PhysicalDeviceObject);
  } /* successful creation */
 return status;
}
```

Creating a WDM Device Object

The real work of creating a Device Object is encapsulated in the following routine. The key parameter here is the instance counter, which we use to keep track of the number of Device Objects. This simplistic code allows us to create up to ten devices, with single-digit suffixes 0 through 9. The generalization should be obvious. We also use this field to formulate the logical device names. The name of our device is declared as

```
#define DEVICE_NAME L"Sample"
```

This is a parameter that is changed to the name of your device. Since there are no C runtime routines such as the familiar lstrcpyW, lstrcatW, wsprintfW, wcscpy, or wcscat, we have to use UNICODE_STRING values. This is a bit clumsier than we would like. However, the overall effect happens only once during initialization, so it is tolerable.

Listing 30.3: *Creating a WDM Device Object*

```
#define DEVICE_ROOT L"\\Device\\"
#define DOS_DEVICE_ROOT L"\\DosDevices\\"
#define MAX_PATH 256

NTSTATUS createDeviceObject(
        IN PDRIVER_OBJECT driverObject,
        IN PDEVICE_OBJECT * deviceObject,
        LONG instance)
    {
    // The following variables are used to form the device name and DOS link name
    WCHAR path[MAX_PATH];
    WCHAR linkpath[MAX_PATH];
```

```
    WCHAR count[4];
    UNICODE_STRING pcount;
    UNICODE_STRING ptemp;
    UNICODE_STRING pname;
    UNICODE_STRING pathString ={0, MAX_PATH, path};
    UNICODE_STRING linkString ={0, MAX_PATH, linkpath};
    UNICODE_STRING countString = {0, sizeof(count)/sizeof(WCHAR), count };
    //----

    RtlIntegerToUnicodeString(instance, 10, &countString);
    RtlInitUnicodeString(&pname, DEVICE_NAME);

    RtlInitUnicodeString(ptemp, DEVICE_ROOT);
    RtlCopyString(pathString, ptemp);   // \\Device\\
    RtlAppendUnicodeStringToString(&pathString, pname);
                                // \\Device\\drivername
    RtlAppendUnicodeStringToString(&pathString,
                           &countString); // \\Device\\drivername0

    status = IoCreateDevice(DriverObject,
                        sizeof(DEVICE_EXTENSION),
                        &pathString,
                        FILE_DEVICE_UNKNOWN,
                        0,
                        FALSE, // Not exclusive access
                        deviceObject);
    if(NT_SUCCESS(status))
       { /* success */
        PDEVICE_EXTENSION extension;

        RtlInitUnicodeString(ptemp, DOS_DEVICE_ROOT);
        RtlCopyUnicodeString(linkString, ptemp);   // \\DosDevices\\
        RtlAppendUnicodeStringToString(&linkString, pname);
                                   // \\DosDevices\\drivername
        RtlAppendUnicodeStringToString(&linkString,
                               &countString);
                               // \\DosDevices\\drivername0
        status = IoCreateSymbolicLink(&linkString, &pathString);
```

At this point, there is no difference between what we've seen here and what we've seen in the traditional DriverEntry *routine of an ordinary NT driver, except for the way we have dynamically formed the names. But now we initialize some fields we've added to support the WDM.*

```
        extension =
              (PDEVICE_EXTENSION) ((*DeviceObject)->DeviceExtension);
        extension->ConfigurationHandle = NULL;
        extension->DeviceDescriptor    = NULL;
        extension->NeedCleanup         = FALSE;
        extension->Interface           = NULL;
       } /* success */

    return status;
    }
```

Calling the USB Driver

We will often need to call the lower-level driver. This USB driver takes a URB that the higher level has created. It creates an IRP, puts a pointer to the URB in it, and calls the lower-level device.

This routine takes a simplistic view of how the communication takes place. It treats the lower-level call as a synchronous call and does not return until that call completes. It does this by waiting on an Event. Another alternative is to use the same sort of I/O completion routine already shown in an NT driver. We show here the use of an Event.

Listing 30.4: *Calling the USB Driver*

```
#define TIMEOUT (5000)
#define MSto100NS (10000)

NTSTATUS callUSBD(IN PDEVICE_OBJECT DeviceObject, IN PURB urb)
    {
      NTSTATUS status;
      PDEVICE_EXTENSION extension;
      PIRP irp;
      KEVENT event;
      IO_STATUS_BLOCK iostatus;
      PIO_STACK_LOCATION next;

      extension = DeviceObject->DeviceExtension;
```

We now need to initialize a kernel Event. This Event will be passed in to the lower level. It becomes the way we are notified of the completion of the I/O request if it cannot be completed immediately.

```
      KeInitializeEvent(&event, NotificationEvent, FALSE);
```

Next, we create an IRP. The code for this IRP is the special `IOCTL_INTERNAL_USB_SUBMIT_URB`, *which causes this message to be sent to the USB device. We provide as additional parameters the pointer to a kernel event and a pointer to an I/O Status Block.*

```
      irp = IoBuildDeviceIoControlRequest(
                            IOCTL_INTERNAL_USB_SUBMIT_URB,
                            deviceExtension->StackDeviceObject,
                            NULL,
                            0,
                            NULL,
                            0,
                            TRUE,    // Internal call
                            &event,  // Notification event
                            &ioStatus);
```

Having created the IRP, we prepare to send it to the next lower level. We must initialize one of the fields of the IRP to point to the URB we are sending. The USB driver has specified that this is to be set in the `Parameters.Others.Argument1` *field.*

```
next = IoGetNextIrpStackLocation(irp);
ASSERT(next != NULL);
next->Parameters.Others.Argument1 = urb;
```

Next, we establish a completion routine. A completion routine can take an arbitrary 32-bit pointer value as a context parameter, so we pass in the address of the event to be signaled. The last three parameters indicate that we want completion on success, error, and cancel.

```
IoSetCompletionRoutine(irp, USBcomplete, &event, TRUE, TRUE, TRUE);
```

Now we call the driver, passing down the IRP we just created.

```
status = IoCallDriver(deviceExtension->StackDeviceObject, irp);
```

There are essentially three possible return conditions:

- *The IRP completed successfully.*
- *The IRP failed in some way.*
- *The IRP is still being processed.*

Given the nature of the USB, most IRPs will probably be returned in a still-pending condition. If we get a pending status, we simply wait on the specified event. Because we want a robust driver, we also provide a (fairly long, by USB standards) timeout of five seconds. (This can be adjusted by changing the TIMEOUT constant, which is the timeout in milliseconds.) A negative value indicates that the time given is relative to the current time (a positive value specifies an absolute time). Unlike the familiar timeout at the user level, which uses milliseconds, the time interval at the kernel level must be given in a platform-independent 100-ns units. We conveniently have the constant MSto100NS declared as 10,000.

```
if(status == STATUS_PENDING)
    { /* pending */
      LARGE_INTEGER timeout;
      timeout.QuadPart = - ((MSto100NS) * TIMEOUT);
```

Now comes the Wait operation. We are waiting on the event that we created and passed in via the IRP. We will not get control back until either the event is signaled or the timeout interval expires. However, during this time this thread releases control of the processor and other threads can be scheduled. When the event is signaled, our waiting thread will become feasible to run and eventually will be scheduled, based on its priority in the scheduling queue. Because we are at PASSIVE_LEVEL, we preempt any lower priority thread that is running.

```
status = KeWaitForSingleObject( &event, Suspended, KernelMode,
                                FALSE, &timeout);
if(status == STATUS_TIMEOUT)
    { /* timed out */
```

If we have a timeout, the lower-level driver has not yet completed our IRP, yet we expected that it should. Failure to complete the IRP suggests that the device is nonresponsive. We must therefore cancel the IRP. The Cancel operation is itself an asynchronous operation, and we again wait on the event. When the Cancel operation has completed, we again gain control. Note that we do not wait for a timeout, because in a properly written driver, a Cancel operation must succeed.

```
            ioStatus.status = status = STATUS_IO_TIMEOUT;
            IoCancelIrp(irp);
            status = KeWaitForSingleObject(&event, Suspended,
                                           KernelMode,
                                           FALSE, NULL);
        } /* timed out */
    } /* pending */
  else
    { /* completed */
      ioStatus.Status = status;
    } /* completed */
```

The status code returned by IoCallDriver, *or if we are waiting, the status code returned by* KeWaitForSingleObject, *is an NT status code. A much more finely detailed USB error code is contained in the* urb->UrbHeader.Status *field, which in the case of failure, we might wish to print out or log.*

```
  status = ioStatus.Status;

  return status;
}
```

The completion routine is very simple. It simply signals the Event Object.

```
NTSTATUS USBComplete(IN PDEVICE_OBJECT DeviceObject, IN PIRP Irp, LPVOID context)
  {
    PKEVENT event = (PKEVENT)context;

  }
```

The USB and the WDM

The first set of WDM drivers from Microsoft for the USB and for IEEE-1394. These two busses represent families of new devices that would involve considerable effort to implement across the two Windows platforms and across a variety of busses.

The USB Subsystem

Figure 30.7 shows a detailed illustration of how the USB system fits into the WDM.

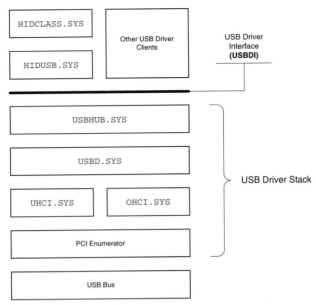

Figure 30.7: *The WDM and the USB Drivers.*

The USB Card MiniDriver

Figure 30.7 illustrates that the USB is actually a card plugged into the PCI Bus. When the PCI Enumerator detects a USB card on the PCI Bus, it causes the rest of the USB Driver Stack to be loaded.

UHCI/OHCI Drivers

UHCI (Universal Host Controller Interface) and OHCI (Open Host Controller Interface) are two standards for a USB interconnect hardware. One of these two drivers is loaded for a particular USB interface card (but it is possible to have two USB interface cards, each with a different driver). These drivers talk to the USB card at the lowest level and to the upper levels using IRPs.

The USB Class Driver

The USB Class Driver, USBD.SYS, handles USB transactions. It does not care about how the USB card is implemented (it's handled at a lower level), and it doesn't care what the semantics of the USB transaction are (it's handled at a higher level). It does handle common USB actions, such as power management and bus enumeration.

The USB Hub Class Driver

The USB Hub Class Driver, USBHUB.SYS, is loaded when USBD.SYS enumerates the root hub. It is also loaded (that is, its reference count is increased and new private data space is allocated) and calls itself recursively whenever it enumerates a downstream hub of any sort. This layer handles all hub transactions, such as port initialization, device initialization of downstream devices on a specific hub, and similar USB administrative functions.

This driver is the highest level of the USB Driver Stack. It defines the USB Device Interface (USBDI). Above this level are the *USB clients*.

The HID/USB Interface

The HID Class is devoted to a variety of input devices, including keyboards, joysticks, mice, game controls, and a variety of similar interface devices. A vendor of a USB device that performs an HID function should create a device that follows a protocol specification of how an HID Class device should behave. For example, all USB mice should follow a single USB mouse protocol. The advantage of this strategy is that a fancy mouse that incorporates, say, a scrolling thumbwheel, ends up having multiple USB "devices", one of which is handled by the scrolling wheel device code. The input to HIDUSB.SYS is a sequence of HID-oriented IRPs; the lower-level calls from HIDUSB.SYS are USB-oriented requests.

Communicating to the USBDI

A WDM-based USB Device Driver communicates to the USB Driver Stack via an IRP interface. There are two kinds of IRPs that may be sent to USBDI.

- The first form has its MajorFunction field set to IRP_MJ_INTERNAL_DEVICE_CONTROL. In the I/O Stack of this IRP, the next location's Parameters.DeviceIoControl.IoControlCode is set to IOCTL_INTERNAL_USB_SUBMIT_URB.
- The second form does not use URBs but uses one of the other function codes shown in Table 30.1.

Table 30.1: *IRP Functions to USBDI*

IRP Major Function Code	Description
IOCTL_INTERNAL_USB_SUBMIT_URB	Submits URBs to the USB stack.
IOCTL_INTERNAL_USB_RESET_PORT	Resets a USB port.
IOCTL_INTERNAL_USB_ENUMERATE	Retrieves a list of all devices on the USB.
IOCTL_INTERNAL_USB_GET_ROOTHUB_PDO	Gets the PDO representing the root hub.

USB Request Blocks

To submit a set of URBs to the USBDI, you pass a pointer to a list of URBs via the IRP using the major function code IOCTL_INTERNAL_USB_SUBMIT_URB. Each URB has a common header format; the remainder of the URB is specific to the type of URB.

The USB and Power Management

The USB provides interfaces for the OnNow power-management operations. The core idea here is that a driver can make its power states visible to the operating system or allow the operating system to specify the current power state, while minimizing the number of states with which the Bus Driver must deal. The power state definitions are given in Table 30.2.

Table 30.2: *Power State Definitions*

OnNow Power State	Device Context	Driver	Consumption	Responsiveness
D0	Fully on.	Fully on.	Highest.	Fastest.
D1	Optional. If used, it is class-specific.	If D1 is used, this is class-specific.	If D1 is used, this is class-specific.	If D1 is used, this is class-specific.
D2	Optional. If used, it is class-specific.	If D2 is used, this is class-specific.	If D2 is used, this is class-specific.	If D2 is used, this is class-specific.
D3	Lost.	Responsible for all device context, including restoration upon leaving D3.	None or very close to none.	Slowest.

The four states, D0, D1, D2, and D3, are what are visible to the operating system. A device is not required to implement the D1 and D2 (intermediate) power states, but it is required to implement D0 and D3 (on and off). Generally, it is expected that the device itself will maintain context in the D0 to D2 states and will lose context in the D3 state, but it is up to the device implementor to specify if this is true for D1 and D2 states. In the intermediate states, it is possible that some, but not all, intermediate state is lost.

The USB specification defines how the USB power-management mechanisms will work. The USB may power down any or all ports on a hub or respond to "remote wakeup" from idle devices (such as a mouse being moved). A *suspended* port continues to supply a limited amount of downstream power to the suspended device, while a *disabled* port is not required to supply any power to downstream devices.

A USB Filter Driver

The code in the following section is adapted from the USB Filter Driver example `valueadd` in the DDK.

This driver is quite interesting and uses a number of advanced techniques. The Filter Driver is controlled by yet another driver, a controller driver, that specifies the parameters to the filter. This controller driver controls no actual hardware; thus there is exactly one Device Object for it in the system. This object is created in `DriverEntry` in the usual way. There also can be any number of instances of controller drivers, one for each USB device that is being filtered. This is shown in Figure 30.8.

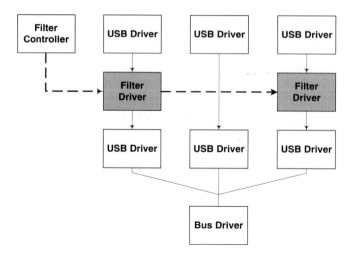

Figure 30.8: *A USB Filter Driver.*

Shown here are three USB Stacks. The first and third are filtered by the Filter Driver. This driver itself is parameterized by the leftmost driver, the Filter Controller, which provides the information required by the Filter Drivers themselves.

Since much of the driver will execute at PASSIVE_LEVEL, we can make much of the driver code pageable.

This driver intercepts each URB packet coming downward and prints it. Of course, you are free to reimplement these features to have it do something else interesting to the USB stream, but this driver as implemented is entirely passive. This is not to say it has no effect on the system. It has considerable effect on the timing because of the delays imposed in printing out the debug strings used to display the information.

The ValueAdd.c File

```
#include <wdm.h>
#include "valueAdd.h"
#include "local.h"
```

The first thing to note is that this is a WDM driver. It includes not ntddk.h, *but* wdm.h. *This header file includes the definitions that are valid for WDM drivers and does not include any definition that the WDM does not support. Thus, when you are compiling your driver, if you get undefined symbol errors for symbols you know are defined and whose documentation you find among the DDK documentation, it means you are trying to use a facility that is not part of the WDM specification. You can get the definition by including* ntddk.h, *but the resulting driver will not be a WDM-compliant driver and will not operate under Windows 9x.*

```
struct _VA_GLOBALS Global;
```

Now this variable is really unusual to find in a driver! It is a global variable in a driver! We've said several times in this book that you mustn't use global variables. Well, one reason for choosing this example is that it violates that restriction and gives us a chance to talk about it. In this case, you will see that DriverEntry *creates the one-and-only-ever Device Object for this driver. How do we know this is the one-and-only-ever Device Object? Because the driver will be loaded only once, and it never does any bus enumeration or otherwise makes any attempt to create more than one Device Object in* DriverEntry. *This Device Object is shared among all of its associated USB Filter Drivers. Thus there is no chance that there will be a conflict.*

Next, we specify which functions are going to be paged. We assign code section names. The DriverEntry *routine is in the section* INIT, *and the remaining functions named here are in the section called* PAGE. *Other functions will be in the default code section and will be nonpaged. If we define the preprocessor symbol* ALLOC_PRAGMA, *we will get a pageable driver; if the symbol is undefined, the entire driver is nonpageable. We also declare* DriverEntry *here because the names of the functions must be defined before the* #pragma *can work. The other functions are declared in the header files that have been included.*

The DriverEntry *Routine*

Listing 30.5: DriverEntry *for a USB Filter Driver*

```
NTSTATUS DriverEntry(PDRIVER_OBJET, PUNICODE_STRING);

#ifdef ALLOC_PRAGMA
#pragma alloc_text (INIT, DriverEntry)
#pragma alloc_text (PAGE, VA_CreateClose)
#pragma alloc_text (PAGE, VA_AddDevice)
#pragma alloc_text (PAGE, VA_Unload)
#endif
```

This is the DriverEntry *routine itself. It looks pretty much like any conventional NT 4.0 driver.*

```
NTSTATUS DriverEntry(IN PDRIVER_OBJECT DriverObject,
                     IN PUNICODE_STRING RegistryPath)
   {
     NTSTATUS status = STATUS_SUCCESS;
     PDEVICE_OBJECT deviceObject;
     UNICODE_STRING NtNameString;
     UNICODE_STRING Win32NameString;
     PVA_CONTROL_DATA deviceData;
     ULONG i;
     PRDRIVER_DISPATCH * dispatch;

     UNREFERENCED_PARAMETER(RegistryPath);

     RtlInitUnicodeString(&NtNameString, VA_FILTER_NTNAME);
```

```
       status = IoCreateDevice(DriverObject,
                               sizeof(VA_CONTROL_DATA), // Extension size
                               &NtNameString,
                               0, // No standard device characteristics
                               FALSE, // Not exclusive
                               &deviceObject);
       if(!NT_SUCCESS(status))
           return status;

       // Create symbolic link

       RtlInitUnicodeString(&Win32NameString, VA_FILTER_SYMNAME);
       status = IoCreateSymbolicLink(&Win32NameString, &NtNameString);
       deviceData = (PVA_CONTROL_DATA)deviceObject->DeviceExtension;
```

So far there are no surprises. Next, we do some device-specific initialization. The intent of this driver is that it will have a list of all of the USB Filter Drivers it controls; this list is maintained as a linked list. We initialize the list, a Spin Lock used to control access to it, and a counter that counts the number of devices.

```
       InitializeListHead(&deviceData->UsbDevices);
       KeInitializeSpinLock(&deviceData->Spin);
       deviceData->NumUsbDevices = 0;
```

We store the one and only Device Object in the one and only global variable.

```
       Global.ControlObject = deviceObject;
```

Because this driver is a WDM driver in a Plug-and-Play, power-managed universe, it must pass on any IRP it doesn't understand. This code initializes the dispatch table to do this. We then selectively override the individual dispatch handlers we actually need. The particular IRP_MJ_ *handler we wish to implement is the* IRP_MJ_INTERNAL_DEVICE_CONTROL, *which is used to pass USB requests downward in the stack.*

```
       for(i = 0; dispatch = DriverObject->MajorFunction;
           i <= IRP_MJ_MAXIMUM_FUNCTION;
           i++, dispatch++)
               *dispatch = VA_Pass;                              // Page 759

       DriverObject->MajorFunction[IRP_MJ_CREATE] =
                                       VA_CreateClose;           // Page 759
       DriverObject->MajorFunction[IRP_MJ_CLOSE]  =
                                       VA_CreateClose;           // Page 759
       DriverObject->MajorFunction[IRP_MJ_INTERNAL_DEVICE_CONTROL] =
                                       VA_FilterURB;             // Page 773
       DriverObject->MajorFunction[IRP_MJ_PNP] = VA_PnP;         // Page 764
       DriverObject->MajorFunction[IRP_MJ_POWER] = VA_Power;     // Page 763
       DriverObject->DriverExtension->AddDevice  = VA_AddDevice; // Page 761
       DriverObject->DriverUnload = VA_Unload;                   // Page 762

       return status;
   }
```

The Pass-Thru Routine

The purpose of the pass-thru function is to pass the IRP down the USB Stack. However, we should never get to this point for any IRP request for the main controller device.

Listing 30.6: *Pass-Thru Function for a USB Filter Driver*

```
NTSTATUS VA_Pass(IN PDEVICE_OBJECT DeviceObject, IN PIRP Irp)
    {
      PVA_USB_DATA usbData;
      NTSTATUS status;
```

Here, we check the input parameter to see if it is the Device Object of the main controller device. If it is, we fail the IRP with STATUS_NOT_SUPPORTED.

```
    if(DeviceObject == Global.ControlObject)
      { /* the main object */
        Irp->IoStatus.Information = 0;
        Irp->IoStatus.Status = STATUS_NOT_SUPPORTED;
        IoCompleteRequest(Irp, IO_NO_INCREMENT);
        return STATUS_NOT_SUPPORTED;
      } /* the main object */
```

If it is not the main Device Object, it is the Device Object for a USB filter. At this point, we pass the IRP downward in the chain. Because we do not want to allow the object to be removed if there are outstanding IRPs, we increment the OutstandingIO *field. We will decrement this when we have finished processing the IRP. If the device has been removed, we cannot pass the IRP down, so we fail it with* STATUS_DELETE_PENDING.

```
    usbData = (PBA_USB_DATA)DeviceObject->DeviceExtension;

    InterlockedIncrement(&usbData->OutstandingIO);
                                    // Increment reference count
    if(usbData->Removed)
      { /* removed */
        status = STATUS_DELETE_PENDING;
        Irp->IoStatus.Information = 0;
        Irp->IoStatus.Status = status;
        IoCompleteRequest(Irp, IO_NO_INCREMENT);
        return status;
      } /* removed */

    IoSkipCurrentIrpStackLocation(Irp);
    status = IoCallDriver(usbData->TopOfStack, Irp);

    if(0 == InterlockedDecrement(&usbData->OutstandingIO))
       KeSetEvent(&usbData->RemoveEvent, 0, FALSE);

    return status;
    }
```

The Create/Close Handler

The Create/Close handler allows a device to be opened or closed. This code is shared between our Filter Controller and the Filter Drivers themselves.

Listing 30.7: *Create/Close Handler for a USB Filter Driver*

```
NTSTATUS VA_CreateClose(IN PDEVICE_OBJECT DeviceObject, IN PIRP Irp)
    {
      PIO_STACK_LOCATION stack;
      NTSTATUS status = STATUS_SUCCESS;
      PVA_USB_DATA usbData;
```

*This is a bit of a diversion, but it indicates a valuable technique for debugging a paged driver. It would be fatal to have a paged handler called at elevated IRQL (*DISPATCH_LEVEL *or higher) while it is paged out. The technique to apply is first to compile the driver without the paging enabled, that is, without the symbol* ALLOC_PRAGMA *defined. This will produce a driver that is entirely nonpaged. For each function you want to have paged, you add the* PAGED_CODE() *call. This simply tests the IRQL with an* ASSERT *that the IRQL is less than* DISPATCH_LEVEL. *If the driver is ever called from an elevated IRQL, you will get a message on the debug output port that a paged driver was called at elevated IRQL. If, by the conclusion of testing, you have not seen any such messages, you know that your driver has not violated the restrictions about calling paged code, and you can compile with the* ALLOC_PRAGMA *option defined and get a pageable driver.*

```
      PAGED_CODE();
```

We test to see if the Device Object is for the global Controller Device Object or is for one of the Filter Drivers. If it is for the global object, we allow the device to be opened or closed. Since opening or closing the Controller Device does not require any specific actions, all we do is complete the IRP here.

```
      if(DeviceObject == Global.ControlObject)
        { /* accessing control object */
         Irp->IoStatus.Information = 0;
         Irp->IoStatus.Status = STATUS_SUCCESS;
         IoCompleteRequest(Irp, IO_NO_INCREMENT);
         return status;
        } /* accessing control object */
```

If it was not the Controller Device, it must be a filter device.

```
      stack = IoGetCurrentIrpStackLocation(Irp);
      usbData - (PVA_USB_DATA) DeviceObject->DeviceExtension;
```

We increment the reference count to indicate that an IRP is active and the device should not be removed.

```
      InterlockedIncrement(&usbData->OutstandingIO); // Increment ref count
```

If the object has been removed, we cannot pass the IRP downward. Instead, we complete it. An IRP_MJ_CREATE *operation fails with* STATUS_DELETE_PENDING, *but an* IRP_MJ_CLOSE *can always successfully complete.*

```
    if(usbData->Removed)
        { /* removed */
          status = (IRP_MJ_CREATE == stack->MajorFunction)
                        ? STATUS_DELETE_PENDING  // Create
                        : STATUS_SUCCESS;        // Close

          Irp->IoStatus.Information = 0;
          Irp->IoStatus.Status = status;
          IoCompleteRequest(Irp, IO_NO_INCREMENT);
        } /* removed */
```

The device has not been removed, so we pass the IRP downward in the chain.
`IoSkipCurrentIrpStackLocation` *will copy the current stack location to the stack*
location used by the next lower-level driver, and `IoCallDriver` *passes the IRP*
downward.

```
    else
        { /* pass it down */
          IoSkipCurrentIrpStackLocation(Irp);
          status = IoCallDriver(usbData->TopOfStack, Irp);
        } /* pass it down */
```

Now that we have completed our processing of the IRP, we can decrement the reference
count. Note that the IRP might have completed as pending at the lower level, but the
lower level now has responsibility for it; this level no longer cares about it and consid-
ers the IRP to be gone. If the reference count should go to 0, the driver can be removed
and the `RemoveEvent` *can be set.*

```
    if(0 == InterlockedDecrement(&usbData->OutstandingIo))
        KeSetEvent(&usbData->RemoveEvent, 0, FALSE);

    return status;
}
```

The `AddDevice` *Function*

The `AddDevice` function is called to add a new Filter Driver to the USB chain. It creates the Filter Driver Device Object and adds it to the Controller Driver's filter list.

Listing 30.8: AddDevice *for a USB Filter Driver*

```
NTSTATUS VA_AddDevice(IN PDRIVER_OBJECT DriverObject,
                      IN PDEVICE_OBJECT PhysicalDeviceObject)
    {
      NTSTATUS status = STATUS_SUCCESS;
      PDEVICE_OBJECT deviceObject = NULL;
      PVA_USB_DATA usbData;
      PVA_CONTROL_DATA controlData =
                  (PVA_CONTROL_DATA)Global.ControlObject->DeviceExtension;

      PAGED_CODE();
```

```
       status = IoCreateDevice(DriverObject,
                               sizeof(VA_USB_DATA),
                               FILE_DEVICE_UNKNOWN,
                               0,
                               FALSE,
                               &deviceObject);

   if(!NT_SUCCESS(status))
       { /* failed */
         return status;
       } /* failed */

   usbData = (PBA_USB_DATA)deviceObject->DeviceExtension;

   usbData->Started = FALSE;
   usbData->Removed = FALSE;
   usbData->PDO = pdo;
   usbData->TopOfStack = NULL;
   usbData->PrintMask = VA_PRINT_ALL;
   deviceObject->Flags &= ~DO_DEVICE_INITIALIZING;
```

This has all been very conventional for a Windows 2000 driver; we create the Device Object and initialize its various data members. Then we add it to the Controller Driver's filter list.

```
   ExInterlockedInsertHeadList(&controlData->UsbDevices,
                               &usbData->List,
                               &controlData->Spin);

   InterlockedIncrement(&controlData->NumUsbDevices);
```

Next, we initialize the Event Object used to determine when the driver can be removed. It is initialized to the Not-Signaled state. We initialize the reference count to 1; it will not go to 0 until the device is about to be removed.

```
   KeInitializeEvent(&usbData->RemoveEvent, SynchronizationEvent, FALSE);
   usbData->OutstandingIO = 1; // Biased to 1
```

Finally, we attach the Filter Driver to the stack, to the PDO that was passed in to AddDevice.

```
   usb->TopOfStack = IoAttachDeviceToDeviceStack(deviceObject, pdo);
   ASSERT(NULL != usbData->TopOfStack);

   return STATUS_SUCCESS;
 }
```

The Unload Function

The Unload function is fairly conventional by Windows NT 4.0 standards; it deletes the Controller Device Object after deleting the symbolic link. But note that it does *not* delete any of the actual USB Filter Drivers! Why? These were already deleted as part of the Plug-and-Play support.

Listing 30.9: *Unload Routine for a USB Filter Driver*

```
VOID VA_Unload(IN PDRIVER_OBJECT DriverObject)
    {
     UNICODE_STRING Win32NameString;

     PAGED_CODE();

     ASSERT(Global.ControlObject == DriverObject->DeviceObject);
     ASSERT(NULL == Global.ControlObject->NextDevice);

     RtlInitUnicodeString(&Win32NameString, VA_FILTER_SYMNAME);
     IoDeleteSymbolicLink(&Win32NameString);

     IoDeleteDevice(DriverObject->DeviceObject);
    }
```

The PnP.c File

```
#include <wdm.h>
#include "local.h"
#include "ValueAdd.h"

#ifdef ALLOC_PRAGMA
#pragma alloc_text (PAGE, VA_Power)
#pragma alloc_text (PAGE, VA_PnP)
#pragma alloc_text (PAGE, VA_StartDevice)
#pragma alloc_text (PAGE, VA_CallUSBD)
```

This material was discussed on page 756.

The Power Dispatch Function

The Power Dispatch Function is an entry point in the driver. This entry point is called by NT to direct the driver to execute a power management function.

Listing 30.10: IRP_MJ_POWER *for a USB Filter Driver*

```
NTSTATUS VA_Power(IN PDEVICE_OBJECT DeviceObject, IN PIRP Irp)
    {
     PVA_USB_DATA usbData;
     NTSTATUS status;

     PAGED_CODE();
```

If this IRP comes in to the Controller Device, it is meaningless, so it is failed as being not supported.

```
     if(DeviceObject == Global.ControlObject)
        { /* controller */
         Irp->IoStatus.Information = 0;
         Irp->IoStatus.Status = STATUS_NOT_SUPPORTED;
         IoCompleteRequest(Irp, IO_NO_INCREMENT);
         return STATUS_NOT_SUPPORTED;
        } /* controller */
```

*The IRP was sent to one of the Filter Drivers controlled by this Controller Driver. If the
Filter Driver is in the process of being removed, we must fail it. However, before doing
so we must start the next power IRP.*

```
if(usbData->Removed)
    { /* fail it */
      status = STATUS_DELETE_PENDING;
      PoStartNextPowerIrp(Irp);
      Irp->IoStatus.Information = 0;
      Irp->IoStatus.Status = status;
      IoCompleteRequest(Irp, IO_NO_INCREMENT);
    } /* fail it */
```

*We have to pass the power IRP downward. First, we must start the next power IRP.
Then we copy the current IRP Stack location to the stack location for the next lower-
level driver and call that driver. Because this is a power IRP, we must use*
`PoCallDriver`, *not* `IoCallDriver`.

```
else
    { /* send it down */
     PoStartNextPowerIrp(Irp);
     IoSkipCurrentIrpStackLocation(Irp);
     status = PoCallDriver(usbData->TopOfStack, Irp);
    } /* send it down */

if(0 == InterlockedDecrement(&usbData->OutstandingIO))
    KeSetEvent(&usbData->RemoveEvent, 0, FALSE);

return status;
}
```

The Plug-and-Play Handler

The Plug-and-Play Handler is a Dispatch Routine called by NT when the system has determined
that a device controlled by this driver must be started, stopped, queried, or controlled.

Listing 30.11: `IRP_MJ_PNP` *Handler for a USB Filter Driver*

```
NTSTATUS VA_PnP(IN PDEVICE_OBJECT DeviceObject, IN PIRP Irp)
    {
      PVA_USB_DATA usbData;
      PIO_STACK_LOCATION stack;
      NTSTATUS status;
      PVA_CONTROL_DATA controlData;
      KIRLQ oldIrql;

      PAGED_CODE();

      usbData = (PVA_USB_DATA)DeviceObject->DeviceExtension;
      stack = IoGetCurrentIrpStackLocation(Irp);
```

*If the Plug-and-Play request came in for the Controller Device, we need to fail it be-
cause it has no meaning.*

```
if(DeviceObject == Global.ControlObject)
   { /* fail it */
    Irp->IoStatus.Information = 0;
    Irp->IoStatus.Status = STATUS_NOT_SUPPORTED;
    IoCompleteRequest(Irp, IO_NO_INCREMENT);
    return STATUS_NOT_SUPPORTED;
   } /* fail it */
```

*If the device has been removed, we have to fail the IRP. However, this would suggest
that another Plug-and-Play IRP has been received after the removal request, which is
(or should be) impossible. The* ASSERT *should catch this during debugging.*

```
if(usbData->Removed)
   { /* removed */
    ASSERT(FALSE); // This should never happen
    Irp->IoStatus.Information = 0;
    Irp->IoStatus.Status = STATUS_DELETE_PENDING;
    IoCompleteRequest(Irp, IO_NO_INCREMENT);
    return STATUS_DELETE_PENDING;
   } /* removed */
```

Next, we increment the reference count of outstanding IRPs.

```
InterlockedIncrement(&usbData->OutstandingIO);

switch(stack->MinorFunction)
      { /* MinorFunction */
```

The **IRP_MN_START_DEVICE** Case

If we are starting the device, we pass the IRP downward in the driver chain. We cannot complete
this operation until all lower-level drivers have completed processing. What we must set up a
completion routine and an event to wait on. When the completion routine is called, it sets the
event, which allows the code to proceed.

Listing 30.12: IRP_MN_START_DEVICE *for a USB Filter Driver*

```
case IRP_MN_START_DEVICE:
     IoCopyCurrentIrpStackLocationToNext(Irp);
     KeInitializeEvent(&usbData->StartEvent, NotificationEvent,
                       FALSE);
     IoSetCompletionRoutine(Irp,
                            VA_PnPComplete,  // Page 768
                            usbData,   // Context
                            TRUE,      // Complete successes
                            TRUE,      // Complete errors
                            TRUE);     // complete cancels
     status = IoCallDriver(usbData->TopOfStack, Irp);
```

*The lower-level driver could succeed immediately, fail immediately, or require addi-
tional processing. If it requires additional processing, it must return* STATUS_PENDING.
*In this case, we wait for the completion routine to be called and set the event we are
about to wait on.*

```
if(STATUS_PENDING == status)
    { /* wait for completion */
    KeWaitForSingleObject(&usbData->StartEvent,
                          Executive,
                          KernelMode,
                          FALSE,    // Not alertable
                          NULL);    // No timeout
    status = Irp->IoStatus.Status;
    } /* wait for completion */
```

At this point, we know the IRP has been processed by all of the lower levels. If it was processed successfully, we can actually start the device.

```
if(NT_SUCCESS(status))
    { /* start it */
    status = VA_StartDevice(usbData, Irp); // Page 769
    } / start it */
```

Next, we complete the IRP and fall out of the switch. *When we fall out, we decrement the reference count.*

```
Irp->IoStatus.Status = status;
Irp->IoStatus.Information = 0;
IoCompleteRequest(Irp, IO_NO_INCREMENT);
break;
```

The IRP_MN_STOP_DEVICE Case

Once the IRP_MN_STOP_DEVICE has been sent down to the lower levels, those levels are "unavailable" until another IRP_MN_START_DEVICE request comes through. This is because the lower levels might no longer be able to perform their actions, such as touching (now unavailable) hardware. So we must call our stop handler first before passing the request downward, in case doing this would require sending other IRPs downward in the chain. After our device-specific stop handler has completed, we can pass the IRP downward.

Listing 30.13: IRP_MN_STOP_DEVICE *for a USB Filter Driver*

```
case IRP_MN_STOP_DEVICE:
    VA_StopDevice(usbData, TRUE);
    IoSkipCurrentIrpStackLocation(Irp);
    status = IoCallDriver(usbData->TopOfStack, Irp);
    break;
```

The IRP_MN_REMOVE_DEVICE Case

The Plug-and-Play system forces the removal of the device. The device must be removed; this is not optional. If there is some reason to not remove the device, implement the IRP_MN_QUERY_REMOVE_DEVICE case and have it return a failure status. Note that it is possible to receive a remove request without first receiving a stop request.

Listing 30.14: `IRP_MN_REMOVE_DEVICE` *Handler for a USB Filter Driver*

```
case IRP_MN_REMOVE_DEVICE:
  usbData->Removed = TRUE;    // Mark as removed to fail future IRPs
    if(usbData->Started)
       VA_StopDevice(usbData, FALSE); // In case not stopped
```

The device is about to be removed. Remove its entry from the Controller Driver.

```
controlData =
     (PVA_CONTROL_DATA)Global.ControlObject->DeviceExtension;
KeAcquireSpinLock(&controlData->Spin, &oldIrql);
RemoveEntryList(&usbData->List);
InterlockedDecrement(&controlData->NumUsbDevices);
KeReleaseSpinLock(&controlData->Spin, oldIrql);
```

We can now pass the removal request downward in the chain.

```
IoSkipCurrentIrpStackLocation(Irp);
status = IoCallDriver(usbData->TopOfStack, Irp);
```

We next decrement the reference count because the IRP has been processed. Then we decrement the reference count one more time. When the reference count goes to 0, there are no outstanding IRPs and the object can be safely removed. If there are other outstanding IRPs to be processed at this level, the second decrement will leave the reference count still above 0, so we must wait for it to go to 0. Note that in all places in which we decrement the reference count, we call `KeSetEvent` *on the* `RemoveEvent` *if the reference count goes to 0. If the reference count does not go to 0 here, we wait on that event until the other pending IRPs have reduced the reference count and the last one eventually releases the event.*

```
InterlockedDecrement(&usbData->OutstandingIO);
if(0 < InterlockedDecrement(&usbData->OutstandingIO))
   { /* wait for completion */
    KeWaitForSingleObject(&usbData->RemoveEvent,
                          Executive,
                          KernelMode,
                          FALSE,
                          NULL);
   } /* wait for completion */

IoDetachDevice(usbData->TopOfStack);

IoDeleteDevice(usbData->Self);
return STATUS_SUCCESS;
```

Unhandled IRP_MN_ Codes

```
case IRP_MN_QUERY_REMOVE_DEVICE:
case IRP_MN_CANCEL_REMOVE_DEVICE:
case IRP_MN_QUERY_STOP_DEVICE:
case IRP_MN_CANCEL_STOP_DEVICE:
case IRP_MN_QUERY_DEVICE_RELATIONS:
case IRP_MN_QUERY_INTERFACE:
case IRP_MN_QUERY_CAPABILITIES:
case IRP_MN_QUERY_RESOURCES:
case IRP_MN_QUERY_RESOURCE_REQUIREMENTS:
```

```
            case IRP_MN_READ_CONFIG:
            case IRP_MN_WRITE_CONFIG:
            case IRP_MN_EJECT:
            case IRP_MN_SET_LOCK:
            case IRP_MN_QUERY_ID:
            case IRP_MN_QUERY_PNP_DEVICE_STATE:
            default:
                    IoSkipCurrentIrpStackLocation(Irp);
                    status = IoCallDriver(usbData->TopOfStack, Irp);
                    break;
            } /* MinorFunction */

    if(0 == InterlockedDecrement(&usbData->OutstandingIO))
        KeSetEvent(&usbData->RemoveEvent, 0, FALSE);
    return status;
}
```

The Plug-and-Play Completion Routine

The completion routine can be used for other purposes, but for this driver it needs to handle only the `IRP_MN_START_DEVICE` request. It handles this by setting the event passed in the Device Extension and that comes in as the `context` parameter. It does not complete the IRP but instead returns the code `STATUS_MORE_PROCESSING_REQUIRED`. The IRP will be completed by the handler that is waiting on the event.

Listing 30.15: *Plug-and-Play Completion for a USB Filter Driver*

```
NTSTATUS VA_PnPComplete(IN PDEVICE_OBJECT DeviceObject,
                        IN PIRP Irp,
                        IN PVOID context)
    {
    PIO_STACK_LOCATION stack;
    PVA_USB_DATA usbData;
    NTSTATUS status;

    UNREFERENCED_PARAMETER(DeviceObject);

    status = STATUS_SUCCESS;
    usbData = (PVA_USB_DATA)context;
    stack = IoGetCurrentIrpStackLocation(Irp);

    if(Irp->PendingReturned)
        IoMarkIrpPending(Irp);

    switch(stack->MajorFunction)
        { /* MajorFunction */
        case IRP_MJ_PNP:
            switch(stack->MinorFunction)
                { /* MinorFunction */
                case IRP_MN_START_DEVICE:
                    KeSetEvent(&usbData->StartEvent, 0, FALSE);
                    return STATUS_MORE_PROCESSING_REQUIRED;
                default:
                    break;
                } /* MinorFunction */
```

```
        break;
    case IRP_MJ_POWER:
    default:
        break;
    } /* MajorFunction */
 return status;
}
```

Starting the Device

The lower level drivers have completed processing the request to start the device. This driver must now initialize the `usbData` structure with the description of the lower level device. This driver does this by queuing a request to the lower level driver to return the device description of the target device.

Listing 30.16: *Starting the USB Filter Driver*

```
NTSTATUS VA_StartDevice(IN PVA_USB_DATA usbData, IN PIRP Irp)
    {
    NTSTATUS status;
    PURB purb;
    struct _URB_CONTROL_DESCRIPTOR_REQUEST urb;

    PAGED_CODE();
```

It would be an error to receive a start request after a remove request, so the ASSERT *checks for that condition. If the device is already started, this request is redundant, so we simply return* STATUS_SUCCESS.

```
    ASSERT(!usbData->Removed); // Should not get here if removed

    if(usbData->Started)
        return STATUS_SUCCESS; // Already started
```

This is our first encounter with a genuine USB request. We don't want to go into a major diversion about this USB call right now, so accept for the moment that this magic builds a request to read the USB descriptor for the device represented by the PDO. We hand it down by calling the function VA_CallUSBD. *The function is described in more detail on page 776.*

```
    purb = (PURB)&urb;

    UsbBuildGetDescriptorRequest( purb,                      // Page 776
                                 (USHORT)sizeof(urb),
                                 USB_DEVICE_DESCRIPTOR_TYPE,
                                 0,      // Index
                                 0,      // Language ID
                                 &usbData->DeviceDesc,
                                 NULL,   // No MDL
                                 sizeof(usbData->DeviceDesc),
                                 NULL);  // No linked URBs
```

```
        status = VA_CallUSBD(usbData, purb, Irp); // Page 771
        if(!NT_SUCCESS(status))
          { /* failed */
           return status;
          } /* failed */

        VA_processDescriptor(usbData, &urb);
        return status;
      }
```

Stopping the Device

This routine is called to notify the filter driver that the device is being stopped. This routine will be called before the lower level driver is notified that it is to shut down so it is possible for this routine to touch hardware. It is, however, possible that this routine will be called multiple times. Therefore, this routine must check that the lower level is still accessible.

Listing 30.17: *Stopping the USB Filter Driver*

```
VOID VA_StopDevice(IN PVA_USB_DATA usbData, IN BOOLEAN touchTheHardware)
    {
      PAGED_CODE();
      ASSERT(!usbData->Removed);
```

If the device is already stopped, we don't need to do anything; we have a redundant stop request.

```
      if(!usbData->Started)
          return;
```

At this point, we can do something to the hardware, provided we have access to it. We could be stopped before the lower-level layers completed their startup, so in the abstract we don't actually know if the hardware is available. However, in practice we do know if the hardware became available, and that state is passed in as a parameter here.

```
      if(touchTheHardware)
          { /* stop it */
```

Here, we would do any required hardware tweaks, possibly to reset state that the Filter Driver introduced to provide its extended capabilities. If no hardware state changes were made during startup, nothing needs to be done here.

```
          } /* stop it */
```

At this point, we do any cleanup required in our own state. Whatever code is written here must not require access to the hardware.

```
      usbData->Started = FALSE;
      }
```

Sending Down the USB Request

The purpose of this code is to synchronously pass a USB request down to the USB Class Driver.

Listing 30.18: *Passing Down a USB Request*

```
NTSTATUS VA_CallUSBD(IN PVA_USB_DATA usbData,
                     IN PURB urb,
                     IN PIRP Irp)
  {
   NTSTATUS status = STATUS_SUCCESS;
   KEVENT  event;
   PIO_STACK_LOCATION next;

   PAGED_CODE();

   KeInitializeEvent(&event, NotificationEvent, FALSE);
```

This is an example of modifying an IRP before sending it onward. We get a pointer to the next stack location and use that pointer to prepare an operation that, in this case, is entirely different from the one that came in with that IRP. By reading the documentation of the USBDI, we know that to send down a new URB we must set the MajorFunction *code to* IRP_MJ_INTERNAL_DEVICE_CONTROL *and set the associated IOCTL value to* IOCTL_INTERNAL_USB_SUBMIT_URB. *The pointer to the URB is placed in the* Parameters.Other.Argument1 *field.*

```
   next = IoGetNextIrpStackLocation(Irp);

   next->MajorFunction = IRP_MJ_INTERNAL_DEVICE_CONTROL;
   next->Parameters.DeviceIoControl.IoControlCode =
           IOCTL_INTERNAL_USB_SUBMIT_URB;
   next->Parameters.Others.Argument1 = urb;
```

We cannot proceed until this request completes. So we set a completion routine that will set the event we are about to wait on. Then we call the lower-level driver.

```
   IoSetCompletionRoutine(Irp,
                  VA_Complete, // Function
                  &event,      // Context pointer
                  TRUE,        // Complete successes
                  TRUE,        // Complete errors
                  TRUE);       // Complete cancels
   status = IoCallDriver(usbData->TopOfStack, Irp);
```

If the IRP was completed immediately, we have its status. If it was deferred and STATUS_PENDING *was returned, we have to wait for it to complete.*

```
   if(STATUS_PENDING == status)
       { /* wait for completion */
        status = KeWaitForSingleObject(&event,
                                    Suspended,
                                    KernelMode,
                                    FALSE,
                                    NULL);
```

```
    } /* wait for completion */

    return Irp->IoStatus.Status;
}
```

The USB Completion Handler

The USB Completion routine will be called when a USB request passed to the lower level has completed processing. This is a simple completion routine which simply signals the completion by setting an Event.

Listing 30.19: *Completion Handler for a USB Filter Driver*

```
NTSTATUS VA_Complete(IN PDEVICE_OBJECT Device, IN PIRP Irp, IN PVOID context)
    {
    UNREFERENCED_PARAMETER(Device);

    KeSetEvent( (PKEVENT)context, 0, FALSE);

    if(Irp->PendingReturned)
        IoMarkIrpPending(Irp);
    return STATUS_MORE_PROCESSING_REQUIRED;
}
```

Processing the USB Descriptor

The following listing is a placeholder for doing whatever you want to do with the USB descriptor. In this case, we do simple printout to the debug port for the various USB descriptor fields. Alternatively, you could keep this information around so that it can be queried by the Controller Device, or you could use it to decide what actions to take based on the nature of the device.

Listing 30.20: *Processing a USB Descriptor in a USB Filter Driver*

```
VOID VA_processDescriptor(IN PVA_USB_DATA usbData,
                          struct _URB_CONTROL_DESCRIPTOR_REQUEST * urb)
    {
    VA_KdPrint (("------------------------\n"));
    VA_KdPrint (("Device Descriptor = %x, len %x\n",
                    &UsbData->DeviceDesc,
                    urb.TransferBufferLength));
    VA_KdPrint (("USB Device Descriptor:\n"));
    VA_KdPrint (("bLength %d\n", UsbData->DeviceDesc.bLength));
    VA_KdPrint (("bDescriptorType 0x%x\n",
                    UsbData->DeviceDesc.bDescriptorType));
    VA_KdPrint (("bcdUSB 0x%x\n", UsbData->DeviceDesc.bcdUSB));
    VA_KdPrint (("bDeviceClass 0x%x\n",
                    UsbData->DeviceDesc.bDeviceClass));
    VA_KdPrint (("bDeviceSubClass 0x%x\n",
                    UsbData->DeviceDesc.bDeviceSubClass));
    VA_KdPrint (("bDeviceProtocol 0x%x\n",
                    UsbData->DeviceDesc.bDeviceProtocol));
    VA_KdPrint (("bMaxPacketSize0 0x%x\n",
                    UsbData->DeviceDesc.bMaxPacketSize0));
    VA_KdPrint (("idVendor 0x%x\n", UsbData->DeviceDesc.idVendor));
    VA_KdPrint (("idProduct 0x%x\n", UsbData->DeviceDesc.idProduct));
```

```
VA_KdPrint (("bcdDevice 0x%x\n", UsbData->DeviceDesc.bcdDevice));
VA_KdPrint (("iManufacturer 0x%x\n",
                    UsbData->DeviceDesc.iManufacturer));
VA_KdPrint (("iProduct 0x%x\n", UsbData->DeviceDesc.iProduct));
VA_KdPrint (("iSerialNumber 0x%x\n",
                    UsbData->DeviceDesc.iSerialNumber));
VA_KdPrint (("bNumConfigurations 0x%x\n",
                    UsbData->DeviceDesc.bNumConfigurations));
VA_KdPrint (("------------------------\n"));
}
```

The `usb.c` File

The actual work of the filter is in the `usb.c` file, as follows.

```
#include <wdm.h>
#include "ValueAdd.h"
#include "local.h"
#include "usbdi.h"
#include "usbdlib.h"
```

The `IRP_MJ_INTERNAL_DEVICE_CONTROL` *Handler*

The `IRP_MJ_INTERNAL_DEVICE_CONTROL` handler intercepts all `IRP_MJ_INTERNAL_DEVICE_CONTROL` requests. If it does not recognize the IOCTL, it simply sends it downward in the stack. No completion routine is required.

The structure of this function raises an important issue in a pageable Device Driver. Because we cannot know which IRPs it is handling, there is no way to know if it is being called at `PASSIVE_LEVEL`. Consequently, the code for this handler must not be pageable.

This driver gives the option, encoded in a bit vector, of printing the URB as it goes down, or as it comes back, or both.

Listing 30.21: `IRP_MJ_INTERNAL_DEVICE_CONTROL` *for a USB Filter Driver*

```
NTSTATUS VA_FilterURB(IN PDEVICE_OBJECT DeviceObject, IN PIRP Irp)
    {
    PVA_USB_DATA usbData;
    NTSTATUS status;
    PIO_STACK_LOCATION stack;
    PURB urb;

    stack = IoGetCurrentIrpStackLocation(Irp);
    usbData = (PVA_USB_DATA)DeviceObject->DeviceExtension;
```

If this is an `IRP_MJ_INTERNAL_DEVICE_CONTROL` *to the main Controller Object, we don't support it. We simply complete the IRP with that notification.*

```
    if(DeviceObject == Global.ControlObject)
        { /* controller */
        Irp->IoStatus.Information = 0;
        Irp->IoStatus.Status = STATUS_NOT_SUPPORTED;
        IoCompleteRequest(Irp, IO_NO_INCREMENT);
        return STATUS_NOT_SUPPORTED;
        } /* controller */
```

Next, we increment the reference count of outstanding IRPs.

```
InterlockedIncrement(&usbData->OutstandingIO); // Up ref count
```

If the device has been removed, we must complete the IRP with
STATUS_DELETE_PENDING. *Note that we don't return here because we want to proceed*
to the end of this conditional and decrement the reference count.

```
if(usbData->Removed)
    { /* removed */
     status = STATUS_DELETE_PENDING;
     Irp->IoStatus.Information = 0;
     Irp->IoStatus.Status = status;
     IoCompleteRequest(Irp, IO_NO_INCREMENT);
    } /* removed */
else
    { /* dispatch it */
     switch(stack->Parameters.DeviceIoControl.IoControlCode)
        { /* IoControlCode */
```

If the IOCTL is the one we are tracing, we handle it here. Otherwise, we pass it straight
through. The routine VA_PrintURB *will print out a URB, which we sketch on page 775.*

- *If the flag is set to print this URB going down, we call this print function.*
- *If the flag is* not *set to print the URB as it comes back, we don't need to know what*
  happens after we send it down.
- *If the flag is set to print the URB as it comes back, we must set a completion routine*
  that will call the VA_PrintURB *handler.*

```
            case IOCTL_INTERNAL_USB_SUBMIT_URB:
                urb = stack->Parameters.Others.Argument1;
                if(VA_PRINT_BEFORE & usbData->PrintMask)
                    VA_PrintURB(urb, usbData->PrintMask);     // Page 775
                if(VA_PRINT_AFTER & usbData->PrintMask)
                    { /* print on completion */
                     IoCopyCurrentIrpStackLocationToNext(Irp);
                     IoSetCompletionRoutine(Irp,
                                    VA_FilterURB_Complete,  // Page 775
                                        usbData, // Context
                                        TRUE,
                                        TRUE,
                                        TRUE);
                    } /* print on completion */
                else
                    { /* simple pass-thru */
                     IoSkipCurrentIrpStackLocation(Irp);
                    } /* simple pass-thru */
```

Either we have either copied the stack location without a completion handler, or we
have copied it and set a completion handler. In either case, we pass the IRP downward
in the driver chain.

```
                status = IoCallDriver(usbData->TopOfStack, Irp);
                break;
```

If we don't recognize the IOCTL, we pass it down transparently.

```
            default:
                IoSkipCurrentIrpStackLocation(Irp);
                status = IoCallDriver(usbData->TopOfStack, Irp);
                break;
        } /* IoControlCode */
    } /* dispatch it */
```

When we get here, we are no longer interested in the IRP. We decrement the reference count. Its going to 0 indicates that we have been waiting for a removal, so we set the removal event so that the removal can proceed.

```
  if(0 == InterlockedDecrement(&usbData->OutstandingIO))
      KeSetEvent(&usbData->RemoveEvent, 0, FALSE);

  return status;
}
```

The URB Handler Completion Routine

This URB completion handler is called when the IRP is completed, and only then if the flag was set to print the URB on the way back.

Listing 30.22: *URB Completion Routine*

```
NTSTATUS VA_FilterURB_Complete(IN PDEVICE_OBJECT DeviceObject,
                               IN PIRP Irp,
                               IN PVOID context)
    {
    UNREFERENCED_PARAMETER(DeviceObject);

    PVA_USB_DATA usbData = (PVA_USB_DATA)context;
    urb = IoGetCurrentIrpStackLocation(Irp)->Parameters.Others.Argument1;
    VA_PrintURB(urb, usbData->PrintMask);
    return STATUS_SUCCESS;
    }
```

The URB Printout Routine

The URB printout routine prints out the details of the URB. It is an incredibly long and tedious function, so rather than reproduce it here (it's on the DDK), we show only a sketch of what it does. The only thing that makes this slightly interesting is the fact that certain URBs can be chained and this function will print out all URBs on the chain.

Listing 30.23: *URB Printout Routine*

```
NTSTATUS VA_PrintURB(IN PURB urb, IN ULONG PrintMask)
    {
    BOOL again = TRUE;
    ULONG i;
```

```
      while(urb & again)
        { /* print each URB */
          again = FALSE; // Assume done unless chained
          switch(urb->UrbHeader.Function)
              { /* Function */
                case URB_FUNCTION_SELECT_INTERFACE:
                    if(PrintMask & VA_PRINT_COMMAND)
                       { /* print */
                       // ...
                       } /* print */
                    break;
                case URB_FUNCTION_SELECT_CONFIGURATION:
                    // ...
                    break;
                case URB_FUNCTION_ABORT_PIPE:
                    // ...
                    break;
                case URB_FUNCTION_RESET_PIPE:
                    // ...
                    break;
                // ...
                case URB_FUNCTION_CONTROL_TRANSFER:
                    // ... Print out next in link
                    urb = urb->UrbControlTransfer.UrbLink;
                    again = TRUE;
                    break;
                case URB_FUNCTION_BULK_OR_INTERRUPT_TRANSFER:
                    // ...
                    urb = urb->UrbBulkOrInterruptTransfer.UrbLink;
                    again = TRUE;
                    break;
                // ...
                default:
                    VA_KdPrint(...); // Warning about unknown URB
                    break;
              } /* Function */
        } /* print each URB */
      }
```

USB Support Functions and Structures

You can build your own URBs by carefully reading the documentation and filling in the fields. There also are fields within fields that must be initialized. A variety of convenience functions are provided to minimize the amount of effort required to accomplish this.

UsbBuildGetDescriptorRequest

```
VOID UsbBuildGetDescriptorRequest(IN OUT PURB Urb,
                                  IN USHORT Length,
                                  IN UCHAR DescriptorType,
                                  IN UCHAR Index,
                                  IN USHORT LanguageId,
                                  IN PVOID TransferBuffer OPTIONAL,
                                  IN PMDL TransferBufferMDL OPTIONAL,
                                  IN ULONG TransferBufferLength,
                                  IN PURB Link OPTIONAL);
```

The UsbBuildGetDescriptorRequest function fills in a
_URB_CONTROL_DESCRIPTOR_REQUEST structure. This structure is essentially a subclass of the general URB structure. Hence the first parameter is a general PURB, but the actual structure must be the _URB_CONTROL_DESCRIPTOR_REQUEST structure. The *Length* parameter is used to ascertain that the block is long enough and initializes a length field within the structure.

The *DescriptorType* parameter can be for a USB_CONFIGURATION_DESCRIPTOR_TYPE, which provides the general USB configuration descriptor (see Chapter 29), a USB_DEVICE_DESCRIPTOR_TYPE. This will provide either the DEVICE descriptor type (which is what we use in our example) or a USB_STRING_DESCRIPTOR_TYPE to get a string from the device. The Index parameter indicates which of several possible available descriptors should be returned. For a DEVICE descriptor, this is set to 0 to get the first descriptor for the device.

The *LanguageId* parameter has no meaning for any descriptor type other than USB_STRING_DESCRIPTOR_TYPE. We can supply either a pointer to a buffer, *TransferBuffer*, or a pointer to a MDL describing the transfer buffer, *TransferBufferMDL*. One or the other of these can be non-NULL. The *TransferBufferLength* parameter indicates the length of the buffer. The *Link* parameter is used to link a chain of URBs, but for our purposes, it is NULL.

Summary

This chapter has given a quick overview of the WDM structure and looked in some detail at how a WDM-style driver is constructed. It is as accurate as it can be given the preliminary information available from Microsoft at the time we are going to press. Details may change with the final release, but the basic structure will probably not change very much.

Appendix

A *Reference*

Support Function Overview

A naming convention has been established for the Kernel-mode support functions. This is shown in Table A.1. The functions that you will normally use are given in Table A.3. Subsequent sections describe these in detail. While some of these descriptions closely parallel the descriptions in the DDK reference found in the DDK documentation (available for download from Microsoft and on the MSDN CD-ROM), we felt that they should be included here because it is more convenient to be able to refer back to them while reading this book. We are deeply opposed to books

Table A.1: *Kernel-Mode Services: Prefixes*

Prefix	Functions
Ex	Executive
Hal	Hardware Abstraction Layer
Io	I/O subsystem
Ke	Kernel
Ks	Kernel streams
Mm	Memory management
Ob	Object management
Po	Power management
Ps	Process subsystem
Rtl	General runtime library (would work in User mode)
Se	Security subsystem
Zw	NT System Service

that require you to be sitting in front of the computer screen with the documentation online in order to understand the material. We tried to make this reference reasonably self-contained, although this is nearly impossible without including all of the DDK reference manual as a subset. We were selective, including only those functions in detail the functions needed to understand the text of this book. This subset includes the functions used for normal Kernel Mode Device Drivers. We did not document those DDK features used by the writers of File System Drivers, Display Drivers, Network Drivers, and other more highly specialized types of drivers.

Microsoft loves to write printed books that, at critical points, refer you to the online documentation, where the same online documentation, at critical points, refers you back to the printed material. This makes it nearly impossible to use their documentation, particularly when you have only the online copy and are at 38,000 feet somewhere over Utah. This is even less useful if you are getting some serious error message from the operating system, and either the online help refers you to the manual (it's in Pittsburgh and I'm at 38,000 feet) or you have a dead system and the printed manual tells you to consult the online help. I've had all of these situations happen to me. *–jmn*

In Table A.2, we index the initial letters of the functions we describe. The "Sum." column refers to the quick function summary in Table A.3, and the "Ref." column refers to the reference documentation.

Table A.2: *Quick Page Index*

Ltr.	Sum.	Ref.	Ltr.	Sum.	Ref.
A	781	864	N	839	969
B			O	839	970
C	781	865	P	841	971
D	782	870	Q		
E	782	876	R	843	975
F			S		
G			T		
H	793	890	U	846	980
I	801	897	V		
J			W	847	983
K	821	934	X		
L	835	963	Y		
M	835	963	Z	849	984

Legal Issues

The material in this section represents a subset of the full DDK documentation. It is intended to be used as a reference while using this book.

The material in this appendix is a snapshot in time of the DDK documentation, which Microsoft updates periodically. This subset is edited by the authors for conciseness; not all the material for each function is included. Comments by the authors have been added. This documentation is not intended to be a replacement for the Microsoft DDK documentation.

The full Microsoft Windows NT DDK is available with the MSDN professional subscription and may be downloaded from the Microsoft Web page `http:\\www.microsoft.com\ddk`.

Support Function and Data Structure Reference

Table A.3: *Important Support Functions and Structures for Device Drivers*

Page Ref.	Function	Parameters and Explanations
864	ASSERT(*expression*)	
		When compiled with the DBG conditional defined, generates an assertion failure if the `expression` is FALSE.
		expression An expression to evaluate. Any FALSE value (0, NULL) will cause the assertion failure.
865	ASSERTMSG(*message, expression*)	
		When compiled with the DBG conditional defined, generates an assertion failure if the `expression` is FALSE.
		message An 8-bit character string to be displayed.
		expression An expression to evaluate. Any FALSE value (0, NULL) will cause the assertion failure.
865	typedef struct {...} CM_FULL_RESOURCE_DESCRIPTOR	
866	typedef struct {...} CM_PARTIAL_RESOURCE_DESCRIPTOR	
867	typedef struct {...} CM_PARTIAL_RESOURCE_LIST	
868	typedef struct {...} CM_RESOURCE_LIST	
868	typedef struct {...} CONFIGURATION_INFORMATION	
869	CONTAINING_RECORD(*address, type, field*)	
869	typedef struct {...} CONTROLLER_OBJECT	

Table A.3: *Important Support Functions and Structures for Device Drivers (continued)*

Page Ref.	Function	Parameters and Explanations
870	VOID DbgBreakPoint()	
		Causes a debug breakpoint. Will stop execution, and the debugger will become active.
870	ULONG DbgPrint(IN PCHAR *fmt*, ...)	
		Writes a formatted string to the debug output port.
		IN PCHAR *fmt* A pointer to an 8-bit formatting string, which uses printf-style formatting.
		... The arguments to the formatting string.
870	typedef struct {...} DEVICE_DESCRIPTION	
872	typedef struct {...} DEVICE_OBJECT	
875	NTSTATUS DriverEntry(IN PDRIVER_OBJECT *driver*, IN PUNICODE_STRING *RegistryPath*);	
		The entry point called when a driver is loaded.
		IN PDRIVER_OBJECT *driver* A reference to a Driver Object.
		IN PUNICODE_STRING *RegistryPath* A reference to the string designating the Registry entry for this driver.
875	typedef struct {...} DRIVER_EXTENSION;	
875	typedef struct {...} DRIVER_OBJECT	
		The basic driver structure passed to the DriverEntry and Unload routines.
876	VOID ExAcquireFastMutex(IN PFAST_MUTEX *FastMutex*);	
		Acquires the indicated Fast Mutex Object. If the Fast Mutex is already acquired, places the thread in a wait state until the Fast Mutex Object is released. Locks out APCs (asynchronous procedure calls) during the wait.
		PFAST_MUTEX *FastMutex* Points to the initialized Fast Mutex Object.
876	VOID ExAcquireFastMutexUnsafe(IN PFAST_MUTEX *FastMutex*);	
		Acquires the indicated Fast Mutex Object. If the Fast Mutex is already acquired, places the thread in a wait state until the Fast Mutex Object is released. Is not safe if APCs (asynchronous procedure calls) occur during the wait.
		PFAST_MUTEX *FastMutex* Points to the initialized Fast Mutex Object.

Table A.3: *Important Support Functions and Structures for Device Drivers (continued)*

Page Ref.	Function	Parameters and Explanations
877		BOOLEAN ExAcquireResourceExclusiveLite(IN PERESOURCE *Resource*, IN BOOLEAN *Wait*);
		Acquires the indicated Executive Resource for exclusive access. If the Executive Resource is already acquired and Wait is TRUE, places the thread in a wait state until the Executive Resource is released. If Wait is FALSE, returns TRUE if it acquired the Executive Resource and FALSE if it failed to acquire the Executive Resource.
		IN PERESOURCE *Resource* Points to the initialized Executive Resource.
		IN BOOLEAN *Wait* TRUE to wait for the resource to come available; FALSE to return immediately if the resource cannot be acquired.
877		BOOLEAN ExAcquireResourceSharedLite(IN PERESOURCE *Resource*, IN BOOLEAN *Wait*);
		Acquires the indicated Executive Resource for shared access. If the resource is already acquired for exclusive access and Wait is TRUE, places the thread in a wait state until the resource is released from its exclusive access. If Wait is FALSE, returns TRUE if it acquired the resource and FALSE if it failed to acquire the resource.
		IN PERESOURCE *Resource* Points to the initialized Executive Resource.
		IN BOOLEAN *Wait* TRUE to wait for the resource to come available; FALSE to return immediately if the resource cannot be acquired.
877		BOOLEAN ExAcquireSharedStarveExclusive(IN PERESOURCE *Resource*, IN BOOLEAN *Wait*);
		Acquires the indicated Executive Resource for shared access. If the Executive Resource is already acquired for exclusive access and Wait is TRUE, places the thread in a wait state until the Executive Resource is released from its exclusive access. If Wait is FALSE, returns TRUE if it acquired the Executive Resource and FALSE if it failed to acquire the Executive Resource. Any exclusive requests in the queue are forced to wait.
		IN PERESOURCE *Resource* Points to the initialized Executive Resource.
		IN BOOLEAN *Wait* TRUE to wait for the resource to come available; FALSE to return immediately if the resource cannot be acquired.
878		BOOLEAN ExAcquireSharedWaitForExclusive(IN PERESOURCE *Resource*, IN BOOLEAN *Wait*);
		Acquires the indicated Executive Resource for shared access. If the Executive Resource is already acquired for exclusive access and Wait is TRUE, places the thread in a wait state until the Executive Resource is released from its exclusive access. If Wait is FALSE, returns TRUE if it acquired the Executive Resource and FALSE if it failed to acquire the resource. Any exclusive requests in the queue take precedence, even if they come in after this request enters the queue.
		IN PERESOURCE *Resource* Points to the initialized Executive Resource.

Table A.3: *Important Support Functions and Structures for Device Drivers (continued)*

Page Ref.	Function	Parameters and Explanations
		IN BOOLEAN `Wait`
		TRUE to wait for the resource to come available; FALSE to return immediately if the resource cannot be acquired.
879		PVOID ExAllocateFromNPagedLookasideList(IN PNPAGED_LOOKASIDE_LIST `Lookaside`)
		Allocates a block of storage from the specified nonpaged lookaside list. If the list is empty, storage is allocated from the Nonpaged Pool. Returns NULL if error.
		IN PNPAGED_LOOKASIDE_LIST `Lookaside`
		Points to the header for the lookaside list.
879		PVOID ExAllocateFromPagedLookasideList(IN PPAGED_LOOKASIDE_LIST `Lookaside`)
		Allocates a block of storage from the specified paged lookaside list. If the list is empty, storage is allocated from the Paged Pool. Returns NULL if an error.
		IN PPAGED_LOOKASIDE_LIST `Lookaside`
		Points to the header for the lookaside list.
879		PVOID ExAllocatePool(IN POOL_TYPE `pooltype`, IN ULONG `NumberOfBytes`);
		Allocates a storage pool, and returns a pointer to the storage allocated, or NULL if an error.
		POOL_TYPE `pooltype`
		One of the values shown next. This tells the allocator what pool to use.

NonPagedPool	Memory is allocated from the Nonpaged Pool. If the memory cannot be allocated, the function returns NULL. Otherwise, returns the virtual memory address of the allocated storage.
NonPagedPoolMustSucceed	Memory is allocated from the Nonpaged Pool. If the memory cannot be allocated, the system dies with the MUST_SUCCEED_POOL_EMPTY BugCheck error (0x41).
NonPagedPoolCacheAligned	Memory is allocated from the Nonpaged Pool. The memory is aligned on a cache-line boundary.
NonPagedPoolCacheAlignedMustS	This odd name is the 31-letter rendition of a "MustSucceed" name. Memory is allocated from the Nonpaged Pool and aligned on a cache-line boundary. If it cannot be allocated, the system dies with the MUST_SUCCEED_POOL_EMPTY BugCheck error (0x41).
PagedPool	Memory is allocated from the Paged Pool.
PagedPoolCacheAligned	Memory is allocated from the Paged Pool and aligned on a cache-line boundary.

Table A.3: *Important Support Functions and Structures for Device Drivers (continued)*

Page Ref.	Function	Parameters and Explanations
		IN ULONG *NumberOfBytes*
		The number of bytes to be allocated. If this is >= PAGE_SIZE, a page-aligned buffer is allocated and consumes an integral number of pages. If this is < PAGE_SIZE, it is allocated on an 8-byte boundary. Allocated memory less than PAGE_SIZE never crosses a page boundary.

Page Ref.	Function	Parameters and Explanations
880	`PVOID ExAllocatePoolWithQuota(IN POOL_TYPE pooltype, IN ULONG NumberOfBytes);`	

Allocates a storage pool, and returns a pointer to the storage allocated, or NULL if an error. The pool space is charged against the quota of the calling thread.

POOL_TYPE *pooltype*

One of the values shown next. This tells the allocator what pool to use.

NonPagedPool	Memory is allocated from the Nonpaged Pool. If the memory cannot be allocated, the function returns NULL. Otherwise, returns the virtual memory address of the allocated storage.
NonPagedPoolMustSucceed	Memory is allocated from the Nonpaged Pool. If the memory cannot be allocated, the system dies with the MUST_SUCCEED_POOL_EMPTY BugCheck error (0x41).
NonPagedPoolCacheAligned	Memory is allocated from the Nonpaged Pool. The memory is aligned on a cache-line boundary.
NonPagedPoolCacheAlignedMustS	This odd name is the 31-letter rendition of a "MustSucceed" name. Memory is allocated from the Nonpaged Pool and aligned on a cache-line boundary. If it cannot be allocated, the system dies with the MUST_SUCCEED_POOL_EMPTY BugCheck error (0x41).
PagedPool	Memory is allocated from the Paged Pool.
PagedPoolCacheAligned	Memory is allocated from the Paged Pool and aligned on a cache-line boundary.

IN ULONG *NumberOfBytes*

The number of bytes to be allocated. If this is >= PAGE_SIZE, a page-aligned buffer is allocated and consumes an integral number of pages. If this is < PAGE_SIZE, it is allocated on an 8-byte boundary. Allocated memory less than PAGE_SIZE never crosses a page boundary.

Table A.3: *Important Support Functions and Structures for Device Drivers (continued)*

Page Ref.	Function	Parameters and Explanations	
881	PVOID ExAllocatePoolWithQuotaTag(IN POOL_TYPE *pooltype*, IN ULONG *NumberOfBytes*, IN ULONG *Tag*);		
		Allocates a storage pool, and returns a pointer to the storage allocated, or NULL if an error. The pool space is charged against the quota of the calling thread. The tag is inserted before the allocation and appears in crash dumps of the system.	
		POOL_TYPE *pooltype*	
		One of the values shown next. This tells the allocator what pool to use.	
		NonPagedPool	Memory is allocated from the Nonpaged Pool. If the memory cannot be allocated, the function returns NULL. Otherwise, returns the virtual memory address of the allocated storage.
		NonPagedPoolMustSucceed	Memory is allocated from the Nonpaged Pool. If the memory cannot be allocated, the system dies with the MUST_SUCCEED_POOL_EMPTY BugCheck error (0x41).
		NonPagedPoolCacheAligned	Memory is allocated from the Nonpaged Pool and aligned on a cache-line boundary.
		NonPagedPoolCacheAlignedMustS	This odd name is the 31-letter rendition of a "MustSucceed" name. Memory is allocated from the Nonpaged Pool and aligned on a cache-line boundary. If it cannot be allocated, the system dies with the MUST_SUCCEED_POOL_EMPTY BugCheck error (0x41).
		PagedPool	Memory is allocated from the Paged Pool.
		PagedPoolCacheAligned	Memory is allocated from the Paged Pool and aligned on a cache-line boundary.
		IN ULONG *NumberOfBytes*	
		The number of bytes to be allocated. If this is >= PAGE_SIZE, a page-aligned buffer is allocated and consumes an integral number of pages. If this is < PAGE_SIZE, it is allocated on an 8-byte boundary. Allocated memory less than PAGE_SIZE never crosses a page boundary.	
		IN ULONG *Tag*	
		The tag to be displayed. Usually four characters, enclosed within single quotation marks, in reverse order.	
882	PVOID ExAllocatePoolWithTag(IN POOL_TYPE *pooltype*, IN ULONG *NumberOfBytes*, IN ULONG *Tag*);		
		Allocates a storage pool and returns a pointer to the storage allocated, or NULL if an error. The tag is inserted before the allocation and appears in crash dumps of the system.	
		POOL_TYPE *pooltype*	
		One of the values shown next. This tells the allocator what pool to use.	

Table A.3: *Important Support Functions and Structures for Device Drivers (continued)*

Page Ref.	Function	Parameters and Explanations
		NonPagedPool	Memory is allocated from the Nonpaged Pool. If the memory cannot be allocated, the function returns NULL. Otherwise, returns the virtual memory address of the allocated storage.

Page Ref.	Function	Parameters and Explanations	
		NonPagedPool	Memory is allocated from the Nonpaged Pool. If the memory cannot be allocated, the function returns NULL. Otherwise, returns the virtual memory address of the allocated storage.
		NonPagedPoolMustSucceed	Memory is allocated from the Nonpaged Pool. If the memory cannot be allocated, the system dies with the MUST_SUCCEED_POOL_EMPTY BugCheck error (0x41).
		NonPagedPoolCacheAligned	Memory is allocated from the Nonpaged Pool and aligned on a cache-line boundary.
		NonPagedPoolCacheAlignedMustS	This odd name is the 31-letter rendition of a "MustSucceed" name. Memory is allocated from the Nonpaged Pool and aligned on a cache-line boundary. If it cannot be allocated, the system dies with the MUST_SUCCEED_POOL_EMPTY BugCheck error (0x41).
		PagedPool	Memory is allocated from the Paged Pool.
		PagedPoolCacheAligned	Memory is allocated from the Paged Pool and aligned on a cache-line boundary.

IN ULONG *NumberOfBytes*

The number of bytes to be allocated. If this is >= PAGE_SIZE, a page-aligned buffer is allocated and consumes an integral number of pages. If this is < PAGE_SIZE, it is allocated on an 8-byte boundary. Allocated memory less than PAGE_SIZE never crosses a page boundary.

IN ULONG *Tag*

The tag to be displayed. Usually four characters, enclosed within single quotation marks, in reverse order.

---

883 | VOID ExConvertExclusiveToSharedLite(IN PERESOURCE *Resource*);

Converts the indicated Executive Resource for shared access. The Executive Resource must be already acquired for exclusive access. The current thread and all threads waiting for shared access will be granted shared access.

IN PERESOURCE *Resource*

Points to the initialized resource object.

---

883 | VOID ExDeleteNPagedLookasideList(IN PNPAGED_LOOKASIDE_LIST *Lookaside*);

Frees a lookaside list allocated by ExInitializeNPagedLookasideList. Any remaining blocks on the list are returned to the pool. The lookaside header itself is not freed.

IN PNPAGED_LOOKASIDE_LIST *Lookaside*

The address of the lookaside header.

Table A.3: *Important Support Functions and Structures for Device Drivers (continued)*

Page Ref.	Function	Parameters and Explanations
884	VOID ExDeletePagedLookasideList(IN PPAGED_LOOKASIDE_LIST *Lookaside*);	
		Frees a lookaside list allocated by ExInitializePagedLookasideList. Any remaining blocks on the list are returned to the pool. The lookaside header itself is not freed.
		IN PPAGED_LOOKASIDE_LIST *Lookaside* The address of the lookaside header.
884	NTSTATUS ExDeleteResourceLite(IN PERESOURCE *Resource*);	
		Deletes the specified Executive Resource. The storage must be freed explicitly after this function returns successfully.
		IN PERESOURCE *Resource* The address of the Executive Resource to be deleted.
884	VOID ExFreePool(IN PVOID *pool*)	
		Frees a pool allocated by ExAllocatePool, ExAllocatePoolWithTag, ExAllocatePoolWithQuota, or ExAllocatePoolWithQuotaTag. The size of the pool is known from the pool address *pool*.
		IN PVOID *pool* The address of the storage allocated by one of the calls listed previously.
884	VOID ExFreeToNPagedLookasideList(IN PNPAGED_LOOKASIDE_LIST *Lookaside*, IN PVOID *Entry*);	
		Frees an entry to a nonpaged lookaside list. If the lookaside list quota is exceeded, frees the storage back to the Nonpaged Pool.
		IN PNPAGED_LOOKASIDE_LIST *Lookaside* The address of the lookaside list header in nonpaged memory.
		IN PVOID *Entry* The address of the entry to be freed.
884	VOID ExFreeToPagedLookasideList(IN PPAGED_LOOKASIDE_LIST *Lookaside*, IN PVOID *Entry*);	
		Frees an entry to a paged lookaside list. If the lookaside list quota is exceeded, frees the storage back to the Paged Pool.
		IN PPAGED_LOOKASIDE_LIST *Lookaside* The address of the lookaside list header in paged memory.
		IN PVOID *Entry* The address of the entry to be freed.
885	ERESOURCE_THREAD ExGetCurrentResourceThread( );	
		Returns a resource thread value for use by ExReleaseResourceForThreadLite.

Table A.3: *Important Support Functions and Structures for Device Drivers (continued)*

Page Ref.	Function	Parameters and Explanations
885	`VOID ExInitializeFastMutex(IN PFAST_MUTEX FastMutex);`	
		Initializes a Fast Mutex Object.
		`IN PFAST_MUTEX FastMutex` The address of the Fast Mutex Object.

885	`VOID ExInitializeNPagedLookasideList(IN PNPAGED_LOOKASIDE_LIST Lookaside,`
	`    IN PALLOCATE_FUNCTION Allocate,`
	`    IN PFREE_FUNCTION Free, IN ULONG Flags, IN ULONG Size,`
	`    IN ULONG Tag, IN USHORT Depth );`	

		Initializes a header to a lookaside list for the Nonpaged Pool.
		`IN PNPAGED_LOOKASIDE_LIST Lookaside` The address of the lookaside list header in nonpaged memory.
		`IN PALLOCATE_FUNCTION Allocate` The address of a function that is called for allocation, or NULL. If NULL, `ExAllocatePoolWithTag` will be used.
		`IN PFREE_FUNCTION Free` The address of a function that is called for deallocation, or NULL. If NULL, `ExFreePool` will be used.
		`IN ULONG Flags` One of the following values.
		0 — Failures (other than from the Must-Succeed pool) return a NULL value.
		`POOL_RAISE_IF_ALLOCATION_FAILURE` — Failures (other than from the Must-Succeed pool) raise an exception.
		`IN ULONG Size` The size of each of the blocks in the list, in bytes.
		`IN ULONG Tag` A 4-byte tag expressed as a four-character ANSI character constant, with the character order reversed; for example, "Temp" would be represented as `'pmeT'`.
		`IN USHORT Depth` The maximum number of free blocks that can be on the lookaside list.

886	`VOID ExInitializePagedLookasideList(IN PNPAGED_LOOKASIDE_LIST Lookaside,`
	`    IN PALLOCATE_FUNCTION Allocate,`
	`    IN PFREE_FUNCTION Free, IN ULONG Flags, IN ULONG Size,`
	`    IN ULONG Tag, IN USHORT Depth );`	

		Initializes a header to a lookaside list for paged memory.

Table A.3: *Important Support Functions and Structures for Device Drivers (continued)*

Page Ref.	Function	Parameters and Explanations
		IN PPAGED_LOOKASIDE_LIST *Lookaside* The address of the lookaside list header, which must be in *nonpaged* memory.
		IN PALLOCATE_FUNCTION *Allocate* The address of a function that is called for allocation, or NULL. If NULL, ExAllocatePoolWithTag will be used.
		IN PFREE_FUNCTION *Free* The address of a function that is called for deallocation, or NULL. If NULL, ExFreePool will be used.
		IN ULONG *Flags* One of the following values.
		0 — Failures (other than from the Must-Succeed pool) return a NULL value.
		POOL_RAISE_IF_ALLOCATION_FAILURE — Failures (other than from the Must-Succeed pool) raise an exception.
		IN ULONG *Size* The size of each of the blocks in the list, in bytes.
		IN ULONG *Tag* A 4-byte tag expressed as a four-character ANSI character constant, with the character order reversed; for example, "Temp" would be represented as 'pmeT'.
		IN USHORT *Depth* The maximum number of free blocks that can be on the lookaside list.
886	NTSTATUS ExInitializeResourceLite(IN PERESOURCE *Resource*);	Initializes the Executive Resource, which must be in nonpaged memory.
		IN PERESOURCE *Resource* Points to the area to be initialized, which must be at least sizeof(ERESOURCE).
887	VOID ExInitializeWorkItem(IN PWORK_QUEUE_ITEM *Item*, IN PWORKER_THREAD_ROUTINE *Routine*, IN PVOID *Context*);	Initializes a WorkItem.
		IN WORK_QUEUE_ITEM *Item* A pointer to the queue item to be initialized. This item must be allocated out of nonpaged memory.
		IN PWORKER_THREAD_ROUTINE *Routine* A pointer to the function to be executed when the thread runs.

Table A.3: *Important Support Functions and Structures for Device Drivers (continued)*

Page Ref.	Function	Parameters and Explanations
		IN PVOID *Context*
		A pointer that is passed into the execution function when the thread is called. This pointer must be valid in any thread context.
887	PLIST_ENTRY ExInterlockedInsertHeadList(IN PLIST_ENTRY *ListHead*, IN PLIST_ENTRY *ListEntry*, IN PKSPIN_LOCK *Lock*);	
		Inserts a list entry at the head of a doubly linked list in a multiprocessor-safe fashion.
		IN PLIST_ENTRY *ListHead*
		The head of the list into which the insertion is made.
		IN PLIST_ENTRY *ListEntry*
		The entry to be added.
		IN PKSPIN_LOCK *Lock*
		The address of the Spin Lock used for synchronization.
887	PLIST_ENTRY ExInterlockedInsertTailList(IN PLIST_ENTRY *ListHead*, IN PLIST_ENTRY *ListEntry*, IN PKSPIN_LOCK *Lock*);	
		Inserts a list entry at the end of a doubly linked list in a multiprocessor-safe fashion.
		IN PLIST_ENTRY *ListHead*
		The head of the list into which the insertion is made.
		IN PLIST_ENTRY *ListEntry*
		The entry to be added.
		IN PKSPIN_LOCK *Lock*
		The address of the Spin Lock used for synchronization.
887	PLIST_ENTRY ExInterlockedRemoveHeadList(IN PLIST_ENTRY *ListHead*, IN PKSPIN_LOCK *Lock*);	
		Removes the list entry at the head of a doubly linked list in a multiprocessor-safe fashion. Returns a pointer to that entry, or NULL if the list was empty.
		IN PLIST_ENTRY *ListHead*
		The head of the list into which the insertion is made.
		IN PKSPIN_LOCK *Lock*
		The address of the Spin Lock used for synchronization.
888	BOOLEAN ExIsResourceAcquiredExclusiveLite(IN PERESOURCE *Resource*);	
		Checks to see if the thread has exclusive access to the Executive Resource. Returns TRUE if it does and FALSE if not.
		IN PERESOURCE *Resource*
		The Executive Resource to be tested.

Table A.3: *Important Support Functions and Structures for Device Drivers (continued)*

Page Ref.	Function	Parameters and Explanations	
888	USHORT ExIsResourceAcquireSharedLite(IN PERESOURCE *Resource*);		
		Checks to see if the thread has shared access to the Executive Resource. Returns the number of times the thread has already acquired shared access to the resource.	
		IN PERESOURCE *Resource* The resource to be acquired.	
888	VOID ExQueueWorkItem(IN PWORK_QUEUE_ITEM *WorkItem*, IN WORK_QUEUE_TYPE *QueueType*);		
		Queues an entry for a System Worker Thread.	
		IN PWORK_QUEUE_ITEM *WorkItem* The item to be inserted in the queue. Must be prepared with ExInitializeWorkItem.	
		IN WORK_QUEUE_TYPE *QueueType* The type of the item to be inserted.	
		CriticalWorkQueue	The thread will execute with real-time priority.
		DelayedWorkQueue	The thread will run with a dynamically assigned nonreal-time priority.
		HyperCriticalWorkQueue	This is a special value for File System work queue items. It runs at very high priority, and the thread must not block.
888	VOID ExReleaseFastMutex(IN PFAST_MUTEX *FastMutex*);		
		Releases the indicated Fast Mutex Object, and allows APCs (asynchronous procedure calls) to occur.	
		IN PFAST_MUTEX *FastMutex* Points to the initialized Fast Mutex Object.	
889	VOID ExReleaseFastMutexUnsafe(IN PFAST_MUTEX *FastMutex*);		
		Releases the indicated Fast Mutex Object.	
		IN PFAST_MUTEX *FastMutex* Points to the initialized Fast Mutex Object.	
889	VOID ExReleaseResourceForThreadLite(IN PERESOURCE *Resource*, IN ERESOURCE_THREAD *ResourceThreadId*)		
		Releases an Executive Resource. The resource may have been acquired exclusively or non-exclusively.	
		IN PERESOURCE *Resource* The Executive Resource to be released.	
		IN ERESOURCE_THREAD *ResourceThreadId* The thread ID of the thread that originally acquired the resource.	

Table A.3: *Important Support Functions and Structures for Device Drivers (continued)*

Page Ref.	Function	Parameters and Explanations
889	`VOID ExTryToAcquireFastMutex(IN PFAST_MUTEX FastMutex);`	
		Tries to acquire the indicated Fast Mutex Object. If successful, acquires the Fast Mutex with APCs (asynchronous procedure calls) locked out and returns TRUE. Otherwise, returns FALSE and does not enter a wait state.
		`IN PFAST_MUTEX FastMutex` Points to the initialized Fast Mutex Object.
889	`BOOLEAN ExTryToAcquireResourceExclusiveLite(IN PERESOURCE Resource);`	
		Attempts to acquire the specified resource for exclusive access. Returns TRUE if successful and FALSE if unsuccessful. Does not wait if the resource is not available for exclusive access.
		`IN PERESOURCE Resource` The resource to be acquired.
890	`PVOID HalAllocateCommonBuffer(IN PADAPTER_OBJECT AdapterObject, IN ULONG Length, OUT PPHYSICAL_ADDRESS LogicalAddress, IN BOOLEAN CacheEnabled);`	
		Allocates a buffer that can be accessed simultaneously by a DMA device and the processor.
		`IN PADAPTER_OBJECT AdapterObject` Points to the Adapter Object that will be used for the DMA.
		`IN ULONG Length` The length of the buffer. Space is allocated in page-sized chunks.
		`OUT PPHYSICAL_ADDRESS LogicalAddress` Points to the place to put a physical address that can be used to program the device.
		`IN BOOLEAN CacheEnabled` TRUE to make the allocated pages cacheable; FALSE to disable caching.
891	`NTSTATUS HalAssignSlotResources(IN PUNICODE_STRING RegistryPath, IN PUNICODE_STRING DriverClassName, IN PDRIVER_OBJECT DriverObject, IN PDEVICE_OBJECT DeviceObject, IN INTERFACE_TYPE BusType, IN ULONG BusNumber, IN ULONG SlotNumber, IN OUT PCM_RESOURCE_LIST * AllocatedResources);`	
		For drivers of devices connected to dynamically configurable I/O busses of a type with a published standard interface, `HalAssignSlotResources` determines the resource requirements of the target device, calls `IoAssignResources` to allocate them, sets the target device with its assigned resources, and returns the assignments to the caller. Returns one of the values given next.
		`STATUS_SUCCESS` A set of resources was claimed for the caller under the Registry \ResourceMap key.

Table A.3: *Important Support Functions and Structures for Device Drivers (continued)*

Page Ref.	Function	Parameters and Explanations
		IN PUNICODE_STRING *RegistryPath*
		The RegistryPath pointer passed in to the DriverEntry routine during initialization if the DeviceObject pointer is NULL. The buffered Unicode string is read-only, giving access to the driver-specific Registry key \Registry\Machine\System\CurrentControlSet\Services *DriverName* with its \parameters subkey(s). The caller is responsible for creating and updating the RegistryPath string if it calls this routine to claim one or more sets of device-specific resources for the device(s) on a multifunction adapter at the given SlotNumber.
		IN PUNICODE_STRING *DriverClassName*
		Points to a Unicode string that describes the class of driver under which driver-specific information should be stored in the Registry. A default type of Other is used if none is given, and a new key is created in the Registry if a unique name is supplied. If this pointer is non-NULL, the caller is claiming a set of resources that it uses in common for the device(s) at the given SlotNumber.
		IN PDRIVER_OBJECT *DriverObject*
		Points to the Driver Object that was input into the DriverEntry routine.
		IN PDEVICE_OBJECT *DeviceObject*
		Points to the driver-created Device Object representing the physical device for which the driver is attempting to claim device-specific resources. If this pointer is non-NULL, the caller usually supports more than one device on a multifunction adapter at the given SlotNumber. For each non-NULL DeviceObject, such a driver's calls to this routine must write resource data into the Registry under a unique, device-specific subkey of the *RegistryPath* pointer that was input into the DriverEntry routine.
		IN INTERFACE_TYPE *BusType*
		Specifies the type of bus on which the device is connected. Currently, this value can be the following: PCIBus. However, additional types of dynamically configurable busses will be supported in future versions of Windows NT. The upper bound on the interface types supported is always MaximumInterfaceType.
		IN ULONG *BusNumber*
		Specifies the zero-based and system-assigned number of the bus.
		IN ULONG *SlotNumber*
		Specifies the logical slot number at which the driver found its device(s) when it called HalGetBusData.
		IN OUT PCM_RESOURCE_LIST * *AllocatedResources*
		Specifies a pointer to an uninitialized pointer. If the call is successful, HalAssignSlotResources allocates a buffer, fills in the assigned resource list, and resets the embedded pointer to the start of the CM_RESOURCE_LIST buffer.
891	VOID HalFreeCommonBuffer(IN PADAPTER_OBJECT *AdapterObject*, IN ULONG *Length*, IN PHYSICAL_ADDRESS *LogicalAddress*, IN PVOID *VirtualAddress*, IN BOOLEAN *CacheEnabled*);	
		Frees a buffer that has been allocated by HalAllocateCommonBuffer.

Table A.3: *Important Support Functions and Structures for Device Drivers (continued)*

Page Ref.	Function	Parameters and Explanations
		IN PADAPTER_OBJECT *AdapterObject* Points to the Adapter Object that was used for HalAllocateCommonBuffer.
		IN ULONG *Length* The length of the buffer. Must be the same value that was passed in to HalAllocateCommonBuffer.
		IN PHYSICAL_ADDRESS *LogicalAddress* The physical address that was returned by HalAllocateCommonBuffer.
		IN PVOID *VirtualAddress* The virtual address that was returned by HalAllocateCommonBuffer.
		IN BOOLEAN *CacheEnabled* The same value that was passed in to HalAllocateCommonBuffer.
891	PADAPTER_OBJECT HalGetAdapter(IN PDEVICE_DESCRIPTION *DeviceDescription*, IN OUT PULONG *NumberOfMapRegisters*);	Returns via the *NumberOfMapRegisters* parameter the maximum number of mapping registers that the Device Driver can allocate for any DMA transfer operation.
		Returns a pointer to the requested Adapter Object, or NULL if an Adapter Object could not be created.
		IN PDEVICE_OBJECT *DeviceDescriptor* Specifies the Device Object that describes the device.
		IN OUT PULONG *NumberOfAdapterRegisters* Specifies the zero-based and system-assigned number of the bus.
892	ULONG HalGetBusData(IN BUS_DATA_TYPE *BusDataType*, IN ULONG *BusNumber*, IN ULONG *SlotNumber*, IN PVOID *Buffer*, IN ULONG *Length*);	Gets information describing the bus structure. Returns one of the values shown next.
		0 The specified PCI Bus does not exist.
		2 The specified PCI Bus exists, but there is no device at the given PCI *SlotNumber*. The *Buffer* also contains the value PCI_INVALID_VENDOR_ID at the PCI_COMMON_CONFIG VendorId member.
		IN BUS_DATA_TYPE *BusDataType* Specifies the type of bus data to be retrieved. Currently, its value can be one of the following: Cmos, EisaConfiguration, Pos, or PCIConfiguration. However, additional types of bus configuration will be supported in future versions of Windows NT. The upper bound on the types supported is always MaximumBusDataType.
		IN ULONG *BusNumber* Specifies the zero-based and system-assigned number of the bus in systems with several busses of the same *BusDataType*.

Table A.3: *Important Support Functions and Structures for Device Drivers (continued)*

Page Ref.	Function	Parameters and Explanations
		IN ULONG *SlotNumber* Specifies the logical slot number or location of the device. If PCIConfiguration is specified as the *BusDataType*, this is specified as a PCI_SLOT_NUMBER-type value.
		IN PVOID *Buffer* Points to a caller-supplied buffer for configuration information specific to *BusDataType*. If Cmos is specified, the buffer will contain the contents of the CMOS (*BusNumber* equals 0) or ECMOS (*BusNumber* equals 1) locations starting with the location specified for *SlotNumber*. If EisaConfiguration is specified, the buffer will contain the CM_EISA_SLOT_INFORMATION structure followed by zero or more CM_EISA_FUNCTION_INFORMATION structures for the specified slot. If Pos is specified, the buffer will contain a CM_MCA_POS_DATA structure for the specified slot. If PCIConfiguration is specified, the buffer will contain the PCI_COMMON_CONFIG information for the given *SlotNumber*.
		IN ULONG *Length* Specifies the maximum number of bytes to return in *Buffer*.
892	ULONG HalGetBusDataByOffset(IN BUS_DATA_TYPE *BusDataType*, IN ULONG *BusNumber*, IN ULONG *SlotNumber*, IN PVOID *Buffer*, IN ULONG *Offset*, IN ULONG *Length*);	
		Gets information describing the bus structure. Returns one of the values shown next.
		0 The specified PCI Bus does not exist.
		2 The specified PCI Bus exists, but there is no device at the given PCI *SlotNumber*. The *Buffer* also contains the value PCI_INVALID_VENDOR_ID at the PCI_COMMON_CONFIG VendorId member.
		IN BUS_DATA_TYPE *BusDataType* Specifies the type of bus data to be retrieved. Currently, its value can be one of the following: Cmos, EisaConfiguration, Pos, or PCIConfiguration. However, additional types of bus configuration will be supported in future versions of Windows NT. The upper bound on the types supported is always *MaximumBusDataType*.
		IN ULONG *BusNumber* Specifies the zero-based and system-assigned number of the bus in systems with several busses of the same *BusDataType*.
		IN ULONG *SlotNumber* Specifies the logical slot number or location of the device. If PCIConfiguration is specified as the *BusDataType*, this is specified as a PCI_SLOT_NUMBER-type value.
		IN PVOID *Buffer* Points to a caller-supplied buffer for configuration information specific to *BusDataType*. If Cmos is specified, the buffer will contain the contents of the CMOS (*BusNumber* equals 0) or ECMOS (*BusNumber* equals 1) locations starting with the location specified for *SlotNumber*. If EisaConfiguration is specified, the buffer will contain the CM_EISA_SLOT_INFORMATION structure followed by zero or more CM_EISA_FUNCTION_INFORMATION structures for the specified slot. If Pos is specified, the buffer will contain a CM_MCA_POS_DATA structure for the specified slot. If PCIConfiguration is specified, the buffer will contain the PCI_COMMON_CONFIG information for the given *SlotNumber*.

Table A.3: *Important Support Functions and Structures for Device Drivers (continued)*

Page Ref.	Function	Parameters and Explanations
		IN ULONG *Offset* Specifies 0 if the *BusDataType* is EisaConfiguration or Pos. Otherwise, specifies the byte offset in the PCI_COMMON_CONFIG structure for which the requested information should be returned. Callers can use the system-defined constant PCI_COMMON_HDR_LENGTH to specify the device-specific area of PCI_COMMON_CONFIG.
		IN ULONG *Length* Specifies the maximum number of bytes to return in *Buffer*.

893	ULONG HalGetInterruptVector(IN INTERFACE_TYPE *InterfaceType*, IN ULONG *BusNumber*,
	    IN ULONG *BusInterruptLevel*, IN ULONG *BusInterruptVector*,
	    OUT PKIRQL *Irql*, OUT PKAFFINITY *Affinity*);
		Returns a mapped system interrupt vector, interrupt level, and processor affinity mask that Device Drivers must pass to IoConnectInterrupt.

		IN INTERFACE_TYPE *InterfaceType* Specifies the bus interface type, which can be one of the following: Internal, Isa, Eisa, MicroChannel, TurboChannel, or PCIBus. However, additional types of busses will be supported in future versions of Windows NT. The upper bound on the types of busses supported is always MaximumInterfaceType.
		IN ULONG *BusNumber* Specifies the zero-based and system-assigned number of the bus in systems with several busses of the same *BusDataType*.
		IN ULONG *BusInterruptLevel* Specifies the bus-specific interrupt level.
		IN ULONG *BusInterruptVector* Specifies the bus-specific interrupt vector.
		OUT PKIRQL *Irql* Points to a variable that is set to the bus-relative IRQL. On return, this is reset to the DIRQL for the mapped vector.
		OUT PKAFFINITY *Affinity* Points to a variable that is set to the system-assigned affinity mask. This mask determines the set of processors on which the device can interrupt.
893	ULONG HalSetBusData(IN BUS_DATA_TYPE *BusDataType*, IN ULONG *BusNumber*, IN ULONG *SlotNumber*, IN PVOID *Buffer*, IN ULONG *Length*);	Sets bus-configuration data for a device on a dynamically configurable I/O bus with a published, standard interface.
		Returns the number of bytes of data successfully set for the given *SlotNumber*. If the given *BusDataType* is not valid for the current platform or if the supplied information is invalid, this routine returns 0.

Table A.3: *Important Support Functions and Structures for Device Drivers (continued)*

Page Ref.	Function	Parameters and Explanations
		IN BUS_DATA_TYPE *BusDataType*
		Specifies the type of bus data to be retrieved. Currently, its value can be one of the following: Cmos or PCIConfiguration. However, additional types of bus configuration will be supported in future versions of Windows NT. The upper bound on the types supported is always MaximumBusDataType.
		IN ULONG *BusNumber*
		Specifies the zero-based and system-assigned number of the bus in systems with several busses of the same *BusDataType*.
		IN ULONG *SlotNumber*
		Specifies the logical slot number or location of the device. If PCIConfiguration is specified as the *BusDataType*, this is specified as a PCI_SLOT_NUMBER-type value.
		IN PVOID *Buffer*
		Points to a caller-supplied buffer containing information specific to *BusDataType*. When Cmos is specified, the buffer contains data to be written to CMOS (*BusNumber* equals 0) or ECMOS (*BusNumber* equals 1) locations, starting with the location specified by the *SlotNumber*. When PCIConfiguration is specified, the buffer contains some or all of the PCI_COMMON_CONFIG information for the given *SlotNumber*. The specified *Length* determines how much information is supplied. Certain members of PCI_COMMON_CONFIG have read-only values. The caller is responsible for preserving the system-supplied values of read-only members.
		IN ULONG *Length*
		Specifies the maximum number of bytes of configuration data in *Buffer*.
893	ULONG HalSetBusDataByOffset(IN BUS_DATA_TYPE *BusDataType*, IN ULONG *BusNumber*, IN ULONG *SlotNumber*, IN PVOID *Buffer*, IN ULONG *Offset*, IN ULONG *Length*);	
		Sets bus-configuration data for a device on a dynamically configurable I/O bus with a published, standard interface.
		Returns the number of bytes of data successfully set for the given *SlotNumber*. If the given *BusDataType* is not valid for the current platform or if the supplied information is invalid, this routine returns 0.
		IN BUS_DATA_TYPE *BusDataType*
		Specifies the type of bus data to be retrieved. Currently, its value can be one of the following: Cmos or PCIConfiguration. However, additional types of bus configuration will be supported in future versions of Windows NT. The upper bound on the types supported is always MaximumBusDataType.
		IN ULONG *BusNumber*
		Specifies the zero-based and system-assigned number of the bus in systems with several busses of the same *BusDataType*.
		IN ULONG *SlotNumber*
		Specifies the logical slot number or location of the device. If PCIConfiguration is specified as the *BusDataType*, this is specified as a PCI_SLOT_NUMBER-type value.

Table A.3: *Important Support Functions and Structures for Device Drivers (continued)*

Page Ref.	Function	Parameters and Explanations
		IN PVOID *Buffer* When PCIConfiguration is specified, the buffer contains some or all of the PCI_COMMON_CONFIG information for the given *SlotNumber*. The specified *Offset* and *Length* determine how much information is supplied. Certain members of PCI_COMMON_CONFIG have read-only values. The caller is responsible for preserving the system-supplied values of read-only members.
		IN ULONG *Offset* Specifies the byte offset in the PCI_COMMON_CONFIG structure at which the caller-supplied configuration values begin. Callers can use the system-defined constant PCI_COMMON_HDR_LENGTH to specify the device-specific area of PCI_COMMON_CONFIG.
		IN ULONG *Length* Specifies the maximum number of bytes of configuration data in *Buffer*.
894	BOOLEAN HalTranslateBusAddress(IN INTERFACE_TYPE *InterfaceType*, IN ULONG *BusNumber*, IN PHYSICAL_ADDRESS *BusAddress*, IN OUT PULONG *AddressSpace*, OUT PPHYSICAL_ADDRESS *TranslatedAddress*);	
		Translates a bus-specific address into the corresponding system logical address.
		A return value of TRUE indicates that the system logical address corresponding to the given *BusNumber* and *BusAddress* has been returned in *TranslatedAddress*.
		IN INTERFACE_TYPE *InterfaceType* Specifies the bus interface type, which can be one of the following: Internal, Isa, Eisa, MicroChannel, TurboChannel, or PCIBus. However, additional types of busses will be supported in future versions of Windows NT. The upper bound on the types of busses supported is always MaximumInterfaceType.
		IN ULONG *BusNumber* Specifies the zero-based and system-assigned bus number for the device, used together with *InterfaceType* to identify the bus for systems with more than one bus of the same type.
		IN PHYSICAL_ADDRESS *BusAddress* Specifies the bus-relative physical address.
		IN OUT PULONG *AddressSpace* In cross-platform-portable drivers, specifies whether the address is a port number or a memory address; *AddressSpace* 0x0 indicates memory, 0x1 indicates I/O space.
		OUT PPHYSICAL_ADDRESS *TranslatedAddress* A pointer to the translated, system physical address. This value is valid only if the function returns TRUE.
895	HKEY_LOCAL_MACHINE\registry\machine\system\currentcontrolset\services\servicename	
		This Registry key contains the relevant information for loading a driver.

Table A.3: *Important Support Functions and Structures for Device Drivers (continued)*

Page Ref.	Function	Parameters and Explanations
		Type = REG_DWORD *value*
		A description of the type of driver being loaded. Although there are C symbols defined for these values, the symbolic names are not stored in the Registry.
		0x00000001 — SERVICE_KERNEL_DRIVER
		0x00000002 — SERVICE_FILE_SYSTEM_DRIVER
		0x00000008 — SERVICE_RECOGNIZER_DRIVER
		Start = REG_DWORD *value*
		A description of when the driver should be started. Although there are C symbols defined for these values, the symbolic names are not stored in the Registry.
		0x00000000 — SERVICE_BOOT_START
		0x00000001 — SERVICE_FILE_SYSTEM_DRIVER
		0x00000002 — SERVICE_AUTO_START
		0x00000003 — SERVICE_DEMAND_START
		0x00000004 — SERVICE_DISABLED
		ErrorControl = REG_DWORD *value*
		A code indicating the way in which the system should respond to an error return from the DriverEntry routine. Although there are C symbols for these values, the numeric values are stored in the Registry.
		0x00000000 — SERVICE_ERROR_IGNORE
		0x00000001 — SERVICE_ERROR_NORMAL
		0x00000002 — SERVICE_ERROR_SEVERE
		0x00000003 — SERVICE_ERROR_CRITICAL
		Group = REG_SZ *value*
		A description of the "load group" to which this driver belongs. All of the drivers in a group will be loaded at the same time. The groups are as follows.
		System Bus Extender
		SCSI miniport
		Port
		Primary disk
		SCSI class
		SCSI CDROM class
		Filter
		Boot file system

Table A.3: *Important Support Functions and Structures for Device Drivers (continued)*

Page Ref.	Function	Parameters and Explanations
		Base
		Pointer port
		Keyboard port
		Pointer Class
		Keyboard Class
		Video Init
		Video
		Video Save
		file system
		Event log
		Streams Drivers
		PNP_TDI
		NDIS
		TDI
		NetBIOSGroup
		SpoolerGroup
		NetDDEGroup
		Parallel arbitrator
		Extended base
		Remote validation
		PCI Configuration
		Tag = REG_DWORD *value* A specification of the "load order" of this driver within each group.
897	VOID InitializeListHead(IN PLIST_ENTRY *ListHead*);	
		Initializes any doubly linked, driver-managed interlocked queue or driver-maintained doubly linked list.
		In PLIST_ENTRY *ListHead* A pointer to the OBJECT_ATTRIBUTES structure to be initialized.

Table A.3: *Important Support Functions and Structures for Device Drivers (continued)*

Page Ref.	Function	Parameters and Explanations
898	VOID InitializeObjectAttributes(OUT POBJECT_ATTRIBUTES *InitializedAttributes*, IN PUNICODE_STRING ObjectName, IN ULONG *Attributes*, IN HANDLE *RootDirectory*, IN PSECURITY_DESCRIPTOR *SecurityDescriptor*);	

Initializes an OBJECT_ATTRIBUTES parameter for use in subsequent ZwOpen... or ZwCreate... calls.

OUT POBJECT_ATTRIBUTES *InitializedAttributes*
> A pointer to the OBJECT_ATTRIBUTES structure to be initialized.

IN PUNICODE_STRING *ObjectName*
> The name of the object that will be operated on. This *must* be a Unicode (L"...") string. This string must be the full pathname of the object.

IN ULONG *Attributes*
> A set of bits indicating the desired attributes. The value can be one or more of the values shown below. Note that the validity or effectiveness of a particular attribute is a function of the type of object being opened.

OBJ_INHERIT	The object can be inherited by a spawned process. Not relevant for most Device Driver code.
OBJ_PERMANENT	
OBJ_EXCLUSIVE	
OBJ_CASE_INSENSITIVE	The name lookup will ignore case. In most cases, because almost all of NT is case-insensitive, this flag should be supplied.
OBJ_OPENIF	

Page Ref.	Function / Parameters and Explanations
898	VOID InsertHeadList(IN PLIST_ENTRY *ListHead*, IN PLIST_ENTRY *Entry*);

Inserts an entry at the head of a doubly linked, driver-managed list.

IN PLIST_ENTRY *ListHead*
> A pointer to the head of a doubly linked list.

IN PLIST_ENTRY *Entry*
> The entry to be added to the list.

Page Ref.	Function / Parameters and Explanations
898	VOID InsertTailList(IN PLIST_ENTRY *ListHead*, IN PLIST_ENTRY *Entry*);

Inserts an entry at the end of a doubly linked, driver-managed list.

IN PLIST_ENTRY *ListHead*
> A pointer to the head of a doubly linked list.

IN PLIST_ENTRY *Entry*
> The entry to be added to the list.

Page Ref.	Function / Parameters and Explanations
899	typedef enum { ... } INTERFACE_TYPE

Table A.3: *Important Support Functions and Structures for Device Drivers (continued)*

Page Ref.	Function	Parameters and Explanations
899	`LONG InterlockedDecrement(PLONG Addend)`	
		Performs a multiprocessor-safe decrement of the referenced value.
		`IN PLONG Addend` A pointer to the value to be decremented.
899	`LONG InterlockedExchange(IN OUT PLONG Target, IN LONG Value);`	
		Performs a multiprocessor-safe setting of a value, returning the previous setting of the value.
		`IN OUT PLONG Target` A pointer to the value to be set.
		`IN LONG Value` The new value to set.
899	`LONG InterlockedExchangeAdd(IN OUT PLONG Target, IN LONG Delta);`	
		Performs a multiprocessor-safe increment of a value by a specified amount, returning the previous setting of the value.
		`IN OUT PLONG Target` A pointer to the value to be modified.
		`IN LONG Delta` The amount to add to the value.
900	`LONG InterlockedIncrement(IN PLONG Addend)`	
		Performs a multiprocessor-safe increment of the referenced value.
		`IN PLONG Addend` A pointer to the value to be incremented.
900	`VOID IoAcquireCancelSpinLock(OUT PKIRQL Irql);`	
		Acquires the IRP queue Cancel Spin Lock. The current IRQL is raised to `DISPATCH_LEVEL`.
		`OUT PKIRQL Irql` A pointer to the location where the current IRQL is stored. This is used on the subsequent `IoReleaseCancelSpinLock`.
900	`NTSTATUS IoAllocateAdapterChannel(IN PADAPTER_OBJECT AdapterObject, IN PDEVICE_OBJECT DeviceObject, IN ULONG NumberOfMapRegisters, IN PDRIVER_CONTROL ExecutionRoutine, IN PVOID Context);`	
		Synchronizes the use of an Adapter Object.
		`IN PADAPTER_OBJECT AdapterObject` The Adapter Object to which you are synchronizing.

Table A.3: *Important Support Functions and Structures for Device Drivers (continued)*

Page Ref.	Function	Parameters and Explanations
		IN PDEVICE_OBJECT *DeviceObject* The Device Object associated with the Adapter Object.
		IN ULONG *NumberOfMapRegisters* Specifies the number of map registers to be used for the I/O operation.
		IN PDRIVER_CONTROL *ExecutionRoutine* The function to be executed when the Adapter Object has been allocated.
		IN PVOID *Context* A user-specified pointer that is passed into ExecutionRoutine.

900	VOID IoAllocateController(IN PCONTROLLER_OBJECT *ControllerObject*,
	          IN PDEVICE_OBJECT *DeviceObject*,
	          IN PDRIVER_CONTROL *ExecutionRoutine*, IN PVOID *Context*);	

		Synchronizes the use of a Controller Object.
		IN PCONTROLLER_OBJECT *ControllerObject* The Controller Object to which you are synchronizing.
		IN PDEVICE_OBJECT *DeviceObject* The Device Object associated with the Controller Object.
		IN PDRIVER_CONTROL *ExecutionRoutine* The function to be executed when the Controller Object has been allocated.
		IN PVOID *Context* A user-specified pointer that is passed into ExecutionRoutine.
901	_PVOID IoAllocateErrorLogEntry(IN PVOID *IoObject*, IN UCHAR *EntrySize*);	
		Allocates an error log entry packet that can be written via IoWriteErrorLogEntry. Returns a pointer to an IO_ERROR_LOG_PACKET, or NULL.
		IN PVOID *IoObject* A pointer to a Device Object representing the device that had the error or a Driver Object that represents the driver that had the error.
		IN UCHAR *EntrySize* The size in bytes of the packet to be allocated. This value cannot exceed ERROR_LOG_MAXIMUM_SIZE.
901	PIRP IoAllocateIrp(IN CCHAR *StackSize*, IN BOOLEAN *ChargeQuota*);	
		Allocates an IRP, and returns either its address, or NULL if the allocation failed.
		IN CCHAR *StackSize* The desired number of IRP Stack locations. This value must be at least equal to the StackSize of the next lower-level driver's Device Object but can be 1 greater than this value. The calling driver need not allocate a stack location in the IRP for itself.

Table A.3: *Important Support Functions and Structures for Device Drivers (continued)*

Page Ref.	Function	Parameters and Explanations
		IN BOOLEAN *ChargeQuota*
		Must be set to FALSE by intermediate drivers. This can be set to TRUE only by highest-level drivers that are called in the context of the thread that originates the I/O request for which the driver is allocating another IRP. It indicates if the IRP should be charged against the process's quota.
902	MDL IoAllocateMdl(IN PVOID *VirtualAddress*, IN ULONG *Length*, IN BOOLEAN *SecondaryBuffer*, IN BOOLEAN *ChargeQuota*, IN OUT PIRP *Irp*);	
		Creates a MDL large enough to map a buffer, given its starting address and length.
		IN PVOID *VirtualAddress*
		The base virtual address that the MDL is intended to describe.
		IN ULONG *Length*
		The length (in bytes) of the buffer the MDL is intended to describe.
		IN BOOLEAN *SecondaryBuffer*
		Indicates whether the buffer is a primary or secondary buffer. This parameter determines how the MDL is to be linked to the IRP, if one is specified. All buffers except the first one described by a MDL in an IRP are considered secondary buffers. This field must be FALSE if no IRP is associated with the MDL.
		IN BOOLEAN *ChargeQuota*
		Must be set to FALSE by all drivers below the highest-level driver. This can be set to TRUE only by highest-level drivers that are called in the context of the thread that originates the I/O request for which the driver is allocating another IRP.
		IN OUT PIRP *Irp*
		If the buffer is to be associated with an IRP, the IRP reference must be supplied; otherwise, this parameter is NULL. The *SecondaryBuffer* parameter determines if this MDL is a primary or secondary buffer for the IRP.
		IN HANDLE *RootDirectory*
		This specifies the handle for the root of the directory in which an object will be created or looked up. Or it can be NULL.
		IN PSECURITY_DESCRIPTOR *SecurityDescriptor*
		An initialized absolute security descriptor, or NULL.
902	NTSTATUS IoAssignResources(IN PUNICODE_STRING *RegistryPath*, IN PUNICODE_STRING *DriverClassName*, IN PDRIVER_OBJECT *DriverObject*, IN PDEVICE_OBJECT *DeviceObject*, IN PIO_RESOURCE_REQUIREMENTS_LIST *RequestedResources*, IN OUT PCM_RESOURCE_LIST * *AllocatedResources*);	
		Attempts to assign resources such as memory, IRQ level(s), and/or I/O address space to the indicated device. Creates a nonconflicting assignment and returns STATUS_SUCCESS or returns some other status code indicating failure.
		IN PUNICODE_STRING *RegistryPath*
		The Registry path passed in to DriverEntry.

Table A.3: *Important Support Functions and Structures for Device Drivers (continued)*

Page Ref.	Function	Parameters and Explanations
		IN PUNICODE_STRING *DriverClassName* The name of the driver used in the Registry, or NULL, which uses the name Other.
		IN PDRIVER_OBJECT *DriverObject* The Driver Object passed into DriverEntry.
		IN PDEVICE_OBJECT *DeviceObject* A pointer to the Device Object that has been created, or NULL.
		IN PIO_RESOURCE_REQUIREMENTS_LIST *RequestedResources* A descriptor that indicates the needed resources and the permissible ranges that can be accepted by the device.
		IN OUT PCM_RESOURCE_LIST * *AllocatedResources* A pointer to an uninitialized pointer to resources. Upon successful completion of the function, this will contain a pointer to a CM_RESOURCE_LIST structure. The caller must free this structure upon completion by using ExFreePool.

902	NTSTATUS IoAttachDevice(IN PDEVICE_OBJECT *SourceDevice*,
	    IN PUNICODE_STRING *TargetDevice*,
	    OUT PDEVICE_OBJECT * *AttachedDevice*);	

		Attaches the specified device to a lower-level device. Sets the AlignmentRequirement of *SourceDevice* to that of the next lower-level driver and the StackSize to the StackSize of the next lower-level driver, plus 1. Returns one of the following values.
		STATUS_SUCCESS — The operation was successful.
		STATUS_INVALID_PARAMETER — One of the parameters is invalid.
		STATUS_OBJECT_NAME_INVALID — The name specified for *TargetDevice* is not a valid device name. Check the load order.
		STATUS_OBJECT_TYPE_MISMATCH — The *SourceDevice* parameter does not refer to a Device Object.
		STATUS_INSUFFICIENT_RESOURCES — Unable to allocate necessary resources.
		IN PDEVICE_OBJECT *SourceDevice* A pointer to the Device Object that is to be linked into a driver chain.
		IN PUNICODE_STRING *TargetDevice* The name of the device to which to attach.
		OUT PDEVICE_OBJECT * *AttachedDevice* A pointer to a place to put the Device Object to which the attachment has been done.

Table A.3: *Important Support Functions and Structures for Device Drivers (continued)*

Page Ref.	Function	Parameters and Explanations
903	PDEVICE_OBJECT IoAttachDeviceToDeviceStack(IN PDEVICE_OBJECT *SourceDevice*, IN PDEVICE_OBJECT *TargetDevice*);	
		Attaches the specified device to a lower-level device. Sets the AlignmentRequirement of the *SourceDevice* to that of the next lower-level driver and the StackSize to the StackSize of the next lower-level driver, plus 1. Returns a pointer to the actual Device Object to which the attachment was made (which can be different from *TargetDevice* if there is already layering of drivers).
		IN PDEVICE_OBJECT *SourceDevice*
		A pointer to the Device Object that is to be linked into a driver chain.
		IN PDEVICE_OBJECT *TargetDevice*
		A pointer to the Device Object to which the attachment is to be done.
904	PIRP IoBuildAsynchronousFsdRequest(IN ULONG *MajorFunction*, IN PDEVICE_OBJECT *DeviceObject*, IN OUT PVOID *Buffer* OPTIONAL, IN ULONG *Length* OPTIONAL, IN PLARGE_INTEGER *StartingOffset* OPTIONAL, IN PIO_STATUS_BLOCK *IoStatusBlock* OPTIONAL);	
		Builds an IRP to be used for an asynchronous File System Driver request, or, for convenience, any other type of lower-level driver.
		IN ULONG *MajorFunction*
		The value for the I/O request: IRP_MJ_READ, IRP_MJ_WRITE, IRP_MJ_FLUSH_BUFFERS, or IRP_MJ_SHUTDOWN.
		IN PDEVICE_OBJECT *DeviceObject*
		A pointer to the Device Object for the next lower-level driver.
		IN OUT PVOID *Buffer*
		A pointer to the buffer to be used for the I/O operation. Set to NULL for IRP_MJ_FLUSH_BUFFERS or IRP_MJ_SHUTDOWN.
		IN ULONG *Length*
		The length of *Buffer*. Set to 0 for IRP_MJ_FLUSH_BUFFERS or IRP_MJ_SHUTDOWN. For some devices, this value may be constrained. For example, for disk drives it must be a multiple of 512 bytes.
		IN PLARGE_INTEGER *StartingOffset*
		The offset on the device of the file operation. Set to NULL for IRP_MJ_FLUSH_BUFFERS or IRP_MJ_SHUTDOWN.
		IN PIO_STATUS_BLOCK *IoStatusBlock*
		A pointer to an I/O Status Block that is used to return the status from the lower-level driver.
905	PIRP IoBuildDeviceIoControlRequest(IN ULONG *IoControlCode*, IN PDEVICE_OBJECT *DeviceObject*, IN PVOID *InputBuffer* OPTIONAL, IN ULONG *InputBufferLength*, IN OUT PVOID *OutputBuffer* OPTIONAL, IN ULONG *OutputBufferLength*, IN BOOLEAN *InternalDeviceIoControl*, IN PKEVENT *Event*, IN PIO_STATUS_BLOCK *IoStatusBlock*);	
		Builds an IRP to be used for a Device Control operation sent to a lower-level driver.

Table A.3: *Important Support Functions and Structures for Device Drivers (continued)*

Page Ref.	Function	Parameters and Explanations
		IN ULONG *IoControlCode* The value for the IOCTL to be sent down.
		IN PDEVICE_OBJECT *DeviceObject* A pointer to the Device Object for the next lower-level driver.
		IN PVOID *InputBuffer* A pointer to the input buffer to be used for the I/O operation. Set to NULL if the lower-level driver does not require any input.
		IN ULONG *InputBufferLength* The length of *InputBuffer*. Set to 0 if *InputBuffer* is NULL.
		IN OUT PVOID *OutputBuffer* A pointer to the output buffer to be used for the I/O operation. Set to NULL if the lower-level driver does not produce any output.
		IN ULONG *OutputBufferLength* The length of *OutputBuffer*. Set to 0 if *OutputBuffer* is NULL.
		IN BOOLEAN *InternalDeviceIoControl* TRUE to call the lower-level driver with IRP_MJ_INTERNAL_DEVICE_CONTROL or IRP_MJ_SCSI. FALSE to call the lower-level driver with IRP_MJ_DEVICE_CONTROL.
		IN PKEVENT *Event* A pointer to an initialized Event Object. This event will be set to the Signaled state when the I/O operation has completed.
		IN PIO_STATUS_BLOCK *IoStatusBlock* A pointer to an I/O Status Block that is used to return the status from the lower-level driver.
906	VOID IoBuildPartialMdl(IN PMDL *SourceMdl*, IN OUT PMDL *TargetMdl*, IN PVOID *VirtualAddress*, IN ULONG *Length*);	Builds a MDL that maps a subrange of the memory described by another MDL.
		IN PMDL *SourceMdl* A pointer to a MDL that describes a region of memory.
		IN OUT PMDL *TargetMdl* A pointer to a MDL that will map the subrange described. This MDL must be large enough to hold the MDL information.
		IN PVOID *VirtualAddress* The base address of storage in *SourceMdl* that is to be mapped by *TargetMdl*.
		IN ULONG *Length* The length of the region to be mapped. The range specified by *VirtualAddress* and *Length* must be a proper subrange of the memory described by *SourceMdl*.

Table A.3: *Important Support Functions and Structures for Device Drivers (continued)*

Page Ref.	Function	Parameters and Explanations
906	`PIRP IoBuildSynchronousFsdRequest(IN ULONG MajorFunction, IN PDEVICE_OBJECT DeviceObject, IN OUT PVOID Buffer OPTIONAL, IN ULONG Length OPTIONAL, IN PLARGE_INTEGER StartingOffset OPTIONAL, IN PKEVENT Event, OUT PIO_STATUS_BLOCK IoStatusBlock);`	
		Builds an IRP to be used for a synchronous File System Driver request, or, for convenience, to any other type of lower-level driver.
		`IN ULONG MajorFunction`
		The value for the I/O request: `IRP_MJ_READ`, `IRP_MJ_WRITE`, `IRP_MJ_FLUSH_BUFFERS`, or `IRP_MJ_SHUTDOWN`.
		`IN PDEVICE_OBJECT DeviceObject`
		A pointer to the Device Object for the next lower-level driver.
		`IN OUT PVOID Buffer`
		A pointer to the buffer to be used for the I/O operation. Set to NULL for `IRP_MJ_FLUSH_BUFFERS` or `IRP_MJ_SHUTDOWN`.
		`IN ULONG Length`
		The length of *Buffer*. Set to 0 for `IRP_MJ_FLUSH_BUFFERS` or `IRP_MJ_SHUTDOWN`. For some devices, this value may be constrained. For example, for disk drives it must be a multiple of 512 bytes.
		`IN PLARGE_INTEGER StartingOffset`
		The offset on the device of the file operation. Set to NULL for `IRP_MJ_FLUSH_BUFFERS` or `IRP_MJ_SHUTDOWN`.
		`IN PKEVENT Event`
		A pointer to an initialized Event Object. This event will be set to the Signaled state when the I/O operation has completed.
		`IN PIO_STATUS_BLOCK IoStatusBlock`
		A pointer to an I/O Status Block that is used to return the status from the lower-level driver.
907	`NTSTATUS IoCallDriver(IN PDEVICE_OBJECT DeviceObject, IN OUT PIRP Irp);`	
		Calls the next lower-level driver in a chain of Device Drivers. The caller must set up any required values in the next lower-level driver's I/O Stack before making the call. Returns one of the values given next.
		value set by lower-level driver — Any NTSTATUS code returned by the callee.
		`STATUS_PENDING` — Indicates that the lower-level driver could not process the request immediately but has queued it for later processing.
		`IN PDEVICE_OBJECT DeviceObject`
		Pointer to the next lower-level driver's Device Object.
		`IN OUT PIRP Irp`
		Pointer to the IRP to be sent to the next lower-level driver. This IRP will be modified by the driver.

Table A.3: *Important Support Functions and Structures for Device Drivers (continued)*

Page Ref.	Function	Parameters and Explanations
907	`BOOLEAN IoCancelIrp(IN PIRP Irp);`	
		Marks the IRP as being canceled, and calls its Cancel Routine. If the IRP is canceled, this function returns TRUE. If the IRP has no Cancel Routine, it is marked as canceled and the function returns FALSE.
		`IN PIRP Irp` Pointer to the IRP that is to be canceled.
908	`VOID IoCompleteRequest(IN PIRP Irp, IN CCHAR PriorityBoost);`	
		Marks the IRP as being completed, and passes it back to the I/O Manager. If any higher-level drivers have specified `IoCompletion` routines, these will be called before the I/O system returns control to the application.
		`IN PIRP Irp` Pointer to the IRP that has been completed.
		`IN CCHAR PriorityBoost` The amount by which to boost the priority.

908	`NTSTATUS IoConnectInterrupt(OUT PKINTERRUPT * InterruptObject,`
	`           IN PKSERVICE_ROUTINE ServiceRoutine, IN PVOID ServiceContext,`
	`           IN PKSPIN_LOCK SpinLock, IN ULONG Vector, IN KIRQL Irql,`
	`           IN KIRQL SynchronizeIrql, IN KINTERRUPT_MODE InterruptMode,`
	`           IN BOOLEAN ShareVector, IN KAFFINITY ProcessorEnableMask,`
	`           IN BOOLEAN FloatingSave);`	

		Registers a Device Driver's ISR to be called when its device interrupts on any of a given set of processors.
		`STATUS_SUCCESS` — The interrupt is connected.
		`STATUS_INVALID_PARAMETER`
		`STATUS_INSUFFICIENT_RESOURCES` — There are insufficient resources (typically memory) to connect the ISR to the interrupt.
		`OUT PKINTERRUPT * InterruptObject` Points to the address of driver-supplied storage for a pointer to a set of Interrupt Objects that was obtained by calling `HalGetInterruptVector`. This pointer must also be passed in subsequent calls to `KeSynchronizeExecution`.
		`IN PKSERVICE_ROUTINE ServiceRoutine` Points to the entry point for the driver-supplied ISR.
		`IN PVOID ServiceContext` Points to the driver-determined context with which the specified ISR will be called.
		`IN PKSPIN_LOCK SpinLock` Points to an initialized Spin Lock that will be used to synchronize access to driver-determined data shared by other driver routines.

Table A.3: *Important Support Functions and Structures for Device Drivers (continued)*

Page Ref.	Function	Parameters and Explanations
		IN ULONG *Vector*
		Specifies the interrupt vector returned by the driver's call to HalGetInterruptVector.
		IN KIRQL *Irql*
		Specifies the DIRQL returned by HalGetInterruptVector for the Vector.
		IN KIRQL *SynchronizeIrql*
		Specifies the DIRQL at which the ISR will execute. If the ISR handles more than one interrupt vector or the driver has more than one ISR, this value must be the highest of the IRQL values returned by calls to HalGetInterruptVector for each vector. Otherwise, the *Irql* and *SynchronizeIrql* values are identical.
		IN KINTERRUPT_MODE *InterruptMode*
		Specifies the device interrupt type.
		Latched Edge-triggered interrupt.
		LevelSensitive Level-sensitive interrupt.
		IN BOOLEAN *ShareVector*
		Specifies whether the interrupt vector is shareable.
		IN KAFFINITY *ProcessorEnableMask*
		Specifies the set of processors on which device interrupts can occur in this platform. This value also is returned by HalGetInterruptVector.
		IN BOOLEAN *FloatingSave*
		Specifies whether to save the floating-point stack when the driver's device interrupts. For *x86*-based platforms, this value must be set to FALSE.
909	VOID IoCopyCurrentIrpStackLocationToNext(IN PIRP *Irp*)	
		Copies the contents of the current IRP Stack location to the next IRP Stack location. Allows a completion routine to be set. *NT 5.0 beta/Windows 2000*.
		IN PIRP *Irp*
		A pointer to the IRP whose Stack location is to be copied.
909	PCONTROLLER_OBJECT IoCreateController(IN ULONG *Size*)	
		Creates a Controller Object.
		IN ULONG *Size*
		Specifies the size of the Controller Extension. Can be 0.
909	NTSTATUS IoCreateDevice(IN PDRIVER_OBJECT *DriverObject*, IN ULONG *DeviceExtensionSize*, IN PUNICODE_STRING *DeviceName*, IN DEVICE_TYPE *DeviceType*, IN ULONG *DeviceCharacteristics*, IN BOOLEAN *Exclusive*, OUT PDEVICE_OBJECT * *DeviceObject*);	
		Creates a Device Object. Normally called from the DriverEntry function. Returns one of the following values.

Table A.3: *Important Support Functions and Structures for Device Drivers (continued)*

Page Ref.	Function	Parameters and Explanations	
		STATUS_SUCCESS	The Device Object has been created.
		STATUS_INSUFFICIENT_RESOURCES	There are insufficient resources.
		STATUS_OBJECT_NAME_EXISTS	A Device Object of this name has already been created.
		STATUS_OBJECT_NAME_COLLISION	
		IN PDRIVER_OBJECT *DriverObject*	
		The pointer to the Driver Object that came into the `DriverEntry` function.	
		IN ULONG *DeviceExtensionSize*	
		The number of bytes required by this Device Driver for its private data.	
		IN PUNICODE_STRING *DeviceName*	
		Points to a buffer containing a NUL-terminated Unicode string that names the Device Object. The string must be a full pathname.	
		IN DEVICE_TYPE *DeviceType*	
		Specifies one of the system-defined FILE_DEVICE_*XXX* constants indicating the type of device.	
		IN ULONG *DeviceCharacteristics*	
		Specifies one or more (ORed) of the following system-defined constants describing the nature of the driver's device, if appropriate. Other types of drivers can ignore this field.	
		FILE_REMOVABLE_MEDIA	The device is removable.
		FILE_READ_ONLY_DEVICE	The device is read-only, for example, a CD-ROM.
		FILE_FLOPPY_DISKETTE	The device is a floppy disk.
		FILE_WRITE_ONCE_MEDIA	The device can be written only once.
		FILE_REMOTE_DEVICE	This is a redirector to a device on the network.
		IN BOOLEAN *Exclusive*	
		Indicates whether the Device Object represents an exclusive device. That is, only a single thread at a time can open the device.	
		OUT PDEVICE_OBJECT * *DeviceObject*	
		Points to the newly created Device Object, if the call succeeds.	
910	PKEVENT IoCreateNotificationEvent(IN PUNICODE_STRING *EventName*, OUT PHANDLE *EventHandle*);		
		Creates or opens a named synchronization event for use in the serialization of access to hardware between two otherwise unrelated drivers. The event, once set, remains set until explicitly cleared.	
		IN PUNICODE_STRING *EventName*	
		Points to a buffer containing a NUL-terminated Unicode string that names the event.	

Table A.3: *Important Support Functions and Structures for Device Drivers (continued)*

Page Ref.	Function	Parameters and Explanations
		OUT PHANDLE *EventHandle* Points to a location in which to return a handle for the Event Object.
911	NTSTATUS IoCreateSymbolicLink(IN PUNICODE_STRING *SymbolicLinkName*, IN PUNICODE_STRING *DeviceName*);	Creates a symbolic link between a device name and the DOS-compatible device name.
		IN PUNICODE_STRING *SymbolicLinkName* The desired symbolic name to be used by applications.
		IN PUNICODE_STRING *DeviceName* The full pathname to the device.
911	PKEVENT IoCreateSynchronizationEvent(IN PUNICODE_STRING *EventName*, OUT PHANDLE *EventHandle*);	Creates or opens a named synchronization event for use in serializing access to hardware between two otherwise unrelated drivers. The synchronization event will allow one thread to pass each time it is set.
		IN PUNICODE_STRING *EventName* Points to a buffer containing a NUL-terminated Unicode string that names the event.
		OUT PHANDLE *EventHandle* Points to a location in which to return a handle for the Event Object.
912	VOID IoDeleteController(IN PCONTROLLER_OBJECT *ControllerObject*)	Deletes a Controller Object.
		IN PCONTROLLER_OBJECT *ControllerObject* A pointer to the Controller Object to be freed.
912	VOID IoDeleteDevice(IN PDEVICE_OBJECT *DeviceObject*);	Deletes a Device Object.
		IN PDEVICE_OBJECT *DeviceObject* A pointer to the Device Object to be freed.
913	NTSTATUS IoDeleteSymbolicLink(IN PUNICODE_STRING *SymbolicLinkName*);	Deletes a symbolic link. Returns STATUS_SUCCESS if successful.
		IN PUNICODE_STRING *SymbolicLinkName* A pointer to the name of the symbolic link.
913	VOID IoDetachDevice(IN OUT PDEVICE_OBJECT *TargetDevice*);	Detaches a driver from the lower-level *TargetDevice*.

Table A.3: *Important Support Functions and Structures for Device Drivers (continued)*

Page Ref.	Function	Parameters and Explanations
		`IN OUT PDEVICE_OBJECT TargetDevice` The Device Object that is being detached from the caller.
913	`VOID IoDisconnectInterrupt(IN PKINTERRUPT InterruptObject);`	
		Disconnects an interrupt from the device.
		`IN PKINTERRUPT InterruptObject` A pointer to the interrupt to be freed.
913	`typedef struct {...} IO_ERROR_LOG_PACKET`	

914	`BOOLEAN IoFlushAdapterBuffers(IN PADAPTER_OBJECT AdapterObject, IN PMDL Mdl,`
	`                IN PVOID MapRegisterBase, IN PVOID CurrentVa, IN ULONG Length,`
	`                IN BOOLEAN WriteToDevice);`	

		Flushes any data that remains in the System DMA controller's or bus master's internal cache. Returns TRUE if successful.
		`IN PADAPTER_OBJECT AdapterObject` The Adapter Object on which DMA was performed.
		`IN PMDL Mdl` The MDL on which DMA was performed (the MDL passed to `IoMapTransfer`).
		`IN PVOID MapRegisterBase` The mapping register base returned by `IoAllocateAdapterChannel`.
		`IN PVOID CurrentVa` The system logical address on which the I/O operation was performed.
		`IN ULONG Length` The length of the transfer, in bytes.
		`IN BOOLEAN WriteToDevice` TRUE for a Write operation; FALSE for a Read operation.
916	`VOID IoFreeAdapterChannel(IN PADAPTER_OBJECT AdapterObject);`	
		Frees a DMA channel allocated by `IoAllocateAdapterChannel`.
		`IN PADAPTER_OBJECT AdapterObject` The Adapter Object from which the channel was allocated.
916	`VOID IoFreeController(IN PCONTROLLER_OBJECT ControllerObject);`	
		Frees the Controller Object.
		`IN PCONTROLLER_OBJECT ControllerObject` A pointer to the Controller Object to be freed.

Table A.3: *Important Support Functions and Structures for Device Drivers (continued)*

Page Ref.	Function	Parameters and Explanations
916	VOID IoFreeIrp(IN PIRP *Irp*);	
		Frees an IRP.
		IN PIRP *Irp* A pointer to the IRP to be freed.
916	VOID IoFreeMapRegisters(IN PADAPTER_OBJECT *AdapterObject*, IN PVOID *MapRegisterBase*, IN ULONG *NumberOfMapRegisters*);	
		Frees the mapping registers allocated in the Adapter Object allocated by IoAllocateAdapterChannel.
		IN PADAPTER_OBJECT *AdapterObject* The Adapter Object to which the map registers were allocated.
		IN PVOID *RegisterBase* The register base returned as a handle by IoAllocateAdapterChannel.
		IN ULONG *NumberOfMapRegisters* The number of registers to be freed. This number must match the number passed to IoAllocateAdapterChannel.
917	VOID IoFreeMdl(IN PMDL *Mdl*);	
		Frees a caller-allocated MDL.
		IN PMDL *Mdl* A pointer to the MDL to be freed.
917	PCONFIGURATION_INFORMATION IoGetConfigurationInformation( );	
		Returns a pointer to the I/O Manager's global configuration information structure.
917	PIO_STACK_LOCATION IoGetCurrentIrpStackLocation(IN PIRP *Irp*)	
		Obtains a pointer to the current stack location of the IRP. This location is the one that belongs to the current driver.
		IN PIRP *Irp* A pointer to the IRP whose current stack location is desired.
917	PEPROCESS IoGetCurrentProcess( );	
		Returns a reference to the current process.

918	NTSTATUS IoGetDeviceObjectPointer(IN PUNICODE_STRING *ObjectName*,
	    IN ACCESS_MASK *DesiredAccess*, OUT PFILE_OBJECT * *FileObject*,
	    OUT PDEVICE_OBJECT * *DeviceObject*);	

		Obtains a pointer to a Device Object and a corresponding File Object.
		IN PUNICODE_STRING *ObjectName* The Device Object that represents the device that generates interrupts.

Table A.3: *Important Support Functions and Structures for Device Drivers (continued)*

Page Ref.	Function	Parameters and Explanations
		IN ACCESS_MASK *DesiredAccess* A bitmask of access rights, such as FILE_READ_DATA, FILE_WRITE_DATA, or FILE_ALL_ACCCESS.
		OUT PFILE_OBJECT * *FileObject* A pointer to a location at which to put a File Object pointer for the Device Object.
		OUT PDEVICE_OBJECT * *DeviceObject* A pointer to a location at which to put a Device Object pointer for the Device Object.
918	PIO_STACK_LOCATION IoGetNextIrpStackLocation(IN PIRP *Irp*)	Obtains a pointer to the stack location in the IRP that will be used by the next driver to be called, or which was called. This allows the current driver to establish values for the lower-level driver or to obtain the results set by the lower-level driver.
		IN PIRP *Irp* A pointer to the IRP whose next stack location is desired.
918	NTSTATUS IoInitializeDpcRequest(IN PDEVICE_OBJECT *DeviceObject*, IN PIO_DPC_ROUTINE *DpcRoutine*);	Registers a driver-supplied DpcForIsr routine. Normally called when the Device Driver initializes.
		IN PDEVICE_OBJECT *DeviceObject* The Device Object that represents the device that generates interrupts.
		IN PIO_DPC_ROUTINE *DpcRoutine* The address of the DPC Routine.
918	VOID IoInitializeIrp(IN OUT PIRP *Irp*, IN USHORT *PacketSize*, IN CCHAR *StackSize*);	Initializes a caller-allocated IRP.
		IN PIRP *Irp* The IRP to be initialized.
		IN USHORT *PacketSize* The size of the IRP.
		IN CCHAR *StackSize* The number of IRP Stack locations allocated. Must be the same value used in computing the allocation.
919	NTSTATUS IoInitializeTimer(IN PDEVICE_OBJECT *DeviceObject*, IN PIO_TIMER_ROUTINE *TimerRoutine*);	Registers a driver-supplied IoTimer routine. Normally called when the Device Driver initializes.
		IN PDEVICE_OBJECT *DeviceObject* The Device Object that represents the device that generates interrupts.

Table A.3: *Important Support Functions and Structures for Device Drivers (continued)*

Page Ref.	Function	Parameters and Explanations
		IN PIO_TIMER_ROUTINE *TimerRoutine* The address of the IoTimer routine.
919	PIRP IoMakeAssociatedIrp(IN PIRP *Irp*, IN CCHAR *StackSize*);	Creates an Associated IRP. Returns a pointer to the Associated IRP, or NULL if there was an error creating it.
		IN PIRP *Irp* The IRP for which the Associated IRP will be created.
		IN CCHAR *StackSize* The stack size of the Associated IRP. This size must be at least the StackSize of the next lower-level driver, but it may be larger.
920	PHYSICAL_ADDRESS IoMapTransfer(IN PADAPTER_OBJECT *AdapterObject*, IN PMDL *Mdl*, IN PVOID *MapRegisterBase*, IN PVOID *CurrentVa*, IN OUT PULONG *Length*, IN BOOLEAN *WriteToDevice*);	Sets up a collection of mapping registers for a DMA transfer.
		IN PADAPTER_OBJECT *AdapterObject* The Adapter Object pointer returned by HalGetAdapter and already passed in a call to IoAllocateAdapterChannel for the current IRP's transfer request.
		IN PMDL *Mdl* The MDL representing the buffer to be mapped.
		IN PVOID *MapRegisterBase* The handle returned by IoAllocateAdapterChannel, which the driver already called for the current IRP.
		IN PVOID *CurrentVa* Pointer to the current virtual address in the buffer, described by the MDL, to be mapped for a DMA transfer operation.
		IN OUT PULONG *Length* Specifies the length, in bytes, to be mapped. If the driver indicated that its device was a bus master with scatter/gather support when it called HalGetAdapter, the value of Length on return from IoMapTransfer indicates how many bytes were mapped. Otherwise, the input and output values of Length are identical.
		IN BOOLEAN *WriteToDevice* TRUE to write to the device; FALSE to read from it.
920	VOID IoMarkIrpPending(IN OUT PIRP *Irp*);	Marks an IRP as pending. A handler that calls this must return STATUS_PENDING.
		IN OUT PIRP *Irp* The IRP that is marked as pending.

Table A.3: *Important Support Functions and Structures for Device Drivers (continued)*

Page Ref.	Function	Parameters and Explanations
920	NTSTATUS IoRegisterShutdownNotification(IN PDEVICE_OBJECT *DeviceObject*);	
		Registers a Device Object to receive shutdown notifications.
		IN PDEVICE_OBJECT *DeviceObject* The Device Object that is to receive the IRP_MJ_SHUTDOWN notification.
921	VOID IoReleaseCancelSpinLock(IN KIRQL *Irql*);	
		Releases the global Cancel Spin Lock.
		IN KIRQL *Irql* The IRQL level returned by IoAcquireCancelSpinLock.
921	VOID IoRequestDpc(IN PDEVICE_OBJECT *DeviceObject*, IN PIRP *Irp*, IN PVOID *Context*)	
		Unregisters a Device Object to receive shutdown notifications.
		IN PDEVICE_OBJECT *DeviceObject* A pointer to the Device Object (passed into the interrupt handler).
		IN PIRP *Irp* A pointer to the IRP for the current interrupt event.
		IN PVOID *Context* A pointer to appropriate context (state values) required to process the DPC. This must be in nonpaged memory.
921	typedef struct {...} IO_RESOURCE_DESCRIPTOR;	
923	typedef struct {...} IO_RESOURCE_LIST;	
923	typedef struct {...} IO_RESOURCE_REQUIREMENTS_LIST;	
924	PDRIVER_CANCEL IoSetCancelRoutine(IN PIRP *Irp*, IN PDRIVER_CANCEL *CancelRoutine*);	
		Sets the address of a Cancel Routine to be called if the IRP is canceled.
		IN PIRP *Irp* A pointer to the IRP whose Cancel Routine is to be set.
		IN PDRIVER_CANCEL *CancelRoutine* The address of the Cancel Routine.
924	VOID IoSetCompletionRoutine(IN PIRP *Irp*, IN PIO_COMPLETION_ROUTINE *CompletionRoutine*, IN PVOID *Context*, IN BOOLEAN *InvokeOnSuccess*, IN BOOLEAN *InvokeOnError*, IN BOOLEAN *InvokeOnCancel*);	
		Sets the address of an I/O completion routine to be called by the next lower-level driver.
		IN PIRP *Irp* A pointer to the IRP whose completion routine is to be set.

Table A.3: *Important Support Functions and Structures for Device Drivers (continued)*

Page Ref.	Function	Parameters and Explanations
		IN PIO_COMPLETION_ROUTINE *CompletionRoutine* A pointer to the completion routine.
		IN PVOID *Context* A pointer to a driver-specific context to be passed to the completion routine.
		IN BOOLEAN *InvokeOnSuccess* If TRUE, the routine will be called for a STATUS_SUCCESS report.
		IN BOOLEAN *InvokeOnError* If TRUE, the routine will be called for all STATUS_* codes that indicate errors.
		IN BOOLEAN *InvokeOnCancel* If TRUE, the routine will be called for a STATUS_CANCELLED report.
925	VOID IoSetNextIrpStackLocation(IN OUT PIRP *Irp*)	
		Sets the contents of the next IRP Stack location to be a copy of that of the current IRP Stack location.
		IN OUT PIRP *Irp* A pointer to the IRP whose stack location is to be set.
925	USHORT IoSizeOfIrp(IN CCHAR *StackSize*);	
		Returns the number of bytes required for an IRP, given the desired number of IRP Stack locations.
		IN CCHAR *StackSize* The desired number of IRP Stack locations. Either the StackSize of the next lower-level driver, or that value plus 1.
926	VOID IoSkipCurrentIrpStackLocation(IN PIRP *Irp*)	
		Copies the contents of the current IRP Stack location to the next IRP Stack location. Does not allow a completion routine to be set. *NT 5.0 beta/Windows 2000.*
		IN PIRP *Irp* A pointer to the IRP whose stack location is to be copied.
926	typedef struct {...} IO_STACK_LOCATION	
931	VOID IoStartNextPacket(IN PDEVICE_OBJECT *DeviceObject*, IN BOOLEAN *Cancelable*);	
		Dequeues the next packet from the StartIo queue that matches Key, and causes it to dispatch to the StartIo handler.
		IN PDEVICE_OBJECT *DeviceObject* The Device Object whose StartIo queue is to be dispatched.
		IN BOOLEAN *Cancelable* TRUE if the request can be canceled; FALSE if it cannot be.

Table A.3: *Important Support Functions and Structures for Device Drivers (continued)*

Page Ref.	Function	Parameters and Explanations
931	`VOID IoStartNextPacketByKey(IN PDEVICE_OBJECT` *DeviceObject*`, IN BOOLEAN` *Cancelable*`, IN ULONG` *Key*`);`	
		Dequeues the next packet from the `StartIo` queue that matches `Key`, and causes it to dispatch to the `StartIo` handler.
		`IN PDEVICE_OBJECT` *DeviceObject* The Device Object whose `StartIo` queue is to be dispatched.
		`IN BOOLEAN` *Cancelable* TRUE if the request can be canceled; FALSE if it cannot be.
		`IN ULONG` *Key* A key value to be matched.
931	`VOID IoStartPacket(IN PDEVICE_OBJECT` *DeviceObject*`, IN PIRP` *Irp*`, IN PULONG` *Key*`, IN PDRIVER_CANCEL` *CancelFunction*`);`	
		Enters an IRP in the device's `StartIo` queue.
		`IN PDEVICE_OBJECT` *DeviceObject* The Device Object whose `StartIo` queue gets the IRP.
		`IN PIRP` *Irp* The IRP to be entered in the queue.
		`IN PULONG` *Key* A pointer to a location that contains a 32-bit value that determines where the entry is inserted into the `StartIo` queue. This key value is also used for `IoStartNextPacketByKey`. If this pointer is NULL, the entry is inserted at the end of the `StartIo` queue.
		`IN PDRIVER_CANCEL` *CancelFunction* If non-NULL, a pointer to a function to be called if the IRP is canceled.
931	`VOID IoStartTimer(IN PDEVICE_OBJECT` *DeviceObject*`)`	
		Enables the timer associated with the specified Device Object. This object must have an `IoTimer` routine established by `IoInitializeTimer`.
		`IN PDEVICE_OBJECT` *DeviceObject* The Device Object whose `IoTimer` entry will receive the timer notification.
931	`typedef struct {...} IO_STATUS_BLOCK`	
932	`VOID IoStopTimer(IN PDEVICE_OBJECT` *DeviceObject*`)`	
		Disables the timer associated with the specified Device Object.
		`IN PDEVICE_OBJECT` *DeviceObject* The Device Object that will no longer receive the `IoTimer` notification.

Table A.3: *Important Support Functions and Structures for Device Drivers (continued)*

Page Ref.	Function	Parameters and Explanations
932	NTSTATUS IoUnregisterShutdownNotification(IN PDEVICE_OBJECT *DeviceObject*);	
		Unregisters a Device Object to receive shutdown notifications.
		IN PDEVICE_OBJECT *DeviceObject* The Device Object that will no longer receive the IRP_MJ_SHUTDOWN notification.
931	VOID IoWriteErrorLogEntry(IN PVOID *ElEntry*);	
		Writes an error log entry to the log.
		IN PVOID *ElEntry* A pointer to an IO_ERROR_LOG_PACKET structure. The length is computed from the fields in the structure.
932	typedef {...} IRP	
932	VOID IsListEmpty(IN PLIST_ENTRY *ListHead*);	
		Tests the list, and returns TRUE if the list is empty and FALSE if not.
		IN PLIST_ENTRY *ListHead* A pointer to the head of a doubly linked list.
934	ULONG KdPrint(*message*)	
		If compiled with DBG defined, writes the message to the debug output port.
		message A parenthesized list that includes the format string and a variable number of arguments.
934	VOID KeAcquireSpinLock(IN PKSPIN_LOCK *SpinLock*, OUT PKIRQL *OldIrql*);	
		"Acquires" a Spin Lock. If the Spin Lock is acquired, control returns; if the Spin Lock has been acquired, this call does not return until the acquisition is made. When control returns, the thread is running at DISPATCH_LEVEL. The former IRQL is stored in the location referenced by *OldIrql*.
		IN PKSPIN_LOCK *SpinLock* Points to an initialized Spin Lock for which the storage is already provided.
		OUT PKIRQL *OldIrql* The previous IRQL is stored in this location.
935	VOID KeAcquireSpinLockAtDpcLevel(IN PKSPIN_LOCK *SpinLock*);	
		"Acquires" a Spin Lock. If the Spin Lock is acquired, control returns; if the Spin Lock has been acquired, this call does not return until the acquisition is made. This call is valid only when executed at IRQL == DISPATCH_LEVEL.
		IN PKSPIN_LOCK *SpinLock* Points to an initialized Spin Lock for which the storage is already provided.

Table A.3: *Important Support Functions and Structures for Device Drivers (continued)*

Page Ref.	Function	Parameters and Explanations
935	`VOID KeBugCheck(IN ULONG BugCheckCode);`	
		This brings the system down in a controlled fashion when continued execution would (potentially) corrupt the system.
		`IN ULONG BugCheckCode` The BugCheck code that is displayed. The predefined KeBugCheck codes and their meanings are shown in Appendix C.

936	`VOID KeBugCheckEx(IN ULONG BugCheckCode, IN ULONG BugCheckParameter1,`
	`            IN ULONG BugCheckParameter2, IN ULONG BugCheckParameter3,`
	`            IN ULONG BugCheckParameter4);`	

		This brings the system down in a controlled fashion when continued execution would (potentially) corrupt the system. In addition to the BugCheck code, up to four additional parameters may be used to encode useful information about the nature of the BugCheck.
		`IN ULONG BugCheckCode` The BugCheck code that is displayed. The predefined KeBugCheckEx codes and their meanings are shown in Appendix C.

		`ULONG BugCheckParameter1`
		`ULONG BugCheckParameter2`
		`ULONG BugCheckParameter3`
		`ULONG BugCheckParameter4`

		Additional parameters to the BugCheck, whose meanings depend on the BugCheck code.
936	`BOOLEAN KeCancelTimer(IN PKTIMER Timer);`	
		Cancels the specified Timer Object. The Timer Object is removed from the system timer queue. Its DPC, if specified, is not called.
		`IN PKTIMER Timer` A pointer to an initialized Timer Object.
936	`VOID KeClearEvent(IN PKEVENT Event);`	
		Sets the given event to the Not-Signaled state.
		`IN PKEVENT Event` A pointer to an initialized object of type Event for which the caller supplies the storage in nonpaged memory.
936	`NTSTATUS KeDelayExecutionThread(IN KPROCESSOR_MODE WaitMode, IN BOOLEAN Alertable,` `            IN PLARGE_INTEGER Interval);`	
		Delays the current thread by a specified interval.
		`IN KPROCESSOR_MODE WaitMode` The mode in which the wait will take place. One of the following values.
		`KernelMode` — The wait is executed in Kernel mode.
		`UserMode` — The wait is executed in User mode.

Table A.3: *Important Support Functions and Structures for Device Drivers (continued)*

Page Ref.	Function	Parameters and Explanations
		IN BOOLEAN *Alertable* TRUE if the wait is alertable; FALSE if not alertable.
		IN PLARGE_INTEGER *Interval* The delay interval in 100-ns units.
937	BOOLEAN KeDeregisterBugCheckCallback(IN PKBUGCHECK_CALLBACK_RECORD *CallbackRecord*);	
		Unregisters a BugCheck callback function.
		IN PKBUGCHECK_CALLBACK_RECORD *CallbackRecord* A pointer to the callback record used to register the callback.
937	VOID KeFlushIoBuffers(IN PMDL *Mdl*, IN BOOLEAN *ReadOperation*, IN BOOLEAN *DmaOperation*);	
		Guarantees that the address range specified by the MDL is flushed from all caches in all processors.
		IN PMDL *Mdl* A pointer to the MDL whose addresses are to be flushed.
		IN BOOLEAN *ReadOperation* TRUE if the flush is being performed prior to a Read operation.
		IN BOOLEAN *DmaOperation* TRUE if the I/O operation will be DMA; FALSE if the I/O will be done by programmed I/O.
937	KIRQL KeGetCurrentIrql( );	
		Returns the current IRQL.
938	ULONG KeGetCurrentProcessorNumber( );	
		Returns the processor number for the processor running the thread that places this call.
938	ULONG KeGetDcacheFillSize( );	
		Returns the current cache line size.
938	VOID KeInitializeCallbackRecord(IN PKBUGCHECK_CALLBACK_RECORD *CallbackRecord*);	
		Initializes a callback record for KeRegisterBugCheckCallback.
		IN PKBUGCHECK_CALLBACK_RECORD *CallbackRecord* A pointer to the callback record that will be used to register the callback.
938	VOID KeInitializeDeviceQueue(IN PKDEVICE_QUEUE *DeviceQueue*)	
		Initializes a Device Queue. The Device Queue is initialized to "empty and not busy".
		IN PKDEVICE_QUEUE *DeviceQueue* A pointer to the Device Queue Object. This must be in nonpaged memory.

Table A.3: *Important Support Functions and Structures for Device Drivers (continued)*

Page Ref.	Function	Parameters and Explanations
938	`VOID KeInitializeDpc(IN PKDPC Dpc, IN PKDEFERRED_ROUTINE DeferredRoutine, IN PVOID DeferredContext);`	
		Initializes a DPC.
		`IN PKDPC Dpc` A pointer to the DPC Object to be initialized. This must be in nonpaged memory.
		`IN PKDEFERRED_ROUTINE DeferredRoutine` A pointer to the routine to be executed when the DPC is dequeued.
		`IN PVOID DeferredContext` A pointer to a value that is passed in to the deferred routine when it is called. This pointer must be valid at the time the deferred routine is called.
939	`VOID KeInitializeEvent(IN PKEVENT Event, IN EVENT_TYPE Type, IN BOOLEAN State);`	
		Initializes an Event Object as a Synchronization (single waiter) Event or Notification Event, and sets its initial state to Signaled or Not-Signaled.
		`IN PKEVENT Event` A pointer to the Event Object to be initialized. Must be in nonpaged memory.
		`IN EVENT_TYPE Type` The type of the event, one of the following.
		`NotificationEvent` — The event is a Notification Event. Once set, it will remain set until reset.
		`SynchronizationEvent` — The event is a Synchronization Event. Once set, it will allow one thread to pass, after which it will automatically reset.
		`IN BOOLEAN State` The initial state to set in the event. TRUE to have the event be set; FALSE to have the event reset.
939	`VOID KeInitializeMutex(IN PKMUTEX Mutex, IN ULONG Level)`	
		Initializes the Mutex Object, sets it to the Signaled state, and sets its IRQL.
		`IN PKMUTEX Mutex` A pointer to the Semaphore to be initialized.
		`IN LONG Level` The initial IRQL level.
940	`VOID KeInitializeSemaphore(IN PKSEMAPHORE Semaphore, IN LONG Count, IN LONG Limit);`	
		Initializes the Semaphore Object.
		`IN PKSEMAPHORE Semaphore` A pointer to the Semaphore to be initialized.

Table A.3: *Important Support Functions and Structures for Device Drivers (continued)*

Page Ref.	Function	Parameters and Explanations
		IN LONG `Count` The initial count to be set for the Semaphore.
		IN LONG `Limit` The maximum value the Semaphore can have.
940	VOID KeInitializeSpinLock(IN PKSPIN_LOCK `SpinLock`);	Initializes a Spin Lock. The Spin Lock must be in nonpageable memory allocated by the caller.
		IN PKSPIN_LOCK `SpinLock` A pointer to the Spin Lock.
940	VOID KeInitializeTimer(IN PKTIMER `Timer`);	Initializes a timer. The timer must be in nonpageable memory allocated by the caller.
		IN PKTIMER `Timer` A pointer to the timer.
940	VOID KeInitializeTimerEx(IN PKTIMER `Timer`, IN TIMER_TYPE `Type`);	Initializes a timer. The timer must be in nonpageable memory allocated by the caller.
		IN PKTIMER `Timer` A pointer to the timer.
		IN TIMER_TYPE `Type` The type of the timer, one of the following.
		NotificationTimer — All waiting threads will be released, and the timer remains Signaled until reset.
		SynchronizationTimer — One waiting thread is released, and the timer is automatically reset until the next interval expires. If the timer is a recurring timer, no effort is required for this; otherwise, the timer must be explicitly requeued.
941	BOOLEAN KeInsertByKeyDeviceQueue(IN PKDEVICE_QUEUE `DeviceQueue`, IN PKDEVICE_QUEUE_ENTRY `DeviceQueueEntry`, IN ULONG `SortKey`);	Attempts to insert the *DeviceQueueEntry* in the specified *DeviceQueue*. If the queue is empty and not busy, the operation fails and the function returns FALSE. If the queue is nonempty or busy, the operation succeeds and the function returns TRUE.
		IN PKDEVICE_QUEUE `DeviceQueue` A pointer to the Device Queue in which the entry is to be inserted.
		IN PKDEVICE_QUEUE_ENTRY `DeviceQueueEntry` A pointer to the Device Queue entry to be inserted.

Table A.3: *Important Support Functions and Structures for Device Drivers (continued)*

Page Ref.	Function	Parameters and Explanations
		IN ULONG `SortKey` The sort-key value that determines the position in the device queue in which to insert the entry.
941	BOOLEAN KeInsertDeviceQueue(IN PKDEVICE_QUEUE `DeviceQueue`, IN PKDEVICE_QUEUE_ENTRY `DeviceQueueEntry`);	Attempts to insert the `DeviceQueueEntry` in the specified `DeviceQueue`. If the queue is empty and not busy, the operation fails and the function returns FALSE. If the queue is nonempty or busy, the operation succeeds and the function returns TRUE. IN PKDEVICE_QUEUE `DeviceQueue` A pointer to the Device Queue in which the entry is to be inserted. IN PKDEVICE_QUEUE_ENTRY `DeviceQueueEntry` A pointer to the Device Queue entry to be inserted.
941	BOOLEAN KeInsertQueueDpc(IN PKDPC `Dpc`, IN PVOID `SystemArgument1`, IN PVOID `SystemArgument2`);	Enqueues a DPC request in the DPC queue to be executed at DISPATCH_LEVEL. IN PKDPC `Dpc` A pointer to the DPC that is to be queued. IN PVOID `SystemArgument1` IN PVOID `SystemArgument2` Pointers to arbitrary data. Passed in to the DPC when it is dispatched. Valid at the time the DPC executes.
942	VOID KeLowerIrql(IN KIRQL `NewIrql`);	Lowers the IRQL to the specified value, and returns the current IRQL. IN KIRQL `NewIrql` The desired IRQL.
942	extern PCCHAR KeNumberProcessors;	A pointer to a variable that is the number of processors in the system.
942	LARGE_INTEGER KeQueryPerformanceCounter(IN PLARGE_INTEGER `PerformanceFrequency` OPTIONAL);	Returns the performance counter value in ticks. Optionally returns the frequency in hertz. IN PLARGE_INTEGER `PerformanceFrequency` A pointer to where to put the performance frequency, or NULL.
943	VOID KeQuerySystemTime(OUT PLARGE_INTEGER `CurrentTime`);	Returns the number of ticks that have elapsed since January 1, 1601.

Table A.3: *Important Support Functions and Structures for Device Drivers (continued)*

Page Ref.	Function	Parameters and Explanations
		OUT PLARGE_INTEGER *CurrentTime* A pointer to where to put the system time.
943	VOID KeQueryTickCount(OUT PLARGE_INTEGER *TickCount*);	
		Returns the number of ticks that have elapsed since the system booted.
		OUT PLARGE_INTEGER *TickCount* A pointer to where to put the number of ticks.
943	ULONG KeQueryTimeIncrement( );	
		Returns the number of 100-ns units added to the system time whenever the system timer interrupts.
943	VOID KeRaiseIrql(IN KIRQL *NewIrql*, OUT PKIRQL *OldIrql*);	
		Raises the IRQL to the specified value, and returns the current IRQL.
		IN KIRQL *NewIrql* The desired IRQL.
		OUT PKIRQL *OldIrql* A pointer to a location to store the previous IRQL.
944	LONG KeReadStateEvent(IN PKEVENT *Event*);	
		Returns the current state, Signaled or Not-Signaled, of a given Event Object.
		IN PKEVENT *Event* A pointer to the event whose state is to be returned.
944	LONG KeReadStateMutex(IN PKMUTEX *Mutex*);	
		Returns the current state, Signaled or Not-Signaled, of a given Mutex Object.
		IN PKMUTEX *Mutex* A pointer to the Mutex whose state is to be returned.
944	LONG KeReadStateSemaphore(IN PKSEMAPHORE *Semaphore*);	
		Returns the current state, Signaled or Not-Signaled, of a given Semaphore Object.
		IN PKSEMAPHORE *Semaphore* A pointer to the Semaphore whose state is to be returned.
944	BOOLEAN KeReadStateTimer(IN PKTIMER *Timer*);	
		Returns the current state, Signaled or Not-Signaled, of a given Timer Object. Returns TRUE if Signaled.
		IN PKTIMER *Timer* A pointer to the Timer whose state is to be returned.

Table A.3: *Important Support Functions and Structures for Device Drivers (continued)*

Page Ref.	Function	Parameters and Explanations

945	`BOOLEAN KeRegisterBugCheckCallback(IN PKBUGCHECK_CALLBACK_RECORD CallbackRecord,`
	`IN PKBUGCHECK_CALLBACK_ROUTINE CallbackRoutine, IN PVOID Buffer,`
	`IN ULONG Length, IN PUCHAR Component);`	

		Registers a function to be called when a BugCheck occurs.
		`IN PKBUGCHECK_CALLBACK_RECORD CallbackRecord` A pointer to a callback record initialized with `KeInitializeCallbackRecord`.
		`IN PKBUGCHECK_CALLBACK_ROUTINE CallbackRoutine` A pointer to the function to be called on a BugCheck.
		`IN PVOID Buffer` A pointer to a programmer-allocated buffer in the Nonpaged Pool.
		`IN ULONG Length` The length of `Buffer`.
		`IN PUCHAR Component` A pointer to the NUL-terminated, 8-bit character string that identifies the component.
945	`LONG KeReleaseMutex(IN PKMUTEX Mutex, IN BOOLEAN Wait);`	
		Releases a Mutex.
		`IN PKMUTEX Mutex` A pointer to a Mutex.
		`IN BOOLEAN Wait` TRUE if this call will be immediately followed by a `KeWait...` function call; FALSE otherwise.
945	`LONG KeReleaseSemaphore(IN PKSEMAPHORE Semaphore, IN KPRIORITY Increment,` `IN ULONG Adjustment, IN BOOLEAN Wait);`	
		Releases a Semaphore.
		`IN PKSEMAPHORE Semaphore` A pointer to a Semaphore.
		`IN KPRIORITY Increment` The amount of priority boost to give to any thread whose wait is satisfied.
		`IN ULONG Adjustment` The amount to add to the Semaphore code.
		`IN BOOLEAN Wait` TRUE if this call will be immediately followed by a `KeWait...` function call; FALSE otherwise.

Table A.3: *Important Support Functions and Structures for Device Drivers (continued)*

Page Ref.	Function	Parameters and Explanations
946	`VOID KeReleaseSpinLock(IN PKSPIN_LOCK SpinLock, IN KIRQL NewIrql);`	
		Releases a Spin Lock and restores the IRQL.
		`IN PKSPIN_LOCK SpinLock` A pointer to a Spin Lock.
		`IN KIRQL NewIrql` The IRQL at which the thread is to be running after the release. This is the *OldIrql* value stored in KeAcquireSpinLock.
946	`VOID KeReleaseSpinLockFromDpcLevel(IN PKSPIN_LOCK SpinLock);`	
		Releases a Spin Lock acquired by KeAcquireSpinLockAtDpcLevel.
		`IN PKSPIN_LOCK SpinLock` The lock to be released.
947	`PKDEVICE_QUEUE_ENTRY KeRemoveByKeyDeviceQueue(IN PKDEVICE_QUEUE DeviceQueue, IN ULONG SortKey);`	
		Removes an entry from the specified *DeviceQueue* whose position is determined by *SortKey*. If the queue is empty and busy, returns NULL and sets the state to "nonbusy".
		`IN PKDEVICE_QUEUE DeviceQueue` The Device Queue from which the entry is to be retrieved.
947	`PKDEVICE_QUEUE_ENTRY KeRemoveDeviceQueue(IN PKDEVICE_QUEUE DeviceQueue);`	
		Removes an entry from the head of the specified *DeviceQueue*. If the queue is empty and busy, returns NULL and sets the state to "nonbusy".
		`IN PKDEVICE_QUEUE DeviceQueue` The Device Queue from which the entry is to be retrieved.
947	`BOOLEAN KeRemoveEntryDeviceQueue(IN PKDEVICE_QUEUE DeviceQueue, IN PKDEVICE_QUEUE_ENTRY DeviceQueueEntry);`	
		Removes the specified *DeviceQueueEntry* from the specified *DeviceQueue*.
		`IN PKDEVICE_QUEUE DeviceQueue` The Device Queue from which the entry is to be retrieved.
		`IN PKDEVICE_QUEUE_ENTRY DeviceQueueEntry` The entry to be removed from the list.
947	`BOOLEAN KeRemoveQueueDpc(IN PKDPC Dpc);`	
		Removes the DPC from the PDC queue. If in the queue and removed, returns TRUE. If not in the queue, returns FALSE.

Table A.3: *Important Support Functions and Structures for Device Drivers (continued)*

Page Ref.	Function	Parameters and Explanations
		IN PKDPC *Dpc* A pointer to the DPC to be removed from the DPC queue.
948	LONG KeResetEvent(IN PKEVENT *Event*);	Sets the state of *Event* to Not-Signaled.
		IN PKEVENT *Event* A pointer to the event whose state is to be set to Not-Signaled.
948	LONG KeSetEvent(IN PKEVENT *Event*, IN KPRIORITY *Increment*, IN BOOLEAN *Wait*);	Sets the specified event to the Signaled state. Returns the previous state.
		IN PKEVENT *Event* A pointer to the event to be signaled.
		IN KPRIORITY *Increment* The priority increment to be added to a process if its wait is satisfied.
		IN BOOLEAN *Wait* TRUE if the operation will be immediately followed by a KeWait*Xxx* operation.
948	KPRIORITY KeSetPriorityThread(IN PKTHREAD *Thread*, IN KPRIORITY *Priority*);	Sets the priority of the thread.
		IN PKTHREAD *Thread* A pointer to the thread whose priority is to be set.
		IN KPRIORITY *Priority* The desired priority for the thread.
948	BOOLEAN KeSetTimer(IN PKTIMER *Timer*, IN LARGE_INTEGER *DueTime*, IN PKDPC *Dpc* OPTIONAL);	Enqueues a request in the system timer queue for a timer, possibly recurring. When the timer interval is satisfied, the Timer Object is set to the Signaled state. If the DPC pointer is non-NULL, the DPC will be called when the interval is satisfied.
		IN PKTIMER *Timer* A pointer to the timer to be signaled.
		IN LARGE_INTEGER *DueTime* The time at which the timer should be satisfied. A positive value represents absolute time, and a negative value represents relative time.
		IN PKDPC *Dpc* OPTIONAL A pointer to a DPC to be invoked when the timer is satisfied, or NULL.

Table A.3: *Important Support Functions and Structures for Device Drivers (continued)*

Page Ref.	Function	Parameters and Explanations
949	BOOLEAN KeSetTimerEx(IN PKTIMER *Timer*, IN LARGE_INTEGER *DueTime*, IN LONG *Period* OPTIONAL, IN PKDPC *Dpc* OPTIONAL);	Enqueues a request in the system timer queue for a timer, possibly recurring. When the timer interval is satisfied, the Timer Object is set to the Signaled state. If the DPC pointer is non-NULL, the DPC will be called when the interval is satisfied.
		IN PKTIMER *Timer* A pointer to the timer to be signaled.
		IN LARGE_INTEGER *DueTime* The time at which the timer should be satisfied. A positive value represents absolute time, and a negative value represents relative time.
		IN LONG *Period* OPTIONAL The period at which this timer should repeat; 0 means the timer is nonrecurring.
		IN PKDPC *Dpc* OPTIONAL A pointer to a DPC to be invoked when the timer is satisfied, or NULL.
950	VOID KeStallExecutionProcessor(IN ULONG *MicroSeconds*);	Causes the executing processor to delay for a brief period.
		IN ULONG *MicroSeconds* The number of microseconds to stall the processor.
950	BOOLEAN KeSynchronizeExecution(IN PKINTERRUPT *Interrupt*, IN PKSYNCHRONIZE_ROUTINE *SynchronizeRoutine*, IN PVOID *SynchronizeContext*);	Synchronizes the execution of a given routine with that of the ISR associated with the given Interrupt Object pointer.
		IN PKINTERRUPT *Interrupt* A pointer to a set of Interrupt Objects. This pointer was returned by IoConnectInterrupt.
		IN PKSYNCHRONIZE_ROUTINE *SynchronizeRoutine* The entry point for a caller-supplied SynchCritSection routine whose execution is to be synchronized with the execution of the ISR associated with the Interrupt Object(s).
		IN PVOID *SynchronizeContext* Points to a caller-supplied context area to be passed to *SynchronizeRoutine* when it is called.
951	NTSTATUS KeWaitForMultipleObjects(IN ULONG *Count*, IN PVOID *Objects*[], IN WAIT_TYPE *WaitType*, IN KWAIT_REASON *WaitReason*, IN KPROCESSOR_MODE *WaitMode*, IN BOOLEAN *Alertable*, IN PLARGE_INTEGER *Timeout*, IN PKWAIT_BLOCK *WaitBlockArray*);	Waits for one or all specified synchronization objects to enter the Signaled state. Returns one of the following values.

Table A.3: *Important Support Functions and Structures for Device Drivers (continued)*

Page Ref.	Function	Parameters and Explanations	
		STATUS_SUCCESS	Depending on the specified *WaitType*, one or all of the dispatcher objects in the *Objects* array satisfied the wait.
		STATUS_ALERTED	The wait is completed because of an alert to the thread.
		STATUS_USER_APC	A user APC was delivered to the current thread before the specified timeout interval expired.
		STATUS_TIMEOUT	A timeout occurred before the specified set of wait conditions was met. This value can be returned when an explicit timeout value of 0 is specified, but the specified set of wait conditions cannot be met immediately.
		IN ULONG *Count* The number of synchronization objects referenced by the *Objects* array pointer.	
		IN PVOID *Objects*[] An array of pointers to synchronization objects.	
		IN WAIT_TYPE *WaitType* The type of wait to be performed.	
		WaitAll	Requires that all dispatcher objects are satisfied before the wait can complete.
		WaitAny	Requires that only one dispatcher object be satisfied before the wait can complete.
		IN KWAIT_REASON *WaitReason* The reason for the wait.	
		Executive	Most drivers should use this value.
		UserRequest	A driver that is performing a request within a User thread should use this value.
		IN KPROCESSOR_MODE *WaitMode* The mode in which the wait is performed.	
		KernelMode	Intermediate and lowest-level drivers should specify this value.
		UserMode	May be used in a top-level driver running in the context of a user-level thread.
		IN BOOLEAN *Alertable* Specifies whether a wait is alertable.	

Table A.3: *Important Support Functions and Structures for Device Drivers (continued)*

Page Ref.	Function	Parameters and Explanations
		IN PLARGE_INTEGER *Timeout* A pointer to a timeout value, or NULL if no timeout is used. A negative timeout is a relative time. A positive value is an absolute timeout and will track any changes in the system time.
		IN PKWAIT_BLOCK *WaitBlockArray* A pointer to a set of wait blocks, or NULL.
953	NTSTATUS KeWaitForMutexObject(IN PKMUTEX *Mutex*, IN KWAIT_REASON *WaitReason*, IN KPROCESSOR_MODE *WaitMode*, IN BOOLEAN *Alertable*, IN PLARGE_INTEGER *Timeout*);	
		Waits for the specified synchronization object to enter the Signaled state. Returns one of the following values.
		STATUS_SUCCESS — The object satisfied the wait.
		STATUS_ALERTED — The wait is completed because of an alert to the thread.
		STATUS_USER_APC — A user APC was delivered to the current thread before the specified timeout interval expired.
		STATUS_TIMEOUT — A timeout occurred before the specified wait condition was met. This value can be returned when an explicit timeout value of 0 is specified, but the specified set of wait conditions cannot be met immediately.
		IN PKMUTEX *Mutex* A pointer to a Mutex Object.
		IN KWAIT_REASON *WaitReason* The reason for the wait.
		Executive — Most drivers should use this value.
		UserRequest — A driver that is performing a request within a User thread should use this value.
		IN KPROCESSOR_MODE *WaitMode* The mode in which the wait is performed.
		KernelMode — Intermediate and lowest-level drivers should specify this value.
		UserMode — May be used in a top-level driver running in the context of a user-level thread.
		IN BOOLEAN *Alertable* Specifies whether a wait is alertable.

Table A.3: *Important Support Functions and Structures for Device Drivers (continued)*

Page Ref.	Function	Parameters and Explanations
		IN PLARGE_INTEGER *Timeout* A pointer to a timeout value, or NULL if no timeout is used. A negative timeout is a relative time. A positive value is an absolute timeout and will track any changes in the system time.
954	NTSTATUS KeWaitForSingleObject(IN PVOID *Object*, IN KWAIT_REASON *WaitReason*, IN KPROCESSOR_MODE *WaitMode*, IN BOOLEAN *Alertable*, IN PLARGE_INTEGER *Timeout*);	

Waits for the specified synchronization object to enter the Signaled state. Returns one of the following values.

STATUS_SUCCESS	The object satisfied the wait.
STATUS_ALERTED	The wait is completed because of an alert to the thread.
STATUS_USER_APC	A user APC was delivered to the current thread before the specified timeout interval expired.
STATUS_TIMEOUT	A timeout occurred before the specified wait condition was met. This value can be returned when an explicit timeout value of 0 is specified, but the specified set of wait conditions cannot be met immediately.

IN PVOID *Object*

A pointer to a synchronization object.

IN KWAIT_REASON *WaitReason*

The reason for the wait.

Executive	Most drivers should use this value.
UserRequest	A driver that is performing a request within a User thread should use this value.

IN KPROCESSOR_MODE *WaitMode*

The mode in which the wait is performed.

KernelMode	Intermediate and lowest-level drivers should specify this value.
UserMode	May be used in a top-level driver running in the context of a user-level thread.

IN BOOLEAN *Alertable*

Specifies whether a wait is alertable.

IN PLARGE_INTEGER *Timeout*

A pointer to a timeout value, or NULL if no timeout is used. A negative timeout is a relative time. A positive value is an absolute timeout and will track any changes in the system time.

Page Ref.	Function
955	typedef struct {...} KEY_BASIC_INFORMATION;

Table A.3: *Important Support Functions and Structures for Device Drivers (continued)*

Page Ref.	Function	Parameters and Explanations
956	`typedef struct {...} KEY_FULL_INFORMATION;`	
957	`typedef struct {...} KEY_NODE_INFORMATION;`	
958	`typedef struct {...} KEY_VALUE_BASIC_INFORMATION;`	
959	`typedef struct {...} KEY_VALUE_FULL_INFORMATION;`	
961	`typedef struct {...} KEY_VALUE_PARTIAL_INFORMATION;`	
962	`typedef UCHAR KIRQL`	
962	`KSYNCHRONIZE_ROUTINE`	
963	`typedef union {...} LARGE_INTEGER;`	
963	`PVOID MmAllocateContiguousMemory(IN ULONG NumberOfBytes, IN PHYSICAL_ADDRESS HighestAcceptableAddress);`	
		Allocates contiguous physical memory of the indicated size and whose entire allocation is below the specified limit. Returns the system logical address of this memory, or `NULL` if the memory cannot be allocated. The memory is allocated cache-aligned in the Nonpaged Pool.
		`IN ULONG NumberOfBytes` The amount of contiguous physical memory to be allocated.
		`IN PHYSICAL_ADDRESS HighestAcceptableAddress` The highest physical address that the allocation is permitted to have.
964	`PVOID MmAllocateNonCachedMemory(IN ULONG NumberOfBytes)`	
		Allocates the requested number of bytes on a cache-aligned boundary. In addition, the memory is allocated from a page whose PTE specifies that the page contents should not be cached. This eliminates any problems of cache consistency that could arise.
		`IN ULONG NumberOfBytes` The number of bytes required.
964	`PMDL MmCreateMdl(IN PMDL MemoryDescriptorList OPTIONAL, IN PVOID Base, IN ULONG Length);`	
		Initializes a MDL, and allocates one if requested.
		`IN PMDL MemoryDescriptorList` A pointer to a preallocated MDL, or `NULL` for `MmCreateMdl` to allocate the space.
		`IN PVOID Base` A pointer to the buffer that the MDL is to represent in system logical space.
		`IN ULONG Length` The length of the buffer, in bytes.
964	`VOID MmFreeContiguousMemory(IN PVOID BaseAddress);`	
		Frees the memory allocated by `MmAllocateContiguousMemory`.

Table A.3: *Important Support Functions and Structures for Device Drivers (continued)*

Page Ref.	Function	Parameters and Explanations
		IN PVOID *BaseAddress* The pointer returned from an MmAllocateContiguousMemory call.
964	PVOID MmFreeNonCachedMemory(IN PVOID *address*, IN ULONG *NumberOfBytes*)	Frees the memory allocated by MmAllocateNonCachedMemory.
		IN PVOID *address* The pointer returned from an MmAllocateNonCachedMemory call.
		IN ULONG *NumberOfBytes* The number of bytes that was specified to the MmFreeNonCachedMemory.
965	ULONG MmGetMdlByteCount(IN PMDL *Mdl*);	Initializes a MDL.
		IN PMDL *Mdl* A pointer to the MDL whose length is to be returned.
965	ULONG MmGetMdlByteOffset(IN PMDL *Mdl*);	Returns the byte offset within the page of the first byte of the buffer represented by the MDL.
		IN PMDL *Mdl* A pointer to a MDL.
965	PVOID MmGetMdlVirtualAddress(IN PMDL *Mdl*);	Returns the virtual address represented by the MDL.
		IN PMDL *Mdl* A pointer to a MDL.
965	PHYSICAL_ADDRESS MmGetPhysicalAddress(IN PVOID *BaseAddress*);	Returns the physical address associated with the virtual address *BaseAddress*.
		IN PVOID *BaseAddress* The virtual address. This must be a valid address in the running thread.
965	PVOID MmGetSystemAddressForMdl(IN PMDL *Mdl*)	Returns a nonpaged virtual address that represents the physical pages described by the MDL. The physical pages described by the MDL are mapped into contiguous virtual memory in system space. If the physical pages have already been mapped, the mapped virtual address is returned.
		IN PMDL *Mdl* The address of a MDL.
966	VOID MmInitializeMdl(IN PMDL *Mdl*, IN PVOID *BaseVa*, IN ULONG *Length*);	Initializes a MDL.

Table A.3: *Important Support Functions and Structures for Device Drivers (continued)*

Page Ref.	Function	Parameters and Explanations
		IN PMDL *Mdl* A pointer to the MDL whose header is to be initialized.
		IN PVOID *BaseVa* The base virtual address to be installed in the MDL.
		IN ULONG *Length* The length in bytes of the buffer described by the MDL.
966	BOOLEAN MmIsAddressValid(IN PVOID *VirtualAddress*);	
		Returns TRUE if the address can be accessed without causing a page fault. Returns FALSE if accessing the address would cause a page fault.
		IN PVOID *VirtualAddress* The address being queried.
966	PVOID MmMapIoSpace(IN PHYSICAL_ADDRESS *phys*, IN ULONG *NumberOfBytes*, IN BOOLEAN *CacheEnable*)	
		Maps a physical address (typically a device address) into the virtual memory space.
		IN PHYSICAL_ADDRESS *phys* A 64-bit physical address.
		IN ULONG *NumberOfBytes* The number of bytes that should be mapped into the virtual address space.
		IN BOOLEAN *CacheEnable* TRUE if the entry should have its PTE cache-enable bit indicate that accesses to these addresses are cacheable. FALSE if the PTE should have its cache-enable bit indicate that accesses to these addresses should not be cached.
967	PVOID MmMapLockedPages(IN PMDL *MemoryDescriptorList*, IN KPROCESSOR_MODE *AccessMode*);	
		Maps a physical address (typically a device address) into the virtual memory space.
		IN PMDL *MemoryDescriptorList* A pointer to a MDL whose pages have been locked by MmProbeAndLockPages.
		IN KPROCESSOR_MODE *AccessMode* KernelMode or UserMode.
967	VOID MmPrepareMdlForReuse(IN PMDL *Mdl*);	
		The MDL fields are prepared for a reinitialization; this saves having to free and then immediately reallocate a MDL.
		IN PMDL *Mdl* The MDL to be reinitialized. Call MmInitializeMdl to reinitialize the MDL.

Table A.3: *Important Support Functions and Structures for Device Drivers (continued)*

Page Ref.	Function	Parameters and Explanations
967	VOID MmProbeAndLockPages(IN OUT PMDL *Mdl*, IN KPROCESSOR_MODE *AccessMode*, IN LOCK_OPERATION *Operation*);	
		This function probes the specified pages, makes them resident, and locks the physical pages mapped by the virtual address range into memory. The MDL is updated to describe the physical pages.
		IN OUT PMDL *Mdl*
		The MDL that describes the pages of the buffer.
		IN KPROCESSOR_MODE *AccessMode*
		Specifies the access mode to use when probing the pages, one of the following values.
		UserMode — The pages are probed with User-mode privileges.
		KernelMode — The pages are probed with Kernel-mode privileges.
		IN LOCK_OPERATION *Operation*
		Specifies the operation that will be performed on the page. It must be one of the following values.
		IoReadAccess — The caller wishes to read the pages.
		IoWriteAccess — The caller wishes to write the pages.
		IoModifyAccess — The caller wishes to both read and write the pages.
968	MM_SYSTEM_SIZE MmQuerySystemSize( );	
		Returns a value suggesting the amount of memory on the system. One of the following values.
		MmSmallSystem — < 12MB
		MmMediumSystem — > 12MB, < 20MB
		MmLargeSystem — > 20MB
968	ULONG MmSizeOfMdl(IN PVOID *Base*, IN ULONG *Length*);	
		Returns the size of a MDL necessary to span the memory described by the input parameters.
		IN PVOID *Base*
		A virtual address. This is the base address of the memory that will be described by a MDL.
		IN ULONG *Length*
		The number of bytes of memory required, starting at *Base*.
969	VOID MmUnlockPages(IN PMDL *Mdl*);	
		Unlocks the pages locked by MmProbeAndLockPages.

Table A.3: *Important Support Functions and Structures for Device Drivers (continued)*

Page Ref.	Function	Parameters and Explanations
		IN PMDL *Mdl* A pointer to a MDL structure. This structure must be a structure whose pages have been locked.
969	VOID MmUnlockPagableImageSection(IN PVOID *ImageSectionHandle*);	
		Decrements the lock count. If the lock count goes to 0, unlocks the pages locked by MmLockPagableCodeSection or MmLockPagableDataSection.
		IN PVOID *ImageSectionHandle* The handle returned by the locking function.
969	VOID MmUnmapIoSpace(IN PVOID *address*, IN ULONG *NumberOfBytes*)	
		Unmaps a virtual address that was assigned using MmMapIoSpace.
		IN PVOID *address* A virtual address. This must be an address that was allocated using MmMapIoSpace.
		IN ULONG *NumberOfBytes* The number of bytes that were mapped into the virtual address space. Must be the same value that was passed to MmMapIoSpace.
969	VOID MmUnmapLockedPages(IN PVOID *BaseAddress*, IN PMDL *MemoryDescriptorList*);	
		Unmaps a set of pages that were locked using MmMapLockedPages.
		IN PVOID *BaseAddress* A virtual address. Must be an address that was returned by MmMapLockedPages.
		IN PMDL *MemoryDescriptorList* The same value that was passed to MmMapLockedPages.
969	typedef ... NTSTATUS	
970	VOID ObDereferenceObject(IN PVOID *Object*);	
		Decrements the reference count of the object. If the reference count goes to 0, the object is deleted.
		IN PVOID *Object* A pointer to the object to be dereferenced.

970	NTSTATUS ObReferenceObjectByHandle(IN HANDLE Handle, IN ACCESS_MASK *DesiredAccess*,
	          IN POBJECT_TYPE *ObjectType*, IN KPROCESSOR_MODE *AccessMode*,
	          OUT PVOID * *Object*,
	          OUT POBJECT_HANDLE_INFORMATION *HandleInformation*);	

		Provides access validation on the object handle, and, if access can be granted, returns the corresponding pointer to the object's body. Returns one of the following values.
		STATUS_SUCCESS
		STATUS_OBJECT_TYPE_MISMATCH

Table A.3: *Important Support Functions and Structures for Device Drivers (continued)*

Page Ref.	Function	Parameters and Explanations
		STATUS_ACCESS_DENIED
		STATUS_INVALID_HANDLE
		IN HANDLE *Handle* The handle of the object to which you want access.
		IN ACCESS_MASK *DesiredAccess* The type of access you desire. Its value depends on the type of object.
		IN POBJECT_TYPE *ObjectType* Pointer to the object type structure for the object. Optional and may be NULL.
		IN KPROCESSOR_MODE *AccessMode* The mode of operation to use for the access check. Must be one of the following values.
		<table><tr><td>UserMode</td><td>The object should be checked for its accessibility from User mode. Returns STATUS_ACCESS_DENIED if not accessible. Only a top-level driver should make this request.</td></tr><tr><td>KernelMode</td><td>The requested access is always permitted for Kernel-mode access. Lower-level drivers should use only this access mode.</td></tr></table>
		OUT PVOID * *Object* A virtual address. Must be an address that was allocated using MmMapIoSpace.
		OUT POBJECT_HANDLE_INFORMATION *HandleInformation* The address of where to place additional information about the handle. If this information is not needed, this parameter may be NULL.
970	NTSTATUS ObReferenceObjectByPointer(IN PVOID *Object*, IN ACCESS_MASK *DesiredAccess*, IN POBJECT_TYPE *ObjectType*, IN KPROCESSOR_MODE *AccessMode*);	Provides access validation on the object referenced by a pointer, and, if access can be granted, returns the corresponding pointer to the object's body. Returns one of the following values.
		STATUS_SUCCESS
		STATUS_OBJECT_TYPE_MISMATCH
		STATUS_ACCESS_DENIED
		IN PVOID *Object* A pointer to the object to which you want access.
		IN ACCESS_MASK *DesiredAccess* The type of access you desire. Its value depends on the type of object.
		IN POBJECT_TYPE *ObjectType* Points the object type structure for the object.

Table A.3: *Important Support Functions and Structures for Device Drivers (continued)*

Page Ref.	Function	Parameters and Explanations		
		IN KPROCESSOR_MODE *AccessMode* The mode of operation to use for the access check. Must be one of the following values.		
			UserMode	The object should be checked for its accessibility from User mode. Returns STATUS_ACCESS_DENIED if not accessible. Only a top-level driver should make this request.
			KernelMode	The requested access is always permitted for Kernel-mode access. Lower-level drivers should use only this access mode.
971	typedef struct {...} PCI_COMMON_CONFIG;			
971	typedef struct {...} PCI_SLOT_NUMBER;			
973	typedef IO_ALLOCATION_ACTION (*PDRIVER_CONTROL)(IN PDEVICE_OBJECT *DeviceObject*, IN PIRP *Irp*, IN PVOID *MapRegisterBase*, IN PVOID *Context*);			
		The prototype for the ExecutionRoutine of IoAllocateAdapterChannel and IoAllocateController. Returns one of the following values:		
		Adapters	DeallocateObjectKeepRegisters	Returned when called by IoAllocateAdapterChannel for a Bus Master adapter, indicating that the adapter will be freed by the I/O Manager when control returns from this function.
			KeepObject	Returned when called by IoAllocateAdapterChannel for a System DMA device. Requires that the driver call IoFreeAdapter when the operation has completed.
		Controllers	DeallocateObject	Returned when called by IoAllocateController. The controller will be freed by the I/O Manager when control returns from this function.
			KeepObject	Returned when called by IoAllocateController. Requires that the driver call IoFreeController when the operation has completed.
		IN PDEVICE_OBJECT *DeviceObject* The Device Object.		
		IN PIRP *Irp* The active IRP.		
		IN PVOID *MapRegisterBase* For IoAllocateAdapterChannel, this is the Map Register handle that was assigned. For IoAllocateController, this parameter has no meaning.		

Table A.3: *Important Support Functions and Structures for Device Drivers (continued)*

Page Ref.	Function	Parameters and Explanations
		`IN PVOID Context`
		The context pointer that was passed into `IoAllocateAdapterChannel` or `IoAllocateController`.
973		`typedef VOID (*PIO_DPC_ROUTINE)(IN PKDPC Dpc, IN PDEVICE_OBJECT DeviceObject, IN PIRP Irp, IN PVOID Context);`
974		`typedef VOID (*PIO_TIMER_ROUTINE)(IN PDEVICE_OBJECT DeviceObject, IN PVOID Context)`
		`typedef VOID (*PKSTART_ROUTINE)(LPVOID Context)`
974		`NTSTATUS PsCreateSystemThread(OUT PHANDLE ThreadHandle, IN ACCESS_MASK DesiredAccess, IN POBJECT_ATTRIBUTES ObjectAttributes, IN HANDLE ProcessHandle, OUT PCLIENT_ID ClientId, IN PKSTART_ROUTINE StartRoutine, IN PVOID StartContext);`
		Creates a driver-dedicated thread.
		`OUT PHANDLE ThreadHandle`
		A thread handle, if the function returns STATUS_SUCCESS.
		`IN ACCESS_MASK DesiredAccess`
		The constant THREAD_ALL_ACCESS.
		`IN POBJECT_ATTRIBUTES ObjectAttributes`
		For driver-created threads, always NULL.
		`IN HANDLE ProcessHandle`
		For driver-created threads, always NULL.
		`OUT PCLIENT_ID ClientID`
		For driver-created threads, always NULL.
		`IN PKSTART_ROUTINE StartRoutine`
		A pointer to the function to be executed.
		`IN PVOID StartContext`
		A value that is passed into the start routine as its only parameter.
975		`PEPROCESS PsGetCurrentProcess( );`
		Returns a pointer to the Process Object representing the process that owns the current running thread.
975		`PETHREAD PsGetCurrentThread( );`
		Returns a pointer to the Thread Object representing the current running thread.
975		`NTSTATUS PsTerminateSystemThread(IN NTSTATUS ExitStatus);`
		Terminates a thread created by `PsCreateSystemThread`.

Table A.3: *Important Support Functions and Structures for Device Drivers (continued)*

Page Ref.	Function	Parameters and Explanations
		IN NTSTATUS *ExitStatus* The status to be returned to the caller.
975	VOID READ_PORT_BUFFER_UCHAR(IN PUCHAR *Port*, IN PUCHAR *Buffer*, IN ULONG *Count*) VOID READ_PORT_BUFFER_USHORT(IN PUSHORT *Port*, IN PUSHORT *Buffer*, IN ULONG *Count*) VOID READ_PORT_BUFFER_ULONG(IN PULONG *Port*, IN PULONG *Buffer*, IN ULONG *Count*)	
		Reads information from a device's port.
		IN P*type Port* The port from which to read data.
		IN P*type Buffer* A pointer to the buffer into which to read the data.
		IN ULONG *Count* The number of units to read.
976	UCHAR READ_PORT_UCHAR(IN PUCHAR *Port*) USHORT READ_PORT_USHORT(IN PUSHORT *Port*) ULONG READ_PORT_ULONG(IN PULONG *Port*)	
		Reads information from a device's port.
		IN P*type Port* The port from which to read data.

976	VOID READ_REGISTER_BUFFER_UCHAR(IN PUCHAR *Register*, IN PUCHAR *Buffer*,
	                IN ULONG *Count*);
	
	VOID READ_REGISTER_BUFFER_USHORT(IN PUSHORT *Register*, IN PUSHORT *Buffer*,
	                IN ULONG *Count*);
	
	VOID READ_REGISTER_BUFFER_ULONG(IN PULONG *Register*, IN PULONG *Buffer*,
	                IN ULONG *Count*);	

		Reads a sequence of values from a specified memory-mapped device register to a buffer.
		IN P*type Register* The register from which to read data. This is a memory-mapped device register.
		IN P*type Buffer* A pointer to the buffer into which to read the data. It must be at least Count units long.
		IN ULONG *Count* The number of units to read.

Table A.3: *Important Support Functions and Structures for Device Drivers (continued)*

Page Ref.	Function	Parameters and Explanations
976	UCHAR READ_REGISTER_UCHAR(IN PUCHAR *Register*) USHORT READ_REGISTER_USHORT(IN PUSHORT *Register*) ULONG READ_REGISTER_ULONG(IN PULONG *Register*)	Reads information from a memory-mapped device register. IN P*type Register* The device register from which to read data.
977	VOID RemoveEntryList(IN PLIST_ENTRY *Entry*);	Removes the entry from the list. The forward and backward pointers of the entry are set to point to the entry. IN PLIST_ENTRY *Entry* The entry to be removed.
977	PLIST_ENTRY RemoveHeadList(IN PLIST_ENTRY *ListHead*);	Removes the entry at the head of the list, and returns a pointer to it. If the list is empty, returns NULL. IN PLIST_ENTRY *ListHead* The head of the list.
977	PLIST_ENTRY RemoveTailList(IN PLIST_ENTRY *ListHead*);	Removes the entry at the end of the list, and returns a pointer to it. If the list is empty, returns NULL. IN PLIST_ENTRY *ListHead* The head of the list.
977	VOID RtlInitUnicodeString(IN OUT PUNICODE_STRING *DestinationString*, IN PCWSTR *SourceString*);	Initializes a UNICODE_STRING structure. IN OUT PUNICODE_STRING *DestinationString* A pointer to the UNICODE_STRING structure to be initialized. IN PCWSTR *SourceString* A pointer to a NUL-terminated Unicode string.

978	NTSTATUS (*PRTL_QUERY_REGISTRY_ROUTINE)(IN PWSTR *ValueName*, IN ULONG *ValueType*,
	                    IN PVOID *ValueData*, IN ULONG *ValueLength*, IN PVOID *Context*,
	                    IN PVOID *EntryContext*)
		The type for an entry in the QueryRoutine field of an RTL_QUERY_REGISTRY_TABLE entry.
		
		IN PWSTR *ValueName*
		A pointer to a NUL-terminated Unicode string. The name of the value to be looked up.

Table A.3: *Important Support Functions and Structures for Device Drivers (continued)*

Page Ref.	Function	Parameters and Explanations
		IN ULONG `ValueType` The type of the value, for example, REG_DWORD.
		IN PVOID `ValueData` A pointer to the location where the data is to be stored.
		IN ULONG `ValueLength` The length of the area referenced by `ValueData`.
		IN PVOID `Context` The `Context` parameter that was passed in to `RtlQueryRegistryValues`.
		IN PVOID `EntryContext` If the RTL_QUERY_REGISTRY_DIRECT flag is set, it is the address of where to place the result. Otherwise it is an arbitrary 32-bit field that is passed uninterpreted each time the `QueryRoutine` is called.
978	`typedef struct {...} RTL_QUERY_REGISTRY_TABLE`	

979	`NTSTATUS RtlQueryRegistryValues(IN ULONG RelativeTo, IN PWSTR Path,`
	`IN PRTL_QUERY_REGISTRY_TABLE QueryTable, IN PVOID Context,`
	`IN PVOID Environment);`	

		Retrieves a specified set of values from the Registry, given the table of keys and defaults.
		IN ULONG `RelativeTo` Specifies how the path is to be interpreted. One of the following values.
		RTL_REGISTRY_ABSOLUTE — *Path* is an absolute path.
		RTL_REGISTRY_CONTROL — *Path* is relative to `\Registry\Machine\System\CurrentControlSet\Control`
		RTL_REGISTRY_DEVICEMAP — *Path* is relative to `\Registry\Machine\Hardware\DeviceMap`
		RTL_REGISTRY_HANDLE — *Path* is not a pointer but a handle to a key.
		RTL_REGISTRY_OPTIONAL — The key referenced by this parameter and the *Path* parameter is optional.
		RTL_REGISTRY_SERVICES — *Path* parameter is relative to `\Registry\Machine\System\CurrentControlSet\Services`
		RTL_REGISTRY_USER — *Path* is relative to `\Registry\User\CurrentUser`
		RTL_REGISTRY_WINDOWS_NT — *Path* is relative to `\Registry\Machine\Software\Microsoft\Windows NT\CurrentVersion`

Table A.3: *Important Support Functions and Structures for Device Drivers (continued)*

Page Ref.	Function	Parameters and Explanations
		IN PWSTR *Path* A pointer to a NUL-terminated Unicode string that defines the path to the keys.
		IN PRTL_QUERY_REGISTRY_TABLE *QueryTable* Specifies the array of keys whose values are to be queried, the location at which to put the result, and the value to use if the key is missing.
		IN PVOID *Context* A 32-bit value, nominally a pointer, which is passed to the query routine specified in the query table.
		IN PVOID *Environment* Points to the environment to be used when REG_EXPAND_SZ Registry values are encountered.
980	NTSTATUS RtlUnicodeStringToAnsiString(IN OUT PANSI_STRING *DestinationString*, IN PUNICODE_STRING *SourceString*, IN BOOLEAN *AllocateDestinationString*);	Converts the string referenced by a UNICODE_STRING structure to an 8-bit ANSI string.
		IN OUT PANSI_STRING *DestinationString* Points to a caller-allocated buffer for the ANSI string or is NULL if *AllocateDestinationString* is set to TRUE. If the translation cannot be done because a character in the Unicode string does not map to an ANSI character in the current system locale, an error is returned. We have not been able to determine how the allocated string returned in this pointer is NULL and suspect a documentation error.
		IN PUNICODE_STRING *SourceString* Points to the Unicode source string to be converted to ANSI.
		IN BOOLEAN *AllocateDestinationString* TRUE if this routine is to allocate the buffer space for *DestinationString*. If it does, the buffer must be deallocated by a call to RtlFreeAnsiString.
980	VOID RtlZeroMemory(IN PVOID *Destination*, IN ULONG *Length*);	Zeroes the block of memory specified by the destination.
		IN PVOID *Destination* The address of the first location to be zeroed.
		IN ULONG *Length* The number of locations to be zeroed.
980	typedef struct {...} UNICODE_STRING	

Table A.3: *Important Support Functions and Structures for Device Drivers (continued)*

Page Ref.	Function	Parameters and Explanations
982	VOID UsbBuildGetDescriptorRequest(IN OUT PURB *Urb*, IN USHORT *Length*, IN UCHAR *DescriptorType*, IN UCHAR *Index*, IN USHORT *LanguageId*, IN PVOID *TransferBuffer* OPTIONAL, IN PMDL *TransferBufferMDL* OPTIONAL, IN ULONG *TransferBufferLength*, IN PURB *Link* OPTIONAL);	
		Fills in a _URB_CONTROL_DESCRIPTOR_REQUEST structure.
		IN OUT PURB *Urb* The address of the URB. It must be at least as large as a _URB_CONTROL_DESCRIPTOR_REQUEST.
		IN USHORT *Length* The length of the URB. It must be at least as large as sizeof(_URB_CONTROL_DESCRIPTOR_REQUEST).
		IN UCHAR *DescriptorType* The descriptor type, one of the following values.
		USB_CONFIGURATION_DESCRIPTOR_TYPE
		USB_DEVICE_DESCRIPTOR_TYPE
		USB_STRING_DESCRIPTOR_TYPE
		IN UCHAR *Index* The index of the descriptor.
		IN USHORT *LanguageId* The ID of the language if the descriptor is USB_STRING_DESCRIPTOR_TYPE; otherwise, 0.
		IN PVOID *TransferBuffer* A pointer to the transfer buffer, or NULL. If NULL, *TransferBufferMDL* must not be NULL.
		IN PMDL *TransferBufferMDL* The address of a MDL for the transfer. If a MDL is not used, should be NULL. If NULL, the *TransferBuffer* pointer must not be NULL.
		IN ULONG *TransferBufferLength* The length of the transfer buffer.
		IN PURB *Link* The address of a linked URB. If there is no linked URB, NULL.
983	VOID WRITE_PORT_BUFFER_UCHAR(IN PUCHAR *Port*, IN PUCHAR *Buffer*, IN ULONG *Count*) VOID WRITE_PORT_BUFFER_USHORT(IN PUSHORT *Port*, IN PUSHORT *Buffer*, IN ULONG *Count*) VOID WRITE_PORT_BUFFER_ULONG(IN PULONG *Port*, IN PULONG *Buffer*, IN ULONG *Count*)	
		Writes information from a device's port.

Table A.3: *Important Support Functions and Structures for Device Drivers (continued)*

Page Ref.	Function	Parameters and Explanations
		IN PUCHAR `Port` The port to which to write data.
		IN P`type` `Buffer` A pointer to the buffer from which to write the data.
		IN ULONG `Count` The number of units of data to write.
983	VOID WRITE_PORT_UCHAR(IN PUCHAR `Port`, IN UCHAR `value`) VOID WRITE_PORT_USHORT(IN PUSHORT `Port`, IN USHORT `value`) VOID WRITE_PORT_ULONG(IN PULONG `Port`, IN ULONG `value`)	
		Reads information from a device's port.
		IN PUCHAR `Port` The port from which to read data.
		IN `type` `Value` The value to be written.

984	VOID WRITE_REGISTER_BUFFER_UCHAR(IN PUCHAR `Register`, IN PUCHAR `Buffer`,
	            IN ULONG `Count`);
	
	VOID WRITE_REGISTER_BUFFER_USHORT(IN PUSHORT `Register`, IN PUSHORT `Buffer`,
	            IN ULONG `Count`);
	
	VOID WRITE_REGISTER_BUFFER_ULONG(IN PULONG `Register`, IN PULONG `Buffer`,
	            IN ULONG `Count`);	

		Writes a sequence of values from a specified memory-mapped device register to a buffer.
		IN P`type` `Register` The register to which to write data. A memory-mapped device register.
		IN P`type` `Buffer` A pointer to the buffer from which to write the data. Must be at least `Count` units long.
		IN ULONG `Count` The number of units to write.
984	VOID WRITE_REGISTER_UCHAR(IN PUCHAR `Register`, IN UCHAR `Value`) VOID WRITE_REGISTER_USHORT(IN PUSHORT `Register`, IN USHORT `Value`) VOID WRITE_REGISTER_ULONG(IN PULONG `Register`, IN ULONG `Value`)	
		Writes information from a memory-mapped device register.
		IN P`type` `Register` A pointer to the memory-mapped device register to which to write the data.

Table A.3: *Important Support Functions and Structures for Device Drivers (continued)*

Page Ref.	Function	Parameters and Explanations
		IN *type Value* The value to be written.
984	NTSTATUS ZwClose(IN HANDLE *Handle*);	
		Closes the object handle. The object handle might be for a file, a directory object, a Registry key, or a section. A named object is not actually deleted until all of its outstanding handles are closed.

STATUS_SUCCESS	The object handle was closed.
STATUS_OBJECT_TYPE_MISMATCH	
STATUS_ACCESS_DENIED	The thread making the call does not have the right to close the handle.
STATUS_INVALID_HANDLE	The handle is not a valid object handle (an attempt to close the same handle twice gives this error, in particular).

IN HANDLE *Handle*

The handle of an object.

Page Ref.	Function

984	NTSTATUS ZwCreateFile(OUT PHANDLE *FileHandle*, IN ACCESS_MASK *DesiredAccess*,
	                     IN POBJECT_ATTRIBUTES *ObjectAttributes*,
	                     OUT PIO_STATUS_BLOCK *IoStatusBlock*,
	                     IN PLARGE_INTEGER *AllocationSize* OPTIONAL,
	                     IN ULONG *FileAttributes*, IN ULONG *ShareAccess*,
	                     IN ULONG *CreateDisposition*, IN ULONG *CreateOptions*,
	                     IN PVOID *EaBuffer* OPTIONAL, IN ULONG *EaLength*);

Creates or opens a file.

OUT PHANDLE *FileHandle*

A pointer to the location to put the file handle on successful return.

IN ACCESS_MASK *DesiredAccess*

Specifies the access. One or more of the flag values shown next or one of the composite values given.

DELETE	The file can be deleted.
FILE_READ_DATA	Data can be read from the file.
FILE_READ_ATTRIBUTES	The *FileAttributes* flags, described later, can be read.
FILE_READ_EA	EAs associated with the file can be read. This flag is irrelevant to Device Drivers and intermediate drivers.
READ_CONTROL	The ACL and ownership information associated with the file can be read.
FILE_WRITE_DATA	Data can be written to the file.

Table A.3: *Important Support Functions and Structures for Device Drivers (continued)*

Page Ref.	Function	Parameters and Explanations	
		FILE_WRITE_ATTRIBUTES	The *FileAttributes* flags, described later, can be written.
		FILE_WRITE_EA	EAs associated with the file can be written. This flag is irrelevant to Device Drivers and intermediate drivers.
		FILE_APPEND_DATA	Data can be appended to the file.
		WRITE_DAC	The discretionary access control list associated with the file can be written.
		WRITE_OWNER	Ownership information associated with the file can be written.
		SYNCHRONIZE	The returned *FileHandle* can be waited on to synchronize with the completion of an I/O operation.
		FILE_EXECUTE	Data can be read into memory from the file using system paging I/O. This flag is irrelevant to device and intermediate drivers.
		FILE_LIST_DIRECTORY	The directory can be listed.
		FILE_TRAVERSE	The directory name can be part of a pathname descriptor.
		STANDARD_RIGHTS_READ	FILE_READ_DATA | FILE_READ_ATTRIBUTES | FILE_READ_EA
		STANDARD_RIGHTS_WRITE	FILE_WRITE_DATA | FILE_WRITE_ATTRIBUTES | FILE_WRITE_EA | FILE_APPEND_DATA
	IN POBJECT_ATTRIBUTES *ObjectAttributes* A pointer to a structure containing, among other attributes, the filename. The fields of the OBJECT_ATTRIBUTES structure are defined as follows.		
		ULONG Length	sizeof(OBJECT_ATTRIBUTES)
		HANDLE RootDirectory	Handle of a directory object, or NULL if *ObjectName* specifies a complete path.
		PUNICODE_STRING ObjectName	The name of the file to be created/opened.
		ULONG Attributes	OBJ_CASE_INSENSITIVE
		PSECURITY_DESCRIPTOR SecurityDescriptor	NULL
		PSECURITY_QUALITY_OF_SERVICE SecurityQualityOfService	NULL

Table A.3: *Important Support Functions and Structures for Device Drivers (continued)*

Page Ref.	Function	Parameters and Explanations
		OUT PIO_STATUS_BLOCK *IoStatusBlock* A pointer to an I/O Status Block. The *Information* field will contain additional information upon return. One of the following values.

FILE_CREATED	The file did not exist and was created.
FILE_OPENED	The file already existed and was opened.
FILE_OVERWRITTEN	The file already existed and was overwritten.
FILE_SUPERSEDED	The file already existed and was superseded.
FILE_EXISTS	The file already existed, and the operation failed.
FILE_DOES_NOT_EXIST	The file did not exist, and the operation failed.

IN PLARGE_INTEGER *AllocationSize*

A pointer to the desired initial allocation size. Normally NULL, thereby indicating there is no initial allocation.

IN ULONG *FileAttributes*

A value that represents the attributes to be associated with the file. One of the following values.

FILE_ATTRIBUTE_NORMAL	A file with standard attributes should be created.
FILE_ATTRIBUTE_READONLY	A read-only file should be created.
FILE_ATTRIBUTE_HIDDEN	A hidden file should be created.
FILE_ATTRIBUTE_SYSTEM	A system file should be created.
FILE_ATTRIBUTE_ARCHIVE	The file should be marked so that it will be archived.
FILE_ATTRIBUTE_TEMPORARY	A temporary file should be created.
FILE_ATTRIBUTE_ATOMIC_WRITE	An atomic-write file should be created. This flag is irrelevant to Device Drivers and intermediate drivers.
FILE_ATTRIBUTE_XACTION_WRITE	A transaction-write file should be created. This flag is irrelevant to Device Drivers and intermediate drivers.

IN ULONG *ShareAccess*

A pointer to an I/O Status Block. The *Information* field will contain additional information upon return. One of the following values.

0	The file cannot be accessed by any other thread until it is closed.
FILE_SHARE_READ	The file can be opened for read access by the calls of other threads to ZwCreateFile.

Table A.3: *Important Support Functions and Structures for Device Drivers (continued)*

Page Ref.	Function	Parameters and Explanations	
		FILE_SHARE_WRITE	The file can be opened for write access by the calls of other threads to ZwCreateFile.
		FILE_SHARE_DELETE	The file can be opened for delete access by the calls of other threads to ZwCreateFile.
		IN ULONG *CreateDisposition* A value that indicates the action to take based on the type of open and whether the file already exists.	
		FILE_SUPERSEDE	Exists: Replace it. Does not exist: Create it.
		FILE_CREATE	Exists: Fail. Does not exist: Create it.
		FILE_OPEN	Exists: Open it. Does not exist: Fail.
		FILE_OPEN_IF	Exists: Open it. Does not exist: Create it.
		FILE_OVERWRITE	Exists: Open it, and overwrite it. Does not exist: Fail.
		FILE_OVERWRITE_IF	Exists: Open it, and overwrite it. Does not exist: Create it.
		IN PVOID *EaBuffer* A pointer to a buffer to hold EAs. For drivers, this value should be NULL.	
		IN ULONG *EaLength* The length of *EaBuffer*; should be 0.	
991	NTSTATUS ZwCreateKey(OUT PHANDLE *KeyHandle*, IN ACCESS_MASK *DesiredAccess*, IN POBJECT_ATTRIBUTES *ObjectAttributes*, IN ULONG *TitleIndex*, IN PUNICODE_STRING *Class*, IN ULONG *CreateOptions*, OUT PULONG *Disposition*);		
		Creates or opens a key in the Registry. Returns one of the following values.	
		STATUS_SUCCESS	The operation is a success. *KeyHandle* represents the newly created or successfully opened key.
		STATUS_INVALID_HANDLE	The operation failed because the directory handle was invalid.
		STATUS_ACCESS_DENIED	The thread making the call does not have the right to access the specified key in the way requested.
		OUT PHANDLE *KeyHandle* The location to which the handle is written on successful completion.	

Table A.3: *Important Support Functions and Structures for Device Drivers (continued)*

Page Ref.	Function	Parameters and Explanations
		IN ACCESS_MASK *DesiredAccess*

Specifies the access. One or more of the flag values shown next or one of the composite values given.

KEY_ALL_ACCESS	STANDARD_RIGHTS_ALL | KEY_QUERY_VALUE | KEY_SET_VALUE | KEY_CREATE_SUB_KEY | KEY_ENUMERATE_SUBKEYS | KEY_NOTIFY | KEY_CREATE_LINK
KEY_CREATE_LINK	A symbolic link to the key can be created. This flag is irrelevant to Device Drivers and intermediate drivers.
KEY_CREATE_SUB_KEY	Subkeys for the key can be created.
KEY_ENUMERATE_SUB_KEYS	All subkeys for the key can be read.
KEY_NOTIFY	This flag is irrelevant to Device Drivers and intermediate drivers and to other Kernel-mode code.
KEY_EXECUTE	KEY_READ. Irrelevant to Device Drivers and intermediate drivers.
KEY_QUERY_VALUE	Value entries for the key can be read.
KEY_READ	STANDARD_RIGHTS_READ | KEY_QUERY_VALUE | KEY_ENUMERATE_SUB_KEYS | KEY_NOTIFY
KEY_SET_VALUE	Value entries for the key can be written.
KEY_WRITE	STANDARD_RIGHTS_WRITE | KEY_SET_VALUE | KEY_CREATE_SUB_KEY

IN POBJECT_ATTRIBUTES *Object_Attributes*

A pointer to the object that describes the key name and the root of the Registry directory in which it is found. The root directory is optional. A name should be an object name in the Registry space and begin with the name \Registry.

IN ULONG *TitleIndex*

Device Drivers and intermediate drivers should set this to 0.

IN PUNICODE_STRING *Class*

Points to the object class of the key. Normally NULL.

IN ULONG *CreateOptions*

The options specifying the nature of the key. This parameter is ignored if the key already exists.

Table A.3: *Important Support Functions and Structures for Device Drivers (continued)*

Page Ref.	Function	Parameters and Explanations	
		REG_OPTION_BACKUP_RESTORE	The key is being opened or created with special privileges that allow backup/restore operations. Irrelevant to Device Drivers and intermediate drivers.
		REG_OPTION_CREATE_LINK	The created key is a symbolic link. Irrelevant to Device Drivers and intermediate drivers.
		REG_OPTION_NON_VOLATILE	The key is preserved when the system is rebooted.
		REG_OPTION_VOLATILE	The key is not to be stored across boots.
		OUT PULONG *Disposition* A pointer to a location that gets a value indicating how the key was opened. If this is NULL, no status is returned indicating the way in which the open succeeded. If the parameter is non-NULL, the specified address will get one of the following values.	
		REG_CREATED_NEW_KEY	A new key object was created.
		REG_OPENED_EXISTING_KEY	An existing key object was opened.
991	NTSTATUS ZwDeleteKey(IN HANDLE *KeyHandle*);		
		Deletes the key specified by *KeyHandle*. If not a top-level key, all subkeys and their associated values are also deleted. Returns one of the following values.	
		STATUS_SUCCESS	The operation is a success. *KeyHandle* is now invalid.
		STATUS_INVALID_HANDLE	The operation failed because the key handle was invalid.
		STATUS_ACCESS_DENIED	The thread making the call does not have the right to delete the specified key.
		IN HANDLE *KeyHandle* The handle of the key that is to be deleted, as obtained by ZwCreateKey or ZwOpenKey.	

992	NTSTATUS ZwEnumerateKey(IN HANDLE *KeyHandle*, IN ULONG *Index*,
	    IN KEY_INFORMATION_CLASS *KeyInformationClass*,
	    OUT PVOID *KeyInformation*, IN ULONG *Length*,
	    OUT PULONG *ResultLength*);		

		Provides information about the subkeys of a specified key. Returns one of the following values.	
		STATUS_SUCCESS	The operation succeeded; *KeyInformation* and *ResultLength* are valid values.
		STATUS_NO_MORE_VALUES	The *Index* value is out of range for the number of subkeys.
		STATUS_BUFFER_OVERFLOW	The operation failed because *Length* was too small. The contents of *ResultLength* give the needed length.

Table A.3: *Important Support Functions and Structures for Device Drivers (continued)*

Page Ref.	Function	Parameters and Explanations	
		IN HANDLE *KeyHandle*	
		The handle of a key. Must have KEY_ENUMERATE_SUB_KEYS access.	
		IN ULONG *Index*	
		The index into the subkeys of the selected key specified by *KeyHandle*.	
		IN KEY_INFORMATION_CLASS *KeyInformationClass*	
		The type of value required. Must be one of the following values.	
		KeyBasicInformation	Returns a sequence of KEY_BASIC_INFORMATION structures. See page 955.
		KeyFullInformation	Returns a sequence of KEY_FULL_INFORMATION structures. See page 956.
		KeyNodeInformation	Returns a sequence of KEY_NODE_INFORMATION structures. See page 957.
		OUT PVOID *KeyInformation*	
		A pointer to a user-allocated buffer that will receive the key information.	
		IN ULONG *Length*	
		The length of the allocated *KeyInformation* buffer, in bytes. If too short, the operation will fail with a STATUS_BUFFER_OVERFLOW error and the *ResultLength* will contain the required length.	
		OUT PULONG *ResultLength*	
		If the return code is STATUS_SUCCESS, the location referenced by this parameter will hold the actual length of the data returned, which will be <= Length. If the return code is RESULT_BUFFER_OVERFLOW, the location referenced by this parameter will hold the required length.	
992	NTSTATUS ZwEnumerateValueKey(IN HANDLE KeyHandle, IN ULONG *Index*, IN KEY_VALUE_INFORMATION_CLASS *KeyValueInformationClass*, OUT PVOID *KeyValueInformation*, IN ULONG Length, OUT PULONG *ResultLength*);		
		Allows the selection of specific subkey values from the key whose handle is presented. Returns one of the following values.	
		STATUS_SUCCESS	The operation succeeded; *KeyInformation* and *ResultLength* are valid values.
		STATUS_NO_MORE_VALUES	The *Index* value is out of range for the number of subkeys.
		STATUS_INVALID_PARAMETER	
		STATUS_BUFFER_OVERFLOW	The operation failed because *Length* was too small. The contents of *ResultLength* give the needed length.

Table A.3: *Important Support Functions and Structures for Device Drivers (continued)*

Page Ref.	Function	Parameters and Explanations	
		IN HANDLE *KeyHandle*	
		The handle of a key. This handle must have KEY_QUERY_KEY access.	
		IN ULONG *Index*	
		The index into the subkeys of the selected key specified by *KeyHandle*.	
		IN KEY_VALUE_INFORMATION_CLASS *KeyValueInformationClass*	
		The type of value required. Must be one of the following values.	
		KeyValueBasicInformation	Returns a sequence of KEY_VALUE_BASIC_INFORMATION values. See page 958.
		KeyValueFullInformation	Returns a sequence of KEY_VALUE_FULL_INFORMATION values. See page 959.
		KeyValuePartialInformation	Returns a sequence of KEY_VALUE_PARTIAL_INFORMATION values. See page 961.
		OUT PVOID *KeyValueInformation*	
		Pointer to a user-allocated buffer that will receive the value information.	
		IN ULONG *Length*	
		The length of the allocated *KeyValueInformation* buffer, in bytes. If too short, the operation will fail with a STATUS_BUFFER_OVERFLOW error and *ResultLength* will contain the required length.	
		OUT PULONG *ResultLength*	
		If the return code is STATUS_SUCCESS, the location referenced by this parameter will hold the actual length of the data returned: <= Length. If the return code is STATUS_BUFFER_OVERFLOW, the location referenced by this parameter will hold the required length.	
992	NTSTATUS ZwFlushKey(IN HANDLE *KeyHandle*);		
		Flushes the key specified by *KeyHandle* to disk. If not a top-level key, all subkeys and their associated values are also flushed to disk. Returns one of the following values.	
		STATUS_SUCCESS	The operation is a success. *KeyHandle* represents the newly created or successfully opened key.
		STATUS_INVALID_HANDLE	The operation failed because the directory handle was invalid.
		IN HANDLE *KeyHandle*	
		The handle of the key that is to be flushed, as obtained by ZwCreateKey or ZwOpenKey.	

Table A.3: *Important Support Functions and Structures for Device Drivers (continued)*

Page Ref.	Function	Parameters and Explanations
993	`NTSTATUS ZwMapViewOfSection(IN HANDLE SectionHandle, IN HANDLE ProcessHandle, IN OUT PVOID *BaseAddress, IN ULONG ZeroBits, IN ULONG CommitSize, IN OUT PLARGE_INTEGER SectionOffset, IN OUT PULONG ViewSize, IN SECTION_INHERIT InheritDisposition, IN ULONG AllocationType, IN ULONG Protect);`	

Given a section handle, maps a piece or all of the section into the virtual address space. Returns one of the following values.

STATUS_SUCCESS	The operation is a success. *BaseAddress* contains a valid base address. *SectionOffset*, if specified, contains a valid section offset. *ViewSize* contains an updated view size.
STATUS_ACCESS_DENIED	The operation failed because the thread does not have sufficient rights to access the section.
STATUS_INVALID_HANDLE	The handle supplied is invalid.

IN HANDLE *SectionHandle*

The section handle returned from ZwOpenSection or ZwCreateSection.

IN HANDLE *ProcessHandle*

The handle of the process whose address space will get the requested mapping.

IN OUT PVOID * *BaseAddress*

A pointer to a PVOID variable that will receive the base address of the newly mapped view. This variable must be initialized to NULL or to a desired memory address. If initialized to a desired address, the actual address will be the specified address rounded down to the nearest 64K boundary. If initialized to NULL, the function will choose some available virtual address for the mapping and store that address back.

IN ULONG *ZeroBits*

Specifies the number of high-order address bits that must be 0 in the base address of the section view. The value of this argument must be less than 21 (you can't map anything into virtual page 0) and is used only when the operating system determines where to allocate the view, that is, when *BaseAddress* is NULL.

IN ULONG *CommitSize*

Specifies the size, in bytes, of the initially committed region of the view. *CommitSize* is meaningful only for page-file-backed sections. For mapped sections, such as physical memory, both the data and the image are always committed when the section is created. This parameter is ignored for mapped files. Its value is rounded up to the next page boundary.

IN OUT PLARGE_INTEGER *SectionOffset*

A pointer to the 64-bit offset, expressed in bytes, from the beginning of the section to the view, or NULL. If *not* NULL, the given value is rounded down to the next allocation granularity size boundary. The allocation granularity may not be assumed, as it might change between platforms or even releases.

Table A.3: *Important Support Functions and Structures for Device Drivers (continued)*

Page Ref.	Function	Parameters and Explanations
		IN OUT PULONG *ViewSize* A pointer to a variable that specifies the desired size of the view, in bytes, and that will receive the *actual* size, in bytes. If the value of this parameter is 0 on input, a view of the section will be mapped starting at the specified *SectionOffset* and continuing to the end of the section. Otherwise, the initial value of this argument specifies the size of the view, in bytes, and is rounded up to the next page boundary.
		IN SECTION_INHERIT *InheritDisposition* Specifies how the view is to be shared by a child process created with a create process operation. Device Drivers and intermediate drivers should set this parameter to 0.
		IN ULONG *AllocationType* A set of flags that describes the type of allocation to be performed for the specified region of pages.
		IN ULONG *Protect* Specifies the protection for the region of initially committed pages. Device Drivers and intermediate drivers should set this value to PAGE_READWRITE.
994	NTSTATUS ZwOpenKey(OUT PHANDLE *KeyHandle*, IN ACCESS_MASK *DesiredAccess*, IN POBJECT_ATTRIBUTES *ObjectAttributes*);	
		Opens an existing key in the Registry. Returns one of the following values.

	STATUS_SUCCESS	The operation is a success. *KeyHandle* represents the newly created or successfully opened key.
	STATUS_INVALID_HANDLE	The operation failed because the directory handle was invalid.
	STATUS_ACCESS_DENIED	The thread making the call does not have the right to access the specified key in the way requested.

OUT PHANDLE *KeyHandle*

The location to which the handle is written on successful completion.

IN ACCESS_MASK *DesiredAccess*

Specifies the access. Can be one or more of the following flag values or one of the composite values given.

	KEY_ALL_ACCESS	STANDARD_RIGHTS_ALL | KEY_QUERY_VALUE | KEY_SET_VALUE | KEY_CREATE_SUB_KEY | KEY_ENUMERATE_SUB_KEYS | KEY_NOTIFY | KEY_CREATE_LINK
	KEY_CREATE_LINK	A symbolic link to the key can be created. Irrelevant to Device Drivers and intermediate drivers.
	KEY_CREATE_SUB_KEY	Subkeys for the key can be created.

Table A.3: *Important Support Functions and Structures for Device Drivers (continued)*

Page Ref.	Function	Parameters and Explanations	
		KEY_ENUMERATE_SUB_KEYS	All subkeys for the key can be read.
		KEY_NOTIFY	Irrelevant to Device Drivers and intermediate drivers and to other Kernel-mode code.
		KEY_EXECUTE	KEY_READ. Irrelevant to Device Drivers and intermediate drivers.
		KEY_QUERY_VALUE	Value entries for the key can be read.
		KEY_READ	STANDARD_RIGHTS_READ | KEY_QUERY_VALUE | KEY_ENUMERATE_SUB_KEYS | KEY_NOTIFY
		KEY_SET_VALUE	Value entries for the key can be written.
		KEY_WRITE	STANDARD_RIGHTS_WRITE | KEY_SET_VALUE | KEY_CREATE_SUB_KEY

IN POBJECT_ATTRIBUTES *ObjectAttributes*

A pointer to the object that describes the key name and the root of the Registry directory in which it is found. The root directory is optional. A name should be an object name in the Registry space and begin with the name \Registry.

995	NTSTATUS ZwOpenSection(OUT PHANDLE *SectionHandle*, IN ACCESS_MASK *DesiredAccess*, IN POBJECT_ATTRIBUTES *ObjectAttributes*);	

Opens a handle to an existing section object. Returns one of the following values.

	STATUS_SUCCESS	The operation is a success, and *SectionHandle* contains a valid section handle.
	STATUS_ACCESS_DENIED	The operation failed because the thread does not have sufficient rights to access the section.
	STATUS_INVALID_HANDLE	The handle supplied in the OBJECT_ATTRIBUTES structure is invalid.

OUT PHANDLE *SectionHandle*

Pointer to the location where a section handle will be placed if the function succeeds.

IN ACCESS_MASK *DesiredAccess*

The desired access to the section. One or more of the following values, combined using the bitwise OR operator.

	SECTION_MAP_WRITE	When a view is mapped, it will be writable.
	SECTION_MAP_READ	When a view is mapped, it will be readable.
	SECTION_ALL_ACCESS	SECTION_MAP_WRITE | SECTION_MAP_READ | STANDARD_RIGHTS_REQUIRED

Table A.3: *Important Support Functions and Structures for Device Drivers (continued)*

Page Ref.	Function	Parameters and Explanations
		IN POBJECT_ATTRIBUTES *ObjectAttributes* Reference to the initialized attributes of the section to be opened.
995	NTSTATUS ZwQueryKey(IN HANDLE *KeyHandle*, IN KEY_INFORMATION_CLASS *KeyInformationClass*, OUT PVOID *KeyInformation*, IN ULONG *Length*, OUT PULONG *ResultLength*);	

Queries a key for its class and the number and sizes of its subkeys. Returns one of the following values.

STATUS_SUCCESS	The operation succeeded; *KeyInformation* and *ResultLength* are valid values.
STATUS_INVALID_PARAMETER	
STATUS_BUFFER_OVERFLOW	The operation failed because *Length* was too small. The contents of *ResultLength* give the needed length.

IN HANDLE *KeyHandle*

The handle of the key whose properties are to be queried. This key must have KEY_QUERY_KEY access.

IN KEY_INFORMATION_CLASS *KeyInformationClass*

Specifies the type of information to be returned. Must be one of the following values.

KeyBasicInformation	Returns a sequence of KEY_BASIC_INFORMATION structures. See page 955.
KeyFullInformation	Returns a sequence of KEY_FULL_INFORMATION structures. See page 956.
KeyNodeInformation	Returns a sequence of KEY_NODE_INFORMATION structures. See page 957.

OUT PVOID *KeyInformation*

A pointer to a user-allocated buffer that will receive the key information.

IN ULONG *Length*

The length of the allocated *KeyInformation* buffer, in bytes. If too short, the operation will fail with a STATUS_BUFFER_OVERFLOW error and *ResultLength* will contain the required length.

OUT PULONG *ResultLength*

If the return code is STATUS_SUCCESS, the location referenced by this parameter will hold the actual length of the data returned: <= Length.
If the return code is STATUS_BUFFER_OVERFLOW, the location referenced by this parameter will hold the required length.

Table A.3: *Important Support Functions and Structures for Device Drivers (continued)*

Page Ref.	Function	Parameters and Explanations
996	NTSTATUS ZwQueryValueKey(IN HANDLE *KeyHandle*, IN PUNICODE_STRING *ValueName*, IN KEY_VALUE_INFORMATION_CLASS *KeyValueInformationClass*, OUT PVOID *KeyValueInformation*, IN ULONG *Length*, OUT PULONG *ResultLength*);	

Retrieves the values for an open key. Returns one of the following values.

STATUS_SUCCESS	The operation succeeded; *KeyValueInformation* and *ResultLength* are valid values.
STATUS_INVALID_PARAMETER	
STATUS_OBJ_NAME_NOT_FOUND	The specified value name was not found for the key specified by the handle.
STATUS_BUFFER_OVERFLOW	The operation failed because *Length* was too small. The contents of *ResultLength* give the needed length.

IN HANDLE *KeyHandle*

The handle of the key whose properties are to be queried. This key must have KEY_QUERY_KEY access.

IN PUNICODE_STRING *ValueName*

The name of the value to be queried.

IN KEY_VALUE_INFORMATION_CLASS *KeyValueInformationClass*

The type of information desired for the class. Can be one of the following values.

KeyValueBasicInformation	Returns a sequence of KEY_VALUE_BASIC_INFORMATION values. See page 958.
KeyValueFullInformation	Returns a sequence of KEY_VALUE_FULL_INFORMATION values. See page 959.
KeyValuePartialInformation	Returns a sequence of KEY_VALUE_PARTIAL_INFORMATION values. See page 961.

OUT PVOID *KeyValueInformation*

A pointer to a user-allocated buffer that will receive the value information.

IN ULONG *Length*

The length of the allocated *KeyValueInformation* buffer, in bytes. If too short, the operation will fail with a STATUS_BUFFER_OVERFLOW error and *ResultLength* will contain the required length.

Table A.3: *Important Support Functions and Structures for Device Drivers (continued)*

Page Ref.	Function	Parameters and Explanations
		OUT PULONG *ResultLength*
		If the return code is STATUS_SUCCESS, the location referenced by this parameter will hold the actual length of the data returned: <= Length. If the return code is STATUS_BUFFER_OVERFLOW, the location referenced by this parameter will hold the required length.

996	NTSTATUS ZwSetInformationThread(IN HANDLE *ThreadHandle*,
	    IN THREADINFOCLASS *ThreadInformationClass*,
	    IN PVOID *ThreadInformation*,
	    IN ULONG *ThreadInformationLength*);	

		Sets information for the thread. Consult table Table A.44 on page 997.
		IN HANDLE *ThreadHandle*
		A handle to the thread whose values are to be modified.
		IN THREADINFOCLASS *ThreadInformationClass*
		The type of information to be set.
		ThreadPriority Sets the priority of the thread.
		ThreadBasePriority Sets the base priority of the thread.
		IN PVOID *ThreadInformation*
		A pointer to the information to be set.
		IN ULONG *ThreadInformationLength*
		The length of the information.

998	NTSTATUS ZwSetValueKey(IN HANDLE *KeyHandle*, IN PUNICODE_STRING *ValueName*,
	    IN ULONG *TitleIndex*, IN ULONG *Type*, IN PVOID *Data*,
	    IN ULONG *DataSize*);	

		Sets the value for the key described by *KeyHandle*. Returns one of the following values.
		STATUS_SUCCESS The operation is a success, and *SectionHandle* contains a valid section handle.
		STATUS_ACCESS_DENIED The operation failed because the thread does not have sufficient rights to access the section.
		STATUS_INVALID_HANDLE The handle supplied in the OBJECT_ATTRIBUTES structure is invalid.
		IN HANDLE *KeyHandle*
		The handle of the key whose value is to be set. This key must have KEY_WRITE_KEY access.
		IN PUNICODE_STRING *ValueName*
		The name of the value to set for the key. If the key already has a value by this name, the value is replaced.
		IN ULONG *TitleIndex*
		Should be set to 0 for Device Drivers and intermediate drivers.

Table A.3: *Important Support Functions and Structures for Device Drivers (continued)*

Page Ref.	Function	Parameters and Explanations	
		IN ULONG *Type*	
		The type of the value. It should be one of the following constants.	
		REG_BINARY	Binary data in any form.
		REG_DWORD	A 4-byte numerical value.
		REG_DWORD_LITTLE_ENDIAN	A 4-byte numerical value whose least significant byte is at the lowest address.
		REG_DWORD_BIG_ENDIAN	A 4-byte numerical value whose least significant byte is at the highest address.
		REG_EXPAND_SZ	A zero-terminated Unicode string, containing unexpanded references to environment variables, such as "%PATH%".
		REG_LINK	A Unicode string naming a symbolic link. This type is irrelevant to Device Drivers and intermediate drivers.
		REG_MULTI_SZ	An array of zero-terminated strings, terminated by another zero.
		REG_NONE	Data with no particular type.
		REG_SZ	A zero-terminated Unicode string.
		REG_RESOURCE_LIST	A Device Driver's list of hardware resources, used by the driver or one of the physical devices it controls, in the \ResourceMap tree.
		REG_RESOURCE_REQUIREMENTS_LIST	A Device Driver's list of possible hardware resources it or one of the physical devices it controls can use, from which the system writes a subset into the \ResourceMap tree.
		REG_FULL_RESOURCE_DESCRIPTOR	A list of hardware resources that a physical device is using, detected and written into the \HardwareDescription tree by the system.
		IN PVOID *Data*	
		The data to be stored with the key. The data must be in a form consistent with *Type*.	
		IN ULONG *DataSize*	
		The length of the data. The length must be consistent with *Type*.	
998		NTSTATUS ZwUnmapViewOfSection(IN HANDLE *ProcessHandle*, IN PVOID *BaseAddress*);	
		Unmaps a view of a section that was established by ZwMapViewOfSection. Returns one of the following values.	

Table A.3: *Important Support Functions and Structures for Device Drivers (continued)*

Page Ref.	Function	Parameters and Explanations	
		STATUS_SUCCESS	The operation is a success. The view formerly at *BaseAddress* is now unmapped, and that address is invalid.
		STATUS_INVALID_PARAMETER	The operation failed because one of the parameters is invalid.
		STATUS_NO_ACCESS	
		IN HANDLE *ProcessHandle* The handle of the process that contains the view.	
		IN PVOID *BaseAddress* A pointer to the base address to be unmapped. This can be any address in the view.	

ANSI_STRING

```
typedef struct _STRING {
                USHORT Length;
                USHORT MaximumLength;
                PCHAR  Buffer;
} ANSI_STRING, * PANSI_STRING;
```

An ANSI_STRING is a counted string and is used to pass strings around as parameters to some functions. An ordinary NUL-terminated 8-bit string can be converted to a ANSI_STRING with the RtlInitAnsiString function.

Table A.4 shows the fields of the ANSI_STRING structure.

Table A.4: *Fields of the* ANSI_STRING *Structure*

Field	Meaning
USHORT Length	The length in bytes of the string stored in Buffer.
USHORT MaximumLength	The maximum length in bytes of Buffer.
PCHAR Buffer	Points to a buffer used to contain a string of 8-bit characters.

ASSERT

```
#ifdef DBG
#define ASSERT(expression) // ... Actual definition (not shown)
#else
#define ASSERT(expression)
#endif
```

The ASSERT macro, whose implementation details we don't show here, is conditionally compiled based on the definition of the DBG preprocessor symbol. If it is defined and the expression evaluates to FALSE, this will cause the attached debugger to display the text of the expression, the source file's name, and the source line number. The debugger also queries whether the assertion failure should be ignored, cause a break into the debugger, or cause the thread that caused the assertion failure to terminate.

Be cautious with termination. An assertion failure in an ISR or DPC Routine might be executing in the context of some thread you've never heard of.

ASSERTMSG

```
#ifdef DBG
#define ASSERTMSG(message, expression) // ... Actual definition (not shown)
#else
#define ASSERTMSG(message, expression)
#endif
```

The ASSERTMSG macro, whose implementation details we don't show here, is conditionally compiled based on the definition of the DBG preprocessor symbol. If it is defined and the expression evaluates to FALSE, this will cause the attached debugger to display the text of the expression, the text of the *message*, the source file's name, and the source line number. The debugger also queries whether the assertion failure should be ignored, cause a break into the debugger, or cause the thread that caused the assertion failure to terminate.

Be cautious with termination. An assertion failure in an ISR or DPC Routine might be executing in the context of some thread you've never heard of.

The parameter *message* must be a pointer to an 8-bit NUL-terminated character string.

CM_FULL_RESOURCE_DESCRIPTOR

```
typedef struct _CM_FULL_RESOURCE_DESCRIPTOR {
        INTERFACE_TYPE InterfaceType;
        ULONG BusNumber;
        CM_PARTIAL_RESOURCE_LIST PartialResourceList;
} CM_FULL_RESOURCE_DESCRIPTOR, *PCM_FULL_RESOURCE_DESCRIPTOR;
```

CM_FULL_RESOURCE_DESCRIPTOR defines an array element in a CM_RESOURCE_LIST.

BusNumber and InterfaceType are redundant information, included so that a driver need not append this information when creating a resource list that could possibly span more than one bus.

Table A.5 lists the fields for CM_FULL_RESOURCE_DESCRIPTOR.

Table A.5: CM_FULL_RESOURCE_DESCRIPTOR *Fields*

Field	Meaning
INTERFACE_TYPE InterfaceType	Specifies the bus interface type, which can be one of the following: Internal, Isa, Eisa, MicroChannel, TurboChannel, or PCIBus. However, additional types of busses will be supported in future versions of Windows NT. The upper bound on the types of busses supported is always MaximumInterfaceType.
ULONG BusNumber	The system-assigned and zero-based number for this bus of the given InterfaceType.
CM_PARTIAL_RESOURCE_DESCRIPTOR PartialResourceList	The partial resource list information.

CM_PARTIAL_RESOURCE_DESCRIPTOR

```
typedef struct _CM_PARTIAL_RESOURCE_DESCRIPTOR {
    UCHAR Type;
    UCHAR ShareDisposition;
    USHORT Flags;
    union {
        struct {
                PHYSICAL_ADDRESS Start;    // 8-byte physical address
                ULONG Length;
                } Port;

        struct {
                ULONG Level;
                ULONG Vector;
                ULONG Affinity;
                } Interrupt;

        struct {
                PHYSICAL_ADDRESS Start;    // 8-byte physical address
                ULONG Length;
                } Memory;

        struct {
                ULONG Channel;
                ULONG Port;
                ULONG Reserved1;
                } Dma;

        struct {
                ULONG DataSize;
                ULONG Reserved1;
                ULONG Reserved2;
                } DeviceSpecificData;
    } u;
} CM_PARTIAL_RESOURCE_DESCRIPTOR, *PCM_PARTIAL_RESOURCE;
```

Each CM_PARTIAL_RESOURCE_DESCRIPTOR defines an element of an array within a CM_PARTIAL_RESOURCE_LIST. Each CM_PARTIAL_RESOURCE_DESCRIPTOR describes only one type of resource used by a driver or device controlled by that driver. Table A.6 lists the fields for CM_PARTIAL_RESOURCE_DESCRIPTOR.

Table A.6: CM_PARTIAL_RESOURCE_DESCRIPTOR *Fields*

Field	Meaning
UCHAR Type	Specifies which of the following is described by this partial descriptor: CmResourceTypePort, CmResourceTypeInterrupt, CmResourceTypeMemory, CmResourceTypeDma, or CmResourceTypeDeviceSpecific.
UCHAR ShareDisposition	Specifies whether or how the particular resource can be shared as one of the following: CmResourceShareDeviceExclusive, CmResourceShareDriverExclusive, or CmResourceShareShared.
USHORT Flags	Specifies type-dependent information about this descriptor.

Table A.6: `CM_PARTIAL_RESOURCE_DESCRIPTOR` *Fields (continued)*

Field	Meaning	
`u.Port`	Describes a range of device ports in I/O space. The range of port numbers, inclusive. These are physical and bus-relative values, which should be passed, unchanged, to `HalTranslateBusAddress` to get the mapped logical port range that the driver uses to communicate with its device.	
	`PHYSICAL_ADDRESS Start`	Bus-specific, 8-byte base physical address for the range.
	`ULONG Length`	The length, in bytes, of the range.
`u.Interrupt`	Describes a bus-relative interrupt. Defines the bus-relative IRQL or vector and affinity, which are returned by `IoQueryDeviceDescription` or `HalGetBusData` and passed, unchanged, to `HalGetInterruptVector` and/or `IoReportResourceUsage`.	
	`ULONG Level`	The IRQL at which the bus interrupts.
	`ULONG Vector`	The vector at which the bus interrupts.
	`ULONG Affinity`	The set of processors to which bus interrupts are dispatched. Set this to −1 in any partial resource descriptor describing interrupt configuration information that is passed to `IoReportResourceUsage`.
`u.Memory`	Describes a bus-relative range of device memory, which is in system memory space. The range of device memory, inclusive. These are physical and bus-relative values, which should be passed, unchanged, to `HalTranslateBusAddress` to get the mapped logical address. This, in turn, can be passed to `MmMapIoSpace` to get the virtual address range that the driver uses to communicate with its device. The value is the following.	
	`PHYSICAL_ADDRESS Start`	Bus-specific, 8-byte base physical address for the range.
	`ULONG Length`	Size in bytes of the range.
`u.Dma`	Describes a bus-relative DMA setting, as one of the following.	
	`ULONG Channel`	Number of the DMA channel on a system DMA controller that the device can use.
	`ULONG Port`	Number of the DMA port that an MCA-type device can use.
`u.DeviceSpecificData`	Describes how much device-specific data follows immediately after the Reserved2 member, as the following.	
	`ULONG DataSize`	The size in bytes of the device-specific data area.

CM_PARTIAL_RESOURCE_LIST

```
typedef struct _CM_PARTIAL_RESOURCE_LIST {
    USHORT Version;
    USHORT Revision;
    ULONG Count;
    CM_PARTIAL_RESOURCE_DESCRIPTOR PartialDescriptors[1];
} CM_PARTIAL_RESOURCE_LIST, *PCM_PARTIAL_RESOURCE_LIST;
```

A partial resource list is collected from the ARC firmware or constructed by NTDETECT. The Configuration Manager transforms this structure into a full resource descriptor when it is about to store it in the Registry.

The CM_PARTIAL_RESOURCE_LIST structure allows drivers for the same types of devices to follow a convention for the ordering of common configuration information, which should be defined on a device-by-device basis. Table A.7 lists the fields for CM_PARTIAL_RESOURCE_LIST.

Table A.7: CM_PARTIAL_RESOURCE_LIST *Fields*

Field	Meaning
USHORT Version	The version number of this structure.
USHORT Revision	The revision of this structure.
ULONG Count	The number of partial resource descriptors in the following array.
CM_PARTIAL_RESOURCE_DESCRIPTOR PartialDescriptors[1]	An array of partial resource descriptors.

CM_RESOURCE_LIST

```
typedef struct _CM_RESOURCE_LIST {
                             ULONG Count;
                             CM_FULL_RESOURCE_DESCRIPTOR List[1];
                             } CM_RESOURCE_LIST, * PCM_RESOURCE_LIST;
```

The CM_RESOURCE_LIST is an input parameter to IoReportResourceUsage. Its nested CM_FULL_RESOURCE_DESCRIPTOR array contains a CM_PARTIAL_RESOURCE_LIST with a nested CM_PARTIAL_RESOURCE_DESCRIPTOR array. Table A.8 lists the fields for CM_RESOURCE_LIST.

Table A.8: CM_RESOURCE_LIST *Fields*

Field	Description
ULONG Count	The number of full resource descriptors in the following array.
CM_FULL_RESOURCE_DESCRIPTOR List[1]	An array of full resource descriptors.

CONFIGURATION_INFORMATION

```
typedef struct _CONFIGURATIONAL_INFORMATION{
        ULONG DiskCount;
        ULONG FloppyCount;
        ULONG CDRomCount;
        ULONG TapeCount;
        ULONG ScsiPortCount;
        ULONG SerialCount;
        ULONG ParallelCount;
        BOOLEAN AtDiskPrimaryAddressClaimed;
        BOOLEAN AtDiskSecondaryAddressClaimed;
} CONFIGURATION_INFORMATION, * PCONFIGURATION_INFORMATION
```

This is the result of the `IoGetConfiguration` call. Table A.9 lists the fields for `CONFIGURATION_INFORMATION`.

Table A.9: `CONFIGURATION_INFORMATION` *Fields*

Field	Description
Each field indicates the total number of physical devices of a particular type in the machine. The value should be used by the driver to determine the digit suffix for Device Object names. Each field must be updated as the driver finds new devices of its own.	
ULONG DiskCount	Count of hard disk drives found so far.
ULONG FloppyCount	Count of floppy disk drives found so far.
ULONG CDRomCount	Count of CD-ROM drives found so far.
ULONG TapeCount	Count of tape drives found so far.
ULONG ScsiPortCount	Count of SCSI HBAs found so far.
ULONG SerialCount	Count of serial ports found so far.
ULONG ParallelCount	Count of parallel ports found so far.
The following two fields indicate the ownership of either of the two I/O address spaces used by WD1003-compatible disk controllers.	
BOOLEAN AtDiskPrimaryAddressClaimed	Primary AT bus address claimed by this device, 0x1F0–0x1FF.
BOOLEAN AtDiskSecondaryAddressClaimed	Secondary AT bus address claimed by this device, 0x170–0x17F.

Note that this structure is not WDM-compatible, since it does not support counts for USB or IEEE-1394 devices.

CONTAINING_RECORD

```
#define CONTAINING_RECORD(address, type, field)
```

This `CONTAINING_RECORD` macro computes the start of a record containing a field. The *address* parameter is a pointer to the field. The *type* parameter is the name of the structure, and the *field* parameter is the access to the field. By a series of intricate type casts,[1] this macro returns a pointer of type *type* *, which is the pointer to the start of the structure.

CONTROLLER_OBJECT

```
typedef struct _CONTROLLER_OBJECT {
    // ... Opaque fields
    PVOID ControllerExtension;
    // ... Opaque fields
    } CONTROLLER_OBJECT, *PCONTROLLER_OBJECT;
```

---

[1] `((type *)((PCHAR)(address) - (PCHAR)(&((type *)0)->field)))`. You didn't really want to see this.

The CONTROLLER_OBJECT data structure is "opaque", except for the pointer to the ControllerExtension, which can be NULL if the *Size* specified by the IoCreateController is 0.

DbgBreakPoint

VOID DbgBreakPoint( );

DbgBreakPoint causes a break into the attached debugger. The debugger is given control.

DbgPrint

ULONG DbgPrint(IN PCHAR *fmt*, ...);

Takes a pointer to an 8-bit printf-style formatting string and zero or more additional arguments depending on the formatting requests in the string. The output will be an 8-bit character string sent to the debug output port. The attached debugger will display this string.

You may use the %1s format to cause a Unicode string to be formatted for output as an 8-bit string. Note that this might produce strange transliterations if the character codes are not in the range 0x0000 through 0x00FF.

DEVICE_DESCRIPTION

```
typedef struct _DEVICE_DESCRIPTION {
        ULONG    Version;
        BOOLEAN Master;
        BOOLEAN ScatterGather;
        BOOLEAN DemandMode;
        BOOLEAN AutoInitialize;
        BOOLEAN Dma32BitAddresses;
        BOOLEAN IgnoreCount;
        BOOLEAN Reserved1;
        BOOLEAN Reserved2;
        ULONG    BusNumber;
        ULONG    DmaChannel;
        INTERFACE_TYPE InterfaceType;
        DMA_WIDTH DmaWidth;
        DMA_SPEED DmaSpeed;
        ULONG    MaximumLength;
        ULONG    DmaPort;
} DEVICE_DESCRIPTION, * PDEVICE_DESCRIPTION;
```

This structure is used to specify the properties of a DMA device to HalGetAdapter. Table A.10 lists the fields for DEVICE_DESCRIPTION.

Table A.10: `DEVICE_DESCRIPTION` *Fields*

Field	Meaning	
`ULONG Version`	Version ID of the data structure, one of the following values.	
	`DEVICE_DESCRIPTION_VERSION`	Normal device description structure.
	`DEVICE_DESCRIPTION_VERSION1`	Description for the device that must use `IgnoreCount`.
`BOOLEAN Master`	TRUE if a bus mastering adapter; FALSE if a slave DMA device.	
`BOOLEAN ScatterGather`	TRUE if the device supports scatter/gather; FALSE if not.	
`BOOLEAN DemandMode`	TRUE if the device uses the system DMA controller's demand mode.	
`BOOLEAN AutoInitialize`	TRUE if the device uses the system DMA controller's autoinit mode.	
`BOOLEAN Dma32BitAddresses`	TRUE if the DMA can use full 32-bit addresses; FALSE if limited to 24-bit addresses.	
`BOOLEAN IgnoreCount`	TRUE if the DMA controller in this platform does not maintain an accurate transfer counter and so requires a workaround. `Version` must be `DEVICE_DESCRIPTION_VERSION1`. The HAL ignores the DMA counter but must take extra precautions to maintain data integrity during transfer operations. Using this workaround to compensate for such a deficient DMA controller degrades the speed of DMA transfers.	
`BOOLEAN Reserved1` `BOOLEAN Reserved2`	These must be FALSE.	
`ULONG BusNumber`	System-assigned value for the I/O bus.	
`ULONG DmaChannel`	If the device is a slave DMA device, this is the DMA channel that it uses.	
`INTERFACE_TYPE InterfaceType`	The type of the interface. One of the following values.	
	`Eisa`	Extended ISA bus.
	`Internal`	Internal (motherboard) bus.
	`Isa`	ISA bus.
	`MicroChannel`	MicroChannel (MCA) bus.
	`PciBus`	PCI Bus.
	`TurboChannel`	TurboChannel bus.
`DMA_WIDTH DmaWidth`	DMA transfer width. One of 8, 16, or 32 bits encoded as shown next.	
	`Width8Bits`	8-bit DMA transfers are supported.
	`Width16Bits`	16-bit DMA transfers are supported.
	`Width32Bits`	32-bit DMA transfers are supported.

Table A.10: DEVICE_DESCRIPTION *Fields (continued)*

Field	Meaning
DMA_SPEED DmaSpeed	DMA speed. Must be one of the following undocumented values:
	Compatible
	TypeA
	TypeB
	TypeC
ULONG MaximumLength	Maximum number of bytes a device can handle per DMA operation.
ULONG DmaPort	MicroChannel-type bus port number.

DEVICE_OBJECT

```
typedef struct _DEVICE_OBJECT {
          PDRIVER_OBJECT DriverObject;
          struct _DEVICE_OBJECT * NextDevice;
          struct _IRP * CurrentIrp;
          ULONG Flags;
          ULONG Characteristics;
          PVOID DeviceExtension;
          DEVICE_TYPE DeviceType;
          CCHAR StackSize;
          ULONG AlignmentRequirement;
          // ...Many other private fields, not documented
     } DEVICE_OBJECT;
```

DEVICE_OBJECT is a "semi-opaque" type. Not all of the fields of a DEVICE_OBJECT are available to you. We show here *only* those fields that Microsoft has documented.

Table A.11 lists the fields for DEVICE_OBJECT.

Table A.11: DEVICE_OBJECT *Fields*

Field	Description
PDRIVER_OBJECT DriverObject	A reference to the Driver Object. It is the input parameter to IoCreateDevice and is set by that function when the Device Object is created.
PDEVICE_OBJECT NextDevice	Points to the next Device Object for this driver. The I/O Manager updates this list when IoCreateDevice is called. This chain is used when the Unload routine is called.
PIRP CurrentIrp	A reference to the current IRP. This is used only if the driver has a StartIo routine whose entry point is set in the Driver Object and if the driver is currently processing IRPs. Otherwise, the value is NULL.
ULONG Flags	This field must be set using the bitwise OR operation (	). After you have created a Device Object, you should OR into this field one of the following values. Other status bits apply to removable file media and are not discussed here.

Table A.11: DEVICE_OBJECT *Fields (continued)*

Field	Description	
	DO_BUFFERED_IO	The device will do buffered I/O. The I/O Manager will copy the application buffers into system buffers for output and copy system buffers to application buffers for input.
	DO_DIRECT_IO	The device will do direct I/O. The I/O Manager will prepare a MDL that describes the application buffers.
	DO_UNLOAD_PENDING	An Unload operation is in progress.
	DO_VERIFY_VOLUME	
	DO_EXCLUSIVE	The device supports only exclusive access.
	DO_DEVICE_HAS_NAME	The device has a name (Filter Drivers usually do not).
	DO_DEVICE_INITIALIZING	The device is initializing. This bit is cleared automatically when DriverEntry returns but must be explicitly cleared for Device Objects created outside DriverEntry, for example, in NT 5.0 beta/Windows 2000, when AddDevice is called.
	DO_LONG_TERM_REQUESTS	
	DO_NEVER_LAST_DEVICE	
	DO_SHUTDOWN_REGISTERED	A shutdown request has been registered with IoRegisterShutdownNotification.
	DO_SYSTEM_BOOT_PARTITION	
	DO_MAP_IO_BUFFER	
ULONG Characteristics	Used only by removable-media File System devices.	
PVOID DeviceExtension	A pointer to the Device Extension block that is at the end of this structure.	
DEVICE_TYPE DeviceType	One of the following values or a programmer-defined device type.	
	FILE_DEVICE_SCREEN	A display device.
	FILE_DEVICE_SOUND	A general audio output device.
	FILE_DEVICE_STREAMS	
	FILE_DEVICE_TAPE	A "raw" tape drive.
	FILE_DEVICE_TAPE_FILE_SYSTEM	A tape drive that supports a tape File System.
	FILE_DEVICE_TRANSPORT	

Table A.11: DEVICE_OBJECT *Fields (continued)*

Field	Description	
	FILE_DEVICE_UNKNOWN	Any other device. Unless you have compelling reasons to use one of the values in the range 32768..65535, you should use this device type for your device.
	FILE_DEVICE_VIDEO	A video (NTSC, PAL, and so on) device.
	FILE_DEVICE_VIRTUAL_DISK	A virtual disk.
	FILE_DEVICE_WAVE_IN	Audio input device.
	FILE_DEVICE_WAVE_OUT	Audio output device.
	FILE_DEVICE_8042_PORT	8042 keyboard controller.
	FILE_DEVICE_NETWORK_REDIRECTOR	Network redirector (File Systems only).
	FILE_DEVICE_BATTERY	Laptop battery monitor.
	FILE_DEVICE_BUS_EXTENDER	A bus extender or repeater.
	FILE_DEVICE_MODEM	A modem.
	FILE_DEVICE_VDM	A virtual DOS machine.
	32768..65535	Programmer-defined.
CCHAR StackSize	Specifies the minimum number of stack locations in IRPs that are sent to this driver. In a newly created Device Object, this value is 1. Normally, a higher-level driver that connects to a lower-level driver (such as a WDM driver hierarchy) must explicitly set this value to the value of the lower-level driver plus 1. A driver that calls IoAttachDevice or IoAttachDeviceToDeviceStack will automatically set the correct stack size (this is not how WDM drivers work).	
ULONG AlignmentRequired	Specifies the alignment restrictions of the data buffers. These restrictions might be due to processor requirements (for example, RISC machines that require LONG alignment are common) or due to restrictions imposed by the devices themselves (some DMA controllers require WORD or other alignments).	
	FILE_BYTE_ALIGNMENT	No alignment restriction.
	FILE_WORD_ALIGNMENT	Address must be a multiple of 2.
	FILE_LONG_ALIGNMENT	Address must be a multiple of 4.
	FILE_QUAD_ALIGNMENT	Address must be a multiple of 8 (a quadword).
	FILE_OCTA_ALIGNMENT	Address must be a multiple of 16 (an octaword).
	FILE_32_BYTE_ALIGNMENT	Address must be a multiple of 32.
	FILE_64_BYTE_ALIGNMENT	Address must be a multiple of 64.
	FILE_128_BYTE_ALIGNMENT	Address must be a multiple of 128.
	FILE_256_BYTE_ALIGNMENT	Address must be a multiple of 256.

DriverEntry

```
NTSTATUS DriverEntry(IN PDRIVER_OBJECT driver,
                     IN PUNICODE_STRING RegistryPath);
```

DriverEntry is the main driver entry point called when a driver is loaded. It receives as input parameters a pointer to the DRIVER_OBJECT that has been allocated for the driver and a pointer to the Registry path for that driver.

DRIVER_EXTENSION

```
typedef struct _DRIVER_EXTENSION {
    PDRIVER_OBJECT DriverObject;
    PDRIVER_ADD_DEVICE AddDevice;
    ULONG Count;
    UNICODE_STRING ServiceKeyName;
} DRIVER_EXTENSION, *PDRIVER_EXTENSION;
```

A Driver Extension has been added to Windows NT 5.0 beta/Windows 2000 to support the additional features of Plug-and-Play. The fields are shown in Table A.12.

Table A.12: DRIVER_EXTENSION *Fields*

Field	Description
PDRIVER_OBJECT DriverObject	A pointer to the DRIVER_OBJECT whose extension this is.
PDRIVER_ADD_DEVICE AddDevice	The AddDevice routine is called by the Plug-and-Play manager to inform the driver when a new device instance arrives that this driver must control.
ULONG Count	Used to count the number of times the driver has had its registered reinitialization routine invoked.
UNICODE_STRING ServiceKeyName	Used by the Plug-and-Play manager to determine where the driver-related info is stored in the registry.

DRIVER_OBJECT

A DRIVER_OBJECT is created by the system whenever a driver is loaded.

The DriverEntry routine receives a pointer to the DRIVER_OBJECT as its first parameter. Not all fields of the DRIVER_OBJECT are documented. Consequently, what we show here is *not* the actual struct, but rather the documented subset.

```
typedef struct {
        PDEVICE_OBJECT DeviceObject;
        PUNICODE_STRING HardwareDatabase;
        PDRIVER_EXTENSION DriverExtension;
        PFAST_IO_DISPATCH FastioDispatch;
        PDRIVER_INITIALIZE DriverInit;
        PDRIVER_STARTIO DriverStartIo;
        PDRIVER_UNLOAD DriverUnload;
        PDRIVER_DISPATCH MajorFunction[IRP_MJ_MAXIMUM_FUNCTION+1];
        } DRIVER_OBJECT, * PDRIVER_OBJECT;
```

Table A.13 lists the documented fields of `DRIVER_OBJECT`.

Table A.13: *Documented Fields of* `DRIVER_OBJECT`

Field	Description
`PDEVICE_OBJECTDeviceObject`	A pointer to the Device Object(s) created by the driver. This field is automatically updated whenever the `DriverEntry` routine successfully calls `IoCreateDevice`.
`PUNICODE_STRING HardwareDatabase`	Points to a string that is the subkey in the `HKEY_LOCAL_MACHINE\Hardware` key that contains hardware configuration information.
`PDRIVER_EXTENSION DriverExtension`	*NT 5.0 beta/Windows 2000 only.* A pointer to a Driver Extension.
`PFAST_IO_DISPATCH FastioDispatch`	Used only by File System Drivers and network drivers.
`PDRIVER_INITIALIZE DriverInit`	Contains the address of the driver's `DriverEntry` routine.
`PDRIVER_STARTIO DriverStartIo`	The address of the `StartIo` routine. This is set by the `DriverEntry` routine when the driver is initializing. If there is no `StartIo` routine, this entry is NULL.
`PDRIVER_UNLOAD DriverUnload`	The address of the driver's Unload routine. This is called whenever the driver is unloaded and is initialized by the `DriverEntry` routine. If there are no special unload requirements, this is NULL.
`PDRIVER_DISPATCH MajorFunction[ ]`	An array of addresses of various Dispatch Routines in the driver. Each driver, when it initializes in `DriverEntry`, sets one or more of these addresses to reference routines in the driver itself.

ExAcquireFastMutex

```
VOID ExAcquireFastMutex(IN PFAST_MUTEX FastMutex);
```

Acquires the given Fast Mutex, with APCs to the current thread disabled.

The *FastMutex* parameter points to an initialized Fast Mutex for which the caller provides the storage.

This function puts the caller into a wait state if the given Fast Mutex cannot be acquired immediately. Otherwise, the caller is given ownership of the Fast Mutex, with APCs to the current thread disabled until it releases the Fast Mutex.

Use `ExTryToAcquireFastMutex` if the current thread wishes to do other work before it waits on the acquisition of the given Mutex.

Any Fast Mutex acquired with `ExAcquireFastMutex` or `ExTryToAcquireFastMutex` must be released with `ExReleaseFastMutex`.

Callers of `ExAcquireFastMutex` must be running at IRQL < `DISPATCH_LEVEL`.

ExAcquireFastMutexUnsafe

```
VOID ExAcquireFastMutexUnsafe(IN PFAST_MUTEX FastMutex);
```

Acquires the given Fast Mutex for the current thread.

The *FastMutex* parameter points to an initialized Fast Mutex for which the caller provides the storage.

This routine puts the caller into a wait state if the given Fast Mutex cannot be acquired immediately. Otherwise, the caller is given ownership of the Fast Mutex and exclusive access to the resource it protects until it releases the Fast Mutex.

It can be called only if APCs will not be delivered to the current thread while it is holding the Fast Mutex. For example, while the thread is running within a critical region, APCs to that thread are disabled.

Any Fast Mutex acquired with ExAcquireFastMutexUnsafe must be released with ExReleaseFastMutexUnsafe.

A thread that calls this function must be running at IRQL < DISPATCH_LEVEL.

ExAcquireResourceExclusiveLite

```
BOOLEAN ExAcquireResourceExclusiveLite(IN PERESOURCE Resource,
                                       IN BOOLEAN Wait);
```

Acquires the given Executive Resource for exclusive access by the calling thread.

The *Resource* parameter points to the Executive Resource to acquire. The *Wait* parameter is TRUE if the caller should be put into a wait state until the Executive Resource can be acquired, if it cannot be acquired immediately.

This routine returns TRUE if the resource is acquired. It returns FALSE if the input *Wait* is FALSE and exclusive access cannot be granted immediately.

For better performance when testing for a conditional acquisition, call ExTryToAcquireResourceExclusiveLite, rather than ExAcquireResourceExclusiveLite with *Wait* set to FALSE.

A thread that calls this function must be running at IRQL < DISPATCH_LEVEL.

ExAcquireResourceSharedLite

```
BOOLEAN ExAcquireResourceSharedLite(IN PERESOURCE Resource,
                                    IN BOOLEAN Wait);
```

Acquires the given Executive Resource for shared access by the calling thread.

Any number of threads can have concurrent shared access to an Executive Resource. Shared access cannot be acquired if any thread already has exclusive access to the Executive Resource. The *Resource* parameter points to the Executive Resource to acquire. The *Wait* parameter is TRUE if the caller should be put into a wait state until the resource can be acquired, if it cannot be acquired immediately.

This routine returns TRUE if the Executive Resource is acquired. It returns FALSE if the input *Wait* is FALSE and exclusive access cannot be granted immediately.

A thread that calls this function must be running at IRQL < DISPATCH_LEVEL.

ExAcquireSharedStarveExclusive

```
BOOLEAN ExAcquireSharedStarveExclusive(IN PERESOURCE Resource,
                                       IN BOOLEAN Wait);
```

Acquires the given Executive Resource for shared access by the calling thread.

Any number of threads can have concurrent shared access to an Executive Resource. Shared access cannot be acquired if any thread already has exclusive access to the Executive Resource. If there are threads waiting for exclusive access, they will be forced to wait, as this function violates the FIFO ordering normally used for queueing requests to an Executive Resource.

The *Resource* parameter points to the resource to acquire. The *Wait* parameter is TRUE if the caller should be put into a wait state until the resource can be acquired, if it cannot be acquired immediately.

This routine returns TRUE if the resource is acquired. It returns FALSE if the input *Wait* is FALSE and exclusive access cannot be granted immediately.

Whether or when the caller is given shared access to the given resource depends on the following.

- If the Executive Resource is currently unowned, shared access is granted immediately to the current thread.

- If the caller already has acquired the Executive Resource, the current thread is granted the same type of access recursively. Note that making this call does not convert a caller's exclusive ownership of a given Executive Resource to shared.

- If the Executive Resource is currently owned as shared by another thread, shared access is granted to the caller immediately, even if another thread is waiting for exclusive access to that Executive Resource.

- If the Executive Resource is currently owned as exclusive by another thread, either the caller is put into a wait state (*Wait* is TRUE) or the call returns FALSE.

A thread that calls this function must be running at IRQL < DISPATCH_LEVEL.

ExAcquireSharedWaitForExclusive

```
BOOLEAN ExAcquireSharedWaitForExclusive(IN PERESOURCE Resource,
                                        IN BOOLEAN Wait);
```

Acquires the given Executive Resource for shared access by the calling thread.

Any number of threads can have concurrent shared access to an Executive Resource. Shared access cannot be acquired if any thread already has exclusive access to the Executive Resource. If there are threads waiting for exclusive access, they will be given preference, even if they enter the queue after this request. This is because this function violates the FIFO ordering normally used for queueing requests to an Executive Resource.

The *Resource* parameter points to the resource to acquire. The *Wait* parameter is TRUE if the caller should be put into a wait state until the resource can be acquired, if it cannot be acquired immediately.

This routine returns TRUE if the Executive Resource is acquired. It returns FALSE if the input *Wait* is FALSE and exclusive access cannot be granted immediately.

Whether or when the caller is given shared access to the given Executive Resource depends on the following.

- If the Executive Resource is currently unowned, shared access is granted immediately to the current thread.

- If the caller already has exclusive access to the Executive Resource, the current thread is granted the same type of access recursively.
- If the Executive Resource is currently owned as shared and there are no pending attempts to acquire exclusive access, shared access is granted to the caller immediately.
- If the Executive Resource is currently owned as shared but there is a pending attempt to acquire exclusive access, either the caller is put into a wait state (*Wait* set to TRUE) or the function returns FALSE.

A thread that calls this function must be running at IRQL < DISPATCH_LEVEL.

ExAllocateFromNPagedLookasideList

PVOID ExAllocateFromNPagedLookasideList(IN PNPAGED_LOOKASIDE_LIST *Lookaside*)

Allocates a block of memory from a nonpaged lookaside list. If a block is available on the lookaside list, it is removed and its pointer is returned. If the lookaside list is empty, a new block is allocated from the Nonpaged Pool and a pointer to it is returned. If storage cannot be allocated, the return value is NULL.

A thread that calls this function must be running at IRQL <= DISPATCH_LEVEL.

ExAllocateFromPagedLookasideList

PVOID ExAllocateFromPagedLookasideList(IN PPAGED_LOOKASIDE_LIST *Lookaside*)

Allocates a block of memory from a paged lookaside list. If a block is available on the lookaside list, it is removed and its pointer is returned. If the lookaside list is empty, a new block is allocated from the Paged Pool and a pointer to it is returned. If storage cannot be allocated, the return value is NULL.

A thread that calls this function must be running at IRQL <= DISPATCH_LEVEL.

ExAllocatePool

PVOID ExAllocatePool (POOL_TYPE *pooltype*, IN ULONG *NumberOfBytes*);

ExAllocatePool allocates a block of memory according to the specified pool type. The pool types are represented by one of the constants shown in Table A.14.

Table A.14: *Allocation Pool Types*

Pool Type Name	Meaning
NonPagedPool	Memory is allocated from the Nonpaged Pool. If the memory cannot be allocated, the function returns NULL. Otherwise, returns the virtual memory address of the allocated storage.
NonPagedPoolMustSucceed	Memory is allocated from the Nonpaged Pool. If the memory cannot be allocated, the system dies with the MUST_SUCCEED_POOL_EMPTY BugCheck error (0x41).

Table A.14: *Allocation Pool Types (continued)*

Pool Type Name	Meaning
NonPagedPoolCacheAligned	Memory is allocated from the Nonpaged Pool. The memory is aligned on a cache-line boundary.
NonPagedPoolCacheAlignedMustS	This odd name is the 31-letter rendition of a "MustSucceed" name. Memory is allocated from the Nonpaged Pool and aligned on a cache-line boundary. If it cannot be allocated, the system dies with the MUST_SUCCEED_POOL_EMPTY BugCheck error (0x41).
PagedPool	Memory is allocated from the Paged Pool.
PagedPoolCacheAligned	Memory is allocated from the Paged Pool and aligned on a cache-line boundary.

For all but the MustS(ucceed) variants, the call can return NULL if there is no memory to allocate. *You must always check the return value for these calls*. If NULL is returned, you will need to take whatever action is appropriate to your driver. The MustS(ucceed) variants guarantee that when the function returns, you *will* have a valid virtual memory address.

If the pool type is one of the MustS(ucceed) variants, the call will succeed if there is *any* available memory to allocate. Normally, memory is allocated from the general Nonpaged Pool, but there are a small number of pages held aside as a "must-succeed last-resort pool". Must-succeed allocations will allocate from this pool if there is no general nonpaged memory to allocate. Such allocations must be for amounts smaller than PAGE_SIZE. These variants should be used only when you are in a state in which you will be in such deep trouble if you can't get this memory allocated that you can respond only by crashing the system. Memory allocated in the must-succeed mode is a precious resource. It should be used only for transient purposes and be released as quickly as possible. This memory should not be retained for any significant length of time. This is because eventually, you could deplete the must-succeed pool and cause some other driver to crash the system. As a strategy, it is best to write your driver so that you don't depend on must-succeed memory.

If there is insufficient memory available to satisfy a MustS(ucceed) request, the system crashes. The BugCheck code is MUST_SUCCEED_POOL_EMPTY. This is typically caused by a driver that has allocated this type of memory and not released it. Note that the driver that gets this error and crashes the system is not necessarily the driver that caused the problem; some other driver could be hoarding must-succeed memory.

This function can be called only if the thread is running at IRQL <= DISPATCH_LEVEL. If IRQL == DISPATCH_LEVEL, the pool type *must* be one of the NonPaged... options. If IRQL < DISPATCH_LEVEL, either paged or nonpaged memory can be allocated.

If the function returns NULL, you can respond by returning the NTSTATUS value STATUS_INSUFFICIENT_RESOURCES or by delaying processing.

ExAllocatePoolWithQuota

```
PVOID ExAllocatePoolWithQuota(IN POOL_TYPE pooltype, IN ULONG NumberOfBytes);
```

Allocates a pool of memory according to the specified pool type. The pool types are shown in Table A.14 on page 879.

Each process has a quota setting a current maximum allowable Paged Pool and Nonpaged Pool use. These quotas are assigned dynamically and will automatically be increased, if possible, when an attempt to allocate from a pool would exceed its quota (taking into account the other active processes). Optionally these quotas may be set (for all processes) via the Registry. The Registry technique is seldom used.

The `ExAllocatePoolWithQuotaTag` and `ExAllocatePoolWithQuota` functions will charge the quota of the current process with the size of the allocation. Note that these routines must not be called in any context other than the context of the appropriate user mode process. Lower-level drivers should call the routines that do not charge quota, since they are running in an arbitrary context.

For all but the `MustS(ucceed)` variants, the call can return `NULL` if there is no memory to allocate. *You must always check the return value for these calls*. If `NULL` is returned, you will need to take whatever action is appropriate to your driver. The `MustS(ucceed)` variants guarantee that when the function returns, you *will* have a valid virtual memory address.

If the pool type is one of the `MustS(ucceed)` variants, the call will succeed if there is *any* available memory to allocate. Normally, memory is allocated from the general Nonpaged Pool, but there are a small number of pages held aside as a "must-succeed last-resort pool". Must-succeed allocations will allocate from this pool if there is no general nonpaged memory to allocate. Such allocations must be for amounts smaller than `PAGE_SIZE`. These variants should be used only when you are in a state in which you will be in such deep trouble if you can't get this memory allocated that you can respond only by crashing the system. Memory allocated in the must-succeed mode is a precious resource. It should be used only for transient purposes and be released as quickly as possible. This memory should not be retained for any significant length of time. This is because eventually, you could deplete the must-succeed pool and cause some other driver to crash the system. As a strategy, it is best to write your driver so that you don't depend on must-succeed memory.

If there is insufficient memory available to satisfy a `MustS(ucceed)` request, the system crashes. The BugCheck code is `MUST_SUCCEED_POOL_EMPTY`. This is typically caused by a driver that has allocated this type of memory and not released it. Note that the driver that gets this error and crashes the system is not necessarily the driver that caused the problem; some other driver could be hoarding must-succeed memory.

This function can be called only if the thread is running at IRQL < `DISPATCH_LEVEL`. Note that this is more restrictive than `ExAllocatePool`.

If the function returns `NULL`, you can respond by returning the `NTSTATUS` value `STATUS_INSUFFICIENT_RESOURCES` or by delaying processing.

ExAllocatePoolWithQuotaTag

```
PVOID ExAllocatePoolWithQuotaTag(IN POOL_TYPE pooltype,
                                 IN ULONG NumberOfBytes,
                                 IN ULONG Tag);
```

Allocates a pool of memory according to the specified pool type. The pool types are shown in Table A.14 on page 879.

Each process has a quota setting a current maximum allowable Paged Pool and Nonpaged Pool use. These quotas are assigned dynamically and will automatically be increased, if possible, when an attempt to allocate from a pool would exceed its quota (taking into account the other active processes). Optionally these quotas may be set (for all processes) via the Registry. The Registry technique is seldom used.

The ExAllocatePoolWithQuotaTag and ExAllocatePoolWithQuota functions will charge the quota of the current process with the size of the allocation. Note that these routines must not be called in any context other than the context of the appropriate user mode process. Lower-level drivers should call the routines that do not charge quota, since they are running in an arbitrary context.

For all but the MustS(ucceed) variants, the call can return NULL if there is no memory to allocate. *You must always check the return value for these calls.* If NULL is returned, you will need to take whatever action is appropriate to your driver. The MustS(ucceed) variants guarantee that when the function returns, you *will* have a valid virtual memory address.

If the pool type is one of the MustS(ucceed) variants, the call will succeed if there is *any* available memory to allocate. Normally, memory is allocated from the general Nonpaged Pool, but there are a small number of pages held aside as a "must-succeed last-resort pool". Must-succeed allocations will allocate from this pool if there is no general nonpaged memory to allocate. Such allocations must be for amounts smaller than PAGE_SIZE. These variants should be used only when you are in a state in which you will be in such deep trouble if you can't get this memory allocated that you can respond only by crashing the system. Memory allocated in the must-succeed mode is a precious resource. It should be used only for transient purposes and be released as quickly as possible. This memory should not be retained for any significant length of time. This is because eventually, you could deplete the must-succeed pool and cause some other driver to crash the system. As a strategy, it is best to write your driver so that you don't depend on must-succeed memory.

If there is insufficient memory available to satisfy a MustS(ucceed) request, the system crashes. The BugCheck code is MUST_SUCCEED_POOL_EMPTY. This is typically caused by a driver that has allocated this type of memory and not released it. Note that the driver that gets this error and crashes the system is not necessarily the driver that caused the problem; some other driver could be hoarding must-succeed memory.

The *Tag* parameter is a string of up to four characters, expressed as a "character value", in reverse order. This tag will appear in any crash dumps or debugger output. Thus an area called "Temp" would have a tag value of 'pmeT'. Note that this value is in 8-bit characters, not Unicode.

This function can be called only if the thread is running at IRQL < DISPATCH_LEVEL. Note that this is more restrictive than ExAllocatePool.

If the function returns NULL, you can respond by returning the NTSTATUS value STATUS_INSUFFICIENT_RESOURCES or by delaying processing.

ExAllocatePoolWithTag

```
PVOID ExAllocatePoolWithTag(POOL_TYPE pooltype,
                            IN ULONG NumberOfBytes,
                            IN ULONG Tag);
```

Allocates a pool of memory according to the specified pool type. The pool types are shown in Table A.14 on page 879.

For all but the MustS(ucceed) variants, the call can return NULL if there is no memory to allocate. *You must always check the return value for these calls.* If NULL is returned, you will need to take whatever action is appropriate to your driver. The MustS(ucceed) variants guarantee that when the function returns, you *will* have a valid virtual memory address.

If the pool type is one of the MustS(ucceed) variants, the call will succeed if there is *any* available memory to allocate. Normally, memory is allocated from the general Nonpaged Pool, but there are a small number of pages held aside as a "must-succeed last-resort pool". Must-succeed allocations will allocate from this pool if there is no general nonpaged memory to allocate. Such allocations must be for amounts smaller than PAGE_SIZE. These variants should be used only when you are in a state in which you will be in such deep trouble if you can't get this memory allocated that you can respond only by crashing the system. Memory allocated in the must-succeed mode is a precious resource. It should be used only for transient purposes and be released as quickly as possible. This memory should not be retained for any significant length of time. This is because eventually, you could deplete the must-succeed pool and cause some other driver to crash the system. As a strategy, it is best to write your driver so that you don't depend on must-succeed memory.

If there is insufficient memory available to satisfy a MustS(ucceed) request, the system crashes. The BugCheck code is MUST_SUCCEED_POOL_EMPTY. This is typically caused by a driver that has allocated this type of memory and not released it. Note that the driver that gets this error and crashes the system is not necessarily the driver that caused the problem; some other driver could be hoarding must-succeed memory.

The *Tag* parameter is a string of up to four characters, expressed as a "character value", in reverse order. This tag will appear in any crash dumps or debugger output. Thus an area called "Temp" would have a tag value of 'pmeT'. Note that this value is in 8-bit characters, not Unicode.

This function can be called only if the thread is running at IRQL <= DISPATCH_LEVEL. If IRQL == DISPATCH_LEVEL, the pool type *must* be one of the NonPaged... options. If IRQL < DISPATCH_LEVEL, either paged or nonpaged memory can allocated.

If the function returns NULL, you can respond by returning the NTSTATUS value STATUS_INSUFFICIENT_RESOURCES or by delaying processing.

ExConvertExclusiveToSharedLite

VOID ExConvertExclusiveToSharedLite(IN PERESOURCE *Resource*);

Converts a given Executive Resource from acquired for exclusive access to acquired for shared access.

The *Resource* parameter points to the Executive Resource for which the access should be converted. The caller must have exclusive access to the given Executive Resource. During this conversion, the current thread and any other threads waiting for shared access to the Executive Resource are given shared access.

A thread that calls this function must be running at IRQL < DISPATCH_LEVEL.

ExDeleteNPagedLookasideList

VOID ExDeleteNPagedLookasideList(IN PNPAGED_LOOKASIDE_LIST *Lookaside*);

Deletes the lookaside list specified. Any blocks remaining on the lookaside list are deleted by using the supplied or default Free routine. The list header itself is not freed.

A thread that calls this function must be running at IRQL <= DISPATCH_LEVEL.

ExDeletePagedLookasideList

```
VOID ExDeletePagedLookasideList(IN PPAGED_LOOKASIDE_LIST Lookaside);
```

Deletes the lookaside list specified. Any blocks remaining on the lookaside list are deleted by using the supplied or default Free routine. The list header itself is not freed.

A thread that calls this function must be running at IRQL < DISPATCH_LEVEL.

ExDeleteResourceLite

```
NTSTATUS ExDeleteResourceLite(IN PERESOURCE Resource);
```

Deletes an Executive Resource from the system resource list.

This routine returns STATUS_SUCCESS if it completes successfully. It does not free the storage that had been allocated for the resource; you must explicitly delete the storage after a successful return.

A thread that calls this function must be running at IRQL < DISPATCH_LEVEL.

ExFreePool

```
VOID ExFreePool(IN PVOID pool);
```

Frees the pool that was allocated via one of the allocation functions.

The thread that calls this function must be at IRQL <= DISPATCH_LEVEL. If IRQL == DISPATCH_LEVEL, the memory must have been allocated with one of the NonPaged... options. Otherwise, the function can be called only if IRQL < DISPATCH_LEVEL. Once the memory is freed, it must not be accessed again.

ExFreeToNPagedLookasideList

```
VOID ExFreeToNPagedLookasideList(IN PNPAGED_LOOKASIDE_LIST Lookaside,
                                 IN PVOID Entry);
```

Returns an entry in nonpaged memory to the specified lookaside list. If the list has reached its maximum size, the entry is returned to the Nonpaged Pool.

A thread that calls this function must be running at IRQL <= DISPATCH_LEVEL.

ExFreeToPagedLookasideList

```
VOID ExFreeToPagedLookasideList(IN PNPAGED_LOOKASIDE_LIST Lookaside,
                                IN PVOID Entry);
```

Returns an entry to the specified lookaside list in paged memory. If the list has reached its maximum size, the entry is returned to the Paged Pool.

A thread that calls this function must be running at IRQL < DISPATCH_LEVEL.

ExGetCurrentResourceThread

`ERESOURCE_THREAD ExGetCurrentResourceThread( );`

Returns the Executive Resource thread required as a parameter to `ExReleaseResourceForThreadLite`.

A thread that calls this function must be running at IRQL <= DISPATCH_LEVEL.

ExInitializeFastMutex

`VOID ExInitializeFastMutex(IN PFAST_MUTEX FastMutex);`

Initializes a Fast Mutex variable. It is used to synchronize mutually exclusive access to a shared resource by a set of threads.

The `FastMutex` parameter points to the caller-supplied storage, which must be at least `sizeof(FAST_MUTEX)`, for the Fast Mutex variable being initialized. Typically this is allocated in an extension object, such as a Device Extension or Controller Extension. It must be in the Nonpaged Pool.

This function must be called before any calls to other `Ex...FastMutex` routines occur.

Although the caller supplies the storage for the given Fast Mutex, the FAST_MUTEX structure is "opaque". That is, its members are reserved for system use.

For better performance, use the `Ex...FastMutex` routines instead of the `Ke...Mutex` routines. However, a Fast Mutex cannot be acquired recursively, as a kernel Mutex can.

A thread that calls this function must be running at IRQL <= DISPATCH_LEVEL.

ExInitializeNPagedLookasideList

```
VOID ExInitializeNPagedLookasideList(
                        IN PNPAGED_LOOKASIDE_LIST Lookaside,
                        IN PALLOCATE_FUNCTION Allocate OPTIONAL,
                        IN PFREE_FUNCTION Free OPTIONAL,
                        IN ULONG Flags,
                        IN ULONG Size,
                        IN ULONG Tag,
                        IN USHORT Depth);
```

Initializes a lookaside list for storage in the Nonpaged Pool.

The `Lookaside` parameter references a block of storage in nonpaged memory that has been allocated or assigned and is of type NPAGED_LOOKASIDE_LIST. The `Allocate` parameter and `Free` parameter are pointers to user-supplied allocation or free routines. If these routines are not used, you can specify NULL as the value for these parameters. If the `Allocate` parameter is NULL, allocation is done using `ExAllocatePoolWithTag`; if the `Free` parameter is NULL, the deallocation is done using `ExFreePool`.

The `Flags` value can be 0 or POOL_RAISE_IF_ALLOCATION_FAILURE, which will cause the allocation to raise an exception. The `Size` parameter specifies the size of objects in the lookaside list, in bytes.

The `Tag` parameter supplies a four-character ASCII tag, given as a single-quoted string of four characters in reverse order. For example, the name "Temp" would be supplied as `'pmeT'`.

The *Depth* parameter specifies the maximum number of free blocks that will be maintained in the lookaside list.

This function initializes the list header, including the Spin Lock, but does not actually allocate any storage. Storage is allocated "on demand" as needed. As blocks are freed, they are added to the lookaside list until there are at most *Depth* free blocks on the list. Allocations are preferentially taken from the lookaside list instead of from the general pool.

A thread that calls this function must be running at IRQL <= DISPATCH_LEVEL.

ExInitializePagedLookasideList

```
VOID ExInitializePagedLookasideList(
                    IN PPAGED_LOOKASIDE_LIST Lookaside,
                    IN PALLOCATE_FUNCTION Allocate OPTIONAL,
                    IN PFREE_FUNCTION Free OPTIONAL,
                    IN ULONG Flags,
                    IN ULONG Size,
                    IN ULONG Tag,
                    IN USHORT Depth);
```

Initializes a lookaside list for storage in the Paged Pool.

The *Lookaside* parameter references a block of storage in nonpaged memory (yes, nonpaged memory, even for a paged lookaside list, because the header contains a Spin Lock) that has been allocated or assigned and is of type PAGED_LOOKASIDE_LIST. The *Allocate* parameter and *Free* parameter are pointers to user-supplied allocation or free routines. If these routines are not used, you can specify NULL as the value for these parameters. If the *Allocate* parameter is NULL, allocation is done using ExAllocatePoolWithTag; if the *Free* parameter is NULL, the deallocation is done using ExFreePool.

The *Flags* value can be 0 or POOL_RAISE_IF_ALLOCATION_FAILURE, which will cause the allocation to raise an exception. The *Size* parameter specifies the size of objects in the lookaside list, in bytes.

The *Tag* parameter supplies a four-character ASCII tag, given as a single-quoted string of four characters in reverse order. For example, the name "Temp" would be supplied as 'pmeT'.

The *Depth* parameter specifies the maximum number of free blocks that will be maintained in the lookaside list.

This function initializes the list header, including the Spin Lock, but does not actually allocate any storage. Storage is allocated "on demand" as needed. As blocks are freed, they are added to the lookaside list until there are at most *Depth* free blocks on the list. Allocations are preferentially taken from the lookaside list instead of from the general pool.

A thread that calls this function must be running at IRQL < DISPATCH_LEVEL.

ExInitializeResourceLite

```
NTSTATUS ExInitializeResourceLite(IN PERESOURCE Resource);
```

Initializes an Executive Resource that is allocated in nonpaged memory.

The storage must be at least sizeof(ERESOURCE). This routine returns STATUS_SUCCESS.

A thread that calls this function must be running at IRQL <= DISPATCH_LEVEL.

ExInitializeWorkItem

```
VOID ExInitializeWorkItem(IN PWORK_QUEUE_ITEM Item,
                          IN PWORKER_THREAD_ROUTINE Routine,
                          IN PVOID Context);
```

Initializes the data structure that is the WORK_QUEUE_ITEM.

This is an "opaque" data structure that must be allocated out of nonpaged memory. The *Routine* parameter points to a function that has the prototype

```
VOID (*PWORKER_THREAD_ROUTINE)(IN PVOID Parameter);
```

Note that only one parameter is passed in. This is typically a pointer to DEVICE_OBJECT, since otherwise, DEVICE_OBJECT would be inaccessible in the thread routine. Alternatively, the parameter could be a pointer to a structure that contains a DEVICE_OBJECT pointer.

A thread that calls this function must be running at IRQL <= DISPATCH_LEVEL.

ExInterlockedInsertHeadList

```
PLIST_ENTRY ExInterlockedInsertHeadList(IN PLIST_ENTRY ListHead,
                                        IN PLIST_ENTRY ListEntry,
                                        IN PKSPIN_LOCK Lock);
```

Inserts the specified *ListEntry* into the list specified by *ListHead*, using *Lock* to provide multiprocessor-safe synchronization.

If all threads that manipulate the list use *only* ExInterlocked..List routines to do so, then these routines can be called from a single IRQL <= DIRQL. If other driver routines access the list using any other routines, such as the noninterlocked InsertHeadList, then callers of ExInterlockedInsertHeadList must be at IRQL <= DISPATCH_LEVEL.

ExInterlockedInsertTailList

```
PLIST_ENTRY ExInterlockedInsertTailList(IN PLIST_ENTRY ListHead,
                                        IN PLIST_ENTRY ListEntry,
                                        IN PKSPIN_LOCK Lock);
```

Inserts the specified *ListEntry* into the list specified by *ListHead*, using *Lock* to provide multiprocessor-safe synchronization.

If all threads that manipulate the list use *only* ExInterlocked..List routines to do so, then these routines can be called from a single IRQL <= DIRQL. If other driver routines access the list using any other routines, such as the noninterlocked InsertHeadList, then callers of ExInterlockedInsertTailList must be at IRQL <= DISPATCH_LEVEL.

ExInterlockedRemoveHeadList

```
PLIST_ENTRY ExInterlockedRemoveHeadList(IN PLIST_ENTRY ListHead,
                                        IN PKSPIN_LOCK Lock);
```

Removes a LIST_ENTRY from the head of the list specified by *ListHead*, using *Lock* to provide multiprocessor-safe synchronization.

If all threads that manipulate the list use *only* `ExInterlocked..List` routines to do so, then these routines can be called from a single IRQL <= DIRQL. If other driver routines access the list using any other routines, such as the noninterlocked `InsertHeadList`, then callers of `ExInterlockedRemoveHeadList` must be at IRQL <= DISPATCH_LEVEL.

ExIsResourceAcquiredExclusiveLite

`BOOLEAN ExIsResourceAcquiredExclusiveLite(IN PERESOURCE Resource);`

Returns TRUE if the thread already has exclusive access to the specified *Resource*. A thread that calls this function must be running at IRQL <= DISPATCH_LEVEL.

ExIsResourceAcquiredSharedLite

`USHORT ExIsResourceAcquiredSharedLite(IN PERESOURCE Resource);`

Returns a count of the number of times the thread already has acquired shared access to the specified *Resource*.
A thread that calls this function must be running at IRQL <= DISPATCH_LEVEL.

ExQueueWorkItem

```
VOID ExQueueWorkItem(IN PWORK_QUEUE_ITEM WorkItem,
                     IN WORK_QUEUE_TYPE QueueType);
```

Enqueues a WorkItem for a System Worker Thread.
The *WorkItem* parameter is the `WORK_QUEUE_ITEM`, which must be allocated from the Non-paged Pool and which has been initialized with `ExInitializeWorkItem`. The *QueueType* can be one of `CriticalWorkQueue`, `DelayedWorkQueue`, or `HyperCriticalWorkQueue`. A thread used for `CriticalWorkQueue` will run the WorkItem in a system thread with a real-time priority. A thread used for `DelayedWorkQueue` will run the WorkItem in a system thread with a variable priority. The hypercritical queue, documented only in the Installable File System (IFS) sources, is used for high-priority WorkItems that never block. The hypercritical WorkItem must not wait for any object.
A thread that calls this function must be running at IRQL <= DISPATCH_LEVEL.

ExReleaseFastMutex

`VOID ExReleaseFastMutex(IN PFAST_MUTEX FastMutex);`

Releases ownership of a Fast Mutex that was acquired with `ExAcquireFastMutex` or `ExTryToAcquireFastMutex`. It is *not* used to release a Fast Mutex Object acquired with `ExAcquireFastMutexUnsafe`.
The *FastMutex* parameter points to the Fast Mutex to be released. This routine releases ownership of the given Fast Mutex and reenables the delivery of APCs to the current thread.
It is a programming error to call `ExReleaseFastMutex` with a Fast Mutex that was acquired with `ExAcquireFastMutexUnsafe`.
Callers of `ExReleaseFastMutex` must be running at IRQL < DISPATCH_LEVEL.

ExReleaseFastMutexUnsafe

VOID ExReleaseFastMutexUnsafe(IN PFAST_MUTEX *FastMutex*);

Releases ownership of a Fast Mutex that was acquired with ExAcquireFastMutexUnsafe. The *FastMutex* parameter points to the Fast Mutex to be released.

It is a programming error to call ExReleaseFastMutexUnsafe with a Fast Mutex that was acquired with ExAcquireFastMutex or ExTryToAcquireFastMutex.

A thread that calls this function must be running at IRQL < DISPATCH_LEVEL.

ExReleaseResourceForThreadLite

VOID ExReleaseResourceForThreadLite(IN PERESOURCE *Resource*,
                                    IN ERESOURCE_THREAD *ResourceThreadId*);

Releases the specified Executive Resource.

The *Resource* parameter indicates which resource is to be released. The *ResourceThreadId* parameter is the thread ID of the thread that originally acquired the resource.

A thread that calls this function must be running at IRQL <= DISPATCH_LEVEL.

ExTryToAcquireFastMutex

BOOLEAN ExTryToAcquireFastMutex(IN PFAST_MUTEX *FastMutex*);

Tries to acquire the given Fast Mutex, if possible.

If the Fast Mutex is acquired, APCs to the current thread are disabled and this function returns TRUE. If the Fast Mutex cannot be acquired, it returns FALSE but does not put the calling thread into a wait.

The *FastMutex* parameter points to the Fast Mutex to be acquired if it is not currently owned by another thread.

Use ExAcquireFastMutex if the current thread must wait on the acquisition of the given Fast Mutex before it can do useful work.

Any Fast Mutex acquired with ExTryToAcquireFastMutex or ExAcquireFastMutex must be released with ExReleaseFastMutex.

A thread that calls this function must be running at IRQL < DISPATCH_LEVEL.

ExTryToAcquireResourceExclusiveLite

BOOLEAN ExTryToAcquireResourceExclusiveLite(IN PERESOURCE *Resource*);

Attempts to acquire the specified resource for exclusive access.

This routine returns TRUE if the resource has been successfully acquired. It will not wait if the resource cannot be acquired but will return FALSE immediately.

A thread that calls this function must be running at IRQL < DISPATCH_LEVEL.

HalAllocateCommonBuffer

```
PVOID HalAllocateCommonBuffer(IN PADAPTER_OBJECT AdapterObject,
                              IN ULONG Length,
                              OUT PPHYSICAL_ADDRESS LogicalAddress,
                              IN BOOLEAN CacheEnabled);
```

Allocates memory and maps it so that it is simultaneously accessible from both the processor and a device for DMA operations. This memory appears contiguous to the device.

The *AdapterObject* parameter points to the Adapter Object representing the bus mastering adapter or DMA controller channel. This pointer was returned by calling HalGetAdapter. The *Length* parameter specifies the number of bytes to allocate. The *LogicalAddress* parameter points to a variable that receives the logical address that the device can use to access the allocated buffer. You should use this address rather than calling MmGetPhysicalAddress because the HAL can take into account any platform-specific memory restrictions. The *CacheEnabled* parameter specifies whether the allocated memory can be cached. This function returns the base virtual address of the allocated range. If the buffer cannot be allocated, it returns NULL.

This function is used to support DMA in which the device and the processor are continuously communicating through system memory, as in a control structure for a Bus Master DMA device. It can also be used to support slave devices whose drivers use a system DMA controller's "autoinitialize" mode.

HalAllocateCommonBuffer allocates mapping registers to map the buffer, if required by the system, and sets up a translation for the device, including loading mapping registers if necessary.

To use resident system memory economically, drivers should allocate as few of these buffers per device as possible. This function allocates at least a page of memory, whatever the requested *Length*. For successful allocations that request less than PAGE_SIZE, only the given *Length* can be accessed by the caller. For successful allocations requesting more than an integral multiple of PAGE_SIZE, any remaining bytes on the last allocated page are inaccessible to the caller.

If a driver needs several pages of common buffer space, but the pages need not be contiguous, the driver should make several one-page requests to HalAllocateCommonBuffer rather than one large request. This approach conserves contiguous memory.

Drivers typically call HalAllocateCommonBuffer during driver initialization. After initialization, it is possible that only one-page requests will succeed, if any. As far as we can tell, the assumption is that the driver is loaded early in the boot sequence. A demand-start driver might not be able to allocate any storage larger than a one-page request due to fragmentation of the Nonpaged Pool.

A thread that calls this function is typically running at IRQL PASSIVE_LEVEL. When called from this level, HalAllocateCommonBuffer makes several attempts to locate the requested memory.

A thread that calls this function can also be running at IRQL == DISPATCH_LEVEL. However, less effort is made to locate a block suitable for satisfying the requested memory, and it is possible that only one-page requests will succeed. It is also possible that when HalAllocateCommonBuffer is called from DISPATCH_LEVEL, any allocation request will fail.

HalAssignSlotResources

```
NTSTATUS HalAssignSlotResources(
                IN PUNICODE_STRING RegistryPath,
                IN PUNICODE_STRING DriverClassName,
                IN PDRIVER_OBJECT DriverObject,
                IN PDEVICE_OBJECT DeviceObject,
                IN INTERFACE_TYPE BusType,
                IN ULONG BusNumber,
                IN ULONG SlotNumber,
                IN OUT PCM_RESOURCE_LIST * AllocatedResources);
```

For drivers of devices connected to dynamically configurable I/O buses of a type with a published standard interface, HalAssignSlotResources determines the resource requirements of the target device, calls IoAssignResources to allocate them, sets the target device with its assigned resources, and returns the assignments to the caller.

A driver cannot call this routine unless its device(s) are connected to a dynamically configurable I/O bus of a type that has a defined, publicly documented, industry-standard interface. Drivers of devices that do not meet this condition can instead call IoAssignResources or IoReportResourceUsage.

The driver should save pertinent values from the AllocatedResources list so that it can pass the appropriate values in calls to other configuration routines, such as HalGetInterrupt and HalGetAdapter. The caller is responsible for releasing the AllocatedResources buffer by using ExFreePool.

A thread that calls this function must be running at IRQL == PASSIVE_LEVEL.

HalFreeCommonBuffer

```
VOID HalFreeCommonBuffer(IN PADAPTER_OBJECT AdapterObject,
                IN ULONG Length,
                IN PHYSICAL_ADDRESS LogicalAddress,
                IN PVOID VirtualAddress,
                IN BOOLEAN CacheEnabled);
```

Frees a buffer allocated by HalAllocateCommonBuffer.

The VirtualAddress and LogicalAddress values must be the values that were returned from HalAllocateCommonBuffer. The AdapterObject, Length, and CacheEnabled values must be the same values that were passed to HalAllocateCommonBuffer.

A thread that calls this function must be running at IRQL <= DISPATCH_LEVEL. It is normally called at PASSIVE_LEVEL in the Unload routine.

HalGetAdapter

```
PADAPTER_OBJECT HalGetAdapter(IN PDEVICE_DESCRIPTION DeviceDescription,
                IN OUT PULONG NumberOfMapRegisters);
```

Returns a pointer to the adapter object for the DMA device defined in the device description structure. The caller should fill in values for all members of the device description structure that are pertinent to its device. All other members must be set to 0 before calling HalGetAdapter.

A successful caller must save the returned Adapter Object pointer in resident memory because this pointer is a required parameter to the DMA support routines. Usually, Device Drivers save this pointer in their Device Extensions.

This routine returns the maximum number of Mapping Registers that the Device Driver can allocate for any DMA transfer operation. The MaximumLength specified in the *DeviceDescription* parameter effectively constrains the input value to no more than (MaximumLength / PAGE_SIZE + 1), a value readily computed by the ADDRESS_AND_SIZE_TO_SPAN_PAGES macro. On return, the updated value of this parameter can be less than the maximum possible input value that was requested. The returned value must be stored somewhere for later use. Note that if a particular DMA transfer requires more Mapping Registers than the returned value, the transfer will have to be broken up into a number of smaller transfers that fit within the available set of Mapping Registers and those transfers must be done piecewise.

HalGetAdapter must be called only during initialization when the thread is running at IRQL == PASSIVE_LEVEL.

HalGetBusData

```
ULONG HalGetBusData(IN BUS_DATA_TYPE BusDataType,
                    IN ULONG BusNumber,
                    IN ULONG SlotNumber,
                    IN PVOID Buffer,
                    IN ULONG Length);
```

Device Drivers call HalGetBusData during initialization to locate their devices on a particular I/O bus in the machine. The bus-type-specific configuration data returned is later used in calls to other configuration and initialization routines, such as HalTranslateBusAddress, HalGetInterrupt, HalGetAdapter, IoAssignResources, and so on.

Calling HalGetBusData with any *BusDataType* except Cmos is the same as calling HalGetBusDataByOffset with an input *Offset* of 0.

If the input *BusDataType* is PCIConfiguration, the thread that calls HalGetBusData can be running at IRQL <= DISPATCH_LEVEL. Otherwise, the thread that calls HalGetBusData must be running at IRQL == PASSIVE_LEVEL.

HalGetBusDataByOffset

```
ULONG HalGetBusDataByOffset(IN BUS_DATA_TYPE BusDataType,
                            IN ULONG BusNumber,
                            IN ULONG SlotNumber,
                            IN PVOID Buffer,
                            IN ULONG Offset,
                            IN ULONG Length);
```

Device Drivers call HalGetBusDataByOffset during initialization to locate their devices on a particular I/O bus in the machine. The bus-type-specific configuration data returned is later used in calls to other configuration and initialization routines, such as HalTranslateBusAddress, HalGetInterrupt, HalGetAdapter, IoAssignResources, and so on.

Calling `HalGetBusDataByOffset` with an input offset of 0 and any *BusDataType* except `Cmos` is the same as calling `HalGetBusData`.

When accessing the device-specific area of the PCI configuration space, `HalGetBusDataByOffset` guarantees the following.

- This routine never reads or writes data outside the range specified by the inputs *Offset* and *Length*.
- Even if the input *Length* is exactly 1 byte or a (2-byte) word, this routine never accesses any data outside the requested range.

If the input *BusDataType* is `PCIConfiguration`, the thread that calls `HalGetBusData` can be running at IRQL <= DISPATCH_LEVEL. Otherwise, the thread that calls `HalGetBusData` must be running at IRQL == PASSIVE_LEVEL.

HalGetInterruptVector

```
ULONG HalGetInterruptVector(IN INTERFACE_TYPE InterfaceType,
                            IN ULONG    BusNumber,
                            IN ULONG    BusInterruptLevel,
                            IN ULONG    BusInterruptVector,
                            OUT PKIRQL Irql,
                            OUT PKAFFINITY Affinity);
```

Returns the system-assigned interrupt vector, system-assigned DIRQL, and processor affinity for the corresponding bus-relative interrupt level and/or vector of the device.

Callers can obtain the input values for these parameters with `HalGetBusData`, `HalGetBusDataByOffset`, `IoQueryDeviceDescription`, `IoAssignResources`, or `HalAssignSlotResources` by querying the device or by using default values if they cannot get hardware configuration information by other means.

Each bit set in the returned processor affinity mask indicates a processor to which the interrupt can be dispatched.

A Device Driver calls `IoConnectInterrupt` to initialize and connect an Interrupt Object and to register its ISR. This call includes parameters for the mapped vector, *Irql*, and for *Affinity*, both of which are obtained from `HalGetInterruptVector`. The call also includes the address of the ISR and additional interrupt information. The mapped system vector, *Irql*, and *Affinity* values that `HalGetInterruptVector` returns must be passed, unchanged, to `IoConnectInterrupt`.

This function is of little interest to USB Class Driver writers or USB MiniDriver writers, since this task is handled by the underlying USB support.

The thread that calls `HalGetInterruptVector` must be running at IRQL == PASSIVE_LEVEL.

HalSetBusData

```
ULONG HalSetBusData(IN BUS_DATA_TYPE BusDataType,
                    IN ULONG BusNumber,
                    IN ULONG SlotNumber,
                    IN PVOID Buffer,
                    IN ULONG Length);
```

Calling `HalSetBusData` is the same as calling `HalSetBusDataByOffset` with a *BusDataType* of `PCIConfiguration` and an input *Offset* of 0.

If the input *BusDataType* is `PCIConfiguration`, the thread that calls `HalSetBusData` can be running at IRQL <= DISPATCH_LEVEL. Otherwise, the thread that calls `HalSetBusData` must be running at IRQL == PASSIVE_LEVEL.

HalSetBusDataByOffset

```
ULONG HalSetBusDataByOffset(IN  BUS_DATA_TYPE BusDataType,
                            IN  ULONG BusNumber,
                            IN  ULONG SlotNumber,
                            IN  PVOID Buffer,
                            IN  ULONG Length);
```

Calling `HalSetBusDataByOffset` with a *BusDataType* of `PCIConfiguration` and an input *Offset* of 0 is the same as calling `HalSetBusData`.

If the input *BusDataType* is `PCIConfiguration`, the thread that calls `HalSetBusDataByOffset` can be running at IRQL <= DISPATCH_LEVEL. Otherwise, the thread that calls `HalSetBusDataByOffset` must be running at IRQL == PASSIVE_LEVEL.

HalTranslateBusAddress

```
BOOLEAN HalTranslateBusAddress(IN  INTERFACE_TYPE InterfaceType,
                               IN  ULONG BusNumber,
                               IN  PHYSICAL_ADDRESS BusAddress,
                               IN  OUT PULONG AddressSpace,
                               OUT PPHYSICAL_ADDRESS TranslatedAddress);
```

Translates a bus-specific address into the corresponding system logical address. If the *AddressSpace* value of 0 is returned, the value returned for the *TranslatedAddress* parameter must be used in a subsequent call to `MmMapIoSpace`. The translated address is a physical address.

There are many ways to connect a peripheral bus into a system. The memory address space of the bus, referred to as the logical address space, can be directly merged with the physical address space of the host, or some mapping might be involved. Also, some machines can have more than one bus, or a bus can have more than one address space, that is, they have separate memory and I/O addresses.

A Device Driver calls `HalTranslateBusAddress` to perform this translation. The parameters to this routine include a bus number to support platforms with more than one bus of the same *InterfaceType*, the bus address to be translated, and an *AddressSpace* specifier typically used to differentiate between memory and I/O space, if these are separate, *as far as the device itself is concerned*. The driver might obtain these parameters from the Registry either by calling `HalGetBusData` or `HalGetBusDataByOffset` and interrogating the device hardware, or by calling `IoAssignResources` or `HalAssignSlotResources`, or by using defaults and claiming them in the Registry.

This function called with the value referenced by *AddressSpace* set to 1 (I/O space) can return with that value set to 0, meaning the HAL has translated the address from I/O space to memory space. In this case, *TranslatedAddress* must be translated from a physical address to a system logical address by using `MmMapIoSpace`. However, this value must *still* be used with the PORT forms of the macros (for example, READ_PORT_UCHAR), not the REGISTER forms (for example, READ_REGISTER_UCHAR). If *AddressSpace* is 1 upon return from this call, the .LowPart of *TranslatedAddress* is the value to be used with the PORT macros.

A thread that calls this function must be running at IRQL <= DISPATCH_LEVEL. Usually, the thread is running at IRQL == PASSIVE_LEVEL because this routine is seldom called except when a driver is initializing.

HKEY_LOCAL_MACHINE

The HKEY_LOCAL_MACHINE Registry base contains a large number of entries of interest to the Device Driver writer. We list many of them here.

> \System\CurrentControlSet\Services*drivername*\DependOnGroup

This key indicates the order in which a driver is started. It can be one of the group names found in the ServiceGroupOrder entry.

> \System\CurrentControlSet\Services*drivername*\DependOnService

This key indicates the order in which a driver is started. It can be one of the service names found in the Registry.

> \System\CurrentControlSet\Services*drivername*\DisplayName

This key provides the name that is used to display the driver in the driver display list of the Control Panel. If this key is omitted, the name of the driver is used.

> \System\CurrentControlSet\Services*drivername*\ErrorControl

This key indicates the way in which a driver is started. It can be one of the values given in Table A.15.

> \System\CurrentControlSet\Services*drivername*\ImagePath

This key indicates the path that is used to find the Device Driver. If this key is not specified, the following path is used:

```
%system%\Drivers\drivername.sys
```

> \System\CurrentControlSet\Services*drivername*\Parameters

This key may be used to hold any driver-specific parameters. You can store under this key any persistent state, user-configurable state, or anything else you want. It is up to you to define what the subkeys, their types, and their values are and what effects they have in parameterizing your driver. You may then use the Registry functions such as ZwQueryKey to obtain these values.

`\System\CurrentControlSet\Services\`*`drivername`*`\Start`

This key indicates the way in which a driver is started. It can be one of the values shown in Table A.16.

Table A.15: `\System\CurrentControlSet\Services\`*`drivername`*`\ErrorControl` *Values*

Value		Meaning
Symbolic	**Numeric**	
SERVICE_ERROR_IGNORE	0x00000000	Any driver load errors are ignored. No notification is given, and nothing is logged.
SERVICE_ERROR_NORMAL	0x00000001	If a driver has a load error, the error is logged in the Event Log, but the boot operation continues.
SERVICE_ERROR_SEVERE	0x00000002	Logs the error. If the boot is coming from the "last known good" configuration, then the boot operation continues. If the boot is not coming from the "last known good" configuration, the system is restarted using the "Last Known Good" configuration.
SERVICE_ERROR_CRITICAL	0x00000003	Logs the error. If the boot is coming from the "last known good" configuration, then the boot operation fails. If the boot is not coming from the "Last Known Good" configuration, the system is restarted using the "last known good" configuration.

Table A.16: `\System\CurrentControlSet\Services\`*`drivername`*`\Start` *Values*

Value		Meaning
Symbolic	**Numeric**	
SERVICE_BOOT_START	0x00000000	The Device Driver is started by the NTLDR component.
SERVICE_SYSTEM_START	0x00000001	The Device Driver is started as part of the essential, or "core", set of drivers.
SERVICE_AUTO_START	0x00000002	The Device Driver will be started by the SCM.
SERVICE_DEMAND_START	0x00000003	The Device Driver is started "manually" (that is, on explicit user request or via the equivalent SCM).
SERVICE_DISABLED	0x00000004	The device will not be started.

`\System\CurrentControlSet\Services\`*`drivername`*`\Tag`

This key indicates the order in which a driver is started within its group. The exact values that are permitted here depend on the values valid for the group and are found as an array of DWORD values stored in the `GroupOrderList`. This is stored under the key

`HKEY_LOCAL_MACHINE\System\CurrentControlSet\Control\GroupOrderList`

`\System\CurrentControlSet\Services\`*`drivername`*`\Type`

This key indicates the way in which a driver is started. It can be one of the values shown in Table A.17.

Table A.17: `\System\CurrentControlSet\Services\`*`drivername`*`\Type` *Values*

Symbolic	Numeric	Condition
SERVICE_KERNEL_DRIVER	0x00000001	The driver is a kernel Device Driver.
SERVICE_FILE_SYSTEM_DRIVER	0x00000002	The driver is a File System Driver. We do not discuss File System Drivers in this book.
SERVICE_ADAPTER	0x00000004	The driver is an Adapter driver.
SERVICE_RECOGNIZER_DRIVER	0x00000008	The driver is a Recognizer driver.

InitializeListHead

`VOID InitializeListHead(IN PLIST_ENTRY `*`ListHead`*`);`

Initializes any doubly linked, driver-managed interlocked queue or driver-maintained, doubly linked list.

The *`ListHead`* parameter points to the driver-allocated storage for the head of the interlocked queue or list. For an interlocked queue, the storage must be resident and the driver also must provide storage for a Spin Lock.

The *`ListHead`* of type LIST_ENTRY is doubly linked. Entries in an interlocked queue can be queued and dequeued by calling `ExInterlockedInsert..List` and `ExInterlockedRemoveHeadList`. Entries can be inserted into and removed from a driver-maintained list with `Insert..List` and `Remove..List`.

For an interlocked queue, a driver must provide resident storage either in the Device Extension of a driver-created Device Object, in the Controller Extension of a driver-created Controller Object, or in a Nonpaged Pool allocated by the driver. The driver also must provide storage for a Spin Lock. This Spin Lock must be initialized with `KeInitializeSpinLock` before the driver's initial call to `ExInterlockedXxx` with the Spin Lock.

For a driver-maintained list, the driver must synchronize access to the list so that in SMP machines it is impossible for any two routines to be inserting and/or removing entries from the list simultaneously. Consequently, most drivers use the ExInterlocked*Xxx* routines to manage the necessary synchronization, rather than setting up a driver-managed list, which also is likely to require Spin Lock protection.

A thread that calls this function must be running at IRQL == PASSIVE_LEVEL.

InitializeObjectAttributes

```
VOID InitializeObjectAttributes(
                    OUT POBJECT_ATTRIBUTES InitializedAttributes,
                    IN PUNICODE_STRING ObjectName,
                    IN ULONG Attributes,
                    IN HANDLE RootDirectory,
                    IN PSECURITY_DESCRIPTOR SecurityDescriptor);
```

Initializes the OBJECT_ATTRIBUTES structure that is used by the ZwOpen . . . and ZwCreate . . . functions.

Note that the string passed in for the *ObjectName* parameter *must* be a UNICODE_STRING string, for example,

```
L"\Device\PhysicalMemory"
L"\Registry\MyFunkyDevice"
```

The RtlInitUnicodeString function can be used to convert a literal string to a UNICODE_STRING.

A thread that calls this function must be running at IRQL == PASSIVE_LEVEL.

InsertHeadList

```
VOID InsertHeadList(IN PLIST_ENTRY ListHead, IN PLIST_ENTRY Entry);
```

Inserts an entry at the head of a doubly linked, driver-managed list.

The *ListHead* parameter references the head of the list, and the *Entry* parameter references the item to be added to the list.

A thread that calls this function can be running at IRQL >= DISPATCH_LEVEL only if the caller-allocated storage for *ListHead* is resident and only if pointers to every list entry remain valid at IRQL >= DISPATCH_LEVEL as well.

InsertTailList

```
VOID InsertTailList(IN PLIST_ENTRY ListHead, IN PLIST_ENTRY Entry);
```

Inserts an entry at the end of a doubly linked, driver-managed list.

The *ListHead* parameter references the head of the list, and the *Entry* parameter references the item to be added to the list.

A thread that calls this function can be running at IRQL >= DISPATCH_LEVEL only if the caller-allocated storage for *ListHead* is resident and only if pointers to every list entry remain valid at IRQL >= DISPATCH_LEVEL as well.

INTERFACE_TYPE

```
typedef enum _INTERFACE_TYPE {
    InterfaceTypeUndefined = -1,
    Internal,
    Isa,
    Eisa,
    MicroChannel,
    TurboChannel,
    PCIBus,
    VMEBus,
    NuBus,
    PCMCIABus,
    CBus,
    MPIBus,
    MPSABus,
    ProcessorInternal,
    InternalPowerBus,
    PNPISABus,
    MaximumInterfaceType
}INTERFACE_TYPE, * PINTERFACE_TYPE;
```

INTERFACE_TYPE specifies the interface type required in various calls, such as HalGetInterruptVector.

InterlockedDecrement

LONG InterlockedDecrement(PLONG *Addend*)

Subtracts 1 from the value referenced by the *Addend* parameter.

Returns the decremented value. This subtraction is multiprocessor-safe with respect to other Interlocked... operations.

A thread that calls this function can be running at any IRQL.

InterlockedExchange

LONG InterlockedExchange(IN OUT PLONG *Target*, IN LONG *Value*);

Sets the specified *Target* value to the specified *Value* and returns the previous value. This operation is multiprocessor-safe with respect to other Interlocked... operations.

A thread that calls this function can be running at any IRQL.

InterlockedExchangeAdd

LONG InterlockedExchangeAdd(IN OUT PLONG *Target*, IN LONG *Delta*);

Adds the specified value *Delta* to the specified *Target* and returns the previous value. This operation is multiprocessor-safe with respect to other Interlocked... operations.

A thread that calls this function can be running at any IRQL.

InterlockedIncrement

LONG InterlockedIncrement(PLONG *Addend*)

Adds 1 to the value referenced by the *Addend* parameter.

This function returns the incremented value. This addition is multiprocessor-safe with respect to other `Interlocked...` operations.

A thread that calls this function can be running at any IRQL.

IoAcquireCancelSpinLock

VOID IoAcquireCancelSpinLock(OUT PKIRQL *Irql*);

Synchronizes cancelable-state transitions for IRPs in a multiprocessor-safe way.

The *Irql* parameter points to a variable in which to save the current IRQL for a subsequent call to `IoReleaseCancelSpinLock`. Usually, *Irql* is saved on the stack as a local variable.

A driver that uses the I/O-Manager-supplied Device Queues in the Device Object must be holding the Cancel Spin Lock whenever it changes the cancelable state of an IRP with `IoSetCancelRoutine`.

A driver that manages its own queue(s) of IRPs does not need to hold the Cancel Spin Lock when calling `IoSetCancelRoutine`.

The holder of the Cancel Spin Lock should release it promptly by calling `IoReleaseCancelSpinLock`.

A driver-supplied Cancel Routine is called with the Cancel Spin Lock held. It must release the Cancel Spin Lock when it has completed the IRP to be canceled.

A thread that calls this function must be running at IRQL <= DISPATCH_LEVEL.

IoAllocateAdapterChannel

```
NTSTATUS IoAllocateAdapterChannel(IN PADAPTER_OBJECT AdapterObject,
                                  IN PDEVICE_OBJECT DeviceObject,
                                  IN ULONG NumberOfMapRegisters,
                                  IN PDRIVER_CONTROL ExecutionRoutine,
                                  IN PVOID Context);
```

Synchronizes the use of an Adapter controller using its Adapter Object.

This routine takes a pointer to the *AdapterObject* whose use is being controlled and its corresponding *DeviceObject* and *NumberOfMapRegisters*. The *ExecutionRoutine* is queued up in the *AdapterObject* for later execution. When the Adapter Object comes available, the *ExecutionRoutine* is dequeued and is executed. It is then passed the specified *Context* pointer. The Adapter Object remains allocated until `IoFreeAdapterChannel` is called.

A thread that calls this function must be running at IRQL == DISPATCH_LEVEL.

IoAllocateController

```
VOID IoAllocateController(IN PCONTROLLER_OBJECT ControllerObject,
                          IN PDEVICE_OBJECT DeviceObject,
                          IN PDRIVER_CONTROL ExecutionRoutine,
                          IN PVOID Context);
```

Synchronizes execution between any number of drivers sharing a Controller Object.

The parameters include the *ControllerObject* and the *DeviceObject*. The *ExecutionRoutine* is queued up for later execution when the *ControllerObject* can be acquired. When the *ExecutionRoutine* is called, the *Context* pointer is passed in as one of its parameters. The Controller Object remains allocated until IoFreeController is called.

A thread that calls this function must be running at IRQL == DISPATCH_LEVEL.

IoAllocateErrorLogEntry

PVOID IoAllocateErrorLogEntry(IN PVOID *IoObject*, IN UCHAR *EntrySize*);

Allocates an error log packet that can be used with IoWriteErrorLogEntry to write an error log.

The *EntrySize* parameter specifies the size of the entry and may not exceed ERROR_LOG_MAXIMUM_SIZE. The function returns NULL if the packet could not be allocated.

The value supplied for *EntrySize* depends on how much DumpData the driver includes in the error log packet, as well as any InsertionStrings it provides for the error. In general, the value of *EntrySize* is the following, where n depends on how much DumpData the driver supplies with the error.

$$
\begin{aligned}
& \texttt{sizeof(IO\_ERROR\_LOG\_PACKET)} \\
& + \texttt{(n * sizeof(ULONG))} \\
& + \sum_{i=1}^{NumberOfStrings} (lstrlenW(InsertionStrings[i-1]) + 1) \times sizeof(WCHAR))
\end{aligned}
$$

If this function returns NULL, the driver should continue to run and assume that if the same error occurs again, the driver can log the error at that point.

A thread that calls this function must be running at IRQL <= DISPATCH_LEVEL.

IoAllocateIrp

PIRP IoAllocateIrp(IN CCHAR StackSize, IN BOOLEAN *ChargeQuota*);

Allocates an IRP.

If this is a top-level driver, the *ChargeQuota* parameter indicates if the IRP should be charged against the process's IRP quota (in general, it should be). For lower-level drivers, the *ChargeQuota* parameter should be FALSE.

The stack depth can be determined by examining the StackDepth field of the device block of the next lower-level Device Driver. The calling driver does not need to allocate an IRP Stack location for itself; this is done automatically by the allocator.

The return value is a pointer to an IRP, or NULL if the IRP could not be allocated. IRPs are allocated out of nonpaged space.

An intermediate or highest-level driver can call IoAllocateIrp to create IRPs for requests that it sends to lower-level drivers. Such a driver must initialize the IRP and must set its IoCompletion routine in the IRP it creates so that the caller can dispose of the IRP when lower-level drivers have completed processing the request.

An intermediate or highest-level driver also can call `IoBuildDeviceIoControlRequest`, `IoBuildAsynchronousFsdRequest`, or `IoBuildSynchronousFsdRequest` to set up requests it sends to lower-level drivers. Only a highest-level driver can call `IoMakeAssociatedIrp`. You will generally not call the `IoBuild...FsdRequest` functions because these build File System Driver requests, and we do not address File System Drivers in this book.

A thread that calls this function should be executing at IRQL <= DISPATCH_LEVEL.

IoAllocateMdl

```
MDL IoAllocateMdl(IN PVOID VirtualAddress,
                  IN ULONG Length,
                  IN BOOLEAN SecondaryBuffer,
                  IN BOOLEAN ChargeQuota,
                  IN OUT PIRP Irp);
```

Allocates a MDL for a given base address and length. This initializes the MDL structure base address and length fields (shown in Figure A.7).

A thread that calls this function must be running at IRQL <= DISPATCH_LEVEL.

IoAssignResources

```
NTSTATUS IoAssignResources(
                  IN PUNICODE_STRING RegistryPath,
                  IN PUNICODE_STRING DriverClassName,
                  IN PDRIVER_OBJECT DriverObject,
                  IN PDEVICE_OBJECT DeviceObject,
                  IN PIO_RESOURCE_REQUIREMENTS_LIST RequestedResources,
                  IN OUT PCM_RESOURCE_LIST * AllocatedResources);
```

Takes an input list of requested hardware resources for a driver or device, claims an available set of hardware resources, such as an interrupt vector, device memory range and/or I/O port range, and possibly a particular DMA controller channel, in the \Registry\Hardware\Machine\ResourceMap tree, and returns a list of allocated hardware resources for the driver or device. As an alternative, drivers of PCI-type devices can call `HalAssignSlotResources`.

The `RegistryPath` parameter is passed into the `DriverEntry` routine. `DriverClassName` is a pointer to a UNICODE_STRING defining the class name under which this device will be stored in the Registry, or NULL, in which case the name will default to `OtherDevices`. The `DriverObject` and `DeviceObject` parameters are the objects associated with the resource assignments.

IoAttachDevice

```
NTSTATUS IoAttachDevice(IN PDEVICE_OBJECT SourceDevice,
                        IN PUNICODE_STRING TargetDevice,
                        OUT PDEVICE_OBJECT * AttachedDevice);
```

Attaches the caller's Device Object to a named target Device Object so that I/O requests bound for the target device are routed first to the caller.

The *SourceDevice* parameter references the device to be attached. The *TargetDevice* parameter points to a string that defines the name of the target device to which the source device is to be attached. The *AttachedDevice* parameter points to a PDEVICE_OBJECT variable that is set to the Device Object of the device to which the attachment is done (if the result is STATUS_SUCCESS). This function returns one of the values shown in Table A.18.

Table A.18: `IoAttachDevice` *Return Values*

Return Value	Meaning
STATUS_SUCCESS	The attachment succeeded. The AttachDevice value contains a pointer to the attached device.
STATUS_INVALID_PARAMETER	One of the parameters is invalid.
STATUS_OBJECT_TYPE_MISMATCH	The SourceDevice parameter does not refer to a valid Device Object.
STATUS_OBJECT_NAME_INVALID	The specified TargetDevice name is not a valid name. This might be due to an error in the load order—this driver was loaded ahead of the driver to which it was supposed to connect. Change the load order control information in the Registry.
STATUS_INSUFFICIENT_RESOURCES	There was not enough memory to allocate the requisite data structures.

IoAttachDevice establishes layering between drivers so that the same IRPs can be sent to each driver in the chain. This routine is used by intermediate drivers during initialization. It allows such a driver to attach its own Device Object to another device in such a way that any requests being made to the original device are given first to the intermediate driver. The caller can be layered only at the top of an existing chain of layered drivers. IoAttachDevice searches for the highest Device Object layered over *TargetDevice* and attaches to that object (that can be *TargetDevice*). Thus this routine must not be called if a driver that must be higher-level has already layered itself over the target device. This routine sets the AlignmentRequirement in *SourceDevice* to the value in the next lower-level Device Object and sets the StackSize to the value in the next lower object, plus 1.

A thread that calls this function must be running at IRQL == PASSIVE_LEVEL.

IoAttachDeviceToDeviceStack

```
PDEVICE_OBJECT IoAttachDeviceToDeviceStack(IN PDEVICE_OBJECT SourceDevice,
                                           IN PDEVICE_OBJECT TargetDevice);
```

Attaches the caller's Device Object to the highest Device Object in the chain and returns a pointer to the previously highest Device Object. I/O requests bound for the target device are routed first to the caller.

The *SourceDevice* parameter points to the caller-created Device Object. The *TargetDevice* parameter points to another driver's Device Object, such as a pointer returned by a preceding call to IoGetDeviceObjectPointer.

This routine returns a pointer to the Device Object to which *SourceDevice* was attached. The returned Device Object pointer can differ from *TargetDevice* if *TargetDevice* had additional drivers layered on top of it. The routine returns NULL if it could not attach the Device Object, for example because the target device was being unloaded.

IoAttachDeviceToDeviceStack establishes layering between drivers so that the same IRPs are sent to each driver in the chain. An intermediate driver can use this routine during initialization to attach its own Device Object to another driver's Device Object. Subsequent I/O requests sent to *TargetDevice* are sent first to the intermediate driver.

This routine sets the AlignmentRequirement in *SourceDevice* to the value in the next lower-level Device Object and sets the StackSize to the value in the next lower object, plus 1. A Device Driver writer must take care to call this routine before any drivers layer on top of the driver. IoAttachDeviceToDeviceStack attaches *SourceDevice* to the highest Device Object currently layered in the chain and has no way to determine whether drivers are being layered in the correct order.

A driver that acquired a pointer to *TargetDevice* by calling IoGetDeviceObjectPointer should call ObDereferenceObject with the File Object pointer that was returned by IoGetDeviceObjectPointer. This is the same pointer that IoGetDeviceObjectPointer returned to release its reference to the File Object. The driver should do this before it detaches its own Device Object, for example, when such a higher-level driver is unloaded.

A thread that calls this function must be running at IRQL == PASSIVE_LEVEL.

IoBuildAsynchronousFsdRequest

```
PIRP IoBuildAsynchronousFsdRequest(
                    IN ULONG MajorFunction,
                    IN PDEVICE_OBJECT DeviceObject,
                    IN OUT PVOID Buffer OPTIONAL,
                    IN ULONG Length OPTIONAL,
                    IN PLARGE_INTEGER StartingOffset OPTIONAL,
                    IN PIO_STATUS_BLOCK IoStatusBlock OPTIONAL);
```

IoBuildAsynchronousFsdRequest allocates and sets up an IRP to be sent to lower-level drivers.

The *MajorFunction* parameter specifies the major function code to be set in the IRP, one of IRP_MJ_READ, IRP_MJ_WRITE, IRP_MJ_FLUSH_BUFFERS, or IRP_MJ_SHUTDOWN. The *DeviceObject* parameter points to the next lower-level driver's Device Object, which represents the target device for the Read, Write, flush, or shutdown operation. The *Buffer* parameter points to a buffer into which data is read or from which data is written. The value of this argument is NULL for flush and shutdown requests. The *Length* parameter specifies the length in bytes of *Buffer*. The value of this argument is 0 for flush and shutdown requests. The *StartingOffset* parameter points to the starting offset on the input/output media. The value of this argument is 0 for flush and shutdown requests. The *IoStatusBlock* parameter points to the address of an I/O Status Block in which the to-be-called driver(s) return the final status about the requested operation.

This routine returns a pointer to an IRP or a NULL pointer if the IRP cannot be allocated.

Intermediate or highest-level drivers can call IoBuildAsynchronousFsdRequest to set up IRPs for requests sent to lower-level drivers. Such a driver must set its IoCompletion routine in the IRP so that the IRP can be deallocated with IoFreeIrp.

The IRP that gets built contains only enough information to get the operation started and to complete the IRP. No other context information is tracked because an asynchronous request is context-independent.

A thread that calls this function must be running at IRQL <= DISPATCH_LEVEL.

An intermediate or highest-level driver also can call `IoBuildDeviceIoControlRequest`, `IoAllocateIrp`, or `IoBuildSychronousFsdRequest` to set up requests it sends to lower-level drivers. Only a highest-level driver can call `IoMakeAssociatedIrp`.

IoBuildDeviceIoControlRequest

```
PIRP IoBuildDeviceIoControlRequest(IN ULONG IoControlCode,
                                   IN PDEVICE_OBJECT DeviceObject,
                                   IN PVOID InputBuffer OPTIONAL,
                                   IN ULONG InputBufferLength,
                                   IN OUT PVOID OutputBuffer OPTIONAL,
                                   IN ULONG OutputBufferLength,
                                   IN BOOLEAN InternalDeviceIoControl,
                                   IN PKEVENT Event,
                                   OUT PIO_STATUS_BLOCK IoStatusBlock);
```

`IoBuildDeviceIoControlRequest` allocates and sets up an IRP for a Device Control request, optionally with an I/O buffer if the I/O control code requires the caller to supply an input or output buffer.

The *IoControlCode* parameter specifies the IOCTL to be set up. The *DeviceObject* parameter points to the next lower-level driver's Device Object, which represents the target device. The *InputBuffer* parameter points to an input buffer to be passed to the lower-level driver or is NULL if the request does not pass input data to lower-level driver(s). The *InputBufferLength* parameter specifies the length in bytes of the input buffer. If *InputBuffer* is NULL, this value must be 0. The *OutputBuffer* parameter points to an output buffer in which the lower-level driver is to return data or is NULL if the request does not require lower-level driver(s) to return data. The *OutputBufferLength* parameter specifies the length in bytes of the output buffer. If *OutputBuffer* is NULL, this value must be 0. The *InternalDeviceIoControl* parameter specifies how the IOCTL is to be interpreted. If *InternalDeviceControl* is TRUE, the target driver's Dispatch Routine for IRP_MJ_INTERNAL_DEVICE_CONTROL or IRP_MJ_SCSI is called; otherwise, the Dispatch Routine for IRP_MJ_DEVICE_CONTROL is called. The *Event* parameter points to an initialized Event Object for which the caller provides the storage. The event is set to the Signaled state when the lower-level driver(s) have completed the requested operation. The caller can wait on the Event Object for the completion of the IRP allocated by this routine. The *IoStatusBlock* specifies an I/O Status Block to be set when the request is completed by lower-level drivers.

This routine returns a pointer to an IRP with the next lower-level driver's I/O Stack location partially set up from the supplied parameters. The returned pointer is NULL if an IRP cannot be allocated.

An intermediate or highest-level driver can call `IoBuildDeviceIoControlRequest` to set up IRPs for requests sent to lower-level drivers. The next lower-level driver's I/O Stack location is set up with the given `IoControlCode` at `Parameters.DeviceIoControl.IoControlCode`. Because the caller can wait on the completion of this driver-allocated IRP by calling `KeWaitForSingleObject` on the given *Event*, the caller need not set an `IoCompletion` routine in the IRP before calling `IoCallDriver`. When the next lower-level driver completes this IRP, the I/O Manager releases it.

A thread that calls this function must be running at IRQL == PASSIVE_LEVEL.

IoBuildPartialMdl

```
VOID IoBuildPartialMdl(IN PMDL SourceMdl,
                       IN OUT PMDL TargetMdl,
                       IN PVOID VirtualAddress,
                       IN ULONG Length);
```

`IoBuildPartialMdl` maps a portion of a buffer described by another MDL into a MDL.

The *SourceMdl* parameter points to a MDL that describes the original buffer, of which a subrange is to be mapped. The *TargetMdl* parameter points to a caller-allocated MDL. The MDL must be large enough to map the subrange specified by the *VirtualAddress* and *Length* parameters. *VirtualAddress* is the base virtual address for the subrange to be mapped by *TargetMdl*, and *Length* specifies the length in bytes to be mapped by *TargetMdl*. This value must be a proper subrange of the buffer described by *SourceMdl*. If *Length* is 0, the subrange to be mapped starts at *VirtualAddress* and includes the remaining range described by *SourceMdl*.

Drivers that must split large transfer requests can use this routine. The caller must release the partial MDL it allocated once it has transferred all of the requested data or completed the IRP with an error status.

A thread that calls this function must be running at IRQL == PASSIVE_LEVEL.

IoBuildSynchronousFsdRequest

```
PIRP IoBuildSynchronousFsdRequest(
                    IN ULONG MajorFunction,
                    IN PDEVICE_OBJECT DeviceObject,
                    IN OUT PVOID Buffer OPTIONAL,
                    IN ULONG Length OPTIONAL,
                    IN PLARGE_INTEGER StartingOffset OPTIONAL,
                    IN PKEVENT Event,
                    OUT PIO_STATUS_BLOCK IoStatusBlock);
```

Allocates and sets up an IRP to be sent synchronously to lower-level drivers.

The *MajorFunction* parameter specifies the major function code to be set in the IRP, one of IRP_MJ_READ, IRP_MJ_WRITE, IRP_MJ_FLUSH_BUFFERS, or IRP_MJ_SHUTDOWN. The *DeviceObject* parameter points to the next lower-level driver's Device Object, which represents the target device for the Read, Write, flush, or shutdown operation. The *Buffer* parameter points to a buffer into which data is read or from which data is written. The value of this argument is NULL for flush and shutdown requests. The *Length* parameter specifies the length in bytes of *Buffer*. The value of this argument is 0 for flush and shutdown requests. The *StartingOffset* parameter points to the starting offset on the input/output media. The value of this argument is 0 for flush and shutdown requests. The *Event* parameter points to an event that is set to the Signaled state when the lower-level driver has completed its operation. The *IoStatusBlock* parameter points to the address of an I/O Status Block in which the to-be-called driver(s) return the final status about the requested operation.

This routine returns a pointer to an IRP, or a NULL pointer if the IRP cannot be allocated.

Intermediate or highest-level drivers can call IoBuildAsynchronousFsdRequest to set up IRPs for requests sent to lower-level drivers, but this can be done only if the caller is running in a nonarbitrary thread context and at IRQL PASSIVE_LEVEL.

IoBuildSynchronousFsdRequest allocates and sets up an IRP that can be sent to a Device Driver to perform a synchronous Read, Write, flush, or shutdown operation. The IRP contains only enough information to get the operation started.

The caller can determine when the I/O has completed by calling KeWaitForSingleObject with *Event*. Performing this Wait operation causes the current thread to wait. Thus this operation can be requested during the initialization of an intermediate driver or from a file system driver in the context of a thread requesting a synchronous I/O operation. A driver cannot wait for a nonzero interval on *Event* at raised IRQL in an arbitrary thread context.

Because the caller can wait on a given *Event*, the caller need not set an IoCompletion routine in the caller-allocated IRP before calling IoCallDriver. When the caller completes the IRP, the I/O Manager releases it.

IoCallDriver

NTSTATUS IoCallDriver(IN PDEVICE_OBJECT *DeviceObject*, IN OUT PIRP *Irp*);

Sends an IRP to the next-lower-level driver after the caller has set up the I/O stack location in the IRP for that driver. The return value is the value set in the I/O Status Block by the lower-level driver, or STATUS_PENDING if additional processing was required.

Assigns the *DeviceObject* input parameter to the Device Object field of the IRP Stack location for the next lower-level driver.

An IRP passed in a call to this function becomes inaccessible to the higher-level driver, unless that driver has set up its IoCompletion routine for the IRP with IoSetCompletionRoutine. If that driver has done this, the IRP input to the driver-supplied IoCompletion routine has its I/O Status Block set by the lower-level driver(s) and by all the IRP Stack locations which had been used by lower level driver(s) are filled with zeros.

A thread that calls this function must be running at IRQL <= DISPATCH_LEVEL.

IoCancelIrp

BOOLEAN IoCancelIrp(IN PIRP *Irp*);

Cancels the specified IRP. It returns TRUE if the IRP was successfully canceled.

If the IRP has a Cancel Routine, IoCancelIrp sets the cancel bit and calls the Cancel Routine. If the IRP has no Cancel Routine (Irp->CancelRoutine is NULL), and therefore the IRP is not cancelable, IoCancelIrp sets the IRP's cancel bit and returns FALSE. The IRP should be canceled later when it becomes cancelable.

If a driver that does not own the IRP calls IoCancelIrp, the results are unpredictable. The IRP might be completed with a successful status even though its cancel bit was set.

An intermediate driver should not arbitrarily call IoCancelIrp unless that driver created the IRP that passed in the call. Otherwise, the intermediate driver might cancel an IRP that some higher-level driver is tracking for purposes of its own.

A thread that calls this function must be running at IRQL <= DISPATCH_LEVEL.

IoCompleteRequest

```
VOID IoCompleteRequest(IN PIRP Irp, IN CCHAR PriorityBoost);
```

This routine is called by a driver when it has finished all processing for a given IRP. The I/O Manager checks the IRP to determine whether any higher-level drivers have set up an IoCompletion routine for the IRP. If so, each IoCompletion routine is called, in turn, until every layered driver in the chain has completed the IRP.

When all drivers have completed a given IRP, the I/O Manager returns the status to the original requestor of the operation. Note that a higher-level driver that sets up a driver-created IRP must supply an IoCompletion routine to release the IRP it created.

This routine specifies a system-defined constant by which to increment the runtime priority of the original thread that requested the operation. This value is IO_NO_INCREMENT if the original thread requested an operation that the driver could complete quickly (so the requesting thread is not compensated for its assumed wait on I/O) or if the IRP is completed with an error. Otherwise, the set of *PriorityBoost* constants are device-type-specific. A priority boost will not be given to a thread that is already in the real-time scheduling class.

A thread that calls this function must be running at IRQL <= DISPATCH_LEVEL.

IoConnectInterrupt

```
NTSTATUS IoConnectInterrupt(OUT PKINTERRUPT * InterruptObject,
                            IN PKSERVICE_ROUTINE ServiceRoutine,
                            IN PVOID ServiceContext,
                            IN PKSPIN_LOCK SpinLock,
                            IN ULONG Vector,
                            IN KIRQL Irql,
                            IN KIRQL SynchronizeIrql,
                            IN KINTERRUPT_MODE InterruptMode,
                            IN BOOLEAN ShareVector,
                            IN KAFFINITY ProcessorEnableMask,
                            IN BOOLEAN FloatingSave);
```

Connects a physical interrupt with a piece of code that handles it. You must first call HalGetInterruptVector to get the appropriate interrupt vector information to pass to this function.

The *ServiceRoutine* parameter is a pointer to the function to be called when the interrupt is taken. The signature of the function is defined as follows.

```
BOOLEAN (*PKSERVICE_ROUTINE)(IN PKINTERRUPT Interrupt,
                             IN PVOID ServiceContext);
```

The *ServiceContext* value points to an area that must be in resident memory, either in the Device Extension of a driver-created Device Object, in the Controller Extension of a driver-created Controller Object, or in a Nonpaged Pool allocated by the Device Driver. This value is stored and is passed as the second argument to the actual ISR when the interrupt is taken.

The *SpinLock* parameter points to a Spin Lock that has been allocated in resident memory and initialized by KeInitializeSpinLock. This Spin Lock will be used to synchronize access to driver-determined data shared by other driver routines. This parameter is required if the ISR handles more than one vector or if the driver has more than one ISR. If neither of these conditions is true, the driver need not allocate storage for an ISR Spin Lock and the input pointer is NULL.

A thread that calls this function must be running at IRQL == PASSIVE_LEVEL.

IoCopyCurrentIrpStackLocationToNext

```
VOID IoCopyCurrentIrpStackLocationToNext(IN PIRP Irp);
// NT 5.0 beta/Windows 2000
```

IoCopyCurrentIrpStackLocationToNext copies the contents of the current IRP Stack location to the next I/O Stack location of the specified IRP.

This routine allows a completion routine to be set. This function is defined only for NT 5.0 beta and Windows 2000.

A thread that calls this function must be running at IRQL <= DISPATCH_LEVEL.

IoCreateController

```
PCONTROLLER_OBJECT IoCreateController(IN ULONG Size)
```

Creates a Controller Object.

The *Size* parameter is the size of the Controller Extension and can be 0. A return value of NULL means the Controller Object could not be created. In this case, the driver should fail loading and free up any resources already allocated.

A thread that calls this function must be running at IRQL == PASSIVE_LEVEL.

IoCreateDevice

```
NTSTATUS IoCreateDevice(IN PDRIVER_OBJECT DriverObject,
                        IN ULONG DeviceExtensionSize,
                        IN PUNICODE_STRING DeviceName,
                        IN DEVICE_TYPE DeviceType,
                        IN ULONG DeviceCharacteristics,
                        IN BOOLEAN Exclusive,
                        OUT PDEVICE_OBJECT * DeviceObject);
```

Creates the Device Object or objects required by the hardware device. This is called either in the DriverEntry routine of an NT 4.0 (or monolithic NT 5.0 beta/Windows 2000) driver, or in AddDevice for a Windows 2000-compliant driver.

The *DriverObject* parameter is the pointer to the *DriverObject* passed into the DriverEntry function. The *DeviceExtensionSize* parameter is the size of the Device Extension. This is where you keep your private data for the device and is usually defined by an appropriate structure, so the sizeof of the structure is the usual value to place here.

The device name string is the external name by which the device is known to the system. It must be a full pathname, for example,

```
L"\\Device\\devicename"
```

and must be converted to a counted UNICODE_STRING. If the name already exists, the return value will be STATUS_OBJECT_NAME_EXISTS. Note that this is *not* the name by which an application opens the device; that name is established by a separate operation. See `IoCreateSymbolicLink`.

The *DeviceType* parameter specifics the nature of the device. The *DeviceCharacteristics* parameter can be used if any of the specified characteristics apply to your device, but for most specialized devices, this value can be set to 0. The *Exclusive* flag indicates if more than one thread can perform a `CreateFile` operation on this device. Some devices are, by their very nature, shared (for example, disks), while some make sense only when opened in exclusive mode (for example, a printer port—you wouldn't want two separate threads arbitrarily sending interleaved bytes to a printer). Unless you have a shareable device, set this parameter to TRUE. If the operation succeeds, a pointer to the newly created Device Object will be placed in the location referenced by the *DeviceObject* parameter.

This routine allocates space in the Nonpaged Pool for the driver-defined Device Extension associated with the Device Object so that the Device Extension is accessible to the driver in any execution context and at any IRQL. The returned Device Extension is initialized with zeros.

Device Objects for disks, tapes, CD-ROMs, and RAM disks are given a Volume Parameter Block (VPB) that is initialized to indicate that the volume was never mounted on the device.

Each driver must create at least one named Device Object by calling `IoCreateDevice`. Otherwise, no I/O requests can be sent to the driver. An unnamed Device Object is invisible to other drivers except, possibly, FSDs, and to User-mode, protected subsystems. This is because a symbolic link cannot be set up for an unnamed Device Object. Consequently, higher-level drivers cannot attach their Device Objects to an unnamed Device Object. Nor can the unnamed object be the target of an IRP.

If a driver's call to `IoCreateDevice` returns an error, it should release any resources it allocated for that device. If the driver cannot set up a Device Object to represent any of the devices it controls, that driver should not load.

Certain Device Drivers call `IoCreateDevice` from a Dispatch Routine. In particular, disk drivers must call `IoCreateDevice` in response to a Device Control request to repartition a disk dynamically.

A thread that calls this function must be running at IRQL == PASSIVE_LEVEL.

IoCreateNotificationEvent

```
PKEVENT IoCreateNotificationEvent(IN PUNICODE_STRING EventName,
                                  OUT PHANDLE EventHandle);
```

`IoCreateNotificationEvent` creates or opens a named Notification Event used to notify one or more threads of execution that an event has occurred. When a Notification Event is set to the Signaled state, it remains in that state until it is explicitly cleared.

The *EventName* parameter points to a buffer containing a NUL-terminated Unicode string that names the event. The *EventHandle* parameter points to a location in which to return a handle for the Event Object.

This function returns a pointer to the created or opened Event Object, or NULL if the Event Object could not be created or opened.

The Event Object is created if it does not already exist, and the handle of the newly created object is returned via *EventHandle*. If the Event Object exists, a new handle to the existing object is returned. `IoCreateSynchronizationEvent` sets the state of a new, Synchronization Event to Signaled. If the Event Object already exists, it is simply opened and the state is left unchanged. The two drivers that use a Synchronization Event call `KeWaitForSingleObject` with the PKEVENT pointer returned by this routine. Use `ZwClose` to close the handle.

Notification Events, like Synchronization Events, are used to coordinate execution. Unlike a Synchronization Event, a Notification Event is *not* autoresetting. Once a Notification Event is in the Signaled state, it remains in that state until it is explicitly reset (via a call to `KeClearEvent` or `KeResetEvent`).

A thread that calls this function must be running at IRQL == PASSIVE_LEVEL.

IoCreateSymbolicLink

```
NTSTATUS IoCreateSymbolicLink(IN PUNICODE_STRING SymbolicLinkName,
                              IN PUNICODE_STRING DeviceName);
```

`IoCreateSymbolicLink` creates a symbolic link from the name specified to a "user-visible" name for a device.

```
#define NT_DEVICE_NAME L"\\Devices\\devicename"
#define DOS_DEVICE_NAME L"\\DosDevices\\devicename"
//...
NTSTATUS DriverEntry(IN PDRIVER_OBJECT DriverObject,
                     IN PUNICODE_STRING RegistryPath)
   {
    UNICODE_STRING NtNameString;
    UNICODE_STRING DosNameString;
    NTSTATUS status;
    PDEVICE_OBJECT device;

    RtlInitUnicodeString(&NtNameString, NT_DEVICE_NAME);
    RtlInitUnicodeString(&DosNameString, DOS_DEVICE_NAME);
    status = IoCreateDevice(DriverObject, 0, &NtNameString,
                            0, TRUE, &device);
    if(NT_SUCCESS(status))
       { /* initialize device parameters */
        // .. Lots of stuff here
        status = IoCreateSymbolicLink(&DosNameString, &NtNameString);
        if(!NT_SUCCESS(status))
           { /* failed to link */
            IoDeleteDevice(DriverObject->DeviceObject);
           } /* failed to link */
       } /* initialize device parameters */
    return status;
   }
```

A thread that calls this function must be running at IRQL == PASSIVE_LEVEL.

IoCreateSynchronizationEvent

```
PKEVENT IoCreateSynchronizationEvent(IN PUNICODE_STRING EventName,
                                     OUT PHANDLE EventHandle);
```

Creates or opens a named synchronization event for use in serialization of access to hardware between two otherwise unrelated drivers.

The *EventName* parameter points to a buffer containing a NUL-terminated Unicode string that names the event. The *EventHandle* parameter points to a location in which to return a handle for the Event Object.

The return value is a pointer to the created or opened Event Object, or NULL if the Event Object could not be created or opened.

The Event Object is created if it does not already exist, and the handle of the newly created object is returned via *EventHandle*. If it exists, a new handle to the existing object is returned. IoCreateSynchronizationEvent sets the state of a new synchronization event to Signaled. If the Event Object already exists, it is simply opened and the state is left unchanged. The pair of drivers that use a synchronization event call KeWaitForSingleObject with the PKEVENT pointer returned by this routine. Use ZwClose to close the handle.

When a synchronization event is set to the Signaled state, a single thread of execution that was waiting on the event is released and the event is automatically reset to the Not-Signaled state.

A thread that calls this function must be running at IRQL == PASSIVE_LEVEL.

IoDeleteController

VOID IoDeleteController(IN PCONTROLLER_OBJECT *ControllerObject*);

Deletes a Controller Object and should be called in the Unload handler, or in response to a Plug-and-Play removal notification.

Note that you normally have several pointers to a Controller Object, but you should call IoDeleteController on exactly *one* of them. It is your responsibility to not call it twice. Any resources stored in the Controller Extension must be freed before this function is called.

A thread that calls this function must be running at IRQL == PASSIVE_LEVEL.

IoDeleteDevice

VOID IoDeleteDevice(IN PDEVICE_OBJECT *DeviceObject*);

Deletes a Device Object.

This routine must be called when a driver that created the Device Object is being unloaded or when the DriverEntry routine encounters a fatal initialization error, such as being unable to properly initialize a physical device. This routine also is called when a driver reconfigures its devices dynamically. In NT 5.0 beta/Windows 2000, this is called to handle Plug-and-Play removal notifications.

Before a driver calls IoDeleteDevice, it must release certain resources for which it supplied storage in its Device Extension. For example, if the driver stores the pointer to its Interrupt Object(s) in the Device Extension, it must call IoDisconnectInterrupt before calling IoDeleteDevice.

When IoDeleteDevice is called, there cannot be any outstanding references to the device that is being deleted or to any attached devices. If there are, a system error occurs.

A thread that calls this function must be running at IRQL == PASSIVE_LEVEL.

IoDeleteSymbolicLink

`NTSTATUS IoDeleteSymbolicLink(IN PUNICODE_STRING SymbolicLinkName);`

    `IoDeleteSymbolicLink` deletes a passive link referenced by the UNICODE_STRING. This is normally called in conjunction with, and immediately preceding, an `IoDeleteDevice` call.

    A thread that calls this function must be running at IRQL == PASSIVE_LEVEL.

IoDetachDevice

`VOID IoDetachDevice(IN OUT PDEVICE_OBJECT TargetDevice);`

    Decrements the reference count of the `TargetDevice` object. If the reference count goes to 0 and the lower-level driver has been marked for an Unload operation, the lower-level driver is unloaded.

    A thread that calls this function must be running at IRQL == PASSIVE_LEVEL.

IoDisconnectInterrupt

`VOID IoDisconnectInterrupt(IN PKINTERRUPT InterruptObject);`

    Disconnects an interrupt established by `IoConnectInterrupt`. A driver should disable interrupts from its device before calling `IoDisconnectInterrupt`.

    If the driver stored the pointer to its Interrupt Object(s) in the Device Extension of its Device Object or in the Controller Extension of its Controller Object, it must call `IoDisconnectInterrupt` before it calls `IoDeleteDevice` or `IoDeleteController`.

    A thread that calls this function must be running at IRQL == PASSIVE_LEVEL.

IO_ERROR_LOG_PACKET

```
typedef struct _IO_ERROR_LOG_PACKET (
    UCHAR MajorFunctionCode;
    UCHAR RetryCount;
    USHORT DumpDataSize;
    USHORT NumberOfStrings;
    USHORT StringOffset;
    USHORT EventCategory;
    NTSTATUS ErrorCode;
    ULONG UniqueErrorValue;
    NTSTATUS FinalStatus;
    ULONG SequenceNumber;
    ULONG IoControlCode;
    LARGE_INTEGER DeviceOffset;
    ULONG DumpData[1];
}IO_ERROR_LOG_PACKET, * PIO_ERROR_LOG_PACKET;
```

    Table A.19 lists the Error Log fields. Its structure is shown in Figure A.1.

Table A.19: `IO_ERROR_LOG_PACKET` *Fields*

Field	Meaning
UCHAR MajorFunctionCode	The IRP_MJ_*XXX* of the current IRP.
UCHAR RetryCount	A count of how many times the caller has retried the operation and encountered the same error.
USHORT DumpDataSize	The number of bytes of caller-supplied DumpData, if any.
USHORT NumberOfStrings	The number of insertion strings supplied following the DumpData. The initial string, if any, is assumed to be the driver name or that of the target Device Object.
USHORT StringOffset	The offset, immediately following any DumpData, of the caller-supplied, zero-terminated Unicode insertion strings, if any.
USHORT EventCategory	A caller-determined value matching that in the caller's message file for categories if the driver set itself up in the Registry as an event-logging component; otherwise, 0.
NTSTATUS ErrorCode	An IO_ERR_*XXX* value.
ULONG UniqueErrorValue	A driver-determined value that indicates where in the driver the error was encountered.
NTSTATUS FinalStatus	The STATUS_*XXX* value to be set in the I/O Status Block of the IRP or a STATUS_*XXX* returned by a support routine.
ULONG SequenceNumber	A driver-assigned number for the current IRP. Constant for the life of the request.
ULONG IoControlCode	An IOCTL_*XXX* if MajorFunctionCode is IRP_MJ_DEVICE_CONTROL, IRP_MJ_INTERNAL_DEVICE_CONTROL, or IRP_MJ_SCSI; otherwise, 0.
LARGE_INTEGER DeviceOffset	The offset on the device where the error occurred, or 0.
ULONG DumpData[1]	Caller-supplied data, such as device register contents, if DumpDataSize is nonzero.

IoFlushAdapterBuffers

```
BOOLEAN IoFlushAdapterBuffers(IN PADAPTER_OBJECT AdapterObject,
                              IN PMDL Mdl,
                              IN PVOID MapRegisterBase,
                              IN PVOID CurrentVa,
                              IN ULONG Length,
                              IN BOOLEAN WriteToDevice);
```

Flushes any remaining data in the System DMA internal cache or in a Bus Master DMA buffer internal cache. The implementation is device-specific.

This routine is normally called upon completion of a DMA operation. The *AdapterObject* parameter is the adapter from which the DMA channel was allocated. The *Mdl* parameter is the same MDL that was passed to *IoMapTransfer*. The *MapRegisterBase* register is the handle that was returned from IoAllocateAdapterChannel. The *CurrentVa* parameter is the virtual address in the buffer described by the MDL where the I/O operation took place. The *Length*

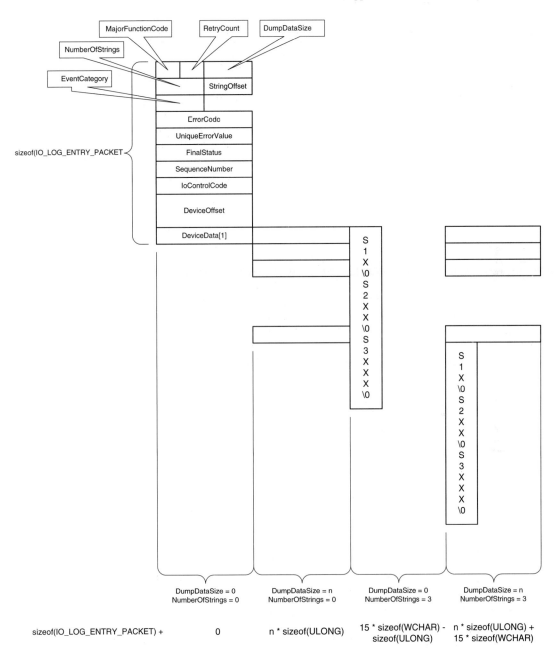

Figure A.1: `IO_ERROR_LOG_PACKET` *structure.*

parameter is the length of that transfer. The *WriteToDevice* parameter is TRUE for a write and FALSE for a read.

This function returns TRUE if the flush operation succeeded.

A thread that calls this function must be running at IRQL <= DISPATCH_LEVEL.

IoFreeAdapterChannel

VOID IoFreeAdapterChannel(IN PADAPTER_OBJECT *AdapterObject*);

Frees the adapter channel allocated by IoAllocateAdapterChannel. This only needs to be called explicitly if the function called by IoAllocateAdapterChannel returned the value KeepObject.

A thread that calls this function must be running at IRQL == DISPATCH_LEVEL.

IoFreeController

VOID IoFreeController(IN PCONTROLLER_OBJECT *ControllerObject*);

Releases the Controller Object that was allocated by IoAllocateController. Other requests that have been pending on the Controller Object can now be dequeued. This only needs to be called explicitly if the function called by IoAllocateController returned the value KeepObject.

A thread that calls this function must be running at IRQL == DISPATCH_LEVEL.

IoFreeIrp

VOID IoFreeIrp(IN PIRP Irp);

IoFreeIrp is the inverse of IoAllocateIrp or IoBuildAsynchronousFsdRequest. The released IRP must have been allocated by the caller. You should never explicitly release an IRP you have not allocated. In particular, you must never release an IRP created by the I/O Manager.

This routine also releases an IRP allocated with IoMakeAssociatedIrp in which the caller sets up its IoCompletion routine that returns STATUS_MORE_PROCESSING_REQUIRED for the Associated IRP.

A thread that calls this function must be running at IRQL <= DISPATCH_LEVEL.

IoFreeMapRegisters

VOID IoFreeMapRegisters(IN PADAPTER_OBJECT *AdapterObject*,
                        IN PVOID *MapRegisterBase*,
                        IN ULONG *NumberOfMapRegisters*);

Releases a set of mapping registers that were saved from a call to IoAllocateAdapterChannel when the driver of a bus mastering device completes the current packet-based DMA transfer request.

The *AdapterObject* parameter points to the Adapter Object representing the bus mastering adapter. This pointer was returned by HalGetAdapter when the driver initialized. The *MapRegisterBase* parameter points to the handle returned by the driver's call to

`IoAllocateAdapterChannel`. The *NumberOfMapRegisters* parameter specifies the number of mapping registers to be released, which must match the number specified in the preceding call to `IoAllocateAdapterChannel`.

A thread that calls this function must be running at IRQL == DISPATCH_LEVEL.

IoFreeMdl

```
VOID IoFreeMdl(IN PMDL Mdl);
```

Releases a driver-allocated MDL. Do not call this for MDLs created by the I/O Manager.

A thread that calls this function must be running at IRQL <= DISPATCH_LEVEL.

IoGetConfiguationInformation

```
PCONFIGURATION_INFORMATION IoGetConfigurationInformation( );
```

Returns a pointer to the I/O Manager's global configuration information structure, which contains the current values for how many devices—physical disk, floppy, CD-ROM, tape, SCSI HBA, USB, IEEE-1394, serial, and parallel—have Device Objects created to represent them by drivers as they are loaded.

Certain types of Device Drivers can use the values of the configuration information structure to construct Device Object names with appropriate digit suffixes when each driver creates its Device Objects. Note that the digit suffix for Device Object names is a zero-based count, while the counts maintained in the configuration information structure represent the number of Device Objects of a particular type already created. That is, the configuration information counts are 1-based.

Any driver that calls `IoGetConfigurationInformation` must increment the count for its kind of device in this structure when it creates a Device Object to represent a physical device.

The system-supplied SCSI Port Driver supplies the count of SCSI HBAs present in the machine. SCSI Class Drivers can read this value to determine how many HBA-specific Miniport Drivers might control a SCSI Bus that has an attached device of the Class Driver's type.

The configuration information structure also contains a value indicating whether an already-loaded driver has claimed either of the "AT" disk I/O address ranges.

A thread that calls this function must be running at IRQL == PASSIVE_LEVEL.

IoGetCurrentIrpStackLocation

```
PIO_STACK_LOCATION IoGetCurrentIrpStackLocation(IN PIRP Irp)
```

`IoGetCurrentIrpStackLocation` is the only valid way to get a pointer to the IO_STACK_LOCATION object that describes the current driver level.

The *Irp* parameter is the IRP, and the result is a pointer to the appropriate data structure.

IoGetCurrentProcess

```
PEPROCESS IoGetCurrentProcess( );
```

Returns a pointer to the current process. There is little reason to execute this in other than the top-level driver because there is no meaning in having a handle for a process other than the process that initiated the I/O transaction.

A thread that calls this function must be running at IRQL == PASSIVE_LEVEL.

IoGetDeviceObjectPointer

```
NTSTATUS IoGetDeviceObjectPointer(IN PUNICODE_STRING ObjectName,
                                  IN ACCESS_MASK DesiredAccess,
                                  OUT PFILE_OBJECT * FileObject,
                                  OUT PDEVICE_OBJECT * DeviceObject);
```

IoGetDeviceObjectPointer, when given the name of a device, *ObjectName*, returns a pointer to the corresponding DEVICE_OBJECT via the *DeviceObject* parameter.

The *DesiredAccess* parameter specifies the type of access: FILE_READ_DATA, FILE_WRITE_DATA, or FILE_ALL_ACCESS. The *FileObject* parameter receives a pointer to the File Object that represents this device to the user-level code.

If the driver that calls this function is going to chain itself into the target driver's driver stack, the caller must set its StackSize to the stack size of the *DeviceObject*, plus 1.

A thread that calls this function must be running at IRQL == PASSIVE_LEVEL.

IoGetNextIrpStackLocation

```
PIO_STACK_LOCATION IoGetNextIrpStackLocation(IN PIRP Irp)
```

IoGetNextIrpStackLocation is the only valid way to get a pointer to the IO_STACK_LOCATION object describing the next lower driver level.

The *Irp* parameter is the IRP, and the result is a pointer to the appropriate data structure.

IoInitializeDpcRequest

```
NTSTATUS IoInitializeDpcRequest(IN PDEVICE_OBJECT DeviceObject,
                                IN PIO_DPC_ROUTINE DpcRoutine );
```

Associates a driver-supplied DpcForIsr routine with the specified Device Object. When the IoRequestDpc function is called in the ISR, the DPC Routine specified here will be scheduled for execution.

A thread that calls this function must be running at IRQL == PASSIVE_LEVEL.

To initialize a DPC at IRQL <= DISPATCH_LEVEL, use KeInitializeDpc.

IoInitializeIrp

```
VOID IoInitializeIrp(IN OUT PIRP Irp,
                     IN USHORT PacketSize,
                     IN CCHAR StackSize);
```

Initializes a given IRP that was allocated by the caller.

The *Irp* parameter points to the IRP to be initialized. The *PacketSize* parameter specifies the size in bytes of the IRP. The *StackSize* parameter specifies the number of stack locations in the IRP. This must be the same stack size value that was used to allocate the IRP (see IoSizeOfIrp).

If a driver calls IoAllocateIrp, it also must call IoInitializeIrp with the same *StackSize* value and the pointer returned by IoAllocateIrp. If the driver associates a MDL with the IRP it allocated, the driver is responsible for releasing the MDL when the IRP is completed. An intermediate or highest-level driver also can call IoBuildDeviceIoControlRequest, IoBuildAsynchronousFsdRequest, or IoBuildSynchronousFsdRequest to set up requests it sends to lower-level drivers. Only a highest-level driver can call IoMakeAssociatedIrp.

A thread that calls this function must be running at IRQL <= DISPATCH_LEVEL.

IoInitializeTimer

```
NTSTATUS IoInitializeTimer(IN PDEVICE_OBJECT DeviceObject,
                           IN PIO_TIMER_ROUTINE TimerRoutine );
```

Sets up a driver-supplied IoTimer routine associated with a given device object. The *DeviceObject* parameter associates a driver-supplied IoTimer routine with the specified Device Object. When the IoStartTimer function is called, the IoTimer routine specified here will be scheduled for execution approximately once per second. This routine must be called before any other IoTimer operations are called.

A thread that calls this function must be running at IRQL == PASSIVE_LEVEL.

IoMakeAssociatedIrp

```
PIRP IoMakeAssociatedIrp(IN PIRP Irp,
                         IN CCHAR StackSize);
```

Allocates and initializes an IRP to be associated with a master IRP sent to a highest-level driver. This allows the caller to split the original request and send Associated IRPs on to lower-level drivers.

The *Irp* parameter points to the master IRP that was input to a highest-level driver's Dispatch Routine. The *StackSize* parameter specifies the number of stack locations to be allocated for the Associated IRP. The value must be at least equal to the StackSize of the next lower-level driver's Device Object, but the Associated IRP can have an additional stack location for the caller. This function returns a pointer to the Associated IRP, or a NULL pointer if an IRP cannot be allocated.

Only a highest-level driver can call this routine. The I/O Manager completes the master IRP automatically when lower-level drivers have completed all Associated IRPs as long as the caller has not set its IoCompletion routine in an Associated IRP and returned STATUS_MORE_PROCESSING_REQUIRED from its IoCompletion routine. In these circumstances, the caller must explicitly complete the master IRP when that driver has determined that all Associated IRPs were completed.

A thread that calls this function must be running at IRQL <= DISPATCH_LEVEL.

IoMapTransfer

```
PHYSICAL_ADDRESS IoMapTransfer(IN PADAPTER_OBJECT AdapterObject,
                               IN PMDL Mdl,
                               IN PVOID MapRegisterBase,
                               IN PVOID CurrentVa,
                               IN OUT PULONG Length,
                               IN BOOLEAN WriteToDevice);
```

Sets up a number of mapping registers (up to the number returned by HalGetAdapter) for the given Adapter Object to map a transfer from a locked-down buffer specified by Mdl, the given CurrentVa into the MDL, the Length in bytes to be transferred, and the transfer direction.

The AdapterObject parameter points to the Adapter Object pointer returned by HalGetAdapter and already passed in a call to IoAllocateAdapterChannel for the current IRP's transfer request. The MapRegisterBase parameter points to the handle returned by IoAllocateAdapterChannel, which the driver already called for the current IRP. The WriteToDevice parameter specifies TRUE for a Write operation and FALSE for a Read operation.

The initial CurrentVa value for the start of a packet-based DMA transfer can be obtained by calling MmGetMdlVirtualAddress. However, the value returned is an index into the Mdl parameter, rather than a valid virtual address. If the driver must split a large transfer request into more than one DMA operation, CurrentVa and Length must be updated for each DMA operation.

The driver of a bus mastering device with scatter/gather support can use the returned logical address and updated Length value to build a scatter/gather list. It can call IoMapTransfer repeatedly until it has used all available mapping registers for the transfer operation.

A thread that calls this function must be running at IRQL <= DISPATCH_LEVEL.

IoMarkIrpPending

```
VOID IoMarkIrpPending(IN OUT PIRP Irp);
```

Marks the given IRP, indicating that a driver's Dispatch Routine is about to return STATUS_PENDING because further processing is required by other driver routines.

Unless a driver calls IoCompleteRequest from its Dispatch Routine with a given IRP or passes the IRP on to lower-level drivers, it must call IoMarkIrpPending with the IRP. Otherwise, the I/O Manager attempts to complete the IRP as soon as the Dispatch Routine returns control.

A routine that calls IoMarkIrpPending *must* return STATUS_PENDING.

A thread that calls this function must be running at IRQL <= DISPATCH_LEVEL.

IoRegisterShutdownNotification

```
NTSTATUS IoRegisterShutdownNotification(IN PDEVICE_OBJECT DeviceObject);
```

Registers the Device Object so that it will receive shutdown notifications.

Only a top-level driver can receive shutdown notifications. It then performs any operations to cause lower-level drivers to perform shutdown operations.

A thread that calls this function must be running at IRQL == PASSIVE_LEVEL.

IoReleaseCancelSpinLock

```
VOID IoReleaseCancelSpinLock(IN KIRQL Irql);
```

Releases the Cancel Spin Lock after the driver has changed the cancelable state of an IRP. This routine also releases the Cancel Spin Lock from the driver's Cancel Routine.

The *Irql* parameter points to the IRQL returned by `IoAcquireCancelSpinLock`.

The holder of the Cancel Spin Lock executes at IRQL == DISPATCH_LEVEL after calling `IoAcquireCancelSpinLock`. `IoReleaseCancelSpinLock` restores the original IRQL of its caller.

A thread that calls this function must be running at IRQL == DISPATCH_LEVEL.

IoRequestDpc

```
void IoRequestDpc(IN PDEVICE_OBJECT DeviceObject,
                  IN PIRP Irp,
                  IN PVOID Context);
```

Enqueues the driver-specified `DpcForIsr` routine for execution at DPC_LEVEL.

The *Context* parameter is a pointer to any block of information required by the DPC to complete the interrupt. For simple synchronous I/O, this could be a pointer to the Device Extension. The *Context* pointer must be in nonpaged memory.

Note that the context must be fully established *before* this function is called. This is because in a multiprocessor system, the DPC Routine could begin execution before the `IoRequestDpc` returns.

A thread that calls this function must be running at a DIRQL > DISPATCH_LEVEL. Note that a DPC may be queued by a thread running at IRQL >= DISPATCH_LEVEL by using the Ke...Dpc functions.

IO_RESOURCE_DESCRIPTOR

```
typedef struct _IO_RESOURCE_DESCRIPTOR {
    UCHAR Option;
    UCHAR Type;
    UCHAR ShareDisposition;
    UCHAR Spare1;                              // Reserved for system use
    USHORT Flags;
    USHORT Spare2;                             // Reserved for system use

    union{
        struct {
            ULONG Length;
            ULONG Alignment;
            PHYSICAL_ADDRESS MinimumAddress;
            PHYSICAL_ADDRESS MaximumAddress;
        } Port;
        struct {
            ULONG Length;
            ULONG Alignment;
            PHYSICAL_ADDRESS MinimumAddress;
            PHYSICAL_ADDRESS MaximumAddress;
        } Memory;
```

```
        struct {
            ULONG MinimumVector;
            ULONG MaximumVector;
        } Interrupt;
        struct {
            ULONG MinumumChannel;
            ULONG MaximumChannel;
        } Dma;
    } u;
} IO_RESOURCE_DESCRIPTOR, * PIO_RESOURCE_DESCRIPTOR
```

Table A.20 lists the fields for IO_RESOURCE_DESCRIPTION.

Table A.20: IO_RESOURCE_DESCRIPTION *Fields*

Field	Meaning	
UCHAR Option	Indicates the nature of the resource list entry.	
	0	No choice; the resources specified must be allocated.
	IO_RESOURCE_PREFERRED	The allocation is the preferred allocation of resources. This implies that there are IO_RESOURCE_ALTERNATIVE entries as well.
	IO_RESOURCE_ALTERNATIVE	The allocation is an alternative allocation of resources that will be acceptable.
UCHAR Type	The type of the resource. Controls how the union is interpreted. One of CmResourceTypePort, CmResourceTypeMemory, CmResourceTypeInterrupt, or CmResourceTypeDma.	
UCHAR ShareDisposition	Specifies whether or how this resource can be shared as one of the following: CmResourceShareDeviceExclusive, CmResourceShareDriverExclusive, or CmResourceShareShared.	
UCHAR Spare1	Not used; if set, should be set to 0.	
USHORT Flags	Indicates options based on Type.	
	CmResourceTypePort	CM_RESOURCE_PORT_MEMORY or CM_RESOURCE_PORT_IO
	CmResourceTypeMemory	CM_RESOURCE_MEMORY_READ_WRITE, CM_RESOURCE_MEMORY_READ_ONLY, or CM_RESOURCE_MEMORY_WRITE_ONLY
	CmResourceTypeInterrupt	CM_RESOURCE_INTERRUPT_LEVEL_SENSITIVE or CM_RESOURCE_INTERRUPT_LATCHED
USHORT Spare2	Not used; if set, should be set to 0.	
u.Port	.Length	The length of the I/O register set, in bytes.
	.Alignment	The alignment multiple for the I/O registers.
	.MinimumAddress	8-byte bus-relative physical address.
	.MaximumAddress	8-byte bus-relative physical address.

Table A.20: `IO_RESOURCE_DESCRIPTION` *Fields (continued)*

Field	Meaning	
u.Memory	.Length	The length of the memory block, in bytes.
	.Alignment	The alignment value.
	.MinimumAddress	8-byte bus-relative physical address.
	.MaximumAddress	8-byte bus-relative physical address.
u.Interrupt	.MinimumVector	4-byte lower bound on the IRQ value.
	.MaximumVector	4-byte upper bound on the IRQ value.
u.Dma	.MinimumChannel	4-byte lower bound on the DMA channel value.
	.MaximumChannel	4-byte upper bound on the DMA channel value.

IO_RESOURCE_LIST

```
typedef struct _IO_RESOURCE_LIST {
    USHORT Version;                         // Of this structure, currently 1
    USHORT Revision;                        // Of this structure, currently 1
    ULONG Count;                            // Of IO_RESOURCE_DESCRIPTORs in array
    IO_RESOURCE_DESCRIPTOR Descriptors[1];
} IO_RESOURCE_LIST, *PIO_RESOURCE_LIST
```

Table A.21 lists the fields for `IO_RESOURCE_LIST`.

Table A.21: `IO_RESOURCE_LIST` *Fields*

Field	Meaning
USHORT Version	The version of this structure. Currently, the only version implemented is 1.
USHORT Revision	The revision number of this structure. Currently, the only revision implemented is 1.
ULONG Flags	The count of the number of resource descriptors in the array.
IO_RESOURCE_DESCRIPTOR Descriptors[1]	This is the first entry of an array of variable length of resource descriptors.

IO_RESOURCE_REQUIREMENTS_LIST

```
typedef struct _IO_RESOURCE_REQUIREMENTS_LIST {
    ULONG Listless;                    // In bytes
    INTERFACE_TYPE interface_type;     // System-defined enum for the bus, one of
                                       // Internal, Isa, Eisa, MicroChannel,
                                       // TurboChannel, or PCIBus
    ULONG BusNumber;                   // System-assigned and zero-based bus
                                       // number
    ULONG SlotNumber;                  // Logical slot or location of the device
    ULONG Reserved[3];                 // For system use
    ULONG AlternativeLists;            // Count of alternative IO_RESOURCE_LIST
                                       // elements with IO_RESOURCE_DESCRIPTORs
```

```
    IO_RESOURCE_LIST List[1];          // Contains a variable-sized array of
                                       // descriptors
} IO_RESOURCE_REQUIREMENTS_LIST, *PIO_RESOURCE_REQUIREMENTS_LIST
```

IoSetCancelRoutine

```
PDRIVER_CANCEL IoSetCancelRoutine(IN PIRP Irp,
                                  IN PDRIVER_CANCEL CancelRoutine);
```

Sets up a driver-supplied Cancel Routine to be called if a given IRP is canceled.

This routine can disable the Cancel Routine currently set in an IRP. The `Irp` parameter points to the IRP being put into or removed from a cancelable state. The `CancelRoutine` parameter specifies the entry point of the caller-supplied Cancel Routine to be called if the specified IRP is canceled, or is NULL if the given IRP is being removed from the cancelable state. Returns the previous value of `Irp->CancelRoutine`. This routine is declared as follows.

```
VOID (*PDRIVER_CANCEL)(IN PDEVICE_OBJECT DeviceObject,
                       IN PIRP Irp);
```

A driver must hold the system Cancel Spin Lock when calling this routine if the driver uses the I/O Manager-supplied Device Queue in the Device Object. The driver executes at IRQL == DISPATCH_LEVEL after calling `IoAcquireCancelSpinLock` until it releases the Cancel Spin Lock with `IoReleaseCancelSpinLock`.

If the driver manages its own queue(s) of IRPs, then it does not need to hold the Cancel Spin Lock when calling this routine. `IoSetCancelSpinLock` uses an interlocked exchange intrinsic to set the address of the Cancel Routine as an atomic operation. Reduced usage of the Cancel Spin Lock can improve driver performance and overall system performance.

Driver Cancel Routines are called at IRQL == DISPATCH_LEVEL with the Cancel Spin Lock held. The Cancel Routine must release the Cancel Spin Lock before it returns control.

IoSetCompletionRoutine

```
VOID IoSetCompletionRoutine(IN PIRP Irp,
                            IN PIO_COMPLETION_ROUTINE CompletionRoutine,
                            IN PVOID Context,
                            IN BOOLEAN InvokeOnSuccess,
                            IN BOOLEAN InvokeOnError,
                            IN BOOLEAN InvokeOnCancel);
```

Establishes a completion routine to be called by a lower-level driver. This completion routine has the following signature.

```
NTSTATUS (*PIO_COMPLETION_ROUTINE)(IN PDEVICE_OBJECT DeviceObject,
                                   IN PIRP Irp,
                                   IN PVOID Context);
```

The parameters should all be obvious, except for `Context`. This is a pointer that is established by the `IoSetCompletionRoutine` `Context` parameter and is passed to the completion routine. In this way, a driver can pass additional information to its completion routine. Note that the `Context` pointer must be guaranteed to be valid at the time the completion routine is called and consequently must not reference a stack location. The *Context* parameter to `IoSetCompletionRoutine` can be NULL.

The lowest-level driver of a chain cannot call this function.

Higher-level drivers that allocate IRPs with `IoAllocateIrp` must call this routine with all *InvokeOn* parameters set to TRUE before passing the driver-allocated IRP to `IoCallDriver`. (Higher-level drivers also can allocate IRPs with `IoBuildAsynchronousFsdRequest`, but we don't deal with File System Drivers in this book.) When the completion routine is called with such an IRP, it must free the driver-allocated IRP and any other resources that the driver set up for the request, such as MDLs, by using `IoBuildPartialMdl`. Such a driver should return `STATUS_MORE_PROCESSING_REQUIRED` when it calls `IoFreeIrp` to forestall the I/O Manager's completion processing for the driver-allocated IRP.

A thread that calls this function must be running at IRQL <= DISPATCH_LEVEL.

IoSetNextIrpStackLocation

`VOID IoSetNextIrpStackLocation(IN OUT PIRP Irp);`

Sets the IRP Stack location in a driver-allocated IRP to that of the caller.

The *Irp* parameter points to the IRP whose stack location is to be set.

In general, this routine is seldom used by drivers. It is primarily used by drivers that require their own stack location in an IRP that they have allocated on their own to send to another driver.

`IoSetNextIrpStackLocation` is generally not needed, for either of the following reasons.

- The driver received the IRP that it is passing from another, higher-level driver, so it already owns a stack location.

- The driver allocated the IRP but does not need its own stack location because it can keep everything that it needs in a context block whose address can be passed to its `IoCompletion` routine.

Care should be taken if this routine is called, especially when allocating the IRP with `IoAllocateIrp` or `IoMakeAssociatedIrp`. The writer of the allocating driver must remember that a caller-specific stack location is not included in the number of stack locations required by the lower-level drivers to which the allocating driver sends IRPs with `IoCallDriver`. A driver must explicitly specify a stack location for itself in its call to `IoAllocateIrp` or `IoMakeAssociatedIrp` if it calls `IoSetNextIrpStackLocation` with the IRP returned by either routine.

A driver cannot call `IoSetNextIrpStackLocation` with any IRP it allocates by calling `IoBuildAsynchronousFsdRequest`, `IoBuildDeviceIoControlRequest`, or `IoBuildSynchronousFsdRequest`.

A thread that calls this function must be running at IRQL <= DISPATCH_LEVEL.

IoSizeOfIrp

`USHORT IoSizeOfIrp(IN CCHAR StackSize);`

Determines the size in bytes for an IRP, given a desired number of stack locations in the IRP.

The *StackSize* parameter specifies the number of stack locations for the IRP. IoSizeOfIrp returns the size, in bytes, of the IRP. The input *StackSize* value is either that of the next lower-level driver's Device Object or that value plus 1.

A thread that calls this function can be running at any IRQL level.

IoSkipCurrentIrpStackLocation

```
VOID IoSkipCurrentIrpStackLocation(IN PIRP Irp); // NT 5.0/Windows 2000
```

Copies the contents of the current IRP Stack location to the stack location for the next lower-level driver. This function does not allow a completion routine to be set.

A thread that calls this function must be running at IRQL <= DISPATCH_LEVEL.

IO_STACK_LOCATION

```
typedef struct _IO_STACK_LOCATION {
    UCHAR MajorFunction;
    UCHAR MinorFunction;
    UCHAR Flags;
    UCHAR Control;
    //
    // The following parameters depend on the IRP_MJ_XXX that is set
    // in MajorFunction. This declaration shows examples for IRP_MJ_READ,
    // IRP_MJ_WRITE, and IRP_MJ_DEVICE_CONTROL or, possibly,
    // IRP_MJ_INTERNAL_DEVICE_CONTROL requests, as well as for IRP_MJ_SCSI,
    // which is equivalent to IRP_MJ_INTERNAL_DEVICE_CONTROL.
    //
    union {
        .
        .
        struct {
            ULONG Length;
            ULONG Key;
            LARGE_INTEGER ByteOffset;
        } Read;

        struct {
            ULONG Length;
            ULONG Key;
            LARGE_INTEGER ByteOffset;
        } Write;
        .
        .
        struct {
            ULONG OutputBufferLength;
            ULONG InputBufferLength;
            ULONG IoControlCode;        // IOCTL_XXX
            PVOID Type3InputBuffer;
        } DeviceIoControl;
        .
        .
        struct {
            struct _SCSI_REQUEST_BLOCK *Srb;
        } Scsi;
        .
        .
```

```
    struct {                                  // NT 5.0 beta/Windows 2000
        CONST GUID * InterfaceType;           // NT 5.0 beta/Windows 2000
        USHORT Size;                          // NT 5.0 beta/Windows 2000
        USHORT Version;                       // NT 5.0 beta/Windows 2000
        PINTERFACE Interface;                 // NT 5.0 beta/Windows 2000
        PVOID InterfaceSpecificData;          // NT 5.0 beta/Windows 2000
    } QueryInterface;                         // NT 5.0 beta/Windows 2000

    struct {                                  // NT 5.0 beta/Windows 2000
        PPOWER_SEQUENCE PowerSequence;        // NT 5.0 beta/Windows 2000
    } PowerSequence;                          // NT 5.0 beta/Windows 2000

    struct {                                  // NT 5.0 beta/Windows 2000
        ULONG SystemContext;  // Reserved     // NT 5.0 beta/Windows 2000
        POWER_STATE_TYPE Type;                // NT 5.0 beta/Windows 2000
        POWER_STATE State;                    // NT 5.0 beta/Windows 2000
    } Power;                                  // NT 5.0 beta/Windows 2000
    } Parameters;
    PDEVICE_OBJECT DeviceObject;
    PFILE_OBJECT FileObject;
    .
    .
    .
} IO_STACK_LOCATION, *PIO_STACK_LOCATION;
```

An IO_STACK_LOCATION is obtained by calling the function
IoGetCurrentIrpStackLocation to get the current stack location of the IRP or by calling the
function IoGetNextIrpStackLocation to get the stack location of the next lower-level driver.
Table A.22 lists the fields for IO_STACK_LOCATION.

Table A.22: IO_STACK_LOCATION *Fields*

Field	Meaning	
UCHAR MajorFunction	The major function code. Although typically selected from the following list, some major function codes are device-dependent. You will define these for your specific device.	
	IRP_MJ_CREATE	Called whenever the application issues a CreateFile call. Every driver must support an entry port.
	IRP_MJ_CREATE_NAMED_PIPE	
	IRP_MJ_CLOSE	Called whenever the application issues a CloseHandle call that releases the last handle to a device.
	IRP_MJ_READ	Called whenever the application issues a ReadFile call.
	IRP_MJ_WRITE	Called whenever the application issues a WriteFile call.
	IRP_MJ_QUERY_INFORMATION	
	IRP_MJ_SET_INFORMATION	
	IRP_MJ_QUERY_EA	

Table A.22: IO_STACK_LOCATION *Fields (continued)*

Field	Meaning	
	IRP_MJ_SET_EA	
	IRP_MJ_FLUSH_BUFFERS	
	IRP_MJ_QUERY_VOLUME_INFORMATION	
	IRP_MJ_SET_VOLUME_INFORMATION	
	IRP_MJ_DIRECTORY_CONTROL	
	IRP_MJ_FILE_SYSTEM_CONTROL	
	IRP_MJ_DEVICE_CONTROL	Called for a DeviceIoControl call issued from the application.
	IRP_MJ_INTERNAL_DEVICE_CONTROL	Called for an IRP that, for internal purposes, is generated within the I/O system. These IRPs can never be directly generated by an application. Use of this technique allows for internal IoControl operations that should not be visible to the application level.
	IRP_MJ_SHUTDOWN	A shutdown request. This entry point is called whenever the system is shutting down, provided the Device Object has been registered using IoRegisterShutdownNotification.
	IRP_MJ_LOCK_CONTROL	
	IRP_MJ_CLEANUP	A driver with a Cancel Routine must handle Cleanup requests as well. This is called when the open handle reference count goes to 0 and the File Object reference count is nonzero.
	IRP_MJ_CREATE_MAILSLOT	
	IRP_MJ_QUERY_SECURITY	
	IRP_MJ_SET_SECURITY	
	IRP_MJ_POWER	*NT 5.0 beta/Windows 2000*; see Chapter 28.
	IRP_MJ_DEVICE_CHANGE	
	IRP_MJ_QUERY_QUOTA	
	IRP_MJ_SET_QUOTA	
	IRP_MJ_PNP	*NT 5.0 beta/Windows 2000*; see Chapter 28.
	IRP_MJ_MAXIMUM_FUNCTION	The largest legitimate value of a MajorFunction index.
UCHAR MinorFunction	A subfunction code, dependent on the major function code. Used almost exclusively by File System Drivers and SCSI drivers.	

Table A.22: `IO_STACK_LOCATION` *Fields (continued)*

Field	Meaning			
`UCHAR Flags`	A set of flags, used almost exclusively by File System Drivers.			
`UCHAR Control`	Can be checked by drivers to determine whether it is set with `SL_PENDING_RETURNED`. Drivers have read-only access to this member.			
`union {...} parameters`	A set of parameters that depend on the `MajorFunction`.			
	`Read`	`IRP_MJ_READ` parameters		
		`ULONG Length`	Number of bytes to transfer.	
		`ULONG Key`		
		`LARGE_INTEGER ByteOffset`	The position in the device at which to perform the operation (might not be meaningful for all devices).	
	`Write`	`IRP_MJ_WRITE` parameters		
		`ULONG Length`	Number of bytes to transfer.	
		`ULONG Key`		
		`LARGE_INTEGER ByteOffset`	The position in the device at which to perform the operation (might not be meaningful for all devices).	
	`DeviceIoControl`	`IRP_MJ_DEVICE_CONTROL` `IRP_MJ_INTERNAL_DEVICE_CONTROL`		
		`ULONG OutputBufferLength`	The length of the output buffer.	
		`ULONG InputBufferLength`	The length of the input buffer.	
		`ULONG IoControlCode`	An `IOCTL_XXX` code.	

Table A.22: `IO_STACK_LOCATION` *Fields (continued)*

Field	Meaning		
		`PVOID Type3InputBuffer`	
	Power	`IRP_MJ_POWER parameters`	*NT 5.0 beta/Windows 2000 only.*
		`ULONG SystemContext`	Reserved.
		`POWER_STATE_TYPE Type`	`SystemPowerState` or `DevicePowerState`.
		`POWER_STATE State`	The power state value. The value depends on the Type field and can be one of the following values.
		`SystemPowerState`	`PowerSystemWorking`
			`PowerSystemSleeping1`
			`PowerSystemSleeping2`
			`PowerSystemSleeping3`
			`PowerSystemHibernate`
			`PowerSystemShutdown`
		`DevicePowerState`	`PowerDeviceD0`
			`PowerDeviceD1`
			`PowerDeviceD2`
			`PowerDeviceD3`
	Scsi	`IRP_MJ_SCSI`	
		`struct _SCSI_REQUEST_BLOCK * Srb`	A pointer to a SCSI control block.

IoStartNextPacket

```
VOID IoStartNextPacket(IN PDEVICE_OBJECT DeviceObject,
                       IN BOOLEAN Cancelable);
```

Takes the IRP at the end of the `StartIo` queue and dispatches it.

The queue is dispatched in FIFO order. The *Cancelable* parameter tells if the IRP can be canceled.

A thread that calls this function must be running at IRQL <= DISPATCH_LEVEL.

IoStartNextPacketByKey

```
VOID IoStartNextPacketByKey(IN PDEVICE_OBJECT DeviceObject,
                            IN BOOLEAN Cancelable,
                            IN ULONG Key);
```

Searches the `StartIo` queue for a packet matching the specified *Key* value and dispatches it.

The *Cancelable* parameter tells if the IRP can be canceled.

A thread that calls this function must be running at IRQL <= DISPATCH_LEVEL.

IoStartPacket

```
VOID IoStartPacket(IN PDEVICE_OBJECT DeviceObject,
                   IN PIRP Irp,
                   IN PULONG Key,
                   IN PDRIVER_CANCEL CancelFunction);
```

Enters an IRP in the `StartIo` queue.

The *DeviceObject* and *Irp* parameters specify, respectively, the Device Object whose `StartIo` queue is to handle the IRP and the IRP itself. The *Key* parameter is a pointer to a value that determines where in the queue the IRP will be inserted. If it is specified as NULL, the IRP will be inserted at the end of the queue. The *CancelFunction* parameter is a pointer to a function to be called when the IRP is canceled. It is stored in the IRP as the IRP's Cancel function. If no Cancel function is required, this parameter would be NULL.

A thread that calls this function must be running at IRQL <= DISPATCH_LEVEL.

IoStartTimer

```
VOID IoStartTimer(IN PDEVICE_OBJECT DeviceObject)
```

Enables the timer established for *DeviceObject* by `IoInitializeTimer`. The `IoTimer` routine specified will be called approximately once per second.

A thread that calls this function must be running at IRQL <= DISPATCH_LEVEL.

IO_STATUS_BLOCK

```
typedef struct _IO_STATUS_BLOCK {
    NTSTATUS Status;
    ULONG Information;
} IO_STATUS_BLOCK, *PIO_STATUS_BLOCK;
```

IoStopTimer

```
VOID IoStoptimer(IN PDEVICE_OBJECT DeviceObject);
```

Disables the timer for the specified Device Object. It cannot be called from within the IoTimer routine.

A thread that calls this routine must be running at IRQL <= DISPATCH_LEVEL.

IoUnregisterShutdownNotification

```
NTSTATUS IoUnregisterShutdownNotification(IN PDEVICE_OBJECT DeviceObject);
```

Unregisters the Device Object that was registered by IoRegisterShutdownNotification so that it no longer receives shutdown notifications.

A thread that calls this function must be running at IRQL == PASSIVE_LEVEL.

IoWriteErrorLogEntry

```
VOID IoWriteErrorLogEntry(IN PVOID ElEntry);
```

Writes the error log entry.

A thread that calls this function must be running at IRQL <= DISPATCH_LEVEL.

IsListEmpty

```
BOOL IsListEmpty(IN PLIST_ENTRY ListHead);
```

Indicates whether a doubly linked, driver-maintained list is empty.

This function returns TRUE if it is empty and FALSE if it is not.

A thread that calls this function can be running at IRQL >= DISPATCH_LEVEL only if the caller-allocated storage for *ListHead* is resident and only if pointers to every list entry remain valid at IRQL >= DISPATCH_LEVEL as well.

IRP

The IRP is a "semi-opaque" data structure. Only certain fields, shown in Table A.23, are publicly available. No other fields of the IRP should be used.

```
typedef struct _IRP {
    // ... Private fields
    PMDL MdlAddress;
    ULONG Flags;
    union {
            struct _IRP *MasterIrp;
            // ... Private fields
            PVOID SystemBuffer;
        } AssociatedIrp;
    IO_STATUS_BLOCK IoStatus;
    KPROCESSOR_MODE RequestorMode;
    BOOLEAN Cancel;
    KIRQL CancelIrql;
```

```
        PDRIVER_CANCEL CancelRoutine;
        PVOID UserBuffer;
        union {
              struct {
                    // ... Private fields
                    union {
                          KDEVICE_QUEUE_ENTRY DeviceQueueEntry;
                          struct {
                                PVOID DriverContext[4];
                                };
                          };
                    // Private fields
                    PETHREAD Thread;
                    LIST_ENTRY ListEntry;
                  } Overlay;
            } Tail;
      } IRP, *PIRP;
```

Table A.23: IRP *Fields*

Field	Meaning	
UCHAR MajorFunction	The major function code. Although typically selected from the following list, some major function codes are device-dependent. You will define these for your specific device.	
	IRP_MJ_CREATE	Opens the target Device Object for I/O.
	IRP_MJ_READ	Transfers data from the device.
	IRP_MJ_WRITE	Transfers data to the device.
	IRP_MJ_DEVICE_CONTROL	Sets up, resets, modifies behavior, or otherwise operates on the device according to a device-type-specific control code.
	IRP_MJ_SCSI IRP_INTERNAL_DEVICE_CONTROL	
	IRP_MJ_CLOSE	Closes the Device Object.
UCHAR MinorFunction	A subfunction code, dependent on the major function code. Used almost exclusively by File System Drivers and SCSI drivers.	
UCHAR Flags	A set of flags, used almost exclusively by File System Drivers.	
PVOID AssociatedIrp.SystemBuffer	A pointer to the system buffer that is used for Buffered I/O.	
PMDL MdlAddress	A pointer to the MDL that is used for Direct I/O.	
BOOLEAN Cancel	Set to TRUE if the IRP has been canceled. If there was no Cancel Routine set, this must be explicitly checked for cancellation.	
KIRQL CancelIrql	The value that must be passed to IoReleaseCancelSpinLock.	
UCHAR Control	Can be checked by drivers to determine whether it is set with SL_PENDING_RETURNED. Drivers have read-only access to this member.	

Table A.23: IRP *Fields (continued)*

Field	Meaning	
IOSTATUS_BLOCK IoStatus	Used to return status to the I/O Manager. The visible fields are defined as follows.	
	.Status	Returns STATUS_ values.
	.Information	The number of bytes transferred on STATUS_SUCCESS; otherwise 0.
PLIST_ENTRY Tail.Overlay.ListEntry	Used to manage the StartIo and device-managed queueing of IRPs.	

KdPrint

```
#ifdef DBG
#define KdPrint(message) // Actual definition (not shown)
#else
#define KdPrint(message)
#endif
```

If the DBG preprocessor symbol is defined, the KdPrint macro will cause *message* to be written to the debug output port. If the DBG preprocessor symbol is not defined, this macro will not compile any code. *message* must be a parenthesized list that consists of a formatting string, which is an 8-bit NUL-terminated character string, and zero or more parameters to be formatted.

```
KdPrint( ("There are %d items in the list", itemCount) );
```

KeAcquireSpinLock

```
VOID KeAcquireSpinLock(IN PKSPIN_LOCK SpinLock, OUT PKIRQL OldIrql);
```

Acquires a Spin Lock.

The Spin Lock referenced must be initialized with KeInitializeSpinLock and be in the Nonpaged Pool allocated by the programmer. When control returns from this call, this means the Spin Lock has been acquired, the thread was reset to run at IRQL == DISPATCH_LEVEL, and the previous IRQL level was stored in the location referenced by the *OldIrql* parameter.

Spin Locks are multiprocessor-safe. Once a lock is acquired, no other processor in a multiprocessor environment can acquire it until the thread that acquired it releases it.

A Spin Lock is a potential serious abuse of a thread's power. Typically, a Spin Lock should be released within 25 microseconds. There are several critical restrictions on the code executed within the scope of a Spin Lock, as follows.

- The code must not be pageable.
- The code must not access pageable memory or in any other way cause a page fault.
- The code must not call any external function that might be in pageable memory or that accesses pageable data.

- The code must not call any function that could raise an exception.
- The code must not, itself, raise an exception.

A thread that calls this function must be running at IRQL <= DISPATCH_LEVEL.

KeAcquireSpinLockAtDpcLevel

VOID KeAcquireSpinLockAtDpcLevel(IN PKSPIN_LOCK *SpinLock*);

Acquires a Spin Lock. This special version of KeAcquireSpinLock can be used when the thread is known to be running at IRQL == DISPATCH_LEVEL. It optimizes this special case and consequently imposes less overhead.

The Spin Lock referenced must be initialized with KeInitializeSpinLock and be in the Nonpaged Pool allocated by the programmer. When control returns from this call, this means the Spin Lock has been acquired.

Spin Locks are multiprocessor-safe. Once a lock is acquired, no other processor in a multiprocessor environment can acquire it until the thread that acquired it releases it.

A Spin Lock is a potential serious abuse of a thread's power. Typically, a Spin Lock should be released within 25 microseconds. There are several critical restrictions on the code executed within the scope of a Spin Lock, as follows.

- The code must not be pageable.
- The code must not access pageable memory or in any other way cause a page fault.
- The code must not call any external function that might be in pageable memory or that accesses pageable data.
- The code must not call any function that could raise an exception.
- The code must not, itself, raise an exception.

A thread that calls this function must be running at IRQL == DISPATCH_LEVEL.

KeBugCheck

VOID KeBugCheck(IN ULONG *BugCheckCode*);

Brings the system down in a controlled fashion when things have gotten so bad that an attempt to continue would only corrupt the system.

This routine should be used with care in production code, but it is often a technique of last resort for some kinds of debugging.

If possible, all Kernel-mode components should log an error and continue to run, rather than calling KeBugCheck, unless the system itself could become corrupted by the inconsistency discovered. Most system components call KeBugCheckEx, which provides more information than KeBugCheck about the cause of such an inconsistency.

A thread that calls this function can be running at any IRQL level.

KeBugCheckEx

```
VOID KeBugCheckEx(IN ULONG BugCheckCode,
                  IN ULONG BugCheckParameter1,
                  IN ULONG BugCheckParameter2,
                  IN ULONG BugCheckParameter3,
                  IN ULONG BugCheckParameter4);
```

Brings the system down in a controlled fashion when things have gotten so bad that an attempt to continue would only corrupt the system.

This function should be used with care in production code, but it is often a technique of last resort for some kinds of debugging. It will display the BugCheck code, as well as information about up to four additional parameters. The meaning of these parameters depends on the BugCheck code. Information about all four will be displayed, so if you need fewer than four you can set the unused ones to 0.

If possible, all Kernel-mode components should log an error and continue to run, rather than calling KeBugCheckEx, unless the system itself could become corrupted by the inconsistency discovered.

A thread that calls this function can be running at any IRQL level.

KeCancelTimer

```
BOOLEAN KeCancelTimer(IN PKTIMER Timer);
```

Dequeues a Timer Object before the timer interval, if any was set, expires.

If the specified Timer Object was in the system timer queue, KeCancelTimer returns TRUE. If the Timer Object is currently in the system timer queue, it is removed from the queue. If a DPC Object is associated with the timer, it is canceled. Otherwise, no operation is performed.

A thread that calls this function must be running at IRQL <= DISPATCH_LEVEL.

KeClearEvent

```
VOID KeClearEvent(IN PKEVENT Event);
```

Sets the given event to the Not-Signaled state.

The *Event* parameter points to an initialized object of type *Event* for which the caller supplies the storage in nonpaged memory. The state of *Event* is set to Not-Signaled, meaning its value is set to 0.

KeClearEvent is more efficient if the caller does not need the value returned by KeResetEvent to determine what to do next.

A thread that calls this function must be running at IRQL <= DISPATCH_LEVEL.

KeDelayExecutionThread

```
NTSTATUS KeDelayExecutionThread(IN KPROCESSOR_MODE WaitMode,
                                IN BOOLEAN Alertable,
                                IN PLARGE_INTEGER Interval);
```

Causes the executing thread to be delayed by a specified interval. During this time, other threads can run.

The *WaitMode* parameter is either KernelMode or UserMode. Low-level drivers should specify KernelMode. The *Alertable* parameter specifies whether the wait is alertable; low-level drivers should specify FALSE. The interval is specified by a pointer to a LARGE_INTEGER, which gives the wait time in 100-ns intervals. The return value specifies the status of the wait. STATUS_SUCCESS indicates that the Wait operation completed successfully. The value STATUS_ALERTED is possible only if *Alertable* is TRUE; it indicates that the thread was alerted. The value STATUS_APC is possible only if the *WaitMode* parameter is UserMode and indicates that a User-mode APC was delivered before the interval expired.

Note that the time given is a *minimum* interval. The actual delay time will be the specified *Interval*, rounded up to the next system time interval, plus any scheduling delays, plus waiting for higher-priority threads to complete, plus any delays caused by threads running at DIRQL or DISPATCH_LEVEL. There is absolutely no guarantee about the latency between the time the *Interval* expires and the thread actually runs. This function cannot be used when precise timing is required, or regularly-spaced timing with very little jitter.

A thread that calls this function must be running at IRQL < DISPATCH_LEVEL.

KeDeregisterBugCheckCallback

```
BOOLEAN KeDeregisterBugCheckCallback(
                IN PKBUGCHECK_CALLBACK_RECORD CallbackRecord);
```

Unregisters a BugCheck callback. (Why it is called *De*register rather than *Un*register like every other unregister-function is one of those inexplicable quirks of history.) It is traditionally called in the Unload routine.

A thread that calls this function can be running at any IRQL.

KeFlushIoBuffers

```
VOID KeFlushIoBuffers(IN PMDL Mdl,
                IN BOOLEAN ReadOperation,
                IN BOOLEAN DmaOperation);
```

Guarantees that the data specified in the MDL is flushed from all caches on all processors. This is typically done before a DMA operation is initiated.

The implementation of this function is platform-dependent and can range all the way from flushing all data from all caches on all processors to flushing only the data specified to doing absolutely nothing (because cache snooping will handle the write-back selectively).

A thread that calls this function must be running at IRQL <= DISPATCH_LEVEL.

KeGetCurrentIrql

```
KIRQL KeGetCurrentIrql( );
```

Returns the current IRQL level.
A thread that calls this function can be running at any IRQL level.

KeGetCurrentProcessorNumber

```
ULONG KeGetCurrentProcessorNumber();
```

Returns the processor number for the processor running the thread that places this call.

A thread that calls this function should be running at IRQL >= DISPATCH_LEVEL. If it is running at IRQL < DISPATCH_LEVEL, it can be rescheduled to another processor at any time; the return value of this function is therefore unreliable.

KeGetDcacheFillSize

```
ULONG KeGetDcacheFillSize( );
```

Returns information that drivers that do DMA can use to avoid cache-line tearing during DMA transfer operations.

Such a driver can use the value that this function returns to allocate cache-aligned buffers for DMA. It also can use the value during DMA transfer operations.

For example, in a platform with the processor's data cache aligned on a 16-byte boundary, a DMA Device Driver should, if at all possible, transfer data as an integral number of 16-byte blocks to or from a buffer aligned on a 16-byte boundary. Otherwise, cache-line tearing occurs during DMA transfers. This can cause data integrity problems for both the driver and the system.

There appears to be no restriction on the IRQL level of a thread calling this function.

KeInitializeCallbackRecord

```
VOID KeInitializeCallbackRecord(
                    IN PKBUGCHECK_CALLBACK_RECORD CallbackRecord);
```

Initializes the callback record that will be used in a KeRegisterBugCheckCallback function. The callback record must be in nonpaged memory.

A thread that calls this function can be running at any IRQL.

KeInitializeDeviceQueue

```
VOID KeInitializeDeviceQueue(IN PKDEVICE_QUEUE DeviceQueue);
```

Initializes the specified queue to be empty and nonbusy. The storage for the DeviceQueue parameter must be in nonpaged memory.

While there is no explicit restriction on when this function can be called, the documentation suggests that it is usually called at PASSIVE_LEVEL during DriverEntry.

KeInitializeDpc

```
VOID KeInitializeDpc(IN PKDPC Dpc,
                    IN PKDEFERRED_ROUTINE DeferredRoutine,
                    IN PVOID DeferredContext);
```

Initializes a DPC Object, setting up a deferred procedure that can be called with a given programmer-supplied context.

The *Dpc* parameter points to a DPC Object for which the caller provides the storage. The *DeferredRoutine* parameter specifies the function to be called when the DPC entry is removed from the DPC queue. The *DeferredContext* parameter is an arbitrary pointer to storage that the DPC Routine will need.

The caller can queue an initialized DPC with `KeInsertQueueDpc`. The caller also can set up a Timer Object associated with the initialized DPC Object and queue the DPC with `KeSetTimer`.

Storage for the DPC Object must be resident either in the Device Extension of a driver-created Device Object, in the Controller Extension of a driver-created Controller Object, or in a Nonpaged Pool allocated by the caller.

The `PKDEFERRED_ROUTINE` is defined as follows.

```
VOID (*PKDEFERRED_ROUTINE)(IN PKDPC Dpc,
                           IN PVOID DeferredContext,
                           IN PVOID SystemArgument1,
                           IN PVOID SystemArgument2);
```

The parameters *SystemArgument1* and *SystemArgument2* are provided when the DPC is queued using `KeInsertQueueDpc`.

A thread that calls this function must be running at IRQL == PASSIVE_LEVEL.

KeInitializeEvent

```
VOID KeInitializeEvent(IN PKEVENT Event,
                       IN EVENT_TYPE Type,
                       IN BOOLEAN State);
```

Initializes an Event Object as a Synchronization (single waiter) Event or Notification Event and sets its initial state to Signaled or Not-Signaled.

The *Event* parameter points to an Event Object, for which the caller provides the storage. The *Type* parameter specifies the event type, one of the constants `NotificationEvent` or `SynchronizationEvent`. The *State* parameter specifies the initial state of the event: TRUE for Signaled and FALSE for Not-Signaled.

Storage for an Event Object must be resident, such as in the Device Extension of a driver-created Device Object, in the Controller Extension of a driver-created Controller Object, or in a Nonpaged Pool allocated by the caller.

A thread that calls this function must be running at IRQL == PASSIVE_LEVEL.

KeInitializeMutex

```
VOID KeInitializeMutex(IN PKMUTEX Mutex, IN ULONG Level)
```

Initializes a Mutex Object at a given level number, setting it to the Signaled state.

The *Mutex* parameter points to a Mutex Object, for which the caller provides the storage. The *Level* parameter specifies the level number to be assigned to the Mutex.

For better performance, use the `Ex..FastMutex` routines instead of the `Ke..Mutex` routines. However, a Fast Mutex cannot be acquired recursively, as a kernel Mutex can.

Storage for a Mutex Object must be resident in the Device Extension of a driver-created Device Object, in the Controller Extension of a driver-created Controller Object, or in a Nonpaged Pool allocated by the caller.

A thread that calls this function must be running at IRQL == PASSIVE_LEVEL.

KeInitializeSemaphore

```
VOID KeInitializeSemaphore(IN PKSEMAPHORE Semaphore,
                           IN LONG Count,
                           IN LONG Limit);
```

Initializes the Semaphore Object to have the value `Count`.

The maximum value of the Semaphore is `Limit`. The storage allocated for the Semaphore must be in the Nonpaged Pool.

A thread that calls this function must be running at IRQL == PASSIVE_LEVEL.

KeInitializeSpinLock

```
VOID KeInitializeSpinLock(IN PKSPIN_LOCK SpinLock);
```

Initializes a Spin Lock.

The caller must have the Spin Lock allocated in the Nonpaged Pool. This function must be called before any other function that operates on a Spin Lock. The Spin Lock is initialized so that the first attempt to acquire it will be successful (for higher-level synchronization structures, this is called the Signaled state). A Spin Lock cannot be initialized to a blocking (Not-Signaled) state.

A thread that calls this function can be running at any IRQL level. Typically, it is called in the `DriverEntry` routine at IRQL == DISPATCH_LEVEL.

KeInitializeTimer

```
VOID KeInitializeTimer(IN PKTIMER Timer);
```

Initializes a Timer Object.

The `Timer` parameter points to a Timer Object, for which the caller provides the storage. The Timer Object is initialized with a state of Not-Signaled. Storage for a Timer Object must be resident in the Device Extension of a driver-created Device Object, in the Controller Extension of a driver-created Controller Object, or in a Nonpaged Pool allocated by the caller.

`KeInitializeTimer` can initialize only a Notification Timer. To initialize a Synchronization Timer, use `KeInitializeTimerEx`. (`KeInitializeTimerEx` also will initialize a Notification Timer.)

A thread that calls this function should be running at IRQL <= DISPATCH_LEVEL. It is best to initialize timers at IRQL == PASSIVE_LEVEL.

KeInitializeTimerEx

```
VOID KeInitializeTimerEx(IN PKTIMER Timer, IN TIMER_TYPE Type);
```

Initializes a Timer Object.

The Timer Object may be initialized as a Notification Timer (all threads released, manual reset) by specifying `NotificationTimer` or as a Synchronization Timer (one thread released, automatic reset) by specifying `SynchronizationTimer`. Storage for a Timer Object must be resident in the Device Extension of a driver-created Device Object, in the Controller Extension of a driver-created Controller Object, or in a Nonpaged Pool allocated by the caller.

A thread that calls this function must be running at IRQL <= DISPATCH_LEVEL. Timers are best initialized at IRQL == PASSIVE_LEVEL.

KeInsertByKeyDeviceQueue

```
BOOLEAN KeInsertByKeyDeviceQueue(IN PKDEVICE_QUEUE DeviceQueue,
                                 IN PKDEVICE_QUEUE_ENTRY DeviceQueueEntry,
                                 IN ULONG SortKey);
```

Tries to insert the specified *DeviceQueueEntry* in the *DeviceQueue*.

If the Device Queue is empty and not busy, this function returns FALSE and the entry is *not* queued. In this case, you must start the desired I/O operation immediately yourself. An attempt to insert a *DeviceQueueEntry* in a nonbusy, empty *DeviceQueue* will set the state of the Device Queue to *busy*. All operations on the Device Queue are synchronized by a Spin Lock. The entry is inserted in the queue in an order determined by the *SortKey* parameter. The new entry is positioned in the Device Queue *after* any entries in the queue that have *SortKey* values less than or equal to its *SortKey* value and *preceding* any entries that have *SortKey* values that are greater.

A thread that calls this function must be executing at IRQL == DISPATCH_LEVEL.

KeInsertDeviceQueue

```
BOOLEAN KeInsertDeviceQueue(IN PKDEVICE_QUEUE DeviceQueue,
                            IN PKDEVICE_QUEUE_ENTRY DeviceQueueEntry);
```

Tries to insert the specified *DeviceQueueEntry* in the *DeviceQueue*.

If the Device Queue is empty and not busy, this function returns FALSE and the entry is *not* queued. In this case, you must start the desired I/O operation immediately yourself. An attempt to insert a *DeviceQueueEntry* in a nonbusy, empty *DeviceQueue* will set the state of the Device Queue to *busy*. All operations on the Device Queue are synchronized by a Spin Lock.

A thread that calls this function must be executing at IRQL == DISPATCH_LEVEL.

KeInsertQueueDpc

```
BOOLEAN KeInsertQueueDpc(IN PKDPC Dpc,
                         IN PVOID SystemArgument1,
                         IN PVOID SystemArgument2);
```

Queues a DPC for execution when the IRQL of a processor drops below DISPATCH_LEVEL.

The *Dpc* parameter points to an initialized control object of type KDPC, for which the caller provides the storage. The parameters *SystemArgument1* and *SystemArgument2* represent additional values that can be passed in to the DPC Routine, in addition to the *Context* pointer that is established by `KeInitializeDpc`. If these parameters are interpreted as pointers, the storage they reference must be defined and available at the time the DPC executes. If the specified DPC

Object is not currently in the queue, `KeInsertQueueDpc` queues the DPC and returns TRUE. If the specified DPC Object is already in the DPC queue, no operation is performed except to return FALSE. Otherwise, the DPC Object is inserted in the DPC queue and a software interrupt is requested at IRQL == DISPATCH_LEVEL on the current processor. This interrupt will be seen, and the DPC dequeued, when the processor IRQL drops to DISPATCH_LEVEL. If the processor, or the target processor in a multiprocessor system, is already at or below DISPATCH_LEVEL, the DPC Routine could either execute before `KeInsertQueueDpc` returns or be into execution (but not completed) when this function returns.

Note that a given DPC Object and the function it represents can each be queued for execution only once at any given moment.

Microsoft's documentation states that "The deferred procedure is run when IRQL on the current processor drops below DISPATCH_LEVEL". This is not true on NT 5.0 beta/Windows 2000 if you have used `KeSetTargetProcessorDpc` to set the desired processor and that processor is already below DISPATCH_LEVEL. Therefore you cannot depend on the DPC's not executing until your current thread has completed its work at elevated IRQL and drops to DISPATCH_LEVEL.

KeLowerIrql

```
VOID KeLowerIrql(IN KIRQL NewIrql);
```

Lowers the hardware priority to a given IRQL value, thereby masking off interrupts of equivalent or lower IRQL on the current processor.

The *NewIrql* parameter specifies the new IRQL to which the hardware priority is to be lowered. This should be the *OldIrql* from a previous call to `KeRaiseIrql`. If the new IRQL is not the IRQL returned by an immediately preceding `KeRaiseIrql`, a BugCheck occurs. Otherwise, the current IRQL is set to the specified value. The Microsoft documentation seems to imply that this is tracked. We do not know if this implies that you cannot nest IRQL changes (raise, (raise, lower), lower), so you should be cautious if this appears to be what you need.

A thread that calls this function should be running at the IRQL set by an immediately preceding `KeRaiseIrql`.

KeNumberProcessors

```
extern PCCHAR KeNumberProcessors;
```

`KeNumberProcessors` is one of the few global variables in the system. It contains a pointer to the number of processors in the system. This pointer must be dereferenced to get the actual number of processors.

KeQueryPerformanceCounter

```
LARGE_INTEGER KeQueryPerformanceCounter(
                    IN PLARGE_INTEGER PerformanceFrequencyOPTIONAL);
```

Returns the performance counter value.

If the *PerformanceFrequency* parameter is not NULL, it returns the performance frequency value in the indicated location.

This is intended for a very fine-grain performance measurement. However, it briefly keeps all interrupts masked off, so if it is called too often, it will seriously affect system performance, thus actually perturbing the very thing it is trying to measure. It is intended strictly for performance measurement.

The value returned is platform-specific and is usually the number of processor clock ticks since boot time.

A thread that calls this function can be running at any IRQL.

KeQuerySystemTime

VOID KeQuerySystemTime(OUT PLARGE_INTEGER *CurrentTime*);

The *CurrentTime* parameter points to a value which is set to the the current time on return from KeQuerySystemTime. The time is a count of 100-ns intervals since January 1, 1601. This time can be rendered into a more usable form by RtlTimeToTimeFields.

A thread that calls this function can be running at any IRQL.

KeQueryTickCount

VOID KeQueryTickCount(OUT PLARGE_INTEGER *TickCount*);

Maintains a count of the interval timer interrupts that have occurred since the system was booted.

The *TickCount* parameter is a pointer that will be set to the value of the system tick count. The *TickCount* value is incremented by 1 at each interval timer interrupt while the system is running.

The use of KeQueryTickCount is the preferred method of determining elapsed time, for measuring relative timing, and for time stamps.

A thread that calls this function can be running at any IRQL.

KeQueryTimeIncrement

ULONG KeQueryTimeIncrement();

Returns the number of 100-ns units that are added to the system time each time the interval clock interrupts.

A thread that calls this function can be running at any IRQL.

KeRaiseIrql

VOID KeRaiseIrql(IN KIRQL *NewIrql*, OUT PKIRQL *OldIrql*);

Raises the hardware priority to a given IRQL value, thereby masking off interrupts of equivalent or lower IRQL on the current processor. The *NewIrql* parameter specifies the new IRQL to which the hardware priority is to be raised. The *OldIrql* parameter points to the storage for the original (unraised) IRQL value to be used in a subsequent call to KeLowerIrql.

If the new IRQL is less than the current IRQL, a BugCheck occurs. Otherwise, the current IRQL is set to the specified value.

A thread that calls this function can be running at any IRQL as long as `NewIrql` <= `CurrentIrql`.

KeReadStateEvent

`LONG KeReadStateEvent(IN PKEVENT Event);`

Returns the current state, Signaled or Not-Signaled, of a given Event Object specified by the `Event` parameter.

If the current state of the Event Object is Signaled, a nonzero value is returned. Otherwise, 0 is returned.

It is also possible to read the state of an event from a driver's ISR at DIRQL, if the following conditions are met: The driver's Event Object is resident (probably in its Device Extension), and any other function that accesses the event synchronizes its access with the ISR.

A thread that calls this function must be running at IRQL <= `DISPATCH_LEVEL`.

KeReadStateMutex

`LONG KeReadStateMutex(IN PKMUTEX Mutex);`

Returns the current state, Signaled or Not-Signaled, of a given Mutex Object.

The `Mutex` parameter points to an initialized Mutex Object for which the caller provides the storage. `KeReadStateMutex` returns `TRUE` if the Mutex is signaled and `FALSE` if the Mutex is Not-Signaled.

A thread that calls this function must be running at IRQL <= `DISPATCH_LEVEL`.

KeReadStateSemaphore

`LONG KeReadStateSemaphore(IN PKSEMAPHORE Semaphore);`

Returns the current state, Signaled or Not-Signaled, of a given Semaphore Object specified by the `Semaphore` parameter.

If the current state of the Semaphore Object is Signaled, a nonzero value is returned. Otherwise, 0 is returned.

It is also possible to read the state of an event from a driver's ISR at DIRQL, if the following conditions are met: The driver's Event Object is resident (probably in its Device Extension), and any other function that accesses the event synchronizes its access with the ISR.

A thread that calls this function must be running at IRQL <= `DISPATCH_LEVEL`.

KeReadStateTimer

`BOOLEAN KeReadStateTimer(IN PKTIMER Timer);`

Reads the current state of a given Timer Object.

The `Timer` parameter points to an initialized Timer Object, for which the caller provides the storage. If the current state of the Timer Object is Signaled, `TRUE` is returned.

A thread that calls this function must be running at IRQL <= `DISPATCH_LEVEL`.

KeRegisterBugCheckCallback

```
BOOLEAN KeRegisterBugCheckCallback(
                    IN PKBUGCHECK_CALLBACK_RECORD CallbackRecord,
                    IN PKBUGCHECK_CALLBACK_ROUTINE CallbackRoutine,
                    IN PVOID Buffer,
                    IN ULONG Length,
                    IN PUCHAR Component);
```

Registers a callback function to be called when a BugCheck occurs.

The *CallBackRecord* parameter points to a callback record that has been initialized with KeInitializeCallbackRecord. The *CallBackRoutine* is the pointer to the function to be called. The *Buffer* supplied must be allocated in the Nonpaged Pool and must not be freed until *after* KeDeregisterBugCheckCallback is called (if the buffer is in the Device Extension, this will not be a problem). If *CallbackRoutine* is called, it will get a pointer to this buffer and may write any information into it that you specify; the nature and format of this information is entirely up to you. The *Component* string is a pointer to a NUL-terminated 8-bit character string that can be used as an aid in analyzing a crash dump.

A thread that calls this function can be running at any IRQL. Traditionally, it is called from PASSIVE_LEVEL during DriverEntry setup.

KeReleaseMutex

```
LONG KeReleaseMutex(IN PKMUTEX Mutex, IN BOOLEAN Wait);
```

Releases a given Mutex Object.

The *Wait* parameter should be TRUE if the thread is immediately going to perform a KeWait... call and should be FALSE otherwise. KeReleaseMutex returns 0 if the Mutex has become Signaled.

A thread that calls this function must be running at IRQL == PASSIVE_LEVEL.

KeReleaseSemaphore

```
LONG KeReleaseSemaphore(IN PKSEMAPHORE Semaphore,
                    IN KPRIORITY Increment,
                    IN LONG Adjustment,
                    IN BOOLEAN Wait);
```

Releases a given Semaphore Object.

This routine supplies a runtime priority boost for waiting threads. If this call sets the Semaphore to the Signaled state, the Semaphore count is augmented by the given value. The caller can also specify whether it will call one of the KeWait... routines as soon as KeReleaseSemaphore returns control.

The *Semaphore* parameter points to an initialized Semaphore Object, for which the caller provides the storage. The *Increment* parameter specifies the priority increment to be applied if releasing the Semaphore causes a wait to be satisfied. The *Adjustment* parameter specifies a value to be added to the current Semaphore count. This value must be positive and most often is 1. The *Wait* parameter specifies whether the call to KeReleaseSemaphore is to be followed immediately by a call to one of the KeWait... functions. This optimizes the performance of the system for this case. If the return value is 0, the previous state of the Semaphore Object is Not-Signaled.

Releasing a Semaphore Object causes the Semaphore count to be augmented by the value of the *Adjustment* parameter. If the resulting value is greater than the limit of the Semaphore Object, the count is not adjusted and an exception, STATUS_SEMAPHORE_COUNT_EXCEEDED, is raised.

Augmenting the Semaphore Object count causes the Semaphore to attain a state of Signaled. An attempt then is made to satisfy as many waits as possible on the Semaphore Object.

If the value of the *Wait* parameter is TRUE, the return to the caller is executed without lowering the IRQL or releasing the dispatcher database Spin Lock. Therefore the call to KeReleaseSemaphore must be followed immediately by a call to one of the KeWait... functions. This capability allows the caller to release a Semaphore and to wait, all as one atomic operation, thus preventing a possibly superfluous context switch. However, the caller cannot wait at raised IRQL or in an arbitrary thread context for a nonzero interval on a Semaphore Object.

A thread that calls this function must be running at IRQL <= DISPATCH_LEVEL, provided that *Wait* is set to FALSE. Otherwise, the caller must be running at IRQL == PASSIVE_LEVEL.

KeReleaseSpinLock

```
VOID KeReleaseSpinLock(IN PKSPIN_LOCK SpinLock, IN KIRQL NewIrql);
```

KeReleaseSpinLock releases a Spin Lock.

The thread is set to run at the specified new IRQL, which is usually the value that was saved as the *OldIrql* parameter when the Spin Lock was acquired. If any threads are waiting to acquire the Spin Lock, one of them will successfully acquire it. If no threads are waiting, the next thread that attempts to acquire the Spin Lock will be able to do so.

If threads are waiting to acquire the Spin Lock, there is no guarantee as to which thread will successfully acquire it. Spin Locks are multiprocessor-safe.

A thread that calls this function must be running at IRQL == DISPATCH_LEVEL. After the function returns, the thread will be running at the *NewIrql* level, <= DISPATCH_LEVEL.

KeReleaseSpinLockFromDpcLevel

```
VOID KeReleaseSpinLockFromDpcLevel(IN PKSPIN_LOCK SpinLock);
```

Releases a Spin Lock that was acquired by KeAcquireSpinLockAtDpcLevel.

If any threads are waiting to acquire the Spin Lock, one of them will successfully acquire it. If no threads are waiting, the next thread that attempts to acquire the Spin Lock will be able to do so.

If threads are waiting to acquire the Spin Lock, there is no guarantee as to which thread will successfully acquire it. Spin Locks are multiprocessor-safe.

A thread that calls this function must be running at IRQL == DISPATCH_LEVEL. After the function returns, the thread will still be running at DISPATCH_LEVEL.

KeRemoveByKeyDeviceQueue

```
PKDEVICE_QUEUE_ENTRY KeRemoveByKeyDeviceQueue(
                                        IN PKDEVICE_QUEUE DeviceQueue,
                                        IN ULONG SortKey);
```

Removes a queue entry whose position is determined by *SortKey* and returns a pointer to it.

It is unspecified what happens if an entry matching *SortKey* does not exist in the queue. If the queue is empty and busy, the value returned is NULL and the queue is marked as not-busy. It is "an error" to call this function on an empty, nonbusy queue (although the consequences are not defined). A Spin Lock in *DeviceQueue* provides for multiprocessor-safe access.

A thread that calls this function must be running at IRQL == DISPATCH_LEVEL.

KeRemoveDeviceQueue

```
PKDEVICE_QUEUE_ENTRY KeRemoveDeviceQueue(IN PKDEVICE_QUEUE DeviceQueue);
```

Removes the queue entry at the head of the queue and returns a pointer to it.

If the queue is empty and busy, the value returned is NULL and the queue is marked as not-busy. It is "an error" to call this function on an empty, nonbusy queue (although the consequences are not defined). A Spin Lock in *DeviceQueue* provides for multiprocessor-safe access.

A thread that calls this function must be running at IRQL == DISPATCH_LEVEL.

KeRemoveEntryDeviceQueue

```
BOOLEAN KeRemoveEntryDeviceQueue(IN PKDEVICE_QUEUE DeviceQueue,
                                 IN PKDEVICE_QUEUE_ENTRY DeviceQueueEntry);
```

The specified *DeviceQueueEntry* is removed from the *DeviceQueue*. If the entry is not in the Device Queue, the function returns FALSE and the entry is not removed. Before this operation is performed, the IRQL is raised to DISPATCH_LEVEL and the Spin Lock is acquired. This provides multiprocessor-safe access even when the function is called from PASSIVE_LEVEL, as it might be during a Cancel operation. When the operation has completed, the Spin Lock is released and the IRQL is returned to its state at the time of the call.

A thread that calls this function must be running at IRQL <= DISPATCH_LEVEL.

KeRemoveQueueDpc

```
BOOLEAN KeRemoveQueueDpc(IN PKDPC Dpc);
```

Removes the specified DPC from the DPC queue.

If the DPC was in the queue and was removed, this routine returns TRUE; if the DPC was not in the queue, it returns FALSE.

A thread that calls this function can be running at any IRQL.

KeResetEvent

```
LONG KeResetEvent(IN PKEVENT Event);
```

Resets the state of a specified Event Object to Not-Signaled and returns the previous state of that Event Object.

This function returns the previous state of the given Event, nonzero for Signaled. Unless the caller uses the value returned by KeResetEvent, KeClearEvent is faster.

A thread that calls this function must be running at IRQL <= DISPATCH_LEVEL.

KeSetEvent

```
LONG KeSetEvent(IN PKEVENT Event,
                IN KPRIORITY Increment,
                IN BOOLEAN Wait);
```

Sets the state of an Event Object to Signaled if the event was not already signaled and returns the previous state of the Event Object.

The *Event* parameter points to an initialized Event Object, for which the caller provides the storage. The *Increment* parameter specifies the priority increment to be applied if setting the event causes a wait to be satisfied. The *Wait* parameter specifies whether the call to KeSetEvent is to be followed immediately by a call to a KeWait... function.

If the *Wait* parameter is TRUE, the return to the caller is executed without lowering the IRQL or releasing the dispatcher database Spin Lock. Therefore the call to KeSetEvent must be followed immediately by a call to one of the KeWait... functions. This allows the caller to set an event and wait, all as one atomic operation, thus preventing a possibly superfluous context switch. However, the caller cannot wait at raised IRQL or in an arbitrary thread context for a nonzero interval on an Event Object.

If *Wait* is set to FALSE, the caller can be running at IRQL <= DISPATCH_LEVEL. Otherwise, callers of KeSetEvent must be running at IRQL == PASSIVE_LEVEL and in a nonarbitrary thread context.

KeSetPriorityThread

```
KPRIORITY KeSetPriorityThread(IN PKTHREAD Thread,
                              IN KPRIORITY Priority);
```

Changes the priority of the specified *Thread*.

The *Priority* parameter is usually the constant LOW_REALTIME_PRIORITY.

A thread that calls this function must be running at IRQL == PASSIVE_LEVEL.

KeSetTimer

```
BOOLEAN KeSetTimer(IN PKTIMER Timer, IN LARGE_INTEGER DueTime, IN PKDPC Dpc);
```

Sets the absolute or relative interval at which a Timer Object is to be set to the Signaled state and, optionally, supplies a CustomTimerDpc routine to be executed when that interval expires.

The *Timer* parameter points to a Timer Object that was initialized with KeInitializeTimer or KeInitializeTimerEx. The *DueTime* parameter specifies the absolute or relative time at which the timer is to expire. If the value of *DueTime* is negative, the expiration time is relative to the current system time. Otherwise, the expiration time is absolute. The expiration time is expressed in system time units (100-ns intervals). Absolute expiration times track any changes in the system time; relative expiration times are not affected by system time changes. The *Dpc* parameter points to a DPC Object that was initialized by *KeInitializeDpc*. This parameter is optional. If the Timer Object was already in the system timer queue, *KeSetTimer* returns TRUE. This function

- computes the expiration time,
- sets the state of the timer to Not-Signaled, and
- inserts the Timer Object in the system timer queue.

If the Timer Object was already in the timer queue, it is implicitly canceled before being set to the new expiration time. A call to KeSetTimer before the previously specified *DueTime* has expired cancels both the timer and the call to the DPC, if any, associated with the previous call.

If *Dpc* is specified, a DPC Object is associated with the Timer Object. When the timer expires, the Timer Object is removed from the system timer queue and its state is set to Signaled. If a DPC Object was associated with the timer when it was set, the DPC Object is inserted in the system DPC queue, to be executed as soon as conditions permit after the timer interval expires.

Only one instantiation of a given DPC Object can be queued at any given moment. To avoid potential race conditions, the DPC passed to KeSetTimer should not be passed to KeInsertQueueDpc.

A caller cannot wait at raised IRQL or in an arbitrary thread context for a timer to expire by calling a KeWait... function.

Callers of KeSetTimer specify a timer that times out once. To set a recurring timer, use KeSetTimerEx.

A thread that calls this function must be running at IRQL <= DISPATCH_LEVEL.

KeSetTimerEx

```
BOOLEAN KeSetTimerEx(IN PKTIMER Timer,
                     IN LARGE_INTEGER DueTime,
                     IN LONG Period OPTIONAL,
                     IN PKDPC Dpc OPTIONAL);
```

Sets the absolute or relative interval at which a Timer Object is to be set to the Signaled state. It also optionally supplies a custom timer DPC Routine to be executed when that interval expires and optionally supplies a recurring interval for the timer. It queues the Timer Object in the system timer queue.

The *Timer* parameter points to a Timer Object that was initialized with KeInitializeTimer or KeInitializeTimerEx. The *DueTime* parameter specifies the absolute or relative time at which the timer is to expire. If the value of *DueTime* is negative, the expiration time is relative to the current system time. Otherwise, the expiration time is absolute. The expiration time is expressed in system time units (100-ns intervals). Absolute expiration times track any changes in the system time; relative expiration times are not affected by system time changes. The *Period* parameter specifies an optional period for the timer, in milliseconds. This value must be less than or equal to MAXLONG. The *Dpc* parameter points to a DPC Object that was initialized by KeInitializeDpc. This parameter is optional. If the Timer Object was already in the system timer queue, KeSetTimerEx returns TRUE. This function

- computes the expiration time,
- sets the state of the timer to Not-Signaled,
- sets the recurring interval for the timer, if one was specified, and
- inserts the Timer Object in the system timer queue.

If the Timer Object was already in the timer queue, it is implicitly canceled before being set to the new expiration time. A call to KeSetTimerEx before the previously specified *DueTime* has expired cancels both the timer and the call to the DPC, if any, associated with the previous call.

If *Dpc* is specified, a DPC Object is associated with the Timer Object. When the timer expires, the Timer Object is removed from the system timer queue (unless it is a recurring timer) and its state is set to Signaled. If a DPC Object was associated with the timer when it was set, the DPC Object is inserted in the system DPC queue, to be executed as soon as conditions permit after the timer interval expires.

A DPC Routine cannot deallocate a periodic timer but can deallocate a nonperiodic timer.

Only one instantiation of a given DPC Object can be queued at any given moment. To avoid potential race conditions, the DPC passed to KeSetTimerEx should not be passed to KeInsertQueueDpc.

A caller cannot wait at raised IRQL or in an arbitrary thread context for a timer to expire by calling a KeWait*Xxx* function.

A thread that calls this function must be running at IRQL <= DISPATCH_LEVEL.

KeStallExecutionProcessor

```
VOID KeStallExecutionProcessor(IN ULONG MicroSeconds);
```

Delays the execution by at least the indicated number of microseconds specified. The processor remains at its current IRQL.

Microsoft recommends that this interval not exceed 50μsec. The main purpose of this function is to handle delays of less than a clock tick in order to deal with very short device-dependent delays.

KeSynchronizeExecution

```
BOOLEAN KeSynchronizeExecution(IN PKINTERRUPT Interrupt,
                               IN PKSYNCHRONIZE_ROUTINE SynchronizeRoutine,
                               IN PVOID SynchronizeContext);
```

When KeSynchronizeExecution is called, the following occurs:

- The IRQL is raised to the *SynchronizeIrql* specified in the call to IoConnectInterrupt.

- Access to *SynchronizeContext* is synchronized with the corresponding ISR by acquiring the associated Interrupt Object Spin Lock.

- The specified *SynchronizeRoutine* is called with the input pointer to *SynchronizeContext*.

The caller-supplied *SynchronizeRoutine* runs at DIRQL, so it must execute very quickly.

A thread that calls this function must be running at IRQL <= DIRQL, that is, less than or equal to the value of the *SynchronizeIrql* parameter specified when the caller registered its ISR(s) with IoConnectInterrupt.

KeWaitForMultipleObjects

```
NTSTATUS KeWaitForMultipleObjects(IN ULONG Count,
                                  IN PVOID Object[],
                                  IN WAIT_TYPE WaitType,
                                  IN KWAIT_REASON WaitReason,
                                  IN KPROCESSOR_MODE WaitMode,
                                  IN BOOLEAN Alertable,
                                  IN PLARGE_INTEGER Timeout,
                                  IN PKWAIT_BLOCK WaitBlockArray);
```

Puts the current thread into an alertable or nonalertable wait state until any or all of a number of dispatcher objects are set to the Signaled state or (optionally) until the wait times out.

The *Object* parameter points to an array of pointers to dispatcher objects (events, Mutexes, Semaphores, threads, and timers) for which the caller supplies the storage. The *Count* parameter specifies how many objects are in the array. The *WaitType* is either the constant WaitAll, which indicates that all of the events must be satisfied, or WaitAny, which indicates that only one needs to be satisfied.

The *WaitReason* parameter specifies the reason for the wait. Drivers should set this value to Executive. Alternatively, if the driver is doing work on behalf of a user and is running in the context of a User thread, this parameter should be set to UserRequest. The *WaitMode* parameter specifies whether the caller waits in KernelMode or UserMode. Intermediate and lowest-level drivers should specify KernelMode. If the set of objects waited on includes a Mutex, the caller must specify KernelMode.

The *Alertable* parameter specifies a Boolean value that indicates whether the thread can be alerted while in the waiting state. The *Timeout* parameter points to an absolute or relative value representing the upper limit for the wait. A negative value specifies an interval relative to the current system time. The value should be expressed in 100-ns units. Absolute expiration times track any changes in the system time; relative expiration times are not affected by system time changes. The *WaitBlockArray* parameter points to an optional array of wait blocks that describe the Wait operation. If the parameter is NULL, the *Count* parameter must be less than or equal to the value THREAD_WAIT_OBJECTS, as described immediately following Table A.24.

This function can return one of the values given in Table A.24.

For convenience and to efficiently handle the most common cases, each Thread Object has a built-in array of wait blocks that can be used to wait on several objects concurrently. Whenever possible, this array should be used in a wait-multiple operation because no additional wait block storage needs to be allocated and later deallocated. However, if the number of objects to be waited on concurrently is greater than the number of built-in wait blocks, you must allocate an

Table A.24: KeWaitForMultipleObjects *Values*

Value	Meaning
STATUS_SUCCESS	For a WaitAll, indicates that all of the objects have satisfied their Signaled conditions.
0..MAXIMUM_WAIT_OBJECTS - 1	For a WaitAny, indicates the index in the object array of the lowest-numbered object that has satisfied the Signaled condition. The following special values are defined.
	STATUS_WAIT_0 0
	STATUS_WAIT_1 1
	STATUS_WAIT_2 2
	STATUS_WAIT_3 3
	STATUS_WAIT_63 63 (MAXIMUM_WAIT_OBJECTS - 1)
STATUS_ALERTED	The wait is completed because of an alert to the thread.
STATUS_USER_APC	A user APC was delivered to the current thread before the specified timeout interval expired.
STATUS_TIMEOUT	A timeout occurred before the specified set of wait conditions was met. This value can be returned when an explicit timeout value of 0 is specified, but the specified set of wait conditions cannot be met immediately.

array of *Count* * sizeof(KWAITBLOCK) bytes and use the *WaitBlockArray* parameter to specify this alternate set of wait blocks to be used in the Wait operation. The number of built-in blocks is defined by the symbol THREAD_WAIT_OBJECTS. If the number of wait objects you need exceeds this value, you must allocate an array of wait blocks that the call will use for synchronization.

If the *WaitBlockArray* parameter is NULL, the *Count* parameter must be less than or equal to THREAD_WAIT_OBJECTS; otherwise, a BugCheck will occur.

If the *WaitBlockArray* pointer is non-NULL, *Count* must be less than or equal to MAXIMUM_WAIT_OBJECTS. Otherwise, a BugCheck will occur, with the code MAXIMUM_WAIT_OBJECTS_EXCEEDED.

The current state for each of the specified objects is examined to determine whether the wait can be satisfied immediately. If the necessary side effects are performed on the objects, an appropriate value is returned.

If the wait cannot be satisfied immediately and either no *Timeout* value or a nonzero *Timeout* value was specified, the current thread is put in a wait state and a new thread is selected for execution on the current processor. If no timeout is supplied, the calling thread will remain in a wait state until the conditions specified by *Object* and *WaitType* are satisfied.

If *Timeout* is specified, the wait will be automatically satisfied if none of the specified wait conditions is met when the given interval expires. A *Timeout* value of 0 allows the testing of a set of wait conditions, conditionally performing any side effects if the wait can be immediately satisfied, as in the acquisition of a Mutex.

The *Alertable* parameter specifies whether the thread can be alerted in the wait state. If its value is TRUE and the thread is alerted for a mode that is equal to or more privileged than the given *WaitMode*, the thread's wait will be satisfied with a completion status of STATUS_ALERTED.

If *WaitMode* is UserMode and *Alertable* is TRUE, the thread can also be awakened to deliver a User-mode APC. Kernel-mode APCs always cause the subject thread to be awakened if the wait IRQL is PASSIVE_LEVEL and no kernel APC is in progress.

Callers of KeWaitForMultipleObjects can be running at IRQL <= DISPATCH_LEVEL. However, the caller cannot wait at raised IRQL for a nonzero interval or in an arbitrary thread context on any dispatcher object, so callers usually are running at IRQL == PASSIVE_LEVEL. A call while running at IRQL == DISPATCH_LEVEL is valid if, and only if, the caller specifies a *Timeout* of 0. That is, a driver must not wait for a nonzero interval at IRQL == DISPATCH_LEVEL.

KeWaitForMutexObject

```
NTSTATUS KeWaitForMutexObject(IN PKMUTEX Mutex,
                              IN KWAIT_REASON WaitReason,
                              IN KPROCESSOR_MODE WaitMode,
                              IN BOOLEAN Alertable,
                              IN PLARGE_INTEGER Timeout);
```

Puts the current thread into an alertable or nonalertable wait state until the given Mutex Object is set to the Signaled state or (optionally) until the wait times out.

The *Mutex* parameter references a Mutex Object for which storage has been allocated and initialized. The *WaitReason* parameter is usually Executive, but it can be UserMode if the wait is being done in a User thread for the user. The *WaitMode* parameter must be KernelMode. The *Alertable* parameter is TRUE if the wait is alertable and FALSE otherwise (it will almost always be FALSE). The *Timeout* parameter is NULL if there is no timeout. Otherwise, it is a pointer to a *Timeout* value expressed as a signed, 64-bit integer representing 100-ns units. A negative value represents a relative time; a positive value represents an absolute time. The function returns one of the values given in Table A.25.

This function is a macro that expands to a call on KeWaitForSingleObject.

A thread that calls this function must be running at IRQL <= DISPATCH_LEVEL.

Table A.25: KeWaitForMutexObject *Values*

Value	Meaning
STATUS_SUCCESS	The Mutex satisfied the wait.
STATUS_ALERTED	The wait is completed because of an alert to the thread.
STATUS_USER_APC	A user APC was delivered to the current thread before the specified Timeout interval expired.
STATUS_TIMEOUT	A timeout occurred before the Mutex wait was met. This value can be returned when an explicit Timeout value of 0 is specified, but the specified wait condition cannot be met immediately.

KeWaitForSingleObject

```
NTSTATUS KeWaitForSingleObject(IN PVOID Object,
                               IN KWAIT_REASON WaitReason,
                               IN KPROCESSOR_MODE WaitMode,
                               IN BOOLEAN Alertable,
                               IN PLARGE_INTEGER Timeout);
```

Puts the current thread into an alertable or nonalertable wait state until the given dispatcher object is set to the Signaled state or (optionally) until the wait times out.

The *Object* parameter points to an initialized dispatcher object (event, Mutex, Semaphore, thread, or timer) for which the caller supplies the storage. The *WaitReason* parameter specifies the reason for the wait, which should be set to Executive by drivers. Alternatively, if the driver is doing work on behalf of a user and is running in the context of a User thread, this parameter should be set to UserRequest. The *WaitMode* parameter specifies whether the caller waits in KernelMode or UserMode. Lowest-level and intermediate drivers should specify KernelMode. If the given *Object* is a Mutex, the caller must specify KernelMode. The *Alertable* parameter specifies whether the wait is alertable. The *Timeout* parameter is optional and may be NULL. If specified, it points to a *Timeout* value that specifies the absolute or relative time at which the wait is to be completed. A negative value specifies an interval relative to the current time. The value should be expressed in 100-ns units. Absolute expiration times track any changes in the system time; relative expiration times are not affected by system time changes.

This function can return one of the values given in Table A.26.

Table A.26: KeWaitForSingleObject *Values*

Value	Meaning
STATUS_SUCCESS	The dispatcher object satisfied the wait.
STATUS_ALERTED	The wait is completed because of an alert to the thread.
STATUS_USER_APC	A user APC was delivered to the current thread before the specified timeout interval expired.
STATUS_TIMEOUT	A timeout occurred before the object wait was met. This value can be returned when an explicit Timeout value of 0 is specified, but the specified wait condition cannot be met immediately.

The current state of the specified *Object* is examined to determine whether the wait can be satisfied immediately. If so, the necessary side effects are performed on the object. Otherwise, the current thread is put in a waiting state and a new thread is selected for execution on the current processor.

The *Alertable* parameter specifies whether the thread can be alerted in the wait state. If its value is TRUE and the thread is alerted for a mode that is equal to or more privileged than the given *WaitMode*, the thread's wait will be satisfied with a completion status of STATUS_ALERTED.

If *WaitMode* is UserMode and *Alertable* is TRUE, the thread can also be awakened to deliver a User-mode APC. Kernel-mode APCs always cause the subject thread to be awakened if the wait IRQL is PASSIVE_LEVEL and no kernel APC is in progress.

If no timeout is supplied, the calling thread will remain in a wait state until the object is signaled. A *Timeout* of 0 allows the testing of a set of wait conditions and for conditionally performing any side effects if the wait can be immediately satisfied, as in the acquisition of a Mutex. Note that a *Timeout* of 0 is *not* the same as a *Timeout* pointer of NULL. The latter means that there is no timeout interval.

Callers of KeWaitForSingleObject must be running at IRQL <= DISPATCH_LEVEL. Usually, the caller must be running at IRQL == PASSIVE_LEVEL and in a nonarbitrary thread context. A call while running at IRQL == DISPATCH_LEVEL is valid if, and only if, the caller specifies a *Timeout* of 0. That is, a driver must not wait for a nonzero interval at IRQL == DISPATCH_LEVEL.

KEY_BASIC_INFORMATION

```
typedef struct _KEY_BASIC_INFORMATION {
    LARGE_INTEGER LastWriteTime;
    ULONG    TitleIndex;
    ULONG    NameLength;
    WCHAR    Name[1];                // Variable-length string
} KEY_BASIC_INFORMATION, * PKEY_BASIC_INFORMATION;
```

Table A.27 lists the KEY_BASIC_INFORMATION fields. The structure is shown in Figure A.2.

Table A.27: KEY_BASIC_INFORMATION *Fields*

Field	Meaning
LARGE_INTEGER LastWriteTime	The last time the value was changed.
ULONG TitleIndex	Device Drivers and intermediate drivers should ignore this field.
ULONG NameLength	The length of the name that follows, including the terminating NUL character, expressed in bytes.
WCHAR Name[1]	The first character of the Unicode character string that is the key name. Additional bytes will follow the structure.

The structure of the information returned will depend on the *KeyInformationClass* parameter. It will be one of the structures discussed next. It does not return an *array* of these structures because the last member of each structure is a variable-length name. You must add sizeof(KEY_BASIC_INFORMATION) + p->NameLength – sizeof(WCHAR) to the current address (starting with the *KeyInformation* pointer value as p). Note that since one character is included in the structure size and NameLength contains the number of *bytes* (not *characters*), including the terminating NUL character, you need to do the sizeof(WCHAR) adjustment.

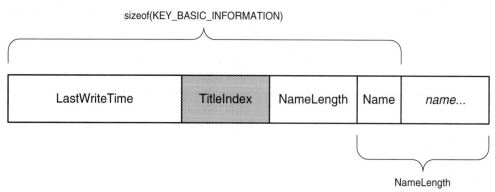

Figure A.2: KEY_BASIC_INFORMATION *structure.*

KEY_FULL_INFORMATION

```
typedef _KEY_FULL_INFORMATION {
    LARGE_INTEGER LastWriteTime;
    ULONG TitleIndex;
    ULONG ClassOffset;
    ULONG ClassLength;
    ULONG SubKeys;
    ULONG MaxNameLen;
    ULONG MaxClassLen;
    ULONG Values;
    ULONG MaxValueNameLen;
    ULONG MaxValueDataLen;
    WCHAR Class[1];
} KEY_FULL_INFORMATION, * PKEY_FULL_INFORMATION;
```

Table A.28 lists the fields for KEY_FULL_INFORMATION.

Table A.28: KEY_FULL_INFORMATION *Fields*

Field	Meaning
LARGE_INTEGER LastWriteTime	The last time the value was changed.
ULONG TitleIndex	Should be ignored by Device Drivers and intermediate drivers.
ULONG ClassOffset	The offset from the start of this structure to the Class member.
ULONG ClassLength	The length of the name that follows, including the terminating NUL character, expressed in bytes.
ULONG SubKeys	The number of subkeys this key has.
ULONG MaxNameLen	The maximum length of a name for any of the subkeys.
ULONG Values	The number of value entries for this key.
ULONG MaxValueNameLen	The maximum length of any value entry name.

Table A.28: KEY_FULL_INFORMATION *Fields (continued)*

Field	Meaning
ULONG MaxValueDataLen	The maximum length of any value data string.
WCHAR Class[1]	The first character of the Unicode character string that is the class name. Additional bytes will follow the structure.

KEY_NODE_INFORMATION

```
typedef struct _KEY_NODE_INFORMATION {
    LARGE_INTEGER LastWriteTime;
    ULONG    TitleIndex;
    ULONG    ClassOffset;
    ULONG    ClassLength;
    ULONG    NameLength;
    WCHAR    Name[1];             // Variable-length string
} KEY_NODE_INFORMATION, * PKEY_NODE_INFORMATION;
```

Table A.29 lists the fields for KEY_NODE_INFORMATION.

Table A.29: KEY_NODE_INFORMATION *Fields*

Field	Meaning
LARGE_INTEGER LastWriteTime	The last time the value was changed.
ULONG TitleIndex	Should be ignored by Device Drivers and intermediate drivers.
ULONG ClassOffset	The offset from the beginning of the structure to the beginning of the class name, which follows the node name.
ULONG ClassLength	The number of bytes in the class name, including the termination NUL character.
ULONG NameLength	The length of the name that follows, including the terminating NUL character, expressed in bytes.
WCHAR Name[1]	The first character of the Unicode character string that is the key name. Additional bytes will follow the structure.

This is a fairly complicated structure, so we give you a visual instance in Figure A.3.

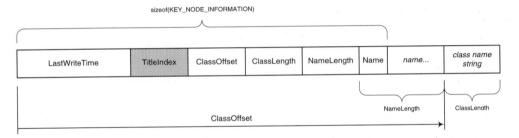

Figure A.3: KEY_NODE_INFORMATION *structure.*

KEY_VALUE_BASIC_INFORMATION

```
typedef struct _KEY_VALUE_BASIC_INFORMATION {
    ULONG    TitleIndex;
    ULONG    Type;
    ULONG    NameLength;
    WCHAR    Name[1];              // Variable size
} KEY_VALUE_BASIC_INFORMATION, * PKEY_VALUE_BASIC_INFORMATION;
```

Table A.30 lists the fields for KEY_VALUE_BASIC_INFORMATION.

Table A.30: KEY_VALUE_BASIC_INFORMATION *Fields*

Field	Meaning	
ULONG TitleIndex	Ignored by Device Drivers and intermediate drivers.	
ULONG Type	The type of the value, one of the following codes.	
	REG_BINARY	Binary data in any form.
	REG_DWORD	A 4-byte numerical value.
	REG_DWORD_LITTLE_ENDIAN	A 4-byte numerical value whose least significant byte is at the lowest address.
	REG_DWORD_BIG_ENDIAN	A 4-byte numerical value whose least significant byte is at the highest address.
	REG_EXPAND_SZ	A zero-terminated Unicode string, containing unexpanded references to environment variables, such as "%PATH%".
	REG_LINK	A Unicode string naming a symbolic link. This type is irrelevant to Device Drivers and intermediate drivers.
	REG_MULTI_SZ	An array of zero-terminated strings, terminated by another 0.
	REG_NONE	Data with no particular type.
	REG_SZ	A zero-terminated Unicode string.
	REG_RESOURCE_LIST	A Device Driver's list of hardware resources, used by the driver or one of the physical devices it controls, in the \ResourceMap tree.
	REG_RESOURCE_REQUIREMENTS_LIST	A Device Driver's list of possible hardware resources that it, or one of the physical devices it controls, can use and from which the system writes a subset into the \ResourceMap tree.
	REG_FULL_RESOURCE_DESCRIPTOR	A list of hardware resources that a physical device is using, detected and written into the \HardwareDescription tree by the system.

Table A.30: KEY_VALUE_BASIC_INFORMATION *Fields (continued)*

Field	Meaning
ULONG NameLength	The length of the Name field, in bytes.
WCHAR Name[1]	The name of the value, a Unicode string terminated with a NUL character.

The Name field is a Unicode string of variable length. To compute the start of the next basic value entry, you must take the current pointer p and add to it sizeof(KEY_VALUE_BASIC_INFORMATION) + p->NameLength - sizeof(WCHAR). You can't treat the values as an array of structures. The layout of a single structure is shown in Figure A.4. The Type field describes the type of the value.

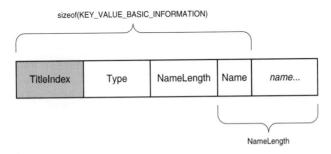

Figure A.4: KEY_VALUE_BASIC_INFORMATION *structure.*

KEY_VALUE_FULL_INFORMATION

```
KEY_VALUE_FULL_INFORMATION
typedef struct _KEY_VALUE_FULL_INFORMATION {
    ULONG    TitleIndex;
    ULONG    Type;
    ULONG    DataOffset;
    ULONG    DataLength;
    ULONG    NameLength;
    WCHAR    Name[1];             // Variable size
} KEY_VALUE_FULL_INFORMATION, * PKEY_VALUE_FULL_INFORMATION;
```

Table A.31 lists the fields for KEY_VALUE_FULL_INFORMATION. A layout of its structure is shown in Figure A.5.

Table A.31: KEY_VALUE_FULL_INFORMATION *Fields*

Field	Meaning	
ULONG TitleIndex	Ignored by Device Drivers and intermediate drivers.	
ULONG Type	The type of the value, one of the following codes.	
	REG_BINARY	Binary data in any form.

Table A.31: KEY_VALUE_FULL_INFORMATION *Fields (continued)*

Field	Meaning	
	REG_DWORD	A 4-byte numerical value.
	REG_DWORD_LITTLE_ENDIAN	A 4-byte numerical value whose least significant byte is at the lowest address.
	REG_DWORD_BIG_ENDIAN	A 4-byte numerical value whose least significant byte is at the highest address.
	REG_EXPAND_SZ	A zero-terminated Unicode string, containing unexpanded references to environment variables, such as "%PATH%".
	REG_LINK	A Unicode string naming a symbolic link. This type is irrelevant to Device Drivers and intermediate drivers.
	REG_MULTI_SZ	An array of zero-terminated strings, terminated by another 0.
	REG_NONE	Data with no particular type.
	REG_SZ	A zero-terminated Unicode string.
	REG_RESOURCE_LIST	A Device Driver's list of hardware resources, used by the driver or one of the physical devices it controls, in the \ResourceMap tree.
	REG_RESOURCE_REQUIREMENTS_LIST	A Device Driver's list of possible hardware resources that it, or one of the physical devices it controls, can use and from which the system writes a subset into the \ResourceMap tree.
	REG_FULL_RESOURCE_DESCRIPTOR	A list of hardware resources that a physical device is using, detected and written into the \HardwareDescription tree by the system.
ULONG DataOffset	The offset from the start of the structure to the data string that immediately follows the Name string.	
ULONG DataLength	The length of the data value.	
ULONG NameLength	The length of the Name field, in bytes.	
WCHAR Name[1]	The name of the value, a Unicode string terminated with a NUL character.	

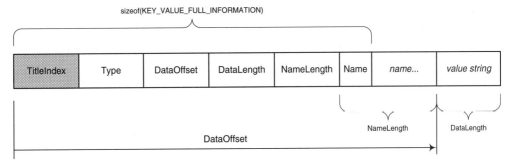

Figure A.5: KEY_VALUE_FULL_INFORMATION *structure.*

KEY_VALUE_PARTIAL_INFORMATION

```
typedef struct _KEY_VALUE_PARTIAL_INFORMATION {
    ULONG    TitleIndex;
    ULONG    Type;
    ULONG    DataLength;
    UCHAR    Data[1];                 // Variable size
} KEY_VALUE_PARTIAL_INFORMATION, * PKEY_VALUE_PARTIAL_INFORMATION;
```

Table A.32 lists the fields for KEY_VALUE_FULL_INFORMATION. A layout of its structure is shown in Figure A.6.

Table A.32: KEY_VALUE_PARTIAL_INFORMATION *Fields*

Field	Meaning	
ULONG TitleIndex	Ignored by Device Drivers and intermediate drivers.	
ULONG Type	The type of the value, one of the following codes.	
	REG_BINARY	Binary data in any form.
	REG_DWORD	A 4-byte numerical value.
	REG_DWORD_LITTLE_ENDIAN	A 4-byte numerical value whose least significant byte is at the lowest address.
	REG_DWORD_BIG_ENDIAN	A 4-byte numerical value whose least significant byte is at the highest address.
	REG_EXPAND_SZ	A zero-terminated Unicode string, containing unexpanded references to environment variables, such as "%PATH%".
	REG_LINK	A Unicode string naming a symbolic link. This type is irrelevant to Device Drivers and intermediate drivers.
	REG_MULTI_SZ	An array of zero-terminated strings, terminated by another 0.

Table A.32: KEY_VALUE_PARTIAL_INFORMATION *Fields (continued)*

Field	Meaning	
	REG_NONE	Data with no particular type.
	REG_SZ	A zero-terminated Unicode string.
	REG_RESOURCE_LIST	A Device Driver's list of hardware resources, used by the driver or one of the physical devices it controls, in the \ResourceMap tree.
	REG_RESOURCE_REQUIREMENTS_LIST	A Device Driver's list of possible hardware resources that it, or one of the physical devices it controls, can use and from which the system writes a subset into the \ResourceMap tree.
	REG_FULL_RESOURCE_DESCRIPTOR	A list of hardware resources that a physical device is using, detected and written into the \HardwareDescription tree by the system.
ULONG DataLength	The length of the Data field, in bytes.	
WCHAR Data[1]	The data.	

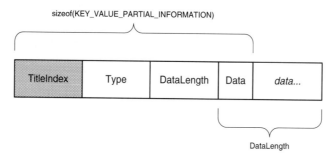

Figure A.6: KEY_VALUE_PARTIAL_INFORMATION *structure.*

KIRQL

typedef UCHAR KIRQL;

A value used to represent kernel IRQL levels.

KSYNCHRONIZE_ROUTINE

BOOLEAN (*PKSYNCHRONIZE_ROUTINE) (IN PVOID *SynchronizeContext*);

This is the prototype for a SynchCritSection routine whose execution is to be synchronized with the execution of the ISR associated with the interrupt object(s). A pointer to a routine of this type is passed in to KeSynchronizeExecution, and when the Interrupt Object becomes available, the specified function is called.

What we find odd is that although this routine is specified as a BOOLEAN, nowhere in the documentation can we determine what effect, if any, occurs if you return TRUE or FALSE. The return value is not specified at all. In examples within the DDK that we have read, Microsoft appears to consistently return FALSE.

The specified routine is always executed at the maximum DIRQL associated with the Interrupt Object.

LARGE_INTEGER

```
typedef union _LARGE_INTEGER {
    struct {
            DWORD LowPart;
            LONG HighPart;
            };
    LONGLONG QuadPart;   // For Intel platform, LONGLONG is __int64
} LARGE_INTEGER;
```

The LARGE_INTEGER type is an unfortunate legacy of the days when the compiler did not have a built-in 64-bit integer type. This is an even more egregious legacy of the design flaw of the C language that stated that the size of an int was the "natural word size" of the target platform (thus rendering nonsense the idea that you can write portable code in C, a myth that has persisted for decades in spite of all evidence to the contrary).[2] It was a composite data type that was used to pass two 32-bit values to functions that manipulated the two 32-bit values as 64-bit values. Because it existed, it is now required to continue to exist for compatibility reasons. Although the __int64 data type is now well established, it cannot be used directly in calls on the various NT support functions, but must be embedded in a LARGE_INTEGER data type to keep the compiler happy.

MmAllocateContiguousMemory

```
PVOID MmAllocateContiguousMemory(
                        IN ULONG NumberOfBytes,
                        IN PHYSICAL_ADDRESS HighestAcceptableAddress);
```

Attempts to allocate contiguous physical memory that is of the indicated size and that is entirely below the specified *HighestAcceptableAddress* parameter.

This function returns the system logical address of this memory, or NULL if the allocation request could not be satisfied.

A thread that calls this function must be running at IRQL == PASSIVE_LEVEL.

---

[2] I have ported a large number of C applications between 16-bit and 32-bit platforms, as far back as the days of the PDP-11 and VAX. In all cases, the int was the major stumbling block in porting. In Win16, the NEAR/FAR/HUGE pointer distinction added additional misery. So I believe that while it is certainly *possible* to write portable code in C, it is never *easy*, and some aspects of the run-time libraries mitigate against it . . . such as requiring int parameters. *–jmn*

MmAllocateNonCachedMemory

PVOID MmAllocateNonCachedMemory(IN ULONG *NumberOfBytes*)

Allocates memory that is not subject to processor caching.

A typical use of this function might be for off-screen frame buffers. This memory is allocated out of one (or more) pages that are not subject to caching. On Intel architectures, these pages have their PTE PCD bit set. (For example, see the *i486 Processor Reference Manual*, page 12-4.) The address is also on a cache-aligned boundary. The storage returned will include an integral number of cache-line units, independent of the actual number of bytes requested.

Memory that is allocated with this function should be allocated during the DriverEntry routine because memory tends to fragment over time, thus making it difficult or impossible to satisfy the request later.

A thread that calls this function must be running at IRQL < DISPATCH_LEVEL.

MmCreateMdl

PMDL MmCreateMdl(IN PMDL *MemoryDescriptorList* OPTIONAL,
                 IN PVOID *Base*,
                 IN ULONG *Length*);

Initializes a MDL. If the *MemoryDescriptorList* parameter is NULL, this function allocates storage for the MDL and returns a pointer to the storage. If *MemoryDescriptorList* is non-NULL, it initializes the MDL referenced and returns a pointer to it. The *Base* parameter references the start of the buffer represented by the MDL, and the *Length* parameter is the length of the buffer.

A thread that calls this function must be running at IRQL < DISPATCH_LEVEL, if the caller passes a NULL pointer for *MemoryDescriptorList* and expects MmCreateMdl to allocate the storage.

If the call to MmCreateMdl occurs while running at IRQL >= DISPATCH_LEVEL, the caller must allocate memory for the MDL from the Nonpaged Pool and must supply a non-NULL pointer for *MemoryDescriptorList*.

MmFreeContiguousMemory

VOID MmFreeContiguousMemory(IN PVOID *BaseAddress*);

Frees the memory at *BaseAddress* allocated by MmAllocateContiguousMemory.
A thread that calls this function must be running at IRQL == PASSIVE_LEVEL.

MmFreeNonCachedMemory

PVOID MmFreeNonCachedMemory(IN PVOID *address*, IN ULONG *NumberOfBytes*)

Frees memory allocated with MmAllocateNonCachedMemory.
It is normally called when a driver is being unloaded.
A thread calling this function must be running at IRQL < DISPATCH_LEVEL.

MmGetMdlByteCount

ULONG MmGetMdlByteCount(IN PMDL *Mdl*)

Returns the length of the buffer represented by the *Mdl* parameter.

Usually, a thread that calls this function runs at IRQL <= DISPATCH_LEVEL.

MmGetMdlByteOffset

ULONG MmGetMdlByteOffset(IN PMDL *Mdl*);

Returns the byte offset within the page of the first byte of the buffer described by the *Mdl* parameter.

A thread that calls this function can be running at any IRQL. Usually, callers are running at IRQL <= DISPATCH_LEVEL.

MmGetMdlVirtualAddress

PVOID MmGetMdlVirtualAddress(IN PMDL *Mdl*);

Returns the initial virtual address for a buffer described by a given MDL.

The returned address, used as an index to a physical address entry in the MDL, can be input to IoMapTransfer. This virtual address is not necessarily valid in the current thread context. Lower-level drivers should not attempt to use the returned virtual address to access memory, particularly user-space memory.

A thread that calls this function can be running at any IRQL. Usually, the caller is running at IRQL == DISPATCH_LEVEL because this routine is commonly called to obtain the *CurrentVa* parameter to IoMapTransfer.

MmGetPhysicalAddress

PHYSICAL_ADDRESS MmGetPhysicalAddress(IN PVOID *BaseAddress*);

Returns the physical address associated with the virtual memory *BaseAddress*.

A thread that calls this function can be running at any IRQL, provided *BaseAddress* is a valid address.

MmGetSystemAddressForMdl

PVOID MmGetSystemAddressForMdl(IN PMDL *mdl*)

Obtains a nonpaged virtual memory address for the base of the storage referenced by the MDL.

There is no corresponding unmap call; the address will be automatically unmapped by a call to MmUnlockPages.

Drivers of programmed I/O devices need to call this routine to translate a virtual address range, described by the MDL at Irp->MdlAddress, in order to get a user buffer mapped to a system-space address range.

A caller running at IRQL == DISPATCH_LEVEL must supply a MDL that maps nonpageable virtual addresses. The input MDL must describe either an already locked-down, user-space buffer returned by MmProbeAndLockPages, a locked-down buffer returned by MmBuildMdlForNonPagedPool, or system-space memory allocated from the Nonpaged Pool, contiguous memory, noncached memory, or a zone buffer.

The returned base address has the same offset as the virtual address in the MDL.

Callers of MmGetSystemAddressForMdl must be running at IRQL <= DISPATCH_LEVEL.

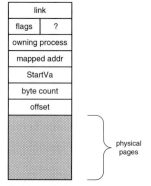

Figure A.7: *MDL structure.*

MmInitializeMdl

VOID MmInitializeMdl(IN PMDL *mdl*, IN PVOID *BaseVa*,
                                IN ULONG *Length*);

Initializes the MDL header, shown in Figure A.7, in particular the virtual address and byte count fields. The layout shown in the figure is indicative rather than definitive because the MDL structure is an opaque type, whose internal structure can change from release to release. All of the fields of the MDL can be manipulated by Mm-prefix functions, such as MmInitializeMdl.

A thread that calls this function must be running at IRQL <= DISPATCH_LEVEL.

MmIsAddressValid

BOOLEAN MmIsAddressValid(IN PVOID *VirtualAddress*);

Tests the *VirtualAddress* to see if it is valid. This function returns TRUE if the address is currently in memory and FALSE if accessing the address would cause a page fault. Note that even if it returns TRUE, preemption could change the status between the time the accessibility is checked and the time an access is actually made, unless the memory has been locked down or is in the Nonpaged Pool.

A thread that calls this function must be running at IRQL <= DISPATCH_LEVEL.

MmMapIoSpace

PVOID MmMapIoSpace(IN PHYSICAL_ADDRESS *phys*,
                    IN ULONG *NumberOfBytes*,
                    IN BOOLEAN *CacheEnable*)

Maps a physical address to a virtual address, returning the mapped virtual address. If it cannot map the address, it returns NULL.

This function is normally called during initialization if a call to HalTranslateBusAddress indicates that the bus-relative device address is mapped to a physical memory address.

There is no way in Windows NT to directly access any physical memory address. The only way you can do this is by mapping the address into your virtual memory. The function might not always return the same virtual address, when given a physical address, but the mapping will give *a* valid virtual address by which the contents of the physical buffer can actually be accessed.

A thread that calls this function must be running at IRQL == PASSIVE_LEVEL.

MmMapLockedPages

```
PVOID MmMapLockedPages(IN PMDL MemoryDescriptorList,
                       IN KPROCESSOR_MODE AccessMode);
```

Returns a virtual address for the pages defined by a MDL. The pages must already be locked down by MmProbeAndLockPages. The *AccessMode* parameter describes whether this should be done in KernelMode or UserMode. Lower-level drivers should use KernelMode. The address returned is the base address for the memory described by the MDL.

A thread that calls this function can be running at IRQL <= DISPATCH_LEVEL if *AccessMode* is KernelMode and at IRQL < DISPATCH_LEVEL if *AccessMode* is UserMode.

MmPrepareMdlForReuse

```
VOID MmPrepareMdlForReuse(IN PMDL mdl);
```

Reinitializes the fields of a MDL so that it can be reused. This saves the overhead of freeing a MDL and immediately allocating and initializing another.

After this call, MmInitializeMdl must be called to reinitialize the MDL. The MDL must be a driver-allocated MDL (not one allocated by the I/O Manager implicitly). This function is very rarely used.

A thread that calls this function must be running at IRQL <= DISPATCH_LEVEL.

MmProbeAndLockPages

```
VOID MmProbeAndLockPages(IN OUT PMDL mdl,
                         IN KPROCESSOR_MODE AccessMode,
                         IN LOCK_OPERATION Operation);
```

Causes all pages associated with the MDL to be brought into memory (if they were pageable) and locks the physical pages into memory.

This is particularly important for doing DMA transfers because the various DMA controllers require physical memory addresses in order to operate.

This function is normally called by the highest-level driver that is doing Direct I/O. It is not called for a driver that does Buffered I/O.

Note that the return value of this function is VOID. If this function fails, it will raise an access failure exception, STATUS_ACCESS_VIOLATION. Therefore you should call it using a structured exception handler around the call. A lower-level driver must not attempt to pass such an exception on to a higher-level driver. It cannot assume anything about a higher-level driver's exception handling capabilities. In particular, the driver cannot call ExRaiseStatus to pass on such an exception.

Once this function is called, it doesn't matter if another thread that has a MDL to the same pages is terminated. Since the physical pages are locked down for this thread, they will remain intact.

The nature of the *Operation* indicates the type of access desired. If it is IoReadAccess, the pages do not need to be writable; this is particularly significant if the Access parameter is UserMode. There is a subtle distinction between IoWriteAccess and IoModifyAccess. Both will permit the driver to write to the buffer. They differ in that IoWriteAccess assumes that the entire contents of the buffer will be rewritten and does not guarantee that the contents of the buffers are left intact, while IoModifyAccess guarantees that the contents of the buffers are left intact. This subtlety applies primarily when the pages are pageable. IoWriteAccess will not necessarily page the previous contents of a page back into memory when doing the mapping and locking; it might just map the page frame to the physical page. IoModifyAccess will force a page's contents to be reloaded if the page had been swapped out. IoWriteAccess is clearly more efficient if the entire buffer contents are to be rewritten.

A process has a quota for the number of pages it can have locked concurrently. An attempt to lock more pages than the process's quota permits will generate an insufficient resource exception.

Once a process locks pages in a MDL, it must make sure it unlocks them using the MmUnlockPages function. If it fails to do so, then when the process is being cleaned up, the system will crash with a PFN_SHARE_CHECK (0x1B) BugCheck. Therefore you must keep track of all MDLs you explicitly allocated (this does not include the one implicitly allocated by the I/O system, if you've chosen that method) so that you can unlock them.

The thread that calls this function must be running at IRQL < DISPATCH_LEVEL if the pages referenced by the MDL were pageable and at IRQL <= DISPATCH_LEVEL if the pages referenced by the MDL were nonpageable.

MmQuerySystemSize

MM_SYSTEM_SIZE MmQuerySystemSize( );

Returns an estimate of the amount of memory on the system. (Mostly) meaningless.

The value returned is MmSmallSystem, MmMediumSystem, or MmLargeSystem. The actual numbers associated with these levels are not documented, but we have seen, within the lifetime of NT 4.0, a set of values that suggest that the returned MM_SYSTEM_SIZE values are completely meaningless. Consequently, the value of this call is questionable. (The information we have tracked down indicates that "small" meant <= 12MB, "medium" meant > 12MB, <= 20MB, and "large" meant > 20MB. In an era in which consumer-level machines from your local discount TV/stereo store come with a base memory of 32MB and a standard option of 64MB, these discriminants seem to be pointless.)

A thread that calls this function must be running at IRQL == PASSIVE_LEVEL.

MmSizeOfMdl

ULONG MmSizeOfMdl(IN PVOID *Base*, IN ULONG *Length*);

Returns the number of bytes necessary for a MDL to describe *Length* bytes starting at address *Base*.

Use this routine if you are allocating your own MDL for a "Neither" mode of buffering or you have to split up a MDL in order to support software scatter/gather.

A thread that calls this function can be running at any IRQL. Note, however, that if you plan to allocate memory you must be running at an IRQL suitable for doing the allocation (<= DISPATCH_LEVEL for the Nonpaged Pool and < DISPATCH_LEVEL for the Paged Pool).

MmUnlockPages

```
VOID MmUnlockPages(IN PMDL mdl);
```

Unlocks any pages locked by `MmProbeAndLockPages`.

The MDL is updated as the pages are unlocked. This function *must* be called before the process that owns the MDL terminates. If it is not, the system will crash with a `PFN_SHARE_COUNT` BugCheck (`0x1B`).

You should call this function only for MDLs you have allocated. You must not call it if the MDL was allocated by the I/O system for your driver.

A thread that calls this function must be running at IRQL <= DISPATCH_LEVEL.

MmUnlockPagableImageSection

```
VOID MmUnlockPagableImageSection(IN PVOID ImageSectionHandle);
```

Unlocks a pageable code or data section locked by `MmLockPagableCodeSection` or `MmLockPagableDataSection`.

The *ImageSectionHandle* parameter is the handle returned by the locking function. This function decrements the lock count and makes the section pageable when the lock count goes to 0.

A thread that calls this function must be running at IRQL == PASSIVE_LEVEL.

MmUnmapIoSpace

```
VOID MmUnmapIoSpace(IN PVOID address, IN ULONG NumberOfBytes)
```

Unmaps any virtual addresses that were allocated by `MmMapIoSpace`.

This routine is normally called when the Device Driver is unloaded.

A thread calling this function must be running at IRQL == PASSIVE_LEVEL.

MmUnmapLockedPages

```
VOID MmUnmapLockedPages(
                    IN PVOID BaseAddress, IN PMDL MemoryDescriptorList);
```

Unmaps pages previously locked by `MmMapLockedPages`.

The *MemoryDescriptorList* parameter must be the same one that was passed to `MmMapLockedPages`.

A thread that calls this function can be running at IRQL <= DISPATCH_LEVEL if the pages were locked in `KernelMode` and must be running at IRQL < DISPATCH_LEVEL if the pages were locked in `UserMode`.

NTSTATUS

This data type represents a 32-bit value that represents a result inside the kernel. When returned as the completion value for an IRP, these values will be converted to an *application-level* error code, which the application discovers by using the `GetLastError` function. A complete listing

of all the NTSTATUS codes, and their corresponding application codes, can be found in
Appendix B.

ObDereferenceObject

```
VOID ObDereferenceObject(IN PVOID Object);
```

Decrements the reference count for the specified `Object`. When the reference count goes to
0, the object will be deleted.

A thread that calls this function must be running at IRQL == PASSIVE_LEVEL.

ObReferenceObjectByHandle

```
NTSTATUS ObReferenceObjectByHandle(IN HANDLE Handle,
                                   IN ACCESS_MASK DesiredAccess,
                                   IN POBJECT_TYPE ObjectType,
                                   IN KPROCESSOR_MODE AccessMode,
                                   OUT PVOID * Object,
                                   OUT POBJECT_HANDLE_INFORMATION
                                                      HandleInformation);
```

A pointer to the object body is retrieved from the object table entry and returned to the caller
via the `Object` parameter. This routine provides access validation on the object handle, and, if
access can be granted, returns the corresponding pointer to the object's body.

If the `AccessMode` parameter is `KernelMode`, the requested access is always allowed. If
`AccessMode` is `UserMode`, the requested access is compared to the granted access for the object.
Only highest-level drivers can safely specify `UserMode` for the input `AccessMode`.

If the call succeeds, a pointer to the object body is returned to the caller and the pointer reference count is incremented. Incrementing this count prevents the object from being deleted
while the pointer is being referenced. You will have to dereference this object to decrement its
reference count when you are done with it.

A thread that calls this function must be running at IRQL == PASSIVE_LEVEL.

ObReferenceObjectByPointer

```
NTSTATUS ObReferenceObjectByPointer(IN PVOID Object,
                                    IN ACCESS_MASK DesiredAccess,
                                    IN POBJECT_TYPE ObjectType,
                                    IN KPROCESSOR_MODE AccessMode);
```

Increments the reference count for the specified `Object`.

The `DesiredAccess` parameter is the desired access to the object. Its values are specific to
the type of object. The `AccessMode` parameter controls whether the access is controlled in
`UserMode` or `KernelMode`. The `ObjectType` parameter is a pointer to an object Type structure.

This routine returns STATUS_SUCCESS or STATUS_TYPE_MISMATCH.

A thread that calls this function must be running at IRQL == PASSIVE_LEVEL.

PCI_COMMON_CONFIG

```
typedef struct _PCI_COMMON_CONFIG {
    USHORT VendorID;
    USHORT DeviceID;
    USHORT Command;
    USHORT Status;
    UCHAR RevisionID;
    UCHAR ProgIf;
    UCHAR SubClass;
    UCHAR BaseClass;
    UCHAR CacheLineSize;
    UCHAR LatencyTimer;
    UCHAR HeaderType;
    UCHAR BIST;
    union {
        struct _PCI_HEADER_TYPE_0 {
            ULONG   BaseAddresses[PCI_TYPE0_ADDRESSES];
            ULONG   CIS;
            USHORT  SubVendorID;
            USHORT  SubSystemID;
            ULONG   ROMBaseAddress;
            ULONG   Reserved2[2]
            UCHAR   InterruptLine;
            UCHAR   InterruptPin;
            UCHAR   MinimumGrant;
            UCHAR   MaximumLatency;
        } type0;
    } u;
    UCHAR DeviceSpecific[192];
} PCI_COMMON_CONFIG, * PPCI_COMMON_CONFIG;
```

This data structure represents the PCI configuration data. Only Type 0 PCI devices are defined by this (currently there are no other types), and the device-specific information is left uninterpreted. This structure is used by operations such as HalGetBusData and HalSetBusData. The PCI configuration fields are given in Table A.33.

Table A.33: PCI_COMMON_CONFIG *Fields*

Field	Meaning
VendorID	The globally unique 16-bit identifier for the vendor, as assigned by the PCI SIG.
DeviceID	The 16-bit device ID, as assigned by the vendor.
Command	The 16-bit PCI Command register.
Status	The 16-bit PCI Status register.
RevisionID	The 8-bit revision ID.
ProgIf	The low-order 8 bits of the 24-bit class code.
SubClass	The middle 8 bits of the 24-bit class code, the subclass code.
BaseClass	The high-order 8 bits of the 24-bit class code, the base class code; 0 for pre-2.1 devices.

Table A.33: `PCI_COMMON_CONFIG` *Fields (continued)*

Field	Meaning
`CacheLineSize`	The cache line size.
`LatencyTimer`	The latency timer.
`HeaderType`	The type of this header. Currently, only Type 0 is defined.
`BIST`	The Built-In-Self-Test Control register.
`u.type0.BaseAddresses`	The six base address registers defined by the PCI Type 0 standard.
`u.type0.CIS`[1]	The CardBus CIS Pointer. The second of these reserved words contains the two 16-bit values, the subsystem ID and the subsystem vendor ID, and are apparently unsupported.
`u.type0.SubVendorID`[1]	The subsystem vendor ID. This usually represents an integration of several PCI parts.
`u.type0.SubSystemID`[1]	The subsystem system ID. This is the equivalent to `DeviceID`.
`u.type0.RomBaseAddress`	The base address of any device-specific ROM, or 0.
`u.type0.Reserved2`	Reserved; must be 0.
`u.type0.InterruptLine`	A read/write register that indicates to which of the IRQ lines the interrupt is connected. In a non-APIC machine, this must be in the range 0..15; in an APIC environment, it can be in the range 0..254. The value 0xFF (255) is used to indicate "unknown" or "no connection".
`u.type0.InterruptPin`	A read-only register that indicates to which of the $\overline{\text{INT}x}$ lines the device is connected. The values are as follows.
	00 Device does not use interrupts.
	01 Device uses $\overline{\text{INTA}}$.
	02 Device uses $\overline{\text{INTB}}$.
	03 Device uses $\overline{\text{INTC}}$.
	04 Device uses $\overline{\text{INTD}}$.
`u.type0.MinimumGrant`	A read-only register specified for bus masters only. If set to 0, the device has no requirements on the minimum grant time. Otherwise, it is the device's opinion of its "ideal" grant time, expressed in 250-ns units.
`u.type0.MaximumLatency`	A read-only register that suggests how often the device will need access to the PCI Bus. A value of 0 means there are no constraints. Otherwise, it is the desired time in 250-ns units.

Fields highlighted are those that are mandatory according to the standard.

[1]These fields are not in the NT DDK documentation but are in the actual structure declared in `ntddk.h`.

PCI_SLOT_NUMBER

```
typedef struct _PCI_SLOT_NUMBER {
    union {
        struct {
            ULONG DeviceNumber:5;
            ULONG FunctionNumber:3;
            ULONG Reserved:24;
        } bits;
        ULONG AsULONG;
    } u;
} PCI_SLOT_NUMBER, * PPCI_SLOT_NUMBER;
```

PCI_SLOT_NUMBER describes the *SlotNumber* parameter for various HAL functions that manipulate bus data. Table A.34 lists the parameter fields.

Table A.34: PCI_SLOT_NUMBER *Fields*

Field	Meaning
u.bits.DeviceNumber	The device number within the slot.
u.bits.FunctionNumber	The function number within the device.
u.type0.Reserved	Reserved; must be 0.
u.AsULONG	The value used as the parameter to the Hal...BusData functions.

PDRIVER_CONTROL

```
IO_ALLOCATION_ACTION (*PDRIVER_CONTROL)(IN PDEVICE_OBJECT DeviceObject,
                                        IN PIRP Irp,
                                        IN PVOID MapRegisterBase,
                                        IN PVOID Context);
```

PDRIVER_CONTROL is the prototype for a function that is called when an IoAllocateAdapterChannel or IoAllocateController request is dequeued.

The function so designated is passed a pointer to the *DeviceObject* and the current *Irp*. If the request was queued from IoAllocateAdapterChannel, the *MapRegisterBase* parameter indicates the base of the set of mapping registers that was made available to the Adapter Object. If the request was queued from IoAllocateController, *MapRegisterBase* has no meaning.

PIO_DPC_ROUTINE

```
typedef VOID (*PIO_DPC_ROUTINE)(IN PKDPC Dpc,
                    IN PDEVICE_OBJECT DeviceObject,
                    IN PIRP Irp,
                    IN PVOID Context);
```

PIO_DPC_ROUTINE is the prototype of the DPC function that is passed to IoInitializeDpcRequest and is called when IoRequestDpc is called.

When the DPC is called, then after DpcForIsr has queued the request, it is called with a reference to the Device Object that requested the DPC, a pointer to the IRP that was active at the

time, and an arbitrary *Context* pointer that was established when the
IoInitializeDpcRequest was called.

PIO_TIMER_ROUTINE

```
typedef VOID (*PIO_TIMER_ROUTINE) (IN PDEVICE_OBJECT DeviceObject,
                                   IN PVOID Context);
```

A timer routine is established by calling IoInitializeTimer and passing in the address of
a function with this prototype. When IostartTimer is executed, this function is then called
approximately once a second. The *Context* parameter is the value passed to
IoInitializeTimer and refers to whatever information the IoTimer routine needs for proper
execution.

PKDEFERRED_ROUTINE

```
VOID (*PKDEFERRED_ROUTINE)(IN PKDPC Dpc;
                           IN PVOID DeferredContext;
                           IN PVOID SystemArgument1;
                           IN PVOID SystemArgument2;);
```

This is the prototype for a DPC routine, whether invoked from an ISR or a timer.

The *DeferredContext* parameter is set up by KeInitializeDpc. In addition, up to two
arguments can be supplied by the KeInsertQueueDpc call when the DPC is queued. These are
passed in as *SystemArgument1* and *SystemArgument2*. These last two parameters cannot be
specified for a Timer DPC.

PKSTART_ROUTINE

```
typedef VOID (*PKSTART_ROUTINE)(LPVOID Context);
```

This is a prototype of the function that is called to start executing a thread created by
PsCreateSystemThread.

The *Context* parameter is the *StartContext* parameter passed to
PsCreateSystemThread.

PsCreateSystemThread

```
NTSTATUS PsCreateSystemThread(OUT PHANDLE ThreadHandle,
                              IN ACCESS_MASK DesiredAccess,
                              IN POBJECT_ATTRIBUTES ObjectAttributes,
                              IN HANDLE ProcessHandle,
                              OUT PCLIENT_ID ClientId,
                              IN PKSTART_ROUTINE StartRoutine,
                              IN PVOID StartContext);
```

Creates a Worker Thread. The handle to the Worker Thread is placed in the location referenced by the *ThreadHandle* parameter and is valid if the return status is STATUS_SUCCESS. The
DesiredAccess parameter is typically THREAD_ALL_ACCESS, or more simply (ACCESS_MASK)0
for a Driver Thread. OBJECT_ATTRIBUTES is largely meaningless for driver-created threads, and

the *ObjectAttributes* parameter should be NULL. The *ProcessHandle* parameter is not used for driver-created threads and must be NULL. The *ClientId* parameter is not used for driver-created threads and must be NULL. The *StartRoutine* parameter must be a pointer to a function that has the prototype

```
typedef VOID (PKSTART_ROUTINE *)(LPVOID Context);
```

When the thread is created, this function is called. This thread is responsible for terminating the thread by calling PsTerminateSystemThread after it completes its work.

A thread that calls this function must be running at IRQL == PASSIVE_LEVEL.

PsGetCurrentProcess

```
PEPROCESS PsGetCurrentProcess( );
```

Returns a reference to the current process.

This function can be called only by a highest-level driver. Lower-level drivers, which might not be running in the context of the original caller, should use IoGetCurrentProcess.

A thread that calls this function must be running at IRQL == PASSIVE_LEVEL.

PsGetCurrentThread

```
PETHREAD PsGetCurrentThread();
```

Returns a pointer to the Thread Object representing the current executing thread.

A thread that calls this function must be running IRQL <= DISPATCH_LEVEL.

PsTerminateSystemThread

```
NTSTATUS PsTerminateSystemThread(IN NTSTATUS ExitStatus);
```

Terminates a caller-created system thread.

The *ExitStatus* parameter specifies the status of the terminating system thread to the thread creator.

This function returns the STATUS_*XXX* supplied by the caller-created thread, usually STATUS_SUCCESS.

A driver that creates a device-dedicated thread calls this routine, either when the driver is unloaded or when the thread decides that it wishes to terminate, for example, when there are no outstanding I/O requests for the driver to process. For such a driver, PsTerminateSystemThread must be called in the context of the driver's thread; that is, the thread must terminate itself by making this call.

A thread that calls this function must be running at IRQL == PASSIVE_LEVEL.

READ_PORT_BUFFER_*type*

```
VOID READ_PORT_BUFFER_UCHAR(PUCHAR Port, PUCHAR Buffer, ULONG Count)
VOID READ_PORT_BUFFER_USHORT(PUCHAR Port, PUSHORT Buffer, ULONG Count)
VOID READ_PORT_BUFFER_ULONG(PUCHAR Port, PULONG Buffer, ULONG Count)
```

The READ_PORT_BUFFER_*type* reads a sequence of data values of the indicated type from the specified *Port*, which is a mapped I/O port.

The *Count* parameter tells how many values to copy. The *Buffer* parameter must be available. That is, it must exist at the time the operation is executed (typically it is either in nonpaged memory or locked down) and must be long enough to hold *Count* units.

A thread that calls this function can be running at any IRQL.

READ_PORT_*type*

```
UCHAR  READ_PORT_UCHAR(PUCHAR Port)
USHORT READ_PORT_USHORT(PUSHORT Port)
ULONG  READ_PORT_ULONG(PULONG Port)
```

READ_PORT_*type* reads a single value of the specified type from a device port.

The *Port* parameter is a mapped port address for the device. The result is the value read.

A thread that calls this function can be running at any IRQL.

READ_REGISTER_BUFFER_*type*

```
VOID READ_REGISTER_BUFFER_UCHAR(IN PUCHAR Register,
                                IN PUCHAR Buffer,
                                IN ULONG Count);
VOID READ_REGISTER_BUFFER_USHORT(IN PUSHORT Register,
                                 IN PUSHORT Buffer,
                                 IN ULONG Count);
VOID READ_REGISTER_BUFFER_ULONG(IN PULONG Register,
                                IN PULONG Buffer,
                                IN ULONG Count);
```

The READ_REGISTER_BUFFER_*type* functions read a sequence of values from a memory-mapped device register or mapped device memory to a memory buffer.

The *Register* parameter is the address of a memory-mapped register of the appropriate size. The *Buffer* parameter points to a location in memory that is at least *Count* units in length.

The source for each operation is the *Register* parameter; this value is not incremented during the transfer. The *Buffer* value is incremented successively during the transfer. The specified number of units is always transferred.

These functions can be called at any IRQL level, provided *Register* is a memory-mapped device register and *Buffer* is in nonpaged memory.

READ_REGISTER_*type*

```
UCHAR  READ_REGISTER_UCHAR(PUCHAR Register)
USHORT READ_REGISTER_USHORT(PUSHORT Register)
ULONG  READ_REGISTER_ULONG(PULONG Register)
```

These functions read a single data value of the indicated type from a memory-mapped device register or mapped device memory.

The *Register* parameter is a memory-mapped register for the device. The result is the value read.

A thread that calls this function can be running at any IRQL.

RemoveEntryList

VOID RemoveEntryList(IN PLIST_ENTRY *Entry*);

Removes the specified *Entry* from the list in which it is located. The forward and backward links of the removed entry are set to reference the entry.

A thread that calls this function must be running at IRQL == PASSIVE_LEVEL if any of the entries can be in paged memory. It can run at any IRQL >= DISPATCH_LEVEL if all of the entries are in nonpaged memory.

RemoveHeadList

PLIST_ENTRY RemoveHeadList PLIST_ENTRY *ListHead*);

Removes the entry at the head of the list referenced by the *ListHead* parameter and returns a pointer to it. If the list is empty, this function returns NULL.

A thread that calls this function can be running at IRQL >= DISPATCH_LEVEL only if the caller-allocated storage for *ListHead* is resident and only if pointers to every list entry remain valid at IRQL >= DISPATCH_LEVEL as well.

RemoveTailList

PLIST_ENTRY RemoveTailList(IN PLIST_ENTRY *ListHead*);

Removes the entry at the tail of the list referenced by the *ListHead* parameter and returns a pointer to it. If the list is empty, this function returns NULL.

A thread that calls this function can be running at IRQL >= DISPATCH_LEVEL only if the caller-allocated storage for *ListHead* is resident and only if pointers to every list entry remain valid at IRQL >= DISPATCH_LEVEL as well.

RtlCopyMemory

```
VOID RtlCopyMemory(IN VOID UNALIGNED * Destination,
                   IN CONST VOID UNALIGNED * Source,
                   IN ULONG Length);
```

Copies the contents specified by the *Source* parameter to the location specified by the *Destination* parameter.

The operation copies *Length* bytes. The source and the destination must not overlap.

This function is the kernel support equivalent of the common C library function memcpy(*Destination*, *Source*, *Length*). When it is used, the source and destination areas must not overlap, whereas RtlMoveMemory will work correctly if the areas overlap.

A thread that calls this function can be running at any IRQL if both memory blocks are resident. Otherwise, the caller must be running at IRQL < DISPATCH_LEVEL.

RtlInitUnicodeString

```
VOID RtlInitUnicodeString(IN OUT PUNICODE_STRING DestinationString,
                          IN PCWSTR SourceString);
```

The *DestinationString* parameter is initialized to point to the *SourceString* parameter. The length and maximum length for *DestinationString* are initialized to the length of *SourceString*. If *SourceString* is NULL, the length is 0.

A thread that calls this function can be running at IRQL <= DISPATCH_LEVEL if the *DestinationString* buffer is nonpageable. Usually, callers run at IRQL == PASSIVE_LEVEL because most other Rtl..String routines cannot be called at raised IRQL.

RtlMoveMemory

```
VOID RtlMoveMemory(IN PVOID Destination,
                   IN CONST VOID * Source,
                   IN ULONG Length);
```

Copies the contents specified by the *Source* parameter to the location specified by the *Destination* parameter.

The operation copies *Length* bytes. Whenever possible, this function optimizes its performance by copying aligned 4-byte blocks, taking special care for the possibly misaligned blocks or any blocks that are fewer than 4 bytes to be copied at the beginning or end. The source and the destination may overlap.

This function is the kernel support equivalent of the common C library function memmove(Destination, Source, Length). When it is used, the source and destination areas may overlap, whereas RtlCopyMemory requires disjoint areas. Thus RtlCopyMemory is faster if the regions are known to be disjoint.

A thread that calls this function can be running at any IRQL if both memory blocks are resident. Otherwise, the caller must be running at IRQL < DISPATCH_LEVEL.

RTL_QUERY_REGISTRY_ROUTINE

```
NTSTATUS
(*PRTL_QUERY_REGISTRY_ROUTINE)(
                            IN PWSTR ValueName,
                            IN ULONG ValueType,
                            IN PVOID ValueData,
                            IN ULONG ValueLength,
                            IN PVOID Context,
                            IN PVOID EntryContext)
```

This is the prototype for the query routine which is specified in an RTL_QUERY_REGISTRY_TABLE.

RTL_QUERY_REGISTRY_TABLE

```
typedef struct _RTL_QUERY_REGISTRY_TABLE {
            PRTL_QUERY_REGISTRY_ROUTINE QueryRoutine;
            ULONG Flags;
            PWSTR Name;
            PVOID EntryContext;
            ULONG DefaultType;
            PVOID DefaultData;
            ULONG DefaultLength;
} RTL_QUERY_REGISTRY_TABLE, * PRTL_QUERY_REGISTRY_TABLE;
```

A Query Table is referenced by the `RtlQueryRegistryValues` function. A valid Query Table must contain at least two entries. The first is a valid entry, and the last must be an entry in which both the `QueryRoutine` field and the `Name` field are *both* NULL. It is valid to have an entry in which the `QueryRoutine` entry is NULL but the `Name` is non-NULL if the `Flags` field specifies the flag `RTL_QUERY_REGISTRY_DIRECT`.

If the key is not found, the information will be treated as if the value with `DefaultDataType`, `DefaultData`, and `DefaultDataLength` had been found. Note that `DefaultData` is *not* the value but rather a *pointer* to the value. Thus, to make a DWORD value default value of 0, you must do something like the following.

```
DWORD zero = 0;
DWORD MyValue;
RTL_QUERY_REGISTRY_TABLE query[] = {
{ NULL, RTL_QUERY_REGISTRY_DIRECT, L"MyValueName", &MyValue, REG_DWORD, &zero, sizeof(DWORD) },
{ NULL, 0,                         NULL,          NULL,     0,         NULL,  0 } // EOT
      } ;
```

RtlQueryRegistryValues

```
NTSTATUS RtlQueryRegistryValues(IN ULONG RelativeTo,
                                IN PWSTR Path,
                                IN PRTL_QUERY_REGISTRY_TABLE QueryTable,
                                IN PVOID Context,
                                IN PVOID Environment);
```

This function is a convenient "wrapper" around the more primitive Zw-functions for Registry management. It permits you to read several values from a general key in a single operation.

The *QueryTable* parameter defines a list of names to be found, the place to put the result, and the default value/type/size to be used in case the requested subkey is not found. The *RelativeTo* parameter allows you to specify one of several standard locations that a Device Driver is likely to care about, such that *Path* is taken to be relative to the indicated path. In addition, you can specify a complete path or even give a handle that you have obtained by using ZwOpenKey.

Note that *Path* is a PWSTR, not a PUNICODE_STRING. If you have in hand a UNICODE_STRING, *there is no guarantee that it is NUL-terminated.* This is very important. You *must* ensure the NUL termination. To do this, you might need to allocate memory large enough to hold the UNICODE_STRING, plus its terminating NUL. Although you can specify a query function in *QueryTable*, there is usually little need to do so. That entry is NULL, and the `Flags` entry for that table entry is set to `RTL_QUERY_REGISTRY_DIRECT`.

The *Context* parameter is passed to the query function and is usually 0, since you generally will not be using one. If a REG_EXPAND_SZ entry can be found, you might wish to pass in an environment list to be used to expand the string.

A thread that calls this function must be running at IRQL == PASSIVE_LEVEL.

We have discovered conditions that seem to indicate that if the data types of the values in the Registry disagree with the data types in the QueryTable, a system thread you've never heard of will crash; if the debugger is not running, this takes NT down. We find this result surprising, but it happened when the Registry contained a string value and the table specified an integer value. We suspect this is a bug, but we found it in NT 4.0 Service Pack 3. Since we do not have NT source available to us, we were unable to investigate this further, but it was absolutely reproducible. Correcting the erroneous value in the Registry fixed the problem. A student had failed to specify REG_DWORD before a numeric value and it was entered as a string value.

RtlUnicodeStringToAnsiString

```
NTSTATUS RtlUnicodeStringToAnsiString(
                        IN OUT PANSI_STRING DestinationString,
                        IN PUNICODE_STRING SourceString,
                        IN BOOLEAN AllocateDestinationString);
```

The *DestinationString* parameter points to an ANSI_STRING structure, or NULL if the *AllocateDestinationString* parameter is TRUE. The input is the *SourceString* parameter, which references a UNICODE_STRING. If *AllocateDestinationString* is FALSE, this destination string must be large enough to hold the converted string.

It is not at all clear that if *AllocateDestinationString* is TRUE, how the value is returned if *DestinationString* is NULL. We believe that this documentation is incorrect. Studying the details suggests that the correct statement is that *DestinationString* does not need to be initialized if *AllocateDestinationString* is TRUE—this is quite different from the parameter's being NULL.

A thread that calls this function must be running at IRQL == PASSIVE_LEVEL.

RtlZeroMemory

```
VOID RtlZeroMemory(IN PVOID Destination,
                   IN ULONG Length);
```

Zeros memory starting at the specified *Destination* and proceeding in ascending addresses for *Length* bytes.

This routine provides the functionality equivalent to the familiar C runtime library call memset(Destination, 0, Length).

A thread that calls this function can be running at any IRQL if the *Destination* block is in the Nonpaged Pool. Otherwise, the caller must be running at IRQL < DISPATCH_LEVEL.

UNICODE_STRING

```
typedef struct _UNICODE_STRING {
                        USHORT Length;
                        USHORT MaximumLength;
                        PWSTR  Buffer;
} UNICODE_STRING * PUNICODE_STRING;
```

A UNICODE_STRING is a counted string that is used to pass strings around as parameters to many functions. An ordinary long string can be converted to a UNICODE_STRING with the RtlInitUnicodeString function.

Table A.35 lists the fields of the UNICODE_STRING structure.

Table A.35: *Fields of the* UNICODE_STRING *Structure*

Field	Meaning
Length	The length in bytes[*] of the string stored in Buffer. *Note that unlike most Unicode representations, this is a byte count, not a character count!*
MaximumLength	The maximum length in bytes[*] of Buffer.
Buffer	Pointer to a buffer used to contain a string of wide characters.

[*]Early documentation provided by Microsoft states that these sizes are the lengths in *words*; this is an error. A later update, Knowledge Base article Q149272, corrects this error and states that the lengths are in *characters*. This update is erroneous, too. Inspection with a debugger demonstrates that the length is in *bytes*. Current documentation from Microsoft gives the correct specification.

_URB_CONTROL_DESCRIPTOR_REQUEST

```
struct _URB_CONTROL_DESCRIPTOR_REQUEST {    // NT 5.0 beta/Windows 2000
    struct _URB_HEADER Hdr;                 // NT 5.0 beta/Windows 2000
    ULONG TransferBufferLength;             // NT 5.0 beta/Windows 2000
    PVOID TransferBuffer;                   // NT 5.0 beta/Windows 2000
    PMDL TransferBufferMDL;                 // NT 5.0 beta/Windows 2000
    struct _URB * UrbLink;                  // NT 5.0 beta/Windows 2000
    UCHAR Index;                            // NT 5.0 beta/Windows 2000
    UCHAR DescriptorType;                   // NT 5.0 beta/Windows 2000
    USHORT LanguageId;                      // NT 5.0 beta/Windows 2000
    // ... Many hidden fields                // NT 5.0 beta/Windows 2000
    };
```

URB_CONTROL_DESCRIPTOR_REQUEST is used to read or write the descriptors of a USB device. The fields of the contained _URB_HEADER, shown in Table A.36, must also be initialized.

Table A.36: _URB_CONTROL_DESCRIPTOR_REQUEST *Fields*

Field	Meaning
TransferBufferLength	The length, in bytes, of the TransferBuffer or the buffer described by TransferBufferMDL.
TransferBuffer	A pointer to a nonpaged memory block, or NULL if a MDL will be used.
TransferBufferMDL	A pointer to a MDL that describes a buffer, or NULL if the buffer is supplied in TransferBuffer.
UrbLink	A pointer to a caller-initialized URB that is the next in a chain of URBs.
Index	The device-defined index of the descriptor that is being retrieved or sent.
DescriptorType	The type of descriptor that is being retrieved or set, one of the following.

Table A.36: _URB_CONTROL_DESCRIPTOR_REQUEST *Fields (continued)*

Field	Meaning	
	USB_DEVICE_DESCRIPTOR_TYPE	The descriptor for a particular USB device.
	USB_CONFIGURATION_DESCRIPTOR_TYPE	The descriptor for the USB configuration.
	USB_STRING_DESCRIPTOR_TYPE	The descriptor for a string.
LanguageId	The language ID of the descriptor to be retrieved when the DescriptorType is USB_STRING_DESCRIPTOR_TYPE.	

_URB_HEADER

```
struct _URB_HEADER {                       // NT 5.0 beta/Windows 2000
                USHORT Length;             // NT 5.0 beta/Windows 2000
                USHORT Function;           // NT 5.0 beta/Windows 2000
                USBD_STATUS Status;        // NT 5.0 beta/Windows 2000
                PVOID UsbdDeviceHandle;    // NT 5.0 beta/Windows 2000
                ULONG UsbdFlags;};         // NT 5.0 beta/Windows 2000
```

Table A.37 lists the fields for URB_HEADER.

Table A.37: _URB_HEADER *Fields*

Field	Meaning
Length	The length of the specific URB request structure.
Function	The URB_FUNCTION_*xxx* for the specific device.
Status	A USB_STATUS_*xxx* code for the request.
UsbdDeviceHandle	Reserved for the USB stack management.
UsbdFlags	Reserved for the USB stack management.

UsbBuildGetDescriptorRequest

```
VOID UsbBuildGetDescriptorRequest(              // NT 5.0 beta/Windows 2000
            IN OUT PURB Urb,                     // NT 5.0 beta/Windows 2000
            IN USHORT Length,                    // NT 5.0 beta/Windows 2000
            IN UCHAR DescriptorType,             // NT 5.0 beta/Windows 2000
            IN UCHAR Index,                      // NT 5.0 beta/Windows 2000
            IN USHORT LanguageId,                // NT 5.0 beta/Windows 2000
            IN PVOID TransferBuffer OPTIONAL,    // NT 5.0 beta/Windows 2000
            IN PMDL TransferBufferMDL OPTIONAL,  // NT 5.0 beta/Windows 2000
            IN ULONG TransferBufferLength,       // NT 5.0 beta/Windows 2000
            IN PURB Link OPTIONAL);              // NT 5.0 beta/Windows 2000
```

You can build your own request blocks for USB by carefully reading the documentation and filling in the fields, but there are fields within fields that must also be initialized. A variety of convenience functions are provided to minimize the amount of effort required to accomplish this.

UsbBuildGetDescriptorRequest fills in a _URB_CONTROL_DESCRIPTOR_REQUEST structure, which is essentially a subclass of the general URB structure. Hence, the *URB* parameter is a general PURB, but the actual structure must be the _URB_CONTROL_DESCRIPTOR_REQUEST.

The *Length* parameter is used to ascertain that the block is long enough; it initializes a length field within the structure. The *DescriptorType* parameter can be for a USB_CONFIGURATION_DESCRIPTOR_TYPE, which provides the general USB configuration descriptor; a USB_DEVICE_DESCRIPTOR_TYPE, which will provide the device descriptor type (which is what we use in our example); or a USB_STRING_DESCRIPTOR_TYPE, which will get a string from the device. The Index parameter indicates which of several possible descriptors should be returned. For a device descriptor, this is set to 0 to get the first descriptor for the device. The *LanguageId* parameter has no meaning for any descriptor type other than the USB_STRING_DESCRIPTOR_TYPE. We can supply either a pointer to a buffer, *TransferBuffer*, or a pointer to a MDL describing the transfer buffer, *TransferBufferMDL*. One or the other of these can be non-NULL. The *TransferBufferLength* parameter indicates the length of the buffer. The *Link* parameter is used to link a chain of URBs, but for our purposes is NULL.

A thread that calls this function must be running at IRQL <= DISPATCH_LEVEL.

WRITE_PORT_BUFFER_*type*

```
VOID WRITE_PORT_BUFFER_UCHAR(PUCHAR Port,
                             PUCHAR Buffer,
                             ULONG Count)
VOID WRITE_PORT_BUFFER_USHORT(PUCHAR Port,
                              PUSHORT Buffer,
                              ULONG Count)
VOID WRITE_PORT_BUFFER_ULONG(PUCHAR Port,
                             PULONG Buffer,
                             ULONG Count)
```

The WRITE_PORT_BUFFER_*type* functions write a sequence of data values of the indicated type to the specified *Port*, which is a mapped I/O port.

The *Count* parameter tells how many values to copy. The *Buffer* parameter must be available. That is, it must exist at the time the operation is executed (typically it is either in nonpaged memory or locked down) and must be long enough to hold *Count* units.

A thread that calls this function can be running at any IRQL.

WRITE_PORT_*type*

```
void WRITE_PORT_UCHAR(PUCHAR Port, UCHAR Value)
void WRITE_PORT_USHORT(PUSHORT Port, USHORT Value)
void WRITE_PORT_ULONG(PULONG Port, ULONG Value)
```

The WRITE_PORT_*type* functions write a singe value of the indicated type to a mapped I/O port.

The *Port* parameter is a mapped port address for the device. The *Value* parameter is the value to write.

A thread that calls this function can be running at any IRQL.

WRITE_REGISTER_BUFFER_*type*

```
VOID WRITE_REGISTER_BUFFER_UCHAR(PUCHAR Register, PUCHAR Buffer, ULONG Count)
VOID WRITE_REGISTER_BUFFER_USHORT(PUSHORT Register, PUSHORT Buffer, ULONG Count)
VOID WRITE_REGISTER_BUFFER_ULONG(PULONG Register, PULONG Buffer, ULONG Count)
```

The WRITE_REGISTER_BUFFER_*type* functions write a sequence of data values of the indicated type to the specified *Register*, which is a memory-mapped device register.

The *Count* parameter tells how many values to copy. The *Buffer* must be available. That is, it must exist at the time the operation is executed (typically it is either in nonpaged memory or locked down) and must be long enough to hold *Count* units.

A thread that calls this function can be running at any IRQL.

WRITE_REGISTER_*type*

```
void WRITE_REGISTER_UCHAR(PUCHAR Register, UCHAR Value)
void WRITE_REGISTER_USHORT(PUSHORT Register, USHORT Value)
void WRITE_REGISTER_ULONG(PULONG Register, ULONG Value)
```

The WRITE_REGISTER_*type* functions write a single data value of the indicated type to a memory-mapped device register or mapped device memory. The *Register* parameter is a memory-mapped device register address for the device. The *Value* parameter is the value to write.

A thread that calls this function can be running at any IRQL.

ZwClose

```
NTSTATUS ZwClose(IN HANDLE Handle);
```

Closes a named object that was opened with one of the Zw-prefix calls.

A thread calling this function must be running at IRQL == PASSIVE_LEVEL.

ZwCreateFile

```
NTSTATUS ZwCreateFile(OUT PHANDLE FileHandle,
                IN ACCESS_MASK DesiredAccess,
                IN POBJECT_ATTRIBUTES ObjectAttributes,
                OUT PIO_STATUS_BLOCK IoStatusBlock,
                IN PLARGE_INTEGER AllocationSize OPTIONAL,
                IN ULONG FileAttributes,
                IN ULONG ShareAccess,
                IN ULONG CreateDisposition,
                IN ULONG CreateOptions,
                IN PVOID EaBuffer OPTIONAL,
                IN ULONG EaLength);
```

Creates or opens a named file.

The *FileHandle* parameter refers to a location that will receive the file handle on successful return. The *DesiredAccess* parameter can be any of the values in Table A.38 or any bitwise combination. The GENERIC_READ flag of the user level translates directly into

STANDARD_RIGHTS_READ for ZwCreateFile, and the GENERIC_WRITE flag of the user level translates directly into STANDARD_RIGHTS_WRITE.

Table A.38: *DesiredAccess Flags for* ZwCreateFile

Flag	Meaning
DELETE	The file can be deleted.
FILE_READ_DATA	Data can be read from the file.
FILE_READ_ATTRIBUTES	The FileAttributes flags, described later, can be read.
FILE_READ_EA	EAs associated with the file can be read. This flag is irrelevant to Device Drivers and intermediate drivers.
READ_CONTROL	The ACL and ownership information associated with the file can be read.
FILE_WRITE_DATA	Data can be written to the file.
FILE_WRITE_ATTRIBUTES	The FileAttributes flags can be written.
FILE_WRITE_EA	EAs associated with the file can be written. This flag is irrelevant to Device Drivers and intermediate drivers.
FILE_APPEND_DATA	Data can be appended to the file.
WRITE_DAC	The DACL associated with the file can be written.
WRITE_OWNER	Ownership information associated with the file can be written.
SYNCHRONIZE	The returned FileHandle can be waited on to synchronize with the completion of an I/O operation.
FILE_EXECUTE	Data can be read into memory from the file by using system paging I/O. This flag is irrelevant to Device Drivers and intermediate drivers.
FILE_LIST_DIRECTORY	The directory can be listed.
FILE_TRAVERSE	The directory name can be part of a pathname descriptor.
STANDARD_RIGHTS_READ	FILE_READ_DATA | FILE_READ_ATTRIBUTES | FILE_READ_EA
STANDARD_RIGHTS_WRITE	FILE_WRITE_DATA | FILE_WRITE_ATTRIBUTES | FILE_WRITE_EA | FILE_APPEND_DATA

Certain *DesiredAccess* flags and combinations of flags have the following effects.

- For a caller to synchronize an I/O completion by waiting on the returned *FileHandle*, the SYNCHRONIZE flag must be set. Otherwise, a caller that is a Device Driver or intermediate driver must synchronize an I/O completion by using an Event Object.

- If only the FILE_APPEND_DATA and SYNCHRONIZE flags are set, the caller can write only to the end of the file, and any offset information on writes to the file is ignored. However, the file will automatically be extended as necessary for this type of Write operation.

- Setting the FILE_WRITE_DATA flag for a file also allows writes beyond the end of the file to occur. The file is automatically extended for this type of write, as well.

- If only the FILE_EXECUTE and SYNCHRONIZE flags are set, the caller cannot directly read or write any data in the file by using the returned *FileHandle*. That is, all operations on the file occur through the system pager in response to instruction and data accesses. Device Drivers and intermediate drivers should not set the FILE_EXECUTE flag in *DesiredAccess*.

The *ObjectAttributes* parameter references an OBJECT_ATTRIBUTES structure that must supply the name of the file to create along with other attributes.

```
typedef struct _OBJECT_ATTRIBUTES {
    ULONG Length;
    HANDLE RootDirectory;                      // Optional
    PUNICODE_STRING ObjectName;
    ULONG Attributes;                          // 0 or OBJ_CASE_INSENSITIVE
    PSECURITY_DESCRIPTOR SecurityDescriptor; // Optional
    PSECURITY_QUALITY_OF_SERVICE SecurityQualityOfService; // Optional
} OBJECT_ATTRIBUTES, * POBJECT_ATTRIBUTES;
```

The Length field must be set to sizeof(OBJECT_ATTRIBUTES). The RootDirectory value is optional. If it is NULL, the ObjectName must specify a full path for the file to be opened. If it is non-NULL, it is a handle to a directory obtained by an earlier call to ZwCreateFile, and ObjectName is a name interpreted relative to that path. The Attributes field should be set to OBJ_CASE_INSENSITIVE to make your request compatible with the standard Windows NT File System conventions. We suggest that you set the SecurityDescriptor and SecurityQualityOfService both to NULL.

The *IoStatusBlock* parameter is a pointer to an IO_STATUS_BLOCK. Upon completion of the operation, the Information field of this block will contain one of the values shown in Table A.39. These should be self-explanatory.

Table A.39: Information *Field Values from* ZwCreateFile

FILE_CREATED
FILE_OPENED
FILE_OVERWRITTEN
FILE_SUPERSEDED
FILE_EXISTS
FILE_DOES_NOT_EXIST

The *AllocationSize* parameter can be used to specify an initial file allocation. This has no effect for an existing file that is being opened for reading. Normally, this value can be set to 0.

Next are a set of file attribute flags. These are the same as the user-level flags, but for most applications within Device Drivers, FILE_ATTRIBUTE_NORMAL suffices. They are summarized in Table A.40.

Table A.40: *FileAttribute Flags for* ZwCreateFile

File Attribute Flag	Interpretation
FILE_ATTRIBUTE_NORMAL	A file with standard attributes should be created.
FILE_ATTRIBUTE_READONLY	A read-only file should be created.
FILE_ATTRIBUTE_HIDDEN	A hidden file should be created.
FILE_ATTRIBUTE_SYSTEM	A system file should be created.
FILE_ATTRIBUTE_ARCHIVE	The file should be marked so that it will be archived.
FILE_ATTRIBUTE_TEMPORARY	A temporary file should be created.
FILE_ATTRIBUTE_ATOMIC_WRITE	An atomic-write file should be created. This flag is irrelevant to Device Drivers and intermediate drivers.
FILE_ATTRIBUTE_XACTION_WRITE	A transaction-write file should be created. This flag is irrelevant to Device Drivers and intermediate drivers.

The *ShareAccess* parameter is identical to that of the user level and uses the same names as the user-level CreateFile operation. Generally, you will specify 0 for this flag, which gives your driver exclusive access to the file as long as it is open. The *ShareAccess* flags are summarized in Table A.41.

Table A.41: *ShareAccess Values for* ZwCreateFile

ShareAccess flag	Meaning
0	The file cannot be accessed by any other thread until it is closed.
FILE_SHARE_READ	The file can be opened for read access by other threads' calls to ZwCreateFile.
FILE_SHARE_WRITE	The file can be opened for write access by other threads' calls to ZwCreateFile.
FILE_SHARE_DELETE	The file can be opened for delete access by other threads' calls to ZwCreateFile.

ShareAccess determines whether separate threads can access the same file, possibly simultaneously. The file can be successfully opened and shared, provided that both file openers have the privilege to access a file in the specified manner. If the original caller of ZwCreateFile does not specify FILE_SHARE_READ, FILE_SHARE_WRITE, or FILE_SHARE_DELETE, no other open operations can be performed on the file. That is, the original caller is given exclusive access to the file.

For a shared file to be successfully opened, the requested *DesiredAccess* to the file must be compatible with both the *DesiredAccess* and *ShareAccess* specifications of all preceding opens that have not yet been released with ZwClose. That is, the *DesiredAccess* specified to ZwCreateFile for a given file must not conflict with the accesses that other openers of the file have disallowed.

The *CreateDisposition* parameter tells how to handle the case of the file already existing, or not existing, for this call. The possible values are summarized in Table A.42.

Table A.42: *CreateDisposition Values for* ZwCreateFile

CreateDisposition **Flag**	**File Exists**	**File Does Not Exist**
FILE_SUPERSEDE	Replace it.	Create it.
FILE_CREATE	Fail.	Create it.
FILE_OPEN	Open it.	Fail.
FILE_OPEN_IF	Open it.	Create it.
FILE_OVERWRITE	Open it, and overwrite it.	Fail.
FILE_OVERWRITE_IF	Open it, and overwrite it.	Create it.

The *CreateDisposition* value FILE_SUPERSEDE requires that the caller have DELETE access to a existing File Object. If it does, a successful call to ZwCreateFile with FILE_SUPERSEDE on an existing file effectively deletes that file and then recreates it. This implies that if the file has already been opened by another thread, then it opened the file by specifying a *ShareAccess* parameter with the FILE_SHARE_DELETE flag set. Note that this type of disposition is consistent with the POSIX style of overwriting files.

The *CreateDisposition* values FILE_OVERWRITE_IF and FILE_SUPERSEDE are similar. If ZwCreateFile is called with an existing file and either of these *CreateDisposition* values, the file will be replaced.

Overwriting a file is semantically equivalent to a supersede operation, except for the following.

- The caller must have write access to the file, rather than delete access. This implies that if the file has already been opened by another thread, it opened the file with the FILE_SHARE_WRITE flag set in the input *ShareAccess*.

- The specified file attributes are logically ORed with those already on the file. This implies that if the file has already been opened by another thread, a subsequent caller of ZwCreateFile cannot disable existing *FileAttributes* flags but can enable additional flags for the same file. Note that this style of overwriting files is consistent with MS-DOS, with DOS-based Windows, and with OS/2.

The *CreateOptions* flags, discussed in Table A.43, generally deal with how Windows NT will handle the file internally.

Table A.43: *CreateOptions Flags for* ZwCreateFile

CreateOptions **Flag**	**Meaning**
FILE_DIRECTORY_FILE	The file being created or opened is a directory file. With this flag, the *CreateDisposition* parameter must be set to one of FILE_CREATE, FILE_OPEN, or FILE_OPEN_IF. With this flag, other compatible *CreateOptions* flags include only the following: FILE_SYNCHRONOUS_IO_ALERT, FILE_SYNCHRONOUS_IO_NONALERT, FILE_WRITE_THROUGH, FILE_OPEN_FOR_BACKUP_INTENT, and FILE_OPEN_BY_FILE_ID.

Table A.43: *CreateOptions Flags for* ZwCreateFile *(continued)*

CreateOptions **Flag**	**Meaning**
FILE_NON_DIRECTORY_FILE	The file being opened must not be a directory file, or this call will fail. The File Object being opened can represent a data file; a logical, virtual, or physical device; or a volume.
FILE_WRITE_THROUGH	System services, FSDs, and drivers that write data to the file must actually transfer the data into the file before any requested Write operation is considered complete. This flag is automatically set if the *CreateOptions* flag FILE_NO_INTERMEDIATE_BUFFERING is set.
FILE_SEQUENTIAL_ONLY	All accesses to the file will be sequential.
FILE_RANDOM_ACCESS	Accesses to the file can be random, so no sequential read-ahead operations should be performed on the file by FSDs or the system.
FILE_NO_INTERMEDIATE_BUFFERING	The file cannot be cached or buffered in a driver's internal buffers. This flag is incompatible with the *DesiredAccess* FILE_APPEND_DATA flag.
FILE_SYNCHRONOUS_IO_ALERT	All operations on the file are performed synchronously. Any wait on behalf of the caller is subject to premature termination from alerts. This flag also causes the I/O system to maintain the file position context. If this flag is set, the *DesiredAccess* SYNCHRONIZE flag also must be set.
FILE_SYNCHRONOUS_IO_NONALERT	All operations on the file are performed synchronously. Waits in the system to synchronize I/O queueing and completion are not subject to alerts. This flag also causes the I/O system to maintain the file position context. If this flag is set, the *DesiredAccess* SYNCHRONIZE flag also must be set.
FILE_CREATE_TREE_CONNECTION	A tree connection is created for this file so that it can be opened over the network. This flag is irrelevant to Device Drivers and intermediate drivers.
FILE_COMPLETE_IF_OPLOCKED	This operation is completed immediately with an alternate success code if the target file is oplocked, rather than blocking the caller's thread. If the file is oplocked, another caller already has access to the file over the network. This flag is irrelevant to Device Drivers and intermediate drivers.
FILE_NO_EA_KNOWLEDGE	If the EAs on an existing file that is being opened indicate that the caller must understand EAs in order to properly interpret the file, fail this request because the caller does not understand how to deal with EAs. Device Drivers and intermediate drivers can ignore this flag.
FILE_DELETE_ON_CLOSE	The file is deleted when the last handle to it is passed to ZwClose.
FILE_OPEN_BY_FILE_ID	The filename contains the name of a device and a 64-bit ID to be used to open the file. This flag is irrelevant to Device Drivers and intermediate drivers.

Table A.43: *CreateOptions Flags for* ZwCreateFile *(continued)*

CreateOptions **Flag**	**Meaning**
FILE_OPEN_FOR_BACKUP_INTENT	The file is being opened for backup intent. Hence, the system should check for certain access rights and grant the caller the appropriate accesses to the file before checking the input *DesiredAccess* against the file's security descriptor. This flag is irrelevant to Device Drivers and intermediate drivers.

The *CreateOptions* FILE_DIRECTORY_FILE value specifies that the file to be created or opened is a directory file. When a directory file is created, the File System creates an appropriate structure on the disk to represent an empty directory for that particular File System's on-disk structure. The call to ZwCreateFile will fail if this option was specified and the given file to be opened is not a directory file or if the caller specified an inconsistent *CreateOptions* or *CreateDisposition* value.

The *CreateOptions* FILE_NO_INTERMEDIATE_BUFFERING flag prevents the File System from performing any intermediate buffering on behalf of the caller. Specifying this value places certain restrictions on the caller's parameters to other Zw..File routines, including the following.

- Any optional *ByteOffset* passed to ZwReadFile or ZwWriteFile must be an integral of the sector size.

- The *Length* passed to ZwReadFile or ZwWriteFile must be an integral of the sector size. Note that specifying a Read operation to a buffer whose length is exactly the sector size might result in a lesser number of significant bytes being transferred to that buffer if the end of the file was reached during the transfer.

- Buffers must be aligned in accordance with the alignment requirement of the underlying device. This information can be obtained by calling ZwCreateFile to get a handle for the File Object that represents the physical device and then calling ZwQueryInformationFile with that handle. For a list of the system FILE_*xxx*_ALIGNMENT values, see DEVICE_OBJECT.

- Calls to ZwSetInformationFile with the *FileInformationClass* parameter set to FilePositionInformation must specify an offset that is an integral of the sector size.

The *CreateOptions* FILE_SYNCHRONOUS_IO_ALERT and FILE_SYNCHRONOUS_IO_NONALERT, which are mutually exclusive, as their names suggest, specify that all I/O operations on the file are to be synchronous as long as they occur through the File Object referred to by the returned *FileHandle*. All I/O on such a file is serialized across all threads using the returned handle. With either of these *CreateOptions*, the *DesiredAccess* SYNCHRONIZE flag must be set so that the I/O Manager will use the File Object as a synchronization object. With either of these *CreateOptions* set, the I/O Manager maintains the "file position context" for the File Object, an internal, current file position offset. This offset can be used in calls to ZwReadFile and ZwWriteFile. Its position also can be queried or set with ZwQueryInformationFile and ZwSetInformationFile.

The *EaBuffer* and *EaLength* parameters are used if you want to get the EAs back from ZwCreateFile. Microsoft states that you should set these to NULL (0).

ZwCreateKey

```
NTSTATUS ZwCreateKey(OUT PHANDLE KeyHandle,
                     IN ACCESS_MASK DesiredAccess,
                     IN POBJECT_ATTRIBUTES ObjectAttributes,
                     IN ULONG TitleIndex,
                     IN PUNICODE_STRING Class,
                     IN ULONG CreateOptions,
                     OUT PULONG Disposition);
```

ZwCreateKey is used to create or open a key in the Registry. The key is specified by an OBJECT_ATTRIBUTES structure (which you initialize using InitializeObjectAttributes). You can work in a specific subdirectory of the directory tree. In this case, either you also specify the handle that specifies the root of the tree used or you specify NULL, which requires that the ObjectName specified in the *ObjectAttributes* be a full path starting with "\". The *Class* value is always NULL for all of the examples we found. In fact, very little documentation is available on the meaning of the object class.

For example, to register the DOS device name of your device, you first need to create a key. You then set the name. Following is a function that registers a device name.

```
NTSTATUS RegisterMyDevice(IN PUNICODE_STRING name)
    {
     OBJECT_ATTRIBUTES attr;
     HANDLE keyhandle;
     NTSTATUS result;

     InitializeObjectAttributes(&attr, L"\Registry\MyDesiredKey",
                                OBJ_CASE_INSENSITIVE,
                                NULL, NULL);
     result = ZwCreateKey(&keyhandle, KEY_WRITE, &attr, 0, NULL,
                          REG_OPTION_VOLATILE, NULL);
     if(result == STATUS_SUCCESS)
        { /* have key */
         // ... Do something interesting here
         ZwClose(keyhandle);
        } /* have key */
     return result;
    }
```

A thread calling this function must be executing at IRQL == PASSIVE_LEVEL.

ZwDeleteKey

```
NTSTATUS ZwDeleteKey(IN HANDLE KeyHandle);
```

ZwDeleteKey deletes a key from the Registry, given its handle.

After this function completes successfully, the key handle is invalid and may not be used for any purpose. There is no need to call ZwClose on a key handle for a key that has been deleted. Doing so will cause that function to fail with a STATUS_INVALID_HANDLE error; the key had to have been opened with delete access. The KEY_ALL_ACCESS constant includes delete access via the STANDARD_RIGHTS_ALL constant.

A thread calling this function must be executing at IRQL == PASSIVE_LEVEL.

ZwEnumerateKey

```
NTSTATUS ZwEnumerateKey(IN HANDLE KeyHandle,
                        IN ULONG Index,
                        IN KEY_INFORMATION_CLASS KeyInformationClass,
                        OUT PVOID KeyInformation,
                        IN ULONG Length,
                        OUT PULONG ResultLength);
```

Provides a list of all of the subkeys of a specified key.

The *Index* parameter is used to distinguish between subkeys. Two successive calls to this function with the same *Index* are not guaranteed to return the same result. The documentation does not state explicitly why. However, the fact that this function must be called at PASSIVE_LEVEL suggests that other threads that have preempted execution of the thread that calls this function may modify the Registry and thus change the meaning of *Index*. Or, alternatively, modifications done by the thread itself can change the meaning of the contents of the Registry at the *Index* position.

This function and the similar Rtl...Registry functions differ in that the latter are required to provide the name of the key. Drivers can call ZwEnumerateKey to get unknown names of the subkeys for a key with a known name.

A thread calling this function must be executing at IRQL == PASSIVE_LEVEL.

ZwEnumerateValueKey

```
NTSTATUS ZwEnumerateValueKey(IN HANDLE KeyHandle,
                             IN ULONG Index,
                             IN KEY_VALUE_INFORMATION_CLASS
                                                KeyValueInformationClass,
                             OUT PVOID KeyValueInformation,
                             IN ULONG Length,
                             OUT PULONG ResultLength );
```

This function allows you to enumerate all of the values stored under a specific key. The *Index* parameter is used to distinguish between subkeys. Two successive calls to this function with the same *Index* are not guaranteed to return the same result. The documentation does not state explicitly why. However, the fact that this function must be called at PASSIVE_LEVEL suggests that other threads that have preempted execution of the thread that calls this function may modify the Registry and thus change the meaning of *Index*. Or, alternatively, modifications done by the thread itself can change the meaning of the contents of the Registry at the *Index* position.

A thread calling this function must be executing at IRQL == PASSIVE_LEVEL.

ZwFlushKey

```
NTSTATUS ZwFlushKey(IN HANDLE KeyHandle);
```

Forces the indicated key (and all of its subkeys) to be immediately committed to disk.

The system automatically flushes keys to disk every few seconds. It is rare to need to use this function. This function could cause the entire Registry to be flushed to disk. Thus it could take a significant amount of time and cause a large number of possibly unnecessary disk accesses. The function will not return until the key (and all of its subkeys) have been success-fully committed to disk.

A thread calling this function must be executing at IRQL == PASSIVE_LEVEL.

ZwMapViewOfSection

```
NTSTATUS ZwMapViewOfSection(IN HANDLE SectionHandle,
                            IN HANDLE ProcessHandle,
                            IN OUT PVOID * BaseAddress,
                            IN ULONG ZeroBits,
                            IN ULONG CommitSize,
                            IN OUT PLARGE_INTEGER SectionOffset,
                            IN OUT PULONG ViewSize,
                            IN SECTION_INHERIT InheritDisposition,
                            IN ULONG AllocationType,
                            IN ULONG Protect);
```

This is one of the key functions for addressing physical memory. In particular, it is the only way to make physical memory addressable by a user-level process.

To address physical memory, you provide the handle for L"\Device\PhysicalMemory", which you get from ZwOpenSection. In this case, the section offset you provide, which is a ref-erence to a LARGE_INTEGER, is the physical memory address.

A typical example familiar to many PC programmers is the VGA frame buffer, which lives at physical address 0x000A0000 and is usually 128K long. There is no way to access this physi-cal address unless it is first mapped into the logical address space. Then the entire physical address space of the VGA card is available. Note that for any given process, the virtual address of the VGA frame buffer could appear at different virtual addresses than in some other process, depending on how many drivers might have been loaded and consumed virtual addresses before the mapping was done.

You provide the process handle for the process whose virtual address space is to receive the view. You can map the view into a specific virtual address range or let the system decide which virtual addresses will be assigned to the view. You pass in a pointer to a PVOID value. This value must be set to NULL, which indicates the system should select the base address in the process vir-tual memory. Or it should be a process virtual memory address. If it is not NULL, the actual address assigned will be the address you give, rounded down to the next lower 64K boundary. Upon a successful return, the actual base address will be returned in the location referenced by this pointer.

If the value of the desired location is set to NULL, the *ZeroBits* parameter gives some guidelines to the virtual machine allocator as to where the page should be placed. This parame-ter, ignored if *BaseAddress is non-NULL, specifies the number of high-order bits that *must* be 0 in the resulting virtual address actually chosen. This value must be < 21. If it is set to 1, the sys-tem is free to assign the virtual address anywhere in the user space. Note that this only indicates the number that *must* be 0. The system is free to assign *more* high-order bits 0 than this parame-ter specifies.

The *CommitSize* parameter applies only to sections that have page-file-backed views. As a Device Driver writer, you won't see these, and although this parameter is ignored, you should probably set it to 0.

The *SectionOffset* parameter is a reference to a 64-bit LARGE_INTEGER. This is the offset into the section and, for \Device\PhysicalMemory, is the physical memory address. Note that this is a value larger than 32 bits. Some RISC machines support physical addresses greater than 32 bits.[3]

The *ViewSize* parameter is optional. If it is NULL, the section that is mapped in starts at the specified address and continues to the end of the section. You will not want this to be NULL when you are using it to map physical memory. So you point to a location that holds the desired size, in bytes. Upon successful return, this location will be (possibly) modified so that the actual length is a multiple of the page size of the processor (for example, 4K on Intel and 8K on Alpha). The size you specify will be rounded up to the next page-size boundary.

The *InheritDisposition* parameter tells whether this view should be inherited by child processes. For Device Drivers, set this to 0.

The *AllocationType* parameter indicates the type of allocation to be done for these pages.

The *Protection* parameter specifies the page-level protection for the allocated and initially committed pages. For Device Drivers, use the value PAGE_READWRITE.

Several different views, of possibly overlapping regions, can be mapped into any one process at any time. In addition, many different processes may concurrently have mapped views of the same section. Only when the last view is unmapped will the section be destroyed. (In the case of physical memory, only the *section* would be destroyed, not the memory. But there are enough outstanding physical memory handles in the system that this will, in practice, never occur except as the system is shutting down.)

A thread that calls this function must be at IRQL == PASSIVE_LEVEL.

ZwOpenKey

```
NTSTATUS ZwOpenKey(OUT PHANDLE KeyHandle,
                   IN ACCESS_MASK DesiredAccess,
                   IN POBJECT_ATTRIBUTES ObjectAttributes);
```

Opens an existing Registry key. If you aren't sure if the key actually exists, you should use ZwCreateKey. This will create a new key if the one specified does not exist or open the key if it is already defined.

The *ObjectAttributes* object defines the key to be retrieved and the directory from which it is to be retrieved. If the Registry directory handle in the OBJECT_ATTRIBUTES is NULL, the key must be a full pathname starting with "\".

---

[3] When IBM introduced the System/360, it came under serious criticism for wasting so many bits on a large address space. They actually allowed for a *full 24-bit address space*, addressing a nearly inconceivable 16MB of physical memory! Some years ago (in the late 1970s, to the best of my recollection), the designer of the S-1 multiprocessor architecture said that he realized that he had been too conservative; he had designed a machine with "only" a 32-bit address space. "I realize now that this could be fully populated for only about $10,000,000. That's nothing to the Department of Energy". At mid-1998 memory prices, you could populate a full 32-bit address space for under $5,000, a nominal sum for a small-sized company (or even an individual!). Today, it is common for corporate file servers with a terabyte of rotating magnetic storage to have a gigabyte (30 bits worth) of physical memory. Microsoft realized this trend early on when Windows NT was first being written, so NT was written to support very large physical memories . . . 64 bits of address are supported uniformly in the kernel. At the time we write this, Microsoft has announced a forthcoming 64-bit user-space version of NT. *–jmn*

```
NTSTATUS ReadSomeUsefulInteger(IN PUNICODE_STRING key, OUT PLONG val)
    {
    OBJECT_ATTRIBUTES attr;
    NTSTATUS result;

    InitializeObjectAttributes(
                    &attr, L"\Registry\MyDesiredKey",
                    OBJ_CASE_INSENSITIVE, // No case sensitivity
                    NULL, NULL);
    result = ZwOpenKey(&handle, &attr, KEY_READ);
    if(result == STATUS_SUCCESS)
        { /* get desired value */
        // ... // Do something useful here
        } /* get desired result */
    return result;
    }
```

A thread that calls this function must be at IRQL == PASSIVE_LEVEL.

ZwOpenSection

```
NTSTATUS ZwOpenSection(OUT PHANDLE SectionHandle,
                    IN ACCESS_MASK DesiredAccess,
                    IN POBJECT_ATTRIBUTES ObjectAttributes);
```

Calling the ZwOpenSection is the first step in gaining access to physical memory.

The *ObjectAttributes* parameter is a pointer to an OBJECT_ATTRIBUTES structure. This is an opaque data type that must be initialized using InitializeObjectAttributes. In particular, to obtain physical memory, you specify the string

```
L"\Device\PhysicalMemory"
```

Next, you must use ZwMapViewOfSection to map some piece of the section into your virtual address space. Note that once you have a handle, you can map several disjoint pieces of the physical memory referenced by this section into your virtual address space. See the description of ZwMapViewOfSection for more details.

A thread that calls this function must be running at IRQL == PASSIVE_LEVEL.

ZwQueryKey

```
NTSTATUS ZwQueryKey(IN HANDLE KeyHandle,
                    IN KEY_INFORMATION_CLASS KeyInformationClass,
                    OUT PVOID KeyInformation,
                    IN ULONG Length,
                    OUT PULONG ResultLength);
```

Returns information in the location pointed to by the *KeyInformation* parameter. *KeyInformation* must be large enough to hold all of the requested information.

If you aren't sure how many subkeys are present, and consequently how much memory is required, you can call this function with a *Length* of 0. It will fail with a STATUS_BUFFER_OVERFLOW error, but it will set the *ResultLength* parameter to the required length. You can then allocate this amount of space and repeat the call with the new length. The

KeyInformationClass value specifies one of the following, to indicate the type of information to be returned: KeyBasicInformation, KeyFullInformation, or KeyNodeInformation.

The function does not return an *array* of structures. The structures are of variable lengths, and consequently you must iterate through the buffer, accounting for each length in turn. See the descriptions of KEY_BASIC_INFORMATION, KEY_FULL_INFORMATION, or KEY_NODE_INFORMATION, based on the type requested by the *KeyInformationClass* request.

A thread that calls this function must be running at IRQL == PASSIVE_LEVEL.

ZwQueryValueKey

```
NTSTATUS ZwQueryValueKey(
                IN HANDLE KeyHandle,
                IN PUNICODE_STRING ValueName,
                IN KEY_VALUE_INFORMATION_CLASS KeyValueInformationClass,
                OUT PVOID KeyValueInformation,
                IN ULONG Length,
                OUT PULONG ResultLength);
```

ZwQueryValueKey retrieves the value for a key whose handle is provided.

The value is placed in a buffer allocated by the user. If the buffer is not long enough to hold the value, the function fails with a STATUS_BUFFER_OVERFLOW error, but it will set the *ResultLength* parameter to the desired length.

If you aren't sure how many bytes are required for the values, you can call this function with a *Length* of 0. It will fail with a STATUS_BUFFER_OVERFLOW error, but it will set *ResultLength* to the required length. You can then allocate this amount of space and repeat the call with the new length.

The type of value returned depends on the *KeyValueType* parameter. You can get basic, full, or partial information about the key, by specifying KeyBasicInformation, KeyFullInformation, or KeyNodeInformation.

A thread that calls this function must be running at IRQL == PASSIVE_LEVEL.

ZwSetInformationThread

```
NTSTATUS ZwSetInformationThread(IN HANDLE ThreadHandle,
                                IN THREADINFOCLASS ThreadInformationClass,
                                IN PVOID ThreadInformation,
                                IN ULONG ThreadInformationLength);
```

Sets the parameters of a thread for which the caller has a handle.

The *ThreadHandle* parameter is the open handle for a thread. The *ThreadInformationClass* parameter is the type of the information to be set by the parameters in Table A.44. It is one of the system-defined values shown in the table.

The *ThreadInformation* parameter is a pointer to the information to be set for the thread. What it points to depends on the value of *ThreadInformationClass*. Other constraints might apply, as shown in Table A.44. The *ThreadInformationLength* parameter specifies the (minimum) length of the information, in bytes. If the length is incorrect, the function will return STATUS_INFO_LENGTH_MISMATCH. If the value is not correct for *ThreadInformationClass*, the function will return STATUS_INVALID_PARAMETER.

Table A.44: `ZwSetInformationThread` *Options*

ThreadInformationClass	*ThreadInformation*	*ThreadInformationLength*
`ThreadPriority`	PKPRIORITY. Pointer to the thread priority value. This value must be in the range `LOW_PRIORITY` < value <= `HIGH_PRIORITY`.	`sizeof(KPRIORITY)`
`ThreadBasePriority`	PKPRIORITY. Pointer to the thread base priority value. This value must fall within the system's valid base priority range and the original priority class for the given thread. That is, if a thread's priority class is variable, that thread's base priority cannot be reset to a real-time priority value and vice versa.	`sizeof(KPRIORITY)`
The following values are not documented in the DDK but are present in the header file.		
`ThreadBasicInformation`		
`ThreadTimes`		
`ThreadAffinityMask`		
`ThreadImpersonationToken`		
`ThreadDescriptorTableEntry`		
`ThreadEnableAlignmentFaultFixup`		
`ThreadEventPair`		
`ThreadQuerySetWin32StartAddress`		
`ThreadZeroTlsCell`		
`ThreadPerformanceCount`		
`ThreadAmILastThread`		
`ThreadIdealProcessor`		
`ThreadPriorityBoost`		
`ThreadSetTlsArrayAddress`		
`MaxThreadInfoClass`		

To call this routine, the caller must have `THREAD_SET_INFORMATION` access rights for the given thread.

Usually, Device Drivers and intermediate drivers that set up driver-created threads call `KeSetBasePriorityThread` or `KeSetPriorityThread` from their driver-created threads, rather than `ZwSetInformationThread`. However, a driver can call `ZwSetInformationThread` to raise the priority of a driver-created thread before that thread is run.

A thread that calls this function must be running at IRQL == `PASSIVE_LEVEL`.

ZwSetValueKey

```
NTSTATUS ZwSetValueKey(IN HANDLE KeyHandle,
                       IN PUNICODE_STRING ValueName,
                       IN ULONG TitleIndex,
                       IN ULONG Type,
                       IN PVOID Data,
                       IN ULONG DataSize);
```

Given a key handle and the name of a value, sets the value for that key. If the key already has a value by the same name, that value is replaced; otherwise, the value name is added to the key. The key must have been opened or created with the KEY_SET_VALUE attribute.

The value is described by its name, its type, a pointer to the bits that will be assigned to the value, and the length of the value in bytes. The value name is optional and may be specified as NULL for an unnamed value.

Drivers need not, and should not attempt to, call ZwSetValueKey directly to write value entries in a subkey of the \Registry..\ResourceMap key. Only the system can write value entries to the \Registry..\HardwareDescription tree.

For any string type value (a type ending in _SZ), the data size must include the terminating zero character(s). Remember that this is Unicode, so for n zero characters you must add n * sizeof(WCHAR).

Key names are case-preserving when they are created and are treated as case-insensitive if OBJ_CASE_INSENSITIVE is specified. Since the application-level API calls that manipulate the Registry are all case-preserving but case-insensitive, you should not use case-sensitive keys in your driver.

At any given level in the Registry, a key value name must be unique. However, the same key value name may be used many times in the tree, as long as it is unique within a single level.

A thread that calls this function must be running at IRQL == PASSIVE_LEVEL.

ZwUnmapViewOfSection

```
NTSTATUS ZwUnmapViewOfSection(IN HANDLE ProcessHandle,
                              IN PVOID BaseAddress);
```

The entire view of the section specified by the *BaseAddress* parameter is removed from the virtual address space of the process whose handle is supplied. Note that there can be many mappings, possibly even of the same piece of a section, in the process, but only one of them will contain *BaseAddress*. Other mappings are left untouched by this function.

The virtual address region occupied by the view is no longer reserved and is available to map other views or private pages. If the view was the last reference to the underlying section, then all committed pages in the section are decommitted and the section is deleted.

A thread executing this function must be running at IRQL == PASSIVE_LEVEL.

Further Reading

Custer, Helen, *Inside Windows NT*, Microsoft Press, 1993. ISBN 155615481X

> This book is primarily of historical interest. It has been superseded by the Solomon book, cited later in these references, which is the second edition of the book.

Intel Corporation, *i486 Microprocessor Reference Manual*, McGraw-Hill, 1990. ISBN 0-07-881674-2

Microsoft Corporation, *Microsoft Windows NT Device Driver Kit Design Guide*, Microsoft Developer Network (MSDN) CD-ROM

Mindshare, Inc: Don Anderson, and Tom Shanley, *Pentium™Processor System Architecture, Second Edition*, Addison-Wesley, 1995. ISBN 0-201-40992-5

Mindshare, Inc: Tom Shanley, *Pentium® Pro and Pentium® II System Architecture, Second Edition*, Addison Wesley Longman, 1997. ISBN 0-201-30973-4

Solomon, David A., *Inside Windows NT (Second Edition)*, Microsoft Press, 1998. ISBN 1-57231-677-2

> This book is the revision of the Custer book and is considered now to be the definitive edition.

Appendix

B *Error Codes and NTSTATUS Codes*

Several reviewers of this book's early drafts pointed out that there was no easy way to figure out how to generate a specific application-level error return value to an I/O operation since Microsoft does not document this mapping. We quickly decided that determining this is trivial and decided to experiment. First, we would write a driver that uses an IOCTL to pass in an NTSTATUS value. The driver then would set the NTSTATUS value as the completion code for the IRP and return. At the application level, we detect that the IOCTL failed and use GetLastError to obtain the error code and FormatMessage to obtain the text of the error. The results of that experiment are in this appendix, as Table B.1, Table B.2 and Table B.3.

We must emphasize that *these are not official lists*. They are the lists produced by Windows NT Workstation version 4.0 under Service Pack 3. They are the version of The Truth for this version, and this version only. However, the software distribution for this book includes the source and executable versions of the application and driver we used to create these tables, so to get the values for your version, you only need to re-run the programs. We discuss the programs and how to use them at the end of this chapter.

The program can produce several lists, of which we include the "interesting subset" here. The program also produces the output both in a "plaintext" format and in a format that is suitable for a word processor's "Convert To Table" function (Word or FrameMaker both have this command). So the only "hand work" was to adjust the fonts and column widths.

Some interesting anomalies showed up as we were creating these lists. For example, some NTSTATUS codes produce GetLastError codes, which are unrecognized by FormatMessage. Some error codes that were returned were not found in the winerror.h file.

If you have an application-level error code name and want to know what NTSTATUS code produced it, or you want to produce a specific application-level error code and want to know what NTSTATUS code to use, Table B.1 is arranged in alphabetical order of application error name. If you have an application-level error code number and want to know what NTSTATUS code produced it, Table B.2 (page 1028) is arranged in numeric order of application error code values. If you want to see what application-level error code will come from a specific NTSTATUS code, Table B.3 (page 1053) is arranged in alphabetical order of NTSTATUS name. Table B.4 has a summary of all the NTSTATUS codes, including their symbolic name and text explanation, in numeric order by NTSTATUS code value.

Note that because of the large amount of information to be displayed, we violated our rule used in this book that no name be hyphenated or split across a line. For some of the longer names, we have split them at the underscore.

When we get an error code back from the I/O operation that forces the NTSTATUS value, we use GetLastError to obtain the actual user-level error number. We then call FormatMessage to convert this to a printable string. It turns out that FormatMessage does *not* recognize all of the error codes from the kernel, and when this happens, our program prints a "?" for the conversion text.

GetLastError Codes (alphabetic) to NTSTATUS Codes

This list is sorted alphabetically by the application error code symbolic name.

Table B.1: *Application Error Codes (alphabetic) to* NTSTATUS *Values*

Application Error Code		Explanation	NTSTATUS Name
Name	Value		
	0x80000001	Not implemented.	STATUS_GUARD_PAGE_VIOLATION
	0x80000003	One or more arguments are invalid.	STATUS_BREAKPOINT
	0x80000004	No such interface supported.	STATUS_SINGLE_STEP
	0xc000001d	?	STATUS_ILLEGAL_INSTRUCTION
	0xc0000025	?	STATUS_NONCONTINUABLE_ EXCEPTION
	0xc0000026	?	STATUS_INVALID_DISPOSITION
	0xc000002b	?	STATUS_PARITY_ERROR
	0xc000008c	?	STATUS_ARRAY_BOUNDS_EXCEEDED
	0xc000008d	?	STATUS_FLOAT_DENORMAL_OPERAND
	0xc000008e	?	STATUS_FLOAT_DIVIDE_BY_ZERO
	0xc000008f	?	STATUS_FLOAT_INEXACT_RESULT
	0xc0000090	?	STATUS_FLOAT_INVALID_ OPERATION
	0xc0000091	?	STATUS_FLOAT_OVERFLOW
	0xc0000092	?	STATUS_FLOAT_STACK_CHECK
	0xc0000093	?	STATUS_FLOAT_UNDERFLOW
	0xc0000094	?	STATUS_INTEGER_DIVIDE_BY_ZERO
	0xc0000096	?	STATUS_PRIVILEGED_INSTRUCTION
	0xc000022a	?	STATUS_DUPLICATE_OBJECTID
	0xc000022b	?	STATUS_OBJECTID_EXISTS
EPT_S_CANT_CREATE	1899	The endpoint mapper database could not be created.	EPT_NT_CANT_CREATE

Table B.1: *Application Error Codes (alphabetic) to* NTSTATUS *Values (continued)*

Application Error Code		Explanation	NTSTATUS Name
Name	**Value**		
EPT_S_CANT_PERFORM_OP	1752	The server endpoint cannot perform the operation.	EPT_NT_CANT_PERFORM_OP
EPT_S_INVALID_ENTRY	1751	The entry is invalid.	EPT_NT_INVALID_ENTRY
EPT_S_NOT_REGISTERED	1753	There are no more endpoints available from the endpoint mapper.	EPT_NT_NOT_REGISTERED
ERROR_ACCESS_DENIED	5	Access is denied.	STATUS_THREAD_IS_TERMINATING
			STATUS_DELETE_PENDING
			STATUS_FILE_IS_A_DIRECTORY
			STATUS_PROCESS_IS_TERMINATING
			STATUS_CANNOT_DELETE
			STATUS_INVALID_LOCK_SEQUENCE
			STATUS_INVALID_VIEW_SIZE
			STATUS_ALREADY_COMMITTED
			STATUS_ACCESS_DENIED
			STATUS_PORT_CONNECTION_REFUSED
			STATUS_FILE_DELETED
ERROR_ACCOUNT_DISABLED	1331	Logon failure: account currently disabled.	STATUS_ACCOUNT_DISABLED
ERROR_ACCOUNT_EXPIRED	1793	The user's account has expired.	STATUS_ACCOUNT_EXPIRED
ERROR_ACCOUNT_LOCKED_OUT	1909	The referenced account is currently locked out and may not be logged on to.	STATUS_ACCOUNT_LOCKED_OUT
ERROR_ACCOUNT_RESTRICTION	1327	Logon failure: user account restriction.	STATUS_ACCOUNT_RESTRICTION
ERROR_ACTIVE_CONNECTIONS	2402	Active connections still exist.	STATUS_ALREADY_DISCONNECTED
ERROR_ADAP_HDW_ERR	57	A network adapter hardware error occurred.	STATUS_ADAPTER_HARDWARE_ERROR
ERROR_ADDRESS_ALREADY_ASSOCIATED	1227	The network transport endpoint already has an address associated with it.	STATUS_ADDRESS_ALREADY_ASSOCIATED
ERROR_ADDRESS_NOT_ASSOCIATED	1228	An address has not yet been associated with the network endpoint.	STATUS_ADDRESS_NOT_ASSOCIATED
ERROR_ALIAS_EXISTS	1379	The specified local group already exists.	STATUS_ALIAS_EXISTS
ERROR_ALLOTTED_SPACE_EXCEEDED	1344	No more memory is available for security information updates.	STATUS_ALLOTTED_SPACE_EXCEEDED
ERROR_ALREADY_EXISTS	183	Cannot create a file when that file already exists.	STATUS_OBJECT_NAME_COLLISION
ERROR_ARITHMETIC_OVERFLOW	534	Arithmetic result exceeded 32 bits.	STATUS_INTEGER_OVERFLOW

Table B.1: *Application Error Codes (alphabetic) to* NTSTATUS *Values (continued)*

Application Error Code		Explanation	NTSTATUS Name
Name	**Value**		
ERROR_BAD_COMMAND	22	The device does not recognize the command.	STATUS_INVALID_DEVICE_STATE
ERROR_BAD_DESCRIPTOR_FORMAT	1361	A security descriptor is not in the right format (absolute or self-relative).	STATUS_BAD_DESCRIPTOR_FORMAT
ERROR_BAD_DEV_TYPE	66	The network resource type is not correct.	STATUS_BAD_DEVICE_TYPE
ERROR_BAD_EXE_FORMAT	193	?	STATUS_INVALID_IMAGE_WIN_16
			STATUS_IMAGE_CHECKSUM_MISMATCH
			STATUS_BAD_INITIAL_PC
			STATUS_INVALID_FILE_FOR_SECTION
			STATUS_INVALID_IMAGE_FORMAT
			STATUS_INVALID_IMAGE_NE_FORMAT
			STATUS_INVALID_IMAGE_LE_FORMAT
			STATUS_INVALID_IMAGE_NOT_MZ
			STATUS_INVALID_IMAGE_PROTECT
			STATUS_IMAGE_MP_UP_MISMATCH
ERROR_BAD_IMPERSONATION_LEVEL	1346	Either a required impersonation level was not provided, or the provided impersonation level is invalid.	STATUS_BAD_IMPERSONATION_LEVEL
ERROR_BAD_INHERITANCE_ACL	1340	The inherited access control list (ACL) or access control entry (ACE) could not be built.	STATUS_BAD_INHERITANCE_ACL
ERROR_BAD_LENGTH	24	The program issued a command but the command length is incorrect.	STATUS_INFO_LENGTH_MISMATCH
ERROR_BAD_LOGON_SESSION_STATE	1365	The logon session is not in a state that is consistent with the requested operation.	STATUS_BAD_LOGON_SESSION_STATE
ERROR_BAD_NET_NAME	67	The network name cannot be found.	STATUS_BAD_NETWORK_NAME
ERROR_BAD_NET_RESP	58	The specified server cannot perform the requested operation.	STATUS_INVALID_NETWORK_RESPONSE
ERROR_BAD_NETPATH	53	The network path was not found.	STATUS_BAD_NETWORK_PATH
ERROR_BAD_PATHNAME	161	The specified path is invalid.	STATUS_OBJECT_PATH_INVALID
			STATUS_OBJECT_PATH_SYNTAX_BAD
ERROR_BAD_PIPE	230	The pipe state is invalid.	STATUS_INVALID_PIPE_STATE
			STATUS_INVALID_READ_MODE
ERROR_BAD_REM_ADAP	60	The remote adapter is not compatible.	STATUS_BAD_REMOTE_ADAPTER
ERROR_BAD_TOKEN_TYPE	1349	The type of the token is inappropriate for its attempted use.	STATUS_BAD_TOKEN_TYPE

Table B.1: *Application Error Codes (alphabetic) to* NTSTATUS *Values (continued)*

Application Error Code		Explanation	NTSTATUS Name
Name	**Value**	**Explanation**	NTSTATUS **Name**
ERROR_BAD_VALIDATION_CLASS	1348	The validation information class requested was invalid.	STATUS_BAD_VALIDATION_CLASS
ERROR_BADDB	1009	The configuration registry database is corrupt.	STATUS_REGISTRY_CORRUPT
ERROR_BEGINNING_OF_MEDIA	1102	Beginning of tape or partition was encountered.	STATUS_BEGINNING_OF_MEDIA
ERROR_BROKEN_PIPE	109	The pipe has been ended.	STATUS_PIPE_BROKEN
ERROR_BUS_RESET	1111	The I/O bus was reset.	STATUS_BUS_RESET
ERROR_BUSY	170	The requested resource is in use.	STATUS_DEVICE_BUSY
ERROR_CANNOT_IMPERSONATE	1368	Unable to impersonate via a named pipe until data has been read from that pipe.	STATUS_CANNOT_IMPERSONATE
ERROR_CANT_ACCESS_DOMAIN_INFO	1351	Indicates a Windows NT Server could not be contacted or that objects within the domain are protected such that necessary information could not be retrieved.	STATUS_CANT_ACCESS_DOMAIN_INFO
ERROR_CANT_DISABLE_MANDATORY	1310	The group may not be disabled.	STATUS_CANT_DISABLE_MANDATORY
ERROR_CANT_OPEN_ANONYMOUS	1347	Cannot open an anonymous level security token.	STATUS_CANT_OPEN_ANONYMOUS
ERROR_CHILD_MUST_BE_VOLATILE	1021	Cannot create a stable subkey under a volatile parent key.	STATUS_CHILD_MUST_BE_VOLATILE
ERROR_COMMITMENT_LIMIT	1455	The paging file is too small for this operation to complete.	STATUS_COMMITMENT_LIMIT
ERROR_CONNECTION_ABORTED	1236	The network connection was aborted by the local system.	STATUS_CONNECTION_ABORTED
ERROR_CONNECTION_ACTIVE	1230	An invalid operation was attempted on an active network connection.	STATUS_CONNECTION_ACTIVE
ERROR_CONNECTION_COUNT_LIMIT	1238	A connection to the server could not be made because the limit on the number of concurrent connections for this account has been reached.	STATUS_CONNECTION_COUNT_LIMIT
ERROR_CONNECTION_INVALID	1229	An operation was attempted on a nonexistent network connection.	STATUS_CONNECTION_INVALID
ERROR_CONNECTION_REFUSED	1225	The remote system refused the network connection.	STATUS_CONNECTION_REFUSED
ERROR_CRC	23	Data error (cyclic redundancy check).	STATUS_CRC_ERROR
			STATUS_DATA_ERROR
			STATUS_DEVICE_DATA_ERROR
ERROR_DEV_NOT_EXIST	55	The specified network resource or device is no longer available.	STATUS_DEVICE_DOES_NOT_EXIST
ERROR_DEVICE_IN_USE	2404	The device is in use by an active process and cannot be disconnected.	STATUS_CONNECTION_IN_USE

Table B.1: *Application Error Codes (alphabetic) to NTSTATUS Values (continued)*

Application Error Code			
Name	**Value**	**Explanation**	**NTSTATUS Name**
ERROR_DEVICE_NOT_PARTITIONED	1107	Tape partition information could not be found when loading a tape.	STATUS_DEVICE_NOT_PARTITIONED
ERROR_DIR_NOT_EMPTY	145	The directory is not empty.	STATUS_DIRECTORY_NOT_EMPTY
ERROR_DIRECTORY	267	The directory name is invalid.	STATUS_NOT_A_DIRECTORY
ERROR_DISK_CORRUPT	1393	The disk structure is corrupt and non-readable.	STATUS_DISK_CORRUPT_ERROR
ERROR_DISK_FULL	112	There is not enough space on the disk.	STATUS_DISK_FULL
ERROR_DISK_OPERATION_FAILED	1127	While accessing the hard disk, a disk operation failed even after retries.	STATUS_DISK_OPERATION_FAILED
ERROR_DISK_RECALIBRATE_FAILED	1126	While accessing the hard disk, a recalibrate operation failed, even after retries.	STATUS_DISK_RECALIBRATE_FAILED
ERROR_DISK_RESET_FAILED	1128	While accessing the hard disk, a disk controller reset was needed, but even that failed.	STATUS_DISK_RESET_FAILED
ERROR_DLL_INIT_FAILED	1114	A dynamic link library (DLL) initialization routine failed.	STATUS_DLL_INIT_FAILED
ERROR_DOMAIN_CONTROLLER_NOT_FOUND	1908	Could not find the domain controller for this domain.	STATUS_DOMAIN_CONTROLLER_NOT_FOUND
ERROR_DOMAIN_EXISTS	1356	The specified domain already exists.	STATUS_DOMAIN_EXISTS
ERROR_DOMAIN_LIMIT_EXCEEDED	1357	An attempt was made to exceed the limit on the number of domains per server.	STATUS_DOMAIN_LIMIT_EXCEEDED
ERROR_DOMAIN_TRUST_INCONSISTENT	1810	The name or security ID (SID) of the domain specified is inconsistent with the trust information for that domain.	STATUS_DOMAIN_TRUST_INCONSISTENT
ERROR_DUP_NAME	52	A duplicate name exists on the network.	STATUS_DUPLICATE_NAME
			STATUS_ADDRESS_ALREADY_EXISTS
ERROR_EA_LIST_INCONSISTENT	255	The extended attributes are inconsistent.	STATUS_EA_LIST_INCONSISTENT
			STATUS_INVALID_EA_FLAG
			STATUS_EA_TOO_LARGE
ERROR_END_OF_MEDIA	1100	The physical end of the tape has been reached.	STATUS_END_OF_MEDIA
ERROR_ENVVAR_NOT_FOUND	203	The system could not find the environment option that was entered.	STATUS_VARIABLE_NOT_FOUND
ERROR_EOM_OVERFLOW	1129	Physical end of tape encountered.	STATUS_EOM_OVERFLOW
ERROR_EVENTLOG_CANT_START	1501	No event log file could be opened, so the event logging service did not start.	STATUS_EVENTLOG_CANT_START
ERROR_EVENTLOG_FILE_CHANGED	1503	The event log file has changed between reads.	STATUS_EVENTLOG_FILE_CHANGED
ERROR_EVENTLOG_FILE_CORRUPT	1500	The event log file is corrupt.	STATUS_EVENTLOG_FILE_CORRUPT

Table B.1: *Application Error Codes (alphabetic) to* NTSTATUS *Values (continued)*

Application Error Code		Explanation	NTSTATUS Name
Name	Value		
ERROR_FILE_CORRUPT	1392	The file or directory is corrupt and non-readable.	STATUS_EA_CORRUPT_ERROR
			STATUS_NONEXISTENT_EA_ENTRY
			STATUS_NO_EAS_ON_FILE
			STATUS_FILE_CORRUPT_ERROR
ERROR_FILE_INVALID	1006	The volume for a file has been externally altered such that the opened file is no longer valid.	STATUS_FILE_INVALID
			STATUS_MAPPED_FILE_SIZE_ZERO
ERROR_FILE_NOT_FOUND	2	The system cannot find the file specified.	STATUS_NO_SUCH_DEVICE
			STATUS_NO_SUCH_FILE
			STATUS_OBJECT_NAME_NOT_FOUND
ERROR_FILEMARK_DETECTED	1101	A tape access reached a filemark.	STATUS_FILEMARK_DETECTED
ERROR_FILENAME_EXCED_RANGE	206	The filename or extension is too long.	STATUS_NAME_TOO_LONG
ERROR_FLOPPY_BAD_REGISTERS	1125	The floppy disk controller returned inconsistent results in its registers.	STATUS_FLOPPY_BAD_REGISTERS
ERROR_FLOPPY_ID_MARK_NOT_FOUND	1122	No ID address mark was found on the floppy disk.	STATUS_FLOPPY_ID_MARK_NOT_FOUND
ERROR_FLOPPY_UNKNOWN_ERROR	1124	The floppy disk controller reported an error that is not recognized by the floppy disk driver.	STATUS_FLOPPY_UNKNOWN_ERROR
ERROR_FLOPPY_WRONG_CYLINDER	1123	Mismatch between the floppy disk sector ID field and the floppy disk controller track address.	STATUS_FLOPPY_WRONG_CYLINDER
ERROR_FULLSCREEN_MODE	1007	The requested operation cannot be performed in full-screen mode.	STATUS_FULLSCREEN_MODE
ERROR_GEN_FAILURE	31	A device attached to the system is not functioning.	STATUS_UNSUCCESSFUL
ERROR_GENERIC_NOT_MAPPED	1360	Generic access types were contained in an access mask which should already be mapped to non-generic types.	STATUS_GENERIC_NOT_MAPPED
ERROR_GRACEFUL_DISCONNECT	1226	The network connection was gracefully closed.	STATUS_GRACEFUL_DISCONNECT
ERROR_GROUP_EXISTS	1318	The specified group already exists.	STATUS_GROUP_EXISTS
ERROR_HANDLE_EOF	38	Reached end of file.	STATUS_END_OF_FILE
			STATUS_FILE_FORCED_CLOSED
ERROR_HOST_UNREACHABLE	1232	The remote system is not reachable by the transport.	STATUS_HOST_UNREACHABLE
			STATUS_PATH_NOT_COVERED
ERROR_ILL_FORMED_PASSWORD	1324	Unable to update the password. The value provided for the new password contains values that are not allowed in passwords.	STATUS_ILL_FORMED_PASSWORD

Table B.1: *Application Error Codes (alphabetic) to* NTSTATUS *Values (continued)*

Application Error Code		Explanation	NTSTATUS Name
Name	**Value**		
ERROR_INSUFFICIENT_BUFFER	122	The data area passed to a system call is too small.	STATUS_BUFFER_TOO_SMALL
ERROR_INTERNAL_DB_CORRUPTION	1358	Unable to complete the requested operation because of either a catastrophic media failure or a data structure corruption on the disk.	STATUS_INTERNAL_DB_CORRUPTION
ERROR_INTERNAL_DB_ERROR	1383	The local security authority database contains an internal inconsistency.	STATUS_INTERNAL_DB_ERROR
ERROR_INTERNAL_ERROR	1359	The security account database contains an internal inconsistency.	STATUS_INTERNAL_ERROR
			STATUS_LPC_REPLY_LOST
ERROR_INVALID_ACCOUNT_NAME	1315	The name provided is not a properly formed account name.	STATUS_INVALID_ACCOUNT_NAME
ERROR_INVALID_ACL	1336	The access control list (ACL) structure is invalid.	STATUS_INVALID_ACL
ERROR_INVALID_ADDRESS	487	Attempt to access invalid address.	STATUS_NOT_COMMITTED
			STATUS_NOT_MAPPED_DATA
			STATUS_FREE_VM_NOT_AT_BASE
			STATUS_NOT_MAPPED_VIEW
			STATUS_CONFLICTING_ADDRESSES
			STATUS_UNABLE_TO_DECOMMIT_VM
			STATUS_MEMORY_NOT_ALLOCATED
ERROR_INVALID_BLOCK_LENGTH	1106	When accessing a new tape of a multi-volume partition, the current blocksize is incorrect.	STATUS_INVALID_BLOCK_LENGTH
ERROR_INVALID_COMPUTERNAME	1210	The format of the specified computer name is invalid.	STATUS_INVALID_COMPUTER_NAME
ERROR_INVALID_DOMAIN_ROLE	1354	This operation is only allowed for the Primary Domain Controller of the domain.	STATUS_INVALID_DOMAIN_ROLE
ERROR_INVALID_DOMAIN_STATE	1353	The domain was in the wrong state to perform the security operation.	STATUS_INVALID_DOMAIN_STATE
ERROR_INVALID_EA_NAME	254	The specified extended attribute name was invalid.	STATUS_INVALID_EA_NAME
ERROR_INVALID_FUNCTION	1	Incorrect function.	STATUS_INVALID_DEVICE_REQUEST
			STATUS_NOT_IMPLEMENTED
			STATUS_INVALID_SYSTEM_SERVICE
			STATUS_ILLEGAL_FUNCTION
ERROR_INVALID_GROUP_ ATTRIBUTES	1345	The specified attributes are invalid, or incompatible with the attributes for the group as a whole.	STATUS_INVALID_GROUP_ ATTRIBUTES

Table B.1: *Application Error Codes (alphabetic) to* NTSTATUS *Values (continued)*

Application Error Code		Explanation	NTSTATUS Name
Name	**Value**		
ERROR_INVALID_HANDLE	6	The handle is invalid.	STATUS_INVALID_PORT_HANDLE
			STATUS_PORT_DISCONNECTED
			STATUS_FILE_CLOSED
			STATUS_HANDLE_NOT_CLOSABLE
			RPC_NT_INVALID_BINDING
			RPC_NT_SS_IN_NULL_CONTEXT
			STATUS_INVALID_HANDLE
			STATUS_OBJECT_TYPE_MISMATCH
			RPC_NT_SS_CONTEXT_MISMATCH
ERROR_INVALID_ID_AUTHORITY	1343	The value provided was an invalid value for an identifier authority.	STATUS_INVALID_ID_AUTHORITY
ERROR_INVALID_LEVEL	124	The system call level is not correct.	STATUS_INVALID_LEVEL
ERROR_INVALID_LOGON_HOURS	1328	Logon failure: account logon time restriction violation.	STATUS_INVALID_LOGON_HOURS
ERROR_INVALID_LOGON_TYPE	1367	A logon request contained an invalid logon type value.	STATUS_INVALID_LOGON_TYPE
ERROR_INVALID_MEMBER	1388	A new member could not be added to a local group because the member has the wrong account type.	STATUS_INVALID_MEMBER
ERROR_INVALID_NAME	123	The filename, directory name, or volume label syntax is incorrect.	STATUS_OBJECT_NAME_INVALID
ERROR_INVALID_NETNAME	1214	The format of the specified network name is invalid.	STATUS_INVALID_ADDRESS_COMPONENT
			STATUS_INVALID_ADDRESS_WILDCARD
ERROR_INVALID_ORDINAL	182	?	STATUS_DRIVER_ORDINAL_NOT_FOUND
			STATUS_ORDINAL_NOT_FOUND
ERROR_INVALID_OWNER	1307	This security ID may not be assigned as the owner of this object.	STATUS_INVALID_OWNER
ERROR_INVALID_PARAMETER	87	The parameter is incorrect.	STATUS_BAD_WORKING_SET_LIMIT
			STATUS_DEVICE_CONFIGURATION_ERROR
			STATUS_INCOMPATIBLE_FILE_MAP
			STATUS_INVALID_CID
			STATUS_INVALID_INFO_CLASS
			STATUS_INVALID_PAGE_PROTECTION
			STATUS_INVALID_PARAMETER
			STATUS_INVALID_PARAMETER_1
			STATUS_INVALID_PARAMETER_2

Table B.1: *Application Error Codes (alphabetic) to* NTSTATUS *Values (continued)*

Application Error Code			
Name	**Value**	**Explanation**	**NTSTATUS Name**
ERROR_INVALID_PARAMETER *(continued)*			STATUS_INVALID_PARAMETER_3
			STATUS_INVALID_PARAMETER_4
			STATUS_INVALID_PARAMETER_5
			STATUS_INVALID_PARAMETER_6
			STATUS_INVALID_PARAMETER_7
			STATUS_INVALID_PARAMETER_8
			STATUS_INVALID_PARAMETER_9
			STATUS_INVALID_PARAMETER_10
			STATUS_INVALID_PARAMETER_11
			STATUS_INVALID_PARAMETER_12
			STATUS_INVALID_PARAMETER_MIX
			STATUS_PORT_ALREADY_SET
			STATUS_SECTION_NOT_IMAGE
			STATUS_SECTION_PROTECTION
			STATUS_UNABLE_TO_DELETE_ SECTION
			STATUS_UNABLE_TO_FREE_VM
ERROR_INVALID_PASSWORD	86	The specified network password is not correct.	STATUS_WRONG_PASSWORD
			STATUS_WRONG_PASSWORD_CORE
ERROR_INVALID_PRIMARY_GROUP	1308	This security ID may not be assigned as the primary group of an object.	STATUS_INVALID_PRIMARY_GROUP
ERROR_INVALID_SECURITY_DESCR	1338	The security descriptor structure is invalid.	STATUS_INVALID_SECURITY_DESCR
ERROR_INVALID_SERVER_STATE	1352	The security account manager (SAM) or local security authority (LSA) server was in the wrong state to perform the security operation.	STATUS_INVALID_SERVER_STATE
ERROR_INVALID_SID	1337	The security ID structure is invalid.	STATUS_INVALID_SID
ERROR_INVALID_SUB_AUTHORITY	1335	The subauthority part of a security ID is invalid for this particular use.	STATUS_INVALID_SUB_AUTHORITY
ERROR_INVALID_USER_BUFFER	1784	The supplied user buffer is not valid for the requested operation.	STATUS_INVALID_BUFFER_SIZE
			STATUS_INVALID_USER_BUFFER
ERROR_INVALID_WORKSTATION	1329	Logon failure: user not allowed to log on to this computer.	STATUS_INVALID_WORKSTATION

Table B.1: *Application Error Codes (alphabetic) to* NTSTATUS *Values (continued)*

Application Error Code		Explanation	NTSTATUS Name
Name	**Value**		
ERROR_IO_DEVICE	1117	The request could not be performed because of an I/O device error.	STATUS_DATA_LATE_ERROR
			STATUS_DATA_OVERRUN
			STATUS_DEVICE_PROTOCOL_ERROR
			STATUS_DRIVER_INTERNAL_ERROR
			STATUS_FT_MISSING_MEMBER
			STATUS_FT_ORPHANING
			STATUS_IO_DEVICE_ERROR
ERROR_IRQ_BUSY	1119	Unable to open a device that was sharing an interrupt request (IRQ) with other devices. At least one other device that uses that IRQ was already opened.	STATUS_SHARED_IRQ_BUSY
ERROR_KEY_DELETED	1018	Illegal operation attempted on a Registry key which has been marked for deletion.	STATUS_KEY_DELETED
ERROR_KEY_HAS_CHILDREN	1020	Cannot create a symbolic link in a Registry key that already has subkeys or values.	STATUS_KEY_HAS_CHILDREN
ERROR_LABEL_TOO_LONG	154	The volume label you entered exceeds the label character limit of the target file system.	STATUS_INVALID_VOLUME_LABEL
ERROR_LAST_ADMIN	1322	The last remaining administration account cannot be disabled or deleted.	STATUS_LAST_ADMIN
ERROR_LICENSE_QUOTA_EXCEEDED	1395	The service being accessed is licensed for a particular number of connections. No more connections can be made to the service at this time because there are already as many connections as the service can accept.	STATUS_LICENSE_QUOTA_EXCEEDED
ERROR_LM_CROSS_ENCRYPTION_REQUIRED	1390	A cross-encrypted password is necessary to change this user password.	STATUS_LM_CROSS_ENCRYPTION_REQUIRED
ERROR_LOCK_VIOLATION	33	The process cannot access the file because another process has locked a portion of the file.	STATUS_FILE_LOCK_CONFLICT
			STATUS_LOCK_NOT_GRANTED
ERROR_LOG_FILE_FULL	1502	The event log file is full.	STATUS_LOG_FILE_FULL
ERROR_LOGIN_TIME_RESTRICTION	1239	Attempting to login during an unauthorized time of day for this account.	STATUS_LOGIN_TIME_RESTRICTION
ERROR_LOGIN_WKSTA_RESTRICTION	1240	The account is not authorized to login from this station.	STATUS_LOGIN_WKSTA_RESTRICTION
ERROR_LOGON_FAILURE	1326	Logon failure: unknown user name or bad password.	STATUS_LOGON_FAILURE
ERROR_LOGON_NOT_GRANTED	1380	Logon failure: the user has not been granted the requested logon type at this computer.	STATUS_LOGON_NOT_GRANTED

Table B.1: *Application Error Codes (alphabetic) to* NTSTATUS *Values (continued)*

Application Error Code		Explanation	NTSTATUS Name
Name	**Value**		
ERROR_LOGON_SESSION_COLLISION	1366	The logon session ID is already in use.	STATUS_LOGON_SESSION_COLLISION
ERROR_LOGON_SESSION_EXISTS	1363	Cannot start a new logon session with an ID that is already in use.	STATUS_LOGON_SESSION_EXISTS
ERROR_LOGON_TYPE_NOT_GRANTED	1385	Logon failure: the user has not been granted the requested logon type at this computer.	STATUS_LOGON_TYPE_NOT_GRANTED
ERROR_LUIDS_EXHAUSTED	1334	No more local user identifiers (LUIDs) are available.	STATUS_LUIDS_EXHAUSTED
ERROR_MAPPED_ALIGNMENT	1132	The base address or the file offset specified does not have the proper alignment.	STATUS_MAPPED_ALIGNMENT
ERROR_MEDIA_CHANGED	1110	Media in drive may have changed.	STATUS_MEDIA_CHANGED
			STATUS_VERIFY_REQUIRED
ERROR_MEMBER_IN_ALIAS	1378	The specified account name is already a member of the local group.	STATUS_MEMBER_IN_ALIAS
ERROR_MEMBER_IN_GROUP	1320	Either the specified user account is already a member of the specified group, or the specified group cannot be deleted because it contains a member.	STATUS_MEMBER_IN_GROUP
ERROR_MEMBER_NOT_IN_ALIAS	1377	The specified account name is not a member of the local group.	STATUS_MEMBER_NOT_IN_ALIAS
ERROR_MEMBER_NOT_IN_GROUP	1321	The specified user account is not a member of the specified group account.	STATUS_MEMBER_NOT_IN_GROUP
ERROR_MEMBERS_PRIMARY_GROUP	1374	The user cannot be removed from a group because the group is currently the user's primary group.	STATUS_MEMBERS_PRIMARY_GROUP
ERROR_MOD_NOT_FOUND	126	The specified module could not be found.	STATUS_DLL_NOT_FOUND
ERROR_MORE_DATA	234	More data is available.	STATUS_BUFFER_OVERFLOW
			STATUS_MORE_PROCESSING_REQUIRED
ERROR_MR_MID_NOT_FOUND	317	? This error code seems to indicate that an error code corresponding to a status code to the right cannot be found. Therefore, it appears that the status codes to the right have no meaningful user-level error code when returned as the completion status of an IRP. You should not use any of these codes unless your own tests indicate otherwise (based on later versions of NT or new Service Packs).	STATUS_ALLOCATE_BUCKET
			STATUS_ABIOS_INVALID_COMMAND
			STATUS_ABIOS_INVALID_LID
			STATUS_ABIOS_INVALID_SELECTOR
			STATUS_ABIOS_LID_ALREADY_OWNED
			STATUS_ABIOS_LID_NOT_EXIST
			STATUS_ABIOS_NOT_LID_OWNER
			STATUS_ABIOS_NOT_PRESENT
			STATUS_ABIOS_SELECTOR_NOT_AVAILABLE
			STATUS_APP_INIT_FAILURE

Table B.1: *Application Error Codes (alphabetic) to* NTSTATUS *Values (continued)*

Application Error Code		Explanation	NTSTATUS Name
Name	**Value**		
ERROR_MR_MID_NOT_FOUND *(continued)*			STATUS_AUDIT_FAILED
			STATUS_BACKUP_CONTROLLER
			STATUS_BAD_COMPRESSION_BUFFER
			STATUS_BAD_DLL_ENTRYPOINT
			STATUS_BAD_FUNCTION_TABLE
			STATUS_BAD_MASTER_BOOT_RECORD
			STATUS_BAD_SERVICE_ENTRYPOINT
			STATUS_BAD_STACK
			STATUS_BIOS_FAILED_TO_CONNECT_INTERRUPT
			STATUS_CANNOT_LOAD_REGISTRY_FILE
			STATUS_CANT_TERMINATE_SELF
			STATUS_CANT_WAIT
			STATUS_CLIENT_SERVER_PARAMETERS_INVALID
			STATUS_CONTROL_C_EXIT
			STATUS_CONVERT_TO_LARGE
			STATUS_COULD_NOT_INTERPRET
			STATUS_DATA_NOT_ACCEPTED
			STATUS_DEBUG_ATTACH_FAILED
			STATUS_DEVICE_ALREADY_ATTACHED
			STATUS_DFS_UNAVAILABLE
			STATUS_DLL_INIT_FAILED_LOGOFF
			STATUS_DOMAIN_CTRLR_CONFIG_ERROR
			STATUS_DRIVER_CANCEL_TIMEOUT
			STATUS_DRIVER_UNABLE_TO_LOAD
			STATUS_EAS_NOT_SUPPORTED
			STATUS_EVALUATION_EXPIRATION
			STATUS_EXTRANEOUS_INFORMATION
			STATUS_FAIL_CHECK
			STATUS_FILE_IS_OFFLINE
			STATUS_FILE_RENAMED
			STATUS_FILES_OPEN
			STATUS_FLOPPY_VOLUME
			STATUS_FOUND_OUT_OF_SCOPE

Table B.1: *Application Error Codes (alphabetic) to* NTSTATUS *Values (continued)*

Application Error Code		Explanation	NTSTATUS Name
Name	**Value**		
ERROR_MR_MID_NOT_FOUND *(continued)*			STATUS_FS_DRIVER_REQUIRED
			STATUS_GUID_SUBSTITUTION_MADE
			STATUS_HANDLES_CLOSED
			STATUS_ILL_FORMED_SERVICE_ENTRY
			STATUS_ILLEGAL_CHARACTER
			STATUS_ILLEGAL_DLL_RELOCATION
			STATUS_ILLEGAL_FLOAT_CONTEXT
			STATUS_INSTRUCTION_MISALIGNMENT
			STATUS_INSUFFICIENT_LOGON_INFO
			STATUS_INVALID_HW_PROFILE
			STATUS_INVALID_LDT_DESCRIPTOR
			STATUS_INVALID_LDT_OFFSET
			STATUS_INVALID_LDT_SIZE
			STATUS_INVALID_OPLOCK_PROTOCOL
			STATUS_INVALID_PLUGPLAY_DEVICE_PATH
			STATUS_INVALID_PORT_ATTRIBUTES
			STATUS_INVALID_QUOTA_LOWER
			STATUS_INVALID_UNWIND_TARGET
			STATUS_INVALID_VARIANT
			STATUS_IO_PRIVILEGE_FAILED
			STATUS_IP_ADDRESS_CONFLICT1
			STATUS_IP_ADDRESS_CONFLICT2
			STATUS_LICENSE_VIOLATION
			STATUS_LOGON_SERVER_CONFLICT
			STATUS_LONGJUMP
			STATUS_LOST_WRITEBEHIND_DATA
			STATUS_MARSHALL_OVERFLOW
			STATUS_MEDIA_CHECK
			STATUS_MESSAGE_NOT_FOUND
			STATUS_MISSING_SYSTEMFILE
			STATUS_MUTANT_LIMIT_EXCEEDED
			STATUS_NO_CALLBACK_ACTIVE
			STATUS_NO_EVENT_PAIR

Table B.1: *Application Error Codes (alphabetic) to* NTSTATUS *Values (continued)*

Application Error Code		Explanation	NTSTATUS Name
Name	**Value**		
ERROR_MR_MID_NOT_FOUND *(continued)*			STATUS_NO_GUID_TRANSLATION
			STATUS_NO_LDT
			STATUS_NO_PAGEFILE
			STATUS_NOT_FOUND
			STATUS_NOT_TINY_STREAM
			STATUS_OPEN_FAILED
			STATUS_OPLOCK_NOT_GRANTED
			STATUS_PAGEFILE_CREATE_FAILED
			STATUS_PAGEFILE_QUOTA_ EXCEEDED
			STATUS_PORT_MESSAGE_TOO_LONG
			STATUS_PROFILING_AT_LIMIT
			STATUS_PROFILING_NOT_STARTED
			STATUS_PROFILING_NOT_STOPPED
			STATUS_PROPSET_NOT_FOUND
			STATUS_PWD_HISTORY_CONFLICT
			STATUS_PWD_TOO_RECENT
			STATUS_PWD_TOO_SHORT
			STATUS_QUOTA_LIST_ INCONSISTENT
			STATUS_RECOVERY_FAILURE
			STATUS_REDIRECTOR_HAS_ OPEN_HANDLES
			STATUS_REDIRECTOR_STARTED
			STATUS_REGISTRY_QUOTA_LIMIT
			STATUS_REPLY_MESSAGE_MISMATCH
			STATUS_RETRY
			STATUS_RXACT_COMMIT_NECESSARY
			STATUS_SERVER_HAS_OPEN_ HANDLES
			STATUS_STACK_OVERFLOW_READ
			STATUS_SYNCHRONIZATION_ REQUIRED
			STATUS_SYSTEM_PROCESS_ TERMINATED
			STATUS_THREAD_NOT_IN_PROCESS
			STATUS_TIME_DIFFERENCE_AT_DC
			STATUS_TIMER_NOT_CANCELED

Table B.1: *Application Error Codes (alphabetic) to* NTSTATUS *Values (continued)*

Application Error Code		Explanation	NTSTATUS **Name**
Name	**Value**		
ERROR_MR_MID_NOT_FOUND *(continued)*			STATUS_TIMER_RESOLUTION_ NOT_SET
			STATUS_TOO_MANY_THREADS
			STATUS_UNDEFINED_CHARACTER
			STATUS_UNEXPECTED_IO_ERROR
			STATUS_UNEXPECTED_MM_ CREATE_ERR
			STATUS_UNEXPECTED_MM_ EXTEND_ERR
			STATUS_UNEXPECTED_MM_MAP_ ERROR
			STATUS_UNHANDLED_EXCEPTION
			STATUS_UNSUPPORTED_ COMPRESSION
			STATUS_UNWIND
			STATUS_VDM_HARD_ERROR
			STATUS_VOLUME_DISMOUNTED
			STATUS_WAKE_SYSTEM_DEBUGGER
			STATUS_WOW_ASSERTION
			STATUS_WX86_FLOAT_STACK_CHECK
			STATUS_WX86_INTERNAL_ERROR
ERROR_NET_WRITE_FAULT	88	A write fault occurred on the network.	STATUS_NET_WRITE_FAULT
ERROR_NETLOGON_NOT_STARTED	1792	An attempt was made to logon, but the network logon service was not started.	STATUS_NETLOGON_NOT_STARTED
ERROR_NETNAME_DELETED	64	The specified network name is no longer available.	STATUS_ADDRESS_CLOSED
			STATUS_CONNECTION_ DISCONNECTED
			STATUS_CONNECTION_RESET
			STATUS_LOCAL_DISCONNECT
			STATUS_NETWORK_NAME_DELETED
			STATUS_REMOTE_DISCONNECT
ERROR_NETWORK_ACCESS_DENIED	65	Network access is denied.	STATUS_NETWORK_ACCESS_DENIED
ERROR_NETWORK_BUSY	54	The network is busy.	STATUS_NETWORK_BUSY
ERROR_NETWORK_UNREACHABLE	1231	The remote network is not reachable by the transport.	STATUS_NETWORK_UNREACHABLE
ERROR_NO_BROWSER_SERVERS_ FOUND	6118	The list of servers for this workgroup is not currently available.	STATUS_NO_BROWSER_SERVERS_ FOUND
ERROR_NO_DATA	232	The pipe is being closed.	STATUS_PIPE_CLOSING
			STATUS_PIPE_EMPTY

Table B.1: *Application Error Codes (alphabetic) to* NTSTATUS *Values (continued)*

Application Error Code		Explanation	NTSTATUS Name
Name	Value		
ERROR_NO_DATA_DETECTED	1104	No more data is on the tape.	STATUS_NO_DATA_DETECTED
ERROR_NO_IMPERSONATION_TOKEN	1309	An attempt has been made to operate on an impersonation token by a thread that is not currently impersonating a client.	STATUS_NO_IMPERSONATION_TOKEN
ERROR_NO_INHERITANCE	1391	Indicates an ACL contains no inheritable components.	STATUS_NO_INHERITANCE
ERROR_NO_LOG_SPACE	1019	System could not allocate the required space in a Registry log.	STATUS_NO_LOG_SPACE
ERROR_NO_LOGON_SERVERS	1311	There are currently no logon servers available to service the logon request.	STATUS_NO_LOGON_SERVERS
ERROR_NO_MEDIA_IN_DRIVE	1112	No media in drive.	STATUS_NO_MEDIA
ERROR_NO_MORE_FILES	18	There are no more files.	STATUS_NO_MORE_FILES
ERROR_NO_MORE_ITEMS	259	No more data is available.	STATUS_AGENTS_EXHAUSTED
			STATUS_GUIDS_EXHAUSTED
			STATUS_NO_MORE_EAS
			STATUS_NO_MORE_ENTRIES
ERROR_NO_SECURITY_ON_OBJECT	1350	Unable to perform a security operation on an object which has no associated security.	STATUS_NO_SECURITY_ON_OBJECT
ERROR_NO_SPOOL_SPACE	62	Space to store the file waiting to be printed is not available on the server.	STATUS_NO_SPOOL_SPACE
ERROR_NO_SUCH_ALIAS	1376	The specified local group does not exist.	STATUS_NO_SUCH_ALIAS
ERROR_NO_SUCH_DOMAIN	1355	The specified domain did not exist.	STATUS_NO_SUCH_DOMAIN
ERROR_NO_SUCH_GROUP	1319	The specified group does not exist.	STATUS_NO_SUCH_GROUP
ERROR_NO_SUCH_LOGON_SESSION	1312	A specified logon session does not exist. It may already have been terminated.	STATUS_NO_SUCH_LOGON_SESSION
ERROR_NO_SUCH_MEMBER	1387	A new member could not be added to a local group because the member does not exist.	STATUS_NO_SUCH_MEMBER
ERROR_NO_SUCH_PACKAGE	1364	A specified authentication package is unknown.	STATUS_NO_SUCH_PACKAGE
ERROR_NO_SUCH_PRIVILEGE	1313	A specified privilege does not exist.	STATUS_NO_SUCH_PRIVILEGE
ERROR_NO_SUCH_USER	1317	The specified user does not exist.	STATUS_NO_SUCH_USER
ERROR_NO_SYSTEM_RESOURCES	1450	Insufficient system resources exist to complete the requested service.	STATUS_INSUFFICIENT_RESOURCES
ERROR_NO_TOKEN	1008	An attempt was made to reference a token that does not exist.	STATUS_NO_TOKEN
ERROR_NO_TRUST_LSA_SECRET	1786	The workstation does not have a trust secret.	STATUS_NO_TRUST_LSA_SECRET

Table B.1: *Application Error Codes (alphabetic) to* NTSTATUS *Values (continued)*

Application Error Code			
Name	**Value**	**Explanation**	**NTSTATUS Name**
ERROR_NO_TRUST_SAM_ACCOUNT	1787	The SAM database on the Windows NT Server does not have a computer account for this workstation trust relationship.	STATUS_NO_TRUST_SAM_ACCOUNT
ERROR_NO_UNICODE_TRANSLATION	1113	No mapping for the Unicode character exists in the target multi-byte code page.	STATUS_UNMAPPABLE_CHARACTER
ERROR_NO_USER_SESSION_KEY	1394	There is no user session key for the specified logon session.	STATUS_NO_USER_SESSION_KEY
ERROR_NOACCESS	998	Invalid access to memory location.	STATUS_DATATYPE_MISALIGNMENT
			STATUS_ACCESS_VIOLATION
ERROR_NOLOGON_INTERDOMAIN_TRUST_ACCOUNT	1807	The account used is an interdomain trust account. Use your global user account or local user account to access this server.	STATUS_NOLOGON_INTERDOMAIN_TRUST_ACCOUNT
ERROR_NOLOGON_SERVER_TRUST_ACCOUNT	1809	The account used is a server trust account. Use your global user account or local user account to access this server.	STATUS_NOLOGON_SERVER_TRUST_ACCOUNT
ERROR_NOLOGON_WORKSTATION_TRUST_ACCOUNT	1808	The account used is a Computer Account. Use your global user account or local user account to access this server.	STATUS_NOLOGON_WORKSTATION_TRUST_ACCOUNT
ERROR_NONE_MAPPED	1332	No mapping between account names and security IDs was done.	STATUS_NONE_MAPPED
ERROR_NOT_ENOUGH_MEMORY	8	Not enough storage is available to process this command.	STATUS_NO_MEMORY
			STATUS_SECTION_TOO_BIG
			STATUS_TOO_MANY_PAGING_FILES
ERROR_NOT_ENOUGH_QUOTA	1816	Not enough quota is available to process this command.	STATUS_QUOTA_EXCEEDED
ERROR_NOT_ENOUGH_SERVER_MEMORY	1130	Not enough server storage is available to process this command.	STATUS_INSUFF_SERVER_RESOURCES
ERROR_NOT_LOCKED	158	The segment is already unlocked.	STATUS_NOT_LOCKED
			STATUS_RANGE_NOT_LOCKED
ERROR_NOT_LOGON_PROCESS	1362	The requested action is restricted for use by logon processes only. The calling process has not registered as a logon process.	STATUS_NOT_LOGON_PROCESS
ERROR_NOT_OWNER	288	Attempt to release mutex not owned by caller.	STATUS_MUTANT_NOT_OWNED
			STATUS_RESOURCE_NOT_OWNED

Table B.1: *Application Error Codes (alphabetic) to* NTSTATUS *Values (continued)*

Application Error Code		Explanation	NTSTATUS Name
Name	**Value**		
ERROR_NOT_READY	21	The device is not ready.	STATUS_DEVICE_NOT_CONNECTED
			STATUS_DEVICE_NOT_READY
			STATUS_DEVICE_OFF_LINE
			STATUS_DEVICE_POWER_FAILURE
			STATUS_DEVICE_POWERED_OFF
			STATUS_NO_MEDIA_IN_DEVICE
ERROR_NOT_REGISTRY_FILE	1017	The system has attempted to load or restore a file into the Registry, but the specified file is not in a Registry file format.	STATUS_NOT_REGISTRY_FILE
ERROR_NOT_SAME_DEVICE	17	The system cannot move the file to a different disk drive.	STATUS_NOT_SAME_DEVICE
ERROR_NOT_SUPPORTED	50	The network request is not supported.	STATUS_NOT_SERVER_SESSION
			STATUS_CTL_FILE_NOT_SUPPORTED
			STATUS_NOT_CLIENT_SESSION
			STATUS_NOT_SUPPORTED
ERROR_NT_CROSS_ENCRYPTION_REQUIRED	1386	A cross-encrypted password is necessary to change a user password.	STATUS_NT_CROSS_ENCRYPTION_REQUIRED
ERROR_OPERATION_ABORTED	995	The I/O operation has been aborted because of either a thread exit or an application request.	STATUS_CANCELLED
ERROR_OUT_OF_PAPER	28	The printer is out of paper.	STATUS_DEVICE_PAPER_EMPTY
ERROR_OUTOFMEMORY	14	Not enough storage is available to complete this operation.	STATUS_SECTION_NOT_EXTENDED
ERROR_PAGEFILE_QUOTA	1454	Insufficient quota to complete the requested service.	STATUS_PAGEFILE_QUOTA
ERROR_PARTIAL_COPY	299	Only part of a Read/WriteProcessMemory request was completed.	STATUS_PARTIAL_COPY
ERROR_PARTITION_FAILURE	1105	Tape could not be partitioned.	STATUS_PARTITION_FAILURE
ERROR_PASSWORD_EXPIRED	1330	Logon failure: the specified account password has expired.	STATUS_PASSWORD_EXPIRED
ERROR_PASSWORD_MUST_CHANGE	1907	The user must change his password before he logs on the first time.	STATUS_PASSWORD_MUST_CHANGE
ERROR_PASSWORD_RESTRICTION	1325	Unable to update the password because a password update rule has been violated.	STATUS_PASSWORD_RESTRICTION
ERROR_PATH_NOT_FOUND	3	The system cannot find the path specified.	STATUS_DFS_EXIT_PATH_FOUND
			STATUS_OBJECT_PATH_NOT_FOUND
			STATUS_REDIRECTOR_NOT_STARTED

Table B.1: *Application Error Codes (alphabetic) to* NTSTATUS *Values (continued)*

Application Error Code		Explanation	NTSTATUS Name
Name	**Value**		
ERROR_PIPE_BUSY	231	All pipe instances are busy.	STATUS_INSTANCE_NOT_AVAILABLE
			STATUS_PIPE_BUSY
			STATUS_PIPE_NOT_AVAILABLE
ERROR_PIPE_CONNECTED	535	There is a process on other end of the pipe.	STATUS_PIPE_CONNECTED
ERROR_PIPE_LISTENING	536	Waiting for a process to open the other end of the pipe.	STATUS_PIPE_LISTENING
ERROR_PIPE_NOT_CONNECTED	233	No process is on the other end of the pipe.	STATUS_PIPE_DISCONNECTED
ERROR_PORT_UNREACHABLE	1234	No service is operating at the destination network endpoint on the remote system.	STATUS_PORT_UNREACHABLE
ERROR_POSSIBLE_DEADLOCK	1131	A potential deadlock condition has been detected.	STATUS_POSSIBLE_DEADLOCK
ERROR_PRINT_CANCELLED	63	Your file waiting to be printed was deleted.	STATUS_PRINT_CANCELLED
ERROR_PRINTQ_FULL	61	The printer queue is full.	STATUS_PRINT_QUEUE_FULL
ERROR_PRIVILEGE_NOT_HELD	1314	A required privilege is not held by the client.	STATUS_PRIVILEGE_NOT_HELD
ERROR_PROC_NOT_FOUND	127	The specified procedure could not be found.	STATUS_DRIVER_ENTRYPOINT_NOT_FOUND
			STATUS_ENTRYPOINT_NOT_FOUND
			STATUS_PROCEDURE_NOT_FOUND
ERROR_PROTOCOL_UNREACHABLE	1233	The remote system does not support the transport protocol.	STATUS_PROTOCOL_UNREACHABLE
ERROR_REDIR_PAUSED	72	The specified printer or disk device has been paused.	STATUS_REDIRECTOR_PAUSED
ERROR_REGISTRY_IO_FAILED	1016	An I/O operation initiated by the Registry failed unrecoverably. The Registry could not read in, or write out, or flush, one of the files that contain the system's image of the Registry.	STATUS_REGISTRY_IO_FAILED
ERROR_REM_NOT_LIST	51	The remote computer is not available.	STATUS_REMOTE_NOT_LISTENING
			STATUS_REMOTE_RESOURCES
ERROR_REMOTE_SESSION_LIMIT_EXCEEDED	1220	An attempt was made to establish a session to a network server, but there are already too many sessions established to that server.	STATUS_REMOTE_SESSION_LIMIT
ERROR_REQ_NOT_ACCEP	71	No more connections can be made to this remote computer at this time because there are already as many connections as the computer can accept.	STATUS_REQUEST_NOT_ACCEPTED
ERROR_REQUEST_ABORTED	1235	The request was aborted.	STATUS_REQUEST_ABORTED

Table B.1: *Application Error Codes (alphabetic) to* NTSTATUS *Values (continued)*

Application Error Code		Explanation	NTSTATUS Name
Name	**Value**		
ERROR_RESOURCE_DATA_NOT_FOUND	1812	The specified image file did not contain a resource section.	STATUS_RESOURCE_DATA_ NOT_FOUND
ERROR_RESOURCE_LANG_NOT_FOUND	1815	The specified resource language ID cannot be found in the image file.	STATUS_RESOURCE_LANG_ NOT_FOUND
ERROR_RESOURCE_NAME_NOT_FOUND	1814	The specified resource name cannot be found in the image file.	STATUS_RESOURCE_NAME_ NOT_FOUND
ERROR_RESOURCE_TYPE_NOT_FOUND	1813	The specified resource type cannot be found in the image file.	STATUS_RESOURCE_TYPE_ NOT_FOUND
ERROR_REVISION_MISMATCH	1306	Indicates two revision levels are incompatible.	STATUS_REVISION_MISMATCH
ERROR_RXACT_COMMIT_FAILURE	1370	An internal security database corruption has been encountered.	STATUS_RXACT_COMMIT_FAILURE
ERROR_RXACT_INVALID_STATE	1369	The transaction state of a Registry sub-tree is incompatible with the requested operation.	STATUS_RXACT_INVALID_STATE
ERROR_SECRET_TOO_LONG	1382	The length of a secret exceeds the maximum length allowed.	STATUS_SECRET_TOO_LONG
ERROR_SECTOR_NOT_FOUND	27	The drive cannot find the sector requested.	STATUS_NONEXISTENT_SECTOR
ERROR_SEM_TIMEOUT	121	The semaphore timeout period has expired.	STATUS_IO_TIMEOUT
ERROR_SERIAL_NO_DEVICE	1118	No serial device was successfully initialized. The serial driver will unload.	STATUS_SERIAL_NO_DEVICE_ INITED
ERROR_SERVER_DISABLED	1341	The server is currently disabled.	STATUS_SERVER_DISABLED
ERROR_SERVER_NOT_DISABLED	1342	The server is currently enabled.	STATUS_SERVER_NOT_DISABLED
ERROR_SERVICE_ALREADY_RUNNING	1056	An instance of the service is already running.	STATUS_IMAGE_ALREADY_LOADED
ERROR_SERVICE_DISABLED	1058	The specified service is disabled and cannot be started.	STATUS_PLUGPLAY_NO_DEVICE
ERROR_SESSION_CREDENTIAL_ CONFLICT	1219	The credentials supplied conflict with an existing set of credentials.	STATUS_NETWORK_CREDENTIAL_ CONFLICT
ERROR_SETMARK_DETECTED	1103	A tape access reached the end of a set of files.	STATUS_SETMARK_DETECTED
ERROR_SHARING_PAUSED	70	The remote server has been paused or is in the process of being started.	STATUS_SHARING_PAUSED
ERROR_SHARING_VIOLATION	32	The process cannot access the file because it is being used by another process.	STATUS_SHARING_VIOLATION
ERROR_SIGNAL_REFUSED	156	The recipient process has refused the signal.	STATUS_SUSPEND_COUNT_EXCEEDED
ERROR_SPECIAL_ACCOUNT	1371	Cannot perform this operation on built-in accounts.	STATUS_SPECIAL_ACCOUNT

Table B.1: *Application Error Codes (alphabetic) to* NTSTATUS *Values (continued)*

Application Error Code			
Name	**Value**	**Explanation**	**NTSTATUS Name**
ERROR_SPECIAL_GROUP	1372	Cannot perform this operation on this built-in special group.	STATUS_SPECIAL_GROUP
ERROR_SPECIAL_USER	1373	Cannot perform this operation on this built-in special user.	STATUS_SPECIAL_USER
ERROR_STACK_OVERFLOW	1001	Recursion too deep, stack overflowed.	STATUS_BAD_INITIAL_STACK
			STATUS_STACK_OVERFLOW
ERROR_SWAPERROR	999	Error performing inpage operation.	STATUS_IN_PAGE_ERROR
ERROR_TOKEN_ALREADY_IN_USE	1375	The token is already in use as a primary token.	STATUS_TOKEN_ALREADY_IN_USE
ERROR_TOO_MANY_CMDS	56	The network BIOS command limit has been reached.	STATUS_TOO_MANY_COMMANDS
ERROR_TOO_MANY_CONTEXT_IDS	1384	During a logon attempt, the user's security context accumulated too many security IDs.	STATUS_TOO_MANY_CONTEXT_IDS
ERROR_TOO_MANY_LINKS	1142	An attempt was made to create more links on a file than the file system supports.	STATUS_TOO_MANY_LINKS
ERROR_TOO_MANY_LUIDS_REQUESTED	1333	Too many local user identifiers (LUIDs) were requested at one time.	STATUS_TOO_MANY_LUIDS_REQUESTED
ERROR_TOO_MANY_NAMES	68	The name limit for the local computer network adapter card was exceeded.	STATUS_TOO_MANY_ADDRESSES
			STATUS_TOO_MANY_GUIDS_REQUESTED
			STATUS_TOO_MANY_NAMES
			STATUS_TOO_MANY_NODES
ERROR_TOO_MANY_OPEN_FILES	4	The system cannot open the file.	STATUS_TOO_MANY_OPENED_FILES
ERROR_TOO_MANY_POSTS	298	Too many posts were made to a semaphore.	STATUS_SEMAPHORE_LIMIT_EXCEEDED
ERROR_TOO_MANY_SECRETS	1381	The maximum number of secrets that may be stored in a single system has been exceeded.	STATUS_TOO_MANY_SECRETS
ERROR_TOO_MANY_SESS	69	The network BIOS session limit was exceeded.	STATUS_TOO_MANY_SESSIONS
ERROR_TOO_MANY_SIDS	1389	Too many security IDs have been specified.	STATUS_TOO_MANY_SIDS
ERROR_TRUST_FAILURE	1790	The network logon failed.	STATUS_TRUST_FAILURE
ERROR_TRUSTED_DOMAIN_FAILURE	1788	The trust relationship between the primary domain and the trusted domain failed.	STATUS_TRUSTED_DOMAIN_FAILURE
ERROR_TRUSTED_RELATIONSHIP_FAILURE	1789	The trust relationship between this workstation and the primary domain failed.	STATUS_TRUSTED_RELATIONSHIP_FAILURE
ERROR_UNABLE_TO_LOCK_MEDIA	1108	Unable to lock the media eject mechanism.	STATUS_UNABLE_TO_LOCK_MEDIA

Table B.1: *Application Error Codes (alphabetic) to* NTSTATUS *Values (continued)*

Application Error Code		Explanation	NTSTATUS Name
Name	**Value**		
ERROR_UNABLE_TO_UNLOAD_MEDIA	1109	Unable to unload the media.	STATUS_UNABLE_TO_UNLOAD_MEDIA
ERROR_UNEXP_NET_ERR	59	An unexpected network error occurred.	STATUS_INVALID_ADDRESS
			STATUS_INVALID_CONNECTION
			STATUS_LINK_FAILED
			STATUS_LINK_TIMEOUT
			STATUS_TRANSACTION_ABORTED
			STATUS_TRANSACTION_INVALID_ID
			STATUS_TRANSACTION_INVALID_TYPE
			STATUS_TRANSACTION_NO_MATCH
			STATUS_TRANSACTION_NO_RELEASE
			STATUS_TRANSACTION_RESPONDED
			STATUS_TRANSACTION_TIMED_OUT
			STATUS_UNEXPECTED_NETWORK_ERROR
			STATUS_USER_SESSION_DELETED
ERROR_UNKNOWN_REVISION	1305	The revision level is unknown.	STATUS_UNKNOWN_REVISION
ERROR_UNRECOGNIZED_MEDIA	1785	The disk media is not recognized. It may not be formatted.	STATUS_UNRECOGNIZED_MEDIA
ERROR_UNRECOGNIZED_VOLUME	1005	The volume does not contain a recognized file system. Please make sure that all required file system drivers are loaded and that the volume is not corrupt.	STATUS_UNRECOGNIZED_VOLUME
ERROR_USER_EXISTS	1316	The specified user already exists.	STATUS_USER_EXISTS
ERROR_USER_MAPPED_FILE	1224	The requested operation cannot be performed on a file with a user-mapped section open.	STATUS_USER_MAPPED_FILE
ERROR_VC_DISCONNECTED	240	The session was cancelled.	STATUS_VIRTUAL_CIRCUIT_CLOSED
ERROR_WORKING_SET_QUOTA	1453	Insufficient quota to complete the requested service.	STATUS_WORKING_SET_QUOTA
ERROR_WRITE_PROTECT	19	The media is write protected.	STATUS_MEDIA_WRITE_PROTECTED
			STATUS_TOO_LATE
ERROR_WRONG_DISK	34	?	STATUS_WRONG_VOLUME
RPC_S_ADDRESS_ERROR	1768	An addressing error occurred in the RPC server.	RPC_NT_ADDRESS_ERROR
RPC_S_ALREADY_LISTENING	1713	The RPC server is already listening.	RPC_NT_ALREADY_LISTENING
RPC_S_ALREADY_REGISTERED	1711	The object universal unique identifier (UUID) has already been registered.	RPC_NT_ALREADY_REGISTERED

Table B.1: *Application Error Codes (alphabetic) to NTSTATUS Values (continued)*

Application Error Code		Explanation	NTSTATUS Name
Name	**Value**		
RPC_S_BINDING_HAS_NO_AUTH	1746	The binding does not contain any authentication information.	RPC_NT_BINDING_HAS_NO_AUTH
RPC_S_BINDING_INCOMPLETE	1819	The binding handle does not contain all required information.	RPC_NT_BINDING_INCOMPLETE
RPC_S_CALL_CANCELLED	1818	The server was altered while processing this call.	RPC_NT_CALL_CANCELLED
RPC_S_CALL_FAILED	1726	The remote procedure call failed.	RPC_NT_CALL_FAILED
RPC_S_CALL_FAILED_DNE	1727	The remote procedure call failed and did not execute.	RPC_NT_CALL_FAILED_DNE
RPC_S_CALL_IN_PROGRESS	1791	A remote procedure call is already in progress for this thread.	RPC_NT_CALL_IN_PROGRESS
RPC_S_CANNOT_SUPPORT	1764	The requested operation is not supported.	RPC_NT_CANNOT_SUPPORT
RPC_S_CANT_CREATE_ENDPOINT	1720	The endpoint cannot be created.	RPC_NT_CANT_CREATE_ENDPOINT
RPC_S_COMM_FAILURE	1820	Communications failure.	RPC_NT_COMM_FAILURE
RPC_S_DUPLICATE_ENDPOINT	1740	The endpoint is a duplicate.	RPC_NT_DUPLICATE_ENDPOINT
RPC_S_ENTRY_ALREADY_EXISTS	1760	The entry already exists.	RPC_NT_ENTRY_ALREADY_EXISTS
RPC_S_ENTRY_NOT_FOUND	1761	The entry is not found.	RPC_NT_ENTRY_NOT_FOUND
RPC_S_FP_DIV_ZERO	1769	A floating-point operation at the RPC server caused a division by zero.	RPC_NT_FP_DIV_ZERO
RPC_S_FP_OVERFLOW	1771	A floating-point overflow occurred at the RPC server.	RPC_NT_FP_OVERFLOW
RPC_S_FP_UNDERFLOW	1770	A floating-point underflow occurred at the RPC server.	RPC_NT_FP_UNDERFLOW
RPC_S_GROUP_MEMBER_NOT_FOUND	1898	The group member was not found.	RPC_NT_GROUP_MEMBER_NOT_FOUND
RPC_S_INCOMPLETE_NAME	1755	The entry name is incomplete.	RPC_NT_INCOMPLETE_NAME
RPC_S_INTERFACE_NOT_FOUND	1759	The interface was not found.	RPC_NT_INTERFACE_NOT_FOUND
RPC_S_INTERNAL_ERROR	1766	An internal error occurred in a remote procedure call (RPC).	RPC_NT_INTERNAL_ERROR
RPC_S_INVALID_AUTH_IDENTITY	1749	The security context is invalid.	RPC_NT_INVALID_AUTH_IDENTITY
RPC_S_INVALID_BOUND	1734	The array bounds are invalid.	RPC_NT_INVALID_BOUND
RPC_S_INVALID_ENDPOINT_FORMAT	1706	The endpoint format is invalid.	RPC_NT_INVALID_ENDPOINT_FORMAT
RPC_S_INVALID_NAF_ID	1763	The network address family is invalid.	RPC_NT_INVALID_NAF_ID
RPC_S_INVALID_NAME_SYNTAX	1736	The name syntax is invalid.	RPC_NT_INVALID_NAME_SYNTAX
RPC_S_INVALID_NET_ADDR	1707	The network address is invalid.	RPC_NT_INVALID_NET_ADDR
RPC_S_INVALID_NETWORK_OPTIONS	1724	The network options are invalid.	RPC_NT_INVALID_NETWORK_OPTIONS

Table B.1: *Application Error Codes (alphabetic) to* NTSTATUS *Values (continued)*

Application Error Code		Explanation	NTSTATUS Name
Name	**Value**		
RPC_S_INVALID_OBJECT	1900	The object universal unique identifier (UUID) is the nil UUID.	RPC_NT_INVALID_OBJECT
RPC_S_INVALID_RPC_PROTSEQ	1704	The RPC protocol sequence is invalid.	RPC_NT_INVALID_RPC_PROTSEQ
RPC_S_INVALID_STRING_BINDING	1700	The string binding is invalid.	RPC_NT_INVALID_STRING_BINDING
RPC_S_INVALID_STRING_UUID	1705	The string universal unique identifier (UUID) is invalid.	RPC_NT_INVALID_STRING_UUID
RPC_S_INVALID_TAG	1733	The tag is invalid.	RPC_NT_INVALID_TAG
RPC_S_INVALID_TIMEOUT	1709	The timeout value is invalid.	RPC_NT_INVALID_TIMEOUT
RPC_S_INVALID_VERS_OPTION	1756	The version option is invalid.	RPC_NT_INVALID_VERS_OPTION
RPC_S_MAX_CALLS_TOO_SMALL	1742	The maximum number of calls is too small.	RPC_NT_MAX_CALLS_TOO_SMALL
RPC_S_NAME_SERVICE_UNAVAILABLE	1762	The name service is unavailable.	RPC_NT_NAME_SERVICE_UNAVAILABLE
RPC_S_NO_BINDINGS	1718	There are no bindings.	RPC_NT_NO_BINDINGS
RPC_S_NO_CALL_ACTIVE	1725	There is not a remote procedure call active in this thread.	RPC_NT_NO_CALL_ACTIVE
RPC_S_NO_CONTEXT_AVAILABLE	1765	No security context is available to allow impersonation.	RPC_NT_NO_CONTEXT_AVAILABLE
RPC_S_NO_ENDPOINT_FOUND	1708	No endpoint was found.	RPC_NT_NO_ENDPOINT_FOUND
RPC_S_NO_ENTRY_NAME	1735	The binding does not contain an entry name.	RPC_NT_NO_ENTRY_NAME
RPC_S_NO_INTERFACES	1817	No interfaces have been registered.	RPC_NT_NO_INTERFACES
RPC_S_NO_MORE_BINDINGS	1806	There are no more bindings.	RPC_NT_NO_MORE_BINDINGS
RPC_S_NO_MORE_MEMBERS	1757	There are no more members.	RPC_NT_NO_MORE_MEMBERS
RPC_S_NO_PRINC_NAME	1822	No principal name registered.	RPC_NT_NO_PRINC_NAME
RPC_S_NO_PROTSEQS	1719	There are no protocol sequences.	RPC_NT_NO_PROTSEQS
RPC_S_NO_PROTSEQS_REGISTERED	1714	No protocol sequences have been registered.	RPC_NT_NO_PROTSEQS_REGISTERED
RPC_S_NOT_ALL_OBJS_UNEXPORTED	1758	There is nothing to unexport.	RPC_NT_NOT_ALL_OBJS_UNEXPORTED
RPC_S_NOT_CANCELLED	1826	Thread is not cancelled.	RPC_NT_NOT_CANCELLED
RPC_S_NOT_LISTENING	1715	The RPC server is not listening.	RPC_NT_NOT_LISTENING
RPC_S_NOT_RPC_ERROR	1823	The error specified is not a valid Windows NT RPC error code.	RPC_NT_NOT_RPC_ERROR
RPC_S_NOTHING_TO_EXPORT	1754	No interfaces have been exported.	RPC_NT_NOTHING_TO_EXPORT
RPC_S_OBJECT_NOT_FOUND	1710	The object universal unique identifier (UUID) was not found.	RPC_NT_OBJECT_NOT_FOUND

Table B.1: *Application Error Codes (alphabetic) to NTSTATUS Values (continued)*

Application Error Code		Explanation	NTSTATUS Name
Name	**Value**		
RPC_S_OUT_OF_RESOURCES	1721	Not enough resources are available to complete this operation.	RPC_NT_OUT_OF_RESOURCES
RPC_S_PROCNUM_OUT_OF_RANGE	1745	The procedure number is out of range.	RPC_NT_PROCNUM_OUT_OF_RANGE
RPC_S_PROTOCOL_ERROR	1728	A remote procedure call (RPC) protocol error occurred.	RPC_NT_PROTOCOL_ERROR
RPC_S_PROTSEQ_NOT_FOUND	1744	The RPC protocol sequence was not found.	RPC_NT_PROTSEQ_NOT_FOUND
RPC_S_PROTSEQ_NOT_SUPPORTED	1703	The RPC protocol sequence is not supported.	RPC_NT_PROTSEQ_NOT_SUPPORTED
RPC_S_SEC_PKG_ERROR	1825	A security package specific error occurred.	RPC_NT_SEC_PKG_ERROR
RPC_S_SERVER_TOO_BUSY	1723	The RPC server is too busy to complete this operation.	RPC_NT_SERVER_TOO_BUSY
RPC_S_SERVER_UNAVAILABLE	1722	The RPC server is unavailable.	RPC_NT_SERVER_UNAVAILABLE
RPC_S_STRING_TOO_LONG	1743	The string is too long.	RPC_NT_STRING_TOO_LONG
RPC_S_TYPE_ALREADY_REGISTERED	1712	The type universal unique identifier (UUID) has already been registered.	RPC_NT_TYPE_ALREADY_REGISTERED
RPC_S_UNKNOWN_AUTHN_LEVEL	1748	The authentication level is unknown.	RPC_NT_UNKNOWN_AUTHN_LEVEL
RPC_S_UNKNOWN_AUTHN_SERVICE	1747	The authentication service is unknown.	RPC_NT_UNKNOWN_AUTHN_SERVICE
RPC_S_UNKNOWN_AUTHN_TYPE	1741	The authentication type is unknown.	RPC_NT_UNKNOWN_AUTHN_TYPE
RPC_S_UNKNOWN_AUTHZ_SERVICE	1750	The authorization service is unknown.	RPC_NT_UNKNOWN_AUTHZ_SERVICE
RPC_S_UNKNOWN_IF	1717	The interface is unknown.	RPC_NT_UNKNOWN_IF
RPC_S_UNKNOWN_MGR_TYPE	1716	The manager type is unknown.	RPC_NT_UNKNOWN_MGR_TYPE
RPC_S_UNSUPPORTED_AUTHN_LEVEL	1821	The requested authentication level is not supported.	RPC_NT_UNSUPPORTED_AUTHN_LEVEL
RPC_S_UNSUPPORTED_NAME_SYNTAX	1737	The name syntax is not supported.	RPC_NT_UNSUPPORTED_NAME_SYNTAX
RPC_S_UNSUPPORTED_TRANS_SYN	1730	The transfer syntax is not supported by the RPC server.	RPC_NT_UNSUPPORTED_TRANS_SYN
RPC_S_UNSUPPORTED_TYPE	1732	The universal unique identifier (UUID) type is not supported.	RPC_NT_UNSUPPORTED_TYPE
RPC_S_UUID_NO_ADDRESS	1739	No network address is available to use to construct a universal unique identifier (UUID).	RPC_NT_UUID_NO_ADDRESS
RPC_S_WRONG_KIND_OF_BINDING	1701	The binding handle is not the correct type.	RPC_NT_WRONG_KIND_OF_BINDING
RPC_S_ZERO_DIVIDE	1767	The RPC server attempted an integer division by zero.	RPC_NT_ZERO_DIVIDE
RPC_X_BAD_STUB_DATA	1783	The stub received bad data.	RPC_NT_BAD_STUB_DATA

Table B.1: *Application Error Codes (alphabetic) to* NTSTATUS *Values (continued)*

Application Error Code		Explanation	NTSTATUS Name
Name	**Value**		
RPC_X_BYTE_COUNT_TOO_SMALL	1782	The byte count is too small.	RPC_NT_BYTE_COUNT_TOO_SMALL
RPC_X_ENUM_VALUE_OUT_OF_RANGE	1781	The enumeration value is out of range.	RPC_NT_ENUM_VALUE_OUT_OF_RANGE
RPC_X_INVALID_ES_ACTION	1827	Invalid operation on the encoding/decoding handle.	RPC_NT_INVALID_ES_ACTION
RPC_X_INVALID_PIPE_OBJECT	1830	The idl pipe object is invalid or corrupted.	RPC_NT_INVALID_PIPE_OBJECT
RPC_X_INVALID_PIPE_OPERATION	1831	The operation is invalid for a given idl pipe object.	RPC_NT_INVALID_PIPE_OPERATION
RPC_X_NO_MORE_ENTRIES	1772	The list of RPC servers available for the binding of auto handles has been exhausted.	RPC_NT_NO_MORE_ENTRIES
RPC_X_NULL_REF_POINTER	1780	A null reference pointer was passed to the stub.	RPC_NT_NULL_REF_POINTER
RPC_X_SS_CANNOT_GET_CALL_HANDLE	1779	The stub is unable to get the remote procedure call handle.	RPC_NT_SS_CANNOT_GET_CALL_HANDLE
RPC_X_SS_CHAR_TRANS_OPEN_FAIL	1773	Unable to open the character translation table file.	RPC_NT_SS_CHAR_TRANS_OPEN_FAIL
RPC_X_SS_CHAR_TRANS_SHORT_FILE	1774	The file containing the character translation table has fewer than 512 bytes.	RPC_NT_SS_CHAR_TRANS_SHORT_FILE
RPC_X_SS_CONTEXT_DAMAGED	1777	The context handle changed during a remote procedure call.	RPC_NT_SS_CONTEXT_DAMAGED
RPC_X_SS_HANDLES_MISMATCH	1778	The binding handles passed to a remote procedure call do not match.	RPC_NT_SS_HANDLES_MISMATCH
RPC_X_WRONG_ES_VERSION	1828	Incompatible version of the serializing package.	RPC_NT_WRONG_ES_VERSION
RPC_X_WRONG_PIPE_VERSION	1832	The idl pipe version is not supported.	RPC_NT_WRONG_PIPE_VERSION
RPC_X_WRONG_STUB_VERSION	1829	Incompatible version of the RPC stub.	RPC_NT_WRONG_STUB_VERSION

GetLastError Codes (numeric) to NTSTATUS Values

Table B.2: *Application Error Codes (numeric) to* NTSTATUS *Values*

Application Error Code			
Value	**Name**	**Explanation**	**NTSTATUS Name**
1	ERROR_INVALID_FUNCTION	Incorrect function.	STATUS_ILLEGAL_FUNCTION
			STATUS_INVALID_DEVICE_REQUEST
			STATUS_INVALID_SYSTEM_SERVICE
			STATUS_NOT_IMPLEMENTED
2	ERROR_FILE_NOT_FOUND	The system cannot find the file specified.	STATUS_NO_SUCH_DEVICE
			STATUS_NO_SUCH_FILE
			STATUS_OBJECT_NAME_NOT_FOUND
3	ERROR_PATH_NOT_FOUND	The system cannot find the path specified.	STATUS_DFS_EXIT_PATH_FOUND
			STATUS_OBJECT_PATH_NOT_FOUND
			STATUS_REDIRECTOR_NOT_STARTED
4	ERROR_TOO_MANY_OPEN_FILES	The system cannot open the file.	STATUS_TOO_MANY_OPENED_FILES
5	ERROR_ACCESS_DENIED	Access is denied.	STATUS_ACCESS_DENIED
			STATUS_ALREADY_COMMITTED
			STATUS_CANNOT_DELETE
			STATUS_DELETE_PENDING
			STATUS_FILE_DELETED
			STATUS_FILE_IS_A_DIRECTORY
			STATUS_INVALID_LOCK_SEQUENCE
			STATUS_INVALID_VIEW_SIZE
			STATUS_PORT_CONNECTION_REFUSED
			STATUS_PROCESS_IS_TERMINATING
			STATUS_THREAD_IS_TERMINATING
6	ERROR_INVALID_HANDLE	The handle is invalid.	RPC_NT_INVALID_BINDING
			RPC_NT_SS_CONTEXT_MISMATCH
			RPC_NT_SS_IN_NULL_CONTEXT
			STATUS_FILE_CLOSED
			STATUS_HANDLE_NOT_CLOSABLE
			STATUS_INVALID_HANDLE
			STATUS_INVALID_PORT_HANDLE
			STATUS_OBJECT_TYPE_MISMATCH
			STATUS_PORT_DISCONNECTED

Table B.2: *Application Error Codes (numeric) to* NTSTATUS *Values (continued)*

Application Error Code		Explanation	NTSTATUS Name
Value	Name		
8	ERROR_NOT_ENOUGH_MEMORY	Not enough storage is available to process this command.	STATUS_NO_MEMORY
			STATUS_SECTION_TOO_BIG
			STATUS_TOO_MANY_PAGING_FILES
14	ERROR_OUTOFMEMORY	Not enough storage is available to complete this operation.	STATUS_SECTION_NOT_EXTENDED
17	ERROR_NOT_SAME_DEVICE	The system cannot move the file to a different disk drive.	STATUS_NOT_SAME_DEVICE
18	ERROR_NO_MORE_FILES	There are no more files.	STATUS_NO_MORE_FILES
19	ERROR_WRITE_PROTECT	The media is write protected.	STATUS_MEDIA_WRITE_PROTECTED
			STATUS_TOO_LATE
21	ERROR_NOT_READY	The device is not ready.	STATUS_DEVICE_NOT_CONNECTED
			STATUS_DEVICE_NOT_READY
			STATUS_DEVICE_OFF_LINE
			STATUS_DEVICE_POWER_FAILURE
			STATUS_DEVICE_POWERED_OFF
			STATUS_NO_MEDIA_IN_DEVICE
22	ERROR_BAD_COMMAND	The device does not recognize the command.	STATUS_INVALID_DEVICE_STATE
23	ERROR_CRC	Data error (cyclic redundancy check).	STATUS_CRC_ERROR
			STATUS_DATA_ERROR
			STATUS_DEVICE_DATA_ERROR
24	ERROR_BAD_LENGTH	The program issued a command but the command length is incorrect.	STATUS_INFO_LENGTH_MISMATCH
27	ERROR_SECTOR_NOT_FOUND	The drive cannot find the sector requested.	STATUS_NONEXISTENT_SECTOR
28	ERROR_OUT_OF_PAPER	The printer is out of paper.	STATUS_DEVICE_PAPER_EMPTY
31	ERROR_GEN_FAILURE	A device attached to the system is not functioning.	STATUS_UNSUCCESSFUL
32	ERROR_SHARING_VIOLATION	The process cannot access the file because it is being used by another process.	STATUS_SHARING_VIOLATION
33	ERROR_LOCK_VIOLATION	The process cannot access the file because another process has locked a portion of the file.	STATUS_FILE_LOCK_CONFLICT
			STATUS_LOCK_NOT_GRANTED
34	ERROR_WRONG_DISK	?	STATUS_WRONG_VOLUME
38	ERROR_HANDLE_EOF	Reached end of file.	STATUS_END_OF_FILE
			STATUS_FILE_FORCED_CLOSED

Table B.2: *Application Error Codes (numeric) to* NTSTATUS *Values (continued)*

Application Error Code		Explanation	NTSTATUS Name
Value	Name		
50	ERROR_NOT_SUPPORTED	The network request is not supported.	STATUS_CTL_FILE_NOT_SUPPORTED
			STATUS_NOT_CLIENT_SESSION
			STATUS_NOT_SERVER_SESSION
			STATUS_NOT_SUPPORTED
51	ERROR_REM_NOT_LIST	The remote computer is not available.	STATUS_REMOTE_NOT_LISTENING
			STATUS_REMOTE_RESOURCES
52	ERROR_DUP_NAME	A duplicate name exists on the network.	STATUS_ADDRESS_ALREADY_EXISTS
			STATUS_DUPLICATE_NAME
53	ERROR_BAD_NETPATH	The network path was not found.	STATUS_BAD_NETWORK_PATH
54	ERROR_NETWORK_BUSY	The network is busy.	STATUS_NETWORK_BUSY
55	ERROR_DEV_NOT_EXIST	The specified network resource or device is no longer available.	STATUS_DEVICE_DOES_NOT_EXIST
56	ERROR_TOO_MANY_CMDS	The network BIOS command limit has been reached.	STATUS_TOO_MANY_COMMANDS
57	ERROR_ADAP_HDW_ERR	A network adapter hardware error occurred.	STATUS_ADAPTER_HARDWARE_ERROR
58	ERROR_BAD_NET_RESP	The specified server cannot perform the requested operation.	STATUS_INVALID_NETWORK_RESPONSE
59	ERROR_UNEXP_NET_ERR	An unexpected network error occurred.	STATUS_INVALID_ADDRESS
			STATUS_INVALID_CONNECTION
			STATUS_LINK_FAILED
			STATUS_LINK_TIMEOUT
			STATUS_TRANSACTION_ABORTED
			STATUS_TRANSACTION_INVALID_ID
			STATUS_TRANSACTION_INVALID_TYPE
			STATUS_TRANSACTION_NO_MATCH
			STATUS_TRANSACTION_NO_RELEASE
			STATUS_TRANSACTION_RESPONDED
			STATUS_TRANSACTION_TIMED_OUT
			STATUS_UNEXPECTED_NETWORK_ERROR
			STATUS_USER_SESSION_DELETED
60	ERROR_BAD_REM_ADAP	The remote adapter is not compatible.	STATUS_BAD_REMOTE_ADAPTER
61	ERROR_PRINTQ_FULL	The printer queue is full.	STATUS_PRINT_QUEUE_FULL
62	ERROR_NO_SPOOL_SPACE	Space to store the file waiting to be printed is not available on the server.	STATUS_NO_SPOOL_SPACE

Table B.2: *Application Error Codes (numeric) to NTSTATUS Values (continued)*

Application Error Code		Explanation	NTSTATUS Name
Value	Name		
63	ERROR_PRINT_CANCELLED	Your file waiting to be printed was deleted.	STATUS_PRINT_CANCELLED
64	ERROR_NETNAME_DELETED	The specified network name is no longer available.	STATUS_ADDRESS_CLOSED
			STATUS_CONNECTION_ DISCONNECTED
			STATUS_CONNECTION_RESET
			STATUS_LOCAL_DISCONNECT
			STATUS_NETWORK_NAME_DELETED
			STATUS_REMOTE_DISCONNECT
65	ERROR_NETWORK_ACCESS_DENIED	Network access is denied.	STATUS_NETWORK_ACCESS_DENIED
66	ERROR_BAD_DEV_TYPE	The network resource type is not correct.	STATUS_BAD_DEVICE_TYPE
67	ERROR_BAD_NET_NAME	The network name cannot be found.	STATUS_BAD_NETWORK_NAME
68	ERROR_TOO_MANY_NAMES	The name limit for the local computer network adapter card was exceeded.	STATUS_TOO_MANY_ADDRESSES
			STATUS_TOO_MANY_GUIDS_ REQUESTED
			STATUS_TOO_MANY_NAMES
			STATUS_TOO_MANY_NODES
69	ERROR_TOO_MANY_SESS	The network BIOS session limit was exceeded.	STATUS_TOO_MANY_SESSIONS
70	ERROR_SHARING_PAUSED	The remote server has been paused or is in the process of being started.	STATUS_SHARING_PAUSED
71	ERROR_REQ_NOT_ACCEP	No more connections can be made to this remote computer at this time because there are already as many connections as the computer can accept.	STATUS_REQUEST_NOT_ACCEPTED
72	ERROR_REDIR_PAUSED	The specified printer or disk device has been paused.	STATUS_REDIRECTOR_PAUSED
86	ERROR_INVALID_PASSWORD	The specified network password is not correct.	STATUS_WRONG_PASSWORD
			STATUS_WRONG_PASSWORD_CORE
87	ERROR_INVALID_PARAMETER	The parameter is incorrect.	STATUS_BAD_WORKING_SET_LIMIT
			STATUS_DEVICE_CONFIGURATION_ ERROR
			STATUS_INCOMPATIBLE_FILE_MAP
			STATUS_INVALID_CID
			STATUS_INVALID_INFO_CLASS
			STATUS_INVALID_PAGE_ PROTECTION
			STATUS_INVALID_PARAMETER
			STATUS_INVALID_PARAMETER_1

Table B.2: *Application Error Codes (numeric) to* NTSTATUS *Values (continued)*

Application Error Code		Explanation	NTSTATUS Name
Value	**Name**		
	ERROR_INVALID_PARAMETER *(continued)*		STATUS_INVALID_PARAMETER_2
			STATUS_INVALID_PARAMETER_3
			STATUS_INVALID_PARAMETER_4
			STATUS_INVALID_PARAMETER_5
			STATUS_INVALID_PARAMETER_6
			STATUS_INVALID_PARAMETER_7
			STATUS_INVALID_PARAMETER_8
			STATUS_INVALID_PARAMETER_9
			STATUS_INVALID_PARAMETER_10
			STATUS_INVALID_PARAMETER_11
			STATUS_INVALID_PARAMETER_12
			STATUS_INVALID_PARAMETER_MIX
			STATUS_PORT_ALREADY_SET
			STATUS_SECTION_NOT_IMAGE
			STATUS_SECTION_PROTECTION
			STATUS_UNABLE_TO_DELETE_SECTION
			STATUS_UNABLE_TO_FREE_VM
88	ERROR_NET_WRITE_FAULT	A write fault occurred on the network.	STATUS_NET_WRITE_FAULT
109	ERROR_BROKEN_PIPE	The pipe has been ended.	STATUS_PIPE_BROKEN
112	ERROR_DISK_FULL	There is not enough space on the disk.	STATUS_DISK_FULL
121	ERROR_SEM_TIMEOUT	The semaphore timeout period has expired.	STATUS_IO_TIMEOUT
122	ERROR_INSUFFICIENT_BUFFER	The data area passed to a system call is too small.	STATUS_BUFFER_TOO_SMALL
123	ERROR_INVALID_NAME	The filename, directory name, or volume label syntax is incorrect.	STATUS_OBJECT_NAME_INVALID
124	ERROR_INVALID_LEVEL	The system call level is not correct.	STATUS_INVALID_LEVEL
126	ERROR_MOD_NOT_FOUND	The specified module could not be found.	STATUS_DLL_NOT_FOUND
127	ERROR_PROC_NOT_FOUND	The specified procedure could not be found.	STATUS_DRIVER_ENTRYPOINT_NOT_FOUND
			STATUS_ENTRYPOINT_NOT_FOUND
			STATUS_PROCEDURE_NOT_FOUND
145	ERROR_DIR_NOT_EMPTY	The directory is not empty.	STATUS_DIRECTORY_NOT_EMPTY

Table B.2: *Application Error Codes (numeric) to* NTSTATUS *Values (continued)*

Application Error Code		Explanation	NTSTATUS Name
Value	Name		
154	ERROR_LABEL_TOO_LONG	The volume label you entered exceeds the label character limit of the target file system.	STATUS_INVALID_VOLUME_LABEL
156	ERROR_SIGNAL_REFUSED	The recipient process has refused the signal.	STATUS_SUSPEND_COUNT_EXCEEDED
158	ERROR_NOT_LOCKED	The segment is already unlocked.	STATUS_NOT_LOCKED
			STATUS_RANGE_NOT_LOCKED
161	ERROR_BAD_PATHNAME	The specified path is invalid.	STATUS_OBJECT_PATH_INVALID
			STATUS_OBJECT_PATH_SYNTAX_BAD
170	ERROR_BUSY	The requested resource is in use.	STATUS_DEVICE_BUSY
182	ERROR_INVALID_ORDINAL	?	STATUS_DRIVER_ORDINAL_NOT_FOUND
			STATUS_ORDINAL_NOT_FOUND
183	ERROR_ALREADY_EXISTS	Cannot create a file when that file already exists.	STATUS_OBJECT_NAME_COLLISION
193	ERROR_BAD_EXE_FORMAT	?	STATUS_BAD_INITIAL_PC
			STATUS_IMAGE_CHECKSUM_MISMATCH
			STATUS_IMAGE_MP_UP_MISMATCH
			STATUS_INVALID_FILE_FOR_SECTION
			STATUS_INVALID_IMAGE_FORMAT
			STATUS_INVALID_IMAGE_LE_FORMAT
			STATUS_INVALID_IMAGE_NE_FORMAT
			STATUS_INVALID_IMAGE_NOT_MZ
			STATUS_INVALID_IMAGE_PROTECT
			STATUS_INVALID_IMAGE_WIN_16
203	ERROR_ENVVAR_NOT_FOUND	The system could not find the environment option that was entered.	STATUS_VARIABLE_NOT_FOUND
206	ERROR_FILENAME_EXCED_RANGE	The filename or extension is too long.	STATUS_NAME_TOO_LONG
230	ERROR_BAD_PIPE	The pipe state is invalid.	STATUS_INVALID_PIPE_STATE
			STATUS_INVALID_READ_MODE
231	ERROR_PIPE_BUSY	All pipe instances are busy.	STATUS_INSTANCE_NOT_AVAILABLE
			STATUS_PIPE_BUSY
			STATUS_PIPE_NOT_AVAILABLE
232	ERROR_NO_DATA	The pipe is being closed.	STATUS_PIPE_CLOSING
			STATUS_PIPE_EMPTY

Table B.2: *Application Error Codes (numeric) to* NTSTATUS *Values (continued)*

Application Error Code		Explanation	NTSTATUS Name
Value	Name		
233	ERROR_PIPE_NOT_CONNECTED	No process is on the other end of the pipe.	STATUS_PIPE_DISCONNECTED
234	ERROR_MORE_DATA	More data is available.	STATUS_BUFFER_OVERFLOW
			STATUS_MORE_PROCESSING_ REQUIRED
240	ERROR_VC_DISCONNECTED	The session was cancelled.	STATUS_VIRTUAL_CIRCUIT_CLOSED
254	ERROR_INVALID_EA_NAME	The specified extended attribute name was invalid.	STATUS_INVALID_EA_NAME
255	ERROR_EA_LIST_INCONSISTENT	The extended attributes are inconsistent.	STATUS_EA_LIST_INCONSISTENT
			STATUS_EA_TOO_LARGE
			STATUS_INVALID_EA_FLAG
259	ERROR_NO_MORE_ITEMS	No more data is available.	STATUS_AGENTS_EXHAUSTED
			STATUS_GUIDS_EXHAUSTED
			STATUS_NO_MORE_EAS
			STATUS_NO_MORE_ENTRIES
267	ERROR_DIRECTORY	The directory name is invalid.	STATUS_NOT_A_DIRECTORY
288	ERROR_NOT_OWNER	Attempt to release mutex not owned by caller.	STATUS_MUTANT_NOT_OWNED
			STATUS_RESOURCE_NOT_OWNED
298	ERROR_TOO_MANY_POSTS	Too many posts were made to a semaphore.	STATUS_SEMAPHORE_LIMIT_ EXCEEDED
299	ERROR_PARTIAL_COPY	Only part of a Read/WriteProcessMem-ory request was completed.	STATUS_PARTIAL_COPY
317	ERROR_MR_MID_NOT_FOUND	? This error code seems to indicate that an error code corresponding to a status code to the right cannot be found. Therefore, it appears that the status codes to the right have no meaningful user-level error code when returned as the completion status of an IRP. You should not use any of these codes unless your own tests indicate otherwise (based on later versions of NT or new Service Packs).	STATUS_ABIOS_INVALID_COMMAND
			STATUS_ABIOS_INVALID_LID
			STATUS_ABIOS_INVALID_SELECTOR
			STATUS_ABIOS_LID_ALREADY_ OWNED
			STATUS_ABIOS_LID_NOT_EXIST
			STATUS_ABIOS_NOT_LID_OWNER
			STATUS_ABIOS_NOT_PRESENT
			STATUS_ABIOS_SELECTOR_ NOT_AVAILABLE
			STATUS_ALLOCATE_BUCKET
			STATUS_APP_INIT_FAILURE
			STATUS_AUDIT_FAILED
			STATUS_BACKUP_CONTROLLER
			STATUS_BAD_COMPRESSION_BUFFER
			STATUS_BAD_DLL_ENTRYPOINT

Table B.2: *Application Error Codes (numeric) to* NTSTATUS *Values (continued)*

Application Error Code		Explanation	NTSTATUS Name
Value	**Name**		
	ERROR_MR_MID_NOT_FOUND *(continued)*		STATUS_BAD_FUNCTION_TABLE
			STATUS_BAD_MASTER_BOOT_RECORD
			STATUS_BAD_SERVICE_ENTRYPOINT
			STATUS_BAD_STACK
			STATUS_BIOS_FAILED_TO_CONNECT_INTERRUPT
			STATUS_CANNOT_LOAD_REGISTRY_FILE
			STATUS_CANT_TERMINATE_SELF
			STATUS_CANT_WAIT
			STATUS_CLIENT_SERVER_PARAMETERS_INVALID
			STATUS_CONTROL_C_EXIT
			STATUS_CONVERT_TO_LARGE
			STATUS_COULD_NOT_INTERPRET
			STATUS_DATA_NOT_ACCEPTED
			STATUS_DEBUG_ATTACH_FAILED
			STATUS_DEVICE_ALREADY_ATTACHED
			STATUS_DFS_UNAVAILABLE
			STATUS_DLL_INIT_FAILED_LOGOFF
			STATUS_DOMAIN_CTRLR_CONFIG_ERROR
			STATUS_DRIVER_CANCEL_TIMEOUT
			STATUS_DRIVER_UNABLE_TO_LOAD
			STATUS_EAS_NOT_SUPPORTED
			STATUS_EVALUATION_EXPIRATION
			STATUS_EXTRANEOUS_INFORMATION
			STATUS_FAIL_CHECK
			STATUS_FILE_IS_OFFLINE
			STATUS_FILE_RENAMED
			STATUS_FILES_OPEN
			STATUS_FLOPPY_VOLUME
			STATUS_FOUND_OUT_OF_SCOPE
			STATUS_FS_DRIVER_REQUIRED
			STATUS_GUID_SUBSTITUTION_MADE
			STATUS_HANDLES_CLOSED

Table B.2: *Application Error Codes (numeric) to* NTSTATUS *Values (continued)*

Application Error Code		Explanation	NTSTATUS Name
Value	Name		
	ERROR_MR_MID_NOT_FOUND *(continued)*		STATUS_ILL_FORMED_SERVICE_ENTRY
			STATUS_ILLEGAL_CHARACTER
			STATUS_ILLEGAL_DLL_RELOCATION
			STATUS_ILLEGAL_FLOAT_CONTEXT
			STATUS_INSTRUCTION_MISALIGNMENT
			STATUS_INSUFFICIENT_LOGON_INFO
			STATUS_INVALID_HW_PROFILE
			STATUS_INVALID_LDT_DESCRIPTOR
			STATUS_INVALID_LDT_OFFSET
			STATUS_INVALID_LDT_SIZE
			STATUS_INVALID_OPLOCK_PROTOCOL
			STATUS_INVALID_PLUGPLAY_DEVICE_PATH
			STATUS_INVALID_PORT_ATTRIBUTES
			STATUS_INVALID_QUOTA_LOWER
			STATUS_INVALID_UNWIND_TARGET
			STATUS_INVALID_VARIANT
			STATUS_IO_PRIVILEGE_FAILED
			STATUS_IP_ADDRESS_CONFLICT1
			STATUS_IP_ADDRESS_CONFLICT2
			STATUS_LICENSE_VIOLATION
			STATUS_LOGON_SERVER_CONFLICT
			STATUS_LONGJUMP
			STATUS_LOST_WRITEBEHIND_DATA
			STATUS_MARSHALL_OVERFLOW
			STATUS_MEDIA_CHECK
			STATUS_MESSAGE_NOT_FOUND
			STATUS_MISSING_SYSTEMFILE
			STATUS_MUTANT_LIMIT_EXCEEDED
			STATUS_NO_CALLBACK_ACTIVE
			STATUS_NO_EVENT_PAIR
			STATUS_NO_GUID_TRANSLATION
			STATUS_NO_LDT
			STATUS_NO_PAGEFILE

Table B.2: *Application Error Codes (numeric) to* NTSTATUS *Values (continued)*

Application Error Code		Explanation	NTSTATUS Name
Value	**Name**		
	ERROR_MR_MID_NOT_FOUND *(continued)*		STATUS_NOT_FOUND
			STATUS_NOT_TINY_STREAM
			STATUS_OPEN_FAILED
			STATUS_OPLOCK_NOT_GRANTED
			STATUS_PAGEFILE_CREATE_FAILED
			STATUS_PAGEFILE_QUOTA_ EXCEEDED
			STATUS_PORT_MESSAGE_TOO_LONG
			STATUS_PROFILING_AT_LIMIT
			STATUS_PROFILING_NOT_STARTED
			STATUS_PROFILING_NOT_STOPPED
			STATUS_PROPSET_NOT_FOUND
			STATUS_PWD_HISTORY_CONFLICT
			STATUS_PWD_TOO_RECENT
			STATUS_PWD_TOO_SHORT
			STATUS_QUOTA_LIST_ INCONSISTENT
			STATUS_RECOVERY_FAILURE
			STATUS_REDIRECTOR_HAS_ OPEN_HANDLES
			STATUS_REDIRECTOR_STARTED
			STATUS_REGISTRY_QUOTA_LIMIT
			STATUS_REPLY_MESSAGE_MISMATCH
			STATUS_RETRY
			STATUS_RXACT_COMMIT_NECESSARY
			STATUS_SERVER_HAS_ OPEN_HANDLES
			STATUS_STACK_OVERFLOW_READ
			STATUS_SYNCHRONIZATION_ REQUIRED
			STATUS_SYSTEM_PROCESS_ TERMINATED
			STATUS_THREAD_NOT_IN_PROCESS
			STATUS_TIME_DIFFERENCE_AT_DC
			STATUS_TIMER_NOT_CANCELED
			STATUS_TIMER_RESOLUTION_ NOT_SET
			STATUS_TOO_MANY_THREADS
			STATUS_UNDEFINED_CHARACTER

Table B.2: *Application Error Codes (numeric) to* NTSTATUS *Values (continued)*

Application Error Code		Explanation	NTSTATUS Name
Value	**Name**		
	ERROR_MR_MID_NOT_FOUND *(continued)*		STATUS_UNEXPECTED_IO_ERROR
			STATUS_UNEXPECTED_MM_CREATE_ERR
			STATUS_UNEXPECTED_MM_EXTEND_ERR
			STATUS_UNEXPECTED_MM_MAP_ERROR
			STATUS_UNHANDLED_EXCEPTION
			STATUS_UNSUPPORTED_COMPRESSION
			STATUS_UNWIND
			STATUS_VDM_HARD_ERROR
			STATUS_VOLUME_DISMOUNTED
			STATUS_WAKE_SYSTEM_DEBUGGER
			STATUS_WOW_ASSERTION
			STATUS_WX86_FLOAT_STACK_CHECK
			STATUS_WX86_INTERNAL_ERROR
487	ERROR_INVALID_ADDRESS	Attempt to access invalid address.	STATUS_CONFLICTING_ADDRESSES
			STATUS_FREE_VM_NOT_AT_BASE
			STATUS_MEMORY_NOT_ALLOCATED
			STATUS_NOT_COMMITTED
			STATUS_NOT_MAPPED_DATA
			STATUS_NOT_MAPPED_VIEW
			STATUS_UNABLE_TO_DECOMMIT_VM
534	ERROR_ARITHMETIC_OVERFLOW	Arithmetic result exceeded 32 bits.	STATUS_INTEGER_OVERFLOW
535	ERROR_PIPE_CONNECTED	There is a process on other end of the pipe.	STATUS_PIPE_CONNECTED
536	ERROR_PIPE_LISTENING	Waiting for a process to open the other end of the pipe.	STATUS_PIPE_LISTENING
995	ERROR_OPERATION_ABORTED	The I/O operation has been aborted because of either a thread exit or an application request.	STATUS_CANCELLED
998	ERROR_NOACCESS	Invalid access to memory location.	STATUS_ACCESS_VIOLATION
			STATUS_DATATYPE_MISALIGNMENT
999	ERROR_SWAPERROR	Error performing inpage operation.	STATUS_IN_PAGE_ERROR
1001	ERROR_STACK_OVERFLOW	Recursion too deep, stack overflowed.	STATUS_BAD_INITIAL_STACK
			STATUS_STACK_OVERFLOW

Table B.2: *Application Error Codes (numeric) to* NTSTATUS *Values (continued)*

Application Error Code		Explanation	NTSTATUS Name
Value	Name		
1005	ERROR_UNRECOGNIZED_VOLUME	The volume does not contain a recognized file system. Please make sure that all required file system drivers are loaded and that the volume is not corrupt.	STATUS_UNRECOGNIZED_VOLUME
1006	ERROR_FILE_INVALID	The volume for a file has been externally altered such that the opened file is no longer valid.	STATUS_FILE_INVALID STATUS_MAPPED_FILE_SIZE_ZERO
1007	ERROR_FULLSCREEN_MODE	The requested operation cannot be performed in full-screen mode.	STATUS_FULLSCREEN_MODE
1008	ERROR_NO_TOKEN	An attempt was made to reference a token that does not exist.	STATUS_NO_TOKEN
1009	ERROR_BADDB	The configuration registry database is corrupt.	STATUS_REGISTRY_CORRUPT
1016	ERROR_REGISTRY_IO_FAILED	An I/O operation initiated by the Registry failed unrecoverably. The Registry could not read in, or write out, or flush, one of the files that contain the system's image of the Registry.	STATUS_REGISTRY_IO_FAILED
1017	ERROR_NOT_REGISTRY_FILE	The system has attempted to load or restore a file into the Registry, but the specified file is not in a Registry file format.	STATUS_NOT_REGISTRY_FILE
1018	ERROR_KEY_DELETED	Illegal operation attempted on a Registry key which has been marked for deletion.	STATUS_KEY_DELETED
1019	ERROR_NO_LOG_SPACE	System could not allocate the required space in a Registry log.	STATUS_NO_LOG_SPACE
1020	ERROR_KEY_HAS_CHILDREN	Cannot create a symbolic link in a Registry key that already has subkeys or values.	STATUS_KEY_HAS_CHILDREN
1021	ERROR_CHILD_MUST_BE_VOLATILE	Cannot create a stable subkey under a volatile parent key.	STATUS_CHILD_MUST_BE_VOLATILE
1056	ERROR_SERVICE_ALREADY_RUNNING	An instance of the service is already running.	STATUS_IMAGE_ALREADY_LOADED
1058	ERROR_SERVICE_DISABLED	The specified service is disabled and cannot be started.	STATUS_PLUGPLAY_NO_DEVICE
1100	ERROR_END_OF_MEDIA	The physical end of the tape has been reached.	STATUS_END_OF_MEDIA
1101	ERROR_FILEMARK_DETECTED	A tape access reached a filemark.	STATUS_FILEMARK_DETECTED
1102	ERROR_BEGINNING_OF_MEDIA	Beginning of tape or partition was encountered.	STATUS_BEGINNING_OF_MEDIA
1103	ERROR_SETMARK_DETECTED	A tape access reached the end of a set of files.	STATUS_SETMARK_DETECTED
1104	ERROR_NO_DATA_DETECTED	No more data is on the tape.	STATUS_NO_DATA_DETECTED

Table B.2: *Application Error Codes (numeric) to NTSTATUS Values (continued)*

Application Error Code		Explanation	NTSTATUS Name
Value	Name		
1105	ERROR_PARTITION_FAILURE	Tape could not be partitioned.	STATUS_PARTITION_FAILURE
1106	ERROR_INVALID_BLOCK_LENGTH	When accessing a new tape of a multi-volume partition, the current block size is incorrect.	STATUS_INVALID_BLOCK_LENGTH
1107	ERROR_DEVICE_NOT_PARTITIONED	Tape partition information could not be found when loading a tape.	STATUS_DEVICE_NOT_PARTITIONED
1108	ERROR_UNABLE_TO_LOCK_MEDIA	Unable to lock the media eject mechanism.	STATUS_UNABLE_TO_LOCK_MEDIA
1109	ERROR_UNABLE_TO_UNLOAD_MEDIA	Unable to unload the media.	STATUS_UNABLE_TO_UNLOAD_MEDIA
1110	ERROR_MEDIA_CHANGED	Media in drive may have changed.	STATUS_VERIFY_REQUIRED
			STATUS_MEDIA_CHANGED
1111	ERROR_BUS_RESET	The I/O bus was reset.	STATUS_BUS_RESET
1112	ERROR_NO_MEDIA_IN_DRIVE	No media in drive.	STATUS_NO_MEDIA
1113	ERROR_NO_UNICODE_TRANSLATION	No mapping for the Unicode character exists in the target multi-byte code page.	STATUS_UNMAPPABLE_CHARACTER
1114	ERROR_DLL_INIT_FAILED	A dynamic link library (DLL) initialization routine failed.	STATUS_DLL_INIT_FAILED
1117	ERROR_IO_DEVICE	The request could not be performed because of an I/O device error.	STATUS_DATA_LATE_ERROR
			STATUS_DATA_OVERRUN
			STATUS_DEVICE_PROTOCOL_ERROR
			STATUS_DRIVER_INTERNAL_ERROR
			STATUS_FT_MISSING_MEMBER
			STATUS_FT_ORPHANING
			STATUS_IO_DEVICE_ERROR
1118	ERROR_SERIAL_NO_DEVICE	No serial device was successfully initialized. The serial driver will unload.	STATUS_SERIAL_NO_DEVICE_INITED
1119	ERROR_IRQ_BUSY	Unable to open a device that was sharing an interrupt request (IRQ) with other devices. At least one other device that uses that IRQ was already opened.	STATUS_SHARED_IRQ_BUSY
1122	ERROR_FLOPPY_ID_MARK_NOT_FOUND	No ID address mark was found on the floppy disk.	STATUS_FLOPPY_ID_MARK_NOT_FOUND
1123	ERROR_FLOPPY_WRONG_CYLINDER	Mismatch between the floppy disk sector ID field and the floppy disk controller track address.	STATUS_FLOPPY_WRONG_CYLINDER
1124	ERROR_FLOPPY_UNKNOWN_ERROR	The floppy disk controller reported an error that is not recognized by the floppy disk driver.	STATUS_FLOPPY_UNKNOWN_ERROR
1125	ERROR_FLOPPY_BAD_REGISTERS	The floppy disk controller returned inconsistent results in its registers.	STATUS_FLOPPY_BAD_REGISTERS

Table B.2: *Application Error Codes (numeric) to NTSTATUS Values (continued)*

Application Error Code		Explanation	NTSTATUS Name
Value	Name		
1126	ERROR_DISK_RECALIBRATE_FAILED	While accessing the hard disk, a recalibrate operation failed, even after retries.	STATUS_DISK_RECALIBRATE_ FAILED
1127	ERROR_DISK_OPERATION_FAILED	While accessing the hard disk, a disk operation failed, even after retries.	STATUS_DISK_OPERATION_FAILED
1128	ERROR_DISK_RESET_FAILED	While accessing the hard disk, a disk controller reset was needed, but even that failed.	STATUS_DISK_RESET_FAILED
1129	ERROR_EOM_OVERFLOW	Physical end of tape encountered.	STATUS_EOM_OVERFLOW
1130	ERROR_NOT_ENOUGH_SERVER_ MEMORY	Not enough server storage is available to process this command.	STATUS_INSUFF_SERVER_ RESOURCES
1131	ERROR_POSSIBLE_DEADLOCK	A potential deadlock condition has been detected.	STATUS_POSSIBLE_DEADLOCK
1132	ERROR_MAPPED_ALIGNMENT	The base address or the file offset specified does not have the proper alignment.	STATUS_MAPPED_ALIGNMENT
1142	ERROR_TOO_MANY_LINKS	An attempt was made to create more links on a file than the file system supports.	STATUS_TOO_MANY_LINKS
1210	ERROR_INVALID_COMPUTERNAME	The format of the specified computer name is invalid.	STATUS_INVALID_COMPUTER_NAME
1214	ERROR_INVALID_NETNAME	The format of the specified network name is invalid.	STATUS_INVALID_ADDRESS_ COMPONENT
			STATUS_INVALID_ADDRESS_ WILDCARD
1219	ERROR_SESSION_CREDENTIAL_ CONFLICT	The credentials supplied conflict with an existing set of credentials.	STATUS_NETWORK_CREDENTIAL_ CONFLICT
1220	ERROR_REMOTE_SESSION_ LIMIT_EXCEEDED	An attempt was made to establish a session to a network server, but there are already too many sessions established to that server.	STATUS_REMOTE_SESSION_LIMIT
1224	ERROR_USER_MAPPED_FILE	The requested operation cannot be performed on a file with a user-mapped section open.	STATUS_USER_MAPPED_FILE
1225	ERROR_CONNECTION_REFUSED	The remote system refused the network connection.	STATUS_CONNECTION_REFUSED
1226	ERROR_GRACEFUL_DISCONNECT	The network connection was gracefully closed.	STATUS_GRACEFUL_DISCONNECT
1227	ERROR_ADDRESS_ALREADY_ ASSOCIATED	The network transport endpoint already has an address associated with it.	STATUS_ADDRESS_ALREADY_ ASSOCIATED
1228	ERROR_ADDRESS_NOT_ASSOCIATED	An address has not yet been associated with the network endpoint.	STATUS_ADDRESS_NOT_ASSOCIATED
1229	ERROR_CONNECTION_INVALID	An operation was attempted on a nonexistent network connection.	STATUS_CONNECTION_INVALID
1230	ERROR_CONNECTION_ACTIVE	An invalid operation was attempted on an active network connection.	STATUS_CONNECTION_ACTIVE

Table B.2: *Application Error Codes (numeric) to* NTSTATUS *Values (continued)*

Application Error Code		Explanation	NTSTATUS Name
Value	**Name**		
1231	ERROR_NETWORK_UNREACHABLE	The remote network is not reachable by the transport.	STATUS_NETWORK_UNREACHABLE
1232	ERROR_HOST_UNREACHABLE	The remote system is not reachable by the transport.	STATUS_HOST_UNREACHABLE
			STATUS_PATH_NOT_COVERED
1233	ERROR_PROTOCOL_UNREACHABLE	The remote system does not support the transport protocol.	STATUS_PROTOCOL_UNREACHABLE
1234	ERROR_PORT_UNREACHABLE	No service is operating at the destination network endpoint on the remote system.	STATUS_PORT_UNREACHABLE
1235	ERROR_REQUEST_ABORTED	The request was aborted.	STATUS_REQUEST_ABORTED
1236	ERROR_CONNECTION_ABORTED	The network connection was aborted by the local system.	STATUS_CONNECTION_ABORTED
1238	ERROR_CONNECTION_COUNT_LIMIT	A connection to the server could not be made because the limit on the number of concurrent connections for this account has been reached.	STATUS_CONNECTION_COUNT_LIMIT
1239	ERROR_LOGIN_TIME_RESTRICTION	Attempting to login during an unauthorized time of day for this account.	STATUS_LOGIN_TIME_RESTRICTION
1240	ERROR_LOGIN_WKSTA_RESTRICTION	The account is not authorized to login from this station.	STATUS_LOGIN_WKSTA_ RESTRICTION
1305	ERROR_UNKNOWN_REVISION	The revision level is unknown.	STATUS_UNKNOWN_REVISION
1306	ERROR_REVISION_MISMATCH	Indicates two revision levels are incompatible.	STATUS_REVISION_MISMATCH
1307	ERROR_INVALID_OWNER	This security ID may not be assigned as the owner of this object.	STATUS_INVALID_OWNER
1308	ERROR_INVALID_PRIMARY_GROUP	This security ID may not be assigned as the primary group of an object.	STATUS_INVALID_PRIMARY_GROUP
1309	ERROR_NO_IMPERSONATION_TOKEN	An attempt has been made to operate on an impersonation token by a thread that is not currently impersonating a client.	STATUS_NO_IMPERSONATION_TOKEN
1310	ERROR_CANT_DISABLE_MANDATORY	The group may not be disabled.	STATUS_CANT_DISABLE_MANDATORY
1311	ERROR_NO_LOGON_SERVERS	There are currently no logon servers available to service the logon request.	STATUS_NO_LOGON_SERVERS
1312	ERROR_NO_SUCH_LOGON_SESSION	A specified logon session does not exist. It may already have been terminated.	STATUS_NO_SUCH_LOGON_SESSION
1313	ERROR_NO_SUCH_PRIVILEGE	A specified privilege does not exist.	STATUS_NO_SUCH_PRIVILEGE
1314	ERROR_PRIVILEGE_NOT_HELD	A required privilege is not held by the client.	STATUS_PRIVILEGE_NOT_HELD
1315	ERROR_INVALID_ACCOUNT_NAME	The name provided is not a properly formed account name.	STATUS_INVALID_ACCOUNT_NAME
1316	ERROR_USER_EXISTS	The specified user already exists.	STATUS_USER_EXISTS

Table B.2: *Application Error Codes (numeric) to* NTSTATUS *Values (continued)*

Application Error Code		Explanation	NTSTATUS Name
Value	Name		
1317	ERROR_NO_SUCH_USER	The specified user does not exist.	STATUS_NO_SUCH_USER
1318	ERROR_GROUP_EXISTS	The specified group already exists.	STATUS_GROUP_EXISTS
1319	ERROR_NO_SUCH_GROUP	The specified group does not exist.	STATUS_NO_SUCH_GROUP
1320	ERROR_MEMBER_IN_GROUP	Either the specified user account is already a member of the specified group, or the specified group cannot be deleted because it contains a member.	STATUS_MEMBER_IN_GROUP
1321	ERROR_MEMBER_NOT_IN_GROUP	The specified user account is not a member of the specified group account.	STATUS_MEMBER_NOT_IN_GROUP
1322	ERROR_LAST_ADMIN	The last remaining administration account cannot be disabled or deleted.	STATUS_LAST_ADMIN
1324	ERROR_ILL_FORMED_PASSWORD	Unable to update the password. The value provided for the new password contains values that are not allowed in passwords.	STATUS_ILL_FORMED_PASSWORD
1325	ERROR_PASSWORD_RESTRICTION	Unable to update the password because a password update rule has been violated.	STATUS_PASSWORD_RESTRICTION
1326	ERROR_LOGON_FAILURE	Logon failure: unknown user name or bad password.	STATUS_LOGON_FAILURE
1327	ERROR_ACCOUNT_RESTRICTION	Logon failure: user account restriction.	STATUS_ACCOUNT_RESTRICTION
1328	ERROR_INVALID_LOGON_HOURS	Logon failure: account logon time restriction violation.	STATUS_INVALID_LOGON_HOURS
1329	ERROR_INVALID_WORKSTATION	Logon failure: user not allowed to log on to this computer.	STATUS_INVALID_WORKSTATION
1330	ERROR_PASSWORD_EXPIRED	Logon failure: the specified account password has expired.	STATUS_PASSWORD_EXPIRED
1331	ERROR_ACCOUNT_DISABLED	Logon failure: account currently disabled.	STATUS_ACCOUNT_DISABLED
1332	ERROR_NONE_MAPPED	No mapping between account names and security IDs was done.	STATUS_NONE_MAPPED
1333	ERROR_TOO_MANY_LUIDS_REQUESTED	Too many local user identifiers (LUIDs) were requested at one time.	STATUS_TOO_MANY_LUIDS_REQUESTED
1334	ERROR_LUIDS_EXHAUSTED	No more local user identifiers (LUIDs) are available.	STATUS_LUIDS_EXHAUSTED
1335	ERROR_INVALID_SUB_AUTHORITY	The subauthority part of a security ID is invalid for this particular use.	STATUS_INVALID_SUB_AUTHORITY
1336	ERROR_INVALID_ACL	The access control list (ACL) structure is invalid.	STATUS_INVALID_ACL
1337	ERROR_INVALID_SID	The security ID structure is invalid.	STATUS_INVALID_SID
1338	ERROR_INVALID_SECURITY_DESCR	The security descriptor structure is invalid.	STATUS_INVALID_SECURITY_DESCR

Table B.2: *Application Error Codes (numeric) to* NTSTATUS *Values (continued)*

Application Error Code		Explanation	NTSTATUS Name
Value	Name		
1340	ERROR_BAD_TNHFRTTANCE_ACL	The inherited access control list (ACL) or access control entry (ACE) could not be built.	STATUS_BAD_INHERITANCE_ACL
1341	ERROR_SERVER_DISABLED	The server is currently disabled.	STATUS_SERVER_DISABLED
1342	ERROR_SERVER_NOT_DISABLED	The server is currently enabled.	STATUS_SERVER_NOT_DISABLED
1343	ERROR_INVALID_ID_AUTHORITY	The value provided was an invalid value for an identifier authority.	STATUS_INVALID_ID_AUTHORITY
1344	ERROR_ALLOTTED_SPACE_EXCEEDED	No more memory is available for security information updates.	STATUS_ALLOTTED_SPACE_EXCEEDED
1345	ERROR_INVALID_GROUP_ATTRIBUTES	The specified attributes are invalid, or incompatible with the attributes for the group as a whole.	STATUS_INVALID_GROUP_ATTRIBUTES
1346	ERROR_BAD_IMPERSONATION_LEVEL	Either a required impersonation level was not provided, or the provided impersonation level is invalid.	STATUS_BAD_IMPERSONATION_LEVEL
1347	ERROR_CANT_OPEN_ANONYMOUS	Cannot open an anonymous level security token.	STATUS_CANT_OPEN_ANONYMOUS
1348	ERROR_BAD_VALIDATION_CLASS	The validation information class requested was invalid.	STATUS_BAD_VALIDATION_CLASS
1349	ERROR_BAD_TOKEN_TYPE	The type of the token is inappropriate for its attempted use.	STATUS_BAD_TOKEN_TYPE
1350	ERROR_NO_SECURITY_ON_OBJECT	Unable to perform a security operation on an object which has no associated security.	STATUS_NO_SECURITY_ON_OBJECT
1351	ERROR_CANT_ACCESS_DOMAIN_INFO	Indicates a Windows NT Server could not be contacted or that objects within the domain are protected such that necessary information could not be retrieved.	STATUS_CANT_ACCESS_DOMAIN_INFO
1352	ERROR_INVALID_SERVER_STATE	The security account manager (SAM) or local security authority (LSA) server was in the wrong state to perform the security operation.	STATUS_INVALID_SERVER_STATE
1353	ERROR_INVALID_DOMAIN_STATE	The domain was in the wrong state to perform the security operation.	STATUS_INVALID_DOMAIN_STATE
1354	ERROR_INVALID_DOMAIN_ROLE	This operation is allowed only for the Primary Domain Controller of the domain.	STATUS_INVALID_DOMAIN_ROLE
1355	ERROR_NO_SUCH_DOMAIN	The specified domain did not exist.	STATUS_NO_SUCH_DOMAIN
1356	ERROR_DOMAIN_EXISTS	The specified domain already exists.	STATUS_DOMAIN_EXISTS
1357	ERROR_DOMAIN_LIMIT_EXCEEDED	An attempt was made to exceed the limit on the number of domains per server.	STATUS_DOMAIN_LIMIT_EXCEEDED

Table B.2: *Application Error Codes (numeric) to* NTSTATUS *Values (continued)*

Application Error Code		Explanation	NTSTATUS Name
Value	Name		
1358	ERROR_INTERNAL_DB_CORRUPTION	Unable to complete the requested operation because of either a catastrophic media failure or a data structure corruption on the disk.	STATUS_INTERNAL_DB_CORRUPTION
1359	ERROR_INTERNAL_ERROR	The security account database contains an internal inconsistency.	STATUS_INTERNAL_ERROR
			STATUS_LPC_REPLY_LOST
1360	ERROR_GENERIC_NOT_MAPPED	Generic access types were contained in an access mask which should already be mapped to non-generic types.	STATUS_GENERIC_NOT_MAPPED
1361	ERROR_BAD_DESCRIPTOR_FORMAT	A security descriptor is not in the right format (absolute or self-relative).	STATUS_BAD_DESCRIPTOR_FORMAT
1362	ERROR_NOT_LOGON_PROCESS	The requested action is restricted for use by logon processes only. The calling process has not registered as a logon process.	STATUS_NOT_LOGON_PROCESS
1363	ERROR_LOGON_SESSION_EXISTS	Cannot start a new logon session with an ID that is already in use.	STATUS_LOGON_SESSION_EXISTS
1364	ERROR_NO_SUCH_PACKAGE	A specified authentication package is unknown.	STATUS_NO_SUCH_PACKAGE
1365	ERROR_BAD_LOGON_SESSION_STATE	The logon session is not in a state that is consistent with the requested operation.	STATUS_BAD_LOGON_SESSION_STATE
1366	ERROR_LOGON_SESSION_COLLISION	The logon session ID is already in use.	STATUS_LOGON_SESSION_COLLISION
1367	ERROR_INVALID_LOGON_TYPE	A logon request contained an invalid logon type value.	STATUS_INVALID_LOGON_TYPE
1368	ERROR_CANNOT_IMPERSONATE	Unable to impersonate via a named pipe until data has been read from that pipe.	STATUS_CANNOT_IMPERSONATE
1369	ERROR_RXACT_INVALID_STATE	The transaction state of a Registry subtree is incompatible with the requested operation.	STATUS_RXACT_INVALID_STATE
1370	ERROR_RXACT_COMMIT_FAILURE	An internal security database corruption has been encountered.	STATUS_RXACT_COMMIT_FAILURE
1371	ERROR_SPECIAL_ACCOUNT	Cannot perform this operation on built-in accounts.	STATUS_SPECIAL_ACCOUNT
1372	ERROR_SPECIAL_GROUP	Cannot perform this operation on this built-in special group.	STATUS_SPECIAL_GROUP
1373	ERROR_SPECIAL_USER	Cannot perform this operation on this built-in special user.	STATUS_SPECIAL_USER
1374	ERROR_MEMBERS_PRIMARY_GROUP	The user cannot be removed from a group because the group is currently the user's primary group.	STATUS_MEMBERS_PRIMARY_GROUP
1375	ERROR_TOKEN_ALREADY_IN_USE	The token is already in use as a primary token.	STATUS_TOKEN_ALREADY_IN_USE
1376	ERROR_NO_SUCH_ALIAS	The specified local group does not exist.	STATUS_NO_SUCH_ALIAS

Table B.2: *Application Error Codes (numeric) to NTSTATUS Values (continued)*

Application Error Code		Explanation	NTSTATUS Name
Value	**Name**		
1377	ERROR_MEMBER_NOT_IN_ALIAS	The specified account name is not a member of the local group.	STATUS_MEMBER_NOT_IN_ALIAS
1378	ERROR_MEMBER_IN_ALIAS	The specified account name is already a member of the local group.	STATUS_MEMBER_IN_ALIAS
1379	ERROR_ALIAS_EXISTS	The specified local group already exists.	STATUS_ALIAS_EXISTS
1380	ERROR_LOGON_NOT_GRANTED	Logon failure: the user has not been granted the requested logon type at this computer.	STATUS_LOGON_NOT_GRANTED
1381	ERROR_TOO_MANY_SECRETS	The maximum number of secrets that may be stored in a single system has been exceeded.	STATUS_TOO_MANY_SECRETS
1382	ERROR_SECRET_TOO_LONG	The length of a secret exceeds the maximum length allowed.	STATUS_SECRET_TOO_LONG
1383	ERROR_INTERNAL_DB_ERROR	The local security authority database contains an internal inconsistency.	STATUS_INTERNAL_DB_ERROR
1384	ERROR_TOO_MANY_CONTEXT_IDS	During a logon attempt, the user's security context accumulated too many security IDs.	STATUS_TOO_MANY_CONTEXT_IDS
1385	ERROR_LOGON_TYPE_NOT_GRANTED	Logon failure: the user has not been granted the requested logon type at this computer.	STATUS_LOGON_TYPE_NOT_GRANTED
1386	ERROR_NT_CROSS_ENCRYPTION_REQUIRED	A cross-encrypted password is necessary to change a user password.	STATUS_NT_CROSS_ENCRYPTION_REQUIRED
1387	ERROR_NO_SUCH_MEMBER	A new member could not be added to a local group because the member does not exist.	STATUS_NO_SUCH_MEMBER
1388	ERROR_INVALID_MEMBER	A new member could not be added to a local group because the member has the wrong account type.	STATUS_INVALID_MEMBER
1389	ERROR_TOO_MANY_SIDS	Too many security IDs have been specified.	STATUS_TOO_MANY_SIDS
1390	ERROR_LM_CROSS_ENCRYPTION_REQUIRED	A cross-encrypted password is necessary to change this user password.	STATUS_LM_CROSS_ENCRYPTION_REQUIRED
1391	ERROR_NO_INHERITANCE	Indicates an ACL contains no inheritable components.	STATUS_NO_INHERITANCE
1392	ERROR_FILE_CORRUPT	The file or directory is corrupt and non-readable.	STATUS_EA_CORRUPT_ERROR
			STATUS_FILE_CORRUPT_ERROR
			STATUS_NO_EAS_ON_FILE
			STATUS_NONEXISTENT_EA_ENTRY
1393	ERROR_DISK_CORRUPT	The disk structure is corrupt and non-readable.	STATUS_DISK_CORRUPT_ERROR
1394	ERROR_NO_USER_SESSION_KEY	There is no user session key for the specified logon session.	STATUS_NO_USER_SESSION_KEY

Table B.2: *Application Error Codes (numeric) to* NTSTATUS *Values (continued)*

Application Error Code		Explanation	NTSTATUS Name
Value	Name		
1395	ERROR_LICENSE_QUOTA_EXCEEDED	The service being accessed is licensed for a particular number of connections. No more connections can be made to the service at this time because there are already as many connections as the service can accept.	STATUS_LICENSE_QUOTA_EXCEEDED
1450	ERROR_NO_SYSTEM_RESOURCES	Insufficient system resources exist to complete the requested service.	STATUS_INSUFFICIENT_RESOURCES
1453	ERROR_WORKING_SET_QUOTA	Insufficient quota to complete the requested service.	STATUS_WORKING_SET_QUOTA
1454	ERROR_PAGEFILE_QUOTA	Insufficient quota to complete the requested service.	STATUS_PAGEFILE_QUOTA
1455	ERROR_COMMITMENT_LIMIT	The paging file is too small for this operation to complete.	STATUS_COMMITMENT_LIMIT
1500	ERROR_EVENTLOG_FILE_CORRUPT	The event log file is corrupt.	STATUS_EVENTLOG_FILE_CORRUPT
1501	ERROR_EVENTLOG_CANT_START	No event log file could be opened, so the event logging service did not start.	STATUS_EVENTLOG_CANT_START
1502	ERROR_LOG_FILE_FULL	The event log file is full.	STATUS_LOG_FILE_FULL
1503	ERROR_EVENTLOG_FILE_CHANGED	The event log file has changed between reads.	STATUS_EVENTLOG_FILE_CHANGED
1700	RPC_S_INVALID_STRING_BINDING	The string binding is invalid.	RPC_NT_INVALID_STRING_BINDING
1701	RPC_S_WRONG_KIND_OF_BINDING	The binding handle is not the correct type.	RPC_NT_WRONG_KIND_OF_BINDING
1703	RPC_S_PROTSEQ_NOT_SUPPORTED	The RPC protocol sequence is not supported.	RPC_NT_PROTSEQ_NOT_SUPPORTED
1704	RPC_S_INVALID_RPC_PROTSEQ	The RPC protocol sequence is invalid.	RPC_NT_INVALID_RPC_PROTSEQ
1705	RPC_S_INVALID_STRING_UUID	The string universal unique identifier (UUID) is invalid.	RPC_NT_INVALID_STRING_UUID
1706	RPC_S_INVALID_ENDPOINT_FORMAT	The endpoint format is invalid.	RPC_NT_INVALID_ENDPOINT_FORMAT
1707	RPC_S_INVALID_NET_ADDR	The network address is invalid.	RPC_NT_INVALID_NET_ADDR
1708	RPC_S_NO_ENDPOINT_FOUND	No endpoint was found.	RPC_NT_NO_ENDPOINT_FOUND
1709	RPC_S_INVALID_TIMEOUT	The timeout value is invalid.	RPC_NT_INVALID_TIMEOUT
1710	RPC_S_OBJECT_NOT_FOUND	The object universal unique identifier (UUID) was not found.	RPC_NT_OBJECT_NOT_FOUND
1711	RPC_S_ALREADY_REGISTERED	The object universal unique identifier (UUID) has already been registered.	RPC_NT_ALREADY_REGISTERED
1712	RPC_S_TYPE_ALREADY_REGISTERED	The type universal unique identifier (UUID) has already been registered.	RPC_NT_TYPE_ALREADY_REGISTERED
1713	RPC_S_ALREADY_LISTENING	The RPC server is already listening.	RPC_NT_ALREADY_LISTENING

Table B.2: *Application Error Codes (numeric) to* NTSTATUS *Values (continued)*

Application Error Code		Explanation	NTSTATUS Name
Value	Name		
1714	RPC_S_NO_PROTSEQS_REGISTERED	No protocol sequences have been registered.	RPC_NT_NO_PROTSEQS_REGISTERED
1715	RPC_S_NOT_LISTENING	The RPC server is not listening.	RPC_NT_NOT_LISTENING
1716	RPC_S_UNKNOWN_MGR_TYPE	The manager type is unknown.	RPC_NT_UNKNOWN_MGR_TYPE
1717	RPC_S_UNKNOWN_IF	The interface is unknown.	RPC_NT_UNKNOWN_IF
1718	RPC_S_NO_BINDINGS	There are no bindings.	RPC_NT_NO_BINDINGS
1719	RPC_S_NO_PROTSEQS	There are no protocol sequences.	RPC_NT_NO_PROTSEQS
1720	RPC_S_CANT_CREATE_ENDPOINT	The endpoint cannot be created.	RPC_NT_CANT_CREATE_ENDPOINT
1721	RPC_S_OUT_OF_RESOURCES	Not enough resources are available to complete this operation.	RPC_NT_OUT_OF_RESOURCES
1722	RPC_S_SERVER_UNAVAILABLE	The RPC server is unavailable.	RPC_NT_SERVER_UNAVAILABLE
1723	RPC_S_SERVER_TOO_BUSY	The RPC server is too busy to complete this operation.	RPC_NT_SERVER_TOO_BUSY
1724	RPC_S_INVALID_NETWORK_OPTIONS	The network options are invalid.	RPC_NT_INVALID_NETWORK_OPTIONS
1725	RPC_S_NO_CALL_ACTIVE	There is not a remote procedure call active in this thread.	RPC_NT_NO_CALL_ACTIVE
1726	RPC_S_CALL_FAILED	The remote procedure call failed.	RPC_NT_CALL_FAILED
1727	RPC_S_CALL_FAILED_DNE	The remote procedure call failed and did not execute.	RPC_NT_CALL_FAILED_DNE
1728	RPC_S_PROTOCOL_ERROR	A remote procedure call (RPC) protocol error occurred.	RPC_NT_PROTOCOL_ERROR
1730	RPC_S_UNSUPPORTED_TRANS_SYN	The transfer syntax is not supported by the RPC server.	RPC_NT_UNSUPPORTED_TRANS_SYN
1732	RPC_S_UNSUPPORTED_TYPE	The universal unique identifier (UUID) type is not supported.	RPC_NT_UNSUPPORTED_TYPE
1733	RPC_S_INVALID_TAG	The tag is invalid.	RPC_NT_INVALID_TAG
1734	RPC_S_INVALID_BOUND	The array bounds are invalid.	RPC_NT_INVALID_BOUND
1735	RPC_S_NO_ENTRY_NAME	The binding does not contain an entry name.	RPC_NT_NO_ENTRY_NAME
1736	RPC_S_INVALID_NAME_SYNTAX	The name syntax is invalid.	RPC_NT_INVALID_NAME_SYNTAX
1737	RPC_S_UNSUPPORTED_NAME_SYNTAX	The name syntax is not supported.	RPC_NT_UNSUPPORTED_NAME_SYNTAX
1739	RPC_S_UUID_NO_ADDRESS	No network address is available to use to construct a universal unique identifier (UUID).	RPC_NT_UUID_NO_ADDRESS
1740	RPC_S_DUPLICATE_ENDPOINT	The endpoint is a duplicate.	RPC_NT_DUPLICATE_ENDPOINT
1741	RPC_S_UNKNOWN_AUTHN_TYPE	The authentication type is unknown.	RPC_NT_UNKNOWN_AUTHN_TYPE

Table B.2: *Application Error Codes (numeric) to* NTSTATUS *Values (continued)*

Application Error Code		Explanation	NTSTATUS Name
Value	**Name**		
1742	RPC_S_MAX_CALLS_TOO_SMALL	The maximum number of calls is too small.	RPC_NT_MAX_CALLS_TOO_SMALL
1743	RPC_S_STRING_TOO_LONG	The string is too long.	RPC_NT_STRING_TOO_LONG
1744	RPC_S_PROTSEQ_NOT_FOUND	The RPC protocol sequence was not found.	RPC_NT_PROTSEQ_NOT_FOUND
1745	RPC_S_PROCNUM_OUT_OF_RANGE	The procedure number is out of range.	RPC_NT_PROCNUM_OUT_OF_RANGE
1746	RPC_S_BINDING_HAS_NO_AUTH	The binding does not contain any authentication information.	RPC_NT_BINDING_HAS_NO_AUTH
1747	RPC_S_UNKNOWN_AUTHN_SERVICE	The authentication service is unknown.	RPC_NT_UNKNOWN_AUTHN_SERVICE
1748	RPC_S_UNKNOWN_AUTHN_LEVEL	The authentication level is unknown.	RPC_NT_UNKNOWN_AUTHN_LEVEL
1749	RPC_S_INVALID_AUTH_IDENTITY	The security context is invalid.	RPC_NT_INVALID_AUTH_IDENTITY
1750	RPC_S_UNKNOWN_AUTHZ_SERVICE	The authorization service is unknown.	RPC_NT_UNKNOWN_AUTHZ_SERVICE
1751	EPT_S_INVALID_ENTRY	The entry is invalid.	EPT_NT_INVALID_ENTRY
1752	EPT_S_CANT_PERFORM_OP	The server endpoint cannot perform the operation.	EPT_NT_CANT_PERFORM_OP
1753	EPT_S_NOT_REGISTERED	There are no more endpoints available from the endpoint mapper.	EPT_NT_NOT_REGISTERED
1754	RPC_S_NOTHING_TO_EXPORT	No interfaces have been exported.	RPC_NT_NOTHING_TO_EXPORT
1755	RPC_S_INCOMPLETE_NAME	The entry name is incomplete.	RPC_NT_INCOMPLETE_NAME
1756	RPC_S_INVALID_VERS_OPTION	The version option is invalid.	RPC_NT_INVALID_VERS_OPTION
1757	RPC_S_NO_MORE_MEMBERS	There are no more members.	RPC_NT_NO_MORE_MEMBERS
1758	RPC_S_NOT_ALL_OBJS_UNEXPORTED	There is nothing to unexport.	RPC_NT_NOT_ALL_OBJS_ UNEXPORTED
1759	RPC_S_INTERFACE_NOT_FOUND	The interface was not found.	RPC_NT_INTERFACE_NOT_FOUND
1760	RPC_S_ENTRY_ALREADY_EXISTS	The entry already exists.	RPC_NT_ENTRY_ALREADY_EXISTS
1761	RPC_S_ENTRY_NOT_FOUND	The entry is not found.	RPC_NT_ENTRY_NOT_FOUND
1762	RPC_S_NAME_SERVICE_ UNAVAILABLE	The name service is unavailable.	RPC_NT_NAME_SERVICE_ UNAVAILABLE
1763	RPC_S_INVALID_NAF_ID	The network address family is invalid.	RPC_NT_INVALID_NAF_ID
1764	RPC_S_CANNOT_SUPPORT	The requested operation is not supported.	RPC_NT_CANNOT_SUPPORT
1765	RPC_S_NO_CONTEXT_AVAILABLE	No security context is available to allow impersonation.	RPC_NT_NO_CONTEXT_AVAILABLE
1766	RPC_S_INTERNAL_ERROR	An internal error occurred in a remote procedure call (RPC).	RPC_NT_INTERNAL_ERROR
1767	RPC_S_ZERO_DIVIDE	The RPC server attempted an integer division by zero.	RPC_NT_ZERO_DIVIDE

Table B.2: *Application Error Codes (numeric) to* NTSTATUS *Values (continued)*

Application Error Code		Explanation	NTSTATUS Name
Value	**Name**		
1768	RPC_S_ADDRESS_ERROR	An addressing error occurred in the RPC server.	RPC_NT_ADDRESS_ERROR
1769	RPC_S_FP_DIV_ZERO	A floating-point operation at the RPC server caused a division by zero.	RPC_NT_FP_DIV_ZERO
1770	RPC_S_FP_UNDERFLOW	A floating-point underflow occurred at the RPC server.	RPC_NT_FP_UNDERFLOW
1771	RPC_S_FP_OVERFLOW	A floating-point overflow occurred at the RPC server.	RPC_NT_FP_OVERFLOW
1772	RPC_X_NO_MORE_ENTRIES	The list of RPC servers available for the binding of auto handles has been exhausted.	RPC_NT_NO_MORE_ENTRIES
1773	RPC_X_SS_CHAR_TRANS_OPEN_FAIL	Unable to open the character translation table file.	RPC_NT_SS_CHAR_TRANS_ OPEN_FAIL
1774	RPC_X_SS_CHAR_TRANS_ SHORT_FILE	The file containing the character translation table has fewer than 512 bytes.	RPC_NT_SS_CHAR_TRANS_ SHORT_FILE
1777	RPC_X_SS_CONTEXT_DAMAGED	The context handle changed during a remote procedure call.	RPC_NT_SS_CONTEXT_DAMAGED
1778	RPC_X_SS_HANDLES_MISMATCH	The binding handles passed to a remote procedure call do not match.	RPC_NT_SS_HANDLES_MISMATCH
1779	RPC_X_SS_CANNOT_GET_ CALL_HANDLE	The stub is unable to get the remote procedure call handle.	RPC_NT_SS_CANNOT_GET_ CALL_HANDLE
1780	RPC_X_NULL_REF_POINTER	A null reference pointer was passed to the stub.	RPC_NT_NULL_REF_POINTER
1781	RPC_X_ENUM_VALUE_OUT_OF_RANGE	The enumeration value is out of range.	RPC_NT_ENUM_VALUE_OUT_OF_ RANGE
1782	RPC_X_BYTE_COUNT_TOO_SMALL	The byte count is too small.	RPC_NT_BYTE_COUNT_TOO_SMALL
1783	RPC_X_BAD_STUB_DATA	The stub received bad data.	RPC_NT_BAD_STUB_DATA
1784	ERROR_INVALID_USER_BUFFER	The supplied user buffer is not valid for the requested operation.	STATUS_INVALID_USER_BUFFER
			STATUS_INVALID_BUFFER_SIZE
1785	ERROR_UNRECOGNIZED_MEDIA	The disk media is not recognized. It may not be formatted.	STATUS_UNRECOGNIZED_MEDIA
1786	ERROR_NO_TRUST_LSA_SECRET	The workstation does not have a trust secret.	STATUS_NO_TRUST_LSA_SECRET
1787	ERROR_NO_TRUST_SAM_ACCOUNT	The SAM database on the Windows NT Server does not have a computer account for this workstation trust relationship.	STATUS_NO_TRUST_SAM_ACCOUNT
1788	ERROR_TRUSTED_DOMAIN_FAILURE	The trust relationship between the primary domain and the trusted domain failed.	STATUS_TRUSTED_DOMAIN_FAILURE
1789	ERROR_TRUSTED_RELATIONSHIP_ FAILURE	The trust relationship between this workstation and the primary domain failed.	STATUS_TRUSTED_RELATIONSHIP_ FAILURE
1790	ERROR_TRUST_FAILURE	The network logon failed.	STATUS_TRUST_FAILURE

Table B.2: *Application Error Codes (numeric) to* NTSTATUS *Values (continued)*

Application Error Code		Explanation	NTSTATUS Name
Value	Name		
1791	RPC_S_CALL_IN_PROGRESS	A remote procedure call is already in progress for this thread.	RPC_NT_CALL_IN_PROGRESS
1792	ERROR_NETLOGON_NOT_STARTED	An attempt was made to log on, but the network logon service was not started.	STATUS_NETLOGON_NOT_STARTED
1793	ERROR_ACCOUNT_EXPIRED	The user's account has expired.	STATUS_ACCOUNT_EXPIRED
1806	RPC_S_NO_MORE_BINDINGS	There are no more bindings.	RPC_NT_NO_MORE_BINDINGS
1807	ERROR_NOLOGON_INTERDOMAIN_TRUST_ACCOUNT	The account used is an interdomain trust account. Use your global user account or local user account to access this server.	STATUS_NOLOGON_INTERDOMAIN_TRUST_ACCOUNT
1808	ERROR_NOLOGON_WORKSTATION_TRUST_ACCOUNT	The account used is a Computer Account. Use your global user account or local user account to access this server.	STATUS_NOLOGON_WORKSTATION_TRUST_ACCOUNT
1809	ERROR_NOLOGON_SERVER_TRUST_ACCOUNT	The account used is a server trust account. Use your global user account or local user account to access this server.	STATUS_NOLOGON_SERVER_TRUST_ACCOUNT
1810	ERROR_DOMAIN_TRUST_INCONSISTENT	The name or security ID (SID) of the domain specified is inconsistent with the trust information for that domain.	STATUS_DOMAIN_TRUST_INCONSISTENT
1812	ERROR_RESOURCE_DATA_NOT_FOUND	The specified image file did not contain a resource section.	STATUS_RESOURCE_DATA_NOT_FOUND
1813	ERROR_RESOURCE_TYPE_NOT_FOUND	The specified resource type cannot be found in the image file.	STATUS_RESOURCE_TYPE_NOT_FOUND
1814	ERROR_RESOURCE_NAME_NOT_FOUND	The specified resource name cannot be found in the image file.	STATUS_RESOURCE_NAME_NOT_FOUND
1815	ERROR_RESOURCE_LANG_NOT_FOUND	The specified resource language ID cannot be found in the image file.	STATUS_RESOURCE_LANG_NOT_FOUND
1816	ERROR_NOT_ENOUGH_QUOTA	Not enough quota is available to process this command.	STATUS_QUOTA_EXCEEDED
1817	RPC_S_NO_INTERFACES	No interfaces have been registered.	RPC_NT_NO_INTERFACES
1818	RPC_S_CALL_CANCELLED	The server was altered while processing this call.	RPC_NT_CALL_CANCELLED
1819	RPC_S_BINDING_INCOMPLETE	The binding handle does not contain all required information.	RPC_NT_BINDING_INCOMPLETE
1820	RPC_S_COMM_FAILURE	Communications failure.	RPC_NT_COMM_FAILURE
1821	RPC_S_UNSUPPORTED_AUTHN_LEVEL	The requested authentication level is not supported.	RPC_NT_UNSUPPORTED_AUTHN_LEVEL
1822	RPC_S_NO_PRINC_NAME	No principal name registered.	RPC_NT_NO_PRINC_NAME
1823	RPC_S_NOT_RPC_ERROR	The error specified is not a valid Windows NT RPC error code.	RPC_NT_NOT_RPC_ERROR

Table B.2: *Application Error Codes (numeric) to* NTSTATUS *Values (continued)*

Application Error Code		Explanation	NTSTATUS Name
Value	Name		
1825	RPC_S_SEC_PKG_ERROR	A security package specific error occurred.	RPC_NT_SEC_PKG_ERROR
1826	RPC_S_NOT_CANCELLED	Thread is not cancelled.	RPC_NT_NOT_CANCELLED
1827	RPC_X_INVALID_ES_ACTION	Invalid operation on the encoding/decoding handle.	RPC_NT_INVALID_ES_ACTION
1828	RPC_X_WRONG_ES_VERSION	Incompatible version of the serializing package.	RPC_NT_WRONG_ES_VERSION
1829	RPC_X_WRONG_STUB_VERSION	Incompatible version of the RPC stub.	RPC_NT_WRONG_STUB_VERSION
1830	RPC_X_INVALID_PIPE_OBJECT	The idl pipe object is invalid or corrupted.	RPC_NT_INVALID_PIPE_OBJECT
1831	RPC_X_INVALID_PIPE_OPERATION	The operation is invalid for a given idl pipe object.	RPC_NT_INVALID_PIPE_OPERATION
1832	RPC_X_WRONG_PIPE_VERSION	The idl pipe version is not supported.	RPC_NT_WRONG_PIPE_VERSION
1898	RPC_S_GROUP_MEMBER_NOT_FOUND	The group member was not found.	RPC_NT_GROUP_MEMBER_NOT_FOUND
1899	EPT_S_CANT_CREATE	The endpoint mapper database could not be created.	EPT_NT_CANT_CREATE
1900	RPC_S_INVALID_OBJECT	The object universal unique identifier (UUID) is the nil UUID.	RPC_NT_INVALID_OBJECT
1907	ERROR_PASSWORD_MUST_CHANGE	The user must change his password before he logs on the first time.	STATUS_PASSWORD_MUST_CHANGE
1908	ERROR_DOMAIN_CONTROLLER_NOT_FOUND	Could not find the domain controller for this domain.	STATUS_DOMAIN_CONTROLLER_NOT_FOUND
1909	ERROR_ACCOUNT_LOCKED_OUT	The referenced account is currently locked out and may not be logged on to.	STATUS_ACCOUNT_LOCKED_OUT
2402	ERROR_ACTIVE_CONNECTIONS	Active connections still exist.	STATUS_ALREADY_DISCONNECTED
2404	ERROR_DEVICE_IN_USE	The device is in use by an active process and cannot be disconnected.	STATUS_CONNECTION_IN_USE
6118	ERROR_NO_BROWSER_SERVERS_FOUND	The list of servers for this workgroup is not currently available.	STATUS_NO_BROWSER_SERVERS_FOUND
0x80000001		Not implemented.	STATUS_GUARD_PAGE_VIOLATION
0x80000003		One or more arguments are invalid.	STATUS_BREAKPOINT
0x80000004		No such interface supported.	STATUS_SINGLE_STEP
0xc000001d		?	STATUS_ILLEGAL_INSTRUCTION
0xc0000025		?	STATUS_NONCONTINUABLE_EXCEPTION
0xc0000026		?	STATUS_INVALID_DISPOSITION
0xc000002b		?	STATUS_PARITY_ERROR
0xc000008c		?	STATUS_ARRAY_BOUNDS_EXCEEDED

Table B.2: *Application Error Codes (numeric) to* NTSTATUS *Values (continued)*

Application Error Code		Explanation	NTSTATUS **Name**
Value	**Name**		
0xc000008d		?	STATUS_FLOAT_DENORMAL_OPERAND
0xc000008e		?	STATUS_FLOAT_DIVIDE_BY_ZERO
0xc000008f		?	STATUS_FLOAT_INEXACT_RESULT
0xc0000090		?	STATUS_FLOAT_INVALID_ OPERATION
0xc0000091		?	STATUS_FLOAT_OVERFLOW
0xc0000092		?	STATUS_FLOAT_STACK_CHECK
0xc0000093		?	STATUS_FLOAT_UNDERFLOW
0xc0000094		?	STATUS_INTEGER_DIVIDE_BY_ZERO
0xc0000096		?	STATUS_PRIVILEGED_INSTRUCTION
0xc000022a		?	STATUS_DUPLICATE_OBJECTID
0xc000022b		?	STATUS_OBJECTID_EXISTS

NTSTATUS Codes (alphabetic) to GetLastError Codes

This list is sorted alphabetically by NTSTATUS code name.

Table B.3: NTSTATUS *(alphabetic) to Application Error Codes*

NTSTATUS Code		Application Error		Explanation
Name	**Value**	**Value**	**Name**	
EPT_NT_CANT_CREATE	0xc002004c	1899	EPT_S_CANT_CREATE	The endpoint mapper database could not be created.
EPT_NT_CANT_PERFORM_OP	0xc0020035	1752	EPT_S_CANT_PERFORM_OP	The server endpoint cannot perform the operation.
EPT_NT_INVALID_ENTRY	0xc0020034	1751	EPT_S_INVALID_ENTRY	The entry is invalid.
EPT_NT_NOT_REGISTERED	0xc0020036	1753	EPT_S_NOT_REGISTERED	There are no more endpoints available from the endpoint mapper.
RPC_NT_ADDRESS_ERROR	0xc0020045	1768	RPC_S_ADDRESS_ERROR	An addressing error occurred in the RPC server.
RPC_NT_ALREADY_LISTENING	0xc002000e	1713	RPC_S_ALREADY_LISTENING	The RPC server is already listening.
RPC_NT_ALREADY_REGISTERED	0xc002000c	1711	RPC_S_ALREADY_REGISTERED	The object universal unique identifier (UUID) has already been registered.
RPC_NT_BAD_STUB_DATA	0xc003000c	1783	RPC_X_BAD_STUB_DATA	The stub received bad data.
RPC_NT_BINDING_HAS_ NO_AUTH	0xc002002f	1746	RPC_S_BINDING_HAS_NO_AUTH	The binding does not contain any authentication information.

Table B.3: *NTSTATUS (alphabetic) to Application Error Codes (continued)*

NTSTATUS Code		Application Error		Explanation
Name	**Value**	**Value**	**Name**	**Explanation**
RPC_NT_BINDING_INCOMPLETE	0xc0020051	1819	RPC_S_BINDING_INCOMPLETE	The binding handle does not contain all required information.
RPC_NT_BYTE_COUNT_ TOO_SMALL	0xc003000b	1782	RPC_X_BYTE_COUNT_ TOO_SMALL	The byte count is too small.
RPC_NT_CALL_CANCELLED	0xc0020050	1818	RPC_S_CALL_CANCELLED	The server was altered while processing this call.
RPC_NT_CALL_FAILED	0xc002001b	1726	RPC_S_CALL_FAILED	The remote procedure call failed.
RPC_NT_CALL_FAILED_DNE	0xc002001c	1727	RPC_S_CALL_FAILED_DNE	The remote procedure call failed and did not execute.
RPC_NT_CALL_IN_PROGRESS	0xc0020049	1791	RPC_S_CALL_IN_PROGRESS	A remote procedure call is already in progress for this thread.
RPC_NT_CANNOT_SUPPORT	0xc0020041	1764	RPC_S_CANNOT_SUPPORT	The requested operation is not supported.
RPC_NT_CANT_CREATE_ ENDPOINT	0xc0020015	1720	RPC_S_CANT_CREATE_ ENDPOINT	The endpoint cannot be created.
RPC_NT_COMM_FAILURE	0xc0020052	1820	RPC_S_COMM_FAILURE	Communications failure.
RPC_NT_DUPLICATE_ENDPOINT	0xc0020029	1740	RPC_S_DUPLICATE_ENDPOINT	The endpoint is a duplicate.
RPC_NT_ENTRY_ALREADY_ EXISTS	0xc002003d	1760	RPC_S_ENTRY_ALREADY_ EXISTS	The entry already exists.
RPC_NT_ENTRY_NOT_FOUND	0xc002003e	1761	RPC_S_ENTRY_NOT_FOUND	The entry is not found.
RPC_NT_ENUM_VALUE_ OUT_OF_RANGE	0xc003000a	1781	RPC_X_ENUM_VALUE_ OUT_OF_RANGE	The enumeration value is out of range.
RPC_NT_FP_DIV_ZERO	0xc0020046	1769	RPC_S_FP_DIV_ZERO	A floating-point operation at the RPC server caused a division by zero.
RPC_NT_FP_OVERFLOW	0xc0020048	1771	RPC_S_FP_OVERFLOW	A floating-point overflow occurred at the RPC server.
RPC_NT_FP_UNDERFLOW	0xc0020047	1770	RPC_S_FP_UNDERFLOW	A floating-point underflow occurred at the RPC server.
RPC_NT_GROUP_MEMBER_ NOT_FOUND	0xc002004b	1898	RPC_S_GROUP_MEMBER_ NOT_FOUND	The group member was not found.
RPC_NT_INCOMPLETE_NAME	0xc0020038	1755	RPC_S_INCOMPLETE_NAME	The entry name is incomplete.
RPC_NT_INTERFACE_ NOT_FOUND	0xc002003c	1759	RPC_S_INTERFACE_NOT_FOUND	The interface was not found.
RPC_NT_INTERNAL_ERROR	0xc0020043	1766	RPC_S_INTERNAL_ERROR	An internal error occurred in a remote procedure call (RPC).
RPC_NT_INVALID_AUTH_ IDENTITY	0xc0020032	1749	RPC_S_INVALID_AUTH_ IDENTITY	The security context is invalid.
RPC_NT_INVALID_BINDING	0xc0020003	6	ERROR_INVALID_HANDLE	The handle is invalid.
RPC_NT_INVALID_BOUND	0xc0020023	1734	RPC_S_INVALID_BOUND	The array bounds are invalid.
RPC_NT_INVALID_ENDPOINT_ FORMAT	0xc0020007	1706	RPC_S_INVALID_ENDPOINT_ FORMAT	The endpoint format is invalid.
RPC_NT_INVALID_ES_ACTION	0xc0030059	1827	RPC_X_INVALID_ES_ACTION	Invalid operation on the encoding/decoding handle.

Table B.3: NTSTATUS *(alphabetic) to Application Error Codes (continued)*

NTSTATUS Code		Application Error		Explanation
Name	**Value**	**Value**	**Name**	
RPC_NT_INVALID_NAF_ID	0xc0020040	1763	RPC_S_INVALID_NAF_ID	The network address family is invalid.
RPC_NT_INVALID_NAME_SYNTAX	0xc0020025	1736	RPC_S_INVALID_NAME_SYNTAX	The name syntax is invalid.
RPC_NT_INVALID_NET_ADDR	0xc0020008	1707	RPC_S_INVALID_NET_ADDR	The network address is invalid.
RPC_NT_INVALID_NETWORK_OPTIONS	0xc0020019	1724	RPC_S_INVALID_NETWORK_OPTIONS	The network options are invalid.
RPC_NT_INVALID_OBJECT	0xc002004d	1900	RPC_S_INVALID_OBJECT	The object universal unique identifier (UUID) is the nil UUID.
RPC_NT_INVALID_PIPE_OBJECT	0xc003005c	1830	RPC_X_INVALID_PIPE_OBJECT	The idl pipe object is invalid or corrupted.
RPC_NT_INVALID_PIPE_OPERATION	0xc003005d	1831	RPC_X_INVALID_PIPE_OPERATION	The operation is invalid for a given idl pipe object.
RPC_NT_INVALID_RPC_PROTSEQ	0xc0020005	1704	RPC_S_INVALID_RPC_PROTSEQ	The RPC protocol sequence is invalid.
RPC_NT_INVALID_STRING_BINDING	0xc0020001	1700	RPC_S_INVALID_STRING_BINDING	The string binding is invalid.
RPC_NT_INVALID_STRING_UUID	0xc0020006	1705	RPC_S_INVALID_STRING_UUID	The string universal unique identifier (UUID) is invalid.
RPC_NT_INVALID_TAG	0xc0020022	1733	RPC_S_INVALID_TAG	The tag is invalid.
RPC_NT_INVALID_TIMEOUT	0xc002000a	1709	RPC_S_INVALID_TIMEOUT	The timeout value is invalid.
RPC_NT_INVALID_VERS_OPTION	0xc0020039	1756	RPC_S_INVALID_VERS_OPTION	The version option is invalid.
RPC_NT_MAX_CALLS_TOO_SMALL	0xc002002b	1742	RPC_S_MAX_CALLS_TOO_SMALL	The maximum number of calls is too small.
RPC_NT_NAME_SERVICE_UNAVAILABLE	0xc002003f	1762	RPC_S_NAME_SERVICE_UNAVAILABLE	The name service is unavailable.
RPC_NT_NO_BINDINGS	0xc0020013	1718	RPC_S_NO_BINDINGS	There are no bindings.
RPC_NT_NO_CALL_ACTIVE	0xc002001a	1725	RPC_S_NO_CALL_ACTIVE	There is not a remote procedure call active in this thread.
RPC_NT_NO_CONTEXT_AVAILABLE	0xc0020042	1765	RPC_S_NO_CONTEXT_AVAILABLE	No security context is available to allow impersonation.
RPC_NT_NO_ENDPOINT_FOUND	0xc0020009	1708	RPC_S_NO_ENDPOINT_FOUND	No endpoint was found.
RPC_NT_NO_ENTRY_NAME	0xc0020024	1735	RPC_S_NO_ENTRY_NAME	The binding does not contain an entry name.
RPC_NT_NO_INTERFACES	0xc002004f	1817	RPC_S_NO_INTERFACES	No interfaces have been registered.
RPC_NT_NO_MORE_BINDINGS	0xc002004a	1806	RPC_S_NO_MORE_BINDINGS	There are no more bindings.
RPC_NT_NO_MORE_ENTRIES	0xc0030001	1772	RPC_X_NO_MORE_ENTRIES	The list of RPC servers available for the binding of auto handles has been exhausted.
RPC_NT_NO_MORE_MEMBERS	0xc002003a	1757	RPC_S_NO_MORE_MEMBERS	There are no more members.
RPC_NT_NO_PRINC_NAME	0xc0020054	1822	RPC_S_NO_PRINC_NAME	No principal name registered.
RPC_NT_NO_PROTSEQS	0xc0020014	1719	RPC_S_NO_PROTSEQS	There are no protocol sequences.

Table B.3: NTSTATUS *(alphabetic) to Application Error Codes (continued)*

NTSTATUS Code		Application Error		Explanation
Name	**Value**	**Value**	**Name**	**Explanation**
RPC_NT_NO_PROTSEQS_REGISTERED	0xc002000f	1714	RPC_S_NO_PROTSEQS_REGISTERED	No protocol sequences have been registered.
RPC_NT_NOT_ALL_OBJS_UNEXPORTED	0xc002003b	1758	RPC_S_NOT_ALL_OBJS_UNEXPORTED	There is nothing to unexport.
RPC_NT_NOT_CANCELLED	0xc0020058	1826	RPC_S_NOT_CANCELLED	Thread is not cancelled.
RPC_NT_NOT_LISTENING	0xc0020010	1715	RPC_S_NOT_LISTENING	The RPC server is not listening.
RPC_NT_NOT_RPC_ERROR	0xc0020055	1823	RPC_S_NOT_RPC_ERROR	The error specified is not a valid Windows NT RPC error code.
RPC_NT_NOTHING_TO_EXPORT	0xc0020037	1754	RPC_S_NOTHING_TO_EXPORT	No interfaces have been exported.
RPC_NT_NULL_REF_POINTER	0xc0030009	1780	RPC_X_NULL_REF_POINTER	A null reference pointer was passed to the stub.
RPC_NT_OBJECT_NOT_FOUND	0xc002000b	1710	RPC_S_OBJECT_NOT_FOUND	The object universal unique identifier (UUID) was not found.
RPC_NT_OUT_OF_RESOURCES	0xc0020016	1721	RPC_S_OUT_OF_RESOURCES	Not enough resources are available to complete this operation.
RPC_NT_PROCNUM_OUT_OF_RANGE	0xc002002e	1745	RPC_S_PROCNUM_OUT_OF_RANGE	The procedure number is out of range.
RPC_NT_PROTOCOL_ERROR	0xc002001d	1728	RPC_S_PROTOCOL_ERROR	A remote procedure call (RPC) protocol error occurred.
RPC_NT_PROTSEQ_NOT_FOUND	0xc002002d	1744	RPC_S_PROTSEQ_NOT_FOUND	The RPC protocol sequence was not found.
RPC_NT_PROTSEQ_NOT_SUPPORTED	0xc0020004	1703	RPC_S_PROTSEQ_NOT_SUPPORTED	The RPC protocol sequence is not supported.
RPC_NT_SEC_PKG_ERROR	0xc0020057	1825	RPC_S_SEC_PKG_ERROR	A security package specific error occurred.
RPC_NT_SERVER_TOO_BUSY	0xc0020018	1723	RPC_S_SERVER_TOO_BUSY	The RPC server is too busy to complete this operation.
RPC_NT_SERVER_UNAVAILABLE	0xc0020017	1722	RPC_S_SERVER_UNAVAILABLE	The RPC server is unavailable.
RPC_NT_SS_CANNOT_GET_CALL_HANDLE	0xc0030008	1779	RPC_X_SS_CANNOT_GET_CALL_HANDLE	The stub is unable to get the remote procedure call handle.
RPC_NT_SS_CHAR_TRANS_OPEN_FAIL	0xc0030002	1773	RPC_X_SS_CHAR_TRANS_OPEN_FAIL	Unable to open the character translation table file.
RPC_NT_SS_CHAR_TRANS_SHORT_FILE	0xc0030003	1774	RPC_X_SS_CHAR_TRANS_SHORT_FILE	The file containing the character translation table has fewer than 512 bytes.
RPC_NT_SS_CONTEXT_DAMAGED	0xc0030006	1777	RPC_X_SS_CONTEXT_DAMAGED	The context handle changed during a remote procedure call.
RPC_NT_SS_CONTEXT_MISMATCH	0xc0030005	6	ERROR_INVALID_HANDLE	The handle is invalid.
RPC_NT_SS_HANDLES_MISMATCH	0xc0030007	1778	RPC_X_SS_HANDLES_MISMATCH	The binding handles passed to a remote procedure call do not match.
RPC_NT_SS_IN_NULL_CONTEXT	0xc0030004	6	ERROR_INVALID_HANDLE	The handle is invalid.
RPC_NT_STRING_TOO_LONG	0xc002002c	1743	RPC_S_STRING_TOO_LONG	The string is too long.

Table B.3: NTSTATUS *(alphabetic) to Application Error Codes (continued)*

NTSTATUS Code		Application Error		Explanation
Name	**Value**	**Value**	**Name**	**Explanation**
RPC_NT_TYPE_ALREADY_REGISTERED	0xc002000d	1712	RPC_S_TYPE_ALREADY_REGISTERED	The type universal unique identifier (UUID) has already been registered.
RPC_NT_UNKNOWN_AUTHN_LEVEL	0xc0020031	1748	RPC_S_UNKNOWN_AUTHN_LEVEL	The authentication level is unknown.
RPC_NT_UNKNOWN_AUTHN_SERVICE	0xc0020030	1747	RPC_S_UNKNOWN_AUTHN_SERVICE	The authentication service is unknown.
RPC_NT_UNKNOWN_AUTHN_TYPE	0xc002002a	1741	RPC_S_UNKNOWN_AUTHN_TYPE	The authentication type is unknown.
RPC_NT_UNKNOWN_AUTHZ_SERVICE	0xc0020033	1750	RPC_S_UNKNOWN_AUTHZ_SERVICE	The authorization service is unknown.
RPC_NT_UNKNOWN_IF	0xc0020012	1717	RPC_S_UNKNOWN_IF	The interface is unknown.
RPC_NT_UNKNOWN_MGR_TYPE	0xc0020011	1716	RPC_S_UNKNOWN_MGR_TYPE	The manager type is unknown.
RPC_NT_UNSUPPORTED_AUTHN_LEVEL	0xc0020053	1821	RPC_S_UNSUPPORTED_AUTHN_LEVEL	The requested authentication level is not supported.
RPC_NT_UNSUPPORTED_NAME_SYNTAX	0xc0020026	1737	RPC_S_UNSUPPORTED_NAME_SYNTAX	The name syntax is not supported.
RPC_NT_UNSUPPORTED_TRANS_SYN	0xc002001f	1730	RPC_S_UNSUPPORTED_TRANS_SYN	The transfer syntax is not supported by the RPC server.
RPC_NT_UNSUPPORTED_TYPE	0xc0020021	1732	RPC_S_UNSUPPORTED_TYPE	The universal unique identifier (UUID) type is not supported.
RPC_NT_UUID_NO_ADDRESS	0xc0020028	1739	RPC_S_UUID_NO_ADDRESS	No network address is available to use to construct a universal unique identifier (UUID).
RPC_NT_WRONG_ES_VERSION	0xc003005a	1828	RPC_X_WRONG_ES_VERSION	Incompatible version of the serializing package.
RPC_NT_WRONG_KIND_OF_BINDING	0xc0020002	1701	RPC_S_WRONG_KIND_OF_BINDING	The binding handle is not the correct type.
RPC_NT_WRONG_PIPE_VERSION	0xc003005e	1832	RPC_X_WRONG_PIPE_VERSION	The idl pipe version is not supported.
RPC_NT_WRONG_STUB_VERSION	0xc003005b	1829	RPC_X_WRONG_STUB_VERSION	Incompatible version of the RPC stub.
RPC_NT_ZERO_DIVIDE	0xc0020044	1767	RPC_S_ZERO_DIVIDE	The RPC server attempted an integer division by zero.
STATUS_ABIOS_INVALID_COMMAND	0xc0000113			
STATUS_ABIOS_INVALID_LID	0xc0000114			
STATUS_ABIOS_INVALID_SELECTOR	0xc0000116			
STATUS_ABIOS_LID_ALREADY_OWNED	0xc0000111	317	ERROR_MR_MID_NOT_FOUND	? (see note, page 1012)
STATUS_ABIOS_LID_NOT_EXIST	0xc0000110			
STATUS_ABIOS_NOT_LID_OWNER	0xc0000112			
STATUS_ABIOS_NOT_PRESENT	0xc000010f			
STATUS_ABIOS_SELECTOR_NOT_AVAILABLE	0xc0000115			

Table B.3: NTSTATUS *(alphabetic) to Application Error Codes (continued)*

NTSTATUS Code		Application Error		
Name	**Value**	**Value**	**Name**	**Explanation**
STATUS_ACCESS_DENIED	0xc0000022	5	ERROR_ACCESS_DENIED	Access is denied.
STATUS_ACCESS_VIOLATION	0xc0000005	998	ERROR_NOACCESS	Invalid access to memory location.
STATUS_ACCOUNT_DISABLED	0xc0000072	1331	ERROR_ACCOUNT_DISABLED	Logon failure: account currently disabled.
STATUS_ACCOUNT_EXPIRED	0xc0000193	1793	ERROR_ACCOUNT_EXPIRED	The user's account has expired.
STATUS_ACCOUNT_LOCKED_OUT	0xc0000234	1909	ERROR_ACCOUNT_LOCKED_OUT	The referenced account is currently locked out and may not be logged on to.
STATUS_ACCOUNT_RESTRICTION	0xc000006e	1327	ERROR_ACCOUNT_RESTRICTION	Logon failure: user account restriction.
STATUS_ADAPTER_HARDWARE_ERROR	0xc00000c2	57	ERROR_ADAP_HDW_ERR	A network adapter hardware error occurred.
STATUS_ADDRESS_ALREADY_ASSOCIATED	0xc0000238	1227	ERROR_ADDRESS_ALREADY_ASSOCIATED	The network transport endpoint already has an address associated with it.
STATUS_ADDRESS_ALREADY_EXISTS	0xc000020a	52	ERROR_DUP_NAME	A duplicate name exists on the network.
STATUS_ADDRESS_CLOSED	0xc000020b	64	ERROR_NETNAME_DELETED	The specified network name is no longer available.
STATUS_ADDRESS_NOT_ASSOCIATED	0xc0000239	1228	ERROR_ADDRESS_NOT_ASSOCIATED	An address has not yet been associated with the network endpoint.
STATUS_AGENTS_EXHAUSTED	0xc0000085	259	ERROR_NO_MORE_ITEMS	No more data is available.
STATUS_ALIAS_EXISTS	0xc0000154	1379	ERROR_ALIAS_EXISTS	The specified local group already exists.
STATUS_ALLOCATE_BUCKET	0xc000022f	317	ERROR_MR_MID_NOT_FOUND	? (see note, page 1012)
STATUS_ALLOTTED_SPACE_EXCEEDED	0xc0000099	1344	ERROR_ALLOTTED_SPACE_EXCEEDED	No more memory is available for security information updates.
STATUS_ALREADY_COMMITTED	0xc0000021	5	ERROR_ACCESS_DENIED	Access is denied.
STATUS_ALREADY_DISCONNECTED	0x80000025	2402	ERROR_ACTIVE_CONNECTIONS	Active connections still exist.
STATUS_APP_INIT_FAILURE	0xc0000145	317	ERROR_MR_MID_NOT_FOUND	? (see note, page 1012)
STATUS_ARRAY_BOUNDS_EXCEEDED	0xc000008c	0xc000008c		?
STATUS_AUDIT_FAILED	0xc0000244	317	ERROR_MR_MID_NOT_FOUND	? (see note, page 1012)
STATUS_BACKUP_CONTROLLER	0xc0000187			
STATUS_BAD_COMPRESSION_BUFFER	0xc0000242	317	ERROR_MR_MID_NOT_FOUND	? (see note, page 1012)
STATUS_BAD_DESCRIPTOR_FORMAT	0xc00000e7	1361	ERROR_BAD_DESCRIPTOR_FORMAT	A security descriptor is not in the right format (absolute or self-relative).
STATUS_BAD_DEVICE_TYPE	0xc00000cb	66	ERROR_BAD_DEV_TYPE	The network resource type is not correct.
STATUS_BAD_DLL_ENTRYPOINT	0xc0000251	317	ERROR_MR_MID_NOT_FOUND	? (see note, page 1012)
STATUS_BAD_FUNCTION_TABLE	0xc00000ff			

Table B.3: NTSTATUS *(alphabetic) to Application Error Codes (continued)*

NTSTATUS Code		Application Error		Explanation
Name	**Value**	**Value**	**Name**	**Explanation**
STATUS_BAD_IMPERSONATION_ LEVEL	0xc00000a5	1346	ERROR_BAD_IMPERSONATION_ LEVEL	Either a required impersonation level was not provided, or the provided impersonation level is invalid.
STATUS_BAD_INHERITANCE_ ACL	0xc000007d	1340	ERROR_BAD_INHERITANCE_ACL	The inherited access control list (ACL) or access control entry (ACE) could not be built.
STATUS_BAD_INITIAL_PC	0xc000000a	193	ERROR_BAD_EXE_FORMAT	?
STATUS_BAD_INITIAL_STACK	0xc0000009	1001	ERROR_STACK_OVERFLOW	Recursion too deep, stack overflowed.
STATUS_BAD_LOGON_SESSION_ STATE	0xc0000104	1365	ERROR_BAD_LOGON_SESSION_ STATE	The logon session is not in a state that is consistent with the requested operation.
STATUS_BAD_MASTER_BOOT_ RECORD	0xc00000a9	317	ERROR_MR_MID_NOT_FOUND	? (see note, page 1012)
STATUS_BAD_NETWORK_NAME	0xc00000cc	67	ERROR_BAD_NET_NAME	The network name cannot be found.
STATUS_BAD_NETWORK_PATH	0xc00000be	53	ERROR_BAD_NETPATH	The network path was not found.
STATUS_BAD_REMOTE_ADAPTER	0xc00000c5	60	ERROR_BAD_REM_ADAP	The remote adapter is not compatible.
STATUS_BAD_SERVICE_ ENTRYPOINT	0xc0000252	317	ERROR_MR_MID_NOT_FOUND	? (see note, page 1012)
STATUS_BAD_STACK	0xc0000028			
STATUS_BAD_TOKEN_TYPE	0xc00000a8	1349	ERROR_BAD_TOKEN_TYPE	The type of the token is inappropriate for its attempted use.
STATUS_BAD_VALIDATION_ CLASS	0xc00000a7	1348	ERROR_BAD_VALIDATION_ CLASS	The validation information class requested was invalid.
STATUS_BAD_WORKING_SET_ LIMIT	0xc000004c	87	ERROR_INVALID_PARAMETER	The parameter is incorrect.
STATUS_BEGINNING_OF_MEDIA	0x8000001f	1102	ERROR_BEGINNING_OF_MEDIA	Beginning of tape or partition was encountered.
STATUS_BIOS_FAILED_TO_ CONNECT_INTERRUPT	0xc000016e	317	ERROR_MR_MID_NOT_FOUND	? (see note, page 1012)
STATUS_BREAKPOINT	0x80000003	0x80000003		One or more arguments is invalid.
STATUS_BUFFER_OVERFLOW	0x80000005	234	ERROR_MORE_DATA	More data is available.
STATUS_BUFFER_TOO_SMALL	0xc0000023	122	ERROR_INSUFFICIENT_BUFFER	The data area passed to a system call is too small.
STATUS_BUS_RESET	0x8000001d	1111	ERROR_BUS_RESET	The I/O bus was reset.
STATUS_CANCELLED	0xc0000120	995	ERROR_OPERATION_ABORTED	The I/O operation has been aborted because of either a thread exit or an application request.
STATUS_CANNOT_DELETE	0xc0000121	5	ERROR_ACCESS_DENIED	Access is denied.
STATUS_CANNOT_IMPERSONATE	0xc000010d	1368	ERROR_CANNOT_IMPERSONATE	Unable to impersonate via a named pipe until data has been read from that pipe.
STATUS_CANNOT_LOAD_ REGISTRY_FILE	0xc0000218	317	ERROR_MR_MID_NOT_FOUND	? (see note, page 1012)

Table B.3: NTSTATUS *(alphabetic) to Application Error Codes (continued)*

NTSTATUS Code		Application Error		
Name	**Value**	**Value**	**Name**	**Explanation**
STATUS_CANT_ACCESS_ DOMAIN_INFO	0xc00000da	1351	ERROR_CANT_ACCESS_ DOMAIN_INFO	Indicates a Windows NT Server could not be contacted or that objects within the domain are protected such that necessary information could not be retrieved.
STATUS_CANT_DISABLE_ MANDATORY	0xc000005d	1310	ERROR_CANT_DISABLE_ MANDATORY	The group may not be disabled.
STATUS_CANT_OPEN_ ANONYMOUS	0xc00000a6	1347	ERROR_CANT_OPEN_ANONYMOUS	Cannot open an anonymous level security token.
STATUS_CANT_TERMINATE_ SELF	0xc00000db	317	ERROR_MR_MID_NOT_FOUND	? (see note, page 1012)
STATUS_CANT_WAIT	0xc00000d8			
STATUS_CHILD_MUST_BE_ VOLATILE	0xc0000181	1021	ERROR_CHILD_MUST_BE_ VOLATILE	Cannot create a stable subkey under a volatile parent key.
STATUS_CLIENT_SERVER_ PARAMETERS_INVALID	0xc0000223	317	ERROR_MR_MID_NOT_FOUND	? (see note, page 1012)
STATUS_COMMITMENT_LIMIT	0xc000012d	1455	ERROR_COMMITMENT_LIMIT	The paging file is too small for this operation to complete.
STATUS_CONFLICTING_ ADDRESSES	0xc0000018	487	ERROR_INVALID_ADDRESS	Attempt to access invalid address.
STATUS_CONNECTION_ABORTED	0xc0000241	1236	ERROR_CONNECTION_ABORTED	The network connection was aborted by the local system.
STATUS_CONNECTION_ACTIVE	0xc000023b	1230	ERROR_CONNECTION_ACTIVE	An invalid operation was attempted on an active network connection.
STATUS_CONNECTION_COUNT_ LIMIT	0xc0000246	1238	ERROR_CONNECTION_COUNT_ LIMIT	A connection to the server could not be made because the limit on the number of concurrent connections for this account has been reached.
STATUS_CONNECTION_ DISCONNECTED	0xc000020c	64	ERROR_NETNAME_DELETED	The specified network name is no longer available.
STATUS_CONNECTION_IN_USE	0xc0000108	2404	ERROR_DEVICE_IN_USE	The device is in use by an active process and cannot be disconnected.
STATUS_CONNECTION_INVALID	0xc000023a	1229	ERROR_CONNECTION_INVALID	An operation was attempted on a non-existent network connection.
STATUS_CONNECTION_REFUSED	0xc0000236	1225	ERROR_CONNECTION_REFUSED	The remote system refused the network connection.
STATUS_CONNECTION_RESET	0xc000020d	64	ERROR_NETNAME_DELETED	The specified network name is no longer available.
STATUS_CONTROL_C_EXIT	0xc000013a	317	ERROR_MR_MID_NOT_FOUND	? (see note, page 1012)
STATUS_CONVERT_TO_LARGE	0xc000022c			
STATUS_COULD_NOT_ INTERPRET	0xc00000b9			
STATUS_CRC_ERROR	0xc000003f	23	ERROR_CRC	Data error (cyclic redundancy check).
STATUS_CTL_FILE_ NOT_SUPPORTED	0xc0000057	50	ERROR_NOT_SUPPORTED	The network request is not supported.

Table B.3: NTSTATUS *(alphabetic) to Application Error Codes (continued)*

NTSTATUS Code		Application Error		Explanation
Name	**Value**	**Value**	**Name**	
STATUS_DATA_ERROR	0xc000003e	23	ERROR_CRC	Data error (cyclic redundancy check).
STATUS_DATA_LATE_ERROR	0xc000003d	1117	ERROR_IO_DEVICE	The request could not be performed because of an I/O device error.
STATUS_DATA_NOT_ACCEPTED	0xc000021b	317	ERROR_MR_MID_NOT_FOUND	? (see note, page 1012)
STATUS_DATA_OVERRUN	0xc000003c	1117	ERROR_IO_DEVICE	The request could not be performed because of an I/O device error.
STATUS_DATATYPE_MISALIGNMENT	0x80000002	998	ERROR_NOACCESS	Invalid access to memory location.
STATUS_DEBUG_ATTACH_FAILED	0xc0000219	317	ERROR_MR_MID_NOT_FOUND	? (see note, page 1012)
STATUS_DELETE_PENDING	0xc0000056	5	ERROR_ACCESS_DENIED	Access is denied.
STATUS_DEVICE_ALREADY_ATTACHED	0xc0000038	317	ERROR_MR_MID_NOT_FOUND	? (see note, page 1012)
STATUS_DEVICE_BUSY	0x80000011	170	ERROR_BUSY	The requested resource is in use.
STATUS_DEVICE_CONFIGURATION_ERROR	0xc0000182	87	ERROR_INVALID_PARAMETER	The parameter is incorrect.
STATUS_DEVICE_DATA_ERROR	0xc000009c	23	ERROR_CRC	Data error (cyclic redundancy check).
STATUS_DEVICE_DOES_NOT_EXIST	0xc00000c0	55	ERROR_DEV_NOT_EXIST	The specified network resource or device is no longer available.
STATUS_DEVICE_NOT_CONNECTED	0xc000009d	21	ERROR_NOT_READY	The device is not ready.
STATUS_DEVICE_NOT_PARTITIONED	0xc0000174	1107	ERROR_DEVICE_NOT_PARTITIONED	Tape partition information could not be found when loading a tape.
STATUS_DEVICE_NOT_READY	0xc00000a3	21	ERROR_NOT_READY	The device is not ready.
STATUS_DEVICE_OFF_LINE	0x80000010			
STATUS_DEVICE_PAPER_EMPTY	0x8000000e	28	ERROR_OUT_OF_PAPER	The printer is out of paper.
STATUS_DEVICE_POWER_FAILURE	0xc000009e	21	ERROR_NOT_READY	The device is not ready.
STATUS_DEVICE_POWERED_OFF	0x8000000f			
STATUS_DEVICE_PROTOCOL_ERROR	0xc0000186	1117	ERROR_IO_DEVICE	The request could not be performed because of an I/O device error.
STATUS_DFS_EXIT_PATH_FOUND	0xc000009b	3	ERROR_PATH_NOT_FOUND	The system cannot find the path specified.
STATUS_DFS_UNAVAILABLE	0xc000026d	317	ERROR_MR_MID_NOT_FOUND	? (see note, page 1012)
STATUS_DIRECTORY_NOT_EMPTY	0xc0000101	145	ERROR_DIR_NOT_EMPTY	The directory is not empty.
STATUS_DISK_CORRUPT_ERROR	0xc0000032	1393	ERROR_DISK_CORRUPT	The disk structure is corrupt and non-readable.
STATUS_DISK_FULL	0xc000007f	112	ERROR_DISK_FULL	There is not enough space on the disk.
STATUS_DISK_OPERATION_FAILED	0xc000016a	1127	ERROR_DISK_OPERATION_FAILED	While accessing the hard disk, a disk operation failed, even after retries.

Table B.3: NTSTATUS *(alphabetic) to Application Error Codes (continued)*

NTSTATUS Code		Application Error		
Name	**Value**	**Value**	**Name**	**Explanation**
STATUS_DISK_RECALIBRATE_FAILED	0xc0000169	1126	ERROR_DISK_RECALIBRATE_FAILED	While accessing the hard disk, a recalibrate operation failed, even after retries.
STATUS_DISK_RESET_FAILED	0xc000016b	1128	ERROR_DISK_RESET_FAILED	While accessing the hard disk, a disk controller reset was needed, but even that failed.
STATUS_DLL_INIT_FAILED	0xc0000142	1114	ERROR_DLL_INIT_FAILED	A dynamic link library (DLL) initialization routine failed.
STATUS_DLL_INIT_FAILED_LOGOFF	0xc000026b	317	ERROR_MR_MID_NOT_FOUND	? (see note, page 1012)
STATUS_DLL_NOT_FOUND	0xc0000135	126	ERROR_MOD_NOT_FOUND	The specified module could not be found.
STATUS_DOMAIN_CONTROLLER_NOT_FOUND	0xc0000233	1908	ERROR_DOMAIN_CONTROLLER_NOT_OUND	Could not find the domain controller for this domain.
STATUS_DOMAIN_CTRLR_CONFIG_ERROR	0xc000015e	317	ERROR_MR_MID_NOT_FOUND	? (see note, page 1012)
STATUS_DOMAIN_EXISTS	0xc00000e0	1356	ERROR_DOMAIN_EXISTS	The specified domain already exists.
STATUS_DOMAIN_LIMIT_EXCEEDED	0xc00000e1	1357	ERROR_DOMAIN_LIMIT_EXCEEDED	An attempt was made to exceed the limit on the number of domains per server.
STATUS_DOMAIN_TRUST_INCONSISTENT	0xc000019b	1810	ERROR_DOMAIN_TRUST_INCONSISTENT	The name or security ID (SID) of the domain specified is inconsistent with the trust information for that domain.
STATUS_DRIVER_CANCEL_TIMEOUT	0xc000021e	317	ERROR_MR_MID_NOT_FOUND	? (see note, page 1012)
STATUS_DRIVER_ENTRYPOINT_NOT_FOUND	0xc0000263	127	ERROR_PROC_NOT_FOUND	The specified procedure could not be found.
STATUS_DRIVER_INTERNAL_ERROR	0xc0000183	1117	ERROR_IO_DEVICE	The request could not be performed because of an I/O device error.
STATUS_DRIVER_ORDINAL_NOT_FOUND	0xc0000262	182	ERROR_INVALID_ORDINAL	?
STATUS_DRIVER_UNABLE_TO_LOAD	0xc000026c	317	ERROR_MR_MID_NOT_FOUND	? (see note, page 1012)
STATUS_DUPLICATE_NAME	0xc00000bd	52	ERROR_DUP_NAME	A duplicate name exists on the network.
STATUS_DUPLICATE_OBJECTID	0xc000022a	0xc000022a		?
STATUS_EA_CORRUPT_ERROR	0xc0000053	1392	ERROR_FILE_CORRUPT	The file or directory is corrupt and non-readable.
STATUS_EA_LIST_INCONSISTENT	0x80000014	255	ERROR_EA_LIST_INCONSISTENT	The extended attributes are inconsistent.
STATUS_EA_TOO_LARGE	0xc0000050			
STATUS_EAS_NOT_SUPPORTED	0xc000004f	317	ERROR_MR_MID_NOT_FOUND	? (see note, page 1012)
STATUS_END_OF_FILE	0xc0000011	38	ERROR_HANDLE_EOF	Reached end of file.
STATUS_END_OF_MEDIA	0x8000001e	1100	ERROR_END_OF_MEDIA	The physical end of the tape has been reached.
STATUS_ENTRYPOINT_NOT_FOUND	0xc0000139	127	ERROR_PROC_NOT_FOUND	The specified procedure could not be found.

Table B.3: NTSTATUS *(alphabetic)* to *Application Error Codes (continued)*

NTSTATUS Code		Application Error		Explanation
Name	**Value**	**Value**	**Name**	**Explanation**
STATUS_EOM_OVERFLOW	0xc0000177	1129	ERROR_EOM_OVERFLOW	Physical end of tape encountered.
STATUS_EVALUATION_ EXPIRATION	0xc0000268	317	ERROR_MR_MID_NOT_FOUND	? (see note, page 1012)
STATUS_EVENTLOG_CANT_ START	0xc000018f	1501	ERROR_EVENTLOG_CANT_START	No event log file could be opened, so the event logging service did not start.
STATUS_EVENTLOG_FILE_ CHANGED	0xc0000197	1503	ERROR_EVENTLOG_FILE_ CHANGED	The event log file has changed between reads.
STATUS_EVENTLOG_FILE_ CORRUPT	0xc000018e	1500	ERROR_EVENTLOG_FILE_ CORRUPT	The event log file is corrupt.
STATUS_EXTRANEOUS_ INFORMATION	0x80000017	317	ERROR_MR_MID_NOT_FOUND	? (see note, page 1012)
STATUS_FAIL_CHECK	0xc0000229			
STATUS_FILE_CLOSED	0xc0000128	6	ERROR_INVALID_HANDLE	The handle is invalid.
STATUS_FILE_CORRUPT_ERROR	0xc0000102	1392	ERROR_FILE_CORRUPT	The file or directory is corrupt and non-readable.
STATUS_FILE_DELETED	0xc0000123	5	ERROR_ACCESS_DENIED	Access is denied.
STATUS_FILE_FORCED_CLOSED	0xc00000b6	38	ERROR_HANDLE_EOF	Reached end of file.
STATUS_FILE_INVALID	0xc0000098	1006	ERROR_FILE_INVALID	The volume for a file has been externally altered such that the opened file is no longer valid.
STATUS_FILE_IS_A_ DIRECTORY	0xc00000ba	5	ERROR_ACCESS_DENIED	Access is denied.
STATUS_FILE_IS_OFFLINE	0xc0000267	317	ERROR_MR_MID_NOT_FOUND	? (see note, page 1012)
STATUS_FILE_LOCK_CONFLICT	0xc0000054	33	ERROR_LOCK_VIOLATION	The process cannot access the file because another process has locked a portion of the file.
STATUS_FILE_RENAMED	0xc00000d5	317	ERROR_MR_MID_NOT_FOUND	? (see note, page 1012)
STATUS_FILEMARK_DETECTED	0x8000001b	1101	ERROR_FILEMARK_DETECTED	A tape access reached a filemark.
STATUS_FILES_OPEN	0xc0000107	317	ERROR_MR_MID_NOT_FOUND	? (see note, page 1012)
STATUS_FLOAT_DENORMAL_ OPERAND	0xc000008d	0xc000008d		?
STATUS_FLOAT_DIVIDE_ BY_ZERO	0xc000008e	0xc000008e		?
STATUS_FLOAT_INEXACT_ RESULT	0xc000008f	0xc000008f		?
STATUS_FLOAT_INVALID_ OPERATION	0xc0000090	0xc0000090		?
STATUS_FLOAT_OVERFLOW	0xc0000091	0xc0000091		?
STATUS_FLOAT_STACK_CHECK	0xc0000092	0xc0000092		?
STATUS_FLOAT_UNDERFLOW	0xc0000093	0xc0000093		?

Table B.3: NTSTATUS *(alphabetic) to Application Error Codes (continued)*

NTSTATUS Code		Application Error		
Name	**Value**	**Value**	**Name**	**Explanation**
STATUS_FLOPPY_BAD_REGISTERS	0xc0000168	1125	ERROR_FLOPPY_BAD_REGISTERS	The floppy disk controller returned inconsistent results in its registers.
STATUS_FLOPPY_ID_MARK_NOT_FOUND	0xc0000165	1122	ERROR_FLOPPY_ID_MARK_NOT_FOUND	No ID address mark was found on the floppy disk.
STATUS_FLOPPY_UNKNOWN_ERROR	0xc0000167	1124	ERROR_FLOPPY_UNKNOWN_ERROR	The floppy disk controller reported an error that is not recognized by the floppy disk driver.
STATUS_FLOPPY_VOLUME	0xc0000164	317	ERROR_MR_MID_NOT_FOUND	? (see note, page 1012)
STATUS_FLOPPY_WRONG_CYLINDER	0xc0000166	1123	ERROR_FLOPPY_WRONG_CYLINDER	Mismatch between the floppy disk sector ID field and the floppy disk controller track address.
STATUS_FOUND_OUT_OF_SCOPE	0xc000022e	317	ERROR_MR_MID_NOT_FOUND	? (see note, page 1012)
STATUS_FREE_VM_NOT_AT_BASE	0xc000009f	487	ERROR_INVALID_ADDRESS	Attempt to access invalid address.
STATUS_FS_DRIVER_REQUIRED	0xc000019c	317	ERROR_MR_MID_NOT_FOUND	? (see note, page 1012)
STATUS_FT_MISSING_MEMBER	0xc000015f	1117	ERROR_IO_DEVICE	The request could not be performed because of an I/O device error.
STATUS_FT_ORPHANING	0xc000016d			
STATUS_FULLSCREEN_MODE	0xc0000159	1007	ERROR_FULLSCREEN_MODE	The requested operation cannot be performed in full-screen mode.
STATUS_GENERIC_NOT_MAPPED	0xc00000e6	1360	ERROR_GENERIC_NOT_MAPPED	Generic access types were contained in an access mask which should already be mapped to non-generic types.
STATUS_GRACEFUL_DISCONNECT	0xc0000237	1226	ERROR_GRACEFUL_DISCONNECT	The network connection was gracefully closed.
STATUS_GROUP_EXISTS	0xc0000065	1318	ERROR_GROUP_EXISTS	The specified group already exists.
STATUS_GUARD_PAGE_VIOLATION	0x80000001	0x80000001		Not implemented.
STATUS_GUID_SUBSTITUTION_MADE	0x8000000c	317	ERROR_MR_MID_NOT_FOUND	? (see note, page 1012)
STATUS_GUIDS_EXHAUSTED	0xc0000083	259	ERROR_NO_MORE_ITEMS	No more data is available.
STATUS_HANDLE_NOT_CLOSABLE	0xc0000235	6	ERROR_INVALID_HANDLE	The handle is invalid.
STATUS_HANDLES_CLOSED	0x8000000a	317	ERROR_MR_MID_NOT_FOUND	? (see note, page 1012)
STATUS_HOST_UNREACHABLE	0xc000023d	1232	ERROR_HOST_UNREACHABLE	The remote system is not reachable by the transport.
STATUS_ILL_FORMED_PASSWORD	0xc000006b	1324	ERROR_ILL_FORMED_PASSWORD	Unable to update the password. The value provided for the new password contains values that are not allowed in passwords.

Table B.3: NTSTATUS *(alphabetic) to Application Error Codes (continued)*

NTSTATUS Code		Application Error		Explanation
Name	**Value**	**Value**	**Name**	
STATUS_ILL_FORMED_SERVICE_ENTRY	0xc0000160	317	ERROR_MR_MID_NOT_FOUND	? (see note, page 1012)
STATUS_ILLEGAL_CHARACTER	0xc0000161			
STATUS_ILLEGAL_DLL_RELOCATION	0xc0000269			
STATUS_ILLEGAL_FLOAT_CONTEXT	0xc000014a			
STATUS_ILLEGAL_FUNCTION	0xc00000af	1	ERROR_INVALID_FUNCTION	Incorrect function.
STATUS_ILLEGAL_INSTRUCTION	0xc000001d	0xc000001d		?
STATUS_IMAGE_ALREADY_LOADED	0xc000010e	1056	ERROR_SERVICE_ALREADY_RUNNING	An instance of the service is already running.
STATUS_IMAGE_CHECKSUM_MISMATCH	0xc0000221	193	ERROR_BAD_EXE_FORMAT	?
STATUS_IMAGE_MP_UP_MISMATCH	0xc0000249			
STATUS_IN_PAGE_ERROR	0xc0000006	999	ERROR_SWAPERROR	Error performing inpage operation.
STATUS_INCOMPATIBLE_FILE_MAP	0xc000004d	87	ERROR_INVALID_PARAMETER	The parameter is incorrect.
STATUS_INFO_LENGTH_MISMATCH	0xc0000004	24	ERROR_BAD_LENGTH	The program issued a command but the command length is incorrect.
STATUS_INSTANCE_NOT_AVAILABLE	0xc00000ab	231	ERROR_PIPE_BUSY	All pipe instances are busy.
STATUS_INSTRUCTION_MISALIGNMENT	0xc00000aa	317	ERROR_MR_MID_NOT_FOUND	? (see note, page 1012)
STATUS_INSUFF_SERVER_RESOURCES	0xc0000205	1130	ERROR_NOT_ENOUGH_SERVER_MEMORY	Not enough server storage is available to process this command.
STATUS_INSUFFICIENT_LOGON_INFO	0xc0000250	317	ERROR_MR_MID_NOT_FOUND	? (see note, page 1012)
STATUS_INSUFFICIENT_RESOURCES	0xc000009a	1450	ERROR_NO_SYSTEM_RESOURCES	Insufficient system resources exist to complete the requested service.
STATUS_INTEGER_DIVIDE_BY_ZERO	0xc0000094	0xc0000094		?
STATUS_INTEGER_OVERFLOW	0xc0000095	534	ERROR_ARITHMETIC_OVERFLOW	Arithmetic result exceeded 32 bits.
STATUS_INTERNAL_DB_CORRUPTION	0xc00000e4	1358	ERROR_INTERNAL_DB_CORRUPTION	Unable to complete the requested operation because of either a catastrophic media failure or a data structure corruption on the disk.
STATUS_INTERNAL_DB_ERROR	0xc0000158	1383	ERROR_INTERNAL_DB_ERROR	The local security authority database contains an internal inconsistency.
STATUS_INTERNAL_ERROR	0xc00000e5	1359	ERROR_INTERNAL_ERROR	The security account database contains an internal inconsistency.
STATUS_INVALID_ACCOUNT_NAME	0xc0000062	1315	ERROR_INVALID_ACCOUNT_NAME	The name provided is not a properly formed account name.

Table B.3: NTSTATUS *(alphabetic) to Application Error Codes (continued)*

NTSTATUS Code		Application Error		
Name	**Value**	**Value**	**Name**	**Explanation**
STATUS_INVALID_ACL	0xc0000077	1336	ERROR_INVALID_ACL	The access control list (ACL) structure is invalid.
STATUS_INVALID_ADDRESS	0xc0000141	59	ERROR_UNEXP_NET_ERR	An unexpected network error occurred.
STATUS_INVALID_ADDRESS_COMPONENT	0xc0000207	1214	ERROR_INVALID_NETNAME	The format of the specified network name is invalid.
STATUS_INVALID_ADDRESS_WILDCARD	0xc0000208			
STATUS_INVALID_BLOCK_LENGTH	0xc0000173	1106	ERROR_INVALID_BLOCK_LENGTH	When accessing a new tape of a multivolume partition, the current block size is incorrect.
STATUS_INVALID_BUFFER_SIZE	0xc0000206	1784	ERROR_INVALID_USER_BUFFER	The supplied user buffer is not valid for the requested operation.
STATUS_INVALID_CID	0xc000000b	87	ERROR_INVALID_PARAMETER	The parameter is incorrect.
STATUS_INVALID_COMPUTER_NAME	0xc0000122	1210	ERROR_INVALID_COMPUTERNAME	The format of the specified computer name is invalid.
STATUS_INVALID_CONNECTION	0xc0000140	59	ERROR_UNEXP_NET_ERR	An unexpected network error occurred.
STATUS_INVALID_DEVICE_REQUEST	0xc0000010	1	ERROR_INVALID_FUNCTION	Incorrect function.
STATUS_INVALID_DEVICE_STATE	0xc0000184	22	ERROR_BAD_COMMAND	The device does not recognize the command.
STATUS_INVALID_DISPOSITION	0xc0000026	0xc0000026		?
STATUS_INVALID_DOMAIN_ROLE	0xc00000de	1354	ERROR_INVALID_DOMAIN_ROLE	This operation is allowed only for the Primary Domain Controller of the domain.
STATUS_INVALID_DOMAIN_STATE	0xc00000dd	1353	ERROR_INVALID_DOMAIN_STATE	The domain was in the wrong state to perform the security operation.
STATUS_INVALID_EA_FLAG	0x80000015	255	ERROR_EA_LIST_INCONSISTENT	The extended attributes are inconsistent.
STATUS_INVALID_EA_NAME	0x80000013	254	ERROR_INVALID_EA_NAME	The specified extended attribute name was invalid.
STATUS_INVALID_FILE_FOR_SECTION	0xc0000020	193	ERROR_BAD_EXE_FORMAT	?
STATUS_INVALID_GROUP_ATTRIBUTES	0xc00000a4	1345	ERROR_INVALID_GROUP_ATTRIBUTES	The specified attributes are invalid, or incompatible with the attributes for the group as a whole.
STATUS_INVALID_HANDLE	0xc0000008	6	ERROR_INVALID_HANDLE	The handle is invalid.
STATUS_INVALID_HW_PROFILE	0xc0000260	317	ERROR_MR_MID_NOT_FOUND	? (see note, page 1012)

Table B.3: NTSTATUS *(alphabetic) to Application Error Codes (continued)*

NTSTATUS Code		Application Error		Explanation
Name	**Value**	**Value**	**Name**	
STATUS_INVALID_ID_ AUTHORITY	0xc0000084	1343	ERROR_INVALID_ID_ AUTHORITY	The value provided was an invalid value for an identifier authority.
STATUS_INVALID_IMAGE_ FORMAT	0xc000007b	193	ERROR_BAD_EXE_FORMAT	?
STATUS_INVALID_IMAGE_LE_ FORMAT	0xc000012e			
STATUS_INVALID_IMAGE_NE_ FORMAT	0xc000011b			
STATUS_INVALID_IMAGE_ NOT_MZ	0xc000012f			
STATUS_INVALID_IMAGE_ PROTECT	0xc0000130			
STATUS_INVALID_IMAGE_ WIN_16	0xc0000131			
STATUS_INVALID_INFO_CLASS	0xc0000003	87	ERROR_INVALID_PARAMETER	The parameter is incorrect.
STATUS_INVALID_LDT_ DESCRIPTOR	0xc000011a	317	ERROR_MR_MID_NOT_FOUND	? (see note, page 1012)
STATUS_INVALID_LDT_OFFSET	0xc0000119			
STATUS_INVALID_LDT_SIZE	0xc0000118			
STATUS_INVALID_LEVEL	0xc0000148	124	ERROR_INVALID_LEVEL	The system call level is not correct.
STATUS_INVALID_LOCK_ SEQUENCE	0xc000001e	5	ERROR_ACCESS_DENIED	Access is denied.
STATUS_INVALID_LOGON_ HOURS	0xc000006f	1328	ERROR_INVALID_LOGON_HOURS	Logon failure: account logon time restriction violation.
STATUS_INVALID_LOGON_TYPE	0xc000010b	1367	ERROR_INVALID_LOGON_TYPE	A logon request contained an invalid logon type value.
STATUS_INVALID_MEMBER	0xc000017b	1388	ERROR_INVALID_MEMBER	A new member could not be added to a local group because the member has the wrong account type.
STATUS_INVALID_NETWORK_ RESPONSE	0xc00000c3	58	ERROR_BAD_NET_RESP	The specified server cannot perform the requested operation.
STATUS_INVALID_OPLOCK_ PROTOCOL	0xc00000e3	317	ERROR_MR_MID_NOT_FOUND	? (see note, page 1012)
STATUS_INVALID_OWNER	0xc000005a	1307	ERROR_INVALID_OWNER	This security ID may not be assigned as the owner of this object.

Table B.3: NTSTATUS *(alphabetic) to Application Error Codes (continued)*

NTSTATUS Code		Application Error		Explanation
Name	**Value**	**Value**	**Name**	**Explanation**
STATUS_INVALID_PAGE_ PROTECTION	0xc0000045	87	ERROR_INVALID_PARAMETER	The parameter is incorrect.
STATUS_INVALID_PARAMETER	0xc000000d			
STATUS_INVALID_PARAMETER_ 1	0xc00000ef			
STATUS_INVALID_PARAMETER_ 2	0xc00000f0			
STATUS_INVALID_PARAMETER_ 3	0xc00000f1			
STATUS_INVALID_PARAMETER_ 4	0xc00000f2			
STATUS_INVALID_PARAMETER_ 5	0xc00000f3			
STATUS_INVALID_PARAMETER_ 6	0xc00000f4			
STATUS_INVALID_PARAMETER_ 7	0xc00000f5			
STATUS_INVALID_PARAMETER_ 8	0xc00000f6			
STATUS_INVALID_PARAMETER_ 9	0xc00000f7			
STATUS_INVALID_PARAMETER_ 10	0xc00000f8			
STATUS_INVALID_PARAMETER_ 11	0xc00000f9			
STATUS_INVALID_PARAMETER_ 12	0xc00000fa			
STATUS_INVALID_PARAMETER_ MIX	0xc0000030			
STATUS_INVALID_PIPE_STATE	0xc00000ad	230	ERROR_BAD_PIPE	The pipe state is invalid.
STATUS_INVALID_PLUGPLAY_ DEVICE_PATH	0xc0000261	317	ERROR_MR_MID_NOT_FOUND	? (see note, page 1012)
STATUS_INVALID_PORT_ ATTRIBUTES	0xc000002e	317	ERROR_MR_MID_NOT_FOUND	? (see note, page 1012)
STATUS_INVALID_PORT_ HANDLE	0xc0000042	6	ERROR_INVALID_HANDLE	The handle is invalid.
STATUS_INVALID_PRIMARY_ GROUP	0xc000005b	1308	ERROR_INVALID_PRIMARY_ GROUP	This security ID may not be assigned as the primary group of an object.
STATUS_INVALID_QUOTA_ LOWER	0xc0000031	317	ERROR_MR_MID_NOT_FOUND	? (see note, page 1012)
STATUS_INVALID_READ_MODE	0xc00000b4	230	ERROR_BAD_PIPE	The pipe state is invalid.
STATUS_INVALID_SECURITY_ DESCR	0xc0000079	1338	ERROR_INVALID_SECURITY_ DESCR	The security descriptor structure is invalid.
STATUS_INVALID_SERVER_ STATE	0xc00000dc	1352	ERROR_INVALID_SERVER_ STATE	The security account manager (SAM) or local security authority (LSA) server was in the wrong state to perform the security operation.

Table B.3: NTSTATUS *(alphabetic) to Application Error Codes (continued)*

Name	Value	Value	Name	Explanation
STATUS_INVALID_SID	0xc0000078	1337	ERROR_INVALID_SID	The security ID structure is invalid.
STATUS_INVALID_SUB_AUTHORITY	0xc0000076	1335	ERROR_INVALID_SUB_AUTHORITY	The subauthority part of a security ID is invalid for this particular use.
STATUS_INVALID_SYSTEM_SERVICE	0xc000001c	1	ERROR_INVALID_FUNCTION	Incorrect function.
STATUS_INVALID_UNWIND_TARGET	0xc0000029	317	ERROR_MR_MID_NOT_FOUND	? (see note, page 1012)
STATUS_INVALID_USER_BUFFER	0xc00000e8	1784	ERROR_INVALID_USER_BUFFER	The supplied user buffer is not valid for the requested operation.
STATUS_INVALID_VARIANT	0xc0000232	317	ERROR_MR_MID_NOT_FOUND	? (see note, page 1012)
STATUS_INVALID_VIEW_SIZE	0xc000001f	5	ERROR_ACCESS_DENIED	Access is denied.
STATUS_INVALID_VOLUME_LABEL	0xc0000086	154	ERROR_LABEL_TOO_LONG	The volume label you entered exceeds the label character limit of the target file system.
STATUS_INVALID_WORKSTATION	0xc0000070	1329	ERROR_INVALID_WORKSTATION	Logon failure: user not allowed to log on to this computer.
STATUS_IO_DEVICE_ERROR	0xc0000185	1117	ERROR_IO_DEVICE	The request could not be performed because of an I/O device error.
STATUS_IO_PRIVILEGE_FAILED	0xc0000137	317	ERROR_MR_MID_NOT_FOUND	? (see note, page 1012)
STATUS_IO_TIMEOUT	0xc00000b5	121	ERROR_SEM_TIMEOUT	The semaphore timeout period has expired.
STATUS_IP_ADDRESS_CONFLICT1	0xc0000254	317	ERROR_MR_MID_NOT_FOUND	?
STATUS_IP_ADDRESS_CONFLICT2	0xc0000255			
STATUS_KEY_DELETED	0xc000017c	1018	ERROR_KEY_DELETED	Illegal operation attempted on a Registry key that has been marked for deletion.
STATUS_KEY_HAS_CHILDREN	0xc0000180	1020	ERROR_KEY_HAS_CHILDREN	Cannot create a symbolic link in a Registry key that already has subkeys or values.
STATUS_LAST_ADMIN	0xc0000069	1322	ERROR_LAST_ADMIN	The last remaining administration account cannot be disabled or deleted.
STATUS_LICENSE_QUOTA_EXCEEDED	0xc0000259	1395	ERROR_LICENSE_QUOTA_EXCEEDED	The service being accessed is licensed for a particular number of connections. No more connections can be made to the service at this time because there are already as many connections as the service can accept.
STATUS_LICENSE_VIOLATION	0xc000026a	317	ERROR_MR_MID_NOT_FOUND	? (see note, page 1012)
STATUS_LINK_FAILED	0xc000013e	59	ERROR_UNEXP_NET_ERR	An unexpected network error occurred.
STATUS_LINK_TIMEOUT	0xc000013f			
STATUS_LM_CROSS_ENCRYPTION_REQUIRED	0xc000017f	1390	ERROR_LM_CROSS_ENCRYPTION_REQUIRED	A cross-encrypted password is necessary to change this user password.
STATUS_LOCAL_DISCONNECT	0xc000013b	64	ERROR_NETNAME_DELETED	The specified network name is no longer available.

Table B.3: NTSTATUS *(alphabetic) to Application Error Codes (continued)*

NTSTATUS Code		Application Error		
Name	**Value**	**Value**	**Name**	**Explanation**
STATUS_LOCK_NOT_GRANTED	0xc0000055	33	ERROR_LOCK_VIOLATION	The process cannot access the file because another process has locked a portion of the file.
STATUS_LOG_FILE_FULL	0xc0000188	1502	ERROR_LOG_FILE_FULL	The event log file is full.
STATUS_LOGIN_TIME_RESTRICTION	0xc0000247	1239	ERROR_LOGIN_TIME_RESTRICTION	Attempting to login during an unauthorized time of day for this account.
STATUS_LOGIN_WKSTA_RESTRICTION	0xc0000248	1240	ERROR_LOGIN_WKSTA_RESTRICTION	The account is not authorized to login from this station.
STATUS_LOGON_FAILURE	0xc000006d	1326	ERROR_LOGON_FAILURE	Logon failure: unknown user name or bad password.
STATUS_LOGON_NOT_GRANTED	0xc0000155	1380	ERROR_LOGON_NOT_GRANTED	Logon failure: the user has not been granted the requested logon type at this computer.
STATUS_LOGON_SERVER_CONFLICT	0xc0000132	317	ERROR_MR_MID_NOT_FOUND	? (see note, page 1012)
STATUS_LOGON_SESSION_COLLISION	0xc0000105	1366	ERROR_LOGON_SESSION_COLLISION	The logon session ID is already in use.
STATUS_LOGON_SESSION_EXISTS	0xc00000ee	1363	ERROR_LOGON_SESSION_EXISTS	Cannot start a new logon session with an ID that is already in use.
STATUS_LOGON_TYPE_NOT_GRANTED	0xc000015b	1385	ERROR_LOGON_TYPE_NOT_GRANTED	Logon failure: the user has not been granted the requested logon type at this computer.
STATUS_LONGJUMP	0x80000026			
STATUS_LOST_WRITEBEHIND_DATA	0xc0000222	317	ERROR_MR_MID_NOT_FOUND	? (see note, page 1012)
STATUS_LPC_REPLY_LOST	0xc0000253	1359	ERROR_INTERNAL_ERROR	The security account database contains an internal inconsistency.
STATUS_LUIDS_EXHAUSTED	0xc0000075	1334	ERROR_LUIDS_EXHAUSTED	No more local user identifiers (LUIDs) are available.
STATUS_MAPPED_ALIGNMENT	0xc0000220	1132	ERROR_MAPPED_ALIGNMENT	The base address or the file offset specified does not have the proper alignment.
STATUS_MAPPED_FILE_SIZE_ZERO	0xc000011e	1006	ERROR_FILE_INVALID	The volume for a file has been externally altered such that the opened file is no longer valid.
STATUS_MARSHALL_OVERFLOW	0xc0000231	317	ERROR_MR_MID_NOT_FOUND	? (see note, page 1012)
STATUS_MEDIA_CHANGED	0x8000001c	1110	ERROR_MEDIA_CHANGED	Media in drive may have changed.
STATUS_MEDIA_CHECK	0x80000020	317	ERROR_MR_MID_NOT_FOUND	? (see note, page 1012)
STATUS_MEDIA_WRITE_PROTECTED	0xc00000a2	19	ERROR_WRITE_PROTECT	The media is write protected.
STATUS_MEMBER_IN_ALIAS	0xc0000153	1378	ERROR_MEMBER_IN_ALIAS	The specified account name is already a member of the local group.
STATUS_MEMBER_IN_GROUP	0xc0000067	1320	ERROR_MEMBER_IN_GROUP	Either the specified user account is already a member of the specified group, or the specified group cannot be deleted because it contains a member.

Table B.3: NTSTATUS *(alphabetic) to Application Error Codes (continued)*

NTSTATUS Code		Application Error		
Name	**Value**	**Value**	**Name**	**Explanation**
STATUS_MEMBER_NOT_IN_ALIAS	0xc0000152	1377	ERROR_MEMBER_NOT_IN_ALIAS	The specified account name is not a member of the local group.
STATUS_MEMBER_NOT_IN_GROUP	0xc0000068	1321	ERROR_MEMBER_NOT_IN_GROUP	The specified user account is not a member of the specified group account.
STATUS_MEMBERS_PRIMARY_GROUP	0xc0000127	1374	ERROR_MEMBERS_PRIMARY_GROUP	The user cannot be removed from a group because the group is currently the user's primary group.
STATUS_MEMORY_NOT_ALLOCATED	0xc00000a0	487	ERROR_INVALID_ADDRESS	Attempt to access invalid address.
STATUS_MESSAGE_NOT_FOUND	0xc0000109	317	ERROR_MR_MID_NOT_FOUND	? (see note, page 1012)
STATUS_MISSING_SYSTEMFILE	0xc0000143			
STATUS_MORE_PROCESSING_REQUIRED	0xc0000016	234	ERROR_MORE_DATA	More data is available.
STATUS_MUTANT_LIMIT_EXCEEDED	0xc0000191	317	ERROR_MR_MID_NOT_FOUND	? (see note, page 1012)
STATUS_MUTANT_NOT_OWNED	0xc0000046	288	ERROR_NOT_OWNER	Attempt to release mutex not owned by caller.
STATUS_NAME_TOO_LONG	0xc0000106	206	ERROR_FILENAME_EXCED_RANGE	The filename or extension is too long.
STATUS_NET_WRITE_FAULT	0xc00000d2	88	ERROR_NET_WRITE_FAULT	A write fault occurred on the network.
STATUS_NETLOGON_NOT_STARTED	0xc0000192	1792	ERROR_NETLOGON_NOT_STARTED	An attempt was made to logon, but the network logon service was not started.
STATUS_NETWORK_ACCESS_DENIED	0xc00000ca	65	ERROR_NETWORK_ACCESS_DENIED	Network access is denied.
STATUS_NETWORK_BUSY	0xc00000bf	54	ERROR_NETWORK_BUSY	The network is busy.
STATUS_NETWORK_CREDENTIAL_CONFLICT	0xc0000195	1219	ERROR_SESSION_CREDENTIAL_CONFLICT	The credentials supplied conflict with an existing set of credentials.
STATUS_NETWORK_NAME_DELETED	0xc00000c9	64	ERROR_NETNAME_DELETED	The specified network name is no longer available.
STATUS_NETWORK_UNREACHABLE	0xc000023c	1231	ERROR_NETWORK_UNREACHABLE	The remote network is not reachable by the transport.
STATUS_NO_BROWSER_SERVERS_FOUND	0xc000021c	6118	ERROR_NO_BROWSER_SERVERS_FOUND	The list of servers for this workgroup is not currently available.
STATUS_NO_CALLBACK_ACTIVE	0xc0000258	317	ERROR_MR_MID_NOT_FOUND	? (see note, page 1012)
STATUS_NO_DATA_DETECTED	0x80000022	1104	ERROR_NO_DATA_DETECTED	No more data is on the tape.
STATUS_NO_EAS_ON_FILE	0xc0000052	1392	ERROR_FILE_CORRUPT	The file or directory is corrupt and non-readable.
STATUS_NO_EVENT_PAIR	0xc000014e	317	ERROR_MR_MID_NOT_FOUND	? (see note, page 1012)
STATUS_NO_GUID_TRANSLATION	0xc000010c			
STATUS_NO_IMPERSONATION_TOKEN	0xc000005c	1309	ERROR_NO_IMPERSONATION_TOKEN	An attempt has been made to operate on an impersonation token by a thread that is not currently impersonating a client.

Table B.3: NTSTATUS *(alphabetic)* to *Application Error Codes (continued)*

NTSTATUS Code		Application Error		
Name	**Value**	**Value**	**Name**	**Explanation**
STATUS_NO_INHERITANCE	0x8000000b	1391	ERROR_NO_INHERITANCE	Indicates an ACL contains no inheritable components.
STATUS_NO_LDT	0xc0000117	317	ERROR_MR_MID_NOT_FOUND	? (see note, page 1012)
STATUS_NO_LOG_SPACE	0xc000017d	1019	ERROR_NO_LOG_SPACE	System could not allocate the required space in a Registry log.
STATUS_NO_LOGON_SERVERS	0xc000005e	1311	ERROR_NO_LOGON_SERVERS	There are currently no logon servers available to service the logon request.
STATUS_NO_MEDIA	0xc0000178	1112	ERROR_NO_MEDIA_IN_DRIVE	No media in drive.
STATUS_NO_MEDIA_IN_DEVICE	0xc0000013	21	ERROR_NOT_READY	The device is not ready.
STATUS_NO_MEMORY	0xc0000017	8	ERROR_NOT_ENOUGH_MEMORY	Not enough storage is available to process this command.
STATUS_NO_MORE_EAS	0x80000012	259	ERROR_NO_MORE_ITEMS	No more data is available.
STATUS_NO_MORE_ENTRIES	0x8000001a			
STATUS_NO_MORE_FILES	0x80000006	18	ERROR_NO_MORE_FILES	There are no more files.
STATUS_NO_PAGEFILE	0xc0000147	317	ERROR_MR_MID_NOT_FOUND	? (see note, page 1012)
STATUS_NO_SECURITY_ON_OBJECT	0xc00000d7	1350	ERROR_NO_SECURITY_ON_OBJECT	Unable to perform a security operation on an object which has no associated security.
STATUS_NO_SPOOL_SPACE	0xc00000c7	62	ERROR_NO_SPOOL_SPACE	Space to store the file waiting to be printed is not available on the server.
STATUS_NO_SUCH_ALIAS	0xc0000151	1376	ERROR_NO_SUCH_ALIAS	The specified local group does not exist.
STATUS_NO_SUCH_DEVICE	0xc000000e	2	ERROR_FILE_NOT_FOUND	The system cannot find the file specified.
STATUS_NO_SUCH_DOMAIN	0xc00000df	1355	ERROR_NO_SUCH_DOMAIN	The specified domain did not exist.
STATUS_NO_SUCH_FILE	0xc000000f	2	ERROR_FILE_NOT_FOUND	The system cannot find the file specified.
STATUS_NO_SUCH_GROUP	0xc0000066	1319	ERROR_NO_SUCH_GROUP	The specified group does not exist.
STATUS_NO_SUCH_LOGON_SESSION	0xc000005f	1312	ERROR_NO_SUCH_LOGON_SESSION	A specified logon session does not exist. It may already have been terminated.
STATUS_NO_SUCH_MEMBER	0xc000017a	1387	ERROR_NO_SUCH_MEMBER	A new member could not be added to a local group because the member does not exist.
STATUS_NO_SUCH_PACKAGE	0xc00000fe	1364	ERROR_NO_SUCH_PACKAGE	A specified authentication package is unknown.
STATUS_NO_SUCH_PRIVILEGE	0xc0000060	1313	ERROR_NO_SUCH_PRIVILEGE	A specified privilege does not exist.
STATUS_NO_SUCH_USER	0xc0000064	1317	ERROR_NO_SUCH_USER	The specified user does not exist.
STATUS_NO_TOKEN	0xc000007c	1008	ERROR_NO_TOKEN	An attempt was made to reference a token that does not exist.
STATUS_NO_TRUST_LSA_SECRET	0xc000018a	1786	ERROR_NO_TRUST_LSA_SECRET	The workstation does not have a trust secret.
STATUS_NO_TRUST_SAM_ACCOUNT	0xc000018b	1787	ERROR_NO_TRUST_SAM_ACCOUNT	The SAM database on the Windows NT Server does not have a computer account for this workstation trust relationship.

Table B.3: NTSTATUS *(alphabetic) to Application Error Codes (continued)*

NTSTATUS Code		Application Error		Explanation
Name	**Value**	**Value**	**Name**	**Explanation**
STATUS_NO_USER_SESSION_KEY	0xc0000202	1394	ERROR_NO_USER_SESSION_KEY	There is no user session key for the specified logon session.
STATUS_NOLOGON_INTERDOMAIN_TRUST_ACCOUNT	0xc0000198	1807	ERROR_NOLOGON_INTERDOMAIN_TRUST_ACCOUNT	The account used is an interdomain trust account. Use your global user account or local user account to access this server.
STATUS_NOLOGON_SERVER_TRUST_ACCOUNT	0xc000019a	1809	ERROR_NOLOGON_SERVER_TRUST_ACCOUNT	The account used is a server trust account. Use your global user account or local user account to access this server.
STATUS_NOLOGON_WORKSTATION_TRUST_ACCOUNT	0xc0000199	1808	ERROR_NOLOGON_WORKSTATION_TRUST_ACCOUNT	The account used is a Computer Account. Use your global user account or local user account to access this server.
STATUS_NONCONTINUABLE_EXCEPTION	0xc0000025	0xc0000025		?
STATUS_NONE_MAPPED	0xc0000073	1332	ERROR_NONE_MAPPED	No mapping between account names and security IDs was done.
STATUS_NONEXISTENT_EA_ENTRY	0xc0000051	1392	ERROR_FILE_CORRUPT	The file or directory is corrupt and non-readable.
STATUS_NONEXISTENT_SECTOR	0xc0000015	27	ERROR_SECTOR_NOT_FOUND	The drive cannot find the sector requested.
STATUS_NOT_A_DIRECTORY	0xc0000103	267	ERROR_DIRECTORY	The directory name is invalid.
STATUS_NOT_CLIENT_SESSION	0xc0000217	50	ERROR_NOT_SUPPORTED	The network request is not supported.
STATUS_NOT_COMMITTED	0xc000002d	487	ERROR_INVALID_ADDRESS	Attempt to access invalid address.
STATUS_NOT_FOUND	0xc0000225	317	ERROR_MR_MID_NOT_FOUND	? (see note, page 1012)
STATUS_NOT_IMPLEMENTED	0xc0000002	1	ERROR_INVALID_FUNCTION	Incorrect function.
STATUS_NOT_LOCKED	0xc000002a	158	ERROR_NOT_LOCKED	The segment is already unlocked.
STATUS_NOT_LOGON_PROCESS	0xc00000ed	1362	ERROR_NOT_LOGON_PROCESS	The requested action is restricted for use by logon processes only. The calling process has not registered as a logon process.
STATUS_NOT_MAPPED_DATA	0xc0000088	487	ERROR_INVALID_ADDRESS	Attempt to access invalid address.
STATUS_NOT_MAPPED_VIEW	0xc0000019			
STATUS_NOT_REGISTRY_FILE	0xc000015c	1017	ERROR_NOT_REGISTRY_FILE	The system has attempted to load or restore a file into the Registry, but the specified file is not in a Registry file format.
STATUS_NOT_SAME_DEVICE	0xc00000d4	17	ERROR_NOT_SAME_DEVICE	The system cannot move the file to a different disk drive.
STATUS_NOT_SERVER_SESSION	0xc0000216	50	ERROR_NOT_SUPPORTED	The network request is not supported.
STATUS_NOT_SUPPORTED	0xc00000bb			
STATUS_NOT_TINY_STREAM	0xc0000226	317	ERROR_MR_MID_NOT_FOUND	? (see note, page 1012)
STATUS_NT_CROSS_ENCRYPTION_REQUIRED	0xc000015d	1386	ERROR_NT_CROSS_ENCRYPTION_REQUIRED	A cross-encrypted password is necessary to change a user password.
STATUS_OBJECT_NAME_COLLISION	0xc0000035	183	ERROR_ALREADY_EXISTS	Cannot create a file when that file already exists.

Table B.3: NTSTATUS *(alphabetic) to Application Error Codes (continued)*

NTSTATUS Code		Application Error		
Name	**Value**	**Value**	**Name**	**Explanation**
STATUS_OBJECT_NAME_INVALID	0xc0000033	123	ERROR_INVALID_NAME	The filename, directory name, or volume label syntax is incorrect.
STATUS_OBJECT_NAME_NOT_FOUND	0xc0000034	2	ERROR_FILE_NOT_FOUND	The system cannot find the file specified.
STATUS_OBJECT_PATH_INVALID	0xc0000039	161	ERROR_BAD_PATHNAME	The specified path is invalid.
STATUS_OBJECT_PATH_NOT_FOUND	0xc000003a	3	ERROR_PATH_NOT_FOUND	The system cannot find the path specified.
STATUS_OBJECT_PATH_SYNTAX_BAD	0xc000003b	161	ERROR_BAD_PATHNAME	The specified path is invalid.
STATUS_OBJECT_TYPE_MISMATCH	0xc0000024	6	ERROR_INVALID_HANDLE	The handle is invalid.
STATUS_OBJECTID_EXISTS	0xc000022b	0xc000022b		?
STATUS_OPEN_FAILED	0xc0000136	317	ERROR_MR_MID_NOT_FOUND	? (see note, page 1012)
STATUS_OPLOCK_NOT_GRANTED	0xc00000e2			
STATUS_ORDINAL_NOT_FOUND	0xc0000138	182	ERROR_INVALID_ORDINAL	?
STATUS_PAGEFILE_CREATE_FAILED	0xc0000146	317	ERROR_MR_MID_NOT_FOUND	? (see note, page 1012)
STATUS_PAGEFILE_QUOTA	0xc0000007	1454	ERROR_PAGEFILE_QUOTA	Insufficient quota to complete the requested service.
STATUS_PAGEFILE_QUOTA_EXCEEDED	0xc000012c	317	ERROR_MR_MID_NOT_FOUND	? (see note, page 1012)
STATUS_PARITY_ERROR	0xc000002b	0xc000002b		?
STATUS_PARTIAL_COPY	0x8000000d	299	ERROR_PARTIAL_COPY	Only part of a Read/WriteProcessMemory request was completed.
STATUS_PARTITION_FAILURE	0xc0000172	1105	ERROR_PARTITION_FAILURE	Tape could not be partitioned.
STATUS_PASSWORD_EXPIRED	0xc0000071	1330	ERROR_PASSWORD_EXPIRED	Logon failure: the specified account password has expired.
STATUS_PASSWORD_MUST_CHANGE	0xc0000224	1907	ERROR_PASSWORD_MUST_CHANGE	The user must change his password before he logs on the first time.
STATUS_PASSWORD_RESTRICTION	0xc000006c	1325	ERROR_PASSWORD_RESTRICTION	Unable to update the password because a password update rule has been violated.
STATUS_PATH_NOT_COVERED	0xc0000257	1232	ERROR_HOST_UNREACHABLE	The remote system is not reachable by the transport.
STATUS_PIPE_BROKEN	0xc000014b	109	ERROR_BROKEN_PIPE	The pipe has been ended.
STATUS_PIPE_BUSY	0xc00000ae	231	ERROR_PIPE_BUSY	All pipe instances are busy.
STATUS_PIPE_CLOSING	0xc00000b1	232	ERROR_NO_DATA	The pipe is being closed.
STATUS_PIPE_CONNECTED	0xc00000b2	535	ERROR_PIPE_CONNECTED	There is a process on the other end of the pipe.
STATUS_PIPE_DISCONNECTED	0xc00000b0	233	ERROR_PIPE_NOT_CONNECTED	No process is on the other end of the pipe.
STATUS_PIPE_EMPTY	0xc00000d9	232	ERROR_NO_DATA	The pipe is being closed.

Table B.3: NTSTATUS *(alphabetic) to Application Error Codes (continued)*

NTSTATUS Code		Application Error		Explanation
Name	**Value**	**Value**	**Name**	
STATUS_PIPE_LISTENING	0xc00000b3	536	ERROR_PIPE_LISTENING	Waiting for a process to open the other end of the pipe.
STATUS_PIPE_NOT_AVAILABLE	0xc00000ac	231	ERROR_PIPE_BUSY	All pipe instances are busy.
STATUS_PLUGPLAY_NO_DEVICE	0xc000025e	1058	ERROR_SERVICE_DISABLED	The specified service is disabled and cannot be started.
STATUS_PORT_ALREADY_SET	0xc0000048	87	ERROR_INVALID_PARAMETER	The parameter is incorrect.
STATUS_PORT_CONNECTION_ REFUSED	0xc0000041	5	ERROR_ACCESS_DENIED	Access is denied.
STATUS_PORT_DISCONNECTED	0xc0000037	6	ERROR_INVALID_HANDLE	The handle is invalid.
STATUS_PORT_MESSAGE_TOO_ LONG	0xc000002f	317	ERROR_MR_MID_NOT_FOUND	? (see note, page 1012)
STATUS_PORT_UNREACHABLE	0xc000023f	1234	ERROR_PORT_UNREACHABLE	No service is operating at the destination network endpoint on the remote system.
STATUS_POSSIBLE_DEADLOCK	0xc0000194	1131	ERROR_POSSIBLE_DEADLOCK	A potential deadlock condition has been detected.
STATUS_PRINT_CANCELLED	0xc00000c8	63	ERROR_PRINT_CANCELLED	Your file waiting to be printed was deleted.
STATUS_PRINT_QUEUE_FULL	0xc00000c6	61	ERROR_PRINTQ_FULL	The printer queue is full.
STATUS_PRIVILEGE_NOT_HELD	0xc0000061	1314	ERROR_PRIVILEGE_NOT_HELD	A required privilege is not held by the client.
STATUS_PRIVILEGED_ INSTRUCTION	0xc0000096	0xc0000096		?
STATUS_PROCEDURE_ NOT_FOUND	0xc000007a	127	ERROR_PROC_NOT_FOUND	The specified procedure could not be found.
STATUS_PROCESS_IS_ TERMINATING	0xc000010a	5	ERROR_ACCESS_DENIED	Access is denied.
STATUS_PROFILING_AT_LIMIT	0xc00000d3	317	ERROR_MR_MID_NOT_FOUND	? (see note, page 1012)
STATUS_PROFILING_ NOT_STARTED	0xc00000b7			
STATUS_PROFILING _NOT_STOPPED	0xc00000b8			
STATUS_PROPSET_NOT_FOUND	0xc0000230			
STATUS_PROTOCOL_ UNREACHABLE	0xc000023e	1233	ERROR_PROTOCOL_ UNREACHABLE	The remote system does not support the transport protocol.
STATUS_PWD_HISTORY_ CONFLICT	0xc000025c	317	ERROR_MR_MID_NOT_FOUND	? (see note, page 1012)
STATUS_PWD_TOO_RECENT	0xc000025b			
STATUS_PWD_TOO_SHORT	0xc000025a			
STATUS_QUOTA_EXCEEDED	0xc0000044	1816	ERROR_NOT_ENOUGH_QUOTA	Not enough quota is available to process this command.
STATUS_QUOTA_LIST_ INCONSISTENT	0xc0000266	317	ERROR_MR_MID_NOT_FOUND	? (see note, page 1012)
STATUS_RANGE_NOT_LOCKED	0xc000007e	158	ERROR_NOT_LOCKED	The segment is already unlocked.

Table B.3: NTSTATUS *(alphabetic) to Application Error Codes (continued)*

NTSTATUS Code		Application Error		
Name	**Value**	**Value**	**Name**	**Explanation**
STATUS_RECOVERY_FAILURE	0xc0000227	317	ERROR_MR_MID_NOT_FOUND	? (see note, page 1012)
STATUS_REDIRECTOR_HAS_OPEN_HANDLES	0x80000023			
STATUS_REDIRECTOR_NOT_STARTED	0xc00000fb	3	ERROR_PATH_NOT_FOUND	The system cannot find the path specified.
STATUS_REDIRECTOR_PAUSED	0xc00000d1	72	ERROR_REDIR_PAUSED	The specified printer or disk device has been paused.
STATUS_REDIRECTOR_STARTED	0xc00000fc	317	ERROR_MR_MID_NOT_FOUND	? (see note, page 1012)
STATUS_REGISTRY_CORRUPT	0xc000014c	1009	ERROR_BADDB	The configuration registry database is corrupt.
STATUS_REGISTRY_IO_FAILED	0xc000014d	1016	ERROR_REGISTRY_IO_FAILED	An I/O operation initiated by the Registry failed unrecoverably. The Registry could not read in, or write out, or flush one of the files that contains the system's image of the Registry.
STATUS_REGISTRY_QUOTA_LIMIT	0xc0000256	317	ERROR_MR_MID_NOT_FOUND	? (see note, page 1012)
STATUS_REMOTE_DISCONNECT	0xc000013c	64	ERROR_NETNAME_DELETED	The specified network name is no longer available.
STATUS_REMOTE_NOT_LISTENING	0xc00000bc	51	ERROR_REM_NOT_LIST	The remote computer is not available.
STATUS_REMOTE_RESOURCES	0xc000013d			
STATUS_REMOTE_SESSION_LIMIT	0xc0000196	1220	ERROR_REMOTE_SESSION_LIMIT_EXCEEDED	An attempt was made to establish a session to a network server, but there are already too many sessions established to that server.
STATUS_REPLY_MESSAGE_MISMATCH	0xc000021f	317	ERROR_MR_MID_NOT_FOUND	? (see note, page 1012)
STATUS_REQUEST_ABORTED	0xc0000240	1235	ERROR_REQUEST_ABORTED	The request was aborted.
STATUS_REQUEST_NOT_ACCEPTED	0xc00000d0	71	ERROR_REQ_NOT_ACCEP	No more connections can be made to this remote computer at this time because there are already as many connections as the computer can accept.
STATUS_RESOURCE_DATA_NOT_FOUND	0xc0000089	1812	ERROR_RESOURCE_DATA_NOT_FOUND	The specified image file did not contain a resource section.
STATUS_RESOURCE_LANG_NOT_FOUND	0xc0000204	1815	ERROR_RESOURCE_LANG_NOT_FOUND	The specified resource language ID cannot be found in the image file.
STATUS_RESOURCE_NAME_NOT_FOUND	0xc000008b	1814	ERROR_RESOURCE_NAME_NOT_FOUND	The specified resource name cannot be found in the image file.
STATUS_RESOURCE_NOT_OWNED	0xc0000264	288	ERROR_NOT_OWNER	Attempt to release mutex not owned by caller.
STATUS_RESOURCE_TYPE_NOT_FOUND	0xc000008a	1813	ERROR_RESOURCE_TYPE_NOT_FOUND	The specified resource type cannot be found in the image file.
STATUS_RETRY	0xc000022d	317	ERROR_MR_MID_NOT_FOUND	? (see note, page 1012)

Table B.3: NTSTATUS *(alphabetic) to Application Error Codes (continued)*

NTSTATUS Code		Application Error		
Name	**Value**	**Value**	**Name**	**Explanation**
STATUS_REVISION_MISMATCH	0xc0000059	1306	ERROR_REVISION_MISMATCH	Indicates two revision levels are incompatible.
STATUS_RXACT_COMMIT_ FAILURE	0xc000011d	1370	ERROR_RXACT_COMMIT_ FAILURE	An internal security database corruption has been encountered.
STATUS_RXACT_COMMIT_ NECESSARY	0x80000018	317	ERROR_MR_MID_NOT_FOUND	? (see note, page 1012)
STATUS_RXACT_INVALID_ STATE	0xc000011c	1369	ERROR_RXACT_INVALID_STATE	The transaction state of a Registry subtree is incompatible with the requested operation.
STATUS_SECRET_TOO_LONG	0xc0000157	1382	ERROR_SECRET_TOO_LONG	The length of a secret exceeds the maximum length allowed.
STATUS_SECTION_NOT_ EXTENDED	0xc0000087	14	ERROR_OUTOFMEMORY	Not enough storage is available to complete this operation.
STATUS_SECTION_NOT_IMAGE	0xc0000049	87	ERROR_INVALID_PARAMETER	The parameter is incorrect.
STATUS_SECTION_PROTECTION	0xc000004e			
STATUS_SECTION_TOO_BIG	0xc0000040	8	ERROR_NOT_ENOUGH_MEMORY	Not enough storage is available to process this command.
STATUS_SEMAPHORE_LIMIT_ EXCEEDED	0xc0000047	298	ERROR_TOO_MANY_POSTS	Too many posts were made to a semaphore.
STATUS_SERIAL_NO_DEVICE_ INITED	0xc0000150	1118	ERROR_SERIAL_NO_DEVICE	No serial device was successfully initialized. The serial driver will unload.
STATUS_SERVER_DISABLED	0xc0000080	1341	ERROR_SERVER_DISABLED	The server is currently disabled.
STATUS_SERVER_HAS_OPEN_ HANDLES	0x80000024	317	ERROR_MR_MID_NOT_FOUND	? (see note, page 1012)
STATUS_SERVER_NOT_ DISABLED	0xc0000081	1342	ERROR_SERVER_NOT_DISABLED	The server is currently enabled.
STATUS_SETMARK_DETECTED	0x80000021	1103	ERROR_SETMARK_DETECTED	A tape access reached the end of a set of files.
STATUS_SHARED_IRQ_BUSY	0xc000016c	1119	ERROR_IRQ_BUSY	Unable to open a device that was sharing an interrupt request (IRQ) with other devices. At least one other device that uses that IRQ was already opened.
STATUS_SHARING_PAUSED	0xc00000cf	70	ERROR_SHARING_PAUSED	The remote server has been paused or is in the process of being started.
STATUS_SHARING_VIOLATION	0xc0000043	32	ERROR_SHARING_VIOLATION	The process cannot access the file because it is being used by another process.
STATUS_SINGLE_STEP	0x80000004	0x80000004		No such interface supported.
STATUS_SPECIAL_ACCOUNT	0xc0000124	1371	ERROR_SPECIAL_ACCOUNT	Cannot perform this operation on built-in accounts.
STATUS_SPECIAL_GROUP	0xc0000125	1372	ERROR_SPECIAL_GROUP	Cannot perform this operation on this built-in special group.
STATUS_SPECIAL_USER	0xc0000126	1373	ERROR_SPECIAL_USER	Cannot perform this operation on this built-in special user.
STATUS_STACK_OVERFLOW	0xc00000fd	1001	ERROR_STACK_OVERFLOW	Recursion too deep, stack overflowed.

Table B.3: NTSTATUS *(alphabetic) to Application Error Codes (continued)*

NTSTATUS Code		Application Error		
Name	**Value**	**Value**	**Name**	**Explanation**
STATUS_STACK_OVERFLOW_ READ	0xc0000228	317	ERROR_MR_MID_NOT_FOUND	? (see note, page 1012)
STATUS_SUSPEND_COUNT_ EXCEEDED	0xc000004a	156	ERROR_SIGNAL_REFUSED	The recipient process has refused the signal.
STATUS_SYNCHRONIZATION_ REQUIRED	0xc0000134	317	ERROR_MR_MID_NOT_FOUND	? (see note, page 1012)
STATUS_SYSTEM_PROCESS_ TERMINATED	0xc000021a			
STATUS_THREAD_IS_ TERMINATING	0xc000004b	5	ERROR_ACCESS_DENIED	Access is denied.
STATUS_THREAD_NOT_IN_ PROCESS	0xc000012a	317	ERROR_MR_MID_NOT_FOUND	? (see note, page 1012)
STATUS_TIME_DIFFERENCE_ AT_DC	0xc0000133			
STATUS_TIMER_NOT_CANCELED	0xc000000c			
STATUS_TIMER_RESOLUTION_ NOT_SET	0xc0000245			
STATUS_TOKEN_ALREADY_ IN_USE	0xc000012b	1375	ERROR_TOKEN_ALREADY_ IN_USE	The token is already in use as a primary token.
STATUS_TOO_LATE	0xc0000189	19	ERROR_WRITE_PROTECT	The media is write protected.
STATUS_TOO_MANY_ADDRESSES	0xc0000209	68	ERROR_TOO_MANY_NAMES	The name limit for the local computer network adapter card was exceeded.
STATUS_TOO_MANY_COMMANDS	0xc00000c1	56	ERROR_TOO_MANY_CMDS	The network BIOS command limit has been reached.
STATUS_TOO_MANY_CONTEXT_ IDS	0xc000015a	1384	ERROR_TOO_MANY_CONTEXT_ IDS	During a logon attempt, the user's security context accumulated too many security IDs.
STATUS_TOO_MANY_GUIDS_ REQUESTED	0xc0000082	68	ERROR_TOO_MANY_NAMES	The name limit for the local computer network adapter card was exceeded.
STATUS_TOO_MANY_LINKS	0xc0000265	1142	ERROR_TOO_MANY_LINKS	An attempt was made to create more links on a file than the file system supports.
STATUS_TOO_MANY_LUIDS_ REQUESTED	0xc0000074	1333	ERROR_TOO_MANY_LUIDS_ REQUESTED	Too many local user identifiers (LUIDs) were requested at one time.
STATUS_TOO_MANY_NAMES	0xc00000cd	68	ERROR_TOO_MANY_NAMES	The name limit for the local computer network adapter card was exceeded.
STATUS_TOO_MANY_NODES	0xc000020e			
STATUS_TOO_MANY_OPENED_ FILES	0xc000011f	4	ERROR_TOO_MANY_OPEN_FILES	The system cannot open the file.
STATUS_TOO_MANY_PAGING_ FILES	0xc0000097	8	ERROR_NOT_ENOUGH_MEMORY	Not enough storage is available to process this command.
STATUS_TOO_MANY_SECRETS	0xc0000156	1381	ERROR_TOO_MANY_SECRETS	The maximum number of secrets that may be stored in a single system has been exceeded.
STATUS_TOO_MANY_SESSIONS	0xc00000ce	69	ERROR_TOO_MANY_SESS	The network BIOS session limit was exceeded.
STATUS_TOO_MANY_SIDS	0xc000017e	1389	ERROR_TOO_MANY_SIDS	Too many security IDs have been specified.

Table B.3: NTSTATUS *(alphabetic) to Application Error Codes (continued)*

NTSTATUS Code		Application Error		Explanation
Name	**Value**	**Value**	**Name**	
STATUS_TOO_MANY_THREADS	0xc0000129	317	ERROR_MR_MID_NOT_FOUND	? (see note, page 1012)
STATUS_TRANSACTION_ ABORTED	0xc000020f	59	ERROR_UNEXP_NET_ERR	An unexpected network error occurred.
STATUS_TRANSACTION_ INVALID_ID	0xc0000214			
STATUS_TRANSACTION_ INVALID_TYPE	0xc0000215			
STATUS_TRANSACTION_ O_MATCH	0xc0000212			
STATUS_TRANSACTION_ NO_RELEASE	0xc0000211			
STATUS_TRANSACTION_ RESPONDED	0xc0000213			
STATUS_TRANSACTION_ TIMED_OUT	0xc0000210			
STATUS_TRUST_FAILURE	0xc0000190	1790	ERROR_TRUST_FAILURE	The network logon failed.
STATUS_TRUSTED_DOMAIN_ FAILURE	0xc000018c	1788	ERROR_TRUSTED_DOMAIN_ FAILURE	The trust relationship between the primary domain and the trusted domain failed.
STATUS_TRUSTED_ RELATIONSHIP_FAILURE	0xc000018d	1789	ERROR_TRUSTED_ RELATIONSHIP_FAILURE	The trust relationship between this workstation and the primary domain failed.
STATUS_UNABLE_TO_ DECOMMIT_VM	0xc000002c	487	ERROR_INVALID_ADDRESS	Attempt to access invalid address.
STATUS_UNABLE_TO_DELETE_ SECTION	0xc000001b	87	ERROR_INVALID_PARAMETER	The parameter is incorrect.
STATUS_UNABLE_TO_FREE_VM	0xc000001a			
STATUS_UNABLE_TO_LOCK_ MEDIA	0xc0000175	1108	ERROR_UNABLE_TO_LOCK_ MEDIA	Unable to lock the media eject mechanism.
STATUS_UNABLE_TO_UNLOAD_ MEDIA	0xc0000176	1109	ERROR_UNABLE_TO_UNLOAD_ MEDIA	Unable to unload the media.
STATUS_UNDEFINED_ CHARACTER	0xc0000163	317	ERROR_MR_MID_NOT_FOUND	? (see note, page 1012)
STATUS_UNEXPECTED_IO_ ERROR	0xc00000e9			
STATUS_UNEXPECTED_MM_ CREATE_ERR	0xc00000ea			
STATUS_UNEXPECTED_MM_ EXTEND_ERR	0xc00000ec			
STATUS_UNEXPECTED_MM_ MAP_ERROR	0xc00000eb			
STATUS_UNEXPECTED_ NETWORK_ERROR	0xc00000c4	59	ERROR_UNEXP_NET_ERR	An unexpected network error occurred.
STATUS_UNHANDLED_ EXCEPTION	0xc0000144	317	ERROR_MR_MID_NOT_FOUND	? (see note, page 1012)
STATUS_UNKNOWN_REVISION	0xc0000058	1305	ERROR_UNKNOWN_REVISION	The revision level is unknown.
STATUS_UNMAPPABLE_ CHARACTER	0xc0000162	1113	ERROR_NO_UNICODE_ TRANSLATION	No mapping for the Unicode character exists in the target multi-byte code page.

Table B.3: NTSTATUS *(alphabetic) to Application Error Codes (continued)*

NTSTATUS Code		Application Error		Explanation
Name	**Value**	**Value**	**Name**	**Explanation**
STATUS_UNRECOGNIZED_MEDIA	0xc0000014	1785	ERROR_UNRECOGNIZED_MEDIA	The disk media is not recognized. It may not be formatted.
STATUS_UNRECOGNIZED_VOLUME	0xc000014f	1005	ERROR_UNRECOGNIZED_VOLUME	The volume does not contain a recognized file system. Please make sure that all required file system drivers are loaded and that the volume is not corrupt.
STATUS_UNSUCCESSFUL	0xc0000001	31	ERROR_GEN_FAILURE	A device attached to the system is not functioning.
STATUS_UNSUPPORTED_COMPRESSION	0xc000025f	317	ERROR_MR_MID_NOT_FOUND	? (see note, page 1012)
STATUS_UNWIND	0xc0000027			
STATUS_USER_EXISTS	0xc0000063	1316	ERROR_USER_EXISTS	The specified user already exists.
STATUS_USER_MAPPED_FILE	0xc0000243	1224	ERROR_USER_MAPPED_FILE	The requested operation cannot be performed on a file with a user-mapped section open.
STATUS_USER_SESSION_DELETED	0xc0000203	59	ERROR_UNEXP_NET_ERR	An unexpected network error occurred.
STATUS_VARIABLE_NOT_FOUND	0xc0000100	203	ERROR_ENVVAR_NOT_FOUND	The system could not find the environment option that was entered.
STATUS_VDM_HARD_ERROR	0xc000021d	317	ERROR_MR_MID_NOT_FOUND	?
STATUS_VERIFY_REQUIRED	0x80000016	1110	ERROR_MEDIA_CHANGED	Media in drive may have changed.
STATUS_VIRTUAL_CIRCUIT_CLOSED	0xc00000d6	240	ERROR_VC_DISCONNECTED	The session was cancelled.
STATUS_VOLUME_DISMOUNTED	0xc000026e	317	ERROR_MR_MID_NOT_FOUND	? (see note, page 1012)
STATUS_WAKE_SYSTEM_DEBUGGER	0x80000007			
STATUS_WORKING_SET_QUOTA	0xc00000a1	1453	ERROR_WORKING_SET_QUOTA	Insufficient quota to complete the requested service.
STATUS_WOW_ASSERTION	0xc0009898	317	ERROR_MR_MID_NOT_FOUND	? (see note, page 1012)
STATUS_WRONG_PASSWORD	0xc000006a	86	ERROR_INVALID_PASSWORD	The specified network password is not correct.
STATUS_WRONG_PASSWORD_CORE	0xc0000149	86	ERROR_INVALID_PASSWORD	The specified network password is not correct.
STATUS_WRONG_VOLUME	0xc0000012	34	ERROR_WRONG_DISK	?
STATUS_WX86_FLOAT_STACK_CHECK	0xc0000270	317	ERROR_MR_MID_NOT_FOUND	? (see note, page 1012)
STATUS_WX86_INTERNAL_ERROR	0xc000026f			

NTSTATUS Codes (numeric) with Explanations

Table B.4 lists the NTSTATUS codes, sorted numerically by code value.

Table B.4: *Numeric List of* NTSTATUS *Codes*

Code	Value	Meaning
0x0000nnnn		
STATUS_SUCCESS STATUS_WAIT_0	0x00000000L	The operation completed successfully, or the wait completed successfully. If the wait is a multiple-wait, if the option is WaitAny, this value means that the 0th item has been signaled; if the option is WaitAll, this value means all the items have been signaled.
STATUS_WAIT_1	0x00000001L	The operation is a multiple-wait and the wait option was WaitAny. The wait item at index position 1 is signaled.
STATUS_WAIT_2	0x00000002L	The operation is a multiple-wait and the wait option was WaitAny. The wait item at index position 2 is signaled.
STATUS_WAIT_63	0x0000003FL	The operation is a multiple-wait and the wait option was WaitAny. The wait item at index position 63 is signaled. This value is primarily useful to detect if any wait item became signaled; the successful return for a signaled wait will be in the range from STATUS_WAIT_0 to STATUS_WAIT_63.
STATUS_ABANDONED	0x00000080L	A wait operation on a Mutex terminated because the Mutex was destroyed.
STATUS_ABANDONED_WAIT_0	0x00000080L	
STATUS_ABANDONED_WAIT_63	0x000000BFL	
STATUS_USER_APC	0x000000C0L	The wait operation completed because a User-level APC was received.
STATUS_KERNEL_APC	0x00000100L	The wait operation completed because a Kernel-level APC was received.
STATUS_ALERTED	0x00000101L	The wait operation completed because of an alert.
STATUS_TIMEOUT	0x00000102L	The wait operation completed because the timeout value expired.
STATUS_PENDING	0x00000103L	The operation that was requested is pending completion.
STATUS_REPARSE	0x00000104L	A reparse should be performed by the Object Manager because the filename resulted in a symbolic link.
STATUS_MORE_ENTRIES	0x00000105L	This is returned by enumeration APIs to indicate that more information is available to successive calls.
STATUS_NOT_ALL_ASSIGNED	0x00000106L	Not all privileges referenced are assigned to the caller. This allows, for example, all privileges to be disabled without having to know exactly which privileges are assigned.
STATUS_SOME_NOT_MAPPED	0x00000107L	Some of the information to be translated has not been translated.
STATUS_OPLOCK_BREAK_IN_ PROGRESS	0x00000108L	An Open/Create operation completed while an oplock break is underway.
STATUS_VOLUME_MOUNTED	0x00000109L	A new volume has been mounted by a File System.
STATUS_RXACT_COMMITTED	0x0000010AL	This success level status indicates that the transaction state already exists for the Registry subtree, but a transaction commit was previously aborted. The commit has now been completed. This status value is returned by the runtime library (RTL) Registry transaction package (RXact).
STATUS_NOTIFY_CLEANUP	0x0000010BL	A notify change request has been completed due to closing the handle that made the notify change request.
STATUS_NOTIFY_ENUM_DIR	0x0000010CL	A notify change request is being completed, and the information is not being returned in the caller's buffer. The caller now needs to enumerate the files to find the changes.
STATUS_NO_QUOTAS_FOR_ ACCOUNT	0x0000010DL	No system quota limits are specifically set for this account.

Table B.4: *Numeric List of* NTSTATUS *Codes (continued)*

Code	Value	Meaning
STATUS_PRIMARY_TRANSPORT_CONNECT_FAILED	0x0000010EL	An attempt was made to connect to the remote server *name* on the primary transport, but the connection failed. The computer *was* able to connect on a secondary transport.
STATUS_PAGE_FAULT_TRANSITION	0x00000110L	The page fault was a transition fault.
STATUS_PAGE_FAULT_DEMAND_ZERO	0x00000111L	The page fault was a demand zero fault.
STATUS_PAGE_FAULT_COPY_ON_WRITE	0x00000112L	
STATUS_PAGE_FAULT_GUARD_PAGE	0x00000113L	
STATUS_PAGE_FAULT_PAGING_FILE	0x00000114L	The page fault was satisfied by reading from a secondary storage device.
STATUS_CACHE_PAGE_LOCKED	0x00000115L	The cached page was locked during the operation.
STATUS_CRASH_DUMP	0x00000116L	The crash dump exists in the paging file.
STATUS_BUFFER_ALL_ZEROS	0x00000117L	The specified buffer contains all zeros.
STATUS_REPARSE_OBJECT	0x00000118L	A reparse should be performed by the Object Manager because the filename resulted in a symbolic link.
0x4000*nnnn*		
STATUS_OBJECT_NAME_EXISTS	0x40000000L	An attempt was made to create an object, but the object name already existed.
STATUS_THREAD_WAS_SUSPENDED	0x40000001L	A thread termination occurred while the thread was suspended. The thread was resumed, and termination proceeded.
STATUS_WORKING_SET_LIMIT_RANGE	0x40000002L	An attempt was made to set the working set minimum or maximum to values that are outside the allowable range.
STATUS_IMAGE_NOT_AT_BASE	0x40000003L	An image file could not be mapped at the address specified in the image file. Local fix-ups must be performed on this image.
STATUS_RXACT_STATE_CREATED	0x40000004L	This informational level status indicates that a specified Registry subtree transaction state did not yet exist and had to be created. This status value is returned by the runtime library (RTL) Registry transaction package (RXact).
STATUS_SEGMENT_NOTIFICATION	0x40000005L	A VDM is loading, unloading, or moving an MS-DOS or Win16 program segment image. An exception is raised so that a debugger can load, unload, or track symbols and breakpoints within these 16-bit segments.
STATUS_LOCAL_USER_SESSION_KEY	0x40000006L	A user session key was requested for a local RPC connection. The session key returned is a constant value and not unique to this connection.
STATUS_BAD_CURRENT_DIRECTORY	0x40000007L	The process cannot switch to the startup current directory *name*. Select OK to set the current directory to *newname* or CANCEL to exit.
STATUS_SERIAL_MORE_WRITES	0x40000008L	A serial I/O operation was completed by another write to a serial port. (The IOCTL_SERIAL_XOFF_COUNTER reached 0.)
STATUS_REGISTRY_RECOVERED	0x40000009L	One of the files containing the system's Registry data had to be recovered by use of a log or alternate copy. The recovery was successful.
STATUS_FT_READ_RECOVERY_FROM_BACKUP	0x4000000AL	To satisfy a read request, the NT fault-tolerant File System successfully read the requested data from a redundant copy. This was done because the File System encountered a failure on a member of the fault tolerant volume but was unable to reassign the failing area of the device.
STATUS_FT_WRITE_RECOVERY	0x4000000BL	To satisfy a write request, the NT fault-tolerant File System successfully wrote a redundant copy of the information. This was done because the File System encountered a failure on a member of the fault-tolerant volume but was unable to reassign the failing area of the device.
STATUS_SERIAL_COUNTER_TIMEOUT	0x4000000CL	A serial I/O operation completed because the timeout period expired. (The IOCTL_SERIAL_XOFF_COUNTER had not reached 0.)

Table B.4: *Numeric List of* NTSTATUS *Codes (continued)*

Code	Value	Meaning
STATUS_NULL_LM_PASSWORD	0x4000000DL	The NT password is too complex to be converted to a LAN Manager password. The LAN Manager password returned is a NULL string.
STATUS_IMAGE_MACHINE_TYPE_MISMATCH	0x4000000EL	The image file *name* is valid, but it is for a machine type other than the current machine. Select OK to continue or CANCEL to fail the DLL load.
STATUS_RECEIVE_PARTIAL	0x4000000FL	The network transport returned partial data to its client. The remaining data will be sent later.
STATUS_RECEIVE_EXPEDITED	0x40000010L	The network transport returned data to its client that was marked as expedited by the remote system.
STATUS_RECEIVE_PARTIAL_EXPEDITED	0x40000011L	The network transport returned partial data to its client, and this data was marked as expedited by the remote system. The remaining data will be sent later.
STATUS_EVENT_DONE	0x40000012L	The TDI indication completed successfully.
STATUS_EVENT_PENDING	0x40000013L	The TDI indication has entered the pending state.
STATUS_CHECKING_FILE_SYSTEM	0x40000014L	Checking File System on *drive*.
STATUS_FATAL_APP_EXIT	0x40000015L	
STATUS_PREDEFINED_HANDLE	0x40000016L	The specified Registry key is referenced by a predefined handle.
STATUS_WAS_UNLOCKED	0x40000017L	The page protection of a locked page was changed to "No Access", and the page was unlocked from memory and from the process.
STATUS_SERVICE_NOTIFICATION	0x40000018L	
STATUS_WAS_LOCKED	0x40000019L	One of the pages to lock is already locked.
STATUS_LOG_HARD_ERROR	0x4000001AL	
STATUS_ALREADY_WIN32	0x4000001BL	
STATUS_WX86_UNSIMULATE	0x4000001CL	This is an exception status code used by the Win32 *x86* emulation subsystem.
STATUS_WX86_CONTINUE	0x4000001DL	This is an exception status code used by the Win32 *x86* emulation subsystem.
STATUS_WX86_SINGLE_STEP	0x4000001EL	This is an exception status code used by the Win32 *x86* emulation subsystem.
STATUS_WX86_BREAKPOINT	0x4000001FL	This is an exception status code used by the Win32 *x86* emulation subsystem.
STATUS_WX86_EXCEPTION_CONTINUE	0x40000020L	This is an exception status code used by the Win32 *x86* emulation subsystem.
STATUS_WX86_EXCEPTION_LASTCHANCE	0x40000021L	This is an exception status code used by the Win32 *x86* emulation subsystem.
STATUS_WX86_EXCEPTION_CHAIN	0x40000022L	This is an exception status code used by the Win32 *x86* emulation subsystem.
STATUS_IMAGE_MACHINE_TYPE_MISMATCH_EXE	0x40000023L	The image file *name* is valid, but it is for a machine type other than the current machine.
STATUS_NO_YIELD_PERFORMED	0x40000024L	A yield execution was performed, and no thread was available to run.
STATUS_TIMER_RESUME_IGNORED	0x40000025L	The resumeable flag to a timer API was ignored.
0x8000*nnnn*		
STATUS_GUARD_PAGE_VIOLATION	0x80000001L	A page of memory that marks the end of a data structure, such as a stack or an array, was accessed.
STATUS_DATATYPE_MISALIGNMENT	0x80000002L	A data type misalignment was detected in a load or store instruction.
STATUS_BREAKPOINT	0x80000003L	A breakpoint was reached.
STATUS_SINGLE_STEP	0x80000004L	A single step or trace operation has just completed.
STATUS_BUFFER_OVERFLOW	0x80000005L	The data is too large to fit into the specified buffer.

Table B.4: *Numeric List of* NTSTATUS *Codes (continued)*

Code	Value	Meaning
STATUS_NO_MORE_FILES	0x80000006L	No more files were found that matched the file specification.
STATUS_WAKE_SYSTEM_DEBUGGER	0x80000007L	The system debugger was awakened by an interrupt.
STATUS_HANDLES_CLOSED	0x8000000AL	Handles to objects have been automatically closed as a result of the requested operation.
STATUS_NO_INHERITANCE	0x8000000BL	An ACL contains no components that can be inherited.
STATUS_GUID_SUBSTITUTION_MADE	0x8000000CL	During the translation of a GUID to a Windows NT security ID (SID), no administratively defined GUID prefix was found. A substitute prefix was used, which will not compromise system security. However, this might provide a more restrictive access than intended.
STATUS_PARTIAL_COPY	0x8000000DL	Not all of the requested bytes could be copied due to protection conflicts.
STATUS_DEVICE_PAPER_EMPTY	0x8000000EL	The printer is out of paper.
STATUS_DEVICE_POWERED_OFF	0x8000000FL	The printer power was turned off.
STATUS_DEVICE_OFF_LINE	0x80000010L	The printer was taken offline.
STATUS_DEVICE_BUSY	0x80000011L	The device is currently busy.
STATUS_NO_MORE_EAS	0x80000012L	No more EAs were found for the file.
STATUS_INVALID_EA_NAME	0x80000013L	The specified EA name contains at least one illegal character.
STATUS_EA_LIST_INCONSISTENT	0x80000014L	The EA list is inconsistent.
STATUS_INVALID_EA_FLAG	0x80000015L	An invalid EA flag was set.
STATUS_VERIFY_REQUIRED	0x80000016L	The media has changed, and a verify operation is in progress, so no reads or writes may be performed to the device, except those used in the verify operation.
STATUS_EXTRANEOUS_INFORMATION	0x80000017L	The specified ACL contains more information than was expected.
STATUS_RXACT_COMMIT_NECESSARY	0x80000018L	This warning level status indicates that the transaction state already exists for the Registry subtree but that a transaction commit was previously aborted. The commit has *not* been completed, but it has not been rolled back either (so it might still be committed if desired). This status value is returned by the runtime library (RTL) Registry transaction package (RXact).
STATUS_NO_MORE_ENTRIES	0x8000001AL	No more entries are available from an enumeration operation.
STATUS_FILEMARK_DETECTED	0x8000001BL	A filemark was detected.
STATUS_MEDIA_CHANGED	0x8000001CL	The media might have changed.
STATUS_BUS_RESET	0x8000001DL	An I/O bus reset was detected.
STATUS_END_OF_MEDIA	0x8000001EL	The end of the media was encountered.
STATUS_BEGINNING_OF_MEDIA	0x8000001FL	The beginning of the tape or partition was detected.
STATUS_MEDIA_CHECK	0x80000020L	The media might have changed.
STATUS_SETMARK_DETECTED	0x80000021L	A tape access reached a setmark.
STATUS_NO_DATA_DETECTED	0x80000022L	During a tape access, the end of the data written was reached.
STATUS_REDIRECTOR_HAS_OPEN_HANDLES	0x80000023L	The redirector is in use and cannot be unloaded.
STATUS_SERVER_HAS_OPEN_HANDLES	0x80000024L	The server is in use and cannot be unloaded.
STATUS_ALREADY_DISCONNECTED	0x80000025L	The specified connection has already been disconnected.
STATUS_LONGJUMP	0x80000026L	

Table B.4: *Numeric List of* NTSTATUS *Codes (continued)*

Code	Value	Meaning
		0xC000nnnn
STATUS_UNSUCCESSFUL	0xC0000001L	The requested operation was unsuccessful.
STATUS_NOT_IMPLEMENTED	0xC0000002L	The requested operation was not implemented.
STATUS_INVALID_INFO_CLASS	0xC0000003L	The specified information class was not a valid information class for the specified object.
STATUS_INFO_LENGTH_MISMATCH	0xC0000004L	The specified information record length did not match the length required for the specified information class.
STATUS_ACCESS_VIOLATION	0xC0000005L	The instruction at 0x*nnnnnnnn* referenced memory at 0x*nnnnnnnn*. The memory could not be "*read/written*".
STATUS_IN_PAGE_ERROR	0xC0000006L	The instruction at 0x*nnnnnnnn* referenced memory at 0x*nnnnnnnn*. The required data was not placed into memory because of an I/O error status of "*nnn*".
STATUS_PAGEFILE_QUOTA	0xC0000007L	The pagefile quota for the process has been exhausted.
STATUS_INVALID_HANDLE	0xC0000008L	An invalid HANDLE was specified.
STATUS_BAD_INITIAL_STACK	0xC0000009L	An invalid initial stack was specified in a call to NtCreateThread.
STATUS_BAD_INITIAL_PC	0xC000000AL	An invalid initial start address was specified in a call to NtCreateThread.
STATUS_INVALID_CID	0xC000000BL	An invalid client ID was specified.
STATUS_TIMER_NOT_CANCELED	0xC000000CL	An attempt was made to cancel or set a timer that has an associated APC, and the subject thread was not the thread that originally set the timer with an associated APC routine.
STATUS_INVALID_PARAMETER	0xC000000DL	An invalid parameter was passed to a service or function.
STATUS_NO_SUCH_DEVICE	0xC000000EL	A device that does not exist was specified.
STATUS_NO_SUCH_FILE	0xC000000FL	The file *name* does not exist.
STATUS_INVALID_DEVICE_REQUEST	0xC0000010L	The specified request is not a valid operation for the target device.
STATUS_END_OF_FILE	0xC0000011L	The EOF (end-of-file) marker was reached. There is no valid data in the file beyond this marker.
STATUS_WRONG_VOLUME	0xC0000012L	The wrong volume is in the drive. Please insert volume *ID* into drive *name*.
STATUS_NO_MEDIA_IN_DEVICE	0xC0000013L	There is no disk in the drive. Please insert a disk into drive *name*.
STATUS_UNRECOGNIZED_MEDIA	0xC0000014L	The disk in drive *name* is not formatted properly. Please check the disk, and reformat if necessary.
STATUS_NONEXISTENT_SECTOR	0xC0000015L	The specified sector does not exist.
STATUS_MORE_PROCESSING_REQUIRED	0xC0000016L	The specified IRP (I/O request packet) cannot be disposed of because the I/O operation is not complete.
STATUS_NO_MEMORY	0xC0000017L	Not enough virtual memory or paging file quota is available to complete the specified operation.
STATUS_CONFLICTING_ADDRESSES	0xC0000018L	The specified address range conflicts with the address space.
STATUS_NOT_MAPPED_VIEW	0xC0000019L	The address range to unmap is not a mapped view.
STATUS_UNABLE_TO_FREE_VM	0xC000001AL	Virtual memory cannot be freed.
STATUS_UNABLE_TO_DELETE_SECTION	0xC000001BL	The specified section cannot be deleted.
STATUS_INVALID_SYSTEM_SERVICE	0xC000001CL	An invalid system service was specified in a system service call.
STATUS_ILLEGAL_INSTRUCTION	0xC000001DL	An attempt was made to execute an illegal instruction.

Table B.4: *Numeric List of* NTSTATUS *Codes (continued)*

Code	Value	Meaning
STATUS_INVALID_LOCK_SEQUENCE	0xC000001EL	An attempt was made to execute an invalid lock sequence.
STATUS_INVALID_VIEW_SIZE	0xC000001FL	An attempt was made to create a view for a section that is bigger than the section.
STATUS_INVALID_FILE_FOR_SECTION	0xC0000020L	The attributes of the specified mapping file for a section of memory cannot be read.
STATUS_ALREADY_COMMITTED	0xC0000021L	The specified address range is already committed.
STATUS_ACCESS_DENIED	0xC0000022L	A process has requested access to an object, but it has not been granted those access rights.
STATUS_BUFFER_TOO_SMALL	0xC0000023L	The buffer is too small to contain the entry. No information has been written to the buffer.
STATUS_OBJECT_TYPE_MISMATCH	0xC0000024L	There is a mismatch between the type of object required by the requested operation and the type of object that is specified in the request.
STATUS_NONCONTINUABLE_EXCEPTION	0xC0000025L	Windows NT cannot continue from this exception.
STATUS_INVALID_DISPOSITION	0xC0000026L	An invalid exception disposition was returned by an exception handler.
STATUS_UNWIND	0xC0000027L	There was an unwind exception code.
STATUS_BAD_STACK	0xC0000028L	An invalid or unaligned stack was encountered during an unwind operation.
STATUS_INVALID_UNWIND_TARGET	0xC0000029L	An invalid unwind target was encountered during an unwind operation.
STATUS_NOT_LOCKED	0xC000002AL	An attempt was made to unlock a page of memory that was not locked.
STATUS_PARITY_ERROR	0xC000002BL	There was a device parity error on I/O operation.
STATUS_UNABLE_TO_DECOMMIT_VM	0xC000002CL	An attempt was made to decommit uncommitted virtual memory.
STATUS_NOT_COMMITTED	0xC000002DL	An attempt was made to change the attributes on memory that has not been committed.
STATUS_INVALID_PORT_ATTRIBUTES	0xC000002EL	Invalid object attributes were specified to NtCreatePort or invalid port attributes were specified to NtConnectPort.
STATUS_PORT_MESSAGE_TOO_LONG	0xC000002FL	The length of the message passed to NtRequestPort or NtRequestWaitReplyPort is longer than the maximum message allowed by the port.
STATUS_INVALID_PARAMETER_MIX	0xC0000030L	An invalid combination of parameters was specified.
STATUS_INVALID_QUOTA_LOWER	0xC0000031L	An attempt was made to lower a quota limit below the current usage.
STATUS_DISK_CORRUPT_ERROR	0xC0000032L	The File System structure on the disk is corrupt and unusable. Please run the Chkdsk utility on the volume *name*.
STATUS_OBJECT_NAME_INVALID	0xC0000033L	The object name is invalid.
STATUS_OBJECT_NAME_NOT_FOUND	0xC0000034L	The object name was not found.
STATUS_OBJECT_NAME_COLLISION	0xC0000035L	The object name already exists.
STATUS_PORT_DISCONNECTED	0xC0000037L	An attempt was made to send a message to a disconnected communication port.
STATUS_DEVICE_ALREADY_ATTACHED	0xC0000038L	An attempt was made to attach to a device that was already attached to another device.
STATUS_OBJECT_PATH_INVALID	0xC0000039L	Object path component was not a directory object.
STATUS_OBJECT_PATH_NOT_FOUND	0xC000003AL	The pathname does not exist.
STATUS_OBJECT_PATH_SYNTAX_BAD	0xC000003BL	Object path component was not a directory object.
STATUS_DATA_OVERRUN	0xC000003CL	A data overrun error occurred.
STATUS_DATA_LATE_ERROR	0xC000003DL	A data late error occurred.

Table B.4: *Numeric List of* NTSTATUS *Codes (continued)*

Code	Value	Meaning
STATUS_DATA_ERROR	0xC000003EL	An error in reading or writing data occurred.
STATUS_CRC_ERROR	0xC000003FL	A CRC checksum error occurred.
STATUS_SECTION_TOO_BIG	0xC0000040L	The specified section is too big to map the file.
STATUS_PORT_CONNECTION_REFUSED	0xC0000041L	The NtConnectPort request was refused.
STATUS_INVALID_PORT_HANDLE	0xC0000042L	The type of port handle is invalid for the operation requested.
STATUS_SHARING_VIOLATION	0xC0000043L	A file cannot be opened because the share access flags are incompatible.
STATUS_QUOTA_EXCEEDED	0xC0000044L	Insufficient quota exists to complete the operation.
STATUS_INVALID_PAGE_PROTECTION	0xC0000045L	The specified page protection is not valid.
STATUS_MUTANT_NOT_OWNED	0xC0000046L	An attempt to release a mutant object was made by a thread that was not the owner of the mutant object.
STATUS_SEMAPHORE_LIMIT_EXCEEDED	0xC0000047L	An attempt was made to release a Semaphore such that its maximum count would have been exceeded.
STATUS_PORT_ALREADY_SET	0xC0000048L	An attempt was made to set a process's DebugPort or ExceptionPort, but a port already exists in the process.
STATUS_SECTION_NOT_IMAGE	0xC0000049L	An attempt was made to query image information on a section that does not map an image.
STATUS_SUSPEND_COUNT_EXCEEDED	0xC000004AL	An attempt was made to suspend a thread whose suspend count was at its maximum.
STATUS_THREAD_IS_TERMINATING	0xC000004BL	An attempt was made to suspend a thread that has begun termination.
STATUS_BAD_WORKING_SET_LIMIT	0xC000004CL	An attempt was made to set the working set limit to an invalid value (minimum greater than maximum, and so on).
STATUS_INCOMPATIBLE_FILE_MAP	0xC000004DL	A section was created to map a file that is not compatible to an already existing section that maps the same file.
STATUS_SECTION_PROTECTION	0xC000004EL	A view to a section specifies a protection that is incompatible with the initial view's protection.
STATUS_EAS_NOT_SUPPORTED	0xC000004FL	An operation involving EAs failed because the File System does not support EAs.
STATUS_EA_TOO_LARGE	0xC0000050L	An EA operation failed because the EA set is too large.
STATUS_NONEXISTENT_EA_ENTRY	0xC0000051L	An EA operation failed because the name or EA index is invalid.
STATUS_NO_EAS_ON_FILE	0xC0000052L	The file for which EAs were requested has no EAs.
STATUS_EA_CORRUPT_ERROR	0xC0000053L	The EA is corrupt and nonreadable.
STATUS_FILE_LOCK_CONFLICT	0xC0000054L	A requested read/write cannot be granted due to a conflicting file lock.
STATUS_LOCK_NOT_GRANTED	0xC0000055L	A requested file lock cannot be granted due to other existing locks.
STATUS_DELETE_PENDING	0xC0000056L	A nonclose operation has been requested of a File Object that has a delete pending.
STATUS_CTL_FILE_NOT_SUPPORTED	0xC0000057L	An attempt was made to set the control attribute on a file. This attribute is not supported in the target File System.
STATUS_UNKNOWN_REVISION	0xC0000058L	A revision number encountered or specified is not known by the service. It might be a more recent revision than the service is aware of.
STATUS_REVISION_MISMATCH	0xC0000059L	Two revision levels are incompatible.
STATUS_INVALID_OWNER	0xC000005AL	A particular SID (security ID) might not be assigned as the owner of an object.
STATUS_INVALID_PRIMARY_GROUP	0xC000005BL	A particular SID (security ID) might not be assigned as the primary group of an object.

Table B.4: *Numeric List of* NTSTATUS *Codes (continued)*

Code	Value	Meaning
STATUS_NO_IMPERSONATION_TOKEN	0xC000005CL	An attempt was made to operate on an impersonation token by a thread that is not currently impersonating a client.
STATUS_CANT_DISABLE_MANDATORY	0xC000005DL	A mandatory group might not be disabled.
STATUS_NO_LOGON_SERVERS	0xC000005EL	There are currently no logon servers available to service the logon request.
STATUS_NO_SUCH_LOGON_SESSION	0xC000005FL	A specified logon session does not exist. It might already have been terminated.
STATUS_NO_SUCH_PRIVILEGE	0xC0000060L	A specified privilege does not exist.
STATUS_PRIVILEGE_NOT_HELD	0xC0000061L	A required privilege is not held by the client.
STATUS_INVALID_ACCOUNT_NAME	0xC0000062L	The name provided is not a properly formed account name.
STATUS_USER_EXISTS	0xC0000063L	The specified user already exists.
STATUS_NO_SUCH_USER	0xC0000064L	The specified user does not exist.
STATUS_GROUP_EXISTS	0xC0000065L	The specified group already exists.
STATUS_NO_SUCH_GROUP	0xC0000066L	The specified group does not exist.
STATUS_MEMBER_IN_GROUP	0xC0000067L	The specified user account is already in the specified group account. This code is also used to indicate that a group cannot be deleted because it contains a member.
STATUS_MEMBER_NOT_IN_GROUP	0xC0000068L	The specified user account is not a member of the specified group account.
STATUS_LAST_ADMIN	0xC0000069L	The requested operation would disable or delete the last remaining administration account. This is not allowed in order to prevent a situation in which the system cannot be administrated.
STATUS_WRONG_PASSWORD	0xC000006AL	When an attempt is made to update a password, this return status indicates that the value provided as the current password is not correct.
STATUS_ILL_FORMED_PASSWORD	0xC000006BL	When an attempt is made to update a password, this return status indicates that the value provided for the new password contains values that are not allowed in passwords.
STATUS_PASSWORD_RESTRICTION	0xC000006CL	When an attempt is made to update a password, this return status indicates that some password update rule has been violated. For example, the password might not meet length criteria.
STATUS_LOGON_FAILURE	0xC000006DL	The attempted logon is invalid. This is due either to a bad username or bad authentication information.
STATUS_ACCOUNT_RESTRICTION	0xC000006EL	A referenced user name and the authentication information are valid, but some user account restriction has prevented successful authentication (such as time-of-day restrictions).
STATUS_INVALID_LOGON_HOURS	0xC000006FL	The user account has time restrictions and might not be logged onto at this time.
STATUS_INVALID_WORKSTATION	0xC0000070L	The user account is restricted such that it may not be used to log on from the source workstation.
STATUS_PASSWORD_EXPIRED	0xC0000071L	The user account's password has expired.
STATUS_ACCOUNT_DISABLED	0xC0000072L	The referenced account is currently disabled and might not be logged onto.
STATUS_NONE_MAPPED	0xC0000073L	None of the information to be translated has been translated.
STATUS_TOO_MANY_LUIDS_REQUESTED	0xC0000074L	The number of LUIDs (local user IDs) requested may not be allocated with a single allocation.
STATUS_LUIDS_EXHAUSTED	0xC0000075L	There are no more LUIDs (local user IDs) to allocate.
STATUS_INVALID_SUB_AUTHORITY	0xC0000076L	The subauthority value is invalid for the particular use.
STATUS_INVALID_ACL	0xC0000077L	The ACL structure is not valid.
STATUS_INVALID_SID	0xC0000078L	The SID (security ID) structure is not valid.

Table B.4: *Numeric List of* NTSTATUS *Codes (continued)*

Code	Value	Meaning
STATUS_INVALID_SECURITY_DESCR	0xC0000079L	The SECURITY_DESCRIPTOR structure is not valid.
STATUS_PROCEDURE_NOT_FOUND	0xC000007AL	The specified procedure address cannot be found in the DLL.
STATUS_INVALID_IMAGE_FORMAT	0xC000007BL	The application or DLL *name* is not a valid Windows NT image. Check this against the installation diskette.
STATUS_NO_TOKEN	0xC000007CL	An attempt was made to reference a token that doesn't exist. This is typically done by referencing the token associated with a thread when the thread is not impersonating a client.
STATUS_BAD_INHERITANCE_ACL	0xC000007DL	An unsuccessful attempt was made to build either an inherited ACL or an ACE. This can result from a number of things. One of the more probable causes is the replacement of a CreatorId with an SID (security ID) that didn't fit into the ACL or ACE.
STATUS_RANGE_NOT_LOCKED	0xC000007EL	The range specified in NtUnlockFile is not locked.
STATUS_DISK_FULL	0xC000007FL	An operation failed because the disk is full.
STATUS_SERVER_DISABLED	0xC0000080L	The GUID allocation server is (already) disabled.
STATUS_SERVER_NOT_DISABLED	0xC0000081L	The GUID allocation server is (already) enabled.
STATUS_TOO_MANY_GUIDS_REQUESTED	0xC0000082L	Too many GUIDs were requested from the allocation server at once.
STATUS_GUIDS_EXHAUSTED	0xC0000083L	The GUIDs could not be allocated because the Authority Agent is exhausted.
STATUS_INVALID_ID_AUTHORITY	0xC0000084L	The value provided was an invalid value for an identifier authority.
STATUS_AGENTS_EXHAUSTED	0xC0000085L	There are no more Authority Agent values available for the given identifier authority value.
STATUS_INVALID_VOLUME_LABEL	0xC0000086L	An invalid volume label was specified.
STATUS_SECTION_NOT_EXTENDED	0xC0000087L	A mapped section could not be extended.
STATUS_NOT_MAPPED_DATA	0xC0000088L	The specified section to flush does not map a data file.
STATUS_RESOURCE_DATA_NOT_FOUND	0xC0000089L	The specified image file did not contain a resource section.
STATUS_RESOURCE_TYPE_NOT_FOUND	0xC000008AL	The specified resource type cannot be found in the image file.
STATUS_RESOURCE_NAME_NOT_FOUND	0xC000008BL	The specified resource name cannot be found in the image file.
STATUS_ARRAY_BOUNDS_EXCEEDED	0xC000008CL	Array bounds were exceeded.
STATUS_FLOAT_DENORMAL_OPERAND	0xC000008DL	This indicates the floating-point denormal operand.
STATUS_FLOAT_DIVIDE_BY_ZERO	0xC000008EL	This indicates floating-point division by zero.
STATUS_FLOAT_INEXACT_RESULT	0xC000008FL	This indicates the floating-point inexact result.
STATUS_FLOAT_INVALID_OPERATION	0xC0000090L	This indicates an floating-point invalid operation.
STATUS_FLOAT_OVERFLOW	0xC0000091L	This indicates the floating-point overflow.
STATUS_FLOAT_STACK_CHECK	0xC0000092L	This indicates the floating-point stack check.
STATUS_FLOAT_UNDERFLOW	0xC0000093L	This indicates the floating-point underflow.
STATUS_INTEGER_DIVIDE_BY_ZERO	0xC0000094L	This indicates integer division by zero.
STATUS_INTEGER_OVERFLOW	0xC0000095L	This indicates integer overflow.
STATUS_PRIVILEGED_INSTRUCTION	0xC0000096L	This indicates a privileged instruction.

Table B.4: *Numeric List of* NTSTATUS *Codes (continued)*

Code	Value	Meaning
STATUS_TOO_MANY_PAGING_FILES	0xC0000097L	An attempt was made to install more paging files than the system supports.
STATUS_FILE_INVALID	0xC0000098L	The volume for a file has been externally altered such that the opened file is no longer valid.
STATUS_ALLOTTED_SPACE_EXCEEDED	0xC0000099L	When a block of memory is allotted for future updates, such as the memory allocated to hold discretionary access control and primary group information, successive updates might exceed the amount of memory originally allotted. Since the quota might already have been charged to several processes that have handles to the object, it is not reasonable to alter the size of the allocated memory. Instead, a request that requires more memory than has been allotted must fail and the STATUS_ALLOTTED_SPACE_EXCEEDED error returned.
STATUS_INSUFFICIENT_RESOURCES	0xC000009AL	Insufficient system resources exist to complete the API.
STATUS_DFS_EXIT_PATH_FOUND	0xC000009BL	An attempt was made to open a DFS exit path control file.
STATUS_DEVICE_DATA_ERROR	0xC000009CL	
STATUS_DEVICE_NOT_CONNECTED	0xC000009DL	
STATUS_DEVICE_POWER_FAILURE	0xC000009EL	
STATUS_FREE_VM_NOT_AT_BASE	0xC000009FL	Virtual memory cannot be freed because the base address is not the base of the region and a region size of 0 was specified.
STATUS_MEMORY_NOT_ALLOCATED	0xC00000A0L	An attempt was made to free virtual memory that is not allocated.
STATUS_WORKING_SET_QUOTA	0xC00000A1L	The working set is not big enough to allow the requested pages to be locked.
STATUS_MEDIA_WRITE_PROTECTED	0xC00000A2L	The disk cannot be written to because it is write-protected. Remove the write protection from the volume *name* in drive *id*.
STATUS_DEVICE_NOT_READY	0xC00000A3L	The drive is not ready for use; its door might be open. Check drive *name*, and make sure that a disk is inserted and that the drive door is closed.
STATUS_INVALID_GROUP_ATTRIBUTES	0xC00000A4L	The specified attributes are either invalid or incompatible with the attributes for the group as a whole.
STATUS_BAD_IMPERSONATION_LEVEL	0xC00000A5L	A specified impersonation level is invalid. This code is also used to indicate that a required impersonation level was not provided.
STATUS_CANT_OPEN_ANONYMOUS	0xC00000A6L	An attempt was made to open an Anonymous-level token. Anonymous-level tokens may not be opened.
STATUS_BAD_VALIDATION_CLASS	0xC00000A7L	The validation information class requested was invalid.
STATUS_BAD_TOKEN_TYPE	0xC00000A8L	The type of a token object is inappropriate for its attempted use.
STATUS_BAD_MASTER_BOOT_RECORD	0xC00000A9L	The type of a token object is inappropriate for its attempted use.
STATUS_INSTRUCTION_MISALIGNMENT	0xC00000AAL	An attempt was made to execute an instruction at an unaligned address, and the host system does not support unaligned instruction references.
STATUS_INSTANCE_NOT_AVAILABLE	0xC00000ABL	The maximum named pipe instance count has been reached.
STATUS_PIPE_NOT_AVAILABLE	0xC00000ACL	An instance of a named pipe cannot be found in the listening state.
STATUS_INVALID_PIPE_STATE	0xC00000ADL	The named pipe is not in the connected or closing state.
STATUS_PIPE_BUSY	0xC00000AEL	The specified pipe is set to complete operations, and there are current I/O operations queued, so the pipe cannot be changed to queue operations.
STATUS_ILLEGAL_FUNCTION	0xC00000AFL	The specified handle is not open to the server end of the named pipe.
STATUS_PIPE_DISCONNECTED	0xC00000B0L	The specified named pipe is in the disconnected state.
STATUS_PIPE_CLOSING	0xC00000B1L	The specified named pipe is in the closing state.

Table B.4: *Numeric List of* NTSTATUS *Codes (continued)*

Code	Value	Meaning
STATUS_PIPE_CONNECTED	0xC00000B2L	The specified named pipe is in the connected state.
STATUS_PIPE_LISTENING	0xC00000B3L	The specified named pipe is in the listening state.
STATUS_INVALID_READ_MODE	0xC00000B4L	The specified named pipe is not in message mode.
STATUS_IO_TIMEOUT	0xC00000D5L	The specified I/O operation on *device* was not completed before the timeout period expired.
STATUS_FILE_FORCED_CLOSED	0xC00000B6L	The specified file has been closed by another process.
STATUS_PROFILING_NOT_STARTED	0xC00000B7L	Profiling was not started.
STATUS_PROFILING_NOT_STOPPED	0xC00000B8L	Profiling was not stopped.
STATUS_COULD_NOT_INTERPRET	0xC00000B9L	The passed ACL did not contain the minimum required information.
STATUS_FILE_IS_A_DIRECTORY	0xC00000BAL	The file that was specified as a target is a directory, and the caller specified that it could be anything but a directory.
STATUS_NOT_SUPPORTED	0xC00000BBL	The network request is not supported.
STATUS_REMOTE_NOT_LISTENING	0xC00000BCL	This remote computer is not listening.
STATUS_DUPLICATE_NAME	0xC00000BDL	A duplicate name exists on the network.
STATUS_BAD_NETWORK_PATH	0xC00000BEL	The network path cannot be located.
STATUS_NETWORK_BUSY	0xC00000BFL	The network is busy.
STATUS_DEVICE_DOES_NOT_EXIST	0xC00000C0L	This device does not exist.
STATUS_TOO_MANY_COMMANDS	0xC00000C1L	The network BIOS command limit has been reached.
STATUS_ADAPTER_HARDWARE_ERROR	0xC00000C2L	An I/O adapter hardware error occurred.
STATUS_INVALID_NETWORK_RESPONSE	0xC00000C3L	The network responded incorrectly.
STATUS_UNEXPECTED_NETWORK_ERROR	0xC00000C4L	An unexpected network error occurred.
STATUS_BAD_REMOTE_ADAPTER	0xC00000C5L	The remote adapter is not compatible.
STATUS_PRINT_QUEUE_FULL	0xC00000C6L	The printer queue is full.
STATUS_NO_SPOOL_SPACE	0xC00000C7L	Space to store the file waiting to be printed is not available on the server.
STATUS_PRINT_CANCELLED	0xC00000C8L	The requested print file was canceled.
STATUS_NETWORK_NAME_DELETED	0xC00000C9L	The network name was deleted.
STATUS_NETWORK_ACCESS_DENIED	0xC00000CAL	Network access is denied.
STATUS_BAD_DEVICE_TYPE	0xC00000CBL	The specified device type (LPT, for example) conflicts with the actual device type on the remote resource.
STATUS_BAD_NETWORK_NAME	0xC00000CCL	The specified share name cannot be found on the remote server.
STATUS_TOO_MANY_NAMES	0xC00000CDL	The name limit for the local computer network adapter card was exceeded.
STATUS_TOO_MANY_SESSIONS	0xC00000CEL	The network BIOS session limit was exceeded.
STATUS_SHARING_PAUSED	0xC00000CFL	File sharing has been temporarily paused.
STATUS_REQUEST_NOT_ACCEPTED	0xC00000D0L	No more connections can be made to this remote computer at this time because there are already as many connections as the computer can accept.
STATUS_REDIRECTOR_PAUSED	0xC00000D1L	Print or disk redirection is temporarily paused.
STATUS_NET_WRITE_FAULT	0xC00000D2L	A network data fault occurred.

Table B.4: *Numeric List of* NTSTATUS *Codes (continued)*

Code	Value	Meaning
STATUS_PROFILING_AT_LIMIT	0xC00000D3L	The number of active profiling objects is at the maximum, and no more may be started.
STATUS_NOT_SAME_DEVICE	0xC00000D4L	The target file of a rename request is located on a different device than the source of the rename request.
STATUS_FILE_RENAMED	0xC00000D5L	The file specified has been renamed and thus cannot be modified.
STATUS_VIRTUAL_CIRCUIT_CLOSED	0xC00000D6L	The session with a remote server has been disconnected because the timeout interval for a request has expired.
STATUS_NO_SECURITY_ON_OBJECT	0xC00000D7L	An attempt was made to operate on the security of an object that does not have security associated with it.
STATUS_CANT_WAIT	0xC00000D8L	An operation cannot continue without blocking for I/O.
STATUS_PIPE_EMPTY	0xC00000D9L	A Read operation was done on an empty pipe.
STATUS_CANT_ACCESS_DOMAIN_INFO	0xC00000DAL	A Windows NT Server could not be contacted, or objects within the domain are protected such that necessary information could not be retrieved.
STATUS_CANT_TERMINATE_SELF	0xC00000DBL	A thread attempted to terminate itself by default (it called NtTerminateThread with NULL), and it was the last thread in the current process.
STATUS_INVALID_SERVER_STATE	0xC00000DCL	The SAM (Security Access Manager) Server was in the wrong state to perform the desired operation.
STATUS_INVALID_DOMAIN_STATE	0xC00000DDL	The domain was in the wrong state to perform the desired operation.
STATUS_INVALID_DOMAIN_ROLE	0xC00000DEL	This operation is allowed only for the Primary Domain Controller of the domain.
STATUS_NO_SUCH_DOMAIN	0xC00000DFL	The specified domain does not exist.
STATUS_DOMAIN_EXISTS	0xC00000E0L	The specified domain already exists.
STATUS_DOMAIN_LIMIT_EXCEEDED	0xC00000E1L	An attempt was made to exceed the limit on the number of domains per server for this release.
STATUS_OPLOCK_NOT_GRANTED	0xC00000E2L	An oplock request was denied.
STATUS_INVALID_OPLOCK_PROTOCOL	0xC00000E3L	An invalid oplock acknowledgment was received by a File System.
STATUS_INTERNAL_DB_CORRUPTION	0xC00000E4L	The requested operation cannot be completed due to a catastrophic media failure or on-disk data structure corruption.
STATUS_INTERNAL_ERROR	0xC00000E5L	The SAM (Security Access Manager) Server has encountered an internal consistency error in its database. This catastrophic failure will prevent further operation of the SAM.
STATUS_GENERIC_NOT_MAPPED	0xC00000E6L	Generic access types were contained in an access mask that should already be mapped to nongeneric access types.
STATUS_BAD_DESCRIPTOR_FORMAT	0xC00000E7L	A security descriptor is not in the necessary format (absolute or self-relative).
STATUS_INVALID_USER_BUFFER	0xC00000E8L	An access to a user buffer failed at an "expected" point in time. This code is defined, since the caller does not want to accept STATUS_ACCESS_VIOLATION in its filter.
STATUS_UNEXPECTED_IO_ERROR	0xC00000E9L	If an I/O error is returned that is not defined in the standard FsRtl filter, it is converted to the following error that is guaranteed to be in the filter. In this case, information is lost; however, the filter correctly handles the exception.
STATUS_UNEXPECTED_MM_CREATE_ERR	0xC00000EAL	If an MM error is returned that is not defined in the standard FsRtl filter, it is converted to one of the following errors that is guaranteed to be in the filter. In this case, information is lost; however, the filter correctly handles the exception.
STATUS_UNEXPECTED_MM_MAP_ERROR	0xC00000EBL	If an MM error is returned that is not defined in the standard FsRtl filter, it is converted to one of the following errors that is guaranteed to be in the filter. In this case, information is lost; however, the filter correctly handles the exception.

Table B.4: *Numeric List of* NTSTATUS *Codes (continued)*

Code	Value	Meaning
STATUS_UNEXPECTED_MM_EXTEND_ERR	0xC00000ECL	If an MM error is returned that is not defined in the standard FsRtl filter, it is converted to one of the following errors that is guaranteed to be in the filter. In this case, information is lost; however, the filter correctly handles the exception.
STATUS_NOT_LOGON_PROCESS	0xC00000EDL	The requested action is restricted for use by logon processes only. The calling process has not registered as a logon process.
STATUS_LOGON_SESSION_EXISTS	0xC00000EEL	An attempt was made to start a new session manager or LSA (Local Security Authority) logon session with an ID that is already in use.
STATUS_INVALID_PARAMETER_1	0xC00000EFL	An invalid parameter was passed to a service or a function as the first argument.
STATUS_INVALID_PARAMETER_2	0xC00000F0L	An invalid parameter was passed to a service or a function as the second argument.
STATUS_INVALID_PARAMETER_3	0xC00000F1L	An invalid parameter was passed to a service or a function as the third argument.
STATUS_INVALID_PARAMETER_4	0xC00000F2L	An invalid parameter was passed to a service or a function as the fourth argument.
STATUS_INVALID_PARAMETER_5	0xC00000F3L	An invalid parameter was passed to a service or a function as the fifth argument.
STATUS_INVALID_PARAMETER_6	0xC00000F4L	An invalid parameter was passed to a service or a function as the sixth argument.
STATUS_INVALID_PARAMETER_7	0xC00000F5L	An invalid parameter was passed to a service or a function as the seventh argument.
STATUS_INVALID_PARAMETER_8	0xC00000F6L	An invalid parameter was passed to a service or a function as the eighth argument.
STATUS_INVALID_PARAMETER_9	0xC00000F7L	An invalid parameter was passed to a service or a function as the ninth argument.
STATUS_INVALID_PARAMETER_10	0xC00000F8L	An invalid parameter was passed to a service or function as the tenth argument.
STATUS_INVALID_PARAMETER_11	0xC00000F9L	An invalid parameter was passed to a service or a function as the eleventh argument.
STATUS_INVALID_PARAMETER_12	0xC00000FAL	An invalid parameter was passed to a service or a function as the twelfth argument.
STATUS_REDIRECTOR_NOT_STARTED	0xC00000FBL	An attempt was made to access a network file, but the network software was not yet started.
STATUS_REDIRECTOR_STARTED	0xC00000FCL	An attempt was made to start the redirector, but the redirector was already started.
STATUS_STACK_OVERFLOW	0xC00000FDL	A new guard page for the stack cannot be created.
STATUS_NO_SUCH_PACKAGE	0xC00000FEL	A specified authentication package is unknown.
STATUS_BAD_FUNCTION_TABLE	0xC00000FFL	A malformed function table was encountered during an unwind operation.
STATUS_VARIABLE_NOT_FOUND	0xC0000100L	The specified environment variable name was not found in the specified environment block.
STATUS_DIRECTORY_NOT_EMPTY	0xC0000101L	The directory to be deleted is not empty.
STATUS_FILE_CORRUPT_ERROR	0xC0000102L	The file or directory *name* is corrupt and unreadable. Run the Chkdsk utility.
STATUS_NOT_A_DIRECTORY	0xC0000103L	A requested opened file is not a directory.
STATUS_BAD_LOGON_SESSION_STATE	0xC0000104L	The logon session is not in a state that is consistent with the requested operation.
STATUS_LOGON_SESSION_COLLISION	0xC0000105L	An internal LSA (Local Security Authority) error has occurred. An authentication package has requested the creation of a Logon Session, but the ID of an already existing Logon Session has been specified.
STATUS_NAME_TOO_LONG	0xC0000106L	A specified name string is too long for its intended use.
STATUS_FILES_OPEN	0xC0000107L	The user attempted to force close the files on a redirected drive, but there were opened files on the drive, and the user did not specify a sufficient level of force.
STATUS_CONNECTION_IN_USE	0xC0000108L	The user attempted to force close the files on a redirected drive, but there were opened directories on the drive, and the user did not specify a sufficient level of force.

Table B.4: *Numeric List of* NTSTATUS *Codes (continued)*

Code	Value	Meaning
STATUS_MESSAGE_NOT_FOUND	0xC0000109L	RtlFindMessage could not locate the requested message ID in the message table resource.
STATUS_PROCESS_IS_TERMINATING	0xC000010AL	An attempt was made to duplicate an object handle into or out of an exiting process.
STATUS_INVALID_LOGON_TYPE	0xC000010BL	An invalid value was provided for the logon type requested.
STATUS_NO_GUID_TRANSLATION	0xC000010CL	An attempt was made to assign protection to a File System file or directory and one of the SIDs (security IDs) in the security descriptor could not be translated into a GUID that could be stored by the File System. This causes the protection attempt to fail; this might cause a file creation attempt to fail.
STATUS_CANNOT_IMPERSONATE	0xC000010DL	An attempt was made to impersonate via a named pipe that has not yet been read from.
STATUS_IMAGE_ALREADY_LOADED	0xC000010EL	The specified image is already loaded.
STATUS_ABIOS_NOT_PRESENT	0xC000010FL	
STATUS_ABIOS_LID_NOT_EXIST	0xC0000110L	
STATUS_ABIOS_LID_ALREADY_OWNED	0xC0000111L	
STATUS_ABIOS_NOT_LID_OWNER	0xC0000112L	
STATUS_ABIOS_INVALID_COMMAND	0xC0000113L	
STATUS_ABIOS_INVALID_LID	0xC0000114L	
STATUS_ABIOS_SELECTOR_NOT_AVAILABLE	0xC0000115L	
STATUS_ABIOS_INVALID_SELECTOR	0xC0000116L	
STATUS_NO_LDT	0xC0000117L	An attempt was made to change the size of the LDT (Local Descriptor Table) for a process that has no LDT.
STATUS_INVALID_LDT_SIZE	0xC0000118L	An attempt was made to grow an LDT (Local Descriptor Table) by setting its size, or the size was not an even number of selectors.
STATUS_INVALID_LDT_OFFSET	0xC0000119L	The starting value for the LDT (Local Descriptor Table) information was not an integral multiple of the selector size.
STATUS_INVALID_LDT_DESCRIPTOR	0xC000011AL	The user supplied an invalid descriptor when trying to set up LDT (Local Descriptor Table) descriptors.
STATUS_INVALID_IMAGE_NE_FORMAT	0xC000011BL	The specified image file did not have the correct format. It appears to be NE format.
STATUS_RXACT_INVALID_STATE	0xC000011CL	The transaction state of a Registry subtree is incompatible with the requested operation. For example, a request was made to start a new transaction when a transaction was already in progress or a request was made to apply a transaction when one is not currently in progress. This status value is returned by the runtime library (RTL) Registry transaction package (RXact).
STATUS_RXACT_COMMIT_FAILURE	0xC000011DL	An error occurred during a Registry transaction commit. The database was left in an unknown, but probably inconsistent, state. The state of the Registry transaction was left as COMMITTING. This status value is returned by the runtime library (RTL) Registry transaction package (RXact).
STATUS_MAPPED_FILE_SIZE_ZERO	0xC000011EL	An attempt was made to map a file of size 0 when the maximum size specified is 0.
STATUS_TOO_MANY_OPENED_FILES	0xC000011FL	Too many files are opened on a remote server. This error should be returned only by the NT redirector on a remote drive.
STATUS_CANCELLED	0xC0000120L	The I/O request was canceled.
STATUS_CANNOT_DELETE	0xC0000121L	An attempt was made to remove a file or directory that cannot be deleted.
STATUS_INVALID_COMPUTER_NAME	0xC0000122L	A name specified as a remote computer name is syntactically invalid.

Table B.4: *Numeric List of* NTSTATUS *Codes (continued)*

Code	Value	Meaning
STATUS_FILE_DELETED	0xC0000123L	An I/O request other than close was performed on a file after it had been deleted. This can happen only to a request that did not complete before the last handle was closed via NtClose.
STATUS_SPECIAL_ACCOUNT	0xC0000124L	An operation was attempted on a built-in (special SAM, Security Access Manager) account that is incompatible with built-in accounts. For example, built-in accounts cannot be deleted.
STATUS_SPECIAL_GROUP	0xC0000125L	The operation requested might not be performed on the specified group because the group is a built-in special group.
STATUS_SPECIAL_USER	0xC0000126L	The operation requested might not be performed on the specified user because the user is a built-in special user.
STATUS_MEMBERS_PRIMARY_GROUP	0xC0000127L	A member cannot be removed from a group because the group is currently the member's primary group.
STATUS_FILE_CLOSED	0xC0000128L	An I/O request other than close and several other special-case operations were attempted using a File Object that had already been closed.
STATUS_TOO_MANY_THREADS	0xC0000129L	A process has too many threads to perform the requested action. For example, assignment of a primary token may be performed only when a process has zero or one thread.
STATUS_THREAD_NOT_IN_PROCESS	0xC000012AL	An attempt was made to operate on a thread within a specific process, but the thread specified is not in the process specified.
STATUS_TOKEN_ALREADY_IN_USE	0xC000012BL	An attempt was made to establish a token for use as a primary token, but the token is already in use. A token can be the primary token of only one process at a time.
STATUS_PAGEFILE_QUOTA_EXCEEDED	0xC000012CL	The page file quota was exceeded.
STATUS_COMMITMENT_LIMIT	0xC000012DL	The system is running low on virtual memory. Close some applications, and then start the System option in the Control Panel, choosing the Virtual Memory button to create an additional paging file or to increase the size of the current paging file.
STATUS_INVALID_IMAGE_LE_FORMAT	0xC000012EL	The specified image file does not have the correct format. It appears to be LE format.
STATUS_INVALID_IMAGE_NOT_MZ	0xC000012FL	The specified image file does not have the correct format. It lacks an initial MZ.
STATUS_INVALID_IMAGE_PROTECT	0xC0000130L	The specified image file does not have the correct format. It lacks a proper e_lfarlc in the MZ header.
STATUS_INVALID_IMAGE_WIN_16	0xC0000131L	The specified image file does not have the correct format. It appears to be a 16-bit Windows image.
STATUS_LOGON_SERVER_CONFLICT	0xC0000132L	The Netlogon service cannot start because another Netlogon service running in the domain conflicts with the specified role.
STATUS_TIME_DIFFERENCE_AT_DC	0xC0000133L	The time at the Primary Domain Controller is different than the time at the Backup Domain Controller or member server by too large an amount.
STATUS_SYNCHRONIZATION_REQUIRED	0xC0000134L	The SAM (Security Access Manager) database on a Windows NT Server is significantly out of synchronization with the copy of the database on the Domain Controller. A complete synchronization is required.
STATUS_DLL_NOT_FOUND	0xC0000135L	The DLL *name* cannot be found in the specified path *path*.
STATUS_OPEN_FAILED	0xC0000136L	The NtCreateFile API failed. This error should never be returned to an application. It is a placeholder for the NT Lan Manager Redirector to use in its internal error mapping routines.
STATUS_IO_PRIVILEGE_FAILED	0xC0000137L	The I/O permissions for the process could not be changed.
STATUS_ORDINAL_NOT_FOUND	0xC0000138L	The ordinal *n* could not be located in the DLL *name*.
STATUS_ENTRYPOINT_NOT_FOUND	0xC0000139L	The procedure entry point *proc* could not be located in the DLL *name*.
STATUS_CONTROL_C_EXIT	0xC000013AL	The application terminated as a result of a CTRL+C.

Table B.4: *Numeric List of* NTSTATUS *Codes (continued)*

Code	Value	Meaning
STATUS_LOCAL_DISCONNECT	0xC000013BL	The network transport on the computer closed a network connection. There might or might not be I/O requests outstanding.
STATUS_REMOTE_DISCONNECT	0xC000013CL	The network transport on a remote computer closed a network connection. There might or might not be I/O requests outstanding.
STATUS_REMOTE_RESOURCES	0xC000013DL	The remote computer has insufficient resources to complete the network request. For instance, there might not be enough memory available on the remote computer to carry out the request at this time.
STATUS_LINK_FAILED	0xC000013EL	An existing connection (virtual circuit) was broken at the remote computer. There is probably something wrong with the network software protocol or the network hardware on the remote computer.
STATUS_LINK_TIMEOUT	0xC000013FL	The network transport on your computer has closed a network connection because it had to wait too long for a response from the remote computer.
STATUS_INVALID_CONNECTION	0xC0000140L	The connection handle given to the transport was invalid.
STATUS_INVALID_ADDRESS	0xC0000141L	The address handle given to the transport was invalid.
STATUS_DLL_INIT_FAILED	0xC0000142L	The initialization of the DLL *name* failed. The process is terminating abnormally.
STATUS_MISSING_SYSTEMFILE	0xC0000143L	The required system file *name* is bad or missing.
STATUS_UNHANDLED_EXCEPTION	0xC0000144L	The exception *name* (*value*) occurred in the application at location *address*.
STATUS_APP_INIT_FAILURE	0xC0000145L	The application failed to initialize properly (*errornum*). Click OK to terminate the application.
STATUS_PAGEFILE_CREATE_FAILED	0xC0000146L	The creation of the paging file *name* failed (*errornum*). The requested size was *value*.
STATUS_NO_PAGEFILE	0xC0000147L	No paging file was specified in the system configuration.
STATUS_INVALID_LEVEL	0xC0000148L	An invalid level was passed into the specified system call.
STATUS_WRONG_PASSWORD_CORE	0xC0000149L	An incorrect password was specified to a LAN Manager 2.*x* or MS-NET server.
STATUS_ILLEGAL_FLOAT_CONTEXT	0xC000014AL	A real-mode application issued a floating-point instruction, but floating-point hardware is not present.
STATUS_PIPE_BROKEN	0xC000014BL	The pipe operation failed because the other end of the pipe was closed.
STATUS_REGISTRY_CORRUPT	0xC000014CL	The structure of one of the files that contains Registry data is corrupt, or the image of the file in memory is corrupt, or the file could not be recovered because the alternate copy or log was absent or corrupt.
STATUS_REGISTRY_IO_FAILED	0xC000014DL	An I/O operation initiated by the Registry failed unrecoverably. The Registry could not read in, or write out, or flush, one of the files that contain the system's image of the Registry.
STATUS_NO_EVENT_PAIR	0xC000014EL	An event pair synchronization operation was performed using the thread-specific client/server event pair object, but no event pair object was associated with the thread.
STATUS_UNRECOGNIZED_VOLUME	0xC000014FL	The volume does not contain a recognized File System. Make sure that all required File System Drivers are loaded and that the volume is not corrupt.
STATUS_SERIAL_NO_DEVICE_INITED	0xC0000150L	No serial device was successfully initialized. The serial driver will unload.
STATUS_NO_SUCH_ALIAS	0xC0000151L	The specified local group does not exist.
STATUS_MEMBER_NOT_IN_ALIAS	0xC0000152L	The specified account name is not a member of the local group.
STATUS_MEMBER_IN_ALIAS	0xC0000153L	The specified account name is already a member of the local group.
STATUS_ALIAS_EXISTS	0xC0000154L	The specified local group already exists.
STATUS_LOGON_NOT_GRANTED	0xC0000155L	A requested type of logon (for example, Interactive, Network, Service) is not granted by the target system's local security policy. Ask the system administrator to grant the necessary form of logon.

Table B.4: *Numeric List of* NTSTATUS *Codes (continued)*

Code	Value	Meaning
STATUS_TOO_MANY_SECRETS	0xC0000156L	The maximum number of secrets that may be stored in a single system was exceeded. The length and number of secrets is limited to satisfy United States State Department export restrictions.
STATUS_SECRET_TOO_LONG	0xC0000157L	The length of a secret exceeds the maximum length allowed. The length and number of secrets is limited to satisfy United States State Department export restrictions.
STATUS_INTERNAL_DB_ERROR	0xC0000158L	The LSA (Local Security Authority) database contains an internal inconsistency.
STATUS_FULLSCREEN_MODE	0xC0000159L	The requested operation cannot be performed in full-screen mode.
STATUS_TOO_MANY_CONTEXT_IDS	0xC000015AL	During a logon attempt, the user's security context accumulated too many SIDs (security IDs). This is a very unusual situation. Remove the user from some global or local groups to reduce the number of SIDs to incorporate into the security context.
STATUS_LOGON_TYPE_NOT_GRANTED	0xC000015BL	A user has requested a type of logon (for example, interactive or network) that has not been granted to the user. An administrator has control over who may logon interactively and through the network.
STATUS_NOT_REGISTRY_FILE	0xC000015CL	The system attempted to load or restore a file into the Registry, and the specified file was not in the format of a Registry file.
STATUS_NT_CROSS_ENCRYPTION_REQUIRED	0xC000015DL	An attempt was made to change a user password in the security account manager without providing the necessary NT cross-encrypted password.
STATUS_DOMAIN_CTRLR_CONFIG_ERROR	0xC000015EL	A Windows NT Server has an incorrect configuration.
STATUS_FT_MISSING_MEMBER	0xC000015FL	An attempt was made to explicitly access the secondary copy of information via a device control to the Fault Tolerance driver, and the secondary copy was not present in the system.
STATUS_ILL_FORMED_SERVICE_ENTRY	0xC0000160L	A configuration Registry node representing a driver service entry was ill-formed and did not contain required value entries.
STATUS_ILLEGAL_CHARACTER	0xC0000161L	An illegal character was encountered. For a multibyte character set, this includes a lead byte without a succeeding trail byte. For the Unicode character set, this includes the characters 0xFFFF and 0xFFFE.
STATUS_UNMAPPABLE_CHARACTER	0xC0000162L	No mapping for the Unicode character exists in the target multibyte code page.
STATUS_UNDEFINED_CHARACTER	0xC0000163L	The Unicode character is not defined in the Unicode character set installed on the system.
STATUS_FLOPPY_VOLUME	0xC0000164L	The paging file cannot be created on a floppy diskette.
STATUS_FLOPPY_ID_MARK_NOT_FOUND	0xC0000165L	While a floppy disk was being accessed, an ID address mark was not found.
STATUS_FLOPPY_WRONG_CYLINDER	0xC0000166L	While a floppy disk was being accessed, the track address from the sector ID field was found to differ from that maintained by the controller.
STATUS_FLOPPY_UNKNOWN_ERROR	0xC0000167L	The floppy disk controller reported an error that is not recognized by the floppy disk driver.
STATUS_FLOPPY_BAD_REGISTERS	0xC0000168L	While a floppy disk was being accessed, the controller returned inconsistent results via its registers.
STATUS_DISK_RECALIBRATE_FAILED	0xC0000169L	While a hard disk was being accessed, a recalibrate operation failed, even after retries.
STATUS_DISK_OPERATION_FAILED	0xC000016AL	While a hard disk was being accessed, a disk operation failed, even after retries.
STATUS_DISK_RESET_FAILED	0xC000016BL	While a hard disk was being accessed, a disk controller reset was needed, but even that failed.
STATUS_SHARED_IRQ_BUSY	0xC000016CL	An attempt was made to open a device that was sharing an IRQ with other devices. At least one other device that uses that IRQ was already opened. Two concurrent opens of devices that share an IRQ and that work only via interrupts is not supported for the particular bus type that the devices use.
STATUS_FT_ORPHANING	0xC000016DL	A disk that is part of a fault-tolerant volume can no longer be accessed.

Table B.4: *Numeric List of NTSTATUS Codes (continued)*

Code	Value	Meaning
STATUS_BIOS_FAILED_TO_CONNECT_INTERRUPT	0xC000016EL	The system BIOS failed to connect a system interrupt to the device or bus for which the device is connected.
STATUS_PARTITION_FAILURE	0xC0000172L	The tape could not be partitioned.
STATUS_INVALID_BLOCK_LENGTH	0xC0000173L	When a new tape of a multivolume partition was being accessed, the current block size was incorrect.
STATUS_DEVICE_NOT_PARTITIONED	0xC0000174L	When a tape was being loaded, the tape partition information could not be found.
STATUS_UNABLE_TO_LOCK_MEDIA	0xC0000175L	An attempt to lock the eject media mechanism failed.
STATUS_UNABLE_TO_UNLOAD_MEDIA	0xC0000176L	An attempt to unload media failed.
STATUS_EOM_OVERFLOW	0xC0000177L	The physical end of the tape was detected.
STATUS_NO_MEDIA	0xC0000178L	There is no media in the drive. Insert media into drive *name*.
STATUS_NO_SUCH_MEMBER	0xC000017AL	A new member could not be added to a local group because the member does not exist.
STATUS_INVALID_MEMBER	0xC000017BL	A new member could not be added to a local group because the member has the wrong account type.
STATUS_KEY_DELETED	0xC000017CL	An illegal operation that was attempted on a Registry key has been marked for deletion.
STATUS_NO_LOG_SPACE	0xC000017DL	The system could not allocate required space in a Registry log.
STATUS_TOO_MANY_SIDS	0xC000017EL	Too many SIDs (security IDs) have been specified.
STATUS_LM_CROSS_ENCRYPTION_REQUIRED	0xC000017FL	An attempt was made to change a user password in the security account manager without providing the necessary LM cross-encrypted password.
STATUS_KEY_HAS_CHILDREN	0xC0000180L	An attempt was made to create a symbolic link in a Registry key that already has sub-keys or values.
STATUS_CHILD_MUST_BE_VOLATILE	0xC0000181L	An attempt was made to create a stable subkey under a volatile parent key.
STATUS_DEVICE_CONFIGURATION_ERROR	0xC0000182L	The I/O device was configured incorrectly, or the configuration parameters to the driver were incorrect.
STATUS_DRIVER_INTERNAL_ERROR	0xC0000183L	An error was detected between two drivers or within an I/O driver.
STATUS_INVALID_DEVICE_STATE	0xC0000184L	The device is not in a valid state to perform this request.
STATUS_IO_DEVICE_ERROR	0xC0000185L	The I/O device reported an I/O error.
STATUS_DEVICE_PROTOCOL_ERROR	0xC0000186L	A protocol error was detected between the driver and the device.
STATUS_BACKUP_CONTROLLER	0xC0000187L	This operation is allowed only for the Primary Domain Controller of the domain.
STATUS_LOG_FILE_FULL	0xC0000188L	Log file space is insufficient to support this operation.
STATUS_TOO_LATE	0xC0000189L	A Write operation was attempted to a volume after the volume was dismounted.
STATUS_NO_TRUST_LSA_SECRET	0xC000018AL	The workstation does not have a trust secret for the primary domain in the local LSA (Local Security Authority) database.
STATUS_NO_TRUST_SAM_ACCOUNT	0xC000018BL	The SAM (Security Access Manager) database on the Windows NT Server does not have a computer account for this workstation trust relationship.
STATUS_TRUSTED_DOMAIN_FAILURE	0xC000018CL	The logon request failed because the trust relationship between the primary domain and the trusted domain failed.
STATUS_TRUSTED_RELATIONSHIP_FAILURE	0xC000018DL	The logon request failed because the trust relationship between this workstation and the primary domain failed.
STATUS_EVENTLOG_FILE_CORRUPT	0xC000018EL	The Event Log log file is corrupt.

Table B.4: *Numeric List of* NTSTATUS *Codes (continued)*

Code	Value	Meaning
STATUS_EVENTLOG_CANT_START	0xC000018FL	No Event Log file could be opened. The Event Log service did not start.
STATUS_TRUST_FAILURE	0xC0000190L	The network logon failed. This might be because the validation authority could not be reached.
STATUS_MUTANT_LIMIT_EXCEEDED	0xC0000191L	An attempt was made to acquire a mutant such that its maximum count would have been exceeded.
STATUS_NETLOGON_NOT_STARTED	0xC0000192L	An attempt was made to log on, but the net logon service was not started.
STATUS_ACCOUNT_EXPIRED	0xC0000193L	The user's account has expired.
STATUS_POSSIBLE_DEADLOCK	0xC0000194L	A possible deadlock condition exists.
STATUS_NETWORK_CREDENTIAL_ CONFLICT	0xC0000195L	The credentials supplied conflict with an existing set of credentials.
STATUS_REMOTE_SESSION_LIMIT	0xC0000196L	An attempt was made to establish a session to a network server, but there are already too many sessions established to that server.
STATUS_EVENTLOG_FILE_ CHANGED	0xC0000197L	The log file was changed between reads.
STATUS_NOLOGON_INTERDOMAIN_ TRUST_ACCOUNT	0xC0000198L	The account used is an Interdomain Trust account. Use a global user account or local user account to access this server.
STATUS_NOLOGON_WORKSTATION_ TRUST_ACCOUNT	0xC0000199L	The account used is a Computer Account. Use a global user account or local user account to access this server.
STATUS_NOLOGON_SERVER_TRUST_ ACCOUNT	0xC000019AL	The account used is a Server Trust account. Use a global user account or local user account to access this server.
STATUS_DOMAIN_TRUST_ INCONSISTENT	0xC000019BL	The name or SID (security ID) of the domain specified is inconsistent with the trust information for that domain.
STATUS_FS_DRIVER_REQUIRED	0xC000019CL	A volume was accessed for which a File System Driver is required that has not yet been loaded.
STATUS_NO_USER_SESSION_KEY	0xC0000202L	There was no user session key for the specified logon session.
STATUS_USER_SESSION_DELETED	0xC0000203L	The remote user session has been deleted.
STATUS_RESOURCE_LANG_NOT_ FOUND	0xC0000204L	The specified resource language ID could not be found in the image file.
STATUS_INSUFF_SERVER_ RESOURCES	0xC0000205L	Insufficient server resources exist to complete the request.
STATUS_INVALID_BUFFER_SIZE	0xC0000206L	The size of the buffer was invalid for the specified operation.
STATUS_INVALID_ADDRESS_ COMPONENT	0xC0000207L	The transport rejected as invalid the network address specified.
STATUS_INVALID_ADDRESS_ WILDCARD	0xC0000208L	The transport rejected the network address specified due to an invalid use of a wildcard.
STATUS_TOO_MANY_ADDRESSES	0xC0000209L	The transport address could not be opened because all the available addresses are in use.
STATUS_ADDRESS_ALREADY_ EXISTS	0xC000020AL	The transport address could not be opened because it already exists.
STATUS_ADDRESS_CLOSED	0xC000020BL	The transport address is now closed.
STATUS_CONNECTION_ DISCONNECTED	0xC000020CL	The transport connection is now disconnected.
STATUS_CONNECTION_RESET	0xC000020DL	The transport connection has been reset.
STATUS_TOO_MANY_NODES	0xC000020EL	The transport cannot dynamically acquire any more nodes.
STATUS_TRANSACTION_ABORTED	0xC000020FL	The transport aborted a pending transaction.
STATUS_TRANSACTION_ TIMED_OUT	0xC0000210L	The transport timed out a request waiting for a response.

Table B.4: *Numeric List of* NTSTATUS *Codes (continued)*

Code	Value	Meaning
STATUS_TRANSACTION_NO_RELEASE	0xC0000211L	The transport did not receive a release for a pending response.
STATUS_TRANSACTION_NO_MATCH	0xC0000212L	The transport did not find a transaction matching the specified token.
STATUS_TRANSACTION_RESPONDED	0xC0000213L	The transport had previously responded to a transaction request.
STATUS_TRANSACTION_INVALID_ID	0xC0000214L	The transport did not recognized the specified transaction request identifier.
STATUS_TRANSACTION_INVALID_TYPE	0xC0000215L	The transport did not recognize the specified transaction request type.
STATUS_NOT_SERVER_SESSION	0xC0000216L	The transport can process the specified request only on the server side of a session.
STATUS_NOT_CLIENT_SESSION	0xC0000217L	The transport can process the specified request only on the client side of a session.
STATUS_CANNOT_LOAD_REGISTRY_FILE	0xC0000218L	The Registry could not load the hive (file) *name* or its log or alternate. They were corrupt, absent, or not writable.
STATUS_DEBUG_ATTACH_FAILED	0xC0000219L	An unexpected failure occurred while a DebugActiveProcess API request was being processed. Choose OK to terminate the process or CANCEL to ignore the error.
STATUS_SYSTEM_PROCESS_TERMINATED	0xC000021AL	The *name* system process terminated unexpectedly with a status of 0x*nnnnnnnn* 0x*nnnnnnnn* 0x*nnnnnnnn*. The system has been shut down.
STATUS_DATA_NOT_ACCEPTED	0xC000021BL	The TDI client could not handle the data received during an indication.
STATUS_NO_BROWSER_SERVERS_FOUND	0xC000021CL	The list of servers for this workgroup is not currently available.
STATUS_VDM_HARD_ERROR	0xC000021DL	NTVDM encountered a hard error.
STATUS_DRIVER_CANCEL_TIMEOUT	0xC000021EL	The driver *name* failed to complete a canceled I/O request in the allotted time.
STATUS_REPLY_MESSAGE_MISMATCH	0xC000021FL	An attempt was made to reply to an LPC message, but the thread specified by the client ID in the message was not waiting on that message.
STATUS_MAPPED_ALIGNMENT	0xC0000220L	An attempt was made to map a view of a file, but either the specified base address or the offset into the file was not aligned on the proper allocation granularity.
STATUS_IMAGE_CHECKSUM_MISMATCH	0xC0000221L	The image *name* is possibly corrupt. The header checksum does not match the computed checksum.
STATUS_LOST_WRITEBEHIND_DATA	0xC0000222L	The system was attempting to transfer file data from buffers to *name*. The Write operation failed, and only some of the data may have been written to the file.
STATUS_CLIENT_SERVER_PARAMETERS_INVALID	0xC0000223L	The parameter(s) passed to the server in the client/server shared memory window were invalid. Too much data might have been put in the shared memory window.
STATUS_PASSWORD_MUST_CHANGE	0xC0000224L	The user must change his or her password before logging on the first time.
STATUS_NOT_FOUND	0xC0000225L	The object was not found.
STATUS_NOT_TINY_STREAM	0xC0000226L	The stream is not a tiny stream.
STATUS_RECOVERY_FAILURE	0xC0000227L	A transaction recover failed.
STATUS_STACK_OVERFLOW_READ	0xC0000228L	The request must be handled by the stack overflow code.
STATUS_FAIL_CHECK	0xC0000229L	A consistency check failed.
STATUS_DUPLICATE_OBJECTID	0xC000022AL	The attempt to insert the object ID in the index failed because the ID is already in the index.
STATUS_OBJECTID_EXISTS	0xC000022BL	The attempt to set the object ID failed because the object already has an ID.
STATUS_CONVERT_TO_LARGE	0xC000022CL	These are internal OFS status codes indicating how an allocation operation is handled. Either the operation is retried after the containing onode is moved, or the extent stream is converted to a large stream.

Table B.4: *Numeric List of* NTSTATUS *Codes (continued)*

Code	Value	Meaning
STATUS_RETRY	0xC000022DL	The request needs to be retried.
STATUS_FOUND_OUT_OF_SCOPE	0xC000022EL	The attempt to find the object found an object matching by ID on the volume, but it is out of the scope of the handle used for the operation.
STATUS_ALLOCATE_BUCKET	0xC000022FL	The bucket array must be grown. After the array is grown, retry the transaction.
STATUS_PROPSET_NOT_FOUND	0xC0000230L	The property set specified did not exist on the object.
STATUS_MARSHALL_OVERFLOW	0xC0000231L	The user/kernel marshaling buffer has overflowed.
STATUS_INVALID_VARIANT	0xC0000232L	The supplied variant structure contained invalid data.
STATUS_DOMAIN_CONTROLLER_ NOT_FOUND	0xC0000233L	A domain controller for this domain could not be found.
STATUS_ACCOUNT_LOCKED_OUT	0xC0000234L	The user account was automatically locked because too many invalid logon attempts or password change attempts were made.
STATUS_HANDLE_NOT_CLOSABLE	0xC0000235L	NtClose was called on a handle that was protected from closing via NtSetInformationObject.
STATUS_CONNECTION_REFUSED	0xC0000236L	The transport connection attempt was refused by the remote system.
STATUS_GRACEFUL_DISCONNECT	0xC0000237L	The transport connection was gracefully closed.
STATUS_ADDRESS_ALREADY_ ASSOCIATED	0xC0000238L	The transport endpoint already had an address associated with it.
STATUS_ADDRESS_NOT_ ASSOCIATED	0xC0000239L	An address has not yet been associated with the transport endpoint.
STATUS_CONNECTION_INVALID	0xC000023AL	An operation was attempted on a nonexistent transport connection.
STATUS_CONNECTION_ACTIVE	0xC000023BL	An invalid operation was attempted on an active transport connection.
STATUS_NETWORK_UNREACHABLE	0xC000023CL	The remote network was not reachable by the transport.
STATUS_HOST_UNREACHABLE	0xC000023DL	The remote system was not reachable by the transport.
STATUS_PROTOCOL_UNREACHABLE	0xC000023EL	The remote system does not support the transport protocol.
STATUS_PORT_UNREACHABLE	0xC000023FL	No service is operating at the destination port of the transport on the remote system.
STATUS_REQUEST_ABORTED	0xC0000240L	The request was aborted.
STATUS_CONNECTION_ABORTED	0xC0000241L	The transport connection was aborted by the local system.
STATUS_BAD_COMPRESSION_ BUFFER	0xC0000242L	The specified buffer contained ill-formed data.
STATUS_USER_MAPPED_FILE	0xC0000243L	The requested operation could not be performed on a file with a user-mapped section open.
STATUS_AUDIT_FAILED	0xC0000244L	An attempt to generate a security audit failed.
STATUS_TIMER_RESOLUTION_ NOT_SET	0xC0000245L	The timer resolution was not previously set by the current process.
STATUS_CONNECTION_COUNT_ LIMIT	0xC0000246L	A connection to the server could not be made because the limit on the number of concurrent connections for this account was reached.
STATUS_LOGIN_TIME_ RESTRICTION	0xC0000247L	An attempt was made to log on during an unauthorized time of day for this account.
STATUS_LOGIN_WKSTA_ RESTRICTION	0xC0000248L	The account is not authorized to log on from this station.
STATUS_IMAGE_MP_UP_MISMATCH	0xC0000249L	The image *name* was modified for use on a uniprocessor system, but it is being run on a multiprocessor machine. Reinstall the image file.
STATUS_INSUFFICIENT_LOGON_ INFO	0xC0000250L	There was insufficient account information to log on.

Table B.4: *Numeric List of* NTSTATUS *Codes (continued)*

Code	Value	Meaning
STATUS_BAD_DLL_ENTRYPOINT	0xC0000251L	The DLL *name* was not written correctly. The stack pointer was left in an inconsistent state. The entry point should be declared as WINAPI or STDCALL. Select YES to fail the DLL load or NO to continue execution. Selecting NO might cause the application to operate incorrectly.
STATUS_BAD_SERVICE_ENTRYPOINT	0xC0000252L	The *name* service was not written correctly. The stack pointer was left in an inconsistent state. The callback entry point should be declared as WINAPI or STDCALL. Select OK to cause the service to continue operation. However, the service process might operate incorrectly.
STATUS_LPC_REPLY_LOST	0xC0000253L	The server received the messages but did not send a reply.
STATUS_IP_ADDRESS_CONFLICT1	0xC0000254L	The system detected an IP address conflict with another system on the network. The local interface was disabled. More details are available in the system Event Log. Consult the network administrator to resolve the conflict.
STATUS_IP_ADDRESS_CONFLICT2	0xC0000255L	The system detected an IP address conflict with another system on the network. Network operations on this system might be disrupted as a result. More details are available in the system Event Log. Consult the network administrator immediately to resolve the conflict.
STATUS_REGISTRY_QUOTA_LIMIT	0xC0000256L	The system is running low on Registry quota. To increase the Registry quota, start the System option in the Control Panel and choose the Change button in the Virtual Memory section of the Performance tab.
STATUS_PATH_NOT_COVERED	0xC0000257L	The contacted server does not support the indicated part of the DFS namespace.
STATUS_NO_CALLBACK_ACTIVE	0xC0000258L	A callback return system service cannot be executed when no callback is active.
STATUS_LICENSE_QUOTA_EXCEEDED	0xC0000259L	The service being accessed is licensed for a particular number of connections. No more connections can be made to the service at this time because there are already as many connections as the service can accept.
STATUS_PWD_TOO_SHORT	0xC000025AL	The password provided is too short to meet the policy of the user's account. Choose a longer password.
STATUS_PWD_TOO_RECENT	0xC000025BL	The policy of the user account does not allow changing passwords too often. This is done to prevent users from changing back to a familiar, but potentially discovered, password. A user who feels his or her password has been compromised should contact the administrator immediately to have a new one assigned.
STATUS_PWD_HISTORY_CONFLICT	0xC000025CL	An attempt was made to change a password to one used in the past. The policy of the user account does not allow this. Select a password that has not been previously used.
STATUS_PLUGPLAY_NO_DEVICE	0xC000025EL	An attempt was made to load a legacy Device Driver while its device instance was disabled.
STATUS_UNSUPPORTED_COMPRESSION	0xC000025FL	The specified compression format is unsupported.
STATUS_INVALID_HW_PROFILE	0xC0000260L	The specified hardware profile configuration is invalid.
STATUS_INVALID_PLUGPLAY_DEVICE_PATH	0xC0000261L	The specified Plug-and-Play Registry device path is invalid.
STATUS_DRIVER_ORDINAL_NOT_FOUND	0xC0000262L	The *name* Device Driver could not locate the ordinal *number* in driver *name*.
STATUS_DRIVER_ENTRYPOINT_NOT_FOUND	0xC0000263L	The *name* Device Driver could not locate the entry point *name* in driver *name*.
STATUS_RESOURCE_NOT_OWNED	0xC0000264L	The application attempted to release a resource it did not own. Select OK to terminate the application.
STATUS_TOO_MANY_LINKS	0xC0000265L	An attempt was made to create more links on a file than the File System supports.
STATUS_QUOTA_LIST_INCONSISTENT	0xC0000266L	The specified quota list is internally inconsistent with its descriptor.
STATUS_FILE_IS_OFFLINE	0xC0000267L	The specified file was relocated to offline storage.
STATUS_EVALUATION_EXPIRATION	0xC0000268L	The evaluation period for this installation of Windows NT has expired. This system will shut down in one hour. To restore access to this installation of Windows NT, upgrade this installation using a licensed distribution of this product.

Table B.4: *Numeric List of* NTSTATUS *Codes (continued)*

Code	Value	Meaning
STATUS_ILLEGAL_DLL_RELOCATION	0xC0000269L	The system DLL *name* was relocated in memory. The application will not run properly. The relocation occurred because the DLL *name* occupied an address range reserved for Windows NT system DLLs. The vendor supplying the DLL should be contacted for a new DLL.
STATUS_LICENSE_VIOLATION	0xC000026AL	The system detected tampering with a registered product type. Tampering with product type is not permitted. This is a violation of the software license.
STATUS_DLL_INIT_FAILED_LOGOFF	0xC000026BL	The application failed to initialize because the window station is shutting down.
STATUS_DRIVER_UNABLE_TO_LOAD	0xC000026CL	*Name* Device Driver could not be loaded. The error Status was *value*.
STATUS_DFS_UNAVAILABLE	0xC000026DL	DFS is unavailable on the contacted server.
STATUS_VOLUME_DISMOUNTED	0xC000026EL	An operation was attempted to a volume after it was dismounted.
STATUS_WX86_INTERNAL_ERROR	0xC000026FL	An internal error occurred in the Win32 *x*86 emulation subsystem.
STATUS_WX86_FLOAT_STACK_CHECK	0xC0000270L	This is a Win32 *x*86 emulation subsystem floating-point stack check.
STATUS_VALIDATE_CONTINUE	0xC0000271L	The validation process needs to continue to the next step.
STATUS_NO_MATCH	0xC0000272L	There was no match for the specified key in the index.
STATUS_NO_MORE_MATCHES	0xC0000273L	There are no more matches for the current index enumeration.
STATUS_INVALID_VLM_OPERATION	0xC0000274L	The specified Very Large Memory (64-bit Virtual Addressing) operation is invalid.
STATUS_WOW_ASSERTION	0xC0009898L	This is a WOW Assertion Error.

The NTSTATUS Explorer

The code we used to produce Table B.1, Table B.2, and Table B.3 accompanies this book. It is called the "NTSTATUS Explorer". It has two components:

- A Device Driver that generates the error
- An application that calls this driver

A screen snapshot of the running application is shown in Figure B.1.

To run the program, you must install the STATUSR.sys driver and start it. Otherwise, the only error you get is "Service Unavailable". Click the **Add** button to load in an NTSTATUS header file, such as ntstatus.h from the DDK include subdirectory. The symbols are added to the list of symbols to be tested. Then click the **Winerror.h** button to add in the current version of WinError.h from the normal C/C++ include directory. The radio buttons on the left control how the sorting is done.

An example of the plaintext file format is shown in Figure B.2.

The list box is a multiple-selection list box, so you can select whatever codes you want to see. Or you can click the **Select All** button to select all of the items in the box. Clicking **Go** will then perform the experiment for each of the selected NTSTATUS codes. The **Save** button will save the resulting text. You use the **Output Options** button to bring up a dialog that determines some details of the output. This is shown in Figure B.3.

The format of the save, either **Formatted** or **Plain Text**; the **Formatted** option is designed for conversion to a table inside a word processor. Usually, codes that have not generated an error

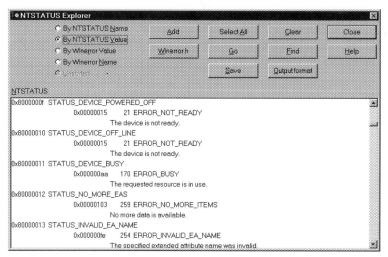

Figure B.1: *The NTSTATUS Explorer.*

```
0x80000001 STATUS_GUARD_PAGE_VIOLATION
           0x80000001
                      Not implemented
0x80000002 STATUS_DATATYPE_MISALIGNMENT
                      998 ERROR_NOACCESS
                      Invalid access to memory location.
0x80000003 STATUS_BREAKPOINT
           0x80000003
                      One or more arguments are invalid
0x80000004 STATUS_SINGLE_STEP
           0x80000004
                      No such interface supported
0x80000005 STATUS_BUFFER_OVERFLOW
                      234 ERROR_MORE_DATA
                      More data is available.
0x80000006 STATUS_NO_MORE_FILES
                      18 ERROR_NO_MORE_FILES
                      There are no more files.
```

Figure B.2: *Plaintext output*

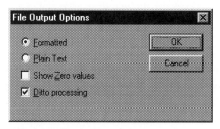

Figure B.3: *NTSTATUS Explorer output options.*

are ignored, but you can select the option to **Show Zero values** as well. The **Ditto procesing** option drops redundant information when there are multiple results (this applies only when the dominant sort is the WinError code or value).

The STATUSR Driver

The STATUSR driver is not much more complex than the "Hello World" driver. We add a handler for the IRP_MJ_DEVICE_CONTROL dispatch, which is shown in Listing B.1. The action is fairly simple. Once we get the stack location, we have the input buffer. We retrieve the desired NTSTATUS return code and set it as the IRP->IoStatus.Status field, and return it as the value of the handler.

Listing B.1: DeviceIoControl *Handler for StatusReturn Driver*

```
NTSTATUS statusRDeviceControl(IN PDEVICE_OBJECT DeviceObject,
                              IN PIRP Irp )
{
    NTSTATUS  ret = STATUS_SUCCESS;
    PIO_STACK_LOCATION irpStack = IoGetCurrentIrpStackLocation(Irp);
    ULONG    *pInBuffer;

    pInBuffer = (ULONG *)Irp->AssociatedIrp.SystemBuffer;  // buffered i/o
    switch(irpStack->Parameters.DeviceIoControl.IoControlCode)
        {
        case  IOCTL_FAIL_WITH:
            ret = *pInBuffer;
            break;
        default:
            ret = STATUS_SUCCESS;
        }
    //
    // Fill these in before calling IoCompleteRequest.
    //
    Irp->IoStatus.Status = ret;
    Irp->IoStatus.Information = 0;
    IoCompleteRequest( Irp, IO_NO_INCREMENT );
    return ret;
}
```

Appendix

C *BugCheck Codes*

This table is a summary of the BugCheck error codes. It includes an explanation for all those codes for which we have information, primarily from the Microsoft Knowledge Base article Q103059. In the explanation column, if the displayed parameters have meaning, the values are explained by parameter number. Those errors that are most common are highlighted in gray.

Table C.1: *BugCheck Error Codes*

Code	Name	Meaning
0x00000001	APC_INDEX_MISMATCH	
0x00000002	DEVICE_QUEUE_NOT_BUSY	
0x00000003	INVALID_AFFINITY_SET	
0x00000004	INVALID_DATA_ACCESS_TRAP	
0x00000005	INVALID_PROCESS_ATTACH_ATTEMPT	
0x0000006	INVALID_PROCESS_DETACH_ATTEMPT	
0x00000007	INVALID_SOFTWARE_INTERRUPT	
0x00000008	IRQL_NOT_DISPATCH_LEVEL	You called a function that was valid only at IRQL == DISPATCH_LEVEL from a higher IRQL, such as a DIRQL.
0x00000009	IRQL_NOT_GREATER_OR_EQUAL	You called a function that was valid only at IRQL >= current level from a lower IRQL.

Table C.1: *BugCheck Error Codes (continued)*

Code	Name	Meaning
0x0000000A	IRQL_NOT_LESS_OR_EQUAL	You called a function that was valid only at IRQL <= current level from a higher IRQL, such as a DIRQL, and it has touched a page that was paged out. 1. The address that was referenced (this is an address in paged memory) 2. The IRQL value that was active at the time of the reference 3. The type of access: 0 for read, 1 for write 4. The address of the instruction that was executing when the error occurred
0x0000000B	NO_EXCEPTION_HANDLING_SUPPORT	
0x0000000C	MAXIMUM_WAIT_OBJECTS_EXCEEDED	You called KeWaitForMultipleObjects with a count of more than THREAD_WAIT_OBJECTS, but you have not allocated your own KWAIT_BLOCK array.
0x0000000D	MUTEX_LEVEL_NUMBER_VIOLATION	An attempt was made to acquire a Mutex that has the wrong level number. 1. The current thread's Mutex level 2. The Mutex level attempting to acquire
0x0000000E	NO_USER_MODE_CONTEXT	
0x0000000F	SPIN_LOCK_ALREADY_OWNED	
0x00000010	SPIN_LOCK_NOT_OWNED	A thread attempted to release a Spin Lock it did not set.
0x00000011	THREAD_NOT_MUTEX_OWNER	An attempt has been made to release a Mutex that was set by some other thread.
0x00000012	TRAP_CAUSE_UNKNOWN	
0x00000013	EMPTY_THREAD_REAPER_LIST	
0x00000014	CREATE_DELETE_LOCK_NOT_LOCKED	
0x00000015	LAST_CHANCE_CALL_FROM_KMODE	
0x00000016	CID_HANDLE_CREATION	

Table C.1: *BugCheck Error Codes (continued)*

Code	Name	Meaning
0x00000017	CID_HANDLE_DELETION	
0x00000018	REFERENCE_BY_POINTER	
0x00000019	BAD_POOL_HEADER	The header for the storage pool was corrupted, or the reference was not to a storage pool.
0x0000001A	MEMORY_MANAGEMENT	The heap was corrupted.
0x0000001B	PFN_SHARE_COUNT	
0x0000001C	PFN_REFERENCE_COUNT	
0x0000001D	NO_SPIN_LOCK_AVAILABLE	
0x0000001E	KMODE_EXCEPTION_NOT_HANDLED	An exception occurred in the kernel. 1. The exception code; the usual exception code values apply, as defined by winerror.h. (see also Table 9.7) 2. The address of the instruction that caused exception 3. The first parameter of the exception 4. The second parameter of the exception
0x0000001F	SHARED_RESOURCE_CONV_ERROR	
0x00000020	KERNEL_APC_PENDING_DURING_EXIT	
0x00000021	QUOTA_UNDERFLOW	
0x00000022	FILE_SYSTEM	
0x00000023	FAT_FILE_SYSTEM	
0x00000024	NTFS_FILE_SYSTEM	
0x00000025	NPFS_FILE_SYSTEM	
0x00000026	CDFS_FILE_SYSTEM	
0x00000027	RDR_FILE_SYSTEM	
0x00000028	CORRUPT_ACCESS_TOKEN	
0x00000029	SECURITY_SYSTEM	

Table C.1: *BugCheck Error Codes (continued)*

Code	Name	Meaning
0x0000002A	INCONSISTENT_IRP	The IRP contains two or more members that conflict. This is most likely caused by mistakenly using the IRP pointer for another kind of access. 1. The address of the IRP
0x0000002B	PANIC_STACK_SWITCH	Kernel-mode stack overflow. This can be caused by large arrays or objects being allocated on the stack and/or too much (or infinite) recursion.
0x0000002C	PORT_DRIVER_INTERNAL	
0x0000002D	SCSI_DISK_DRIVER_INTERNAL	
0x0000002E	DATA_BUS_ERROR	This error is normally caused by a parity error in system memory. It can also be caused by a driver that is accessing an address in the range 0x8xxxxxxx that does not exist. 1. The virtual address that caused the fault 2. The physical address that caused the fault 3. Processor Status Register (PSR) 4. Faulting Instruction Register (FIR)
0x0000002F	INSTRUCTION_BUS_ERROR	
0x00000030	SET_OF_INVALID_CONTEXT	
0x00000031	PHASE0_INITIALIZATION_FAILED	
0x00000032	PHASE1_INITIALIZATION_FAILED	
0x00000033	UNEXPECTED_INITIALIZATION_CALL	
0x00000034	CACHE_MANAGER	
0x00000035	NO_MORE_IRP_STACK_LOCATIONS	You created an IRP that does not have enough stack locations for the layers of drivers it is being processed by. Make sure you have allocated the correct stack size. 1. The address of the IRP

Table C.1: *BugCheck Error Codes (continued)*

Code	Name	Meaning
0x00000036	DEVICE_REFERENCE_COUNT_NOT_ZERO	IoDeleteDevice has detected that the Device Object has a non-zero reference count. 1. The address of the Device Object
0x00000037	FLOPPY_INTERNAL_ERROR	
0x00000038	SERIAL_DRIVER_INTERNAL	
0x00000039	SYSTEM_EXIT_OWNED_MUTEX	
0x0000003A	SYSTEM_UNWIND_PREVIOUS_USER	
0x0000003B	SYSTEM_SERVICE_EXCEPTION	
0x0000003C	INTERRUPT_UNWIND_ATTEMPTED	
0x0000003D	INTERRUPT_EXCEPTION_NOT_HANDLED	
0x0000003E	MULTIPROCESSOR_CONFIGURATION_NOT_SUPPORTED	The processor chips of a multi-processor are not identical. Processor chips cannot be mixed.
0x0000003F	NO_MORE_SYSTEM_PTES	The system page table is full. The most likely cause is a driver that has not properly released pages. It may also be due to a page table that is too small. A technique for increasing the number of PTEs is discussed in Chapter 12 on page 274.
0x00000040	TARGET_MDL_TOO_SMALL	IoBuildPartialMdl has been passed a target MDL that is too small for the range of addresses required.
0x00000041	MUST_SUCCEED_POOL_EMPTY	You did an allocation from the must-succeed pool, and there are so many outstanding allocations that there is no space left. Make certain you have released any must-succeed allocations you have made. 1. The size of the request that failed 2. The number of pages in use in the Nonpaged Pool 3. The number of too-large PAGE_SIZE requests from the Nonpaged Pool 4. The number of pages available

Table C.1: *BugCheck Error Codes (continued)*

Code	Name	Meaning
0x00000042	ATDISK_DRIVER_INTERNAL	
0x00000043	NO_SUCH_PARTITION	
0x00000044	MULTIPLE_IRP_COMPLETE_REQUESTS	The IRP received a second IoCompleteRequest call. 1. Address of the IRP
0x00000045	INSUFFICIENT_MAP_REGS	
0x00000046	DEREF_UNKNOWN_LOGON_SESSION	
0x00000047	REF_UNKNOWN_LOGON_SESSION	
0x00000048	CANCEL_STATE_IN_COMPLETED_IRP	IoCompleteRequest was called for an IRP that has an outstanding Cancel function. 1. Address of the IRP
0x00000049	PAGE_FAULT_WITH_INTERRUPTS_OFF	An attempt was made to a nonresident or nonexistent page at a very high IRQL. This error is often caused by an access from within a Spin-Lock-protected area.
0x0000004A	IRQL_GT_ZERO_AT_SYSTEM_SERVICE	
0x0000004B	STREAMS_INTERNAL_ERROR	
0x0000004C	FATAL_UNHANDLED_HARD_ERROR	

0x0000004D	NO_PAGES_AVAILABLE	There are no more free pages left in the system. If WinDbg is active, typing the following commands will give more-useful information.
		
		`!process 0 7`
		`!vm`
		`dd mmpagingfiles`
		`dd @$p`
		
		1. The number of dirty pages
		
		2. The number of physical pages in machine
		
		3. The extended commit value, in pages
		
		4. The total commit value, in pages

Table C.1: *BugCheck Error Codes (continued)*

Code	Name	Meaning
0x0000004E	PFN_LIST_CORRUPT	The most likely cause is that a MDL was trashed. 1. The constant 1 2. The ListHead that was corrupted 3. The number of pages available 4. The constant 0 or 1. The constant 2 2. Entry in list being removed 3. Highest physical page number 4. Reference count of entry being removed
0x0000004F	NDIS_INTERNAL_ERROR	
0x00000050	PAGE_FAULT_IN_NONPAGED_AREA	
0x00000051	REGISTRY_ERROR	The most likely cause is that the Registry was corrupted by an earlier crash. You will probably have to reinstall NT.
0x00000052	MAILSLOT_FILE_SYSTEM	
0x00000053	NO_BOOT_DEVICE	
0x00000054	LM_SERVER_INTERNAL_ERROR	
0x00000055	DATA_COHERENCY_EXCEPTION	
0x00000056	INSTRUCTION_COHERENCY_EXCEPTION	
0x00000057	XNS_INTERNAL_ERROR	
0x00000058	FTDISK_INTERNAL_ERROR	The system was booted from a revived primary partition, so the hives say the mirror is all right, when in fact it is not. The real images of the hives are on the shadow. You must boot from the shadow.
0x00000059	PINBALL_FILE_SYSTEM	
0x0000005A	CRITICAL_SERVICE_FAILED	
0x0000005B	SET_ENV_VAR_FAILED	

Table C.1: *BugCheck Error Codes (continued)*

Code	Name	Meaning
0x0000005C	HAL_INITIALIZATION_FAILED	
0x0000005D	UNSUPPORTED_PROCESSOR	
0x0000005E	OBJECT_INITIALIZATION_FAILED	
0x0000005F	SECURITY_INITIALIZATION_FAILED	
0x00000060	PROCESS_INITIALIZATION_FAILED	
0x00000061	HAL1_INITIALIZATION_FAILED	
0x00000062	OBJECT1_INITIALIZATION_FAILED	
0x00000063	SECURITY1_INITIALIZATION_FAILED	
0x00000064	SYMBOLIC_INITIALIZATION_FAILED	
0x00000065	MEMORY1_INITIALIZATION_FAILED	
0x00000066	CACHE_INITIALIZATION_FAILED	
0x00000067	CONFIG_INITIALIZATION_FAILED	
0x00000068	FILE_INITIALIZATION_FAILED	
0x00000069	IO1_INITIALIZATION_FAILED	
0x0000006A	LPC_INITIALIZATION_FAILED	
0x0000006B	PROCESS1_INITIALIZATION_FAILED	
0x0000006C	REFMON_INITIALIZATION_FAILED	
0x0000006D	SESSION1_INITIALIZATION_FAILED	
0x0000006E	SESSION2_INITIALIZATION_FAILED	
0x0000006F	SESSION3_INITIALIZATION_FAILED	
0x00000070	SESSION4_INITIALIZATION_FAILED	
0x00000071	SESSION5_INITIALIZATION_FAILED	
0x00000072	ASSIGN_DRIVE_LETTER_FAILED	
0x00000073	CONFIG_LIST_FAILED	
0x00000074	BAD_SYSTEM_CONFIG_INFO	
0x00000075	CANNOT_WRITE_CONFIGURATION	

Table C.1: *BugCheck Error Codes (continued)*

Code	Name	Meaning
0x00000076	PROCESS_HAS_LOCKED_PAGES	A process is terminating, but it still has locked pages. This is usually due to a failure to unlock pages in the Unload or Shutdown handlers. 1. The process address 2. The number of locked pages 3. The number of private pages 4. The constant 0
0x00000077	KERNEL_STACK_INPAGE_ERROR	I/O error occurred while reading a page of the Kernel-mode stack.
0x00000078	PHASE0_EXCEPTION	
0x00000079	MISMATCHED_HAL	The kernel and the HAL images are not consistent. This inconsistency can result from improper use of the /kernel and /hal switches in BOOT.INI. See Knowledge Base article Q103059 for a more detailed explanation.
0x0000007A	KERNEL_DATA_INPAGE_ERROR	I/O error occurred while reading pageable kernel data. 1. The lock type that was held (value is 1, 2, 3, or the PTE address) 2. The error status (normally an I/O status code) 3. The current process (virtual address for lock type 3 or the PTE) 4. The virtual address that could not be paged in

Table C.1: *BugCheck Error Codes (continued)*

Code	Name	Meaning
0x0000007B	INACCESSIBLE_BOOT_DEVICE	During the initialization of the I/O system, the driver for the boot device may have failed to initialize the device that the system is attempting to boot from, or the file system that is supposed to read that device may have either failed its initialization or simply not recognized the data on the boot device as a file system structure. In the former case, the first argument is the address of a Unicode string data structure that is the ARC name of the device from which the boot was being attempted. In the latter case, the first argument is the address of the Device Object that could not be mounted. This error can also be caused by certain configurations of devices that are incompatible, software that is incompatible with NT, a boot-sector virus, or by removing or reconfiguring an ATAPI CD-ROM drive. See also Knowledge Base articles Q103069, Q105026, Q115339, Q120744, Q124307, Q126423, Q131337, Q131712, Q136074, Q137860, Q153296, Q156168, and Q161960.
0x0000007D	INSTALL_MORE_MEMORY	Insufficient memory is available to boot the system. This could be caused by specifying the BOOT.INI /maxmem switch with too small a value. Or you could really have too little memory. 1. The number of physical pages found 2. The lowest physical page 3. The highest physical page 4. The constant 0
0x0000007F	UNEXPECTED_KERNEL_MODE_TRAP	(Intel platforms only) The hardware generated a trap that cannot be handled. 1. The trap code
0x00000080	NMI_HARDWARE_FAILURE	

Table C.1: *BugCheck Error Codes (continued)*

Code	Name	Meaning
0x00000081	SPIN_LOCK_INIT_FAILURE	The Spin Lock could not be initialized. The conditions that cause this are not well-defined, but they always represent a programming error.
0x00000082	DFS_FILE_SYSTEM	
0x00000083	OFS_FILE_SYSTEM	
0x00000084	RECOM_DRIVER	
0x00000085	SETUP_FAILURE	
0x00000086	AUDIT_FAILURE	
0x0000008A	THREAD_TERMINATE_HELD_MUTEX	
0x0000008B	MBR_CHECKSUM_MISMATCH	This message occurs during the boot process when the Master Boot Record (MBR) checksum the system calculates does not match the checksum passed in by the loader. This is usually an indication of a virus. There are many forms of viruses, and not all can be detected. The newer ones usually can be detected only by a virus scanner that has recently been upgraded. Boot a write-protected disk containing a virus scanner and attempt to clean out the infection. 1. The disk signature from the MBR 2. The MBR checksum computed by the OS Loader 3. The MBR checksum calculated by the system
0x0000008F	PP0_INITIALIZATION_FAILED	
0x00000090	PP1_INITIALIZATION_FAILED	
0x00000091	WIN32K_INIT_OR_RIT_FAILURE	
0x00000092	UP_DRIVER_ON_MP_SYSTEM	
0x00000093	INVALID_KERNEL_HANDLE	
0x00000094	KERNEL_STACK_LOCKED_AT_EXIT	
0x00000095	PNP_INTERNAL_ERROR	
0x00000096	INVALID_WORK_QUEUE_ITEM	

Table C.1: *BugCheck Error Codes (continued)*

Code	Name	Meaning
0x00000097	BOUND_IMAGE_UNSUPPORTED	
0x00000098	END_OF_NT_EVALUATION_PERIOD	
0x00000099	INVALID_REGION_OR_SEGMENT	
0x0000009A	SYSTEM_LICENSE_VIOLATION	
0x0000009B	UDFS_FILE_SYSTEM	
0x0000009C	MACHINE_CHECK_EXCEPTION	

Index

Addison-Wesley Computer and Engineering Publishing Group

How to Interact with Us

1. Visit our Web site

http://www.awl.com/cseng

When you think you've read enough, there's always more content for you at Addison-Wesley's web site. Our web site contains a directory of complete product information including:

- Chapters
- Exclusive author interviews
- Links to authors' pages
- Tables of contents
- Source code

You can also discover what tradeshows and conferences Addison-Wesley will be attending, read what others are saying about our titles, and find out where and when you can meet our authors and have them sign your book.

2. Subscribe to Our Email Mailing Lists

Subscribe to our electronic mailing lists and be the first to know when new books are publishing. Here's how it works: Sign up for our electronic mailing at http://www.awl.com/cseng/mailinglists.html. Just select the subject areas that interest you and you will receive notification via email when we publish a book in that area.

3. Contact Us via Email

cepubprof@awl.com
Ask general questions about our books.
Sign up for our electronic mailing lists.
Submit corrections for our web site.

bexpress@awl.com
Request an Addison-Wesley catalog.
Get answers to questions regarding your order or our products.

innovations@awl.com
Request a current Innovations Newsletter.

webmaster@awl.com
Send comments about our web site.

jcs@awl.com
Submit a book proposal.
Send errata for an Addison-Wesley book.

cepubpublicity@awl.com
Request a review copy for a member of the media interested in reviewing new Addison-Wesley titles.

We encourage you to patronize the many fine retailers who stock Addison-Wesley titles. Visit our online directory to find stores near you or visit our online store: http://store.awl.com/ or call 800-824-7799.

Addison Wesley Longman
Computer and Engineering Publishing Group
One Jacob Way, Reading, Massachusetts 01867 USA
TEL 781-944-3700 • FAX 781-942-3076